Contemporary
Literary Criticism

Guide to Gale Literary Criticism Series

For criticism on	Consult these Gale series
Authors now living or who died after December 31, 1959	*CONTEMPORARY LITERARY CRITICISM (CLC)*
Authors who died between 1900 and 1959	*TWENTIETH-CENTURY LITERARY CRITICISM (TCLC)*
Authors who died between 1800 and 1899	*NINETEENTH-CENTURY LITERATURE CRITICISM (NCLC)*
Authors who died between 1400 and 1799	*LITERATURE CRITICISM FROM 1400 TO 1800 (LC)* *SHAKESPEAREAN CRITICISM (SC)*
Authors who died before 1400	*CLASSICAL AND MEDIEVAL LITERATURE CRITICISM (CMLC)*
Black writers of the past two hundred years	*BLACK LITERATURE CRITICISM (BLC)*
Authors of books for children and young adults	*CHILDREN'S LITERATURE REVIEW (CLR)*
Dramatists	*DRAMA CRITICISM (DC)*
Hispanic writers of the late nineteenth and twentieth centuries	*HISPANIC LITERATURE CRITICISM (HLC)*
Native North American writers and orators of the eighteenth, nineteenth, and twentieth centuries	*NATIVE NORTH AMERICAN LITERATURE (NNAL)*
Poets	*POETRY CRITICISM (PC)*
Short story writers	*SHORT STORY CRITICISM (SSC)*
Major authors from the Renaissance to the present	*WORLD LITERATURE CRITICISM, 1500 TO THE PRESENT (WLC)*

ISSN 0091-3421

Volume 102

Contemporary Literary Criticism

Excerpts from Criticism of the Works
of Today's Novelists, Poets, Playwrights,
Short Story Writers, Scriptwriters, and
Other Creative Writers

Deborah A. Schmitt
EDITOR

Jeffrey W. Hunter
COORDINATOR

Tim Akers
Pamela S. Dear
Daniel Jones
John D. Jorgenson
Jerry Moore
Polly A. Vedder
Tim White
Thomas Wiloch
Kathleen Wilson
ASSOCIATE EDITORS

GALE

DETROIT • NEW YORK • TORONTO • LONDON

STAFF

Deborah A. Schmitt, *Editor*

Jeffrey W. Hunter, *Coordinator*

Tim Akers, Pamela S. Dear, Daniel Jones, John D. Jorgenson, Jerry Moore,
Polly A. Vedder, Timothy White, Thomas Wiloch, and Kathleen Wilson, *Associate Editors*

Tracy Arnold-Chapman, John P. Daniel, Chris Giroux,
Linda Quigley, and Janet Witalec, *Contributing Editors*

Susan Trosky, *Permissions Manager*
Margaret A. Chamberlain, Maria Franklin, and Kimberly F. Smilay, *Permissions Specialists*
Sarah Chesney, Edna Hedblad, Michele Lonoconus, and Shalice Shah, *Permissions Associates*

Victoria B. Cariappa, *Research Manager*
Julia C. Daniel, Tamara C. Nott, Michele P. Pica, Tracie A. Richardson,
Norma Sawaya, and Cheryl L. Warnock, *Research Associates*
Laura C. Bissey, Alfred A. Gardner I, and Sean R. Smith, *Research Assistants*

Mary Beth Trimper, *Production Director*
Deborah L. Milliken, *Production Assistant*

Barbara J. Yarrow, *Graphic Services Manager*
Sherrell Hobbs, *Macintosh Artist*
Randy Bassett, *Image Database Supervisor*
Robert Duncan and Mikal Ansari, *Scanner Operators*
Pamela Reed, *Photography Coordinator*

Library of Congress Catalog Card Number 76-46132
ISBN 0-7876-1192-1
ISSN 0091-3421

Printed in the United States of America
10 9 8 7 6 5 4 3 2 1

Contents

Preface vii

Acknowledgments xi

Preface

A Comprehensive Information Source
on Contemporary Literature

Named "one of the twenty-five most distinguished reference titles published during the past twenty-five years" by *Reference Quarterly,* the *Contemporary Literary Criticism (CLC)* series provides readers with critical commentary and general information on more than 2,000 authors now living or who died after December 31, 1959. Previous to the publication of the first volume of *CLC* in 1973, there was no ongoing digest monitoring scholarly and popular sources of critical opinion and explication of modern literature. *CLC,* therefore, has fulfilled an essential need, particularly since the complexity and variety of contemporary literature makes the function of criticism especially important to today's reader.

Scope of the Series

CLC presents significant passages from published criticism of works by creative writers. Since many of the authors covered by *CLC* inspire continual critical commentary, writers are often represented in more than one volume. There is, of course, no duplication of reprinted criticism.

Authors are selected for inclusion for a variety of reasons, among them the publication or dramatic production of a critically acclaimed new work, the reception of a major literary award, revival of interest in past writings, or the adaptation of a literary work to film or television.

Attention is also given to several other groups of writers-authors of considerable public interest—about whose work criticism is often difficult to locate. These include mystery and science fiction writers, literary and social critics, foreign writers, and authors who represent particular ethnic groups within the United States.

Format of the Book

Each *CLC* volume contains about 500 individual excerpts taken from hundreds of book review periodicals, general magazines, scholarly journals, monographs, and books. Entries include critical evaluations spanning from the beginning of an author's career to the most current commentary. Interviews, feature articles, and other published writings that offer insight into the author's works are also presented. Students, teachers, librarians, and researchers will find that the generous excerpts and supplementary material in *CLC* provide them with vital information required to write a term paper, analyze a poem, or lead a book discussion group. In addition, complete bibliographical citations note the original source and all of the information necessary for a term paper footnote or bibliography.

Features

A *CLC* author entry consists of the following elements:

- The **Author Heading** cites the author's name in the form under which the author has most commonly published, followed by birth date, and death date when applicable. Uncertainty as to a birth or death date is indicated by a question mark.

- A **Portrait** of the author is included when available.

- A brief **Biographical and Critical Introduction** to the author and his or her work precedes the excerpted criticism. The first line of the introduction provides the author's full name, pseudonyms (if applicable), nationality, and a listing of genres in which the author has written. To provide users with easier access to information, the biographical and critical essay included in each author entry is divided into four categories: "Introduction," "Biographical Information," "Major Works," and "Critical Reception." The introductions to single-work entries—entries that focus on well known and frequently studied books, short stories, and poems—are similarly organized to quickly provide readers with information on the plot and major characters of the work being discussed, its major themes, and its critical reception. Previous volumes of *CLC* in which the author has been featured are also listed in the introduction.

- A list of **Principal Works** notes the most important writings by the author. When foreign-language works have been translated into English, the English-language version of the title follows in brackets.

- The **Excerpted Criticism** represents various kinds of critical writing, ranging in form from the brief review to the scholarly exegesis. Essays are selected by the editors to reflect the spectrum of opinion about a specific work or about an author's literary career in general. The excerpts are presented chronologically, adding a useful perspective to the entry. All titles by the author featured in the entry are printed in boldface type, which enables the reader to easily identify the works being discussed. Publication information (such as publisher names and book prices) and parenthetical numerical references (such as footnotes or page and line references to specific editions of a work) have been deleted at the editor's discretion to provide smoother reading of the text.

- Critical essays are prefaced by **Explanatory Notes** as an additional aid to readers. These notes may provide several types of valuable information, including: the reputation of the critic, the importance of the work of criticism, the commentator's approach to the author's work, the purpose of the criticism, and changes in critical trends regarding the author.

- A complete **Bibliographical Citation** designed to help the user find the original essay or book precedes each excerpt.

- Whenever possible, a recent, previously unpublished **Author Interview** accompanies each entry.

- A concise **Further Reading** section appears at the end of entries on authors for whom a significant amount of criticism exists in addition to the pieces reprinted in *CLC*. Each citation in this section is accompanied by a descriptive annotation describing the content of that article. Materials included in this section are grouped under various headings (e.g., Biography, Bibliography, Criticism, and Interviews) to aid users in their search for additional information. Cross-references to other useful sources published by Gale Research in which the author has appeared are also included: *Authors in the News, Black Writers, Children's Literature Review, Contemporary Authors, Dictionary of Literary Biography, DISCovering Authors, Drama Criticism, Hispanic Literature Criticism, Hispanic Writers, Native North American Literature, Poetry Criticism, Something about the Author, Short Story Criticism, Contemporary Authors Autobiography Series,* and *Something about the Author Autobiography Series.*

Other Features

CLC also includes the following features:

- An **Acknowledgments** section lists the copyright holders who have granted permission to reprint material in this volume of *CLC*. It does not, however, list every book or periodical reprinted or consulted during the preparation of the volume.

- Each new volume of *CLC* includes a **Cumulative Topic Index,** which lists all literary topics treated in *CLC, NCLC, TCLC,* and *LC 1400-1800.*

- A **Cumulative Author Index** lists all the authors who have appeared in the various literary criticism series published by Gale Research, with cross-references to Gale's biographical and autobiographical series. A full listing of the series referenced there appears on the first page of the indexes of this volume. Readers will welcome this cumulated author index as a useful tool for locating an author within the various series. The index, which lists birth and death dates when available, will be particularly valuable for those authors who are identified with a certain period but whose death dates cause them to be placed in another, or for those authors whose careers span two periods. For example, Ernest Hemingway is found in *CLC,* yet F. Scott Fitzgerald, a writer often associated with him, is found in *Twentieth-Century Literary Criticism.*

- A **Cumulative Nationality Index** alphabetically lists all authors featured in *CLC* by nationality, followed by numbers corresponding to the volumes in which the authors appear.

- An alphabetical **Title Index** accompanies each volume of *CLC.* Listings are followed by the author's name and the corresponding page numbers where the titles are discussed. English translations of foreign titles and variations of titles are cross-referenced to the title under which a work was originally published. Titles of novels, novellas, dramas, films, record albums, and poetry, short story, and essay collections are printed in italics, while all individual poems, short stories, essays, and songs are printed in roman type within quotation marks; when published separately (e.g., T. S. Eliot's poem *The Waste Land),* the titles of long poems are printed in italics.

- In response to numerous suggestions from librarians, Gale has also produced a **Special Paperbound Edition** of the *CLC* title index. This annual cumulation, which alphabetically lists all titles reviewed in the series, is available to all customers and is typically published with every fifth volume of *CLC.* Additional copies of the index are available upon request. Librarians and patrons will welcome this separate index: it saves shelf space, is easy to use, and is recyclable upon receipt of the next edition.

Citing *Contemporary Literary Criticism*

When writing papers, students who quote directly from any volume in the Literary Criticism Series may use the following general forms to footnote reprinted criticism. The first example pertains to material drawn from periodicals, the second to material reprinted in books:

[1]Alfred Cismaru, "Making the Best of It," *The New Republic,* 207, No. 24, (December 7, 1992), 30, 32; excerpted and reprinted in *Contemporary Literary Criticism,* Vol. 85, ed. Christopher Giroux (Detroit: Gale Research, 1995), pp. 73-4.

[2]Yvor Winters, *The Post-Symbolist Methods* (Allen Swallow, 1967); excerpted and reprinted in *Contemporary Literary Criticism,* Vol. 85, ed. Christopher Giroux (Detroit: Gale Research, 1995), pp. 223-26.

Suggestions Are Welcome

The editors hope that readers will find *CLC* a useful reference tool and welcome comments about the work. Send comments and suggestions to: Editors, *Contemporary Literary Criticism,* Gale Research, Penobscot Building, Detroit, MI 48226-4094.

Acknowledgments

The editors wish to thank the copyright holders of the excerpted criticism included in this volume and the permissions managers of many book and magazine publishing companies for assisting us in securing reproduction rights. We are also grateful to the staffs of the Detroit Public Library, the Library of Congress, the University of Detroit Mercy Library, Wayne State University Purdy/Kresge Library Complex, and the University of Michigan Libraries for making their resources available to us. Following is a list of the copyright holders who have granted us permission to reproduce material in this volume of *CLC*. Every effort has been made to trace copyright, but if omissions have been made, please let us know.

COPYRIGHTED EXCERPTS IN *CLC*, VOLUME 102, WERE REPRODUCED FROM THE FOLLOWING PERIODICALS:

Afterimage, v. 15, October, 1987 for "Topos Noir: The Spacialization and Recuperation of Disorder" by Michael Renov. © Visual Studies Workshop 1987. Reproduced by permission of the publisher and the author.—*American Anthropologist,* v. 84, December, 1982 for a review of "Divine Horsemen" by George M. Epple. Copyright 1982 by the American Anthropological Association. All Rights Reserved. Reproduced by permission of the American Anthropological Association and the author.—*American Studies,* v. 14, Spring, 1981; v. 21, Spring, 1988; v. 24, Spring, 1991; v. 24, Winter, 1991; v. 33, Fall, 1992; v. 26, Spring, 1993; v. 26, Summer, 1993; v. 26, Winter, 1993; v. 27, Summer, 1994; v. 29, Winter, 1996. Copyright © Mid-American Studies Association, 1981, 1988, 1991, 1992, 1993, 1994, 1996. All reprinted by permission of the publisher and the authors.—*ASSAPH: Studies in the Theatre,* v. C, 1986. Reproduced by permission.—*The Atlanta Journal/Constitution,* November 26, 1995. Reproduced by permission.—*The Bloomsbury Review,* v. 11, June, 1991 for a review of "The Price of Salt" by Pat Wagner. Copyright © by Owaissa Communications Company, Inc. 1991. Reproduced by permission of the author.—*Book World--The Washington Post,* v. XV, October 6, 1985; March 15, 1987; February 21, 1988; February 5, 1989; November 19, 1989; v. 20, April 15, 1990; November 18, 1990; November 17, 1991; October 17, 1993; Setpember 18, 1994; v. XXV, November 5, 1995. © 1985, 1987, 1988, 1989, 1990, 1991, 1993, 1994, 1995, Washington Post Book World Service/Washington Post Writers Group. All reproduced with permission.—*Books In Canada,* v. 13, June-July, 1984 for "Findlay's People" by Alberto Manguel/ v. 15, January/February, 1986, for "Sins of the Father," by Volker Strunk/ v. 24, April, 1995 for "The Past Recaptured" by Gary Draper. All reproduced by permission of the authors.—*Canadian Drama,* Fall, 1976. Reproduced by permission.—*Canadian Literature,* v. 103, for a review of "Thérèse and Pierrette and the Little Hanging Angel" by Jane Moss/ n. 91, Winter, 1981 for "Look! Listen! Mark My Words!: Paying Attention to Timothy Findley's Fictions" by John F. Hulcoop/ v. 128, Spring, 1991 for a review of "Le Premier Quartier de la lune" by Eva-Marie Kroller/ v. 134, Winter, 1992 for "Poet's Dilemma" by Kathy Mezei/ v. 144, Spring, 1995 for "The Bingocentric Worlds of Michel Tremblay and Tomson Highway" by Renate Usmiani. All reproduced by permission of the authors.—*Chicago Tribune,* March 6, 1988 for "Dick Francis' Latest A Good Bet" by Frederick Busch. © copyrighted 1999, Chicago Tribune Company. All rights reserved. Reproduced by permission of the author.—*Chicago Tribune--Books,* November 22, 1987 for "'Silence' is Golden" by Jack Fuller/ June 4, 1989 for "Two Numbed Vietnam Vets Turn to the Soil" by Greg Johnson/ May 30, 1993 for "Poised Between Hell and Purgatory" by Andy Solomon. © copyrighted 1987, 1989, 1993 Chicago Tribune Company. All rights reserved. All reproduced by permission of the authors.—*The Christian Science Monitor,* July 25, 1989; v. 86, October 27, 1994. © 1989, 1994 The Christian Science Publishing Society. All rights reserved. Both reproduced by permission from The Christian Science Monitor.—*Clues: A Journal of Detection,* v. 5, Spring-Summer, 1984. Copyright 1984 by Pat Browne. Reproduced by permission.—*Concerning Poetry,* v. 18, 1985. Copyright © 1985, Western Washington University. Reproduced by permission.—*English Studies in Canada,* v. XV, September, 1989 for "Civilian Conflict: Systems of Warfare in Timothy Findley's Early Fiction" by Lorraine M. York. © Association of Canadian University Teachers of English 1989. Reproduced by permission of the publisher and the author.—*Essays on Canadian Writing,* Summer, 1978. © 1978 Essays on Canadian Writing Ltd. Reproduced by permission.—*Film Library Quarterly,* v. 5, Winter, 1971-72. © Copyright, Film Library Information Council, 1971.

228, August 23, 1985. Copyright © 1985 by Xerox Corporation. Reproduced from Publishers Weekly, published by R. R. Bowker Company, a Xerox company, by permission.—*Punch,* v. 29, October 15, 1986. © 1986 by Punch Publications Ltd. All rights reserved. May not be repirnted without permission.—*Queen's Quarterly,* v. 95, Winter, 1988 for a review of "Albertine in Five Times" by Catherine Paul. Copyright © 1988 by the author. Reprinted by permission of the author.—*Quill and Quire,* v. 54, November, 1988 for "Findley's Fine Line Between Untidy Life and Orderly Art" by Keith Garebian/ v. 59, March, 1993 for "The Horror and the River" by Sandra Martin. Both reproduced by permission of the author.—*Reviews in American History,* Vol. 23, March, 1995, "Christopher Lasch, The New Radicalism, and the Vocation of Intellectuals" by Robert W. Westbrook. © 1995. Reproduced by permission of The Johns Hopkins University Press.—*Salmagundi,* Winter, 1992; Spring-Summer, 1995. Copyright © 1992, 1995 by Skidmore College. Both reproduced by permission.—*Seminar,* v. 20, November, 1984. Reproduced by permission.—*The Sewanee Review,* v. XCII, Spring, 1984 for "Other Voices, Other Runes" by Mark Royden Winchell. Copyright © 1984 by The University of the South. Reproduced with the permission of The Sewanee Review and the author.—*Southern Humanities Review,* v. XX, Spring, 1986 for a review of The Minimal Self: Psychie Survival in Troubled Times by Joseph Voelker. Reproduced by permission.—*The Southern Review,* Louisana State University, v. 17, July, 1981 for "Three Poets in Mid Career" by Dana Gioia/ January, 1994 for an interview with Madison Smartt Bell by Mary Louise Weaks. Copyright, 1981, 1994, by the authors. Both reproduced by permission of the authors.—*The Spectator,* v. 263, November 18, 1989. © 1989 by The Spectator. Reproduced by permission of The Spectator.—*THALIA: Studies in Literary Humor,* v. II, Spring-Fall, 1979. Copyright © 1979 by Jacqueline Tavernier-Courbin. Reproduced by permission.—*Theatre Journal,* v. 32, March, 1980. © 1980, University and College Theatre Association of the American Theatre Association. Reproduced by permission of The Johns Hopkins University Press.—*Time,* v. 131, March 21, 1988. Copyright 1988 Time Warner Inc. All rights reserved. Reproduced by permission from Time.—*U.S. News & World Report,* v. 104, March 28, 1988. Copyright © 1988, by U.S. News & World Report, Inc. All rights reserved. Reproduced by permission.—*Verse,* v. 8, Winter,-Spring, 1992 for "Essays" by Robert Mezey, Paul Ramsey, Bruce Bawer, Dana Gioia, William Logan and Michale Peich. © 1992 Copyright by the authors. Reproduced by permission.—*The Village Voice,* v. XV, December 10, 1970 for "The Voodoo Gods of Haiti," by Hant Heifetz/ v. XXIII, May 15, 1978 for "The Maya Mystique" by J. Hoberman. Copyright © V. V. Publishing Corporation, 1970, 1978. Both reproduced by permission of the authors.—*Wide Angle,* v. 8, 1986. © 1986. Reproduced by permission of The John Hopkins University Press.—*World Literature Today,* v. 55, Autumn, 1981; v. 58, Summer, 1984; v. 66, Autumn, 1992; v. 69, Winter, 1995. Copyright © 1981, 1984, 1992, 1995 by the University of Oklahoma Press. All reproduced by permission.—*Yale French Studies,* n. 65, 1983. Copyright © Yale French Studies 1983. Reproduced by permission.

COPYRIGHTED EXCERPTS IN *CLC,* VOLUME 102, WERE REPRODUCED FROM THE FOLLOWING BOOKS:

Birkerts, Sven. From *American Energies: Essays on Fiction.* William Morrow and Company, Inc., 1992. Copyright © 1992 by Sven Birkerts. All rights reserved. Reproduced by permission.—Gioia, Dana. From *Can Poetry Matter?: Essays on Poetry and American Culture.* Graywolf Press, 1992. Copyright © 1992 by Dana Gioia. Reprinted with the permission of Graywolf Press, Saint Paul, Minnesota.—Justice, Donald. From "Meters and Memory" in *The Structure of Verse: Modern Essays on Prosody.* Revised Edition. Edited by Harvey Gross. Copyright © 1966 by Fawcett Publications, Inc. Copyright © 1979 by Harvey Gross. All rights reserved. Reprinted by permission of the author and The Ecco Press.—Klein, Kathleen Gregory. From "Patricia Highsmith" in *And Then There Were Nine: More Women of Mystery.* Edited by Jane S. Bakerman. Bowling Green State University Popular Press, 1985. Copyright © 1985 by Bowling Green State University Popular Press. All rights reserved. Reproduced by permission.—L'Henry Evans, Odette. From "A Feminist Approach to Patricia Highsmith's Fiction" in *American Horror Fiction: From Brockden Brown to Stephen King.* Edited by Brian Docherty. St. Martin's Press, 1990. © the Editorial Board, Lumiere (Co-operative) Press Ltd. 1990. All rights reserved. Reproduced by permission.—Mahoney, MaryKay. From "A Train Running on Two Sets of Tracks: Highsmith's and Hitchcock's Strangers on a Train" in *It's a Print!: Detective Fiction from Page to Screen.* Edited by William Reynolds and Elizabeth A. Trembley. Bowling Green State University Popular Press, 1994. Copyright © 1994 by Bowling Green State University Popular Press. Reproduced by permission.—Van Hooft, Karen S. From *Theory and Practice of*

Madison Smartt Bell
1957-

American novelist and short story writer.

The following entry presents an overview of Bell's career. For further information on his life and works, see *CLC,* Volume 41.

INTRODUCTION

In his novels and short stories Bell has depicted sordid, urban underworlds of drugs, violence, and weird pathologies. His fiction is usually set in New York City and peopled by uprooted Southerners, although the milieus of his later work have ranged from his native, rural American South to London and Haiti. Bell is sometimes connected to the Southern literary tradition because of his heritage and his concern with the sociological motivations of misfits and outcasts. While he has been faulted for using contrived literary devices, trendy subject matter, and occasionally flat characterizations, Bell possesses an imaginative depth, considerable narrative skills, and an evocative style uniquely his own. Andy Solomon has called Bell "one of our most prolific and precocious talents," adding that his "unique wedding of intelligence and craft to a signature angle of vision . . . marks him as one of our more courageous and large-souled talents as well."

Biographical Information

Born August 1, 1957, in Nashville, Tennessee, Bell was raised on his family's farm in Williamson County. He attended Princeton University, where he won several literary prizes for fiction writing and received a summa cum laude B.A. degree in English literature in 1979; he earned a master's degree from Hollins College in 1981. Employed by film and publishing enterprises during his college days, Bell read manuscript and wrote copy for Berkley Publishing Corporation in New York upon graduation from Hollins until 1983, when he published his first novel, *The Washington Square Ensemble*. In 1984 he accepted an assistant professorship in English at Goucher College, where he wrote two novels, *Waiting for the Ending of the World* (1985) and *Straight Cut* (1986). During the academic year 1987-88, Bell participated in the Iowa Writers' Workshop and finished writing the short story collection *Zero db and Other Stories* (1987) and the novel *The Year of Silence* (1987). After returning to his position at Goucher, Bell attended the 1989 Johns Hopkins Writing Seminars, which yielded the novel *Soldier's Joy* (1989). During the 1990s Bell expanded his oeuvre with the publication of another short story collection, *Barking Man and Other Stories* (1990), and three novels, *Doctor Sleep*

(1991), *Save Me, Joe Louis* (1993), and *All Souls' Rising* (1995), which was nominated for the National Book Award.

Major Works

The Washington Square Ensemble is a fast-paced and occasionally violent portrait of the New York City heroin trade. Resembling a jazz composition in its stream-of-consciousness narration by five alternating voices, the novel chronicles one day in the lives of drug dealer Johnny B. Goode and his associates. *Waiting for the End of the World* concerns a group of social misfits who plot to destroy Times Square with a homemade nuclear device, while *Straight Cut,* a highbrow thriller, focuses on a pair of degenerate New York film-makers, Tracy Bateman and Kevin Carter, caught up in a financially lucrative international drug deal, which involves Carter's duped, estranged wife, Lauren, and a double-crossed Bateman. *The Year of Silence* centers on the suicide of a young Manhattan illustrator, Marian, whose tale is recounted by those who knew her at different times in her life. *Soldier's Joy,* Bell's first novel set entirely in the South, relates the story of Thomas Laidlaw, who is white, and his childhood friend Rodney Redmon, who is black. Both men are freshly turned-out Vietnam War veterans trying to sort out their lives in their native Tennessee, but they instead find themselves embroiled in a conflict with the Ku Klux Klan. *Doctor Sleep,* billed as a thinking-man's thriller and set in London, concerns a practicing American hypnotherapist and recovered heroin addict whose insomnia leads him into some freakish encounters while employed by Scotland Yard. *Save Me, Joe Louis* is an episodic novel about two grifting and doomed drifters: Macrea, a young petty thief, and Charlie, an older psychopath. The novel recounts their violent, criminal escapades from New York through Baltimore to Tennessee and South Carolina. *All Souls' Rising,* an historical novel, tells of the brutal and grisly Haitian slave revolt of 1791 as seen through the eyes of several characters. Bell's short story collections display his virtuosity in the form, most notably in "Holding Together" from *Barking Dog,* in which a wise laboratory mouse tries to find solace from the indignities of science in the *I Ching.*

Critical Reception

Bell's novels and short stories generally have received enthusiastic critical acclaim, although some reviewers have wondered why, as did Sven Birkerts who emphatically pronounced, "Bell's every sentence is *not* a joy." Most critics have commented on "his conspicuous sympathy for the alienated and the bruised," as Solomon has stated, but Roberta Silman has noted that Bell displays "an uncanny understanding of the way many people must struggle to live." While David Montrose and others have suggested that some of Bell's characters were "cardboard-flat and forgettable," Alan Davis has remarked that Bell's "sense of character and place is always sure-handed." Some critics, like Davis, have preferred "the compressed dazzle" of Bell's short fiction; Paul D. McCarthy has called his short stories "a splendid testament to Bell's superb narrative, stylistic gifts and passionate humanity." Although Bell has earned the reputation of "one of the South's most promising young writers," as Greg Johnson observed, others have questioned the regional character of Bell's work. Dwight Garner has indicated the significance of *All Souls' Rising* to Bell's literary development: "In earlier novels . . . Bell demonstrated that he was a young American novelist of the first rank. *All Souls' Rising,* however, puts him on another level as an artist."

PRINCIPAL WORKS

CRITICISM

Jack Fuller (review date 22 November 1987)

SOURCE: "'Silence' Is Golden," in *Chicago Tribune Books,* November 22, 1987, p. 9.

[*In the positive review below, Fuller focuses on the structure of* The Year of Silence.]

A promising but elusive young woman, admired for all the usual reasons, dies of an overdose in Manhattan. Whether the story of this sadly ordinary event comes to anything depends on how the writer decides to tell it.

He can make it a melodrama or a cocaine thriller. He can find in it a tragedy of innocence or the embodiment of the emptiness of existence. He can lapse into cynical black humor or succumb to the sentimentality of despair. Or if he is good enough, he can make something new, reveal things we hadn't known before.

For Madison Smartt Bell in his latest book, *The Year of Silence,* the death is like a crystal, a transparent, sharp-edged fact that refracts all light and separates the colors. The story becomes many stories, a collection, each of them in its own way pure and whole.

The most trivial way to describe Bell's approach is to say that every chapter examines the death of the young woman known as Marian from a different point of view: that of her lover, her drug connection, the street freak she gives money to, the cop who is called to the scene.

This technique leaves obscure the forces that propel Marian to her death. The voices are confused; none of them can tell us what we want to know about the meaning of Marian's life and death.

Even when, midway through the book, she speaks to us, she does not know herself. Yet there is no sense of the author's having forsaken the real work of fiction, its justification and its truth. *The Year of Silence* is not empty. It is ambiguous but plentiful, as full and yet unresolved as life.

In a deeper sense, the book opens out beyond the confines of Marian and those with whom she comes in contact.

Without once becoming cynical, Bell's stories give a view of the modern city more uncompromising than most of the more straightforward urban narratives I have read. It is Hugh Selby's *Last Exit to Brooklyn* with the brutality brought down to a scale that anyone can identify with. It is not minimalist, but it is an example of how less can be more.

Bell's restraint with violence and squalor magnifies the effect, the power to reshape the way we see the world.

And it is a measure of the strength of Bell's book that, although it is a collection of fragments, we never once feel that, by calling it a novel, the publishers deceived us. Instead, we are forced to examine whether the deception is really in those other works called novels that in effect say, "Here is the story. Here is all of it. It happened just this way."

The irony of conventional taste and marketing is that *The Year of Silence* will in all likelihood be a modest book, read principally by other writers and by that undaunted band of pure readers who are willing to take a chance.

But while the story of Marian's death does not make for a big book in length or publicity, it is capable of rewarding a very wide audience.

Anyone who values grace in language, elegance of structure and the magic of finding meaning in literature's subtle ordering of fact will find in *The Year of Silence* a book that is worth the price of a dozen others that, for whatever reasons of enterprise, are thrust before the public as the best that American publishing sells.

Mark Royden Winchell (review date Spring 1989)

SOURCE: "Other Voices, Other Runes," in *Sewanee Review*, Vol. XCII, No. 2, Spring, 1989, pp. xliii-xliv.

[*In the following excerpt, Winchell focuses on Bell's role as author of* The Washington Square Ensemble.]

The novelist starts out as God, creating a world that he knows and controls. In deciding how to use his powers, he makes a metaphysical choice. With the rise of modernism and the more recent emergence of that hybrid known as postmodernism, we have seen the demise of the author-as-God. All notable exceptions conceded, the dominant point of view in twentieth-century fiction has been limited and unreliable. In Ron Loewinsohn's *Magnetic Field* (*s*) and Madison Smart Bell's *The Washington Square Ensemble* we find two cur-

rent examples of this trend. Both novels use multiple narration to convey the elusiveness of reality, but they ultimately make very different epistemological statements. . . .

In Bell's *The Washington Square Ensemble* we are far removed from the intellectual games that dominate Ron Loewinsohn's novel. Bell's characters do not live in a model-train village, but in New York City. They make their living dealing in heroin and, for the most part, speculate only about their own lives. They also have voices. Bell has his characters speak for themselves in distinctive rhythms and cadences. Although they all have different perspectives, the reality that they apprehend is not meant to be the product of anyone's imagination. When they seek to escape that reality, it is through such normal opiates as booze, drugs, and religion.

Bell's protagonist is Johnny Dellacroce, a free-lance hood who smokes Kools, calls himself Johnny B. Goode, and generally seeks to emulate Norman Mailer's paradigm of the white negro. Johnny's lieutenants include a former hit man who is called Holy Mother because of his childhood piety, a gentle seven-foot Black Muslim named Yusuf Ali, and a voodoo-crazed Puerto Rican known as Santa Barbara. The other major character is an alcoholic jazz artist whom Johnny has dubbed Porco Miserio (in his role as name-giver Johnny is an American Adam). Although each of these characters takes his turn in telling the story (toward the end they are assisted by dialogues between two cops), we are led to believe that they are acting under the spell of Porco's magic storytelling rock. This entails what Wayne Booth might call the "implied author."

Topical references to recent gang wars, an extended account of the Attica uprising, and convincing local geography help to ground *The Washington Square Ensemble* in time and place. This novel, however, is intended to be more than another tale of urban depravity. Owing to their belief in the supernatural, Bell's characters sometimes resemble big-city versions of the God-haunted freaks of Flannery O'Connor (like O'Connor's The Misfit, Holy Mother is a potential saint turned pathological killer). By the end of the novel even the hard-boiled Johnny B. has experienced a moral education. When Yusuf Ali and Santa Barbara risk their own safety to rescue him from danger, they violate Johnny's rules and save his life.

In Robert Penn Warren's "Old Nigger on One-Mule Cart" God is described as a magnet who gives shape to the iron filings of our lives. For Ron Loewinsohn there is no single magnet—only many possible magnetic field(s). What saves us from solipsism is those moments when our fields intersect (thus eliminating the optional *s*). Such moments occur considerably more frequently in Madison Smartt Bell's novel because he sees the world not as colliding fields of perception but as a place as solid and mysterious as a story-telling rock.

Greg Johnson (review date 4 June 1989)

SOURCE: "Two Numbed Vietnam Vets Turn to the Soil," in *Chicago Tribune Books,* June 4, 1989, sec. 14, p. 5.

[*In the following review, Johnson faults the "moribund" characterization and "somnolent" pacing of* Soldier's Joy, *but concludes that "the determination and risk-taking evident in* Soldier's Joy *are likely to bear fruit in [Bell's] future work."*]

Madison Smartt Bell has earned a reputation as one of the South's most promising young writers. In four previous novels and one story collection, he has written skillfully about the Northeast—especially New York City and urban New Jersey—as well as his native South.

His first novel, *Washington Square,* was a harrowing tale of New York's drug underworld, while *Waiting for the End of the World* focused on a disturbed group of men—including a drug dealer and a Vietnam veteran—who plot to blow up Times Square. The stories collected in *Zero db* clearly illustrated Bell's dual focus—neo-Faulknerian tales of race relations in a declining South appearing alongside briskly paced stories set in New York, Newark and Hoboken.

It is clear that Bell's allegiance is still divided between the urban Northeast and his Southern heritage. His new novel, *Soldier's Joy,* is an unsatisfying return to Southern soil.

It is clear that Bell's allegiance is still divided between the urban Northeast and his Southern heritage.
—Greg Johnson

Lengthy and slow-paced, *Soldier's Joy* focuses on Thomas Laidlaw, a Vietnam veteran who returns from the war to sort out his life on a Tennessee farm, and Rodney Redmon, a black man who served alongside Laidlaw and has spent time in prison on a trumped-up charge. Redmon also ends up in the South, almost penniless, and takes a demeaning warehouse job.

Because Bell's previous novels have been so fast-paced, one is puzzled and then annoyed by this book's somnolent pace. The first 100 pages are devoted to Laidlaw's life on the farm, which consists of little more than his walking through woods and pastures, picking his banjo and keeping his mind as blank as possible. He prefers doing nothing at all, and the novel follows his every move as he does it.

At least the second section, which focuses on Redmon, contains some dramatic conflict, since Redmon has a temper

and often clashes with his white fellow employees. But his inner life is nearly as moribund as Laidlaw's: "The time had passed slowly, though nothing much had happened in it that seemed worth remembering now."

Evidently Bell is attempting to portray the numbing after-effects of the war upon his two heroes. But by detailing the ordinary physical routine of their daily lives and giving the reader almost nothing of their past experiences and emotions, he has produced a turgid novel whose characters never manage to come to life.

Laidlaw's sections are particularly wearing, since his attitude toward his war experience is pseudo-stoic. The writing here often suggests Hemingway on a bad day, as when Laidlaw muses upon "his spell in the Mekong Delta, where he had not had a pleasant time."

We are halfway through the novel before Laidlaw and Redmon find one another. The remaining chapters focus on their friendship and the racial hatred that threatens to erupt as a result. Near the end of the book, the two men are pitted against a violent group of Klansmen, a confrontation that serves as a potentially effective analogue to Laidlaw and Redmon's Vietnam experience. But this dramatic scene is too little, too late.

It seems likely that Bell's title is an allusion to William Faulkner's first novel, *Soldiers' Pay,* for some of Bell's short stories show Faulkner's influence. Yet the allusion may be more meaningful than Bell intended, for *Soldiers' Pay,* which deals with the after-effects of World War I upon another moribund "hero," is one of Faulkner's most contrived and least convincing works.

Only 32, Madison Smartt Bell is clearly still struggling to find his voice. This novel and certain of his short stories suggest that he does best when he avoids Southern settings and sticks to what he knows best. (Bell was a schoolboy during the Vietnam conflict). Despite this disappointing performance, however, the determination and risk-taking evident in *Soldier's Joy* are likely to bear fruit in his future work.

Rick DeMarinis (review date 8 April 1990)

SOURCE: "The Hero Is a Mouse," in *The New York Times Book Review,* Vol. 95, April 8, 1990, p. 11.

[*In the following review, DeMarinis analyzes the themes of pain and search-and-rescue in* Barking Man.]

A collection of short stories that work well together has the effect of standing the reader in a world he recognizes but is no longer on comfortably familiar terms with. *Barking Man,* Madison Smartt Bell's second collection of stories and seventh book, satisfies the standard with unwavering compassion. The world these 10 stories conjure is a shifty, dangerous place, requiring of its inhabitants small acts of daily heroism. That these heroic deeds sometimes resemble madness or criminal mischief does not compromise their necessity or moral authenticity. If anything, they are all the more laudable because the odds for success are always dismally low. In each case, the reader finds himself cheering for these outgunned characters because Mr. Bell himself cares so deeply about them.

I hesitate to describe the wonderful opening story, **"Holding Together"**, for fear of undermining the gravity of what I've just said. It is a story of heroism and suffering, and of blind injustice. The imprisoned hero is not only subjected to mental torture and physical disfigurement at the "hands" of his fellow prisoners, he also experiences a devastating crisis of belief. His drinking water is laced with insidious, mind-fragmenting drugs and, worse, he gradually comes to realize that he is intended for grievous biological experimentation.

A collection of short stories that work well together has the effect of standing the reader in a world he recognizes but is no longer on comfortably familiar terms with. *Barking Man* . . . satisfies the standard with unwavering compassion.
—*Rick DeMarinis*

The hero of **"Holding Together"** is a white mouse. Not your ordinary white mouse—but then who is so knowledgeable about the perception and sensitivity of other creatures as to insist on their ordinariness? This mouse is, rather, an Oriental white mouse who, having committed to memory the entire *I Ching*, divines his fate by studying the hexagrams revealed by his makeshift yarrow stalks. In hands as skilled as Mr. Bell's, the short story is the most dynamic and flexible of literary forms, and **"Holding Together"** proves this out. We not only care about this bookish mouse, we suffer his pain and are humbled by his steadfast devotion to his fellow mice and to the values that have made his survival not merely possible but necessary. A story with a more humanistic theme is hard to imagine.

As the stories in *Barking Man* make plain, survival can be a triumph of the spirit—but it can also be a siege of cruelty. In **"Black and Tan,"** a tobacco farmer suffers, in under two years, the deaths of his wife and his two grown children. When a minister, at the funeral of the man's daughter, tries to console him by saying, "You're surviving. Today's today and then there'll be tomorrow," the farmer replies, "That's

right, and it's a curse." Oblivion is preferable to such pain, but the farmer, who has no observable religious views that might see him through his agony, becomes, by pure contrariness and grit, an existential hero who leads a productive and exemplary life, first by breeding dogs and then by turning his home into a shelter for unmanageably delinquent boys.

Pain is the hard stylus that engraves the world of these stories. We see this not only in the duress endured by most of the characters but in the fine line details of their struggles, for which Mr. Bell has a sharp and loving eye. Someone's version of paradise might be the south of France but, like severe sunburn and a beach full of foot bruising pebbles, the French Riviera of **"Petit Cachou"** is grained with hurt. This Mediterranean vacationland is the stage for a California family's brief descent into purgatory. **"Petit Cachou"** is an astringent novella in which the lives of utterly dissimilar characters are cleverly braided together in a comedy of adolescent libido and parental dismay. As the expatriate peddler Ton-Ton Detroit, the one character in the story who believes in and respects the treacherous magic of his unpredictable surroundings, reflects, "The world was full of a number of things, many of them possible."

This cautionary proposition can be extended to many of Mr. Bell's stories, subverting and controlling a reality that has lost predictability and definition. In **"Dragon's Seed,"** an impoverished old woman of questionable stability, Mackie Loudon, tries to save a boy from a sadistic child pornographer. Both Mackie and the pornographer live on the crumbling urban fringe, an area indifferently policed and mostly invisible to the selective eye of mainstream society. This isolation provides the setting for a life-and-death struggle that has the moral dimensions of myth.

Many of Mr. Bell's heroes dwell in this disposable outland that exists alongside conspicuous prosperity. Their stories are often about the attempted search and rescue, against impossible odds, of a lost mate or child. In **"Move On Up,"** Mr. Bell puts us squarely on the side of a drifter named Hal, one of society's forgotten members. Such people are not lovable—Mr. Bell is no sentimentalist—but they are observed so acutely and with such brave affection that we suspend our judgment and are compelled to walk the streets in their salvaged shoes. Mr. Bell can convey in a single image—in a park, for example, where "a statue of a man in a three piece suit made an expansive gesture toward the pile of litter at its base"—the inflexibility and blindness of the urban landscape, and in a manner that speaks with the economy of poetry.

The would-be searcher and rescuer in **"Finding Natasha"** says: "I feel responsible . . . for everybody. . . . It's got to be like a long chain of people, see? I take hold of her and she takes hold of somebody else and finally somebody takes hold of you, maybe, and then if every body holds on tight, we all get out of here." This effectively describes the spirit that travels through these admirable stories. It is a spirit that insists there is something in all of us that is still worthy of rescue. And it is what makes *Barking Man* such a humane and mature book, the work of an important and talented writer.

Patrick McGrath (review date 15 April 1990)

SOURCE: "Misfits and Outcasts," in *Washington Post Book World,* April 15, 1990, pp. 7-8.

[*In the mixed review below, McGrath ponders the themes of abuse and vulnerability in* Barking Man, *suggesting that "the events that befall Bell's misfits and outcasts lack significant power in either existential or literary terms."*]

Madison Smartt Bell has been publishing fiction at a very smart clip since 1983—five novels and two collections in a mere seven years. In much of that work he has depicted characters both urban and rural whose lives are marked by poverty, failure, madness and futility.

Most of the stories in *Barking Man* work the same territory, and one begins to wonder why Bell returns so doggedly to the dirt and dinge of existences scraped to the bone. For his approach to his subject matter lacks the engaged analytic vigor that Orwell brought to the down-and-out, and the only Beckettian impulse apparent, the only suggestion, that is, of the derelict as epitome of modern godless man, is contained in the idea that even those who've hit rock-bottom must construct some sort of meaning for their lives. For the most part these stories tend to concentrate on the simple behavioral routines of street life, and in the end the events that befall Bell's misfits and outcasts lack significant power in either existential or literary terms.

"Move On Up" is about a man called Hal. As readers of Bell's novel *Waiting for the End of the World,* and some of the stories in *Zero db,* will recall, the author likes to devote many paragraphs to solitary figures walking city streets and encountering empty beer cans and other trash. Hal wanders about downtown Manhattan making a buck here and there unloading trucks. Nothing very much happens. It emerges that he is listlessly looking for a woman called Judith whom he slept with once or twice and who has since probably died as a result of her addiction to crack. In the course of his search he gives Judith's son half his small stash of cash. Then he hits a crack dealer with a bit of metal railing. By the end of the story he has wandered up to Grand Central, and still hasn't established for certain that Judith is dead, and if so, where her body has been taken.

Another story, **"Finding Natasha,"** works the same theme,

the fruitless search for a lost woman, in the same mode of conventional third-person realism, and here too the assumption seems to be that it's enough merely to sketch a few days in the life of a loser engaged in a somewhat aimless quest purely for its own sake. The final image, of Natasha slumped on a bench in Washington Square Park with infected needle tracks in her arms, is bleak and stark and arresting. The irony here, that this is what our man has been looking for all along, is as black as it comes; but merely to illustrate the horror feels like little more than an exercise in gratuitous nihilism.

The fiction improves when an attempt is made to suggest not only how but why lives get blighted, why people get trapped in vicious downward spirals, "Sometimes you don't get but one mistake," says the woman who narrates **"Customs of the Country,"** "if the one you pick is bad enough." She has been in a relationship with a minor drug dealer and has become hooked on Dilaudid. When her man is arrested she goes into withdrawal, in the course of which she falls into a rage with her little boy and hurts him badly. The child is taken into foster care, and the mother lives a blameless life for a year in the hope of getting him back. Meanwhile the man in the next apartment is regularly beating his wife.

When the narrator at last realizes she has lost her child for good she goes next door and hits the man hard in the face with a frying pan. She then invites the abused woman to leave town with her, but the woman cannot. "I just didn't know what difference it had made, and chances were it had made none at all," reflects the narrator. This line could be spoken by many of Bell's characters, but here it has real depth and poignance, for here an attempt is made to set the character's misery in the context of the larger social forces shaping her fate. Also, the splicing of the two instances of abuse has solid psychological resonance: It is a telling example of the displacement of guilt, and it imposes on the story a strong formal design.

"Black and Tan" is the nicely handled tale of a tobacco farmer called Peter Jackson who, after losing his family, takes to training both Dobermans and delinquent punks, the latter sent to him by a local judge. Jackson gradually emerges as a fully rounded and enigmatic figure, but the story is finally disappointing. Asked why he has decided to give up his work with the delinquents, Jackson says that "a man is not an animal," and this rather banal truism is all we're left with. **"Dragon's Seed"** is a gothic tale about an old, mad, woman sculptor called Mackie Loudon who befriends a little boy and who, like the narrator of **"Customs of the Country,"** wreaks violent revenge on an abusive man, the man who'd been sexually exploiting the child for profit.

But these few aside, the stories in *Barking Man* are unsatisfying. The title story has nothing to commend it—a man begins behaving like a dog for no clear reason and to no clear purpose—and **"Petit Cachou,"** which runs over 60 pages, is the tiresomely dull description of a small set of Americans in the south of France. Almost nothing happens, and much attention is paid to the simplest activities and thought processes of the few thin characters. By the end one has no clear idea why this story needed to be told.

The twin themes of vulnerability and abuse fuel the best work in this collection, and the quirkiest instance of this is the first story, **"Holding Together."** A small band of Chinese laboratory mice is being subjected to a nasty experimental procedure, probably ingestion of caffeine, and the task facing their leader, our narrator, is how to maintain morale and solidarity. He consults what he can remember of the *I Ching*, a venerable Oriental philosophy that explains and dignifies the suffering of tiny creatures victimized by a power too vast for them to understand, a power which, in this case, makes the mice turn their violence on one another rather than upon their oppressor. Our narrator contemplates the possibility that the universe may not in fact be ordered according to the wise constructs of the *I Ching*, but may instead be random, meaningless and chaotic; he wonders if all attempts to find meaning are delusional. "At times I've been tempted to wonder what offense I could possibly have committed to bring such a punishment down on me," he says, and a little later: "What if . . . every geometric figure of my so carefully constructed memory would mean no more than an idiot's unintended scrawl. . ."

The predicament of the three little mice, with their arcane trove of inherited wisdom, would seem to stand as a paradigm for many of Bell's characters, who tend to be similarly helpless in the face of fate, similarly prone to constructing meanings where none exist, and similarly inclined to displace their aggression on their fellow-suffers. This is a familiar analysis of the human condition; to render it fresh, and fictively redeem the victims, requires a copious infusion of literary grace and a keen sense of the social determinants of misery, both of which are only intermittently present here.

Paul D. McCarthy (review date 30 September 1990)

SOURCE: "Pounding Out the Dents," in *Los Angeles Times Book Review,* September 30, 1990, p. 12.

[*Below, McCarthy considers the moral progression of the stories in* Barking Man, *calling the collection "a splendid testament to Bell's superb narrative, stylistic gifts and passionate humanity."*]

Light, shadows and light. That is the moral progression that novelist Madison Smartt Bell develops in the 10 tales of *Barking Man and Other Stories,* his haunting, protean, compassionate second collection.

Through the five stories that comprise Part I, the characters, human and nonhuman—the narrator of the opening story, **"Holding Together,"** is a scholarly white mouse—are beaten by life. They suffer, struggle, are defeated, make tragic mistakes, but somehow endure. At their core, they find courage and hope, sometimes even honor. Their inner dignity may get battered, but they pound most of the dents out.

The tone darkens when we enter Part II. Alf, the **"Barking Man,"** educated and highly intelligent, is unable to bear the responsibility of being a human adult, and while he evolves a way of coping with life that has him retreating into canine fantasy, he simultaneously sacrifices one of his most important capacities—being able to love—because that too carries responsibility, of which he wants no part.

Bell's profound compassion and his wise, forgiving vision that avoids contempt and harsh judgment but is never blind to the world's ugliness, are given wondrously varied and eloquent expression in these stories. His voice and style is so natural, so brilliantly authentic and individual, that we immediately enter the mind of the narrator or the world of the characters.

Evidence of Bell's stylistic virtuosity in the face of technical difficulty is the perfect pitch of **"Holding Together."** In this story of three white mice of superior cultural breeding, sharing the ancestral "Legend of the Voyage from the Orient" and recently bought by a laboratory to be fed an experimental drug, the narrator, a mouse of the Scrivener class, watches with horror as the drug begins to make his companions psychotic. Bringing all of his philosophical resources to bear to hold the three together, the narrator mouse thinks: "Put aside those dreams of owls and snakes, for death must come to all mice finally, in one form or another. No, what I fear far more deeply is chaos." The mind of this credible mouse is the most intellectually refined of the whole collection.

The other stories, though sharing an omniscient point of view, reveal different tones, rhythms and levels of complexity and elegance, as the settings shift from the French Riviera to New York, Alabama, London.

Another dimension of this collection is the powerful recurrence of certain motifs which, compellingly, are always directly or indirectly related to the unifying moral principle.

For example **"Finding Natasha"** and **"Move On Up"** are about men looking for women. Stuart, a newly cleaned-up drug addict, wanders through Manhattan and Brooklyn hoping to find Natasha. At one point, he explains to a sympathetic hooker that he feels a survivor's responsibility. If he can help just one person, even Natasha, an almost hopeless junkie, who then can help someone else, perhaps he can precipitate a chain reaction of assistance.

Hal, homeless and unemployed, is seeking Judith's body in **"Move On Up"** because he suspects she's killed herself in a crack attack, and he wants to bury her with a little dignity.

Both Hal and Stuart are near the bottom materially but they shine spiritually.

The entire extraordinary collection is a splendid testament to Bell's superb narrative, stylistic gifts and passionate humanity.

Elizabeth Tallent (review date 6 January 1991)

SOURCE: "Hypnotist, Heal Thyself," in *The New York Times Book Review,* Vol. 96, January 6, 1991, p. 11.

[*In the review below, Tallent discusses the interplay of the ordinary with the extraordinary in* Doctor Sleep.]

A harrowing wakefulness sets the tone for Madison Smartt Bell's sixth novel. Adrian Strother is an American living in London, a recovered heroin addict and practicing hypnotherapist who is expertly gentle with his clientele of insomniacs and phobics; on eight hours a night, he'd make quite a trustworthy narrator. He has the tolerant cool that is characteristic of Mr. Bell's protagonists, an observant detachment backed, in his case, by his prowess in the martial arts. But as *Doctor Sleep* begins, Adrian, his sleeplessness resisting his own mesmeric powers, is treading delicately along an insomniac edge where consciousness dissolves two ways—into manic hallucination or dulled, drifting numbness. Slyly, this "thriller," as its jacket copy has it, shines a speculative light on the shadowy interplay of perception with delusion, dream with reason.

Mr. Bell's prose, which generally moves at a nimble narrative clip, has the habit of rising now and then to set pieces that lyrically detail a particular process. In *Soldier's Joy,* it is the traditional claw-hammer method of banjo playing; in *The Year of Silence,* the performance of the 21st Goldberg Variation. In *Doctor Sleep,* oddly enough, the set pieces include the mercy killing of a white mouse and the dramatic appeal by which a roomful of heroin addicts are stirred to their first wan hope of recovery, as well as a hypnotist's stage trick of anesthetizing a subject before forcing a spike between his jaws: "Just where a horse's bit would go, the space glittered damply against the back of his throat." The incongruousness of this list reflects Mr. Bell's fascination with those times when, as a character in *The Year of Silence*

phrases it, "the extraordinary mixed and blended so thoroughly with the ordinary that it could not be distinguished in the end."

Madison Smartt Bell renders the marginal, the underground, the twisted or seedy with quirky attentiveness. His array of lost souls gets onto the page without the least pre-emptive hint of authorial sympathy, yet he catches the poignant in the freakish. In *Doctor Sleep* the agoraphobic Eleanor Peavey, "hair done in very early Princess Di and a Sloane Ranger pearl string around her neck," displays under hypnosis the multiple personalities of a foul-mouthed tart and a terrified sexually abused child. Another client appears in a "black leather jacket, naturally, scuffed and cracked, with swastikas and other inspiriting devices daubed on it at random in white house paint." He wants Adrian's expertise—which Adrian can't grant—to help him kick heroin.

> **Madison Smartt Bell renders the marginal, the underground, the twisted or seedy with quirky attentiveness. His array of lost souls gets onto the page without the least pre-emptive hint of authorial sympathy, yet he catches the poignant in the freakish.**
> **—*Elizabeth Tallent***

The ranker of these lost souls are dangerous. Adrian is followed down slum streets by a pair of punks employed by Karnock, a notorious drug trafficker. Adrian's talents are required by someone called the Dutchman, possibly an Interpol policeman, who is after Karnock; to secure Adrian's cooperation the Dutchman threatens him with deportation, when for Adrian a return to New York would guarantee a return to heroin. Stirred into this mix are the running newspaper accounts of the deaths of little girls, victims of a serial killer, whose portraits keep turning up in the London tabloids and for whom Adrian feels a bleak sort of pity.

Unfortunately, some of the elements in the novel's mix of the ordinary and the extraordinary fail to convince. Adrian's habit of recondite apocryphal quotation is hard to reconcile with his essentially sardonic, street-smart voice, and less comes of his otherworldly flights than from his roundhouse kicks. And Adrian's relationship with his now-you-see-her-now-you-don't girlfriend, Clara, has a hollowness that comes not from her most recent disappearance but from the unconvincing quality of the scenes and exchanges between them.

Soon after Clara leaves him, there appears in Adrian's mailbox the small metal cog that his New York lover, Nicole, used as a signal that she'd be in touch with him. ("Nicole and I had decided to exchange *bone* rings," Adrian says, explaining his bond with her, "because they had no monetary value and therefore couldn't be converted into scag.") Adrian's last meeting with Nicole in a London hotel, though interestingly wary, ends with him easing her to sleep: "I saw her eyes roll under the lids, looking at something in a dream. I could do that so easily sometimes . . . to someone else."

Eventually, exhaustion and the surrealistic brutality that he has witnessed bring Adrian to the lowest possible point—death is the biggest Doctor Sleep, and the last remaining piece of consciousness, begging for erasure, is despair. Now someone else, someone as magical as he has aimed to be, is needed to save him. Lofty though his spiritual ambitions have been, it's the value of the ordinary that strikes Adrian as a revelation. Dark though its vision has been, this vivid insomniac jag of a novel ends healingly in sleep.

Gabrielle Donnelly (review date 20 January 1991)

SOURCE: "In the Wake of Dr. Strother," in *Los Angeles Times Book Review,* January 20, 1991, p. 8.

[*In the following review, Donnelly admires the unreal, dreamlike narrative and atmosphere of* Doctor Sleep.]

To say that an air of unreality hangs over a book is not usually a compliment. To say it about *Doctor Sleep,* the new novel by Madison Smartt Bell, is to describe one of its greatest strengths.

Let's start with the title. Adrian Strother is not a doctor—although people persist in addressing him as one—but a hypnotherapist: as for the sleep, he spends most of the long weekend of the book trying to break a bout of insomnia which has for several days been driving him to the edge of sanity. He is a displaced person anyway, a hip young New Yorker who left America to escape a drug addiction, now lives in London's seedy Notting Hill, and during the book travels all over London from the British Museum reading room to a pub in Chelsea to Harrods tea room to Wapping docks to, well, you name the part of London, he goes there.

When he does go out, he is followed—or is he?—by two hoods, one of whom sports a Statue of Liberty haircut; when he stays near his home, he is blasted by the famously jubilant—and potentially violent—Notting Hill carnival, which is going on. His girlfriend has left him; his pet snake refuses to eat the live mouse he has given it for dinner. He has conversations with people who are not there, and occasionally cures wounds by self-hypnosis. Often, he stops to ponder on his real specialty, the Hermetic myth and the writings of 16th-Century philosopher Giordano Bruno. It's none of it quite like real life.

It is, on the other hand, an extremely vivid account of the way real life seems when you can't quite handle it. Adrian Strother simply never has the time to catch up with himself. During three days, he finds himself chasing his girlfriend, being chased by a drug trafficker, dealing with a former junkie friend from New York now turned anti-drug evangelist, resurrecting an old love affair, taking on a new client with multiple personalities, performing a magic show, half-killing himself practicing an Oriental kind of self-defense . . . the list goes on and on. Always, he is remembering he is late for an appointment; always he is side-tracked somehow into another. Throughout the book, his eyes itch; he tries to eat and cannot; he drinks and regrets it; he longs for and dreads the night. As a portrait of a man on the brink, it is remarkable.

The book has not one story line but several, and—inevitably with so much crammed into 304 pages—some are more successful than others. A subplot involving a brutal series of murders is brought to a too-pat ending, but adds a nice frisson of suspense on the way there. The Hermetic myth is invoked constantly and with an air of great significance, but since the myth never is explained precisely, it is difficult to see quite what point is being made by it. On the other hand, Strothers' confusion about why his girlfriend has left him is both realistic and moving; and a story about a woman with multiple personalities packs a real wallop.

> **[*Doctor Sleep* is] an extremely vivid account of the way real life seems when you can't quite handle it. . . . As a portrait of a man on the brink, it is remarkable.**
> **—Gabrielle Donnelly**

If all this is beginning to sound either confusing or depressing, it is neither: It's a rip-roaring good read.

Even the book's great failing, its portrait of the English, ends up by adding to the atmosphere. Bell is an American who clearly has lived in, and loves, London: His portrayal of the city itself—accurate down to the names of the most obscure alleys, the nightmarish rock and bump of the tube trains, the flowers in the churchyard by Putney Bridge—is such as can only be born of deep affection. But its inhabitants, the Londoners, are no more than cartoons. They are called names which no one has been called for years, like Sid, or Nell, and their dialogue—lots of "or-right, Guv" and "you shut your bloody hole"—is straight out of the worst of bad movies. In other books, this would seriously impede the enjoyment; in the strange dreamlike world of Adrian Strother, it actually becomes part of it.

Apart from this, the language of the book is a joy. Listen to this for a miserable morning: "It was gray, grim gray, in the cold bedroom, and the air had the feel of wet cement." Or this for a crowd scene: "I felt like a particle of a lot of toothpaste being slowly rolled toward the top of the tube." Or this for two karate partners: "Trust someone to almost kill you barehanded, but not quite; trust yourself to do the same for him . . . There's nothing that feels quite like that, though perhaps a couple of things come close."

All in all, *Doctor Sleep* is an extraordinary book, haunting, overwhelming, sometimes confusing, altogether unforgettable. You may find some of its passages too long; you might be irritated by the frequent, not always explained, jumps from reality to fantasy and back again. But there is a pretty good guarantee, when you have read it, that the next time you have insomnia, or jet lag, or a hangover, or are simply feeling too stressed to cope, you will find yourself thinking of Adrian Strother.

Mary Louise Weaks and Madison Smartt Bell (interview date August 1992)

SOURCE: An interview with Madison Smartt Bell, in *Southern Review,* Vol. 30, No. 1, January, 1994, pp. 1-12.

[*In the following interview, which originally took place in August, 1992, Weaks questioned Bell about the southernness of his fiction, the influence of the Fugitives/Agrarians on his work, and the future of southern literature.*]

[*Mary Louise Weaks:*] *You've told me several times that you consider yourself a southern writer, yet so many places and people that you create are alien to southerners.*

[Madison Smartt Bell:] Well, maybe not so much as you think. I didn't write in southern settings for a long time because I've read so much work by southerners that did use southern settings. There were two generations of writers before me who were very good, that I greatly admired. So I felt released when I discovered urban life, which I didn't know anything about as a literary subject. Not that it hadn't been written about; I just hadn't read it. So it was then easy for me to start that way. And I think that was a good thing, because to that urban landscape and society, I brought a southern literary approach and stylistic conventions and also some attitudes that I got from southern writers.

What sort of attitudes?

I think a lot of what I ended up feeling about city life is stated in the abstract in Walker Percy's essays, in *The Message in the Bottle* and so on. His whole idea about apocalypse, which in its way I think is related—even though he

comes at it from a very different angle—to the whole Agrarian idea about the way the world is going because of certain decisions that were made about how society would become increasingly technological and industrial. And the Agrarians (I think) saw those as being deliberate decisions capable of being made or not rather than as an inexorable teleological process in history. And I think that they were right. So you have those two things meeting each other in a way in a lot of my work, including all the urban stuff.

So you see your freaks in the city as very much related to southern freaks?

Well, they just seem to be like people to me. I thought they were people with whom I felt a certain kinship a lot of times. It was pointed out to me by reviewers just how fringy and in many ways socially undesirable these people were. I wasn't really thinking about it that way. I think that was naive, but there we are. I also think my association with fringe characters is a little bit inaccurate really—if you look at all the books—because not all of them are really like that.

Your ability to create voices has been very much praised by the critics. I wonder how much that ability has been influenced by your southern background.

Yes, at that point all the clichés pop out of your mouth automatically. It's something that has been highlighted for me by being married to someone who is not a southerner, and it drives her really crazy sometimes that all conversation takes place in the form of anecdotes, a kind of complicated exchange of anecdotes. I'm sure you're familiar with that, too. Elsewhere in the country it is apparently just not like that. You don't get a shaggy-dog story when you simply ask what time it is, or which way it is to the mall, in Topeka. Whereas in the South you very likely will, and that influences everyone. That's a kind of approach to wrapping the language around the world, I guess.

Do you find yourself thinking about place and community as you write?

Not consciously, no. But if I look back at the New York City stuff, which I think seems anomalous to a lot of people who are trying to figure out what to make of my claim to be, truly, a southern writer, you do see that those books are repeatedly drawn to communities of one kind or another that are trying to hold themselves together in a situation of diaspora, like the Russian Orthodox/White Russian community in New Jersey that figures in *Waiting for the End of the World.* Black Islam and the very specialized Puerto Rican religion Santería that is practiced in New York. The Mafia is like that too (less benign). I look back on this now and I see it makes a certain kind of sense for me to be drawn to that, being who I am. I was in some ways in a similar situation, except that there were no cliques or claques of southerners around that I particularly wanted to get into. In fact, I tended to steer clear of them—the identifiable little southern subsets at Princeton University, and then in New York, too, I was pretty much out of that kind of thing.

I certainly wasn't thinking about it then. But it comes up in the books over and over again: the ways in which people do remain faithful to their origins.

It seems that with the publication of each of your books you're turning back more and more to the South. Do you see this turning to the South as a sort of personal escape and return?

What it is more for me is that I needed to do some books that were not set in the South to prevent me from just turning out imitations of southern writings I admire because, like I said before, I'm much, much better-informed about southern writers up to 1945 than I am about anybody else, or, at any rate, I was at the time that I wrote those first books because of the nature of my education. So now—and indeed around the time I started writing *Soldier's Joy* I thought of this—I can write a novel that takes place on a Tennessee farm that will still sound like me, will sound like I wrote it and not like a bad Robert Penn Warren imitator wrote it, which is my fear.

It was nice to see I could do it. That was in a lot of ways a kind of strange mnemonic exercise I had done. I wrote about half of *Soldier's Joy* in England and the other half in Iowa City. I deliberately did not put it on my family's farm, but I put it on one that's quite nearby. I made an imaginary place by taking different features of this little valley and scrambling them up together so none of it is really totally recognizable, but it does all come out of my own experience—I was trying to reconstruct it at a distance, which is a kind of weird thing to do.

Is that typical of your work? Do you work from places you know or people you know?

Yes, places especially. I think settings are hard to invent, but usually it's best when I'm not actually in them. In most of the New York books, I would make better progress on them if I was not actually in New York at the time. I think if you're in a big city in particular, it's surrounding you, you can't see the edge of it. It's difficult to figure out a way to contain it. Distance in a sense produces clarity: you're more able to see the forest and less distracted by the trees. I think almost everything is based on places that I really know. I can't think of any instance where I didn't do that. I wrote a story about the Battle of Little Big Horn, and I've actually been out there and looked at the Custer monument, which is very interesting. It's one of the most interesting, in fact, *the* most inter-

esting battlefield memorial I've ever seen. When they came a day later what they did was they picked up all these bodies and buried them in a mass grave, but they planted stakes where the soldiers fell. They were going up a coulee to the top of a hill, where they were eventually all killed. There's just a little monument up there on the top—on top of the mass grave—and then these tiny little Arlington-style stones, where the stakes had been, coming up the hill. But in any case, I couldn't be there at the right time . . . but I did go see this.

That story seems very different from your other stories, just because it is historically based. Did that visit prompt the story?

Well, yes, I made that visit when I was nineteen and I did write a novella that's part contemporary and part historical, and it had Crazy Horse in it as a character. It was terrible. It's the worst thing I've ever done. But I was very interested in the subject, and I wanted to do something with it. Ten years later I tried it again. What I wanted to do was write it from the inside with an Indian point of view. I couldn't do that; I could not get that to work.

Did you do research?

I did a lot of research. I read a lot of accounts. I was interested in oral histories and firsthand accounts, including some by people who were there as kids. They were kids who were old enough to scalp and kill people, and were very proud of that. You know some of those people were still alive in the '30s telling stories, which are very interesting. If I try it again, I might have better luck. At the time, I couldn't get that to work, and so what I ultimately decided to do was turn my ignorance into the linchpin for the story. I created a character who doesn't belong there: first of all because he's on the opposing team, and secondly he's not really even supposed to be with that regiment. So he doesn't know anything. All his ignorance is really mine. It works, I think, for the purposes of that story.

If you had taken the point of view of the Indian, how might the story have been changed?

Well, hell, I don't know. I mean, like I say, I was never able to get it to work. I don't know. A lot of people have a sort of messianic fascination with Crazy Horse and I do too, and I was trying to make him be a fictional character. I think at the time I was trying to do that I would no more have been able to create a fictional Oglala Sioux to stand next to him and observe him than I could get him to be real. That's different. I sort of pride myself on the ability to project myself into alien personalities, but I really had trouble with that one. I'm doing a novel now about the Haitian slave revolt of 1791 which requires a great deal of that sort of thing.

What brought about that novel?

Well, I have a messianic fascination with Toussaint Louverture. Since we're on the southern thing, I would say too that it's a way for me—I realized this after fooling with it for five years or so—to write about slavery without having to write about slavery in Middle Tennessee. It's an indirect approach to that whole subject.

It seems there are many young southern writers who are part of the last wave of writers who are called "southern."

Yes, I don't know what's going to happen. I think you may be, in fact, getting another sort of wave of the thing that Allen Tate said about the Southern Renascence at the very beginning, which was that this was an intrinsically temporary phenomenon because it has to do with the perception that we have lost our culture. In that sense at least, historically, he was a fatalist. The whole vision we have of ourselves is about the disappearance of our culture, and that has created what he called the "strange burst of intelligence that we get at the crossing of the ways."

I think we may be getting a kind of second run on that now. It's a little bit different because it seems to me that if there's a large, powerful group of southern writers now, they're mostly women, and they mostly are not writing about any kind of Agrarian pastoral situation. They're writing about small-town life, which is, I think, quite a bit different from the central subject matter that you have for the first generation of southern writers. The person who really understood the Agrarian idea better than anyone else was Andrew Lytle. The South really was a farm culture. It was a culture of small farms. That, I think, is no longer a factor in the work of somebody like Jill McCorkle or Mary Hood, Lee Smith and so on and so forth. Sometimes some of these people get a little bit historical where they're turning up some farm folks, but their small towns are not the same kind of small towns that crop up in Faulkner and Flannery O'Connor. For one thing they're much much more influenced by national culture. I suppose a lot of the interest in those novels comes out of a kind of friction between the national culture and the insular quality of the place itself. Whether or not that's going to be temporary is hard to guess. In some ways I think those southern small towns are somewhat like China in the sense that they can absorb people endlessly without really changing. You see that happening with some of these women writers I've talked about.

Perhaps as long as there are older generations to tell stories and to keep the type of culture going that has been there . . .

Well, that I think you truly will lose. It's kind of depressing. The person who I think was truly aware of the interest of this as a literary subject was Allan Gurganus. What's happening

right now is the living memory of the Civil War is dying out for the second time because now it's not only that the last people who were in it, who were alive at that time or who were old enough to be cognizant of what was going on have died, but the last people who *talked* to those people are now dying. So it's a second kind of attenuation of the connection to that event, and that for better or worse is going to weaken the separate southern identity. There's no helping it.

Has your family been in Middle Tennessee for several generations?

Yes, two sides of it have been, and then if you go back to grandparents, the Bells have been there for a long time and the Wiggintons—my mother's side of the family—have been there for a long time. The distaff side of the grandparents are both from the deep South: my father's mother was from Georgia, my mother's mother was from Tupelo.

Were they in the Middle Tennessee region during the Civil War?

Yes, the Bells would have been. So would the Wiggintons, I reckon. I don't know what all they did. I do know in the Mississippi connection they had some fairly famous folks. John Allen, who was a spy as a child.

A child spy?

Yes, he was one of those guys that would go selling cookies to Union troops and count the cannon. They took that very seriously. They killed them for it, and they tried to kill him.

When you were growing up, what were your connections with Tate and Lytle?

My parents knew them from before I was born, from being students at Vanderbilt. I think mainly my mother, because she was an English major; my father was in the law school. And they were still a presence there when she was in school. I'm not sure if they were actually teaching, but they were around. And then there was a period where Tate and Lytle were at Sewanee together.

Did you know them well?

I saw Mr. Lytle and Mr. Tate fairly frequently when I was a small child, and when I got a little older I kept on seeing them. I was fascinated with the idea that they were writers, even when I was tiny. And Donald Davidson, too, he was another one. He died before I was old enough to get to know him as an adult, but Mr. Tate lived until I was in my twenties, and I used to visit him whenever I could. And I still go to see Mr. Lytle when I get a chance.

Did you think very early on that you wanted to become a writer?

By the time I was sixteen—seventeen—eighteen I was really interested in those people. I wanted to be a writer. I wanted to be that *kind* of writer. My original idea was that the thing for me to do would be to continue the Agrarian/Fugitive pattern in my own work and write books that were southern in setting as well as in vision. And that's what I wanted to do, but I was having some difficulty doing that. I was trying to write material like that when I was in college, and it just didn't turn out. I think it was fortunate for me that I got distracted because of the whole problem of derivativeness that I talked about before. You know there's just such an imitation problem. Well, look what happens!

How do you imitate southern writers without having it appear that that's what you're doing? I mean, the woods are full of Hemingway imitators who don't even know that they are Hemingway imitators. Amy Hempel, in a certain way, is a lineal descendant of Hemingway, though I don't think it would please her to hear me say that. But people who are imitating Faulkner—it's very apparent. People who are imitating Robert Penn Warren are very apparent, and this is a bad thing. It means they've never come out from under the weight of that influence, and very few people have done that successfully. I think Cormac McCarthy has taken some of Faulkner's things, and he was strong enough to transform them. In a way, too, George Garrett. But most people just are not that strong, and instead you get somebody like William Humphries, who just sort of sounds like Faulkner all the time. What I was thinking was I was going to try to hit some kind of position between Madison Jones and Harry Crews, who were second-generation writers that I greatly admired, and whom I wrote a lot of critical stuff about when I was in college. I don't think that would have been a good thing. It's not a good idea to consciously start off with that kind of derivative attitude.

Have you moved away from the Fugitive/Agrarian view of the South?

I don't think I have that much, really. In certain senses no. The feeling of embitterment, I think, gets less with every generation. The sort of emotional values that first had to do with resentment of things like Sherman's March through Georgia, and things that happened specifically during Reconstruction, then became a kind of resentment, which could be projected on an outside enemy, about how the world was changing. You have to admit that perhaps this is specious. It's very hard to make a plausible argument that it would still be a pastoral paradise down there if we'd won the war. I don't quite see how that was going to work. You look anywhere in the world, I don't see that. But still and all, one of the peculiar situations in the South has been that it's pos-

sible to project the anxiety and the fear you have about the destruction of the natural rhythms of life in connection to the land. This is the whole problem. It's a national problem; it's not just the South. We get to blame somebody else, and we've done that for a long, long time, but I think it's becoming harder and harder to do so.

I think the people of the Madison Jones/Harry Crews generation felt more personally affronted by the fact that the national cultural process was apparently eating up the South and changing it, in very bad ways in a lot of cases. It was a new, demographic wave of carpetbagging. Now I think it's harder to feel that way because a lot of it has already been accomplished. What happens is that peculiarly southern feeling results in—Al Gore, to put it politically, coming out of the South as a red-hot environmentalist. I admire him for that (Tipper notwithstanding). This is not a peculiarly southern concern. It's actually national and global, and it's exactly the same thing that Wendell Berry is talking about in his kind of Nouvelle Agrarianism, which is much more national in its scope and in its analysis than the original Agrarian thing was. He's thinking about the whole country. He's thinking about the Midwest and the farm crisis there and agribusiness and all that stuff. Those other guys would have too if they had been around when he was, but it hadn't happened yet. They thought it was going to happen. They were right. They thought it could be stopped. I don't think we'll ever know if they were right about that. I would like to think that it can be reversed.

Were you primarily drawn to the Fugitive/Agrarian movement by the reading that you had done or because of any particular conversation with any of these writers?

I think their whole ideology. I do not know whether those ideas consciously influenced my parents in the way they chose to live their lives, or whether they just happened to be in sympathy with them. But what they did—and this affected everything about the way I grew up—was decide very early in their marriage that they wanted to live on a farm. And at that point land was quite cheap and they were able to buy 90-some-odd acres with some forest and pasture and an old house and a falling-down barn. And there was a tenant house and somebody who was willing to live in it and work on the farm for their job, and that was cheap too then.

A cattle farm, then?

No, it was just a subsistence farm. My mother kept horses. She was not like a show-circuit person. She was running a little kind of scrub riding school. We had a milk cow, and we had sheep and hogs and a garden out of which we got all our food. They lived there six years before I was born, so by the time I was born even, they were just doing all this stuff. They were getting all their food out of the garden; Mother would can and freeze everything for the winter. She never bought any vegetables. We had a smokehouse for pork and all that. We did buy beef and chicken, but about seventy-five percent of our food was produced on the farm. When I was eight or nine the man who worked for us kind of fell apart and left, and he couldn't be replaced. So then we just did it ourselves. This was like the mid-'60s.

Either white or black, there are no longer any people who want to do that kind of agricultural labor for hire. There's nobody that has the skill. You know, the only people who know that kind of stuff now are hippies. Hippies are going to be the great repository of craft information.

Did you ever feel like a lot of kids who were raised on the farm, that you just wanted to leave that way of life?

Yes. I certainly made a beeline to New York City. I went there right after college. I ended up in this place as far away as you could possibly imagine, and now in some ways I regret it. But there are certain things about farming that I just didn't like, although in a way the disadvantages are also the virtues. Nothing's ever finished.

Well, what it really gets down to is this, and this you can find in Andrew Lytle too: If you're going to be a working artist, it's not good to also try to really be a farmer. If you're rich, you can live on a farm and have somebody else do it for you. But if you're going to be trying to do it yourself and be personally responsible, you can forget about doing anything else. And you have to have the temperament that just wants to do that exclusively, and I don't really have that.

The Tates tried to do that.

Well, the Tates! The person who seriously tried to do that was Andrew Lytle. Lytle is very funny on Tate's effort to do that. He was completely incapable of even—I mean, you can't imagine a more cerebral personality really. Tate didn't know anything about farming. Lytle did know a lot about it because his father had a big farm—Cornsilk—and he managed that place during his young adulthood. One of the reasons he has a small body of work is that he spent so much time actually farming, and out of all those people he's the only one who did. He doesn't recommend it, I guess, as a life for an artist.

Did you consider a career that combined work in creative writing and literary scholarship, as Tate and Warren did?

I did at one time think that I would be the sort of academician that Tate was. That was my objective when I was in college—that I would go on and get a Ph.D., and I did well in school so I was a good candidate for those programs. What I did was forget to fill out the applications until it was too late. I wrote off for them all, got their forms, and I had a bale of these things in my room. I was going to take them home and do them over Christmas, and I just left them. And when I realized I'd forgotten them I thought, "God, this is great. I don't have to do this." Because I hadn't realized I didn't want to do it. I thought I did want to do it, but whenever I thought about it I would get really depressed. So I didn't do it, and I think it's better, because in a certain way I don't have the patience to be a good Ph.D. student. But I'm now in the position where I can write a literary essay, which is nice.

Could you be more specific about your attraction to the Fugitives?

Well, my first really strong infatuation with a serious author was with Robert Penn Warren. It started when I was about fifteen. I gobbled up all the Robert Penn Warren novels, which I really thought were wonderful—I still do. And then a little bit later I began to read quite a bit of Faulkner, and I read Flannery O'Connor over and over.

What drew you to Warren?

I don't know. I think both style and subject. He's a very powerful stylist. The first one I read was *All the King's Men*, and I was very taken with the momentum of the language and the worldliness of that narrator. And then I just got more and more involved.

And O'Connor?

Well, if you think of those two together: he's a very lush writer and she's very spare. So in a way she's like an antidote. If you get an overdose of the rush of words that you find with Warren, then the kind of crabby, spare style of Flannery O'Connor is really nice to go to. So those two writers were working on me quite strongly when I was in high school, and with, again, a fair amount of Faulkner being pulled along in the background. And then by the time I got to college I read more across the whole base. I read Tate's novel and was starting to read the essays, which I still use as a critical Bible.

I became very interested in the ideological position of the Fugitive/Agrarian movement as it was expressed in a lot of literature, which had to do with a sense of something gone radically wrong. I now think about this in a different way than I did then. In fact, the whole thing has affected my work quite a bit. Walker Percy talks about this too, but he talks about it in broader religious-philosophical terms. In his language, there is a general sense that most people still have—whether they practice religion or not—that things are not going the way they're supposed to. You're not in your ideal position. And, in fact, that's a sort of general quality of human experience, I guess, but southerners have had a stronger sense of this, I think. It was focused for them in what happened to the South, in the worst possible way. In Percy's language, the sense of unease, of not being at home, the sense that things are awry, comes from what he calls an "aboriginal catastrophe," which is remembered. In the Judeo-Christian religion, that's the fall. But for southerners, it's the Civil War. That's the whole thing that's underwriting the Fugitive/Agrarian movement.

Now my sense of this is, I guess, a little bit broader than it was twenty years ago or even ten years ago. I don't see this any more as a kind of uniquely southern phenomenon. It's really general to our whole society, but I do think that southerners have had a peculiarly potent understanding of it and have had this ability to make it into art. They have a particular sense that something happened, though blaming it on the Yankees is increasingly hard to do. But because of the whole nature of industrial progress, which, of course, did have a lot to do with the war and losing it, we have now come to a very vexatious point in national history and in human history: Do we have the power to destroy our world completely? And I think we're now to the point where it's not just can we crush some particular culture and eradicate it, which is the southern subject—can you destroy yourselves on a global level? Can you destroy, stamp out certain groups of people completely? And indeed you can. That's been proven.

But now the question that's so much broader is, is it possible to commit species suicide? And I think, in a way, that is the southern question in a broader form. The Agrarians didn't know that's what they were looking at when they predicted the kinds of disasters that would come about as the result of hegemony of an industrial society over an agrarian society, but their sense of danger had a lot to do with where we're at now. And, of course, they were really right about that. Whether their strategy for preventing it would have worked, I really don't know, but it all has to do with eschatology and the sense that you have of being at the end of your culture or at the end of your life or at the end of your race. Now the species itself is in some real jeopardy.

People know this, and they're very reluctant to think about it. But it's part of the unconscious makeup of most people. That, in a way, if you want the Fugitive/Agrarian influence on me stated in the abstract, is what it's been. It certainly made me sensitive to those issues, and it gave me a peculiar way of seeing things. And out of that eschatology comes a good situation for art, because the very terror of that, as it's sublimated, makes for good fiction and poetry, for strong narratives. That is the phenomenon that produced all the great southern literature, and I think we're now going into a phase where it'll be a national literature that turns on that problem. A universal eschatology that says we are living in the last days. That really is what's happening now, and I think that's

the big motor that is going to turn out a lot of literary art. In the future it will be interesting to see if there's anyone around to read it.

Sven Birkerts (review date 1992)

SOURCE: "Madison Smartt Bell/Debra Spark," in his *American Energies: Essays on Fiction,* Morrow & Co., 1992, pp. 380-85.

[*In the excerpt below, Birkerts detects a "moviemaking" quality about* Straight Cut, *remarking: "I have no problem with that. Entertainment is entertainment. What bothers me is that the idea of literature got mixed in."*]

On the desk in front of me are two books, *20 Under 30: Best Stories by America's New Young Writers,* edited by Debra Spark and **Straight Cut,** a novel by Madison Smartt Bell. The dust jacket of the latter features a cut-in color photograph of a handsome and brooding young man, and the author's biography begins: "Born in 1957 . . ." The note on the other book has me reaching for my cane: "Debra Spark was born in 1962. . ." No doubt about it, the marketing mind has decided to locate the cutoff line between prodigy and ordinary adulthood at a round three-zero.

This is something new, and a quick retrospective glance will confirm it. Joyce had written *Dubliners* and most of *A Portrait of the Artist as a Young Man* before he was thirty, Lawrence published *Sons and Lovers* at twenty-eight, and when Hemingway affixed the date—September 21, 1925—to the manuscript of *The Sun Also Rises,* he was a mere twenty-six. Nobody exclaimed over their precocity, or flashed their numbers at the public. These were adult artists; they had long since put sweet youth behind them.

The changed perception, I'm certain, stems in part from the demographics of what has come to be called a youth culture. But the real explanation goes deeper. Quite simply, it's become extraordinarily difficult for a writer—any writer—to give comprehensive expression to our times. The forces are too various and incalculable. The rate and magnitude of change have outstripped the integrating powers of the psyche. Even older, proven writers are at a loss. The *feel* of life out there in the present seems to elude their verbal net. With the possible exception of Don DeLillo's *White Noise,* I can't think of a single recent work that has managed to get a narrative frame around the ambient sensations of the cultural moment. And DeLillo is no beginner. The near impossibility of achieving significant art has raised the threshold—*any* literary attainment before the age of thirty starts to look remarkable.

Madison Bell touched on some aspects of this malaise in his essay **"Less Is Less: The Dwindling American Short Story"** in the April issue of *Harper's*. Although he deplored the "low-key noncommittal presentation" that characterizes the fiction of writers like Ann Beattie, David Leavitt, and Bobbie Ann Mason, Bell did not pay sufficient heed to the conditions that foster it. Against the engulfing insubstantiality, he raised the example of Peter Taylor, "arguably the best American short story writer of all time." But Taylor does not write toward the present, he turns against it; his work is an ongoing time capsule of Southern mores in the forties and fifties. Bell noted this, of course. Nevertheless, it was Taylor he invoked to bolster his final point: "Literature might as well undertake certain responsibilities abandoned by the rest of the entertainment industry." The syllables scarcely chime with conviction.

When I first ran up against that phrase yoking literature to "the rest of the entertainment industry," I assumed that Bell was being deliberately wry. But now, after reading **Straight Cut,** I realize that my impulse was too charitable. The book is a straightforward middle-brow page-turner that has been dressed up to look like something more: an existential thriller, an investigation of fast-lane morality. Forget the pretense. Starve it for a day, and it will reveal its true shape—a screenplay.

I have no problem with that. Entertainment is entertainment. What bothers me is that the idea of literature has got mixed in. I hear Bell touted in certain circles as a comer, a serious writer. And then he goes public with big diagnostic pronouncements, raises a call for a responsible fiction. When a man takes the time to build his own gallows, we ought at least to do him the courtesy of hanging him.

Straight Cut is actually Bell's third novel. He won the terrifying moniker of "promising" (Cyril Connolly: "Whom the gods would destroy, they first call 'promising'") with *The Washington Square Ensemble* and *Waiting for the End of the World*. Both were praised for their energy and their openness to the edges of culture. Both were also criticized for their shapelessness and excess. Bell has evidently taken those reactions to heart—*Straight Cut* is pure narrative.

The plot begins simply enough. The protagonist, Tracy, who's living in numbed estrangement from his wife, Lauren, gets a call from his old moviemaking and drug-dealing partner, Kevin. Kevin wants him to fly to Rome immediately to edit a film. Tracy is suspicious—he knows just how duplicitous his "friend" can be, and he's being given far too much money up front—but he agrees anyway. Deadlocked souls love a promise of trouble. The project turns out to be small potatoes. Living in a borrowed apartment, Tracy falls into an automaton routine of work and sleep, hiding from everything. Until one day he comes back and finds Lauren

in his room and a mysteriously locked briefcase parked by the door. As this is, ultimately, a genre novel, I dare not take away the sole reader incentive by divulging any more. The staples are all there: drugs, sex, guns, stakeouts, smuggling, betrayal, death . . . And yes, the usual gritty location shots in Brussels and London.

Take away the plot, and the critic has nothing left to bite into. Characterization is nonexistent. Whether this is by design or just a result of hasty execution I can't say. Possibly Bell wanted Tracy to be one of those hard-hurting iceberg narrators—he is given a drinking problem and a penchant for Kierkegaard. But there is an enormous, if superficially subtle, difference between an understated character like Jake Barnes and an undeveloped cutout like Tracy. And without a sense of who Tracy is, you can make nothing of the dark vibrations that he claims to feel for Kevin, or the wavering passion that Lauren seems to elicit.

I go on at this length only because *Straight Cut* is being sold to us as something that it's not. The back of the jacket features the *New Yorker* seal of approval: "Every sentence he writes is a joy." And other critics weigh in with phrases like "ennobled vision" and "Between your screams of delight are his overtures with death . . ." This is just blurbing, I know. But every so often we need to blow the whistle on it—after all, *you* might be the one tricked into buying the book. Bell's every sentence is *not* a joy. I open the book blind and find: "In Kevin's entryway I waited five minutes before I could stop shaking. Another drink would have gone down good but I didn't have one handy." The pages are filled with this kind of unshaven prose. Anyone capable of reading Kierkegaard ought to know that *good* should be *well*. For that matter any writer who can celebrate Peter Taylor as our living master should be well aware of how the line between literature and the entertainment industry gets drawn.

Andy Solomon (review date 30 May 1993)

SOURCE: "Poised between hell and purgatory: The fiction of Madison Smartt Bell," in *Chicago Tribune Books,* May 30, 1993, p. 6.

[*In the review below, Solomon focuses on the detailed descriptions and realistic characters of* Save Me, Joe Louis, *especially "Bell's sharp insights into, and extraordinary compassion for, his outcast protagonists."*]

The seven novels and two story collections that comprise the oeuvre of Madison Smartt Bell at age 35 make him one of our most prolific and precocious talents. What grows clearer with each book is Bell's unique wedding of intelligence and craft to a signature angle of vision that marks him as one of our more courageous and large-souled talents as well.

Bell might be described as a regional writer—his region being the foggy border that buffers purgatory from hell in the sootiest creases of contemporary society. The plots he sets in motion there, if merely described, would sound as sensational and bizarre as Stephen King's. What places them well within the sphere of art, however, are Bell's sharp insights into, and extraordinary compassion for, his outcast protagonists.

Since his first novel, *The Washington Square Ensemble,* with its cluster of heroin dealers, Bell has always written with conspicuous sympathy for the alienated and the bruised. He searches for characters beaten down by a combination of life and poor choices yet who retain, however vaguely or unconsciously, a desire to seek affirmation.

In *Save Me, Joe Louis,* Macrae, age 23, is AWOL from the army and living in New York's Hell's Kitchen. He hasn't enjoyed much of anything since his teen years in Tennessee, when he was in love without knowing it with a spirited photographer named Lacy. Broke and wandering in Manhattan's Battery Park, Macrae spots Charlie. They ask each other for a handout and "circle each other like two strange dogs," then team up to rob the first of a series of victims carrying ATM cards. No guns, no violence, just forced withdrawals of $400, the maximum allowed. "Relax," Macrae tells female victims, "I'm not a rapist. I'm a thief." Charlie prefers the term "aggressive solicitation."

> **Since his first novel, *The Washington Square Ensemble,* with its cluster of heroin dealers, Bell has always written with conspicuous sympathy for the alienated and the bruised.**
> **—*Andy Solomon***

Petulant and lost, Macrae often forms unfortunate attachments, one to a prostitute whose pimp decides to blow half her head off. His most dangerous alliance is with the increasingly unstable Charlie, whose rationale is, "Ain't nobody cares that much what you do."

After they've made New York too hot for their comfort, they head south to Baltimore where they add a third partner, a benign, dog-loving young black man named Porter, fresh off a jail term for a bar fight that inadvertently turned gory. The three hold up an armored car, but police arrive, bullets fly and the trio heads full speed for Macrae's blind father's farm outside of Nashville.

Were trigger-happy Charlie not with him, Macrae might feel he's returned from far east of Eden. There's the potential for a wholesome life in Tennessee. Adjacent to Macrae's land is the farm of Thomas Laidlaw, the hero of Bell's 1989 *Soldier's Joy,* who'd done much two decades earlier to rid the area of injustice. Not only is Laidlaw there, still playing banjo with his bluegrass band; but also the beautiful Lacy has returned home from art school in Philadelphia. That she still loves Macrae is clear to everyone but him, as he keeps stumbling aimlessly in restless confusion.

After a robbery attempt even more botched than the Baltimore fiasco, Macrae, Charlie and Porter flee to the South Carolina coast. There it grows obvious that Macrae may have outlived his usefulness to Charlie, and that the book's final page won't be big enough to hold both of them.

Bell has visited most of these settings and walked with these dangerous drifters many times before. Over the last decade, he has put before us heroin addicts, murderers who plot to set off nuclear bombs in New York City, alcoholics, unemployed sound men slipping from the human community in dingy Greenwich Village bars and insomniac hypnotists who keep pet boa constrictors and stalk nighttime streets while haunted by Renaissance mystics. He invites us to care about characters who offer scarcely an inch of ground to build affection on—no more than, say, some foolish old man who gives his kingdom to two satanic women while disowning the only child who loves him.

Yet, by combining subtle technique and native compassion, Bell inevitably succeeds. Here he establishes his authority immediately by the careful accretion of accurate detail. Whether he describes audio equipment or tae kwon do or the Port Authority Terminal, his minute realism wins the reader's suspension of disbelief. Holding fast to that trust, he edges us into the murky world his people inhabit, like Porter's gin mill where "most of the seats at the bar had been taken by the ageless career boozers, damp tangled clothing twisted into their wrinkled skin, leaning in tight to their ashtrays and glasses." From there he gradually draws us into the smoky and dark caverns of the characters' minds. He makes us feel Macrae's discomfort, his reluctance to hurt people, his affection for those close to him, his unvoiced hope to know a simpler world he can inhabit with Lacy. And she, the potential healing agent, blends an allure, vitality, loyalty and self-possession that again reflect Bell's affection and respect for women, even when they sleep with killers.

As Bell descends with Macrae into his underworld, he takes us with him, and we see that the crucible that forged Macrae held our trials too. Here lies Bell's trademark gift, how he moves among modern thieves and lepers with charity. His is a Robert Browning empathy that creates no character so defiled that Bell cannot ask, "What is at the heart of this man that is in me as well?" In Macrae, Bell once again takes a character you'd be disturbed to find living anywhere near your neighborhood, then moves relentlessly against the grain of popular thought to find the embers of Macrae's humanity beneath the ashes of his pain.

Harry Crews (review date 20 June 1993)

SOURCE: "A Couple of Predators," in *The New York Times Book Review,* Vol. 98, June 20, 1993, p. 9.

[*In the positive review below, Crews commends the true-to-life narrative and characterization in* Save Me, Joe Louis, *observing that Bell is "an exceptional novelist. . . [capable] of occasionally turning a miracle."*]

Madison Smartt Bell has written an episodic novel of two grifters and drifters, Charlie and Macrae, whose only thought seems to be to drink and dope a bit today and tomorrow. After tomorrow, they'll turn their attention toward relieving an unsuspecting citizen of enough money so they can drink and dope a bit one more time. Always one more time. Charlie, in his early 40's, is an ex-con and Macrae, hardly more than 20, is AWOL from the Marines.

Never once in *Save Me, Joe Louis* do they have a thought of getting a job, or of giving up the grift, quitting the scam, abandoning the occasional low-rent mugging or dropping the habit of stealing a car for a few days. While these two men are not stupid, they are not very bright either. To make it worse, they are totally alienated from society, alienated from the criminal subculture in which they live their lives and, most devastatingly, alienated from their own selves.

These two predators on the weak and unsuspecting think of themselves as pretty good guys. I don't find that very strange. As James Baldwin put it in his introduction to his play *Blues for Mr. Charlie,* "No man is a villain in his own heart." Just so. Charlie and Macrae have their own valid—at least to them—reasons for what they do. Their view of the world, and their understanding of it, seems reasonable to them. It is the quintessentially recidivist con's mentality, a mentality so ordinary and common in this society that it keeps all our jails full to overflowing.

Save Me, Joe Louis is Mr. Bell's ninth book in a decade—he's published seven novels and two collections of short stories—and it is not his first trip to the hairy underbelly of society in search of a story. He seems to have an overwhelming affinity for that level of existence where the qualities of which novels are normally made are missing—qualities of mercy and love and compassion and sacrifice and most of the other abstractions you've ever heard.

It would seem reasonable that the next sentence I ought to write would be something like: "And consequently, Madison Smartt Bell has written another bad novel." Not so. He has not to this point written his *first* bad novel, so far as I'm concerned. In *Save Me, Joe Louis,* Mr. Bell has taken the artist's shaping magic and transformed a totally unpromising narrative into something of value.

The narrative of *Save Me, Joe Louis* is sorry enough. Charlie and Macrae meet in the dead of winter in New York's Battery Park, where they try to panhandle each other. Neither of them has any "spare" change for the other, so they decide to do what they do best: take the money from the next people they meet, in this case a couple of college kids out on a date. Charlie and Macrae become friends and steal together, dope together and drink together. In the process, a teen-age prostitute is brutally slain, and so is her pimp, Big Tee. It is not long before they draw so much heat (they are not the most skillful bad guys in the world) that they have to steal a car and head south. They end up in Baltimore, where they meet a black ex-con named Porter and the three of them steal (among a great many other things) a lot of guns and Charlie blows away some cops.

This is when Porter tells a too-good-to-be-true story you often hear in the Deep South: "'I heard this story,' Porter said,' Back when the gas chamber was new, you know? Go back 40 years or whatever. First dude they threw in there, one of the first. Somewhere down south, I guess it was. Anyway, they wanted to see how it would go, so they had some kind of a window they could look at him through, and they put a microphone in there with him. . . .

"'Save me, Joe Louis,' Porter said. 'That's all they got. Over and over, just like that. *Save me, Joe Louis. Save me, Joe Louis.*'"

There's nothing to do but steal another car and run again, this time to a little farm in the hills of Tennessee where Macrae was raised and where his blind daddy still lives. There, and in South Carolina, where Charlie was born, the novel is resolved, insofar as such a story line admits of resolution. The men are doomed, they know it, they have always known it, and they accept it.

Macrae is left with the greatest possibilities. He is back home with a woman who may or may not save him. Most important, he likes being back home and has no desire to return to the dirty, bloody, noisy big cities, and certainly he has no desire for the life he has left behind him on the mean streets of those cities. But the trail he has left behind him is hot. He knows it and we know it. He, too, is doomed.

The two men at the heart of this story are not the first doomed men to populate a novel and make it pulse with life. Mr.

Bell's ability to render the look and smell and sound and even at times the taste or place, his vision of human experience being no more than dust blown in the winds of chance, and finally his determination never to make the life of the novel have more symmetry and sense than flesh and blood normally have, make him the exceptional novelist he is, and also make him capable—in his best moments—of occasionally turning a miracle. *Save Me, Joe Louis* is a remarkable read. I encourage people everywhere to go out and put their money down and take this book home.

Garry Abrams (review date 11 July 1993)

SOURCE: "Bad, Bad Buddies," in *Los Angeles Times Book Review,* July 11, 1993, p. 7.

[*In the following review, Abrams offers a favorable assessment of* Save Me, Joe Louis.]

When two guys with criminal tendencies go skidding across the country like a souped-up car with bad brakes and a bald set of tires, bad things are bound to happen. Talk about that American pastime, random violence—*Save Me, Joe Louis* has got it: shotgun killings, baseball-bat mayhem and what may be the only armed robbery ever committed to save a captured fox. It is the perfect vehicle for a sociopathic buddy movie—*Thelma and Louise* without the extenuating circumstances.

That said, it must be stressed that Madison Smartt Bell's latest novel is richer in subtlety and nuance and a lot less romantic than might be expected in a genre that thrives on bold strokes and the frequent glorification of hard cases. It is both a good read and an ambitious, informed exploration of the underbelly of America.

The two chief characters, Charlie, an ex-con with a penchant for spur-of-the moment robbery, and Macrae, a hillbilly army deserter, are already loaded with deadly personal cargo before they meet on a cold autumn night in New York's Battery Park. The chemistry between them creates the foul brew of their tale.

The two begin by perpetuating a common urban nightmare—forcing selected Manhattan pedestrians to visit the nearest bank machine and withdraw the daily cash limit, or all of their money, whichever comes first. This is a relatively innocent avocation compared with what comes later.

Charlie and Macrae use the proceeds from these early crimes to rent an apartment and hang out at bars and greasy spoons in the Times Square area. It is as close as they ever get to bliss. Naturally, things fall apart pretty quick. Macrae and a

prostitute woo each other, angering the hooker's pimp. After a bar fight and other grim preliminaries, the pimp kills the prostitute, executing her in front of Macrae with a heavy caliber pistol that splatters brains all over an alley.

Macrae, who usually is just along for the ride with Charlie, finds the will to act on his own. He carefully manufactures a lead-weighted baseball bat and begins stalking the pimp. The revenge is horrific.

Soon after, an impulsive holdup fails when the Korean store owner gives Macrae an educational flesh wound. Now wise enough to leave New York, Charlie and Macrae head south, landing first in Baltimore where they find haven with Porter, an ex-con whose duplex adjoins a crack house.

The three musketeers steal a few cars and then decide to hold up a liquor store. By now, Charlie and Macrae are using guns. The liquor store robbery fails, Charlie turns his shotgun on the cops, they escape by the skin of their gnashing teeth and flee southwest to Tennessee. There, the gang holes up on the hardscrabble farm of Macrae's father, an old man in his last decline but still wily, unsentimental and inscrutable.

As a rural interlude, the Tennessee sojourn is anything but bucolic. Macrae meets an old nemesis at a barbecue and finds an old flame there, too. Meanwhile, Macrae begins to distance himself from Charlie. In his inchoate way Macrae is seeking redemption as he finds a small flicker of decency still burning in his heart.

But it is a tiny flicker, indeed.

Bell seems to know intimately the seedy sides of New York, Baltimore and the ex-urban south of housing developments and shopping centers abutting old, dying farms. He renders each locale exquisitely and seems as familiar with street jive as redneck vernacular. For fans of symbolism, Bell throws in an elaborate and deft use of legendary boxer Joe Louis as an icon for the down and out. In fact, the novel's title derives from an anecdote about Louis and a condemned criminal.

There are many fine passages, including one tracing the steps of a successful crabbing expedition and another about the grittiness of a Tennessee hog roast:

> The men around the smoking pits were tired and sooty, a processed bourbon smell leaking out of their pores along with the green hickory smoke. Two whole hogs, cloven from jowl to tail, lay blackening on wire screens across the pits. A fat man seemed to be in charge. Sunburn ran all under his crew cut and down to the neck of his football jersey, a flashy

acetate thing with a mesh curling flirtatiously over his guts. He reached on the rack and lifted a hind trotter, woggling the bone in the loosening meat.

Help yourself.

John Vernon (review date 29 October 1995)

SOURCE: "The Black Face of Freedom," in *The New York Times Book Review*, Vol. 100, October 29, 1995, p. 12.

[*In the review below, Vernon appraises* All Souls' Rising, *concluding that there "are flaws, but flaws dwarfed by a powerful and intelligent novel."*]

Haiti's 18th-century slave rebellion—an object lesson for slave owners in the United States—played itself out against the unfolding revolution in the colony's mother country, France. The result was a complex struggle among Haitian groups trying to align themselves with a shifting template 5,000 miles away with each arriving wave of rumor and news, loyalties switched, authority changed hands, the last became first, retribution threatened. It takes a skillful rage for order to make sense of the moral and political morass that was Haiti in the midst of its historic uprising. Toward the end of Madison Smartt Bell's novel about the revolt, *All Souls' Rising,* his central character notes that the corpses unaccountably dragged from the middle of a Haitian street and lined against the walls represent an exotic "impulse to bring order into hell's worst chaos." We may conclude the same about this epic novel constructed on the moving avalanche of history. The order Mr. Bell brings to his novelistic chaos is never fixed, always provisional; yet, alert readers will not lose their way following his carefully drawn road map through hell.

On May 15, 1791, the French National Assembly granted full political rights to free mulattoes in Haiti. As a response in the May 15th degree, Mr. Bell's Haitian royalists decide to stage an insurrection of the African slaves, who are the population's vast majority. Their thinking is that this will drive all revolutionary nonsense out of the colony's white Jacobins and the free mulattoes. Let them see the black face of freedom, says a royalist, and you'll see the end of politics.

But politics in this centrifugal world, charged with racial division, has a way of quickly flying out of control. The black uprising is Grand Guignol come to life. Two thousand whites are killed, 180 sugar plantations burned, and a 14-year military struggle set in motion. Mr. Bell's protagonist, a French doctor named Antoine Hébert, wanders through the resulting flames while searching for his sister, the wife of a dead planter. Hébert is not unlike Tolstoy's Pierre adrift in burning Moscow, an adult child fortified with the proper degree

of innocence in his perceptions. He becomes our guide through a tunnel of horrors.

All Souls' Rising is historical fiction in the monumental manner, heavily prefaced, prologued, glossaried and chronologized. It admirably diagrams the complex muddle of 18th-century Haiti, a slave society constructed along clearly racist lines but with surprising alliances. Haitian whites, split into royalists and revolutionaries, alternately compete for and spurn the loyalties of free mulattoes, for whom gradations of color are of central importance. Mr. Bell informs us in his preface that 64 different colors had been identified and named among the mulattoes of Haiti, with social rank predicated upon lightness of shade. Lacking such bodily marks of distinction, the whites adopt identifying tokens: white cockades in their hats for the royalists, red ones for the revolutionaries. Meanwhile, the rebellious blacks, led by, among others, Toussaint L'Ouverture, think the French King will free them, and adopt the royalist uniforms and the tactical strategies of European armies.

This bizarre and rich stew is the perfect stuff of fiction, whose subject is never reality but competing realities; but it is also clearly the stuff of history and readers will undoubtedly be reminded of chalk marks on doors, Jews forced to wear stars and the whole sad sweep through history's alleys of differences marked out for excision. In *All Souls' Rising,* the acts of excision on every side are bloody, torturous and mind-numbing in their repetitive insistence. Beneath the social and political collusions and betrayals, the real subject of the novel—and the ground-floor perspective for its understanding of history—is the human body and its fragile relation to human identity under conditions of torture and mutilation.

For much of the novel, the violence is relentless. There are entrails galore, mutilations by the bucketful, multiple rapes in pools of blood. A man throws himself across the mouth of a cannon, clinging with arms and legs to its barrel, and is blown across a field "in a bloody net." Two men remove a soldier's eye with a corkscrew. One group of rebel slaves carries as its banner into battle a white baby impaled on a spear, arms and legs weakly waving. A female slave nailed through the wrists and feet to a pole is removed with an ax. This is strong stuff and threatens to numb by repetition into a handbook of splatter-punk.

To his credit, Mr. Bell knows that violence may be the writer's hedge against mawkishness, but it also threatens to become mere slush, the sentimentality of gore. The most telling moment in *All Souls' Rising* occurs when Doctor Hébert observes through a thicket a man bound to a tree being skinned alive.

> The operator was a mulatto, oddly freckled—the doctor felt he'd seen him somewhere before. The sub-

ject, on the other hand, was skinless now, deracinated, transmogrified into the internal self he possibly had always been, raw human nature laid bare to greasy viscera and a scream. The doctor had seen the assembly of these parts of ten times before in his own chilly dissections—but this was life itself. Unconsciously he mutilated the vine he'd plucked between his fingers; new fragrance rose from the crushed leaves. He felt through his nausea and terror that he was witnessing something well beyond torture or murder. Though he could not understand or grasp it, he was seeing what it meant to be human. This was a sincere inquiry into the nature of man, not how a man is made and how his parts cooperate, but what a man is, in his essence, and who, in the final analysis, would be allowed to be one.

This is merciless and perhaps a bit portentous, but not heartless. It may help to know that the victim is the white plantation owner who conceived of the staged insurrection, and the flayer is his mulatto son. In passages like this one, Mr. Bell appears to test his characters' limits in order to make readers test their own. And he knows that readers only care about violence when they care about the characters on whom the human meat is tacked.

The characters in *All Souls' Rising,* Mr. Bell's eighth novel, are an uneven bunch, but they grow on you. The dazed Doctor Hébert, for example, accumulates an appropriately befuddled human reality as the novel progresses. But the most memorable character is the one around whom the violence most often swirls, like smoke or spinning flies: the wife of a vicious slaveowner. Against all odds, Mr. Bell succeeds in making us, if not admire, surely marvel at this woman, Claudine Arnaud, as we marvel at a monstrous spectacle of nature. She and her husband become horribly redeemed by violence, their own and that of the historical moment that they have helped to create. The passages describing them are some of the most startling—because disturbingly lyrical—in the novel.

The black characters are less successful. Toussaint L'Ouverture is by turns saintly, foolish, canny and paternally benevolent. Mr. Bell can't quite seem to penetrate his mystery and allows him to stand, as it were, in unassembled pieces that the historical imagination despairs of putting together. Part of the problem surely is the generally hagiographic manner in which Toussaint is presented. When we first meet him, he heroically rescues his children from wild dogs, then later, like a black Joseph Smith, becomes anointed by God in a jungle clearing. We see Toussaint held so beautifully in a nimbus of sunlight that "he would have the power, when he chose, to give it forth as a healing light."

Similarly, a runaway slave named Riau—whose chapters in this otherwise omniscient novel are narrated in the first person—strikes me as a failed experiment. Through Riau we learn about voodoo (or, properly, vodoun) and its role in the Haitian uprising, but in thus instructing us Mr. Bell must violate the first-person authenticity of his character with clumsy passages of exposition. He never quite finds the right voice for Riau. Mr. Bell tries to show Riau as torn between identities—pagan and Christian, black and white, illiterate and literate—but the terms with which the character portrays himself are often leaden versions of Western anthropological formulas. "The words were thinking in my head that they were like the corrupted kings of Guinee," he says, sounding like a ventriloquized Tonto describing his own alternation. "I, Riau, I hated all of this," he says. "Riau wanted Ogun in his head again instead of all the shadowy thinking words." Language like this perilously skirts the slippery slope to *Ungawa, Bwana!'*

These are flaws, but flaws dwarfed by a powerful and intelligent novel. Mr. Bell can manage epic slabs of action remarkably well, has a feel for the panoramic and iconic, and, above all, seeks to understand and probe the mysterious intersection of history and flesh by which historical forces become incarnate. *All Souls' Rising,* refreshingly ambitious and maximalist in its approach, takes enormous chances, and consequently will haunt readers long after plenty of flawless books have found their little slots on their narrow shelves.

Dwight Garner (review date 5 November 1995)

SOURCE: "Nothing to Lose But Their Chains," in *Washington Post Book World,* Vol. XXV, No. 45, November 5, 1995, p. 4.

[*Below, Garner marvels at the erudition and literary skill of* All Souls' Rising, *finding that Bell's "gifts have never been more fully on display."*]

Madison Smartt Bell's sprawling and masterful new novel, about political and racial turmoil in French colonial Haiti during the late 18th century, is not for the squeamish. The book's first scene is an exacting depiction of the crucifixion of a black female slave by a wealthy French landowner. That's merely a primer. In the ensuing 200 pages or so, up until about the novel's midway point, we learn much, much more about the terrors regularly inflicted upon African slaves by their French masters, including the fact that "it was nothing to lop an ear or gouge an eye, even to cut off a hand, thrust a burning stake up a rectum, roast a slave in an oven alive, or roll one down a hill in a barrel studded with nails."

And then, when the political tables turn in the book's second half and the slaves stage a successful rebellion, equally gruesome forms of revenge—such as the removal of a captive's eyeballs by means of a corkscrew—are visited upon the French. There is a description of a man being flayed from head to foot, while very much alive, that will have even hardened readers peeking between the cracks in their fingers.

The massive erudition Bell displays about methods of torture in *All Souls' Rising* is worth noting because it reflects his massive erudition about just about everything else in this ambitious and audaciously complex novel. Most historical novelists are content merely to unfold their plots against what's often referred to as a "historical backdrop," as if they were talking about wallpaper. *All Souls' Rising* on the other hand, is a remarkable feat of historical imagination—one that tells a compelling tale from several competing points of view and that digs fully into the emotional, intellectual and historical realities that made up Haiti in the late 1700s.

> **Madison Smartt Bell's sprawling and masterful new novel, about political and racial turmoil in French colonial Haiti during the late 18th century, is not for the squeamish.**
> —*Dwight Garner*

Bell unspools this saga on an intimate, human scale, which is impressive given the complexity of his subject matter. The Haiti he writes about was torn not only by political divides (the French colonials versus Haitian and African slaves of shifting allegiances) but racial ones; as Bell notes, 64 different shades of color were identified among the island's many mulattos, "and social status depended on the lightness of the shade." Combine the anger and confusion caused by both situations, add the fact of the concurrent French Revolution, and you've got a volatile brew. Bell keeps his facts straight—the book includes a preface that provides historical context, a chronology of historical events, and a glossary of terms—while keeping the book's sensibility loose enough that he can garnish chapter headings with apt lines from Bob Marley's songs.

The book's narrative revolves around the slave rebellion that effectively ended white rule in Haiti. Bell tells this story through the eyes of several characters, including a freethinking French doctor named Antoine Hebert, an African slave named Riau, and a particularly cruel French landowner and his rebellious wife, Michel and Claudine Arnaud. Perhaps the most notable character, however, is the historical figure Toussaint-Louverture, a self-educated, second-generation African slave who led the rebellion while attempting to prevent grisly mob violence against the French.

As *All Souls' Rising* hurtles towards its close, the battle scenes and skirmishes grow more furious, and the bodies seem to pile up and up. Yet Bell's narrative never feels rushed or cramped, and away from the heat of battle there is plenty of room for human interaction and often a kind of wry humor. Bell has always been a muscular writer, a kind of Martin Amis without the fripperies, and his gifts have never been more fully on display. In his hands, even a simple sex scene—here between the shy French doctor Hebert and a mulatto woman—takes on an heightened intensity: "He'd lost all sense of his identity; the last vestige of the personality he'd brought into the room eddied somewhere high above like a flake of ash from some great conflagration. Perhaps it had an eye and watched the scene. He'd slipped his boundaries; there were capabilities in him he'd never known. This was vertigo."

In earlier novels such as *Soldier's Joy* and *Waiting for the End of the World,* Bell demonstrated that he was a young American novelist of the first rank. *All Souls' Rising,* however, puts him on another level as an artist. It's a big, morally intricate book that grows, deepens and shifts as the narrative progresses. At more than 500 pages, too, *All Souls' Rising,* a finalist for the National Book Award, sits lightly on the lap. It is that increasing rarity: a serious historical novel that reads like a dream.

Diane Roberts (review date 26 November 1995)

SOURCE: "Stature of Bell Is Uplifted in Gothic 'All Souls' Rising,'" in *The Atlanta Journal-Constitution,* November 26, 1995, p. K11.

[*In the following review, Roberts compares* All Soul's Rising *to William Faulkner's* Absalom, Absalom!, *noting that Bell's novel "suffers only a little in comparison."*]

Madison Smartt Bell is a Southerner, a Tennessean, but he's not what you'd call a Southern writer. Since 1987, he has produced nine books, novels and short story collections, occasionally set in the South, occasionally peopled with deracinated Southerners in the big cities of the North, often more about the weird pathologies of late 20th-century American life than meditations on the ever-present painful past of the nation's most romanticized and vilified region.

But his cornucopian *All Souls' Rising,* nominated for the National Book Award, is a Southern novel—of a sort. It is about slavery, about revolution, about class, about the past, about racial hatred, about the Byzantine mechanics of oppression. The novel is set in Haiti, not Mississippi, and it is a historical novel the way William Faulkner's great *Absalom, Absalom!* is a historical novel. Indeed, *All Souls' Rising* is kin to *Absalom, Absalom!* somewhat in the way Toni

Morrison's *Beloved* is a mirror revision of *Uncle Tom's Cabin.* Both Bell and Faulkner explore the mysteries of slavery, miscegenation and the decline of the plantation system, but where Faulkner is most passionately interested in the fall of the Big House white folks, Bell tells of the rise of a self-made black hero, the Haitian patriot Toussaint L'Ouverture. But both Faulkner and Bell give us their best prose on the bleeding tragedy of race in the New World, the unquiet ghost that haunts our bright egalitarian national edifice. *Absalom, Absalom!* stands as an undisputed masterpiece of American (not just Southern) fiction; without claiming too much for it, *All Souls' Rising* suffers only a little in comparison.

Bell's style can be as evocative and eerie as a cathedral full of candles, or as luminous as a rainbow. And he has a way with a Gothic image that would make Faulkner (or Poe) proud: "Madame Arnaud, or no, it was Elise herself, younger than she ought to have been, her face at sixteen, seventeen. Her gown was hanging off one shoulder. Blood squirted mightily from her severed wrists, and as she reached out to embrace her brother, she opened her mouth and howled like a wolf."

The novel is Gothic—but it is also political, social, tough and lyrical all at the same time. Bell does some of his most impressive writing about the runaway slaves hiding in the Haitian hills, who, with the ex-coachman Toussaint, fostered the revolution that took from France the richest colony in the Atlantic. Bell balances his various stories—which are large—with the exquisite and unobtrusive precision of a master choreographer. We deal in turn with Doctor Hebert, newly arrived from France, as he searches for his sister Elise, who has fled from her husband's great plantation, or Riau, who has escaped from a vicious master to join the rebels and is possessed at times by the gods, or Nanona, beautiful mulatto with a political agenda of her own.

> **Like all "historical novels,"** *All Souls' Rising* **is really about us, our times, our prejudices, our race wars. And in the telling of our story, it is as powerful as a hurricane.**
> *—Dwight Garner*

The Haiti that Bell spreads out for us, like a gorgeous and busy tapestry, is both familiar and tantalizingly strange. There is the violence, the magic, the decadence, the sweltering heat, the passion, the rage that marked the country then—and colors it still. But there is also an uncanny sense that this is a place like no other, a place we cannot quite grasp, a New World where everything is actually very old, almost a myth, like the transcendent Africa or Guinee the slaves believe lies at the bottom of the ocean.

Like all "historical novels," *All Souls' Rising* is really about us, our times, our prejudices, our race wars. And in the telling of our story, it is as powerful as a hurricane.

FURTHER READING

Criticism

Davis, Alan. A review of *Save Me, Joe Louis. The Hudson Review* 47, No. 1 (Spring 1994): 145-46.
  Claims that "this baggy novel often reads more like a true-crime study than like fiction."

Johnson, George. A review of *Straight Cut. The New York Times Book Review* 92 (27 December 1987): 24.
  Brief, positive notice.

Mesic, Penelope. "The Fire That Time." *Chicago Tribune* (22 October 1995): sec. 14, pp. 1, 11.
  Considers the violence and racial themes in *All Souls' Rising,* observing that the "scope of this ambitious narrative is heroic."

A review of *The Year of Silence. The New York Times Book Review* 94 (5 February 1989): 34.
  Notes Bell's understanding of "the way many people must struggle to live."

A review of *Soldier's Joy. The New York Times Book Review* 95 (8 July 1990): 28.
  Brief commendation for Bell's narrative tack.

A review of *Barking Man. The New York Times Book Review* 96 (2 June 1991): 34.
  Sees the collection as "a humane and mature work."

A review of *Doctor Sleep. The New York Times Book Review* 96 (9 June 1991): 28.
  Notes that the novel "once more captures the poignant in the freakish."

A review of *Straight Cut. The Observer,* No. 10272 (21 August 1988): 41.
  Calls Bell "an original mix of radical chic, sleaze and Kierkegaard."

A review of *The Year of Silence. The Observer,* No. 10300 (12 March 1989): 44.
  Finds that Bell "has not lost his knack for sharp language, or his taste for sleaze."

Yardley, Jonathan. A review of *The Year of Silence. Washington Post Book World* 19, No. 8 (19 February 1989): 12.
    Compares the novel's effect to "a little like throwing a stone into a pool and watching the ripples flow outward from the center."

————. A review of *Soldier's Joy. Washington Post Book World* 20, No. 27 (8 July 1990): 12.
    Brief summary of plot.

Additional coverage of Bell's life and career is contained in the following sources published by Gale Research: *Contemporary Authors,* **Vol. 111, and** *Contemporary Authors New Revision Series,* **Vol. 28.**

Maya Deren
1917-1961

Russian-born American filmmaker, dancer, essayist, and film critic.

The following entry presents an overview of Deren's career. For further information on her life and works, see *CLC*, Volume 16.

INTRODUCTION

An important figure in American avant-garde filmmaking of the 1940s, Deren created the trend towards and the marketplace for avant-garde films in the United States. She wrote extensively about her own work and film theory in general. In 1959 she wrote an article defining what she considered truly independent films: films made by one person. In the article, she praises amateur filmmakers and what they stand for: "[That] very word—from the Latin 'amateur'—'lover' means one who does something for the love of the thing rather than for economic reasons or necessity." Her profound respect for independent films inspired her own work and she became involved in promoting the work of others. To this end, she established the Creative Film Foundation in 1954 to give financial aid to filmmakers.

Biographical Information

Deren was born to liberal, Russian-Jewish parents in Kiev in 1917. Her father was a psychiatrist, and Deren's exposure to this discipline shaped her intellectual outlook. In New York in the mid- to late 1930s she was a part of the Trotskyist youth movement and had strong Marxist beliefs. She had an early marriage to a member of the movement which ended in divorce. In 1941 she became the assistant to choreographer Katherine Dunham and travelled with Dunham's dance tour *Cabin in the Sky*. The experience with the dance company helped shape Deren's vision and throughout her career she displayed a fascination with the form and movement of dance. After ending the tour in Los Angeles she met and married the filmmaker Alexander Hammid, and she became interested in the medium of film herself. Hammid is credited with teaching Deren the technical aspects of filmmaking and collaborated with her on her first film, *Meshes of the Afternoon* (1943), in which Deren starred. The couple later divorced. Deren made three more films before sharing the first Guggenheim Fellowship awarded for creative filmmaking. The film she proposed was about Haitian dance and in 1947 she traveled to Haiti to begin filming. When she arrived, however, she found that the dance itself could not be captured without putting it in the context of the Voudoun cul-

ture. She immersed herself in this culture and even experienced the ultimate expression of Voudoun, possession by a voodoo god. The end result of her time in Haiti was a book, *Divine Horsemen: The Voodoo Gods of Haiti* (1953), rather than a film. She made two more films when she returned from Haiti and left several works in progress. Deren died suddenly in 1961 at the age of 44 from a brain hemorrhage. During her life she worked to make the avant-garde accessible in this country by finding venues to show her work. She promoted her films at college campuses and museums and managed to find an audience for her work. In 1946 she rented the Provincetown Playhouse to show her films. It was the first time that a public theater screened privately produced 16mm films. It was this self-promotion and leadership that set Deren apart from other filmmakers of the avant-garde.

Major Works

Deren had a very specific vision of her filmic technique. She always visualized and mapped out her films in advance, which enabled her to create films on shoestring budgets. Deren's early films were surrealistic and fantastic, constructed to portray a dream rather than tell a traditional story. In *At Land* (1945), Deren used editing techniques to create a continuous, impossible landscape out of several different locations. Drawing on her experience with Katherine Dunham's dance company, Deren used dance as the structural dynamic in *A Study in Choreography for Camera* (1944) and *Ritual in Transfigured Time* (1946). Deren also displayed an effective use of freeze-framing in *Ritual in Transfigured Time*. In her last two films, *Meditation on Violence* (1948) and *The Very Eye of Night* (1955), she abandoned her somewhat narrative style, unstructured as it was, in favor of a purely physical expression in free form.

Critical Reception

Deren's work is widely considered difficult and obscure, and the reaction to her films is sometimes negative. Reviewers often point out the social dimension to Deren's work. Although some argue that it is autobiographical, most agree her films are not focused inward; instead they open up her world to the viewer. Reviewers discuss the importance of ritual and myth to Deren and many assert that she uses dance as a ritual expression of myth. *The Very Eye of Night* is often cited as Deren's weakest film; some critics complain that it is more formal than her earlier films. However, *Meshes of the Afternoon* is considered one of the finest independent films to evoke the surrealist tradition. Several critics refer to Deren as the "Mother of the Underground Film" and credit her with legitimizing the use of 16mm film as an artistic medium.

PRINCIPAL WORKS

Meshes of the Afternoon (film) 1943
A Study in Choreography for Camera (film) 1944
At Land (film) 1945
An Anagram of Ideas on Art, Form and Film (essay) 1946
Ritual in Transfigured Time (film) 1946
Meditation on Violence (film) 1948
Divine Horsemen: The Voodoo Gods of Haiti (nonfiction) 1953
The Very Eye of Night (film) 1955
Divine Horsemen [edited by Cherel and Teiji Ito after Deren's death] (film) c. 1982
Witch's Cradle [produced posthumously] (film) c. 1988

CRITICISM

Hank Heifetz (review date 10 December 1970)

SOURCE: A review of *Divine Horsemen: The Voodoo Gods of Haiti,* in *The Village Voice,* Vol. XV, No. 50, December 10, 1970, pp. 6, 16.

[*In the following review, Heifetz praises Deren's* Divine Horsemen: The Voodoo Gods of Haiti *as a careful and intelligent portrayal of its subject.*]

Maya Deren's profound, loving study of the Voodoo religion is a very rare kind of book. In it, as in Alexandra David-Neel's books on Tibetan Buddhism, a famous system of practice and belief about the deep psyche and its relation to ultimate reality is portrayed from the inside by a highly intelligent, carefully honest and passionate observer. The Chelsea House edition is a handsome book, illustrated, with big type and nice paper and expensive. It's worth the money if you have it but I hope the book eventually gets into a reasonably priced paperback edition, for the good of all those it can feed at a lower price.

A book like this is the farthest thing possible from the kind of pseudo-occult phrase-dripping that passes itself off as mystic literature on the newsstands next to the astrology weeklies. For Maya Deren, Voodoo was a genuine matter of life and death. An early "underground" film-maker, she origi-nally went to Haiti in 1947 to spend eight months shooting a film on Haitian dance. But Voodoo, the religion, the reality of it, overwhelmed her artistic intentions. The film was never finished. Instead she returned to Haiti twice more to learn about Voodoo, spending a total of 18 months there before she wrote this book (first printed in 1952, in a limited edition). She did not formally become a Voodoo initiate but spoke to many devotees and attended many ceremonies, participating often in the dances. And, as the last chapter of her book tells us, she became one of the very few people from outside the Haitian culture known to have experienced possession by a Voodoo god. In all, "seven or eight times," she was "mounted" by Erzulie, the Goddess of Love and Beauty.

Possession by the gods, the loas (a Congo word for spirits), is the central experience of the Voodoo religion. It is normal for there to be one or more or many possessions at almost every ceremony. Those mounted become, during the period of possession, *les chevaux,* the horses of the gods. The experience, when fully authentic, is accompanied by amnesia. In one sense the person vanishes, or as Maya Deren says, "To understand that the self must leave if the loa is to enter is to understand that one cannot be man and god at once." What is left then, what is there, dancing, speaking, performing whatever customary actions are expected when He or She appears, is the embodiment of an archetypal principle, not a symbol with a narrow meaning but a many-sided image developed over time through a consensus of insights and feelings that can be called the art of communal religion. There are many loas, and the individual loas can appear under diverse aspects. But in each case, a unity like a magnetic field of traits and powers seems to have been compounded from mythological elements out of various parts of Africa, influences from the now extinct Haitian Indians, and features of later Haitian history as well as contemporary life. A Ghede, God of Death, puts on a black top hat and dark sunglasses, gives information and advice from the dead, eats ravenously and continuously because death eats up the world and is the only being who can swallow his own drink ("a crude rum steeped in 21 of the hottest spices known"). An Ogoun, origi-nally a Nigerian god of the thunderbolt and war, may appear as a raging, swearing general, greeted with a military salute and the national anthem. An Erzulie comports herself like a woman of boundless wealth and immeasurable grace, the best dancer of all the loas and a generous giver of gifts, as befits Love.

But there is another way to look at the loas, existentially, as beings intensely personal to the individual devotee, the serviteur. A loa to whom a person is particularly devoted is known as his mait-tete, the master of his head. The mait-tete may be passed down in a family, exemplifying hereditary or conditioned psychological characteristics, or else a man's true loa may be discovered in the course of his life; "Matu-rity is a condition for the manifestation of the loa mait-tete. . . .

The apparently ambivalent relationship of a man to his loa is a delicate and dynamic balance between devotion to and mastery of one's principles; possession can be understood, in this light, as a transitory period of exalted and exclusive obsession with a principle." Maya Deren's own mait-tete Erzulie clearly makes sense in this way, crystallizing her woman artist's love of beauty and the senses.

The long chapter describing the characteristics of the loas is the centerpiece of the book. Practically all the other material is intensely interesting as well: on the rites, the congregations, the priesthood, the drums and the formalized dances, as well as the final chapter which describes the "white darkness" of her own possession. But the loas are the core of it, and Maya Deren presents them in careful, personalized detail, each one coming over as a character, a mighty if often bizarre friend. And her general treatment of Voodoo is as a great life-enhancing image system, as a work of deepest art. Her own position, an experimental artist in a society where commerce cuts like corroding smog into the manifestations of the spirit, gave her a strong sympathy for this "primitive" society where art and the spirit are still one, fused in religion, where it seemed to her possible to serve and renew the spirit by becoming part of an expressive collective instead of developing as a lonely, defiant ego.

So the book is basically a hymn of praise to the loa, with an artist's feeling for the central importance of the emotions. The dark side of Voodoo is mentioned—black magic and the manipulation of powers—and some interesting comments are made on it, but it is treated as distinctly secondary. The author was not greatly interested in the negative uses of Voodoo. This is certainly a limitation of breadth but it is a conscious choice. Voodoo as a system is seen as providing psychic access to the reality of principles that underlie the working of life and death. It is possible that men may misuse the energy thus tapped, but that is the fault of men. For the author, "religion presumes that the major forces of the universe (which, after all, created life) are essentially benevolent in nature. . . . Religion, being a collective enterprise, is concerned with directing the cosmic forces toward a collective public good." And in this sense she sees the significance of Voodoo for the Haitians as overwhelmingly positive.

[*Divine Horsemen*] is basically a hymn of praise to the loa, with an artist's feeling for the central importance of the emotions.
—Hank Heifetz

Similarly, the function of possession as a kind of psychological compensation is mentioned but not considered pri-

mary. She does not interpret possession by a god or goddess as essentially a device by which the Haitian, for a while, forgets his or her powerless and impoverished condition. The loas give life force. A loa which becomes a mait-tete is a person's strength, available to him in whatever fields life offers him. A person possessed by a loa is not a weakling in a dream of strength—because daydreaming is a sentimental pushing of obvious buttons, with no coherent base in any depth of feeling or action. But when you really go deep and come back up again you come up strong, or at least stronger.

Contemporary hip society is full of people looking for access to the depths of the spirit. But because real access means taking chances, and putting your psyche on the line (and also knowing where to look), too much time is wasted paying attention to various occult fakes, roaming around in the comfortable boredom of astrology, talking about witches and psychics. Books like *Divine Horsemen,* on the other hand, can be of use toward developing the spiritual side of what the community of the future will have to be (if life makes it). Not that everybody should promptly begin practicing Voodoo in the East Village or on the commune. But there are lessons to be learned from knowing about it, the way Maya Deren makes you know about it. She gives the example of a collectivity committed to continual renewal and enhancement of the emotional life; a society where the individual is valued for taking psychic chances, searching diligently and maturely for his or her mait-tete and serving that loa; a society where religion involves a sense of the history of the collective, and where the spiritual power and unity deriving from it have been, in the past at least, a fuel for revolution—in 1791, when the wretched of the Haitian earth came pouring down on the plantations.

At times, in her less descriptive, more analytical sections, the writing, though never bad and never unclear, can become a little too winding and latinate, under the influence, it seems to me, of certain surrealist prose (an influence also evident in her films). But most of the time even this mild criticism can't be laid against the writing. On the whole the style shines, because the words and rhythms are really born from a relentless devotion to their subject. The book is full of rich things, to be read over and over, which is a groove when you consider that even most so-called creative fiction around now is written to be skimmed once, at most, and thrown away. To pull just one quiet, beautiful passage out, see how this one, about the drummers, builds: "It is the drums and the drum beats, per se, which are the sacred sound, and although one man may articulate the drum's voice more fluently, brilliantly, and invocatively than another, he is but a minor part of the mechanism of that speech. If he beats anything except the sacred beats, his most brilliant virtuosity produces not one loa. But the loa will come to a merely adequate rendition of the sacred beats, and to the call of the asson (a sacred rattle); to just the voices lifted in song or invocation; in answer to ritual gesture; and even, on their own initiative, in answer to silent need."

Regina Cornwell (essay date Winter 1971-72)

SOURCE: "Maya Deren and Germaine Dulac: Activists of the Avant-Garde," in *Film Library Quarterly,* Vol. 5, No. 1, Winter, 1971-72, pp. 29-38.

[In the following essay, Cornwell asserts that Deren is important to filmmaking for both her work as a female director and for her role as a film activist.]

In "The Woman as Film-Director," Harry Alan Potamkin writes:

> I have been asked a number of times, "Can a woman become a film-director?" My answer takes two forms. First, I make the obvious retort that women are in demand as players, as scenario writers, and as film editors. Then I go on to say how few women have ever created films themselves. (*American Cinematographer,* XII, January, 1932, p. 10)

After a brief enumeration of women directors, Potamkin concentrates on Germaine Dulac, identified with both the commercial and the avant-garde film. If there have been few women directors in commercial cinema, proportionately there have been and still are fewer women working within the avant-garde. Along with Germaine Dulac, one can cite Maya Deren, Marie Menken, Shirley Clarke, Storm de Hirsch, Joyce Wieland and Gunvor Nelson. Dulac and Deren can be singled out for they are important in the history of film not solely for their directing but also and perhaps equally for their roles as film activists—propagandists for the film as a serious art form.

Deren, whose name is familiar, is identified with the American avant-garde of the '40's. She is acclaimed as important; yet, seldom is the real significance of her role as an activist in this avant-garde explained. Her film career began in 1943 at the age of 26 when she made her first work in conjunction with her husband, filmmaker, Alexander Hammid. From 1943 until her sudden death in 1961 at the age of forty-four, Deren completed six films: *Meshes of the Afternoon* (1943), *A Study in Choreography for Camera* (1944), *At Land* (1945), *Ritual in Transfigured Time* (1946), *Meditation on Violence* (1948), and *The Very Eye of Night* (1955). If Deren was influential through her filmmaking it was only so because she began the process of establishing, almost single-handedly, a milieu for the avant-garde film in this country—ways and means by which her work could be seen, ways and means taken up in turn by other artists.

In 1943, 16mm was still considered a substandard or inferior film gauge suitable only for educational, documentary and amateur work. But Deren seized upon the notion of "amateur" and happily applied it in its original meaning to herself and her work. She wrote later in 1959, in an article entitled "Amateur Versus Professional": "The very classification 'amateur' has an apologetic ring. But that very word—from the Latin 'amateur'—'lover' means one who does something for the love of the thing rather than for economic reasons or necessity." (Reprinted in *Film Culture*, No. 39, Winter, 1965, p. 45) The avant-garde in Europe and America in the '20's had, of course, worked in 35mm. There may have been in this country in the '30's, a few filmmakers who at one time or another worked in 16mm; but, Deren served to legitimatize it as a film gauge in which one could work artistically, analogous to the way in which Stan Brakhage, who started working with 8mm in 1964, has begun to legitimatize its artistic use. Others in the '40s, such as Sidney Peterson, Willard Maas, James Broughton and Kenneth Anger, then followed her example; and, today the American avant-garde is principally identified with 16mm.

At the time that Deren began there were no channels of distribution, let alone exhibition, for *new* avant-garde work. In 1945, having completed three films, she sent out leaflets to colleges, universities, art schools and museums around the country, advertising her work. She began renting her films, using her home as a distribution base. Often she would accompany her showings with a lecture. The following year Deren set up what is credited as the first showings in a public theatre in the U.S. of privately made 16mm film. These two Provincetown Playhouse screenings of her work even prompted reviews in major publications, including one by James Agee in *The Nation.* Thus she paved the way for Frank Stauffacher's avant-garde "Art in Cinema" series which began in 1947 at the San Francisco Museum of Art and for Amos Vogel's "Cinema 16" begun the same year, followed up three years later by his distribution center of the same name which finally provided a professional rental outlet for avant-garde work.

But Deren did not stop with showing and promoting her work. She had, in 1946, shared the distinction with the Whitney brothers of receiving the first Guggenheim Fellowships ever awarded for creative filmmaking; she had attempted a renewal of her grant the following year but was unsuccessful. In 1954, based on her years of experience with the difficulties of obtaining grants and raising money in order to pursue independent filmmaking, she established the Creative Film Foundation which continued until two years after her death. Among those awarded grants that first year were Shirley Clarke and Stan Brakhage. As a writer, Deren spoke frequently and at length of her own work, but also about the art of the independent film in general. Very much of a dogmatist and polemicist, Deren rigidly maintained her ideas about the art of the personal film, persuading many to her camp.

She had begun her career at a time when there was negligible interest in film as an art form in this country and she provided through her active dedication an example, a hope to others for the possibilities of independent filmmaking. To call Maya Deren "Mother of the Underground Film," as Sheldon Renan does in *An Introduction to the American Underground Film,* characterizes the debt which American avant-garde filmmakers since the forties continue to owe to her.

Cecile Starr (essay date 2 May 1976)

SOURCE: "The Mother of the American Avant-Garde Film," in *The New York Times,* May 2, 1976, pp. 13, 22.

[*In the following essay, Starr discusses how Deren's films influenced a generation of avant-garde filmmakers.*]

The gospel of the low-budget, personal, experimental film was first preached in this country by an explosive, dedicated young woman named Maya Deren. From the early 1940's until her death in 1961, Miss Deren both invoked and exemplified the American avant-garde movement, virtually by herself—as filmmaker, distributor, lecturer, theorist, and promoter, all in one fiery personality. In the 15 years since her death, hundreds of new experimental filmmakers have shown their films around the country; yet, in contrast to modern music, dance, architecture, and painting, the avant-garde film has remained almost invisible to the American public. This week, a series of avant-garde films at The Museum of Modern Art ushers in what may be a new era of visibility.

Starting on Tuesday, and continuing each evening at 8:30 until May 11 (except Thursday, May 6), a 30-year History of American Avant-Garde Cinema is being presented at the Museum, free of charge, under the auspices of The American Federation of Arts, with support from the National Endowment for the Arts. This comprehensive retrospective marks the first nationwide effort to cultivate new audiences for an art that may at times be exasperating, incomprehensible, or even maddening. The series, comprised of 39 films selected by John Hanhardt, Film and Video Curator of The Whitney Museum of American Art, will travel to Boston, Philadelphia, Baltimore, St. Louis and other cities.

It's a far cry from the days when Maya Deren took to the road alone, with her handful of films, and startled college audiences. She was unmistakably a woman with a cause, and she defined that cause in many ways, on many esthetic levels. In basic terms, it was to achieve recognition for the personal film as the magical creation of the solitary artist, a truly

independent art form comparable to a poem one reads and rereads, or a painting to which one returns many times. "A radio is not a louder voice," she pointed out, "an airplane is not a faster car, and the motion picture should not be thought of as a faster painting or a more real play."

She set up the Creative Film Foundation, through which she focused attention on outstanding younger film-makers—Stan Brakhage, Stan VenDerBeek, and Robert Breer, whose works are generously represented in the current exhibition. Her own first film, *Meshes of the Afternoon,* which opens the first program of the MOMA's current series, was actually a collaborative work between Miss Deren, who supplied the poetic concepts, and Alexander Hammid—then her husband—who was responsible for the technical polish. Filmed and edited in 1943 in about three weeks, *Meshes* depicts various experiences of reality and dreams. The Deren-figure walks (feet and shadow first) down a path, enters a house, observes and examines its disordered objects, sits down and dreams, and sees herself and other figures walking down the path, entering the house, and so forth.

Maya Deren believed that each film has its own logic, separate from the logic of causes and events in the outside world. "*Meshes of the Afternoon,*" she said, derived from "the logic of ideas and emotions," within the poetic mode. Although—or possibly because—she was a psychiatrist's daughter, she consistently refused easy interpretations of the film's recurring symbols—the fully open hibiscus flower, the tortuous stairway, the black-garbed figure with a mirror for a face. Such imagery she embraced for its own mythic values.

Meshes of the Afternoon set the tone of American avant-garde films for a decade, and linked the movement to the older European avant-garde films of Cocteau and Bunuel. James Broughton's *Mother's Day,* Willard Maas's *Geography of the Body,* Kenneth Anger's *Fireworks,* all made in the 1940's, had in common with Miss Deren's films an intimate, sometimes intense physicality. And as Susan Sontag has noted, this group of films was also "technically studied . . . as professional as possible," within their modest means.

Meshes of the Afternoon **set the tone of American avant-garde films for a decade, and linked the movement to the older European avant-garde films of Cocteau and Bunuel.**

—Cecile Starr

In contrast to Miss Deren's meticulous approach, the second wave of avant-gardists, led by her friends Stan Brakhage and Jonas Mekas in the 1950's, made long, almost unedited diary-style films, seemingly careless works in which these technically proficient moviemakers deliberately cultivated the amateur's mistakes (over-and under-exposures, out-of-focus shots, wild panning movements). They did this partly as an act of rebellion, but mainly to achieve a greater sense of freedom and spontaneity. There experimentalists, in turn, were followed by younger filmmakers who looked into the very elements of film itself: Tony Conrad, with his ominous film, *The Flicker,* made up only of intermittent dark and bright flashing frames, and George Landow, with his almost self-descriptive *Film in Which There Appear Sprocket Holes, Edge Lettering, Dirt Particles, Etc.*

When Maya Deren showed her films in New York City in 1946, at the small Provincetown Playhouse which she herself had rented, such a large crowd gathered outside, the story goes, that a policeman stopped to ask if it were a demonstration, and someone answered, "No, it's a revolution in filmmaking."
—Cecile Starr

Other young experimenters have concentrated upon a single scene. Michael Scow's *Wavelength,* for example, is built entirely upon the "logic" of the zoom shot, extended for 45 minutes, making its mechanical advance into a room which slowly, slowly, is consumed and made to vanish into a picture of the ocean. Slowness is almost totally sustained in the shorter films of Barry Gerson, who has created rich filmic episodes from such common elements as the shadow of a lucent curtain moving back and forth across a brightly polished floor. Ernie Gehr's *Sublime Velocity* gives rapid pulsation to a deserted hallway, by manipulation of the zoom lens every few frames. Harry Smith's hand-made animations, and the brilliant symmetries of Jordan Belson and James Whitney, offer diversion in abstract color and design.

When Maya Deren showed her films in New York City in 1946, at the small Provincetown Playhouse which she herself had rented, such a large crowd gathered outside, the story goes, that a policeman stopped to ask if it were a demonstration, and someone answered, "No, it's a revolution in filmmaking." Now it's past history. And Maya Deren has taken her place as Mother of the American Avant-Garde Film.

J. Hoberman (essay date 15 May 1978)

SOURCE: "The Maya Mystique," in *The Village Voice,* Vol. XXIII, No. 20, May 15, 1978, p. 50.

[*In the following essay, Hoberman explains how Deren was an innovator in filmmaking for her generation.*]

Seventeen years after her death, Maya Deren's films (at the Film Forum, May 11 through 14) continue to provoke a violently mixed response. A pioneer working in a virtual vacuum, she invented the two genres—psychodrama and dance-film—that most characterize American personal cinema from World War II through the late 1950s. So many of Deren's devices have grown shopworn in other hands that it takes an active imagination to recognize just how innovative her work really was.

Of the six films Deren completed, her three psychodramas are the most substantial. *Meshes of the Afternoon* (1943) was the first and, *Un Chien Andalou* aside, probably the most widely seen avant-garde film ever made. Like that film, Deren's has the logic of a dream; but while Bunuel and Dali used an irrational narrative to mimic the general structure of the unconscious mind, Deren attempted to depict the specific internal world of her film's protagonist, played by herself. In fact, *Meshes* seems less related to European surrealism than to the Freudian flashbacks and sinister living-rooms that typify Hollywood's wartime "noir" films. Located in some hilly L.A. suburb, the house where Deren's erotic, violent fantasy was filmed might be around the corner from Barbara Stanwyck's place in *Double Indemnity*.

The film's haunting power is derived, not so much from its symbolism, as from a brilliant use of matched cuts, elliptical editing, and slow-motion to reorder time and space. Many of its effects have yet to be bettered. The vision was Deren's, but the skill of its execution was due, in part, to the expertise of Alexander Hammid, the Czech filmmaker who was then her husband. One need only compare the film to the kitsch-arama dream sequence concocted by Dali two years later for *Spellbound* to see how effectively Deren and Hammid could work with little more than home-movie means.

Deren continued to refine these techniques in her subsequent psychodramas, *At Land* (1944) and *Ritual in Transfigured Time* (1946). Although neither has the sustained visual complexity or tension of *Meshes of the Afternoon,* both contain passages as potent as anything in the earlier piece. *At Land,* in particular, is a superb exposition of the kind of editing Soviet montage-theorists called "creative geography"—constructing a continuous, impossible landscape out of a number of different locations. In her ambitious *Ritual in Transfigured Time* (which features Anais Nin among other Village residents), Deren adds an effective use of freeze-framing to her already established film vocabulary.

Perhaps because they are denied the intensity of her own performances, Deren's dance-films are less compelling than her psychodramas. In *A Study in Choreography for Camera* (1945), she match-cuts a male dancer as he leaps in slow motion from the woods to an apartment to the Egyptian room of the Metropolitan Museum of Art and back. One has to struggle past the near self-parody of this literal evocation of "art and beauty" to appreciate the graceful economy with which Deren demonstrates the cinema's power to delete space while expanding time. *Choreography* was not only the first real dance-film, it also—as P. Adams Sitney has pointed out—"introduced the possibility of isolating a single gesture as a complete film."

After *Meditation on Violence* (1948), a kind of kungfu remake of *Choreography* (more successful in its choice of subject though less concise in its form), Deren became the first filmmaker to receive a Guggenheim fellowship and left for Haiti to make a film on voodoo ritual. She never edited the footage (which will be screened at the Anthology Film Archives on May 27, 30, and 31), and, in fact, completed only one other film before her death at 44. This last work, *The Very Eye of Night* (1959), is generally held to be her weakest film; certainly it is her most naive. Over a simulated starry sky, Deren superimposed negative images of ethereal, gravity-free dancers. Though the film is far less structured than its predecessors, it reveals a new interest in flat cinematic space and something of the sweet fetish-quality of a Joseph Cornell box.

The essential vulnerability of Deren's oeuvre stems from her apparent need to justify the value of her work by burdening it with a load of extraneous cultural baggage. But if Deren was over-earnest, she probably had to be. As America's first real avant-garde filmmaker, and a woman as well, she was not about to find people lined up around the block waiting to take her seriously. The text of a 1953 symposium on "Poetry and Film" (reprinted in *Film Culture Reader*) is indicative of the cultural climate she was up against. The only filmmaker on the panel, she resolutely contends with Dylan Thomas's shameless hot-dogging and Arthur Miller's windy pontifications. When Gay Talese—who covered the New York City oddball beat for the *Times* in the late '50s—wrote Deren up, he mentioned her interest in voodoo, her Japanese husband, her cats—everything but her film work. Fortunately, Deren was a determined, vigorous polemicist and organizer for what, in a 1961 *Voice* article, she called the "chamber film." The best of her work has yet to be exhausted, but it is primarily for the chances she took with her life that every independent filmmaker in America remains in her debt.

George M. Epple (review date December 1982)

SOURCE: A review of *Divine Horsemen: The Voodoo Gods of Haiti,* in *American Anthropologist,* Vol. 84, No. 4, December, 1982, pp. 979-80.

[*In the following review, Ehrenreich discusses the film* Divine Horsemen, *based on Deren's book by the same name. He asserts that the film has a limited usefulness for a general audience, but provides a thrilling visual document of Haiti for the informed viewer.*]

Divine Horsemen preserves and makes available to a wider audience some of the intriguing and valuable film footage shot by the American filmmaker/anthropologist Maya Deren between 1947 and 1951 in Haiti. Cherel and Teiji Ito have edited the film and sound track and have added narration. The narration is adapted from Deren's book, *Divine Horsemen* (1953), and provides an adequate description of the more important aspects of the Voudoun (voodoo) rituals shown (I have chosen to use Deren's spellings for technical terms). At some points in the film a second narrator quotes from Deren's personal descriptions of the ceremonies, providing an interesting insight into the observer's perspective.

The film begins with a general introduction to some of the elements of the Voudoun belief system and its rituals. We are acquainted with the *loa,* or divine spirits, who are most important in the lives of individuals, including Legba the God of the Crossroads and one of the primary figures in the Haitian pantheon. The narration also identifies and provides some explanation for the central features of the rituals and belief system. The major portion of the film presents a sequence of rituals which portray the major Voudoun cult complexes of Rada, Congo, and Petro. Each of these sections is initiated with a shot of the *vever (veve)* or symbol of the major divinity of the cult. This is followed in each segment by a series of rituals appropriate to the worship of the *loa* of that cult. Major *loa* appearing in the ceremonies include Damballah (The Serpent), Agwe (The Sovereign of the Seas), Ogun (The Warrior), Ghede (The Clown), and Erzulie (The Goddess of Love). Explanations are given for the progression typical of each ritual, and through this technique the viewer is made aware of the significant stages of the service and the roles and personalities of the participants. The footage includes examples of various types and stages of possession and animal sacrifices; these scenes are handled sensitively, and their integration into the rituals is clear. The film concludes with examples of secular dances from the Rara festival and masked bands from Haitian Carnival celebrations in Port-au-Prince. This documentary presentation of Haitian ritual and ceremony is exciting in its visual impact and informative in its description.

The technical quality of the film is surprisingly fine. Deren's film exudes an artistic quality which far overshadows any limitations inherent in the equipment of her day. The editors have managed to maintain the very good image quality and have done an excellent job of synching the sound. A few minor flaws were present in the print including awkwardly slowed down segments, some abrupt cuts and flashes, and minor focus problems. It might have been helpful also if the editors had inserted subtitles containing the *loa's* names with each of the *vever,* an obvious aid to identification for those unfamiliar with the Voudoun religion.

The major problem with the film is that it fails to provide an adequate sociocultural and historical context for the fascinating performances of the sacred and secular rituals, thus limiting the usefulness of the film for general audiences. The film would require considerable explanation and discussion by an instructor familiar with the literature on Haitian Voudoun. This might inhibit the use of the film in relevant courses in religion, psychological anthropology, art, and others if the instructor is unable to do the necessary research. For the general viewer, this film should raise more questions than it answers. For example, we are told little about the people who are participants in the rituals. Nor are we informed about the social structure of Haiti and its relationship to Voudoun. The broader role of religion in Haitian life and culture is only hinted at. Moreover, the transition from presentation of Voudoun rituals to the scenes from Carnival is not clearly indicated, although it will be obvious to most viewers that a dichotomy between wealthy and poor has suddenly appeared in the film. The editors have apparently chosen to remain faithful to Deren's intuitive and artistic approach and have directed the film at an evocative portrait of fragments of the Voudoun belief system. For the informed viewer and researcher this provides a marvelously thrilling and rare visual document on Haiti. The usefulness of the film could be enhanced, however, by providing a reasonably thorough study guide for the interested user.

Lauren Rabinovitz (review date 1986)

SOURCE: A review of *The Legend of Maya Deren: A Documentary Biography and Collected Works,* in *Wide Angle,* Vol. 8, No. 3, 1986, pp. 131-33.

[*In the following review, Rabinovitz discusses* The Legend of Maya Deren *as a biography which presents the relationship of a female artist to a male-dominated system.*]

The Legend of Maya Deren is the first book on the most frequently mentioned woman filmmaker of the postwar avant-garde cinema. Maya Deren (1917-1961) made short, modernist films that initially addressed an individual woman's subjective experiences but which later expanded to celebrations of myth and ritual. Unable to secure continued financial backing for her films, Deren became a lecturer,

teacher, publicist and organizational administrator in order to create and to promote a more sympathetic climate for American independent filmmaking in the Forties and Fifties. Acknowledging Deren's central role in the New York avant-garde cinema, *The Legend of Maya Deren* constructs a psychological biography of Deren so as to make her a role model for contemporary women.

Calling themselves *The Legend of Maya Deren* Project, authors Clark, Hodson, Neiman and director of photography Francine Bailey Price began their proposed three-volume biography of Deren's life and works in 1973. At that time, an auteurist study establishing a pre-feminist tradition in cinema and arranging one woman artist's life (both interior and exterior) as a model narrative for contemporary women typified feminist film criticism and history in its preliminary stage of development. The Berkeley-based magazine *Women and Film* (1972-1975) was uncovering an archaeology of such women directors as Germaine Dulac, Leontine Sagan and Agnes Varda. Other articles by Regina Cornwell and Francis Lacassin reinserted into mainstream film history obscured female directors like Dulac, Deren, or Alice Guy-Blaché. But when, in the mid-Seventies, British critics Claire Johnston and Pam Cook examined the work of Hollywood film director Dorothy Arzner, they redirected feminist film criticism to textual-based analysis demonstrating how women's covert discourses may act subversively upon the dominant patriarchal discourse. Their work reflected a larger shift in film scholarship from Romantic-based auteurism to Marxist-oriented criticism informed by semiotics, structuralism and psychoanalytic theories.

While progressing on their book, *The Legend of Maya Deren* Project reformed their feminist practice within the new direction of feminist criticism. In a *Camera Obscura* interview conducted in 1977, the *Legend* authors stated that their goal was to understand how "legends" about Maya Deren had created discourses surrounding the reception of a woman artist, her films, and ideas. They said that their decision to do a documentary biography was an effort to collect and to juxtapose multiple narratives about a woman's life so that "the reader can weigh alternative points of view." Although they maintained their aim of creating a cultural heroine, they now infused their discussion with an implicit understanding of new interpretive methods for the primary texts that would comprise their biography.

Such a biography promised not only a chronicle of one individual's role in an independent artisanal system; more importantly, it proposed new understanding of the processes which inform a woman artist's relationships to a male-dominated system and to the public-at-large. The first major books on the relationship between feminism and cinema addressed the critical need for a discussion of the issues. E. Ann Kaplan's *Women and Film: Both Sides of the Camera* (1983) called for future studies which would examine the ways that theory, cinematic strategies and reception have affected filmic interpretation and the economic base for women's independent film production. Annette Kuhn's *Women's Pictures: Feminism and Cinema* (1982) outlined as a productive area for further feminist investigation the independent cinema's interconnectedness between meaning construction and relations of production and reception. In the early Eighties, both books pointed to the way that a woman filmmaker's biography could raise timely questions about political practice—whether feminist or otherwise—in independent cinema frameworks.

Acknowledging Deren's central role in the New York avant-garde cinema, *The Legend of Maya Deren* constructs a psychological biography of Deren so as to make her a role model for contemporary women.
—*Lauren Rabinovitz*

But *The Legend of Maya Deren* does not address the social formation of women's participation and reception in the institutions that form the economic base for independent artisanal practices. It fails to do so not because the authors challenge Kaplan's or Kuhn's models inasmuch as they do not see how such concerns are relevant to their feminist history. Rather than explore the relationships between institutional structures and discursive strategies in Deren's film and theories, they attempt "to see the world through Deren's eyes."

A self-proclaimed history written from the inside of a woman artist's life, *The Legend* posits a phenomenological approach to Maya Deren herself as a metaphor for feminist consciousness. The authors' introduction makes clear the tacit approach: "Maya Deren was a model our generation was seeking. She had raised the political, cultural, and many of the personal questions all of us had been formulating in the early Seventies." What follows then is a herculean attempt to reconstruct Deren's life and thoughts from more than 30 boxes of materials in the Maya Deren Papers (Special Collections, Mugar Memorial Library, Boston University) and from more than 100 interviews conducted by the authors.

It is even more unfortunate that the authors selected as the first volume for publication one covering the period in Deren's life from birth up to her first film. Although the decision is consistent with a psychoanalytic approach in which Deren's family relationships, childhood, and adolescence would have deep significance, the 500-page volume period predates any of Deren's film-making or theoretical activi-

ties and, as such, the effect of her early life on her mature work is not elucidated. Among the three volumes scheduled for publication, the documents contained herein are likely to hold the least interest for film scholars or enthusiasts.

A more serious problem though lies in *The Legend*'s approach to the materials. After effusive commentary about handling archival materials originally owned and touched by Deren herself, the authors treat the documents as valuable heirlooms in and of themselves. They reproduce Deren family photographs, school records and transcripts, letters, facsimiles of early diaries, drawings, college newspaper clippings, high school and college essays, course notes, adolescent poetry and short stories.

They also insert snapshots that they made taking pilgrimages to the various sites of Deren's early life. Included are photos of the entrance to a camp that Deren attended when she was 10, the facade of a school in Syracuse, New York, and the street sign from Deren's block in Syracuse. The value of this documentation is never made any clearer than the extent to which all materials from her life or which reflect back on her life offer traces of Deren's conscious presence. Idealized as the original sources for Deren's representation, the materials become fetishized objects, and they, rather than a representation of Deren, provide the book's focus.

Although the authors acknowledge that they made selections from greater numbers of documents, they do not so much examine their processes for selection as offer two alternative narrative commentaries. The first consists of interviews with Deren's mother, husbands, relatives and friends interspersed throughout the volume. The authors annotate the interviews with a commentary meant to be self-revelatory. For example, they describe their encounters with Marie Deren (Maya's mother), "When she 'played' history for us, Marie 'played' between the black and white keys—it was a different sound, subtle, often too sharp or too flat for the ears of three post World War Two 'youngsters.'" A few pages later, they switch from self-deprecation to condescension regarding the elderly Deren, "She was a far more engaging individual than we persons under 35 years of age had expected her to be." Even when they analyze their own processes for making history, they swing between hyperbole and conceit.

A second narrative commentary consists of the organizational structure superimposed on the primary materials. The authors explain that because language—its acquisition and mastery—was the guiding force of Deren's youth, they organize her first 16 years according to the Muntu Scheme that the German literary historian Janheinz Jahn developed in 1958 when he was classifying the Bantu-speaking tribes of Africa. They defend their model saying childhood is a "modern-day oral societ[y] which show[s] certain similarities to traditional societies in Africa today." One has to question whether a primarily anthropological model for language acquisition can be so easily transferred from a primitive, oral society to a highly technologized industrial society.

The authors themselves contradict their own justification—that both are oral societies—when the primary materials that they present as evidence for Deren's mastery of language are all *written*. The documents reflect not the "verbal world in which children live" but Deren's increasing mastery of a reality where "the written word is law." The authors' recognition of language acquisition and mastery in childhood development seems far more dependent on the well-established theories of French psychoanalyst Jacques Lacan, and their argument would have profited from a review of discussions concerning woman's mastery of written language as her inscription inside patriarchal law.

The second organizational device that the authors employ is Deren's astrological natal chart. Relying upon the chart as "a source of information more reliable than the recollections of persons who had been emotionally involved with [her]," the authors interject an astrologer's interpretations so as to provide a narrative commentary on Deren's familial relationships and psychological profile. The authors tacitly accept that astrology is both an objective and valuable biographical methodology. Albeit this is not the proper forum for a discussion of astrology's merits as a science; yet one cannot help but wonder why they chose such a highly unorthodox methodology and why they did not more thoroughly justify its use.

The Legend of Maya Deren's greatest value, however, may be that the volume makes generally available to interested scholars a wealth of documents otherwise unobtainable or accessible only in archival collections. In this regard, the book continues—after a long interruption—the effort that *Film Culture* began in 1965 when it published a special issue of Deren's writings. In fact, *Film Culture* together with its offspring organization Anthology Film Archives is the volume's publisher, and the authors dedicated the book to Jonas Mekas, founder of both *Film Culture* and Anthology Film Archives. In light of the publication relationship, it is less surprising then that *The Legend of Maya Deren* perpetuates the auteurist-based phenomenological approach which these two organizations heralded in the Sixties and Seventies.

The Legend of Maya Deren Project has ultimately overlooked not only the relationships among institutions, discourses and reception in Deren's life and work but also those among its own practices and politics. Without remarking on the significance of their relationship with *Film Culture* and Anthology Film Archives, *The Legend* authors have affiliated with the one institution considered the prime "canonizer" for a narrowly auteurist cinema favoring formalist concerns

of certain male filmmakers over all others. More importantly, they have adopted the very same critical attitude that made Anthology the target for numerous feminist critiques in the Seventies, the most notable of which was Constance Penley's and Janet Bergstrom's 1978 *Screen* article. Representing the Camera Obscura editorial collective, Penley and Bergstrom attacked not only what they felt were Anthology's elitist, misogynous policies regarding its archival selections but also the ways in which auteurism and phenomenology intellectually supported Anthology's political position. Because *The Legend* authors have failed to see themselves or their work inside a history of feminist criticism, they have contradictorily problematized their project's feminist goals.

Michael Renov (essay date October 1987)

SOURCE: "The Spacialization and Recuperation of Disorder," in *Afterimage,* Vol. 15, No. 3, October, 1987, pp. 12-3.

[*In the following excerpt, Renov discusses Deren's film and writing as "most clearly evok[ing] as well as theoriz[ing] the heterotopic effects that have been attributed to the* film noir, *primarily through their elaboration of the horizontal and vertical axes of meaning potential to cinema."*]

The work and writing of Maya Deren most clearly evoke as well as theorize the heterotopic effects that have been attributed to the *film noir,* primarily through their elaboration of the horizontal and vertical axes of meaning potential to cinema. During a now-famous symposium on the poetic film held in New York City in 1953, Deren described the functioning of these twin paradigms in the meaning construction of the avant-garde film form by relating filmic inscription to literary practice:

> The poetic construct arises from the fact . . . that it is a "vertical" investigation of a situation in that it probes the ramifications of the moment, and is concerned with its qualities and its depth, so that you have poetry concerned, in a sense, not with what is occurring but with what it feels like or what it means. . . . Now [a poem] may also include action, but its attack is what I would call the "vertical" attack, and this may be a little clearer if you will contrast it to what I would call the "horizontal" attack of drama, which is concerned with the development, let's say, within a very small situation from feeling to feeling.

For Deren, then, filmmaking that aspired to the poetic would explore paradigmatic as well as syntagmatic relations. The vertical axis, the retardation of event, the domain of metaphor—all allude to a logic exterior to action and the hermeneutic drive, to a figuration that, in certain instances, achieves a kind of relative autonomy.

> **In Deren's films, the locus of formal tension is frequently the frontier between abstraction and, if not realism, at least a kind of (sur)realism.**
> —*Michael Renov*

The question remains, in part, to what degree this relative autonomy of the figurative impulse indicates a departure from the limits of a representationalism that fosters the much-discussed illusion of reality. Again, Deren offers the clearest explication in word and image. In a lucidly argued essay entitled "Cinematography: The Creative Use of Reality," Deren theorizes the delicate balance between realisms and abstraction evidenced in such creative works as *Meshes of the Afternoon* and *Ritual in Transfigured Time* (1946):

> The motion picture medium [is] a form in which the meaning of the image originates in our recognition of a known reality and derives its authority from the direct relationship between reality and image in the photographic process. While the process permits some intrusion by the artist as a modifier of that image, the limits of its tolerance can be defined as that point at which the original reality becomes unrecognizable or is irrelevant (as when a red reflection in a pond is used for its shape and color only and without contextual concern for the water or the pond).

Deren argues for the efficacy of a residual referentiality that enriches abstract expression "like a strip of memory unrolling beneath the images of the film itself, [forming] the invisible underlayer of an implicit double exposure."

In Deren's films, the locus of formal tension is frequently the frontier between abstraction and, if not realism, at least a kind of (sur)realism. Verisimilitude, however, is otherwise encoded within dominant cinema so that the split between abstraction and (sur)realism present in her work would be situated wholly within the figurative domain. Nevertheless, a sense of spatial disjunction (with space defined in both its concrete and more abstract, Foucauldian sense) and hence "disorder" is generated in *Meshes* or in *Ritual*. In the former, architectural space is, at times, problematized to so radical a degree that, through the sinuous spiralling of the camera, horizontal and vertical are vanquished as meaningful categories of visual organization. Such a formal strategy can only be said to achieve an effect of disorder, however, if it is contradicted elsewhere within the text. (A film shot in a weightless state would be homogeneous in its effect of disorientation without producing a heteroclitic state.) While *Meshes* elsewhere obeys the laws of gravity, the rendering of space and of temporality is so profoundly disruptive, faithful only to the demands of the dream work's associative powers, that it is difficult to invoke the principle of verisimilitude in any meaningful sense. The notion of representational disorder developed in this essay, insofar as it depends on an assumption of textual logics held in tension, is applicable to Deren's films only when the logical categories are shifted from those of classical narrative (verisimilitude/figuration) to more actively avant-garde axes of meaning (abstraction/representationalism).

Ritual in Transfigured Time offers further evidence of the variance of effects generated within the problematic of the classical film text and in Deren's explorations of filmic potential. Again, as in *Meshes,* the claims of verisimilitude are not at issue. In *Ritual,* a level of mediation or authorial intervention sustained throughout the film is most frequently expressed through the use of stop-action or slow-motion effects, functions of the camera as "time microscope." The final image floats through the frame in a mesmerizing vertical movement, a figure suspended in a purely negative space. This is the wedding-dress-cum-shroud of Deren's multiple protagonist; death and ritual celebration are both fused and rendered cyclical. In her use of a stripped-down decor, solitary figures wielding objects charged with a symbolic weight, and slow-motion effects that alternately produce a sense of solemnity and of desperation. Deren creates a world apart, which overwhelms by the sum of its indeterminacy. Deren's film work, while posing the problem of textual logics in conflict quite vividly, outflanks the relatively limited domain of formal conditions (Hollywood's *vraisemblable*) incumbent on those working within the mainstream. And, in choosing to function beyond the constraints of the "brute reality" that the classical cinema takes as its given. Deren's films fail to generate that concussive effect of heterogeneity achieved by certain Hollywood films in which isolated, transgressive moments or muted counterstrategies assail the dominion of verisimilitude.

Annette Kuhn (review date June 1988)

SOURCE: A review of *Meshes of the Afternoon,* in *Monthly Film Bulletin*, Vol. 55, No. 653, June, 1988, pp. 186-87.

[*In the following review, Kuhn praises Deren's* Meshes of the Afternoon *for revealing "a memorable inner world of stunning imagery and powerful emotion."*]

A sunny, steep-walled lane, a large, delicate flower in full bloom, a woman's sandalled feet, sharp shadows, a cloaked figure glimpsed disappearing around a corner, steps to a house door. Within, a series of everyday objects—mirror, armchair, knife. The scene is set, the stage empty: what will happen? The enigmatic opening of *Meshes of the Afternoon,* Maya Deren's first film—made in collaboration with her husband, Alexander Hammid—introduces the protagonist (played by Deren herself) without actually showing her. The point of view is the woman's, and through it the viewer is drawn into a world which combines reassuring and threatening aspects of the familiar to produce an uneasy sense that things are not quite right, not quite as they seem.

This could easily be a scaled-down setting for the 'Gothic' melodramas so popular in 40s Hollywood: a young woman marries a man about whom she knows little and, brought to his house, begins to feel threatened by her new surroundings. Films of this genre—from *Rebecca* (1940) to *Secret Beyond the Door* (1948)—ask to be read in popularised Freudian terms: a bride, at once frightened and fascinated by her newly discovered sexuality, projects these ambivalent feelings on to their object and their scene. The home, besides representing that combination of safe haven and prison that marriage can be for a woman, takes on the fearful qualities of a potentially uncontrollable sexuality.

But if in these respects *Meshes* has more in common than is often acknowledged with the commercial cinema of the time, their expression is quite distinct. The empty house of Deren's film is a scene of reflection, not of action. Elements of the opening are repeated with variations in several sequences, giving the film a kind of spiral structure, in that events/images are always nearly-but-not-quite returning to the starting point. The opening sequence comes to an end as the woman sits in an armchair. Her face appears on screen for the first time. Her eyes close and, as if from her point of view, we see a veil descending over the window opposite: a classic cue for a dream sequence, 40s style. The rest of the film both plays on, and overturns, any assumption that what we are seeing is the sleeper's dream.

Outside the house, the woman's double pursues the cloaked figure, (re-)enters the house and climbs the stairs. Some of the objects evident in the first sequence are now in the 'wrong' place—the knife, for example, is in the bed—and so take on a more menacing aspect. At the close of this second sequence, the 'double' returns to the sleeping figure in the chair, and a new sequence begins with yet another double pursuing the cloaked figure in the lane outside the house.

A classic resolution is duplicitously promised when one of the doubles returns to the armchair for the fourth time, now aggressively grasping the knife. Awakened, the sleeper sees not a murderous double but a smiling man (played by Alexander Hammid), a complex figure functioning on one

level as the Prince awakening the Sleeping Beauty, but also standing both for the woman's destructive self and for the mysterious other, the cloaked figure (though since the figure's face has been shown to be a mirror, it/he too can be regarded as an aspect of the woman's self). As it turns out, however, this is not the end of the story, but the beginning of yet another twist in the spiral of repetition/variation, this one ending not in salvation but in death.

Meshes of the Afternoon can be regarded as an expression of Maya Deren's dictum that poetry in film is "a 'vertical' investigation of a situation, in that it probes the ramifications of the moment". The 'moment' in *Meshes* comprises what the protagonist sees on her approach and entry to the house, recounted in cinematic 'first person'. The rest of the film—readable as the woman's inner reflection upon, or unconscious reworking of, this material—is organised very much like a dream, with the half-logical associations, the displacements, doublings, repetitions and spatial dislocations characteristic of dream language.

In histories of the U.S. avant-garde, *Meshes* is invariably credited with being the point of origin, and its maker the 'mother', of what was to become a male-dominated movement. But if the avant-garde has understandably placed its own history firmly outside that of commercial cinema, it must be conceded that even a pioneering film like *Meshes of the Afternoon* does not spring from nowhere. The film's impulse, its desire, its very distinctiveness, is rooted in preoccupations which also find expression—albeit in very different ways—in other cinemas of the period. Deren's particular contribution is the brilliance with which her films explore and exploit the potential of the film image, though never for its own sake. In *Meshes,* the cracks fissuring the smooth surface of the everyday are prised open to reveal a memorable inner world of stunning imagery and powerful emotion.

Michael O'Pray (essay date June 1988)

SOURCE: "Maya Deren 9 Times a Life," in *Monthly Film Bulletin,* Vol. 55, No. 653, June, 1988, pp. 183-85.

[In the following essay, O'Pray presents an overview of Deren's life and career and discusses the legacy of Deren's work.]

1. Maya Deren had a rich, eventful life, cut tragically short when she died of a brain haemorrhage at the age of forty-four in 1961. A legendary figure of the American avant-grade cinema, which she was so instrumental in founding and nurturing, she was also active in dance, literature, anthropology, photography and politics. Astonishingly, her reputation as a filmmaker rests on a mere six completed short films,

only five of which have been available in this country until recently, when the remaining one, *The Very Eye of Night,* was brought into distribution by the BFI. Her film footage of Haitian voodoo dances and rituals was edited by others after her death under the title *Divine Horsemen,* and has had questionable status. Other films in distribution are out-takes from *A Study in Choreography for Camera* and the uncompleted *Witch's Cradle,* again put together after her death.

2. Not a small part of the myth of Maya Deren is her beauty. To ignore this on sexist grounds would be a distortion. The fact that she appears as the protagonist in the early films has made her physical presence an important factor in any study of the films, and has been a prime element in the uncanny fascination they have held for generations of viewers. The famous photograph, taken from her first film, *Meshes of the Afternoon,* of her looking through a window, has become one of the few cult images from the avant-garde cinema (only surpassed by the razored eye of Buñuel's *Un chien andalou*), and has served, perhaps unhappily, as a nexus of associations, beliefs and desires, a condensation of projected fantasies peculiar to the myth of Deren.

3. Born of liberal, educated Russian-Jewish parents in Kiev, in the fateful year of 1917, Maya Deren seemed, throughout her life, to have a strong sense of being an outsider—strengthened, no doubt, by her Russian roots—and in many ways the ideas and practices in which she became involved gave shape to this feeling. An active Trotskyist in the mid to late 1930s, she moved from early attempts at writing to work with the innovative black dance theatre of Katherine Dunham, to field study of voodoo ritual in Haiti under the influence of Gregory Bateson and Margaret Mead, and finally to the displaced world of avant-garde cinema in the 40s and after until her untimely death. Nevertheless, her ideas and life were of a piece, distinguished throughout by a connection with movement and psychic way. All her films and writings have a hard-edged intelligence that completely eschews sentimentality or emotional indulgence.

> **The famous photograph, taken from her first film, *Meshes of the Afternoon,* of her looking through a window, has become one of the few cult images from the avant-garde cinema . . . , and has served, perhaps unhappily, as a nexus of associations, beliefs and desires, a condensation of projected fantasies peculiar to the myth of Deren.**
> **—*Michael O'Pray***

Her father's occupation as a psychiatrist and her own attachment to—and what at times appears to be an identification with—him would imply an intellectual approach to her subject matter. This is not to deny the role of the emotions which was central to her overall artistic and cultural practice, but it is to distinguish her involvement from that of the dilettante or the sensationalist. Her book on voodoo, *Divine Horsemen,* never succumbs to cheap journalism or superficial ghoulishness. Quite the opposite, it reveals Deren as the academic, a profession she flirted with at university only to reject it (although her methodology in the book ran against the prevailing 'scientific' methods of anthropology). More interestingly, the Haiti episode was to have an enormous impact on everything that followed. The study is also imbued, in spirit at least, with her early Marxism.

4. Deren's political activities are neglected in most writing about her, but thanks to the documents, interviews and articles collected in *The Legend of Maya Deren* (edited by Clark, Hodson and Neiman in three volumes, only the first, dealing with the years 1917-1942, has been published, and has been extensively used by this article), we have a fuller picture of her as a young woman in her late teens, completely submerged in the Trotskyist circles of New York. She joined the Young People's Socialist League in 1934 and remained a card-carrying member until 1937. This commitment was to collapse under the impact of the 'show' trials in the Soviet Union in the 30s, the Soviet invasion of Finland and the Nazi-Soviet pact, together with, one feels, her own development away from the narrow sectarian confines of American Communism. This background, shared by many intellectuals at the time, formed a radical generation, from Clement Greenberg to Saul Bellow, which had an enormous influence on American culture (as did its counterpart in this country).

Deren's activities during this period seem to have marked her for life so that her work never loses a social dimension, a progressive notion of self-development, and an integrity of purpose that was not limited by the egotism of much of the American underground film movement that followed. It would explain, for example, what distinguishes Deren's film work from Kenneth Anger's, and it might have been one of the sources of her discomfort with Stan Brakhage's work, where exploration of the self moves inwards rather than outwards. Deren's work, for all its symbolism and dream-state qualities, is never subjectivist, never hermetic and cabalistic as is Anger's. In *Meshes of the Afternoon,* one is not drawn into her world so much as her world is opened out to us.

5. The late and much under-rated American critic Parker Tyler (who appears as one of the figures seated around the long table in *At Land*) once said of Maya Deren's 'best' films that they "provide mind work that expressed "filmic ideas about feelings". Generally speaking, for Tyler, Ameri-

can underground cinema failed this criterion; either it showed too much feeling and no form or too much form and no feeling. In a similar vein, Deren made clear in a letter to Jonas Mekas in 1961 that she had no time for the dominance of the passions in art; 'pseudo-primitivism', she called it. For her, an intelligence and a technical professionalism were necessary conditions for art, if not sufficient. Art for her was inextricably tied to form—"a scream is not a song" she once said.

Of course, Tyler's model was a surrealist-symbolist one, of sorts, and to that extent was not dissimilar to Deren's own aesthetic proclivities (despite her justifiable denial of being a surrealist *per se*). She found much that troubled her in the avant-garde cinema she energetically defended and supported. She was never a purveyor of anti-art sentiments, and it is no accident that she came to the fore in this country in the late 70s and early 80s, when feminist film-making and criticism was burgeoning and many avant-garde women filmmakers were becoming disillusioned with the formalist and anti-art projects of the 60s.

6. Deren's first film, the classic *Meshes of the Afternoon,* was made in 1943, the year after she married her second husband, Alexander Hammid. They met while Deren was personal assistant (1941-2) to Katherine Dunham, whose black dance and theatre group was touring *Cabin in the Sky* in the U.S. at the time. Deren was still busily writing between 1938 and 1942—a novel, radio scripts, articles—and translating. In fact, her break with the Trotsky coincided with her translation of the book *Conquered City* by the Belgian socialist, Victor Serge, and her enrolment as a graduate student at Smith College (1938-9) where she finally rejected an academic career. Her poems at the time, e.g., **"I Cannot Place the Face"** (1941), have a toned-down, T.S. Eliot quality and point towards *Meshes* with their symbolism and fragmentation of time and space (cf. "The Waste Land").

In many ways, this possible influence would lend support to the view of her work as not surrealist but essentially modernist-symbolist. After all, Deren's dissertation at Smith College had been on the nineteenth-century Symbolist school's influence on American and British poetry, particularly that of Pound and Eliot. In her film notes to *Meshes,* Deren cites her prior (and unsuccessful) poetry writing as a major factor in the film's success. She also credits Hammid with "teaching me the mechanics of film expression".

7. Most of her work was completed in the years 1943 to 1948: *Meshes of the Afternoon* (1943), *At Land* (1944), *A Study in Choreography for Camera* (1945), *Ritual in Transfigured Time* (1946), *Meditation on Violence* (1948). *The Very Eye of Night,* more controversial in critical terms, appeared in 1959. In September 1947, Deren arrived in Haiti to begin her study of its folk beliefs and rituals, producing not a film as originally planned but a standard text on voodoo, *Divine*

Horsemen (1953), published in this country as *The Voodoo Gods.* Her interest in dance, film, ritual and society came together, it seems, in this period, but interestingly it did not result in the film she had planned. Instead, she made *Meditation on Violence,* a film on Chinese boxing which eschews the 'narrative' complexities of her earlier work. Instead, it has the form of a document, albeit a mesmeric one, echoing the 'trance' themes of *At Land, Meshes of the Afternoon* and *Ritual in Transfigured Time.*

8. If Deren's intellect and imagination were too fluid and probing for her to restrict herself to a single area of activity, there is an integral and almost systematic exploration of time, space and movement in her films which has rarely been surpassed since and, surprisingly, has not influenced as many film-makers as one would expect. In Britain, for example, Jayne Parker's films have a certain Derenesque quality, but in their narrative-symbolist aspects rather than their formal interests. Tina Keane has explored play and ritual in her films, videos and installation work, in ways that are reminiscent of Deren's ideas as she set them out, for example, in her Guggenheim grant application for her Haiti study (childhood rituals, like not stepping on cracks in paving stones, are discussed in terms of wish-fulfilment, separateness of ritual from objective, and the secrecy of the performance).

9. Such ideas were to infiltrate women's work almost twenty years after Deren's death. But there is no substantial critical writing on Deren in this country and her own writings, particularly the fascinating essay **"An Anagram of Ideas on Art, Form and Film",** have been virtually ignored. The sooner the hypnotic, and ultimately crude, myth of Deren is replaced by a serious confrontation and engagement with her life, work and ideas, the better it will be for our understanding of the relationships that exist between her films and other arts (dance and music, for example) and the social and political context in which they were made. The return in this country in recent years to the image, to expression and 'narrative', after the excesses of the formal, will hopefully create the space and sympathy for more extensive research. In the meantime, Maya Deren's films stand as a stark reminder of the creative possibilities of film and of the uncompromising nature of her own practice, at a time when rampant commercialism and Thatcherite values, even within the so-called independent sector, threaten to dampen the ability and, more importantly, the desire to experiment.

Michael O'Pray (review date June 1988)

SOURCE: A review of *Witch's Cradle,* in *Monthly Film Bulletin,* Vol. 55, No. 653, June, 1988, p. 187.

[*In the following review, O'Pray asserts that editing was so important to Maya Deren's work that a film of hers that is put together by someone else, in this case* Witch's Cradle, *is "automatically less interesting."*]

As Maya Deren remarked, **Witch's Cradle** "was inspired by the architectural structure and paintings and objects" of the Surrealist Exhibition at the "Art of This Century" gallery in New York in 1942. The film was never completed and seems to have been made between the Hammid-influenced **Meshes of the Afternoon** and **At Land** in 1943. (Very little documentation exists on the film; it is not mentioned by P. Adams Sitney in his book *Visionary Film*.) Its main focus is Marcel Duchamp's string 'installation', which evoked for Deren the idea that surrealist work was the alchemy of the twentieth century, an idea with which Duchamp himself toyed. Deren did programme notes for the film at some unspecified date, and they were published in *Film Culture*, No. 39, in 1965.

One is even puzzled as to whether Deren ever showed the film, which is described as 'out-takes' by its distributors and in the American Anthology Film Archives. The existence of programme notes would suggest that she did, but it seems that whatever she showed, in an incomplete state, was different from the film that we have here. Given Deren's low output, it is worth quibbling about this, as her stress on editing makes anything not actually put together by Deren automatically less interesting.

Witch's Cradle gives the impression of someone discovering, with excitement, a new medium, as Deren obviously was at that time. The images of the installation, of Duchamp's wheel, fleetingly of Duchamp himself near the beginning, are elliptical. In her notes, Deren speaks of surrealist artists being like "feudal magicians and witches" who were "motivated by a desire to deal with *real* forces underlying events". Interestingly, she saw **At Land** as a twentieth-century conception of space and time, and **Witch's Cradle** as being 'feudal'. Given her later antagonism to certain forms of surrealism, it perhaps also points to some of the problems she found with that aesthetic.

Although in Deren's view the film exemplified the 'defiance' of normal time and space, the major formal theme of all her films, **Witch's Cradle** does not have the fluidity and formal coherence she was to achieve later. Her restless search for the *image juste* with which to express the "cabalistic symbols" of surreal magic has none of the magic that would itself be characteristic of Deren's editing. One can only guess at her reasons for not completing the film, but it is a measure of her integrity and self-criticism that she remained dissatisfied with it.

Deke Dusinberre (review date July 1988)

SOURCE: A review of *Ritual in Transfigured Time*, in

Monthly Film Bulletin, Vol. 55, No. 654, July, 1988, pp. 217-18.

[*In the following review, Dusinberre discusses the place of individual and collective identity in Deren's* Ritual in Transfigured Time.]

Maya Deren's **Ritual in Transfigured Time** merits special attention for a number of reasons. First, it synthesises all the major elements found in Deren's other films: psychodramatic condensation/displacement of time and space, the recourse to myth, and the use of dance as ritual expression of that myth. In addition, it represents the last of her truly 'accomplished' films (her subsequent work never quite attaining the same intensity and clarity). Finally, the film is strikingly relevant in the context of today's social trend towards serial monogamy; what Deren described as a woman's rite of passage from "widow into bride" could be pertinently paraphrased as 'the (cyclical) loss of one lover and the search for another'.

The film can be divided, somewhat schematically, into three distinct sequences. In the first, an essentially 'interior' passage, a woman (played by Deren herself) induces a younger woman (Rita Christiani) to participate in the timeless feminine rite of winding a skein of yarn into a ball. The second section represents a transitional sequence in which the young woman, already 'widowed' (dressed and veiled in black), enters the social whirlwind (in this case a lively and urbane party), apparently seeking a partner. Her encounter with that partner leads to the third, 'exterior' sequence, involving an ambivalent dance of seduction and domination, a chase which becomes a flight towards and away from love and sexuality.

This ambivalent quest for a lost partner is rendered in Deren's own highly refined idiom, which stresses perpetual transformation, a multiplicity of meanings, and an interweaving of histories. The various narrative threads are too complex to recount here, but Deren's characteristic melding of spatio-temporal boundaries is signalled at the outset when Deren herself, seen framed in the doorway of a backlit room, passes magically to another doorway, traversing a wall (unseen, but assumed to exist) separating two rooms. This reframing, this traversing of barriers, tugs us away from quotidian reality towards the psychological reality of our human 'imaginative faculty'. Space is once again subtly reframed the first time we see Rita Christiani's face, in a dark and ambiguous but presumably interior setting; for the light scarf on her shoulders is tickled by a breeze unmistakeably evoking the exterior (Deren is seen wearing this same scarf some seconds later, still wind-blown, establishing a level of identification between Deren and Christiani, between 'nymph' and 'maiden').

As the young woman is encouraged to wind the skein of yarn (or 'thread of life') held out by Deren, she notices a third, older woman on the threshold. This seems to complete the mythological trinity of the three Fates—who also represent maiden, nymph, crone. A rare deep-focus shot shows Christiani 'assuming her place' between Deren in the foreground and the crone in the distance. This first scene, then, established the co-existence of psychological space within a mythological framework. Once the skein has been finished, Deren 'disappears', and Christiani leaves the room, passing the crone and entering the neighbouring room where we discover a party in full swing.

The following sequence is ushered in by a formal device which serves as motif for this second section: the freeze frame. The young woman, dressed in black, stands in the doorway. Though her veil suggests mourning, the cross hanging from her neck simultaneously suggests a vow of chastity; she also cradles a bouquet of white arum lilies against her breast. The image unfreezes and the young woman enters a room full of people milling and greeting. A limited number of shots, usually involving swirling motion, are rhythmically presented and repeated, punctuated by freeze frames, lending a highly choreographed feel to this ritual of human encounter and separation. Eventually, a young man is singled out, consistently moving right to left in counterpoint to the young woman's movement left to right; the shot/countershot editing suggests that they are seeking and approaching one another. When they finally meet, once again 'framed' in a doorway, a smooth cut on a close-up of their faces suddenly transfers us outside to a classical sculpture garden.

Which is where the dance of seduction, of approach and avoidance, begins. The young man (played by Frank Westbrook) has become a bare-chested satyr. He flings Christiani into the air (she literally 'falls at his feet'), then gives an impetuous leap. Three dancing women mimicking the three Graces (echoing the Fates of the first section) are in turn flung into statuesque poses (via freeze frames). Christiani leaves, wearing a white shawl, and as she turns to look back, another smooth cut shows Deren completing the turn, wearing the same shawl—their identities have now been twinned. Though Christiani moves farther into the distance, she winds up (in typical Deren fashion) at her point of departure: the sculpture garden, complete with a real statue of the three Graces and a freeze-frame statue of Westbrook on a pedestal. As Christiani gazes up at him, he 'comes to life' in fits and starts. She flees, and this time Westbrook gives chase. During the chase, Christiani and Deren again twin as the nymph, and though she runs at normal speed and the satyr follows in slow motion, she cannot outdistance him. Deren finally runs under a pier out into the sea. Twisting and sinking into the water, she becomes Christiani once again, now seen in negative, so that her widow's black garb is transformed into a white bridal gown. In the final shot, the 'drowned' bride, clutching her arum lilies, lifts her veil and opens her eyes.

Through a remarkable series of transpositions and metamorphoses, Deren's personal vision achieves a universal human resonance. This is even signalled on a racial level, insofar as Rita Christiani, Deren's counterpart in the film, is black—as was Talley Beatty, the dancer with whom Deren made *A Study in Choreography for Camera* (Deren had previously worked with Katherine Dunham's black dance theatre); the assimilation of racial difference is just part of her internationalism, the party sequence also being conspicuously cosmopolitan. The combined Christiani/Deren identity, the conflating of Fates and Graces and other mythological figures, is obviously also emblematic of a larger social merger, the coming together of the group to form a single entity. This, indeed, is one of the very functions of 'ritual', to bind the group into a collective identity. As such, it represents an important departure from the 'splitting of the self' which characterised the earlier *Meshes of the Afternoon* and *At Land*. It tends to support Deren's professed interest in the "minimisation of personal identity", and perhaps partially spurred her subsequent lengthy research into Haitian voodoo.

> **Through a remarkable series of transpositions and metamorphoses, Deren's personal vision achieves a universal human resonance.**
> *—Deke Dusinberre*

Deren's oeuvre is personal to the extent of being almost autobiographical, clearly stemming from her experience of successive marriages and divorces. But she tried to comprehend and transcend that experience by setting it in a context not of resolution and closure, but of contradiction and assimilation (loss and gain, mourning and restitution, death and survival); the widow, drowned, is also a bride, alive, alone. The strength of Deren's presence in her own films never eclipses, fortunately, the complexity and intensity of her vision, her attempt at a resolutely modern reformulation of that primal, universal rite of passage: the search for the other, a partner, oneself.

Annette Kuhn (review date July 1988)

SOURCE: A review of *The Very Eye of Night,* in *Monthly Film Bulletin,* Vol. 55, No. 654, July, 1988, p. 219.

[In the following review, Kuhn asserts that Deren's The Very Eye of Night *has "a more formal, abstract—even a more modernist—quality than any of Deren's other films."]*

The Very Eye of Night is the last of Maya Deren's six completed films. Ten years separate it from her penultimate work, *Meditation on Violence,* and Deren herself announced that this would be her final film (fateful words—she was to die just three years afterwards). It is in consequence often treated as an after-thought: the film has received little critical attention—it has only recently become available in Britain—and rather less acclaim. Described by its maker as "cool and classicist", it has a certain detached quality although it is by no means merely a formal exercise. Nor, in any real sense, does it constitute a break from Deren's output of the 1940s.

Against a starry night sky, human forms, male and female, move and revolve as if weightless. The bright, unindividuated figures shimmer in negative images which perhaps represent night's opposition to day, the utter otherness of the world of sleep. Here favourite Deren themes (dreaming, sleepwalking) already evident in her first film, *Meshes of the Afternoon,* re-emerge, but now organised and expressed quite differently. Any concern with the transition between the world of the ordinary, the everyday, and the world of dream, trance and ritual; any concern with the permeability of the 'mesh' that separates one from the other, is abandoned in favour of a 'metaphysical' exploration of that other world. For it is entirely to this world that *The Very Eye of Night* confines itself.

This is also the last of a line of cinechoreography pieces. The human figures—students of the Metropolitan Opera Ballet School—perform a series of dance movements representing various archetypal characters (Noctambulo, the sleepwalker; Gemini, the twins; Uranus, father of Heaven, and Urania, his female aspect) in a kind of inner journeying. The choreography is complemented by the relentless and complex movement of the camera, although its choreography is barely perceptible as such: the negative-black background obscures all depth cues, so that the dance of the camera is 'transferred' to the movement of the figures within the frame. This particular relation of figure and frame—deriving from an absence of perspective in the image and an intricate interweaving of dancers and camera—gives rise to an illusion of gravity-free movement: the figures seem to float and tumble across the space bound by the frame. The 'free fall' of dream itself, perhaps.

Despite its metaphysical theme and quasinarrative trajectory, and despite its continuing preoccupation with the filmic expression of dance and ritual, *The Very Eye of Night* does have a more formal, abstract—even a more modernist—quality than any of Deren's other films. Jonas Mekas, referring to the loss of depth, the breakdown of horizontal/vertical

centrality, and the affirmation of surface in the film, has pointed to its 'late Cubist' quality. Other commentators have suggested that its apparent formalism represents a deliberate reaction against the U.S. avant-garde's flirtation at this time with 'direct cinema'. Whatever the case, *The Very Eye of Night* in some ways foreshadows the self-reflexive concern with the materiality of film as a medium which was to preoccupy avant-garde film-makers in the 60s and 70s—though, like all Deren's work, it is never simply a film about film.

Michael O'Pray (review date July 1988)

SOURCE: "Out-takes from Maya Deren's *Study in Choreography for Camera*," in *Monthly Film Bulletin,* Vol. 55, No. 654, July, 1988, p. 217.

[In the following review, O'Pray asserts that the out-takes from Deren's A Study in Choreography for the Camera *should be shown with the completed film to show how the film was edited and constructed.]*

An assembly of out-takes, running about eight times the length, from Deren's *A Study in Choreography for Camera.* In one way, with their repetition, the out-takes seem to foreshadow the minimalism and serial structures of what came to be called structural film-making as practised by Michael Snow, Peter Gidal and Malcolm Le Grice in the 60s and later. But such reflexivity, and its concomitant anti-content aesthetics, were foreign to Deren; they smacked too much of anti-art and the draining of meaning from film, tendencies for which she had little sympathy. For this reason alone, the out-takes should be shown with the completed film, also to demonstrate editing techniques and film construction—in other words, the raw materials of artistic production.

Part of the film was shot in the Egyptian Hall of the Metropolitan Museum of Art. Deren later discussed her use of the wide-angle lens in order to achieve effects of scale and internal speed within the sequence. The out-takes, it is worth pointing out, reveal Deren's insistence on meticulous planning of the visual ideas for her films prior to shooting. The strong rationalist, classicist trait in Deren's aesthetic is no more clearly demonstrated than in this selection, as it were, from the director's sketchpad.

Michael O'Pray (review date July 1988)

SOURCE: A review of *A Study in Choreography for Camera,* in *Monthly Film Bulletin,* Vol. 55, No. 654, July, 1988, pp. 218-19.

[In the following review, O'Pray praises Deren's A Study in Choreography for Camera as being an innovative and unsurpassed film on movement.]

With the exception of perhaps the early single-take 'primitive' films of the Lumières, Maya Deren's *A Study in Choreography for Camera* was probably the simplest film, at least thematically if not formally, to have been made at the time, 1945. Nothing in the 1920s German avant-garde work of Richter, Ruttmann, et al., prepares us for its formal purity and rigour. It is also as far removed from the 'other' 20s avant-garde film movement—the surrealist-cum-dadaist work of Cocteau, Man Ray, Dulac, Clair and Buñuel—as *Meshes of the Afternoon,* Deren's first film, was close to that same movement. However, there is a sense in which all Deren's films are choreographed, all draw on a sense of movement even when not explicitly concerned with dance.

Choreography depicts a dancer's leap passing through different locations in filmically constructed space and time. Five of Deren's six completed films were concerned with 'dance', partly fostered, one imagines, by her involvement with the Katherine Dunham Dance Company in the early 1940s, and later deepened in her studies of Haitian voodoo rituals. It might be argued that *Choreography* was genuinely avant-garde insofar as it took many years for its formalism and anti-narrative concerns to be taken up by others.

The film broke with narrative and metaphor quite decidedly, laying the way open, in its celebration of a single movement, for Kenneth Anger's *Eaux d'Artifice* and such major works of Stan Brakhage's as *Dog Star Man.* For the same reason, it also constitutes some kind of break with Deren's own psychodramas, while obviously extending ideas contained in the repetition structures and spatial and temporal displacements of *Meshes of the Afternoon* and *At Land.* In Deren's own words. *Choreography* "was an effort to isolate and celebrate the principle of the power of movement which was contained in *At Land*".

The film depicts a run, a pirouette and a leap. It begins with a slow pan from right to left of a clearing in a wood. During the almost 360-degree pan, the dancer, Talley Beatty, appears four times, each time having gone further in his slow spiralling movement from a dancer's crouch, and each time coming closer to the camera. The dancer then extends his foot to place it inside a room. In his run, he passes through different locations—rooms, woodlands, a museum courtyard—until the pirouette, during which he passes from a slowed-down speed to a very fast one. The film ends with a slow leap, fractured by edits so that time is extended as if the dancer were slowly and impossibly soaring through the air. He lands magically back in the woodland clearing.

For P. Adams Sitney, the film has a 'perfection' which Deren achieved nowhere else. This may be the case, but there is perhaps still too much of the formalist aspiration in *Choreography* for it to have the broad appeal of *Meshes of the Afternoon,* with its dreamscape, symbolism and the charismatic figure of Deren herself. What is important about *Choreography* is its demonstration of Deren's ability to switch from complex elliptical narrative forms, with highly constructed scenarios, to a film that has an unflinching formal integrity in relation to its subject matter. For Deren, the dancer's leap is a unified 'primitive' form of expression, in which she allows no element of filmic or personal indulgence to interfere—its own completeness, and universality, is enough. The innovatory nature of Deren's film on the ancient art of movement remains unsurpassed.

A. L. Rees (review date July 1988)

SOURCE: A review of *Meditation on Violence,* in *Monthly Film Bulletin,* Vol. 55, No. 654, July, 1988, pp. 216-17.

[In the following review, Rees discusses how the changes in film style in Deren's Meditation on Violence match the changes in the film's action.]

Against a blank studio wall, a half-naked Chinese boxer performs in two traditional modes. To a solo flute, balletically flowing movements (Wu-tang) are captured by similarly fluid camerawork. This turns into a more erratic and jagged movement (Shaolin), reflected in the abrupt editing for the boxer's jabs and kicks. A drum is added to the flute, the music and action quicken, until the boxer makes a jump-cut leap to a flat rooftop where, now armed and in a warrior's robes, he enacts dramatic swordplay to the sound of rapid drumbeats. At his climactic jump, midway through this section and at the apex of the film, the boxer is held in mid-air in a long silent freeze frame. Finally the boxer is back in the room, where in reverse motion (so continuous as to be barely perceptible) he moves from the aggressive style back to the fluid kind of movement. With its cycle complete, the film ends.

Meditation on Violence has never shared the popularity of Maya Deren's psychodramas, being too stylised and preconceived for some critics, and too objective and impersonal for others. Perhaps in protest at the over-psychological interpretation which she felt her earlier films had received, Deren seems to abandon symbolic narrative here to concentrate on a single figure and on cinematic gesture. These aspects may link the film to Action painting of the period, as does the camera's insistently frontal view of the leaping swordsman, and the 'push-pull' filming of the boxer in shallow space. But, in highly abstracted form, it also echoes a major theme of *Meshes of the Afternoon,* in which imagination (here the stylised fantasy of ritual fighting) becomes action. The role of the film's style is to evoke metaphors for consciousness from a physical process.

Narrative drama and lyrical images are replaced by a spartan style which suggests not only a search for the essence of the medium but also defiantly asserts the poverty of this film's funding. Like Deren's earlier works, it is characterised by fragmentation, a mood of threat and dream, and a camera which participates in the action. But Deren's characteristic fusion of sorcery and aggression is here transposed to the abstract form of the film, so that its overall shape, not its episodes, make up an erotic metaphor (the rise and fall of a climactic moment). In these respects, it is related to other films which expand on a single moment or gesture, made by Deren's younger contemporaries from the 1940s onwards, some of them inspired by her own earlier example, *A Study in Choreography for Camera* (1945). Makers of such 'imagist' films (as P. Adams Sitney called them) include Kenneth Anger, Bruce Baillie, Gregory Markopoulos, Charles Boultenhouse, Stan Brakhage and, in Europe in the 1950s, Kurt Kren and Peter Kubelka.

Like *Meditation,* their dynamic is based on the expansion of space, with mini-narratives composed from changes in body movement. Often they serve as analogies for the movement of an imaginative consciousness by which (in Deren's words) "a person is first one place and then another without travelling between". This amounts to what Deren saw as essential to film, "the change from instant to instant". In *Meditation,* changes in film style are systematically matched with changes in the action, from flowingly holistic camerawork for the opening dance-like gestures to abruptly fragmented shots in the aggressive sequence. What also lends the film an added contemporary resonance is its stress on performance, the body, trance-like rhythm, and an exotic display of biomechanics in an open cross-cultural mix: Haitian music, Chinese martial arts, and Deren's Western modernism.

William C. Wees (review date Winter 1989-90)

SOURCE: A review of *The Legend of Maya Deren: A Documentary Biography and Collected Works.* Vol. 1, Part 2, in *Film Quarterly,* Vol. 43, No. 2, Winter, 1989-90, pp. 56-8.

[*In the following review, Wees asserts that* The Legend of Maya Deren *"is not only for fans of Maya Deren, but for everyone interested in the development of the avant-garde film movement in North America."*]

With photographs, letters, interviews, articles by and about Maya Deren, and unpublished documents of many sorts, including sketches and scripts for her films—all held together by the clear and intelligent commentary of Catrina Neiman—

the second installment of *The Legend of Maya Deren* chronicles the years during which Deren made her first four films and became a well-known figure among the artists and intellectuals of New York. The angst-ridden images and themes of isolation in her early films give no hint of the energetic, outgoing, exceedingly practical, and socially accomplished person who created an audience for her films and, in the process, prepared the way for successive waves of American avant-garde film-makers. For the first time we have a clear sense of Deren's public presence and a fuller but far from complete picture of her private life, at the beginning of her career.

As Deren learned film-making quickly, so she also quickly arrived at a theoretical position on film, a position that changed very little during the rest of her life, as can be seen by comparing **"Cinema as an Art Form,"** published in 1946, with **"Cinematography: The Creative Use of Reality,"** which appeared less than a year before her death in 1961. One indication of how her theories took shape is the change in labels she applied to her early films: from "abandoned" (in the spirit of Valéry: "A work is never completed, but merely abandoned"), to "classicist" (by which she meant films which subordinate personal expression to the demands of "form"), to "ritualistic" (implying for Deren "depersonalization of the individual" and stylization of action so that its meaning becomes "forever valid for all time and place").

Ritual and "de-personalization" had become Deren's guiding principles by the time she completed *Ritual in Transfigured Time.* One can only speculate on the reasons for this, but it is notable that with the exception of a few of Deren's poems, there is very little in *The Legend* that could be called truly personal. What Deren herself referred to as her habitual "intellectualizations and labored analysis" proved to be excellent strategies for keeping the personal at bay and avoiding the spontaneous, deeply personal, and revealingly autobiographical dimensions of art.

Why was it so important for her to separate the artist from her art? Was the nearly obsessive orderliness she imposed on her daily life (to which several of *The Legend's* interviewees attest) evidence of her fear of unruly and disruptive thoughts and feelings? Was her stubborn dismissal of psychoanalytic or even autobiographical readings of *Meshes of the Afternoon* an after-the-fact recognition that the film was, indeed, too personal? Was her impromptu dancing at parties the one release of emotions she regarded as safe? *The Legend* does not ask, let alone answer, questions of this sort, but they will have to be answered eventually, if we are to have a proper biography of Maya Deren.

On the other hand, *The Legend* is informative and forthright on another controversial aspect of Deren's career: her indebtedness to her second husband, Alexander Hammid. The years covered in this volume are precisely the years she and Hammid were married, and the editors draw extensively—and uncritically—on his comments and those of his wife, Hella Heyman Hammid, who was Deren's principal cinematographer for *At Land* and *Ritual in Transfigured Time.* Their evidence indicates that Hammid not only taught Deren the basic of cinematography and editing while they were making *Meshes of the Afternoon,* but shared equally in all aspects of the film's conception and execution. "One of those perfect collaborations," Deren called it later. Hammid also continued to assist Deren on her subsequent films, though his help is not recognized in the films' credits. Not only had Hammid made his own personal and lyrical films before he met Deren, but his admiration for independent, experimental work in film was as great as hers and no doubt encouraged her to stick to her convictions about film as an independent art form. Hammid's essay, "New Fields—New Techniques," published in 1946, could easily be mistaken for one of Deren's, and demonstrated that husband and wife shared, in Neiman's words, "the same vision for the future of their art." If Deren had not met and married Hammid, it is quite possible that her "legend"—were it to exist at all—would not include film.

> **What Deren herself referred to as her habitual "intellectualizations and labored analysis" proved to be excellent strategies for keeping the personal at bay and avoiding the spontaneous, deeply personal, and revealingly autobiographical dimensions of art.**
> **—William C. Wees**

Thanks to the work of Clark, Hodson, and Neiman, we are able to watch that legend taking shape, even as Deren's film career begins. The films made their contribution, of course, but equally important was the powerful impression Deren made as a person, which is preserved in the vivid impression of her appearance and personality recorded in this volume—compounded by her own tireless efforts to promote her films and disseminate her ideas through letters, lectures, and articles, also well represented here. In these efforts Deren singlehandedly created (or re-created, if one recalls the similar efforts of Germaine Dulac a generation earlier) the model followed by later film artists seeking a receptive and knowledgeable audience for avant-garde films. This volume is not only for fans of Maya Deren, but for everyone interested in the development of the avant-garde film movement in North America.

Jacqueline R. Smetak (essay date Winter 1990)

SOURCE: "Continuum or Break? *Divine Horsemen* and the Films of Maya Deren," in *New Orleans Review,* Vol. 17, No. 4, Winter, 1990, pp. 86-97.

[*In the following essay, Smetak explores how Deren's* Divine Horsemen *fits in with the aesthetic set forth by her films.*]

In 1947 Maya Deren, a New York based film-maker, received the first Guggenheim Fellowship awarded for creative work in the field of motion pictures. The result of this, however, was not a film but a book, *Divine Horsemen: The Living Gods of Haiti.* Deren's original intention had been to go to Haiti to film indigenous dance. She had, as she says in the preface to the book, "deliberately refrained from learning anything about the underlying meaning of the dance movements, so that such knowledge should not prejudice [her] evaluation of their purely visual impact." But she soon discovered that "the dance could not be considered independently of the mythology," and she was thus forced to spend most of the eight months she stayed in Haiti learning about the culture.

The book, an anthropological study of Voudoun culture, is the work of an amateur. Deren admits that she had "no anthropological background," yet her background as an artist "provided an alternative mode of communication and perception: the subjective level which is the particular province of artistic statement." She says:

> But my detailed and precise interpretations were derived specifically from the fact that, as an artist, my predominant professional concern was with *form.* An artist usually recognizes the integrity of a form, whether or not he agrees with it, if only because he would do unto others as he would desperately hope to have them do unto him.

The implication here is that she saw what she saw without prejudice, without pre-conceived notions which would have warped her observations. Yet her book is not a break from her earlier work but a continuum because what she saw was influenced by ideas she had already formed and expressed through her films made before she went to Haiti. The overall organization of her book reflects what she says about the essential character of the photographic medium in her essay **"Cinematography: The Creative Use of Reality,"** where she states that this medium is "so amorphous that it is not merely unobtrusive but virtually transparent." Her function, as she saw it, was to be as transparent as a camera:

> I, having no . . . commitment, nor professional or intellectual urgency, could permit the culture and

the myth to emerge gradually in its own terms and in its own form.

In keeping with this, her book begins at the beginning. And as in the beginning was the Word, she starts with the Word: "Myth is the twilight speech of an old man to a boy." Our introduction to Voudoun takes the form of an initiation as she first explains the mysteries underlying all myth, the specific forms the mysteries take in this myth, and then allows us to observe, but only observe, a ritual we are not yet ready to understand. The book follows this pattern as she first teaches us the forms and their meanings, then takes us through the actual rituals, each building on each until, at the end, we are ready to participate, to be possessed by the loa as she herself was possessed, through dance.

But the idea that dance exists as a ritual by means of which one could be possessed by something other than one's self was not something she hadn't thought about before. As film critic Parker Tyler notes, "Maya Deren found in dancing a possession by a transcendent spirit," and he felt that her film *Ritual in Transfigured Time* (1945-46) used dance and "its power to confer power, to promote revelation, to initiate the individual into final harmony with the world of nature." Deren's own program notes for this film substantiate Tyler's observation:

> The quality of the movement is not a merely decorative factor; it is the meaning itself of the movement. In this sense, this film is a dance . . . the film confers dance upon the non-dancer . . . the elements of the whole derive their meaning from a pattern which they did not themselves consciously create, just as a ritual . . . fuses all individual elements into a transcendent tribal power toward the achievement of some extraordinary grace.

Also, the fact that she was possessed by the loa Erzulie, the loa of Eros, should come as no surprise. In both *Meshes of the Afternoon* (1943) and *Ritual in Transfigured Time,* the female subject (played in *Meshes* by Deren herself) is as if possessed by the force of Eros. In *Meshes,* this possession leads to suicide as one manifestation of the subject kills her body. In *Ritual,* the subject, escaping the male embodiment of Eros, plunges into the sea, the widow become bride as the film goes into negative.

But *Ritual* is not that easy to read. The widow does run from the male dancer whose attitude toward her is clearly one of courtship, but Deren's program notes for the film indicate that some sort of transference or transformation has occurred:

> Such efforts [that of ritual] are reserved for the accomplishment of some ritual metamorphosis, and above all, for some inversion towards life; the pas-

sage from sterile winter into fertile spring; or, as in this film, the widow into bride.

The conclusion of the film, however, the plunge into water, is ambiguous because the image of water itself is ambiguous. As Joseph Campbell, who served as mentor for *Divine Horsemen,* notes in his own book, *The Masks of God: Primitive Mythology:*

> Every threshold passage . . . is comparable to a birth and has been ritually represented, practically everywhere, through an imagery of re-entry into the womb. . . . The water image in mythology is intimately associated with this motif, and the goddesses, mermaids . . . Ladies of the Lake and other water nixies, may represent either its life-threatening or its life-furthering aspects.

Thus her plunge is either into a new state of being (as the program notes say) or into death, a suicide that resolves all conflicts.

In *Meshes,* water is clearly a death image. During the course of a dream, the subject splits into three selves, one of which will emerge from the sea to walk across a vast expanse of time and kill the body of the three selves. The self who kills seems to be a projection of the unconscious. Deren comments:

> As the girl with the knife rises, there is a close-up of her foot as she begins striding. The first step is in sand (with suggestion of sea behind), the second stride . . . is in grass, third is on the rug, and then the camera cuts up to her head with the hand with the knife descending towards the sleeping girl. What I meant when I planned that four stride sequence was that you have to come a long way—from the very beginning of time—to kill yourself, like the first life emerging from the primeval waters.

But even here the death image contains within itself a core of ambiguity because the film was meant to depict an inner reality and an inner experience. Deren says:

> This film is concerned with the interior experiences of an individual. It does not record an event which could be witnessed by other persons. Rather, it reproduces the way in which the sub-conscious of the individual will develop, interpret and elaborate an apparently simple and casual incident into a critical emotional experience. . . . Part of the achievement of this film consists in the manner in which cinematic techniques are employed to give a malevolent vitality to inanimate objects. This film is culminated by a double-ending in which it would *seem* that the

imagined achieved, for her, such force that it became reality.

In *Divine Horsemen,* death itself has this kind of ambiguity. In *Meshes,* the sea is emblematic of death or perhaps a death wish, Thanatos. In *Divine Horsemen,* however, the sea is the source of all beginnings:

> The microscopic egg rides the red tides of the womb which, like the green tides, still rise and recede with the moon; the latest life, like the first, flows with the sea's chemistry . . . is beached in a surf, its heart reverberates a life-time with the pounding momentum of the primal sea pulse.

No one has witnessed the beginning of life, but death is not so hidden. It is "life's first and final definition," and, as such, it is death that has "first informed the ancestral elders" and has given them "the common inspiration of their common fanfare for origins, their common fiction of initiation, their common metaphors of metamorphous":

> The fictions of the old men are their final fecundity. As their flesh once labored to bring forth flesh, so the minds of the elders labor, with a like passion, to bring forth a mind. By rites of initiation they would accomplish the metamorphosis of matter into man, the evolution of a mind for meaning in the animal which is the issue of their flesh. . . . The rites of this second birth, into the metaphysical cosmos, everywhere mime the conditions of the first physical birth. The novice is purified of past, relieved of possessions, made innocent, placed nascent in the womb solitude of a dark room . . . a man emerges by ordeal, to be newly named, newly rejoiced in.

In other words, the fact of death makes possible the second birth, the animal reborn as a human being. This process of transformation is given form in myth which "is the voyage of exploration in this metaphysical space . . . between the quick and the dead":

> To enter a new myth is a moment of initiation. . . . It is to enter, in one's mind, the room which is both tomb and womb, to become innocent of everything except the motivation for myth, the natural passion of the human mind for meaning.

To note that the fact of death is the motive for and marks the beginning of the myth-making process is not an idea original to Deren. Susanne Langer in *Philosophy in a New Key* defines myth as "a story of the birth, passion, and defeat by death which is man's common fate." Joseph Campbell connects myth to dream: "Through dreams a door is opened to mythology, since myths are of the nature of dream, and that

as dreams arise from an inward world unknown to waking consciousness, so do myths." Freud, using a similar analogy, is more specific:

> But the dream-work knows how to select a condition that will turn even that dreaded event [death] into a wish-fulfillment. . . . In the same way, a man makes forces of nature . . . into gods [whose function is to] reconcile men to the cruelty of fate, particularly as it is shown in death."

Given this context, the origin and function of myth and the function of water in myth, the suicide at the end of both *Meshes* and *Ritual* acquires another meaning. In both cases the highly ritualized self-murder marks not literal death but a transition as both women cross a threshold into another state of being. The old self has died so that the new self may be born. This is clearly the intent in *Ritual* as widow becomes bride, but in *Meshes* the rebirth is displaced. The realization that will enable the subject to cross the threshold is not the subject's but ours as we discover the dangers inherent in denying and repressing the impulses of the unconscious. Deren comments that "*Meshes* is, one might say, almost expressionistic; it externalizes an inner world to the point where it is confounded with the external one." Deren's reaction to watching her own film is one of realization displaced on to the viewer:

> The important thing for me is that, as I used to sit there and watch the film when it was projected for friends in those early days, that one short sequence [the four steps] always rang a bell or buzzed a buzzer in my head. It was like a crack letting the light of another world gleam through. I kept saying to myself, "The walls of this room are solid except right there. That leads to something. There's a door there leading to something. I've got to get it open because through there I can go through to someplace instead of leaving here by the same way I came in."

Since both films deal with the female subject's feelings of repulsion and attraction toward Eros, it could be argued that they represent a continuum, an attempt to resolve certain conflicts within the artist herself. This is, however, a tenuous position to take because a psychoanalytic approach to art cannot be easily transferred to a psychoanalysis of the person who produced the art. Art itself is a cultural censorship mechanism and thus cannot be taken as a purely personal expression of anything. Besides, these films, particularly *Meshes,* were products of collaboration, and P. Adam Sitney argues that *Meshes* is as much Alexander Hammid's film as it is Maya Deren's:

> In recent years commentators on this film have tended to neglect the collaboration of Alexander

Hammid, to consider him a technical assistant rather than an author. We should remember that he photographed the whole film. Maya Deren simply pushed the button on the camera for the two scenes in which he appeared. The general fluidity of the camera style, the free movements, and the surrealistic effects . . . are his contribution. If *Meshes of the Afternoon* is, in the words of Parker Tyler . . . , "The death of her narcissistic youth," it is also Hammid's portrait of his young wife.

But if a thread may be established, it could be said that *Meshes* is about a woman who fails to resolve her conflicting feelings and that *Ritual* is about one who has managed to find a means, that of ritual, toward resolution. Given this context, *At Land* (1944) may be seen as an allegory about a woman, newly emerged or born from the sea, empowering herself by snatching the symbol of power, a chess piece. *At Land* is, however, problematic because the woman (played by Deren, which would encourage a confusion between the fictive woman and the artist herself) snatches power from other women. If the chess piece is taken to have erotic significance—it is phallic—this would lead to a reading that would see the power of Eros, for women, as essentially matrilineal. Feminine sexuality is not something women get from men even though the dominant culture may define female sexuality from a male point of view. It is something women get from, win from, earn from, learn from other women who, given the configuration of the characters in this scene, guard rather than share the secret. It is not, in other words, a power to be taken lightly, nor is it easily obtained. The snatching of the chess piece may thus be taken as an initiation ritual, the second birth of the woman first born from the sea.

If these three films are taken as different steps toward a resolution of inner conflicts regarding sexuality, the final resolution of these conflicts occurs in the last chapter of *Divine Horsemen*, "The White Darkness." *Divine Horsemen* was intended as an anthropological study, that is, a study of another culture, not an expression of the artist's own personal concerns. As Deren says:

> I had begun as an artist, as one who would manipulate the elements of a reality into a work of art in the image of my creative integrity; I end by recording, as humbly as I can, the logics of a reality which has forced me to recognize its integrity, and to abandon my manipulations. . . . I feel that that fact that I was defeated in my original intention assures, to a considerable degree, that what I have here recorded reflects not on my own integrity which, as an artist's had been overcome, but that of the reality that had mastered it.

She had gone there, tabula rasa, but quickly found that that approach was not going to work. She had intended to make a "creative" film but found herself, though she does not discuss this, moving toward a documentary.

Documentaries have their own problems, problems of which she was fully aware and discussed at length in *An Anagram of Ideas on Art, Form and Film*:

> But the documentary film maker is not permitted the emotional freedom of other artists, or the full access to the means and techniques of this form. . . . He is further limited by a set of conventions which originate in the methods of the scientific film. He must photograph "on the scene" . . . even when material circumstances . . . force him to select the accessible rather than the significant.

Thus Deren was forced to change the premise of her project. She could not photograph except what was accessible unless she knew what was significant, but if she knew the culture well enough to know what was significant, her knowledge would prevent her from seeing the Haitian dances as pure form. She would run the risk of creating something not quite art since, for her, art is defined in terms of its form. Further, the documentary, as a form, exists in limbo between the objective and the creative for, as she says, "in order to achieve a 'realism' of effect, it is often necessary to be imaginative in method." The project pulled in two directions, and the tensions of this pull resulted in not a film but a book, a documentary in words of the cultural context of the dance she had originally intended to film.

While the book, *Divine Horsemen,* is impressive as a study of Haitian culture, it also exists as a creative piece which further developed themes and ideas already expressed in the films Deren had made prior to 1947. The three films I have discussed seem to have something to do with erotic power (her personal language makes it difficult to state anything definitively), either possessing it or being possessed by it. "The White Darkness" chapter in *Divine Horsemen* is a description of actual possession. She says, "I have left possession until the end, for it is the center toward which all roads of Voudoun converge." This is also something which could be said of her previous work: that it converges toward the possession she has left for last.

Possession comes through dance, and to prepare us, she preceeds the last chapter with one on the drums. Drums are central to the ritual but not so the drummer. He is a craftsman and "has no position whatsoever in the hounfor [temple]." His music is not a personal expression but that of the tradition:

> The form is the total statement; and its distinctive

quality is that reverent dedication which man brings only to divinity . . . it is therefore characterized by a quality of selflessness, discipline and even of depersonalization. The performer becomes as if anonymous.

This is also how she has described herself as an artist. In Voudoun, which she sometimes explains using analogies with American artists and their world, the reason for this anonymity is functional and a function of the religion:

> A collective religion cannot depend on the vagaries of individual aptitude and persuasion; on the contrary, it must stabilize these vagaries and protect the participants against their own weaknesses, failures and inadequacies. It must provide the generally uncreative, often distracted individual with a prescribed movement and attitude, the very performance of which gradually involves, and perhaps inspires him. . . . The tradition must support the individuals, give them security beyond personal indecision, lift them beyond their own individual creative powers.

There is much here that echoes her own aesthetic theories, and perhaps her break with colleague Stan Brakhage could be explained by the distaste she expresses in this passage for art that exists as pure personal expression. The passage also explains what underlies her belief in the power of dance. This power of dance has been noted by others. Susanne Langer, for example, in *Feeling and Form* felt dance to be "the envisagement of a world beyond the spot and moment of one's animal existence" and that the first move of dance was "the creation of a realm of virtual power." Ecstacy, she further states, "is nothing else than the feeling of entering such a realm. There are dance forms that serve mainly to sever the bonds of actuality and establish the 'otherworldly' atmosphere in which illusory forces operate." Langer uses words such as "virtual" and "illusory" to establish the difference between this world and that other. For Deren, there is a boundary to be crossed, but that other world is neither "virtual" nor "illusory." It is as real and as concrete as this one. For Deren, the loa were not virtual projections of a "primitive" mind but as actual as the person who experienced possession by them.

Deren's description of the dance nevertheless, the final dance in which possession occurs, takes a specific myth-like form which reiterates that of her book as a whole. As life starts with water and as creation myths and initiation rituals foreground this motif so too does her description of this dance:

> Hardly has hearing plunged to encompass this dark dimension, then the high clang of the iron *ogan* [musical instrument] sets in. . . . This towering architecture of sound . . . seems to advance without

movement like a tidal wave so vast that no marker exists to scale its progress for the eye. Then a chorus of voices, having, it would seem, accumulated its force in the trough concealed behind the towering crest, hurls forward over that crest, and the whole structure crashes like a cosmic surf over one's head. . . . Now it is the dance which suggests water.

The actual possession comes suddenly and in two phases. The first is communal:

> What secret source of power flows to them, rocks them and revolves them . . . ? I have but to rise, to step forward, become part of this glorious movement, flowing with it, its motion becoming mine, as the roll of the sea might become the undulation of my own body.

The second phase is frightening, a sudden blow from which she, like the women in her films, flees. She is shaken:

> These are the warning auras of possession, One knows oneself vulnerable. I begin to repeat to myself; "Hold together, hold, hold."

She leaves the dancing but then returns, becomes part of it, never stopping until

> This sound will drown me! Why don't they stop! Why don't they stop! I cannot wrench my leg free. I am caught. . . . There is nothing anywhere except this. There is no way out. The white darkness moves up. . . . It is too much, too bright, too white for me; this is its darkness. "Mercy!" I scream within me. . . . "Erzulie!" The bright darkness floods up through my body, reaches my head, engulfs me. I am sucked down and exploded upward at once. That is all.

This is followed by an image in which all oppositions are reconciled, all divisions made whole:

> The sun-door and the tree-root are the same thing in the same place, seen from below and now from above and named by the seer, for the moment of seeing.

If the subjects of the films are seen as characters suffering from inner division caused by conflicting desires, if *At Land* is seen as one possible solution to these conflicts, the subject aggressively seizing that which could, if others have it, cause division and conflict, then *Divine Horsemen* may be seen as the final resolution. Either Deren is projecting her own psychic conflicts and resolving them through her art or this was a topic that interested her and was finally exhausted in her book. In either case, the nature of her film work changed after her trip to Haiti. She became interested only in form, making, in *Meditation on Violence* (1948) and *The Very Eye of Night* (1952), the film she did not make of Haiti. From her program notes:

> [The camera can] be the meditating mind turned inward upon an idea of movement, and this idea, being an abstraction, takes place nowhere or, as it were, in the very center of space. [*Meditation on Violence*]

> The laws of macro-and microcosm are alike. Travel in the interior is a voyage in outer space: We must in each case cut loose from the anchorage of an absolute, fixed center, enter worlds where the relationship of parts is the sole gravity. [*The Very Eye of Night*]

Her program notes use language similar to that used in *Divine Horsemen* when she attempts to describe what she "saw" as a result of possession. It is as if the film *The Very Eye of Night* were intended as a visual projection of that experience.

She made no films after that, and while this can be explained by the fact that she both ran out of money and got herself embroiled in so many other projects that she ran out of time as well, it is also a fact that her work exists of a piece. If her work is taken as a purely personal expression of purely personal problems (a tenuous but sometimes productive approach), then William James's comments in *Varieties of Religious Experience* on the religious experiences of the divided self are helpful. He says:

> [Religion is characterized by] the contrast between the two ways of looking at life which are characteristic respectively of what we have called the healthy-minded, who need be born only once, and of the sick souls, who must be twice born in order to be happy.

The sick soul is one which is heterogeneous, divided within and against itself. This definition is essentially Freudian (though James was working within his own system), and, like Freud, James saw religion as one of those maneuvers (from which he, like Freud, was distanced) by which some people come to some sort of resolution of their problems. Religious conversion could unify the divided self, a comment that is more Jungian (though James pre-dates Jung) than Freudian. Jung felt that the divided self could be made whole (or at least the impulse of the divided soul was always in that direction), whereas Freud thought that the divided self could achieve only a simulacrum of wholeness through repression, sublimation, reaction formation, and similar tactics.

From this angle, Deren's films could be seen as an effort to achieve wholeness through artistic expression. She made no more films after *The Very Eye of Night* because she no longer needed to. She had already achieved wholeness in Haiti, and her last two films exist as an expression of her interest in form rather than as an expression of personal concerns and problems. On the other hand, since her subsequent life was marked by problems and her personality remained as aggressive and, presumably, as divided as ever, the wholeness she achieved could perhaps better be seen as aesthetic rather than emotional. The idea of conflicting desires was one which interested her, but, with the trip to Haiti, it seems to have run its course. She said no more about it because she may have had nothing more about it to say.

Interestingly enough, however, her book itself is divided against itself because she uses two opposing psychoanalytic approaches. Her definition of myth—"Myth is the facts of the mind made manifest in a fiction of matter"—is Jungian, for what underlies it is the assumption of a collective unconscious. This mind isn't any mind but all minds: "It is to meditate upon the common human experience which is the origin of the human effort to comprehend the human condition." Her approach, however, to the specific culture of Haiti (she makes of Haiti a discrete situation by overlooking Voudoun cultures in Louisiana and Brazil) is Freudian. Her observations are empirical and specific, inductive rather than deductive, and her explanation of the reasons for Voudoun makes use of Freudian ideas of displacement and sublimation:

> Petro was born out of . . . rage. It is not evil; it is the rage against the evil fate which the African suffered, the brutality of his displacement and his enslavement.

and:

> Our general tendency is to regard the psychosomatic act of transferring a difficulty from the psychic to the physical system as "bad." This evaluation reflects . . . a moral dislike of "dishonesty" and a scientific rejection of "untruth." But an organism cares little for such abstract criteria. It is concerned with self-preservation. . . . When a situation is temporarily or permanently and irremediably brutal, the organism behaves like a clever boxer: it shields the mind from the blows which would only destroy it, and absorbs the shock in the muscular and durable flesh.

These are explanations which she both believes and does not believe because, for her, the loa are real. From her first description of a ritual in which the "voices" of the dead are treated as actual and not explained away to her final description of the dance—

I turn back toward the dancers, and join them. I sing, converse with Ogoun [Warrior Hero loa]. Nothing is shaken within me. After many dances Ogoun announces that he is content with the dance, and that now he will leave.

—she speaks as one who has been "born again" and believes totally in the religion she describes. Yet she makes no overt attempt to convert her reader. She wants us to accept the validity of the beliefs of these people much as we accept the validity of any religion, but whether we believe or not does not concern her.

She walks a tightrope, much like the hougan (shamen or "priest"), pulled in one direction by the demands of her culture to be scientific, objective, rational, and in the other by the demands of her aesthetics and personal religious beliefs to commit herself totally to the matter at hand. The book itself moves between, balancing its scholarly apparatus against personal anecdote. Her method of citation reflects this balance for, as she explains in the introduction, notes of interest to the layman are at the bottom of the page, those of interest to the scholar segregated to the back.

This balance could, perhaps, be explained as a defense mechanism because the book is, finally, a personal statement of personal belief, a belief that perhaps she feared might strike the rest of us as odd:

> As the souls of the dead did, so have I, too, come back. I have returned. But the journey around is long and hard, alike for the strong horse, alike for the great rider.

But within its proper context, the journey and what it means is not at all odd. It is, as Joseph Campbell says in the foreword to this book, an epiphany, a "crisis of becoming." Deren's experience, her "countertransference" to another culture, may be nothing more than a projection of personal fantasies; it certainly intersects rather neatly with her other work, but there are too many parallels to similar experiences in many other cultures. It could be argued that since she knew something about such experiences before she went, that she, in spite of her best intentions, was imposing her own desires on what she encountered, forcing these into the a priori mold of her aesthetic theories, but then again, the universality of such experiences would work against such a pat dismissal. She saw what she saw. And if we do not believe, that is our problem not hers.

FURTHER READING

Biography

Cook, Pam. "Chambers and Corridors—Maya Deren." *Monthly Film Bulletin* 55, No. 654 (July 1988): 220.
  Provides a brief biography of Deren and short quotes about her films.

Clark, Veve A. et al. *The Legend of Maya Deren: A Documentary Biography and Collected Works, Part 1.* Anthology Film Archives, 1984.
  A biography of Deren's life and works, from a somewhat subjective viewpoint.

Criticism

Deren, Maya. "Cinema as an Art Form." *New Directions,* No. 9 (Fall 1946): 111-20.
  Discusses film as an independent art form and asserts that it should not be seen as merely a way to illustrate a literary narrative.

————. "Movie Journal." *The Village Voice* V, No. 39 (31 July 1966): 6, 8.
  Compares the creative process to developing a reserve of life experiences and then robbing the bank and depleting one's reserves.

Michelson, Annette. "Camera Lucida/Camera Obscura." *Art Forum* XI, No. 5 (January 1973): 30-7.
  Discusses the careers of Sergei Eisenstein and Stan Brakhage and how Maya Deren's work influenced the interpretation of Eisenstein's films by Brakhage's generation.

Rabinovitz, Lauren. "Maya Deren and an American Avant-garde Cinema." *Women, Power and Politics in the New York Avant-garde Cinema, 1943-71.* Urbana, IL: University of Illinois Press, 1991, 250 p.
  Analyzes Deren's relationship to the development of the avant-garde cinema in America.

Stein, Ellin. A review of *The Legend of Maya Deren: A Documentary Biography and Collected Works. The New York Times Book Review* 134 (29 September 1985): 47.
  Asserts that the first volume of this biography uncovers youthful, embarrassing mementos that are better left buried and that to get to know the artist one must see her films.

Additional coverage of Deren's life and career is contained in the following source published by Gale Research: *Contemporary Authors,* Vol. 111.

Friedrich Dürrenmatt
1921-1990

Swiss dramatist, novelist, short story writer, scriptwriter, essayist, and critic.

The following entry provides an overview of Dürrenmatt's career. For further information on his life and works, see *CLC,* Volumes 1, 4, 8, 11, 15, and 43.

INTRODUCTION

Along with Bertolt Brecht, Dürrenmatt is considered one of the most important German-language dramatists of the 20th century. His plays are largely tragicomedies for, according to Dürrenmatt, true tragedy is impossible to write, but "we can achieve the tragic out of comedy." Paradoxes and irony are predominant in Dürrenmatt's fiction where he uses clever reversals to illustrate the cruelty of the world.

Biographical Information

Dürrenmatt was born in Switzerland in 1921, and grew up in an intellectual family—his father was a minister and his grandfather had been a member of parliament. Many of the biblical and mythological allusions that appear in his work came from his parents' retelling of mythological and biblical tales. Later he studied theology, philosophy, literature, and science at the Universities of Bern and Zurich. He left school without completing a degree in order to pursue writing. In 1943 he wrote his first play, *Komödie,* which, though unproduced, set his style. Three years later he saw his first two plays produced—*Es steht geschrieben* (1947; *It Is Written*) and *Der Blinde* (1948; *The Blind Man*). Dürrenmatt used historical and religious events and people out of context to create these morality plays. *It Is Written* was ill-received by audiences (deemed an overly large and complicated production in both plot and staging), but critics nonetheless recognized Dürrenmatt's talent. With *Romulus der Grosse* (1949; *Romulus the Great*), his self-proclaimed "un-historical historical comedy," Dürrenmatt achieved acceptance by both audiences and critics alike. International recognition came with the production of *Die Ehe des Herrn Mississippi (The Marriage of Mr. Mississippi)* in 1952. This play, about an upper class man and woman committing murders, was followed by a religious parable of selfless love in a material world—*Ein Engel kommt nach Babylon: Eine Fragmentarische Komödie in drei Akten* (1954; *An Angel Comes to Babylon*).

Major Works

With international success, Dürrenmatt had perfected his tragicomic style of writing. Most of his work utilized anachronistic settings or unusual reversals. This trend continued with his two most popular works: *Des Besuch der alten Dame* (1956; *The Visit*) and *Die Physiker* (1962; *The Physicists*). *The Visit* concerns a rich woman returning to the village where she grew up. Upon her return, she offers the citizens millions of dollars to kill her old suitor. The play centers on the moral struggle the impoverished citizens must go through—deciding between financial freedom and the morality of becoming hired killers. *The Physicists* centers around three physicists in an insane asylum. The three pretend to be mad and "believe" that they are Einstein, Newton, and Moebius. In order to keep secret their knowledge of how to destroy the world, they each commit murder. Dürrenmatt was also regarded as a successful fiction writer. As early as 1950, with his detective story *Der Richter und sein Henker (The Judge and His Hangman)*, he had applied his plot-twisting style to novels. *Der Verdacht* (1953; *The Quarry*), a sequel to *The Judge and His Hangman*, and *Das Versprechen* (1958; *The Pledge*) are also considered to be among his more important works.

Critical Reception

Although some critics recognized Dürrenmatt's talent when he wrote *It Is Written*, it wasn't until *Romulus the Great* that he developed widespread critical acclaim. His most praised works continue to be *The Visit*, for which he won the New York Drama Critics Circle Award, and *The Physicists*. Through the years critical reception of his work has varied, though critics have tended to favor him despite often luke-warm receptions from audiences. With his adaptation of August Strindberg's *Dance of Death*, he attained favorable reception for *Play Strindberg* (1969) as well as some critical acceptance for *Koenig Johann* (1968; *King John*) and *Titus Andronicus* (1970)—adaptations of Shakespeare's works. During the 1960s, Dürrenmatt became more and more disillusioned with the direction in which the theater was headed and turned toward fiction. *Der Auftraug* (1986; *The Assignment*) was one of his last works to receive critical praise. Striving to maintain his style of the unusual, Dürrenmatt tells the story of *The Assignment* in twenty-four chapters, each one sentence long. The rest of the narrative runs through twists and turns as the characters are all simultaneously observing and being observed by others in the novel. As Jennifer Michaels notes, "Dürrenmatt creates a powerful image of the alienation and the dehumanization that . . . people experience in the modern world." Throughout his career Dürrenmatt highlighted a world which he saw in chaos and which was, in his own words, something "monstrous, a riddle of misfortunes."

PRINCIPAL WORKS

Es steht geschrieben [*It Is Written*] (play) 1947

Der Blinde [*The Blind Man*] (play) 1948

Romulus der Grosse [*Romulus the Great*] (play) 1949

Der Richter und sein Henker [*The Judge and His Hangman*] (novel) 1950

Die Ehe des Herrn Mississippi [*The Marriage of Mr. Mississippi*] (play) 1952

Der Verdacht [*The Quarry*] (novel) 1953

Ein Engel kommt nach Babylon [*An Angel Comes to Babylon*] (play) 1953

*Herkules und der Stall des Augias (radio play) 1954

Der Besuch der alten Dame [*The Visit*] (play) 1956

Das Versprechen [*The Pledge*] (novel) 1958

Frank der Fuenfte [with Paul Burkhard] (play) 1960

Die Physiker [*The Physicists*] (play) 1962

Der Meteor [*The Meteor*] (play) 1966

Koenig Johann [*King John*] (adaptation) 1968

Play Strindberg (adaptation) 1969

Titus Andronicus (adaptation) 1970

Der Mitmacher, ein Komplex (play) 1976

Achterloo (play) 1983

Der Auftraug [*The Assignment*] (novel) 1986

Midas (novel) 1990

*Herkules und der Stall des Augias was expanded and produced as a play in 1962.

CRITICISM

Gabrielle Robinson (essay date March 1981)

SOURCE: "Justice Breeds Murder: Justice in Dürrenmatt as Theme and as Theatrical Material," in *Modern Drama*, Vol. 24, No. 1, March, 1981, pp. 73-86.

[*In the following essay Robinson examines Dürrenmatt's use of justice. She looks at how justice is depicted as paradox and how the characters "choose to play madmen, clowns or victims in order to achieve their goals."*]

In Dürrenmatt's plays "justice is at stake," as Palamedes tells his father in *The Blind Man*. Dürrenmatt tends to examine every situation and every action from the standpoint of justice, discussing such themes as the possibility of changing the world through justice, the perversion and parody of justice in our world, and man's injustice versus the justice of God. As far as his characters are concerned, they are obsessed with it; it is the idea of justice which makes their existence meaningful. "If there is no justice, one parts easily from it [life]," says the man who is about to die in *Nighttime Talk With A Despised Man*. Dürrenmatt's characters fight to their last breaths for their visions of justice, however distorted. For no matter how elevated or debased their aims, their conflicts arise from their pursuits of justice: whether hunting down a criminal, sentencing a son, robbing a bank, seeking revenge, destroying or saving an empire, they all believe themselves to be fighting for justice and order. Some of them, like the old lady in *The Visit*, seek personal justice for wrongs they have suffered, but most of Dürrenmatt's major heroes pursue absolute social and historical justice. The Emperor in *Romulus the Great* sets himself up as Rome's judge and condemns his corrupt civilization to death in the name of justice. In *The Marriage of Mr. Mississippi*, Mississippi fights to reinstitute iron Mosaic justice in his unjust and chaotic society. The Bastard in *King John* uses all the power of his reason to work for justice and order in his war-torn country, whereas Titus of *Titus Andronicus* seeks justice for Rome as well as for his tortured family.

> **Dürrenmatt's characters fight to their last breaths for their visions of justice, however distorted.**
>
> —*Gabrielle Robinson*

Dürrenmatt's seekers after justice are exceptional men. Most of them hold powerful and outstanding positions; yet they choose to play madmen, clowns or victims in order to achieve their goals. Typically, it is Romulus who focuses on the crucial question: "Do we still have the right to be more than a victim?" In the end-time in which they live, heroism can work only through deliberate self-victimization: Romulus's clowning, Möbius's and Titus's madness, the Bastard's and Bockelson's playacting. But even this reduced form of heroism is ultimately doomed, and the heroes end trapped by their own acts, victims now against their wills, able to prove their greatness only by bearing injustice. In his later plays, Dürrenmatt denies them even this most personal achievement. The monstrous disorder wins. "Nonsense is victor!", "And heroes there are none. Only victims."

Therefore, although both Dürrenmatt and his characters want to light up the world with the "pure ray of justice" (as is said of the four old lawyers in *The Puncture*), thus bringing meaning and dignity to their lives, what they achieve is "justice reflected in the eyeglass of a drunk ... " Not content with showing the hero's victimization, Dürrenmatt demonstrates paradoxical reversal and grotesque parody of justice. Judges turn into executioners, just men into criminals, and justice into farce. ". . . Justice / Breeds murder and does not create an order." Although this quotation stems from the later and more farcically distorted *Titus Andronicus,* its message is inherent in all of Dürrenmatt's plays. It is foreshadowed in Sainte-Claude's reply to Mississippi, who has called him a fool because "There is no justice without God."

> You are the fool. There is justice only without God. . . . We both have spilled blood; you killed three hundred and fifty criminals and I never counted my victims. What we do is murder; therefore we have to do it meaningfully.

As we shall see, Dürrenmatt's idealistic heroes are forced to accept this monstrous paradox and with it their defeats, whereas the cynical characters use it, or play with it, to serve their ends.

The Puncture (1956) offers an ironic combination of these possibilities when four jovial old lawyers sentence a chance visitor to death in the name of the highest ideal of justice. ". . . Only in the act of sentencing . . . does justice become knighted; there can be nothing higher, nobler, greater than when a human being is sentenced to death." Although this is only a game with which the four amuse themselves on their stag night, it causes the death of their victim, Traps, who executes their sentence by hanging himself. Traps believes that they have lit up his world with the pure ray of justice, and he proudly accepts his fate, since it bestows greatness and meaning on his muddled, mediocre existence. So justice breeds murder but also offers meaning to a senseless life.

The same is true of *The Visit* (1956). Here another grotesque version of fate—she might as well be called Clotho instead of Claire—offers to buy justice for a billion, demanding in return the death of Alfred III, the lover who had betrayed her many years before. Her idea of justice is squarely based on capitalistic manipulation, which has determined her life from the start. Claire's lover forsook her when she was pregnant so that he could marry a shopkeeper's daughter, and he bought witnesses to conceal his paternity. Forced into exile and disgrace, she recovered her fortune by selling herself in marriage to a series of millionaires; she then used the money to starve prosperous Güllen economically. At the opening of the play, the town is destitute, and although the worthy citizens begin by protesting Claire's demand for justice and revenge, they go off to buy new yellow shoes—on credit, of course—and end by accepting her bargain. Ill is murdered communally, and the people get their money. Yet they, too, claim to act in the name of justice: to establish a just community, not to tolerate injustice. "It is not a matter of prosperity and good living, nor of luxury; it is a matter of wanting to realize justice. . . ." Like Traps, Ill in the end becomes a willing victim; he accepts his death sentence, which in truth condemns his executioners, and gives content to his empty life.

In order to understand more fully Dürrenmatt's paradoxical view of justice, one has to examine both the nature of his world and his justice-obsessed heroes. Dürrenmatt throws his characters into critical situations and extreme moments; for him it is always A.D. 476, "a ghastly Götterdämmerung of civilization. . . ." His characters have the sense of living in "the last evening of time", when "the end-time has set in."

Therefore, Dürrenmatt's plays focus on moments of crisis. As historical subjects, he has chosen the fall of Rome, the Thirty Years' War, the Anabaptist revolt in Münster; but his nonhistorical plays concentrate no less on critical situations: Claire's fatal visit in *The Visit,* the collapse of a band in *Frank V,* Schwitter's ever repeated dying moment in *The Meteor,* the murder of a political leader in *The Fall.* Not content with selecting such critical situations, Dürrenmatt further augments the effect by distorting, exaggerating, parodying the action to a point where extremes confront each other and turn into paradoxical reversals. Only in this way, he feels, can he fix reality precisely, make it transparent. He wants to think a situation through to its end, which to him means both creating a paradox and presenting the worst possible turn a story can take. The result is, as he says of *King John,* "nasty," but it reveals a truth which is confirmed by our time.

Yet for Dürrenmatt, the worst possible case is not a matter of losing one's head in despair. On the contrary, he relishes the opportunity to tell annoying stories and to challenge his audience with extreme contrasts and paradoxes. Furthermore, as we shall see, the worst possible turn a story can take has its vital and liberating implications, since it constitutes for him the essence of theater and of play; and above all, Dürrenmatt is dedicated to playing with theatrical possibilities and models of the world.

Romulus the Great (1949), set in A.D. 476 with the barbarians at the gates of Rome, shows a world at the point of collapse. Traveling through the country, one finds destroyed cities and smoking villages, men massacred, women ravished and children starving. It is, nevertheless, a parodical world; the Emperor of Rome is a fat, middle-aged clown whose one serious concern is the breeding of hens. While Imperial officials make desperate and often hysterical attempts to save "our civilization," the Emperor concerns himself with his menu—the cook is the only official accorded any importance—and the productivity of his hens, which are named after his Imperial predecessors. The clucking of these fowls disturbs the decrepit but peaceful palace, and hen droppings soil every path of the neglected garden and every crumbling wall. The only source of efficiency—itself grotesque—is the mighty Caesar Rupf, a manufacturer of trousers, who is ready to rescue the moribund empire with his millions if he can marry Romulus's daughter. Romulus, however, scorns such a deal, reminding his servant of a more pressing task: "To our duty, Pyramus. Let's have the chicken feed."

Futile heroism and self-sacrifice abound in this hopeless time. Aemilianus, Romulus's prospective son-in-law, who has just returned, mutilated, from a Gothic prison, is ready for any sacrifice to save the fatherland. "Our shame will feed Italy; through our disgrace it will regain its strength." But Romulus checks him, as he does the messenger who has ridden for a hundred hours without rest to bring the news of another defeat: "Go to sleep, prefect, the times have turned your heroism into a pose." Neither heroism nor wisdom nor planning can alter this "disorderly earth", which will forever be engulfed in wars and upheavals spreading suffering and injustice.

An Angel Comes to Babylon (1953) expresses a similar view of an ever-changing yet also never-changing chaos and confusion. Nebuchadnezzar alternates between ruling and being ruled; using his rival Nimrod as footstool, having his ministers spit at him, and then serving as Nimrod's footstool, being spat at in turn by the ministers. His only creation—or is it Nimrod's?—is the idiot son who hops through the palace. The other permanent element is the suffering and persecution of the people, symbolized in the red garb of the hangman. Heroic deeds and sacrifices are senseless. As the wise Akki tells his friends in his last and most bitter *Macame,* "Bear disgrace, walk any paths, bury, if the times demand it, wild hope, hot love, suffering, grace, and humanity, under a red hangman's grab."

Frank V (1959) is perhaps too blatantly a schematic parody of justice, recounting the fortunes of a dynasty of criminals and their "gangster-bank." (Incidentally, Dürrenmatt draws a parallel between this gangster-bank and the "gangster-monarchy," as he calls it, of Richard III.) At one point, two men invoke the aid of "divine justice" in robbing the bank; after they are discovered, the wife of the bank owner pronounces the verdict: "You are definitely accepted into our bank. The attempted break-in was laudable, even if amateurishly planned; the key was excellent work". When this same lady, after a lifetime of forgery, fornication and murder, confesses all and asks for justice, the president of the country in his turn gives a verdict:

> My old sweetheart, come on, don't take it to heart
> What you confessed may be nasty but
> If I look more closely it's no big thing. . . .

There can be no justice, for that would jeopardize world order and economics. Instead, the lady is complimented for having saved the bank, which continues on its course.

In his other plays, Dürrenmatt builds similar extreme worlds, alienated from order and meaning, and constructed so that justice is reduced to the absurd. However, his *Titus Andronicus,* a play which presents a purely parodical accumulation of monstrosities, paints an even starker picture of this "idiotic course of time". During the course of his career, Dürrenmatt intensifies the parody, the grotesque, the simplification, using these devices to reduce everything to theatrical essence. Personal meaning or individual conscience, even if manifested only in the acceptance of victimization, become less and less possible.

This development begins with *The Physicists* (1962), set in an insane asylum inhabited by three brilliant scientists and run by an insane hunchbacked spinster, a good example of Dürrenmatt's totalized scheme: a mad hero in a mad world. In *King John* (1968), "the comedy of politics" portrays secular and religious rulers caught in a web of pointless wars and equally pointless reconciliations which lead to further injustice and violence. The city of Münster in *The Anabaptists* is yet another place of unreason and injustice, where Catholics and Protestants indiscriminately exchange positions, invariably getting hurt in the process. One knight, for example, on being struck by the falling statue of his patron saint, is converted to Protestantism, while at the same moment his colleague becomes a Catholic, so that once again they find themselves in opposite camps. Those in power are cynical, and the Anabaptists are either deluded fanatics or opportunists. The only rational man, a mathematical monk who believes that "my reason can conquer this unreasonable world", is constantly threatened by the gallows, whether Catholic, Protestant or Anabaptist.

In *Titus Andronicus* (1970), Dürrenmatt goes even further in exemplifying "the farce of politics". The opening lines at once reveal this world of pure parody, when Saturninus appeals to the patricians to elect him, not his brother, emperor of Rome:

> Elect me, and if my brother Bassianus
> Gets elected, stick this lewd pig immediately.

The play ends with the deaths and mutilations of all the characters, and the senselessness of all endeavors:

> What use is justice, what use revenge?
> They are only names for an evil affair
> The globe rolls along in the void
> And dies as senselessly as we all die. . . .

With this background of chaos, accidents and inhumanity, the "monstrous disorder of things", Dürrenmatt concentrates on the actions of characters who make an effort to change "this world of breakdowns" (*Panne*, p. II). His heroes, like Romulus, are remarkable men: emperors, generals, millionaires, artists or scientists of genius, men of extraordinary powers who try to control, improve or order the world according to their visions of justice. They will not accept the injustice of the world as immutable, and reason is the chief weapon in their fights. Often their senses of logic and order are offended as much as their senses of rightness. Thus, Newton of *The Physicists,* finding disorder unbearable, has become a physicist out of love of order: "to reduce the seeming disorder of nature to a higher order"; and Schwitter of *The Meteor* (1966) flees from the "monstrous disorder of things" into a fantasy of reason and logic which he finds in art, which, as Dürrenmatt describes it, is a world closed in itself, with its own geometry. Most of Dürrenmatt's characters, dreaming of a higher order and a higher justice, aspiring to prove that the spirit is stronger than the matter, man, like to think in terms of computations which leave no remainder; but reality corrects their ideas, as Romulus admits at the end. Romulus's true greatness lies in this insight, rather than in his schemes, for as Dürrenmatt says, the only greatness which man can show in these times is to bear injustice.

Don Quixote, whose name is frequently mentioned in the texts, could be the model for all of Dürrenmatt's heroes. "We should all be Don Quixotes, if only our hearts were a little in the right place and we had a grain of sense under our scalps." Dürrenmatt's characters are indeed engaged in Quixotic struggles, against overwhelming odds, to which they dedicate themselves with single-minded enthusiasm, ready for any sacrifice.

But they are Quixotes also in the sense of being madmen and fools, often dangerous and destructive fools who bring disaster on themselves and those around them. They will not see that in the time of crisis in which they live, it is not enough to be sharp-witted, to reason, to plan and be dedicated. A minor character like Charles V in *It Is Written* understands this: "Our deeds," he remarks, "only heighten the confusion". He dreams of retiring from the Imperial throne to a cloister where he can circle all day around a statue of justice in quiet contemplation. In fact, the heroes' fanatical adherence to reason does add to the confusion and lead to such absurdities as an emperor playing a clown and a physicist, a madman. Moreover, their idealism causes them to compound the very chaos and injustice which they set out to destroy. Romulus, Mississippi, Claire, the Bastard and Titus (one could add others, such as Möbius, Knipperdollinck, even Baerlach from *The Suspicion*), are all ready to kill for the sake of their ideals. They are all therefore subjected to paradoxical reversals, when their desires for justice lead to murder and their heroism to victimization. Clearly, for Dürrenmatt it is always a matter of paradox and the worst possible case. Those who sit in judgment over their worlds are themselves judged in the end. As the admittedly opportunistic secretary of justice declares in *The Marriage of Mr. Mississippi*: "The world is bad, but not hopeless; it becomes hopeless only when it is measured by an absolute standard. Justice is not a chopping machine, but an arrangement". For Dürrenmatt, the tragedy of human justice is embodied in Kleist's character Kohlhaas, whom he interprets as a typical Dürrenmatt hero who "refutes the world, but in so doing is himself refuted by the world. . . . But Kohlhaas must be absolute, if he wants to be in the right, and thereby his justice becomes a crime" (*Theater*).

> **Don Quixote, whose name is frequently mentioned in the texts, could be the model for all of Dürrenmatt's heroes.**
> —*Gabrielle Robinson*

Romulus is the best example of this typical Dürrenmatt character; most later heroes resemble him in their aims, methods and in their final failures. At the beginning, we see Romulus as a clown, occupying his time with his hens while Rome is collapsing. But soon we recognize in him the relentless hero who has dedicated himself to justice. Romulus turns out to be the severe moral judge of his society. He condemns Rome for having transgressed his ideal: "it knew truth, but it chose force; it knew humaneness, but it chose tyranny. . . . Justice is at stake." In his fervor, he believes that he can execute justice only through execution, sacrificing his family and delivering his entire civilization to the barbarians, and finally dying himself. Like Mississippi and many other Dürrenmatt heroes, he makes himself into the executioner of his world: "Like a God is such an executioner." Romulus believes that in an end-time such as his, the only just solution is deliberately to become the victim. But his plan fails;

there is no justice as he had envisaged it, only a "disorderly earth." In historical terms, this means that the world will be caught in an endless succession of wars, and in personal terms, that Romulus is forced to end his days in an ignominious retirement. Far from dying a just and heroic death, Romulus is pensioned off, his dream of justice having turned into the farce of his retirement. Having played the clown deliberately and for a purpose, he is finally compelled to play that part against his will. Whereas in the beginning Romulus sits in judgment over the world, in the end the world sits in judgment over him. Through him, Dürrenmatt shows how man's every effort at justice is overthrown by accident and by an ironic fate which annihilates his plans and forces him into a ridiculous defeat. But at the same time, Romulus is one of those terrible simplifiers who bring calamity because they insist on measuring the world with an absolute standard. Holding this ironic double vision, Dürrenmatt can grant his hero greatness only when Romulus willingly accepts his defeat in the face of reality and plays the bitter comedy to the end.

In *The Marriage of Mr. Mississippi* (1957), each character, dialectically developed out of the others, pursues his own vision of justice; they are all united only in their disregard of human life. Under the banner of Mosaic justice, Mississippi passes a record number of death sentences; this practice is frowned upon by the secretary of justice, for whom justice has to be politically feasible: "At times one has to decapitate in God's name, at times be clement for the devil's sake." To bring about a "triumph of justice", Mississippi is prepared to murder his adulterous wife and marry the woman who murdered her husband, and the communist Sainte-Claude is prepared to start revolutions in the name of human rather than divine justice. They generate murder and unrest, but neither man realizes his ideal and both are accidentally killed. They repeat Romulus's fate in that everything they do becomes senseless, but they do not share his insight. Their justice breeds murder and revolutions which "condense to a single monstrous trumpet blast of death."

Nebuchadnezzar in *An Angel Comes to Babylon* has the same aims and the same frustrations as Romulus. He wants to create an empire based on reason and justice, "a new order of things." But all he achieves is a string of executions and wars. It is indifferent whether he or Nimrod reigns. The empire "is carted through our times / On the old rails . . . ", to paraphrase a line from *King John*: the same attempts at reform to combat never-changing grievances, a succession of wars and revolutions, and, above all, executions—in short, the eternal disorder and injustice which no man can change. As the Angel tries to teach Nebuchadnezzar: "ruling worlds befits heaven and begging befits man" (I, 190). Yet, although his impotence is proven by events, he remains defiant in spirit, seeking to oppose "creation out of nothingness with the cre-

ation out of the spirit of man and see which is better: My justice or the injustice of God."

At the beginning of *King John,* the Bastard is confidently "Playing the game I chose . . . " Like Romulus, he plays the clown with a serious purpose: everything he does serves his plan to regulate politics by reason, to make it just. Under his influence, King John himself becomes an advocate of justice, seeking restriction of the royal power, protection from arbitrary laws, freedom for the people. But invariably the crises and accidents of a chaotic world turn the Bastard's plans upside down:

> I interfered
> In the world of the powerful
> Tried to steer them to a better course.
> Yet stupidity pulled the carriage of fate.
> And accident.

The result of his intervention is further chaos and bloodshed. So Dürrenmatt again reaches paradox: the man who plans is most vulnerable to accident and achieves the very opposite of his plans; he who seeks justice is the most destructive. As John tells the Bastard at the end:

> You brought nothing but calamity.
> Improving the world you only made it the
> More damned.

This accusation also fits Dürrenmatt's other seekers of justice and order who turn out to be the perpetrators of the very evils they are trying to root out. The Bastard ends, not unlike Romulus, by withdrawing from the world and playing the part he once had freely chosen as a guise; he is a bastard and his brother's groom.

Although Titus's fate resembles that of the others, Dürrenmatt has so reduced him to the purely farcical that we cannot respond in the same way to his predicament. Titus lacks the wit and fascination of the other heroes, yet he shares their obsessions. A mixture of Romulus and Mississippi, Titus believes that Rome's greatness lies in its law, which he enforces in a single- but also narrow-minded manner. Dürrenmatt denies him the distinction of playing a part; Titus is simply a bigoted advocate of law and order. In an extended interlude—which, although not strictly linked to the plot, expresses Dürrenmatt's concern—Titus asks heaven and hell for justice, chanting together with his invalided soldiers:

> Justice, justice,
> Who sustains you, justice?
> Who greased you, justice?
> With whom do you whore, justice?

This litany continues for another page when, among other things, they plan to stage the tragedy of the missing justice.

Like Möbius before him, Titus plays the madman when all else fails him.

> The nonsense
> Of the world only insanity can still subdue.

He serves a mother her sons for dinner, then stabs her and is finally stabbed himself by the Emperor. So the cycle continues until all the characters are maimed, raped or killed. Justice becomes revenge which demands justice, which again cries out for revenge, and "Thus it goes on in the idiotic course of time." Once m[o]re justice turns to madness and then murder; it does not, finally, subdue the nonsense of the world.

In *The Conformist* (1973), Dürrenmatt continues the farcical reduction of his characters and plot, while still exploring the same themes; indeed, here he gives them a pure schematic form. The gifted scientist Doc, a latter-day Möbius, has been fired from his job during an economic crisis; now he works for Boss, whose business is murder. Doc lives literally underground, where he dissolves the bodies which Boss provides so plentifully. Doc's son Bill seeks justice by trying to destroy the world which has destroyed his father. Having become the richest man in the country, he squanders his fortune in an attempt to wreck the economy and hastens political collapse by arranging the murder of each incoming president. This mixture of Romulus and Claire is finally killed by Cop.

Justice breeds murder also in the case of Cop. He has dedicated his life to convicting Boss; but when at last he lays his evidence before the authorities, every one of the officials is interested only in sharing Boss's profits. Finally Cop "demands justice" from the highest judge; but laughing at Cop, this man demands the largest share of the profit: "Only drunk writers and divorced females babble of justice." Cop realizes the senselessness of his life's work, what a "gigantic nonsense the whole." In a world in which crime is "the form of our civilization," he is the only guilty one, "since I alone sought justice in a world in which justice can be stolen." He then voices one of Dürrenmatt's paradoxical ideas about justice from the aptly named *Monster Lecture about Justice and Law,* where Dürrenmatt had written: "No single man changes reality; reality is changed by all. Reality is all of us and we are always only single men." Indeed Cop, like Romulus, believes that a single man can realize justice which is everyone's business. And this misconception leads him to murder. At the end, however, aware of his mistake and of his powerlessness, he is ready to die himself. His death, at least, will be just, "even if it is a pitiful justice, but that already is much today; there is no other." Clearly, Dürrenmatt

is doing what Charles V desires, always circling around justice.

In *The Anabaptists* (1967), the hero, Bockelson, is spared both the confrontation with paradox and the defeat, since the games he plays have no ulterior purpose. He "lets himself be driven / Wherever his game drives him. . . .", not even trying to steer. He creates parodies of "lofty stories, heroic stories," without ever losing the sense that they are just different versions of his game; he plays king or beggar with equal detachment, out of "loose inspiration." He believes in nothing and uses everything. Somewhat like his creator, Bockelson recites "comedian-like a farce / Interspersed with Biblical passages and dreams of a better world . . . ." So for once a hero remains undefeated; he is even promoted to the first rank of the Cardinal's theatrical company. Only he who plays a game as radically as Bockelson can survive. Those who believe in justice or reason come to grief, and those who are resigned to making compromises are condemned "to patch up a foul order . . . " (III, 126), as the Bishop knows from his own experience. Like the disorderly earth of *Romulus the Great,* this foul order is characterized by a terrible perversion of justice:

> The blessed strung to the wheel; the seducer pardoned
> The seduced butchered, the victors derided by their victory
> The judgment defiled by the judges. . . .

The answers to this injustice are as extreme as the situations themselves. One can accept it in faith, trusting to divine grace. Man is nothing without grace, but grace is incompatible with human justice. Thus, the blind faith of the blind duke, who never defends himself and who gives in to his blindness, wins out over all the horror of this life. He would agree with Knipperdollinck's daughter in *It Is Written* that, "It does not befit man to be just" (III, 141). This is a lesson which the "just" Knipperdollinck learns only after he has sacrificed his wealth and his family in his dedication to justice: "Injustice is your lot, you men, and error. Look at my bloody sword of justice, you Anabaptists. Look at human justice. She cut everything to pieces without knowledge, she beheaded blindly. Be it cursed, human justice" (III, 141). He ends strung to the wheel, praising God: "Lord! Lord! / Look at my broken limbs, crushed by Your justice. . . ."

Another answer, as the ends of both *The Physicists* and *Titus Andronicus* illustrate, is to see only meaningless indifference, monstrous accident, dead matter, "an obscene aberration of carbon . . . and incurable scab." But instead of submission, which is stressed more in the earlier works, and denial, which predominates in the later ones, integrity is an option: man can simply cultivate his own garden, as Augias does in the "garden of his renunciation," surrounded by dung, and the Bishop, amidst wars and slaughter, trying "to remain reasonable amidst unreason." Unable to change the world, these characters are resigned to doing the small things which are within reach. The Jew Gulliver from *The Suspicion* (1961) also teaches Commissioner Bärlach this lesson. Bärlach is another Quixotic seeker after justice, setting out "to combat evil with the mind." Although ingenious and courageous, he is nevertheless "a fool of a detective," who causes the death of an accomplice, and who might have lost his own life, had not Gulliver rescued him at the last minute, with the advice: "As single men we cannot save the world. Therefore we should seek not to save the world but to endure it, the only true adventure which is still left us at this late date." Yet, this awareness of an all-pervasive injustice, which cannot be altered, which can only be borne, does tend to keep these characters from taking any action at all.

Dürrenmatt's plays are built of dialectical reversals, antithetic contrasts, and the grotesque parallels and distortions which constitute his vision. As we have seen, he uses paradox and parody extensively. Seeing everything as its own parody presupposes an attitude of play, but it also implies the collapse of order and meaning, and man's lack of control. Thus, in *The Physicists,* Möbius, playing mad, acts out a parody of Solomon. Once "a prince of peace and justice," Solomon becomes the inspiration for madness and murder, for Möbius invokes this ruler when he turns to insanity and when he kills the nurse whom he loves. Ultimately, however, this parodied "poor king Solomon" is a symbol of our world and man's state. Like parody, paradox confronts man with the limits of his power and understanding, and exposes his impotence in the most striking manner. Both parody and paradox work through ironic reversals, antithetic constellations and developments. This process is crucial for Dürrenmatt, who believes that "the playwright needs a gradient, a contrast."

> **Dürrenmatt's plays are built of dialectical reversals, antithetic contrasts, and the grotesque parallels and distortions which constitute his vision.**
> *—Gabrielle Robinson*

So it seems that parody, paradox, as well as the worst possible turn, the dialectics, the reversals, often so perfectly symmetrical, and the grotesque contrasts, all are ultimately in the service of Dürrenmatt's theatrical conception. "The more paradoxically it can be presented, the better reality is suited as theatrical material." "Justice breeds murder," therefore, can be read as a theatrical rather than a conceptual statement. And, indeed, Dürrenmatt's ideas of justice, however thought-provoking, are perhaps a little simple and absolutist, and do not add up to a philosophy. But they are always

highly theatrical: heroes fighting to the last for justice and humanity, and turning justice into crime; both human inadequacy and monstrous disorder turning idealism destructive. "The disgrace of the times which makes statesmen out of murderers and judges out of executioners, forces the just to die like criminals." Moreover, these ideas are expressed, of course, by Dürrenmatt's grotesque parodical view.

So perhaps what is crucial for Dürrenmatt in the end is not even justice itself, but playing with the theatrical possibilities of this theme, exploiting the material, creating models, possible worlds. In a sense, that is the basic process of writing, but for Dürrenmatt, playing—with ideas and forms, with situations, with a role, with words—is especially important. He is always sharpening his ideas and situations into paradoxical and parodistical formulations, and challenging us with his constructions. This generalization applies to his expository prose as well as to his art; it describes his way of thinking. In the *Monster Lecture about Justice and Law,* for example, Dürrenmatt concludes that: "The world, through our injustice, is with justice unjust." In the same lecture, he says: "I think the world through by playing it through"; he compares the procedure to a game of chess in which it does not matter who wins: "the game alone counts, the theme of the opening, the drama of the endgame." "Every play," Dürrenmatt once said, "almost forces a counterplay. It is an inner dialectical process"; and, "The theater as a world of its own contains as its themes fictional men; it develops contrapuntally. A theme has a countertheme. . . ."

As a result of these views, Dürrenmatt often devises contrasting endings for his stories, as in *Greek Man Seeks Greek Maiden,* or even reworks them completely. In *The Pledge,* subtitled "Requiem of a Mystery Novel," we get a direct glimpse of Dürrenmatt's way of playing with his material. The story concerns Matthäi, a brilliant criminologist, who is convinced of the innocence of a convicted murderer. "Inexorable, obstinate, passionate," like all of Dürrenmatt's heroes, he tracks down the real criminal. Yet he is foiled at the last minute by an accident, literally, a car accident, which prevents the murderer from being caught in Matthäi's trap. Now, says the old police inspector who tells the story, the writer has certain alternatives. He can let Matthäi win after all, thereby establishing the higher idea of justice, the victory of faith, hope and reason. (That is essentially what Dürrenmatt does in the television version of the story, called **"It Happened in Broad Daylight."**) Or, he can make the story even more cruel—"The worst also happens occasionally"—by letting Matthäi believe in the innocence of a guilty man and seek a murderer who does not exist; then all the protagonist's actions and plans, however clever, are absurd. Yet even here man has a choice: he can accept his inadequacy in all humility, aware that accounts do not square in reality, or he can deny reality and end in madness. After suggesting these possible models for his story, Dürrenmatt settles for a compromise: Matthäi, unable to accept the workings of accident and absurdity which have destroyed his life's work, goes mad; but at least the inspector discovers years later that Matthäi was right after all.

Despite the evidence, however, one must guard against making this distinction between concept and theater too neat. Perhaps Dürrenmatt, like so many contemporary writers, sees it the other way round: it is justice that is essentially theatrical and therefore parodical. Hence, he does not simplify and totalize—reality does; he is not theatrical—reality is.

In any case, like their creator, the characters are players in the widest sense; references to playing a game occur in almost every work. Palamedes plays "a lonely game, as it flourishes among ruins on the last evening of time," helping his father maintain his illusion. Da Ponte plays the opposite game, using the whores and derelicts of his army as actors to destroy the blind man's peace. Of course, Romulus, Möbius, Bockelson, the Bastard are all master players. But, as we have seen, their games—and Dürrenmatt likes to use a chess metaphor—end in a checkmate. Yet, though forms of play are always present in Dürrenmatt's art, there is the same change of emphasis and orientation which we have noted before. This tendency becomes apparent, for example, in a comparison of the two Bockelsons. In *It Is Written* (1947), Bockelson says that he plays "with men as with light balls" (II, 23); in *The Anabaptists,* he plays "comedian-like a farce / Interspersed with Biblical passages and dreams of a better world . . . . " In the earlier plays, the characters are more immediately playful, experiencing the wonder and joy of their games: hence, Romulus's fun with his hens, and Bockelson's relish of food: "Blessed and full of grace be what I have just savored! / Russian salad with tuna!" Dürrenmatt stresses the wit and wisdom as well as the courage of these game-playing characters who, like Romulus, have the greatness to accept their defeat. In his later plays, he accentuates the limitations of their games and the futility. The idealist and rebel can survive only as the consummate actor who turns his dreams of a better world into a farce; believing in nothing, he reduces everything to a mere game. Playing now makes reality absurd and alienates man.

A crucial scene alteration in the two Anabaptist plays illustrates Dürrenmatt's development. At the end of *It Is Written,* Bockelson and Knipperdollinck dance on the rooftops under a giant moon and an infinite sky; theirs is a poetically exalted meeting which shows Dürrenmatt to be heavily influenced by the expressionists. In *The Anabaptists,* this scene is moved to a stage on which Bockelson appears, stripped to the waist, carrying paintbrushes and a pail, and wearing an enormous red train and a crown. Dürrenmatt, having forsaken deeper meaning and poetry, shows the world as a stage of grotesque theatricality. A similar reduction is apparent in the endings of *Romulus the Great* and *The Physicists.* At

his abdication, Romulus bids farewell to the world, seeing it as a colored ball with rich provinces, a blue sea with dancing dolphins, yet also a ball dissolving into nothingness. This is a world monstrous at once in its abundance and in its emptiness. The defeated Möbius, on the other hand, sees the universe as a blue shimmering desert, "and somewhere around a small, yellow, nameless star circles senselessly, evermore, the radioactive earth." If formerly the monstrosity of the world stimulated wonder, fear and joy, now its effect is desolate, forsaken, alienated.

In his later plays, Dürrenmatt is working more and more towards reduction and a theatrical essence: "Dramaturgically I try to show things always more simply, to become more and more economical, to leave out more and more, only to hint." In *Play Strindberg* and, even more, in *The Conformist,* characters, dialogue and action begin to resemble the comic strip, and the entire conception, thus reduced, does not yield much stimulation or insight. And yet, however reduced and absurd it may be, playing is itself a liberating force; it creates distance, energy and freedom. The player observes "the doings of men a little detached from earthly encumbrances, in a light . . . in which lines appear more distinctly . . . and shapes stand out clearly against their background." Again, playing is defined as a way of making reality transparent, being precise about it. It not only expresses but also subdues and controls the "nonsense of the world." And it always precludes the sentimentality inherent in a perception of reality which reduces men to victims. In the same ways, seeing and shaping reality through parody and paradox create not only a grotesque perception, but also distance and freedom: clarity of vision—"The grotesque is one of the great possibilities of being precise"—as well as a form which enables one to cope with whatever desperate message it contains. For Dürrenmatt insists that his portrayal does not of necessity lead to despair: "He who despairs loses his head; he who writes comedies, uses it" (*Theater*). In the end, the effect is tragicomedy, although Dürrenmatt prefers to call it comedy. It is comedy for our time, comedy about tragedy, which is the only comedy we can put up with. This concept gives meaning to Romulus's statement, "Someone on his last legs like us can understand only comedies." The writer of comedy, says Dürrenmatt, transforms "a world which is no laughing matter into a stage world about which he laughs . . . " (*Theater*).

Peter Spycher (essay date Autumn 1981)

SOURCE: "Friedrich Dürrenmatt's Story 'Das Sterben der Pythia': Farewell to Theatre and a Return to Fiction and Essays?", in *World Literature Today,* Vol. 55, No. 4, Autumn, 1981, pp. 614-18.

[*In the following essay, Spycher examines Dürrenmatt's use of chance and coincidence, specifically in "Das Sterben der Pythia," in place of fate.*]

For decades after World War II the two Swiss writers Max Frisch (b. 1911; . . .) and Friedrich Dürrenmatt (b. 1921) were regarded as two leading playwrights of the German-language theater. But after his play *Biografie* (1967) Frisch did not write another for some ten years. This new play, *Triptychon,* was published in book form in 1978. Will there be a next one? It is an open question. Dürrenmatt, on the other hand, has kept writing for the theatre at a fairly steady pace. His last success, however, was *Play Strindberg* (1969). His subsequent "comedies" have all been failures with the public: *Porträt eines Planeten* (1970/71), *Der Mitmacher (The Accomplice;* 1972), *Die Frist (The Deadline;* 1977), *Die Panne (The Breakdown;* 1979); also his adaptation of Shakespeare's *Titus Andronicus* (1969/70), as well as his subjective productions of Goethe's *Urfaust* (1969/70), Büchner's *Woyzeck* (1971/72) and Lessing's *Emilia Galotti* (1974/75). He decided not to attend the premiere of *Die Frist,* and he reserved *Die Panne* for a restricted theatrical occasion.

André Müller reports: "Dürrenmatt knows his worth. He is confident that his time, the time of world theatre, will come, after his death at the latest." Rolf R. Bigler seconds: "In recent years [Dürrenmatt] was no longer timely. With his plays he was too far out in the future. He let the spokesmen of the age [*Zeitgeistliche*] do their preaching. Now he is becoming timely again. Not because he has slowed down his pace, but because today's reality shamelessly copies him." But Gerd Jäger voices a different opinion: "*Porträt eines Planeten* (at the very least) . . . shows that Dürrenmatt's theatre world is not the result of a transformation of the real world into theatre but that of his dramaturgic (i.e., increasingly cliché-ridden) conception of the world into theatre." Timo Tiusanen, in his discussion of *Der Mitmacher,* bluntly states what he thinks is wrong with Dürrenmatt's more recent dramatic work: "[*Der Mitmacher*] is a play demonstrating one of Dürrenmatt's basic difficulties. Where and how to find a context for the results of his macabre creative imagination? The grotesque, Dürrenmatt's forte, presupposes some kind of balancing factor, a minimum amount of everyday probability, to be effective." Maybe there is a discrepancy between Dürrenmatt's aspiration to the creation of a *theatrum mundi* and the often lowbrow cabaretistic media and means he employs to this end.

Dürrenmatt has announced his intention of increasingly writing for "an imaginary stage," for "the theatre of [his] imagination"; but as in the case of Frisch, it would be prudent to refrain from making firm predictions. And it is a fact that both Frisch and Dürrenmatt have continued being successfully productive as writers of fiction and of essays,

Dürrenmatt moreover as a graphic artist. In an article on Dürrenmatt's book *Der Mitmacher: Ein Komplex* (1976) the Swiss literary critic Anton Krättli writes: "The games [Dürrenmatt] has played in this . . . book as an aftermath to the comedy '**Der Mitmacher**' are not only richer and more stimulating, they are also more profound, they are games relevant to reality, a relevance that seems to be almost completely missing from the comedy. And in vivid contrast to the compressions and abbreviations which prevented the play from really coming alive, his dramaturgic conclusions and above all his stories ['**Smithy**' and '**Das Sterben der Pythia**'] in his exuberant Postscript to '**Der Mitmacher**' may well constitute one of his major works." Krättli praises the "novella" "**Smithy**" (especially its protagonist, a "courageous human being") and calls the "parodistic story" "**Das Sterben der Pythia**" ("**The Death of the Pythia**") "perhaps the highlight of the book, . . . a small masterpiece." I would like to adopt Krättli's judgment and illustrate it by an analysis of one of the stories, "**Das Sterben der Pythia.**"

In "**Das Sterben der Pythia**" Dürrenmatt deals with a myth, that of Oedipus. In an interview with Heinz Ludwig Arnold he once said that a writer may "suddenly have an idea as to how to choose a myth and reuse it." He did this for and in his *Herkules und der Stall des Augias* and specifically in his "**Dramaturgie des Labyrinths,**" in which the story of the Minotaur is told. In "**Das Sterben der Pythia**" he has conducted something like an experiment with a remarkably flexible myth which had been adapted innumerable times before: he wished to illustrate and demonstrate a concept that had always been close to his heart. "Having told the story of Smithy," he states, "to find out how I come across a subject matter, I told the story of Oedipus to satisfy my curiosity as to what excites me about a subject matter." What is it that excites him? Dürrenmatt: "The plot of Oedipus's story seems to be inseparably connected with the idea of fate." Dürrenmatt wants to replace fate by chance or coincidence or accident (*Zufall*); this is what he calls a "flight" from an action that is controlled by gods and their oracles into the human agents of an action that is continually subjected to coincidences. If there is a fate, then man is simultaneously threatened and guided, and it is at one with him; in a world of coincidences, however, man is exclusively threatened, is exclusively a victim. In *Die Panne* retired Judge Wucht probably speaks in the author's name when he says: "In a world of guiltless-guilty men, fate has exited from the stage, and chance or accident has taken its place. The age of necessities has yielded to the age of catastrophes."

The (hitherto very few) critics have characterized "**Das Sterben der Pythia**" as the author himself has done so. Anton Krättli, for example, writes: "Since Dürrenmatt no longer believes in the possibility of tragedy, he sets out to offer an altered interpretation of the myth: it was not fate but chance that guided Oedipus along his ghastly paths." Jan Knopf, intriguingly enough, formulates a Dürrenmattian "theory of chance" (in a discussion of *König Johann*): "The theory of chance carries itself to an absurd extreme in that chance appears in accordance with a plan whenever a plan made by a human being is to be thwarted. Now the law is the following: the more planning, the more interfering by chance.... Chance assumes the meaningful function of creating madness.

What may the story of the Pythia conceivably have to do with the comedy *Der Mitmacher?* One link may be this statement by Dürrenmatt: "In contrast to the dramaturgic tactic of treating chance with care so that chance would remain what it is, chance, in *Der Mitmacher* chance happens *again and again*" (my emphasis). Is this perhaps conscious or unconscious self-criticism with regard to the comedy? The fact is that in the comedy chance plays too massive a part, whereas in the story chance is parodistically thematized, on the one hand, and unmistakably kept within limits on the other—so much so that the figures here are plausible characters, indeed are apt to arouse a psychological interest. Krättli notes too that there may be something other than just the question of fate or chance involved; he says: "[Dürrenmatt] does not directly aim to refute the thesis that it was the curse of the gods that drove the son of the king of Thebes into a trap. But he harbors doubts and thinks it is possible that a quite different authority, one behind the gods or even farther out in a mysterious realm, is responsible for what happens. Again, he pleads for the existence of a mystery."

In the story an intimate familiarity of the reader with the classical Oedipus matter is obviously presupposed; otherwise the story could not be a parodistic tragicomedy. As far as I am concerned, I have to presuppose the reader's familiarity with Dürrenmatt's parody, which fairly bursts with witty themes and motifs and ingenious variations and metamorphoses; any attempt at a summary would probably fall far short of its purpose and would be too clumsy.

Dürrenmatt's contention that, in his story, "It is no longer the oracle that counts but the person who proclaims it, the priestess of Apollo, the Pythia," and that one could posit, as a point of departure, "that Oedipus might, for instance, fall prey to a Pythia who happens to be in a bad mood" is not altogether correct. What matters is who formulates an oracle, in what spirit, with what intent—and also who hears it and how he reacts to it, as, say, in *Der Meteor,* where the miracle of the divinely ordained resurrections of Schwitter is assessed in very diverse ways by Schwitter himself and the other characters in the comedy. In **"Das Sterben der Pythia"** (as in **"Smithy"**) Dürrenmatt abundantly employs the device of the interior monologue (*erlebte Rede*); seldom does the narrator speak in his own name. It is important for the reader to recognize the different narrative perspectives and to avoid confusing the opinions of individual figures with the fictional facts of the story. The story as a whole, it should be borne in mind, consists of real or imagined conversations held, in retrospect, between actual or potential shades of the characters involved in the history of the kingdom of Thebes with a disillusioned Pythia, Pannychis XI, who is weary of life and looks forward to her death.

The "de-mythologizing," "de-heroicizing," "de-bunking" narrative style naturally recalls that of *Herkules und der Stall des Augias* or *Der Proze um des Esels Schatten* or *Grieche sucht Griechin* but is, by and large, more casual, more mellow, wiser, more cognizant of the "moral frailty of the world." It closely resembles that of **"Dramaturgie des Labyrinths."** The very beginning of the story sets the tone for it as a whole.

> The Delphic priestess, Pannychis XI, tall and haggard like most of her predecessors, being annoyed by the monkey business of her oracles and by the credulity of the Greeks, had listened to the youth Oedipus; ah, again someone who inquired whether or not his parents were his parents, as if that could so easily be ascertained in aristocratic circles, really, after all, there were wives who pretended to have had sexual intercourse with Zeus, and husbands who were even willing to believe this.... Today she was positively disgusted with everything, ... and thus, be it because she wanted to cure him of his superstition with regard to the art of proclaiming oracles, be it because it simply occurred to her, as a byproduct of her momentarily ugly mood, to annoy the blasé prince from Corinth, she prophesied for him something supremely nonsensical and improbable which, she was sure, would never materialize, for, so she thought, who on earth would be able to murder his own father and sleep with his own mother—she considered those incest-laden stories about gods and demigods to be fairy tales anyhow.

We cannot assert that what the oracle Pannychis communicated to Oedipus was a chance oracle. First, Pannychis "wanted to use her oracles to mock those who believed them"; thus she herself does not believe in gods, or certainly not in their faculty of inspiring oracles; but from her longtime experience, she should know that her cocky oracles only tend to make "devout people even more devout" and thereby decisively contribute to Delphi's economic boom with all its gaudily opulent features. Also, those paid-for oracles that seers like Tiresias formulate for or against prominent persons and that the Pythia thereupon has to recite, have nothing to do with chance: "They were meant for a certain purpose; there was corruption behind it all, maybe even politics." We will learn what the political angles of the oracles of Tiresias are. And second, Oedipus, the devout believer in gods and oracles, has strong motives of his own to see the oracle which Pannychis has just communicated to him come true: much later, he confides to her, "I hated my real parents more than anything else; they wanted to cast me before wild beasts, I did not know who they were, but Apollo's oracle solved the problem for me." His parents, "according to the oracle, . . . were bound to be those upon whom the oracle would be executed," and "I wanted to become king of Thebes, and so did the gods, and I triumphantly slept with my mother. . . . The gods had made this monstrous decision, and therefore it was to be implemented." In this sense, Tiresias fittingly says about Oedipus: "It was he himself who chose his fate." (From the point of view of the Pythia, however, who does not believe in gods, let alone in oracles, the fulfillment of her oracle is "a grotesque fluke hit.") Even the trial Oedipus eventually conducted against himself and his subsequent self-punishment were a triumph for him, because from that time on he could give free rein to his hatred for his parents, his ancestors and the gods. As a blind beggar, accompanied by his daughter Antigone, he now wanders around in Greece, "not in order to exalt the power of the gods, but to scoff at them." Hatred and rebellion against his progenitors, this is Oedipus's case, a kind of triumphantly exploding Oedipus complex.

Each one of the figures has psychologically plausible motives and intentions and suffers whatever consequences may derive from them: Menoikeus, who deems himself socially superior to Laios, nourishes "the hope that he or at least his son Creon would accede to the throne." The oracle bought by him for a high price from Tiresias—"If a son is born to [Laios], he will murder [his father]"—is supposed to work for him as a "deterring oracle." His final self-sacrifice, dictated to him through an oracle that has been arranged for by Laios, suits him well because he has irremediably gone bankrupt. Assuming that Tiresias's oracle has been directed against him, Laios nonetheless wants to maintain his autocratic regime for himself and perpetuate it for posterity, but he makes mistakes or has bad luck: his wife Jocasta bears him a son who has been fathered either by him or by the commanding officer of his royal guard, and somewhat irresolutely he has the infant cast out rather than killed; and on an earlier occasion, perhaps it was he who begat the Sphinx with Hippodameia, the wife of Pelops, who thereupon took his revenge by castrating him; he, Laios, forced his carriage driver Polyphontes to rape the Sphinx in order to produce a grandchild that might become his heir and successor, and through all those actions he drew the deadly hatred of the members of his family upon himself. In her first night of love with Oedipus, Jocasta recognizes him as her son but is more than willing to buy his lies about his "parents," Polybos and Merope, in Corinth, and makes no attempt at enlightening him. Why this behavior? She tells Pannychis: "I fainted with sexual delight; never was it more intense than when I gave myself to [Oedipus]." Was this incestuous perversion? Maybe. But certainly also and above all it was satisfaction of her feelings of revenge toward Laios, who once had had

her son cast out. Having taken her revenge, she gladly allows herself to be hanged from the beam of her bedroom door by one of her jealous guard officers. In her encounter with the Pythia Pannychis she proudly claims or pretends always to have acted in accordance with the gods' decrees—which, to be sure, always corresponded to her very own wishes.

The episode about the Sphinx is quite a special matter. One could raise the question whether Dürrenmatt here did not indulge himself too much in spinning his yarn, but it seems to be preferable to suppose that he has both lit up a fireworks of fantasy and intentionally carried the complications of the story to an absurd extreme. Be that as it may, to present a summary of the Sphinx's biography would be tantamount to extinguishing fireworks with water. Suffice it to note that the Sphinx insists her own son is the genuine Oedipus and that she lived with her son, except that she, the Sphinx, and her son Oedipus remained unaware of their mutual identities. Thus we are offered a choice between *two* Oedipuses. But we are thrown into further confusion: "Perhaps there is a third Oedipus," says Tiresias to Pannychis. "We do not know whether or not the Corinthian shepherd handed over to Queen Merope his own son rather than the son of the Sphinx—if he was the son of the Sphinx—after having pierced [his own son's] ankles too, and having cast the genuine Oedipus, who, after all, was not the genuine one either, out to the wild beasts; [and we do not know] whether or not Merope threw the third Oedipus into the sea in order to present her own son, to whom she had secretly given birth—his father possibly having been an officer of the guard too—as a fourth Oedipus to her guileless husband Polybos." Under such circumstances it is probably best to leave alone "what actually was different and will be different again and again the more we investigate."

Where does this uncertainty, mutually experienced among the various figures and also by the reader, come from? Well, all the figures tell either lies or "only the approximate truth," in part on purpose, in part unconsciously, in part out of ignorance. Besides, the author of course enjoys turning the order he has created into disorder so as to have his "labyrinthine reality" and to baffle the reader. In spite of all the psychological plausibilities, which I have deliberately dwelled on, the fact remains that, from a viewpoint negating the existence of gods, the story abounds with chances and coincidences. (One of the more comical ones is the fact that Oedipus happens to kill all his conceivable fathers: Laios, Polyphontes and Mnesippos.) Nevertheless, of the three main oracles pertaining to the Theban monarchy—1) if a son is born to Laios, the son will murder his father; 2) Oedipus will murder his father and marry his mother; 3) the plague in Thebes will go away if Laios's murderer or murderers are found and punished—only the second, the one improvised by Pannychis, is due to chance. Interestingly enough, its effect on Oedipus is not, as in the classical myth, a tragic one but, instead, a deeply satisfying one (Oedipus as the husband of Jocasta satisfies his feelings of revenge against his parents) or an enchanting one (Oedipus as the lover of the Sphinx experiences idyllic happiness with her). Dürrenmatt thinks that he could not penetrate to the center of his own personality by employing psychoanalytical methods, but admits that he could not, of course, prevent other people from psychoanalyzing him. I, for one, suspect that a psychoanalytical interpretation of **"Das Sterben der Pythia"** would yield valuable insights.

But back to the oracles! The first and the third oracle were conceived by Tiresias for a political purpose. Tiresias, like Pannychis and indeed much more than she, is "a rational human being"; "I too do not believe in the gods," he says, "but I believe in reason, and because I believe in reason, I am convinced that irrational faith in the gods has to be used in a rational way." According to his own confession, Tiresias is a "democrat." He takes sides, not so much *for* Laios, a corrupt but nonideological tyrant, as *against* Creon, who would, if he were to become king (Menoikeus's hope!), establish a totalitarian state modeled on Sparta. Tiresias's first oracle was intended to advise the castrated and homosexual Laios to *adopt* a son—for instance, the decent General Amphitryon. Laios, we recall, fails to understand this advice. Tiresias's other oracle (our third one) is based on an error: he mistakenly believes that it was Creon, not Oedipus, who murdered Laios (Jocasta had concealed the truth from the seer). Tiresias would like to use his second oracle to focus the people's attention on Creon as the suspected assassin in order to prevent him from overthrowing Oedipus (the real assassin of his father and husband of his mother!) and replacing him as king of Thebes (262 f.). Unfortunately, Tiresias's oracle has the opposite effect: Oedipus abdicates, and Creon becomes king.

Pannychis and Tiresias, not Oedipus, are the actual protagonists of the story. At the end Tiresias says to Pannychis: "Both of us faced the same monstrous reality, which is as opaque as man, who creates it." If the gods existed (but they do not), they would probably have "a certain, if superficial, general overview." How have Tiresias and Pannychis reacted to this monstrous, opaque reality? Pannychis "with imagination, with whimsicality, with high spirits, even with a virtually irreverent insolence, in short: with blasphemous jocularity"; Tiresias "with cool reflection . . . , with incorruptible logic, again in short: with reason." Paradoxically, Pannychis's "improbable" oracle turn out to be failures. Tiresias has acted as a rationalist, as a "utopian," who perceives the world as "a monster." This, at any rate, is what Dürrenmatt has Tiresias proclaim. Yet Tiresias, in contrast to a rationalistic would-be reformer of society like Bertolt Brecht, recognizes the problematic nature of his philosophy and the desirability of its being supplemented by imagination. At the end of the

story Tiresias explicitly raises the question of Oedipus's fate: is it determined by the gods, or through Oedipus's "breach" of "certain principles that lend support to the society of his times" or through some chance triggered by Pannychis?

It seems to me that what is discussed in **"Das Sterben der Pythia"** is not so much Oedipus's fate (which brings him satisfaction and fulfillment) as the question of the effect of the whimsical imagination of the irreligious Delphic priestess Pannychis XI in a chaotic world; above all, however, is the fact that the irreligious seer Tiresias, a rationalist working for the establishment of a rational and preferably democratic order (under Oedipus's guidance), makes a bad miscalculation, causing the establishment of a tyrannical order under Creon), and thus checkmates himself—not unlike, e.g., the Bastard in **König Johann,** "Exzellenz" in *Die Frist,* the private court and Traps in the comedy *Die Panne* and the dramatis personae in *Der Mitmacher,* To quote Anton Krättli once more, "Here it is again, the theme of *Mitmachen*: to commit or not to commit oneself in the affairs of the world, that is the question." But as I have observed already, "Das Sterben der Pythia" has an advantage over *Der Mitmacher*: the story is told with imagination, wit, urbanity, suspense, elegance and—"with humor!"

A. M. Wright (essay date October 1981)

SOURCE: "Scientific Method and Rationality in Dürrenmatt," in *German Life and Letters,* Vol. 35, No. 1, October, 1981, pp. 64-72.

[*In the following essay, Wright shows how Dürrenmatt explores what is real by juxtaposing scientific method and speculation in his detective novels.*]

Dürrenmatt's work so often presents us with an incalcuable world thwarting man's attempts to shape it, that the world's rationality seems questioned and thus the whole scientific enterprise to understand it. Nowhere does this seem more evident than in the detective novels, where scientific procedures are apparently mocked. In lectures of recent years Dürrenmatt has dealt directly with such philosophical issues, comparing in particular the views of Spinoza and Einstein, and acknowledging the importance that the thought of Karl Popper has come to have for him. An analysis of the detective novels will show just how much of what he now makes explicit was contained in his earlier work, suggesting that underlying his work is a coherent philosophical position that has changed little. While his work constitutes a critique of the Cartesian strand of rationalism, of which Spinoza is an extreme representative, his position remains firmly rationalist.

> **Underlying [Dürrenmatt's] work is a coherent philosophical position that has changed little.**
> —*A. M. Wright*

The novels contain an exploration of scientific method, presenting competing views of it that reflect the battles in physics fought out in Germany between the wars. The contrast that we are shown in *Der Richter und sein Henker* is ostensibly that between the brilliant but unsystematic Bärlach, proceeding by hunch not scientific method, and his superior Lutz, the champion of modern scientific criminology, employing inductive logic and a methodical discovery procedure. It is precisely these rational procedures that the novel seems to mock and Lutz himself, bewildered by the denouement, is made to admit the inadequacy of his science: ". . . wenn es nach der Wissenschaft gegangen wäre, schnüffelten wir jetzt bei fremden Diplomaten herum." Bärlach accepts the role he is cast for, playing teasingly with the accusations of unscientific procedure: ". . . mein Verdacht ist nicht ein kriminalistisch wissenschaftlicher Verdacht. Ich habe keine Gründe, die ihn rechtfertigen." Justification will prove to be a key notion.

Lutz's view of science is the Baconian one of a procedure that starts from firmly established facts and builds on this sure foundation a structure of verified knowledge, discovery being achieved by applying a rigorous method. This view is suspicious above all of hypotheses. It finds bold expression in Newton's "Hypotheses non fingo", which Dürrenmatt put into the mouth of his own Newton in *Die Physiker* and which was a slogan of Philipp Lenard's "Aryan Physics". Above all it is necessary to restrain the imagination, to avoid obscuring the truth of nature with the mind's fantasies. Nature must be viewed without preconceptions and the mind firmly anchored in the "real" world. Nature is thus an open book, revealing itself to any mind unclouded by the fictions produced by the all too fertile imagination. The idea is fostered that the scientist is the man of cold reason who points to a reality we all could see, if we would open unprejudiced eyes and look. With such a method, Bacon even suggested, great intellect was no longer essential: "Not much is left to acuteness and strength of talent." With a pair of compasses, he remarks, anyone can draw a circle. Any of Dürrenmatt's dull policemen, Lutz, Tschanz or Henzi, will suffice; the undisciplined brilliance of a Bärlach is superfluous. The empiricist Bacon was at one with the rationalist Spinoza on this point at least, that truth manifests itself.

Opposed to this is the view argued above all by Popper that science can yield no more than theories that may take us ever closer to the truth but can never be verified or "justified"; they are falsified by one counter-example, but no amount of "confirmatory" evidence can establish their truth, for the very next instance may contradict. Progress is only by the negative way of subjecting theories to the severest tests, in order to reveal inadequacies and suggest better theories. A theory is only as good as the tests it has survived; a good one will not only be consistent with available data but lead to new discoveries. The scientist should not try to prove his theory but to falsify it. On this view it is not only the dramatist but the scientist too who must pursue "die schlimmst mögliche Wendung", which for him means refutation of his theory. In this process of conjectures and refutations hypotheses are essential. It matters little how fantastic the hypothesis, if it yields testable statements; the only hypothesis useless to science is one that cannot be falsified. Reality is not an open book; in Heraclitus' words, Nature loves to hide, and must be tricked into revealing her secrets. Einstein called his world "a world of some objective reality which I try to catch in a wildly speculative way." Dürrenmatt's detective novels bring these two conceptions of science into confrontation.

In *Das Versprechen* the hawker von Gunten, with a previous conviction for indecency involving a fourteen year old girl, is the obvious and only available suspect for the murder of the young child Gritli Moser. Henzi, in charge of the case, jumps at the plausible solution, fitting all the confirmatory evidence to the pattern: the previous conviction; the failure of von Gunten to report tripping over the body he claims he found, until confronted with the bloodstains detected on his trousers; his unwillingness to mention razors in the list of his wares etc. The pattern is impressive, but is it there in the real world or being forced onto it? All the evidence can be fitted into another coherent pattern, that of the hawker's own explanation. Some test is required to show the explanatory power of Henzi's theory. Henzi does not look for such a test; he prefers to squeeze von Gunten till he cracks and confesses. It does not trouble Henzi that not even the confession yields testable information, such as the whereabouts of the murder weapon. His hypothesis has risked nothing and survived no tests. It triumphs only because the alternative is silenced: von Gunten commits suicide.

Yet any serious attempt to refute the hypothesis would have aroused immediate doubts. Matthäi's keener mind had spotted the irrelevance of the previous conviction to a case involving no sexual assault. Dissatisfied, he seeks further evidence and finds it in Gritli's drawing of a man, made shortly before her death. The psychiatrist Locher, to whom he submits it for comment, dismisses it as worthless evidence, because children's drawings are a mixture of fantasy and reality, but coaxed into going along with Matthäi's "fiction" and informed that three girls have been murdered in the same way, he obliges with a hypothesis. When Matthäi proceeds to take it seriously, however, he reacts with horror: "Alles, was er ihm gesagt habe, sei nur eine Spekulation, ein blosses

Gedankenspiel ohne wissenschaftlichen Wert." It is a mere fiction, one possibility in a thousand: "Mit der gleichen Methode könate man beweisen, dass jeder beliebige der Mörder sein könnte." The sober scientist pleads with Matthäi to leave his fantasy world: ". . . nun solle Matthäi auch Manns genug sein, die Realität ohne Hypothesen zu schen."

Locher has however overlooked a vital point: his "wild" speculation has the great merit of being falsifiable, because it has yielded one testable statement, the prediction that the girls will resemble each other. "Prüfen Sie es nach, die Opfer werden sich alle gleichen." The hypothesis leads to the discovery of a significant fact, for Locher is right and the fact had not previously been noticed. Unlike Henzi's plausible hypothesis, Locher's speculative one ran the risk of being refuted; it has probed the world, instead of fitting known facts into a preconceived pattern. Matthäi's next step is equally conjectural. Following painstaking experimental work with children, he suggests that a horned figure in the drawing depicts the ibex motif on a Graubünden car number plate. This conjecture focuses attention on another detail that nobody had noticed: all three murder locations were on the Graubüden—Zurich road, and von Gunten had no car. Further successful predictions finally convince everyone. Matthäi's fiction exposes reality so well that the police chief Dr. H. calls the detective a genius. Locher had pleaded with Matthäi to face reality without hypotheses; Matthäi shows that only with hypotheses can reality be faced.

Locher and Dr. H. had urged Matthäi to be reasonable and accept what was probable. Too often the reasonable and probable are merely what seem plausible to an unimaginative mind. Poor Lutz in *Der Richter und sein Henker* never questions the plausible: at first the master criminal Gastmann is "above all suspicion" and at the end his guilt is "proven". The truth he never suspects. That reality might be surprising never enters his mind. All the scientific paraphernalia in the world is useless, when the thinking is as shoddy and unimaginative as his.

In the Bärlach novels it is Bärlach himself, not Lutz, who displays scientific method. In *Der Richter und sein Henker* this is obscured by the fact of Bärlach's previous knowledge of Gastmann. In *Der Verdacht,* however, Dürrenmatt gives us two examples of scientific reasoning made so explicit that it reads like a textbook. Bärlach characterizes the detective's art for his surgeon friend Hungertobel as follows: "Unsere Kunst setzt sich aus etwas Mathematik zusammen und aus sehr viel Phantasie." This resembles the account given by Einstein and Popper of the scientist's "art". Expounding Einstein, Dürrenmatt has written:

> Damit sind wir auf das wichtigste Dogma der Einsteinschen Erkenntnistheorie gestossen, auf den Glauben, dass sich die Sinnen-Erlebnisse nur

intuitiv, nicht logisch auf ein in sich logisches, aber an sich logisch willkürliches Begriffssystem beziehen lassen.

Bärlach's intuitive processes are stimulated by Hungertobel's astonishment at the close resemblance between a picture of the concentration camp doctor Nehle and a student colleague, Emmenberger, now running a prosperous local sanatorium. To Bärlach's speculative identification of the two Hungertobel reacts with the same horrified protest with which Locher greets Matthäi. He objects to the unrestrained imagination: "Deiner Phantasie sind offenbar nicht die geringsten Grenzen gesetzt." Like Locher and Lutz he prefers to draw the least disturbing conclusion, the one easiest to fit into routine modes of thinking: "Jeder von uns kann einem Mörder gleichen." Bärlach is suspicious of the obvious. He has to seek the solution that is most "wahrscheinlich", for verisimilitude is, as Popper asserts, the most that science can attain, but "Wahrscheinlichkeit", understood as plausibility, is too often the refuge of the lazy mind. With rigorous logic the detective forces the doctor to defend his common-sense theory against alternative hypotheses. Hungertobel greets the suggestion that Emmenberger was in the camp and Nehle in Chile under Emmenberger's name with cries of "Unsinn", "ein unwahrscheinlicher Schluss." This manner of dealing with reality is primitive; it is, he implies, arbitrary and thus unscientific, because it would put everything in doubt, leaving no firm ground on which to stand. Bärlach agrees about the doubt: "Wir müssen in diesem Punkt durchaus wie die Philosophen vorgehen, von denen es heisst, dass sie erst einmal alles bezweifeln."

The detective now proceeds to show that what saves his approach from arbitrariness is the testing of the hypothesis. This is where "Phantasie" gives way to "Mathematik". Close investigation shows the similarity between the two men to be remarkable: both have a scar on the forehead as a result of a far from common operation and in both cases part of the eyebrow is missing, because the operation has not been managed with the usual skill. This is a highly improbable coincidence or a contrived one. The "probable" hypothesis now rests on a highly improbable occurrence, but here "improbability" has a precise meaning: it is not mere implausibility; it can be given a numerical, if approximate, value. Dürrenmatt pursues the demonstration at length, showing the hypothesis leading, like Matthäi's, to the discovery of relevant and quite unpredictable facts. Like Matthäi Bärlach then proves his confidence in his theory by acting upon it. Here, however, we have one of Dürrenmatt's characteristic twists: by sticking his neck out a scientist usually runs the risk of being wrong, but in entering Emmenberger's sanatorium Bärlach only runs a risk if he is right.

This lesson in scientific thinking from Part I of the novel is then balanced and reinforced in Part II by its mirror image, with roles of doctor and detective neatly reversed. Emmenberger, having discovered Bärlach's identity, needs to know whether Hungertobel is involved and needs to be disposed of. The detective now finds himself desperately trying to make his denial of Hungertobel's involvement convincing. Emmenberger subjects Bärlach's arguments to the same rigorous scrutiny to which Bärlach had subjected Hungertobel's. The detective's objections echo his friend's: "Unsinn . . . das sei eine unberechtigte Idee, eine leere Spekulation." Emmenberger carefully tests the opposing hypotheses for their "Wahrscheinlichkeit", attempting to argue the negation of his hypothesis that Hungertobel knows all: "Gehen wir vorher zu andern möglichen Indizien über, die gegen mich vorliegen, versuchen wir ihn reinzuwaschen." The attempted refutation is not convincing: on Bärlach's "hypothesis" the facts simply cannot be made to cohere, but on his own they cohere perfectly. It is not thereby established or justified, but it is the one that has best survived criticism and to act according to the best tested theory is the rational course. It is the only rational strategy in a world without certainty. Doctor and detective show the same capacity for critical thought. With some justice Emmenberger tells Bärlach: "Wir sind beide Wissenschaftler."

Now that Einstein is one of the undisputed "greats", it is easy to forget the bitter struggle his theories provoked. His most virulent opponent was Philipp Lenard (Nobel Prizewinner for Physics, as chance would have it, in 1905, the year in which Einstein made the discovery for which he won the prize in 1921), who championed what he saw as the empiricist view of science, distinguishing between "mere hypothesis" and well founded theory derived from observation and experiment. Relativity theory, he insisted, did not deserve the name theory, because it came not from careful observation of the great judge and teacher Nature, but from the relativists' own fantastic imaginations. We meet here what, in the context of Dürrenmatt's work, is the familiar accusation of distorting reality through the unrestrained and grotesque imagination. For Lenard, Einstein's theories were procreations alien to nature and he scorned the idea that knowledge of the exterior world could come from the notions of human heads. "Makers of hypotheses" was an insult hurled at the "new" physicists. In the Aryan Physics that Lenard attempted to construct, discovery was to be firmly rooted in Nature, with which the nordic researcher was engaged in close dialogue, whereas the Jew was involved in abstractions from his own head, abstruse mathematical constructs deriving from the imagination, supported by "Gedankenexperimente".

Einstein's answer to Lenard at the Bad Nauheim conference on relativity in 1920 had been the now familiar notion that we cannot rely on the intuitively obvious, because what is intuitively obvious changes with time. It is uncomfortable to have our familiar images questioned and the questioner is

resented. Einstein disturbed Lenard, as Bärlach disturbed Hungertobel, and Matthäi disturbed Locher and Dr. H. The world of Dürrenmatt's detective fiction is one in which there is no simple contrast between the imaginative artist and the "rational" or "logical" scientist. In this world writer, detective and scientist are alike dependent on imagination. More recently Dürrenmatt has made the point explicit: "Dagegen ist die Logik der Wissenschaft jene des schöpferischen Menschen." The imagination is essential for the rational exploration of reality, and not for its exploration only: its rational ordering requires the imagination just as urgently. To Lutz, in **Der Verdacht,** Bärlach grumbles: "Die Phantasie, das sei es eben, die Phantasie! . . . Die Welt sei aus Nachlässigkeit schlecht, und daran, aus Nachlässigkeit zum Teufel zu gehen." In a novel concerned with the devils of the concentration camps it is a striking suggestion that the greatest threat to a humane world is unimaginative and slipshod thinking.

Yet despite brilliant thinking, both imaginative and logical, Matthäi fails disastrously, evoking the nightmare thought that we are not in a rational world. It is tempting to ascribe the failure to "the element of unreason in the world", but it is misleading. Matthäi fails because he is ignorant of one fact that he could not possibly have known: the man he seeks is already dead. Writing of the problems of prediction in the social sciences, F.A. von Hayek, whose work has pertinent things to say on Dürrenmatt's perennial theme of "Zufall", states:

> The difficulties which we encounter . . . are not, as one might at first suspect, difficulties about formulating theories for the explanation of the observed events . . . The real difficulty, to the solution of which science has little to contribute, and which is sometimes indeed insoluble, consists in the ascertainment of the particular facts.

To ascribe to a lack of reason in the world man's inability to know all, is a manifestation of human pride, which in Dürrenmatt's work is always punished. Matthäi's failure has disastrous consequences, not despite his rationality, but because he is not rational enough to realize that no theory, however fruitful, can be relied on as true. He presumes to know and acts with absolute faith in his theory.

The rationalism that **Das Versprechen** mocks is the Cartesian rationalism that believes that an absolutely sure foundation can be given to the structure of human knowledge. Descartes wrote: "It seems to me that I can establish as a general rule that all things which I perceive very clearly and distinctly are true." Matthäi too perceives clearly and distinctly: having calmed a lynch mob by daringly offering to hand over the hawker if they insist, he is asked by the horrified Staatsanwalt what he would have done, had the villagers insisted; he replies: "Ich wusste, dass dies nicht der Fall sein würde." The arrogant tone of absolute self-confidence is that of Spinoza's remark (which shows the gulf between him and Einstein, for all the similarities that Dürrenmatt adduces): "I do not presume that I have found the best philosophy, I know that I understand the true philosophy."

The representative of a worthier and more Einsteinian rationalism is Bärlach who, having quite demolished Hungertobel's objections to his hypothesis, concludes his lesson in scientific thinking by emphasizing that it remains a hypothesis:

> Ich habe dir nur die Wahrscheinlichkeit meiner Thesen bewiesen. Aber das Wahrscheinliche ist noch nicht das Wirkliche . . . In dieser Welt ist der Gedanke mit der Wahrheit nicht identisch . . . Zwischen dem Gedanken und der Wirklichkeit steht immer noch das Abenteuer des Daseins.

The scientific enterprise is "ein grandioses Abenteuer des Geistes", requiring both boldness and humility, both the recognition of ultimate ignorance and the refusal despairingly to ascribe to irrationality one's failure to make sense. In comparing Einstein's search for understanding to a chess game played between the scientist and God (or Nature), Dürrenmatt says:

> . . . er nimmt die Partie in der Überzeugung auf, dass auch jene Spielzüge Gottes, die Sinnen-Eindrücke, die den Spielregeln zu widersprechen scheinen, sich auf dem Schachbrett nachspielen lassen; und er beginnt die Partie im Vertrauen, einer fairen Auseinandersetzung entgegenzugehen.

It is assumed that God keeps the rules and any apparent breaking of them is due to "eine fehlerhafte Interpretation des göttlichen Spiels". He quotes Einstein himself: "Die Natur verbirgt ihr Geheimnis durch die Erhabenheit ihres Wesens, nicht durch List." Many years before, in *Das Versprechen,* he had made Dr. H. urge his interlocutor not to draw irrationalist conclusions from the story of Matthäi:

> Unser Verstand erhellt die Welt nur notdürftig. In der Zwielichtzone seiner Grenze siedelt sich alles Paradoxe an. Hüten wir uns davor, diese Gespenster "an sich" zu nehmen, als ob sie ausserhalb des menschlichen Geistes angesiedelt wären.

In Dürrenmatt's works reality mocks those who presume to know her and act arrogantly on the basis of their mistaken epistemology, either with the cruel punishment experienced by Romulus, Matthäi and Möbius, or merely with ignorance. Dürrenmatt ends *Das Versprechen* with a coda that subtly restates a main theme. The grotesque old lady, Frau Schrott,

has an unshakable view of the world. She is obsessed by the conviction of her sister's malice towards her and she keeps secret the murders committed by her mentally sub-normal husband Albert precisely to deny her sister the opportunity to gloat. This malice, she asserts, has been lifelong, but has never shown outwardly. All the sister's actions are fitted into the pattern. She had, it is true, made no comment on the marriage with Albertchen, but:

> wenn ihre Schwester auch nichts dazu bemerkt habe, ja sogar zur Hochzeit nach Chur gekommen sei, geärgert habe sie sich über diese Heirat, das wisse sie bestimmt, wenn die Schwester auch wieder, um sie eben zu ärgern, nichts habe merken lassen.

Of the flowers decorating her hospital room she says: "All diese Blumen . . . schicke ihre Schwester nur, um sie zu ärgern." The circle is closed. Even the absence of positive evidence is regarded as corroboration. Here is a theory like Henzi's, sealed off from any danger of refutation. (Lenard apparently countered the negative result of the Michelson-Morley experiment with the irrefutable theory that each bit of matter carries with it its own ether.) Such theories and such minds run no risk of being proved wrong, nor of probing the world.

In Dürrenmatt's works reality mocks those who presume to know her.
—A. M. Wright

Dürrenmatt has frequently shown the importance of the epistemological issue. He sums up one consequence for action of Spinoza's philosophy as follows: "gut ist der Wissende, schlecht der Unwissende, böses Handeln ist falsches, gutes Handeln ist richtiges Handeln." Many of Dürrenmatt's characters presume to know, and act accordingly, pragmatically rejecting traditional moral constraints in pursuit of their visions, Möbius murdering his nurse and Romulus sacrificing his people. Romulus at least recognizes his error, but disillusionment too can have dangerous consequences. Marlok, having discovered that the knowledge of which Spinoza speaks is impossible, draws the conclusion that good action is no longer possible, leaving her a "Mitmacher", the tool of Emmenberger's evil:

> das Gute und das Böse sind zu sehr ineinander verschlungen . . . um je wieder voneinander getrennt zu werden, um zu sagen: Dies ist wohlgetan und jenes vom Übel, dies führt zum Guten und jenes zum Schlechten. Zu spät! Wir können nicht mehr wissen, was wir tun, welche Handlung unser Gehorsam oder unsere Auflehnung nach sich zieht.

She rejects with scorn Bärlach's desire to uphold the law, failing to see that in rejecting "Gesetze" she rejects precisely those strategies that mankind has unconsciously developed for coping with chance and our ignorance of the consequences of our actions. They are of course as unjustifiable as the scientists' hypotheses; they are just as much in need of constant revision. Bärlach's banal-sounding "das Gesetz ist das Gesetz" is not as intellectually lame as first it seems. Rules prove themselves by their fruitfulness and to reject them because they are "unjustifiable" is as irrational as rejecting a theory for the same reason. Swiss society, Bärlach admits to the iconoclast Fortschig, in *Der Verdacht,* is pretty shabby, but it is not rational to want to destroy it: "gleich das ganze Haus abreissen ist sinnlos und nicht gescheit; denn es ist schwer, in dieser armen lädierten Welt ein neues Haus zu bauen." Neither our systems of theory nor our systems of rules can be perfected. In a world of ignorance the rational course is to accept provisionally a well tested system and to use the imagination to construct theories that mesh better with reality, and institutions that shape it to accord more nearly with our values. Dürrenmatt's early novels suggest a view of the links between science, politics and art that he has made explicit in the following words:

> Ich weiss, wir frösteln, wenn wir von Institutionen hören. Wenn aber die Wissenschaft ein grandioses Abenteuer des Geistes ist, das nicht auf die Entdeckung absolut sicherer Theorien ausgeht, sondern auf die Erfindung immer besserer Theorien, die immer strengeren Prüfungen unterworfen werden können, wie Karl Popper meint, so sollten wir dieses Abenteuer auch für unsere Institutionen entdecken und es auf sie anwenden, indem wir sie immer gerechter und vernünftiger machen, indem wir in ihnen nicht Zwangssysteme sehen, sondern Kunstwerke, die für den Menschen da sind, nicht der Mensch für sie.

Dennis Mueller (essay date Summer 1984)

SOURCE: Review of *Achterloo* in *World Literature Today,* Vol. 58, No. 3, Summer 1984, p. 409.

[*In the following review, Mueller praises Dürrenmatt, but is disappointed by* Achterloo.]

How I greeted the opportunity to review a new Dürrenmatt play when I first unpacked *Achterloo.* As a long-time friend of his story *Der Richter und sein Henker* (which I have taught so often I know entire passages by heart) and the plays *Der Besuch der alten Dame* and *Die Physiker,* I was delighted to receive the playwright's latest work and to have a chance to proclaim its worth. After reading the play, I real-ize that it is not only I who has aged in teaching German literature; it appears that the creators of contemporary German classics have also aged. Dürrenmatt, it seems, is not what he used to be. This potpourri of characters from and allusions to history and the playwright's own earlier plays does not achieve the coherence of before.

Shakespeare said that all the world is a stage; Dürrenmatt seems to be saying the stage is all the world.
—*Dennis Mueller*

Peter Weiss's *Marat/Sade* and Dürrenmatt's own *Physiker* seem to have provided the inspiration to write this play, for in the closing lines we discover that the events have occurred in an insane asylum and that the actors were inmates of the asylum. In *Achterloo* Dürrenmatt continues the demythologizing and deheroicizing of important historical personages that he began in **"Das Sterben der Pythia."** Here Napoleon, Richelieu, Benjamin Franklin, Jan Hus and Karl Marx appear at various points in the play and speak of contemporary phenomena such as nuclear war, the confrontation between East and West and capitalism and communism. In his last major play, *Der Mitmacher,* Dürrenmatt felt compelled to write a "Nachwort" that is longer than the play itself, in at attempt to justify his play and to rationalize its failure. Would that he had written an afterword for this play also, so that we might have some idea of his intent. The setting gives us a clue to one aspect of that intent: "Achterloo in Achterloo somewhere near Waterloo." Dürrenmatt is manipulating historical reality to show us that this is a completely imaginary locale with completely imaginary characters. Interwoven into the dialogue are real and imaginary speeches by historical and fictional characters: for example, Robespierre's famous address to the French Assembly which sent Louis XVI to the guillotine is quoted, and lines from Büchner's *Woyzeck* appear in Woyzeck's conversation with Napoleon.

Shakespeare said that all the world is a stage; Dürrenmatt seems to be saying the stage is all the world. He arbitrarily brings historical personages onto his stage to show us a microcosm of today's world. In the end, Marion, Woyzeck's daughter, emerges as the heroine when she murders Napoleon with her father's razor. Yet it was Napoleon's stated aim to keep the world off-balance by not attacking or starting an international conflict that might widen to a world war. Does this mean that the whore of the world—Marion has slept with all the major figures in the world's history—is dooming us to self-destruction? Would that Dürrenmatt had given us an answer.

Susan Smith Wolfe (essay date November 1984)

SOURCE: "Lovers, Labours, and Cliff Top Meals: The Architectonics of Dürrenmatt's two *Herkules* Dramas," in *Seminar*, Vol. XX, No. 4, November, 1984, pp. 279-89.

[*In the following review, Wolfe compares the love scenes in the 1954 radio drama to the 1963 stage version of Dürrenmatt's* Herkules. *She contends that the love scenes were awkward in the radio drama, but are a more important subplot in the stage play.*]

No other radio play by Friedrich Dürrenmatt has elicited such criticism, no other theater piece such impassioned denials as **Herkules und der Stall des Augias.** Deeply offended by the lampoon of their heroic tradition, and resentful of what appeared as a dark attack on the democratic process itself, Swiss audiences and reviewers alike rejected the two Hercules dramas. This was the emotional, public reaction to Dürrenmatt's playful handling of hallowed institutions; scholarly attention, however, turned inward, to a structural irregularity which seemed to force a "feeble lesson, a comfortable reconciliation of opposites." The love sequences of both the 1954 radio and 1963 stage versions have been unanimously regarded as subordinate and external to the central theme of courageous commitment to evolutionary change, a theme which had found its culmination in the final, garden scene. The critic Renate Usmiani, in considering that final scene in the radio version, voiced the discomfort of her colleagues: "Es ist nicht zu leugnen, da der ernste Ton, mit dem das Stück endet, schwer mit dem spöttisch-frivolen Lustspielcharakter der vorhergehenden Szenen in Einklang zu bringen ist und daher künstlerisch zumindest fragwürdig erscheint." That the same censures were then applied to the stage play reflects a failure—often in production—to detect the modifications in the love story which set the 1963 version on an entirely different course.

The chief obstacle to a successful re-writing was the crucial Augias/"garden" scene, which in the radio play had seemed to surface without dramatic foundation. The love story—a mere subplot in the radio version—had been too deeply rooted in the comic plane to successfully announce the pensive finale. A resolution of the structural dilemma would have to include anchoring the philosophical question firmly in dramatic incident. By exploiting the compressed space of the two campfire dinners atop the rapidly sinking Elian cliffs, as well as the inherent temporal limitations of the meal itself, the 1963 version "forces" the lovers Dejaneira and Herkules into dialogue and an eventual understanding of their relationship to one another. Although a skeleton of the love scenes to be considered is already contained in the radio drama (45% and 62% of their spoken lines respectively), it is the addition of the meal with its highly charged confinement which adds the emotional urgency essential for an intense, and credible, sounding of the lovers' inner motives. What then emerges through the love conversations becomes an eloquent foreshadowing of the final garden scene, for it becomes evident that Dejaneira and the Elian president Augias share the same vision: the Earth, as wasteland, transformed through human endeavour. It is the challenge and failure of that vision—already contained in the two major love scenes—"Auf den Felsen" and "Wieder auf den Felsen"—which successfully anchors the pivotal garden scene in the love conflict.

In Augias' charge to his son to "cultivate a private garden," Christian Jauslin thought he detected the first solution ever dramatically expressed by Dürrenmatt. Yet in the radio drama, that solution surfaced without motivation; its only connection to the love story lay in Herkules' and Dejaneira's role as "that chance of a lifetime which comes and goes," for which the Elians were as yet unprepared. Dejaneira, particularly, personified the lost opportunity: "AUGIAS: Du hast eine Frau geliebt und verloren. Sie war nicht für uns geschaffen. Zu finster ist es noch." When, nine years later, Dürrenmatt chose to excise that oft-quoted line, he accomplished a major shift in tone: no longer would Dejaneira personify "promise"; it would instead become her failure to grasp the same message—"cultivate a garden here"—which would tie the love triangle firmly to the Augias scene.

Herkules and Dejaneira share three scenes; it is in the second and third that Dürrenmatt chooses the vehicle of the meal (quite simply a soup pot warmed over an open fire) to force the lovers into speech and toward a recognition of their inner motives. Both Herkules—for whom self-expression is a flexing of muscle—and Dejaneira—most at home when verbally mothering him—are forced to express and define a love which is nearly ineffable.

As scene ten opens, Dejaneira has just spoken to the young Phyleus of the manifold possibilities awaiting mankind, should it elect to create from the surrounding chaos rather than capitulate; for, much like Elias, her beloved Thebes had once lain a wasteland:

> DEJANEIRA: Dazu ist uns die Erde gegeben: Da wir das Feuer bändigen, die Gewalt des Windes und des Meeres nutzen, da wir das Gestein zerbrechen und aus seinen Trümmern Tempel und Häuser bauen. Und du sollst einmal Theben sehen, meine Heimat, die Stadt mit den sieben Toren und der goldenen Burg Kadmeia.
>
> PHYLEUS (zögernd): Du liebst deine Heimat?
>
> DEJANEIRA: Ich liebe sie, weil sie vom Menschen erschaffen ist. Ohne ihn wäre sie eine Steinwüste geblieben, denn die Erde ist blind und grausam ohne den Menschen.

This is the continuing vision to which Dejaneira repeatedly refers, and therefore the standard by which we must judge her; it will be the forthcoming campfire scenes which test her commitment to the ideal.

It becomes increasingly apparent, as Phyleus runs off and Herkules approaches, that Herkules and Dejaneira are least verbal in one another's presence. The problems of the day, certainly, surface at mealtime in typical domestic fashion: Herkules' difficulties at work, the lack of meat on the table, and Dejaneira's manner of dress. Yet, the real issue flickering through the domestic exchanges is their relationship to one another, and it emerges only through gesture, or through the meal ritual. For the duration of their scene together, the lovers will remain huddled around the soup pot, the length of their conversation determined by the temporal restrictions of the meal, and their remarks punctuated by the rigid formality of Dürrenmatt's particular table etiquette.

Beneath the typical interchanges of this scene lie verbal minefields, heavily charged with what remains unvoiced. The question of Dejaneira's naive state of undress—given a forest full of Elian "voyeurs"—can't be pursued, because it broaches the subject of their own relationship:

> DEJANEIRA: Oh! (Sie bedeckt sich.)
> DEJANEIRA: Mahlzeit.
> HERKULES: Mahlzeit. (Sie beginnen zu essen.)

The domestic dialogue deteriorates further as it brushes the cause of their financial difficulties—Herkules' inability to support them:

> DEJANEIRA: Das elische Nationalgericht.
> HERKULES: Auch wie seit Monaten.
> DEJANEIRA: Sonst gab es doch noch Speck dazu.
> HERKULES: Speck können wir uns nicht mehr leisten. Die Reisespesen sind aufgebraucht.
> DEJANEIRA: Könnten wir nicht einen gewissen Vorschuss-
> HERKULES: Das Finanzamt ist dagegen.
> DEJANEIRA: Essen wir weiter.
> HERKULES: Essen wir weiter. (Sie essen weiter.)

In the background of this conversation lurks the shadow of an earlier disagreement in Thebes, an argument which had resulted in Dejaneira's threatened return to the more lucrative field of prostitution; only the spectre of that very private loss had persuaded Herkules to accept the Elian offer.

The silences which fall between Dejaneira and Herkules in this scene—meticulously punctuated by the mechanics of eating—are heavy with shared emotion. Each of the lovers feels compelled to speak, yet the verbal communication never matches their silent rapport. In their embarrassment and their bewilderment, they are curiously reminiscent of Kleist's Achilles and Penthesilea. Gerhard Bauer considers this phenomenon in his analysis of the love dialogue: "Es fällt allerdings auf—schon Goethe und Tieck haben darauf hingewiesen—da die Liebenden in der deutschen Dichtung nur dann beredt werden, wenn sie Differenzen auszutragen haben, also doch einen Zweck verfolgen, während sie ihre Übereinstimmung mehr durch Wortlosigkeit als durch spielerischen Austausch demonstrieren.

Again Dejaneira attempts to introduce the subject which neither has been able to articulate:

> DEJANEIRA: Herkules.
> HERKULES: Dejaneira?
> DEJANEIRA: Eigentlich sind wir jetzt noch ruinierter als in Theben.
> HERKULES: Eigentlich.

Only the circus director Tantalos' abrupt appearance prevents the anticipated refrain ("DEJANEIRA: Essen wir weiter. / HERKULES: Essen wir weiter."), and the almost certain lapse into silence. In a reference to Brecht's *Kaukasischer Kreidekreis*, Bauer has termed such retreats into formality "das Übergewicht des Zeremoniells." The ceremonial circumlocutions-forming what we might term an increasingly "charged field"—build in intensity toward a central question.

A source of tension in the unfolding scene has been the contrastive compulsion of the two lovers to speak and their preference for silence. Now, as they burst into speech, the silent communion is lost and the lovers begin to speak past one another:

> HERKULES: Hast du gehört, Dejaneira, was dieser unverschämte Kerl vorschlug?
> DEJANEIRA: Gewi .
> HERKULES: Ich hätte ihn den Felsen hinunterschmettern sollen.
> DEJANEIRA (leise): Unser schönes Haus in Theben.
> HERKULES: Ich lehne das Angebot selbstverständlich ab.

While Herkules is incensed at the offer to feature him in the circus and thus resolve their financial difficulties, Dejaneira broods over the beautiful home in Thebes now lost through a foreclosure. Her reaction to Tantalos' report of the news from Thebes—"(entsetzt): Unser Haus in der Kadmosstrasse?"—sounds the first notes of a building theme: "Haus in der Kadmosstrasse" / "goldene Burg Kadmeia" / "Garten."

Having again failed to reach one another through conversation, the lovers take the now familiar retreat into silence:

"DEJANEIRA (seufzend): Essen wir weiter. / HERKULES: Essen wir weiter. / (Sie essen weiter.)" (403). This time it is Herkules who ventures into uncertain territory: "HERKULES: Dejaneira. / DEJANEIRA: Herkules?" Like Brecht's Simon, he has arrived at the real question by a circuitous route: *"Willst du mich eigentlich noch heiraten?"* None of the foregoing passages, so weighted with unexpressed emotion, were included in the radio version, where the love story had been of secondary importance.

It is at this point that the physically oriented Herkules attempts to express the unspeakable—typically, through gesture; for, in the course of his conversation his love for Dejaneira finds expression through a heightened appetite. His extra helpings revealingly occur at particularly painful points in the emotional exchange:

> HERKULES: Willst du mich eigentlich noch heiraten? (Er schöpft sich einen neuen Teller voll.)
> . . .
> HERKULES: Nun, ich fürchte mich etwas davor. Ich bin doch vielleicht nicht sonderlich ein Mann für dich—mein Beruf . . . (Er schöpft sich einen neuen Teller voll.)
> . . .
> HERKULES: Liebst du ihn denn nicht, den Phyleus? (Er nimmt sich einen neuen Teller voll.)

The fact that Herkules can only express his love for Dejaneira through the meal was evident in an earlier discussion of Phyleus's hasty retreat:

> HERKULES: Was hat der Junge? Er scheint verwirrt.
>
> DEJANEIRA: Es gibt Momente im Leben eines jeden Mannes, wo ihm Bohnen und Rindfleisch trivial vorkommen.
>
> HERKULES: Verstehe ich nicht. Als ich dich zum ersten Male sah, a ich nachher vor Begeisterung einen ganzen Ochsen auf.

In their vehicular capacity, the gestures of the meal must often communicate alone, without further elucidation. Bauer, referring to gesture in what he terms the "ungebundener Dialog," concludes: "was sie bedeuten, also dem Dialogpartner mitteilen, ist komplex und lasst sich in keinem anderen Medium vollständig ausdrücken."

Gradually and painfully, Herkules and Dejaneira touch on the possibility that genuine love may be beyond the reach of two such "embodied ideals":

> DEJANEIRA: Ich zögere ja auch ein wenig. Du bist

ein Held, und ich liebe dich. Doch ich frage mich, ob ich für dich nicht ein Ideal bin, so wie du für mich ein Ideal bist.

> HERKULES: Zwischen uns steht dein Geist, deine Schönheit und meine Taten und mein Ruhm, das willst du sagen, nicht wahr, Dejaneira?
> DEJANEIRA: Ja, Herkules.
>
> HERKULES: Siehst du, darum solltest du diesen reizenden Jungen heiraten, diesen Phyleus. Er liebt dich, er hat dich nötig und ihn kannst du lieben nicht als ein Ideal, sondern als einen unkomplizierten jungen Mann, der eine Frau wie dich braucht.

In the radio drama, Herkules' painful proposal had been motivated by his sympathy for the young Phyleus; in the stage play, he is driven by his failures, particularly his inability to rescue Dejaneira's beautiful home from the creditors, but also by his understanding of the nature of their relationship.

The lost paradise of Thebes weighs heavily on them both:

> (Schweigen.)
> (Dejaneira isst nicht weiter.)
>
> DEJANEIRA (ängstlich): *Ich soll hier in Elis bleiben?*
>
> HERKULES: Liebst du ihn denn nicht, den Phyleus? (Er nimmt sich einen Teller voll.)
>
> DEJANEIRA: Doch. Ich liebe ihn.
>
> HERKULES: Es ist deine Bestimmung, zu bleiben und die meine, zu gehen.
>
> DEJANEIRA: *Dieses Land ist so schrecklich.*
>
> HERKULES: Ich miste aus.
> (Schweigen.)
> . . .
> DEJANEIRA: *Ich sehe nie mehr Theben, nie mehr die Gärten, die goldene Burg Kadmeia*, bleibe ich hier.

It is the sacrifice that a love for Phyleus requires—the permanent loss of Thebes—which now begins to obsess Dejaneira.

In the radio piece, Dejaneira's love of homeland had been treated satirically. There had been her tendency to "rave" about the fatherland, "war sie in der Fremde und besonders jetzt natürlich in Elis," while Herkules seemed more inclined to recall the predatory bankers and shopowners who "nested" on the cliffs of her "beloved Kadmeia." In the stage play, Dejaneira's grief over the lost paradise is handled on two levels simultaneously, the satirical and the pathetic:

> O siebentoriges Theben, o meine goldene Burg Kadmeia, wie konnte ich euch verlassen! Eine barbarische und düstere Welt umgibt mich. Ich bin ratlos und verzweifelt. Meine Seele ist voll schrecklicher Bilder . . . (389)

It is Herkules who—as Augias will later caution Phyleus—warns Dejaneira against dwelling in the past, and who reminds her of the "vision" of Thebes: "La fahren, was verloren ist. Errichte *hier* dein Theben, deine goldene Burg Kadmeia." Herkules' admonition is, in fact, a mirror speech of Augias' advice to his disheartened son: "Wage jetzt zu leben und hier zu leben, mitten in diesem gestaltlosen, wüsten Land . . . ." If Dejaneira is true to her vision ("Dazu ist uns die Erde gegeben . . . , dass wir das Gestein zerbrechen und aus seinen Trümmern Tempel und Häuser bauen", she will remain behind to fulfill her awakening love for Phyleus and help him build anew from the wasteland that is Elis.

Momentarily suspended above the rapidly rising dung plains, on what Elisabeth Brock-Sulzer has termed an "oasis on the cliffs," the lovers have been forced into dialogue through the meal's intense compression of time and space. The fearful probing of the nature of their love has included their most intimate moments: "DEJANEIRA: Ich danke dir, mein Freund. / HERKULES: Ich werde dich nie vergessen." In the freedom of her decision, Dejaneira thinks to have found the resolve to pour out Nesso's blood, thus delivering her love for Herkules from the fetters of jealousy.

The challenge of scene ten has been a once-in-a-lifetime opportunity—a call to Dejaneira to descend from the heights of lofty idealism, toward the troubled, yet fertile plains of human endeavour. Her ultimate failure, to which she now bears witness in the thirteenth scene, is a failure to bridge the gulf between aesthetics and life, to anchor her dreams in the Herculean struggle of the everyday.

The degeneration of the meal in the second campfire, from a hearty Elian stew to a pitiful water soup, parallels both the material and emotional decline of the love pair. As Dejaneira crouches beside Herkules to warm her hands at the soup kettle, still in her wedding dress, their conversation takes up the threads of the earlier dinner; the structural character of the dialogue continues as well, each fragmented utterance now the painful attempt to give voice to defeat:

> HERKULES: Dejaneira.

DEJANEIRA: Mein Freund?

HERKULES: Phyleus?

DEJANEIRA: Ich konnte ihn nicht heiraten. Ich habe ihn vor dem Hausaltar verlassen. (Schweigen.)

HERKULES: Du weizsst, wie es um mich steht.

DEJANEIRA: Ich weiss.

HERKULES: Entscheide nun du.

DEJANEIRA: Wir gehen nach Stymphalien.

HERKULES: Dieses Land ist noch schmutziger als Elis.

DEJANEIRA: Ich werde bei dir sein.

HERKULES: Nun müssen wir beieinander bleiben.

Yet, the real grounds for Dejaneira's return defy articulation. She reasons finally: "Wir gehören auch zusammen." Dejaneira's inability to love freely and simply implies a capitulation to Fate, for as Polybios begins to push the pair toward Stymphalus his mistress turns back for the bowl of Nesso's blood: "Fast hätte ich sie vergessen." Herkules and Dejaneira are physically reunited, yet spiritually separated by the bowl.

Perhaps with some justification Timo Tuisanen has assumed: "Whatever Dürrenmatt may be, he is not a great poet of love"; yet in the 1963 Hercules drama, Dürrenmatt has accomplished some of the tenderest love scenes of his career. Such intimate moments would nevertheless be troublingly inadequate had they continued outside the greater philosophical conflict. In contrast to the earlier, radio version, Dürrenmatt plants the motivation for his pivotal dialogue of decision in the cliff-top meals, where the pressures of limited time and space can credibly exert their influence on the nearly mute participants. Thus in the later version, the final garden scene is given firm footing in the crisis of the two lovers; their mutual inability to persevere in a more gradual, evolutionary struggle anticipates the later response by the young Phyleus. As Augias had insisted to Herkules, "Du bist unser aller Prüfstein geworden."

Elyakim Yaron (essay date 1986)

SOURCE: "Space, Scenery and Action in Dürrenmatt's Plays," in *Assaph*, Vol. C, No. 3, 1986, pp. 191-206.

[In the following essay Yaron discusses how Dürrenmatt's use of specific and detailed stage directions yields an allegorical background for his plays.]

> When I undertake the writing of a play, the first step which I make clear to myself is where this play is to take place.
>
> —F. Dürrenmatt

The Swiss playwright, Friedrich Dürrenmatt, attaches great significance to the place of action (*Handlungsort*) in his plays. He deals with this subject in great detail in his essay **"Theater Problems"**, where he also underlines his predilection toward variegated scenery. Indeed, in his stage directions regarding the scenery, Dürrenmatt's love for the colorful setting is distinctly expressed. One manifestation of variegation is the sense of "overflowing", which is shown, for instance, in his detailed demands concerning the scenery of **Ein Engel Kommt Nach Babylon.** In the opening stage directions to the second act we read:

> The second act is to be played beneath one of the Euphrates bridges, in the very heart of Babylon. The sky is shut out by towering skyscrapers and palaces. The orchestra pit again represents the river, and the bridge makes a great vault forwards from the back of the stage, so that it appears in cross-section and from below. High overhead the traffic of the giant city makes itself heard. (. . .) Akki's dwelling is a wild hotch-potch of various objects of every period: sacrophagi, heathen idols, an ancient royal throne, Babylonian bicycles and car tyres and so forth, all covered with the dirt of ages, mouldy, heaped with dust. Above all this mess (. . .) there is a relief of the head of Gilgamish. Beside it, torn copies of the notices about begging with strips pasted across them (. . .) Outside on the right, clear of the bridge, a kitchen range and a kettle. The ground is red sand, littered with jam tins and poetic manuscripts. Everywhere hang parchments and clay tablets closely written with poetry; in short the characters seem to be moving about on an enormous rubbish dump. (. . .)

Dürrenmatt is not contented with merely economical and suggestive stage directions. On the contrary, his descriptions, in which a visible picture of location is portrayed, are particularly lengthy and detailed. The picture as a whole is dominated by a vast number of objects, each of which retains its distinctiveness, but which, at the same time, also contributes to the unmistakable effect of accumulated confusion. However, within all this excess, or overflowing, a characteristic Dürrenmattian trait can be distinguished: this vast mixture of period and places loses its definite historical-geographical nature. The great effort invested in the detailed stage directions, in order to represent a location according to the realistic tradition, actually achieves an inverted result. Precisely because of the huge accumulation, so concrete and realistic, the abstraction is actually indicated. That is precisely because what at first appears to be realistic, allows the emergence of the allegorical, or universal dimension. Dürrenmatt's Babel, for example, is a spacious modern metropolis, but, at the same time, anachronistic, as if a huge pile of urbanistic civilizations has been accumulated. Establishing the scene within a vague time and place allows Dürrenmatt a great deal of liberty in the use of anachronisms. This blurring of the distinctive by way of accumulating real materials is what lends Dürrenmatt's work an allegorical dimension. In spite of the broad use made of particular historical and geographical data, this is no historic or geographic Babel. This strict, realistic-like representation of place has turned extempore to the representation of nowhere, or, perhaps, of everywhere. But this is no single phenomenon in Dürrenmatt's colorful scenic representations.

In spite of the obvious attempt to depict a vivid picture overloaded with details, Dürrenmatt never loses control of his stage-space. Alongside the different details, some of the stage directions deal with the division of space. The different directions of the stage are sharply marked: the foreground (including, by extension, the orchestra) against the background, left and right. The bold drawing of the bridge that crosses the stage from the orchestra toward the rear also makes its decisive contribution to the defining of the space, and even adds to it the dimension of height: above the bridge (traffic noise) and under it (Akki's dwelling). The space is thus not only a scene of unique atmosphere, but the piled-up objects also shape a well-defined space. The sense of confusion that is marked by this overflow of objects, which do not "agree" with each other, works here as some grotesque parody upon the very tradition of the dramatic place (i.e., the realistic school), and this without losing its clear trait as space. The characteristic of creating atmosphere by use of colorful and overloaded objects marks most of Dürrenmatt's stage descriptions. A comparison, for example, between **Romulus der Grosse, Die Ehe des Herrn Mississippi** and **Die Physiker** shows a growth in the number of stage directions. Indeed, the concept of scenery in **Die Ehe** occupies a conspicuous place in Dürrenmatt's *oeuvre*.

> **In spite of the obvious attempt to depict a vivid picture overloaded with details, Dürrenmatt never loses control of his stage-space.**
>
> —*Elyakim Yaron*

Dürrenmatt's **Die Ehe des Herrn Mississippi** has been published in two versions, and the main differences between them do indeed concern stage design. The play uses one set, a room, which not only forms the scenic background to the actions, but occupies a substantial role in it. During the action it goes through considerable changes; eventually it is destroyed, except for one piece of furniture, the round Biedermeier coffee table, which Dürrenmatt refers to as the play's protagonist. The process of the destruction of the room parallels the action: indeed, the conflict between the ideational powers, which constitutes the main part of the action, destroys the room.

After the publication of the first version, Dürrenmatt came out in favor of a certain degree of licence for the director and admitted to the possibility of more than one theatrical interpretation of the play. In the second version however, the author seems to have made a special effort to prevent such freedom and to reduce its likelihood as far as possible. The whole matter is completely manifested in the opening stage directions. In the first version the room is described in terms that specifically allow the stage designer complete artistic freedom:

> Let us imagine in the background (of this room) perhaps two huge windows which are wider at the top than at the bottom like everything in this room, in which the spatial relationships increase with height. The impression is one of profuse insanity as if one were at the bottom of a hellish funnel (Höllentrichter), as if the room had been built for giants at the top and for dwarfs at the bottom—the same principle should be applied to the furniture: However, in spite of the fantasy, the middle-class quality of the room must not be lost. (. . .) In the same manner the landscape (seen through the windows at the rear of the room) is confusing. (. . .)

This version even contains some surrealistic and fantastic suggestions that explicitly aim at the evocation of an atmosphere that does not belong to this world ("profuse insanity"; a "hellish funnel"; a room that has been built for giants at the top and for dwarfs at the bottom; distorted perspective). This atmosphere has completely disappeared from the second version (except for the varied landscapes as seen through the windows). Now the room is expected to be as realistic as possible, for only in this way, says Dürrenmatt, can its visual breaking down be materialized:

> A room whose late-bourgeois magnificence and splendour will not be altogether easy to describe. (. . .) The room stinks to high heaven. In the background are two windows. The view from them is bewildering. To the right the branches of an apple tree, and behind it some northern city with a Gothic cathedral; to the left a cypress, the remains of a classical temple, a bay, a harbour. (. . .) Between the

two windows, but no higher than they are, a grandfather clock. Also Gothic in style. Let us turn to the right-hand wall. Here there are two doors. The door at the back of the stage leads through the veranda into a second room (. . .); the door front stage right leads to an entrance hall and the front door; the kitchen is also situated there, perhaps round the corner to the right of the entrance hall. Let us not bother about the possible lay-out of the house, we will assume that it is a rambling mansion to which many alterations and additions have been made. Between the doors on the right stands a small sideboard; this time I should like to suggest Louis Quinze. On it is a Venus. Of plaster. Naturally. In the left-hand wall there is only one door. It opens between fin-de-siècle mirrors. The door leads into a boudoir (. . .) Front stage left the Louis Seize frame of a second mirror dangles in mid-air, of course without a glass, so anyone looking in it will see the audience. Front stage right there might hang a small, oval, blank picture. In the centre stands a round Biedermeier coffee table; this is really the main character in the play, upon which all the action centers (. . .) it is flanked by two Louis Quatorze chairs. A bit of Empire furniture can undoubtedly be introduced somewhere say, left front stage a small sofa and left back stage a folding screen. (. . .) On the little table stands a Japanese vase containing red roses (. . .) The table is laid for three people. One suggests it is Dresden China. (. . .)

The world of fantasy has disappeared. The special place that the table occupies is also established only in the second version. Dürrenmatt's claim that the fantastic and the unreal would remain in the text only and not intrude into the realm of scenery is thus a decisive warning against any attempt at abstraction.

We are thus faced with a "miniature of the common European cultural heritage," a small-scale museum of European taste. Southern (classical temple) and northern (Gothic cathedral) landscapes are viewed from the windows, and even within the room there is a complexity of styles: Louis Quatorze chairs beside a Gothic grandfather clock, a Louis Quinze sideboard by a Biedermeier coffee table, and so on. Once more we meet the Dürrenmattian overflowing, with the amazing profusion of realistic details that contradict each other stylistically and lend a measure of allegory to the whole scene. Once more there occurs a realistic-like representation, whose main effort is aimed at suspending any appearance of realism: a Dürrenmattian parody on the tradition of drama that usually unfolds within a respectable bourgeois room.

It is possible to accept without difficulty Dürrenmatt's remark that the Biedermeier coffee table is indeed the play's main character. This table is of enormous significance to the characters, but at the same time it also functions as a kind of altar that all seek to grasp by way of the ritualistic ceremonies of coffee drinking. At this table the couple would even drink their poison, while all the characters try to find in it some kind of support for their deeds. But what is most important, while everything breaks into pieces—ideas, people, houses, furniture—only this coffee table survives in its proud wholeness. This, perhaps, has some relation to the play's form, as it is, after all, called a *comedy*. The table is accorded a very detailed position in the stage directions and some of its attributes become conspicuous: (1) that it stands in the center of the room; (2) that it is the only piece of furniture that remains on stage intact: some kind of visual evidence that it is indeed possible to destroy very much, but never everything; and (3) its definite style—Biedermeier—is a possible suggestion of an outward respectable bourgeois appearance, which entails social conventions that seem calm and peaceful (i.e., the coffee ritual) and thus contributes to the creation of a place that contrasts visually with what actually happens around it.

In *Der Besuch der Alten Dame* the author demands many changes from the stage representations. In this instance the overflowing that characterizes most of his plays is somewhat difficult to discern. The epic technique that Dürrenmatt employs here relates not only to *Der Besuch der Alten Dame,* but also to *Herkules und der Stall des Augias* and in a certain way to *Die Ehe des Herrn Mississippi.* Some critics have expressed themselves regarding the relationship Dürrenmatt's drama bears to the epic tradition in the theater and particularly to Brecht. Indeed, the use Dürrenmatt makes of scenery in *Der Besuch der Alten Dame* points to his links with the theater of Brecht and Thornton Wilder.

The first scene takes place in the railway station in the town of Güllen; the second scene occurs in front of the hotel of the Golden Apostle. The transition between the scenes is outlined with great precision and is probably of substantial significance:

> Open scene-change: facade of station and adjacent
> little building soar into flies. Interior of the Golden
> Apostle: an hotel-sign might well be let down from
> above, an imposing gilded Apostle, as emblem, and
> left to hang in mid-air.

The disappearance of parts of the scenery, which constitute the first scene, as well as the apparance of others that are intended as the visual background to the second scene, are thus made in front of the audience. Theater takes over the sheer realism and the scenery acts upon the audience as scenery. Every touch of illusionism is abolished. Moreover, "reality" is only hinted at and a sign or an image suffice to

represent it. Another example perhaps illustrates this point more strongly, as the changes in the scenery take place with the help of the actors:

> Scene-change (. . .) Man Three enters, carries off
> shop-till and shifts counter into position as desk.
> Mayor enters. Puts revolver on table (. . .) A con-
> struction-plan is affixed to wall.

This technique is employed many times with or without the assistance of the actors. But all the changes take place in front of the audience and the scene is always formed by way of hint alone, mostly by means of an inscription, or minimal props. Contrary to Brecht, who harnesses the action to the didactic aspect, Dürrenmatt strives first and foremost toward "indirect theatrical impact." The abolition of naturalistic illusionism and the inclusion of the "realism" of the theater in its stead is thus made evident (1) in the open changes of the scenery; (2) in the transformation that takes place in the scene by means of a sign or inscription; (3) in the simultaneous scene in which Ill's shop is represented against the background of the balcony from which the Old Lady observes everything; and (4) in the charming "forest" scene, in which the actors represent trees and even the voices of animals. In the humorous stage directions the hotel scene vanishes the same way as it appears, and at the end of the "forest" scene "the trees have metamorphosed back into citizens and moved away upstage."

The epic technique attains by Dürrenmatt a more pungent expression in those plays in which the actor appears in the place of the epic story teller. The actor who appears in the prologue of *Herkulos und der Stall des Augias* addresses himself directly to the audience. He relates to the stage machinery and to other technical resources, to the props and to various instruments by means of which the stage is going to be invested with its poetic reality. Dürrenmatt applies a similar technique in other plays, as in *Es Steht Geschrieben* and in *Die Ehe des Herrn Mississippi.* In all these a distinguished dramaturgical effect determines the function of space, which is made evident to the spectator in a double aspect: the shape of reality and the reality of the stage-world. This double function of the character, first as one who takes an active part in the action and then as an epic story teller, probably parallels the double existence of the reality of the stage. Here, certain lines uttered by the epic story teller are, in a way, an extension of the conventional stage directions:

> Well, then, it is May, the windows are slightly open
> (the windows open slightly), on the table stand red
> roses, above the grandfather clock hangs the por-
> trait of the first man who had the good fortune to be
> married to Anastasia, the picture of a beet-sugar
> manufacturer (. . .) (The picture floats down), and

the Moid brings in my old friend Mississippi (the Maid and Mississippi enter right).

These words, spoken by Saint-claude at the opneing of *Die Ehe des Herrn Mississippi,* represent the stage reality the audience watches. Sometimes he relates to matters that are already known from the opening stage directions (e.g., the red roses). On another occasion it is as if he creates this reality by the power of his words (the windows that open as if by themselves; the picture that suddenly appears; Mississippi's entrance.) This duality of the spoken word and the description of the stage directions creates, expectedly, an outstanding humorous effect, so characteristic of Dürrenmatt.

Through his ingenious employment of all available resources of the stage, Dürrenmatt shows a deep awareness of the possibilities the stage offers him. As evidence of Dürrenmatt's consciousness of the stage, his many stage directions delineate its appearance. Very rarely does he use the spoken word to depict a scene, to which he attaches great significance, as can be understood from his lengthy and detailed depictions. In many cases the logic of the play cannot be separated from its scene: thus, the town of Güllen, with all the changes that transform its outward appearance *(Der Besuch der Alten Dame)*; so in the drama of insanity that cannot be enacted out of the walls of the sanatorium *(Die Physiker)*; so when the room and all the furniture in it become a decisive factor in the action *(Die Ehe des Herrn Mississippi)*; so when the theme of the play is the polarity between heaven and earth *(Ein Engel Kommt nach Babylon)*; and so in the visual collapsing of an empire *(Romulus der Grosse)*. In none of these plays is there a reference to the visual background, which is so integral a part of the events, without the stage directions that delineate it so clearly and so explicitly.

Space and Action

> This divorce between man and his life, the actor and his setting, is properly the feeling of absurdity.
> —A. Camus

In a short note at the end of *Die Ehe des Herrn Mississippi,* Dürrenmatt complains that many productions have distorted the play's meaning by employing scenery that tended toward too much abstraction. By doing this, Dürrenmatt claims, they were probably misled by the text itself. Dürrenmatt concludes:

> (. . .) the room in which everything takes place must at the beginning be as real as possible. Only so will it be able to disintegrate. The unreal and fantastic may safely be left to the text, to the author.

Apart from the logical argument that demands that scenery be realistic at the beginning in order to disintegrate later on,

these words also point to the existence of some tension between the space (real) and what happens in it (unreal, fantastic). Moreover, precisely this measure of fantasy that characterizes the action is, so Dürrenmatt claims, what has misled directors and stage designers. Dürrenmatt thus wants this tension to be sustained.

It is also possible, as Murray B. Peppard does, to combine this tension with the well-known grotesque character of Dürrenmatt's drama. But even without drawing upon a conspicuous characteristic in his drama, we can clearly argue that this tension between the space and events, between realistic scenery and fantastic text, cannot exist at all without the extensive significance that the playwright attaches to his stage directions. That this is no trifle with Dürrenmatt we can learn from the fact that he returns to it even in the "Postcript" he published for *Der Besuch der Alten Dame.*

Critics have already noted that in the middle of the play there is a discrepancy between subjective thought and reality. The drama, in this case is conceived as a transformation of values in the world of the people of Güllen—a transformation that should be "transmitted" to the audience without the characters being aware of it. The play's problem is thus in the presentation of a certain rationale by means of the discrepancy between what is said and done by the actors and what is actually conceived by the audience. But what critics seem to have failed to notice is that the presentation of a discrepancy of this kind necessitates a certain amount of autonomy of the theatrical means (i.e., to extend the stage directions) and invest them with a new significance.

In the foreground the people of Güllen are struggling, or at least they pretend they are, to maintain a degree of moral integrity. But reality negates their verbal declarations. This reality, however, is nothing but the reality of the theater. The space—the background that Dürrenmatt refers to—contradicts what happens in the "foreground." The fact that the scenery is part of the play's significance has two essential visual aspects. The first is linked with the scene in which the old Lady acts. This scene has already been explictly fixed in the opening stage directions of the second act:

> The little town. (Only in outline.) In background, the Golden Apostle Hotel, exterior view. (. . .) Balcony. Right, a sign, "Alfred Ill: General Store", above a grimy shop-counter backed by shelves displaying old stock.

From now on the action unfolds as if on two levels. On the first level there is the wretchedness of the people of Güllen who buy at Ill's shop on credit. On the second level there is the "balcony scene," in which the Old Lady makes her ironic comments and shows off her wealth. What the Gülleners say and do cannot be understood if separated from this background. It lends to the events the note of a play-within-play, or rather some theater of marionettes with the Old Lady pulling the strings from above. Only by means of explicit stage directions is it possible for Dürrenmatt to create this visual aspect of the play.

But the collapsing of the world of values of the Gülleners attains a more poignant expression in the second visual aspect. Here is not meant only the direct materialistic manifestations that had control over them: the yellow shoes that the Gülleners have suddenly begun to wear, the new typewriter the mayor buys, the new clock for the church, the new clothes, as well as other signs of prosperity—all these are certainly clear attributes of the materialism that gradually gains control over the Gülleners. But it is the change that the scenery itself undergoes that conveys the transformation that takes place in the values of the Gülleners. At times this change finds its expression in a direct and unequivocal manner: as against the wretched railway station that was presented at the beginning, the appearance of this very station later on is remarkable. The multilated timetable has been changed into a new one and in contrast to the previous wretched appearance there are now touristic posters, while in the background even a few cranes can be observed, as a sign of building activity that is in progress all over the town. Even Ill's shop, so poverty-stricken in the past (a grim shop counter, old stock), reappears according to the prosperity of the times: a new sign, a new shop counter, a new till, and more expensive merchandise. The same applies to the ragged Gülleners themselves (see their depiction at the opening scene), whose last gathering turns into a scene of dazzling evening gowns and dress-suits. This process reaches its climax in the lengthy stage directions that Dürrenmatt delineates toward the end, and in which he actually sums up this transformation of boasting wealth, which has gradually dominated the play as a whole:

> As the clothing, that outward visible form of a mounting standard of living, improves by degrees discreet and unobtrusive yet less and less to be ignored, and as the stage grows more inviting, while rung by rung it scales the social ladder and metamorphoses into wealth, like a gradual change of house from a slum to a well-to-do neighbourhood, so the epitome of that ascent occurs in the concluding tableau. The erstwhile grey and dreary world has been transformed; it has grown rich and dazzling new, a flashy incarnation of up-to-the-minute technics, as if the world and all were ending happily. Flags and streamers, posters, neonlights now surround the renovated railway station, and the men and women of Güllen clad in evening gowns and dress-suits (. . .)

Perhaps this representation exceeds the bounds of ordinary

stage directions. However, one cannot doubt Dürrenmatt's attempt to present this visual process of transformation from shabby wretchedness into dazzling splendour, as an essential factor in his drama. The scenery has not only turned into an active part, but the change that has taken place in it is, in a sense, the play's true theme. Dürrenmatt is thus bound to a new concept of stage directions in order to depict the discrepancy between background and action, between scenery and behavior—a process during which the theatrical reality contradicts the remarks the Gülleners (the actors) incessantly make.

To illustrate this we have to return to the railway station. A big poster reads: "Travel South." Another poster invites the traveller: "Visit the Passion Plays in Oberammergau." Trains are rushing through, the Station Master salutes. Then

> Ill emerges from background, one hand clutching little, old suitcase, and looks around. As if by chance, citizens of Güllen come gradually closing in on him from all sides.

The visual scene depicts how the belt tightens around Ill. The real power of the scene is in its visual vigor, in the movements of the people who gradually close in on Ill, as if on a cornered animal. The Gülleners their "hands in pockets"—against the solitary Ill, who is clutching a little suitcase. But the scene is incomplete without the posters Dürrenmatt has with such great care introduced: the poster of the Oberammergou Passion Plays turns Ill, into a Jesus who is trapped in one of the highest points of his Road to Calvary, while the poster that invites one to visit the South is a clear hint at Ill's end: the Old Lady is indeed going to take his body to Capri! The yellow sun, big and bright, which is seen on one of the posters, becomes a bitter and blood-freezing comment.

Indeed, the stage directions apparently do not contribute any new or essential information. However, the visual and stunning spectacle that concludes the second act is a kind of *tableua vivant*. It lends complexity to the whole scene, invests it with emotional heterogeneity. We imagine the Gülleners surrounding the frightened Ill, the train rushing thunderously through, the Station Master fulfilling his duty and saluting, the posters charged with irony. And in the middle of all this, Ill, motionless, peering fearfully around. Not only does the optic aspect add some information to the dialogue, but, it might be argued, that the dialogue becomes here an illustration of the stunning visual process. In the dialogue there are no posters, no trains rushing through, no Station Master saluting—only the Gülleners with their sweet hypocrisy plead with Ill to remain. The visual spectacle creates a world in itself, some kind of independent action, that speaks a language of its own—the language of the stage.

The tension between the stage and the action reaches its pungent form in *Die Ehe des Herrn Mississippi.* We have already mentioned Dürrenematt's remark about the tension between the realistic scenery and the unreal, or rather fantastic action. We have also noticed that the precise and detailed description turns what seems like an ordinary realistic bourgeois living room into an impossible place, into a "nowhere." Now, the more the details are realistically precise, the more their mere excess neutralizes their specific nature and renders it, both geographically and historically, ineffectual. However, this is still a room. At the beginning the stage directions raise an essential matter worth considering. The play's subject, we recall, is the story of a room. Moreover, as the events that are going to occur in it would indeed, as the stage directions specify, happen in this room alone, it seems as if Dürrenmatt has in mind the traditional unity of place. However, as with other Dürrenmattian expectations, this one should also be considered somewhat sceptically. The play's physical action, it is true, never goes beyond the limits of a room, but one of the play's explicit characteristics is the existence of a persistent tension between the unity of place and its constant violation.

The opening stage directions make it clear how the outside world intrudes, and how the contradictory views from the windows refute the sense of unity of place. The stylistic contradiction of the pieces of furniture, each realistic in itself, again undermines the traditional concept of unity. Even some details that distinguish the characters' behavior contribute to this feeling. One character, we recall, enters through the window, while another bursts out of the grandfather-clock. Some objects, strange as it may sound, descend into the room, or disappear mysteriously. Windows open as if by themselves, while strange, or rather fantastic events take place in a manner that cannot be explained in terms of strict realism. The contrast between the room and the action also amounts to parodistic dimensions, as if we have in mind another type of discrepancy: between the living room, where coffee is being drunk and a maid is summoned by a delicate silver bell, and the violent events that occur there according to the logic of fantasy. What has begun as a respectable bourgeois living room is gradually destroyed visually. The story of the room turns into the story of its physical destruction. The demolishing of most of the furniture becomes a visual statement of the disaster caused by narrow minded idealists who seek to reform, but who, in fact, bring about utter destruction.

The play cannot be separated from its visualization of the sustained destruction of the scenery. Without this visualization, there is mere verbal polemics. The words and acts attain their full significance when they are shown in direct relationship to that grotesque and violent transformation that the room undergoes. The scenery is no mere "background" anymore. It has become an active factor in the play's logic.

A concept such as this is impossible without the extension of the stage directions, which delineate the "behavior" of the scenery, at times even behind the back of the characters. Many actions thus take place autonomously; they are not prompted by the dialogue and the characters have no control over them. Indeed, this lack of control over events is a major theme in the play.

The tension that rises from *Ein Engel Kommt nach Babylon,* however, is of a different kind. Dürrenematt, constantly aware of the process of creativity, mentions the unique question of the concept of space in his essay on the problems of the theater: (. . .) there are two locations in this comedy—the heavens and the city of Babylon. The heavens as the secret starting-point of the action and Babylon as the place where the action happens.

Dürrenmatt's problem is therefore of how to communicate (non-verbally) the feeling of the direct presence of the two poles, heaven and earth. The stage representation has therefore to deliver the feeling of an unattainable and impenetrable Kingdom of Heaven and an earthly level. This contrast between the two worlds lies at the heart of Dürrenmatt's grotesque outlook, in which man is shown in all his limitations in front of infinite space, which the scenery attempts to depict. The unavoidable sense that the play conveys is of the existence of that unbridgeable gap between vast spaces, openness and infinity, on one hand, and enclosed worlds, contracted and imprisoned, on the other. As usual with Dürrenmatt this sense is carried over the heads of the characters, who are unaware of their circumscriptions. As usual with Dürrenmatt this task is ascribed not to the dialogue, but to the detailed stage directions. Without the stage directions this gap, so central to the play, has no existence. Toward the end of the play the infinite space takes up its priority:

> Darkness. The scenery vanishes overhead.
> Vaguely, a measureless desert can be glimpsed, a
> vast wilderness through which Akki and Kurrubi are
> fleeing.

Scenery has made way for the empty space. The only limits are the boundaries of the stage. At the end there is a sand storm. The scenic occurrence, that has by now become autonomous, has completely passed to the stage directions.

The gap between space and scenery in *Romulus der Grosse* does not take on the cosmic dimension of *Ein Engel Kommt nach Babylon.* However, again we are confronted with a contrast between the real situation and the lofty ideals to which the characters try to keep faith. This contrast attains a visual dress by the contradiction between the conventional image of the Emperor's glory and the rural negligence of the royal "court". The grotesqueness of the last Roman Emperor, captured in a filthy yard of cackling hens, strikes one as an original and brilliant image. Pompous declarations and wretched reality become once again an ironic comment (through stage directions) upon the discrepancy of the characters' words and deeds. This is a play at whose center lies the development of the theme of disintegration: the decline of the Roman Empire. At first sight there is again the familiar phenomenon of unity of place. However, Dürrenmatt raises once more his beloved tension of unity of place and its violation. As in the case of *Die Ehe des Herrn Mississippi,* the house does not suffer any change; it is only the objects that underline the change that takes place. The atmosphere of disintegration and decay is accentuated by the collection of statues in the background. After Romulus has sold everything to the Antique Dealer, the porters continue to remove busts during the whole of the first act. This turns into an autonomous background action, which takes place independently of the dialogue. This action exists in the stage directions only. The same applies to the exciting image of the cackling hens, around which a considerable part of the action is woven. One critic has rightly noted the coordination that exists between the ideas pronounced in the play and its scenery, as it is a play at the heart of which lies a visual transformation.

Dürrenmatt's verbal-visual dichotomy therefore attains many faces. By means of placing the words and the actions against the visual image, Dürrenmatt expresses his central belief about man who distorts the evidence of reality. The chaotic world and man's proclaimed actions do not always agree with each other. The poignant sense of the grotesque that comes out of this concept demands that the starting point be well anchored within a familiar model of reality: a model that can be easily identified and that is far from any allegory. Within the most realistic background the most unexpected is due to take place. The source of horror is usually found in the most familiar environment. The contrast between the visual world of the stage and the action that takes place on it becomes, with Dürrenmatt, a poignant ironic comment upon man's words and deeds.

Jennifer E. Michaels (essay date 1988)

SOURCE: "Through the Camera's Eye: An Analysis of Dürrenmatt's *Der Auftrag* . . . ," in *International Fiction Review*, Vol. 15, No. 2, Summer, 1988, pp. 141-147.

[*In the following, Michaels examines Dürrenmatt's use of observation in* Der Auftrag. *Typical of his work, Dürrenmatt's characters are in a dichotomy—this time of not wanting to be observed, yet wanting to observe.*]

In his recent work, *Der Auftrag oder Vom Beobachten des Beobachters der Beobachter: Novelle in vierundzwanzig*

Sätzen (1986), as in his earlier works, Friedrich Dürrenmatt is sharply critical of many trends in modern technological society. The tone of the work is suggested by the introductory quotation from Kierkegaard's *Either/Or* to which Dürrenmatt refers on two further occasions in the novella: "What portends? What will the future bring? I do not know, I have no presentiment. When a spider hurls itself down from some fixed point consistently with its nature, it always sees before it only an empty space wherein it can find no foothold however much it sprawls. And so it is with me: always before me an empty space; what drives me forward is a consistency which lies behind me. This life is topsy-turvy and terrible, not to be endured." This quotation expresses the atmosphere of despair, emptiness, and uncertainty that, despite Dürrenmatt's characteristic grotesque humor and his inventive twists in the plot, pervades the whole work. Dürrenmatt creates a world in which chance reigns, in which God (if He even exists) is a mere onlooker, and in which people, acutely sensing their insignificance, desperately search for meaning.

As the title indicates, the role of observing and being observed is central to the novella. Out of this, Dürrenmatt creates a powerful image of the alienation and the dehumanization that, he believes, people experience in the modern world. In this novella, everyone observes everyone else, and in turn everyone is observed by everyone else: there is no longer any freedom or privacy. Observation reaches into all aspects of life, from the domestic to the political, scientific and even the theological spheres. Observing, for Dürrenmatt, is an indication of callousness and inhumanity. As he remarks elsewhere, to want to be only an observer requires a certain inhumane hardness. Even the genre that Dürrenmatt chooses for his work, that of the suspenseful detective novel, stresses the focus on observation, since in the classic detective novel the detective observes the facts coolly, and logically searches for clues.

In his depiction of the marriage of Tina and Otto von Lambert, Dürrenmatt explores the effect of observing and being observed on human relationships. The novella opens with the burial of Tina who supposedly has been raped and murdered, a crime that has not been solved. Her corpse, which has been badly mauled by jackals, has been found in the Al-Hakim ruins in the desert of M. (The description of M. suggests Morocco but, by refusing to give the country a specific name, Dürrenmatt implies that the events could happen anywhere.) The psychiatrist, Otto von Lambert, has the coffin containing the corpse airlifted by helicopter over the Mediterranean and the Alps, dangling from a cable, and lowered into the grave, a grotesque funeral that the protagonist F. and her film team record. Von Lambert gives F. the mission of reconstructing on film the last days of Tina's life, a film that he intends to show to the prosecutor's office and at professional meetings. Von Lambert holds himself responsible for Tina's death since he believes that she fled from home after reading his case notes about her depression. In these notes, he does not treat her as a woman but as a psychiatric object, devoid of all human qualities. He has turned her into an abstraction, a trend symptomatic of our age which has become, according to Dürrenmatt, an age of abstraction. As her diary shows, Tina is also guilty of such merciless observation. It is as if she has observed her husband under a microscope with increasing magnification, an observation that has stripped him of all individuality. As the logician D. remarks, observing leads to an objectification of people. This marriage, which is typical of many marriages in Dürrenmatt's works, has, however, an untypical happy end since it is discovered that the wrong corpse has been buried and that Tina is still alive.

The observing and being observed that characterizes Otto and Tina von Lambert's relationship is, however, no isolated case, as the logician D. argues. In his house in the mountains, he tells F., he has a telescope. Whenever he looks through the telescope, he sees people looking at him with binoculars. When they realize that he is watching them, they hurriedly turn away: those observing have themselves become the observed. Being caught in the act of observing leads to aggression and humiliation, and some of the people throw stones at D.'s house in revenge. From this experience, D. generalizes that today man is an observed person. People become suspicious of the state which likewise is suspicious of them and observes them with increasingly sophisticated devices. In despair, people try to flee from being observed.

Dürrenmatt explores observation on the state level when F. and her team go to M. to try to reconstruct what happened to Tina. Everywhere they go they are accompanied by the police and filmed by other cameramen. Dürrenmatt shows the insanity of present-day politics in his depiction of this corrupt and brutal system that callously tortures people for its own political ends. The two characters who represent the state in this work are both in positions in which observation plays a key role—in the police and in the secret service. The fat police chief, who resembles Göring, is locked in a power struggle, filled with Machiavellian intrigues, with the "sanfter Schönling" (the gentle little beautiful one) who turns out to be the ruthless head of the secret service. Both use the case of Tina and manipulate F. to gain power and topple the government, although they fail and are later executed. The head of the secret service listens to every conversation of the police chief (there are "bugs" everywhere) and watches everything that he does, although the police chief is unaware that he is being observed—he does not even know who the head of the secret service is. This state, which not only watches its own citizens but also the members of its own government, is itself watched by others: the country is filled with spies from all nations.

In this novella, even war is waged only to be observed, a sharp criticism of the senselessness of war which Dürrenmatt has called on other occasions a reckless crime and a great stupidity. As the cameraman Polyphem tells it, this state relies on the strange mixture of tourism and war for its economic health. For many years, a war that has lost all political meaning has been fought over an insignificant piece of desert, inhabited only by a few bedouins and desert fleas. The war is conducted solely to test the weapons of the arms-producing countries, to observe how these weapons function. This is emphasized towards the end of the novella when Polyphem drives F. to a tank graveyard where the mad Achilles intends to rape and murder her. In addition to the tanks, there are burnt-out floodlight poles, built to illuminate the battle, proof that the battle was staged only to be observed.

Throughout the novella, Dürrenmatt sharply criticizes modern technology for dehumanizing people—and he focuses in particular on the technologies that enable people to observe each other. Initially man has used machines as a prosthesis. Now, however, man himself has become the prosthesis of the machine, and ultimately discardable, an indication of the topsy-turvy world referred to in the quotation from Kierkegaard. Polyphem tells F. that the state launches satellites equipped with computer-controlled cameras to spy on other satellites, likewise equipped with computer-controlled cameras which in turn are watched by other computers. At this point, the individual is fully eliminated. Polyphem himself has been replaced by an automatic video camera. To be observed, Polyphem remarks, is bad enough, but to be observed not by a person but by a computer is worse, a mistrust of the computer that Dürrenmatt expresses in other works.

In this work, the camera in particular expresses the detachment and alienation of people from each other. Most of the characters in the work are connected to the camera. F. is a filmmaker; Polyphem and Björn Olsen are cameramen; Jytte Sörensen (the real corpse) was a television journalist; and there are cameramen everywhere who film F. as she is filming. Those who are not cameramen, like Otto von Lambert and the police chief, want to be filmed. F. has the idea of putting together a complete portrait of our planet by creating a whole out of chance scenes, a satirical reference to Dürrenmatt's *Porträt eines Planeten* (1970; *Portrait of a Planet*), an idea that she later abandons since she begins to mistrust the camera's ability to capture reality. The characters even use film to explain the real world. When F. is alone in the run-down hotel in the desolate mountains, it seems to her as if she is in an unreal film. Dürrenmatt sometimes uses analogies to people to describe the film. When Björn Olsen is killed in the explosion, his films burst out of their tin cans and look like intestines (82).

In his preface to Bernhard Wicki's book *Zwei Gramm Licht*,

Dürrenmatt compares the camera to the human eye. The human eye is fleeting, forgetful, and can be deceived. It sees only what it wants to see and suppresses everything else. It cannot see anything that occurs too swiftly. In contrast, the camera can capture the most fleeting moment. It documents and is incorruptible: it penetrates everything. This is the view that Polyphem—who is so called because, like the Cyclops, he views the world through one eye, the eye of the camera—presents. In his underground observation station, there is a wild confusion of films and the walls are covered with single photographs. Polyphem argues that only the camera can capture reality objectively and aseptically without any feelings that lead to distortion. Without the camera, the experience slips away and becomes just memory, and, like all memories, falsified fiction. Polyphem even believes that the film itself is deceptive since it conjures up a sequence out of single pictures. For this reason, he cuts up his films into single pictures which are for him crystallized reality.

Dürrenmatt is, however, critical of the camera. Polyphem's method of cutting his films into isolated pictures is indicative of a world which, Dürrenmatt believes, has lost the sense of the total picture and has declined into many pictures, a world that has become a series of unrelated, meaningless images. Elsewhere, Dürrenmatt defines the camera as the eye of the human saurian that stares at us coldly and glassily. This glassy, cold stare is typical of many of the cameramen in this work. With the exception of F., they are characterized by their complete detachment from the events they are filming, no matter how much suffering and death they are recording. The most striking example of such detachment is Polyphem himself. F. sees photographs that Polyphem has taken of a burning armored vehicle with a man caught in the turret and burned to death. Polyphem goes beyond such callous observation, however, to actually stage events to film. He blows up Björn Olsen's van because he wants to film the explosion. This is a tragic and terrible accident, he comments, but thanks to the camera it is immortalized. Polyphem also stages Jytte Sörensen's death, partly to satisfy the lust of the mad Achilles whom he normally keeps sedated with Valium, but partly because he wants to capture the murder on film. Even at the end, when Achilles is killed by the police, Polyphem continues filming Achilles whose body is being torn apart by shots. Polyphem is utterly divorced from all feelings, from any sense of humaneness, compassion, or morality. Like Dürrenmatt, F. criticizes Polyphem's views of depicting reality. Since he stages the events he films, he does not record reality, as he claims, but only his twisted perception of reality.

In this vicious circle of observing and being observed, people feel helpless and insignificant, the playthings of powers that they do not understand. They feel at a loss in a hostile and threatening world, a world in which peace is maintained only by atomic and hydrogen bombs. In this world of technology, chance reigns supreme. The logician D. notes that should the arms race unleash an atomic firebrand because of some blunder, this would be nothing more than a senseless manifestation that the earth was once inhabited. It would be a firework that nobody would notice. The world, according to Dürrenmatt's apocalyptic view, is one that can be destroyed by some technical short circuit, by an explosion in an atomic bomb factory caused by an absent-minded technician.

In the world of the novella, a world made up of unconnected fragments, even people have lost their sense of wholeness, of identity, and have themselves become in effect like Polyphem's cut-up films. The logician D. argues that nobody is identical with himself; at each moment in time a person is different. F. reflects that this would mean that there are no whole selves. What one calls the self is only a collection of innumerable past selves, a collection of experiences, memories, and roles, a self that constantly shifts, a self that cannot be captured, as she previously thought, on film. It is also a self that cannot communicate effectively with others. The logician D., for example, gives lectures that nobody can understand. This inability to communicate with others reinforces people's sense of isolation, their sense of estrangement from one another.

People's feeling of isolation is made more acute in the world as Dürrenmatt portrays it because "there does not seem to exist a divine power which will either help or hinder." As D. remarks, a personal god who observes each person, a god who rules the world, a god who is a father, has become unthinkable. The only god who is now possible is god as an abstract principle, a philosophical and literary construct, created to conjure up some meaning in a monstrous whole. Polyphem echoes this view. If God exists, then he is the pure spirit of pure observing without the possibility of becoming involved, rather like Allah in Dürrenmatt's **"Monstervortrag über Gerechtigkeit und Recht" ("Huge Speech on Justice and on Law").**

Dürrenmatt explores people's response to this hostile and threatening world, in which people feel as if they are trapped in a labyrinth, an image that he uses in the novella. Although people flee from being observed, they also *want* to be observed. If people are not observed they feel unimportant and meaningless. People film each other out of fear of their insignificance in a universe, filled with millions of Milky Ways, exploding stars, and collapsing suns, a universe that contains billions of absurd, populated planets like ours, hopelessly separated from each other by enormous distances. Even countries want to be observed. They want to be spied upon, and therefore stage events such as the arms race to ensure that they will be observed, to ensure that they will be considered important.

The desire to be observed, to feel significant, explains for D.

the current trend towards religious and political fundamentalism. Since people cannot bear not being observed, they flee into the notion of a personal god or a similarly metaphysically founded party who or which observes them. From this they derive the right to ensure that others observe the commands of god or the party. D. sees this as people's attempt to thrust on an unobserved mankind some meaning. Man, he comments, cannot live without meaning.

Another response to the dehumanization characteristic of the world as Dürrenmatt sees it is that of the mad Achilles, a former professor of Greek who is so called because he quotes Homer even when he is killing people in air raids in Vietnam or strangling women; a particularly grotesque use of culture. Achilles protests against the automation of war. He feels like a coward, a non-person, in his plane which he terms a flying computer. He kills people by pushing buttons and never comes face to face with his victims. Yet his protest against the inhumanity of modern warfare does not make him protest for peace. Instead, he argues for war filled with hatred and fear in which man becomes an animal and tears apart his enemy. Killing should be filled with hatred, he argues. People should fight like the real Achilles fought at Troy. For Achilles, two possibilities are open to man. He can either become a soulless machine, a camera, a computer, much like Polyphem has become, or an animal. Achilles opts for the latter. He longs to do something really criminal; he longs to become an animal and rape and strangle women, a wish that he later fulfills after he has become severely wounded in an air raid over Vietnam. F.'s behavior when she is faced with death appears to support Achilles's division of people into animals or soulless machines. When she fights for life, she herself becomes a predator, at one with the man who would rape and murder her, at one with the terrible stupidity of the world.

> **Dürrenmatt has commented that it is good to know how far the branch on which we are sitting is sawn through.**
> —*Jennifer E. Michaels*

Unlike his earlier works in which, despite the gloom, flickers of hope appear because of courageous individuals like Romulus in *Romulus the Great* or Akki in *An Angel Comes to Babylon,* Dürrenmatt offers little hope for change, for any improvement in mankind's condition in this work. More than ever he sees his role here as a diagnostician rather than a therapist. In light of the quotation from Kierkegaard that the world is a terrible place and not to be endured, the concluding words by D., who tells F. after she arrives back home that she has been lucky, are particularly grotesque, a happy end that does not often happen in Dürrenmatt's works. Else-

where, Dürrenmatt has commented that it is good to know how far the branch on which we are sitting is sawn through. In this work, the branch on which we are sitting is about to fall.

Sven Birkerts (essay date 5 June 1989)

SOURCE: "Crimes of the Mind," in *New Republic,* Vol. 200, June 5, 1989, pp. 39-41.

[*In the following review, Birkerts looks at the mind games and plot twists which Dürrenmatt has placed in* The Execution of Justice *and* The Assignment.]

Friedrich Dürrenmatt is best known on these shores as one of Switzerland's two world-class playwrights, the other being Max Frisch. Both came to prominence after World War II, tilling the then-fertile soil of European malaise. Both filtered an existential pessimism into refined, often paradoxical investigations of good and evil, guilt and accountability. Politically neutral, culturally Germanized, the status of these Swiss writers seemed to mandate that ambiguity of thought and deed should be their proper subject. Dürrenmatt's two best-known plays, *The Visit* and *The Physicists,* reconnoiter precisely this terrain.

But Dürrenmatt, like Frisch, also turned his hand early on to novels, and to non-fiction prose of various descriptions. *The Execution of Justice,* which appeared in Germany in 1985, addresses many of Dürrenmatt's familiar themes—just as the title suggests. Nothing, however, can prepare us for the innovations of *The Assignment*, which was released the very next year. Careers, too, can make quantum leaps.

In 1950 Dürrenmatt published a short novel, *The Judge and His Hangman,* enormously successful, which was the first of many speculative crime novels, what Graham Greene might call "entertainments." Here, using an intricate pattern of reversals and revelations, Dürrenmatt pried away at appearances to show what quick and unpredictable currents ran beneath the routine procedures of a police investigation. Punishments, like crimes, were matters of destiny: if the criminal always returns to the scene of the crime, it is because his capture is a necessary fulfillment of the deed. The novella was in no way an innovation, but it pressed its episodes forward with a confident rigor.

The Execution of Justice could almost stand as a companion piece to *The Judge and His Hangman.* It, too, marks no great stylistic or conceptual advance. Indeed, it belongs to the era of the earlier book; Dürrenmatt tells us in a short postscript that the work, originally titled *Wheels of Justice* was begun in 1957; he took it up and abandoned it a number of times before rewriting it entirely in 1985. Once again we have a crime and an expectation of the echoing call of justice. But now there is a difference: the killer steps free, apparently untroubled by even the slightest pang of remorse. (In English, the title can be read as a pun on the two meanings of "execution.")

Perhaps by temperament, and perhaps, too, because of his experience as a writer for the stage, Dürrenmatt is impatient with all the niceties of descriptive evocation or transcription of inwardness. *The Execution of Justice,* like the earlier novel, cuts its way forward in the terse, flat cadences of a police report. The conceit, in fact, is that this *is* a report, a confession set down by a dissipated lawyer named Spät in anticipation of his murder of the murderer—an execution he will ultimately be unable to carry out.

The plot (don't be deceived by the slimness of the book) is as complicated, maybe as impossible to pin down, as Faulkner's screenplay of *The Big Sleep.* Time frames and identities keep shifting; new relationships between subsidiary players emerge at every turn. But the motion of this "wheel" revolves around a fairly simple core premise. One March day in 1955, as Spät reports it, a well-known Zurich councilman, Dr. h.c. (*honoris causa*) Isaak Kohler, walks into a crowded downtown restaurant, and after a ritual exchange of greetings, shoots one Professor Winter at his table. Then, as calm as can be, he leaves, and resumes his busy life as a man-about-town. When Kohler is later apprehended at the concert hall, he gives himself up without protest. He is tried, found guilty, sentenced to prison. The whole city is baffled by what seems to be a purely gratuitous crime.

But Kohler, we soon learn, is something of a scientist, an experimenter. One day he summons Spät to the prison and offers him a rather peculiar commission. He asks the lawyer to reinvestigate his case under the presumption that he was *not* the murderer. Spät does not understand. "You are to create a fiction, nothing more," directs Kohler. He then tries to explain his reasoning:

> You see, my dear Spät, we know very well what reality is, that's why I'm in here weaving baskets, but we hardly know what possibility is. Possibility is something almost limitless, while reality is set within strictest limits, since, after all, only one of those possibilities can become reality. Reality is only an exception to the rule of possibility and can therefore be thought of quite differently too. From which follows that we must rethink reality in order to forge ahead into possibility.

In a matter of days, Spät has plunged into a thicket of possible clues and motives so dense that he has no hope of extricating himself. The sequence of revelations defies detailing.

Suffice it to say that Spät is able to construct a tissue of plausible circumstance that implicates another man, whereupon the case is brought to appeal. And when the other man—a former fencing champion named Olympic Heinz—commits suicide, Kohler is freed.

Spät cannot endure the miscarriage of justice that he has abetted. He resolves to murder Kohler and then to take his own life; his confession, he is sure, will explain everything. In the end, his plan fails. He winds up a besotted lawyer in a small farming village, regaling the locals with his extraordinary tale.

Dürrenmatt then appends to Spät's confession an epilogue in his own person (the device, I would guess, that finally allowed the author to finish the novel). He tells how some 30 years later he chanced to be at a gathering where ancient, wheelchair-bound Dr. Kohler was telling the guests the story of his crime and his release. His outrage has become something charming:

> Renewed laughter, people were having a great time, strong coffee was served, cognac. All that was left, the old man began once more, while concentrating on the ash of his cigar, which he had not knocked off but was carefully allowing to grow, was the moral question. Suddenly he was a different person. No longer a hundred years old but timeless. Whether he had killed or only intended to kill, he said, in moral terms it was the intent that counted, not the execution. . . . Everything can be justified dialectically, and thus morally as well.

Kohler continues in this vein long enough to establish the relativity of all moral constraints, then asks his daughter to wheel him away. A fitting place to end. But it is not the end. Dürrenmatt then describes his visit to Kohler's daughter, who was briefly Spät's lover, and she gives him an astonishing account of how she was raped and humiliated by a group that included Professor Winter. The elaborate architecture of her father's supposedly gratuitous crime collapses upon itself: Kohler turns out to have had an excellent motive.

I have not been able to do more than hint at the circles within the circles of connected depravities that Dürrenmatt ultimately parades before us. Perhaps it was his intent to show that the fretwork of social and personal justice cannot be safely supported by any private or collective standard, that all pretense to the contrary is sham. Well, we take the point. But somehow we are not as shocked or as distressed as we ought to be. The whole of the novella feels like a conceit that has been whipped up logically and then set to the page. The characters all have a predictable police-blotter flatness. Their thoughts and arguments, Kohler's especially, read like a writer's notebook musings on the paradoxes of morality.

What's more, we've absorbed all of these reversals and inversions before, by way of Dostovevsky, Sartre, even Frisch, who dissected similar notions in *I'm Not Stiller* and a half-dozen other works—to say nothing of Dürrenmatt himself. *The Execution of Justice* suggests that the provocations of postwar European literature may no longer provoke; that they long ago shattered the complacency that Dürrenmatt would here assault. How startling, then, to turn to Dürrenmatt's next novella. *The Assignment,* which has been subtitled: *On Observing the Observer of the Observers.*

This work is sui generis, a late-modernist legend that pushes past the usual conceptions of self and society and finds a whole new way of rendering disturbance. While the clever circularity of the subtitle (which is not part of the book's German title) suggests the thematic concerns of the narrative, it gives a sportive ring to what is, in fact, a most chilling recognition: that our electronic technology has entirely deformed our self-conception and our behavior. When Rilke wrote in his "Archaic Torso of Apollo" that "there is no place that does not see you," he was not, presumably, referring to electronic surveillance, but his conclusion—"You must change your life"—would still apply. Dürrenmatt would probably say that for the culture at large it's too late.

Reading *The Assignment* is like taking a head-first tumble down a staircase made of words. The book has 24 chapters, each a single sentence that builds velocity from phrase to phrase. Once again we have a murder and a search for a killer. But this time the crime is less a central subject, more a pretext for the creation of a futuristic scenario that will allow Dürrenmatt to expose the changed terms of our contemporary situation.

Psychologist Otto von Lambert, who has written a well-known book on terrorism, learns that his wife's body has been found at the site of the Al-Hakin ruin in an unnamed Arab country. Lambert ships her body home for burial and at the funeral hires the filmmaker F., who is working on an idea of "creating a total portrait, namely a portrait of our planet, by combining random scenes into a whole." F. is to go to the site with her crew to film the investigation of the murder. Not an everyday request, but then F. is clearly a woman who lives for such adventuring—a kind of Laurie Anderson of the dark side. What's more, the hyper-ventilating prose creates a climate wherein the extraordinary seems the expected.

But before jetting off, F. must consult with her friend D., a logician at the university. D. hears her out, then tells a story of his own. He has been watching people through a telescope in his home. He has observed that these same people have been looking at him through field glasses. As soon as they realized that *they* were being watched, they ran off—a

fact that prompts D. to make this Gertrude Steinian peroration:

> anything observed requires the presence of an observer, who, if he is observed by what he is observing, himself becomes an object of observation, a banal logical interaction, which, however, transposed into reality, had a destabilizing effect, for the people observing him and discovering that he was observing them through a mirror telescope felt caught in the act, and since being caught in the act produces embarrassment and embarrassment frequently leads to aggression, more than one of these people, after retreating in haste, had come back to throw rocks at his house.

D.'s little story, his "banal logical interaction," is, in a sense, the metaphorical pivot for the rest of this strangest of novellas: only the scale and application of its point keep changing. Briefly: F. flies to the unnamed Arab country; she instantly finds herself in a nightmare world of cubicles and interrogations. She films, and her filming is filmed. The plot flashes forward, chapter-sentence by chapter-sentence, obeying only the paralogic of dreams. Until at last the intrepid filmmaker finds herself in what might be seen as the Ur-location of our modern world: a fortified, automated monitoring site for high-tech weaponry. World powers are testing their new weapons by proxy in a staged desert war. Everything is filmed—even the satellite filming the site is being filmed by another satellite. In the back room, under lock and key, is a fighter pilot gone mad named Achilles, who reads Homer in the Greek and lives only to rape and destroy.

Trust me, Dürrenmatt's narrative is far more compelling than any precis can indicate. The improbable plot is pressured by a sense of ominous inevitability: F. is led remorselessly to her rendezvous with the rough beast, the extrusion of what Yeats called the "animus mundi." Moreover, the ruling conceit—observer and observed—is true enough to the way things are to activate the paranoid strain in most readers. We bother less with F. and her fate, but we are riveted by the implications of the trope. For Dürrenmatt has hit upon a very real connection between exposure and aggression. D.'s insight about embarrassment leading to violence only grazes the surface.

The real issue, we come to see, revolves around identity and the authentication of existence. The more we watch and are watched watching, the less we are able to hold a self-boundary in place. And the diffusion of the sense of the real, like the sleep of reason, breeds monsters. Marshall McLuhan, the antic theorist of a world transformed by electronic technology, remarked on this very thing: "The meaningless slaying around our streets is the work of people who have lost all identity, and who have to kill in order to know if they're real." *The Assignment* finds this same horrifying logic of compensation at the heart of our late-century doings. Dürrenmatt's edgy musing may seem futuristic, but so does the daily news.

Margaret Scanlan (essay date March 1991)

SOURCE: "Terror as Usual in Friedrich Dürrenmatt's *The Assignment,*" in *Modern Language Quarterly,* Vol. 52, No. 1, March 1991, pp. 86-93.

[*In the following essay on Dürrenmatt's* The Assignment, *Scanlan explores the fragmentation of identity and "the paired themes of terrorism and literary realism."*]

The history of terrorism has been entwined with the history of the novel ever since serialization of Dostoevski's *The Possessed* began in 1871. Perhaps in spite of traditional assumptions, still not entirely lost, about the clear distinctions between literary and political activities, it is inevitable that terrorists sometimes seem to resemble novelists. Marginalized plotters both, they seek to impose their own constructions on a chaotic and resistant reality, relying on their ability to move the emotions of strangers. And though terrorists attract attention through violence, their targets are almost always symbolic, and their aims must finally be explained in language. Moreover, as leftist critics frequently argue, the public perception of terrorism is itself highly constructed. To say so is not to aestheticize the cruel reality of terrorist activities—to gloss over, for example, the fate of the passengers on Pan Am flight 103—but to argue that the ways in which government officials and the press represent terrorism are remarkably similar to the ways in which popular fiction does so. The nature and inadequacy of such representations of terrorism are the subject of Friedrich Dürrenmatt's *The Assignment,* a 1986 novel in which the author's absurdist critique of contemporary politics merges with a postmodern conception of terrorism.

Before turning to Dürrenmatt, we need to look at the public conceptions of terrorism that his novel implicitly criticizes and at some of the alternatives scholars have proposed. In popular representations, the terrorist is always the other, an outsider who—if not a representative of a once-colonized people, a swarthy Islamic archfiend, say, or a grubby chain-smoking product of the Shankill Road—is at the very least a drug-crazed adolescent from a subculture that defies everything the middle class values. Clever enough to elude the police, terrorists are nonetheless usually assumed to be mad bombers, motivated more by their traumatic childhoods and personal failures than by the causes they publicly adopt. It is their deviance from mainstream values and solutions, rather than their connection to a familiar social setting or to recognizable political problems, that defines them.

In this representation, the plot of the terrorist story, whether we find it within the embossed covers of a paperback novel or in the headlines of the *Washington Post,* is almost reassuringly familiar; "terrorist acts are never really news." We know about bombings and hijackings, about SWAT teams and exhausted negotiators, about communiqués issued in halting English by dark-eyed men in ski masks, and we are reasonably sure, most of the time, that in the end the security forces, the orderly state, will triumph. As the other, terrorists gratify a need for an identified enemy that can only increase as differences between communist and capitalist states dissolve.

Seen as a political strategy rather than as a myth, the terrorist deed is perhaps best defined as "a symbolic act designed to influence political behaviour by extranormal means, entailing the use or threat of violence." Terrorism is a behavior of small groups alienated from conventional ways of influencing the political system, incapable of mounting a full-scale military campaign (in which violent acts cease to be symbolic and compel by sheer force alone) and unwilling or unable to take part in, for example, free electoral processes.

While agreeing with Thornton's basic definition, commentators on the political left, such as Edward Said and Noam Chomsky, have expressed their dismay at the tendency to label as terrorist the behavior of what they see as legitimately revolutionary groups—the PLO, say, or the IRA—and to deny the terrorizing activities of the state. Mick Taussig argues that the terrorist myth props up the unstable and violence-ridden regimes of much of the Third World, where "terror in . . . disruption is no less than that of the order it is bent on eliminating." The state's attempt to brainwash the population into accepting its violence as orderly seems even more futile when one recognizes that the state itself is disappearing under the pressures of modern corporations and technologies of knowledge. "Might not the very concept of the social, itself a relatively modern idea, be outdated insofar as it rests on assumptions of stability and structure? In which case what is all the talk about order about?" Terrorists, half-creations of the unstable state, serve to legitimate its own violence. "There may even arise in the political economy of news a certain 'demand' for publicized terrorist activity in order, paradoxically, to continually reaffirm the principle that the use of force rightly belongs only with the state."

Dürrenmatt shares with these political commentators a wish to expose the myths and explore the realities of terrorism. An experimental fiction, *The Assignment* points to the complex reality that lies behind the too-familiar story and suggests as well what factual studies mask, the actual experience of human beings caught up in terrorist activities. Fragmentation of identity in the novel's unstable world leads to a longing for order that asserts itself in totalitarian politics, fundamentalist religion, and documentary realism, all disciplines, in Foucault's sense, that depend on observation. Suggesting the difficulty of distinguishing between the victims and practitioners of terror, Dürrenmatt undermines the usual story of sinister Islamic terrorists. Terrorism in his novel belongs as much to the illusory order as to its half-imagined opposition; it is dispersed through government and business and can be found as well in high culture and in the representational practices taken for granted in realism and mass journalism. Yet while he thoroughly recognizes the popular critique of the letter as terrorizing, Dürrenmatt implicitly argues that a novel about terrorism can suggest what is otherwise "unpresentable" in our experience of public violence. His manipulations of the myth present terror both as an understandable private response to the conditions of late twentieth-century life and as a public practice that intensifies and conditions panic.

Although *The Assignment* begins like a standard thriller, with the funeral of a European woman found "dead and violated at the foot of the Al-Hakim ruin," the briefest survey of its bizarre plot demonstrates how Dürrenmatt borrows from, but quickly revises, the familiar story in order to deny the reader the comfortable satisfaction of identifying the usual culprits and bringing them to an unexamined justice. After Tina von Lambert's funeral, her husband, a psychiatrist, engages another woman, the filmmaker "F.," to find her murderer. F. goes to North Africa, where she interviews two officials, a police chief resembling Göring and a mild-mannered "investigating magistrate" who is actually the head of the secret service. After filming the murder site and the execution of an obviously innocent man condemned for the crime, F. is convinced by the head of the secret service to help him track down the real murderer by impersonating the victim, wearing Tina's red fur coat while another woman plays F.'s part, touring the country with her film crew. On a tip from Björn Olsen, a Danish journalist who is almost immediately murdered, F. discovers that Tina is still alive and that the real victim was another journalist, Jytte Sörensen. Wandering down the road on which she discovered Olsen's body, F. is picked up by a Vietnam veteran who mans a giant observatory intended to keep track of the country's war with its next-door neighbor. This veteran and his brain-damaged friend are the real murderers of Jytte Sörensen and Björn Olsen, and F. is saved from their fate only at the eleventh hour.

F. and, very likely, the reader look for some sinister Arab as Tina von Lambert's killer, because her body was found not only in an Islamic country but at a shrine sacred to Shi'ite Muslims, a group consistently demonized in the Western press for its role in the Iranian revolution. Dürrenmatt, however, immediately complicates the case by presenting Tina's husband as "a man who had defended the Arab resistance movement and hadn't called it a terrorist organization." Although nothing in the book suggests empathy for Islamic culture or political causes—Dürrenmatt's point, indeed, is that nationalist causes have become meaningless—*The Assignment* refuses the stereotype of the Arab terrorist. The Shi'ite "saints" may be fanatics, starving to death as they wait for their caliph to emerge from his stone cube, but they are dangerous only to themselves. The Westernized head of the secret service, lecturing F. about Khomeini and the finer features of Islamic fundamentalism as he sips an Alsatian white wine, is a considerably more sinister figure because he is more European, more powerfully interested in weaving F. into his plots, which include turning his country's war into an "international scandal." Sörensen and Olsen are killed not by the infidel but by Americans, Vietnam veterans with names taken from Homer.

At its simplest level, the novel complicates the terrorist myth by making the identities of the victims as problematic as those of the killers. Nothing is what it seems: Jytte Sörensen, not Tina von Lambert, is the first of Polypheme and Achilles' murder victims; F., the once-detached filmmaker, nearly becomes the third. Surely few readers can have the moral certainty to decide whether a brain-damaged Vietnam veteran-turned-rapist is a victim or a terrorizer. Identity also remains problematic in part because few characters, including the protagonist, have names. The second subtitle of the original text (omitted from the translation), *Novelle in vierundzwanzig Sätzen*, calls the reader's attention to the artifice of constructing a short novel in twenty-four chapters, each consisting of a single long sentence or—to draw on another connotation of the German word—philosophical proposition. And this device, too, by departing from the conventions of realistic fiction and documentary journalism and by at least suggesting an allusion to the twenty-four books of the *Iliad*, reminds us that the text does not correspond neatly to some external reality. Dürrenmatt's mock omniscient narration, presenting everything as summary, refusing to render dialogue directly, to give the protagonist a personal history, to name the country in which the novel is set, and so on, frustrates the reader's desire to master the whole story. If it is true that "the [criminal] under-world is the phantasmagoric paranoid construction of the ruling class," surely the desire for a solid external reality, for the identities and oppositions contemporary thought and events refuse to give us, drives that construction.

Terrorism in the novel deviates, then, from the story we already know to become what Taussig calls "terror as usual," a dispersed and decentered phenomenon of the postcolonial world. His phrase provides a pale suggestion of the nightmarish confusion of the apparently normative and social with terror that Dürrenmatt's novel develops. In the streets of his fictional North African country one finds "a multiracial thicket of travelers all busily photographing and filming each other and forming an unreal contrast to the secret life inside the compound of the police ministry, like two interlocking realities, one of them cruel and demonic, the other as banal as tourism itself." Yet the presence of a Grand Hotel Maréchal Lyautey, with its large portrait of that quintessential empire builder, suggests that tourism is colonialism by other means and as such is not only banal but cruel in its indifference to the "secret life" of local people. The state is unstable: the mild, bespectacled investigating magistrate turns out to be the head of the secret service, locked in a power struggle with the chief of police, "who didn't even know who the head of the secret service was."

One of the accomplishments of *The Assignment* is to depict "terror as usual" as more than a political phenomenon and to communicate to the reader an anxiety corresponding to the symptoms of postmodernism as Jean-François Lyotard diagnoses them. In a world incommensurable with our desires and conceptions, something unrepresentable always remains outside art, and though we long for the consolations of form and order, we must make up the rules as we go along. Such views are not, of course, an invention of the twentieth century—Lyotard himself refers to Montaigne's essays as possessing some of these qualities—and in *The Assignment* they are represented by a passage from Kierkegaard and enacted in the fate of the three Europeans killed in North Africa. When F. discovers the quotation from Kierkegaard, it is in Jytte Sörensen's handwriting and in her native Danish, which F. parses out, believing that she has discovered a code. The fuller quotation forms the novel's epigraph:

> What will come? What will the future bring? I do not know. I have no presentiment. When a spider plunges from a fixed point to its consequences, it always sees before it an empty space where it can never set foot, no matter how it wriggles. It is that way with me: before me always an empty space; what drives me forward is a consequence that lies behind me. This life is perverse and frightful, it is unbearable.

The quotation evokes the conditions of life lived in a period of frequent terrorist attacks, a radical insecurity conditioned by a historical past, as well as the familiar existential angst felt by the human moving forward into a future at once unknowable and deeply determined. The now-dated slogans of "alienation" become fresh in the experience of Europeans encountering in North Africa not oriental romance but the cruelties of a world where they have lost all familiar points of reference and every benign expectation is crushed. Reducing a human being to a short-lived pest is not only unwelcome but Kafkaesque.

More precisely, like Jytte Sörensen, who came to North Af-

rica to track down a story, and F., who came to find the killer of a still-living woman, the spider is a weaver of traps, in popular lore a plotter, in Swift the very image of the "modern" scholar with his dictionaries and footnotes, ready to strip a rich traditional culture of its living grace. It would be hard to construct a better metaphor for a documentary realism that seeks to "capture" the real in its web, at the risk of destroying its mysterious, unpresentable life. And when F., almost as if the message were in code, begins to identify with Jytte Sörensen, walking off "helpless as a spider" along the road that leads to Polypheme's cave, "a consequence of her whole life", she does so as the representative of a certain kind of art, of a documentary realism whose premises began to explode for her the day she filmed the burial of Tina von Lambert.

"I am being watched," writes Tina in her journal, and the problem of being watched and its relationship to identity enters a political and philosophical context when the logician "D." ruminates on these matters. D., apparently a disciple of Derrida, for whom he may even have been named, lectures F. about the impossibility of self-identity, for "everyone was subject to time and was therefore, strictly speaking, a different person at every moment." Given this insight, portrayal becomes impossible; the human self is a fiction, an "accumulation of shreds of experience and memory, comparable to a mound of leaves." The novel then presents the process by which late twentieth-century human beings struggle to understand each other, the world outside the ego, with no certainty of achieving more than "reconstruction, raking together scattered leaves to build up the subject of [a] portrait, never being sure, all the while, whether the leaves . . . actually belonged together, or whether, in fact, [one] wasn't ultimately making a self-portrait."

Therefore, although no novelists stalk Dürrenmatt's pages, although no one ever reads or quotes from a novel or play, *The Assignment* again and again demonstrates a concern with the problematics, and especially with the political implications, of literary realism. The novel's first subtitle, *Or on the Observing of the Observer of the Observers*, recalls a Shakespearean phrase that had, by the late nineteenth century, become ominous; given "the depersonalized relations of the information society . . . the condition of being 'the observed of all observers' [is] no longer a compliment, as it was intended for Hamlet, but a threat of exposure."

Made sensitive to such threats by Michel Foucault, at least two recent critics argue that realism fundamentally depends on a "fantasy of surveillance" that corresponds to nineteenth-century developments in, for example, psychiatry and urban sociology. In the extreme case, the representational practices of realism are seen as another way of policing, enforcing social norms and denying aberrations. Trollope, for example, just because he seems so tolerant, not to say boring, forces the reader to accept his own highly detailed moral code, and the problem in reading him is "to render as such, and not merely repeat, the terroristic effects of the banality that Trollope, as a matter of principle and program, relentlessly cultivates."

> ***The Assignment*** **again and again demonstrates a concern with the problematics, and especially with the political implications, of literary realism.**
> ***—Margaret Scanlan***

One might protest that realistic and naturalistic novels were often destabilizing, that *Hard Times* did help change the divorce laws. Dickens's novels generally might, in the mystery and undecidability they grant to working-class characters such as Jenny Wren of *Our Mutual Friend* (sunbeam? witch?), be taken as rather less complicit with state terror than, say, the Nazi remake of *Jew Süss*. The whole argument that the conventions of nineteenth-century realism reproduce a taken-for-granted consensus about what constitutes reality, and therefore stifle dissent, weakens when we consider Mikhail Bakhtin's persuasive arguments to the contrary. Unlike poetry, which traditionally avoids "actual available social dialects," the realistic novel, says Bakhtin, constantly posits a difference between the narrator's language and intentions and those of the dramatized characters, "a freedom connected with the relativity of literary and language systems." Reproducing in part the variety of the world's languages, the novel brings about "a destruction of any absolute bonding of ideological meaning to language, which is *the* defining factor of mythological and magical thought."

Nonetheless, despite the frequency with which recent theorists cite Bakhtin, the critique of realism as allied with official views of reality and with the suppression of dissent remains a key point in the post-modernist program, for which Lyotard is a prestigious and articulate spokesperson, and it is one that Dürrenmatt obviously takes seriously. In *The Postmodern Condition: A Report on Knowledge*, Lyotard argues that "terror" is "the efficiency gained by eliminating, or threatening to eliminate, a player from the language game one shares with him." In his peroration he argues eloquently for an experimental, postmodern art that preserves the living contradictions and incompletion of the world:

> It is our business not to supply reality but to invent allusions to the conceivable which cannot be presented. And it is not to be expected that this task will effect the last reconciliation between language games (which, under the name of faculties, Kant knew to be separated by a chasm), and that only the transcendental illusion (that of Hegel) can hope to

totalize them into a real unity. But Kant also knew that the price to pay for such an illusion is terror. The nineteenth and twentieth centuries have given us as much terror as we can take. We have paid a high enough price for the nostalgia of the whole and the one, for the reconciliation of the concept and the sensible, of the transparent and the communicable experience. Under the general demand for slackening and for appeasement, we can hear the mutterings of the desire for a return of terror, for the realization of the fantasy to seize reality.

Lyotard's theory goes some way toward explaining the significance of the paired themes of terrorism and literary realism in *The Assignment*. The holes in Dürrenmatt's plot, the unanswered questions about unnamed characters, the fragmentary glimpses of landscapes, interiors, motives, and political contexts are as so many refusals of "the transparent and communicable." The effect is perhaps not so antimimetic as it might seem; refusing transcendent illusions, the novelist suggests an elusive dimension of personality or experience that withers under the harsh floodlights of documentary realism.

F.'s goal for many years has been to create a documentary, a "total portrait . . . of our planet," a goal that leads her to film Tina von Lambert's funeral and then to agree to the psychiatrist Otto von Lambert's request that she find his wife's killers. But even before F. leaves Europe, her faith in representation is shaken by her reading of Tina von Lambert's journal, in which Tina has recorded her husband's every minute action with Balzacian intensity. Yet her descriptions have not given but destroyed her husband's identity, putting into question the old humanistic idea of the unique person:

> Reading this journal was like being immersed in a cloud of pure observations gradually condensing into a lump of hate and revulsion, or like reading a film script for a documentary of every human being, as if every person, if he or she were filmed in this manner, would turn into a von Lambert as he was described by this woman, all individuality crushed out by such ruthless observation.

This terroristic "ruthless observation" that ends by destroying the identity it seeks to establish, what Lyotard might call the "unpresentable" in the person, resembles the medical jargon that turns us into unflattering synecdoches of ourselves, the ruptured appendix in 412B, the morbidly enlarged liver in 413A.

In von Lambert's notes on his wife, whom he fears having seen as a case, we find such observations carried to the point that they are no longer observations at all but literally an abstracting of her humanity, defining depression as a psychosomatic phenomenon resulting from insight into the meaninglessness of existence, which is inherent in existence itself, since the meaning of existence is existence, which insight, once accepted and affirmed, makes existence unbearable, so that Tina's insight into that insight *was* the depression, and so forth, this sort of idiocy page after page.

Neither journal nor case notes—both like documentary-film allotropes of literary realism and the faith in communicating observation—provides F. with insight into Tina's motives for running off to North Africa, and she is left feeling like some adjunct of the contemporary information system, "one of those probes they shoot out into space in the hope that they will transmit back to the earth information about its still unknown composition."

Because its representations are closest to a commonsense, consensus notion of reality, Dürrenmatt sees a realistic art as potentially dangerous. Its illusions appear graphically when F., having found the address of a famous, recently dead painter in Tina's journal, goes to his studio. Its floors and walls are lined with paintings that recall F.'s own project of creating a "total portrait . . . of our planet": a whole gallery of the city's more disreputable citizens. "At the feet of these figures who were no longer present except on canvas stood smaller pictures, representing a streetcar, toilets, pans, wrecked cars, bicycles, umbrellas, traffic policemen, Cinzano bottles, there was nothing the painter had not depicted, the disorder was tremendous."

As in the von Lamberts' writings, but here presumably only because of the riotous juxtaposition of the paintings, a representational art suggests what its critics say it is intended to repress, the underlying chaos of the world. F., turning to let in light from a window, sees a portrait of a woman in a red fur coat that she "at first took for a portrait of Tina von Lambert, but which turned out not to be Tina after all, it could just as well be a portrait of a woman who looked like Tina, and then, with a shock, it seemed to her that this woman standing before her defiantly with wide-open eyes was herself." Yet when she returns later in the day the "portrait" is gone, and the apparently real studio turns out to be a "reconstruction" made for a film crew and intended to "give an impression . . . of how the studio had looked when the artist was using it." And indeed, at the end of the novel, F., who has barely escaped rape and murder in North Africa, realizes that the woman in the portrait must have been Jytte Sörensen and the one standing in front of her Tina von Lambert; "no doubt the director was her lover."

The dangerous illusions of realism have more specifically political implications. F.'s "total portrait . . . of our planet"

would indeed be that kind of totalizing, totalitarian art that Lyotard deplores. In *The Assignment,* the political terrors of realism are seen at their simplest in North Africa when the police chief steals F.'s film of the execution of the Scandinavian prisoner and replaces it with an official "documentary," complete with shots of cheerful cadets at a police training academy, which might be equally convincing to a European audience. Such documentaries seem to carry out the logical implications of nineteenth-century realism:

> Photography did not appear as a challenge to painting from the outside, any more than industrial cinema did to narrative literature. . . . The challenge lay essentially in that photographic and cinematographic processes can accomplish better, faster, and with a circulation a hundred thousand times larger than narrative or pictorial realism, the task which academicism had assigned to realism: to preserve various consciousnesses from doubt.

Indeed film, while clearly an art form for F., often associates itself directly with the police and with surveillance in *The Assignment.* F., to take one example, rides to Al-Hakim in a convoy of "policemen and television people."

More nakedly still, the complex technology on which F.'s art depends can be separated almost entirely from human agency. The ultimate surveillance of the novel's last chapter, for example, depends on a series of cameras, each operated by a computer, watching each other observe the world. Achilles spoke of that nightmare in Vietnam, where he flew a computerized bomber: "Their plane was a flying computer, programmed to start, fly to the target, drop its bombs, all automatic, their only function was to observe." Discipline, in short, becomes the *only* human function, reducing a person to an observer of machines made *pour surveiller et punir.*

Better than any political analyst, Dürrenmatt draws us close to understanding the emotional and intellectual costs of living in the late twentieth century.
—*Margaret Scanlan*

Dürrenmatt clearly agrees with Foucault that such observation is a fundamental condition of twentieth-century life: his Arab jail is positively Benthamite, with its courtyard that looks like a shaft and its series of peepholes. As D. puts it, "A very suitable definition of contemporary man might be that he is man under observation—observed by the state, for one." Yet D. argues that such a Foucauldian discipline is not only necessary but deeply desired. Fundamentalism, both religious and political, has revived because "many, indeed most, people could not stand themselves if they were not observed by someone." Nuclear weaponry, requiring spy satellites and at best eventuating in mutually agreed on-site inspections, enacts the same need, "which was why they basically hoped to be able to keep up the arms race forever, so that they would have to observe one another forever, since without an arms race, the contending powers would sink into insignificance."

If the novel could have a center, then, it would be the terrifying underground observatory, equipped with the latest cameras, from which the half-crazed Vietnam veteran nicknamed Polypheme observes the desert border war that is the mainstay of this unnamed country's economy. It is the ultimate panoptical war, Undershaft-gone-mad, existing only to be observed for the benefit of the people who really run things, that is, the sellers of weapons: "the war effort was constantly seeking out new battlefields, quite logically, since the stability of the market depended on weapons exports." Polypheme himself, the camera his one eye, links the most ancient violence with the problematics of modern identity: "Nobody injured me." His original purpose had been to provide such close documentation of the weapons that he could make "espionage obsolete," but "he really wasn't needed anymore, he had been replaced by fully automated video cameras, then a satellite had been launched to a permanent position above the observation center."

Polypheme exists at a disquieting nexus between immemorial violence and its contemporary manifestations. During the Vietnam war, his life was saved by his closest friend, a classics professor and bomber pilot nicknamed Achilles. In a world of automatic weapons, where computers do most of the work, Achilles had complained that "the idea of a human being was an illusion, man either became a soulless machine, a camera, a computer, or a beast," and he "sometimes wished he could be a real criminal, do something inhuman, be a beast, rape and strangle a woman." Horribly brain-damaged in the war, Achilles is locked in a V.A. hospital, from which he occasionally escapes to rape and murder women, and since it is the only pleasure he is able to feel, Polypheme feels obliged to procure it for him after he liberates his friend and installs him at the observation center. In his case, "terror as usual" takes the form suggested by Robin Morgan, who argues for a direct link between the old classical heroes and modern terrorism, the "sexuality of violence," the capture and rape of women that is, in fact, taken for granted in the *Iliad*. By suggesting that terrorism has an affinity with beautiful and durable monuments of Western, not Islamic, culture, Dürrenmatt reminds us of Benjamin's famous observation that there is "no document of civilization which is not at the same time a document of barbarism."

Better than any political analyst, Dürrenmatt draws us close to understanding the emotional and intellectual costs of living in the late twentieth century, when even terrorism cannot be counted on to correspond to our conceptions of it. Otto von Lambert's insight that "Auschwitz . . . was not the work of terrorists but of state employees" is well supported in this novel. Terrorists serve the need to believe that there are centers of resistance against a well-established order, yet as this novel amply demonstrates, the very notion of a center is illusory. The new physical terror of computerized bombing and the old one of rape correspond to a condition in which late twentieth-century human beings live and move, their identity fragmented by new philosophical conceptions of memory and the self but also by new technologies that violate their privacy or reduce their importance in traditional roles, such as that of the warrior. Surveillance and observation, intended to reduce the likelihood of nuclear war or successful terrorist attacks, are oppressive but desired. F., ironically, is at last saved from Achilles because a camera crew rises up in the desert to film her (Taussig explains how a friend in Bogotá warned him to "always make sure that if anything happens to you there will be publicity. Make sure there are journalists who know where you are going"). Fear of nuclear holocaust feeds the conventional weapons industry; the barbarous high-tech warfare of Vietnam turns a highly civilized man into a primitive rapist; computerized satellites observing other computerized satellites make a mockery of human observers and of the idea of God; "the world [is] spinning back to its origin," that is, to chaos.

Franz P. Haberl (essay date Autumn 1992)

SOURCE: Review of *Midas oder Die schwarze Lenwand*, in *World Literature Today*, Vol. 66, No. 4, Autumn, 1992, pp. 708-709.

[*The following is a favorable review of Dürrenmatt's* Midas oder Die schwarze Lenwand.]

The nucleus of the opusculum **Midas oder Die schwarze Leinwand** is narrated by one of its characters, the writer significantly named F.D. An industrialist appears before his company's board of directors, where it is made clear to him that his firm is bankrupt and that his business practices will land him in jail. His friends on the board are ready to help him. They will take over the company, pay his debts, and provide for his family. They have taken out an insurance policy on his life. All he has to do is sign the policy and step out of his villa punctually at 8 P.M., and a truck will run him over. The industrialist agrees to the scheme and signs the document. He then visits his mistress and a pastor to say a sort of vicarious farewell without telling them what he intends to do. He has a similarly opaque conversation with his family during supper, then steps out of the house, and the truck rolls down the street, "a gigantic, sullen animal."

F.D. states that he intended to develop this nucleus into a filmscript, but "then Midas had to come to my mind. . . . The bankrupt industrialist became a tycoon." F.D. makes these revelations during the last few pages of the work, long after the reader has been told and retold that the character F.D. is the author Friedrich Dürrenmatt. In a brief dust-jacket description of his slim volume Dürrenmatt characterized the work thus: "Not a script for a film, a film to be read."

Bearing that characterization in mind, it is a sheer pleasure to follow the "plots" of this nonfilm. The one agon involves the question of how the immensely rich tycoon Green will die or has died. For die he must, or die he did, depending on which of the purported twelve versions of the script we are following. The other agon involves the process of artistic creation, in this case the creation of a filmscript that has become too convoluted by the addition of the mythical tale of King Midas to the topic of a ruthless billionaire who can no longer be tolerated even in this corrupt world. Some of the nocturnal encounters between the writer F.D. sitting at his desk with a candle and a bottle of Bordeaux and arguing with his characters belong to the wittiest scenes Dürrenmatt ever wrote.

Reading *Midas* evokes fond memories of Dürrenmatt's many excellent plays. Seeing the date when the work was completed (31 July 1990) makes one doubly sad at the author's death less than half a year later.

FURTHER READING

Criticism

Cory, Mark E. "Shakespeare and Dürrenmatt: From Tragedy to Tragicomedy." *Comparative Literature* 32, No.3 (Summer 1980): 253-73.

Examines Dürrenmatt's adaptations and how they reveal his political motivations as well as his mastery of tragicomedy.

Geldrich-Leffman, Hanna. "Vision and Blindness in Dürrenmatt, Buero Vallejo and Lenz." *MLN* 97, No. 3 (April 1982): 671-93.

Explores the use of blindness and its two-sided nature of impairment and link to subconscious, creative powers.

Masuzawa, Tomoko. "Behind the Law: Staging of Guilt in Kafka via Dürrenmatt." *Journal of the American Academy of Religion* LX, No. 1 (Spring 1992): 35-55.

Masuzawa looks at Dürrenmatt, especially his earlier works, as creating variations of Kafkan themes.

Reid, J. H. "Dürrenmatt in the GDR: The Dramatist's Reception up to 1980." *The Modern Language Review* 79, Part 2 (April 1984): 356-371.

Provides an historical review of Dürrenmatt's reception in the former East Germany.

Robinson, Gabrielle. "Nothing Left but Parody: Friedrich Dürrenmatt and Tom Stoppard." *Theatre Journal* 32, No. 1 (March 1980): 85-94.

Compares Dürrenmatt's and Tom Stoppard's adaptations of Shakespeare's works. Robinson notes the common use of parody by both writers in dealing with Shakespeare's plays.

Steer, Alun. "Delusion and Reality in Friedrich Dürrenmatt's *Romulus the Great*." *Journal of European Studies* 18, Part 4, No. 72 (December 1988): 233-51.

Establishes the connection between the comedy of the first three acts with Romulus's error and the tragedy of the end.

Additional coverage of Dürrenmatt's life and career is contained in the following sources published by Gale Research: *Contemporary Authors*, Vol. 17-20R; *Contemporary Authors New Revision Series*, Vol. 33; *Dictionary of Literary Biography*, Vols. 69 and 124; *DISCovering Authors Modules: Dramatists*; and *Major Twentieth Century Writers*.

Timothy Findley
1930-

Canadian novelist, short story writer, playwright, and scriptwriter.

The following entry presents criticism on Findley through 1995. For additional information on his life and works, see *CLC*, Volume 27.

INTRODUCTION

A prize-winning author, Findley is recognized as one of Canada's preeminent literary figures. He frequently makes reference to historical events, figures, and other works of literature, and his writings, according to John F. Hulcoop, are evocative in nature, "[compelling] the critic to recover his senses (*see* more, *hear* more) by making direct appeals to the viewer-listener-reader through sight, sound and style: these are what force us to pay attention—to look and listen and mark his words." Thematically, Findley's works typically focus on the past and history, isolation, identity, war, madness, and authority.

Biographical Information

Born in Toronto, Ontario, Findley learned of sorrow at an early age: a sibling died when he was a child and Findley's father essentially abandoned the family for a time by suddenly enlisting in the Canadian armed forces. Due in part to illness, Findley never formally finished his secondary education and initially pursued—and succeeded in establishing—a career in acting. He worked with such renowned actresses as Ruth Gordon, toured in a production of *The Matchmaker,* and participated in the first season of the renowned Stratford Theater Festival in Stratford, Ontario. He spent some time acting in England at the suggestion of Sir Alec Guinness, whom he had met at Stratford. Eventually, Findley began writing as an adult—he wrote his first story during a time of illness while a teenager—to prove a point to Gordon, with whom he was acting at the time. In Gordon and her friend, the renowned American dramatist Thornton Wilder, Findley found encouragement and advice—and ultimately a second career. In addition to his work as a playwright, fiction writer, and scriptwriter—he was employed at one point as a scriptwriter in California—he also served as a radio broadcast journalist in Canada. Findley has received numerous honors and awards in his career, including the Governor General's Award for the novel *The Wars* (1977), and has served as president of International PEN's English-Canadian Centre and as playwright-in-residence at Canada's National Arts Centre.

Major Works

The past, marginalization, mental illness, and interpersonal conflict are central to Findley's art. In his first novel, *The Last of the Crazy People* (1967), Findley focuses on a dysfunctional family and the tensions and numerous conflicts that arise between its members. The world of the novel's protagonist, eleven-year-old Hooker Winslow, is dramatically shaped by his fear of being left alone, his mother's refusal to leave her bedroom, his father's ineffectuality, and his mentally unbalanced brother—items that eventually culminate in suicide and murder. Conflict and isolation, however, are not limited to domesticity and familial life in Findley's art. For example, the 1976 drama *Can You See Me Yet?* is set in an insane asylum whereas the setting of *The Wars* (1977) is World War I. Described by critics as a powerful account of how war simultaneously defines and destroys the personality, *The Wars* relates, in documentary style, the life of Robert Ross, a Canadian soldier serving overseas who eventually succumbs to desertion, theft, and murder. In *Famous Last Words* (1981), one of Findley's best-known novels, Findley shifts his focus to World War II. Having Hugh

Selwyn Mauberly, a persona created by American poet Ezra Pound, as one of its central characters, this novel is filled with references to historical figures, including Italian dictator Benito Mussolini, German politician Joachim von Ribbentrop, Swedish-born actress Greta Garbo, and the former Duke and Duchess of Windsor. (The novel's publication in England, in fact, had to be delayed until the deaths of Edward and Wallis Simpson for fear of a libel suit.) Mauberly's fascist beliefs and "historical" writings, scrawled on the wall of his hotel room and found by American soldiers, detail a plan to depose the victors of World War II (presumably the Germans) and place the Windsors in a position from which they can rule all of Europe. This book has been praised for its commentary on history and politics, truth and reality, twentieth-century society, and corruption, themes also found in *The Butterfly Plague* (1969), which portrays 1930s Hollywood as a dystopia, and in the 1986 mystery *The Telling of Lies*. Findley's more recent works continue to incorporate themes and techniques employed in earlier writings. In *Not Wanted on the Voyage* (1984) and *Headhunter* (1993), for example, Findley draws characters from other literary works. In the former novel, Findley updates the biblical story of the great flood, Noah's ark, the Jewish god Yahweh's covenant with Noah, and the survival of the human species. In Findley's version, however, Noah is a misogynistic dictator (married to a feminist) who forbids certain species to enter the ark, thereby ensuring their extinction. Also, in this fabulistic rendering of the flood in which Noah entertains his maker with dramas and theatrics, the ark's residents include a unicorn, an angel, and a talking cat. *Headhunter* alludes to a more recent literary work, namely Joseph Conrad's *Heart of Darkness*. Though largely set in a psychiatric hospital in modern-day Toronto, in a world plagued with moral depravity, crime, and disease, *Headhunter,* like *Heart of Darkness,* focuses on the struggle of good versus evil between characters named Marlow and Kurtz. Identity and the past are central to Findley's most recent novel, *The Piano Man's Daughter* (1995), which largely concerns a Canadian man's search for clues about his pyromaniac mother and his ancestry. Findley is also known for his short stories and his work as a playwright and scriptwriter. His short stories share thematic similarities with many of his novels and have been collected in *Dinner along the Amazon* (1984) and *Stones* (1988).

Critical Reception

Regarded as a master stylist and writer of engaging fiction, Findley has been the recipient of numerous awards. In addition to the Governor General's award and numerous other prizes, he has received the Canada Council Senior Arts Award, an ANIK award for the documentary *Dieppe: 1942* (1979) and an Association of Canadian Television and Radio Artists award for *The National Dream* (1974), a series of scripts about the development of the Canadian railway system. Though Findley typically employs Canadian characters and settings, his work has found audiences throughout North America and Europe. He is often praised for his thematic interests, engaging style, and the psychological insight and acuity with which he renders his characters; his portraits of women, children, and marginalized members of society, as well as his focus on conflict and mental health, have been particularly extolled. As John F. Hulcoop has argued, among Canadian writers, Findley's "international reputation [is] second only to that of Margaret Atwood."

PRINCIPAL WORKS

The Last of the Crazy People (novel) 1967
The Paper People (teleplay) 1967
The Butterfly Plague (novel) 1969
Don't Let the Angels Fall (screenplay) 1969
The Journey (radio play) 1970
The Whiteoaks of Jalna [adaptor; from the novels by Mazo de la Roche] (teleplay) 1971-72
The National Dream [with William Whitehead] (teleplay) 1974
Can You See Me Yet? (drama) 1976
The Wars (novel) 1977
Dieppe: 1942 (teleplay) 1979
John A.—Himself! (drama) 1979
Other People's Children [with William Whitehead] (teleplay) 1980
Famous Last Words (novel) 1981
Daybreak at Pisa: 1945 (play) 1982
Strangers at the Door (radio play) 1982
*The Wars (screenplay) 1983
Dinner along the Amazon (short stories) 1984
Not Wanted on the Voyage (novel) 1984
The Telling of Lies: A Mystery (novel) 1986
Stones (short stories) 1988
Inside Memory: Pages from a Writer's Notebook (nonfiction) 1990
Headhunter (novel) 1993
The Stillborn Lover (drama) 1993
The Piano Man's Daughter (novel) 1995

*This is an adaptation of the novel of the same name.

CRITICISM

John F. Hulcoop (essay date Winter 1981)

SOURCE: "'LOOK! LISTEN! MARK MY WORDS!': Paying Attention to Timothy Findley's Fictions," in *Canadian Literature,* No. 91, Winter, 1981, pp. 22-47.

[*In the following essay, Hulcoop provides a stylisticc discussion of Findley's work, examining how Findley uses textual and sensual markers in his early fiction as a means of drawing the reader into the text.*]

> "It's all an attempt not to say what you don't want to say. You've achieved art when you cannot be misconstrued.
>
> (Timothy Findley, in *Conversations with Graeme Gibson*)

In an age of structuralist and deconstructive criticism it may be salutary for the critic to begin by reminding himself of the dangers of misconstruction—despite that cunning cartographer Harold Bloom (author of *A Map of Misreading*) who insists [in *The Anxiety of Influence*] that "[t]here are no interpretations but only misinterpretations." Susan Sontag, in a famous essay [in *Against Interpretation and Other Essays*], inveighs "against interpretation," wittily dismissing it as "the revenge of the intellect upon art." She calls upon commentators to recover their senses: "to *see* more, to *hear* more, to *feel* more." The function of criticism, says Sontag, should be "to show *how* [art] *is what it is*, even that *it is what it is*, rather than to show *what it means.*" Having defined "the aims of interpretation" and demonstrated its "validity," E. D. Hirsch reasons [in *Validity in Interpretation*] that "[u]nderstanding (and therefore interpretation, in the strict sense of the word) is both logically and psychologically prior to criticism." Interpretation is "the construction of textual meaning as such; it explicates . . . those meanings and only those meanings which the text explicitly or implicitly represents."

Conceding that "nothing in the nature of the text itself . . . requires the reader to set up the author's meaning as his normative ideal," and that the reader of any text may easily "construe meanings . . . different from the author's," Hirsch nevertheless believes—and he professes his "simple belief" in the sometimes over-zealous accents of an academic Savonarola—that "a text means what its author means" and that the "interpreter's job is to reconstruct a determinate actual meaning"—namely, the "verbal meaning" which the author "has willed to convey by a particular sequence of linguistic signs and which can be conveyed (shared) by means of those linguistic signs." *Verbal meaning* Hirsch defines as "the content of the author's intention . . . the author's verbal intention," a somewhat slippery definition compelling him to reticulate a casuistical net in order to keep what he's caught in his critical hold. To fulfill his proper function, the interpreter must be able to reconstruct "the author's subjective stance" (meaning "his disposition to engage in particular kinds of intentional acts"), must be able to describe the hori-

zon which defines the author's intention as a whole (meaning the boundary which separates "meanings of which he was explicitly conscious" as he wrote from meanings of which he was only implicitly conscious. Hirsch rejects as a contradiction in terms meanings of which an author was unconscious).

That Hirsch should look with disfavour on a large number of current critics and critical schools is not surprising. His commendation of Frye is cautious; his condemnation of Barthes is peremptory. Barthes' expansive outlook on writer, text and reader is antithetical to Hirsch's straight and narrow view of the reader as reconstructor of the author's verbal intentions. The "goal of literary work," says Barthes in *S/Z*, "is to make the reader no longer a consumer, but a producer of the text . . . . This new operation is *interpretation* (in the Nietzschean sense of the word). To interpret a text is not to give it a (more or less justified, more or less free) meaning, but on the contrary to appreciate what *plural* constitutes it." The "text is a galaxy of signifiers, not a structure of signifieds," and "the more plural the text, the less it is written before I read it. . . . If we want to remain attentive to the plural of a text . . . we must renounce structuring this text in large masses . . . no *construction* of the text: everything signifies ceaselessly and several times, but without being delegated to a great final ensemble, to an ultimate structure."

Bloom, Sontag, Hirsch and Barthes can be taken to represent the cardinal points on the critical compass I shall carry with me on my expedition into the relatively unexplored territory of Timothy Findley's fictions. Findley himself would obviously acknowledge the validity of Hirsch's viewpoint, not only because he believes that art, in order to be art, must be invulnerable to misconstruction, but also because he admits that his "biggest problem" as a writer is the fear of not having made himself clear: "I'll write the same thing into a novel several times so that by the time I've got it said, I've said it eight different ways . . . I don't trust enough—either myself or the reader." One result of Findley's anxiety is that the critic coming fresh to his work will, almost inevitably, respond like Tzvetan Todorov who begins his essay on Artaud by wondering "if it is not superfluous to interpose an exegesis between [Artaud's] text and his reader," since "Artaud said what he 'meant' so well and so abundantly." If we agree with Todorov that a "docile commentary, whose limit is paraphrase, is scarcely justified with regard to a text [or texts] whose initial comprehension does [do] not raise excessive difficulties," then we must align ourselves *with* Susan Sontag and *against* interpretation. On the other hand, if, like Barthes, we want to remain "attentive to the plural of a text"—and *attention* is a key to, a crucial term in any attempt to understand (or interpret) Findley's work—we are bound to offer readings which were not necessarily a part of the author's conscious verbal intentions (explicit or implicit) as he wrote, and which (as Bloom explains) are likely to be misreadings or misinterpretations of the author's *intentions*, though not of the *text* as it stands (or is plurally constituted).

Findley's work compels the critic to recover his senses (*see* more, *hear* more) by making direct appeals to the viewer-listener-reader through sight, sound and style.

—*John F. Hulcoop*

The plurality of Findley's texts, as in all texts, derives not only from the galaxy of verbal signifiers which "signifies ceaselessly and several times," and so creates the complexities of *mythos, ethos*, and *dianoia* (to borrow from Aristotle those terms Frye has proved so useful); the plurality derives equally from those aspects of the signifiers which (Sontag would say) appeal less to the intellect than to the senses: namely, *melos* (the element of sound analogous to the music in opera), *opsis* (the element of spectacle analogous to sets, costumes, lighting and the moulding of movement on stage in opera), and *lexis* (the element of texture, diction, or literary style which is analogous to the *tessitura* of a particular role in opera, or to the singing style—say *bel canto* as distinct from *verismo* or music-drama). The importance of sound, spectacle, and style to a full appreciation of Findley's fictions, whether they be scripts intended to be *listened to* on the radio, scripts intended to be *seen* on television, the movie-screen, or the theatre-stage, or whether they be the texts of short-stories and novels, cannot be overemphasized. His work compels the critic to recover his senses (*see* more, *hear* more) by making direct appeals to the viewer-listener-reader through sight, sound and style: these are what force us to pay attention—to look and listen and mark his words. And the need to pay attention, together with the learning how and why we need to pay attention, is an important theme in all Findley's fictions.

When the curtain rises on the garden of the old Insane Asylum at Britton, Ontario—the setting of Findley's first stage-play, *Can You See Me Yet?*—the audience is forced to look and listen:

> *The garden is empty. The sound of a radio rises in the wings; someone is singing "Where or When," by Rodgers and Hart. Thwack! A large wooden croquet ball rolls across the stage. A dog barks off stage.*

The first character to enter is Doberman, a patient who thinks he's a dog and, like man's best friend, is dumb (until the last minute of the play when he utters a single word twice and stops the central character from killing herself). The second entrance is Enid's. Hearing the dog barking off stage she says, "Yap-yap-yap. Morning, noon and night. *Listen* to 'im.

YAP-YAP-YAP-YAP! Wouldn't you think he'd lose his voice?" (italics mine). Having commanded Doberman (and, by implication, the audience since it, like the dog, cannot speak) to listen, she says, "You shouldn't stare at the sun . . . That's how people go blind. *Mark my words*: blind as a bat" (italics mine). Edward and Clare enter and sit down to play cards. Instantly, Enid interrupts: "Stop! I want attention!" The men ignore her. In the distance, "*the sound of a fire engine is heard approaching.*" Enid shouts, "THE SKY IS FALLING!" Edward tells Clare to "Pay no attention," but Enid persists: "Listen to me. Listen—there's something terrible happening." Other patients join the group; a scene breaks out and their nurse, Alma, enters, trying to calm things down by promising a surprise. "*Watch out!*" Franklin exclaims. "Miss Alma is going to surprise us" (italics mine). At which point Enid resumes her bid for attention, screaming "FIRE! FIRE! FIRE! FIRE!" Alma strikes her. Moments later, Annie enters and announces that something has happened, down by the gate: a dog has been killed. Enid says, "I told you! I warned you! But—oh, no, no. No one listened."

Long before the significantly named central character enters at the beginning of Scene Two, Findley has already made his point. He has made us look at an empty stage, listen to various sound effects, and to Enid's imitating a yapping dog and then shouting. We have heard the repeated imperatives; seen a number of characters behaving oddly and, presumably, tried to figure them out, just as we have tried to follow the non-sequential conversation of the madhouse inmates. Finally, we have been given the explicit warning, "I told you! . . . But . . . no one listened." The fact that Findley withholds Cassandra's name for five or more minutes after she first appears makes its ultimate revelation even more pointed. If we have been listening to what Enid tells us, marking her words, watching out, taking her warning seriously, then we shall certainly not need to have the significance of Cassandra's name spelled out for us.

Edward, who plays Cassandra's father in the psychodrama she acts out with the other inmates, and with Alma, says to his daughter, "You haven't changed, Cassandra. Still a question. Still a riddle." The question she embodies is the same as the play's title, a question she asks three times in the course of the drama's fifteen scenes. It is a question Findley poses in all his fictions, from **"About Effie"** to *The Wars*. It must, therefore, be crucial. So is the riddle. Like the play, which unfolds on two levels (Cassandra's recognition and acceptance of and by her fellow inmates; the psychodrama in which she re-enacts her family relationships from childhood on), the riddle is twofold: Who is the "me" of the play's title-question? or, from the subjective view-point compelled by the psychodrama, Who am *I*? And, *Is* anyone there to see me? or, from the personal point of view, *Who* is there to see me? Both question and riddle clearly relate to a central concern in Findley's work: Does anyone *care enough* to pay me any attention? And if so, *Who* cares enough? And, Do they care enough to see me and accept *me as I am*?

Ontological insecurity—together with the sometimes desperate search for a lovable and therefore acceptable identity—is a constant feature in the variable worlds of Findley fictions. In his first short-story, **"About Effie,"** the insecurity of the young narrator, Neil Cable, is displaced by his acute anxiety about his ability to make the reader identify Effie if and when he meets her:

> I don't know how to begin about Effie, but I've got to because I think you ought to know about her. Maybe you'll meet her one day, and then you'll be glad I told you all this. If I didn't, then maybe you wouldn't know what to do.

The "main thing," Neil continues, "is to watch out for her." If the reader meets an Effie and the name is uncommon), "take a good look because it might be her." She lacks easily identifiable physical characteristics, "but the way you'll know her is this: she'll look at you as if she thought you were someone she was waiting for, and it will probably scare you." (*Waiting*, which creates suspense and heightens anxiety, is another recurrent feature of Findley's fictional world.) The best way to "introduce" Effie so as we shall not forget her is obviously to tell her story; but even when he's finished telling it, Neil is still uncertain about his achievement. "So you can see what I mean. It still worries me. And that's why I want you to be sure—to be *sure*—to recognize her when you see her."

Similarly, in his second-written story, **"Harper's Bazaar,"** the insecurity is again displaced from the main character, eight-year-old Harper Dewey, to his beautiful, alcoholic mother whom he comes to identify with her jewels, which she sells for liquor, and whom he tries to pin into place forever by selling liquor-laced lemonade in order to make enough money to replace his mother's jewellery. He has been told in a letter from his father (killed in World War II) that "his 'Duty' [is] to obey his mother and always 'to love her more dearly than all the earth, dearer still than your own dear life.'" But she dies anyway, even though Harper runs away from home and spends the night in a tree "'to make my mother take attention.'" Says Bertha Millroy, the Dewey's maid, "'I guess we just didn't pray enough. . . . We went and lost her, Harper. . . . We went and lost her to the Lord.'" Gradually overwhelmed by "the deep quiet of loneliness," "the loneliness of an adult, the loneliness defined by remembrance," Harper is confronted by

> Nothing.

> That was all he could grasp. Nothing. Everything

was over—everyone went away—and finally you went away yourself.

"Nothing, as experience," according to R. D. Laing [in his *The Politics of Experience & The Bird of Paradise*], "arises as an absence of someone or something. No friends, no relationships, no pleasure, no meaning in life. . . . The list is, in principle, endless. Take anything and imagine its absence." Laing distinguishes very carefully between "the absence of relationships, and the experience of every relationship as an absence": the difference is that "between loneliness and a perpetual solitude, between provisional hope or hopelessness and a permanent state of despair." He goes on to point out that, in a world without meanings, values, sources of sustenance or help, "man, as creator, must invent, conjure up meanings and values, sustenance and succour out of nothing." But the fate of the creator, says Laing, "after being ignored, neglected, despised, is . . . to be discovered by the non-creative."

> There are sudden, apparently inexplicable suicides that must be understood as the dawn of a hope so horrible and harrowing that it is unendurable.

In *The Last of the Crazy People,* as the title suggests, Findley moves closer than in the two preceding stories to the characters and setting of *Can You See Me Yet?* What "pleases me most about my work as a novelist," Findley has stated in the Gibson interview, "is my own awareness of having that special twisted view which is a dependence on the insane people to do sane things. The ultimate sanity comes from the insane, I believe. Now—be careful! What I mean is—we call the *sane* insane.' In fiction you have to heighten this, treat it symbolically." In *Crazy People,* Findley moves closer to his own confrontation with the kind of nothingness that Harper Dewey glimpses, that R. D. Laing sees as a symptom of ontological insecurity, and that Hooker Winslow, eleven-year-old protagonist of Findley's first novel, faces in the novel's Prologue and obliterates in its Epilogue.

The structure of this first novel is clearly significant: from the Prologue to the Epilogue, Hooker is waiting, alone—"a perpetual solitude." The intervening chapters form a single, extended flashback, a "loneliness defined by remembrance." The dawn described in the Prologue does what Findley says fiction must do; it heightens, by symbolizing, "the dawn of a hope so horrible . . . that it is unendurable." The light (and maybe what "we" call sanity) begins to break in Hooker's mind when he hears his aunt talking to his father about his brother, Gilbert: "'They're going to hold a shotgun over your son, and you just sit there!'" This prompts Hooker to steal the pistol that belonged to John Harris (killed in World War I): "When Gilbert needed a gun, it would be there . . . for him to use when he got in trouble. Then Gilbert would know that he had thought of him kindly." Gilbert, however, commits suicide (a "sudden, apparently inexplicable" suicide), and Hooker, attending the inquest, hears the verdict: "Death by his own hand"—presumably "while of unsound mind." His father is mortally shamed by Gilbert's suicide. "'One of us has killed himself.... It's like having a bloody gun at your head all the time.'" By which point in the novel, Hooker has already seen the light (his mother is a psychopathic recluse; his father is figuratively impotent; his aunt lives in the past; his brother is mentally handicapped; and Hooker suspects that he himself is homosexual): "'I think that we are crazy people,' said Hooker. 'Like those crazies in the asylum. We have a crazy mother, don't we?... It's like a whole list of crazy people, and we're the last of them.'" His brother's suicide is all the confirmation he needs. He holes up in the loft of the stable (which is where we leave him waiting in the Prologue): "Somehow, in the *stable*, they would have to come to *him*" (italics mine). His family will have to search for Hooker. When they do, in the Epilogue, he guns them down and is committed to an insane asylum. Iris, the Winslow's maid and Hooker's closest companion, is told it's best to think of him dead—another of those "sudden, apparently inexplicable suicides that must be understood as the dawn of a hope so horrible ... it is unendurable." As Findley explained to Gibson, with reference to a story he heard of a child who killed one of his parents, his sister and someone else staying in the house: "I was thunderstruck by what I considered the beauty ... of his statement when someone ... said to him: Can you tell me why you did it? He said, Because I loved them so. And for me, that's all he needed to say."

Any attempt to reconstruct Findley's "subjective stance" in relation to a number of given texts returns the attentive reader to his preoccupation with loneliness. As a child, he confesses to [Donald] Cameron [*Conversations with Canadian Novelists*],

> I had no interest in other children, maybe because I was often sick and had no tie with what other kids were doing.... I spent a lot of time with the maid, or just plain by myself, so it got that I sort of feared other kids.... Nothing but surface communication. I was sent to boarding school during the worst part of the war ... my brother got sick ... I was left there all by myself and my mother could hardly ever come to see me. Dad was at war and I just felt—abandoned.

But the loneliness was not confined to his childhood. Asked by Gibson if he enjoys writing, Findley replied that he loves it but hates "all the other stuff that goes with it," meaning loneliness. Though he alludes to Mann's *Death in Venice* because it shows that loneliness has its positive side, Findley concludes that "loneliness perverts":

> I wouldn't attempt to say anything more than lone-

liness perverts, and this is very disturbing, very upsetting and you have to go through that to be a writer ... the way you live very often cuts you off from people that you shouldn't be cut off from.... You're intellectually lonely: no one—hardly anyone "understands" you, because your whole life—maybe I should say your whole existence is an intensified searching—not for your own identity—but for your *work's* identity.

Like Harper Dewey and Hooker Winslow, James Reid Taylor, principal character in *The Paper People*, a film-script written for television in 1967, has an unhappy childhood, was "a lonely boy" born about "eight friends behind everyone else." Taylor, a contemporary artist who expresses "with increasing violence ... his distaste for contemporary life," is the subject of a TV documentary being researched and written by Janet Webb, a fictional TV producer. Janet's "filmic inquiry"—the containing subject of *The Paper People*—is a quest for the identity of Jamie Taylor as revealed in his work: his "work's identity." Jamie's current mode is to make life-size and lifelike models of his friends out of *papier-maché*, and then to burn them ritualistically, reducing both his art and his paper people "to ashes—the ultimate symbol of emptiness." Janet, in the course of compiling her documentary, uncovers important aspects of Taylor's life he would prefer to keep secret but which she insists on including. He reacts by calling her a killer: "I knew you were a killer the moment I laid eyes on those cold, cold hips of yours." Like Hooker, and "[l]ike to the Egyptian thief at point of death," both Jamie and Janet "kill" what they love. The search for and assertion of identity—even the work's identity—results in its extermination: self-consciousness paralyses the self. The quester is left feeling unattended to in innominate loneliness; or, if the critic is quester, he is left to face his own failure and the fact that, as Wordsworth warns, "We murder to dissect."

Not coincidentally, one of the major sequences (entitled "BANG-BANG") in *The Paper People* includes a discussion of the sniper in the tower on the University of Texas campus who shot fifteen and wounded thirty other people. Janet asks why anyone must be killed, "Why kill at all?" "To make a statement," answers one of Jamie's friends, "... what other *new* way is there to express something?"

TONYA: You're setting up killers as artists.

MARCO: Or artists as killers ...

WILFRID: ... Suicide and assassination are the new art forms ....

MARCO: ... All you have to do is look at *In Cold Blood*.

HAROLD: (DREAMILY) Yes,—and those nurses in Chicago,—and Austin,—and Dallas! They're all sort of pointless, unless the point is to say something.

JAMIE: With style.

When Janet objects, reminding them that human lives are at issue here, Marco, who has seen one of Janet's documentaries in which she exposes a distinguished neuro-surgeon as an alcoholic, says, "I've seen you assassinate in your quiet lady-like way!" Suicide, homicide and/or assassination, real or figurative, are not uncommon events in Findley's fictional world over which hangs the "allure of violence" which is also seen to hang in the air over Cheeverland, his satirical model of the United States. After he has seen Lee Harvey Oswald shot, on television, Hooker asks Gilbert what "assassinate" means. "'Usually it's killing for a bigger reason than plain ordinary murder,'" Gilbert explains. "'Like Kennedy and Abe Lincoln and the Archduke Ferdinand. . . . [T]hey decided . . . if they killed the Archduke, that would make something happen. Cause attention and division.'" James Reid Taylor burns his paper people in public; the "fires are what draw public attention to him and, thus, Janet's interest in putting his world on film."

Of the many images people use to describe "ways in which identity is threatened"—being buried, drowned, dragged down into quicksand—that which "recurs repeatedly" (according to Laing) is fire:

> Fire may be the uncertain flickering of the individual's own inner aliveness. It may be a destructive alien power which will devastate him. Some psychotics say in the acute phase that they are on fire, that their bodies are being burned up. A patient describes himself as cold and dry. Yet he dreads any warmth or wet. He will be engulfed by the fire or the water, and either way be destroyed.

This last sentence is immediately relevant to Robert Ross in *The Wars,* who first fears death by drowning and finally dies as a result of injuries sustained in fire; but Laing's observation illuminates more generally the recurrence of fire as event, image and symbol in Findley's fictions.

Gilbert Winslow slams his Jaguar into a tree and is instantly immolated: "Gilbert, on fire, lay back like Peter crucified, hooked by his feet to the cross of the motor car, his arms spread out in a hopeless gesture." The first sequence in *The Paper People* (described entirely in terms of visuals without any dialogue) is a junkyard in which James Reid Taylor's *papier-maché* doll of Tonya is being burned; fire is what draws the public's attention to his work; with fire he reduces both art and life to ashes, "the ultimate symbol of empti-

ness"—of nothingness. For Ruth Damorosch, in *The Butterfly Plague,* 1938 "had been a year of fires. Real fires, imaginary fires, symbolic fires. All burning—all eating—most of them conjuring death." The first fire is a small fire on Topanga Beach, where she lives. By the time she finds it, it is only embers: "There was nothing sinister in the fire at all." But she removes from the ashes "a small piece of blue material" which turns out to be a *memento mori,* the remains of a bathing suit belonging to a girl whose naked body is later washed ashore: the first of many deaths, violent and pacific, in Findley's second novel. The second fire provides the climax and conclusion to the novel's first book: the fire in Alvarez Canyon, due north of Santa Monica, a tourist beauty-spot "known around the globe," and proclaimed "'Paradise'" by the visiting public. Approximately forty acres in area, Alvarez Canyon is a cunning mixture of natural and artificial: "In order to preserve the atmosphere of Paradise in all weathers, some portions of Alvarez were quite unreal. The plants in these places were made of specially treated fabrics and rubber. Thus when elsewhere the acacia leaves were falling they did not fall down in Alvarez." But Paradise is lost at the end of Book One, totally destroyed by fire: "The sanctuary was to become a charnel house." Standing outside the gates of Paradise—their poses a "[s]tillness in the holocaust"—Ruth, her mother, father, brother, and several other characters, turn back to watch the terror, panic and suffering of all the animals trapped inside the sanctuary, "fleeing mindlessly in concerted directions, not knowing what death was, but smelling death—not knowing what fire was, but being burned. Some turned back into the furnace. Some others crept into the flaming trees. Some attempted impossible flight into the sky":

> Naomi said, "They will all die."
>
> And Ruth said. "Pay attention." . . .
>
> "Pay attention. Listen. Watch. Attention . . . .
>
> In the ghettos of Paradise, four thousand creatures had perished.
>
> Against a wall . . . .
>
> Surely someone was there to see it and to pay attention.

Clearly, the fire in Alvarez Canyon is proleptic; in its flames Findley prefigures the fate of the Jews in the German crematoria (the dream of a pure and perfect Aryan race and the evils of Naziism being, of course, a central subject in this novel). Near the end of *The Butterfly Plague,* Ruth sets fire to her dead brother's house wanting to raze to the ground the softly seductive, sweetly dangerous dreams of impossible perfection her brother's life has housed. And the final chronicle in this novel composed of seventeen separate chronicles is entitled "The Fire Chronicle." "We know that history repeats itself." In September of 1968, Ruth's orphaned daughter, Lisa, meets the son of another character on Topanga Beach. They smell smoke. "'Fire is dangerous,'" says Lisa. They go to look for it. "This makes an interesting conclusion," says the narrator. "As always. And thus, this chronicle is over—the last of the chronicles of the Butterfly Plague. The first of the Fire Plague. And . . ." [Findley's ellipsis]. Though the novel stops after one more sentence (which tells that Lisa and the boy don't find the fire), the ellipsis after the additive conjunction invites the reader to anticipate another story chronicling the Fire Plague, which is precisely what Findley's third novel is and does. But between *The Butterfly Plague* and *The Wars* comes the long short-story, **"Hello Cheeverland, Goodbye,"** which has little directly to do with fire until the very last sentence.

Two epigraphs precede **"Hello Cheeverland, Goodbye,"** one from John Cheever's *Bullet Park* (in response to which this story was written) and another from Nicholas Fagan's *Essays and Conversations*. Fagan suggests that Cheever's fictional world is so true-to-life and all-absorbing that people have started forsaking New York, New Jersey and Connecticut in order to "take up residence inside his books . . . they've foundered in this place called Cheeverland." Findley's story (which cannot be summarized because it has no plot) creates a Lilliputian model of Cheeverland located somewhere on Long Island, with a view of the Sound and the sight of William F. Buckley Junior's home on the far shore. The cast of characters is extensive, including another in the significant series of Findley maids, and a young man "innocent of all experience save imagination. . . . Call him Ishmael. . . . He has come a long way to Cheeverland, from Toronto." He has come to the house of Arthur and Alicia Anderson ("on their way up in the world of television") because they want to turn his novel, *Blackwater Falls*, into a "'Film of the Week' (not the same as a FILM)." Ishmael stays in the maid's old room. "After the events in Memphis [in 1968] a meeting was held [of the blacks in Cheeverland regarding those who worked as live-in servants in white folks' houses] and the decision was made to move out. It was one thing to work there and to eat there, but quite another to sleep there, and so their bedrooms . . . were abandoned." Clyde, lover of Rosetta, the Anderson maid, is a leader of "this movement" among the blacks, and he persuades Rosetta to carry a gun. On Saturday morning, his second day in Cheeverland, Ishmael wakes and hears a "distant narrative of fire and lemonade": Rosetta is telling Alicia about "a fire in the night, downtown, and even now the soldiers and the fireman are sifting through the ashes for the victims." Apart from references to Professor Dinstitch, another character who, as a younger man, helped to invent the atomic bomb, Findley lets fire drop until the final sentence which reads: "On Monday Rosetta comes up coatless in the morning, but the fires have moved up be-

fore her and these pages already burn." The revolution, it seems, has already started, and the illusory pseudo-liberal world of Cheeverland browns and crumbles in the reader's hands. Feeling the heat, he drops it, watching it (Findley's art, and life itself) reduced to ashes, ultimate symbol of nothingness.

The Wars begins and ends with fire (even though it is also full of images of water, earth and air, a fact to which the inscription on Robert Ross's gravestone alerts readers):

> *Robert Ross comes riding straight towards the camera. His hat has fallen off. His hands are knotted to the reins. They bleed. The horse is black and wet and falling. Robert's lips are parted. He leans along the horse's neck. His eyes are blank. There is mud on his cheeks and forehead and his uniform is burning—long, bright tails of flame are streaming out behind him. He leaps through the memory without a sound. The archivist sighs. Her eyes are lowered above some book. There is a strand of hair in her mouth. She brushes it aside and turns the page. You lay the fiery image, back in your mind and let it rest. You know it will obtrude again and again until you find its meaning—here.*

The "fiery image" of Robert burning on horseback, "tails of flame . . . streaming out behind him," is carefully paralleled by a watery image of Robert, after he has nearly drowned, swimming on horseback, "almost submerged with his clothes flowing back. . . . Pegasus." Both images are simultaneously elemental and mythical; and attention is drawn, directly or indirectly, to both aspects of both images; directly, in the single-word sentence "Pegasus"; indirectly, with reference to the "fiery image" of Robert, which has to be seen in its chronological context at the end of the novel, the four final sections of Part Five beginning, "Here is where the mythology is muddled." What is important, quite apart from what these images signify in relation to the plot (*mythos*), to Robert's character (*ethos*), and to the thematic content of the novel (*dianoia*), is the fact that in both cases the narrator compels the reader to look at the image (*opsis*), and to hear how the image sounds (*melos*), and carefully to mark his words (*lexis*). From first to last, the unspecified narrator of ***The Wars*** makes his presence felt, addressing the reader, directing the reader's attention, compelling him to mark the narrator's words in a particular way (one may even wonder, at moments, if the unspecified narrator is not a personification of Findley's anxiety about being misconstrued, about not making himself clear, about trusting—or not trusting—the reader).

"You lay the fiery image back in your mind and let it rest. You know it will obtrude again and again until you find its meaning—here." The deictics are tricky since we cannot be

sure if the "you" is really reflexive—the narrator as fictional researcher hypothesizing someone engaged in the same process as himself—or whether he is addressing the reader directly and casting him in a role parallel to the narrator's own. Similarly, the adverb "here" may refer specifically to an *imaginary* photograph (since, so far as we know, no photographer is present to take pictures when Robert breaks out of the fired barn) which the narrator is describing; or, if the "you" is addressed to the reader, "here" could mean "in this image, in this passage of this novel"—or "in this image, *in its proper context* in this novel." The shades of difference in meaning are complementary rather than contradictory. Clearly, the attentive reader now knows that whatever "meaning" (the "author's verbal intention") he is to take from the novel inheres in this "fiery image"—even though the reader must remain attentive to the plurality of the text, aware that everything signifies ceaselessly and several times, that the "fiery image" is only one of the several ways in which the same story is told, simultaneously and sequentially; and is itself a microcosm of the single story which is projected in other elements and *mythoi*, severally and at the same time.

When Robert tries to save the horses at the end of ***The Wars*** (an action which involves the killing of Captain Leather which, in turn, compels him to become a deserter, to shoot Private Cassles and, in some eyes, to become a renegade horse-thief) he fulfills the proper function of a soldier which he wrongly attributes to the unnamed soldier in the early scene in which Teddy Budge is called in to kill Rowena's rabbits after her death. When Robert sees Budge, it takes him "thirty seconds to emerge from his pain and to realize why Teddy Budge was there." Robert turns to the soldier and yells "something like: 'you bastard! Bastard! What are soldiers for?'" The young man's question obviously expects the answer, "To protect the defenceless," not "To kill." *That* answer is something Robert has to learn ("What he wanted was a model. Someone who could teach him, by example, how to kill"). Ironically, his action at the end of the novel repeats the unknown soldier's in the very attempt to do what the latter did not do: protect the defenceless (horses). Robert's final acts are, therefore, open to interpretation, both negative and positive. As the researcher-narrator discovers, when he interviews World War I veterans, and asks about Robert, "they look away." Others weep when he says "'Tell me about the horses.'" And yet others say "'that bastard!'" Marian Turner states simply: "'My opinion was—he was a hero . . . he did the thing that no one else would dare to think of doing.'" Juliet d'Orsey, who falls in love with Robert when she is only twelve, and who looks after him after he's wounded until he dies, asserts neither *hero* nor *bastard*. She says:

> "So what it was we were denied [in the war] was to be ordinary. All our ordinary credos and expectations vanished. *Vanished*. There was so much death.

No one can imagine. These were not *accidents*—or the quiet, expected deaths of the old. These were murders. By the thousands. All your friends were . . . murdered."

The death of Captain Leather is, then, no different from that of Clive d'Orsey, died July 1st, 1916, in the Battle of the Somme; or of Rodwell who walks out into No Man's Land and blows his brains out; or of Clifford Purchas, shot in the back as a deserter; or of the friendly German sniper whom Robert shoots in a moment of panic; or of Robert himself who dies of wounds sustained while performing what he has thought the duty of a soldier ought to be.

In the same way, the "fiery image" is open to both positive and negative interpretations. For the disinterested reader of fiction, it is striking evidence of Findley's imagination; for those who enjoy projecting themselves into fictional worlds, the "fiery image" is a beautiful, Phoenix-like metaphor for the spirit of self-sacrifice embodied in Robert (and all those like him); and for the hope of a whole generation that believed it was fighting the war to end all wars, a hope reduced to ashes in the prolonged and senseless front-line slaughter but resurrected repeatedly in the human heart because it *is* human. For those whose view of human nature is less optimistic (and Findley's view, as revealed in interviews if not in fictions, inclines to be less optimistic), the "fiery image" may well suggest what Laing sees as the recurring image for the threatened identity of the psychotic in the acute stage. This negative interpretation is certainly supported by other aspects of the text, quite apart from the fact that, just before he shoots Leather, Robert's anger rises to such a pitch that he fears he is "going over into madness"; and Major Mickle, responsible for arresting Robert, decides that he is "plainly . . . dealing with a man gone mad." Juliet d'Orsey links Robert with Eugene Taffler and Jamie Villiers: all three become the lover of Barbara d'Orsey who "'had a taste for heroes and athletes. She enjoyed the spectacle of winning.'" Ironically, Taffler, Villiers and Robert are all losers; all suffer extensive injuries in battle. Taffler, the David-like stone-thrower, loses both his arms and tries to kill himself in hospital. Jamie, like Robert, dies of his burns. Robert first sees Barbara when, with Taffler on her arm, she visits Villiers in the hospital where Robert is keeping vigil at Harris's bedside. The visit is brief.

> When they'd gone Robert could feel the man in bandages [Villiers] 'screaming' and the sensation of this silent agony at the other end of the room was so strong that Robert had to go and get one of the nurses. . . . She told him the man had been trapped in a fire and his vocal cords destroyed when he'd swallowed the flames.

Later, Juliet comments on her sister's visit to Villiers:

"Her silence in Jamie's presence. Was it cruel? Of course it was. Not to let him hear her voice. Nothing was left of him, you know. Nothing but nerves and pain and his mind. No voice—no flesh. Nothing. Just his *self*. Later, as you'll see, this forms a sort of pattern . . . well—a very definite pattern." [Findley's ellipsis]

(Here, again, the narrator through Juliet directs reader-attention, compelling us to mark these words in a particular way: to look for a specific pattern.) Robert, like Villiers, is reduced to nothing, to nerve, pain, mind—his *self*, essenced in two words "'Not yet'": "according to the medical testimony—there was virtually no hope that he would ever walk or see or be capable of judgement again." The narrator describes another photo of him, "taken about a year before his death. He wears a close-fitting cap rather like a toque—pulled down over his ears. He has no eyebrows—his nose is disfigured and bent and his face is a mass of scar tissue. . . . Robert is looking directly at the camera."

"*Robert comes riding straight towards the camera*": here, near the beginning of the book, the circle is opened. By the end, "Robert is looking directly at the camera": here the circle is almost closed. "'These are the circles—all drawing inward to the thing Robert did.'" Robert died, his life

> obscured by violence. Lawrence was hurled against a wall—Scott entombed in ice and wind—Mallory blasted on the face of Everest. Lost. We're told Euripides was killed by dogs—and this is all we know. The flesh was torn and scattered—*eaten*. Ross was *consumed* by fire. These are like statements: '*pay attention!*' [First two italics mine.]

The narrator instructs the reader how to pay attention: "You begin at the archives with photographs. Robert and Rowena . . . . Boxes and boxes of snapshots and portraits; maps and letters; cablegrams and clippings from the papers. All you have to do is sign them out and carry them across the room . . . a whole age lies in fragments underneath the lamps. *The war to end all wars*. . . . You hold your breath." You look at the images and listen to the narrator. A series of pictures of 1915: the "year itself looks sepia and soiled." Then comes April, Ypres and six thousand dead. "This is where the pictures alter—fill up with soldiers—horses—wagons. Everyone is waving either at the soldiers or the cameras. More and more people want to be seen . . . want to be remembered." Troops marching down Yonge Street, Sir Sam Hughes taking the salute. Then the "fiery image" of Robert (imagined, in italics); then a series of family photographs: "*Thomas Ross and Family . . . Rowena . . . Mother and Miss Davenport . . . Meg—a Patriotic Pony . . . Peggy Ross with Clinton Brown.*" A picture of the ocean, taken on a trip to England, with a small white dot which is "clearly . . . an iceberg" (conjuring

thoughts of 1912 and that archetypal Canadian image, the *Titanic*).

Two more photos, one early, one late, and the circle is completed. The early one was obviously taken at the end of Robert's training, before he embarked for England:

> Robert Raymond Ross—Second Lieutenant, C.F.A.
>
> He is wearing his uniform. Nothing yet is broken down . . . .
>
> *Dead men are serious*—that's what this photograph is striving to say. Survival is precluded. Death is romantic—got from silent images. I lived—was young—and died. But not real death, of course, because I'm standing here alive with all these lights that shine so brightly in my eyes. . . . *He died for King and Country*—fighting the war to end all wars.
>
> 5 x 9 and framed in silver.

The last picture was taken even earlier and returns us to the beginning: "begin at the archives with photographs. Robert and Rowena":

> The archivist closes her book. . . . It is time to tell us all to go. . . . You begin to arrange your research in bundles—letters—photos—telegrams . This is the last thing you see before you put on your overcoat:
>
> *Robert and Rowena with Meg*: Rowena seated astride the pony—Robert holding her in place. On the back is written, 'Look! You can see our breath.' And you can.

Just as early and late are transposed (the last thing you see is what you began with), so are life and death (Robert standing there alive in his uniform long after he has died); but Robert's death is "not real" because, of course, his life is only imagined (as a novel by Findley). What never really lived can never really die. He exists in a continuous fictional present and only in a series of images—some fiery, some watery, some earthy (Robert in the whore-house, in the dugout), some airy: "'Look! You can see our breath.'" And the attentive reader *can*, if he uses his imagination (Pegasus); if he remains attentive to the text's plurality, has marked the narrator's words with care, he will also understand that the visible breath of Robert and Rowena, which makes them appear so lifelike, is simultaneously an image of death. "'Be quiet,'" says Robert to his men, trapped in the crater under the eye of the German sniper, "and as he said it, he saw in front of them the dreadful phenomenon that could give them all away. His breath." "'Birth I can give you—but life I cannot,'" his mother tells Robert just before he joins up. "'I can't keep anyone alive. Not any more.' . . . This was the last time they breathed in one another's presence." "Rowena and his father and his mother and the whole of his past life—birth and death and childhood. He could breathe them in and breathe them out."

Harris, dying of pneumonia, "said the strangest things. . . . Strange and provocative. Robert didn't know, sometimes, what to do with Harris's sentences: where to fit them in his mind, or how to use them." Having drawn attention to Harris's strange sentences, the narrator makes the reader listen more carefully:

> 'Then I'd slide. Like a seal. Out of the air and into the water. Out of my world and into theirs. And I'd stay there hours. Or so it seemed. I'd think: *I never have to breathe again.* I've changed. It changes you.' . . . And in his sleep his hands would move . . . as if he dreamt of swimming—or of 'breathing' in the other element. . . . 'In that place—there—in *that* element—somehow I was safe—even from choking. . . . But once I'd landed on the shore . . . I nearly died. In the air. . . . in the air . . .

Lying in his bunk, in the dugout, listening to his batman's harsh breathing, Robert is reminded of Harris,"—and that was the last thing he needed reminding of' (since Harris has died). "All he wanted was a dream. Escape. . . . Dreams and distance are the same. If he could run away . . . Like Longboat" [Findley's ellipsis]. Longboat, the Indian marathon runner, is Robert's childhood hero, and he himself is really "a long distance runner." During training at Lethbridge, Robert runs every night by himself. Running, he loses all sense of time. "There was nothing to be won but distance." "Distance was safety. Space was asylum."

From the Prologue until the antepenultimate section of the novel, Robert is on the run (just as Hooker is waiting), trying to put a safe space between himself (his self) and all that threatens destruction. Dreaming of distance, he runs toward asylum; but, like Cassandra's, in the final scene of *Can You See Me Yet?*, Robert's airy dream is dashed or drowned in the mud, destroyed by fire:

> Brothers and sisters: there should be a place to go for safety: asylum, and there's not. There is no safety—none for love, or for the mind. . . . I've failed. I couldn't make a place for safety. *I should be asylum, and I'm not.* . . . Why can't I help? Why can't I get beyond the fire? . . . The world is ending all around us, and we need each other now. And yet there is no sanctuary. Nowhere. None. In all the world. In all the width and breadth and depth of the human heart—where there is room for sanctuary— there is none. I know, because there is none in mine.

In order to know what nothingness is, says Laing, take anything—distance, safety, sanctuary, asylum—and imagine its absence. Even the old asylum at Britton offers no sanctuary. As Alma informs us, in September of 1939 (ominous and symbolic date), it "was destroyed by fire. Cassandra Wakelin died. But . . . she did not die alone. As she had lived." Equally ironic is the fact that, when Robert, near the end of the book, goes to the *Asile Desolé*, where mad Van Gogh was once an inmate and where, in the war, the officers are allowed to take a bath, he is raped by a gang of men he assumes are "crazies" but who turn out to be "his fellow soldiers."

Cassandra cries out that she cannot get beyond the fire. Earlier in the play, like a psychotic in the acute phase, she has declared "I am fire." At Verdun, the Germans used a new weapon, the flame-thrower: "Men . . . carrying tanks of fire on their backs . . . spread the fire with hoses. Water burned and snow went up in smoke. Nothing remained." A silent image, Robert leaps through the memory as a human torch on horseback. Beyond the fire, he is nothing. He is made one with the elements (like the tormented Empedocles whose final leap takes him under the volcano); but the elements themselves, in the infernal world of the wars, suffer unnatural changes and become one: the air is "filled with a fine, grey powder" that turns into mud; men and horses "drowned in mud"; the only water lies "out in the marsh beyond the flaming hedgerows"; gasoline spreads "through the town in rivers of fire."

> Fire storms raged along the front. Men were exploded where they stood—blown apart by the combustion. . . . Wells and springs of water were plugged and stopped by the bodies of men . . . who had gone there for safety. The storms might last for hours— until the clay was baked and the earth was seared and sealed with fire.

Fire, asserts Gaston Bachelard, is "a privileged phenomenon which can explain anything"—and everything; "it is one of the principles of universal explanation." Certainly, a reading of *The Psychoanalysis of Fire* provides a most provocative commentary not only on the "fiery image" in *The Wars,* but also on the phenomenon of fire in all Findley's work. In addition to making the predictable examination of "Sexualized Fire"—"the connecting link for all symbols"—Bachelard comes in his "Conclusion" to identify fire with imagination which "works at the summit of the mind like a flame." *"You lay the fiery image back in your mind . . . until you find its meaning—here"* in the *mind,* in the imagination, that realm to which the winged-horse, Pegasus, transports us. And it is here, in the imagination—with its creative and destructive powers, its complex processes and seemingly simple productions, its instrumentality in enabling the individual to perceive and comprehend, or to distort and run away from, reality—that we confront the primary concern of Findley's imagination, just as (in the works of the greatest writers) narrative is the ultimate theme of narrative, and literature is the first (but not only) context in which to understand the nature of literature.

What Frye says of "the dislocations of narrative" in *Tristram Shandy: "they take our attention away from *looking at* the external situation"—i.e., the story—"to *listening to* the process of its coming into being in the author's mind"—i.e., the imaginative process or discourse. In other words, the almost continuous presence of the narrator in *The Wars*—even in Part Three in which the sections are dated and clocked, rather than simply numbered, so that we are made to feel the narrator was also an eyewitness to these events, documenting or logging them as they occurred—keeps pulling the reader's attention away from what Frye calls "the internal fiction" which is of "primary interest" in the fictional modes, and making him refocus on the external fiction, the relationship established by writer with reader, which "cuts across the story" and is of primary interest in thematic modes of literature. But Findley's "writer" or "narrator" demands a great deal from his relationship with the reader, commanding him to look and listen simultaneously: the story of Robert Ross is shown as a series of photographs or pictures (with which we can do nothing, if not *look* at them); but, at the same time, the narrator is busy telling us about the Archives, the archivist, his progress as a researcher, his methodology, his interviews with Marian Turner and his taping sessions with Juliet d'Orsey, all of which we must *listen* to.

Findley and his narrators are, in some ways, reminiscent of Woolf and at least one of her characters: Bernard in *The Waves*. (Allusions to Woolf appear in **"Hello Cheeverland, Goodbye."** In *The Wars* she appears as a character, a friend of Clive d'Orsey. Juliet records in her diary that "Mrs. Woolf is my idol.") Bernard, who distrusts "'neat designs of life,'" speculates on his problems as a would-be novelist: "'But if there are no stories, what end can there be, or what beginning? Life is not susceptible perhaps to the treatment we give it when we try to tell it.'" Findley's story, **"Losers, Finders: Strangers at the Door,"** opens with what appears to be a lyric poem (and Woolf's fictions, in particular *The Waves*, have frequently been called "poems" or "lyrical novels"):

> Some lives
> are only seen
> through windows
> beyond which
> the appearance
> of laughter
> and of screaming
> is the same.

The second section continues: "2 . . . there are no beginnings,

not even to stories. There are only places where you make an entrance . . . and either stay or turn and go away." The final section reads: "18 . . . nor are there endings. Even to stories. There are only places where you exit from another life. Or turn again and stay. Not knowing why" (Findley's ellipses).

Beginning his summing up in *The Waves*, Bernard says, "'in order to make you understand, to give you my life, I must tell you a story.'" But, tired of stories and neat designs of life, he looks for some new form of narrative "'more in accordance with those moments of humiliation and triumph that come now and then.'" What delights him is the confusion of cloud-formations, ever changing, always in motion:

> "Of story, of design, I do not see a trace then.
>
> But, meanwhile, while we eat let us turn over these scenes as children turn over the pages of a picture-book . . . and I will add, for your amusement, a comment in the margin."

Findley's fascination with stories told in the form of pictures (as in picture-books and films) is obvious. Much of his own story-telling has been done in the medium of television, and a great part of the TV script consists quite literally of visuals, instructions as to how a "scene" or sequence" should be shot, from what angle, what distance, what the individual "frame" (or picture) should include, what objects should be prominent, how the sequence should be separated from or attached to what follows, and so on. In fact, he won more recognition in Canada for his work on *Whiteoaks of Jalna* and *The National Dream* than he did for his first two novels. That *The Paper People,* one of his most important TV film-scripts, should be a TV film about the making of a TV film only intensifies by dramatizing Findley's profound interest in the pictorial modes of narrative. He has also written a film-script for the National Film Board, worked as a script-writer in Hollywood, and is currently engaged in translating *The Wars* into a film-script. *The Butterfly Plague,* set in Hollywood in the first three decades of this century, is very much a novel about movie-making and the impact of the "talking pictures" on people's private lives and political dreams.

But *The Butterfly Plague* is cast in the form of "chronicles" by a chronicler who is anything but unobtrusive and effects a reader-response very similar to that effected by Part Three of *The Wars*. The fourth chronicle of Book Two is entitled "The Chronicle of Evelyn de Foe," one of the new-wave Hollywood starlets. Even the minimally attentive reader is bound to think at once of the Diaries of John Evelyn, and of Daniel Defoe's *Journal of the Plague Year*, a literary forerunner of the year of the butterfly plague recounted in Findley's second novel. Like Bernard, Findley's narrator (and

Findley himself as author of TV scripts) turns over scenes like the pages of a book and directs his audience's attention to the pictures by providing comments in the margin. These comments pull attention away from the story—which every picture tells—and redirects it to the imaginative process by which that story comes into being in the story-teller's mind. Even in his plays, which have strongly literary texts, Findley's thematic concern is largely with looking, as the title *Can You See Me Yet?* indicates. *John A.—Himself!*, the title of his second play, is equally indicative of Findley's preoccupation: namely, the desire to rescue Sir John A. Macdonald, first Prime Minister of Canada, from the great mound of public myths, legends and stories beneath which the private individual has been buried—a passionate desire to make the audience look at and see the man *himself*. And he accomplishes this aim by resorting to many more *spectacular* theatrical effects than he employs in *Can You See Me Yet?*

Findley's theatrical and dramatic talents tend toward the operatic, toward music-drama, a combination of words (or lyrics) and music—and spectacle on a grand scale which, in terms of writing, *is* style.
        —John F. Hulcoop

Like Woolf, and like Oscar Wilde (alluded to in *The Last of the Crazy People,* where he is also quoted, and in *The Wars*), Timothy Findley is a stylist in the same way that Sheila Watson (*The Double Hook*) and Marian Engel (*Bear*) are stylists, but that Robertson Davies (*Fifth Business*) and Margaret Atwood (*Lady Oracle*) are not. "In all important matters, style, not sincerity, is the essential. In all unimportant matters, style, not sincerity, is the essential." Frivolous though Wilde's epigrams may often appear, their truthfulness is taken seriously and fruitfully applied to literary issues by perceptive critics like Frye and Sontag. Wilde, a true descendant of another great aesthetician, Schiller, believed that "Art begins with abstract decoration," which explains why he declares that "art is at once surface and symbol. Those who go beneath the surface do so at their own peril." Only "the superficial qualities last"; and "only shallow people . . . do not judge by appearances. The mystery of the world is the visible, not the invisible." Style is surface and surface *is* symbol; style is what makes the imagined world visible in Findley's fictions, enabling us to see and therefore understand. Style is what Frye calls "ornamental speech" (as distinct from "persuasive speech," the other arm of rhetoric) which "acts on its hearers statically, leading them to admire its own beauty or wit." Developing a mature style takes time; and the chances are that, in risking the venture of style, a writer (like Wilde and Woolf) may well be accused by hostile critics of literary affectation, of sacrificing profound substance to superficial artifice. Findley has inevitably suffered

this fate. Arguing that some subjects "have a built-in intransigence to literary treatment," Michael Taylor, reviewing *The Wars,* reasons that, because Findley "realizes he's dealing with intractable material, . . . he camouflages the fiction of his story by pretending that the novel is a species of historical document." At the same time that he accuses Findley of disguising fiction as history, Taylor illogically explains Findley's failure in *The Wars* by referring us to "the clipped, portentous style" and the fact that this "Hemingwayesque style pitches over into sentimentality."

Nice work if you can get it—but few of us can, both have our critical cake and eat it. In the first place, Findley's style is not like Hemingway's, which may be "clipped" but, if clipped, is not "portentous." In the second, Findley's very conscious development and deployment of style draws attention to the fact that what we are reading *is* fiction, just as his narrative dislocations compel acknowledgement of the imaginative process by which the fiction is brought into being. From his earliest story to his most recent novel, Findley has worked toward perfecting a style that is unmistakably his own—a marvellous mixture of the lyric and dramatic that can be put to narrative purposes. A simple example from **"About Effie"** comes at the end of a scene in which the mysterious maid tells Neil Cable about the man she's waiting for to come and carry her off. A thunderstorm is in progress, which precipitates Effie's telling about the man: "'There has to be thunder, or he won't come.'" The scene ends as follows:

> And it rained and it rained and it rained.
> But there was no more thunder.
> That was over.

The short sentences and abbreviated paragraphs are characteristic. They function in a number of ways: they isolate actions, events, thoughts, emotions, images, or whatever Findley wants to focus on; by isolating an "object" and forcing the reader to focus on it in a single sentence (which may be a single word—"Pegasus"), in a single paragraph, the reading process is slowed down and becomes like a replay (in reverse) of the writing process. When the process is slowed down, the reader's attention is intensified (as in the crucial scenes of Wagner's music-drama, as in arias in general). The movement is clearly toward that *stillness* (or *status* as Kenneth Burke calls it in his *Grammar of Motives*) which characterizes the lyric poem. This is one reason why Findley, at his most characteristic, is less like Hemingway than like Woolf.

At its most exaggerated (as in **"Losers, Finders: Strangers at the Door"**), Findley's style may well prove off-putting (or even offensive) to those who pride themselves on plain-speaking, who prefer Bacon to Lamb, Austen to C. Brontë, Huxley to Carlyle. The concentrated passages of repetition, alliteration, compound epithets, self-conscious puns (often very funny), internal rhymes, line-breaks, and diverse typographical devices are all guaranteed to draw a great deal of attention to themselves. In **"Losers, Finders,"** published in 1975, Findley was undoubtedly testing himself, stretching his style to extremes to see just how much strain it could take, before embarking on *The Wars.* At its most effective, as in *The Wars,* it still draws attention to itself, but this is precisely what Findley wants since his major thematic concern is the necessity of getting attention and the dangers of both getting and failing to get it. In *The Wars,* the stylistic devices are less obtrusive because more subtly paced and varied, and because the style itself wholly absorbs narrative and dramatic purposes as well as achieving a lyric intensity in the expression of moods, emotions and states of mind.

Speaking of style, Frye states that in "all literary structures we are aware of a quality that we may call the quality of a verbal personality or a speaking voice." Sometimes, when this quality is felt to be "the voice of the author himself, we call it style: *le style c'est l'homme.*" In the novel, however, the author has "to speak with the voice of the internal characters . . . and sometimes dialogue and narrative are so far apart as to divide the book into two different languages." The suiting of style to "internal characters or subject" Frye calls "decorum"; and drama he defines as "epos or fiction absorbed by decorum"—or a suitable style. Much about Findley's style may fairly be called *dramatic*; it has been shaped by his writing of many dramas for radio and television, as well as for the stage; by his dramatization of both fiction (the *Whiteoaks* series) and non-fiction (*The National Dream*); and by his early career as an actor. But Findley's theatrical and dramatic talents tend toward the operatic, toward music-drama, a combination of words (or lyrics) and music—and spectacle on a grand scale which, in terms of writing, *is* style. Even suicide and assassination, the new art forms according to Jamie Taylor and his friends, should be undertaken "with style." Certainly, opera goes in for life, love and, above all, death, on a grand scale (the fiery finales of *Die Walküre* and *Gotterdämmerung* have a certain Findleyesque quality about them).

The ultimate irony of Findley's operatic style, his dramatic and often violent stories, his preference for what Browning calls "the dangerous of things"—that borderland between sanity and insanity, between the beautiful and sinister, between political issues and private problems, between social satire and psychological exploration, between dramatic spectacles and lyrical revelations, between story-telling pictures and silent images, between prose and poetry—is that, while Browning believed the lad astride the chimney-stack was a sure attention-getter whom we "must watch" (in contrast to lads who "walk the street / Sixty the minute"); Findley has rarely (if ever) received the kind of attention he merits. He has, rather, been largely ignored by reviewers and critics

alike. He has, like the Cassandra of Canadian novelists, too often spoken without being listened to. This is a sad irony since, again and again, his fictions display the disastrous consequences of not paying attention—consequences that involve not only those who, like lonely children, are never loved enough to be seen and heard, but also those (like the Trojans) who have never cared enough to look or listen or mark Cassandra's words. Iris Pengelli, the psychiatrist in *Other People's Children* (a TV drama written in 1978), works with autistic children who live alone "in their ultra-ordered private worlds": "'These are all "my children." . . . All of them—*look*—are wearing masks. Anger. Fear. Hatred. Single emotions dominate their whole lives'" (italics mine). Dr. Pengelli has a favourite, Jeremy, whom she cannot reach; he starves himself to death. But, as a favour to a friend, she also works with Erin Foley, a teen-ager whose mother has died, who has been raped by her father, and lived most of her young life in foster-homes. In one of the last sequences in the drama, Pengelli confronts Erin: "'Look at me,'" she says. "'Tell me what you see.'" Erin answers, "'An old woman.'" Pengelli presses, "'But who?'" "'You,'" says Erin, refusing to name names. Two sequences are superimposed in the final minutes of the teleplay. Erin, looking in a mirror as she makes up her face, recalls the first sequence in which she was arrested. A policeman is asking her name, age, address, and demanding identification:

> ERIN: (VOICE OFF) Me. Okay? I'm here ain't I? You got to know where I come from? I was found in a brown paper bag.
>
> FREEZE FRAME.
>
> HOLD.
>
> PENGELLI: Tell me what you see.
>
> The FREEZE FRAME MELTS and becomes the PHOTOGRAPH OF EILEEN MARY [Erin's mother] holding ERIN as a BABY—with FOLEY [Erin's father] standing with them. SMILING.
>
> ERIN: (V.O.) Me.
>
> HOLD.

The prerequisite for any answer to the question, "Can you see me yet?" is that the asker know and be able to acknowledge self. The prerequisite for any answer to the question, "Can we see Findley yet?" is that the asker be able to *see* and *hear* Findley, and be willing to *mark his words.* And name names.

Alberto Manguel (review date June-July 1984)

SOURCE: "Findley's People," in *Books in Canada,* Vol. 13, No. 6, June-July 1984, pp. 13-14, 16.

[In the highly favorable review below, Manguel offers a stylistic and thematic overview of Dinner along the Amazon, *noting how this work is representative of and related to Findley's other writings.]*

We always arrive too late or too early in Timothy Findley's stories. The event has already taken place, or will take place sometime later, once we have left the page, or perhaps it will never take place. **"Sometime—Later—Not Now"** is the title of one of the stories in *Dinner Along the Amazon* (which is one of the first four titles in Penguin's new Penguin Short Fiction series), and the title fits almost all pieces in this brilliant book. ". . . There are no beginnings, not even to stories," writes Findley in **"Losers, Finders: Strangers at the Door."** "There are only places where you make an entrance into someone else's life and either stay or turn and go away." This sense of distant continuity, of solidity in all of Findley's work, lends reality to the world he portrays. His characters have lives of their own, lives that come from a past we, the readers, are not asked to witness, and drift toward a future we are not invited to share. Their history, which is also the history of Findley's obsessions, is taken for granted.

The background of Findley's world is ours, however; it is known to us, its features are common to our experience. Suburbia in our time, the world wars in our shared past: this chosen background enjoys the prestige of "having happened," of being true to life. The reader's disbelief is suspended from the very start: of course these houses exist, of course the war took place—and the reader is then left to wander in the maze he has accepted as real. But now comes the realization that the background is *not* the focus of our attention. Against it, in mid-speech, in mid-action, we see Findley's people. They are always occupied, a group obsessed with collecting whatever evidence about themselves is available—photographs, childhood memories, souvenirs in cardboard boxes—trying to understand their world. Suddenly the landscape is questioned, and the reader is made to question it with them.

Chekhov (whom Findley mentions in his introduction as another writer pursued by obsessions) proceeds in the same manner: setting up an acceptable world and peopling it with characters who fail to understand it. The reader then joins the characters in the investigation of the story.

One of the finest stories in this collection, the macabre and moving masterpiece that lends its title to the book—**"Dinner Along the Amazon"**—is remarkable because of the many ways in which it explores the paradox of the reader joining forces with the fictional characters to solve the riddle of their common world, a paradox illustrated by one of the characters, Fabiana:

She began in the middle of some interior monologue that perhaps had occupied her for some time—which yet seemed pertinent to the monologue of each of the others; one long sentence describing their mutual apprehension, whether it be about the past or the present or the future; arising out of the common literature which is the mind, peopled with common characters, moving over a common landscape, like a book they had all read—from which one of their voices began to quote aloud.

Their voices: the plural reveals another aspect of Findley's people. They are a conglomerate, a group functioning as one single being, each part unable to detach itself from the others, each however keeping its individual face, and yet depending on the others for survival, suffering the others' misfortunes and fears. Everything is shared, and yet the characters still feel lonely, like Siamese twins/each speaking a different language, each with his own memory. "Adult loneliness," says Findley "is the loneliness defined by remembrance."

> **In Findley's world there is always a struggle, a war going on: historical or social, political or personal, a combat whose ends are not known.**
> **—Alberto Manguel**

Even when a character succeeds in freeing himself from the knot of his fellow beings (as does the Snow White maid in **"About Effie"**), his influence is still felt by the rest of the group. "I don't know how to begin about Effie," says the child narrator (beginning, as is usual in Findley, *after* the fact), "but I've got to because I think you ought to know about her. Maybe you'll meet her one day, and then you'll be glad I told you all this. If I didn't, then maybe you wouldn't know what to do."

There seem to be two ways of entering Findley's world: through the eyes of a character whose reactions we follow (**"Lemonade," "About Effie"**), or on our own, with no interpreter (**"Hello Cheeverland, Goodbye," "Dinner Along the Amazon"**). In both cases the discovery of this world comes as a shock: we thought we knew it so well, and it is never what we expected. In most cases—unlike Effie—the characters share the shock and fail in their efforts to make sense of what is happening; their struggle, their passionate trying, makes the stories.

In Findley's world there is always a struggle, a war going on: historical or social, political or personal, a combat whose ends are not known. The war means different things to different characters; "war" is the name given to the machineries of fate. For Harper (in "**Lemonade**") war is a dream that has silenced his father; for Neil (in "**War**") it is a broken promise about skating. In "**Hello Cheeverland, Goodbye**" it is a strict code of social graces, fought as absurdly and pathetically as the kind of war fought with guns.

To survive in this world, Findley's characters perform rituals we as readers are made to observe: Harper's morning wakening before he is allowed to kiss his wasting mother; Neil's escape into the hayloft to punish his father for betrayal; T. S. Eliot distilling words from his wife Vivienne in "**Out of the Silence**"; Ezra Pound purging in his cage the sin of visionary poetry in "**Daybreak at Pisa**." Some perform these rituals as imitations of life, as Annie Bogan does in "**The Book of Pins**." Others, especially the children, perform them to find a place in the world of adults.

For Findley's children the world has already happened: the laws and reasons that governed its construction have been forgotten, and what faces them now is an incomprehensible theatre stage. Here actions are mistaken for other actions, and all intentions seem wrong. A poem—reminiscent of Stevie Smith's "Not Waving, Drowning"—introduces "**Losers, Finders: Strangers at the Door**":

> Some lives
> are only seen
> through windows
> beyond which
> the appearance
> of laughter
> and of screaming
> is the same.

The confusion of appearances provides a key to most of Findley's stories. In "**Lemonade**" Harper cannot understand why his mother lets her beauty die away and imagines that the jewels she has sold can restore her lost grace; in "**War**" Neil takes his father's enlistment as an act of unfaithfulness; in "**The People on the Shore**" the narrator assumes that a dying woman's last glance is a revelation. After the confusion comes the disappointment: the jealousy, the rage of unkept promises, the disenchantment. "**Dinner Along the Amazon**" is thickly layered with this sequence: the characters build their hopes on their assumptions, fall from grace, and rise again, in a seemingly everlasting pattern.

Because their assumptions are mistaken, their lives are never fulfilled. In "**Sometime—Later—Not Now**" Diana, the young artist with whom the narrator is in love, never becomes a great pianist. "No. They won't die," she says talking about the babies she will never have. "They just won't happen." It was her own epitaph," the narrator adds. It is also the epitaph of most of Findley's people. In "**Lemonade**" the neighbourhood witch mistakenly supposes that

Harper is setting off on an adventure: "I've been waiting for adventure all my life," she says. "How lucky that you're so young." Adventure will never come to her (perhaps because she never sets out to find it) nor will it come for Harper. The solid background reality is inflexible, and when we leave the story—even though we will never know its true end—we realize that the characters will not succeed. Defeat seems to be the very essence of a Findley being.

The children are encroached by adults, the adults are encroached by war, the countryside (in the least successful of the stories in this collection, a fable called "**What Mrs. Felton Knew**") is encroached by the city. Danger is always there, lurking, ready to spring, bringing change. Change is to be avoided at all costs. The children do not want to become adults, the adults do not want to grow or learn too much: a delicate balance maintains the social structure. Only the present counts: things are as they are, never as they might be. Michael, in "**Dinner Along the Amazon**," hates the future: "He hated anything he could not control: he hated anything he didn't know. Certainty was the only ally you could trust." And then: "The future was his enemy." Fear of change keeps Findley's people alive.

As a group, Findley's people believe they are guilty. They never question why whatever has happened, has happened to *them*; instead they try to explore new ways of living with their guilt. In "**Losers, Finders: Strangers at the Door**" the heroine tries to convince a stranger to come and live in her house and share her [plans] and her anguish; in "**The Book of Pins**" Annie Bogan purges her guilt through memory; in *The Last of the Crazy People* (Findley's first novel) guilt is paid for with death. As in Catholic confession, the assumption is always that we have sinned, that we are never guiltless.

Read after *The Wars* and *Famous Last Words, Dinner Along the Amazon* takes on another significance: it is not only a collection of extraordinary short stories—it is also a showcase of drafts, ideas, new developments, variations on the obsessions that make up Findley's chosen world. In his introduction, Findley says he was surprised to find that certain themes, certain "sounds and images," crop up again and again in his writing. It is true that what Henry James called "the figure in the carpet" repeats itself in Findley's work—dusty roads, solitary children, photographs, silence—but these images are not just samples of a collector's hobby. They constitute the certain, precise landscape of the writer, a dangerous landscape laid thick with traps, through which the characters have to pick their way. The roads have to be dusty because Nature here is not welcoming; the children have to be lonely because within the group speech carries no meaning, no comfort; the photographs are necessary because they are the only tangible evidence of these moments, these stories, with no ending and no beginning, moments snipped out of time; silence is essential because from the lack of words comes the words themselves (as in the Eliot story or in *Famous Last Words*). Silence is all-important. "Our world," says Findley, "had been secured for us by a World War that closed in a parable of silence."

To anyone approaching Canadian literature for the first time, it becomes painfully obvious that the quest for a national identity is a literary obsession. The reader has the overall feeling that most Canadian writers confirm their existence by constantly pinching their nationality, by making statements rather than showing a world. Timothy Findley is never guilty of rhetoric: his stories are wonderfully visual, like plays acted out on the page at a breathtaking pace. When his characters speak, they never explain: they explore, they talk, and their dialogue becomes the characters.

Certain writers, perhaps unwittingly, have defined a country through their literature: Paul Scott's India, García Márquez's Colombia, Malcolm Lowry's Mexico. Findley's world of missed historical events, assumed guilt and contrived ways of survival, of children besieged by paternalistic politics and culture, of adults deeply concerned with, but awed by, art and social graces—all this world seems to me an excellent definition of Canada. In his major novels, in this astounding *Dinner Along the Amazon*, Timothy Findley restores an almost forgotten power to the art of fiction: the creation of a deep, coherent world in which we see our own.

Boyd Tonkin (review date 27 March 1987)

SOURCE: "Hitler's Understudy," in *New Statesman,* Vol. 113, No. 2922, March 27, 1987, p. 33.

[*In the favorable review below, Tonkin discusses Findley's focus on history, historical figures, and nostalgia in* Famous Last Words, *noting the book's contemporary relevance.*]

In this century novelists have their own special Valhalla, a place of mirth and luxury to which many are called but few chosen. It would astonish me if *Famous Last Words* didn't at some stage receive this final accolade: 'soon to be a major motion picture.' What makes it so unmistakably a work of our time is the uncanny sensation that it has already been one.

Published in his native Canada in 1981, Timothy Findley's novel has had to wait for an English edition as a result of what the blurb coyly calls 'legal reasons'. In a multi-national cast that also features Lana Turner, Ezra Pound and Joachim von Ribbentrop, two of its principal figures are the late Duchess and Duke of Windsor. It hints, among other revelations, that Wallis Simpson and the former Edward VIII preferred

to make love under the unsmiling gaze of a photograph of the ex-king's mother, Queen Mary.

Where does gossip end and history begin? Balzac and Tolstoy muddied these waters long before today's theorists of discontinuity started to splash about in them. Presenting the fate of Europe in the age of the dictators as an unlucky-bag of accident and conspiracy, Findley shoots a version of the Thirties and Forties lit by the twin lamps of glamour and chance.

He assumes a readership which no longer tells itself stories of destiny or revolution. Instead, we glimpse the face of Garbo or trade insults with Senor Hemingway, while in the background a little man with a Chaplin moustache makes trouble for the beautiful people. If we no longer believe such events had meaning or direction, only these foolish things can remind us of them. Findley plays on one of the few emotions that the late 20th century can claim to have patented: a heart-stopping nostalgia for a world we never knew.

Alone at the Grand Elysium Hotel, high in the Austrian Alps, in the winter of 1945, the expatriate American writer Hugh Selwyn Mauberley records the secret history of two decades, before the allied armies arrive to punish his flirtation with high-minded Fascism. (I expected him to take tea at some point with J. Alfred Prufrock, but they never meet.) Mauberley scrawls not in his notebooks but on the plaster of his empty suite: American graffiti, the writing on the wall. The inter-war Belshazzar's feast is over. He weighs the guests in the balances, and finds them wanting.

A fastidious pillar of the glitterati, Mauberley has idled away his years trailing redundant royalty around the Caribbean and the Med. As confidant of Wallis Simpson, he watched her take command of the weak-willed Prince of Wales and his shoal of parasites. Now he spills the beans about the global plot, codename Penelope, that sought to replace Hitler as the figurehead of anti-Communism with the spineless and malleable Edward Windsor . . . Compounded of derring-do, cultural name-dropping and bursts of bravura prose, *Famous Last Words* embroiders a fantasy of the past in the manner of Burgess's *Earthly Powers* and Doctorow's *Ragtime*. Such novels refer not so much to a pattern of actualities as to the clutter of cultural artefacts that gather round them.

So Mauberley's Windsors belong squarely in the William Hickey school of historiography: beings brought to life by the light of a thousand flashbulbs. Findley opens the door on a gilded mausoleum of celebrities. As his narrator reflects, 'This was the new mythology . . . Homer might have written it.' The neurasthenic author takes on the job of recording angel for the sins of a generation.

Both symptom and critique of the paranoid theory of history, the action of the novel steams along with the same kind of manic energy that drives all those books about how Josef Mengele killed John Paul I on the orders of Anthony Blunt and the Freemasons. Findley knows better; the final secret is that there is none. Truth 'was just another bit of gossip in amongst the litter of names and dirty jokes on the partitions of a comfort station'. He arranges the fabulous monsters of the *entre-deux-guerres* into a gallery of archetypes, seen hazily through the veils of fame. 'History is made in the electric moment, and its flowering is all in chance.' So writes his hero, as did Nietzsche long ago. Lavish in its disenchantments, *Famous Last Words* holds up a glass, not to the 1930, but to the suspicion and amnesia of the Age of Reagan.

Keith Garebian (review date November 1988)

SOURCE: "Findley's Fine Line Between Untidy Life and Orderly Art," in *Quill & Quire*, Vol. 54, No. 11, November, 1988, p. 17.

[*In the following primarily positive review of* Stones, *Garebian assesses several stories in the collection.*]

Timothy Findley's latest collection of short stories [*Stones*] can be defined by many elements: a theatricality in imagery and characterization, an evocative sense of Toronto (particularly Rosedale and Queen Street West), a compassion for emotional desperadoes, and an urge for retrospective regeneration—a looking back into the details of a past, a gliding in and out of specific moments in a character's life, a dispersing of details within a compass of shifting moods, varieties of human nature, and the inevitability of story-line.

There are two complementary pairs of stories in *Stones*. In **"The Name's the Same"** and **"Real Life Writes Real Bad,"** there are characters we have already met in *Dinner Along the Amazon*, Findley's first short-story collection that, despite its evident virtues, had a somewhat unfinished quality. In this collection Findley's preoccupations, while repetitive in the two sets of stories, justify his implicit question: Why am I obsessed with you? A tentative answer can be found in the configurations of love and desperation. **"Bragg and Minna"** and **"A Gift of Mercy,"** the first two stories in *Stones*, probe the tormented relationship between a husband and wife. **"Bragg and Minna"** begins with a brief prologue from Minna's journal of despair and the image of three men walking up a hill in Australia. One of the three is Stanley Nob, "the sad, mad poet from Sydney." Another is Stuart Bragg, estranged husband of Minna Joyce, who has just died from cancer. The third is Bragg's homosexual lover. They are preparing to scatter Minna's ashes, and from this image proliferate scenes from a woman's struggle to escape her husband. Minna, whose central anarchy and strange power

of compassion are vividly explored in the next story, had been an avowed enemy of "ladyhood." Her life, until she met and married Bragg, was one of "inherited privilege mixed with deliberate squalor." Escaping from Rosedale and its snobberies, she went to Parkdale to do "good works" among "all its resident rubbies and gentle crazies, dressed in all weathers in their summer coats and woollen mittens and all their hair cut straight across in bangs and all with their tam-o'-shanters pulled down over their ears and their eyes as crafty and innocent all at once as the eyes of bears." The sense of place is thrillingly effective, as is the sense of drama. Husband and wife are both writers, though Bragg produces short, terse books at three-year intervals, while Minna writes 11 books before she dies (there are four more in bureau drawers), all told with less ambiguity than Bragg's, "very much the way she had lived."

Minna wants a child desperately, but Bragg, afraid of a genetic curse in the family (he even thinks his homosexuality is a means of frustrating the curse), wishes to avoid procreating. Ultimately, Minna wins. But the marriage is over, and she goes off to Australia with her daughter Stella (born hideously deformed and brain-damaged). Only after Minna's death, when her ashes are scattered over an aboriginal petroglyph (which seems to be an emblem for their freakish child), does Bragg recognize the real monster as himself. The irony is sharp: he, the homosexual outcast in a conservative society, has cast out love from his life.

The pairing of these two stories effectively illustrates the strangeness of Minna's love. **"A Gift of Mercy"** details the dramatic dichotomy between Minna's compassion for strangers who are plagued by demons and her own lack of articulateness. However, the two stories would have been even better had they been fused into a novella.

Findley is best when he doesn't seek glib symmetry or a series of shocks. **"Foxes"** (in which a man identifies with a Japanese theatre mask), **"The Sky"** (in which a paranoid man suffers a breakdown), and **"Dreams"** (another breakdown story that could have been imagined by David Cronenberg) are all interesting in themselves and all stem from a common desire to discover and touch an essential humanity. But they are melodramatic, more contrived than credible. **"Almeyer's Mother"** reveals a woman's long-held secret about her father's incestuous urges. The flick of the underside of a young girl's breast is sexually suggestive enough, but Findley almost overplays his hand in describing the family photograph that reveals an "alarming affection" between father and daughter.

Findley's craft is more assured in other stories. The duo of **"The Name's the Same"** and **"Real Life Writes Real Bad"** explores the chasm between two brothers, the elder of whom is an alcoholic who repudiates reality and whose almost suicidal despair has an acute psychological root. In these stories, Findley glides in and out of the past, achieving his microcosmic focus through lists and minor details, finding emblems of self-destruction and highlighting the sharp division between untidy real life and neatly ordered art.

The best story is **"Stones,"** yet another about breakdown. The narrator, Ben Max, in his early 50s, shuffles time—the prewar days when his parents were successful florists, and the wartime and post-war days when the family began to feel the stress of the father's dishonourable discharge for cowardice at Dieppe. The stones of Dieppe, which had trapped the tanks and precipitated the slaughter of Canadian forces, become a recurring symbol in Max's memory. In a sense, they turn his father to stone, a man whose positive emotions fossilize as he is spiritually broken. After his death his ashes are scattered like powdered stone in the sea at Dieppe. This is a story that attempts to avoid sentimentality in its re-creation of a troubled political period and an anguished family history. Yet there is an inevitability about its final nostalgic image of Mr. and Mrs. Max walking their children on a Sunday afternoon. The past, Findley shows, doesn't have to lie like heavy stones on the heart.

Lorraine M. York (essay date September 1989)

SOURCE: "Civilian Conflict: Systems of Warfare in Timothy Findley's Early Fiction," in *English Studies in Canada*, Vol. XV, No. 3, September, 1989, pp. 336-47.

[*York is an educator. In the essay below, she delineates Findley's focus on war and conflict in* The Last of the Crazy People, *"Lemonade," and other early works.*]

It is no coincidence or quirk of fate that two of Timothy Findley's early works, *The Last of the Crazy People* (1967) and the short story **"Lemonade"** (composed mid-50s; publ. 1980) open with a "stand-to" at dawn. But here the soldier on his lonely vigil is a young child, and the war in which he participates is a domestic one. Nevertheless, these early tales of civilian conflict are war texts; many of the basic strategies and structures of military behaviour inform these works, and even particular wars serve as touchstones or intertexts within them. Indeed, in *The Last of the Crazy People,* Findley's first novel, an entire nineteenth-century war serves as a complex hidden metaphor for the domestic skirmishes of the twentieth-century Winslow family: the American Civil War.

Polarity and conflict have always fascinated Findley as a writer, and both are present in large measure in a very early story of his, **"About Effie"** (1956), a work which has nothing to do with war as we normally conceive of it. The story opens with a veritable domestic attack; young Neil enters his house in the midst of a raging thunderstorm and is immediately ambushed: "Right then I didn't know what it was. It looked like a ghost, you know, and then it looked like a great big crazy overcoat, and it sort of fell at me" (*Dinner Along the Amazon*). The modulation here from the Gothic to the eerie but domestic—from "ghost" to "big gray overcoat"—prepares us for the discovery of the truly "domestic" nature of Neil's attacker: it is the new maid, Effie.

Neil is only the first of many Findley characters who are "attacked by the domestic." The subject of the short story **"War"** (1957-58) is not military war at all, but rather the domestic warfare caused by a father's decision to go to war. Neil retreats to the loft of the barn, from where he fires domestic missiles—golfballs, stones—at his father. But in Findley's fictional world, stone-throwing and shooting are distinctly related. In **"Lemonade"** Harper Dewey, mourning the withdrawal of his mother's affection, hurls a stone through her window. And later, in *The Wars* (1977), we meet Eugene Taffler, who is a practised hand at firing missiles, both on and off the battlefield; Robert and Clifford Purchas see him throwing stones at bottles on the Alberta prairie. "All you get in this war," he complains, "is one little David against another . . . Just a bunch of stone throwers." Already we begin to see the system of interlocking images which forms the fictional wars of Timothy Findley.

In human warfare, missiles are most often fired in order to obtain or to defend territory; indeed, the struggle for territory is endemic to war. This struggle, beginning as early as **"Lemonade"** and forming complex patterns of domestic invasion and retreat in *The Last of the Crazy People* and *The Wars,* is no less basic to Findley's fictions. **"Lemonade"** opens with a careful observation of territorial rules; Harper must wait in the chair outside his mother's room while she is awakened and refreshed by the maid Bertha Millroy. When Renalda Dewey's troubles burst upon the domestic scene, the carefully ordered procedure is upset. Renalda begins a strategic retreat from her son—strategic because it is designed to keep him in the dark about her alcoholism. The first stage of this retreat is the locking away of property—Renalda's locking of the highboy drawer so that Harper cannot ascertain how much jewellery she has sold to supply her alcoholic needs. This act—the first act of denial by his mother—has all the effect, for Harper, of a physical blow: "Gone. Everything was suddenly motionless. Never before had the key not been there." This act of removing the key is merely a prelude, however, to the locking away of a more valuable possession of the young child's: his mother. One morning Bertha suddenly announces that Harper is no longer allowed to see his mother in the mornings, "Upon which she fled, under the protection of shock, into the newly forbidden reaches of the upper floor." The quasi-military withdrawal of both natural and surrogate mothers represents a major retreat in domestic terms, leaving the stunned child alone to brood and to regroup his forces.

Muster his forces Harper does, and in response to the retreating actions of his mother and Bertha he tries, at first, to launch an offensive. The first hint of this advance comes in that crucial episode where Harper is locked out of the highboy drawer. As a form of compensation, he makes incursions into his mother's cosmetics, stirring her powder with his finger:

> It came into his mind that his mother would know by this that he had been there, where he wasn't allowed: but it passed out again: he didn't care: she had locked him out, and he had found his way in, as the wind had found its way back in through the windows.

The gauntlet has been thrown down; Harper is determined to make incursions into enemy territory whenever and wherever possible in order to win back the spoils of his mother's affection. Surveying his mother's room during her absence, he "vehemently" stakes his claim: "I've got to get back in here . . . I've got to get back in this room."

But as all military strategists know, a well-executed and determined defence may easily rebuff or wear away a formidable attack. Renalda's retreats are both artful and absolute. On one occasion, she charms Harper with conversation ("You have a nice day with Bertha, dear"—the very commodity which Harper craves—while she positions herself for a swift escape: the car engine "gave a roar. 'Mother.' She was— 'Good-bye!'—Gone." As for so many of Findley's female characters—Jessie Winslow in *The Last of the Crazy People,* Mrs. Ross in *The Wars*—the family home becomes the final stage for Renalda's retreat; she locks herself alone in her room to suffer the miseries of her condition.

Confronted by such a determined retreat on his mother's part, Harper finally hits upon another strategy: to retreat himself, in order to draw his mother out of her self-imposed exile. In this spirit, he formulates the plan of sleeping overnight in Miss Kennedy's tree. "I had to," he explains to Bertha, "I want her to notice." Unfortunately, a strategic retreat can only be effective when the other party takes note of that retreat. This is where Harper's plan fails; Renalda is too busy making her own retreat from life—staying out all night—to notice her son's absence. One retreat may be strategic; two are utterly useless.

Faced with this preliminary defeat, Harper must once again cast about for a workable strategy. He opts this time for an offensive action, but one which is not well suited to his problem: selling his mother's liquor at his lemonade bazaar. Findley clothes his description of Harper's preparations in appropriate military language: he has "commandeered" several frosted bottles from his mother's favourite hiding place (strategically leaving the partially emptied one behind in order to delay his mother's discovery of his act). "Everything," we hear, "seemed at his command." Explaining his "cover" activity—selling lemonade—to Bertha, he claims that it's merely a diversion" from his problems. A diversion, indeed, but in a military as well as a recreational sense.

Harper does engineer a truce of sorts, but not with his mother. The neighbourhood children and the supposed "witch," Miss Kennedy, feeling the effect of the liquor-laced lemonade, begin to form a companionable, if somewhat tipsy, group. A tearful Harper, unable to bring about any such reconciliation with his mother, resorts to open hostilities: he throws a stone through her window. "She was holding it in her hand when they found her," Findley's narrator informs us, and this linking of the stone and Renalda's act of shooting herself with the Colt revolver draws the images of stone and gun together once more. Harper has become a warlike David, a thrower of stones, but Renalda has made her ultimate retreat in suicide, and it is an irreversible one.

. . . . .

If **"Lemonade"** ends with the ultimate domestic retreat, *The Last of the Crazy People* ends with the ultimate act of domestic attack: murder. One senses that in the novel Findley has confronted what he could not bear to confront in the short story: that domestic war may end in a harmful act of aggression which is, if not entirely justifiable, surely understandable. (He confronts a similar possibility in his sixth novel, *The Telling of Lies* [1986].) Hooker Winslow carries to their logical extreme the stone-throwing impulses of both Harper Dewey and Neil from **"War,"** but here, the stones have been transformed into their military equivalents, bullets.

However, the difference between the systems of war found in **"Lemonade"** and *The Last of the Crazy People* is one of complexity as well as degree. **"Lemonade"** is a blueprint of domestic war; *The Last of the Crazy People* is Findley's first attempt to create a multi-dimensional model from that blueprint. One indication of this growing complexity is the first appearance in his fiction of the famous war theorist, Carl von Clausewitz (1780-1831), whose treatise *On War* (1832) finds its way onto Gilbert Winslow's bookshelf, just as it will later find its way into Levitt's knapsack in the trenches of France in *The Wars*. Findley's inclusion of a theorist of war in his fictional world is a tantalizing clue to his readers that the domestic struggles in that fiction are to be understood in relation to the larger theoretical framework of war.

It is true that one sees in *The Last of the Crazy People* basically the same territorial squabble as in **"Lemonade"**—the retreat of the mother—but in the novel Findley enlarges upon and varies the sorts of stratagems used to halt that retreat. In the short story, we are presented only with Harper's battle against this maternal manoeuvre, but here, the greater scope of the novel form allows Findley to depict and compare several family members' idiosyncratic means of waging war. Nicholas Winslow's part in the territorial wars of his family is essentially passive; gazing at the bedroom door which his wife Jessie has closed against him and the family, he thinks, "This is my room. Why shouldn't I go in there?"—the simple childlike response which we see in Harper Dewey when he is confronted by the occupied territory of his mother's room. Yet Nicholas lacks the childlike exuberance which would allow him to carry this thought into action; throughout the novel he appears a jaded man, aged before his time. Even the thought of breaking down Jessie's door is alien ground to him: "The thought trespassed in his mind, just as he wished that he could be strong enough to trespass beyond the door. But he didn't."

His elder son, Gilbert, on the other hand, represents that thought of trespass put into action with a vengeance. Gilbert is, by temperament and by design, a trespasser. He trespasses on the family's rigid code of silence by getting drunk and inviting conflict to come out into the open. He trespasses in the same way on society's code of silence; faced with the accusation that he has gotten Mr. Parker's daughter pregnant, he breaks in on a highly stylized social ritual—a society ball—to ask, "Will you openly accuse me?" It comes as no surprise, then, that Gilbert's major strategy in the family's territorial battles should be frontal attack. He trespasses beyond the door which even Jessie's husband dares not open: "MOTHER? . . . Are you going to come down? . . . Or am I going to come up? . . . You aren't really sick, you know. . . . What are you going to do about it?" In Clausewitz's terms, Gilbert chooses one of the three ways of wearing out the enemy, "invasion": "*the occupation of the enemy's territory, not with a view to keeping it*, but in order to levy contributions upon it, or to devastate it." But, as Clausewitz himself warns, the defeat of the enemy is not the immediate objective of such a manoeuvre; it is, rather, "to *do him damage in a general way*." This is, in effect, the key to the failure of Gilbert's offensive; it does not bring Jessica to any new resolution as much as it puts her even more solidly on the defensive, and her retreat becomes an outright rejection: "I will not go . . . on . . . giving . . . birth . . . to you . . . and to Hooker . . . and to that . . . god . . . damned . . . baby . . . day . . . after . . . bloody . . . day . . . for the rest of my LIFE! . . . I hate you!" Inflicting "general harm" on an already mentally unbalanced woman is, Gilbert discovers too late, a serious strategical blunder.

If Gilbert represents the option of invasion and Nicholas the passive stance, or what Clausewitz calls "the *wearing out* of

the enemy," there do not seem to be many strategical options left open for Hooker. Indeed, Gilbert and Nicholas, taken together, represent the two forces which are at war within Harper Dewey in **"Lemonade"**: the desire to attack and the desire to retreat. In *The Last of the Crazy People,* therefore, Findley allows himself to study what is the most likely condition of a young child caught up in domestic war:

> the absence of strategy altogether. In the early stages of the novel, Hooker seems almost as determined to avoid Jessie as Gilbert is to confront her. Carrying home his straight-A report card, he vows "not [to] even ask for her." As the novel progresses, he is repeatedly cast in the role of the observer of other family members' strategic moves. He inadvertently witnesses his father's attempt to talk to Jessie at her door and when Gilbert is storming his mother's bastion, Harper remains the alert but passive pair of eyes and ears; he climbs onto the maid Iris's lap and awaits the passing of the verbal storm.

Hooker is most obviously and poignantly the onlooker, bereft of strategy, during the family's most organized and concerted campaign to defeat Jessie's illness: their birthday party for her. Each of the family's presents to Jessie reflects a private campaign to lure her downstairs and into the family for good. Gilbert gives her stockings which are, as Gilbert announces in his frontal-attack manner, "to wear downstairs." Rosetta's gift of bath beads and lipstick is a more veiled appeal to Jessie to reassume her old mask—the mask of traditional femininity. Appropriately, Jessie, with the intuition which often attends the deeply disturbed, "unmasks" the hidden symbolism of Rosetta's gift; she turns these icons of passive womanhood into symbols of phallic intent. "'It reminds me'," she says of the lipstick, "'of something.' Working the dial at its base, raising and lowering the small red tongue of colouring. 'Isn't it funny,' she said, and smiled directly at Nicholas." If the family is going to wage a war of symbolism, Jessie is prepared to fight back with the same weapons.

Nicholas's gift of the nightgown, the "bride's nightie," as Jessie puts it, is the last straw; it provokes in her the same counter-attack which she had earlier been forced to make against Gilbert: "I hate you for this." But Hooker's gift is to be distinguished from this long line of artificial products; he gives Jessie a robin's egg which he naïvely hopes will hatch a bird. In Hooker, therefore, we see one who is without artifice or guile; he is capable of hatching neither bird nor plot.

Unlike Harper Dewey in **"Lemonade,"** who is continually casting about for workable stratagems, Hooker Winslow is devoid of stratagems until his final decisive act—taking the Colt revolver from the Harris home and using it against his family. His direct fall into what Clausewitz calls absolute war thus sets him apart from his strategic-minded family, and Findley, by having the family Hotspur, Gilbert, remove himself from the scene by committing suicide, focuses on Hooker's act. That such an act—the destruction of human beings—could result from even an absence of strategy is shocking proof of the immense power for destructiveness hidden and unacknowledged in our civilian wars.

. . . . .

What we begin to see in *The Last of the Crazy People,* then, is a greater willingness on Findley's part to have various family members and their interactions embody the dynamics of war. Herein lies the three-dimensionality of the novel in contrast to **"Lemonade,"** where we see an elementary conflict: mother retreats, child schemes, retreats, and finally advances. Here all the members of the Winslow family have, as we have seen, wars to wage, and they must be considered both as individuals and as part of a complex dynamic of domestic war. As Findley once reflected [in Graeme Gibson's *Eleven Canadian Novelists*] on *The Last of the Crazy People,* "ultimately I realised that one of the things that I had said in that book had something to do with this impasse, and that the Winslow family, as individuals and collectively, represented a lot of values and things that must go."

This new emphasis on the dynamics of family interaction finds several outlets in the novel, most explicitly in the increased use of war terminology to describe domestic conditions (a phenomenon witnessed only briefly in **"Lemonade,"** when Harper "commandeers" his mother's liquor). Here Findley begins a practise which reaches its heights in *The Wars*—the use of war similes. At one point in a crucial domestic clash, we are told that "Nicholas spoke as he might have if he had been asked, 'Do you know Adolf Hitler?'" After the inquest into Gilbert's suicide, Nicholas is again metaphorically clothed in the terminology of war; his cigarette box "cellophane crunkled like machine-gun fire." Incidentally, the latter simile was singled out for criticism by an early reviewer of the novel, George Bowering, who [in *Canadian Forum* 48 (1968)] christened it "inaccurate." But given the aura of emotional warfare which pervades the Winslow household, such a detail is not simply accurate or inaccurate (similes seldom are), but evocative and apposite. Such a detail highlights the oppressive silences and neuroses of that household, wherein even an ordinary act may take on hostile overtones.

What the simile does linguistically—drawing together two realms of experience often thought quite separate—Findley does symbolically in his first novel as well. Gilbert's bookshelf, filled with the books whose titles he has Hooker read aloud, serves as a type of microcosm or *mise en abyme* of this juxtaposition of two realms—war and domesticity. Byron, Shelley, Arnold and Keats share shelfspace with *"Chums '38 . . . Chums '39 . . . Chums '40 . . . Chums '41 . . . Airplanes of the Future . . . "* and, of course, Clausewitz, whose name Hooker ironically domesticates in translation: "Closets—." The most telling sign, though, that Gilbert is living in an inner world torn between aesthetic pleasures and wartime disillusion is the presence on his shelves of the following titles: *"Tender is the Night . . . The Great Gatsby . . . Tales of the Jazz Age . . . The Far Side of Paradise . . . The Disenchanted . . . This Side of Paradise . . . "* and, most ironically, *"The Crack Up."* As a Fitzgeraldian aesthete disillusioned by a decrepit post-war society, Gilbert finds himself, in the words of one of his older literary mentors, "wandering between two worlds / One lost, the other powerless to be born." This image of intellectual stillbirth—the social equivalent of Jessica Winslow's stillborn child—adds an extra degree of complexity to the wars of *The Last of the Crazy People.* It also foreshadows the fervent cultural concerns of later novels such as *Famous Last Words* and *The Butterfly Plague,* wherein Findley examines in greater detail twentieth-century culture under siege.

. . . . .

Hooker, though no strategist, is by no means unschooled in the ways of war. Several wars are mentioned by family members throughout the novel; Rosetta likens the beleaguered family to "the Jews at Auschwitz," and Gilbert, Iris and Hooker engage in a conversation about political assassinations, including the one which touched off the First World War. But the war which sheds the most light on the family struggles in *The Last of the Crazy People* is not a war between nations, but a civil war, the American Civil War (1861-65). It has become by now a critical commonplace that Findley's first novel was influenced by the writers of the American South; critics of the novel have busied themselves tracing the presence of Faulkner, Welty, or McCullers. But the South inhabits *The Last of the Crazy People* in a much more complex political and textual sense; the war between North and South is a hidden intertext, a war whose details bear in subtle and penetrating ways on the war within a single family unit.

Though Findley has set his novel in Canada, he deliberately invokes the conflict between North and South, between blacks and whites, throughout the work. Hooker upsets the maid Iris by asking why she calls herself Miss Iris Browne on the telephone when anyone would know that she is speaking because, as Hooker puts it, "You speak Negro." Iris senses that she faces not one opponent in this racial war, but two: "You get it from that Gilbert. Sometimes I could take him and hit him so hard he'd split down the middle, he makes me so mad. Where does he think we live—the States?"

Canadian this story certainly is, as Iris and other telling details such as the evening Toronto paper received by the

Winslows remind us. Yet the constant invocation of the United States and racial tensions is present in the novel for a purpose. Later, we meet another black maid, Alberta Perkins, who, her Canadian first name notwithstanding, is closely associated with the South and slavery. Speaking of her present task in the Harris household—going to the dogcatcher's to rescue the family pet—she exclaims, "Time was . . . the dogs chased *us*!" Significantly, it is Alberta who prophesies that Hooker will run away from home, almost as though she recognizes a state of slavery when she sees it, in whatever form. Domestic slavery here finds its historical counterpart—the slavery of the blacks in eighteenth-and nineteenth-century America—and even Iris's threat of splitting Gilbert down the middle begins to take on ominous historical overtones.

Timothy Findley has been writing "the wars" all along.
—*Lorraine M. York*

The actual references to the Civil War in the novel are sparing, but they set up a framework of historical reference within which the reader may forge some intriguing connections. The war surfaces as a topic of conversation in the aforementioned discussion about political assassination; John Wilkes Booth, according to Gilbert, "wanted to divide the nation over Mr. Lincoln's war." Thus the concept of division itself becomes multiplied, subdivided: aiming to divide a nation over a war which quite literally divided a nation.

Division is the central motif of one of the most famous statements to have come out of the Civil War period, and it is a statement rich in implications for Findley's novel. "A house divided against itself cannot stand," Lincoln declared on June 16, 1858. One could imagine no better epigraph for *The Last of the Crazy People* than this pronouncement, with its determined juxtaposition of military and domestic war. One even hears echoes of its apocalyptic message in the conversation between Iris and Gilbert about the Civil War:

> "Now Iris," he said, "I'm reading *Lee's Lieutenants*. And you know what? I've been thinking. If the South—"
>
> . . . "The South of *what*?" said Iris with practiced stupidity. And something else that Hooker could not quite put his finger on. A practiced something else.
>
> It was always the same, every day, now, in the closed-up house. Two people talking, and the rest all silent.

Findley does more here than to evoke a sense of the Winslow house divided; he also introduces an important intertext to

his novel: Douglas Southall Freeman's three-volume study of the Confederate war in the East, *Lee's Lieutenants* (1942-44). In his work Freeman delves into the characters and propensities of the men who worked under Robert E. Lee's command, and what results is as much a work of psychological scrutiny as of military analysis. Lee's lieutenants, taken as a whole, form the military equivalent of a bickering family, full of jealousies and animosities. "In the hearts of Lee's subordinates," Freeman writes, "were all the explosive qualities that existed elsewhere." How appropriate that Gilbert should read and keep on his telltale bookshelf a work which studies military relationships much as a family therapist might study a domestic unit.

Once one is willing to make this connection between the two divided houses of the United States in 1861 and the Winslow family in 1964, other remarkable parallels surface. Jessica's withdrawal into the hermitage of her bedroom is tantamount to a secession from the family state and, as Daniel Webster realized one hundred years before, "There can be no such thing as a peaceable secession." The attempts of the other family members to lure her back into their lives (by buying her birthday gifts, for example) find their historical counterparts in the efforts of politicians such as Daniel Webster and Henry Clay in 1850 to placate the South and keep the Union intact. In both instances, lure and compromises fail, and family members settle the conflict by picking up a gun. As an observer of the Civil War, Mrs. Mary Chestnut from South Carolina wrote, in characteristically domestic terms, "we are divorced, North from South, because we have hated each other so."

Hooker Winslow's obsession with assassination may also owe something to the Civil War aura of the novel and, more specifically, to the John Brown legend. Brown, the fanatical anti-Slavery activist from Kansas, murdered five men from the pro-slavery South who had moved into Kansas, men who, according to some sources, may themselves have been escaping from the social system of the South rather than trying to perpetuate it in Kansas. After these murders and before his abortive attempt to seize Harper's Ferry, Virginia, in October 1859, Brown located his operations in Canada. There he and his cohorts drew up a provisional constitution for the United States as well as a plan for "violent emancipation." The term suits precisely the final acts of Hooker Winslow; his father, shot, is described as "thrown back into violent stillness," a stillness which Hooker by now associates with emancipation from all care. One last detail which draws Brown's campaign for "violent emancipation" even closer to Hooker's is his madness. There was evidence of madness in the maternal line of the Brown family, and Brown had a sibling and a son who went mad. The similarity to Hooker's condition as "the last of the crazy people" is all too evident.

The mention of Harper's Ferry touches off other connections between this violent emancipator and the characters who people Findley's fictions. Harper Dewey's Christian name recalls the government arsenal which Brown tried to seize (an apt connection, given Harper's own seizure of his mother's alcoholic arsenal). His surname is militaristic as well; Commodore George Dewey was the commander of the American naval forces in the Spanish American War, whose rallying cry, "Full speed ahead—damn the torpedoes," has become household parlance.

Hooker himself bears a name which is rich in Civil War associations. The family name, "Winslow," recalls the well-known artist who sketched troops during the Civil War: Winslow Homer. But the name "Hooker" carries even more in the way of Civil War associations. General Joseph ("Fighting Joe") Hooker was one of the leading generals on the Union side, but one with a bizarre history. He commanded the Army of the Potomac from 1863 until the eve of Gettysburg, and his physical demeanour was somewhat reminiscent of Hooker's ("curling blond hair . . . a complexion 'as delicate and silken as a woman's'"). General Hooker's plan, like the Winslows', was one of luring—drawing General Lee out of what military historian Robert Leckie has called his "fortified defenses," a term admirably suited to Jessie Winslow's condition. The perplexing part of Hooker's career arose at Chancellorsville, where he had Lee's forces outnumbered, outflanked—and suddenly retreated, for reasons which still remain somewhat mysterious today. Findley, though, may well have read the account of Hooker's failure which appears in Freeman's *Lee's Lieutenants*, and one of the main reasons postulated there for Hooker's mistake is faulty communications—in short, the wires and signal stations crossed up. Furthermore, Freeman reports, Hooker may have believed rumours to the effect that Lee did not have sufficient numbers to do battle. These problems are precisely those faced by Hooker Winslow on his domestic battlefield in *The Last of the Crazy People*. He believes that the Parker family really will hold a shotgun to Gilbert's head when he hears Rosetta using this figure of speech, and he believes Alberta Perkins when she tells him that Armageddon is near and that the only "answer to per-di-tion . . . is merciful death." Hooker, like his Civil War namesake, is a warrior in a field where messages are unclear and threatening. Faced with such a situation, he can only trust what he hears and resort to merciful death as a means of saving life.

This conclusion, startling though it is to many readers of *The Last of the Crazy People,* is the only outcome possible in the world of domestic warfare which Timothy Findley has created. By setting the young children of his early fiction—from Neil in **"War"** and "About Effie" to Harper in **"Lemonade"** and Hooker in *The Last of the Crazy People*—in domestic situations which become increasingly warlike and increasingly complex in their approximations to war, Findley finally arrives at the point where metaphorical and literal wars intersect—the point where the stones thrown by Neil and Harper become the shots fired by Hooker. It is this moment of intersection, of embarking on our own private and domestic civil wars that both fascinates and terrifies Timothy Findley—"The moment," as Lincoln said of *his* civil war, "when I felt that slavery must die that the nation might live."

This is the same moment of intersection which Findley's Robert Ross will witness in *The Wars;* Robert, too, eventually decides that "slavery must die" when he disobeys his commander and attempts to set the horses free. That novel, which appeared a full decade after *The Last of the Crazy People,* and which heralded, for many Canadian readers, the arrival of an exciting new maker of fictions, is less a beginning than a culmination of the civilian wars which Timothy Findley had already charted in his early fiction. Retreating mothers, stone-throwers and divided houses do indeed make a return appearance ten years later; Timothy Findley, we discover, has been writing "the wars" all along.

Sharon Oard Warner (review date 29 April 1990)

SOURCE: A review of *Stones,* in *The New York Times Book Review,* Vol. 95, April 29, 1990, p. 38.

[*In the following brief review, Warner praises Findley's characterization and focus on isolation in the short fiction collection* Stones.]

Musing on the fervent need of children to love their parents, a middle-aged narrator admits. "I would have loved a stone". He might well be speaking for any of the characters in this new collection of stories [*Stones*] by Timothy Findley. Driven to love, they find that love itself drives them away. "Something in the signature informed him she would always be alone," we are told as one man reflects on a note left by his mother. Couples sleep in separate beds and imagine the infidelities of their mates. Even the animals suffer isolation. While putting his dying brother's house in order, a man wishes he could explain things to the cat that will "wonder, perhaps forever, where all his people had gone and why they had deserted him." In someone else's hands, these characters might provoke merely pity or irritation, but Mr. Findley, the winner of Canada's prestigious Governor-General's Award, has the skilled touch of a surgeon. Under our skins, he reminds us, we all look much the same. Although they occupy the same landscape and frequent the same places, the characters in his stories remain, strangers to one another. Like the stones on the beach at Dieppe, where the middle-aged man in the title story scatters his father's ashes, they are "treacherous" but "also beautiful," together but alone.

Sandra Martin (review date March 1993)

SOURCE: "The Horror and the River," in *Quill & Quire,* Vol. 59, No. 3, March, 1993, p. 47.

[In the excerpt below, Martin offers a primarily negative review of Headhunter.*]*

"On a winter's day, while a blizzard raged through the streets of Toronto, Lilah Kemp inadvertently set Kurtz free from page 92 of *Heart of Darkness.*" That is how Timothy Findley begins his monumental new novel, *Headhunter,* the latest in a list of fictional works that includes half a dozen novels and two collections of short stories, and three plays. Lilah, an out-patient at the Queen Street Mental Health Hospital, is sitting amidst the hangings and the pools in the lobby of Raymond Moriyama's Metropolitan Toronto Reference Library, "framed by the woven jungle of cotton trees and vines that passed for botanic atmosphere," when Kurtz makes his escape from the literary cage Joseph Conrad fashioned for him nearly 100 years ago.

An intriguing beginning, but there is nothing playful in Findley's intent. *Headhunter* is an expedition into the heart of evil as it festers in the male ego in the jungle of post-contemporary Toronto. Kurtz is the chief psychiatrist of an institution that is closely modelled on the Clarke Institute of Psychiatry. His nemesis, Marlow, is a practising psychiatrist in the same facility. Findley's portrait of Kurtz as a sinister, controlling demi-god is all the more devastating for the honour and prestige we lavish on psychiatrists in contemporary society.

Kurtz craves power, which in his case translates as research grants and donations. He gets it by violating his patients—clients as he calls them—using their intimate revelations to escalate their depravities, to blackmail them emotionally, and to subjugate their psyches. His clients, though, are not so much victims as instruments that Kurtz wields for his own nefarious purposes. The real victims in Timothy Findley's eyes are the children who are traumatized and tortured by their own fathers, most of whom are Kurtz's clients.

> **It is time for Findley to throw off these literary shrouds of *Headhunter* and come out as the unadorned and powerful novelist that he is more than capable of being.**
> **—*Sandra Martin***

What a hell-hole Findley has created: the mad are sane, moral and sexual taboos have evaporated; AIDS is rampant, while another plague, called sturnusemia, is even more wanton. Nobody knows how it is transmitted, but because victims turn speckled in the terminal stages of the disease, public health officials, in the absence of a scientific explanation, have in desperation blamed birds, sending extermination squads around the city spraying trees, gardens, and ravines with deadly chemicals. The young, the environment and, by extension, life itself are in mortal danger while men abuse their own children and women douse themselves in alcohol and sex and fling themselves on metaphorical pyres.

This cautionary moral tale is driven by Findley's outrage at the depravity that he sees around him. There are echoes of Robertson Davies in the gossip and theatricality of this novel and in the skilful way Findley depicts old, monied Toronto as a small Ontario town. Ultimately, though, Findley lacks that old magician's bluster and sleight of hand. *Headhunter* dangles too many loose ends and, as in all of Findley's novels that I can think of except *The Wars,* there are too many obeisances to the literary monuments of earlier writers. There is no reason for Findley to invoke Conrad to reinforce his imaginary world. He can stand on his own prose and tell his own story without props or crutches. It is time for him to throw off these literary shrouds and come out as the unadorned and powerful novelist that he is more than capable of being.

James Marcus (review date 5 June 1994)

SOURCE: "Mr. Kurtz—He Back!" in *The New York Times Book Review,* Vol. 99, June 5, 1994, p. 40.

[Marcus is a critic and translator. In the review below, he favorably assesses Headhunter.*]*

With eight books of fiction and a number of plays to his credit, including *Famous Last Words* and *The Telling of Lies,* an Edgar Award winner, the Canadian writer Timothy Findley is something of an institution north of the 49th parallel. In the United States he has achieved much critical attention but little popular success. Perhaps *Headhunter* will remedy the situation. This long, densely populated novel is already a best seller in Canada and its fusion of jeremiad with psychological thriller may win Mr. Findley the American audience he deserves.

Set in Toronto in the near future, *Headhunter* makes the tail end of the millennium look bleak indeed. Gangs of silver-suited skinheads, called Moonmen, rove the streets, pollution has given the sky a permanent yellow tint and a mysterious plague called sturnusemia—transmitted, we are told, by starlings—has begun to take its toll on the population. What's more, this physical decay seems to reflect an ethical and moral collapse. According to one character, the psychiatrist Charles Marlow, "Sturnusemia and AIDS were not the only plagues Civilization—sickened—had itself become a plague And its course . . . could be followed by tracing the patterns of mental breakdown . . . . Psychiatric case loads; everywhere, carried alarming numbers. Broken dreamers, their minds in ruin. This was the human race."

While Mr. Findley's dystopia signifies a shortage of happiness, there is no shortage of characters. The author's large cast constitutes a cross section of Toronto society, from kitchenmaids to painters to press barons, and the city itself is evoked so minutely and with such affection that it, too, becomes a kind of character.

At the center of the novel, however, is an unlikely trio. There is Lilah Kemp, former librarian, spiritualist and schizophrenic, "diagnosed according to her raising of the dead and her conversations with literary characters and famous persons from the past." And there are a pair of psychiatrists, Marlow and Rupert Kurtz, who act as standard bearers for the novel's conceptions of good and evil.

Marlow is no saint, of course, he merely possesses a conscience, which seems to have become a rare commodity in Toronto. But Kurtz is a black hat of memorable proportions. As the director of the city's most prestigious psychiatric institute (and confessor to many of its most powerful miscreants), this "harbinger of darkness," sets all sorts of ugly schemes in motion, involving blackmail, child pornography, torture, suicide and murder. Kurtz intends to "go against the current until he reaches that point where the river rises—the point of absolute power." At first only Lilah Kemp gauges the extent of Kurtz's wickedness, and in the end only Marlow is capable of confronting him with his crimes.

The attentive reader, noting the names and the talk of going upstream, will conclude that a prior work of literature is casting a long shadow over the present one. But Mr. Findley makes no secret of the fact that *Headhunter* is one long gloss on *Heart of Darkness*. Indeed, in the opening scene Lilah Kemp panics at the thought that she may have released Kurtz from the very pages of Joseph Conrad's novel. By updating this century-old parable of power and corruption. Mr. Findley demonstrates its relevance to an age in which both concepts have undergone a great many ghastly refinements. As one character points out, "Conrad was not the first to conjure Kurtz—and not the last. He was merely the first to give him that name."

But Mr. Findley has another purpose in mind, too. After all, *Headhunter* pilfers several other works for its characters, including *The Great Gatsby, Madame Bovary* and *Peter Rabbit*. These borrowings suggest a kind of interpenetration of literature and life, a sense that the best books do not merely tell a good story but add, as R. P. Blackmur once wrote, to our stock of available reality. Fiction seems to enfold the

very act of human intercourse, enabling Marlow to claim that "we write each other's lives—by means of fictions. Sustaining fictions. Uplifting fictions. Lies. This way, we lead one another toward survival."

Like many a loose and baggy saga, *Headhunter* has moments when the proliferation of characters and subplots begins to sap its narrative energy. In addition, Mr. Findley's spare prose occasionally lapses into pulpishness ("If his eyes had been lasers, his gaze would have burned a hole in the glass"). Still, it's rare to find an author in which the moralist and the entertainer cohabit so naturally. And if it is true, as Emerson insisted, that "every age, like every human body, has its own distemper," then Mr. Findley has diagnosed our own with eloquence and indignation.

John Rechy (review date 17 July 1994)

SOURCE: "The Heart of Madness," in *Los Angeles Times Book Review*, July 17, 1994, pp. 2, 8.

[*Rechy is a novelist. In the review below, he provides a laudatory assessment of* Headhunter.]

This exceptional novel [*Headhunter*] opens with a smashing paragraph that elevates a reader's expectations:

> On a winter's day, while a blizzard raged through the streets of Toronto, Lilah Kemp inadvertently set Kurtz free from Page 92 of *Heart of Darkness*. Horror-stricken, she tried to force him back between the covers. The escape took place at the Metropolitan Toronto Reference Library, where Lilah Kemp sat reading beside the rock pool. She had not even said come forth, but there Kurtz stood before her, framed by the woven jungle of cotton trees and vines that passed for botanic atmosphere.

Lilah is a schizophrenic, an outpatient in a psychiatric treatment center. She roams Toronto while pushing a baby carriage containing a copy of *Wuthering Heights*. From childhood she has been able to conjure up characters from her favorite books. Now she believes she has unleashed the evil Kurtz of Joseph Conrad's famous novella onto the streets of Toronto, but Kurtz is not a figment of Lilah's imagination. He's the chief of Toronto's Parkin Institute of Psychiatry.

The prospect of Lilah as substitute Marlow (the pursuer of Conrad's Kurtz) tracking down a sinister psychiatrist is exciting indeed. Alas, Timothy Findley, celebrated Canadian author, opts for more literal parallels with Conrad's novella. Another psychiatrist—named Marlow!—arrives at the center, a forced development that Findley tries to shrug off: "It's just sort of crazy—the kind of coincidence that happens once in a lifetime." Perhaps because of their allegorical function, neither Kurtz nor Marlow is as engaging as Lilah—she is crafty, wickedly likable, expertly drawn but finally not involved as fully as anticipated in bringing Kurtz out of his new station of power.

Findley intends to locate a contemporary heart of darkness: "If there are new forms of human beings, then it follows there must be new forms of madness." In place of the river up which Conrad's Marlow trails his Kurtz, Findley substitutes the convoluted corridors of psychiatric power ruled, godlike, by a modern Kurtz. Findley's Marlow discovers that Kurtz is condoning behavioral experiments in the control of the young. Kurtz is aware of, and even visits, the Club of Men, a group of wealthy Canadians who perpetrate increasing debaucheries.

Another horror is loose in the city. As deadly as AIDS, a new illness, "sturnusemia," is being suspiciously attributed by the government to starlings. D-squads are annihilating birds and wasting the landscape.

Given these grim developments, it's surprising that Findley manages terrific satire along the way: Gallery-opening art-chat becomes uproarious during the unveiling of deranged paintings of mutilation. A "fable" within the novel purports to reveal how Jean-Paul Sartre really died. At a formal dinner, Sartre expounds: "We pay attention to one another in accordance with our functions in one another's lives. . . . I desire wine—I call the waiter. . . . And once my glass is filled, then—poof!—he is gone. The waiter no longer exists." The waiter opens fire and—poof—kills Sartre and Simone de Beauvoir. Findley makes a hilarious, satirically illuminating commentary on existentialism.

Throughout, impeccable sentences and sophisticated insights delight. At the art opening, Kurtz muses:

> Nearly everyone in the room . . . has violence somewhere in the family background—the violence always on an operatic scale—Verdi, not Puccini. Never Wagner. Tasteful—but full-blown; a generation of weddings sung by tenors and sopranos—with all the dark basses and contraltos waiting in the wings . . . La Forza del destino.

Part of this novel's commercial success in Canada may result from its Canadian readers' familiarity with Toronto society. The uninitiated reader may find the book too long and become frustrated by its intended descriptions of city landscapes, its vast cast of glamorously named characters (Fabiana, Julian Slade), each of whom, major and minor, carries loads of unneeded background. There's too much

fussy action. Cigarettes are lit and snuffed, olives recurrently fished out of martinis.

Literary allusions abound, some surely meaningful mainly to the author, others amusing: Emma Berry conducts romantic liaisons in her moving limousine; and Lilah names the invisible baby in her carriage Linton.

> **Findley deserves high praise for his daring to explore grand themes, and to do so in fine, literate writing.**
> —*John Rechy*

Findley does not finally fulfill his own high ambitions: "Every Kurtz must have his Marlow, and Marlow will always come back to take Kurtz home. . . . With every journey up the river, we discover that Kurtz has penetrated just a little farther . . . through darker mysteries."

What Findley locates is more a unique perversion than the universal evil he has promised to explore, mysteries "darker" than Conrad's. The depravity here is too specific to stand as metaphor for the mysteries posed by real, near-ungraspable horrors that have occurred since the original Kurtz appeared: the Holocaust, the slaughter at My Lai, the lingering indifference to AIDS—much more brutal than the sturnusemia Findley imagines—the emergence of "ethnic cleansing," the hundreds of acts of daily brutalities.

Asking why Marlow always appears in order to pursue Kurtz, Findley proposes: ". . . because he is beholden to Kurtz for having provided him, after darkness, with a way to find new light." Findley does not contribute such "new light" of possible redemption. The relative hopefulness of his ending seems imposed. Despite the fact that his novel succeeds only partially, Findley deserves high praise for his daring to explore grand themes, and to do so in fine, literate writing.

Gary Draper (review date April 1995)

SOURCE: "The Past Recaptured," in *Books in Canada,* Vol. 24, No. 3, April, 1995, pp. 35-36.

[*Draper is a librarian. In the review below, he praises* The Piano Man's Daughter *for its focus on the past, its characterization, and its readability.*]

Some books set in the past try to ape the literary conventions of the past; some eschew them altogether. In *The Piano Man's Daughter,* Timothy Findley goes for the fundamentals. Without any suggestion of mimicry, this splendid novel captures the feel of high Victorian Gothic. It tells a multi-layered, multi-generational story of family madness and mysterious births. Attics. Dark secrets.

Melodrama is badly served by plot summary, which throws into visible relief the coincidences, parallels, and ironic twists which, in the context of the book, can be swallowed whole. Briefly, however, the piano man is Tom Wyatt, and his daughter is Lily, a creative, bright, eccentric woman attracted to music and to fire; the novel tells her story, in fragments, from conception to death. Inevitably, it is also a book about the storyteller, her son Charlie, born in her shadow, who spends much of his life in putting together the pieces of Lily's history and his own. And, because the mystery Charlie has to solve is rooted in the past, it is also the story of Lily's mother Ede, and her love for the piano man, and her marriage to his brother Frederick.

The book spans a neat half-century, from 1889 to 1939, though the last two decades are rather more quickly traversed. This is a very Findleyesque recasting of the past, a world of shabby gentility whose nearest Canadian relative might be Mazo de la Roche's *Jalna* (for which Findley wrote the TV adaptation). Whatever its affinities, it is a wonderfully idiosyncratic vision, and it enhances and enriches the way Canadians see themselves.

One of the simplest and most effective ways in which Findley evokes the past is by introducing popular songs of the time. I still find myself humming "Shine on, shine on harvest moon, up in the sky . . . " The reader understands the time and place better for hearing its songs: when you've hummed along with characters, you know a little more of where they come from. Of course the songs also work as reflections of the story, and as part of Lily's very identity:

> My mother believed in continuance—in what she called the songs in the blood; but my definition of those songs is far from benign. No child of mine will ever sing Lily's song. Once—for all its marvels—was once too often.

The Piano Man's Daughter is a veritable catalogue of Findley motifs: fire, photos, a search for the past, imprisonment and freedom. One hallmark of the World of Findley, of course, is the presence—indeed centrality—of exiles and outcasts, people who are different, peripheral, delicate. That means Lily, of course, but also, memorably, Lizzie Wyatt, her husband's younger brother, one of those "men so special they had been given women's names." Like all Findley's best writing, this book is rhythmic and lyrical; appropriately, it sings. Here is Charlie on his mother:

> I was never Lily's keeper. I was only ever her child and, on occasion, her guardian and, on occasion, her

victim and, on occasion, her accomplice. But I was never her keeper. The Keeper in Lily's life was fire. Her jail was her illness, and its key was a box of matches.

Among other things, this is a compellingly readable novel. It opens with a death; and it seems as if each time one mystery is put to bed another springs out. There is a good deal of foreboding. The reader keeps expecting the worst, an expectation that is usually met. The occasions when the clouds clear—as for example in the lovely moment among her Cambridge friends when Lily declares that she is happy—feel like those dangerous moments in real life when you know things are going too well, you know you're about to crash.

One way of looking at the novel is to see it as a series of brilliant set-pieces, as if Findley has imagined with incredible vividness some astonishing tableaux, and then created a narrative that makes sense of them. As a result, the reader assembles the novel's fragments as Charlie assembles the fragments of his past: Ede's first view of the piano man, the kitchen-table surgery, Lizzie waltzing Lily down the canvas rollers of the piano factory.

The story opens in a surreal world and slowly comes to clarity, like the stilling of rough waters. For all the dissolution and dispersal of the conclusion, there is hope for renewal and regeneration. The book moves from not knowing into a degree of knowing, from missing persons to found people, from fragments into a kind of wholeness. In a narrative such as this, the great trick is to weave a conclusion that lives up to the promise of the many mysteries that have been unravelling. The conclusion of *The Piano Man's Daughter* is completely satisfying without being self-evident; like all the best endings, it is also the beginning of another story.

John Bemrose (review date May 1995)

SOURCE: "Rural Roots," in *MacLean's,* Vol. 108, May, 1995, p. 66.

[*In the following, Bemrose assesses the plot and principal theme of* The Piano Man's Daughter.]

So often, Timothy Findley's fiction circles some central image, like a tribe dancing around a fire. In his 1977 novel, *The Wars,* it was horses: horses screaming under the artillery barrages of the First World War, or stampeding away from the madness of the trenches. Findley's 1993 novel, *Headhunter,* offered the image of its heroine, Lilah Kemp, the unforgettable street woman whose schizophrenia harbored an element of strange, life-nourishing sanity. And in his richly layered new novel, *The Piano Man's Daughter,*

Findley conjures up the presence of a simple field in a southern Ontario farm. This field—like both the horses and Lilah Kemp—becomes a touchstone for what is sacred in Findley's vision: a buffer against a society that seems bent on destroying innocence and psychic health.

Findley is, in the best, nondenominational sense, a religious novelist. His books reflect a world where wholeness has been grievously broken, although he occasionally allows a character to catch a glimpse of redemption shining among the fragments. In the opening pages of *The Piano Man's Daughter,* the first-person narrator, Charlie Kilworth, seems afflicted by a peculiarly modern sense of rootlessness and loss. It is 1939, war is looming, and his wife, Alexandra, has left him. His mother, Lily, has just died in a fire at a mental institution where she was a patient. As well, Charlie has no idea who his father was. It seems that Lily was not only mad but sexually profligate, and could never remember which of her couplings produced her son. So, with the help of some old photographs and letters, Charlie sets out to reconstruct his mother's life—with the hope of bringing some meaning into his own.

His search leads him to the closing decades of the 19th century, and the prosperous Ontario farm where Lily was born. He discovers that her penchant for making love to strangers was inherited from *her* mother, Ede Kilworth. Ede, it seems, fell in love with a travelling piano player, Tom Wyatt. She led him into a field that had been special to her as a girl, made love and later gave birth to their daughter, Lily, in the same place. This field—beautifully evoked by Findley with its wildflowers and brooding cows—is her refuge from social and family disapproval, as well as her solace when Tom dies in a trolley-car accident.

Ede's field is both an important symbol and a naturalistic detail woven into the novel's wondrous recreation of late Victorian and Edwardian Canada. For a time, Charlie all but disappears from the story, replaced by Findley's vision of life on the Kilworth farm, and in the big Toronto house where Ede takes her daughter to live after marrying Tom's wealthy brother, Frederick, a manufacturer of pianos. Findley has evoked the spirit of a time and place basking in the late sun of Empire: both its outward confidence and security, and its secret shadows. Lily's stepfather represents the former: he rules his household with a firm paternalism everyone accepts as completely normal, adhering to his demands like trains to a schedule.

The young Lily proves a threat to that tidy world. She is a pyromaniac. She also has violent fits, and when a seizure spoils an important dinner party, Frederick locks her in the attic—the first of several such incarcerations—and later banishes her to a strict boarding school. These two characters are the mythic poles of a tragic imbalance. Frederick embodies an overdeveloped masculine principle, grim and all-controlling, Lily, with her ready sympathy and love of animals, is the repressed feminine. And when the First World War erupts, it is as if Lily's pyromania has taken global revenge.

Those themes are buried in the substructure of the novel. On another, more naturalistic level, Findley's characters are also rounded human beings—here, even Frederick has his more likable side. *The Piano Man's Daughter* works best when both levels support each other, and that happens most impressively in the first two-thirds of the novel. Here, the story feels deeply, mysteriously organic—propelled by a vast, entirely believable web of relationships, from the sprawling Kilworth and Wyatt families themselves, to the servants who look after their houses and horses, to their cats and dogs and even the ants that live in their gardens.

Much of the novel's final third—which evokes Lily's university days at Cambridge, as well as her itinerant years raising Charlie in a series of boarding houses and hotels—feels attenuated and forced by comparison. Removed from the matrix of her family. Lily's character becomes static, while Charlie's search for his father's identity is not particularly compelling. Yet, Findley recovers in the novel's final, elegiac pages, in which Charlie achieves a deepened understanding of his mother's suffering. Here, too, he reconnects with his wife, and together they renew their hopes for the future. The reader last glimpses the characters in the field where Lily was conceived and born: it makes a moving conclusion to a novel that reaches memorably into that crucible of origins and losses we call the past.

FURTHER READING

Criticism

Caldwell, Joan. "Findley, Timothy." In *The Oxford Companion to Canadian Literature,* edited by William Toye, pp. 257-59. Toronto: Oxford University Press, 1983.
    Brief biocritical survey of Findley's career.

D'Haen, Theo. "Timothy Findley: Magical Realism and the Canadian Postmodern." In *Multiple Voices: Recent Canadian Fiction,* edited by Jeanne Delbaere, pp. 217-33. Sydney: Dangaroo Press, 1990.
    Provides a thematic analysis of *The Telling of Lies,* in which the book's postmodernist and magic realist elements are discussed.

Foley, Michael. "Noah's Wife's Rebellion: Timothy Findley's Use of the Mystery Plays of Noah in *Not Wanted on the Voyage*." *Essays on Canadian Writing*, No. 44 (Fall 1991): 175-82.

Studies Findley's use of medieval plays in *Not Wanted on the Voyage*.

Fraser, C. Gerald. Review of *The Last of the Crazy People*, by Timothy Findley. *The New York Times Book Review* 90 (13 October 1985): 38.

Extremely brief, favorable assessment of *The Last of the Crazy People*.

Gabriel, Barbara. "Staging Monstrosity: Genre, Life-Writing, and Timothy Findley's *The Last of the Crazy People*." *Essays on Canadian Writing*, No. 54 (Winter 1994): 168-97.

Examines elements and influences of Gothicism, the American southern literary tradition, homosexuality, the grotesque, and autobiography in *The Last of the Crazy People*.

Grosskurth, Phyllis. "New Canadian Novels." *Canadian Saturday Night* 82, No. 5 (May 1967): 39-40.

Offers a mixed appraisal of *The Last of the Crazy People*.

Kröller, Eva-Marie. "The Exploding Frame: Uses of Photography in Timothy Findley's *The Wars*." *Journal of Canadian Studies/Revue d'études canadiennes* 16, Nos. 3-4 (Fall-Winter 1981): 68-74.

Explores the importance of photography and photographs in *The Wars*.

Nicholson, Mervyn. "God, Noah, Lord Byron—and Timothy Findley." *Ariel: A Review of International English Literature* 23, No. 2 (April 1992): pp. 87-107.

Argues that Findley's examination of the biblical flood myth in *Not Wanted on the Voyage* aims to "reveal, forcefully and clearly, the power relations in the Bible and in any culture that professes to take the Bible literally." Nicholson compares Findley's retelling of the flood with that of Lord Byron's *Heaven and Earth*.

Shields, E. F. "'The Perfect Voice': Mauberly as Narrator in Timothy Findley's *Famous Last Words*." *Canadian Literature* 119 (Winter 1988): 84-98.

Examines the narrative strategies employed in *Famous Last Words*.

Sullivan, Jack. Review of *The Telling of Lies*, by Timothy Findley. *The New York Times Book Review* 93 (9 October 1988): 34.

Highly favorable, albeit short, assessment of *The Telling of Lies*.

Weiss, Allan. "Private and Public in Timothy Findley's *The Wars*." *Canadian Literature/Littérature canadienne*, Nos. 138-39 (Fall-Winter 1993): 91-102.

Examines the relationship between privacy and the public sphere in *The Wars*, asserting that "[the] entire novel, in fact, is in the form of an effort by the researcher-narrator to break through . . . public reticence to discover the real Robert Ross."

W. E. L. Review of *Dinner along the Amazon*, by Timothy Findley. *Kliatt: Young Adult Paperback Book Guide* 20, No. 1 (January 1986): 29.

Offers praise for *Dinner along the Amazon*. The critic briefly notes themes in the volume and argues some young readers may be frustrated with the book.

Interview

Aitken, Johan. "'Long Live the Dead': An Interview with Timothy Findley." *Canadian Fiction*, No. 33 (1982): 79-93.

Interview originally conducted in April, 1980, while Findley was writer-in-residence at the University of Toronto, in which Findley discusses *The Wars*, its composition, characters, and influences, as well as various aspects of Canadian literature and criticism.

Additional coverage of Findley's life and career is contained in the following sources published by Gale Research: *Contemporary Authors,* 25-28R; *Contemporary Authors New Revision Series,* Vols. 12, 42; *Dictionary of Literary Biography,* Vol. 53; *DISCovering Authors: Canadian;* and *DISCovering Authors Modules: Most-studied Authors.*

Dick Francis
1920-

(Born Richard Stanley Francis) Welsh-born English novelist, short story writer, autobiographer, and biographer.

The following entry presents an overview of Francis's career. For further information on his life and works, see *CLC*, Volumes 2, 22, and 42.

INTRODUCTION

A former steeplechase jockey, Francis is famous for his suspense novels as well as his championship career. His thrillers usually focus on corruption in the world of horse racing and feature a hero struggling through various physical and psychological obstacles to return order to that world. Francis produces one novel per year, most of which are bestsellers. He has a strong popular following and most of his work is critically acclaimed.

Biographical Information

Francis comes from a long line of Welsh horsemen. His father was a former jockey and a successful trainer. Although his father discouraged his interest in becoming a jockey, Francis signed up with a stable at the age of eighteen. Francis, however, did not have an opportunity to race before the outbreak of World War II. He became an Air Force pilot, flying Spitfires and then bombers, before returning to England to become a jockey in 1946. He won between 350 and 400 races and suffered from a variety of injuries during his career. He was England's champion jockey in 1954, and in 1957 he was jockey for the Queen Mother's horse Devon Loch in the Grand National. The horse stumbled in the last stretch and was unable to recover. After this great disappointment, Francis retired from his career as a steeplechase jockey. A publisher convinced Francis to write his autobiography, *The Sport of Queens* (1957), while he was still well known. The book was commercially successful and led him to write racing articles for the London Sunday Express for the next sixteen years. An admirer of the popularity of mystery novels, Francis always wanted to write one himself. When Francis's wife became worried about the state of their finances, she finally convinced him to try. He wrote *Dead Cert* (1962) which was accepted by a publisher and became a bestseller. Two years later he wrote *Nerve* (1964) and has continued at a pace of one novel per year since then. He writes from January to May on the balcony of his Ft. Lauderdale apartment, and for the rest of the year he and his wife travel and conduct research for his next novel. Francis has won several literary awards, including Edgar Allan Poe Awards for *For-*

feit (1968) and *Whip Hand* (1979), and his work is among the most commercially successful in the crime and mystery genre.

Major Works

All of Francis's books follow a similar formula: they are written in the first person; the protagonist is a male in his 20s or 30s with some connection to horse racing; and he is drawn into an intrigue caused by a villain whom he works to expose and defeat by the end of the novel. There are a variety of physical and mental obstacles to overcome along the way. Most of Francis's earlier work centers on the horseracing world. *Dead Cert,* his first novel, is the story of a jockey who uncovers and eliminates a race-fixing scheme. *Forfeit* is about a racing journalist whose invalid wife discovers a bookmaking scheme. While horse racing is always part of the story, even if only peripheral to the action, Francis also presents a new topic with each new novel. Subjects of Francis novels have included flying in *Flying Finish* (1966), gold mining in *Smokescreen* (1972), art in *In the Frame* (1976), technology in *Twice Shy* (1981), high finance in

Banker (1982), winemaking in *Proof* (1985), and the gem business in *Straight* (1989). Francis' heroes are men of conscience who uphold values of justice and integrity. Francis asserts that his protagonists are not strictly autobiographical, but they are men he admires and he never makes them do anything he wouldn't do himself. Francis's experience as a steeplechase jockey exposed him to extensive pain and injury. He uses his knowledge of injury to subject his heroes to a variety of physical torments either through racing spills or attacks by villains. While Francis's earlier novels are filled with physical torture, his later work shifts its focus to the psychological aspects of pain and mental torture.

Critical Reception

Critics often point out the influence of Francis's earlier careers on his writing. Reviewers compare the skillful pacing of his narratives to the skillful pacing of racing a horse. His work as a journalist helped him develop a succinct prose which critics praise. Francis is also known for his well-rounded characters, skill at suspense, and the authenticity of his dialogue and setting. Many critics find great humor in Francis's fiction, asserting that it provides relief when things get too grim. Reviewers disagree about the place of class in Francis's books. Several critics accuse him of being too aristocratic, but others assert that his heroes come from all classes. Class conflict is inherent in most of his novels. Some reviewers complain that Francis novels are overly violent and formulaic, but still praise his fast-moving and well-researched plots.

PRINCIPAL WORKS

The Sport of Queens: The Autobiography of Dick Francis (autobiography) 1957
Dead Cert (novel) 1962
Nerve (novel) 1964
For Kicks (novel) 1965
Odds Against (novel) 1965
Best Racing and Chasing Stories 2 vols. [editor; with John Welcome] (short stories) 1966-69
Flying Finish (novel) 1966
Blood Sport (novel) 1967
Forfeit (novel) 1968
Enquiry (novel) 1969
The Racing Man's Bedside Book [editor; with John Welcome] 1969
Rat Race (novel) 1970
Bonecrack (novel) 1971
Smokescreen (novel) 1972
Slay-Ride (novel) 1973
Knockdown (novel) 1974
High Stakes (novel) 1975

In the Frame (novel) 1976
Risk (novel) 1977
Trial Run (novel) 1978
Whip Hand (novel) 1979
Reflex (novel) 1980
Twice Shy (novel) 1981
Banker (novel) 1982
The Danger (novel) 1983
Break In (novel) 1985
Proof (novel) 1985
Lester: The Official Biography (biography) 1986
Bolt (novel) 1987
Hot Money (novel) 1987
The Edge (novel) 1988
Straight (novel) 1989
Longshot (novel) 1990
Comeback (novel) 1991
Driving Force (novel) 1992
Decider (novel) 1993
Wild Horses (novel) 1994

CRITICISM

Denis Pitts (review date 15 October 1986)

SOURCE: "Very Yoff-Yoff," in *Punch Weekly,* Vol. 291, October 15, 1986, p. 55.

[*In the following review, Pitts criticizes Francis's* Bolt *for being snobbish and implausible.*]

My favourite jump-jockey is a minute little fellow with a face like a pruned-up parrot and a voice to match. He's so small that he has to have a leg up on to the barstool; but when he gets there, he's good for many a yarn.

There was the drunken starter at Chepstow who fell off his stand and took off on the favourite's rump; and the semi-delirious rider who took advantage of a St. John's Ambulance lady in the back of a blood-wagon at Newton Abbot (and pleaded concussion); or the desolate, newly-gelded favourite who stopped to graze in a steeplechase at Fontwell.

He retired at the end of last season and the beer which he once declined, has given him a tiny, pimple-like paunch. He says he has broken every bone in his body in his time but there seems to be little mental deterioration—except, maybe, for a mild amnesia of the wallet.

"I suppose you wouldn't care to write my life story." he asked me the other day.

"It'd make great reading." I told him. "But Dick Francis has got the jockey business well sewed up."

I was somewhat taken aback by the fury that followed.

"Bloody Dick bloody Francis." he almost shouted. "What does he bloody know about bloody racing?"

I reminded him of our hero's record of distinction as an amateur jump jockey.

"Oh, he was all right in the saddle but his books . . . he's a bloody yoff-yoff, that's his problem."

(Racing parlance. A yoff-yoff (toff) is the owner. Trainers are guvnors, stewards are right bastards).

More calmly, he claimed that Dick Francis was a snob who never wrote sympathetically about the real racing workers like the lads and lasses and apprentices who did the mucking out while the guvnors swilled champagne with the yoff-yoffs.

I saw his point. Francis does tend to indulge the higher echelons of the great fraternity of the turf—but, to be fair, most of his villains come from that strata, and nasty villains they are, too.

> **Francis does tend to indulge the higher echelons of the great fraternity of the turf—but, to be fair, most of his villains come from that strata, and nasty villains they are, too.**
> —*Denis Pitts*

Then came **Bolt**. I stretched myself out on a beach in Cyprus the other day to enjoy the latest Dick Francis and found myself coming rapidly to the conclusion that my friend was right. This is a very snobbish book and, what's more, it is a very disappointing 25th novel—dead cert though it will be in the bookshops.

Without wishing to give away the plot (though, Lord knows, I don't think I could ever sell it myself), there is this archetypal Dick Francis hero, a jockey who rides for a wealthy countess whose husband is being threatened by a grossly implausible business partner. He (the jockey) has a fiancée called Danielle and she looks like leaving him for a wealthy prince.

Somehow, between riding countless winners at Newbury and the like, the jockey sorts out the countess's problems, gets the girl and disposes of the villain.

To enjoy this book, even the most devout Francis fan will need not just to suspend belief—he'll need to stretch it from Aintree to breakfast-time.

I mean to say, here is a villain who makes the most open and evil threats against a family, who tries to murder the aforesaid prince (you've just got to believe the way our Dick gets him out of that one) and yet no one seems to think of calling in the police like you and I would. No, they are happy to rely on this obsequious, somewhat toady-like, jump-jock who is too clever by half, anyway.

Come to think of it, there's no real climax, either. If there is, I must say I've known more suspenseful moments on *Playschool*.

Sorry (and I speak as a founder member of the DF appreciation society) but **Bolt** seems to have died under Dick Francis, just like Devon Loch died under him in the National.

Nick Kimberley (review date 14 November 1986)

SOURCE: "Knacker's Yard," in *New Statesman*, Vol. 112, No. 2903, November 14, 1986, pp. 28-9.

[*In the following review, Kimberley criticizes Francis's* Bolt *and asserts that thriller writers are not allowed to "retire gracefully" like old race horses when they "no longer cut the mustard."*]

When old race horses no longer cut the mustard, they're allowed to retire gracefully. Not so thriller writers—which brings me to Dick Francis. **Bolt** is his 25th racetracker thriller and, like many of its predecessors, it's taken up with wealth, opulence and lineage. Kit Fielding, a well-bred jockey not at all like those you see interviewed on TV, rides horses for a princess whose family's vast but honourable business is threatened by an uncouth partner. Fielding sees off this loudmouth, and any other villains, while still managing to ride a few winners, take a few falls.

As you might expect from a man whose autobiography is called *The Sport of Queens,* there's little time spent with the lowly punter who, in the real world, makes the jockey's efforts meaningful. In fact, horses and courses are incidental colouring, endearing to those who like racing, off-putting to the rest of us. What matters is protecting the lovely princess and her money. Fielding shows a commendable desire to prevent the weapons industry from sullying that wealth—not, though, because guns in themselves are to be shunned, but simply to ensure that no terrorists are armed out of the family's trading. Terrorists, after all, are unprincipled lunatics whose actions are merely self-serving. Ironic, then, that throughout the novel Fielding insists that the police should not be called in—as he says, he has taken justice into his own hands. Isn't that one definition of terrorism?

Tony Hillerman (review date 15 March 1987)

SOURCE: "Dick Francis And the Racer's Edge," in *Washington Post Book World,* March 15, 1987, p. 9.

[*In the following review, Hillerman asserts that while readers generally do not read Francis's work for his plots, with* Bolt *"Francis finally uses a plot so flawed that it ruins the book."*]

Admirers of Dick Francis don't read him for his plots. We read him for his precise use of the language, for rounded characters, for his skill at suspense and for the authentic trip he gives us through the world of steeplechase racing. When he gives us an outstanding story line, as in *Blood Sport, Odds Against, In the Frame,* etc., it is a bonus. Usually it isn't the plot that keeps us reading long into the night.

In *Bolt,* unfortunately, Francis finally uses a plot so flawed that it ruins the book.

We deal here with a cast even more aristocratic than usual in the expensive world of horses that Francis likes to explore. Roland de Brescou, the target of the dastardly deeds, is half owner of the French industrial conglomerate which bears his family's name. He is husband of Princess Casalia. Prince Listi is wooing his niece. And as Prince Listi reminds us, one of the useful things about being so well connected "is that if one seriously asks, one is seldom refused. Another is that one knows and has met a great many people in useful positions." Such powerful folks can "simply set a few wheels in motion." Yet in *Bolt* we must believe that such powerful people can't get police action even when a roomful of them witness a felony.

> **Admirers of Dick Francis don't read him for his plots. We read him for his precise use of the language, for rounded characters, for his skill at suspense and for the authentic trip he gives us through the world of steeplechase racing.**
> **—Tony Hillerman**

A Frenchman named Nanterre owns the other half of de Brescou's industry. He wants to enter the armaments business and needs de Brescou's signature on pertinent papers. De Brescou considers the venture dishonorable. Nanterre

storms past his butler into his parlor, makes threats and finally, "produced a black and businesslike pistol. With a gliding step he reached the princess and pressed the end of the barrel against her temple, standing behind her and holding her head firmly with his left hand under the chin.

'Now,' he said gratingly to de Brescou, 'sign the form.'"

This assault is done before the eyes of four witnesses, three of whom are hostile to the culprit. Do these people, all of whom have the power "to set a few wheels in motion," have Nanterre arrested, prosecuted and deported? Nope, They call upon Kit Fielding, who rides for the Princess. Why don't they call the police?

It seems Princess Casalia's lawyer had called the police earlier after Nanterre had threatened her at the track. No crime had been committed so the police weren't interested. But now (on page 53) we have felonious assault with threats of more to come. For the next 250 pages *Bolt* struggles under the burden of our impatience, and it increases as the Princess's horses are slaughtered and an attempt is made on the Prince's life. Even prose as clean as Francis' can't hold us when we're wondering why these dolts don't go to the police and sign a complaint.

Bolt asks us to suspend more disbelief than we can manage. But it also contains some of the skill that earned the author fame. The relationship between the lovelorn Fielding and a girl having second thoughts about their involvement is handled with artistry. Aware he is losing her, not knowing why, Fielding leaves her at her bedroom door, remembering a goodnight kiss which "had again been a defense, not a promise." When he finally blurts out the question of what's gone wrong, he instantly withdraws it and scrambles out of his car to avoid the answer. The answer, typically of Francis, is exactly right. The racing scenes which Francis uses to illuminate the character of his rider/hero are tense and lyrical as always. Fielding is perfectly drawn as a decent man who loves what he does, and the animals he rides. Here he is by the body of a horse that had gallantly recovered from a stumble in an earlier race.

"I put a hand down to touch Col's foreleg, and felt its rigidity, its chill. The foreleg that had saved us from disaster at Ascot, that had borne all his weight."

If you haven't read Francis, do so. But don't begin with *Bolt.*

Dick Lochte (review date 7 June 1987)

SOURCE: A review of *Bolt,* in *Los Angeles Times Book Review,* June 7, 1987, p. 13.

[*In the following review, Lochte praises Francis's* Bolt, *noting the exceptional dialogue and faultless storytelling.*]

Steeplechase jockey-turned-author Dick Francis' last racing tale, *Break In,* introduced us to a self-reliant rider named Kit Fielding who had to deal with a violent family feud that threatened him and his twin sister, a budding romance with a headstrong young woman and the navigation of several rather difficult races. The first of many surprises greeting us in Francis' new tale is the discovery that there is an Act Two to Kit's life.

Though many of the novelist's central characters are jockeys or former jockeys, he has gone out of his way to eschew series books, probably in an effort to make the point that, though they may share some common physical traits, jockeys are as individually unique as any other professionals.

Bolt is less a sequel than a continuation of the original book, and yet *Break In* is not required reading. With an almost miraculous economy of words, Francis swiftly sums up as much information as is needed from the earlier book, while simultaneously untying the ends that had been so neatly gathered. As Kit explains: "Winning the lady, back in November, had been unexpected, an awakening, deeply exciting . . . happy. Keeping her, in the frosts before spring, was proving the merry devil. My much-loved dark-haired young woman seemed frighteningly to be switching her gaze from a steeplechase jockey (myself) to an older, richer sophisticate of superior lineage. . . ." Returning also is the malevolent Maynard Allardeck, whose family has despised the Fieldings for generations. Kit cleverly devised a stratagem to keep him at bay in the last book, but Allardeck has not taken his defeat gracefully and, as a racing steward, is in a position to cause trouble.

And there is a powerful new villain, Henri Nanterre, who will stop at nothing, apparently, to convince his partner, Kit's prospective uncle-in-law, to convert their construction company into an armament empire. First he threatens the partner's wife; when Kit checks that challenge, he ups the ante. The wife's championship horses, Kit's mounts, are brutally slain by a bolt gun, a captive-bullet weapon that is supposed to provide a merciful death for animals in pain. And when the jockey's fiancé and even her "older richer sophisticate" are threatened, Kit is forced to devise a particularly devious plan to spike Nanterre's guns.

Francis has said in interviews that his tales aren't thrillers. He prefers to call them "adventure stories." None of them proves his point better than *Bolt.* The sport of kings. The wealthy and titled reacting to stress. The setting of traps to catch evildoers rather than resorting to the police. This is not exactly the stuff that turns the bleak world of John Le Carre so chillingly cold and gray. Actually, it is closer in spirit to the capers that kept "The Saint," Simon Templar, in champagne and caviar for so many decades. Admittedly, the characterizations are a bit sketchier than the author has settled for in the past. And his lead is more idealistically heroic—dashing, wealthy, clever and a great deal more confident—than others who have worn the Francis colors. But the dialogue—from tough talk to drawing-room banter—rings entertainingly true and bristles with edgy energy. The storytelling is faultless. And the track is so fast, it seems as if we have scarcely cleared the starting gate when we are bolting past the finish line. That's how it goes when you ride with a champion who knows the course.

Brigitte Weeks (review date 21 February 1988)

SOURCE: "Of Heroes And Horses," in *Washington Post Book World,* February 21, 1988, pp. 1, 14.

[*In the following review, Weeks discusses Francis's* Hot Money, *focusing on the themes of horses and heroism which are found throughout Francis's work.*]

Dick Francis' mysteries have been published every spring for more than 20 years. They come out in England the previous fall and many of his fans just can't wait those extra few months. Winter travelers last year returned to Washington loaded down with British editions of *Hot Money.* Soon the word was out among aficionados: "A good Francis."

And good it is, up there with *Whip Hand* and *Forfeit.* It is awesome how this 67-year-old former steeplechase jockey (he rode for the Queen Mother until 1957) produces an annual novel of unrivalled consistency and craft. Each one explores a new area of knowledge—ranging from artificial limbs to wine-making—that becomes part of the fabric of the story.

At the center of Francis' 26th thriller are a five-times-married international gold speculator, Malcolm Pembroke, and Ian, his son by his second wife. Ian is an amateur jockey with dreams of turning professional.

Francis once said that his heroes "are the sort of chaps I'd like to meet" and Ian is exactly the kind of young man most of us would love to meet: independent yet responsible, kind yet courageous, full of the moral fiber essential to the kind of chap Dick Francis admires.

> **Francis once said that his heroes "are the sort of chaps I'd like to meet."**
> —*Brigitte Weeks*

So gold bullion trading (at which Malcolm is spectacularly successful) and steeplechase riding are the setting for *Hot Money* and they make a sexy combination. When Malcolm gets interested in his son's avocation, the two come satisfyingly together. Money is a more accessible central gimmick to most readers than the rather technical plastic firearms or humane killing devices that worked less successfully in last year's *Bolt*. Spare gold is also very handy in the horse racing business.

The Pembrokes are not a large and happy family. In fact, they could be the Medici in modern dress. Malcolm's riches have in different ways distorted the lives of his children and their spouses. Ian, a personable bachelor with the usual Franciscan reluctance to commit himself to a serious relationship, is unexpectedly presented with a double task: to keep his father from being murdered and to discover which of his siblings or relatives may have been behind the near-miss car accident or the home-made bomb that destroyed the family home.

As his five marriages might indicate, Malcolm was no boy's dream father. He quarreled violently with Ian over his fifth wife, but even before that Ian tells us, "In a totally confused chaotic upbringing I'd spent scattered unhappy periods with my bitter mother but had mostly been passed from wife to wife in my father's house as part of the furniture or fittings, treated by him throughout with the same random but genuine affection he gave to his dogs."

Despite this inauspicious history, affection and trust reawakens between Ian and his father, haltingly with setbacks, as they are drawn together by danger. "It struck me that he really needed to hear me say I loved him, so although he might scoff at the actual words, and despite the conditioned inhibitions of my upbringing, I said, feeling that desperate situations needed desperate remedies, "You're a great father-. . . . and . . . er . . . I love you." Ian's handling of the shortcomings and problems of his seven half-siblings is enviably laced with compassion and understanding.

To handle this large and intertwined cast of characters without thoroughly confusing his readers, Francis uses a tried and true technique: he introduces a depressed but highly professional private detective by the name of Norman West to investigate the movements and circumstances of everyone in the Pembroke family. West's flat but conscientious reports to Ian fill in many necessary details and his occasional asides provide a wonderful deadpan viewpoint, taking us briefly outside the family. Of Mrs. Ursula Pembroke, the wife of one of Ian's half brothers, he reports "Mrs. U unhappy woman but wouldn't unbutton. Loyal. Any wife of Mr. G likely to be unhappy (my opinion). . . . Does she believe killing Mr. Pembroke could solve her Problems? Does

she believe if Mr. G. becomes richer it will make things right? I could tell her it won't. End of inquiry."

Best-selling suspense fiction relies on many different elements to creep into the hearts and pocketbooks of readers. Sex and violence are standards—some of the latter but not much of the former in Francis—but what is unusual about his immense appeal is that all his books are skilful, elegant variations on a theme of horses and heroism. But they are no more repetitious or monotonous than are a set of Bach variations. We care about his heroes because they are worth caring about. (I'd definitely like to have Ian Pembroke on my side in a crisis.) They represent the best in human nature while struggling convincingly with their own shortcomings and weaknesses. They are never too perfect to identify with and don't win all their races.

Frederick Busch (review date 6 March 1988)

SOURCE: "Dick Francis' Latest a Good Bet," in *Chicago Tribune Books,* March 6, 1988, p. 6.

[*In the following review, Busch describes Francis's* Hot Money *as a thriller with enough suspense to keep the reader interested.*]

"Hot Money," Ian Pembroke explains to his father, consists of "bets made by people in the know. People with inside information." Ian, a horse trainer and amateur jockey, is bodyguarding millionaire Dad, Malcolm—all over their native England, and in parts of Australia and America—because someone is trying to kill the irascible man who by Ian and outrageous to his seven other surviving children and their four surviving mothers, Malcolm's ex-wives.

His fifth has been murdered as the novel opens. It's a fine beginning, in Ian's voice: "I intensely disliked my father's fifth wife, but not to the point of murder." Father and son, estranged for years, become reconciled—become friends—as Ian labors to keep his father alive. For of all his children, Malcolm (their difficulties notwithstanding) trusts Ian. So do we. He's tough, resourceful, unselfish and, as Francis proves in some of his customarily magically stirring racing descriptions, a brave and able rider.

To Ian's credit, he loves his nasty family—the drunkard, the fat failed poet, the brain-damaged accident victim, the shrewish aerobics teacher, and the others. They are crass, small and selfish in their lust for Malcolm's money. And it's clear, as Ian demonstrates, that one of them killed Wife Five, and is bent on killing Ian and Malcolm.

It's really a thriller, not a mystery. The central "clue" is Ian's insight into his family; a secondary clue might be considered unfair by detective-story purists, though it's part of a novel that yields enough fun to forestall complaints.

The novel is really more about money than racing, though its title and central metaphor derive from the horses. Ian is one of those "people with inside information" derived from studying his weak, well-loved, money-hungry kin. He cracks the case as Francis gives us ample suspense, a plenitude of venalities, lots on information on home-made bombs, and perhaps more caviar and champagne than we can digest.

John Skow (review date 21 March 1988)

SOURCE: "Reverse *Lear*," in *Time*, Vol. 131, No. 12, March 21, 1988, p. 78.

[*In the following review, Skow praises Francis's* Hot Money *for its believable characterizations and whodunit puzzle.*]

Psychology is kept decently out of sight in most of the 25 horsey thrillers listed on the op-title page of Dick Francis' new entertainment. It is what goes on—wheels turning in the murky unconscious, and all that—when one of his characters, caught in some awkwardness, says "er . . ." That unmistakable Francis "er . . ." has got author and readers past many a potentially mushy spot and on to the good part, where the hero is gonked by hired gorillas or injected with horse tranquilizer, and then wakes up, aware that something is wrong, inside a locked steamer trunk.

The author's formula has become too predictable, however, and *Hot Money* is especially welcome because it offers a variation. No steamer trunks this trip, though as usual there are a few "ers" in the mixture, for flavor. Only the locked room of the mind (and the odd explosion) vex the hero, an amateur steeplechase rider named Ian Pembroke, as he puzzles out who is trying to murder his rich and autocratic father.

There is no lack of candidates. Malcolm Pembroke, a hugely successful gold speculator, has shed several repellent wives. Recently someone knocked off his loathsome fifth, presumably to keep her from inheriting the family bundle. There are nine children, including Ian, and assorted spouses and their children. All are neurotic, vengeful and desperate for money, because Malcolm refuses to sweeten their small trust funds. The author's scheme neatly turns the *King Lear* plot inside out, observing the wreckage strewn about the heath when an aging tyrant fails to hand over power and wealth to his children.

Ah, but who is playing Goneril and Regan, and who Cordelia?

Could this be one of those *Orient Express* situations in which everyone is the murderer? Everyone has a motive; no question about that. Malcolm goads his whining brood without mercy, taking care to be seen splashing money and champagne in all directions but theirs as he buys racehorses and lolls about the world like a pasha.

Then his house blows up, and he is made to realize that his goading has succeeded. Somebody wants him dead, and may well get his wish. Or hers. Now what? He goes on the run, of course, but flamboyant Malcolm has no talent for keeping his head down. Author Francis is sometimes faulted for wooden characterizations, but here he is believable and chilling as he takes on the pathology of a large, mutually destructive family. The whodunit puzzle at the book's core is unusually good, and its solution, like those the late Ross Macdonald used to devise, takes into account wounds dealt out and suffered decades before.

Dick Francis with Alvin P. Sanoff (interview date 28 March 1988)

SOURCE: "Finding Intrigue Wherever He Goes," in *U.S. News and World Report*, Vol. 104, No. 12, March 28, 1988, p. 56.

[*Below, Sanoff presents Francis' remarks about his work and the research he does for his novels.*]

I write mysteries because I like reading them. I would pick them up at railway stations and airports—and one day said to my wife Mary: "I'm going to write a mystery someday. These Agatha Christie and Edgar Wallace books seem to be doing all right." At the time, I was writing about racing for the *Sunday Express*, but it wasn't quite so lucrative as my career as a successful jockey: There weren't so many dollars coming in. Still, the newspaper work taught me how to write—what words to leave out. After a few years, Mary said: "You always said you were going to write a novel. Now's the time. We don't want to lower our standard of living, and we've got two sons to educate, and the car is beginning to knock. You had better start."

I began in early 1961 and finished *Dead Cert* sometime in the fall. The publishers had it about 10 days and said they would publish it straightaway. It was a great day. The next book, *Nerve,* came out two years later. They made me write two in 1965. God, it was a hard year! There's been one every year since. The recent ones have got a little bit longer. Since I've given up the newspaper work, there's more time to spend on them.

I always start writing a story in January and finish in May.

But I start thinking about what I will write months before. I watch the news a lot and get ideas from it. In fact, I've got an idea for my next book from something that has happened in the news recently, but I'm not going to say what it is other than that it involves the press and probably will be set in the United States.

The next step in the process is the research. I researched the novel I'm now writing, *The Edge,* while I was on a book-promotion trip across Canada last autumn. After I got back home and put quite a few notes down, my wife and I went back to spend time around train yards and went into the engines with the drivers. The main character works for the Racecourse Security Service in England. One of the characters the service is keeping a very close eye on is coming to Canada to take part in an international railway tour taking horses to run at tracks around the country.

In *The Edge,* as in all the others, I know before I start writing what the main crime is going to be and who the culprits and victims are, but the subplots develop as I write. My crooks are an amalgam of a number of people. As for my heroes, I won't say they're autobiographical, but I wouldn't ask them to do anything I wouldn't do myself.

The opening passage and paragraphs take a long time to write because I like to capture my audience straightaway when they open the book and look in. When I'm at home—I live in Fort Lauderdale now—I write about 4 or 5 hours every day, sitting outside on the veranda with a notebook. I find it easier to write over here because not so many people know my telephone number and my whereabouts. Back in England, I can never get through a day without someone telephoning and wanting to know about my social or racing life.

My wife and I travel about the world quite a lot, and are endlessly saying: "You know, that would be a good idea for the next story." Wherever I go, I try to use the scenes I see. About 16 months ago, we went to the Breeders Cup at Santa Anita in California. Then we flew to Australia. We got there just in time for the Melbourne Cup on the following Tuesday. I wrote *Hot Money* around some of these places.

Before I wrote *Blood Sport,* which was set in America, my wife and I went on Greyhound buses and traveled 7,500 miles in three weeks. The people we met around Chicago were foreigners to those who got on the bus near Phoenix: It was like going across Europe and meeting a Greek on one part of the trip and a Belgian on the other.

As we travel, Mary takes a lot of photographs of ordinary, everyday scenes that might be of help in writing. In Oslo, for instance, we'll see the blue buses going down the road, and she'll take a picture. And she'll photograph telephone kiosks about the road, so we know that they use green boxes in Prague. We've got a big library of photographs.

Mary is my one and only editor: If I can get something past her, I hope I can get it past the publishers. In fact, the books ought to be written by "Dick and Mary Francis." But I had a name to start with, and so I have carried it on like that.

Mary loves doing research. She even took up flying for *Flying Finish.* I had been a pilot during the war, but by the time I wrote the book, regulations had changed a lot. I kept going to the local flying-training school at Oxford to get up-to-date. They said: "Why don't you start flying again? In a few hours, you'll soon get your license back." I didn't have time, so the fellow at the school said, "Well, send your wife along for a few lessons, and she'll help." Mary got bitten by the bug. My accountant talked us into buying three airplanes, and we started a little air-charter business. And that was the background for the book *Rat Race.*

Mary took up painting for another book, *In the Frame,* but she wasn't a born artist, so she didn't keep that up. We both spent a lot of time at the laboratories at UCLA to learn all about pharmacology for *Banker.* For the book I called *Proof,* we spent 30 years researching and drinking wine. Writing is hard work, but it's great fun doing the research.

William L. DeAndrea (review date Spring 1988)

SOURCE: A review of *Hot Money,* in *The Armchair Detective,* Vol. 21, No. 2, Spring, 1988, p. 156.

[*In the following excerpt, DeAndrea praises Francis's* Hot Money.]

Last column, I had a few words to say about one of those writers whose mystery-story career is a cause of anguish, someone who has to "write down" to the mystery audience, who is constrained by the plot requirements of the form from doing something Better and Finer.

I kept thinking of this guy as I was reading *Hot Money,* the new Dick Francis novel, which should be out in its American edition just about the time you read this. Now, Francis is someone who adds restrictions of his own to the requirements of the thriller. The books are always first-person. There is always a horse-racing connection, however tenuous. The protagonist is always a man, young to middle-aged, with a trace of melancholy to his character.

And it doesn't constrain him a bit. Dick Francis's books are always filled with believable characters doing things for reasons that make sense in the context of the book. There is frequently violence in a Dick Francis novel, but it is never of the "Let's go for the gross-out" kind. As I have said before, it is there to show the courage and loyalty of the protagonist.

Dick Francis's books are always filled with believable characters doing things for reasons that make sense in the context of the book.
—William L. DeAndrea

In *Hot Money,* there is a lot less violence than usual for a Francis novel. A lot less *physical* violence, at least. There is plenty of emotional violence—cruelty in the family, the most exquisite kind. Who knows better which of your buttons to push? Francis does such a good job of depicting the sniping and relentless ego-destruction that only loved ones can inflict. *Hot Money* is at times uncomfortable to read. No "serious novelist" or "angry young man" could do it better.

Hot Money is the story of an amateur jockey named Ian Pembroke and his much-married millionaire father, Malcolm. Malcolm's fifth wife has been murdered, suffocated in a bag of compost, and Malcolm is the number-one suspect. The police suspect Malcolm because a messy and expensive divorce was in the offing. They don't believe him when he says that an attempt has been made on his own life. Malcolm turns to Ian for help, even though it is apparent that the killer is one of Malcolm's own children . . .

Well, I'm not going to tell you anything more about it. This is not a book review column. I just want to point out that a good writer picks his form and makes it work for him. *Hot Money* is a straight whodunit—the first Francis has done, as far as I can remember—but it is no less of a Real Novel for all that.

Kirkus Reviews (review date 15 December 1988)

SOURCE: A review of *The Edge,* in *Kirkus Reviews,* Vol. LVI, No. 24, December 15, 1988, p. 1758.

[*In the following review, the critic complains that Francis's work has gotten weak and that* The Edge *is "lumpily padded, thinly plotted: a thouroughgoing disappointment for Francis fans."*]

Once upon a time there was an ex-jockey named Dick Francis who wrote taut, fresh action-mysteries about racing (*Dead Cert, Nerve, Forfeit, Bonecrack,* etc.). For the past ten years or so, however, his fame has grown while his work has gotten ragged, strained, unreliable. And this new adventure—a

formula train-thriller that's short on races, and virtually devoid of mystery—may well be Francis' weakest book yet.

Bland narrator-hero Tor Kelsey is a millionaire but, for fun, works as a security-agent for the British Jockey Club. Most recently, he's been on the trail of sleek villain Julius Filmer, who's guilty of extortion and murder—but always manages to walk away scot-free. Then the Jockey Club learns that Filmer has booked passage on "The Great Transcontinental Mystery Race Train," a Canadian PR event that combines a posh rail-ride with special races and a silly "murder game" (complete with hired actors) along the way. What dastardly evil does Filmer have in mind? No one is sure. But young Tor goes undercover—just in case—as a waiter/actor. From Toronto to Vancouver, he watches as Filmer cozies up to a matronly (but shady) Thoroughbred-owner, and to the super-wealthy Lorrimore family. Blackmail, it would seem, is in the air—as is sabotage: all the familiar railroad cliffhangers are played out, halfheartedly. Some of the horses on board may also be in danger. And eventually, after some minor derring-do, Tor foils the foul Filmer at last—and uncovers the truth about the Lorrimore clan's truly ludicrous Deep Dark Secret.

Lumpily padded, thinly plotted: a thoroughgoing disappointment for Francis fans—and not much fun even for fanciers of the luxury-train-in-jeopardy genre.

Donald E. Westlake (review date 5 February 1989)

SOURCE: "Dick Francis: Not Just Horsing Around," in *Washington Post Book World,* February 5, 1989, pp. 1, 6.

[*In the following review, Westlake discusses Francis's "edge" over other writers of the English detective story, focusing on his novel* The Edge.]

What is it, all at once, with Canada? First we had Sondra Gotlieb, wife of the Canadian ambassador, being quoted saying witty things about us and them; then we had the brouhaha up north about our trade agreement with them, making for the first Canadian election in history to be covered seriously in the U.S. press; and now we have Dick Francis, giving us an amiable train ride all across the breadth of Canada, pointing out items of interest long the way. Maybe this is Canada's 15 minutes.

Dick Francis, as everybody knows, gives a good ride. He did so when he first came to fame as a jockey, and he does so now, as one of our premier purveyors of the classic English detective story. *The Edge,* in a way, refers more directly to Francis himself than to anything in the novel; in both of his professions, he is a consistent winner not because of any particular flash or dash, but because he has the edge he is just that little extra bit better than anybody else in the race. And that's enough.

Which he proves again this time, in a novel that combines in a smooth and palatable way three elements that shouldn't mix well at all: a villain-hunter story; a mystery game with actors playing out a trumped-up plot over several days in front of an audience with its attention primarily elsewhere (on horse racing, in fact); and that train ride across Canada, a travelogue that really ought to bore the pants off us, but doesn't.

The Edge, in a way, refers more directly to Francis himself than to anything in the novel; in both of his professions, he is a consistent winner not because of any particular flash or dash, but because he has the edge he is just that little extra bit better than anybody else in the race. And that's enough.
—Donald E. Westlake

Several years ago I took that same train trip, from Toronto to Vancouver, and I can attest that Francis deals with it both accurately and delicately. The scenery across Canada is wild and beautiful and boring—the thousandth mile of great plain looks pretty much like the first, and one tumbled boulderscape can do for them all—and Francis conveys all this without once calling attention to himself calling attention to the scenery. That isn't easy.

Much of what Francis does looks easy and isn't. Here, for instance, is his hero's first sight of the train: "The great train was standing there, faintly hissing, silver, immensely heavy, stretching away in both directions for as far as one could see in the gloom." I've read many train-in-station descriptions— we all have—but I've never before read two words like "immensely heavy" that so effectively lifted me out of my chair and planted me on the platform.

The hero who rides this train is young Tor Kelsey, an undercover investigator for the British Jockey Club, hired because Jockey Club Security needed "someone who knew the racing scene . . . An eyes and ear man . . . A fly on racing's wall that no one would notice." Having recently returned to England to claim a hefty inheritance after several years wandering abroad, Tor takes the job because he's alone and idle and the best times of his life had been spent as a teenager with a race-mad aunt.

His current assignment is to get the goods on a "villain" named Filmer, whose previous bad actions are known but unprovable. (In classic style, Filmer is a villain because he's a villain.) Filmer goes to Canada to join a promotional gimmick for Canadian racing—"Briefly, the enterprise offered to the racehorse owners of the world a chance to race a horse in Toronto, to go by train to Winnipeg and race a horse there . . . and to continue by train to Vancouver, where they might again race a horse"—and Tor follows, disguised on the train as a dining-car waiter.

Also aboard is an acting troupe, performing one or two scenes a day over the course of a week in a mystery story they've concocted: They pretend to be horse owners and trainers and so on, and Francis is, I think, too kind to them. (In real life, it takes much less than a week for such shenanigans to pall.) But, quoting Hamlet's "the play's the thing wherein I'll catch the conscience of the king," Tor eventually takes over the mystery-within-a-mystery and rewrites it to affect the action in his own story.

The recipe includes as well a teaspoon of romance, a walloping tablespoon of action (Tor at one point must save the becalmed Race Train Special from being crashed into fulltilt by the overtaking high-speed regular passenger train, the Canadian), and an oddly real and affecting love story between young Tor and a dying elderly lady he's never met, who is his telephone link to the authorities back in Toronto. The development of that character sidebar is touching, must be sincerely felt, and is just one more way in which Dick Francis demonstrates his edge over the rest of the crowd.

If there's a flaw in **The Edge** it is in Filmer, the villain. His personality and motives remain unclear, and finally we simply have to accept his villainy as a given. Iago at least declared himself; Filmer never does. It may be that Dick Francis is simply too fundamentally decent to give roundly imagined life to someone fundamentally nasty; not a bad flaw to have, really.

At the end of the train ride, Tor and the actors part company, the chief of the troupe saying, "Don't lose touch now . . . Any time you want a job writing mysteries, let me know." "OK," says the narrator. Good. OK, Dick, you've got the job.

Charles Champlin (review date 12 February 1989)

SOURCE: "Bloody Sunday," in *Los Angeles Times Book Review,* February 12, 1989, p. 6.

[*In the following excerpt, Champlin calls the plot of Francis's* The Edge *"contrived and confining," but asserts that the novel "is suspenseful as always and interesting."*]

Dick Francis is now indubitably one of the superstars among mystery/thriller writers: 200,000 first printings, major ad budgets, the works. *The Edge,* by my reckoning his 27th thriller, has a more contrived and confining plot than his others, but it is suspenseful as always and interesting because there is less of the ultra-graphic violence that has been one of Francis' hallmarks.

A bored and wealthy young horse lover has enlivened his life by getting into undercover work around racecourses. Now he is posing as a waiter aboard "The Great Intercontinental Mystery Race Train," bound west from Ottawa with a cargo of prize horses and their owners, aiming toward a kind of Super Derby in Vancouver.

Vile deeds are feared en route. The faked theatrical mystery enacted now and again along the way thus blends conveniently with the "real" perils. The villain is no mystery: a thoroughly nasty self-made man who has been acquiring fine horses by infamous but so far unprosecutable means. The suspense is what he'll get away with, and how, and whether he can be thwarted.

There is at last a thrilling race—Francis at his descriptive best, catching all the passion of the sport. Before that, the plot roars through the Canadian days and nights with action aplenty but the violence muted, as if Francis himself wanted to take life a bit more calmly. Still *The Edge* ranks well up among his titles.

Sue Grafton (review date 12 February 1989)

SOURCE: "Our Money Is on the Waiter," in *The New York Times Book Review,* February 12, 1989, p. 9.

[*In the following review, Grafton praises Francis's* The Edge *for its authenticity.*]

Now and then, a writer's skill and his subject are so perfectly wed that a whole new category of fiction has to be invented to accommodate the offspring. Such is the case with Dick Francis and his love of horse racing, which he's managed to blend into some 29 mystery novels to date. A former champion steeplechase jockey until sidelined by an injury at the age of 36, Mr. Francis has used his passion for the sport as the focus of fiction both polished and engaging. The possibilities are apparently endless for this fine craftsman. One needn't be a race track aficionado oneself to be drawn into the world he creates. (My own relationship with horses ended abruptly when I was 9, after a Calumet Farms thoroughbred bit me in the dress, ripping the waistband beyond redemption. I haven't stopped to give a horse the time of day since.)

The protagonist in a Dick Francis racing tale is inevitably male, ranging in age from his mid-20's to late 30's, competent, decent, dedicated, tough, often a solitary figure operating against great odds. His profession may vary, but he's always connected to the racing game in some guise; owner, trainer, jockey, pilot, photographer. Whatever his hero's occupation, Mr. Francis' research is impeccable and his dedication to the world of racing infuses the narrative with authenticity.

In his latest book, *The Edge,* the protagonist Tor Kelsey has acquired his equine expertise through the tutelage of the "race-mad" maiden aunt who raised him after the death of his parents. Now, at age 29, having come into a sizable inheritance, he's returned to England after several years of world travel and for three years has worked as an undercover investigator for the British Jockey Club. The object of his attention is a man named Julius Apollo Filmer, who's been involved in numerous questionable transactions with Jockey Club members, using any means at his disposal to acquire ownership of certain thoroughbreds. In addition, the ruthless Filmer has been implicated in the death of a stable lad, but has managed to sidestep conspiracy charges.

The Jockey Club, frustrated in its attempts to have Filmer warned off, is alarmed to learn that he's managed to insinuate himself onto the passenger list of the Great Transcontinental Mystery Race Train, which will shortly be crossing Canada on a seven-day junket. Tor Kelsey is assigned to protect both the horses and the passengers. Kelsey joins the staff, using the invisibility of his waiter's uniform, to keep an eye on Filmer, hoping to prevent any acts of sabotage. No easy task. A series of near misses keeps the story moving, along with the shenanigans of a "murder mystery" being enacted en route, which are cleverly incorporated into the plot. He not only evokes the seduction of traveling by train but, as usual, he manages to convey his abiding affection for the racing game itself.

"The jockeys were thrown up like rainbow thistle—down onto the tiny saddles and let their skinny bodies move to the fluid rhythm of the walking thoroughbreds. Out on the track with the horses' gait breaking into a trot or canter they would be more comfortable standing up in the stirrups to let the bumper rhythms flow beneath them, but on the way out from the parade ring they swayed languorously like a camel train. I loved to watch them: never grew tired of it. I loved the big beautiful animals with their tiny brains and their overwhelming instincts and I'd always, all over the world, felt at home tending them, riding them and watching them wake up and perform."

It's obvious Dick Francis had a good time writing *The Edge.* I certainly had a good time reading it.

S. J. Tirrell (review date 25 July 1989)

SOURCE: "Train Thriller Not on Track," in *Christian Science Monitor,* July 25, 1989, p. 13.

[*In the following review, Tirrell discusses the problems with Francis's* The Edge, *including its weak premise, its lack of mystery, and the blandness of the protagonist.*]

His record is impressive. After a near-fatal riding accident "put paid" to his career as a champion steeplechase jockey, Dick Francis took his intimate knowledge of the racing world and translated it into another winning profession, that of writing mystery/thrillers. *The Edge* is Francis's 29th offering and his latest in a string of international best-sellers.

Set aboard a Canadian Transcontinental Mystery Race Train, *The Edge* contains all the components of a classic Dick Francis thriller: a very unctuous, very rich, very evil villain; a nice, ordinary guy turned hero; horses; horse owners; racetracks; and a girl.

Tor Kelsey—the hero—is a Jockey Club investigator with a skill for blending into the background and seeing things that other people might overlook. Disguised as a waiter, he travels from Ottawa to Vancouver for the purpose of thwarting the schemes of the Machiavellian Mr. Julius Filmer, a man with a penchant for blackmail and murder. The difficulty for Tor lies in the fact that he has no idea how or when Mr. Filmer may strike.

Often Francis's novels begin with a bang, with the discovery of some horrific incident that jolts the protagonist into heroic action. But *The Edge* begins slowly and has a hard time getting rolling as Francis meticulously sets the scene and assembles the cast for his drama.

As ever, Francis writers in whistle-clean, economical prose, with a deft turn of phrase. And his first person narrative style is embracing and engaging.

But somewhere between Ottawa and Vancouver, the thrill in this thriller gets derailed.

Perhaps the difficulty lies in the premise—not all people are as unnoticing as Francis wants us to believe, and so the chameleon-man concept doesn't work. Or maybe it's that Francis reveals the villain at the outset, thus diluting this mystery's mystique.

It could be that the hero, Tor Kelsey, is so adept at becoming one with the wallpaper that the reader cannot come to know and like him because there's very little to know and like.

But whether the problem is just one of the above or a combi-

nation of all three, *The Edge* is one racing mystery that doesn't keep suspense on track.

Harriet Waugh (review date 18 November 1989)

SOURCE: "Five Thriller Writers at Their Best," in *The Spectator,* Vol. 263, No. 8419, November 18, 1989, pp. 41-2.

[*In the following review, Waugh lauds Francis's* Straight *as one of his most enjoyable novels.*]

Dick Francis' annual treat for his admirers is out, and it is a good one. The story races along without any phoney plotting to slow it down. The hero of *Straight* is an aging steeplechaser called Derek Franklin who finds he has inherited his much older brother Greville's gem business after he has died in an accident. He only knew his brother slightly and knows nothing about gems. However, since he is temporarily on crutches, owing to a bad racing fall, he decides to spend his time sorting out his brother's affairs, which include a married mistress, two racehorses and the business itself, employing about six people. There is trouble ahead. People constantly clobber him over the head, there are two million pounds worth of missing diamonds which, unless they can be recovered, could mean the business going bust, and then there is the curious behaviour of Greville's trainer. In fact there is so much sculduggery around, and Derek receives so much physical damage, that I began to wonder whether he would be able to ride again. However, Derek is a Real Man and takes it all in his stride until he has everything neatly unravelled. This is one of the most enjoyable books Dick Francis has written in years, and for once (unlike the other crime novels I am reviewing) the villain is arrested and taken off to face justice. Much more satisfactory.

Jean M. White (review date 19 November 1989)

SOURCE: "Dick Francis: Back in Winning Form," *The Washington Post Book World,* November 19, 1989, p. 10.

[*In the following review, White asserts that Francis's* Straight *represents a return to the winner's circle for Francis after a string of disappointing novels.*]

If you read the first paragraph of *Straight,* the latest Dick Francis thriller, I'm willing to wager, whatever the odds, you will sprint to the finish line.

Who can resist this lead-on:

"I inherited my brother's life. Inherited his desk, his

business, his gadgets, his enemies, his horses, and his mistress. I inherited my brother's life, and it nearly killed me."

Derek Franklin, one of the more engaging narrator-heroes in the Franciscan canon of 28 thrillers, is hobbling around on a broken ankle after a steeplechase fall when he receives word that Greville, his older brother, is in the hospital on life-support systems after being injured by falling scaffolding at a construction site.

In the impersonal intensive-care room with a bank of screens showing Greville's brain waves and heartbeats, Derek realizes how little he has shared with Greville (19 years his senior) and wishes that they had been closer.

To Derek's surprise, he is the only beneficiary—inheriting his brother's gem-importing business, two horses (and mistress, whom he must remind later, "I'm not Greville"). And Derek and the reader get to know the dead Greville as he searches through his brother's diary, appointment calendar and computer notations.

Greville loved gadgets, and his collection included a remote car spotter (it sounds the horn and blinks the lights), a sound-enhancer for eavesdropping, spy juice to read letters through envelopes doctored to become transparent, a Geiger counter and secret computer files.

There is one riddle after another. Where did Greville hide $1.5 million in diamonds bought secretly? Why does an alarm go off at precisely 4:20 p.m. each day in the office? What does the scribbled notion "Koningen Beatrix" stand for? Who is ransacking Greville's home and office? Why is the trainer of Greville's two horses so hostile? Who ambushed the car of an American couple (among the fascinating supporting characters) in which Derek was riding?

All is answered satisfactorily as Francis paces the narrative to a smashing finish. The book's title, *Straight,* resonates with meaning. In Britain, the homestretch is called the finishing straight. And Greville had written in his notes that "the crooked despise the straight."

With *Straight,* Francis is back in top form after some rather flat, overbloated recent performances where he succumbed to "novel" writing rather than sticking to the limits of the genre of which he is master. Last year's *The Edge,* saved only by Francis's gift for narration, was an overweight variation on the old theme of murder-on-train and sometimes seemed as long as its trans-continental trip across Canada.

This time Francis is back on his turf. The plot is inventive and beautifully constructed to bring together all the threads of the sub-plots at the end. The characters are real and indi-

vidual. There are poignant, touching moments, such as Derek's realizing the missed opportunities with the brother who followed his steeplechase rides on television and jotted down "Derek won it!" in his diary.

As is all Francis novels, the racing background, although subsidiary in *Straight,* is alive with the sounds and smells and characters at the track and stables. Should a horse be gelded? And why would a kitchen-variety baster be found near the stables?

But it's the world of gems and gadgets that proves most fascinating in *Straight.* Francis is a tireless researcher when he ventures into a new field. Derek's brother ran an import business dealing with semi-precious gems, and we learn how gamma radiation can improve the color of stones and what the formula $CZ=Cx1.7$ signifies.

It seems that all of the Francis heroes have to suffer pain in exploding violence that sometimes borders on the gratuitous. Derek, an easy mark on his crutches, is mugged and bashed, then spends harrowing moments trapped in a car as rescuers attempt to free him before the gas tank catches fire. It's tough to be a Francis hero. But Francis is back in the winner's circle aboard *Straight.*

Marilyn Stasio (review date 3 December 1989)

SOURCE: "Off-Track Villainy," in *The New York Times Book Review,* December 3, 1989, p. 32.

[*In the following review, Stasio asserts that while Francis's* Straight *is well-researched, the sections about horse racing are more compelling than the scenes about gemstones.*]

During the years that Dick Francis rode steeplechase jumps for the Queen Mother, he broke his collarbone a dozen times, fractured multiple ribs and dislocated, sprained, wrenched, twisted and smashed so many other parts of his anatomy that he lost count. It was while recuperating from one of these injuries, in fact, that the onetime champion rider took up writing as a hobby.

Today, 32 years and 28 novels later, the British author can still describe in wincing detail the pain of a broken ankle and the boredom that can send an injured jockey hobbling around on crutches in search of something to occupy his mind. Something like a good adventure with a bit of horseflesh and a spot of danger. Something like *Straight.*

Derek Franklin, the terribly decent hero of this well-told tale, is a steeplechase jockey who breaks his ankle in a miscalculated jump on the last fence at Cheltenham. Two days later, he gets another jolt when his estranged older brother, Greville Saxony Franklin, is killed in a freak accident. As his brother's sole heir and executor, Derek unexpectedly finds himself the head of a thriving gemology firm and owner of two race horses.

But before he can settle the estate, he becomes entangled in his brother's complicated business and personal affairs. Greville's home and office are mysteriously burgled, and Derek himself is attacked. Urgent offers, bordering on threatening demands, are extended by would-be buyers of Dozen Roses and Gemstones, the two race horses. A mistress surfaces. A million-and-a-half dollars worth of missing diamonds does not.

"I inherited my brother's life, and it nearly killed me," observes Derek, who limps through these and other baffling developments with a throbbing ankle and a stiff upper lip, drawn by the new insights he is gaining into his brother's forceful but extremely private identity. "I knew only his taste in clothes, food, gadgets and horses," he mourns "Not very much. Not enough."

In the course of his quest—for the missing diamonds, for more knowledge of his secretive brother, for the shadowy assailants who will reveal themselves as ruthless killers—the unflappable Derek also learns something about the semi-precious gem industry. In the laconic fashion that we have come to identify with Mr. Francis' essentially interchangeable heroes, the jockey even begins to appreciate his brother's collection of high-tech computerized gadgetry, especially when one of these little toys saves his life.

The author delivers his well-researched material in that didactic, politely impressed tone that he often reserves for such literary excursions outside the world of horse racing. The humble reader, however, remains unawed by the technical chitchat about chrysoberyls and peridots, and infinitely more grateful for the rare appearances of Gemstones the horse than for those of gemstones the gemstones. Even those elusive diamonds lack the sparkle and flash of Derek's too-brief encounters with horses and their owners and trainers.

It can be said, without spoiling the story, that Derek eventually overcomes the villain (who has stuck out all along, like an army boot at a cotillion ball) and discovers that his brother was something of a saint, embodying all those values of loyalty and integrity and fair play that Francis heroes live by and die for.

"If home was where the heart was," Derek says, "I really lived out on the windy Downs and in stable yards and on the raucous racetracks." If this nice chap follows doctor's or-

ders, perhaps the author will let him heal in time for the Grand National.

Tim Cahill (review date 14 October 1990)

SOURCE: "Surviving the English Countryside," in *The New York Times Book Review,* October 14, 1990, p. 45.

[*In the following review, Cahill lauds Francis's* Longshot *as a satisfying, read-at-one-sitting novel.*]

They're calling for passengers to board the plane to Tonga and I find that I'm unprepared. I need a book. Something light and entertaining and informative and plot driven. Ah, but there's always Dick Francis at the newsstand, several dozen of him, staring out from the best seller rack. I know that the book will be a mystery, probably a murder mystery, and that it will be set against a racing background. After all, Mr. Francis, once a champion jockey in Britain, has written a string of best selling mysteries, most of which check in regularly at the track.

I'm about as interested in horse racing as I am in dentistry—which is to say not at all. Still, experience has taught me that Mr. Francis is one of our most satisfying read it at one sitting writers. I know that. But I resist him because of the racing. Still, staring at a 16 hour flight, I find the phrase "don't take chances, go with Francis" echoing in my mind. So what if there are horses in this new book? When I look up from the last page, I'll be halfway across the Pacific, and the time will have passed painlessly. I'll know a little more about, ho hum, racing as well.

But *Longshot* turns out to be a bit of a surprise. It opens with a one sentence paragraph that speaks to me as viscerally as anything Mr. Francis has ever written. "I accepted a commission that had been turned down by four other writers, but I was hungry at the time." A writer who will accept any paying job? I find this a credible character.

The writer in question, John Kendall, is the author of such aptly titled survival manuals as *Safari, Jungle* and *Ice.* Ironically, he can't afford the necessities of life in London because he hasn't managed to make much of a living writing about ways to avoid death.

Hey, I write books and articles that sometimes concern themselves with survival. And I currently have a letter on my desk from the mortgage company wondering what happened to the September payment. This is the shock of recognition Writ Large. Either that or Dick Francis has been reading my mail.

Kendall agrees to write the biography of a successful and boorish—yes—horse trainer. He contracts to spend several months at his subject's training facility in rural England, where he will interview him.

Now, the simplest rules of craft suggest that if you introduce a survival expert in the first chapter, he should demonstrate his skills somewhere in the course of the book. However, John Kendall is a man who writes about remote locales, who advises his readers not to eat polar bear liver because "it stores enough vitamin A to kill humans." Rural England, I sensed, would not contain enough challenges for John Kendall.

But no, there's a survival situation in the second chapter. I read it the way doctors read operating room scenes or lawyers read courtroom dramas. Did the author hit the note or is he blowing smoke? Mr. Francis' scene is believable and convincing.

There is, of course, a murder to be solved, and Kendall finds himself dragged, willy-nilly, into the investigation. Meanwhile, the entire cast of suspects—the trainer, his son, the son's wife, an obnoxious amateur jockey—is reading and enjoying Kendall's survival manuals. To help wounds clot, Kendall informs one of them, it is necessary only to apply cobwebs, which are organic and "as sterile as most bandages."

As Kendall gets closer to discovering the identity of the killer, he is ambushed, according to—good Lord—the hunting and trapping instructions in his own books. There is a harrowing and breathless chapter toward the end that is a comment on the entire concept of survival, followed by an ending that wraps everything up in a neat bundle without cheating.

Perfect. I closed the book, satisfied *Longshot* ate up several thousand miles. Sentient human beings know that 16 hour flights are boring unto death. An intelligent, fast-paced mystery is a survival tool. Dick Francis can save your life.

Linda Stewart (review date 18 November 1990)

SOURCE: "Take a Walk on the Wild Side," in *The Washington Post Book World,* November 18, 1990, p. 9.

[*In the following review, Stewart praises Francis's impeccable research for* Longshot, *and comments on how Francis deals with expletives in the novel.*]

There are two kinds of readers: those who like heroes and those who like anti-heroes. The hero, in general, is unswervingly honorable, unquestionably decent, unabash-

edly straight. Ambiguity never pokes a finger in his eye. And unlike his opposite, the anti-hero, he doesn't seem to stumble onto paths of virtue by way of an accidental detour in the existential maze. He's there because it's simply in his bones to be there.

And there, in a nutshell, is the charm (or, depending on your attitude, the drawback) of the Dick Francis hero—the man who keeps appearing, under various names and selected occupations, in Francis's intelligent and well-crafted books.

Longshot, his 29th mystery-thriller, sets writer John Kendall, another of his pleasantly engaging young men, on an R-rated version of a boys' adventure plus country-house murder. The result is a thoroughly appealing whodunit, the kind to go to bed with on a cold winter's night or to take—along with chicken soup, aspirin and honey—at the first signs of flu.

In fact, so adept is Francis at his craft, so properly insistent on the borders of his isolated, civilized world, that even those readers who prefer sterner stuff may find themselves in sudden agreement with the hero: "Though . . . it was odd to find myself living in the lives of all these people, as if I'd stepped into a play that was already in progress and been given a walk-on part in the action . . . I felt drawn in and interested and unwilling to miss any scene."

Kendall, 32, is a between-novels writer who's been alternately starving and freezing in a garret. Author of half a dozen guides to survival (personally researched in the jungles and the wilds), he's tried his hand at fiction and been struck with its rewards: publication, poverty, solitude and dread. Surviving as a writer, he's learned, is as difficult as camping in a swamp.

And so, when he's offered a chance to make some money by writing the biography of one Tremayne Vickers, a man who's convinced he's led a fascinating life ("Childhood . . . growing up . . . success . . . My life had been *interesting,* dammit"), well, it's an offer not easy to refuse. Especially when it's sweetened by the heartwarming (anyway, bone-warming) promise of a month in the country at the Vickers estate.

Vickers (are you waiting for the horses?) is a trainer. His family is charming, his friends are attractive and his world is an oyster—if you don't count the undercurrents roiling all around.

Murder, for one thing. Mayhem, for another. And suddenly Kendall's in the trickiest position of his short happy life.

Francis, whose research is always impeccable, has previously offered us the wine world (in *Proof*) the gem world (in *Straight*) and the art world (in *In the Frame*). This time he offers us the world of survival.

In *Longshot* you can learn how to build your own fire, how to clot your own blood ("Apply cobwebs to the wound. They're . . . as sterile as most bandages"), how to use your watch as a compass ("Point the hour hand at the sun, then halfway between the hand and twelve o'clock is the north-south line").

Obviously, a set-up like that demands a payoff. Something like the hero getting trapped in the forest with a two- (or is it three-) time killer on his trail, and finding rare opportunity to practice what he's preached.

> **I have only one quarrel to pick with Francis, though I understand his problem: How do you write dialogue for tough modern characters and still keep it clean? Francis's solution is to aim for a compromise, with dialogue that's, well, half-buttocked, shall we say. A kind of exercise in curses that never got cursed.**
> **—*Linda Stewart***

I have only one quarrel to pick with Francis, though I understand his problem: How do you write dialogue for tough modern characters and still keep it clean?

Francis's solution is to aim for a compromise, with dialogue that's, well, half-buttocked, shall we say. A kind of exercise in curses that never got cursed.

One of his characters is even self-censored, substituting words like "expletive," "bleep" and "deleted" for the "truly offensive obscene words" he means. Some examples: "'Bleep the lawyer,' Lewis said." and "'Nolan doesn't expletive like you, dear heart.'"

As I say, I'm completely sympathetic to the problem, which is definitely thorny. But then, on the other hand, it's one of those situations where you're bleeped if you do and deleted if you don't.

Michael Killian (essay date 20 November 1990)

SOURCE: "Champion Rider to Champion Writer," in *The Chicago Tribune*, November 20, 1990, pp. 1, 2.

[*In the following essay, Killian describes Francis's life and careers as both a steeplechase jockey and a writer.*]

Dick Francis no longer needs to ride a horse.

He has just issued *Longshot,* his 29th novel and 31st book, and, like previous Francis works, it is being displayed on the best-seller shelves of the nation's bookstores. This puts it in a league with *Straight,* his novel of last year, and *The Edge,* released the year before that.

In January, he'll begin his next one, and a year from now the bookstores very likely will be making a lot of shelf room for that one too.

It's hard to think of a more celebrated and avidly read mystery writer in Francis' adoptive United States or his native England. But he used to ride horses quite a lot, and has many more honors than the designation as England's champion jockey of 1954 to prove it.

Over coffee one bright, brisk recent morning as he prepared to drive out to the Virginia horse country to help preside over the running of the 53rd International Gold Cup steeplechase race, Francis recalled that his trophies have included a few broken bones:

"The collar bones, six times each side. Broke my nose five times. I crushed some vertebrae, and I broke my arms—and my wrist. Not my legs. I've always been able to walk about. But ribs? No end of ribs. Couldn't count those. You'd just strap yourself up and ride if you possibly could. When you got warmed up, you couldn't feel it."

Just turned 70 and an official "resident alien" of the U.S., Francis and his wife of 43 years, Mary, live a sunny, comfortable existence in an oceanfront high-rise in Ft. Lauderdale. He turns up as an honored guest at race meetings all over the fabled, rolling horse country of the U.S. and Britain. This year as last, he helped present the extravagantly grand trophy to the winner of the Virginia International, adding his luster to one of the most prestigious events in American steeplechasing.

But that's about as close as he gets to the intimidating, giant fences he used to take at full gallop, mile after mile, day after day, simply as a way of making an ordinary living.

"I don't ride much at all," he said. "When I go back and stay with my oldest son, Merrick [a British horse trainer], I might go out in the morning and ride one of his horses to watch the others work, but I don't ride enough to say I still ride."

But he sure did. Few of the world's top mystery and thriller writers have lived the lives of their protagonists, relying instead on vivid imaginations and hard research to produce their compelling stories. Mickey Spillane was never a private eye. Freddy Forsyth was a journalist, not a spy (or assassin). Neither was spymaster Len Deighton, who also wrote *Bomber* and another best-seller about fighter pilots called

Goodbye, Mickey Mouse, without benefit of World War II aerial combat experience.

Francis, who incidentally was a fighter pilot *and* bomber pilot in the war, came to novel-writing with 11 years' experience as a jockey, much like those who serve as the heroes of his books, all of which involve horse racing. He once asked his publisher if she'd mind if he wrote a book that wasn't about racing.

"We'll publish anything you write," she said. "We'd rather you didn't, though."

And, yes, he concedes, those dogged, likable guys who always manage to prevail over Francis' rich assortment of villains are based on him.

"I'm not as clever or as brave as they are," he said. "But I never ask my characters to suffer anything or do anything I haven't suffered or done myself. The things that happen to them are the sort of things that happened to me on racecourses. In *Knockdown,* the man suffered from a recurring dislocated shoulder, and it was pulled out when he tried to open a door. That happened to me. I've got a recurring dislocated shoulder, and that's more painful than any break."

In a steeplechasing career lasting from 1946 to 1957, Francis won between 350 and 400 races (he can't recall exactly). He was so good he became jockey for the horses of Elizabeth, England's queen mother, and it was in her service that the extraordinary incident occurred that led to his turning to writing.

He said it was old age (37) that prompted him to retire from the sport. "The breaks were taking longer to heal." But the decision involved the sort of odd twist of fate that figures in his stories.

"I was the queen mother's main jockey," he said, "and was riding her horse Devon Loch. He was winning the race—I was having a wonderful ride on him—and I jumped the last fence and was half a mile to the winning post.

"There were a quarter of a million people there, and they were all yelling for the queen mother. You don't really hear the noise from the sidelines when you're riding, but I heard it when I was jumping the last fence. I thought no more of it, and rode on. About 25 yards from the winning post—I've looked at the film many times—Devon Loch sort of pricked up his ears and this crescendo of cheering hit him.

"I thought, 'God, what's that?' and his hindquarters refused to act for a slight second, and down he went on his belly and slid along the ground. How I didn't fall off him, I didn't know. If he'd got to his feet and I got him going again, I was

still in front enough to have won. But he pulled all the muscles in his hindquarters and more or less collapsed again. I had to get off him and walk away in disgust."

Though he lost the race—the Grand National—the "fantastic happening" made him an instant celebrity. An agent told him it was the perfect time to write his autobiography. It was also, Francis decided, a good time to get out of racing. A friend advised that "if you stop now, you'll get all sorts of things offered to you. If you train, you'll get horses sent."

Francis didn't want to become a horse trainer, but his fame and his progress on his memoir, *The Sport of Queens,* inspired the sports editor of the London Sunday Express to hire him to write a half dozen articles on racing, which led to his becoming a professional journalist and writing a weekly racing commentary for the next 16 years.

Steeplechase jockeys weren't paid very much in those days ("7 pounds, 7 shillings; another 10 pounds if you brought in a winner"), but newspaper writers earned even less. After four years of this, he said, his wife said to him: "'We've got two boys to educate, and the carpet's beginning to wear out. The car's beginning to knock. What are you going to do? You always said you were going to write a novel. Now's the time.'"

Called *Dead Cert,* the novel came out the next year, and Francis has been writing a novel a year ever since.

At 5 foot 8—a typical height for a steeplechase jockey (in racing attire he weighed 140 pounds)—Francis was "born to the saddle," the descendant of a long line of Welsh horsemen and the son of a successful trainer. He began riding ponies at age 3. His father tried to discourage him from becoming a jockey, but at age 18 he signed up with a racing stable. Before he could get into a race, his patron was killed in an automobile accident, and shortly afterward World War II broke out in Europe.

Beginning his military service as an enlisted man in a Royal Air Force ground crew, he was promoted to pilot, flying Spitfires in Africa and over northern Europe, and then transferring to bombers as the pilot of a Lancaster.

He met his wife at a cousin's wedding in the midst of the war. "She said if I had asked her to marry me that day, she'd have married me straight away, but it took me 18 months to persuade her in the end," Francis said.

Leaving the service with the rank of flying officer, he commenced his career as a jockey in 1946.

Their son Merrick now has three children, and their other son, Felix, a schoolmaster, has two. The two families visit the Francises frequently in Ft. Lauderdale, where Francis took up permanent residence several years ago because of his wife's asthmatic aversion to cold.

Their principal recreation is travel. It takes Francis from early January to late May every year to write his books, and he and Mary spend much of the rest of the time wandering about the globe, doing research for the next book.

For example, his latest, *Longshot,* grew out of his son Felix's journey to the jungles of Borneo with a group of his pupils. The hero is a travel writer who gets caught up in a racing mystery.

Francis wouldn't reveal the plans for his next novel. But he did admit that as soon as the Virginia Gold Cup race was over, he was returning to Florida, where he and his wife were joining Felix and his family for their first visit to Disney World.

Hmmmm. Could there be a plot in the works about a jockey who goes to Orlando in search of a horse named Goofy?

Charles Champlin (review date 16 December 1990)

SOURCE: A review of *The Dick Francis Treasury of Great Horseracing Stories,* in *The Los Angeles Times Book Review,* December 16, 1990, p. 7.

[*In the following excerpt, Champlin provides a brief overview of* The Dick Francis Treasury of Great Horseracing Stories.]

The short form demands, and in these selections receives, high dosages of wit and irony as well as surprise. The conjoined spirits of O. Henry and Alfred Hitchcock, so to speak, watch over much of the work, which is to be taken in small doses. One at bedtime, say.

The principal link to crime as such in another anthology is that its co-editor was Dick Francis. He and John Welcome have chosen and introduced *The Dick Francis Treasury of Great Horseracing Stories.* The authorships range from Conan Doyle (his "Silver Blaze," historic if only because it was therein that the dog, curiously, did not bark in the night) to Sherwood Anderson ("I'm a Fool"), John Galsworthy ("Had a Horse") and John P. Marquand whose "What's It Get You?" is a lovely sardonic tale about a caper involving a disguised horse.

Rick Mattos (review date Spring 1991)

SOURCE: A review of *Longshot,* in *The Armchair Detective,* Vol. 24, No. 2, Spring, 1991, p. 228.

[*In the following excerpt, Mattos lauds the "pulse-quickening suspense" of Francis's novels and* Longshot *in particular.*]

In 1962, so the story goes, Dick Francis needed a new carpet for his sitting room. He decided to write a book to get the money. Drawing upon his past as a successful jockey, he wrote a thriller set in the world of horse racing. That was *Dead Cert.* He now has homes in both the U.S. and Great Britain, and I bet they all have fine carpets. In Francis's latest novel, the hero, John Kendall, is a struggling writer. He is down to his last few pence when the pipes freeze in his rooms and he is forced to seek temporary accommodations. About this time, he meets Tremayne Vickers, a successful horse trainer who feels the need to have his biography written. Although Kendall knows little of horses and less of Vickers, he succumbs to the lure of room and board. Kendall arrives at Vickers's estate amid a swirl of controversy about a trial concerning the death of a young lady at a party given there. Tensions mount as the skeleton of another girl, who has been missing for some time, is found in a nearby wood. As the list of suspects narrows to the Vickers group, we find the usual Dick Francis nail-biting, page-turning climax.

Dick Francis does not use a continuing series character in his novels. John Kendall is, however, a typical Francis hero—competent, likable, and decent. He is thrust, reluctantly, into an alien environment where he must use all of his skills to survive. Luckily for this hero, a past job was to research and write a series of survival manuals. Unfortunately, the information in these manuals not only helps Kendall survive, it also provides the killer with a source of deadly ideas.

> **There are few books that I know I will enjoy just from the author's name. The Dick Francis novels are on this list.**
> **—Rick Mattos**

Dick Francis is my favorite writer of thrillers (at least this week he is). His novels can always be counted on for pulse-quickening suspense. His talent is such that you may actually find yourself breathing a little faster, pulling at your hair, and groaning a bit with the characters before you reach the end of the book. There are few books that I know I will enjoy just from the author's name. The Dick Francis novels are on this list. A definite must-read.

Maureen Corrigan (review date 17 November 1991)

SOURCE: "Another Day At the Races," in *Washington Post Book World,* November 17, 1991, p. 10.

[*In the following review, Corrigan briefly discusses Francis's formula and how* Comeback *differs from his previous novels.*]

By now, fans look forward to getting three things in a Dick Francis mystery. First, there's the obligatory "race-with-a-close-finish" scene, in which an unlikely horse with the heart of a champion beats the racetrack favorite by a nostril hair. Francis recycles this scene to establish the moral code of his books. It goes something like this: Racing is like Life. Cowards and cheaters always lose; the good and the brave always win, damn the odds!

Another staple of Francis's books is his reverence for superior bloodlines, not only in horses but in people. The typical thriller restores order to the racing world by restoring power to the aristocracy. Usually a humble but fearless hero (often a jockey) discovers an evil plot against racing. He informs one of the patrician members of the Racing Commission—someone with a name like Sir Nigel Gout. At first, Sir Nigel's judgment is clouded (maybe by decades of guzzling gin and tonics). But Sir Nigel always rallies, the low-class bounder is arrested, and our hero rides off, usually with Sir Nigel's niece.

That's the third trademark element of a Francis mystery—the love interest. To Francis, a desirable woman is a lot like a fine racehorse. Both have glossy manes, firm withers and good breeding. And both secretly want to be reined in and mastered by our heroes.

Comeback, Francis's 30th thriller, serves up his basic winning formula with some exotic touches. Hero Peter Darwin, a young British diplomat who's just been assigned to a posting in London, finds himself caught up in the nightmarish problems of a new friend, veterinary surgeon Ken McClure. It seems that a lot of injured racehorses have died shortly after McClure has operated on them. McClure's reputation is heading to the glue factory—fast—and so Darwin puts his diplomatic skills to work to solve the mysterious deaths.

Francis substitutes suspenseful descriptions of horse surgery here for his usual suspenseful descriptions of horse racing, since most of the action takes place on the grounds of the veterinary practice. *Comeback* also contains one of the creepiest climaxes of any recent Francis novel and, certainly, one of the tackiest propositions ever uttered by a Francis hero—"How about a bonk, then?" says Darwin to a frisky filly, *not* to be confused with the thoroughbred Bishop's daughter he's set to hitch up with by novel's end. The most startling change in *Comeback,* however, is the class background of the villain: for once, I couldn't figure out who the bad guy was simply by noticing which one of the characters didn't know how to use a fingerbowl.

Publishers Weekly (review date 27 July 1992)

SOURCE: A review of *Driving Force,* in *Publishers Weekly,* Vol. 239, No. 34, July 27, 1992, p. 46.

[*In the following review, the critic praises Francis's* Driving Force *for its believable characters and realistic setting.*]

Archetypal Francis hero Freddie Croft is a 35-year-old former champion steeplechase jockey, knowledgeable about the British racing milieu and tolerant of its denizens, a bit of a loner, keen on honor and notably phlegmatic. His phlegm is sorely tested when two of his drivers—he owns 14 vans that transport racehorses from a Hampshire village—arrive with the body of a hitchhiker who died in the backseat during the ride. Before the death is ruled natural Freddie's head mechanic, Jogger, finds odd empty containers hidden on three vans. Freddie chases a midnight prowler, Jogger turns up with his neck broken, the firm's computer system crashes with a virus and Freddie discovers 10cc tubes filled with mysterious liquid in a Thermos that belonged to the dead hitchhiker. Worried that drugs are being smuggled during the vans' regular trips between England and Ireland and the Continent, he enlists help from Jockey Club Security in the undercover form of glamorous, older Nina. Muscle, money and malice threaten our hero in a wonderfully complicated plot centering on a tick virus. Colorful and believable characters, a setting so realistic the book could double as a manual on running a horse-transport firm, a delicious puzzle and a very satisfying ending add up to first-class entertainment. Francis (*Comeback* and 31 other mysteries) is not a brand-name author for nothing.

Elizabeth Tallent (review date 18 October 1992)

SOURCE: "He Gets the Horse Right There," in *The New York Times Book Review,* October 18, 1992, p. 32.

[*In the following review, Tallent offers reserved praise for Francis's* Driving Force *while pointing out some of the novel's flaws.*]

In his autobiography, *The Sport of Queens,* Dick Francis could not be more direct about his latest profession: "When I write any one sentence, I think first of all of what I want to say. Then I think of a way of saying it." The brisk assessment of a situation, the lucid self-reliance, the smart refusal to fuss about what other people fuss a lot about—this confession rings with the elements of style for many a Dick Francis protagonist. Racing journalism was the means for Mr. Francis, in 1957 a retired Champion Jockey in Britain, not only to earn a different kind of living, but also to perfect professionally succinct prose conveying vivid action. Adept hero, dexterous prose—these are the unfailing aspects of Dick Francis' series of 31 novels.

With *Driving Force* he treats his readers to another amiably disillusioned, smart and un-self-pitying ex-jockey narrator. Freddie Croft's current business is transporting horses to English race tracks. "I had told the drivers never on any account to pick up a hitchhiker but of course one day they did, and by the time they reached my house he was dead." "Of course" nonchalantly removes this first sentence from any danger of seeming simply a mystery's obligatory hook.

The "multimillion fortunes on the hoof," as Freddie terms race horses, with their fragile legs and fractious moods, pose tricky problems in transit. Largely by computer, in pinches by intuition, Freddie choreographs the crisscrossing of England by his fleet of huge vans. Mr. Francis, who can turn the nuts and bolts of any profession to fictional gold, sketches a thriving business whose peculiar emergencies include claustrophobic horses, flu-stricken drivers and of course the occasional dead hitchhiker. But horses are fortunes to Freddie, investments to be protected rather than real, errant individuals, and whenever a Dick Francis hero strays too far from actual horseflesh, the novel he's in forfeits a great source of gusto.

My private theory is that horses function as the id, the unruly life force, for Mr. Francis' disciplined sleuths, and that cut off from horses these narrators have the brainy, controlled dryness of too much superego. (I know: this analysis would rate, from any Dick Francis hero, one of those infinitely ambiguous "Mm" s. Or worse, "Right," Brit for "in a pig's eye.") Irkab Athawa, a dazzling 3-year-old, steals those scenes he's in and, briefly, Freddie's heart; the horse could have figured more consistently in the plot as it complicates.

It gets very complicated. Beginning with that dead body, Freddie is confronted with a wicked scam, on the cutting edge in its technology and implications. His vans, he finds, have been transporting something other than horses. *Driving Force* is rich in information—about Cockney rhyming slang, the Michelangelo computer virus, intercontinental smuggling and ticks (yes, ticks), among other subjects. Mr. Francis deals with the potential for boredom in exposition, or at least flatness, by putting the more obscure explanations in the mouths of completely charming, completely obsessed eccentrics ("Guggenheim moved in this mysterious territory [his laboratory] with the certainty of a Rubik round his cube"), and I read merrily along, entranced. It's either hard or impossible to read Mr. Francis without growing pleased with *your self:* not only the thrill of vicarious competence imparted by the company of his heroes, but also the lore you collect as you go, feel like a field trip with the perfect guide.

Driving Force isn't flawless Dick Francis. Too many char-

acters share the quirk of prefacing remarks with "Er." I wanted to kill Freddie the next time he responded to a remark with "Mm." Too many mouths hang open in astonishment. Successive one-sentence paragraphs seem an effort to trump up suspense that isn't coming naturally. Freddie's romance with an undercover agent for the Jockey Club has its moments, but is basically as overshadowed by proliferating plot twists as his romance with Irkab Athawa.

What's wanted in a violent denouement is that it seem boldly improbable but, by a whisker, believable, and because mysteries are ecosystems of right and wrong, fair. The culprit remained too enigmatic to inspire real dislike, and the climax, besides tying up too many loose ends for credibility, was a slightly abstract satisfaction.

"Frenzy," "sly childish impulse to hurt," "destruction and wrecking for its own sake" are names given the danger threatening Freddie. The havoc wreaked by this perverse driving force makes for a read that is (I'm resisting saying "as always") ingeniously entertaining, overall. The author's notes for Mr. Francis' books often observe that as a jockey he rode for the Queen Mother. At this point in his illustrious writing career, the Queen Mother might wish to note in her vita that the writer Dick Francis once rode for her.

Cindy Dampier and Elizabeth Gleick (essay date 23 November 1992)

SOURCE: "As Easy as Falling Off a Horse," in *People Weekly,* Vol. 38, No. 21, November 23, 1992, pp. 139-40.

[*In the following essay, Dampier and Gleick present an overview of Francis's life and career.*]

Dick Francis begins every new year the same way. Each Jan. 1, he rises early, takes a walk on the beach and a quick swim, then repairs to the balcony of his Fort Lauderdale condominium. There the 72-year-old author sits in a pink lawn chair, takes out an empty notebook and waits, pen poised, for inspiration. "It takes quite a time," he says. "I sit out there and think. After a while, you find the words coming."

Another year, another best-seller. Five months after this annual ritual, Francis delivers a manuscript—always a tightly wrought tale of horse racing and gambling, spills, thrills and what he calls "dirty deeds"—to his publisher. And each fall the Welsh-born former jockey's eager public, including Britain's Queen Mother, devours a new Dick Francis mystery. His newest, *Driving Force,* like the 30 preceding it, promptly leapt onto best-seller lists here and in Britain. (Novelist Elizabeth Tallent, in *The New York Times,* called it "ingeniously entertaining"—standard praise for a Francis thriller.) He sells more than 200,000 hardcover copies of each new mystery—and millions more in paperback. "The books have done quite well," says Francis with characteristic understatement.

Francis requires silence to do his daily six or seven hours of writing, but he does not labor in solitude. His wife of 45 years, Mary who is in her 60s, tiptoes around their large, cluttered apartment and, without making a sound, brings her husband lunch; meanwhile, she keeps busy with some detective work of her own. When Francis needed aeronautical details for *Flying Finish* (1966), she took flying lessons. "I had never touched a small airplane before, and I absolutely loved it," says Mary, who ended up starting her own air-charter business—which she later sold—in 1975. For *Reflex* (1980), Mary learned photography—and now she takes her husband's book-jacket photos. For *Driving Force* she hung around the local computer store investigating computer viruses. But, notes Dick, "she's told me she's not going to do any underwater research if I start writing about submerged things."

Mary can also, if needed, pop Dick's shoulder back into place when Francis, who's still fit though no longer rides, dislocates it doing simple tasks—a skill she perfected during his nine-year career as a champion steeplechase jockey. The son of a jockey turned horse dealer, Francis grew up in Pembrokeshire, Wales. After serving as a pilot in Africa during World War II, he returned to Britain and began racing in 1947 at age 25.

That same year, he married Mary Brenchley, an honors graduate of London University who barely knew how to ride. Both sets of parents thought the match would be disastrous, as the two had little in common. But, says Mary, "it didn't matter to us. We just liked being together." In 1953, Francis was appointed jockey for the Queen Mother (with whom he now sometimes sits when he attends races in England), making champion—winning more races than anyone else—that year. Three years later, a spectacular spill in the last few yards of the Grand National cost him the race but also brought Francis to the attention of a literary agent, who suggested he write his autobiography.

Having little formal education, Francis was apprehensive. Mary encouraged her husband to start writing things down "as though you were telling it to your uncle" and promised to check the spelling and grammar. She has been his editor ever since.

In 1957 *The Sport of Queens* appeared, and Francis also began writing a newspaper column. But, Mary told Dick, "we've got two sons to educate, the carpets are wearing thin and the cars are beginning to knock. If you were ever going to write a novel, now's the time." Francis decided to try his hand at a mystery. "I saw people buying them at train stations," he recalls. "And I thought, 'That's the field to get into; I can do that.' And I can, apparently."

In 1962 his first mystery, *Dead Cert,* based in part on his own racing experiences, was an instant success. Best-seller No. 2, *Nerve,* appeared in 1964, and, says the author, "there's been one every fall since." Francis's elder son, Merrick, 42, who owns a horse transport business in England, keeps him up to date on racing matters; son Felix, 39, recently quit his job as a high school physics teacher in England to become his father's business manager.

In 1983, in search of a climate more hospitable to Mary's asthma, the Francises moved from Oxfordshire, England, to Florida. In Francis' off months, the couple travel together, sometimes researching locales for the next book. But when January rolls around, the writer will settle in on his balcony. Francis says he feels like quitting every year, but, as always, Mary urges him on. "I think, 'Oh, I've got all this work to do.' And Mary says, 'Oh, go on, write it.'" At this rate, he admits, "I might go on to the beginning of the next century."

Rachel Schaffer (essay date Spring 1993)

SOURCE: "Dead Funny: The Lighter Side of Dick Francis," in *The Armchair Detective,* Vol. 26, No. 2, Spring, 1993, pp. 76-81.

[*In the following essay, Schaffer discusses the humor found in Francis's novels.*]

Since Dick Francis published his first mystery novel in 1962, he has gained a world-wide audience of devoted readers. The critics who have written articles about him over the years put into words what his fans feel. Paul Bishop, for example, comments on Francis's skillful pacing, attributing that ability to "what he learned about pacing a horse" during his career as a steeplechase jockey. Michael Stanton approves of his "exquisite variations of setting, plot, and psychology" and notes the role violence plays in his novels. Charles Gould praises him for his "tight plotting" and "the strongly-marked and individual style which makes such storytelling into literary art." And Marty Knepper analyzes the considerable literary risk-taking found in his novels.

No reviewer, however, has ever described Francis as a notably *humorous* writer. And yet, humor is as integral a part of his novels as action and violence. Every one of his mysteries is laced with humor, not the slapstick or farcical kind deriving from eccentric characters or absurd situations, but clever verbal humor that most often takes the form of acerbic observations of human nature or clever retorts in dialogue. Whatever shape the humor takes, it contributes integrally to the effective development of character and mood.

In his essay "Comedy and the British Crime Novel," H. R. F. Keating describes five types of comedy found in British crime novels: the traditional, the witty, the donnish, the farcical, and social comment. Of the five, Francis uses traditional and witty forms of humor most often along with less frequent one-liners that clearly constitute social comment. According to Keating, traditional humor incorporates wordplay of all sorts, deflationary humor of the gentle type and whimsy. The witty category includes elegant humor of a lightly darting character and the casually conversational tone of typical British understatement. These characteristics can be seen to a greater or lesser degree in all of Francis's novels, regardless of the uses he puts his humor to, beginning with his first novel, *Dead Cert.*

Dead Cert tells the story of a young steeplechase jockey from (then) Rhodesia, Alan York, and his investigation into the death of a close friend in a racing fall. The action is complicated by Alan's relationship with a wealthy, upper-class woman and her family, while further dimensions of Alan's character emerge through his relationship with the dead jockey's wife and children, with whom he boards when he is in England.

In this novel, as in so many others, Francis uses humor as a method of developing characterizations and relationships between his characters, helping his readers to gain insights into the protagonists' inner lives, especially their motivations and feelings for others. He describes major and even minor characters by what their sense of humor reveals about them.

Dead Cert's protagonist, Alan York, is developed as a character through his use of "typical British understatement," which reveals the jockey's casual professionalism in the face of injury and pain. This is a trait Francis is familiar with firsthand from his racing days, and which he uses to good effect in all of his novels, creating a series of incredibly stout and stoic protagonists. What is especially interesting about this use of humor to reveal character is that it is the narrator himself who does the revealing and must do so without appearing to brag about his strength in the face of pain.

For example, after a serious fall from his horse during a steeplechase, Alan is in the hospital, discussing his condition with his doctor:

> "What is wrong with me, exactly?" I asked.
>
> "Concussion is what has affected your memory. As

to the rest of you," he surveyed me from head to foot, "you have a broken collar-bone, four cracked ribs and multiple contusions."

> "Nothing serious, thank goodness," I croaked.

He opened his mouth and gasped, and then began to laugh. He said, "No, nothing serious. You lot [jockeys] are all the same. Quite mad."

An example of the way Francis uses humor in developing even minor characters can be seen in one of the villains in *Dead Cert,* a fellow jockey named Sandy Mason, who at first seems perfectly harmless (in spite of some unscrupulous dealings in fixing races) thanks in large part to his constant cheerfulness and broad sense of humor. "His aggressiveness in races had got him into hot water more than once with the Stewards, but he was not particularly unpopular with the other jockeys, owing to his irrepressible, infectious cheerfulness."

Even when Sandy makes a mistake, no one blames him for it because he doesn't take it—or himself—seriously and provides a lively source of entertainment in the changing room. In the following incident, Francis uses Sandy's informal vocabulary and lower-class dialect as a further source of amusement, even including Cockney rhyming slang (i.e. "half-inched" for "pinched") as part of the overall humor:

> "Which of you sods has half-inched my balancing pole?" he roared in a voice which carried splendidly above the busy chatter to every corner of the room. To this enquiry into the whereabouts of his whip, he received no reply.
>
> "Why don't you lot get up off your fannies and see if you're hatching it," he said to three or four jockeys who were sitting on a bench pulling on their boots. They looked up appreciatively and waited for the rest of the tirade. Sandy kept up a flow of invective without repeating himself until one of the valets produced the missing whip.
>
> "Where did you find it?" demanded Sandy. "Who had it? I'll twist his bloody arm."
>
> "It was on the floor under the bench, in your own place."
>
> Sandy was never embarrassed by his mistakes. He roared with laughter and took the whip. "I'll forgive you all this time, then."

The true nature of Sandy's humor, however, is a good deal darker; his cheerfulness is a facade to distract others and cover up his less honest tendencies. This is initially revealed by another character, a sleazy jockey named Joe Nantwich, who tells Alan that Sandy tipped him off his horse during a recent race. "'Lucky for me I hit a soft patch or I might have broken my neck. It wasn't funny. And that bloody Sandy,' he choked on the name, 'was laughing. I'll make him laugh on the other side of his bloody face'." This revelation alerts readers that Sandy is not what he seems, and that perhaps other characters in the novel are not, either, no matter how benign they appear.

Dead Cert also illustrates a second major use of humor in Francis novels: to provide comic relief when the going gets grim, as it often does. The relief here takes the form of interludes between the action, giving the reader (and the protagonist) both a breathing space and further insight into the various characters' relationships and environments.

Since Alan York has been living with the family of the jockey recently killed in a racing fall, he has become an intimate part of the household. The dead jockey's three children—uncommonly precocious youngsters—are very attached to him. Each time the mystery takes a nasty turn—a racing injury or a roughing up—Alan returns to the house for a relaxed and whimsical respite with the children. In one such instance, after Alan has been waylaid by the villains and "persuaded" not to investigate his friend's death any further, he returns home to consider what to do next.

> I played poker with the children and lost to Henry because half my mind was occupied with his father's affairs.
>
> Henry said, "You aren't thinking what you're doing, Alan," in a mock sorrowful tone as he rooked me of ten chips with two pairs.
>
> "I expect he's in love," said Polly, turning on me an assessing female eye. There was that, too.
>
> "Pooh," said Henry. He dealt the cards.
>
> "What's in love?" said William, who was playing tiddly-winks with his chips, to Henry's annoyance.
>
> "Soppy stuff," said Henry. "Kissing, and all that slush."
>
> "Mummy's in love with me," said William, a cuddly child.
>
> "Don't be silly," said Polly loftily, from her eleven years. "In love means weddings and brides and confetti and things."

> "Well, Alan," said Henry, in a scornful voice, "you'd better get out of love quick or you won't have any chips left."
>
> William picked up his hand. His eyes and mouth opened wide. This meant he had at least two aces. They were the only cards he ever raised on. I saw Henry give him a flick of a glance, then look back at his own hand. He discarded three and took three more, and at his turn, he pushed away his cards. I turned them over. Two queens and two tens. Henry was a realist. He knew when to give in. And William, bouncing up and down with excitement, won only four chips with three aces and a pair of fives.

Odds Against makes use of another form of comic relief, black humor, both to pace the action and to provide acerbic commentary on it. Ex-jockey Sid Halley, whose hand has been crippled in a racing fall, is learning to cope with his disfigurement, both physical and mental, while working for an investigative firm, the Radnor Agency, as a private investigator. The novel centers on one case in particular: the attempt by a wealthy businessman to take over a racecourse through illegal methods. Sid's sidekick and assistant on the case, Chico Barnes, is a lower-class character designed largely for purposes of comic relief through black humor and large doses of ironic irreverence.

Very early in the novel, Sid has been shot in the stomach by a small-time crook he'd been following, and Chico comes to visit him in the hospital to "cheer him up," revealing at the same time the closeness and mutual understanding between the two characters that allow him to tease Sid in such an apparently callous way:

> [Chico] wandered on [around the hospital room]. "Haven't you got a telly then? Cheer you up a bit, wouldn't it, to see some other silly buggers getting shot?" He looked at the chart on the bottom of the bed. "Your temperature was one hundred and two this morning, did they tell you? Do you reckon you're going to kick it?"
>
> "No."
>
> "Near thing, from what I've heard. Jones-boy [another detective in the Radnor Agency] said there was enough of your life's blood dirtying up the office floor to make a tidy few black puddings."
>
> I didn't appreciate Jones-boy's sense of humor.

Blood Sport also makes use of black humor as comic relief and as a form of running commentary by the narrator/protagonist, who is a suicidal government counter-espionage agent. Things have not gone well for Gene Hawkins, whose wife has left him, whose life is in constant danger from a variety of enemies, and who purposely lives in a depressing flat with dingy furnishings. During the course of the novel, Gene begins to regain an interest in life as he tries to protect a wealthy American horse breeder, Dave Teller, and investigates the reasons for assassination attempts against him.

Early in the novel, Gene saves Teller from drowning in a boating "accident." Peter, the young son of Gene's boss, has been taking pictures all day, but failed to record either the accident or the suspicious couple who may have been responsible for it. Gene comforts Peter about his photography skills through a bit of black humor that may be lost on the boy, but not on the reader:

> "A fire," I agreed seriously, "would anyway make a much better picture than just people drowning, which they mostly do out of sight."
>
> Peter nodded, considering me. "You know, you're really quite sensible, aren't you?"

Blood Sport also exhibits Francis's occasional use of humorous social commentary. In this case, the commentaries are both psychological and social in nature, demonstrating Francis's keen eye for human nature in individuals and in groups. One of the characters, blissfully naive about criminal behavior, is described this way:

> Like most law-abiding citizens, she had not grasped that a criminal mind didn't show, that an endearing social manner could coexist with fraud and murder. "Such a *nice* man," the neighbors say in bewilderment, when Mr. Smith's garden is found to be clogged with throttled ladies. "Always so pleasant."

A much more cutting social observation (not yet outdated in 1967) reflects Francis's ongoing concern with relations (and frictions) between social groups. Gene is breaking into the house of two of the villains for a little sabotage, and as he cases the neighborhood, he notices that "beside one of [the swimming pools] a woman in two scraps of yellow cloth lay motionless on a long chair, inviting heatstroke and adding to a depth of suntan which would have got her reclassified in South Africa."

Blood Sport is one of Francis's darker novels, but even so, there are moments of lighter humor and even a touch of whimsy. For example, a company that rents trailers a la U-Haul is called Snail Express, with the motto: "Carry your house on your back, but let us take the weight." And later in the novel, Gene and his temporary American partner in the investigation, Walt, are finally beginning to like each other,

after a period of getting past some major differences in personality and operating style. Late one night, when Walt invites Gene to his room for a drink, Francis uses an intentionally (and humorously) mixed metaphor to describe his reaction: "I wasn't sure that I wanted to, but he smiled suddenly, wiping out all resentments, and one didn't kick that sort of olive branch in the teeth."

Readers can be sure a Francis character is trouble when he *lacks* a sense of humor. In *The Edge,* which is set on the Great Transcontinental Mystery Race Train across Canada, one of the wealthy horse owners is being blackmailed over a particularly cruel prank his son Sheridan pulled at his private school. Sheridan's more serious character defects are foreshadowed by his nonexistent sense of humor.

> Nell sat opposite Sheridan Lorrimore, who seemed to be telling her that he had wrapped his Lamborghini round a tree recently and had ordered a new one.
>
> "Tree?" Nell said, smiling.
>
> He looked at her uncomprehendingly. Sheridan wasn't a great one for jokes.

In this novel, as in *Dead Cert,* the narrator's own character is revealed through his sense of humor. This time, however, it is another character who comments on the protagonist's humorous personality, providing an insight that illuminates his solitary nature and need for privacy, traits which stem from his inherited wealth and his efforts to deal with it.

"There's something about you that's secret . . . ultra-private. As if you didn't want to be known too well . . . You always have jokes in your eyes," she said. "And you never tell them."

In a Francis novel, written as they are by an eminent ex-jockey, even the horses become characters with distinct personalities that are occasionally revealed through humor. In *Break In,* protagonist Kit Fielding has to ride an extremely stubborn horse, North Face, in a race. The experience is described in ironic, affectionate, gently "deflationary," and very realistic terms:

> Dramatic pictures of Fielding being bucked off before the start were definitely not going to be taken. I called the horse a bastard, a sod and a bloody pig, and in that gentlemanly fashion the race began.
>
> He was mulish and reluctant and we got away slowly, trailing by ten lengths after the first few strides. It didn't help that the start was in plain view of the stands instead of decently hidden in some far corner. He gave another two bronco kicks to entertain the multitude, and there weren't actually many horses

who could manage that while approaching the first fence at Cheltenham.

Hot Money makes good use of several humorous devices. The murder victim, Malcolm Pembroke's unpopular fifth wife Moira, was found suffocated in her greenhouse; in life she was a self-serving gold-digger, the perfect target for Francis's black humor, delivered through the narrator, Malcolm's son Ian:

> Malcolm's personal alibi for Moira's death had been as unassailable as my own, as he'd been in Paris for the day when someone had pushed Moira's retroussé little nose into a bag of potting compost and held it there until it was certain she would take no more geranium cuttings.

This novel also showcases one of Francis's fortes, what Keating calls a traditional humor hallmark: word-play of all sorts. Francis's careful use of language and poetic devices such as similes, metaphors, irony, personification, and synecdoche produces humor and enlightening characterization with economy, mostly taking the form of acerbic one-liners commenting on characters and events in scathing detail.

Describing a private detective, for example, Francis comments, "His gray suit looked old and uncared for and his shoes had forgotten about polish. He looked as much at home in a suite in the Savoy as a punk rocker in the Vatican." And after Malcolm's family manor has been bombed, a flock of reporters descends on the estate and on the family members, going from one to the next, trying to extract juicy tidbits:

"The reporters, having sucked the nectar from Gervase [one of Ian's brothers], advanced on Malcolm and on the gardener and the superintendent."

Over the years, Francis's sense of humor seems to have mellowed slightly, certainly not losing the bite of his early novels, but with more frequent appearances of whimsy, a gentler form of humor. *The Edge* has some of the clearest examples of whimsical humor to be found in Francis's novels. Tor Kelsey, an investigator of racing crimes, is traveling aboard the Great Transcontinental Mystery Race Train, posing as an actor playing a waiter who is part of the mystery being performed for the guests. Before leaving Toronto, Tor takes the event's organizer, Nell, out to dinner at a restaurant called the Fluted Point People.

> The waiter, who must have been asked a thousand times, said the fluted point people had lived on this land ten thousand years ago. Let's not worry about them, he said.

Nell laughed and I thought of ten thousand years and wondered who would be living on this land ten thousand years ahead. Fluted points, it transpired, described the stone tools in use over most of the continent: would our descendants call us the knife and fork people?

On board the train, security around the horse car is fierce, under the guard of a woman whom the conductor calls the "dragon-lady." Francis uses Tor's puckish sense of humor as a whimsical counterbalance to the seriousness of the guard and to the potential danger of the whole journey. Tor's stage name on the train is Tommy.

> [The guard] produced a clipboard with a sheet of ruled paper attached. "Sign here," she said. "Everyone who comes in here has to sign. Put the date and time."
>
> I signed Tommy Titmouse in a scrawl and put the time.

More whimsy is evident in Tor's description of the horse car itself: "A couple of grooms sat around on bales while their charges nibbled their plain fare and thought mysterious equine thoughts."

A colleague of mine, passing my office as I was looking at *Proof,* told me that he'd read that novel and been surprised at how funny it was, particularly the ongoing theme of the hero visiting pub after pub, becoming increasingly tipsy while tasting various wines and liquors for the police. His comment sums up for me the mistaken impression that infrequent readers of Francis often have: all action and no laughs. Those of us who are more familiar with the range of his writing know that, while some of his novels are indeed funnier than others, the thread of humor runs through every one. Francis is a writer who takes neither himself nor the mystery genre so seriously that he doesn't enjoy poking some gentle fun at both and letting his readers in on the joke. Judging by his books, Dick Francis is a very funny man indeed, and failing the company of the man himself, his books are a very close second best.

Doug Simpson (review date Summer 1993)

SOURCE: A review of *Driving Force,* in *The Armchair Detective,* Vol. 26, No. 3, Summer, 1993, p. 103.

[*In the following review, Simpson asserts that "Francis always delivers a story you can bet on" as he does with* Driving Force.]

Like a good race horse that always finishes in the money, Dick Francis always delivers a story you can bet on. His latest, *Driving Force,* is no exception. Again we have that winning formula: a decent, resourceful and courageous hero finds himself pitted against an evil force, which he ultimately overcomes. And, of course, some aspect of the horse racing industry is involved.

In this case, Freddie Croft, an ex-jockey, owns a business that transports horses. It's one thing when a hitchhiker dies of a heart attack in one of Croft's vans. But when an intruder searches the van, Croft knows something is up. Then the mysterious death of his maintenance man is too much of a coincidence. Croft's investigation leads to malicious destruction of his office and computer records, a senseless deliberate collision of his prized Jaguar into his sister's helicopter, and his being assaulted and subsequently dumped into the sea, where he nearly drowns.

Croft knows that some sort of virus is being transported, first because the deceased hitchhiker's thermos contained some tubes holding a liquid virus, and second because of the secret compartments discovered under his vans. The question is what was transported under there and why. The computer records might help discover the truth, but they were destroyed. Only Croft knows that he had a back-up disk locked in his safe. Imagine how a few well-placed viruses can debilitate good horses, and, in turn, affect the outcome of the races.

Francis builds his story skillfully, presenting an interesting variety of characters, some good and appealing, others unpleasant and possessing evil. The title, in fact, refers not to racing a horse, but to man's capacity for evil, that force within that obsessively drives an evil person to do what he or she does. It's always in a Francis novel, and it's always reassuring to see it defeated in the end.

Kirkus Reviews (review date 1 August 1993)

SOURCE: A review of *Decider,* in *Kirkus Reviews,* Vol. LXI, No. 15, August 1, 1993, p. 966.

[*In the following review, the critic lauds Francis's* Decided *as one of his most satisfying recent books.*]

Francis's newest suspenser (his 32nd) is typical not only in its racetrack setting, but in its doubling of the hero's mildly dysfunctional family (he and his diffident wife are held together only by their brood of six sons) with another family of deep-dyed villains.

Because his mother Madeline was once married into the frac-

tious Stratton family, owners of the Stratton Park racecourse, architect/builder Lee Morris, a restorer of ruined houses, owns a small number of voting shares in the course. His long-standing revulsion from Madeline's wife-beating first husband Keith Stratton has kept him away from the family—especially from his half-sister Hannah, a child of marital rape—and, despite the pleas of course manager Roger Gardner, he intends to keep his distance even when Keith's father, Lord William Stratton, dies. But an invitation to a meeting of the shareholders leads to an unexpected request from matriarchal Marjorie Binsham, William's sister—to look into the question of whether the outdated grandstands really need replacing—and while he's poking around along with his five oldest sons, an explosion rocks the stands and nearly kills him. Sabotage, of course; but was the culprit habitual animal-rights picketer Harold Quest, or one of the Stratton heirs—Keith himself, his despised twin Conrad (the new head of the family), their ineffectual brother Ivan—or one of their children—spiteful unwed mother Hannah, sullen jockey Rebecca, insouciant Dart, or troublemaking Forsyth?

Francis's biggest coup here is his success in delineating shades and varieties of wickedness in the superbly monstrous Strattons. Despite an unconvincing hint of May-December romance for his fatalistic hero, this is the most elaborate and satisfying of his recent books—a winner from the starting gate to the last hurdle.

J. P. Donleavy (review date 17 October 1993)

SOURCE: "Racing All the Way to the Bank," in *The New York Times Book Review,* October 17, 1993, p. 40.

[*In the following review, Donleavy compares and contrasts Francis's* Decider *and William Murray's* We're Off to See the Killer.]

My own long-term interpretation of the writing trade has been that it is the turning of one's worst moments into money. And in Dick Francis and William Murray we have two writers who are ambidextrous, so to speak, and indeed are turning both their best and worst moments into revenue. These authors come out of their corners jabbing you instantly in the imagination and setting on edge your state of expectancy as they unfold with complacency-piercing words the contrasting worlds of horse racing on each side of the Atlantic. In *Decider,* Mr. Francis gives his somewhat more polite version, peopled by aristocrats in their country mansions. In *We're Off to See the Killer,* Mr. Murray gives us a rougher picture of lust and venery, peopled by a tougher-sounding brand of folk whose abodes are where their hats hang.

Resentfully blaming the genre because it sells so well and makes its creators rich, one sometimes wonders if the so-called literary world is out to ruin literature that can be so readily read, like these quite gripping books by two of the best writers in the business. For I somehow imagine that this must be the most exacting form for the literary craftsman, with every word you write there on the page forever to be used against you by your admiring but aware-eyed aficionados. But both Mr. Francis and Mr. Murray are clearly expert, even down to one of two stereotypical characters, as you would expect to find in the racing world. And there are no literary nonsense descriptions. Their words are precise, vivid and as brilliant literary as you can get.

Any mention of Dick Francis to one of his readers brings unrestrained eruptions of enthusiasm of every pleasant kind. Of course, Mr. Francis already enjoys the patronage of members of the British royal family, who eagerly devour his words—not a bad recommendation. But then on the other side of the Atlantic I imagine President Clinton to be a fan of William Murray's, and if he isn't yet, let me suggest *We're Off to See the Killer* instead of budget deficits for his bed-side reading. Mr. Murray's hero, Shifty Lou Anderson, is a magician who bets on horses. In Mr. Murray's expert writing, there are many suspicious goings-on that even touch on the contemporary, with a corporation supplying arms to the former Yugoslavia.

We're Off to See the Killer has a much more carnal-minded and complicated plot than *Decider.* However, Mr. Francis is not far behind Mr. Murray in these matters. He comes from behind and rides at his shoulder, as it were, and in the final furlong his fast pace makes up for the lack of Mr. Murray's riotous sexual romping. With his hero an architect restoring ruins, Mr. Francis comes down the stretch with a hint of incest, wife beating and rape, edging up to be nose and nose with Mr. Murray and adding a nice touch of British morality, which, in your best aristocratic family tradition, has always meant keeping scandal quiet and paying to preserve a good name. In *Decider,* we can learn not only of horse racing but also of the behind-the-scenes business of running a racecourse and the internecine family disputes it can involve, which produce a fiery and violent climax.

In reviewing these two highly commendable works, I have to admit an ignorance, not of horses or racing but of this genre. And I would have once imagined that purveyors of this form of fiction had a much easier time than the so-called literary authors in putting together their stories. And I would have thought them a different breed had I not once actually encountered one of these writers and found him to be the most dedicated and serious of literary men. Such types are exemplified by Mr. Murray's and Mr. Francis' rapier use of words and the scrupulous attention paid to their authentic settings and how intimately they examine and know the worlds they write about.

The revelation happened during the more sumptuous days of television years ago, on a rainy Sunday morning in Manchester, England. The previous night, a public relations officer separately invited two writers to appear, representing the opposite, hostile sides on the question of obscenity. The intention of the program was to contrast a so-called serious author whose work had been banned with one who had become noted for his so-called less serious fiction and was not banned. The two antagonists were staying overnight in Manchester's best hotel. Informed that a chauffeured limousine was available to take them separately to the studio the next morning, each man declined, deciding instead to walk and find his own way to the television station through Manchester's then quite grim smog-bound and anonymous streets. In the drizzle the men arrived to confront each other on the entrance steps of the television studio.

I was one of these writers who chose to walk through the gloomy Sunday morning Manchester streets. The other was Ian Fleming. We both stood there wet and dripping, and soon to be contrasted to the nation on that Sunday afternoon, I as a scandalous author published by the Olympia Press in Paris, my book *The Ginger Man* having been recently ordered by a Manchester magistrate to be destroyed, and Fleming to be made an example of an unbanned purveyor of so-called popular pornography, eagerly and widely read by the British public. But Fleming, who knew he was to be used as a scapegoat, instead of recoiling at the sight of me, smiled and seemed relieved, holding out his hand to shake mine in recognition of the fact that we had both chosen to eschew ease and luxury for the discomfort of the rain in order to see the slums of Manchester on a foggy, cold morning. We both knew that we were equally serious authors whose lives were devoted to writing, which is hardly necessary to say of these two authors, Dick Francis and William Murray, whose books stand them in good stead and allow them to continue to turn their worst and best moments into money.

Pat Dowell (review date 17 October 1993)

SOURCE: "Mysteries," in *Washington Post Book World,* October 17, 1993, p. 8.

[*In the following review, Dowell asserts that Francis's De-cider "runs smoothly and efficiently to a tidy conclusion."*]

When you pick up *Decider,* the 34th mystery novel written by Dick Francis, there's no question that you've got a well-established, best-selling author in your hands. The pages are creamy and as thick as cardboard, and the story they tell—

full of proper folk, ancient manses, and "squashy" furniture—runs smoothly and efficiently to a tidy conclusion.

The narrator is Lee Morris, an architect-builder with "Le Corbusier technology and humanist tendencies." His specialty is turning ruins into elegant, comfortable habitats. He houses his increasingly estranged wife and their six sons on-site in a converted double-decker bus while he builds a dwelling. Then they move in while the new place is on the market.

The old tithe barn on the Surrey-Sussex border that is their current abode feels like home, however, and that is where the manager of Stratton Park racecourse (you knew we'd get around to horses) finds Lee. He has an old, unhappy family connection with the Strattons, who own the park. More important, he owns eight shares of their racecourse. The fate of the park is a bone of contention among the snarling aristocrats. Thus is Lee, hated by the family, drawn reluctantly into their lives, and a plot.

One might almost suspect that Francis, in penning the Stratton family, had in mind another, more loftily titled clan. The Strattons are certainly in as much disarray as the royals; they even have to cope with a surreptitiously taped phone call used by a blackmailer. Ruled by "a delicate-looking, tough-minded old lady with a touch of tycoon" and plagued by scandal hushed up with their millions, the various Strattons are milquetoasts, wife-beaters, and inept swindlers. They might even number among themselves a murderer, who would stoop to blow up the racecourse grandstand with Lee Morris inside.

The Strattons are also rather stiff creations, constantly striding about in more of a lather than the thoroughbreds. Lee has to look out in particular for Keith, whose beastly behavior long ago to his first wife, Lee's mother, has much to do with everything that keeps *Decider* trotting along.

Francis far more vividly renders Lee's battalion of boys, who dine on such English delicacies as tinned spaghetti on toast and ultimately become the pawns in a grudge match between their father and his archenemy. There are also some lilting odes to horseflesh.

It's all rather soothing, if not very bright, inspiring the same kind of mysterious affection that settles one down to enjoy a dim but satisfying episode of "Murder, She Wrote." As Lee Morris says of a proper gent who refrains from asking personal questions, "I found his inhibitions restful."

Dick Roraback (review date 19 December 1993)

SOURCE: A review of *Decider,* in *The Los Angeles Times Book Review,* December 19, 1993, p. 6.

[*In the following review, Roraback asserts that despite a slow start Francis's* Decider *is a good bet.*]

A little late out of the gate, *Decider,* Dick Francis' 32nd (!) novel, is still worth a show bet, maybe even a place. Francis, of course, is the former jockey whose nourishing mysteries center about the racetrack. *Decider*'s slow start, then, can be chalked up to its leading man, builder Lee Morris, who doesn't know a bangtail from an I-beam. Naturally he learns; by Page 241 he's good and hooked on horseflesh: "No architect anywhere could have designed anything as functional, economical, superbly proportioned." But it's a way from there to here.

Morris stumbles into the milieu via seven inherited shares in a racecourse 90% owned by the Strattons, a "noble" British family that makes the Jukeses look like your in-laws from Anaheim. Guilty of everything from pride and prejudice to embezzlement and incest, the Strattons are precariously strung together by the Honourable Marjorie—"a delicate-looking tough-minded old lady with a touch of tycoon"—and by ownership of the track. When the stands are torched, identity of the arsonist is elusive: Pick a Stratton, any Stratton.

Meanwhile Francis is freed to do what he does best. First a swipe at animal-rights picketers who eat hamburgers and wear leather shoes: "Horses run and jump because they like to." Next a nod to female jockeys, "rapt in [their] own private world of risk, effort, metaphysics." Finally: Had it not been for the horse, "the seafarers, Vikings and Greeks, might still rule the world."

Christopher Lehmann-Haupt (review date 20 December 1993)

SOURCE: "Mystery and Suspense From Three Old Hands," in *The New York Times,* December 20, 1993, p. C15.

[*In the following excerpt, Lehmann-Haupt praises Francis's* Decider, *asserting that Francis "writes winningly about horses."*]

At the start of Mr. Francis's *Decider,* Lee Morris, an Oxford architect and builder, is asked to help save a race track in nearby Swindon from destruction by the wealthy but violently feuding relatives who have inherited it. Knowing he should stay clear, he nevertheless piles five of his six sons, ages 14 to 7, into the family bus and drives them out for a look at the track. Before he knows it, he and one of the boys are nearly killed by an explosion that destroys the grandstand. Which crazed family remember could have done such a thing?

As always, Mr. Francis, a retired jockey, writes winningly about horses. "Imagine the world without them, I thought: history itself would have been totally different. Land transport wouldn't have existed. Medieval battles wouldn't have been fought. No six hundred to ride into a valley of death. No Napoleon. The seafarers, Vikings and Greeks, might still rule the world."

As always, his humans are immediately likable or detestable, as his strong plotting directs them. And as always, Mr. Francis, whose 34th novel *Decider* is, extends his curiosity to a new interest, here the art of restoring old buildings attractively.

As Lee remarks after riskily rescuing the track's fortunes: "For years I asked hundreds, literally hundreds of people, why they'd bought the old houses they lived in. What was the decider, however irrational, that made them choose that house and no other?"

The deeper question posed by the novel is why people take the crazier chances they do, even to the point of endangering their children.

Dale H. Ross (review date Winter 1993)

SOURCE: A review of *Long Shot,* in *The Armchair Detective,* Vol. 26, No. 1, Winter, 1993, pp. 107-8.

[*In the following review, Ross discusses survival in Francis's* Long Shot.]

Survive is what the first person narrators of Dick Francis' very successful novels do and survival is what *Long Shot* is all about. Thirty-two year old John Kendall, an erstwhile employee of a travel service specializing in strenuous outings for adventure seekers, has published six survival guides for such trips. An expert photographer, helicopter pilot, specialist in wildernesses hot, temperate, and cold, Kendall has had a first novel (about the survival attempts of people isolated by a disaster) accepted. On the strength of that success, he has severed his ties with the travel service and is attempting to make his living as a writer of fiction.

Francis employs a standard convention: a group of people—related by blood and marriage—living together in an English country house in a small village. His narrator (in order to bolster his meager finances) signs on to do an "as told to" autobiography of the owner of the place, a self-made man with an outstanding reputation as a trainer of steeplechase horses.

Arriving in the dead of winter, Kendall is met at the train by

a car that will take him to the country house to meet his employer. The icy roads and a mysterious stray horse combine to put the vehicle and its inhabitants at some peril. Kendall's survival skills are immediately put to the test, and he at once earns the respect of his fellow passengers.

As is always the case in a Francis novel, the reader learns much: here it is about how to use a watch as a compass, or catch trout without fish hooks, or start fires in the rain, or set traps. This lore and more come into play as the plot develops.

Violent death is no stranger to the country house and the disappearance of a promiscuous, young female groom—amidst much business about training horses for the steeplechase and about how one rides in such races—whets the reader's interest. Always inventive, Francis displays here, as he does in his earlier novels, an affinity for the arresting phrase, the novel comparison (e.g. "set nemesis in motion"; "while the combined ghosts of two young women set traps for the flies"; "a pair of binoculars powerful enough to see into the riders' minds").

Kendall is victimized by several assaults, the techniques of which are drawn from the very survival guides he authored. Justice—or at least Dick Francis' version of justice—is finally served, however. As always, Francis' narrative skills hold the reader's attention and provide a strenuous trip for those who prefer to seek their adventures vicariously.

Rachel Schaffer (essay date Summer 1994)

SOURCE: "The Pain: Trials by Fire in the Novels of Dick Francis," in *The Armchair Detective,* Vol. 27, No. 3, Summer, 1994, pp. 349-57.

[*In the following essay, Schaffer discusses the use of violence and injury in Francis's novels.*]

Dick Francis is no stranger to pain. For over a decade (1946 to 1957), as an amateur and then professional steeplechase jockey in England, he suffered countless bruises and 21 broken bones (not counting ribs) from the inevitable racing falls, followed by horses galloping over him. In his autobiography, *The Sport of Queens,* Francis details the variety of injuries he suffered over the years, emphasizing the ability of jockeys to heal rapidly and even to ride with broken bones. He takes an athlete's pride in his high tolerance for pain and injury, shrugging them off casually as merely something to be expected in his profession, yet offering fairly frequent and detailed descriptions of them.

In writing his autobiography, Francis honed his descriptive

skills not only on racing details and action, but also on his first-hand experiences with pain and injury. When he later turned to writing mystery novels, he continued to use with great impact his first-hand knowledge of the world of British horse racing and the effects of pain and injury. Whether Francis uses pain to add color, action, and realism to the pictures of the racing and criminal worlds he so vividly paints, or to explore the deeper psychological effects of fear, pain, and violence on character, for 31 years and 31 novels he has offered readers insights that only personal experience can provide.

In his earlier novels, Francis follows a fairly straightforward formula of pain set pieces of two basic types: scenes in which the protagonists suffer racing injuries of various sorts, and scenes in which they suffer punishment at the hands of the villains. Since many of the heroes are jockeys and have extensive experience with pain already, they exhibit amazing stoicism in the face of the suffering they endure—or at least they appear stoic to outsiders, for as they usually confide to the reader, they suffer as much as anyone, but have too much pride to show it.

Francis's first novel, *Dead Cert,* sets the pattern to come. The protagonist, Alan York, is the son of a wealthy Rhodesian trader and has been living with a jockey friend and his family while racing in England. When his friend is killed in a racing fall, Alan gets involved in the search for the murderer and uncovers a protection racket.

Alan's first encounter with violence occurs when some of the villains waylay him and hold him captive in a horse trailer. Their intent is only to warn him off, but Alan has no way of knowing this—he believes he's been kidnapped for ransom and acts accordingly. When Sonny, a young thug, unbuttons Alan's shirt and holds a knife point against his breastbone, instead of standing still, Alan does precisely the last thing anyone would expect of him: " . . . I thrust forwards and sideways as strongly as I knew how, bringing my knee up hard into Sonny's groin and tearing my arms out of the slackened grasp of the men behind me." He then heads for the door, but doesn't make it. This time the men holding him are not at all gentle, nearly dislocating his shoulders as they pull his arms back. Alan's only reaction to the abuse is to "shut [his] teeth" because "there didn't seem to be much [he] could do about it."

After the thugs have finished delivering their message, they throw Alan from the moving horse-box. Here again, his experience as a jockey serves him well. As he hits the ground, he notes, "It was as well I had had a good deal of practice at falling off horses. Instinctively, I landed on my shoulder and rolled."

A while later, he tells an incredulous local police official why he threw himself into the knife instead of staying still:

> "I wouldn't have been so keen if he'd held the point a bit higher up: but it was against my breastbone. You'd need a hammer to get a knife through that. I reckoned that I'd knock it out of Sonny's hand rather than into me, and that's what happened."

> "Didn't it cut you at all?"

> "Not much," I said.

He shows the inspector a shallow cut with some dried blood and comments to the reader, "Nothing. I hadn't felt it much."

Clearly, Alan's professional experience with injuries has taught him what risks he can safely take and has hardened him to what he considers minor pain or danger. Such stoicism, and the understatement used to express it, is a recurring trait in every Francis protagonist: whether they consider themselves brave or not, outsiders invariably see their actions as courageous.

Dead Cert set the pattern found in many of Francis's subsequent novels of having at least two violent confrontations per book. Much later in the story, the second episode occurs when Alan rides his mount into a wire strung across the racetrack and takes a fall. The fact that he expected the wire to be somewhere on the track and decided to ride anyway plays up his stoicism and sense of duty in the face of danger, another of Francis's favorite character traits. The fall itself isn't so bad, but the horses coming over the fence after him batter him brutally, which, as Francis often points out in his novels, is where the real damage to jockeys most often occurs: "The galloping hooves thudded into my body. One of the horses kicked my head and my helmet split so drastically that it fell off. There were six seconds of bludgeoning, battering chaos, in which I could neither think nor move, but only feel."

Then, to add insult to injury, the villain who had strung the wire across the course walks up to him as he lies on the ground and kicks him: "I heard the ribs crack, and I felt the hot stab in my side"; "He kicked my face, and I went out like a light."

A recurring theme in Francis novels, and one that frequently provides a source of violence, is class conflict. Francis is a keen observer of social manners and attitudes and has mined class differences successfully in most of his books. He plays no favorites, however, when it comes to his protagonists. Sometimes they are lower class, sometimes middle class, and occasionally even members of royalty. *For Kicks* and *Flying Finish* provide mirror images of the heroes' class and the class conflicts—in the form of violence—that they face as a result.

The hero of *For Kicks,* Daniel Roke, may in reality be a successful South African stud farm owner, but his dark coloring and Cockney-sounding accent mark him as lower class to the English upper class, which is exactly why he is offered an undercover job in England investigating the suspiciously energetic performances of certain horses in certain races. Daniel decides to accept the job "for kicks" and is soon working at the stable of one of the suspects in the case, a gentleman trainer named Humber, whose partner in crime, a wealthy sadist named Adams, believes that the lower-class stable hands should be treated like dogs, and who therefore takes great delight in tormenting Daniel. At his first encounter with Daniel, Adams drops his walking stick, and as Daniel bends over to pick it up, pushes him over with his boot, smiling "with malicious enjoyment." Turning to his assistant, Adams says, "'You've got to show them you won't stand any nonsense. Stamp on them whenever you can. This one . . . needs to be taught a lesson.'"

This scene sets the stage for much more physical abuse of Daniel by Adams throughout the novel, including ear boxing and face slapping, all of which must be stoically borne for the sake of his cover (risking personal safety for the greater good). Only at the climax of the novel does Daniel have the freedom to fight back, this time for his life. Even then, the odds are against him, with both villains attacking him while he is unarmed. Fortunately, he has a skill that comes in handy against walking sticks, one that Francis has carefully told the reader about previously: the ability to throw a cricket ball.

> There on the desk was the green glass paperweight. The size of a cricket ball. It slid smoothly into my hand, and in one unbroken movement I picked it up, pivoted on my toes, and flung it straight at Humber where he sprawled off balance barely ten feet away.
>
> It took him centrally between the eyes. A sweet shot. It knocked him unconscious. He fell without a sound.

Francis reverses the social roles of protagonist and villain in a later novel, *Flying Finish,* in which the hero, Henry Grey, the son of an earl, faces the same kind of physical and verbal abuse from someone of a different class that Daniel Roke does, only this time the villain, Billy, is lower class and hates the nobility and the wealthy with vicious passion.

Henry meets Billy when he takes a job as head groom for Yardman Associates, a horse transport firm. On their first trip together, Billy initiates a fistfight with Henry after telling him that "your kind ought not to be allowed." Henry

fights back well and wins that battle, telling Billy, "'I don't see any point in fighting you, but I will if you make me. You can forget I'm an earl's son, Billy, and take me as I am, and this is what I am. . . .' I jerked his arm. 'Hard, Billy, not soft. As tough as necessary. Remember it.'"

Henry's victory only sets the scene for later attempts at revenge. On almost every trip the two take together after that, Billy tries to hurt Henry somehow, first dropping a heavy metal bar on his fingers, then dropping peat into Henry's coffee and pouring sugary coffee over his head, and later hitting him "savagely across the shoulders with a spare tethering chain."

As it later turns out, Billy has an added motivation for tormenting Henry: he is also distracting him from a transport racket that Yardman has designed, smuggling spies out of England. But the more basic hatred Billy feels for the nobility makes him especially sadistic when he finally has Henry to himself.

Billy's plan is to torture Henry until the pilot of a hijacked plane takes him where he wants to go. He therefore ties Henry to a horse box and begins shooting him along the ribs, showing off his shooting ability—not deep enough to break the bone, just enough to hurt like hell. Henry takes this torture stoically, and it's this stoicism that saves his life, for Billy is so determined to make him beg for mercy that he keeps him alive, rather than killing him quickly and surely.

In fact, the fate Billy has planned for Henry is turned against him: he has chained a can of petrol to Henry's ankle and made him dig his own grave. Just as he flicks his cigarette lighter to set Henry ablaze, Henry, who has managed to sever the chain with the shovel he was using, throws the can of petrol at Billy and sets him ablaze. As Billy drops his gun and runs for help, Henry follows.

Billy is burned, but not dead. At this point, Francis departs from the normally ultra-ethical protagonists he usually portrays. Henry has a choice: to shoot or not to shoot. Another true-blue hero might have spared Billy's life and left him alive to possibly interfere with his flight to safety. Henry is more pragmatic than that.

> [Billy] stared unbelievingly at me and then at his gun in my hand. His mouth shut with a snap; and even then he could still raise a sneer.
>
> "You won't do it," he said, panting.
>
> "Earls' sons," I said, "learn to shoot."
>
> "Only birds." He was contemptuous. "You haven't the guts."

"You're wrong, Billy. You've been wrong about me from the start."

I watched the doubt creep in and grow. I watched his eyes and then his head move from side to side as he looked for escape. I watched his muscles bunch to run for it. And when I saw that he finally realized in a moment of stark astonishment that I was going to, I shot him.

On one level, this outcome is highly satisfying, pure revenge against a truly evil character, his own sadistic desires turned back upon him sadistically. There is no doubt that Billy deserves to die, but Francis has made his execution problematic by having Henry shoot him in cold blood, not entirely in self-defense, not in the heat of the moment. Does his victory make Henry a hero or a cold-blooded killer? Whichever, this violent action reflects basic changes in his character: he has done something he never would have done before these events changed his life.

In the sequence of events leading up to Billy's death, Francis illustrates explicitly another theme running through his novels: underestimating the hero's abilities and toughness—the amount of pain and suffering he can take and that he can inflict. Yardman, the chief villain of *Flying Finish,* has the acumen to see beyond Henry's patrician surface, telling him at one point, "'You look so gentle, dear boy. . . . So misleading, isn't it?'" and warning Billy, "'Take no chances, Billy, do you understand? You underestimate this man. He's not one of your fancy nitwits, however much you may want him to be.'" Billy discovers the truth of this the hard way.

In this novel, there is no racing violence, but there is a graphic scene depicting what can happen when a horse goes berserk on an airplane. Some horses become so frightened by the noise and motion that they try to escape their boxes, with possibly fatal consequences in a pressurized cabin at 30,000 feet. Francis carefully lays the groundwork for the later scene by describing several uneventful trips, then pulls out all the stops.

On this particular trip, a horse has begun kicking its box to pieces in its panic, trying desperately to escape and threatening to unbalance the plane or put a hoof through a window. Henry takes decisive action. Because there is no humane killer on board and drugs are unpredictable on horses, Henry uses a carving knife from the galley to slit the horse's throat as it breaks through its box and lunges toward him. He manages to hit the carotid artery,

> [b]ut I couldn't get out of his way afterwards. The colt came down solidly on top of me, pouring blood, flailing his legs and rolling desperately in his attempts to stand up again.

His mane fell in my mouth and across my eyes, and his heaving weight crushed the breath in and out of my lungs like some nightmare form of artificial respiration. . . .

> The blood went on pouring out, hot sticky gallons of it, spreading down the gangways in scarlet streams. Alf cut open one of the hay bales and began covering it up, and it soaked the hay into a sodden crimson-brown mess. I don't know how many pints of blood there should be in a horse; the colt bled to death and his heart pumped out nearly every drop.

This description is graphic, extremely unpleasant, and gut-wrenchingly exciting. It also brings home the dangers of air transportation for large animals, something the average reader is unaware of and therefore will find lends authenticity to the story.

As Albert Wilhelm points out in his analysis of "Fathers and Sons in Dick Francis's *Proof,*" many Francis novels "examine the growth of an individual's character" and "focus on the theme of maturation," following the youthful protagonist as he successfully meets "a series of crucial tests" on his way to attaining a new level of maturity. Henry Grey fits this pattern perfectly, as Wilhelm demonstrates in his article "Finding the True Self: Rites of Passage in Dick Francis's *Flying Finish.*" Wilhelm sees more in the violence of this story than mere background color or action to keep the reader interested. He points out the parallels between Henry's personal growth throughout the novel and classic "stories of initiation documenting the rites of passage of . . . characters." As Wilhelm sees it, Henry Grey is typical of Francis's protagonists, who are "often young men . . . who forge new identities as a result of their involvement with criminal activities." In this interpretation of events, Billy's torture of Henry by shooting along his ribs becomes "scarification on the chest" and "a trial by fire" (which also becomes literal later in the novel), the colt's blood pouring over him becomes "a bath in animal blood," and Henry's shooting of Billy becomes "the killing of a foe," all traditional elements of initiation ceremonies. At the end of the novel, after successfully surviving all of these experiences, Henry has matured; he is ready to take on a new identity as an adult and begin a much more fulfilling life than his earlier, emotionally limited one.

Francis's pain set pieces most often center on beatings that the heroes undergo at the hands of the villains. Occasionally, however, the punishment takes a different form, with added psychological elements. In *Smokescreen,* for example, the protagonist is an actor whose opening scene foreshadows (and in fact inspires) the peculiar form of torture inflicted on him at the novel's climax. Edward Lincoln begins the novel handcuffed to the steering wheel of a car as part of a film he's making, and ends up in the same position in a desert in South Africa after agreeing to help a close family friend investigate the poor performance of some racehorses she owns. For 18 pages, Francis explores every aspect of a man chained in one position, with no water, food, or bathroom facilities, no chance to stretch, and no escape from the heat. He describes, in Link's own words, the physical and mental anguish as they grow more and more unbearable. The passage is a feat of empathy that involves readers completely, far more effectively than the more mundane beatings and shootings normally featured.

Here also, however, Francis emphasizes the physical aspects of the torment. Link describes "legs like lead and ankles swollen to giant puffballs," an abdomen "agonizingly distended with gas," and eyes "like sandpaper when the lachrymal glands dried up." Fortunately, Link has strong reserves of physical strength and mental resourcefulness. He survives physically until help comes by condensing water in a plastic sandwich bag and mentally by writing down a complete account of the crime, which he has now solved. At the end of the novel, Link has learned a great deal about physical suffering and has once again shown the kind of self-sacrifice for the greater good that Francis specializes in: after he's rescued, he insists on getting back in the car (still unwashed) in order to catch the villain, perhaps the hardest thing he's ever done.

Francis earlier explored the themes of maturation and growth through suffering in *Odds Against*. Here again the catalyst is violence, first a racing accident, then a shooting, and then a final act of brutality that changes the life of the protagonist permanently. Sid Halley was a professional steeplechase jockey until a fall from a horse smashed his hand and ended his racing career. Sid keeps his hand, now deformed and useless, carefully hidden in his pocket and works halfheartedly for the Racing section of Hunt Radnor Associates, a private investigation firm.

At the novel's opening, Sid is lying in the hospital, recovering from a gunshot wound from a small-time hood breaking into the firm's building—an event which, Sid says, "left me with fire in my belly in more ways than one" and "was the first step to liberation." Because of that shooting, Sid spends some time with his ex-father-in-law, Charles Roland, recuperating and becoming involved in Charles's attempt to foil a shady plot to take over a nearby racecourse for real estate development. And because in the course of this investigation he meets someone else with an even more disfiguring physical handicap, he is forced to come to grips with his own.

Early in *Odds Against*, Sid's relationship with the primary villain, wealthy, sadistic Howard Kraye, and his masochis-

tic wife, Doria, is established as the source of ongoing conflict that leads eventually to one of Francis's most violent scenes. From the beginning of their relationship, when Sid is introduced to them in his disguise as the disgraced, illegitimate ex-son-in-law of the wealthy and powerful Charles Roland, the Krayes become fascinated with the idea of humiliating him in every way they can, first by making Sid take his deformed hand out of his pocket ("They both saw from my face that I would hate that more than anything. They both smiled.") and then actually attacking the injury itself ("[Kraye] stiffened his free hand and chopped the edge of it down across the worst part, the inside of my wrist. I jerked in his grasp."). For the sake of his investigation, Sid bears the humiliation stoically, as he has always borne his trials, for, as he says at one point in a summary that speaks for most, if not all, of Francis's heroes,

> Always, from my earliest childhood, I had instinctively shied away from too much sympathy. I didn't want it. I distrusted it. It made you soft inside. . . . So [personal problems] had to be passed off with a shrug, and what one really felt about it had to be locked up tightly inside, out of view. Silly, really, but there it was.

The final showdown between Sid and the Krayes is one of the most horrifying Francis has ever written. Normally, his heroes suffer no permanent damage—broken bones and bruises heal. But not so with Sid. The punishment is so horrible, especially to him, that the jockey's stoicism is broken at last.

The Krayes have tied Sid to a chair, and in order to get the information they need out of him, they torture him with the best weapon they have: his deformed hand.

> "We know where he's most easily hurt," [Kraye] said. "That hand."
>
> "No," I said in real horror.
>
> They all smiled.
>
> My whole body flushed with uncontrollable fear. Racing injuries were one thing: they were quick, one didn't expect them, and they were part of the job.
>
> To sit and wait and know that a part of one's self which had already proved a burden was about to be hurt as much as ever was quite something else. Instinctively I put my arm up across my face to hide from them that I was afraid, but it must have been obvious.
>
> Kraye laughed insultingly. "So there's your brave

clever Mr. Halley for you. It won't take much to get the truth."

"What a pity," said Doria.

Even faced with the threat to his hand, Sid still lies, and Kraye smashes his wrist with a poker:

> . . . he used all his strength and with that one first blow smashed the whole shooting match to smithereens. The poker broke through the skin. The bones cracked audibly like sticks.
>
> I didn't scream only because I couldn't get enough breath to do it. Before that moment I would have said I knew everything there was to know about pain, but it seems one can always learn. . . . There had never been anything like it. It was too much, too much. And I couldn't manage any more.

And yet, Sid does manage more. He remains silent when Kraye jerks his wounded hand, telling them "where to go" for the papers they want only when Kraye jolts his hand a second time. The Krayes leave him tied to his chair in the dark, where he has plenty of time to think about the consequences of his capitulation, as well as about torture in general: "To suffer or to talk. The dilemma that stretched back to antiquity. . . . I didn't understand how anyone could keep silent unto death."

The kicker to all this is, of course, that Sid had planned the entire sequence, knowing that Kraye wouldn't believe his story without the punishment appearing to break him. Instead of sending the villains to the real source of information they want, he sends one of them to the home of a colleague well able to take care of himself, and with a code phrase to serve as a warning.

Sid pays a dear price for his stoicism, of course: his hand has been thoroughly destroyed by the torture, and at the novel's end, it has been amputated. Now, however, rather than always trying to hide a deformity, Sid has been relieved of a burden and is considerably freer to put his life back together and learn to live with a prosthesis, in a way a much more honest handicap to cope with. But Sid's worries about his hands have not ended here, for in the sequel to *Odds Against,* the novel *Whip Hand,* they once again play a prominent role in exploring the recurring Francis themes of courage and stoicism in the face of loss, and growth through painful life experiences.

Whip Hand concerns a wealthy aristocrat's plot to impair the performance of top two-year-old racers. As Sid gets closer and closer to the villain, Trevor Deansgate, Deansgate takes matters into his own hands and kidnaps Sid, using a weapon

against him that he at first is powerless to fight against: Deansgate has his men hold Sid down with arms outstretched and puts a shotgun at his one remaining good wrist, threatening to shoot his hand right off if he doesn't leave England until after a crucial race. The thought of being without hands, helpless to live independently and do the things for himself that he can still do with only one hand, is more than Sid can take. This form of mental torture works where no mere beating could. He describes his state of mind with vivid clarity:

> All the fear I'd ever felt in all my life was as nothing compared with the liquefying, mind-shattering disintegration of that appalling minute. It broke me in pieces. Swamped me. Brought me down to a morass of terror, to a whimper in the soul. And instinctively, hopelessly, I tried not to let it show.

Even at this moment of greatest fear, Sid's major concern is to hide any signs of weakness; his stoicism is so deeply ingrained that he is unable to show emotion even then. He does, however, agree to leave town, and then suffers agonies of shame and self-doubt for his "weakness."

However, true to the Francis code of honor, when Sid returns to England and sees Deansgate's plans continuing unimpeded, he decides to pick up the investigation again, although he is still afraid of the results. In another classic Francis fight, Sid is beaten with a chain until his back has turned to "jelly. A living jelly. Red. On fire. Burning, in a furnace." Sid contemplates the nature of pain and people's coping mechanisms for over an hour until some help comes, but he must still drive three and a half hours to a friend's house before he can get safe medical attention.

Eventually, Sid solves the case and effectively ruins Deansgate's life. At the last, he arrives home to find Deansgate waiting for him, shotgun in hand, ready to carry out his threat. Sid refuses to beg for his hand, in spite of the renewed terror he feels—he says, "I thought numbly that I wasn't so sure, either, that I wouldn't rather be dead." To his surprise and relief, Deansgate does not shoot him—he's had too much time to think about the consequences of maiming or killing a national hero, an ex-champion jockey. He had wanted very badly for Sid to beg him not to shoot him, but, he says, "'I'd forgotten . . . what you're like. You've no bloody nerves.'" In spite of Sid's battle with fear, cowardice, and self-doubt, he finally wins back his self-respect when Deansgate says to him, "'Isn't there anything . . . that you're afraid of?'" The answer is yes, but in the end, not enough to make him compromise his unfailing sense of justice.

The variations on Francis's use of pain and violence to provide racing color, supply action to further the plot, and develop themes of growth through suffering have taken increasingly interesting directions over the years. From the earliest beatings, fights, and assaults with deadly weapons, Francis has moved on to concentrate more on disabilities, both physical and psychological, insecurities, and fears of isolation, inadequacy, and loss. Barry Bauska, in a 1978 *TAD* article, observed that "as a focus of tension physical pain is being supplanted by psychological strain as Mr. Francis himself grows farther and farther away from his riding days." This trend away from the purely physical punishment (even torture) of his earlier novels has continued to an even greater extent in recent years: since the late '80s, Francis has been using more distant, impersonal forms of violence—bombings, fires, or violence against animals rather than prolonged physical assault on the protagonists. There has even been a decrease in the number of violent scenes in recent novels, and those still included seem shorter and more peripheral to the action proper.

In *Hot Money,* for example, the most violent scenes are child-hood memories, a house that explodes while the characters are safely away, and a bomb that goes off accidentally. In *The Edge,* there is only one real fight scene, and the hero actually wins it handily with a modicum of damage (there is a later scene, as well, where the hero takes some punches without resisting to make the case's outcome more satisfying, another case of the protagonist making physical sacrifices for the good of others). The protagonist in this novel still grows and matures—he is better able to handle personal relationships—but it is not the violence that has changed him. In *Straight,* much of the violence occurs almost in passing: the hero is mugged, attacked by a woman who believes him to be a burglar, and knocked out by real burglars. (There is, however, a very personal and very exciting fight between protagonist and villain at the end of the novel.) And in *Comeback,* there are fairly brief violent episodes at the very beginning and end of the novel, with punching and kicking the major action involved, but most of the violence in the novel is done offstage to horses rather than people. The protagonist, Peter Darwin, undergoes very little physical punishment, even when his life is threatened. This is indeed fortunate because Peter is a diplomat, not a fighter (he is, quite likely, the most pacific—and static—protagonist Francis has ever created); as he himself says, "Words were my weapons, not arms."

However, Francis has not completely abandoned explorations of pain and suffering in recent novels. *Longshot,* in a return to earlier form, has the protagonist shot through the chest with an arrow, followed by a 20-page tour-de-force examination of his painful journey toward help that is entirely the equal of Edward Lincoln's ordeal in the car in *Smokescreen.*

While there is still plenty of action involved in his more recent mysteries, Francis has also expanded his repertoire of literary techniques to include more development of charac-

ters and relationships without violence as the primary catalyst. The reduced emphasis in later novels on describing suffering in graphic detail is a change from the "tortured" heroes of the early Francis, though admittedly not a complete one. Bauska, in his *TAD* article, sees this widening of focus as a sign of Francis's own growing maturity as a writer, praising him for "becoming less a writer of thrillers and more a creator of literature." Having developed many permutations on scenes of pain, violence, and suffering, Francis is now depending less on the traditional violent elements of detective fiction in order to explore more intently the elements of mainstream fiction: character development, the evolution of relationships, and nonviolent themes of growth, change, and maturation.

Richard Lipez (review date 18 September 1994)

SOURCE: "Mysteries," in *The Washington Post Book World,* September 18, 1994, p. X10.

[*In the following excerpt, Lipez calls Francis's* Wild Horses *"pretty enjoyable."*]

The movie business is . . . the setting of *Wild Horses,* Dick Francis's pretty enjoyable new equestrian thriller. . . . [H]is nice-guy sleuth, Thomas Lyon, is the serious and well-thought-of director of "Unstable Times," a film based on a real-life (in the book) horsey-set mystery. And the eroticism here is not only central to the plot, . . . but it's also much more—I'm tempted to say—English.

Francis's 33rd mystery—which on a Francis scale of one-to-10 I'd rate an entirely respectable eight—gets off to an intriguing start when Lyon, in Newmarket for filming, hears the death-bed confession of Valentine Clark, an aged black-smith and old family friend. To Lyon's amazement, Clark asks for absolution for killing someone long ago. The details, however, are mystifying.

> **Dick Francis, O.B.E., probably has more medals by now than the average field marshal, but he still has a high old time razzing the English upper classes, a race of ninnies throughout his books.**
> **—Richard Lipez**

It soon develops that there's a connection between the confession and the story on which the film is based. Twenty-six years earlier, a young woman named Sonia was found hanged in a stable. In the novel that speculated on the incident, young Sonia's husband is wrongly accused of causing her death and then cleared. The novelist, who is also the screenwriter, is a pretentious artiste who lounges around the set, bemoaning the liberties that are being taken with his screenplay. He's more interested in Sonia's possible fantasy life—centering on wild horses—than on who might have strung her up.

That's all largely academic until Clark's elderly sister is horribly slashed in her house and attempts are made on Lyon's life by someone who wants to stop the film. Solving the crime is no longer a matter of mere art; it's necessary to save the lives of Lyon and maybe others. So the past is dredged up with a vengeance.

Dick Francis, O.B.E., probably has more medals by now than the average field marshal, but he still has a high old time razzing the English upper classes, a race of ninnies throughout his books. In *Wild Horses,* they're the usual rum lot, and it's the self-made who get the work done. Francis has lived in Florida and the Caribbean off and on in recent years, so he's started in on our more democratic tyrannies, especially the American insistence on eternal youth if not eternal life. A British doctor in *Wild Horses* asks a Hollywood actor, "Is it true that in America, if you die of old age, it's your fault?" Francis is so good-natured, the reader may miss the real edge in his consistently interesting voice.

John Mortimer (review date 2 October 1994)

SOURCE: "Back in the Saddle Again," in *The New York Times Book Review,* October 2, 1994, p. 26.

[*In the following review, Mortimer praises Francis's storytelling ability in* Wild Horses.]

In many ways the writer is made by the day job. Where would Chekhov and Conan Doyle have been without their medical training, or Dashiell Hammet if he hadn't learned about the sleazier side of San Francisco as an operative in the Pinkerton detective agency? If Dick Francis' father hadn't been a steeplechase jockey, and if he hadn't decided to follow his father's breathlessly dangerous profession, we certainly shouldn't have had 33 novels that have entertained millions and won the approval of such as Philip Larkin, the fine but notably grumpy English poet, who was by no means easy to please.

"The mingled smells of hot horse and cold river mist filled my nostrils. I could hear only the swish and thud of galloping hooves and the occasional sharp click of horseshoes striking against each other. Behind me, strung out, rode a group of men dressed like myself in white silk breaches and harlequin jerseys, and in front, his body vividly red and green against the pale curtain of fog, one solitary rider steadied his

horse to jump the birch fence stretching blackly across his path." The opening of *Dead Cert,* his first novel, published in 1962, in fact portrays Dick Francis chasing his subject. In this pursuit he reckoned that he hit ground at 30 miles an hour every 12th ride and suffered a fractured skull, six broken collarbones, five broken noses and no end of shattered ribs. To this day his face looks as though it had been blown in by the wind. As a method of acquiring material for a novel this seems a good deal harder than lying in a cork-lined room, remembering a childhood beach or the taste of a madeleine.

Many years ago Dick Francis the jockey was riding the Queen Mother's horse Devon Loch with the Queen watching, and he had established a lead of 10 lengths at the last fence of the Grand National. Suddenly, 30 yards from the winning post, Devon Loch mysteriously sank to the ground. (Several theories were advanced for the collapse, including the possibility that Devon Loch had suffered a sudden, severe muscular cramp in his hindquarters.) After this disappointment, and many injuries, he decided on the even chancier life of a novelist. What he brought with him from the race track were the crowed-pulling powers of suspense, surprise and the shared enthusiasm to discover who's going to win.

He still talks in the voice of an old steeplechaser, cutting off his final g's. Whereas he once said, "My father said a day's huntin' was better than a day's schoolin'," he now says, "I'm writin' a book a year."

> **The excitement as well as the pain of his former life have given Dick Francis an extraordinarily clear view of the racing world and the squalors, as well as the beauties, of the English countryside.**
> **—*John Mortimer***

The excitement as well as the pain of his former life have given Dick Francis an extraordinarily clear view of the racing world and the squalors, as well as the beauties, of the English countryside. It's a place where the fields and downs have been defaced by motorways and the old towns wrecked by shopping malls. The villains, bookmakers or dubious trainers, wear camel's-hair coats, drive Bentleys and live in vast spreads of red brick houses, swimming pools illuminated by carriage lamps and white fences. The jockeys, pulling on laddered nylon stockings under their racing boots, or shivering on early-morning rides on the downs, are Spartan. Their idea of a treat is a plate of bacon and eggs and a cup of strong tea after a long fast. They live in bungalows or mobile homes, and their bodies are broken by falls and the bully boys hired by the villains. Their careers are in the hands of the stewards of the Jockey Club, who are not jockeys but upper-crust, elderly men who treat fearless riders as though they were inferior and frequently dishonest servants. On the whole Dick Francis' view of the racing world is not shaped by any inherent assumptions about class. If a lord appears, wearing a tweed suit and a waxed coat, living in a drafty house that smells of wet dog, he's quite likely to turn out to be the source of all villainy.

Philip Marlowe walked down mean streets, and Mr. Francis' heroes frequent some pretty mean race tracks. Raymond Chandler set out the standards of decency he required of the detective: he must be neither tarnished nor afraid. "He must be, to use a rather weathered phrase, a man of honor, by instinct and inevitability, and certainty without saying it. He must be the best man in his world, and a good enough man for any world." Dick Francis would not express the creed of the mystery-story here so resonantly, but what makes his books attractive is his sense of decency and honorable behavior. He put it more succinctly when he said, "What it comes to is that I never ask my main character to do anything I wouldn't do myself."

One of the results of this is that while in today's world of best sellers you can't get through three pages without stumbling across throbbing members or meeting flowing juices, there's not much sensational sex in the Francis novels. In **Banker,** the hero and the heroine, although passionately in love, don't sleep together until her husband dies, conveniently, of a brain hemorrhage on the last page. In **Dead Cert,** the hero kisses the girl he loves discreetly and, although he feels inclined to carry her off to the downs and "behave likes a cave man," he resists the temptation. Perhaps it's inevitable that more sex has crept into the books, occasionally salted with a twist of sadomasochism, but making love still ranks far lower than racing. In his latest work, *Wild Horses,* the sexual behavior is very rare and exotic; but fortunately it happened long before the book began and the hero, who though a film director is still an extremely decent chap, had absolutely nothing to do with it.

Thomas Lyon has come to Newmarket, "the town long held to be the home and heart of the horse racing industry worldwide," to direct a drama about racing. He has been recruited because he's already made several successful films and because "I'd spent my childhood and teens in racing stables." The film is based on a recent best-selling book, a fictionalized account of a scandal that had occurred in Newmarket 26 years earlier, when the wife of Jackson Wells, a horse trainer, had been found hanging in a stall and her husband was suspected of having killed her. But he was never charged, the film script does not identify a killer and the death remains a mystery that Lyon finds himself increasingly eager to solve.

His pursuit is at first driven by the idea that some sort of resolution would aid the film. And then, inevitably, he finds

that his inquiries have stirred up a variety of unappetizing, smarmy characters, among them a killer. Like many of Mr. Francis' heroes, Lyon finally must find the truth to save his life.

We live in a time when many highly regarded and prize-winning novelists have forsaken plot. Stories are regarded as somewhat down-market and fit only for airport bookstands and poolside reading. Stories go with pina coladas and Ambre Solair suntan lotion, proper novels with arugula salads and chardonnay. But the best writers, as well as the most popular, have always known that telling a story is the only way of inducing the reader to turn the pages. Dick Francis takes from Jan. 1 to May 8 each year to write a novel, and his latest, produced at the age of 73, is as compulsive as ever.

Christopher Lehmann-Haupt (review date 20 October 1994)

SOURCE: "High Life and Low In a Pair of Mysteries," in *The New York Times,* October 20, 1994, p. C19.

[*In the following excerpt, Lehmann-Haupt complains that the characters and plot of Francis's* Wild Horses *are forced.*]

At the opening of Dick Francis's latest racetrack thriller, *Wild Horses,* a dying old man, mistaking a young friend for a priest, asks to be forgiven for killing "the Cornish boy" and leaving "the knife with Derry." The friend goes along with the charade and absolves the dying man, assuming the confession to be senile rambling.

Certainly it would have nothing to do with the movie young man is directing on location nearby in "Newmarket, Suffolk, England, the town long held to be the home and heart of the horseracing industry worldwide." After all, the novel on which the movie is based is only a fictionalized version of a local murder case that remains unsolved. And the film takes such liberties with the book that the novelist is incensed.

So there couldn't be a connection, the narrator thinks at first. "Ah well," he reflects as efforts to stop his film grow increasingly violent. "One can get things wrong."

As always, Mr. Francis has done his homework in telling a story that links his longtime knowledge of horse racing with an unrelated profession, in this case Hollywood film making. In fact, *Wild Horses* is strikingly more ambitious than the usual Dick Francis, as its narrator strives for a cinematic image of the erotomania he discovers lying behind what his dying friend has confessed.

Unfortunately, what's missing from *Wild Horses* is the seductive case of plotting that has made most of Mr. Francis's previous thrillers so much fun to read. Unlike Mr. Francis's usual narrator, this one races around like a circus plate-spinner to keep all the parts of the story moving. The characters are so forced that they become caricatures. The plot machinery clanks and sputters.

The novel even strives for what can be read as a defense of Mr. Francis's craft. As the narrator tells another character: "I'm still an entertainer and always will be, I guess . . . I make the images. I open the door. I can inflame . . . and I can heal . . . and comfort . . . and get people to understand . . . and for God's sake don't remember a word of this. I've just made it up to entertain you."

But given the way *Wild Horses* labors, you can't help but feel that by stretching out for meaning Mr. Francis has stumbled on self-consciousness and taken an unusual fall.

Kristiana Helmick (review date 27 October 1994)

SOURCE: "The Thunder of Racing Hooves Inspires Winning Mysteries," in *The Christian Science Monitor*, Vol. 86, No. 234, October 27, 1994, p. 13.

[*In the following review, Helmick discusses Francis's love of horses and how he uses it in his novels.*]

The Grand National at Aintree is England's greatest steeplechase; in 1956, British jockey Dick Francis lost it in the last 25 yards. The years have not worn away the tinge of regret in his voice as he describes his "darkest day."

But what good fortune for his soon-to-be readers. The loss prompted him to write his autobiography, which in turn has led to a streak of more than 30 best-selling mysteries, most of which incorporate a riding theme.

Indeed, as Francis said when we spoke together recently, horses are never far from his thoughts, and riding has become a kind of allegory for Francis's life: "The main good point of any jockey . . . is loyalty. . . . And in life, you do your best for those nearest to you."

He says that this has become a driving force behind his writing as well: "That is the honesty which I aim to preach."

That code often tips the balance in favor of Francis's protagonists. Francis concedes that he ensures his hero always "knows what is right" and that, in the end, "right comes out on top." This holds true in his latest mystery, *Wild Horses* (currently No. 7 on the Publisher's Weekly fiction bestseller list), in which Thomas Lyon, acting on a friend's dying wish, solves a 25-year-old murder without police help.

Francis needs only to look to the lessons of the track for the persistence he instills in his heroes. The author's own determination led him through numerous defeats and injuries—from which he "always came up smiling"—and earned him status as champion jockey in 1954.

But if Francis were pressed to choose between writing about riding and the rough sport itself, he'd ask for a jockey's life every time.

"There is nothing more satisfying," he says grinning, "than to be on the back of a horse you like very much . . . and jump into the first fence of a race and then you see all the other fences and think, What a thrill it's going to be. . . ."

All the same, writing hasn't been a bad alternative. Though it isn't as easy as being on horseback—"I was born to the saddle," he explains—the reward of writing bestsellers lasts longer.

Francis doesn't have to go it alone as an author. He has long depended on his wife, Mary, to conduct research. She's mastered everything from merchant banking to painting and airplanes to help out.

And the husband-wife team's creativity shows in quite a few non-equine plots: The hero of *The Danger,* for example, is a professional negotiator for the release of kidnapping victims. Although he gladly rescues a famous jockey in distress, horses leave him clammy. Unlocking another mystery, *Twice Shy,* takes physics and Olympic-level riflery. Another book centers on gem smuggling.

Francis's writing has earned him kudos on the racetrack as much as anywhere else, however. The author says several racetracks now sponsor races in his name, adding without fanfare that many British jockeys, who were not yet born when he was champion, view him as a legend. Needless to say, most of them read his books, he says.

Francis's riding success also gave him the opportunity to rub shoulders with royalty. He rode for the Queen Mother for several years, and it was her horse Devon Loch that he rode in the 1956 Grand National that was so important for his writing career.

Francis's love for the track in life and on paper comes down to the horses. *Wild Horses* contains only a brief passage on racing, in which film director Lyon must win the allegiance and trust of local jockeys, extras in his film, by daring them to race. Yet those few pages are among the most gripping in the novel: "There was speed and there was silence. No banter, no swearing from the others. Only the thud of hooves and the brush through the dark birch of the fences. Only the gritting determination and the old exultation," Francis writes.

The "old exultation" lives with Francis, too, though the author falters as he attempts to explain it—as if it were so natural that anyone should understand. Shaking his head impatiently, he stretches to articulate his vast love for riding that permeates his novels. "It isn't actually the fences; it's the way the horse jumps the fences. If you've got a good jumper, it's terrific. You kick him into the fence and throw your heart over and hope you catch it on the other side."

Kirkus Reviews (review date 15 July 1995)

SOURCE: A review of *Come to Grief,* in *Kirkus Reviews,* Vol. LXIII, No. 14, July 15, 1995, p. 986.

[*In the following review, the critic discusses the return of the protagonist Sid Halley in Francis's* Come to Grief.]

Big news for Francis fans: He's broken his rule against recycling heroes and brought back one-handed p.i. Sid Halley (**Odds Against,** 1966; **Whip Hand,** 1980) to investigate a series of mutilations of two-year-old ponies. Sid naturally feels close to the equine victims, who've had their off-forefeet amputated; but he feels even more unnervingly close to the suspect he soon uncovers—his old friend and former racing competitor Ellis Quint, now turned immensely popular TV entertainer. Despite the mountain of evidence that leads to Ellis's arrest, Sid, gagged by England's sub judice rule from discussing the case until the trial begins, falls victim himself to a campaign of smears and revenge so vicious—the weekly paper he's been working with suddenly turns on him in savage columns defending Ellis, and Ellis's father attacks him with an iron bar—that there must be somebody big and well-organized behind the vendetta against him. A world away from the racetracks he used to call home—the closest we get to a race is Sid's laconic comment, "I watched the Derby with inattention. An outsider won"—Sid pokes around after that somebody, risking not only innuendo and hatred, but the loss of his remaining hand.

Francis's 34th novel is grand entertainment with a bittersweet edge his fans haven't seen since his sorely missed hero's last appearance. Welcome back, Sid.

Norma J. Shattuck (review date Winter 1996)

SOURCE: A review of *Come to Grief,* in *The Armchair Detective,* Vol. 29, No. 1, Winter, 1996, pp. 102-3.

[*In the following review, Shattuck asserts that Francis does not fully explore the emotions and motivations of the villain in his* Come to Grief.]

To say that jockey-turned-sleuth Sid Halley solves puzzlers involving horses and horse racing is to repeat what Dick Francis readers know already. To say that he solves them single-handedly is to perpetrate the obvious pun.

Actually, Halley's state-of-prostheses-art left hand comes close to being a co-character in Francis's Halley novels. At some point Sid's amputee status (the hand was lost in a disastrous racing spill) can be expected to become the focus of some character's malicious intent toward Halley-in-whole. A sub-theme of such encounters is people's not uncommon fascination with such physical infirmities. In Sid's dangerous business, morbid interest of this sort can segue to sadism.

Here, the twisted type who's seized by a grim compulsion to wound Halley where he's most vulnerable is a former close friend and fellow jockey who's now an adored media celebrity. What triggers this unsettling episode is Halley's finding and reporting of evidence that Ellis Quint, a genuine charmer, may have perpetrated a series of grotesque mutilations of ponies and horses.

Beleaguered by a pro-Quint public and press—a tabloid paper launches a particularly vicious smear campaign against him—Halley perseveres in pursuing the evidence, even after learning that the mother of the accused has committed suicide, apparently unable to accept what she perceives as Sid's sullying of her innocent son's name.

Steely but not nerveless, Halley suffers both physical danger and guilt for sundering the Quint family, whose patriarch becomes so crazed that he proceeds to stalk his son's accuser with an iron bar, then with a gun.

While dealing with all this, Halley is also striving to give emotional support to another family—that of a woman friend whose nine-year-old daughter is sinking fast from leukemia. Sid's warm rapport with mother and child reminds him poignantly of the failure of his marriage to the beautiful Jenny. Though she has remarried, apparently happily, it's clear that the emotional bond is not completely broken.

> One of the delightful perks of a Francis novel is finding oneself diverted by some character's unusual area of expertise.
> —*Norma J. Shattuck*

One of the delightful perks of a Francis novel is finding oneself diverted by some character's unusual area of expertise. Here, we are introduced to a woman who's a master weaver, known for creating rare, expensive, one-of-a-kind creations from gold and silk. It's a deft Francis touch that one of her museum-worthy pieces, crafted 30 years previously, has ended up wrapped around a pair of shears used to lop off an equine hoof.

Issues of character and morality are also part of the mix. For choosing truth over loyalty to friends, Sid is excoriated. This loss of repute can't help but remind him of earlier, piled-up losses: of the racing career he loved, of his wholeness of body, of the woman he'd married.

Still, as sensitive as Francis seems here to human frailty and to the emotional nuances of his hero, he ends up short-changing readers as to his villain. What impels an otherwise seemingly normal person to commit a series of cruel, bizarre, profitless acts? The explanations contained in the perpetrator's confessional note are unconvincing, and Francis fails to follow through with anything that addresses the psychological riddle. Thus, the book is like an absorbing race with photo-finish in which the central image is too blurred to settle the crucial question.

FURTHER READING

Criticism

Adler, Dick. "Inspector Wexford in top form." *Chicago Tribune Books* (3 September 1995): 4.
  Lauds the well-drawn villains and touching hero of Francis's *Come to Grief.*

Anderson, Michael. A review of *Comeback. The New York Times Book Review* (22 December 1991): 14.
  Lauds Francis's *Comeback* as an enjoyable ride.

Binyon, T. J. "Criminal proceedings." *The Times Literary Supplement,* No. 4374 (30 January 1987): 108.
  Criticizes Francis's *Bolt* for lacking the qualities commonly associated with Francis novels, including "tension, excitement, surprise, atmosphere and characterization."

———. "Crime file." *The Times Literary Supplement,* No. 4421 (25-31 December 1987): 1428.
  Complains that there is too much psychology and not enough action in Francis's *Hot Money.*

———. "Criminal Proceedings." *The Times Literary Supplement,* No. 4471 (9 December 1988): 1376.

Criticizes Francis's *The Edge* for being "thinly plotted" and "carelessly written."

Campbell, Don. "Track, Casino, Newsroom, Squad Car." *The Los Angeles Times Book Review* (24 January 1988): 6.
  Praises Francis's *Hot Money* for being a good mystery and a good read.

Champlin, Charles. A review of *Longshot. The Los Angeles Times Book Review* (11 November 1990): 15.
  Calls *Longshot* one of Francis's best novels in his prolific career.

———. A review of *Driving Force. The Los Angeles Times Book Review* (11 October 1992): 13.
  Lauds Francis for keeping his formula fresh in his *Driving Force.*

———. "Criminal Pursuits." *The Los Angeles Times Book Review* (11 September 1994): 18.
  Praises Francis's research of the movie industry in *Wild Horses.*

Cromie, Alice. "'Poison' You Can't Put Down." *Chicago Tribune Books* (10 May 1987): 6.
  States that Francis's *Bolt* is a winner.

Dretzka, Gary. "Nero Wolfe Leaves His Lair, and Dick Francis Rides Again." *Chicago Tribune Books* (4 October 1992): 6-7.
  Praises Francis's *Driving Force* as a sure best-seller.

———. "Is Scudder Getting Weird on Us?" *Chicago Tribune Books* (2 October 1994): 9.
  Reviews several mystery novels including Francis's *Wild Horses.*

French, Edward. A review of *Driving Force. Books* 6, No. 5 (September/October 1992): 27.
  Praises Francis for his natural storytelling ability and asserts that *Driving Force* is a satisfying read.

Harshaw, Tobin. "Books in Brief." *The New York Times Book Review* (8 October 1995): 26.
  Praises Sid Halley, the hero of Francis's *Come to Grief,* but asserts that Francis has been better.

Hubin, Allen J. A review of *Straight. The Armchair Detective* 24, No. 1 (Winter 1991): 29.
  Praises the plot and characters of Francis's *Straight.*

Kaufman, Gerald. "Bring in the Heavy Guns." *The Listener* 120, No. 3093 (15 December 1988): 34.
  Praises the prose and plot of Francis's *The Edge.*

A review of *Wild Horses. Kirkus Reviews* LXII, No. 14 (15 July 1994): 950.
> Lauds the expertise Francis exhibits about directing in *Wild Horses,* but complains that "the mystery is muddled and the villains muffled."

Moore, Kevin. "From Nero Wolfe's Orchids to a 'Prime Slime' Shamus." *Chicago Tribune Books* (5 November 1989): 6.
> Asserts that Francis has maintained his high standards with his novel *Straight.*

———. "A Cajun Beat and Brit Cool Set the Mood." *Chicago Tribune Books* (14 October 1990): 6.
> Lauds Francis's *Longshot* despite the author's occasional overwriting.

———. "Keeping a Watch on Crime with Francis and Others." *Chicago Tribune* (6 October 1991): 6.
> States that Francis's *Comeback* demonstrates the writing skills that Francis has developed throughout his career.

A review of *Bolt. The New Yorker* LXIII, No. 8 (13 April 1987): 106.
> Asserts that with *Bolt* Francis is back to the quality of his earlier writing.

Rosser, Claire. A review of *Comeback. Kliatt* 27, No. 3 (May 1993): 6.
> Calls Francis's *Comeback* one of Francis's best.

Ryan, Desmond. "In Short." *The New York Times Book Review* (1 May 1988): 22.
> States that although the puzzle of Francis's *Hot Money* is not among his best, Francis displays his gifts for narrative and economical prose.

Shibuk, Charles. A review of *Bolt. The Armchair Detective* 22, No. 1 (Winter 1989): 106.
> Asserts that while Francis's *Bolt* is a good novel, it does not attain the achievement of his previous work *Break In.*

———. A review of *Straight. The Armchair Detective* 24, No. 4 (Fall 1991): 507.
> Calls Francis's *Straight* "so spellbinding that it is almost impossible to put down."

Spitzer, Jane Stewart. "Popular Novels." *Christian Science Monitor* (6 March 1987): B4.
> Asserts that Francis's *Bolt* is far from being his best novel.

———. "Suspense Stories." *The Christian Science Monitor* (23 March 1988): 20.
> Asserts that the resolution of Francis's *Hot Money* does not provide the satisfaction usually associated with the end of a Francis novel.

Stuewe, Paul. "Of Some Import." *Quill & Quire* 55, No. 12 (December 1989): 29.
> Points out the problems with Francis's *Straight* including the author's failed attempt to integrate the gem business into the story line.

A review of *Bolt. Time* 129, No. 17 (27 April 1987): 83.
> States that with Francis's *Bolt,* he "again demonstrates that he is both a win and a nice read."

Watkins, Mel. "In Short." *The New York Times Book Review* (29 March 1987): 22.
> Asserts that Francis's *Bolt* delivers on all of the elements expected from a Francis novel.

Waugh, Harriet. "O, Let Them Not Be Mad!" *The Spectator* 259, No. 8306 (26 September 1987): 34-5.
> States that Francis's *Hot Money* is enough to keep a not very discerning detective reader happy.

———. "Thrills on a Wet Afternoon." *The Spectator* 261, No. 8359 (24 September 1988): 40-1.
> Asserts that *The Edge* suffers from an unnecessary subplot and is not one of Francis's best.

———. "Not Altering When it Alteration Finds." *The Spectator* 266, No. 8467 (20 October 1990): 33-4.
> Asserts that Francis's *Longshot* "is an exceptionally well-plotted novel with convincing characters . . . and is also truly exciting."

———. "Murder Most Enjoyable." *The Spectator* 267, No. 8526 (7 December 1991): 34.
> Complains that Francis's *Comeback* starts slow and is not as good as his *Longshot,* but that by the end, the novel becomes thoroughly engrossing.

———. "English Country Murders." *The Spectator* 275, No. 8721 (2 September 1995): 32.
> Calls Francis's *Come to Grief* an example of "sado-masochistic, action-packed detection."

Additional coverage of the author's life and career is found in the following sources published by Gale Research: *Authors and Artists for Young Adults,* Vol. 5; *Bestsellers,* Vol. 89:3; *Concise Dictionary of Literary Biography,* 1960 to Present; *Contemporary Authors,* Vol. 5-8R; *Contemporary Authors New Revision Series,* Vols. 9, 42; *DISCovering Authors: Popular Fiction and Genre Authors Module; Dictionary of Literary Biography,* Vol. 87; and *Major Twentieth-Century Writers.*

Patricia Highsmith
1921-1995

(Born Patricia Plangman; also wrote under the pseudonym Claire Morgan) American-born novelist, short story writer, and nonfiction writer.

The following entry provides an overview of Highsmith's career. For further information on her life and works, see *CLC*, Volumes 2, 4, 14, and 42.

INTRODUCTION

An American-born author who resided in Europe for most of her adult years, Highsmith is best known for her suspense novels, which challenge many of the conventional precepts of the genre. Highsmith avoided gimmicks and formulaic plots and concentrated on developing the motivations behind criminal behavior rather than apprehending the villain. The presence or absence of guilt for one's actions dominates Highsmith's fiction, and often the innocent characters suffer more than the guilty. Highsmith also frequently employed such dualistic pairings as the weak with the strong, and the sane with the insane to examine such themes as violence, morality, and self-delusion. Although Highsmith wrote numerous novels and short stories, she is most highly regarded for her novels that feature the character Tom Ripley, a charming, intelligent, and sophisticated murderer who is never brought to justice.

Biographical Information

Highsmith was born in Fort Worth, Texas. Her parents separated before she was born, and she was raised by her grandparents, who taught her to read when she was two years old. Highsmith joined her mother and stepfather, Stanley Highsmith, in Greenwich Village, New York, when she was six; she has stated that she had an unhappy childhood and youth and that she was not close to her mother. She attended Julia Richman High School, where she was the editor of the school newspaper and read books by such writers as Leo Tolstoy and Fyodor Dostoyevsky. After earning a B.A. from Barnard College in 1942, Highsmith published her first short story, "The Heroine," in *Harper's Bazaar* in 1945. She had originally submitted the story to the Barnard College magazine, but it was rejected as "too unpleasant." In 1950, Highsmith published her first novel, *Strangers on a Train,* which was an instant success. From 1963 to her death in 1995, Highsmith lived in Europe, mainly in England, France, Italy, and Switzerland. A victim of leukemia, she died in Locarno, Switzerland, in 1995.

Major Works

Strangers on a Train sets the tone for Highsmith's subsequent work. In this novel, Highsmith pairs two men, Bruno and Guy, who, although opposites in many ways, are drawn together into a web of murder and betrayal. The men agree to kill each other's most-hated person—Bruno is to murder Guy's wife, and Guy, Bruno's father—so no one will be able to link them to the murders. This focus on the relationship between two men is common in Highsmith's fiction and is a means by which she explored the nature of good and evil and created psychological tension. *The Blunderer* (1954) also centers on two men. The protagonist, Walter Stackhouse, attempts to copy a murder committed by Melchior Kimmel, resulting in Stackhouse's own death and the capture of Kimmel. *The Two Faces of January* (1964) features a young man, Rydal Kenner, who is compelled to pursue a petty criminal, Chester McFarland, because he resembles his dead father. In *The Story-Teller* (1965), Sidney Bartleby, a writer, is falsely accused of murdering his unfaithful wife after he records his fantasies of killing her. Bartleby's writing partner, Alex, attempts to blackmail Bartleby and eventually turns him in to the police. Highsmith also frequently paired Tom Ripley with another character in her Ripley novels. In *The Talented Mr. Ripley* (1955), the first work in her Ripley series, Highsmith introduces Ripley as an American living in Europe. In this book, Ripley befriends and later murders Dickie Greenleaf, an American heir to a business fortune, and assumes his identity. After forging a will that makes him the beneficiary of Greenleaf's estate, Ripley resumes his own identity and enters Europe's high society. *Found in the Street* (1986) centers on two men living in Greenwich Village. When Jack Sutherland, a happily married book illustrator, drops his wallet on the street, it is later found and returned by Ralph Linderman, a lonely older man who occupies his time walking his dog. After Linderman returns the wallet, both men become obsessed with Elsie Tyler, a beautiful young woman who is temporarily working as a waitress at a local coffee shop. Eventually Linderman comes to believe that Sutherland has sinister intentions toward the woman and begins harassing the younger man with threatening phone calls and letters. In her later novels, Highsmith began to address contemporary social issues. *A Dog's Ransom* (1972) comments on urban America and ineffectual law enforcement agencies; *Edith's Diary* (1977) explores the methods by which society forces women into subservient roles; and *People Who Knock on the Door* (1983) focuses on fundamentalist Christianity and its influence on an ordinary American family. Highsmith, who some have speculated was a lesbian, also wrote novels that focus on homosexual relationships and issues. *The Price of Salt* (1952), which was originally published under the pseudonym Claire Morgan and later reprinted as *Carol* under the name Highsmith, features two women who become involved in a lesbian affair after meeting at a department store. Highsmith's last novel, *Small g* (1995), is set in a nightclub in Zurich. The code "small g" is used in guidebooks to indicate "partly gay," and the work centers on the murder of an HIV-positive gay man, Rickie. Highsmith also published several short story collections, including *Little Tales of Misogyny* (1974), *The Animal-Lover's Book of Beastly Murder* (1975), *The Black House* (1981), and *Mermaids on the Gulf Course* (1985). Some of her better known works of short fiction include "The Heroine," "The Terrapin," and "Not One of Us." "The Heroine" centers on a young woman named Lucille Smith, who is determined to be successful and content after experiencing an unhappy upbringing. After securing a job as a nursemaid in a household with two children, however, she sets the house on fire. "The Terrapin" concerns a lonely boy, Victor, whose mother dresses him in children's clothes. Alienated from his peers, he grows increasingly hysterical until he stabs his mother to death after she boils a turtle alive. "Not One of Us" depicts a circle of friends that tries to drive a young man to suicide. Highsmith is also the author of *Plotting and Writing Suspense Fiction* (1966), which offers an analysis of her own works as well as a description of her approach to writing novels. Many of Highsmith's novels have been adapted for film, most notably *Strangers on a Train,* which was directed by Alfred Hitchcock.

Critical Reception

Although critical reaction to Highsmith's works has been generally positive in the United States, she has gained more critical and popular attention in Europe, where she has not been so readily categorized as a mystery writer. Reviewers have consistently praised her focus on psychological concerns, her rejection of contrived and predictable endings, and her ability to convey emotion, mood, and atmosphere. Most critics, however, have reserved their highest praise for Highsmith's depiction of Tom Ripley. A reviewer in *Armchair Detective,* for example, stated: "For the successful creation of fiction as powerfully attractive as the Ripley novels are, Patricia Highsmith deservedly has earned her place as a crime writer of exceptional achievement." Highsmith's first Ripley novel, *The Talented Mr. Ripley,* won the 1957 Mystery Writers of America Scroll and the Grand Prix de Littérature Policière. Although reaction to Highsmith's work is often laudatory, some have faulted what they consider her detached, matter-of-fact depiction of crime and her negative portrayal of women. Numerous reviewers have noted that female characters in Highsmith's works are often secondary, but some have faulted her short fiction in particular for focusing on brutalized women. The stories in *Little Tales of Misogyny,* for example, have been dismissed by some reviewers as blatantly antifeminist. Others have contended that the stories were intended to satirize present-day attitudes toward women. In general, Highsmith's novels have been more positively received than her short stories, with some reviewers asserting that her short fiction lacks sympathy and is overly satirical and ironic. Despite such criticisms, Highsmith's work as a whole has generated praise for its ability to create a sense of unrest in the reader and for expanding and challenging conventional notions of crime and mystery fiction. Author and critic Graham Greene, for example, observed that "[Highsmith] has created a world of her own—a world claustrophobic and irrational which we enter each time with a sense of personal danger, with the head half-turned over the shoulder, even with a certain reluctance, for these are cruel pleasures we are about to experience." Another critic, Marcia Froelke Coburn, asserted that Highsmith's "work is an inversion of the hard-boiled [mystery] style, an act of turning it upside down and shaking all the hidden fears and neuroses out of it."

PRINCIPAL WORKS

Strangers on a Train (novel) 1950
*The Price of Salt [under pseudonym Claire Morgan] (novel) 1952

†*The Blunderer* (novel) 1954

The Talented Mr. Ripley (novel) 1955

Deep Water (novel) 1957

A Game for the Living (novel) 1958

Miranda the Panda is on the Veranda (juvenilia) 1958

This Sweet Sickness (novel) 1960

The Cry of the Owl (novel) 1962

The Glass Cell (novel) 1964

The Two Faces of January (novel) 1964

‡*The Story-Teller* (novel) 1965

Plotting and Writing Suspense Fiction (nonfiction) 1966

Those Who Walk Away (novel) 1967

The Tremor of Forgery (novel) 1969

Ripley under Ground (novel) 1970

§*The Snail-Watcher and Other Stories* (short stories) 1970

A Dog's Ransom (novel) 1972

Kleine geschichten für weiberfeinde [*Little Tales of Misogyny*] (short stories) 1974

Ripley's Game (novel) 1974

The Animal-Lover's Book of Beastly Murder (short stories) 1975

Edith's Diary (novel) 1977

Slowly, Slowly in the Wind (short stories) 1979

The Boy Who Followed Ripley (novel) 1980

The Black House (short stories) 1981

People Who Knock on the Door (novel) 1983

Mermaids on the Gulf Course and Other Stories (short stories) 1985

§§*The Mysterious Mr. Ripley* (novels) 1985

Found in the Street (novel) 1986

Tales of Natural and Unnatural Catastrophes (short stories) 1987

Ripley under Water (novel) 1992

Small g: A Summer Idyll (novel) 1995

*This title was reprinted in 1984 as *Carol* under the name Patricia Highsmith with a new afterword by the author.

†This work was published as *Lament for a Lover* in 1956.

‡This title was also published as *A Suspension of Mercy* in 1965.

§This work was published as *Eleven* in 1970.

§§This work contains *The Talented Mr. Ripley, Ripley under Ground,* and *Ripley's Game.*

CRITICISM

Patricia Highsmith with Diana Cooper-Clark (interview date 19 August 1980)

SOURCE: An interview with Patricia Highsmith, in *Armchair Detective*, Vol. 14, No. 4, Spring, 1981, pp. 313-20.

[*In the following interview, which was conducted on August 19, 1980, in Moncourt, France, Highsmith discusses such subjects as the philosophy of criminology, her portrayal of female characters, and critical response to her works.*]

[*Cooper-Clark:*] *I recently read, and you can clarify or correct me, that you are not enamoured of the human race. Is that accurate?*

[Highsmith:] Not really. I often talk with a sociologist friend, and her opinion is that most people are quite ordinary, that universal education hasn't brought the happiness and beauty that people had hoped. I think human beings are very interesting, however. It is like talking about "a better life." Not everybody wants it, not everybody likes aesthetic things. Why should they? It is a matter of taste. It is one thing to make millions of people literate, to enact labor laws that provide leisure. The individual then decides how he spends that leisure time.

This particular reporter was from the Observer, *and the slant of the article was that you were misanthropic.*

That isn't true. But like many writers, I like solitude. I have had two rather bad interviews with *Observer* people who shall be nameless. In fact, I don't even remember their names. I remember distinctly that I had a nice lunch, but it was a silly interview. Lots of my friends saw it and said it really wasn't like me. I didn't even keep it in my scrapbook.

You have said: "I like to entertain and to stimulate in an emotional way." Is emotion diametrically opposed to intellect, or are they part of the same thing for you?

It could be part of the same thing, but I know that I write to tell an entertaining story, and that I am not trying to make a point. I am not trying to be an intellectual.

So you really have no particular philosophy of criminology or murder as some people do who write?

No. I think unfortunately that most criminals, in fact, the vast majority of the people who are in jail, have not got a very high IQ. Therefore, they don't interest me very much.

So you don't agree with George Bernard Shaw's idea that the artist is very close to the criminal? Colin Wilson also picks that up.

I can think of only one slight closeness, and that is that an imaginative writer is very free-wheeling; he has to forget about his own personal morals, especially if he is writing about criminals. He has to feel anything is possible. But I don't for this reason understand why an artist should have any criminal tendencies. The artist may simply have an ability to understand.

In A Casebook of Murder, *Colin Wilson wrote that he regarded murder as a response to certain problems of human freedom: not as a social problem, nor a psychological problem, nor even a moral problem, but as an existential problem. Is that what you meant before when you said that you really are writing to entertain, rather than for a didactic purpose?*

Yes, I still stand by what I said. I would much rather be an entertainer than a moralizer, but to call murder not a social problem I think is ridiculous; it certainly is a social problem. The word existentialist has become fuzzy. It's existentialist if you cut a finger with a kitchen knife—because it has happened. Existentialism is self-indulgent, and they try to gloss over this by calling it a philosophy.

In Ritual in the Dark *and some of his earlier novels, Wilson is exploring the idea of the criminal, the murderer who is trying to move away from the boredom of life, searching for the meaning of life, going beyond the taboos of society. I think it is in this sense that he means freedom. He finally comes to the conclusion that murder really is a perversion of freedom, but he is still sympathetic to it as an attempt for freedom.*

Yes, Dostoyevski was toying with this idea too. It is extremely interesting if one writes a story about that, but I wouldn't want to imagine a world in which everybody tried this.

Would you associate Bruno in Strangers on a Train *with some of these notions? He often speaks on this subject.*

Yes, but he is also a psychopath. He is really mentally sick, and either doesn't realize or doesn't care about the consequences of these ideas if he carries out all these projects; he is without a conscience and without any understanding of what he is talking about. He is simply not right in the head.

Often the criminal is the hero in your novels. Is this because, for a while at least, this particular person is not bound by society?

Yes, in fact I once wrote in a book of mine about suspense writing, that a criminal, at least for a short period of time is free, free to do anything he wishes. Unfortunately it sounded as if I admired that, which I don't. If somebody kills somebody, they are breaking the law, or else they are in a fit of temper. While I can't recommend it, it is an awful truth to say that for a moment they are free, yes. And I wrote that in a moment of impatience, I remember distinctly. I get impa-

tient with a certain hidebound morality. Some of the things one hears in church, and certain so-called laws that nobody practices. Nobody can practice them and it is even sick to try. I get impatient with that, and so I made a rather hasty statement that at least for a short period of time the criminal is free.

And many people picked that up.

Yes. Julian Symons has quoted it, and he said the equivalent of what I said, which was neither the law nor nature cares about real justice. I mean frequently in court the guilty person goes free, either through mistakes or a crooked court which is quite possible. In nature it is the survival of the fittest. You cannot call that justice, you just call it a scheme of nature, a jungle.

Many contemporary novels, those of Colin Wilson, James Dickey's Deliverance, *Walker Percy's* Lancelot, *Saul Bellow's* Mr. Sammler's Planet, *Graham Greene's* A Sort of Life, *to name a few, explore the idea that human beings murder and seek violence in a search for meaning, as a relief from ennui, as a challenge to society in order to find the potential in themselves. Although Bruno is a psychopath, these ideas are touched upon in* **Strangers on a Train.** *Is it ever justifiable to convert murder into a philosophical and aesthetic experience?*

I simply don't agree with it. Murder, to me, is a mysterious thing. I feel I do not understand it really. I try to imagine it, of course, but I think it is the worst crime. That is why I write so much about it; I am interested in guilt. I think there is nothing worse than murder, and that there is something mysterious about it, but that isn't to say that it is desirable for any reason. To me, in fact, it is the opposite of freedom, if one has any conscience at all.

I think that is important. Critics just don't pick up on that aversion to murder in your work. They seem to want to create categories of responses. Do they ever say anything that you consider accurate?

> **I suppose I find amorality an interesting contrast to stereotyped morality which is very frequently hypocritical and phony. I also think that to mock lip-service morality and to have a character amoral, such as Tom Ripley, is entertaining.**
> **—*Patricia Highsmith***

In regard to murder I can't think of anything. Just now, I am going over the past two years of reviews. I have neglected them for two or three books, and I'm interested in the negative things. The new book out, *The Boy Who Followed Ripley,* is an interesting case. By the way, Ripley very much resembles Bruno psychologically because Ripley has done about eight murders by now, of which the first was the most important to him. I mean, he thinks back on the first murder and he feels shame. In the later murders he is killing people who—except for one honest man who is about to spill some beans, Murchison—are evil themselves. But he is also singularly lacking in normal conscience. So naturally the critics are going to pick up the similarity or they will make the remark about Ripley that he has no conscience. That is true. But, on the other hand, this is not true in a book like *The Blunderer,* in which the man gets to the brink of killing his wife, when she takes the bus trip, and can't bring himself to do it, only to have the wife throw herself over the cliff. Mostly my heroes are rather like Walter in *The Blunderer,* I think, by which I mean that whether they kill somebody or whether they don't, murder is not a casual thing to them, it is of great importance, it is a very serious crime.

This is exactly what I find interesting, because it is so much at odds with what other people seem to glean from your books. I think that if someone reads all of your work, he or she should see what you are saying. Perhaps part of the problem with reviewing is that many of the reviewers have not read a large quantity of your work. If you read only one of your books, I think it is easy to pick out certain striking features that are quite antithetical to what you are doing on the whole.

Yes, I can hardly blame them now because I have about twenty books.

It is a large undertaking, but a fascinating one. I have read many of the reviews of your latest book, **The Boy Who Followed Ripley,** *and they do seem to stress the negativity. To go back to what you were saying about guilt, you have previously said: "I suppose the reason I write about crime is simply that it is very good for illustrating moral points of life. I am really interested in the behavior of people surrounding someone who has done something wrong, and also whether the person who has done it feels guilty about it, or just, 'so what'." Very often the people in your novels around the killer think that he is mad or close to madness, and very often he is: David in* **This Sweet Sickness,** *Syd in* **Suspension of Mercy** *(in Britain,* **The Story-Teller** *in the United States), Robert in* **The Cry of the Owl,** *Vic in* **Deep Water.** *What interests you about this particular reaction?*

I suppose in the case of Vic it makes the story much more alive. One can identify with a so-called normal person who is looking at Vic and suspecting, because anybody can identify with a person who has a suspicion, you see, in fact more easily than they can identify with Vic. It is just like a "back-

ground" in writing, a necessary element or a very useful element.

Freud and Jung both felt that murder can exact its own punishment in that the murderer feels tremendous guilt and punishes himself. In **Strangers on a Train,** *Guy says that "every man is his own law court and punishes himself enough." Guy certainly is tortured by guilt, but several of your characters do* not *feel guilt: Philip Carter in* **The Glass Cell,** *Victor Van Allen in* **Deep Water,** *Tom Ripley. Do you find the effect of non-guilt just as interesting as guilt in a murderer?*

Yes, I do.

Why?

Ripley as I said before is a little bit sick in the head in this respect of having very little conscience. Vic is becoming deranged in the book, he is a bit schizophrenic at the end. I try to explore as much as I can the part of themselves that these murderers are keeping secret from the public and even their wives. I try to tell how they deal with what they have done.

And Philip?

Philip was changed in prison when he saw the riot and his best friend Max was killed. He became hardened, you might say, and detests the man he kills at the end.

In what way does amorality interest you in a character like Tom Ripley?

I suppose I find it an interesting contrast to stereotyped morality which is very frequently hypocritical and phony. I also think that to mock lip-service morality and to have a character amoral, such as Ripley, is entertaining. I think people are entertained by reading such stories. The murderers that one reads about in the newspaper half the time are mentally deficient in some way, or simply callous. There are young boys, for instance, who pretend to be delivering, or who may help an old lady carrying her groceries home, and then hit her on the head when she invites them in for tea, and rob her. These are forever stupid people, but they exist. Many murderers are like that, and they don't interest me enough to write a book about them. Somebody like Ripley however, who is reasonably intelligent and still has this amoral quality, interests me. I couldn't make an interesting story out of some morons.

It seems to be a sine qua non *of crime fiction that order is restored and good triumphs over evil, but sometimes your murderers do get away with murder; again, Philip Carter and Tom Ripley.*

This is the way life is, and I read somewhere years ago that only 11% of murders are solved. That is unfortunate, but lots of victims are not so important as the President of the United States. The police make a certain effort, and it may be a good effort, but frequently the case is dropped. And so I think, why shouldn't I write about a few characters who also go free?

You have often been accused of carrying your identification with your psychotic characters to the point where you actually seem to be preferring their interesting evil to the mediocre virtue of their victims. Would you agree with that assessment?

Yes. I think it is more interesting to talk about something off the beaten track than it is to talk about a so-called normal person. That's one answer to your question. Another might be, that in some of my books the victims are evil or boring individuals, so the murderer is more important than they. This is a writer's remark, not a legal judge's.

Is this why you might perhaps find amorality more interesting than immorality, because it is more unusual?

Yes. I suppose it is such a subtle question because it is such a subtle difference. Amorality such as Ripley's is rarer than immorality. People in the Mafia, or pimps, people in any kind of wretched occupation, know that they and their work are strictly in the gutter, that their activities are disgusting, and they don't care as long as it puts a little money in their pockets. This is immoral, but the Ripley type is amoral.

In **The Tremor of Forgery,** *the hero is both detective and suspect, accused and accuser. He is faced with the question of whether or not he must recognize the violence within himself. Conventional values and ethics seem lost in Tunisia and he is faced in his own life by the novel's statement: "Whether a person makes his own personality and standards from within himself, or whether he and the standards are the creations of the society around him." Which do you think come first?*

I am quite sure that the standards of morality come from the society around; a child within the jungle is not going to invent his own sense of right and wrong. In *Forgery,* he leaves America and comes to a place where murder is taken a little more lightly.

Your exploration of the criminal mind is ever-fascinating. There have been so many conflicting insights about the criminal mind: murderers are innately evil; Lombroso believed that criminality was a trait inherited from degenerate ancestors; sociologists maintain that criminals are victims of urbanization, family disintegration, poor schooling, unemployment, mental illness; and a recent study by Yachelson

and Samenow stated that there is *a criminal personality. Where do you believe the ability to murder comes from?*

I happen to believe more in heredity than I do in environment. There is certainly such a thing as a no-good family. Families always have a history, and I have heard of families where the grandfather was an old crook, never quite in jail. Within one household, one can find sometimes an atmosphere of flaunting the law to a greater or lesser degree.

Do you believe in the "bad seed" theory?

Yes, I think there is something in that; it doesn't mean the individual would always turn out badly, but as I said, I do believe in heredity more than environment. The phrase "poor schools" makes me laugh. I went to several. What counts is individual motivation. Ambition and drive count.

Do you think it is a mistake to try to reduce the original impulse to murder to one thing or another?

An impulse to murder is surely based on anger. Premeditated murder is different. I think of the two young Australian girls. One was eleven and one was thirteen, and they murdered the mother of one of them on a garden path I believe, for no reason. They just got together and said, "Let's do it." That comes under mental derangement, and as I am not a psychologist, I can't make any intelligent statement about that, except that any court would probably say that the girl who was the leader of the two, was mentally deranged. Where does that get you? It's just a term. But there was something wrong with her brain, even though she was only about thirteen. There is something wrong with anybody who is so inhuman as to kill the mother of a friend.

In P. D. James's novel Death of An Expert Witness, *the murderer states that a murderer sets himself aside from the whole of humanity forever. It's a kind of death. Do you believe that murder is a kind of death for the murderer?*

It certainly would be for me, but I don't know if many murderers take it that seriously. I had two dreams in my life in which I had committed a murder, and only in one could I identify a certain person whom I disliked years ago. But in each dream I was very disturbed by the fact that I was ostracized from society, or at least I felt that I was. In the dream, if I went to a store to buy a newspaper, I felt that people were looking at me and saying, "there goes a murderer." It was a truly dreadful feeling, but I think the world is also full of people walking around the streets in Chicago and Marseilles who have killed somebody and they sleep quite well.

In **Strangers on a Train,** *Bruno tells Guy that "any person can murder." Do you think that is true?*

No, I don't. Maybe I thought it was when I wrote it, but at any rate it comes out of Bruno's mouth. I don't believe that at all. I don't believe that everybody can be coerced into murder. In war, yes, I guess it is different. But I don't think everyone can murder, not even for money. It is all relative, because if you were to go to some primitive place, the Far East or Africa, and offered a fantastic sum to some humble person to kill somebody he doesn't know, then you or your paid agent could do it. You could find maybe the same thing in America if you looked hard, but I think I have to ask myself what kind of people am I talking about; the poor, the middle-class, or people like you and myself. I don't think you could be coerced, you couldn't be persuaded, I dare say you would not be able to kill somebody even for a considerable amount of money or whatever else.

What if we eliminate the question of punishment, jail, so that one would not weigh the consequences against the act? Many people think that it is the spectre of jail and punishment that prevents people from committing acts of violence.

Again one has to ask what intellectual level of person is one talking about. Of course, the more primitive the person is, if you eliminate the punishment, then the more likely the person can kill somebody for money. But I mostly write about middle-class people, and they would have too much awareness of what they had done, just as I had in the dream. It is the awareness of it that is the torture rather than being put into jail. Koestler spent some time campaigning against hanging in England, and with success, because he proved that capital punishment is not a deterrent, but insignificant. Yet its advocates are again trying to call it a deterrent. It's revenge they want, and that's as barbaric as the Old Testament.

I agree. Graham Greene, in his introduction to **Eleven**, *wrote that you create a claustrophobic world which we enter each time with a sense of personal danger. Do you see danger everywhere in life as in your writing?*

No. I am inclined to be naive in my personal dealings, and I am not inclined to lock the door and have padlocks everywhere. I don't know what Graham Greene means, but in my short story, **"The Terrapin,"** about the little boy with the tortoise, the story is seen through his eyes. I don't know why it is so claustrophobic any more than any story, considering that a short story has to be intense, and is usually seen through the eyes of one person. You are within the little boy's atmosphere. I don't know why that is claustrophobic.

Just to continue with that, danger can also lurk under the rules and regulations of society. Vic, in **Deep Water**, *feels that "people who do not behave in an orthodox manner are by definition frightening." This juxtaposition of the ordinary and the respectable with violence, creates a chilling atmo-*

sphere in your books because we are dealing with people who are middle-class, who are respectable. Do you purposely create that kind of atmosphere because you know it is all the more frightening?

No, it is because it is the atmosphere that I know, because it is my own class more-or-less, a very ordinary American. My family was neither rich nor poor, and I couldn't write about peasants. In New York once, when I was a teenager, I tried to write a short short about an Italian family because I went to school with many many Italians. I found I couldn't do it because I had never lived in their households with ten or eleven people sitting at the dining room table. I never finished the story. In other words, I have to write, any writer has to write, about the class of people that he knows. Therefore the contrast between class respectability and murderous thoughts is bound to turn up in most of my books.

You often return to the theme of a pathological conflict between two men, in **Strangers on a Train, Deep Water, The Blunderer, The Glass Cell, The Cry of the Owl** *and others.*

The ideas come to me in that way. The idea for *Strangers on a Train* came as an idea for an exchange of murders. For the exchange, one needs two men, two people.

You don't really explore that conflict with women though.

No, the only female protagonist I suppose in my novels is Edith in **Edith's Diary**. But I have a lot of short stories that have women protagonists.

Are you more interested in the conflict between men as opposed to conflict between women?

No, perhaps I find men more violent by nature than women, or more able to use physical strength, but that is obvious. In the American schools, at least in my generation, around fourteen years of age, they separated the boys from the girls in the Junior High School. It wasn't to keep the birth rate down at all, it was because the boys were difficult to handle, they were disobedient and the teacher would have to slap them in the face in those days and pull their ears. It was much more fun when I was going to school with boys before the age of fourteen, because they have a sense of humor, much better than that of the girls, I must say, and it was amusing. And suddenly from fourteen to seventeen there was a bunch of girls before university learning things by rote. Pretty boring. Young women these days are less passive, thank goodness, but they've still a long way to go.

In a time when people are interested in the portrayal of women in literature, I found your book **Little Tales of Misogyny** *really quite unique.*

That was like a book of jokes.

Yes, but I find that in a number of your novels the women seem despicable in trivial ways. They are often cheats, Melinda in **Deep Water,** *Hazel in* **The Glass Cell,** *Alicia in* **Suspension of Mercy,** *Miriam in* **Strangers on a Train.** *And the women are totally unsympathetic in* **Little Tales of Misogyny.**

I must say that it certainly looks like that, but actually I have quite an esteem for women's strength. I think the women portrayed in my writing have rather bad characters, but I don't think that personally. I think that women can be quite strong. I can remember my grandmother who was the head of the household in a very pleasant way when I was a kid, and my own mother's character was stronger than my stepfather's. Unfortunately in *Strangers on a Train,* Miriam, the wife, happened to be a silly high school girl. The early marriage of Guy and Miriam was based, you might say, on falling in love around high school age. This was a mistake for Guy, and so the girl Miriam is the type who would flirt and make another stupid liaison of some kind. And then Melinda, who was Vic's wife, was always flirting and having two or three lovers. I simply needed that for the story because it gives Vic a motivation for murder. Unfortunately, the whole picture looks as if I suspect that women have narrow characters, which is not really true. It is not my personal feeling at all.

Julian Symons has pointed out that you are drawn to the attraction exerted on the weak by the idea of violence, such as in **The Two Faces of January** *and* **Those Who Walk Away.**

Well, I don't plan these things. When I start to write anything, I think of the story first. I think of the events. Is it interesting or is it amusing or is it unexpected or is it almost unbelievable? That comes first, rather than thinking one character is weak and one character is strong.

Critics often discuss your obsessions and fixations, and the one they usually mention is paranoia. Clearly from what you have said, you don't believe that you particularly have obsessions and fixations in your own life.

Well, maybe there is a bit of paranoia in David in *This Sweet Sickness,* but I don't find it in *The Tremor of Forgery.* Vic, in *Deep Water,* is just the opposite of paranoid; he is quite sure of himself. He kills one man, then the second man, and he thinks he is completely in the clear. As for myself, I don't think I'm paranoid, but as I said before, rather trusting and optimistic about personal and business relationships.

Maurice Richardson has said that you write about men like a spider writing about flies, and another reviewer has main-

tained that reading one of your novels is like having tea with a dangerous witch. Both are compliments, I might add; they weren't meant to be negative. We talked before about reviewers. Do you read, now or in the beginning, material about yourself?

Oh, Definitely! I read reviews as I was beginning to write. Now I finally read the critiques, sometimes after they've been lying around the house for months. It is the last thing I look at in the Sunday paper when I know I have a review out. I am not exactly eager to read my reviews, but I have always been interested in the negative comments.

Do you notice a change in the responses to your work, from your first novel, **Strangers on a Train,** *to your latest,* **The Boy Who Followed Ripley***? Do you see an evolution in the response? Is it the same, is it very different?*

No, I don't find it very different. I don't notice any change in them.

Do you feel that your literary reputation has suffered, as some people think, because crime is at the center of your books? Or do you really worry about your literary reputation?

I don't care about it at all. The publishers always want to categorize you, and they think it helps them to sell books. *Edith's Diary* was rejected by Knopf in New York and because the publishers can't categorize every book I write, this is why in New York I must have been with five publishers by now. I would rather stay with one, but they get so fixed on a certain category, that if I write something out of line, then it is a rejection and my agents have to take it to another publisher which up to now I have always been able to find. In England, Heinemann is less rigid. I won't say they will take anything, but my work has a fair amount of variation, if I consider *Edith's Diary, Little Tales of Misogyny* and the animal stories, but Heinemann is content to publish them all, mainly because they can sell them. So this business of categorizing bores me. I couldn't tailor my inspiration to that.

You mentioned **Edith's Diary,** *which was a departure from the murder that is in most of your books. It was a wonderful novel. Are you interested in writing more novels in the future that don't deal with murder?*

Oh, yes, definitely. In fact, I might go to the States to live for a few months in order to freshen my memory and my information, in which case I might write another American-set book with quite a different theme. I am interested in morale just now, not morals, but how one keeps up one's morale. It doesn't sound like a very exciting theme, and isn't until I attach it to a story.

I think it is crucial to anybody who is alive today.

Sometimes one has the mental habit, well, really tricks, to continue to be cheerful and to continue to imagine that one's making progress when one really isn't. I speak not of myself but of many, many people.

Why have you never written a detective novel as such?

I think it is a silly way of teasing people, "who-done-it." It doesn't interest me in the least and I don't know anything about the police procedure or the detective methods of working; that is an occupation in itself. It is like a puzzle, and puzzles do not interest me.

I am interested in the movies that were done from your novels. What did you think of them?

The Hitchcock film, *Strangers on a Train,* is very dated now but I think it is a good film. *Purple Noon* is an entertaining film even though Ripley gets caught in the end. *The American Friend,* I thought, came off quite well. That's Wim Wenders doing **Ripley's Game** with Dennis Hopper. I saw that twice; I like to see any film that I'm interested in twice. *The American Friend* is a good film. I like it all except the ending. I thought they did the train scene very well.

I know that some writers, once they have sold the rights to their book, don't care what the filmmakers do with the movie after that. Do you like to be involved?

I do care. My agents want to put into the contract that I have the right to see the script, and if I don't like it, I can remove my name. I care quite a lot because I like to have a reputation for not only writing amusing books, but books that are capable of becoming good films. Of course, that depends on the quality of the director and script writer.

Was it an augury that you have the same birthday as Edgar Allan Poe, January 19?

I don't believe in astrology. It is also the birthday of Robert E. Lee, so I used to have a holiday down south in school. They recently stopped having holidays on his birthday though—too Confederate. (Laughs.)

Erlene Hubly (essay date Spring/Summer 1984)

SOURCE: "A Portrait of the Artist: The Novels of Patricia Highsmith," in *Clues: A Journal of Detection,* Vol. 5, No. 1, Spring/Summer, 1984, pp. 115-30.

[*Hubly is an American educator and critic. In the following essay, she discusses how Highsmith's portrayal of artists in her novels advances such themes as identity, homosexuality, and the real versus the imagined. The critic focuses on the character Sydney Bartleby, the protagonist of* A Suspension of Mercy, *and Tom Ripley in* The Talented Mr. Ripley.]

Patricia Highsmith's artists, those characters who create works of art and often themselves in the process, form, even when compared to some of her other protagonists, a unique group of characters. There is Sydney Bartleby, the writer-hero of **A Suspension of Mercy,** who in order to stimulate his imagination, plans the imaginary murder of his wife, an endeavor which he then proceeds to act out as though it were so. His ruse is so successful that both his friends and the authorities think he has murdered his wife, as does he himself at times. There is Howard Ingham, the writer-hero of **The Tremor of Forgery,** who, again, in order to excite his imagination, deliberately lives in a dangerous place, Tunisia, in order to undergo new and dark passions, committing, possibly, even a murder, so that he can write about his experiences. And there is, above all others, the character of Tom Ripley, who if he is not a writer, is an actor, a master of the art of impersonation. It is this art, when coupled with the act of murder, that enables Ripley not only to kill a wealthy young American, Dickie Greenleaf and then to pose as him, but also to provide for his own future security as well, Ripley producing, after Dickie's death, a will, forged, of course, by him, in which Dickie Greenleaf leaves all his money to his good friend, Tom Ripley. Indeed, Highsmith's artists display her ingenuity at its best, allowing her to fashion plots that dazzle the reader with their inventiveness. In addition, Highsmith's artists get the reader closer to the heart of her fictional world perhaps better than any other of her characters. For by examining her artists, we explore some of her major themes: the nature of identity; homosexuality; the real versus the imagined world; the effect of a foreign country on the Americans who live there.

Sydney Bartleby, the protagonist of Highsmith's novel, *A Suspension of Mercy* (1965), defines the type. An American writer living in England, Bartleby is at work, as Highsmith's novel begins, on a television series featuring the sleuth-hero Nicky Campbell, an ordinary young man who keeps running into crime and solving mysteries. Unable to sell any of the Campbell scripts, which are uninspired, Bartleby seems stymied until he hits upon the idea of murder—the imaginary murder of his wife, Alicia, to whom he is rather unhappily married. After all, he thinks, he has already killed her, in his imagination, "at least twenty times." When Alicia, aware of her husband's growing hostility toward her, leaves for a vacation at Brighton, Bartleby is free to act out his murderous plan. Plotting Alicia's murder, he enacts the imaginary crime, pushing Alicia down the stairs, causing her to break her neck as she hits the floor below. Rolling her body up in a carpet, he carries it from the house;

savoring the feelings of guilt and fear that his deed has inspired, he drives to some nearby woods where he buries the carpet, Alicia's body still inside.

His imagination by now on fire, Bartleby returns home, scraps the Nicky Campbell scripts and begins a new series featuring a criminal-hero, The Whip, which prove to be far superior to anything he has yet written. Bartleby is further inspired by the fact that he must continue to play-act: as Alicia stays away from home longer and longer, having met a lover in Brighton and as the police begin to suspect Bartleby of having murdered her, he must master the art of plotting, must both protect himself from a murder charge and yet continue to be, for his own purposes, a murderer. It is a schizophrenic existence, but one which has its rewards: the Whip scripts become better and better and Bartleby finally sells them to a producer for a large sum of money. Murder, then, although here only imaginary, would seem to be a necessary part of the creative process at its most inspired.

If murder stimulates Highsmith's writers' imaginations, it can do so because of their peculiar view of reality. For Highsmith's artists, having manipulated reality for so long through the act of writing, masters at turning the real into fiction, live in a fluid world where few things are clearly defined. Sydney Bartleby, for example, often has difficulty distinguishing the real from the imagined and at times thinks that real conversations he is having with real people are imaginary ones, the words being spoken sounding "like lines in a play they were performing." His efforts at creating fiction, of acting out and experiencing the murder of Alicia, are so successful that he convinces himself that she is dead. And at the height of his difficulties with the police, when asked by Inspector Brockway if he did kill his wife, Bartleby can barely answer "no," feels as if his imagined murder of her is real, that he has "only hours more of freedom" before he is arrested for the crime of murder. The line between the real and the imagined becomes so blurred in Bartleby's mind that later, when he commits a real murder, that of Edward Tilbury, the man with whom Alicia had lived while she was at Brighton, he does so with less effort and with fewer feelings of guilt than he experienced when he committed the imaginary murder of Alicia. Indeed, it is his imagined murder that affects him most deeply.

If Highsmith's artists have difficulty distinguishing between the real and the imagined, they do not, like many of her non-artist protagonists, pay for that difficulty with their lives. For Highsmith has a predilection for her artists: all of them, although warped by their experiences, survive, even prosper. Sydney Bartleby may continue to live in the confusing world of his imagination, may have killed a man and thus risked his own life, but he will not be caught, will continue to write and sell his Whip television scripts, will continue, then, to prosper. Tom Ripley, another of Highsmith's artists,

may not, like Sydney Bartleby, be able to distinguish between the real and the imagined, may thus live perpetually on the fringes of madness, may before his career is over murder eight men and thus continually risk exposure and ruin, but he is never caught, never ruined, indeed, even gains a good deal of money from his misdeeds. Able to manufacture plots, to manipulate people as if they were fictional characters, three steps ahead of everyone else because they, the authors, know the script, having written it, Highsmith's artists literally get away with murder, even prosper because of it. And it is their art, their ability to manipulate reality, which enables them to succeed.

If Sydney Bartleby is an early portrait of Highsmith's artist, Howard Ingham, the writer-protagonist of *The Tremor of Forgery* (1969), enables her to refine and deepen that concept, taking it into new directions. And here, with Howard Ingham, Highsmith employs one of her favorite themes: the effect of a foreign country on the Americans who live there. Highsmith's artists are always Americans and usually in confrontation with a foreign culture. Sydney Bartleby is the exception: living in England, a stable and still Puritan society, he is not threatened by the culture around him. But continental Europe and the Arab countries south of it, are another matter. For Highsmith uses foreign settings, particularly Europe, in the same way that Henry James does, as a place, steeped in centuries of corruption and evil, which offers the American, naive and as yet untested, possibilities heretofore unknown. For Europe is a place in which all inhibitions can be dropped, a place in which an American, no longer under the moral constraints of his homeland, can experience, if he so desires, new and tempting forms of evil. And Highsmith's Americans so desire.

Howard Ingham is such an American. Going to North Africa in order to work on a film with a friend, Ingham, when his friend fails to show up, stays on, fascinated by the country around him. The attraction soon becomes clear: Africa is a place in which all experiences, however evil, seem permissible. A person can murder another and no questions are asked; bodies with their throats cut lie undisturbed in alleys, people barely noticing them as they pass by. There are no restrictions placed on one's sexual activities: homosexual couples openly hold hands as they walk down the street and if a man wants an Arab street boy, he merely singles out one from the many who are willing, for the price of a cigarette, to engage in such sex. "Africa does turn things upside down," Ingham observes early in his stay there and this fact will prove both Africa's attraction and Ingham's near undoing.

Fascinated by Africa's permissive atmosphere, Ingham, a writer, decides to begin work on a novel there. Renting a beach bungalow at Hammamet, a suburb of Tunisia, he is slowly drawn into a life of dark passions. Engaged to a woman, Ina Pallant, back in the States, he, nevertheless, is attracted to a girl he sees in his hotel and begins an affair with her. Drawn to a homosexual Danish artist, Anders Jensen, who makes a pass at him, Ingham stops just short of an affair with him. He does, however, move into Jensen's dirty, run-down apartment building in order to be closer to him and to experience first hand the bohemian life. One night, feeling both sexually excited and lonely, Ingham comes close to taking a young Arab boy home to bed with him. It is an act which he does not accomplish, but which clearly indicates his sexual desires. And, in the central scene of the novel, while his apartment is being robbed, Ingham throws his typewriter at the thief's head and, in all probability, kills him. All things, then, murder, homosexuality, the pleasure of forbidden desires, have become possible for Howard Ingham in Africa.

If *The Tremor of Forgery* is about an American confronting a foreign culture, it is also a novel about the nature of identity. For Howard Ingham, like Highsmith's other artists, is a man without a clear identity. Coming to Africa without a fixed set of principles in which he both believes and practices, he is especially vulnerable to the temptations around him. That this is to be Highsmith's theme she makes clear early in her book, by surrounding her protagonist with a number of characters, each of whom bears a definite relationship to the question of identity. There is Francis J. Adams, a retired American businessman in Hammamet, who if he has a definite and fixed identity—he is an arch conservative who lives by a rigid code of morality—is finally less than admirable because of that rigidity. There is Anders Jensen, the young Danish artist who befriends and hopes to seduce Ingham. The opposite of the American, Adams—amoral and unstable—Jensen is also a less than admirable character for just that reason. And there is Ina Pallant, Ingham's American fiancee. The most admirable character in the book, she stands somewhere between Adams and Jensen, moral without being rigid, wise because balanced in her views and responses. And as Ingham interacts with each of these characters in turn, he is slowly defined.

Fluid, unable to commit himself to any consistent course of action or to any one person, moving in his affections from Anders Jensen to Ina Pallant and then finally back to his former wife, Charlotte, who by the end of the book wants to see him again, doomed to repeat the mistake of his marriage over again because he is unable to grow into a new and more mature relationship, Howard Ingham is finally a man without a stable identity. Thinking of his life late in the story, he wonders who he is:

> He had the awful feeling that in the months he had been here, his own character or principles had collapsed, or disappeared. What was he? Presumably someone with a set of attitudes on which his conduct was based. They formed a character. But Ingham now felt he couldn't think, if his life depended on it, of one principle by which he lived.

Contemplating his own feelings of emptiness, he thinks "it was strangely like a religious experience. It was like becoming nothing and realising that one was nothing anyway, ever. It was a basic truth."

Ingham, does, of course, survive and again, like Sydney Bartleby, because of his art. If Howard Ingham is finally anything, he is a writer, a person who defines himself daily through the words that he writes. At one point in the story he sets himself a working schedule: he must write every day, because if he doesn't, he will "go to pieces." The act of writing then, literally holds him together and, spinning out his tale, he takes form himself. The book he is working on while in Tunisia thus bears an intimate relationship to his own life and becomes the means through which he explores not only his own problems, but also attempts to create a self.

A glamorized version of his own life, Ingham's novel, *Dennison's Lights,* is the story of a man, Dennison, who becomes a bank embezzler, but whose criminality, because his deeds ultimately do more good than harm, he giving away most of the money he steals, is in question. Like his hero, Dennison, Ingham's criminality, his killing of the thief who tried to rob him, is also in doubt. For maybe the typewriter he threw at the thief's head killed him, but, then, maybe it didn't. As he never investigates the consequences of his deed and as no body is ever found, it having been dragged away in the dark by some young Arabs, neither Ingham nor the reader knows for certain what happened to the thief. But both deeds—Dennison's embezzlement and Ingham's possible killing of the thief—force their perpetrators to live in a secret and criminal world, "a world of darkness known only to him." Although Dennison seems, at one point, to be headed downward toward total collapse, as does Ingham himself, Ingham, by making the crucial decision not to have Dennison collapse, thus saves not only Dennison, but also, by extension, himself. Dennison does pay for his crime, by going to prison, as does Ingham suffer for his deed, through a good deal of mental anguish. But both men survive, Ingham through his art saving Dennison and, Dennison, in turn, giving form to Ingham.

Both men, if survivors, are finally forgers, a term which comes to have special meaning in Highsmith's novels. For a forger is both creator and criminal, one who forges, as in "makes" something, but one who forges, as in "forgery," the attempt to pass off that which is false for that which is real. And that Highsmith's artists are forgers and thus basically dishonest, becomes clear. For Ingham is finally a forger both in his life and in his art. Unable to create for himself a genuine identity, drawing his responses from those around him, never sure of what he thinks, refusing to confront the very issues his life raises—his possible killing of another man, his own homosexual desires—Ingham finally can create a self only through the act of writing. Writing itself here becomes a kind of forgery, a means of making a self impossible to achieve in any other way and yet a self which is inauthentic because it is composed of words alone. Ingham finally exists because he is a writer and, defined solely by that which he does, a dealer in artifice, he becomes that in which he traffics, an imitation of the real. And his books, reflections of himself, copies, therefore, of that which is not genuine, can become only that which they imitate, dishonest and second-rate. To be a writer, then, in this kind of world is to be a special kind of criminal, one who evades the real, a forger, then, of life itself.

This theme, the artist as forger, reaches its culmination in Highsmith's novel, *The Talented Mr. Ripley* (1955), the first of the four books which feature her protagonist Tom Ripley. Tom Ripley is Highsmith's ultimate artist, a man who if he does not write, is an actor of immense abilities, gifted in the art of impersonation. As unformed in his identity as Howard Ingham, Ripley can, nevertheless, profit from this very fact, by passing himself off as other men. Like Sydney Bartleby, a master of invention, he can not only think up clever plots, but also turn them into reality. *The Talented Mr. Ripley,* mirroring Highsmith's other two studies of the artist, *A Suspension of Mercy* and *The Tremor of Forgery,* finally surpasses them both in quality and depth, and becomes her most profound study of the artist's personality.

The Talented Mr. Ripley is, on its most immediate level, a suspense story. Like *A Suspension of Mercy,* it is a novel with an ingenious plot which carries the reader at break-neck speed toward the final question: will the murderer, in spite of his cleverness, get caught? Of course, by now, we know the answer to that question. For Tom Ripley, like Sydney Bartleby, is a master artist and thus a certain survivor. Going to Europe at the request of an acquaintance's father, Mr. Herbert Greenleaf, in order to persuade Mr. Greenleaf's son, Dickie, to come back home to the States and to his responsibilities as the Greenleaf heir, Ripley masterminds a plot by which he, similar in size and looks to Dickie Greenleaf, will *become* Dickie Greenleaf, wear his clothes, use his passport, live off his money. Ripley must, of course, get rid of the real Dickie Greenleaf first, a task he accomplishes by killing him while they are out in a boat together. The rest of the novel traces the process by which Ripley does, indeed, literally get away with murder, his efforts to impersonate Dickie Greenleaf so successful that he is able to fool even those who know Dickie best—Marge Sherwood, Dickie's best friend; Dickie's father, Mr. Greenleaf—as well as the bank authorities and police officials of two countries, Italy and America. Ripley's scheme is so ingenious that he is finally able to produce a will, forged, of course, by him, in which Dickie leaves all his money to him, thus ensuring his finan-

cial security for the rest of his life. Tom Ripley is, indeed, as the title of the novel in which he first appears would suggest, a very clever fellow.

If *The Talented Mr. Ripley* is, like *A Suspension of Mercy,* a means through which Highsmith can display the ingenuity of her artists, it is also, like *The Tremor of Forgery,* a way in which she can explore one of her favorite themes: the effect of a foreign country on the Americans who travel there. And that she intends to use, in this case, Europe, in the same way that Henry James does, as a liberating and yet corrupting influence on the lives that are exposed to it, she makes clear early in her novel. As Mr. Greenleaf is seeing Ripley off for Europe, he asks him if he has ever read Henry James' novel, *The Ambassadors?* Ripley has not, but the question remains as a reminder of what Highsmith is up to in her novel. For *The Ambassadors,* like *The Talented Mr. Ripley,* is a book about an American who, at the request of another, goes to Europe in order to bring back home an errant and recalcitrant son. And Tom Ripley's journey, like Lambert Strether's before him, will be one that will expose him to all that Europe can offer the American: liberation from a Puritan upbringing and outlook; exposure to a culture rich in artistic accomplishments and to countries full of romantic places; and an atmosphere in which all actions, however immoral, seem if not actually sanctioned, then certainly accepted. And Tom Ripley, like Lambert Strether, will find the lure of Europe so enticing that he will be unable not only to persuade his quarry to come back to America, but also to return there himself.

The effect of Europe upon Tom Ripley is immediate and lasting. Arriving in Mongibello, Italy, where Dickie Greenleaf has been living for the past few years, Ripley is at once charmed by all that he sees: the town; Dickie's house; the two original Picasso drawings that hang in Dickie's hallway; Dickie Greenleaf himself. But by far the most charming thing that Ripley sees is Dickie's way of life, Dickie pursuing the life an artist, painting in the mornings, sailing in his boat at sundown, drinking aperitifs in the evening in one of the cafes on the beach, taking trips to such cities as Naples, Rome, Paris whenever the mood strikes, answerable to no one for the way he spends his time or money. Ripley, comparing his life to Dickie's, is overcome by feelings of envy and self-pity and vows that he will devote all his efforts to becoming Dickie's best friend and thus a part of his life.

If Europe offers the ideal way of life, it also provides the moral atmosphere in which to attain it. Non-Puritan, seemingly indifferent to questions of morality, thousands of miles from the United States, it can offer the American there—cut off from family and social ties and thus from moral accountability—liberation, release from inhibitions. Tom Ripley was, to be sure, a petty crook in America, but in Europe he is free, if he is so inclined, to become a killer. Successful with Dickie at first, Ripley's hopes for becoming his friend are shattered by Marge Sherwood, an American living in Mongibello and Dickie's best friend. Becoming suspicious of Ripley, warning Dickie that Tom may be a homosexual with designs on him—a charge to which there may be some truth—Marge effectively drives the two men apart. On a trip to San Remo with Dickie, Ripley, sensing Dickie's growing indifference to him, realizing that he has lost his friendship forever, feeling humiliated and rejected, kills Dickie while they are out in a boat together, hitting him in the head with an oar and then weighing his body down in the water with a cement anchor. Dickie's death, however, is not without its practical side. For if Ripley cannot share in Dickie's life, by becoming his friend, he can, once Dickie is dead, become Dickie himself, assuming his very identity.

Ripley is, of course, a man eminently qualified for such a task. Like Howard Ingham in *The Tremor of Forgery,* Tom Ripley is a man without a self. Having no clear identity, he is a man who has rejected himself and all that he is: his unhappy childhood; his upbringing by a cruel and somewhat sadistic aunt; his impoverished emotional life. And in finding Dickie Greenleaf he finds for the first time in his life an identity he can accept, that he would even like for his own.

This transformation, this process by which Ripley absorbs Dickie into his own being, begins slowly. At first it is on a superficial level, Ripley merely copying Dickie's bodily movements, the way he walks, the way he parts his lips when he is out of breath from swimming. Then his efforts become more serious and far more encompassing. Mastering Dickie's voice, the little growl in his throat at the end of phrases, he begins to impersonate the whole man Dickie and in one of the most striking scenes in the book, attempts for the first time literally to become Dickie. Standing in front of a mirror, his hair parted and fashioned as Dickie wears his, dressed in Dickie's clothes, even wearing Dickie's rings, Ripley acts out a scenario in which he, as Dickie, confronts an imaginary Marge Sherwood, first telling her that he, Dickie, does not love her and then strangling her with his bare hands because she threatens to come between Tom and himself. It is a chilling scene in itself, made all the more so because it reveals not only the depth of Ripley's feelings for Dickie, but also the nature of his madness. Identity has become a deadly game, one that he would kill for.

This is, of course, exactly what he does. Wanting a complete union with Dickie—in this sense Ripley is a homosexual—but unable to accomplish it physically—no one can *become* another person—Ripley accomplishes it, like the artist he is, through his imagination. Dickie's body, his physical substance, is, of course, the obstacle. But by removing that obstacle, by destroying Dickie's body, Ripley is then free to incorporate the *idea* of Dickie into his own being—through

his mind. Murder, then, makes the process of attaining an identity complete and Ripley, with Dickie's physical presence removed, can become that which he thinks Dickie is.

There are, of course, several ironies here. For Dickie himself did not have much of an identity himself. Having rejected much of his own background, living off his father, refusing to do any kind of meaningful work, Dickie was a man who had yet to find himself. And Ripley, in modeling himself after Dickie, becomes that which had little substance to begin with. This irony underscores yet another one: Ripley, even after he thinks he has become Dickie, continues to act as Ripley, doing things, his murder of Dickie's friend, Freddie Miles, for example, when Freddie seems about to expose him, that Dickie himself would never have done. But in Ripley's world, where thinking something makes it so, Tom Ripley, thinking he is Dickie Greenleaf, becomes Dickie Greenleaf. Going to Paris, walking the streets, sightseeing, he delights in his new identity: "*Wonderful* to sit in a famous cafe and to think of tomorrow and tomorrow and tomorrow being Dickie Greenleaf! . . . It was impossible ever to be lonely or bored, he thought, so long as he was Dickie Greenleaf!"

Ripley's joy at being Dickie is short-lived, however, for as Ripley, who is now Dickie, continues to act as Ripley, murdering Freddie Miles, for example, he begins to threaten Dickie's identity as well. Furthermore, the boat in which Ripley and Dickie had last been seen together in San Remo is found scuttled, blood stains on its bottom. And as the police cannot find Tom Ripley, who is now Dickie Greenleaf, they suspect Dickie of having murdered Ripley as well as Freddie Miles. Realizing that the time has come when it is more dangerous to be Dickie Greenleaf than to be Tom Ripley, that he must now kill Dickie again, this time for good, Ripley becomes despondent: "This was the end of Dickie Greenleaf, he knew. He hated becoming Thomas Ripley again, hated being nobody, hated putting on his old set of habits again. He hated going back to himself as he would have hated putting on a shabby suit of clothes." Ripley's confusion here—of identity with clothes—is characteristic and will provide the idea by which he gets rid of Dickie once and for all. Packing up Dickie's clothes, storing them in the American Express in Venice under the name of Robert Fanshaw, Ripley, in effect, kills Dickie for a second and final time. For if a person is the clothes he wears, then by disposing of Dickie's clothes, Ripley not only disposes of Dickie, but also makes it impossible for himself to become Dickie again.

If Ripley cannot be Dickie, he must become someone and it is at this point in the novel that Highsmith begins her deepest exploration into the question of identity. For as Tom Ripley begins to put together a new self, Highsmith lets the reader know what a genuine identity is not. For Tom Ripley, as artist, will base his ultimate creation, himself, on a lesson he has learned while posing as Dickie Greenleaf: that the important thing about an identity is not who you are, but who you think you are. Acting out something makes it so: "If you wanted to be cheerful, or melancholic, or wistful, or thoughtful, or courteous," all you had to do was "simply *act* those things with every gesture." Gestures then, have become personality; acting, being; appearance, reality. And Ripley, in creating a self based on such principles, will, like Highsmith's other artists, become a forger, passing off that which is false, a sham-self, for that which is real, a genuine identity.

The fact that he is an American in Europe again aids Ripley's enterprise. Without any family or friends nearby, without any job to define him, with the money to travel and thus the means to escape any fixed existence, he can make himself into anyone he wishes. In such a fluid world, geography can become character; a person, the sum of the places he has been Going to Paris, Ripley begins to absorb that city into himself; walking the streets, he learns the names of its famous places; sitting in a well-known sidewalk cafe, he begins to have a new sense of who he is. It is a practice he will repeat in a number of cities—Rome, Venice, Athens—each place he's visiting adding further to his concept of himself. Sightseeing, then, literally becomes a way of life, the places one has been, the things one has seen, becoming one's self.

What one owns can also help to define one and Ripley sets out to associate himself with those things which best represent that which he would like to become. Ripley, of course, never owns anything; to own something would be to possess something of substance and value, an accomplishment he is at present incapable of. But he does rent. Moving to Venice, he leases a two-story house overlooking San Marco, with a garden "slightly run down," but with an interior which suggests all the splendor and wealth he would like for his own. There is a checkerboard black-and-white marble floor downstairs that extends from the foyer into each of the rooms, pink and white marble floors upstairs and carved wooden furniture so eloquent that it does not resemble furniture at all but rather "an embodiment of cinquecento music played on haut-boys, recorders and violas da gamba." He spends some time—Highsmith slyly points out "at least two weeks"—decorating the house and it reflects his growing good taste: "There was a sureness in his taste now that he had not felt in Rome, that his Rome apartment had not hinted at. "Indeed, Ripley's near-possessions, the house he rents, the way he has decorated it, all give him a new sense of himself: "He felt surer of himself now in every way."

If things can give one an identity, so can the media. The newspaper stories which begin to appear in the Italian press about the "sensational" Dickie Greenleaf case also help to define Ripley. In these stories he is described in some detail,

as the friend of the now missing Dickie Greenleaf, as "a young well-to-do American" now living in a "Palazzo" in Venice. Ripley had never thought of his house as being a "palace" before, but seeing it called such in print must make it so and he immediately feels a new sense of pride. Going to a party, he becomes the center of attention. Recognized immediately, because of the newspaper stories, as being Tom Ripley, his identity is further confirmed; he must be someone because other people know who he is.

Slowly, then, Ripley puts together a self made up of the gestures he affects, the places he has been, the things he is associated with, the newspaper stories which confirm that he does, indeed, exist. A patchwork creation made possible by Dickie Greenleaf's money and held together by his own art—his ability to think up new plots, to act out new roles—Tom Ripley is, then, at the end of *The Talented Mr. Ripley,* the perfect hero for further adventures. Highsmith will, in the three Ripley novels which follow, *Ripley under Ground* (1970), *Ripley's Game* (1974) and *The Boy Who Followed Ripley* (1980), modify her concept of her hero somewhat, even suggest that as Ripley beings to lose his powers of invention—as he does in these novels—as he becomes, then, less of an artist, he becomes more of a human being, even moves toward acquiring a genuine self. But at the end of *The Talented Mr. Ripley,* Tom Ripley is Highsmith's ultimate artist, a man who because he has no real identity, can become all things.

Anthony Channell Hilfer (essay date Summer 1984)

SOURCE: "'Not Really Such a Monster': Highsmith's Ripley as Thriller Protagonist and Protean Man," in *Midwest Quarterly,* Vol. XXV, No. 4, Summer, 1984, pp. 361-74.

[*In the following essay, Hilfer characterizes Tom Ripley as a particularly "subversive variation on the possibilities of a suspense thriller protagonist" as well as a "strikingly original exemplar of a contemporary character type, protean man."*]

Tom Ripley, Patricia Highsmith's most memorable character, is a problem from the conventional point of view, an opinion enunciated, for instance, by Simone Trevanny, a character in Highsmith's *Ripley's Game,* for whom his appeal makes no sense: "'I cannot understand. I cannot,' she said. 'Jon, why do you *see* this monster.'" Her husband, Jon, surrogate to Highsmith's bemused reader, reflects, "Tom was not really such a monster. But how to explain?" How indeed? Tom may not be a monster or at least *such* a monster but Simone's view of him has some warranty. She has, after all, found him hosting two bodies, the death of whom she rightly suspects him of having facilitated. Luckily, Simone is unaware of four earlier murders Tom has accomplished but Tom's attempt to reassure her becomes rather counterproductive when circumstances force him to dispatch two mafiosi with a hammer before her very eyes: "Of all times, Tom thought, when he'd meant to create a peaceable impression on Simone."

What to make of a character like Ripley is not a problem peculiar to the four novels Highsmith devoted to Ripley but one central to the suspense thriller genre. The best definition of this genre is that of Julian Symons, one of its leading practitioners, who emphasizes the genre's concentration on psychology, its unconventional morality (unlike the classic English detective novel, it puts "justice" into quotation marks), and the defining absence of a central detective hero. The protagonist of the suspense thriller is more likely either the victim or perpetrator of violence—sometimes both. So the problem of evoking sympathy where not conventionally placed is intrinsic to the genre. In this essay I shall explore Highsmith's Ripley as a particularly subversive variation on the possibilities of a suspense thriller protagonist and, simultaneously, as a strikingly original exemplar of a contemporary character type, protean man, more usually to be found in high than popular fiction.

First to the problem of a murderer-protagonist. As Highsmith herself puts it, in her how-to book on writing suspense fiction, "I think many suspense writers . . . must have some kind of sympathy and identification with criminals, or they would not become emotionally engrossed in books about them. The suspense book is vastly different from the mystery story in this respect. The suspense writer often deals much more closely with the criminal mind, because the criminal is usually known throughout the book, and the writer has to describe what is going on in his head." If this is imperative for the writer, is it not so, *a fortiori,* for the reader? Not entirely, according to Highsmith. The reader must care about the protagonist but this "is not the same as liking the hero. It is caring whether he goes free, or caring that he is caught rightly at the end, and it is being interested in him, pro or con."

The questions then in the Ripley books are: who is Ripley, what makes him interesting, why do we care about him, and, not least, why does Highsmith protect him always from being "caught rightly at the end." I shall answer these questions by means of a commentary on the first and best of the Ripley novels, *The Talented Mr. Ripley,* with cross references to others in the Ripley series when relevant.

The Talented Mr. Ripley begins with Tom being followed by a man whom he fears is about to arrest him. (Tom has constructed a minor scam with I.R.S. forms. Though criminal, Tom's scam is more a form of play since he has not had the nerve to get money from it. Tom's nerve improves dur-

ing the course of the novel and the series, but it is important to recognize that he is always *playing* at crime.) The man turns out to be Herbert Greenleaf, father of Dickie Greenleaf, whom Herbert mistakenly supposes to be a close friend of Tom's whereas they are merely slight acquaintances. Even after being apprised of his error, Greenleaf proposes that Tom take a leave of absence from his job in order to retrieve Dickie from the Italian seacoast town where Dickie is living a pleasant expatriate life and return him to his responsibilities as scion of a large shipbuilding concern. This presents no problem for Tom since the job he must leave is fictitious, but when he arrives in Italy he finds it more appealing to insinuate himself into Dickie's enjoyable lifestyle than to persuade him to renounce it. The spanner gets into the works when Dickie falls out with Tom due to Tom's jealousy of Dickie's girl friend, Marge. Ultimately, Tom solves the problem by replacing Dickie; he murders him, impersonates him, and forges a will leaving his money to Tom Ripley. He is also forced to murder Dickie's friend, Freddie Miles, who discovers the impersonation.

This brief plot outline necessarily focuses on Tom's actions, especially his murders, but Highsmith's interest is less in Tom as murderer than in Tom as actor, performer, role player, in Tom's ability not merely to escape the limitations of his identity, but the identity itself. Tom is pleased with himself in direct ratio to his ability to stand outside this self, objectify it, play it as a role. Thus, early in the novel we get the first of many mirror images: "Slowly he took off his jacket and untied his tie, watching every move he made as if it were somebody else's movements he were watching. Astonishing how much straighter he was standing now, what a different look there was in his face. It was one of the few times in his life that he felt pleased with himself." On the ship to Europe he signalizes his "starting a new life" with the purchase of a cap reminiscent of the mythical helmet of invisibility: "A cap was the most versatile of headgears, he thought, and wondered why he had never thought of wearing one before? He could look like a country gentleman, a thug, an Englishman, a Frenchman, or a plain American eccentric, depending on how he wore it. Tom amused himself with it in his room in front of the mirror. He had always thought he had the world's dullest face, a thoroughly forgettable face with a look of docility that he could not understand and a look also of vague fright that he had never been able to erase. A real conformist's face, he thought. The cap changed all that." Appearance takes priority over reality or, to be precise, for Tom it *becomes* an effective reality, creating class, moral, and national identity.

Tom's very defects turn out to be functional in his eventual transformation—his other-directed oversensitivity to others, his diffidence, his self-dislike all make it easy for him to shuck off his rather minimal self and become the other he has so well observed. His initial blunder with Dickie is to approach him at the beach in a bathing suit, a self-exposure which goes against Tom's genius and has the reverse effect to that of the versatile cap: "Tom stood there, feeling pale and naked as the day he was born. He hated bathing suits. This one was very revealing." But Tom's other-directed responsiveness soon has him unconsciously copying Dickie's walk as he becomes more and more Dickie's double:

> They sat slumped in the carozza, each with a sandalled foot propped on a knee, and it seemed to Tom that he was looking in a mirror when he looked at Dickie's leg and his propped foot beside him. They were the same height, and very much the same weight, Dickie perhaps a bit heavier, and they wore the same size bathrobe, socks, and probably shirts.

> Dickie even said, "Thank you, Mr. Greenleaf," when Tom paid the carozza driver. Tom felt a little weird.

At this point in the novel, Tom has no thought of murdering Dickie. What he aspires to is a kind of cross between a blood brother and mirror image of Dickie, living Dickie's life concurrently with him. He fantasizes murdering not Dickie but Dickie's friend, Marge, who is the reality principle interfering with Tom's dream of sharing Dickie's life. In the most bizarre scene of the novel, Tom, alone in Dickie's room and dressed in Dickie's clothes, fantasizes himself as Dickie murdering Marge: "'Marge, you must understand that I don't *love* you,' Tom said in the mirror in Dickie's voice, with Dickie's higher pitch on the emphasized words, with the little growl in his throat at the end of the phrase that could be pleasant or unpleasant, intimate or cool, according to Dickie's mood. 'Marge, stop it!' Tom turned suddenly and made a grab in the air as if he were seizing Marge's throat. He shook her, twisted her, while she sank lower and lower, until at last he left her, limp on the floor. . . . 'You know why I had to do that,' he said, still breathlessly, addressing Marge, though he watched himself in the mirror. 'You were interfering between Tom and me—No, not that! But there is a bond between us!'"

What Tom has not yet realized is that he cannot be Dickie or even effectively play Dickie so long as Dickie is alive to be and do so. There cannot be two Napoleons in the same asylum. The conclusion of the scene above is that Dickie explodes Tom's act by catching him in the performance of it. Shortly thereafter Tom has an epiphany of Dickie's (and everyone's) irremediable otherness: "He stared at Dickie's blue eyes that were still frowning, the sun-bleached eyebrows white and the eyes themselves shining and empty, nothing but little pieces of blue jelly with a black dot in them, meaningless, without relation to him. You were supposed to see the soul through the eyes, to see love through the eyes, the one place you could look at another human being and see what really went on inside, and in Dickie's eyes Tom saw

nothing more now than he would have seen if he had looked at the hard bloodless surface of a mirror. Tom felt a painful wrench in his breast, and he covered his face with his hands. It was as if Dickie had been suddenly snatched away from him. They were not friends. They didn't know each other. It struck Tom like a horrible truth, true for all time, true for the people he had known in the past and for those he would know in the future . . . ." To sum up, Tom now envisions relations with others as external and illusory, a matter of surface appearances. His initial response to this vision is to wish to die.

In a way he does this. He dies to himself as Tom and becomes Dickie, after murdering the original claimant to that identity. Tom so throws himself into being Dickie that his Tom-identity becomes more distant to him; he imagines telling Marge something "in Tom's voice." In becoming Dickie, he appropriates not only the latter's clothes but his smile, he packs like Dickie, paints like Dickie, even tries "to think about what Dickie would be thinking about." In sum, "Now, from the moment when he got out of bed and went to brush his teeth, he was Dickie, brushing his teeth with his elbow jutted out, Dickie invariably putting back the first tie he pulled off the rack and selecting a second." Being Dickie is a vast improvement over being Tom: "It was impossible ever to be lonely or bored, he thought, so long as he was Dickie Greenleaf." Finally, in one of Highsmith's nicest moments, Tom-as-Dickie is asked about Tom and responds not untruthfully, that he doesn't know him very well.

But there are problems. As Tom splits Dickie's money between his own and Dickie's bank account, he reflects that "after all, he had two people to take care of." He can only be Dickie to people who have never seen Dickie and he is forced to murder Freddie Miles for stumbling across his impersonation. Worst of all, he must go back to being Tom when Dickie becomes the main suspect in Freddie Miles's murder. This prospect of becoming a real Tom as opposed to a fake Dickie is highly depressing: "He hated going back to himself as he would have hated putting on a shabby suit of clothes, a grease-spotted, unpressed suit of clothes that had not been very good even when it was new." He becomes upset at catching sight of himself in the mirror: "He looked as if he were trying to convey the emotions of fear and shock by his posture and his expression and *because the way he looked was involuntary and real,* he became suddenly twice as frightened" (my italics). It should be remembered that Tom enjoys mirrors when he is practicing a role before them. At this point, Tom arrives at his second major revelation—that "Tom Ripley" is like "Dickie Greenleaf" a role and that he controls the performance of it: "It was senseless to be despondent, anyway, even as Tom Ripley. . . . Hadn't he learned something from these last months? If you wanted to be cheerful, or melancholic, or wistful, or thoughtful, or courteous, you simply had to act those things with every gesture." Settling into the role of Tom Ripley, he finds enjoyment in hamming it up: "He began to feel happy even in his dreary role as Thomas Ripley. He took a pleasure in it, overdoing almost the old Tom Ripley reticence with strangers, the inferiority in every duck of his head and wistful, sidelong glance." Later, Tom sets himself off from the lighter haired Dickie by dyeing his hair "so that it would be even darker than his normal hair." Tom even pulls off the tour de force of successfully playing Tom to the same policemen to whom he had earlier played Dickie.

It is not surprising that Tom "had wanted to be an actor" since the main thematic pattern in *The Talented Mr. Ripley* is Tom's confirmation in the belief that acting creates reality. At this point, a distinction is necessary. It is possible to construe a determinate identity for Tom in terms of two culturally talismanic terms: "Homosexual" and "Schizophrenic." The reader has doubtless picked up intimations of these identities simply in the quotes I've given, especially the one in which Tom, playing Dickie to the mirror, justifies himself to an imaginary Marge. "You were interfering between Tom and me—No, not that!" *That* obviously refers to homosexual attachment and we may suspect that Tom doth protest too much. Both earlier and later, Tom shows notable anxiety about being perceived as effeminate or homosexual and, in the scene where Dickie finds Tom playacting in Dickie's clothes, Tom is accused to his face of being "queer." In what is so far the latest in the Ripley series, *The Boy Who Followed Ripley,* Tom dresses in drag partly as a disguise but more just for the experience. Most suggestive of all, Freddie Miles, before it dawns on him that Tom is impersonating Dickie Greenleaf, suspects that Tom's presence in what is supposedly Dickie's apartment wearing Dickie's cloths and jewelry must indicate a homosexual relation between them. After murdering Freddie, Tom thinks "how sad, stupid, clumsy, dangerous and unnecessary his death had been, and how brutally unfair to Freddie. Of course, one could loathe Freddie, too. A selfish, stupid bastard who had sneered at one of his best friends—Dickie certainly was one of his best friends—just because he suspected him of sexual deviation. Tom laughed at that phrase 'sexual deviation.' Where was the sex? Where was the deviation? He looked at Freddie and said low and bitterly: 'Freddie Miles, You're a victim of your own dirty mind.'"

The above passage also can be read as evincing Tom's schizophrenic tendencies. Tom's indignation at Freddie's suspicions seems curiously displaced. After all, Tom has *murdered* Dickie, surely rather more unfriendly an act than sneering, however unjustly, at supposedly deviant tendencies in him. Equally odd is that Tom, when he returns to his Ripley identity, feels free of guilt for Freddie's murder: "Being Tom Ripley had one compensation at least: it relieved his mind of guilt for the stupid, unnecessary murder of Freddie Miles." This is because Tom was being Dickie at that time. Later, when Marge asks Tom where he had been that winter—we know, of course, that he spent it playing Dickie—Tom suffers a slight identity slippage: "'Well not with Tom, I mean, not with Dickie,' he said laughing, flustered at his slip of the tongue."

But to anchor Tom's identity in latent homosexuality and schizophrenia is to read against the clear indications in Highsmith's novel that Tom's strength is in his indeterminacy of identity, in an emptiness of self that allows the superior performance of roles, eventuating in Tom's finest performance—the role of himself. So my answer to the question I raised at the beginning of this essay, the question of who Tom is, why we are interested in him and care about him is that we are interested in and care about Tom precisely because he is not anybody. It is this negative capability that exempts Tom from detection and exposure. Along, that is, with the author's sympathy for what Tom isn't. Ripley's non-essentiality, his lack of a determinate identity, is the making of him. It is his talent, his vocation, and we may recall that, as Falstaff pointed out, "'Tis no sin for a man to labour in his vocation." Ripley's interest is, in fact, paradigmatic; he refers back to the trickster archetype while traversing the narrow field of post-modern identity, beginning as a sleazy version of Riesman's other-directed man and developing into a sinister version of Lifton's protean man, a player with his own and others' destinies.

Tom's transformation begins with his other-directed need "to make Dickie like him," progresses to imitating Dickie, playing Dickie, and finally to the protean triumph of playing himself. The central feature of protean man, Robert Lifton notes [in "Protean Man," *History and Human Survival* (1971)], is the "repeated, autonomously willed death and rebirth of the self," associated with the theme of "fatherlessness." Tom, whose parents conveniently died in his early childhood, leaving him to the care of an aunt he detests, has carried the protean tendency to its logical extreme, reflecting at one point, "this was the real annihilation of his past and of himself, Tom Ripley, who was made up of that past, and his rebirth as a completely new person." Divested of past and parentage, Tom is remarkably free of the conventional constraints of superego, again matching Lifton's definition of protean man: "What has actually disappeared ... is the *classical* superego, the internalization of clearly defined criteria of right and wrong transmitted within a particular culture by parents to their children." Alisdair McIntyre, in a less sanguine view of protean man than Lifton, could have been describing Highsmith's creation [in *After Virtue* (1981)]: "The self thus conceived, utterly distinct on the one hand from its social embodiments and lacking on the other any rational history of its own, may seem to have a certain abstract and ghostly character." One recalls Iago, whose motto is "I am not what I am not what I am."

Tom's sexual anxieties, then, can be best explained as compounding a conventional enough shame at a socially derogatory label (the novel was published in 1956) with an emergent protean man's dislike of getting fixed in *any* identity. In accord with Diderot's paradox of the actor, Tom is able to be anyone or anything only by way of being detached from the acts and identities he performs. Marge may well be on the right track when she comments in a letter to Dickie—which Tom in his Dickie-role actually receives and reads—"All right, he may not be queer. He's just nothing, which is worse." In the later books, we find Tom happily married to a lady as amoral and as relatively passionless as himself. And though Tom's self-detachment may be taken as schizophrenic, it is questionable if he is any more so than other literary adumbrations or fulfillments of the protean self—say, for a short list, Gide's Lafcadio, Mann's Felix Krull, Barth's Jacob Horner ("In a sense, I am Jacob Horner"), among others. In all these characters, as in Tom, indeterminacy of identity seems, as Lifton argues, less a dysfunction than a survival mechanism. Even when most absorbed in his role of Dickie, Tom never completely loses himself in his role: "He felt alone, yet not at all lonely. It was very much like the feeling on Christmas Eve in Paris, a feeling that everyone was watching him, as if he had an audience made up of the entire world, a feeling that kept him on his mettle, because to make a mistake would be catastrophic. Yet he felt absolutely confident he would not make a mistake. It gave his existence a peculiar, delicious atmosphere of purity, like that, Tom thought, which a fine actor probably feels when he plays an important role on a stage with the conviction that the role he is playing could not be played better by anyone else. He was himself and yet not himself. He felt blameless and free, despite the fact that he consciously controlled every move he made."

Finally, within the conventions of the suspense thriller, Tom's survival and triumph is an evident authorial endorsement. The structure of Highsmith's book is built on the tension between Tom's potential exposure and punishment and his actual evasion and exemption. The novel begins with Tom's fear of arrest and throughout the novel Tom varies between fear of "nemesis" and confidence in luck: "Something always turned up. That was Tom's philosophy." After his murder of Freddie, Tom imagines all the possibilities of disaster he must face in carrying a dead body down several flights of stairs; he "imagined it all with such intensity, writhing upstairs in his apartment, that to have descended all the stairs without a single one of his imaginings happening made him feel that he was gliding down under a magical protection of some kind, with ease in spite of the mass on his shoulder." His magical protector is, of course, Highsmith, a protection she extends on condition that Tom play his roles audaciously and with a kind of artistic lightness. Tom's initial blunder with Dickie is to have come on too seriously, heavily: "Tom cursed himself for having been so heavy-handed and so humorless today. Nothing he took desper-

ately seriously ever worked out. He'd found that out years ago." (Note, again, the paradox of the actor.) Tom's virtù is his joy in risk taking: "Risks were what made the whole thing fun."

Highsmith deliberately and shamelessly evades the conventional morality of crime and punishment. Toward the end of the novel she presents us with a barrage of signs that Tom has pushed his luck too far, has risked too much, that nemesis is finally, if a bit belatedly, approaching. Tom "considered that he had been lucky beyond reason"; he speculates "something was going to happen now . . . and it couldn't be good. His luck had held just too long." Certainly this is the way it ought to be and in the film version of *The Talented Mr. Ripley,* Rene Clement's *Plein Soleil* (*Purple Noon* is the American title), Tom is exposed at the end as Dickie's body literally surfaces. In her how-to book on suspense fiction, Highsmith comments that it "makes a book altogether more eligible for television and movie sales if the criminal is caught, punished, and made to feel awful at the end." So Tom's exemption is a thoroughly calculated flouting of moral and literary expectations, a play against genre since even in the relatively subversive suspense genre a murderer-protagonist usually ends by being hoist on his own petard. Simone Trevanny in *Ripley's Game* stands in for readers shocked by any play with, evasion of, or undercutting of such expectation, though Highsmith rather unfairly characterizes Simone as hysterical and unreasonable for reacting with predictable shock and outrage to the bodies she keeps finding Tom stacking like cordwood. Highsmith can, however, turn back the accusation of immorality on more conventionally proper writers and readers: "The public wants to see the law triumph, or at least the general public does, though at the same time the public likes brutality. The brutality must be on the right side, however. Sleuth-heroes can be brutal, sexually unscrupulous, kickers of women, and still be popular heroes, because they are chasing something worse than themselves, presumably." Tom Ripley, it is true, has never achieved the popularity of Mike Hammer.

Still, he does all right for himself and Highsmith does all right by him. At the conclusion of *The Talented Mr. Ripley,* Tom has gotten off clear from two murders and found his forged will accepted with almost magical ease. It should not be too surprising that Highsmith's ending resembles that of Gide's *Lafcadio's Journey* (*Les Caves du Vatican*) where by a chain of extraordinary coincidences Lafcadio escapes the consequences of a gratuitous murder he has committed. Both endings imply a quasi-providential endorsement of the protagonists' actions with the respective authors in the role of *deus ex machina*. The deity is, of course, Proteus. Both these novels adumbrate a long reign for this usurper deity, an appropriate modern replacement for Zeus with his obsolescent baggage of nemesis and superego. In the last lines of *The*

Talented Mr. Ripley, we see Tom instructing a taxi driver, "'To a hotel, please. . . . Il meglio albergo. Il meglio, il meglio!'"

Washington Post Book World (review date 6 October 1985)

SOURCE: A review of *People Who Knock on the Door,* in *Washington Post Book World,* Vol. XV, No. 40, October 6, 1985, p. 6.

[*Below, the critic offers a negative review of* People Who Knock on the Door.]

Even good novelists occasionally have a lapse, and Patricia Highsmith had a very bad lapse of several hundred pages when she wrote *People Who Knock on the Door.* It's the story of Arthur, 17, and the effects on him and his family when his father becomes a born-again Christian and tries to revise all their lives and impose his moral views on others.

Things come to a head when Arthur's girlfriend reveals that she is pregnant and opts for an abortion. Because Arthur approves the decision, he is put out of the house and denied funds for college. Meanwhile his younger brother Robbie becomes the father's faithful ally. Mom tries to keep peace by keeping everyone well-fed. In the end, inevitably, principles are challenged and hypocrisy revealed, and also inevitably, terrible violence ensues.

Alas, it's all thoroughly unconvincing. For one thing, Robbie is outlandish; when did you last see a normal 15-year-old playing horsey? And how many teen-agers casually drop by to have a cocktail with the old lady next door, or "smooch," or describe something as "kooky," or hang out with their buddies listening to the Beach Boys and Cole Porter? They certainly don't do that on my block. And, besides, has Highsmith never heard of Planned Parenthood? These characters act like nothing more than characters in a novel.

Kathleen Gregory Klein (essay date 1985)

SOURCE: "Patricia Highsmith," in *And Then There Were Nine . . . More Women of Mystery,* edited by Jane S. Bakerman, Bowling Green State University Popular Press, 1985, pp. 170-97.

[*In the following essay, Klein provides a stylistic and thematic overview of Highsmith's works, concluding that the writer challenged the conventions of the mystery genre.*]

In her refusal to be limited by the conventional considerations of the genre, Patricia Highsmith is, quite simply, one of the best and most significant crime writers working today. Critic Blake Morrison notes that "[T]o call her a 'crime writer' sounds limiting, even patronising, since, like Chabrol, Highsmith is less interested in the mechanics of crime than in the psychology behind them;" while Brigid Brophy extends the praise, "as a novelist *tout court* she's excellent. . . . Highsmith and Simenon are alone in writing books which transcend the limits of the genre while staying strictly inside its rules: they alone have taken the crucial step from playing games to creating art." What characterizes Highsmith's work beyond attention to character development and atmosphere is a way of examining human beings which unnerves and disquiets the reader. She takes a grim look at the darker side of human nature, revealing the innate capacity of everyone for violence, even murder. While some readers might deny this assessment of themselves, escaping to the classical puzzle novel with its neat definitions of villainy and while others, preferring those "mean streets," erroneously believe that they are facing death as it really can happen, Highsmith, both obviously and subtly, recognizes a common personality trait. Equally present in everyone, the propensity for evil is inescapable; its execution depends on circumstances, not the will or public posture of the individual.

In accenting dualities, Highsmith further comments on the universal inclination to violence. Her characters' duets of love and hate, power and powerlessness, order and disorder, guilt or guiltlessness never really display the expected results. All virtue can not reside within a single character, not can it invariably triumph. Blended in such a way that lovers hate, ordering disorders, or powerlessness empowers, the dualities are charged with intensity and mystery. Like sexuality, a persistent challenge in Highsmith's works, opposites and pairs reverberate discordantly.

Like only a few of her colleagues, Highsmith has written critically and instructionally about crime fiction. While undoubtedly exaggerating some of her advice and conclusions, nonetheless, she acknowledges the craft involved in writing popular fiction ("popular" is used here to identify that which is widely read and praised, not to make any unnecessary artificial distinctions between "literary" and "popular" fiction). The title of Highsmith's non-fiction, "how-to" book, *Plotting and Writing Suspense Fiction,* provides a significant indication of one approach to her work. It implies that organization of plot elements, development of action and concern for the overall structure of the work are central among Highsmith's concerns. Even a casual consideration of her novels and short stories verifies this obvious fact as the opening paragraph of each work exemplifies perfectly. Succinct, but action-filled, each opening forces itself upon the reader's attention. Four examples from the novels and short stories easily demonstrate the point:

Coleman was saying, "My only child, she was, but it doesn't mean she'll be your only wife. Your last wife."

Those Who Walk Away

"There's no such thing as a perfect murder," Tom said to Reeves. "That's just a parlor game, trying to dream one up. Of course you could say there are a lot of unsolved murders. That's different." Tom was bored. He walked up and down in front of his big fireplace where a small but cozy fire crackled. Tom felt he had spoken in a stuffy, pontificating way. But the point was he couldn't help Reeves, and he'd already told him that.

Ripley's Game

Greta showed Ed the letter as soon as he opened the door. "I couldn't help opening it, Eddie, because I knew it was from that—that creep."

A Dog's Ransom

When Mr. Peter Knoppert began to make a hobby of snail-watching, he had no idea that his handful of specimens would become hundreds in no time.

"The Snail-Watcher"

Like other famous first lines in literary works (eg. *Pride and Prejudice* or *Anna Karenina*), they orient the reader not merely to characters or plot but primarily to atmosphere, the prose setting. Tightly organized yet never hurried, Highsmith's novels and short stories compel the reader's attention through her careful delineation of contrasts between realistic and improbable detail.

Although *Plotting and Writing Suspense Fiction* is extremely varied in its approach—concerned with choosing an agent, expecting advertising of a publisher, recognizing the germ of an idea, or organizing the first page—it is generally chatty and personal in style. Highsmith uses her own ideas and works, her failures as well as her successes to focus the details of her advice. For the reader rather than the writer of fiction, the volume's greatest appeal lies in the important clues it provides to Highsmith's thinking and the perspective on her own work which it articulates; as a volume of criticism of the genre, it is generally unfocused and limited in its concerns.

At the outset, Highsmith claims to accept the trade definition of suspense: "stories with a threat of violent physical action and anger, or danger and action itself." But she re-fuses to concede the usual limitations ascribed to the genre, believing instead that "the beauty of the suspense genre is that a writer can write profound thoughts and have some sections without physical action if he wishes to, because the framework is an essentially lively story." This contrast between the usual expectations and the expanded form of the genre is at the heart of Highsmith's talent and success. More widely praised in England and Europe than in the United States, she is not limited abroad to a narrow category, rigidly defined and briefly reviewed. Instead she is accorded serious consideration; as a result, she encourages young writers to "keep as clear of the suspense label as possible." She indicates her own limitless conception of the possibilities, free of formulaic blandness of gore and brutality, by citing *Crime and Punishment* as a perfect example of the genre's possibilities.

The centrality of character formulation and development as a subject in this book belies the title's insistence on "how" to focus on "why;" not being formulaic mystery or detective novels, her works are never concerned with teasing the reader about "whodunit." In fact, the tantalizing question of why crime is planned or committed is seldom answered with satisfying finality. Instead, the reader is treated to a progress report on the criminal's mind and emotions at work. People, then, rather than plots, are at the center of Highsmith's suspense-filled universe. The crucial pair—character and atmosphere—are both defined and placed through a "bit of action" which is focused at the center or the climax of the story. Although this action—such as an imitated murder (*The Blunderer*) or an exchange of victims (*Strangers on a Train*)—may often first occur to her without the appropriate characters attached. Highsmith notes, its direction and thrust later serve to identify a major facet of the characters' personalities or wills.

As action determines her characters, Highsmith explains, point of view affects her tone. She abandoned first person narrators as a novelistic device when she "got sick and tired of writing the pronoun 'I,'" and recognized that her scheming characters seemed more sympathetic when filtered through the authorial consciousness. Because Highsmith varies even using two different perspectives in a single novel, most of her works, despite their similarities, have a fresh and unique appeal. She is adamant about the importance of good and careful writing, critical of the gimmickry which pervades many novels and most short stories. Nonetheless she is not tediously serious; the writer must acknowledge the game-playing element in his work, she notes.

Highsmith is thus led to acknowledge the recurrent theme in her own works, which she sees in six of her first ten books—the relationship between two men, frequently strangers, occasionally mismatched friends. These two do not always divide neatly into categories of good and evil, right and wrong, criminal and victim; their relationships, whatever overtones of these they may contain, are based on a real or perceived inequality which Highsmith manipulates, blurs, or emphasizes. She reuses this theme easily, believing that "[U]nless one is in danger of repeating oneself, they should be used to the fullest, because a writer will write better making use of what is, for some strange reason, innate."

Because puzzles and mysteries bore her and because she finds "the public passion for justice" artificial, Highsmith believes in the inevitably interesting and dramatic criminal: "I rather like criminals and find them extremely interesting, unless they are monotonously and stupidly brutal." Naturally, then, she is careful to recognize the necessity of suspending moral judgments and even shutting off one's mind to certain strictures and proscriptions which she would unquestionably acknowledge in daily life. Moralizing and censorship are equally unacceptable to her; recognizing the use the artist makes of experience, she rejects artificial judgments.

When all the subjects on which she cautions other writers to take care are considered in view of her own fiction, Highsmith's concern for character presentation, development and unfolding is clearly at the center of her work. Carefully she builds one detail after another, aiming at a portrait of the person himself. His inclinations are probed; his secret musings revealed; his sudden and often unexplained plunge into criminality is charted. The atmosphere and actions which encourage and reinforce him are painted in. Not only the character alone but also the character in contrast draws her attention; in the recurring thematic pattern of pairs of men, the influence of one upon the other is explored. In the recurring pattern of couples of man and woman, the questions of power and powerlessness are presented and reversed, challenged and enacted. Finally, the pattern of the criminal's interaction with his second, sometimes unknown, self is considered.

Highsmith acknowledges an exclusive use of the masculine perspective in her own fiction: "women are not so active as men and not so daring." Not only are her protagonists male (with only one exception), but also their attitudes toward women are conventionally stereotyped. Almost unconsciously Highsmith validates the concept of women as appropriate victims of murder or violence; they are presented as having deserved punishment for being too available or unavailable sexually, too domineering or insufficiently independent, too loving or too hateful. The short stories collected in *Little Tales of Misogyny* with their stereotyped titles (**"The Fully-Licensed Whore," "The Wife," "The Breeder,"** or **"Oona, The Jolly Cave Woman"**) are the most openly anti-women. Inasmuch as women are easy victims, violence and crimes against them are easily justified and rationalized.

II

Highsmith's first novel, **Strangers on a Train,** later filmed by Alfred Hitchcock in his characteristic style, is a model for the rest of her fictional canon; in theme and attitude, action and characters it announces her chief concerns and the direction her work will take. Highsmith's concept of the thriller, its attitude and moral posture, is clearly enunciated here; her concern is not with uncovering the roots of a crime already committed in either the classical or hard-boiled style. She does not accept the legalistic notion of justice; detectives, though both private and official ones are included in many of the novels, are not memorable characters, but are overshadowed by the protagonist himself. In a similar way, detection is overshadowed by criminal activity; despite the presence of both, the focus is skewed. Neither the classical detective story with its focus on the investigated nor the hard-boiled with its concern for the detective's interaction with those he chases forms the basis for Highsmith's novels. Instead the criminal, his mind, and emotions, are minutely dissected. His perspective dominates the novels and comes to dominate the reader as well.

A focal concern of this and Highsmith's other novels is the ordinary individual's capacity for violence and murder. Anyone, the characters come to recognize, can commit murder; it is not that the individual must be right for the task but that the circumstances make anyone right. As Guy Haines comes to realize, contrary to his childhood beliefs in the goodness of human nature, love and hate as well as good and evil live side by side in every human heart. There are not different proportions of each depending on the person's temperament; all good and all evil coexist. To find them, it is only necessary to look a little for either one; anyone can be pushed over the brink. As Anne Faulkner expresses it, "Amazing what goes on in people's lives."

The action and situation of **Strangers** are typical of Highsmith. Two men, meeting accidentally, find themselves, almost without knowing how, caught in a love-hate relationship which puzzles them. As they are almost ignorant of its beginnings, they are unaware of how to bring it to a conclusion even if they were certain they wanted to. The action arises from a simple proposal by Charles Bruno: he will kill Guy Haines' wife if Haines will return the favor by killing Bruno's father; both will be able to escape suspicion since there is no link between them. In conception the plan is successful; its failure comes from both of the men who are to execute it: Guy cannot agree to the plan but can be manipulated five or six months later into meeting his obligation while Charley Bruno cannot keep himself from contacting Guy and trying to be friends. Thus both aspects of the plan's success—mutual consent and complete separation—are jeopardized.

The dualistic male pair is matched in two other all-male combinations: Guy finally confesses his share in his first wife's murder to her lover Owen Markman; Bruno is dogged consistently by Gerard, his father's detective, who eventually overhears Guy's confession. The Guy/Bruno pair thus splits into two less intense and less destructive segments—Guy/Owen and Bruno/Gerard. This is mirrored in the two wives of Guy Haines—Miriam, a redheaded southern girl with limited education, few social graces and too much interest in other men, contrasts with Anne, an intelligent, talented, wealthy woman of tact and sincerity. For all his vacillation, Guy can abandon neither; for all his determined gentlemanliness with Anne, Bruno wants to dispose of both. A pair of mothers, pair of murderers, pairs of houses, parties and hotels carry the point a bit too far in this first novel, but the crucial focus is well-developed and carefully maintained.

Charley Bruno is hardly an appealing character; his physical appearance, personal habits, tendency to whining and self-pity, not to mention his plan for murder, do not appeal to the reader. Yet Guy's tie with him is partially affectionate in nature; not only shared crime and Guy's guilt keep them together. Guy reveals his private feelings and problems believing that Bruno, as a stranger, is an unthreatening listener, but is forced to admit later that this is no ordinary stranger on a train but rather a cruel and corrupt one. Bruno seems incapable of being surprised; details only encourage him to probe for more information. Deciding to kill Miriam, his half of the "deal," he experiences neither guilt nor remorse, only a kind of excitement which gives direction to his life. Afterward he imagines his responses to a radio interview: She was like a rat to be killed; he couldn't say whether he would ever do it again: yes, he rather liked killing her. In the murder, in his plot to have his father killed so he and his mother would be free to live, in his drinking to constant drunkenness and in his reckless pursuit of Guy, Bruno reveals a man who always wants more, who cannot be sated. Although he claims to love Guy like a brother, he fantasizes being rid of Anne so the two men can really be close. His deficiency, Guy notes, is that Bruno does not know how to love, though he needs to learn. "Bruno was too lost, too blind to love or to inspire to love. It seemed all at once tragic." Bruno's only response is to equate love with sex or women and to think that he has never liked either.

Bruno quotes Guy as once having talked about opposites, saying that every person has an opposite, unseen part of himself which is lying in ambush waiting to attack unexpectedly and dangerously. This is clearly how Guy sees the two of them related: and to some degree, Bruno does also. Only metaphorically is it possible to understand the link between these two. Guy Haines is a well-respected young architect who seems to almost fall under the hypnotic spell of another man and his own innate decency. The latter, as much as the former, leads him to murder; because he is racked by guilt

for not having prevented or accused Bruno in Miriam's murder, he equalizes his guilt by murdering Bruno's father. Guy is persistently haunted and reassured by the idea that his destiny, which he has always trusted, holds the answer to his guilt. He is convinced, for example, that atonement is part of his destiny and will find him without his searching for it; or, that the murder he's committed might have been part of his destiny—an improbable mixture of arrogance and humility which compels him to obey only the laws of his own fate.

A key to both *Strangers* and Highsmith's inversion of the standard techniques of the genre can be found in Guy Haines' profession. As an architect he is concerned with design, order, harmony and honesty. When he rejects a beach club commission because of Miriam's new entanglement in his life, Guy is genuinely pained to think of the imitation Frank Lloyd Wright building which will replace his perfect conception; in designing his own Y-shaped house, he refused necessary economies which would truncate the building. His work is, for him, a spiritual act, defined by unity and wholeness; it rejects disorder, fragmentation and shallowness. Contrasted in the two sections of the book are his description of the bridge he hopes to build as the climax of his career and his inability to accept the commission when telegraphed an offer. His dream of a great white bridge with a span like angels' wings is shattered when his feeling of corruption keeps him from his talent.

In Highsmith's fictional world, issues of order, harmony of civilization—whatever it is called—are seldom so simple and traditional. Contrasted with the more stereotyped perspective which Guy accepts is her series character Tom Ripley. His notions of order are equally predictable; Bach, or classical music in general, provide the right stimuli to focus his attention, distill and concentrate his mind. Ripley uses these devices, however sincerely he may value them as entities in themselves, as personal preparations for crime: fraud, theft, murder. Not so amoral, Guy uses them as avoidance mechanisms; he refuses to consider trying to create perfect order out of his own disordered mind. These attitudes toward order mark Highsmith's vacillating and threatening challenge to oversimplified theories of order and disorder, harmony and chaos. Never committing her fiction to either the triumph of order or the inevitability of chaos, she creates worlds which misuse both, locations in which both are equally and simultaneously present; in fact, she suggests that they may be indistinguishable. Highsmith's manipulation of these dualities suggests closer parallels with contemporary absurdists and existentialists than with her colleagues in crime or suspense fiction. Challenging the either or structure of human thinking in a work ostensibly about a pair of murders and murderers is part of Highsmith's conscious expansion of an established genre into a new and provocative form.

Like *Strangers on a Train,* Highsmith's masterful novel,

The Blunderer charts the intersecting lives of two men who plan similar murders. Also filmed, this novel qualifies as one of the 100 best detective novels of all time, according to Julian Symons in the *New York Times Book Review*. "Unworthy friendships" is how Walter Stackhouse defines the subject of a book he considers writing: "A majority of people maintained at least one friendship with someone inferior to themselves because of certain needs and deficiencies that were either mirrored or complemented by the inferior friend." Coming across a newspaper report of an unusual death, Walter saves the clipping in his scrapbook of notes for his essays; later, he begins to consider how the murder might have been committed by the victim's husband. Miserably unhappy with his own wife Clara, he begins to fantasize committing a similar murder. Like Walter, Clara easily recognizes unworthy friends: she considers most of her husband's companions and even their neighbors in that light. Her critical, unfriendly, insulting manner costs Walter many friendships which he cherishes; he simply cannot forgive her.

Walter's fantasy life is rich and full. Because the world in which he lives does not meet his expectations, he creates an alternate reality in which the ordering of both events and motives are within his own command. Having convinced himself through reading newspaper clippings of Melchior Kimmel's guilt, he travels to the man's bookstore just to meet him, scrutinize him and reaffirm his verdict. Circumstances identical to those surrounding Helen Kimmel's death arise for the Stackhouses; Walter behaves exactly as he believes Kimmel had done, except that he does not kill Clara, although she dies. Initially, Highsmith's intermingling of Walter's fantasy with his actions implies murder; gradually, it becomes clear that Clara's death is truly not his responsibility.

The novel's irony develops from this confusion of reality and questions of responsibility. Kimmel has been a very careful killer; the police cannot prove his crime. Although they are suspicious, they cannot charge him. Nonetheless, he is guilty. Walter, not even sufficiently inventive to create his own mode of murder and then not sufficiently calculating or clever to go through with it, is a blunderer. He has left clues and suspicious evidence everywhere for the police to discover. Yet, he is innocent. The police are only reinforced in their unprovable thesis about Kimmel by the plethora of evidence they find against Stackhouse.

Bonding the two men further together in a strange alliance is their response to the police investigation. Initially both protect each other from Corby, a brutal, driven cop who tries to intimidate both Walter (psychologically) and Kimmel (physically). When their mutual protection breaks down, both men rush to betray each other to Corby; only the liar is believed. In a final irony and gesture of angry frustration, Kimmel kills Walter, taking great satisfaction in his death: "There was Stackhouse, any way! Enemy number one!" Captured immediately, Kimmel is caught killing the man who, he believes, murdered him by the blundering imitation which convinced the police.

Ironically, Walter's inability to acknowledge all the truth about his activities to either friends or the police leads to his being shunned. Neighbors too often questioned by the police avoid him; his respectable housekeeper quits; his friend and intended law partner withdraws from the arrangement; finally, his new girlfriend, a sensitive and affectionate violinist and children's music teacher, frustrated by his persistent evasions and new stories, begins to suspect him and ends their relationship. Even as Clara alive had alienated his friends, he too, responding to her death, achieves the same effect. His alienation is both the cause and effect of Walter's being forced into an isolated position where he feels compelled to create his own reality, ordering events which have no apparent basis in fact.

Walter Stackhouse's almost compulsive fascination with his counterpart is part of his cycle of "unworthy friendships." The ones he had documented for his essays clearly invoked an aura of power whereby the superior friend maintained his status through this relationship. And yet, in the pairing of Stackhouse and Kimmel, Highsmith challenges the foundation of so-called friendship which Walter establishes. The surface of an unworthy friendship implies all power and prestige to the superior partner; yet his dependence on the socially, economically, or morally inferior partner puts him under the second man's power. Should the weaker person withdraw even the slightest, the ostensibly stronger personality would be left without a framework in which to judge himself. Kimmel and Stackhouse articulate this exactly; the imaginative, amoral, clever Melchior Kimmel cannot evade Walter Stackhouse's blundering imitation or undesired attachment. Walter's fascination with this unwilling companion alerts the police and marks his power in the relationship. However, prior to this, his similar fascination had so engaged Walter that he felt compelled to imitate Kimmel's supposed wife-murder, implying that he is actually as powerless to resist Kimmel's subconscious, hypnotic influence as he later is to avoid Kimmel's enraged revenge.

Inverting and reversing concepts of power and powerlessness between the two men, Highsmith here indicates even more clearly her view of human conflict. Frequently, the same issue is raised more covertly in the novels and short stories, shown as male-female struggle. Both men in this novel insist on the unreasonable power which their wives have over them; the extent is more fully described in the Stackhouses' marriage but is implicit also with the Kimmels'. The temporary appearance of female power is shattered, however, when the women are threatened by the power-seeking men. Both women, the novel implies, are justifiably punished; Kimmel shares this attitude when he murders Walter. This parallel suggests a second: in establishing "unworthy friendships," men are looking for the male equivalent of a wife—someone whose inferiority is unquestionable, whose "power" can be manipulated, whose defined existence reinforces the ego of the man who chooses him/her. In Highsmith's novels, true and positive friendships are seen as impossible. Characters feed parasitically off each other, destroying the "friend" for their own needs, having sought someone whose destruction they will not really regret. Even when a character, such as Charley Bruno, sees the relationship as symbiotic—mutual rather than one-sided—he does not recognize how enormously different the intentions of the two friends are. As a result, the same alienation and destruction are inevitable.

The link between power and sexuality is clearly enunciated in *The Two Faces of January,* recognized in England as the best foreign crime novel of 1964 by the British Crime Writers Association. Ostensibly based on the criminal-accomplice alliance between Chester McFarland and Rydal Kenner, their relationship actually begins with Rydal's surprised recognition of Chester's physical resemblance to his recently dead father, an archaeology professor at Harvard. Seeing Chester in this context, Rydal vacillates between relating to Chester himself or to Chester as a shadow of his father with Rydal alternating between his fifteen-year-old self and his current adult stage. The novel is told from the alternating perspectives of the two men filtered through a central consciousness so that their reservations and curiosity about each other are both documented. Meanwhile, the authorial voice is weighing both. This pairing is further complicated by Chester's wife's (Colette) resemblance to Rydal's first love, Agnes, who had accused him of raping her, initiating Rydal's serious conflict with his father. Rydal's attraction to Colette generates his conflict with Chester, the father substitute.

The dual identities which these characters have in Rydal's mind are matched by their multiple aliases, assumed under a variety of circumstances and for different reasons. Chester's phoney stock dealing has led him to use various names in the U.S.; his flight from murder in Greece forces him to purchase two false passports. Colette, deciding at the age of fourteen that she did not like her given name Elizabeth, renamed herself; marriage changes her name again as does flight with Chester. Suspected of murder, Rydal not only obtains a false passport but also poses as an Italian, his fluency in languages allowing him to blend into crowds in Greece, Crete and Paris also.

Similar to their manipulation of names—accurate and false—is the author's and characters' dealing with truth. Rydal has a juvenile criminal record because of Agnes' accusation of rape and an attempted grocery robbery in bitterness and anger at being disbelieved; nonetheless, he is no criminal. Chester McFarland, who has escaped suspicion, owes his income to deception and fraud, his continued freedom to

murdering a Greek police officer, and his conflict with Rydal to the killing of his own wife in an attempt to murder Rydal. However, they both protect and expose each other in the police investigation triggered anew by Colette's death; the unspoken and unacknowledged between them keeps each committed to the other. Finally, in his deathbed confession, Chester continues to lie, freeing Rydal from all voluntary participation in either murder or flight to escape arrest.

> **Highsmith takes a grim look at the darker side of human nature, revealing the innate capacity of everyone for violence, even murder.**
> —*Kathleen Gregory Klein*

It is continually clear that Chester's parental resemblance persists in its influence. Chester's protection of him, clearing him of complicity in any of Chester's crimes, demonstrates a faith in Rydal's essential decency and reverses his father's harsher judgment on that same point twelve years earlier. Rydal considers his own behavior, perhaps also reflecting on the past:

> He did not by any means emerge a hero, nor did his behavior appear very intelligent, but none of his actions was labelled criminal.

The final note of reconciliation with his past, father, and himself is signaled in Rydal's decision to attend Chester's funeral although he had deliberately bypassed his own father's, because "Chester deserved more than that." In this, Rydal rounds off his adolescence and frees himself to return to the States. As his paternal grandmother's money, willed as a sign of her belief in him, had freed Rydal to escape to Europe, Chester's money, extorted in exchange for silence and freedom, sends Rydal back home.

In himself, Chester McFarland is not an especially interesting character. A petty criminal in terms of his types of crime if not his financial success, his only complexity comes from Rydal's interest in and confusion about him. Before the police official's death, he is friendly and fairly easygoing; he kills almost by accident, shows little remorse or fear and is surprised by his wife's more emotional response. His attempt to murder Rydal comes from male sexual jealousy and possessiveness over Colette and Rydal's mutual attraction; though he fails to eliminate his rival, Chester does break up the flirtation by killing his wife instead. His reaction is proportionally more one of anger at Rydal for having escaped than of sadness or self-directed anger.

On the other hand, Rydal Kenner is a psychologically complex and even confusing character. Throughout the novel, his actions and reactions are based on a mixture of feelings of anger and betrayal at fifteen and his adult attempt to feel reconciled with his father through an intense attraction to and rejection of Chester McFarland. Immediately involved in Chester's criminal activities, the reverse of his relationship with his own stern father who had him sent to reform school, Rydal begins to confuse the two men, superimposing the image of one over the other. No longer the less knowledgeable child, Rydal assists the unprepared McFarlands, through his knowledge of Greece and the language, to obtain false passports and escape notice; this knowledge is ironically the result of his father's disciplined teaching in Rydal's childhood. Rydal's response to Colette's flirtation because she reminds him of his first love offers him the opportunity to justify his adolescent behavior, avenge the rape charge, punish his father for being wrong, and take advantage of Chester. The mutual seduction of young Rydal and Agnes is superseded by the flirtations seduction of Colette; when she changes her mind, Rydal's acceptance of that decision despite his aroused feelings vindicates his former claims of innocence. Because they never slept together, although Rydal taunts Chester with the idea that they did, he is able to manipulate the sexual situation as Agnes had done, hurting the father substitute/husband.

In most of Highsmith's works sexuality correlates with power and possessiveness. Men generally don't like women as people; Charley Bruno merely speaks more openly than most about the opposite sex as a whole rather than a specific individual:

> ('What significance did it have for you that your victim was female?') . . . Well, the fact that she was female had given him greater enjoyment. No, he did not therefore conclude that his pleasure had partaken of the sexual. No, he did not hate women either. Rather not! Hate is akin to love, you know . . . No, all he would say was that he wouldn't have enjoyed it quite so much, he thought, if he had killed a man (**Stranger**).

This unadmitted hatred is tied to possessiveness in two ways: jealousy and envy. Men wish to possess both women themselves and what women seem to have simultaneously. To do this, it becomes necessary to destroy women physically or psychologically. Chester McFarland insures permanent ownership of his wife through her death and from this he also gains Colette's possession—Rydal Kenner and his fascination. For Rydal, who had never possessed her in either sexual or legal terms, her murder had to be avenged not so much for her loss as for his own.

This stereotyping of male-female relationships as little more than potentially destructive sexual encounters is typical in Highsmith's fiction. Several causes are worth considering:

first, she has totally absorbed social attitudes and is unconscious of the anti-woman tone; second, she is acknowledging a mind-set on the part of her readers which is too strongly ingrained to be easily overthrown; third, having challenged the boundaries of her genre in so many other arenas, she is unwilling to force the issue. Certainly not arguable in most cases is the theory that the portraits of women are ironically inverted as critic Tom Paulin notes of **Misogyny** (and the point is valid elsewhere): "[I]t would be wrong to read these stories as indirectly feminist satires on dependency because the real centre of their inspiration is the delight Patricia Highsmith everywhere shows for the brutal ways in which these unlikely women are first murdered and then 'thrown away as one might throw away a cricket lighter when it is used up.'" Paulin's "everywhere" must, however, be modified, as must any judgment of Highsmith's treatment of women, to acknowledge her 1977 novel **Edith's Diary**. Even here, however, the revisionist treatment of women is covertly presented.

Not usually considered a suspense novel, **Edith's Diary** is unique in Highsmith's canon for its female protagonist. The novel is ostensibly the story of a former New York housewife and writer's move to rural Pennsylvania and of the years which follow during which her son drinks, fantasizes and can't hold a job; her husband divorces her and remarries; his invalid uncle finally dies and Edith's favorite great aunt and supporter dies. Throughout, Edith records these events and others which never happened in a large leather-bound diary she has had since college. It is her confidante and her escape. Finally, her friends and ex-husband accuse her of mental instability and an incomplete grasp of reality; trying to disprove them, she is accidentally killed. In fact, the novel is anything but what it appears to be. Unlike her counterparts in other novels, Edith is never acknowledged as a victim nor is her death seen as murder. While no single individual is actually responsible for killing her, Edith dies as a result of society's pressure to conform to a female stereotype urged on her by her ex-husband. As a representative of the larger community, Brett Howland stifles Edith's psychological life and contributes to the circumstances which lead to her physical death.

In **Edith's Diary,** Highsmith is following in the tradition of nineteenth century women writers who disguised their tales of anger and frustration in the more conventional and acceptable cloak of punishing women for their independent behavior. As recent feminist literary criticism has noted, a pattern of action was developed in which the assertive, strong-willed, intelligent female character suffered one of three inevitable fates: insanity, suicide, or death, as apparently logical outgrowths of and altogether commendable punishment for their behavior. What critics have also noted, however, is the way women writers have used these surface stories to hide their more subversive underlying message. Certainly, Charlotte Bronte and Charlotte Perkins Gilman provide perfect examples of this; Jane Eyre and the nameless narrator-writer of "The Yellow Wallpaper" are Edith Howland's literary ancestors. They write their own stories because they are unable to create their own lives; Edith's diary becomes a novel, like Highsmith's, in which the woman writer tells two stories.

The surface story of Edith's growing madness and apparent personality change is told in two ways: by her ex-husband and her friend, Gert Johnson, and through her diary entries. The people who know her become convinced that she is changing, that she is no longer in control of her own sanity. They verify this change by pointing to four specific activities which they cannot understand and do not wish to accept. Edith, they say, has become unusually and excessively argumentative to the point where she is willing to alienate friends and acquaintances; she has become increasingly conservative in her attitudes and proposes more authoritarian institutions in her writings; she has published parodies or fantasies in underground newspapers. Finally, she has refused a $10,000 check from her husband who offers it as part of the estate of his dead uncle. For the casual reader, Edith's diary entries reinforce the charges of instability: she invents a happy, successful marriage and life for her son Cliffie whose amoral and lazy behavior has remained unchanged since his childhood; and, after their divorce, she writes of her ex-husband Brett's death, not his actual remarriage and new family. In emphasizing her happiness and satisfaction, Edith's diary entries seem directly contradictory to her reality in which anger and frustration surface daily over the divorce and having to continue to care for Brett's invalid, incontinent Uncle George while Brett and his new family avoid the daily responsibility and expense.

If this evidence seems weighted against Edith, it rapidly becomes apparent that the submerged story, carefully revealed and concealed, makes a different point. At the novel's opening, Edith is a young married mother. Her husband wants to live in the country which he believes their child needs and deserves. Although Edith agrees to move, she is not sure she accepts Brett's rationale. Apparently happy in their new home, Edith becomes more tied to her family; even the local newspaper they try to start jointly has Brett, the professional, as the final authority. And, although he delegates the responsibility for their son Cliffie, Brett's advice and criticism make it clear that he still wishes to control how she handles the boy. The pattern is continued when his Uncle George comes to live in the extra room which was to have been Edith's study; almost alone, she cares for the selfish old man. Nonetheless, she has some illusions of control over her own life; she believes she participates in the decisions which direct her life. When Brett divorces her, leaving George and Cliffie behind, pressing money and, later psychiatrists on Edith, she begins to recognize how few of the decisions reflected her own choice.

Unable to change the divorce, Cliffie, or George, Edith takes control of her life in two logical ways: her social opinions alter and her diary records a better life. It is certainly plausible that the liberal Edith should gradually become more conservative and even propose stricter, more authoritarian measures in some of her articles. Even as others have controlled her life, she is demanding a place to control also. Having lost power in her own actual world without being aware of it, she gropes for another part of the world where her knowledge, experience, talent or mere presence will offer her some escape from a powerless position. Yet she also continues to write for *Shove It,* an underground magazine, which accepts a fantasy deliberately more extreme than her actual beliefs, almost as though to demonstrate how varied her opinions are. In this, she seems to believe that by constantly changing the grounds of her argument, by persistently refusing to be forced into any mold, she can avoid the judgment and limitations society—in the pernicious form of family and friends—seeks to impose upon her.

The diary entries, which seem to demonstrate Edith's decline, are actually very carefully introduced, making clear her awareness of the life she is creating for herself in exchange for the one others would like to force on her:

> Edith had in the last month decided that Brett should be dead since about three years now. It didn't matter that this conflicted with George's demise and funeral service. Edith was writing her diary for pleasure, and was taking poetic license, as she put it to herself.

While she does not consistently insist on this fictive approach, occasional reminders do surface to alert the aware reader of her deliberate and conscious creation of an alternative reality. Aware that her husband and friend know that she mistrusts their plotting to get her to see a psychiatrist, Edith, nonetheless, tries to placate them—"make a gesture of goodwill!" Offering to show them a piece of her sculpture, she trips carrying it down the stairs, hits her head and dies. While falling she "thought of injustice, felt her personal sense of injustice combined now with the crazy complex injustice of the Vietnam situation . . . ."

Parallels with the Vietnam war are not inappropriate in this covertly feminist novel; at issue is the repeated question of power and superiority. The traditional American male, secure in the knowledge that his point of view is always accurate, saw himself rushing to defend the smaller and weaker nation of Vietnam as he sees himself hurrying chivalrously to assist the weaker sex, all the time despising these "gooks" and "broads." In unconsciously deliberate power plays, he destroys both. Edith's attempt to placate society, to convince it to leave her alone, are the gestures of the subordinate; her failure to achieve even understanding or an independent life is inevitable. The demands she makes challenge the established order's view of itself and threaten the hierarchical arrangement of power and status.

If *Strangers on a Train* is the model for Highsmith's later work, then *The Storyteller* presents a paradigmatic overview of her non-series novels. Highsmith must have enjoyed writing this compendium of good and bad murder-detective-suspense tales enormously. In a short story, **"The Man Who Wrote Books in his Head,"** she creates a protagonist who so completely wrote and polished his novels mentally that he felt no need of committing them to paper; even on his deathbed he is able to quote passages accurately, although he has obviously remembered only some of his works. It is certainly true that, with the exception of Walter Stackhouse, all of Highsmith's characters are inventive and imaginative, however, in no other work as compared with *The Storyteller* do their stories intersect and yet so completely miss the mark since, after all, the murder they describe here never happens.

The victim is Alicia Bartleby whose accidental death actually follows the investigation of her suspected murder. Accused by a neighbor and his partner is Sidney Bartleby, a novelist and television scriptwriter. Complicating Sid's defense is the diary he kept after Alicia's departure for a secret rendezvous with her lover. Wishing to experience guilt in order to use the material in his writing, Sid has fantasized Alicia's murder and recorded the details in his diary. Hoping to clear himself, he tracks his wife; when she later dies, Sid forces her lover to commit suicide, believing him guilty of Alicia's death.

The novel is an unusual one in Highsmith's canon with far less of the overt brooding and dark atmosphere which marks most of her work; it is even more striking for its apparent lack of or interest in violence until the very end. These factors combine to give a misleading surface impression of the story and the author's intentions. Although the work seems more benign, even positive and relatively harmless, it is actually more negative and critical of human inclination to crime and violence than her more blatant murder novels. Couched almost entirely in stories, fantasies, inventions, novels and TV scripts, the substance of the book seems distinct but unthreatening; the characters seem inventive but non-violent. In fact, the very complex and satisfactory quality of their fantasies seems, through eighty percent of the book, to replace the need for action. Insidiously, Highsmith makes the reader laugh, approve, even easily identify with the story-makers, especially Sid; for who has not imagined what he would never wish to do?

Because Sidney and Alicia Bartleby have marital problems, they decide to separate briefly, she deliberately not telling him that she's going to Brighton where she hopes to meet a new lover, Edward Tilbury. A writer with a growing sense of hostility, Sidney has little success selling his ironically named novel *The Planners*. Having often imagined the details of murdering many people, including his wife, Sidney decides to use Alicia's departure as an opportunity to visualize her dead and himself the murderer. He even keeps a notebook to help him feel like a real criminal, noting actions and reactions as if for a novel: "Sidney thought automatically and as impersonally as if he were thinking about the actions of a character in a story." When the police find the notebook, Sidney explains his view of it: "The narrative—descriptions in the notebook—is not true. You might say the ideas in it are true. I mean, it's not a diary of facts."

Including Sidney's, which is the most elaborate and most imaginative, six different stories intersect throughout this novel, delighting the reader by Highsmith's adroit parallels. The Bartlebys' neighbor, Mrs. Lillybanks, constructs hers around having seen Sid carrying a rolled carpet over his shoulder out of the house at dawn on the day after Alicia had left. Carrying the carpet as though it contained a heavy body, Sid is fantasizing murder; Mrs. Lillybanks suspects him of just that. Sid's partner in writing TV scripts has a much more self-centered version of the story; Alex Polk-Faraday blackmails Sid for a larger share of their joint royalties when the police are investigating. Refused, he tells a version of Alicia's murder story which claims to take seriously his and Sid's joking repartee about wife-murderers. Unlike Mrs. Lillybanks who has cause for suspicion and remains silent, Alex accuses Sid to the police. Meanwhile, Alicia, under an assumed name, and her lover are deliberately hiding out, refusing to respond to police information requests in the newspaper. Alicia's version of events is based on embarrassment at having to admit where she's been and what she's done; the longer she hides, the deeper this difficulty goes. Edward Tilbury, on the other hand, commutes weekly to his office in London where he tells the false story of his weekend whereabouts over several months. Concerned primarily for his reputation, he urges Alicia to respond to the police; she, with the same concern, refuses. Overlying all these inventions is Sid's newest TV character, The Whip:

> The Whip would be a criminal character who did something ghastly in every episode. . . . The audience saw everything through the Whip's eyes, did everything with him, finally plugged for him through thick and thin and hoped the police would fail, which they always did. He wouldn't carry a whip or anything like that, but the nickname would be suggestive of depraved and secret habits. . . . He has no police record, because he has always been too clever for the police. And he started young, of course. No,

that couldn't be conveyed, because The Whip had no intimates with whom he talked. That would be part of the fascination: the audience wouldn't know what was on The Whip's mind until he started doing things.

Sidney thinks about his journal of Alicia's "murder" and episodes of The Whip: the former "gave Sidney a pleasant feeling of both creating something and of being a murderer"; the latter undoubtedly reinforced it.

Eventually Sidney becomes a killer but not as he had expected, nor is Alicia the victim. Instead, he seems to be responsible for Mrs. Lillybanks' heart attack: he believes she may have died from fear of him. He also forces Edward Tilbury to commit suicide, inaccurately suspecting him of having pushed Alicia off a cliff. Neither death is a conventional murder; neither can be attributed to him. Like The Whip, he eludes capture and is more clever than his detractors; he even recognizes that he could safely write the facts of Tilbury's death in his notebook without attracting police suspicion.

Sidney's claim and belief that he is punishing Tilbury is debatable. It seems far more likely that his actions result from sexual jealousy, guilt for suppressed hostility against Alicia, revenge for the difficulties their hiding out cost him and anger for Tilbury's apparently having done, in supposedly murdering Alicia, what Sidney himself is able only to fantasize doing. Finally, moving confidently and aggressively against Tilbury, he is able to become his own character, to create himself.

Rootless or dissatisfied, Highsmith's characters often need, like Sidney Bartleby, to create themselves. In one of two ways, Highsmith defines this self-creation or re-creation through the concept of dualities which regularly appears in her novels. First, two characters are bonded together in a love-hate relationship as one tries to absorb the essential qualities of the other so that the two seem as one. Charley Bruno does this with Guy Haines in *Stranger,* leading both of them to murder and rejection; Walter Stackhouse imposes himself on Melchior Kimmel with both success and failure. Otherwise, a single character, equally unsettled about his own nature and personality, divides into two, becoming both what he was and what he hopes to be. Colette McFarland (*January*) changed her name as a teenager to feel like a different person; Edith Howland writes a second self. In *This Sweet Sickness,* David Kelsey functions normally in his work world while simultaneously constructing a fantasy-marriage, decorating a home and having conversations with his imaginary bride. With unsatisfying self-images, these characters require an alternative mirror to the one which reflects reality. They remake the world to conform to their needs, even if that leads to murder and violence.

In certain ways, they would all like to emulate Sidney's creation, The Whip. Defined in a phrase—"The Whip acts"— this character serves as a standard against which all Highsmith's characters measure themselves. The reader feels much like the projected TV audience; in the latter case motivation is unknown because The Whip shares none of his thoughts with friends. In the novels, psychological and emotional attitudes are presented and analyzed but no conclusion is ever clearly and incontrovertibly reached. Characters often seem to act and especially to kill, for reasons other than those articulated by the text. If The Whip is a model of the unknowable killer-of-action, then his direct and mirror images among Highsmith's protagonists are like him in the acting and unlike him in being as unknown to themselves as to their audiences. Too few see themselves clearly; their self-images are informed by fantasy and desire.

III

Highsmith's only series character, Tom Ripley, appears in four novels published between 1955 and 1980: *The Talented Mr. Ripley,* which won both the Mystery Writers of America Scroll and the Grand Prix de Litterature Policiere, *Ripley under Ground, Ripley's Game* and *The Boy Who Followed Ripley.* Because even the first novel is based more on character alone than on the combination of character development within a self-ending plot and because Tom himself is likeable despite his criminal actions, the Ripley character is one of the few Highsmith creations who can continue. He bears some resemblance to Rydal Kenner in *The Two Faces of January*; in fact, both Ripley and the young man he befriends in *The Boy Who Followed Ripley* are like Rydal in their attempts to escape and yet understand the past, to know themselves and comprehend their own often implausible actions. The Ripley novels are also made more interesting in having the usual traits of a series: the recurring cast of supporting characters including his wife, housekeeper, criminal associates and even his first murder victim, Dickie Greenleaf; familiar and new aspects of the protagonist are developed as former episodes and established traits are woven into each additional novel—music, art, the American-in-Europe character. Tom Ripley remains recognizably familiar yet develops interesting aspects as he matures.

The young Tom Ripley introduced in *The Talented Mr. Ripley,* is gauche, uncertain and not quite immoral or guiltless; he has a strong sense of inferiority and an intense desire to change his lifestyle and himself. Several typical patterns are established here and continue with slight variations in the subsequent novels: the mixture of sympathy and justification Tom feels, his desire to get and then protect exactly what he wants and feels he deserves, his isolation which is not loneliness, and his willingness to kill. The last is the least interesting in itself. The reader's real fascination with Ripley comes from the mixture of all his other tendencies with that one, from questions about the absence of guilt and of any ordinary pangs of conscience.

At the novel's opening, Ripley is reasonably worried about being followed from one bar to another by a stranger since he has been operating an IRS scam. Although the potential difficulty works out well, in accord with Tom's philosophy that "something always turned up," the Ripley status and attitude are established. First, he has cause to be always on guard; secondly, he manages to escape detection. The meeting he has with Dickie Greenleaf's father and the subsequent commission to convince his distant acquaintance, Dickie, to return home from Europe give Tom what he hopes will be an opportunity for a new life. He dwells on his rejection, deprivation, modest and unfulfilled childhood desires and hopes to succeed. Like Lambert Strether in Henry James' *The Ambassadors,* Tom fails completely in his assignment, the results satisfying him and disappointing his employer. Ironically, this "job" does lead him to a new life, but not as he had anticipated—he does not become the smart, well dressed, clever and successful American in Europe.

Perhaps the results of his trip ought to have been apparent from his interview: he lies to the Greenleafs about how well he knows their son, his education, his former jobs and tells them the truth only about having been orphaned and raised by an aunt. Yet, "he had felt uncomfortable, unreal, the way he might have felt if he had been lying, yet it had been practically the only thing he had said that *was* true." Feeling rejected by Dickie and his girlfriend and also by Mr. Greenleaf's businesslike letters when he cannot convince Dickie to return home, Tom assuages his genuinely hurt feelings by imitating Dickie, wearing his clothes and mimicking his voice. Caught at it, he is embarrassed and his hurt, angry feelings grow:

> He hated Dickie, because however he looked at what had happened, his failing had not been his own fault, not due to anything he had done but to Dickie's inhuman stubbornness. And his blatant rudeness! He had offered Dickie friendship, companionship, and respect, everything he had to offer, and Dickie had replied with ingratitude and now hostility. Dickie was just shoving him out in the cold.

For this, he feels justified in murdering Dickie.

Although Tom occasionally, and once in particular, regrets having killed Dickie and wishes he could change what had happened, he is more often pleased with his cleverness in evading discovery by Dickie's friends and family or the police, in masquerading successfully as Dickie and in forging a will making himself Dickie's heir. It is this last success which finally frees Tom from his early awkwardness, feel-

ing of inferiority and needing the world to approve of him; it gratifies his desire for luxury, importance, self-justification and getting away with something.

When he reappears in *Ripley under Ground,* Tom has married the daughter of a wealthy businessman and provided himself with an income by participating in an art fraud where forgeries are passed off as the work of a reclusive painter who actually has committed suicide. Disguise is again an important motif as Tom impersonates the painter Derwatt as he impersonated Dickie Greenleaf. Determined again to protect his possessions, he poses successfully and kills where necessary. In this novel, Ripley's material acquisitions and personal taste form an important part of the development of his character; the opportunity to create himself and his life has been used in ways which satisfy him:

> Tom loved his leisure, however, as only an American could, he thought—once an American got the hang of it, and so few did. It was not a thing he cared to put into words to anyone. He had longed for leisure and a bit of luxury when he had met Dickie Greenleaf, and now that he had attained it, the charm had not palled.

As well as any other example in the novel, this clarifies his state of mind. He is complacent and self-satisfied, almost a bit smug and superior about others who can not achieve as he has; while the stated goal is appreciation, the means to it was murder—which presumably others could also not handle. He demonstrates no pangs of conscience or remorse; his pleasure is not dimmed by the memory of how it was obtained. Like Sid Bartleby, David Kelsey, and Edith Howland, he has assumed another identity in which his actions are reasonable and logical, his rewards deserved and justified.

The three legal and ordinary pleasures which he enjoys are introduced here and developed in subsequent novels: gardening, music and art. His illegally obtained incomes help him build a greenhouse, purchase a harpsichord and collect fine paintings, both real and forged. Music especially becomes a leitmotif as Ripley uses different types or even individual pieces in varying circumstances to alter or improve his mood. Preparing to impersonate the painter Derwatt, he sends his colleague out to purchase a copy of *A Midsummer Night's Dream* to inspire him. Jazz, on the other hand, does nothing for him in crucial moments—"only classical music did something . . . because it had order, and one either accepted that order or rejected it." After a successful shootout with the Mafia and destruction of the bodies, he discusses Bach with his dazed companion, describing the composer's work as instantly civilizing.

Because he is not so frantic for acceptance or affection as he had been with Dickie Greenleaf and because he is now more mature about his role in relationships, Tom can be more introspective about his marriage. Neither sex nor his wife Heloise's family money concern Tom as much as their shared disrespectful partnership, their ability to laugh together at conventional attitudes, their similar though not equal amorality. However, no matter how important she is to him and how much confidence he has in her, he does not tell her what he does or where his money comes from, although she suspects both. Even in lovemaking he preserves a certain separation which might be "shyness or puritanism . . . or some fear of (mentally) giving himself completely" but may also be a positive pleasure experienced from the "inanimate, unreal, from a body without an identity." And yet, humanly contradictory, he does not want to be rejected, salving his ego when people who've heard rumors about his reputation withdraw by the knowledge that most people really liked him when they got to know him better in his own home where he has created an ambiance of culture, taste and friendliness which charms them. The reader shares his neighbors' vacillating judgments of Tom, subtly drawn to like him despite distaste and revulsion for his actions by Highsmith's refusal to relinquish these contradictions in his portrait.

Perhaps one of Highsmith's great strengths is in making readers nervous and uncomfortable with her talent.
—*Kathleen Gregory Klein*

Ripley's contradictions certainly extend to his crimes and murders: while he gives the impression of being willing to bypass violence and additional crime so long as he can protect his safety and income, he also kills without squeamishness or regret and commits minor crimes virtually without thinking about them except when the arrangements inconvenience him. There is a strange quirk of logic in all but the first novel which allows his actions to seem finally justifiable. The cruelest of Ripley's actions is no crime at all: because cancer victim Jonathan Trevanny had, Tom thought, sneered at him, Ripley begins a cruel game in ***Ripley's Game*** to drag the cancer victim into a scheme to murder two Mafia men. He wants to "make Jonathan Trevanny who Tom sensed was priggish and self righteous, uneasy for a time." Ripley succeeds, but Trevanny, who kills one Mafia man alone and three more in Ripley's company, becomes estranged from his wife and child, confused and guilty and finally dies in another shootout. Although Tom recognizes the role of his own curiosity and later tries to help Trevanny accomplish the murders and make peace with his wife, the casual manner in which he sets all this trauma in motion and his suggestion that medical records be falsified to prod Trevanny to further action are thoughtlessly and needlessly callous. In the end, Ripley can even feel virtuous because the victims were Mafia—"there were people

more dishonest, more corrupt, decidedly more ruthless than himself"—and because Trevanny's wife, having not helped the police, seems as corrupt as "much of the rest of the world."

Mixed motives regularly dog Ripley's decisions. To protect the Derwatt forgery schemes, he believes that he would "*lay my soul bare, show him the poems I've written to Heloise, take my clothes off and do a sword dance. . . .*" (***Ripley under Ground***): instead, he murders. Death and deception are justified in the name of Bernard Tufts, Derwatt's close friend, admirer, and forger whose conscience drives him toward suicide. Telling himself that he's going to help Tufts, Ripley half consciously urges him toward death, making Tufts doubt his vision and sanity. With this death, two of Ripley's problems seem solved: Tufts cannot now reveal the forgery scheme and his burned corpse can be falsely identified as Derwatt. Though he thinks he might have preferred another outcome, Tom knows he consciously worked the situation out as he really wanted. Even Ripley's apparently generous offer to help runaway Frank Pierson in ***The Boy Who Followed Ripley*** return to his family and reject his own feelings of guilt at having pushed his crippled father off a cliff is motivated, in part, by Tom's seeing himself in the boy and wanting to recreate and thus justify his own behavior. How far apart the two are is registered in Tom's attitude about guilt:

> How was Frank ever going to achieve the big justification, which would take away all his guilt? He might never find a total justification, but he had to find an attitude. Every mistake in life, Tom thought, had to be met by an attitude, either the right attitude or the wrong one, a constructive or self-destructive attitude. What was tragedy for one man was not for another, if he could assume the right attitude toward it. Frank felt guilt, which was why he had looked up Tom Ripley, curiously Tom had never felt such guilt, never let it seriously trouble him. In this, Tom realized that he was odd. Most people would have experienced insomnia, bad dreams, especially after committing a murder such as that of Dickie Greenleaf, but Tom had not (***Boy***).

Yet, in taking Frank to Berlin, giving him time to plan, rescuing him from kidnappers and flying home to the States with him, Ripley shows understanding and compassion which almost no one else could. However, his inability to understand Frank's guilt and need for personal salvation eventually contribute to the boy's suicide. Tom's sympathy and recognition of his failure to comprehend leave him as vulnerable as he had been with Dickie Greenleaf's rejection and no more certain how to cope with it.

Tom's guiltlessness and apparent inability to comprehend

guilt feelings in others are among the strongest impressions a reader receives from the Ripley series. In the four books Tom participates in over a dozen murders, three extended fraudulent schemes, four major betrayals of trust and dozens of minor crimes. Only infrequently and briefly is he ever even willing to consider the morality of his decisions or the ethical nature of his behavior. Highsmith's conception of the criminal-hero as a superior person (expressed in *Plotting*) is manifest in Tom Ripley's creation of himself. Once he has justified, however briefly and inadequately, lying to Dickie Greenleaf's father in order to secure the trip to Europe, he recreates himself. Rejecting his unpleasant childhood, all the memories and all the lessons learned in it, he becomes a new-born. His schooling both on the ship and in Italy convince Tom of the futility of moral behavior. Not immoral but thoroughly amoral, he accepts no standards of judgment which would undermine his new status and freedom. In the clear-cut contrast between himself and Frank Pierson, Tom is genuinely bewildered. Intellectually, he knows that some people feel guilty; he takes advantage of this in dealing with them. Emotionally, he no longer comprehends the feeling. Self-serving and self-protective, Tom recognizes that to atone himself to guilt would inhibit his financial and criminal success; so he perseveres in his chosen ignorance of guilt and rejects circumstances which would force the sensation upon him.

Because Tom Ripley, like few other Highsmith protagonists, is a calculating criminal whose behavior is both conscious and deliberate, he poses a dilemma for the reader. On the one side, his actions and their consequences are vicious and destructive; he can be neither enjoyed nor admired in that light. On the other, his motivations and choices are clearly and logically debated; there is a certain fascination to the way his mind works which can intrigue and attract a reader who is simultaneously repulsed. Tom's criminality seems to fit him; it is a part of his everyday life. Side by side in his living room hang two "Derwatt" paintings, one real and the other—"in the place of honor"—forged. He recognizes his preference for the forgery despite his judgment that the other is better art. This image may also represent his life where ordinary activities stand next to criminal ones, the latter usurping the primary place in his life. For the reader, the disconcerting blend of real and ordinary with forgery and crime may discompose; but, at least here, readers understand how Tom operates and where his priorities intersect.

IV

Having considered the extraordinary talent and vitality which Highsmith brings to the genre, as well as the innovations and expansions she uses to extend its limits, the conclusion to this essay is an appropriate place to speculate on her reception by readers. Julian Symons, who admires her work, calling her "the most important crime novelist at present in

practice," also recounts an anecdote about mystery publisher and fan Victor Gollancz regarding Highsmith's novels. Having read *The Two Faces of January,* Gollancz declined to read her works further. Symons wryly remarks that Highsmith is an acquired taste which some never manage. It is possible to analyze, admire and value her contributions to fiction without having acquired the taste and, even, without particularly wishing to read her next published work. While admiration and pleasure need not always go hand-in-hand, some consideration of the divergent feelings her work provokes illuminates her intention.

In establishing the novels' frameworks, atmospheres and, often, characters, Highsmith seems to be providing a realistic perspective. Details are sharp and accurate; settings are reliable, characters behave in ways observable in society at large. While readers of classical puzzle-mysteries look for an intellectual challenge and fans of the hard-boiled expect psychological truth and action, no reader of crime or mystery fiction anticipates deliberate violations of realism. In such circumstances, puzzles cannot be solved or criminals' moves anticipated. Nonetheless, Highsmith violates this convention; unbelievable details, actions, psychology or motives sit side-by-side with realistic elements. If the readers were merely confused, disoriented, or annoyed by these juxtapositions, the novels could be rejected as failures. However, although these reactions are shared by Highsmith's audience, this response must be separate from the judgments. Perhaps one of Highsmith's great strengths is in making readers nervous and uncomfortable with her talent.

Chief among Highsmith's deviations is her presentation of psychological motivation. The characters seem so much like known and understood people in the everyday world that their decisions to kill are unanticipated, unpredicted and baffling. Because the murderers are such ordinary people, the readers initially identify and empathize with them. Highsmith uses the narrators' varieties of omniscience to create sympathy for the protagonist; she manipulates readers to like her characters and understand their lives and feelings. She draws her readers into recognizing themselves in most of the characters' action and behavior. Then a character murders; the readers are faced with accepting Guy Haines' discovery that anyone has the capacity for killing given the right circumstances. Rejecting this idea, which would force them to see themselves as potential murders, the readers attempt to retrace the character's psychological state, mental attitude and reasoning patterns which led to the decision to kill. Frequently, there are none; or, more accurately, none really matter. Only the intersection of victim, killer and circumstances make this occasion different from others. The crime-solution game of conventional detective novels becomes a new kind of psychological scavenger hunt in which all the clues either mislead or direct the readers to vacant lots. Without the explanations which allow the readers a comfortable place from which to contrast themselves and the murderer, their avoidance mechanisms are employed for self-protection. They become irritated with the character, seeing ways in which circumstances could have been avoided, loopholes sought and danger eluded. In this process of criticism and distancing, readers often confuse their dislike for the characters and discomfort with the criminal activity for a valid critique of the novel and its author.

In challenging the readers' self-image of safe innocence and protective, benign behavior, Highsmith risks alienating her audience. Her canon of twenty-two crime books indicates more clearly than any single evaluation how willing she is to take such risks. Her characters are too much like and yet too unlike her audience to be attractive and appealing; their behavior is too close to the dark ruthlessly hidden side of human personality; their actions, however, much they may correspond with readers' fantasies, are too disruptive to be allowed. In showing us ourselves, Highsmith takes the elements of her given genre and creates a sharp, new fictional form.

Ursula Hegi (review date 6 April 1986)

SOURCE: A review of *Little Tales of Misogyny*, in *New York Times Book Review*, Vol. 91, April 6, 1986, p. 22.

[*In the following review, Hegi criticizes Highsmith's portrayal of women in* Little Tales of Misogyny.]

Punishment is the central theme of this collection of stories about women that was first published in a German translation in the mid-70s. The titles of the stories give an indication of their content: **"The Mobile Bed-Object," "The Middle-Class Housewife," "The Breeder," "The Fully-Licensed Whore, or, The Wife."** Patricia Highsmith's women destroy men and, as a result, most of them are punished. Yvonne, "The Coquette," is killed by two of her suitors "with various blows about the head." Claudette, "The Dancer," is strangled by her partner for refusing to sleep with him. Mildred, the bed-object, is dumped into a canal and drowned. "She had been thrown away, as one might throw away a cricket lighter when it is used up, like a paperback one has read." Catherine, "The Victim," wears makeup and platform boots though she isn't even 12; her rapes are portrayed as a direct result of her appearance: "As time went on, when Cathy complained about rape, her parents paid not much attention. After all, Cathy had been on The Pill." Patricia Highsmith is the author of several books, including ***The Animal-Lover's Book of Beastly Murder*** and ***Ripley under Ground***. In *Little Tales of Misogyny* she uses her women characters to perpetuate the worst stereotypes. Her selection of titles certainly indicates that she is aware of the

hatred of women that fills the pages of her book, but this awareness does not make up for it. Her tales seem intended to be witty and sarcastic; yet they come across as shallow and vicious.

Christopher Ricks (review date 7 August 1986)

SOURCE: "Death for Elsie," in *London Review of Books*, Vol. 8, No. 14, August 7, 1986, p. 21.

[*In the following excerpt, Ricks provides a positive review of* Found in the Street, *focusing on Highsmith's depiction of crime and her portrayal of the protagonist, Elsie Tyler.*]

Patricia Highsmith has been praised by Graham Greene in the good old way as 'a writer who has created a world of her own'. She can be even better than that—when she takes a world and makes it not only her own but ours. She lurks in the murk where you have to peer to check if this is an—or the—underworld. In her seething city-settings, paranoia may be the saving of you, and yet paranoia does have, too, a hideously masochistic alluring power. She is the poet of these death-bearing pheromones of fear.

Found in the Street is her exact territory; she patrols these Greenwich Village streets as if from a neighbourhood vigilante force. Strangers on a powder-train. She knows crime well, especially in its intimacy with sin and with frustration; she watches for the selfish illiberality of paid-up progressives and for the malfeasances of the Watch Committee, for prurience and high-minded corruption. As a novelist she is herself placed in this grey area or combat zone: should the new Highsmith be sent for review to the supreme fiction people or to the crime squad? She capitalises candidly on these equivocations: Her studies of alienation are at once very literary and allusive and entirely untrammelled by fictive thickenings and alienation-effects. If she is more than admired by, actually is read by, highbrows, this is partly because there is just now a special relief in so unfurrowed a writer from 'the underworld of letters'.

The phrase is T. S. Eliot's. His breach between the underworld of letters and 'serious writers', even though he judged the former (like the music hall as against 'serious' theatre) to be the more healthy in many ways, is one which Highsmith's art both concedes and does something to heal. Their cities, Eliot's and hers, are weightily real and phantasmagorically unreal. 'That subway smell was of old metal-on-metal, of oily dust moist with human breath, the semi-trapped air.' Questions of reality are crucial to Highsmith, but—as to Eliot—they are spiritual questions, not philosophical ones: spiritual, and instinct with the spiritual's fear of an alliance between erotic and economic forces. Elsie Tyler, the victim in *Found in the Street* (or the victim who, unlike the others, has a sudden dying, not a long day's one), is dead-set for success, garish and enslaved, in the world of glossy modelling and of lip-service to art, an underworld of unreality which comes on as the overworld. Highsmith's anger, dismay and pity at such a world, and particularly at what it does to human decision, choice, and therefore reality, are precipitated by the conditions which Eliot enunciated with grim lips, suggesting

> that with the disappearance of the idea of Original Sin, with the disappearance of the idea of intense moral struggle, the human beings presented to us both in poetry and in prose fiction today, and more patently among the serious writers than in the underworld of letters, tend to become less and less real. It is in fact in moments of moral and spiritual struggle depending upon spiritual sanctions, rather than in those 'bewildering minutes' in which we are all very much alike, that men and women come nearest to being real. If you do away with this struggle, and maintain that by tolerance, benevolence, inoffensiveness and a redistribution or increase of purchasing power, combined with a devotion, on the part of an élite, to Art, the world will be as good as anyone could require, then you must expect human beings to become more and more vaporous.

Found in the Street begins with a moment of moral and spiritual struggle depending upon spiritual sanctions: the decision by a shabby-genteel embittered loner to return to its rightful owner a wallet containing, among other things, 263 dollars. This social and spiritual act has falling upon it the shadow of the impure motive, since the proud good citizen is trying to prove not just something but everything, including that his violent principled atheism puts religionists to shame. 'I'm an atheist, by the way, so naturally I returned your wallet.' But the novel's plot is not bent upon the wallet found in the street but upon the person found there in the opening sentences: Elsie Tyler, who is alive, naive, confident of body, staunch of nature, and educable of mind. Ralph Linderman, who found the wallet, and Jack Sutherland, who lost it, vie for her, though neither as a lover exactly: Ralph, to set her apart from the city predators, there in her coffee-bar and in her shared rooms; Jack, to lift her above her pinched contingencies into some larger air (the larger air-conditioning of affluent squalor, it does seem). Others, too, compete for her: her room-mate, gay; an ex-lover, gay; Jack's wife, found playing both sides of the street. The end is death for Elsie. Do a girl in. Her death is like her life—tangential, in a way: if neither Ralph nor Jack is guilty. And they are shown to be—show themselves to each other to be—much more like each other, in their dangerous idealisings of Elsie,

than they dare admit, even though the idealisings are, the one, unworldly, the other, worldly.

It is a question whether the book itself doesn't idealise Elsie. She comes across as oddly vaporous—oddly because that might seem to be a way of not coming across (though one remembers George Eliot's pungent vapour Stephen Guest). Perhaps Highsmith can't quite bear to think that the matter to be contemplated is less that of a liveliness, a life, annulled than of a collusion between something of a personal nullity and modelling's nubile nullities. More likely, though, is that T. S. Eliot's terms apply, and that Elsie is not permitted—not by the book but by something in her and in her society—to become real. 'That was crazy, airy, unreal, his words and his feelings even, as unreal as the Elsie he saw in the photograph in which her face showed largest.' Elsie has something of the vaporousness of the heroine of 'Maud', the heroine loved and competed for and done for: trapped in the wishfulness, not just the wishes, of the driven others. There are gleams, and Highsmith is in her way, like Tennyson in his, a religious writer; I thought of Clough on 'Oh! that 'twere possible', from 'Maud', and on the simmering solitude of the crowded cityscape:

> It seems to satisfy a want that we have long been conscious of, when we see the black streams that welter out of factories, the dreary lengths of urban and suburban dustiness,
>
> The squares and streets,
> And the faces that one meets,
> irradiated with a gleam of divine purity.

The cityscape has its Dickensian gleams, too. When Ralph and Jack slug it out (their quarrel in the street is a thing to be entirely hated, since the energies displayed in it are *not* fine), there is a moment of suspended quotation which would have delighted both Dickens and his modern analyser Mark Lambert:

> 'Adulterer,' Ralph said calmly, 'and murderer'.
> Sutherland said just as calmly, 'Piss off or I'll bust you wide open.'

Just as calmly, but not just as poisedly. Dignity's preposterousness meets indignity's factitiousness. What a world. And what a steely style to indict it with. 'Jack did not exactly hear it, but Elsie had been pronounced dead, the attitude was that she was dead.'

Carol Ames (review date 1 November 1987)

SOURCE: A review of *Found in the Street*, in *Los Angeles Times Book Review*, November 1, 1987, p. 4.

[*In the following review, Ames praises* Found in the Street.]

Found in the Street is a complex character study of New Yorkers brought together by chance. Elsie is a vivid, young waitress with the magnetism and energy to break into the modeling world. Ralph Linderman, an atheist with a dog named God, is the aging security guard who becomes obsessed with protecting Elsie's innocence. And Jack Sutherland is a wealthy, aspiring artist with a mostly happy family life. He has the fortune—or misfortune—to have his wallet returned by Linderman with all $263, as well as credit cards and photographs, still intact.

Written by a longtime American exile, this accomplished and engrossing novel captures the taste and texture of life in Manhattan. From the exhilaration of discovering a previously overlooked Greek take-out restaurant to the feel of jogging through the empty, early-morning streets, "You could never tell what might happen in New York!"

This 19th novel goes far beyond the bounds of the "mystery," a genre label that has stuck to Highsmith's work since her first, *Strangers on a Train,* in 1950. It is time she reached a wider audience.

Richard Burgin (review date 1 November 1987)

SOURCE: A review of *Found in the Street,* in *New York Times Book Review,* November 1, 1987, Vol. 92, p. 24.

[*In the following positive review, Burgin discusses the psychological elements in* Found in the Street.]

Patricia Highsmith writes compellingly about those ambiguous boundaries that are supposed to separate rational behavior from irrationality and beautiful lives from grotesque ones. Her 19th novel [*Found in the Street*] centers on Elsie, a pretty 20-year-old waitress who has moved to Greenwich Village from upstate New York, dreaming of modeling or becoming an actress. Friendly, earnest and preternaturally charismatic, she captivates everyone who meets her, including Jack Sutherland and Ralph Linderman. At the novel's beginning, Ralph is already obsessively following her, warning about the dangerous company she keeps. A lonely night watchman and amateur inventor in his mid-50's, Ralph is at once a moralist and an atheist, an idealist and a spy. He is contrasted with Jack, a wealthy and amenable illustrator in his late 20's, and his wife, Natalia, a quasi-socialite art gallery manager, both of whom befriend and fall in love with Elsie. They help her modeling career by introducing her to the chic social world of the Village and SoHo. Ralph misperceives but is correctly alarmed by Elsie's sudden rise in society. Meanwhile, Elsie, who is gay "just now," also excites the passions

of three other young women. Despite a plethora of coincidences, the novel's violent conclusion is both surprising and esthetically satisfying. Ms. Highsmith keeps her potentially bathetic material under control through a patient unfolding of luminous details. She understands her characters' conflicts and how they are inflamed by the peculiar tensions of their environment. Often misrepresented as a genre writer of thrillers, Ms. Highsmith is a fine psychologist and ironist, and her newest novel is a powerfully disturbing, resonant creation.

Charles Champlin (review date 13 March 1988)

SOURCE: A review of *The Black House,* in *Los Angeles Times Book Review,* March 13, 1988, p. 13.

[*Below, Champlin offers a positive review of* The Black House.]

The Black House is a collection of stories by Patricia Highsmith, the Texas-born author long a resident in Europe. Like Ruth Rendell, she keeps a very, very cold eye on the world. Her protagonists are apt to be as amoral as other writers' villains.

She is at her most characteristically cynical in **"Not One of Us"** in which a circle of his friends conspire in the most subtle ways to drive a decent but boring fellow named Quasthoff to suicide.

In the title story, murder is done by some local chaps simply to preserve the myths they have created for themselves about a deserted house in an Upstate New York village.

In **"Old Folks at Home,"** a man and his wife kindly decide to house an elderly couple from an overcrowded retirement home nearby. The consequences are disastrous and morbidly funny, and you would expect nothing less from Miss Highsmith. Weird, but not *too* weird.

Robert Towers (review date 31 March 1988)

SOURCE: "The Way We Live Now," in *New York Review of Books,* March 31, 1988, Vol. XXXV, No. 5, pp. 36-7.

[*In the following excerpt, Towers offers a mixed assessment of* Found in the Street, *expressing reservations about Highsmith's "downplaying of the dramatic."*]

[Highsmith] is prolific, with nineteen novels to her credit, together with six volumes of short stories. . . . [She] frequently writes from the point of view of one or more of her male characters, who may or may not be "straight"; in fact, taken as a group, Miss Highsmith's characters, male and female, represent a wide spectrum of what used to be called the perverse. . . .

Highsmith is one of those writers of genre fiction who have a following among literary people, especially in England. She has been handsomely praised by Graham Greene, Julian Symons, and Auberon Waugh. In this country she has had enthusiastic readers ever since her first book, *Strangers on a Train,* which was filmed by Hitchcock, but her literary reputation is fairly recent and seems just now to be gaining momentum. *Found in the Street,* which was published in Britain in 1986 and in this country only a few months ago, has been widely and for the most part glowingly reviewed.

The novel begins with the image of a pretty girl with short blond hair and white sneakers making her way, smiling and spirited, down a Greenwich Village street. Suddenly she spots a man "with a rather side to side gait and with a dog on a leash. The girl stopped abruptly, and took the first opportunity to cross the street." We cut immediately to the consciousness of the dog walker, a middle-aged man named Ralph Linderman, who is clearly obsessive and a bore, his head full of angry clichés about dirty streets, littering kids, and muggers. We learn that eighteen years before he had fallen down an elevator shaft in a garage where he worked as a security guard and has felt changed ever since. We learn too that he is preoccupied with a young blond girl, Elsie, whom he met in a coffee shop, and worries about her safety in this dangerous, sordid city. While Ralph is conscientiously scooping up the mess of his dog, a black and white, piglike animal he has named God, he finds a wallet lying in the gutter. Though a cantankerous atheist, Ralph thinks of himself as one of the last moral men, and there is no question that he will return the bulging wallet to its rightful owner.

Thus we meet the second consciousness of the novel—that of a blandly reasonable, agreeable man whose character contrasts in every way with Ralph's. Jack Sutherland is an "up-scale" young book designer and commercial artist who enjoys a coolly modern marriage with a good-looking fairly rich woman named Natalia. "She was the kind of girl, or woman, who would bolt and run off, perhaps forever, if she felt the marital harness chafing even a little." They live in a handsomely decorated apartment on Grove Street in the Village (only a short distance from Ralph's Bleecker Street tenement) and have a bright little girl, Amelia. For the rest of the novel we alternate between Ralph and Jack, following the former from his dingy flat to the garage where he works at night and the latter to conferences about his art work, to parties, gallery openings, and other events in the life of a young New York husband and father. In addition to the returned wallet, Ralph and Jack have a bond in their mutual fascina-

tion with the young blond girl, Elsie, whom Jack, too, has encountered at the coffee shop where she works as a waitress.

Terrified that Elsie might fall into prostitution or get hooked on drugs, Ralph makes a nuisance of himself at the coffee shop, lecturing her on her sex life and issuing baleful warnings. He begins to spy on her, following her to her apartment. Jack, meanwhile, has fallen in love with her looks and spirit and wants to sketch her—all without any acknowledged desire to go to bed with her. When Ralph one day sees Elsie leave Jack's building (she has innocently helped him carry home some groceries), he suspects the worst and writes Jack a letter telling him not to see the girl again. What follows is a situation of mounting paranoia on Ralph's part and growing annoyance on the part of Jack and Elsie. Having set up this situation, Patricia Highsmith complicates it by revealing that this sunny girl of men's dreams is, at least for the present, a lesbian, and that Jack's wife, Natalia, has fallen in love with her. Jack's easy acceptance of his wife's homosexual affair is an example of the passivity that seems to afflict so many of Patricia Highsmith's male characters, including her murderers.

> This downplaying of the dramatic in Highsmith's work has been much praised, as has the ordinariness of the details with which she depicts the daily lives and mental processes of her psychopaths. Both undoubtedly contribute to the domestication of crime in her fiction, thereby implicating the reader further in the sordid fantasy that is being worked out.
> —*Robert Towers*

Interestingly (and typically) the author does not play up the inherent drama in the situation, but mutes it, slows things down, and distracts us with other matters. We are allowed to spend a lot of time with Amelia, watching her being put to bed, listening to her prattle with her parents, particularly her father, who, more than the elusive Natalia, is in charge of domestic arrangements. We tune in on Ralph's reminiscences of his wretched, brief marriage and listen to his misogynous imprecations. From time to time we are allowed to glimpse Elsie's meteorically rising career (aided by Jack and Natalia) as a fashion model. The explosion, when it occurs, is produced not by the bomb that has been quietly ticking away but from another source altogether—the sudden murderous impulse of a jealous "dikey" type whom we have met only once before and may well have forgotten. Murder, in Patricia Highsmith's hands, is made to occur almost as casually as the bumping of a fender or a bout of food poisoning.

This downplaying of the dramatic in her work has been much praised, as has the ordinariness of the details with which she depicts the daily lives and mental processes of her psychopaths. Both undoubtedly contribute to the domestication of crime in her fiction, thereby implicating the reader further in the sordid fantasy that is being worked out. *Found in the Street* is a fairly typical example—less lively than the cycle involving that prince of disguises and offhand murder, Tom Ripley, and less stolid than, say, *Deep Water.* The claustrophobic and obsessional quality that Graham Greene has praised (and that I certainly experienced in other novels going all the way back to the rantings of the polymorphously warped Bruno in *Strangers on a Train*) is here limited to those passages in which we are trapped in the boring mind of Ralph Linderman, but its impact is undeniable. The denouement, when it occurs, is skillfully worked out and its effect is enhanced by the way in which the reader has been led to expect something altogether different.

But I have reservations that apply, in varying degrees, to Patricia Highsmith's other novels as well. The ordinariness—what might be called the calculated banality—of her approach extends to her use of dialogue, which in the case of *Found in the Street* is generally commonplace and often dull. Miss Highsmith's ear seems to fail her when she attempts to reproduce the speech of the contemporary American young—would a girl like Elsie really pepper her speech with "gollys" and "by goshes" and refer to young men as "fellows"? Furthermore, the utilitarian flatness of the novel's prose is such that one is never tempted to quote more than is strictly needed for illustrative purposes. While the characters, here and elsewhere, come equipped with any number of interesting kinks, quirks, and neuroses, their rendering seems to me to lack a certain energy that would make them memorable in their pathology. I suppose I should at this point confess that I find the understated approach to the crime genre that Miss Highsmith's British critics admire less appealing than the fast-paced, vulgarly sensational, and demonically attuned crime novels of a writer like Elmore Leonard.

Alex Raskin (review date 5 February 1989)

SOURCE: A review of *Tales of Natural and Unnatural Catastrophes,* in *Los Angeles Times Book Review,* February 5, 1989, p. 4

[*In the following review, Raskin offers a mixed assessment of* Tales of Natural and Unnatural Catastrophes, *commenting on Highsmith's "wry portrayals of human folly."*]

The catastrophes [in *Tales of Natural and Unnatural Catastrophes*] actually are all "unnatural," prompted when Patricia Highsmith's bizarre, blundering characters attempt to defy nature: the defense tactics of a high-rise crumble against a crawling army that fumigation can't kill; the Nuclear Regulatory Commission finds that its hiding place for nuclear waste isn't so sporting after all; a Japanese whaling ship gets its due after a day harpooning whales.

While best known as a writer of thrillers, Highsmith, a Texas-born author now living in Switzerland, is primarily concerned with crafting stories to evoke the human comedy. Her wry portrayals of human folly sometimes lack sympathy, as in the tasteless piece **"Rent-a-Womb,"** which trivializes the abortion debate. But Highsmith condescends wittily and without favor, and so we soon cease to take offense, enjoying stories we might otherwise have dismissed as prejudiced.

"Mabuti," for example, satirizes the dictator of a small African nation, who frantically tries to prepare for the arrival of a United Nations delegation, burning everything from garbage to corpses and trying to transform Government House, a brothel with "a couple of rooms holding papers with which the country gained its independence," into a "building like the Parthenon." Everything goes awry, of course: The city is shrouded in smoke from the burning when the delegation arrives and the Government house erupts in a conflagration when Mabuti soldiers try to "properly" cremate people who had died in an elevator. The U.N. members are less-than-pleased—so Bomo has them shot.

Odette L'Henry Evans (essay date 1990)

SOURCE: "A Feminist Approach to Patricia Highsmith's Fiction," in *American Horror Fiction: From Brockden Brown to Stephen King,* edited by Brian Docherty, St. Martin's, 1990, pp. 107-19.

[*In the following essay, Evans relates Highsmith's exploration of the unconscious in her novels and short stories to feminist critical theories.*]

A critical examination of the work of Patricia Highsmith from a feminist standpoint unavoidably presents a number of challenges, the first being the difficulty of ascertaining precisely to what genre her novels belong. To see her as a 'crime writer' would be inaccurate as well as limitative, since it would mean ignoring certain elements of her stories which are outside the usual crime-detection-arrest pattern. To call her a mystery writer may be more accurate, since she was once awarded the Edgar Allan Poe Scroll by the Mystery Writers of America, yet the nature of mystery in her novels differs greatly from what is usually expected, in so far as it never comes from wondering who the evildoer is; instead it is connected with what kind of person he is, or more accurately it enfolds the reasons which make him progressively deviate from the norm and become a murderer.

Patricia Highsmith herself stated that she was 'interested in the effect of guilt on [her] heroes' and her study of the invisible 'glass cell' which surrounds and isolates the criminal is one of the remarkable features of her work. It may well be that this is the key to understanding the precise nature of her work, and it will need to be examined in relation to feminist critical theories in order to establish accurately the status of the work defined as woman's writing.

It has been said that there are as many forms of feminism as there are women, and, while this can only be seen as a reduction to the absurd, the fact remains that a number of tendencies exist, some mainly concerned with everyday social issues, and others, more particularly among French women writers and critics, essentially involved in debating the intellectual aspects of feminism. One important element of this approach has been the redefinition of what is meant by women's writings, no longer in relation to male literature (for instance, being 'potentially as good as . . .' or 'indistinguishable from . . .'), but in relation to language itself as a means of expressing the inner consciousness of the female writer, proceeding, in other words, according to what Róisîn Battel calls the 'rejection of phallic discourse'.

This concern with language or, more precisely, with the creation of languages (discourse) can operate at the linguistic level of language, involving considerations of form, organisation, vocabulary, syntax which, in the discourse, reflect female identity, or it can explore the deeper layers of the text to search for a novel apprehension of the unconscious as expression of the female psyche—in other words, a writing of self. The corpus of literary analyses which has been produced during the past twenty years or so has amply demonstrated the value of textual deconstructions at linguistic and at psychoanalytical levels in establishing a formula able to define accurately the specificity of woman.

The advantage of this two-pronged investigation is that it not only covers the manner in which a woman writer expresses herself within a literary text, but also encompasses her selection of plots, and her presentation of episodes and characters, thus highlighting in turns the various strands of a complex pattern.

What criteria should then be considered in this quest for an 'authentic' feminine voice?

Traditionally, women writers have been seen as lacking the sense of logic, universality and objectivity which is commonly thought to characterise the production of male authors, so much so that, if a woman succeeded in that field, as, for example, George Eliot did, she was accused of 'committing atrocities with it that beggar description'. Women were, on the other hand, credited with a gift for immediate empathy with the world around them, as well as an appreciation of each of its separate elements. In that connection it may be interesting to hear Jan Morris, who before undergoing a sex-change was a man, explain that, as far as she is concerned, the most thrilling thing about being a woman is that she no longer feels remote and alienated from her urban surroundings, but is deeply conscious of being part of them.

No such empathy, however, is in evidence in the novels of Patricia Highsmith. At best, the surroundings are indifferent, and not infrequently they are hostile. The comfortable home of Vic and Melinda Van Allen, in *Deep Water,* is never described; there is mention of a 'nice' house, a 'good' phonograph and a 'favourite armchair', and also a dented metal vase, since Melinda is prone to throwing things when annoyed, but nothing more.

Similarly, in *The Glass Cell,* when Carter is released from the penitentiary, it is obvious that his wife has taken particular care to make their flat attractive for his return, yet there is only a brief reference to a rubber plant and to some 'gladioli in a large vase', without even, as one would have expected, a notation of colour. The only colour mentioned, in fact, is that of the 'two thick red books' on the chest of drawers, right in the bedroom. These crimson-coloured law books belong to Sullivan, the lawyer initially commissioned to establish Carter's innocence, who is now Hazel's lover and will eventually be killed by Carter.

Julia Kristeva, a radical feminist as well as a rigorous theorist, realised that there was no single feature that could identify or characterise all feminine texts, and that most texts can dissolve identities, as she illustrates with reference to avant-garde authors such as Joyce and Artaud. Indeed, while postulating a distinction between man's and woman's writing, she asserts that, to the extent that it is not a natural construct, the term 'woman' itself can not be defined: 'La femme ce n'est jamais ça' ('Woman is never what one supposes'). Criteria are therefore to be sought in the social rather than the individual context. Following this line, Kristeva argues that women, because of their social roles, tend to be more mindful of ethics and to create a 'maternal' climate of calm and tenderness, so that, when a woman novelist writes, she either reproduces a real family or, at least, creates a similar imaginary one.

This is rather less easy to identify, but, for all that, there is no evidence that Patricia Highsmith's own affective or moral values play a part in her novels. She does not write in the way, for instance, that Claudine Herrmann suggests: 'As soon as a woman speaks up, it is usually to reclaim the right to the present moment, to affirm the refusal of a life alienated in social time which is so hostile to interior time.' Little of what appears in the novels relates exclusively to the present, the general tendency being to anticipate future events. This is even more apparent in the short stories, where the first words prefigure the tragedies to come. The opening sentence of **'The Birds Poised to Fly'**—'Every morning, Don looked into his mailbox, but there was never a letter for him'—takes the reader to the very centre of the drama, the awaited letter that his girlfriend Rosalind does not write. His frustration tempts him to look into the mailbox next to his own, where a fickle boy friend has left uncollected a love letter from another girl.

Similarly, the words 'Stanley Hubbell painted on Sundays', which open **'The Barbarians'**, identify the relaxing occupation so dreadfully spoilt by the raucous exclamations and shouts of the ball-players under Hubbell's window. He drops a stone from his window onto a player's head, nearly killing him.

By such means, time is made into a continuum. This contradicts also Virginia Woolf's contention that feminine writing explodes time into a series of 'moments', each complete in itself, in an effort to distance the text from the masculine tenets of logic and of strict temporal and causal perspective.

Undoubtedly Virginia Woolf insisted on using that disjointed form herself—in *Mrs Dalloway* for instance, where only one ordinary day in the life of a married woman is depicted. This proved a fitting demonstration of her belief that 'how one writes is more important than what one writes', but the fact remains that many women writers, past and present, have chosen to work within a logical context.

This, at least to some extent, is probably what led to a reappraisal of the question and prompted some radical feminists to wonder whether it made sense, intellectually as well as politically, for women to attempt to write in a 'new' language which, in order to be their own, would reject logic. Such a 'discourse that surpasses the regulated phallocentric system', as Hélène Cixous defines it, may distinguish a feminine text from a masculine one, but at the same time it may prove self-destructive.

It may be more fruitful to accept, as John Stuart Mill, Mary Wollstonecraft and more recently Simone de Beauvoir have maintained that women, like men, are part of the human race and therefore that their writing—meaning the terms they use, their style or the structure of their discourse—is not gender-oriented. The way would then be open to consider Patricia Highsmith's work as part of a feminine corpus of production, and to see whether a psychoanalytical investigation of her plot and character presentation yields elements which can be related to another aspect of feminine writing: that which consists in liberating and expressing the unconscious, as specifically shaped by a woman's perception of it.

A brief survey of Patricia Highsmith's novels shows that the great majority of her central characters—often psychopathic killers—are male. As statistics demonstrate that most violent criminals are men, here selection can legitimately be seen as representative rather than sexually biased, although, to be fair, some of her killers, such as the snails which appear in two of her stories, can hardly be fitted into statistical realism.

In the novels dealing with male criminals, the distinctive function of women can, however, be observed either in gender-oriented social relations or in the woman's distinctive nature. The feminist standpoint, which here can be termed as 'feminine epistemology', goes beyond the appearance of women's function—love, motherhood, care of the home and of the outside world—in order to explore the systemic relations of a sex-gender universe. The Marxist view of gender-related functions sees these as derived from forms of labour, with men, traditionally, dominant in the fields of science and technology, and endowed with cognitive and objective rationality, while women are closer to nature and more subjective and emotional, so that for them labour and love become inextricably mixed.

Women's traditional work primarily involves the bearing and bringing-up of children, and in that connection it can be noted that in Patricia Highsmith's novels children often appear as part of the family unit. The 'care' they receive from their mothers varies greatly, although it never appears as loving and tender. It seems to range from bland duty or indifference to sheer brutality.

In *The Glass Cell,* there is no doubt that the little boy Timmie is reasonably well looked after by his mother, but, for instance, despite the boy's obvious distress at having a father in prison (Carter has been imprisoned for embezzlement, although he is in fact innocent), she writes calmly to her husband that 'Timmie is bearing up pretty well. I lecture him daily, though I try not to make it sound like a lecture. The kids are picking on him at school of course. . . .' When Carter has been released, she does not bother to come home from work on her birthday, but goes straight on to a party, despite the fact that Timmie is waiting expectantly to give her his present: 'Timmie had bought a white slip with brown embroidery . . . quite an expensive item.' By contrast, he is shown real affection by his father, who makes various gifts for him while he is in prison, including 'a good sized chest of oak with [his] initials carved in its lid'.

When the boy accidentally cuts his hand, it is again his father who shows concern, while, on another occasion, he is shown companionably washing the dishes with Timmie drying and putting them away. Obviously, when we compare Carter's attitude towards the boy to that of his wife, who is secretly conducting her longstanding love affair, we have to conclude that Patricia Highsmith depicts the behaviour of the couple towards their child in a non-stereotyped way.

It could be argued, of course, that Carter's caring attitude is meant to stress how fundamentally honest and decent he is, since his arrest has been due to a false testimony. However, if we consider another novel, *Deep Water,* we find a similar contrast between mother and father. The mother, Melinda Van Allen, is indifferent to her daughter Beatrice, known as Trixie: 'She had not wanted to have a child, then she had, then she hadn't, and finally, after four years, she had wanted one again, and finally produced one.' It is left to her father to care for her: 'Just then Trixie's pyjama clad form appeared in the doorway. "Mommie!" Trixie screamed, but Mommie neither heard nor saw her. Vic got up and went to her. "S'matter, Trix?" he asked, stooping by her. "I can't sleep."' The tragedy here is, of course, that the father is a psychopath, and that the story as it develops takes him from the faintest stirring of an unbalanced mind to the full-blown horrors of successive murders, culminating in the strangling of his wife.

Through all this, Trixie is ignored by her mother, but an object of concern for her father. He is sorry for what will happen to her, and at the very end, when he walks out of the house with the police officer who has just arrested him, his befuddled mind conjures a vision of the child: 'He saw Trixie romping up the lawn and stopping in surprise as she saw him with the policeman, but frowning at the lawn, Vic could see that she wasn't really there. The sun was shining and Trixie was alive somewhere.'

We should certainly search in vain for an expression of 'woman's writing' in this novel, if we mean by that writing expressive, even if only subconsciously, of women's feelings of love and tenderness, of role-playing. What is more, in 'The Terrapin' there is a little boy, Victor, whose mother is even more devoid of understanding and affection. She never pays attention to anything he may have to say, never even listens to him, and, despite the fact that she is a professional illustrator of children's books, she has no understanding of his longing to look 'grown up', to wear long trousers and sturdy manly shoes. All she can say, in her stiff foreign accent, is 'Veector, you are seeck. And retarded. You know that?' She makes fun of him, slaps him, and when, one day, she brings a terrapin to cook for the 'ragoût', the boy's show of affection for the poor animal only seems 'seeck' to her and she refuses even to let him take it downstairs to show to his friend. When she cuts up the creature to cook it, his latent hatred for her crystallises:

> He thought of the terrapin, in little pieces now, all
> mixed up in the sauce of cream and egg yolks and
> sherry in the pot in the refrigerator. His mother's
> cry was not silent [like the terrapin's had been], it

seemed to tear his ears off. His second blow was in her body, and then he stabbed her throat again. Only tiredness made him stop.

Giving up the search for maternal care, we might look instead for qualifiers of sexual difference, taking as our point of departure the traditional association of female sexuality with passivity, the opposite of masculine thrusting aggressiveness. Freud, in *The Disappearance of the Oedipus Complex* (1933), equates 'feminine' with vagina and 'virile' with penis, concluding that 'anatomy is destiny'. Feminist theorists usually contradict him by insisting upon a valorisation of individuality, perhaps through refusing marriage: Simone de Beauvoir, for example, remarked that she could have married Sartre, but would thereby have ceased to be herself. Other feminists have sought to assert control of their lives by selecting a variety of lovers and partners, or by aggressively preserving their virginity, or by becoming part of a familial community, as Germaine Greer suggested, or an all-female group, like the women of Greenham Common—in other words, as Dale Spender expressed it, by altering the pattern of relations with men, making the woman an autonomous subject revelling in her regained freedom from sexual bondage; 'Men is an issue over which feminists agonise.'

In Patricia Highsmith's novels, relationship patterns involving women mostly involve married women who indulge in extramarital affairs. One such woman is Hazel in *The Glass Cell,* who, however, writes to her imprisoned husband every day, being supporting, cheering him up through his various unsuccessful appeals and eventually welcoming him home: 'Hazel kissed him on the cheeks, then on the lips. She was crying. She was also laughing. Carter blinked awkwardly at the lights that seemed so bright, at the dazzling colour everywhere.' She retains this fondness to the end, even to the extent of forgiving him for having killed her lover.

Her lover is the lawyer, Sullivan, who seems to hover in the background from the start, offering assistance and organising holiday outings; but, when asked by her husband, she repeatedly denies that they have an adulterous relationship: '"I hear you are seeing Sullivan a lot," he said, and saw in her face that he had hurt her. "I see him as often as I tell you I see him. . . ."' She goes on denying it until caught, when she has recourse to the old traditional formula: 'You don't understand women.' Whether this affair was deliberately initiated by her, or whether she drifted into it because she enjoyed the lawyer's protective presence, felt attracted to him, or could not resist his advances is certainly never made clear; all she will say is 'it happened while you were in prison'.

Initially, one may feel that she was fond of her lover, since she appears 'ravaged with grief' when she hears that he has been killed; she wants his murderer found and punished, and yet, when she realises that her husband is the killer, she only tells him, 'Everything is going to be all right!' The level of natural determinism in her attitude must be seen as rather limited.

Melinda, in *High Water,* is unfaithful on a grander scale and makes clear her evident desire to attract men. She smiles 'a gay catch-me-if-you-can smile' over her shoulder whenever someone she fancies comes near, and, as a result, jealousy will be the motive for a whole series of murders, although the first lover is disposed of simply by a threat. Melinda does not miss him, as she is already having an affair with a not-too-bright instructor at a riding-academy, who is succeeded by a very young record salesman, and others. So, on the surface, there seems to be evidence of feminist self-assertion, in the form of a determination to live to the full. Life for Melinda is 'the pursuit of a good time'.

Her husband's jealously would then present a dreadful, murderous but totally logical reaction. This is, however, not the case, and again the opacity of the character's mind makes a definite judgement impossible. Melinda's husband is unbalanced from the outset, as his passion for bedbugs and snails shows; his soft even voice and his fixed smile ought to give him away, and so should some of his odd statements, such as 'I have an evil side too, but I keep it well hidden', which cause further distortion to the portrait.

There remains, however, the possible argument that, by destroying the masculine image and altering the powerful emotion of jealousy to make it into the pathetic blubberings of a monster, another form of feminist writing is realised, akin to that suggested by a radical French feminist, Annie Leclerc: 'One must not wage war on man. That is his way of attaining value. . . . One must simply deflate his values with the needle of ridicule.' This might also account for the presentation of other male 'heroes' in what seems the same 'destructional' perspective, where apparent logic turns to aberration. Could it be that Patricia Highsmith, as an *Observer* critic once suggested, 'writes about men like a spider writing about flies'?

This is a tempting approach; indeed Peter Knoppert, in the story **'The Snail-Watcher'**, shares Vic Van Allen's sick fascination for snails. He watches and breeds them until they fill the living-room, cover the walls and eventually suffocate him: 'There were snails crawling over his eyes. Then just as he staggered to his feet, something else hit him. . . . He was fainting. His arms felt like leaden weights as he tried to reach his nostrils, his eyes, to free them from the sealing, murderous snail bodies.' Snails in fact appear again as deadly animals, this time in giant form, in the story titled **'The Quest for Blank Claveringi'**, where they deliberately set out to kill the distinguished, but far too arrogant, professor of zoology.

What makes it difficult, nevertheless, to see such effects as a 'destructional' feminist expression is the presence in the novels of female criminals, some of them just as subject to psychopathic disorders as Highsmith's males. Perhaps the most haunting example is that pretty young woman Lucille Smith in **'The Heroine'**, so determined to make good and to lead a happy life, to forget her own mad, wild-eyed mother. Having secured an ideal job as a nursemaid in a beautiful and happy household with two lovely children, she none the less eventually turns pyromaniac and sets fire to the house.

There is also, in **'When the Fleet Was in in Mobile'**, which Graham Greene called his favourite story, the haunting portrait of Geraldine, who reveals in the disconnected form of an interior monologue what seems to be the cruel and obsessive character of her husband, so that her action in killing him seems fully justified. Slowly, however, her own underlying irrationality emerges, together with the echoes of some past nymphomania which drove her to meet the sailors 'when the fleet was in'. In the end, as Graham Greene so pithily put it, 'what seemed at first a simple little case of murder' becomes an unbearably claustrophobic experience.

The fascination of Patricia Highsmith's characters lies precisely in the way their twilight world is painted, in small impressionistic touches. They see themselves as normal and may appear so to casual onlookers, yet, when details of their speech or behaviour are sifted carefully, the flaws in their make-up come to light, and one can foresee the horrors to come.

Similarly, in *Those Who Walk Away,* what begins as the natural grief of a father whose daughter had committed suicide, and his unjustified but understandable anger against his son-in-law, develops progressively into an obsessive stalking of the tragic young husband through the narrow passages and the piazzas of Venice:

> Ray [the young man] had started suddenly, but he had stopped walking. In the shadows ahead emerging from a triangular shadow that clung to a small church like a dark pyramid, he saw Coleman [his father-in-law] looking over both shoulders, obviously looking for something, someone.
>
> 'What is it?' Antonio asked.
>
> 'Nothing. I thought I saw someone.'
>
> 'Who?'
>
> Coleman was still in sight. Then in another second he wasn't. He had vanished in the slit on an alley on the left of the church square.

And it may well be that it is at that level, when the extraordinary accuracy of Highsmith's observation is realised, and when her gift for psychoanalysis is recognised, that one can legitimately re-examine the possibility of a feminine form of writing. It has been said that it is an oppression to force women to adhere to 'the stereotype of a passive powerless and sexually masochistic femininity', yet, as Deborah Cameron states,

> It seems to offer us through its account of the construction of the self in family relations and the unconscious mind, an understanding of how subordination can be internalised deep in our personalities. Moreover it is centrally concerned with the forging of sexual identity and with the extreme importance of the sexual in all aspects of mental life.

In that light, the stories of Geraldine and of Ray's father-in-law, for instance, have all the concepts posited first by Freud and renewed by Lacan in a purely masculine context, and eventually enlarged and 'feminised' by women such as Hélène Cixous, a lecturer in psychology, in *The Laugh of the Medusa,* and Luce Irigaray, initially a member of the Lacanian school. Irigaray, realising how Lacan's theories were limited by their exclusion of women, attempted a reappraisal of women's relation to their unconscious, which she sees as radically different from men's—a belief which leads her to wonder whether women are not in fact *the* unconscious which their writing reveals.

It would seem fair to accept that the wealth of details given to express in terms of language a range of emotions which escape the mould of logical reality, and the empathy which emerges from Patricia Highsmith's pages for the characters who, despite their desire or their illusion, cannot come to terms with others or cope with the outside world, bring her work within the scope of feminine writing.
—*Odette L'Henry Evans*

It is certainly true that in Patricia Highsmith's novels the unconscious is reconstructed through language, to the extent that Coleman, for example, in *Those Who Walk Away,* 'recognises' his dead daughter's scarf in the different, newly bought scarf that he pulls out of his hated son-in-law's pocket, and that Geraldine, in **'When the Fleet Was in in Mobile'**, can 'hear' the words spoken by her father when she was a child, by her friend Marianne when she was young, or, more recently, by her now supposedly dead husband, just as clearly as she hears the woman speaking to her on the bus, or the man that she meets during the ride on the merry-go-round.

Past and present are fused in her mind in such a way that submerged memories partly resurface and she 'recognises' an old boyfriend, far more real to her, in the unknown state policeman who comes to take her back. At the end, her madness taking over, she screams while holding her fists in front of her eyes to blot out reality: 'Then his face [the policeman's] and the lights and the park went out, though she knew as well as she knew she still screamed that her eyes were open under her hands.'

It would seem fair to accept that the wealth of details given to express in terms of language a range of emotions which escape the mould of logical reality, and the empathy which emerges from Patricia Highsmith's pages for the characters who, despite their desire or their illusion, cannot come to terms with others or cope with the outside world, bring her work within the scope of feminine writing—not at the superficial level that some feminist propagandists have surmised, but in the deeper realm of psychoanalysis where the act of writing is an exploration of the unconscious and where women have excelled from time immemorial, in a way which makes them enthralling tellers of tales.

Noel Dorman Mawr (essay date Winter 1991)

SOURCE: "From Villain to Vigilante," in *Armchair Detective,* Vol. 24, No. 1, Winter, 1991, pp. 34-8.

[*Mawr is an American educator and critic who has written works on Romantic poetry. In the following essay, she discusses the development of the character Tom Ripley in Highsmith's Ripley novels, stating that the series shows Ripley's "progression from a villain to a vigilante as the world becomes even too evil for his taste."*]

Have you ever wondered how the criminal mind works? Patricia Highsmith has. Her first novel, ***Strangers on a Train,*** focused on the pathology of a central character; and her only series character, Ripley, is a professional criminal. Some writers might make the hero charming—a bumbling crook, or a swashbuckling villain—but not Highsmith. Ripley is a thief, a murderer; he even takes risks in order to make it all more "fun."

Ripley undergoes some very interesting changes throughout the four-book series. In his debut, he lives in a fantasy world; and Highsmith presents him as the unfortunate product of a corrupt society. By the fourth book, society is presented as a malignant force which makes criminal behavior an inevitability. A close look at this most unusual series, which began in 1956 and was last added to in 1980, shows Ripley's progression from a villain to a vigilante as the world in which he lives becomes even too evil for his taste.

The original Tom Ripley, in the 1956 *The Talented Mr. Ripley,* lives in a society which hardly touches him—which, in fact, he half creates in his imagination. Tom is given a conventional fairy-tale orphan's background, complete with a sadistic aunt who belittled and humiliated him. Apparently as a result of this, Tom is lacking in self-confidence and drive, has identity problems, and creates his own imaginary world. Such a self-created world comes in later life to control him, and he loses his ability to tell real from imaginary. It is this invented "reality," coupled with Tom's weak sense of ego and contempt for the "real" Tom Ripley, which leads him first to attempt to alter his identity and finally to kill another human being with whom he has identified, actually assuming his identity.

Tom's great need to find an identity leads him to attempt to find it through "love": someone will love him, and he will lose himself in the identity of that person. He meets and seizes upon Dickie Greenleaf. "More than anything else in the world," Tom wants Dickie to like him, but in this Tom fails:

> In Dickie's eyes Tom saw nothing more now than he would have seen if he had looked at the hard, bloodless surface of a mirror. Tom felt a painful wrench in his breast, and he covered his face with his hands. It was as if Dickie had been suddenly snatched from him. They were not friends. They didn't know each other. It struck Tom like a horrible truth, true for all time, true for all the people he had known in the past and for those he would know in the future: each had stood and would stand before him, and he would know time and time again that he would never know them, and the worst was that there would always be an illusion, for a time, that he did know them, and that he and they were completely in harmony and alike.

Tom's disappointment finally results in murderous rage toward the would-be object of his love and identification, so Tom kills Dickie and finds after Dickie's death the identity that has eluded him: he assumes Dickie's name, his appearance, his voice, his manner, until it finally comes easier to Tom to be Dickie than to be Tom Ripley.

Tom Ripley's imagination has vast powers over the external world. It can cause "the whole city of New York" to "collapse with a *poof* like a lot of cardboard on a stage." But it does not have the power to give Tom Ripley self-confidence, or cause others to love or even like him. Since Tom could not get Dickie to love him, he killed him, and now he must go on killing in order to protect his new identity as Dickie Greenleaf. He has no doubt that these murders are justified; they are, after all, necessary to protect what simply is *due* him. In these latter respects, Tom becomes more the type, not of the psychotic in his world of delusions, but of the amoral, unfeeling psychopathic criminal—the type he will become in later novels.

Another development within Tom in this first novel is his increasing enjoyment, not only of his masquerade, but of the feeling of danger that goes with it. He has always chosen to "tempt fate," to "take a chance" whenever he can. After the first murder, "it was as if he were really inviting trouble, and couldn't stop himself." He thinks about taking risks and realizes that "risks were what made the whole thing fun" because "he was so bored." What had begun as a need to find a secure and acceptable identity has become a need for stimulation, for excitement to allay the boredom of life. For Tom, in whatever incarnation, cannot really feel very much. His overriding need is always to fill up the void that is Tom Ripley—with another's identity, with the stimulation of danger.

These latter elements are further developed in the second novel, *Ripley under Ground* (1970). The recognizable traits of the psychopathic criminal, which have become evident in Tom by the end of *The Talented Mr. Ripley,* here dominate. Tom is no longer at the mercy of his imagination, and he is now Tom Ripley pretty consistently, and apparently satisfied with this. Tom now prides himself on his sensitivity, sincerity, and moral rectitude, while at the same time emerging as a moral Typhoid Mary. In the first novel, Tom murdered the person closest to him. In the second and third in the series, he becomes a malignant influence on those who are sucked into his orbit. In each novel, someone is driven to suicide through contact with him.

In *Ripley under Ground,* Tom is a creator and part owner of a counterfeit painting racket. Bernard, the counterfeiter, becomes increasingly distraught over his own dishonesty, and Tom realizes that Bernard must die or he will expose the scheme and ruin everyone involved. When, after lengthy pursuit by Tom, Bernard kills himself, "Tom began to realize that he had willed or wished Bernard's suicide." Bernard has accused Tom of being the "origin" of the whole fraud, and Tom's response is to acknowledge—while deriding—the fact that people look upon him as "a mystic origin, a font of evil."

In this novel, Tom is less a prey to his fantasies, more secure in himself, but more in need of external stimulation to alleviate his boredom. Even some of his criminal activities, such as smuggling, cause him to experience "fatigue, contempt, boredom even." Only *danger* can alleviate this boredom, and the excitement of the dangerous game banishes all other concerns. Tom tells himself—and, as is usual with his imaginary constructs, *believes*—that he is concerned with ethics, with right and wrong. He even has feelings of sympathy for the wife of one of his murder victims. But Tom never really feels very much—including a sense of "right" and "wrong."

He "saw the right and wrong, yet both sides of himself were equally sincere," because for Tom the actual reality is still that bottomless pit which is Tom's lack of identity—of any inner self. He is in constant—and increasing—need of stimulation to fill that void. And the more he fills it, the less he feels, and the more he needs. When the art collector first reveals that he is onto the forgeries, Tom does not know if he should feel anything or not: "Tom was unworried. Ought he to be more worried? He shrugged slightly."

Tom is fairly consistently self-confident, he is aware of his lack of a basic sense of right and wrong, but he is also becoming increasingly moralistic and self-righteous, and this characteristic manifests itself in his responses to French society. He thinks with scorn of "French bloody-mindedness, greed, a lie that was not exactly a lie but a deliberate concealment of fact." In Tom's observations about French society, Highsmith initiates the move toward depicting the actual society in which her protagonist functions. In *The Talented Mr. Ripley,* Tom lives in a New York City of his own imagination and in an Italian tourist wonderland. The natives are hardly noticed, and crime is not a significant enough occurrence to be commented on. In *Ripley under Ground,* French society is full of greedy, dishonest people, and crime is a way of life—a business. Tom's new friend, Reeves Minot, is a smuggler by profession, and Tom's "business" interest is art forgery. Even murder is a business in this society, and the "honest" people are not really honest, cheating each other every chance they get. This is a different picture of society from the first Ripley novel, and this Tom is more confident but more criminal, more hardened. These changes will be developed in the next two Ripley novels, but, with the added twist that Tom, while rarely seeing himself as evil (or even criminal), will become increasingly disgusted with criminal activity in society and will begin to direct his efforts *against* other criminals—and simply, he will tell himself, for the sake of foiling professional criminals. At the same time, he will continue to seduce and to destroy ordinary, innocent people—and still see himself as a decent, moral person. In the most recent Ripley novel, Tom does, in fact, see himself as the hero, fighting impersonal crimes in a corrupt society.

In *Ripley's Game* (1974), the focus is divided between Tom and his victim, Jonathan Trevanny, who seems to serve as counterpoint to Tom: against Tom's pretensions to ethics and morality is placed the genuinely ethical and moral Jonathan. And, while Tom always feels that he "understands" Jonathan, Jonathan *never* feels that he understands Tom. While Tom's "understanding" of Trevanny is always skewed, he yet is able to draw Trevanny into his schemes, and finally—while convincing himself that he is Trevanny's benefactor—to destroy him, both morally and physically. Tom's malignancy is stronger than the ordinary man's morality, just as, in society as it is seen in this novel, crime is stronger than

honesty and the lives of criminals are worth more than the lives of ordinary citizens.

The Tom-Jonathan comparison is ubiquitous throughout *Ripley's Game.* Jonathan cannot manage the self-control to lie convincingly to his wife; Tom is still the master of invention, and one of his greatest inventions is his perception of himself as sensitive, ethical, and civilized. It is he who suggests pulling Jonathan into his and Reeves's criminal schemes, but, when Reeves actually acts on the suggestion, Tom calls it "a dirty, humourless trick." Tom's luring Jonathan into crime is soon looked upon by him as an act of beneficence, and he both congratulates himself and feels some empathy with Jonathan, whom he can now view as just a murderer, like himself. As he did with Dickie Greenleaf, Tom identifies with his victim and feels the warmest of feelings for him while never understanding that Jonathan both abhors and is mystified by Tom. Tom engages in crime to allay the boredom of his life—the boredom of being Tom Ripley. Jonathan has no need for stimulation and, in fact, after at first feeling "a bit euphoric" thinking of the money he will earn for his wife and child, is able to feel nothing.

To Tom, it is imperative that he see the rest of the world as no better than himself—as corruptible, as always having something to be ashamed of, as Jonathan must have felt once he became a murderer. Tom constructs a picture of himself as a heroic figure, kindly benefactor to Jonathan Trevanny, and moral superior to most criminals. He has the utmost contempt for large-scale, professional criminals, such as the Mafia, of whom he thinks as "more dishonest, more corrupt, decidedly more ruthless than himself." And, because "the law couldn't get its hands on the bigger bastards among them," he, Tom, will become a vigilante, assassinating criminals whom the law cannot touch.

But, Tom's pretensions to moral righteousness aside, the society portrayed *is* growing more corrupt, at least within the context of the Ripley novels. Organized crime and random violence exist in a society in which governments do not seem to be "aware of the insane actions of some of their spies. Or those whimsical, half-demented men flitting from Bucharest to Moscow and Washington with guns and microfilm." This last is Tom's view, and in such a context Tom's "game" is relatively harmless, his claim to be a force for the good and the right almost credible. It is these claims and this eroding society which become dominant in *The Boy Who Followed Ripley* (1980).

The original Tom Ripley created his own reality. In *The Boy,* the deception is more often on the part of the environment, and Tom is at its mercy. The illusion of wilderness in the Grunewald Forest of West Berlin first leads Tom to wonder if *everything* is not an illusion, and then leads him to succumb to the deceptions of a gang of criminals and to fail to prevent the kidnapping of Frank (the "Boy" of the title). External forces exert an unaccustomed control over Tom. After Frank's kidnapping, Tom feels that he "had never felt thus shaken by something that he himself had done, because in such cases in the past, he had been in control of things. Now he was anything but in control." Unlike the earlier, omnipotent Tom, this Tom becomes "tired of fretting over things he couldn't do anything about."

Tom once again identifies with the male figure in the story but this time seeks to *protect* his alter ego from the society that threatens both of them. No longer does he seduce the innocent into crime (Frank is a murderer before he meets Tom). And, this time, Frank's suicide seems to have nothing to do with Tom's influence. In this case, Tom's identification seems benign, a magnanimous, protective gesture. His perception of his righteousness grows as he opposes the professional criminals who try to kidnap Frank, and his perception seems (for a change) fairly close to reality. Tom initiates no evil, and the forces he is battling do seem more evil than he is. But the old Tom is still there, pursuing criminals finally for the ultimate good: the risk, the danger, the stimulation. And Tom Ripley the heroic crime fighter is still Tom Ripley who thinks like a criminal, anticipating the kidnappers at every turn—and succumbing to the foolhardy out of his abiding love of danger.

The old Tom Ripley is still with us, but the society in which he operates is now so rotten—*really* rotten—that the criminal with a "code" comes off as a hero. *Any* morality is superior to the total depravity into which most of society has sunk.

This view of society is not confined to the later Ripley novels. In her ***The Glass Cell*** (1964), Highsmith depicts a naïve protagonist first victimized by criminals, then corrupted by the prison environment in which he is unjustly confined. That Highsmith's focus on society begins to usurp her earlier vision of isolated criminality is underlined by her using ***The Glass Cell*** as the one extended example of her creative process in her 1966 how-to-book, ***Plotting and Writing Suspense Fiction*** (wherein she speaks of one of the "elements" of the story as "the deleterious effect of exposure to brutality in prison, and how this can lead to anti-social behavior after release"). Her next two novels, excluding the 1970 ***Ripley under Ground*** and the 1974 ***Ripley's Game,*** continue the new interest in social forces: ***The Tremor of Forgery*** (1969) depicts the effects of the alien view of criminality in Tunisian society on an American, and ***A Dog's Ransom*** (1972) is an obsessive portrait of a crime-ridden New York City which corrupts and destroys decent human beings. Three of Highsmith's four most recent novels (***The Boy Who Followed Ripley*** is the exception) are set in the United States (and the latest Ripley novel ends there), and none focuses primarily on criminals. All (***Edith's Diary,*** 1977; ***People who Knock on the Door,*** 1983; and ***Found in the Street,*** 1986)

depict a society in which most people are either obsessed with fanatical religious or political beliefs or are turned inward toward totally self-serving, socially irresponsible behavior. Both orientations can lead to criminality, and they do so in these books. The evolution of the picture of crime and society which occurs in the Ripley novels is consistent with the evolution occurring in Highsmith's other works. But, while Ripley's perception of society seems to parallel Highsmith's, his perception of himself does not.

One must remember the irony: Tom Ripley may be right about the world, but he is still thoroughly lacking in insight into Tom Ripley. His motives are, ultimately, the strictly personal ones of his need for the stimulation of danger and, still, for occasionally losing his identity in a masquerade of some kind. These last Ripley novels are not works of social criticism. Patricia Highsmith remains the novelist of the psychological portrayal of criminal behavior. She simply has moved, over the years, toward a more social orientation— to a greater awareness of the effects of society on behavior.

Susannah Clapp (review date 10 January 1991)

SOURCE: "Lovers on a Train," in *London Review of Books,* Vol. 13, No. 1, January 10, 1991, p. 19.

[*In the following positive review of* Carol, *which was originally published as* The Price of Salt *under the pseudonym Claire Morgan, Clapp discusses the plot of the novel, focusing on Highsmith's depiction of landscape and homosexuality.*]

'Beautifully written' is novel-reviewer's shorthand for 'written by a woman'. So is 'slim'. And 'slender'. I began to note these casual condescensions when I was helping to judge last year's Booker Prize. But then, prizes bring out prickliness. 'Do you think,' asked one contributor to the *London Review of Books,* 'that the Booker panel is as distinguished as it should be?' The question was delivered with a speculative air, worthy of the academic who spoke. 'After all,' he mused on, 'there are probably *dons* who would be prepared to act as judges.'

So it seems. There is, for example, Eric Griffiths, who was beamed onto the television screen cutting the Booker finalists, especially the females, down to size. He blamed A. S. Byatt for producing 'the kind of novel I'd write if I was foolish enough not to know that I couldn't write a novel'; he commended Brian Moore for having included, in one of the most routine sentences Moore has ever written, the words 'a quarter to nine'. Beryl Bainbridge's *An Awfully Big Adventure* he denounced as being a novel 'about a charming little girl written by a charming big girl'. Books don't come slimmer than that.

Some critics seemed to think that male writers must have been strenuously extruded from the short list. Why, one friend asked indignantly, wasn't the 'Amis-Barnes Axis' on it? The explanation that neither writer had published a novel in 1990 was met by a witheringly sceptical silence. Others seemed unnerved by Bainbridge's novel, which was patronised as a 'surprise' finalist. The surprise was partly because her novel had been put out in unfashionable December and skimpily reviewed. It was also expressive of a conventional idea of a Booker book. Bainbridge's novels are short and funny and dark. They are very particular: an inventory of their names and contents—all those loofahs, geysers, murders, Fredas—could not easily be accommodated in another contemporary novel. They are not usually described as 'ambitious'. And ambition, which is easier for people to agree about than, say, a sense of prizes. It is a unisex quality. When Bainbridge was first shortlisted for the Booker in 1973, the prize was won by J. G. Farrell for *The Siege of Krishnapur,* this year it went to A. S. Byatt's *Possession.* Both these good winners were rightly praised for the largeness of their historical reach. Bainbridge's scenes are more claustrophobic—both drabber and more dire. But small does not mean puny. There is a scatter—it is hardly a line—of female wits whose stage is narrow, whose mode is elliptical, and whose secrets are guilty. They are called Ivy Compton-Burnett, Muriel Spark and Beryl Bainbridge. All have crime at the heart of their novels. None of them is a crime novelist.

Patricia Highsmith is. And in making murder her main point, she has avoided being thought of primarily as a woman novelist. She has made a career of producing books of settled menace, in which acts of homicide surface, almost welcomed, as breaks in routine. Her heroes kill not without feeling, but without fear of reprisal. They bash because someone is about to get in their way: 'He remembered his cool thoughts of beating her senseless with his shoe heel.' And they strangle as part of a self-development project:

> If he were interviewed he would say, 'It was terrific! There's nothing in the world like it.' ('Would you do it again, Mr Bruno?') 'Well, I might,' reflectively, with caution, as an arctic explorer when asked if he will winter up north again next year might reply uncommittingly to a reporter.

Highsmith, who has said that she 'never thinks about style', has developed a distinctive prose which catches the obsessions of her protagonists, their dogged attention to detail, and their insulation from the rest of the world. This can go too far. Some of her narration has a stunned, Janet-and-John quality.

But the restaurant served only beer and wine, so they left. Carol did not stop anywhere for her drink as they drove back towards New York. Carol asked her if she wanted to go home or come out to Carol's house for a while, and Therese said to Carol's house. She remembered the Kellys had asked her to drop in on the wine and fruitcake party they were having tonight, and she had promised to, but they wouldn't miss her, she thought.

This passage—a limp note in an atmospheric book—is from Highsmith's second novel, which, under the unsurprising title *Carol,* is now published in Britain for the first time. *Carol* is a novel about a lesbian love-affair, and was written shortly after *Strangers on a Train,* which was branded by Harper as 'A Harper Novel of Suspense'. Anxious not to be relabelled as 'a lesbian-book writer', Highsmith submitted the manuscript under a pseudonym: Harper turned it down. She changed publishers, and the book appeared in 1952. It was called *The Price of Salt* and was said to be by Claire Morgan; it received 'respectable' reviews, piles of fan mail, and sold a million copies in paperback. It is a romance which reads almost exactly like a Patricia Highsmith thriller.

Highsmith got the idea for *Carol* in 1948, when she was 27. She had finished her first novel, was broke and fed up, and had taken a job in a Manhattan department store. She was sent to work in the toy department, on the dolls' counter—where all those floppy or morbidly stiff little limbs and those rows of glassy eyeballs must have appealed to her. One day a blonde woman in a mink coat came into the store. She was elegant and a little uncertain. She bought a doll, gave a delivery name and address, and left. 'It was a routine transaction . . . But I felt cold and swimmy in the head, near to fainting, yet at the same time uplifted, as if I had seen a vision.' Highsmith went home and wrote out the entire plot of *Carol,* which begins with a meeting between a salesgirl and a glamorous older woman in the toy department of a large store, spills out across the North American continent, as the two women decide to go travelling together (at first simply as friends, later as lovers), and ends with the couple looking as if they will try to settle down together. It took Highsmith two hours to plan her book. The next day, still in a strangely swoony condition, she was diagnosed as having chicken pox. Characteristically, she identifies the germ that gave her the fever and pustules with the germ of her idea for a novel: she describes herself dreaming up her love story with a face full of 'bleeding spots . . . as if . . . hit by a volley of air-gun pellets'.

Carol is constructed like a Highsmith thriller, with pages of uneasy eventlessness punctuated by sudden alarms. If anything, these alarms are more frequent and more exciting than those in her suspense novels. The young heroine Therese, infatuated by her companion and beginning to trust her, discovers a gun tucked away in her suitcase; as Therese and Carol travel from Chicago to Salt Lake City, a solitary man seems to follow them from hotel to hotel; in an unfamiliar town, the couple discover a bugging device strapped to their bedside table. There is a car chase through unpeopled hills, a confrontation with a detective, a pay-off and the possibility of a shoot-out. Each incident is given piquancy by the equivocal character of Carol, who is lovely, cool, mocking, given to abrupt silences and unpredictable sweetness. Her attitudes and affections are often in doubt; her impenetrability is as threatening as it is alluring.

But it is the landscape, glimpsed in Hopper-like snatches, at once sharp-edged and one-dimensional, which gives the novel its tang. That and the details of weird animation. Here is a Highsmith character eating a canteen lunch: 'The peaches, like slimy little orange fishes, slithered over the edge of the spoon.' And here is another, downing a wholesome bedtime posset: 'The milk seemed to taste of bone and blood, of warm flesh or hair . . .' This is a world full of the eerie vitality of the miniature. A toy train, freighted with tiny men and little logs, speeds round the department store in which Therese works, 'like something gone mad in imprisonment, something already dead that would never wear out'—or like the funfair roundabout near which a killing takes place in *Strangers on a Train*. A model village fascinates Therese, who wants to design theatre sets, and who pins up tiny cardboard rooms on her walls. Her fascination elicits one of her lover's acerbic observations: 'You so prefer things reflected in glass, don't you? You have your own private conception of everything . . . I wonder if you'll even like seeing real mountains and real people.' Which could be said of Highsmith's murderers.

Like her murderers, Highsmith's lovers make their dreams come true. In *Strangers on a Train* Bruno imagines committing the perfect murder ('the idea of my life'), and then does it. In *Carol* the 19-year-old shop assistant fantasises about kissing the beautiful older woman—who has money, a husband, a child and a huge house—and ends up running off with her. In many novels such success would be punished, but in Highsmith's fiction people get away with things. Tom Ripley begins a murderous career by drowning one acquaintance and battering another—and then swans off to a Greek island. Therese and Carol are vilified and threatened by husbands, lovers and lawyers, but finally decide they can manage a future together. It was this glimmer of a happy ending that attracted early readers of *Carol*. 'Prior to this book', Highsmith reflects, 'homosexuals male and female in American novels had had to pay for their deviation by cutting their wrists, drowning themselves in a swimming-pool, or by switching to heterosexuality (so it was stated), or by collapsing—alone and miserable and shunned—into a depression equal to hell.'

It is unlikely that the sex in the novel drew people to it. Sharing a bed in a town called Waterloo, Therese and Carol kiss and fondle: then, suddenly, white flowers are seen glimmering in water, arrows are sent whizzing, and bodies melt into 'widening circles that leaped further and further, beyond where thought could follow'. This can't be good news. Highsmith can write persuasively about sexual feeling, but she is at her best when she does so obliquely. Before *Carol*, she had written *Strangers on a Train*, with its celebrated exchange of murders by two men, one of them a mother-dependent wheedler who craves the admiration of his counterpart. Immediately after *Carol*, she wrote *The Blunderer*, which featured a similarly charged relationship between two men, whose sexual ambiguity is given even more emphasis: 'Kimmel was aware that he felt intensely feminine, more intensely than when he spied upon his own sensuous curves in the bathroom mirror.' (Melchior Kimmel, who has vulgarly fat lips and a tendency to shrug, is an envier of 'Anglo-Saxon good looks'.) When Highsmith began her Ripley series, with *The Talented Mr Ripley* in 1955, she created a protagonist who dresses up in his host's trousers and prances in front of the mirror, who is disgusted by his chum's girlfriend, and who savours as his most bitter memory an episode in which he was called a sissy at the age of 12. *Carol* has the compulsion of a thriller; Highsmith's thrillers have the lure of romance.

Pat Wagner (review date June 1991)

SOURCE: A review of *The Price of Salt*, in *The Bloomsbury Review*, Vol. 11, No. 4, June, 1991, p. 16

[*In the following review of* The Price of Salt, *which Highsmith published under the pseudonym Claire Morgan, Wagner examines Highsmith's depiction of homosexual love.*]

To risk love is to risk unhappiness, but for those whose love goes against the main currents of society, punishment and tragedy are certain. The only way, in fact, that generations of writers who discussed "forbidden" love could get away with creating three-dimensional and sympathetic characters is to make sure everyone suffered by the final curtain. A publisher, editor, or even a self-censuring author might force an unhappy ending on those fictional couples unfortunate enough to love across racial, political, or socioeconomic barriers or whose passion violated marital or religious vows. The necessity of imparting a lesson by destroying star-crossed lovers is part of indigenous myth, the Bible, Shakespeare, and, of course, the mid-century literature of the gay and lesbian community. To love someone of the same sex was to sin, and sin could only be written about (and enjoyed) if it was punished by death or abandonment. This forty-year-old classic [*The Price of Salt*] broke the rules.

It charts a difficult love between two women, with the complications of a husband, former lovers, and a child. Some of the conflicts will seem a little clichéd to today's readers, who have seen the story recounted in dozens of novels, if not ones nearly as well written. The younger woman learns about life as her passion for the older woman takes her out of herself; it allows her to take risks she would not have taken on her own behalf. The affair affects her relationship with others and even her career; she becomes willing to try to leave the usual dead-end jobs and hasten her success as a stage designer in New York. She begins to know herself.

This is not a perfect couple, and, in some ways, their attraction is a mystery. The younger woman is timid and vague; she seems too young in the beginning to be taken seriously. The older woman, on the other hand, is almost ruthless in her desire to achieve her ends. There is the awkward and dated glamour of her money and power, but this wears a little thin. What works is watching the author develop both characters into better people.

Love as a teacher, particularly between partners of different ages and experiences, is not new. It is not unexpected that the younger woman should become so much wiser by the end of the book. But the surprise at the end, the happy surprises, must have made the original readers cry with joy. Not having to compromise oneself, yet still finding an intimate and positive connection with another human being is rare in fiction, more so in the gay and lesbian fiction written in the "pulp" years of the genre.

Armchair Detective (essay date Summer 1994)

SOURCE: "Past Crimes," in *Armchair Detective*, Vol. 27, No. 3, Summer, 1994, p. 360.

[*In the following essay, the critic discusses Highsmith's five Tom Ripley novels, focusing on Ripley's matter-of-fact attitude toward crime.*]

Through the years we have had the chance to follow the extraordinarily eccentric life of Patricia Highsmith's Thomas Ripley, who surely must be one of the oddest series figures in crime fiction since Raffles, the gentleman crook. The Ripley novels have been appearing since 1955, and the fifth and latest, *Ripley under Water,* came out in 1992.

The first in the series is the strongest and probably the most bizarre. *The Talented Mr. Ripley* (1955) is truly a masterpiece of crime fiction, one to rival in weirdness Highsmith's first novel, *Strangers on a Train*. At the beginning of this on-going saga the impecunious Mr. Ripley is hired to go to Europe to find the wayward son of a wealthy Boston couple.

By the end of the novel, Ripley has not only murdered his quarry, but he has also forged a will in his favor, financially setting himself up for life, and he has done all of this with apparently little cost to his conscience. Tom Ripley has been looking over his shoulder ever since.

By the second novel, *Ripley under Ground* (1970), Tom Ripley has become a silent partner in The Buckminster Gallery in London which specializes, unknown to its customers, in art forgeries of a dead surrealist artist, Derwatt. In addition, he does a few favors to help a friend who runs a high-ticket fencing operation out of Germany and putters in his garden while enjoying the good life with his wife, Heloise, in their suburban villa, Belle Ombre, situated just outside Paris. Through the rest of the books Tom continues to prosper despite the fact that he continues to break the law, on occasion murdering those who threaten his secure existence. Not that all of these crime stories do not have their strange attraction but once Ripley has married and settled down with his wife to live an outwardly bourgeoisie life, the books lose some of their tension. Part of the problem is that as the series progresses, it becomes increasingly unlikely that he will be caught no matter how dangerous the adventures he experiences.

The action of all of the novels after the first takes place from Belle Ombre and although Ripley jets around Europe and even once in a while to America, he always returns to the safety of his wife and house. In this series however safety is conditional. Ever since the questionable events of the first book, Ripley has existed under a cloud of suspicion, watched by the police and always prey to those who would pry into the mysterious disappearances of the increasing number of people who seem to vanish when Ripley is around. He never quite rids himself of the sins of his past, although he does seem to be able to live with his transgressions with little regret.

What makes the books so fascinating and so eerie is the flat, matter-of-fact attitude toward murder and mayhem which Ripley maintains. He suffers momentary pangs of remorse or disquieting thoughts on occasion, but in general, he slips down the bloody trail he walks with a certain ease. And those around him, even if they know about Ripley's crimes, seem little bothered by them. It is as if the world he inhabits is strangely immune from guilt.

These are unsettling works of fiction, full of macabre humor and devilish insouciance, which play on the reader's fantasies of individual power and choice. In a universe so full of nasty people and random, uncontrollable events, it is awkwardly satisfying to watch someone exercise his personal will unfettered by the normal constraints of legality and civilized controls imposed upon the rest of us. For the successful creation of fiction as powerfully attractive as the Ripley novels are, Patricia Highsmith deservedly has earned her place as a crime writer of exceptional achievement.

MaryKay Mahoney (essay date 1994)

SOURCE: "A Train Running on Two Sets of Tracks: Highsmith's and Hitchcock's *Strangers on a Train*," in *It's a Print: Detective Fiction from Page to Screen,* edited by William Reynolds and Elizabeth A. Tremblay, Bowling Green State University Popular Press, 1994, pp. 103-13.

[*In the following essay, Mahoney provides a comparative study of Highsmith's novel* Strangers on a Train *and Alfred Hitchcock's film adaptation of the work, concluding that "the two works are substantially different in focus and direction."*]

Highsmith's *Strangers on a Train* provides a psychological analysis of Guy Haines and Charles Anthony Bruno and their intertwined relationship. Hitchcock transforms the material into a thriller, focusing on action, suspense, and surprise. In the novel, the personalities of the characters, Highsmith's stylistic techniques, and the plot structure emphasize the similarities between Haines and Bruno; in the film, however, the visual links between the two are confused by the transformation of Haines into an innocent hero.

It begins with a casual conversation between two men on a train. When one of them shifts the topic to a "trade" of murders—"I kill your wife and you kill my father"—the first strands are spun of a web of violence that will entangle both men. Readers of suspense fiction and fans of Alfred Hitchcock films will immediately identify this plot: Patricia Highsmith's novel *Strangers on a Train* (1950) and Alfred Hitchcock's 1951 film adaptation of the same name.

Highsmith describes the starting point for her novel [in *Plotting and Writing Suspense Fiction*]: "the germ of the plot for *Strangers on a Train* was: 'Two people agree to murder each other's enemy, thus permitting a perfect alibi to be established.'" Highsmith's own novel deals somewhat ironically with that plot germ, since Guy Haines does not, on the train, "agree" verbally to the trade of murders suggested by his fellow "stranger" Charles Anthony Bruno. In Guy's revelations about his wife, Miriam, to Bruno, and in his silence after Miriam's murder, however, there is an implicit consent, and Guy eventually becomes a full accomplice in the exchange of murders, killing Bruno's father as his part of the trade. In Hitchcock's film, on the other hand, the exchange of murders is far more one-sided, with Bruno Killing Miriam but Guy, in return, attempting instead to warn Bruno's father, the intended second victim.

As suggested by the dramatic plot change in the film, the

two works are substantially different in focus and direction. Highsmith focuses on the psychological analysis of the two men and their intertwined relationship, whereas Hitchcock's transformation of the material into the genre of the thriller means a corresponding focus on action and the characteristic Hitchcock elements of suspense and surprise. According to John Russell Taylor, "In *Strangers on a Train* Hitch had managed, by instinct rather than conscious thought, to find a deeply disturbing subject—that of an exchange of guilt—which could be satisfactorily externalized in thriller form." Hitchcock himself commented, "*Strangers on a Train* wasn't an assignment, but a novel that I selected myself. I felt this was the right kind of material for me to work with."

As various film critics have pointed out, Hitchcock's opening shots for the film capture a sense of the film as a whole:

> Extremely low camera placements in the opening sequence prepare us for a film that will take place largely in a subterranean world of anxiety and nightmare. The credits run over a scene looking back from the inside of a cavernous train station to the brightness of the world outside. As they end, a cab turns into the entrance. It disgorges Bruno, or more accurately, Bruno's garish shoes and trouser legs. A second cab pulls up at the dark curb and unloads Guy's legs, feet, and tennis racquets. The film begins with a movement into darkness from which it will return only at the very end. . . .
>
> As the action of guilt and entrapment commences, images of descent and imprisonment proliferate. The camera stays at knee level for a minute and a half after the credits, until Bruno's foot and Guy's bump under a table in the lounge car. This opening sequence includes an expressive shot of the shadow of the train proceeding along the intersecting and diverging tracks of the railyard. . . . The image of the converging rails at the beginning of *Strangers on a Train* serves as an emblem of the plot, in which characters in a chaos of unconnected human lives coincidentally converge and collide, turn apart, and pursue crucial actions in parallel.

Those opening shots of the two pairs of feet moving towards each other and of the converging railroad tracks emphasize the connection between the two men, the deliberate image of them as doubles. Robin Wood points out that, in the process, our sense of the opposition between the two pairs of shoes seen in the opening sequence—Guy's modest dark shoes and Bruno's flashier two-toned spats—becomes a parallel "imposed by the editing on what would otherwise be pure contrast." This sense of Bruno and Guy as doubles is reinforced both visually and linguistically throughout the scenes that follow by such elements as Guy's lighter with its engraving of crossed tennis racquets, the link between the "doubles" of tennis player Guy and the scotch doubles ordered for them both by Bruno, and Bruno's thoughtful murmurs of "Crisscross" as he lies back in his private compartment, holding the lighter Guy has left behind and contemplating the trade in murders he has just suggested to Guy.

Yet despite the film's technical brilliance in suggesting the idea of doubles, the viewer's sense of Bruno as the representative of Guy's unexamined and repressed desires is shortcircuited by the plot level of the film, resulting in a significant departure from the dynamics of the Highsmith novel. In plot terms, Guy is an innocent man, guilty on a conscious level of neither Miriam's death nor Bruno's plans to have his father killed. Hitchcock's editing techniques visually link Guy and Bruno; for example, when Hitchcock cuts from a scene in a telephone booth where Guy, drowned out at first by a train, shouts about Miriam, "I said I could strangle her!" to a shot of Bruno's curved, upheld hands, the sequence directly links Guy's desire for Miriam's death to the means by which Bruno will accomplish that death. Yet the essence of the film's plot is that Guy, the innocent hero, will eventually emerge uncorrupted from the world of darkness into which Bruno has temporarily plunged him.

When Hitchcock's Guy, having entered Bruno's father's bedroom at night in accordance with Bruno's murderous plan, attempts to warn the father (only to find a suspicious Bruno there in his place), the opposition, rather than the likeness, between the two men becomes marked. Even though Guy carries a gun with him on his nocturnal expedition, the speed with which he pockets the gun outside the bedroom and calls out the name of Bruno's father makes it nearly impossible to believe that Guy is seriously tempted to carry out the killing to protect himself from Bruno's blackmailing threats. As a result, the scene's suspense derives from Hitchcock's deliberately misleading the viewer, rather than from any sense of Guy as a potentially complex and unpredictable character torn between two possible choices. When Guy is confronted on the staircase by an apparently vicious guard-dog and the viewer is swept into fear for Guy's safety, that very anxiety (considering that Guy *may* be about to kill a defenseless old man in cold blood) is designed to force viewers to deal with the moral ambiguity of their own reactions. Yet the viewers' moral dilemma is patently manufactured if there is no real chance of Guy's killing Bruno's father, and this converts the whole sequence to the level of a clever trick. (Interestingly, Wood, in revising his essay on the film, shifts from seeing this problem as simply a "misjudgment" to commenting that "Major lapse in artistic integrity' is perhaps not too strong a description.")

This confrontation between Bruno and Guy reveals to Bruno as well as to viewers that Guy will not succumb to Bruno's

dark desires. In retaliation, Bruno threatens to find an appropriate revenge for the "betrayal": he will falsify evidence of the innocent Guy's guilt. After Bruno's decision, the film moves quickly to two dramatically crosscut races against time: Bruno's attempting to rescue Guy's lighter from a sewer so he can use it to incriminate Guy, and Guy's attempting to win his tennis match at Forest Hills as quickly as possible so he can thwart Bruno's plans. This crosscutting emphasizes the differences between the two men by means of a striking visual contrast: the darkness of the sewer scenes and the open, sunlit scenes of the tennis match represent each character's moral condition.

As the film progresses, viewers clearly discern the men's dramatic opposition despite the chaos of events and the confusion of the police. In the film's climactic scene Guy follows Bruno to the carnival grounds where Bruno killed Guy's wife, Miriam. There the police are misled by the ambiguity of a carnival worker's cry; looking towards the two men, he exclaims: "He's the one. He's the one who killed her." As the accidental shooting of the carousel operator sends the carousel hurtling at top speed, Guy is swept dramatically from the ordered safe world he craves into the instability and disorder linked with Bruno. Nevertheless, the opposition between the two men remains paramount, captured in miniature by a vignette where a young boy attempting to help Guy is pushed viciously by Bruno and nearly falls from the wildly spinning carousel; Guy risks himself to save the child, with the result that he himself is nearly killed by Bruno.

As soon as the carousel's crash and the discovery of Guy's lighter in the dead Bruno's hand have revealed Guy's innocence to the police, Guy is able to return to a harmony with the ordered world beyond the carnival gates. The film ends, however, not with the death of Bruno, but with a humorous parallel that indicates the degree to which Guy is free of Bruno and the threat to Guy's world and his sense of self that Bruno represented. A minister on the same train as Guy and Anne (the woman Guy loves and intends to marry) inadvertently repeats Bruno's opening question, "Aren't you Guy Haines?"; Guy and Anne look at each other and exit the car, leaving behind the bemused minister. The repetition of Bruno's comments by this clearly harmless "stranger" underlines Guy's return to a world of order and normalcy.

Earlier in the film, the use of other minor "strangers" on trains also de-emphasizes the idea that the link between Guy and Bruno is predestined, necessitated by something within Guy himself rather than by random chance. Just as the minister's question is a harmless repetition of Bruno's, so another passenger has earlier nudged the foot of another man accidentally, just as Guy had nudged Bruno's. And Guy's supposed acquiescence to Bruno's murder plot—"Now, you think my theory's okay, Guy? You like it?" "Sure, Bruno, sure. They're all okay"—is humorously repeated, on the same night that Bruno kills Miriam, when Guy casually assures the drunken Professor Collins, in response to a confused question about differential calculus, "Yes, I understand."

The clear separation between Guy and Bruno during the later part of the film is responsible for an element of moral ambiguity in the film as a whole: Guy's pleasant future of marriage to Anne and a political career has been provided for him courtesy of Bruno, who has removed Miriam, the only obstacle to Guy's happiness. Guy's ability both to separate himself from that murderous desire and to profit from its results has been described variously: Spoto calls it "one of Hitchcock's darkest ironies," whereas Wood notes that "the effect seems at times two-dimensional, or like watching the working out of a theorem rather than a human drama."

In contrast to the portrayal in Hitchcock's film, Highsmith's novel makes the link between Guy and Bruno a major component of the book's overall direction. Highsmith's use of both Guy's and Bruno's narrative points of view acts structurally as Hitchcock's crosscutting does in his adaptation: forcing us to picture the two men as inextricably linked doubles, rather than as separate individuals. But whereas in the Hitchcock film this visual fusing runs counter to the development of the plot itself, in Highsmith's novel the personalities of the characters, the stylistic techniques, and the structure of the plot all emphasize the doubling.

The fusing of the two main characters in Highsmith's novel begins, as does Hitchcock's visual linking, with the train journey. The encounter between Highsmith's Guy and Bruno is accidental only in the most superficial way; though the encounter is not planned, the sense of shared identity arises immediately and is reinforced by Guy's denial of its existence: "All he despised, Guy thought, Bruno represented. All the things he would not want to be, Bruno was, or would become." Despite these protests, Highsmith's Guy is quickly drawn to something in his companion, unlike Hithcock's Guy, who is presented as alternately amused, annoyed, or irritated by Bruno and his notions. When Bruno propounds his theory that "a person ought to do everything it's possible to do before he dies, and maybe die trying to do something that's really impossible," Guy's reaction reveals a likeness to Bruno: "Something in Guy responded with a leap, then cautiously drew back. He asked softly, 'Like what?'"

Highsmith continues to stress the psychological links between the two men through her portrayal of Guy's passive vulnerability when he is confronted with Bruno's aggressive curiosity. Hitchcock's adaptation de-emphasizes this sense of passivity, instead presenting Guy as a successful professional tennis player—a career choice which helps emphasize his physical presence and suggests that he is a man of action. In the film, Miriam's threat to Guy is minimal, existing only because it is impossible for Guy to refute her false charge

that the child she is carrying is his and she an abandoned wife. This strong, active, tennis-playing Guy effectively resists Bruno's murder scheme by attempting instead to warn the intended murder victim. In contrast, Highsmith's Guy is not a tennis player but a successful architect with a tendency to live in his mind, to see the world in ideals and abstractions while refusing to recognize or fully acknowledge his own suppressed emotions and needs. Until he meets Bruno, his companion on the train is a volume of Plato, an old high school text that he accidentally leaves in Bruno's compartment and that later becomes a clue to be used against him. He has brought the book as "an indulgence to compensate him, perhaps, for having to make the trip to Miriam." But while the words he reads make sense to him, an inner voice questions, "But what good will Plato do you with Miriam."

Guy's inability to face his tangled feelings about Miriam makes him an easy prey for Bruno, with his cool, unshockable curiosity. Finding in Bruno the stranger to whom he can admit Miriam's unfaithfulness, Guy realizes that "he had never told anyone so much about Miriam." Bruno evokes in Guy the feelings he has tried both to conceal and ignore; when Bruno asks how many lovers Miriam had, Guy, in answering, finds himself caught in a surge of emotion: "'Quite a few. Before I found out.' And just as he assured himself it made no difference at all now to admit it, a sensation as of a tiny whirlpool inside him began to confuse him. Tiny, but realer than the memories somehow, because he had uttered it."

Despite, or perhaps because of, this whirlpool of emotion, Highsmith's Guy remains vulnerable and passive, enabling Miriam to control him through his inability to confront difficult situations. He is willing to give up the chance to bring into actuality the Palmyra, a building he has designed, rather than face the emotional chaos and failure of his relationship with her. Miriam recognizes Guy's weakness and taunts him about his decision to give up the Palmyra to keep her from coming with him: "Running away? . . . Cheapest way out." Guy later tells Anne that, because of Miriam, he had decided the Palmyra simply wasn't part of his "destiny."

While Hitchcock's stronger, more active Guy Haines successfully resists Bruno's attempts to draw him into crime, Highsmith's confused, passive architect fails to resist Bruno because Bruno represents a part of Guy himself. In fact, in the novel the interaction between Guy and Bruno immediately takes on an overtone of mutual sexual attraction downplayed in the film's presentation of their first encounter. In the film, Bruno has no sooner met Guy than he launches into innuendoes about Guy's publicly known relationship with Anne, a senator's daughter, and his desire to get a divorce so that he and Anne can marry. In the novel, Bruno's conversation focuses on Miriam, the hated and destructive other. He knows nothing about Anne, and later feels cheated when he learns about Guy's relationship with her. However, the novel's Anne is significant in her absence, since Guy is thinking about Anne when he initiates the meeting with Bruno: "Suddenly he [Guy] felt helpless without her. He shifted his position, accidentally touched the outstretched foot of the young man asleep, and watched fascinatedly as the lashes twitched and came open." Thus begins the complex triangle as Guy's allegiance shifts between her and Bruno.

Later in the novel, Guy's relationship with Anne and Bruno becomes an almost mystical *ménage à trois*. During his wedding, Guy discovers Bruno in the church: "He [Guy] was standing beside Anne, and Bruno was here with them, not an event, not a moment, but a condition, something that had always been and always would be. Bruno, himself, Anne. And the moving on the tracks. And the lifetime of moving on the tracks until death do us part . . . ." Soon, however, three becomes a crowd. Guy and Anne's home is invaded by an uninvited Bruno, who is as immediately comfortable as if he were one of the inhabitants. Before long, Bruno comes to view Anne as the invasive presence and begins to think and act destructively toward her. Anne's prized sailboat is damaged on a surreptitious sail that Guy and Bruno take together; and Bruno finally considers eliminating Anne as the only obstacle left between himself and Guy: "*Anne is like light to me,* Bruno remembered Guy once saying. If he could strangle Anne, too, then Guy and he could really be together."

Guy's suspension between Anne and Bruno represents the struggle between the creative and destructive elements within himself, a struggle which Hitchcock's secure playboy is never forced to endure. For Guy, his architectural designs represent in concrete from the grace, beauty, and order that he discovers in the act of creation; as Kathleen Klein describes it, "His work is, for him, a spiritual act, defined by unity and wholeness; it rejects disorder, fragmentation and shallowness." His ultimate dream as an architect has always been to build that visible symbol of unity and balance, a bridge—he imagines designing "a white bridge with a span like an angel's wing." Guy's vision of Anne as an ideal—the light opposed to the darkness represented by Bruno—links her directly with the creations of his mind; and at Guy's wedding, Bob Treacher, who later offers Guy a chance to realize his dream, notes that Anne is "as beautiful as a white bridge."

Similarly, Guy recognizes a starker, destructive side of himself mirrored in Bruno. As Guy journeys to Great Neck to kill Bruno's father, he defines the relationship between them quite differently than at their first meeting: "He was like Bruno. Hadn't he sensed it time and time again, and like a coward never admitted it? Hadn't he known Bruno was like himself? Or why had he liked Bruno? He loved Bruno." After the murder, that sense of shared identity tightens; as Guy considers how good and evil, hate and love exist simulta-

neously in the human heart, he thinks, "Bruno, he and Bruno. Each was what the other had not chosen to be, the cast-off self, what he thought he hated but perhaps in reality loved." This insight is confirmed by a dream later that night, in which Guy imagines himself waking to find Bruno springing into his room. To Guy's question, "Who are you?" Bruno finally answers, "You." While he and Bruno are on the train early in the novel, Guy sees how the intelligence and clarity of his creative professional life run counter to the confused emotion and blindness of his personal life; once he has murdered, Guy understands a starker contrast:

> He felt rather like two people, one of whom could create and feel in harmony with God when he created, and the other who could murder. "Any kind of person can murder," Bruno had said on the train. The man who had explained the cantilever principle to Bobbie Cartwright two years ago in Metcalf? No, nor the man who had designed the hospital, or even the department store, or debated half an hour with himself over the colour he would paint a metal chair on the back lawn last week, but the man who had glanced into the mirror just last night and had seen for one instant the murderer, like a secret brother.

Guy is at peace in his work on the Palmyra project because of his belief that it will reach perfection: "And the more he immersed himself in the new effort, the more he felt recreated also in a different and more perfect form." The house that Guy designs for himself and Anne is likewise beautiful in both design and final form. But the idea of that house, like the finished and inhabited house itself, becomes infected and changed by becoming linked with the thought of Bruno. On the night Guy learns that Miriam is dead, he has been visualizing the house he will build, seeing it in his hotel room as "shining white and sharp against the brown bureau across the room." After the phone call reporting Miriam's murder, he looks again at the bureau: "Now, where he had seen the vision of the white house, a laughing face appeared, first the crescent mouth, then the face—Bruno's face."

Symbolically, the design of the house, planned by Guy before his encounter with Bruno on the train, reflects Guy's position as the focal point of a triangle. The house is conceived of as "Y"-shaped; and while Guy has considered dispensing with one of the arms of the "Y" in the interests of economizing, "the idea sang in Guy's head only with both arms." The house is designed to project from a white rock, and to look "as if alchemy had created it from the rock itself, like a crystal"; Guy, in fact, considers naming the house "The Crystal." As Guy imagines the house, it is a work of proportion and balance, in harmony with both itself and the environment from which it has sprung.

The idea of the house as a crystal echoes and contrasts with

Guy's earlier mental description of himself when he thinks about ways in which he has sabotaged himself and chosen to fail: "There was inside him, like a flaw in a jewel, not visible on the surface, a fear and anticipation of failure that he had never been able to mend." The jewel image is repeated when Guy drops overboard the gun he has used to kill Bruno's father. Bruno has sent Guy a Luger for the murder; Guy rejects the gun for its ugliness and ungainliness, and uses instead a gun he had bought as a teenager, an object purchased solely for its cleanness of design and aesthetic appeal. Guy's use of his own gun indicates the degree to which he is fusing what he considers the best of himself, his sense of beauty and design, with this act of destruction; it also emphasizes that he is acting of his own volition, rather than being compelled by Bruno. After the murder, despite the fact that the gun is the one concrete piece of evidence linking him to a crime, Guy is reluctant to eliminate its loveliness: "How intelligent a jewel, he thought, and how innocent it looked now. Himself—." Highsmith's Guy, unlike his creations or the beautifully designed gun, is "flawed," and he is unable to achieve within himself the harmony and balance he values. This inability renders him vulnerable to Bruno's suggestions and makes him utterly unlike the Guy Haines created in Hitchcock's film.

In the opening minutes of the Hitchcock adaptation, the shot of railway tracks coming together, and then diverging, sets the tone for the film: Guy's and Bruno's lives will converge, and then separate. In Highsmith's novel, however, the image of train tracks is used throughout to emphasize Guy's sense of imposed direction, a cessation of choices: "the lifetime of moving on the tracks."

In the film, the encounter with a stranger asking "Aren't you Guy Haines?" can be answered differently (and in a sense replayed) and so escaped. But for Highsmith's Guy, a meeting with another "stranger," Miriam's lover Owen, to whom he goes to confess his guilt, brings a fear of being further swept into a cycle rather than a sense of escaping one; as he describes the murder scheme and hears himself voicing Bruno's ideas, he has "a horrible, an utterly horrible thought all at once, that he might ensnare Owen in the same trap that Bruno had used for him, that Owen in turn would capture another stranger who would capture another, and so on in infinite progression of the trapped and the hunted." Guy can be renewed and escape from the cycle only by capture, confession, and punishment. True to his nature, the novel's Guy achieves a new ending for his script by passivity and acceptance rather than by action. He attempts to purge himself by going to Owen, telling him of the two murders, and waiting for him to make the appropriate decision. When Owen refuses to act—and indeed shows little interest in the whole situation—Guy is rescued from his passivity by the actions of the detective Gerard, who has listened to the confession by means of a telephone connection.

Despite the status of the Hitchcock film as an adaptation of Highsmith's novel, the differences in focus and plot ultimately make the two very different and individual works of art. And in spite of the drastic shift in overall effect caused by Hitchcock's plot changes, Highsmith considers *Strangers on a Train* one of the best of the films made from her novels. Perhaps the key to her ability to accept Hitchcock's vision of her novel as well as her own can be found in a comment Highsmith made on the artistic process:

> Every human being is different from the next, as handwriting and fingerprints prove. Every painter or writer or composer has consequently something different to say from the next (or should have). A Rembrandt or a Van Gogh is identifiable from a distance and at once. I believe in individuality, in being oneself, in using the maximum of one's talent. . . . That is what the public finally loves—something special and individual.

Lorna Sage (review date 13 March 1995)

SOURCE: "Savage Swiss Army Knife," in *The Observer Review,* No. 10612, March 13, 1995, p. 19.

[*In the following review of* Small g: A Summer Idyll, *Sage discusses the plot of the work and examines Highsmith's characterization and depiction of sex.*]

Patricia Highsmith's (posthumous) new novel [*Small g: A Summer Idyll*] starts out in cool, utterly characteristic vein. A beautiful boy, a character we've hardly had a chance to meet, is murdered on page two by strangers who'll never be caught—not in any story she's responsible for. And, to add insult to injury, Lulu, a self-possessed performing dog ('a circus dog, from circus stock'), is introduced as a character in her own right, one who takes up more or less as much space as the humans, and has about as much inner life as most of them, too.

Highsmith once notoriously confessed that if she saw a kitten and a baby starving on the side of the road, she'd feed the kitten first if no-one was looking—and *Small g: A Summer Idyll,* like almost everything she did, builds in the same shocking lack of prejudice in favour of the human race. Although this time, oddly enough, there is a plot which distributes rewards and punishments, it's done in a way that privileges frivolity, fairy-tale style.

Lulu the performing dog, who's dressed up from time to time in dark glasses and a headscarf, like an old-style movie star on a cruise, socialises in the Zurich bar, Jakob's Bierstube, otherwise known as the 'small g', that gives the novel its title. Small g is apparently guidebook code for 'partly gay', and a typically tidy Swiss way of making sure you know where you are. Except that you don't, since Jakob's is where gay and straight worlds border on each other and violence lurks around the corner.

Rickie, Lulu's owner, and the lover of beautiful Petey, dead on page two, is HIV positive, and trying hard—we've cut to a few months later—to get back into his life. Sentimentally (sentimentality is OK for Highsmith, it's claims to profound feeling that she scorns), Rickie resolves to take an interest in a pretty girl, Luisa, who was also in love with Petey. Luisa it turns out, is a sort of prisoner of the couturier Renate, to whom she's apprenticed; and now the plot gets into its stride—a battle between Rickie and Renate over Luisa's destiny.

Renate is an agent of the gender-police, a gay-hater, and a hater of youth and sexual freedom in general; Rickie is on the side of the mildly camp fun that goes on at the 'small g', and sees Luisa as a surrogate self, someone who yearns for the same golden boys as he does. Teddy, a sweet-and-straight Prince Charming, turns up, and Rickie encourages Luisa's interest in him, to Renate's fury . . .

So much for Swiss tidiness. Highsmith (who lived in Switzerland herself during her last years) relishes, clearly, the opportunity to litter the orderly, uptight scene with ambiguities. Again, in characteristic style, you're told some of the most vital-seeming things (Rickie's being HIV positive, Luisa's having been sexually abused by her step-father) in passing. But the most cavalier authorial gesture is the use of fairy-story motifs.

Renate is referred to as 'the old witch', and actually becomes one, complete with club foot ('Clump, scrape') and a half-witted familiar, 'like a classic village idiot of yore', whom she brainwashes into violence against her enemies. Highsmith's famous contempt for justice is here turned inside out—we have fairy-tale revenge, when the witch gets her come-uppance, silly Rickie is 'a knight in armour', and it turns out the doctor who did the HIV test was only teasing.

Doubtless the little dog laughed to see such fun and the dish ran away with the spoon, too. From one angle, this 'happy ending' looks 'mellow'; from another, though, it's full of malice (straights are cripples) and fear and loathing of the surveillance of other people's lives that happens in anything resembling a family. Luisa thinks of Renate's eyes as 'knives cutting her brain open'. Highsmith lived with animals, was bi-sexual, left no known survivors (as the *New York Times* quaintly put it) and once complained that, when she started writing, 'homosexuals in American novels had to pay for

their deviancy by cutting their throats'. In this latest novel she imagined a new generation of golden boys and girls who would escape the gingerbread house of either/or.

Geoffrey Elborn (review date 19 March 1995)

SOURCE: "Mellow at the Last," in *Guardian Weekly*, Vol. 152, No. 12, March 19, 1995, p. 29.

[*In the following positive review of* Small g: A Summer Idyll, *Elborn states that the work "has a serenity rarely found in Highsmith's world."*]

No other crime writer came near to possessing Patricia Highsmith's particular gift. Highsmith, who died last month, had an ability to stretch the nerves by teasing out the tension of some trivial domestic incident, or to describe suffocation by a cluster of snails, was entirely her own. *Small g: A Summer Idyll* is unlike any of her previous books, but from the first page, it is recognisably authentic Highsmith. Perhaps approaching her lesbian novel *Carol* in tenderness and theme, it has a serenity rarely found in Highsmith's world.

This does not mean that the novel is in any way soft. No story that opens with a vicious fatal stabbing by two drug-crazed thugs can be considered comfortable. But the victim, Petey Ritter, becomes a symbol which helps to unite a young Zurich community, both gay and straight. They have a cosy meeting-place in "small g", the codename given by a guide-book to Jakob's Beirstube Restaurant to indicate that at weekends, a partly gay clientele is welcome. The place is a centre for local gossip; Highsmith seems well-informed about the social and sexual habits of gay men, their anxieties about ageing, wearing the "wrong" clothes and fear of ending unattached on the scrapheap.

These are the concerns of Rickie Markwalder, a graphic artist of 46, whose younger boyfriend was the murdered Petey, and who is already unrequitedly in love with a young straight man called Georg. Rickie, who is a daily habitue of the restaurant, seems to know and like everybody, with the exception of two misfit characters. The more extraordinary is Renate, a middle-aged seamstress who employs a few women in a dress-making business. Her hatred of gay men edges on the paranoid. She is a monster, sexually frustrated and lonely.

Renate's behaviour becomes psychopathic when she forms an alliance with Willi, the other misfit. This impressionable, malevolent and retarded lumbering hulk is easily led by Renate into committing an act of violence in the dark of night against a gay man. "Give him a good big scare, Willi. You know how," she says.

Highsmith's dexterity in controlling atmosphere depends on what we know but the characters do not. Scattered hints that Willi is a queer-basher are introduced but deliberately not proved, a classic Highsmith confusion without which her aficionados would feel cheated. The "big scare" results in Georg suffering a nasty, near-fatal "accident".

Nemesis is achieved in a particularly satisfying way, and yet it is not quite the point. If the novel is partly an eloquent appeal for tolerance of a gay society, it also, unusually for Highsmith, shows happy relationships. This is all the more remarkable because those involved at the start love or are loved by either the wrong person or someone of the wrong sex. Fulfilment seems impossible, but the characters in this "summer idyll" surprise themselves.

Highsmith generally planted no "message" in her books, considering that anyone of any sense would realise that there is no natural justice in this world. With *Small g: A Summer Idyll,* she seems to have felt that a statement about loving relationships of all kinds was more important.

Brooks Peters (essay date June 1995)

SOURCE: "Stranger than Fiction," in *Out*, June, 1995, pp. 70, 72, 150.

[*In the following essay, Peters provides an overview of Highsmith's career, focusing on her fascination with death and murder, her lesbianism, and critical reaction to her work.*]

"Sometimes I think that the artistic life is a long and lovely suicide, and I am sorry that is so." This quote, from Oscar Wilde's personal letters, was used by writer Patricia Highsmith in a foreword to one of her 21 extraordinary novels. It might as well have been her epitaph (she died of leukemia at age 74 in Switzerland on February 4), for the statement sums up so simply the eerie melancholy that colored her lifework.

From her first novel, *Strangers on a Train* (immortalized, if bowdlerized, in Hitchcock's classic film), to her last, *Small g: A Summer Idyll,* about a bizarre gay bar in Zurich (published in London, just days after her death), Patricia Highsmith probed the dark depths of paranoia, delving into the minds of homicidal psychopaths and their victims. Very often, in her world, crime *did* pay. Her short stories were horrifying, frequently grotesque: A rat devours the nose of a small child; a snail-lover is smothered to death by millions of his slimy pets; a man saddled with a deformed baby strangles an innocent passerby in a sudden act of revenge.

One treads gingerly in Highsmith's troubled universe, never knowing what waits around the corner. Graham Greene called her "the poet of apprehension." But she was also haunted by her own demons.

Pegged early on as a suspense writer, Highsmith transcended the genre, gaining cult status even as she was ignored by most American literary critics. Those who did pay attention compared her to Henry James, Dostoyevsky, and Poe. Immensely popular in Europe, her books were filmed by Wim Wenders, René Clément, and Claude Miller, and garnered numerous awards. But she never caught on with the American public, no doubt because she didn't portray them in flattering terms and had little patience with middle-class conceptions of good versus evil. To her, justice was a man-made conceit. Novelist and director Michael Tolkin (*The Player, The Rapture*) says. "She was one of the best writers in the world. I have never read a review of her work where there wasn't some hedging on the part of the critic, a slightly superior tone because she was a girl or writing in this genre. But she was a great writer, the last turn of the dial to unlock my novels. I don't think I could have written *The Player* without her."

Few people know, however, that Patricia Highsmith, by all accounts a passionate yet very private lesbian, was also an important figure in gay literature. In 1952, fresh from her success with *Strangers on a Train,* she wrote the ground breaking novel *The Price of Salt.* Perhaps fearful of being branded a "lesbian author" as she had been a "mystery writer," Highsmith wrote under the pseudonym Claire Morgan. For decades this heartfelt romance, one of the first lesbian novels with a happy ending, was required reading for young women (and many men) eager to overcome their isolation and loneliness. Reissued several times, most notably by Naiad Press, the book is still in print. Eventually Naiad publisher Barbara Grier convinced Highsmith to use her own name on the book. "I worshipped that book," Grier says, recalling the thrill of discovering it in 1952 in a department store in Kansas City. "It was a very upbeat, pro-lesbian book, which in itself was a miracle." Highsmith's representative Anne Elisabeth Suter estimates *The Price of Salt* has sold hundreds of thousands of copies worldwide, so its impact cannot be ignored. But none of her obituaries mentioned it, except a personal piece by Tolkin in the *Los Angeles Times.*

> **From her first novel to her last, Patricia Highsmith probed the dark depths of paranoia, delving into the minds of homicidal psychopaths and their victims. Very often, in her world, crime *did* pay.**
> **—*Brooks Peters***

In fact *The New York Times*' obituary did Highsmith another disservice by erroneously calling her "Ms. Ripley," confusing the author with her most diabolical creation, Tom Ripley, an engaging American psychotic living abroad, who continually gets away with murder. No doubt Highsmith, master of irony, was laughing in her grave. She often said that Ripley, not she, had written the first of the five books in which he appears. That novel, *The Talented Mr. Ripley,* is currently being developed as a project for Paramount Pictures by Sydney Pollack and William Horberg. "Highsmith was one of the great postwar novelists," Horberg says. "Her books are impossible to put down. *The Talented Mr. Ripley* is a profound love story. Ripley loves Dickie Greenleaf but can't have him, so, tragically, he destroys him."

For all their psychological intrigue, Highsmith saw her books merely as entertainments. Favoring emotions over style, she wrote in a spare, declarative tone that weaves a terrifying spell. The monotony of quotidian details lulls the reader into a false sense of security. Her protagonists are always cooking, drinking, or making their beds, so that when a murderer suddenly *acts,* the horror is infinitely more dramatic, raw. In *The Boy Who Followed Ripley,* one of her most affecting and disturbing novels, Highsmith grippingly depicts Ripley's growing affection for a handsome young man who has murdered his invalid father by pushing his wheel-chair off a cliff in Maine. He turns to the notorious Ripley for support. Later, Ripley dresses in drag for a rendezvous at a gay bar and commits murder to save the boy's life.

What was behind Highsmith's fascination with death and murder? One can only suspect it stems from her private obsessions. She was born Patricia Plangman in Fort Worth, Texas, in 1921. Her parents, commercial artists, had divorced before she was born. Patricia lived with her maternal grandmother until age six, when she moved with her mother to New York. Her mother remarried a man named Highsmith, who later adopted Patricia. Highsmith didn't meet her natural father until she was 12. In interviews she hinted that her childhood was less than happy. Emotional turmoil was constant.

A clue to her feelings may be gleaned from her early writings, odd little stories about homicidal children. She was inspired by a clinical text her family owned called *The Human Mind,* by Dr. Karl Menninger, filled with vivid case studies about pyromaniacs, sadists, and kleptomaniacs. Highsmith used it throughout her career as a character bible. **"The Terrapin,"** for example, concerns a lonely boy whose mother dresses him in children's clothes. Alienated from his peers, in particular a bully next door, the youth grows increasingly hysterical until he stabs his mother to death after she boils a turtle alive. One wonders, with a chill, if Highsmith's mother ever read that story.

Highsmith attended Barnard College, where she edited the school literary magazine. There she met journalist Kate Kingsley Skattebol, who corresponded with Highsmith the rest of her life and remained a devoted friend. Skattebol recalls Highsmith as a droll, impish wit fond of practical jokes, scatological humor, and bawdy limericks. "Her writing talent was evident in college," she says. One of her earliest tales, **"The Heroine,"** about a deranged nanny who sets fire to a house where she works, was rejected by the Barnard magazine, Skattebol says, because it was "too unpleasant." It later appeared in *Harper's Bazaar* and the short story collection *Eleven,* regaining notoriety decades later during the scandalous Swiss nanny murder trial. Some thought the alleged killer (later acquitted) might have been inspired by Highsmith's story.

An early friend, Truman Capote championed Highsmith, helping her to get into Yaddo, where she rewrote *Strangers on a Train* (it had been rejected by six publishers). Over the years, Highsmith also developed lasting friendships with writers Graham Greene, Gore Vidal, and Paul Bowles. When not writing fiction, Highsmith found odd jobs, writing scenarios for Superman comics or toiling at Bloomingdale's over Christmas. She used that stint as background for *The Price of Salt:* Therese, the main character, whose dark features and shy, dreamy demeanor bear more than a passing resemblance to the young Highsmith, meets her lover, Carol, at a New York department store.

"Every adult has secrets," writes Highsmith at the novel's end. And throughout her life she seemed to enjoy harboring her own. "Pat was nothing if not unobvious," says Gary Fisketjon, her editor at Knopf, her last American publisher. "She was not particularly troubled by the fact that she was gay. She couldn't give a shit—she was Texan until the fucking end. But she preferred leading a private life." Barbara Grier, who never met her in person but corresponded with her frequently, says Highsmith suffered acutely from "internalized homophobia," which was not surprising, she adds, considering the era in which she was raised. Highsmith's own attitude is put rather succinctly in a postscript to *The Price of Salt,* in which she states, "I like to avoid labels."

An expatriate, Highsmith traveled constantly, moving first from New York to Mexico, then to Italy, England, and France, before finally settling near Locarno, in Switzerland. Often cold and close-mouthed with reporters, Highsmith disliked publicity. "She hated to come out of her house," says her Swiss publisher Daniel Keel. On more than one occasion she walked out in the middle of interviews. But her sense of humor was well-known. Larry Ashmead, executive editor at HarperCollins, recalls Highsmith telling him how she once smuggled live snails into France by hiding them under her breasts.

At the end, Highsmith lived alone with her beloved cat, Charlotte. She was by most accounts, a loner who drank and smoked to excess. As a young woman, according to Fisketjon, Highsmith was a "staggeringly beautiful woman." But as she aged, her sturdy, masculine features became more exaggerated, almost forbidding. Duncan Hannah, a New York artist, recalls meeting Highsmith at a book-signing: "She was like a Mandarin, almost Buddha-like," he says, "with a dilapidated, very still quality. Being under her gaze was like being under a microscope. It was spooky."

Highsmith seems to have exorcised her demons with her final and most openly gay work, *Small g: A Summer Idyll.* Sweetly sentimental, with gothic undertones, this dark romance harks back to the young-adults-in-love theme of *The Price of Salt,* but lacks its focus. In fact, *Small g* was rejected by Knopf and poorly reviewed in England. But it has unmistakable Highsmith touches: a club-footed homophobe, a bisexual beauty, a dandy diagnosed as HIV positive, and a clever circus dog named Lulu who upstages everyone else. One wonders what Highsmith might have achieved had she brought her literary villains and herself "out" decades ago. But maybe, for her readers, it's better she didn't. For then we might not have experienced the full rewards of her strange, macabre genius.

FURTHER READING

Criticism

Campbell, James. "Criminal Negligence." *Times Literary Supplement,* No. 4795 (February 24, 1995): 32.
> Negative review of *Small g: A Summer Idyll* in which Campbell states that the work is repetitive and lacks suspense and sympathy.

Dowell, Pat. "Gentleman with a Past." *The Washington Post Book World* XXII, No. 42 (October 18, 1992): 9.
> Positive review of *Ripley under Water* in which Dowell discusses Highsmith's depiction of the character Tom Ripley.

King, Frances. "Perverse and Foolish." *The Spectator* 274, No. 8697 (March 18, 1995): 34.
> Mixed review of *Small g: A Summer Idyll.* King praises the empathy with which Highsmith writes about gay men but faults the work's "slowness and repetitiveness."

Pamuk, Orhan. "A Taste for Death: Patricia Highsmith's Crime Time." *The Village Voice* XXXVII, No. 46 (November 17, 1992): 107-08.
> Mixed assessment of *Ripley under Water* in which Pamuk states that the work lacks "any forceful character to balance the charm of [Tom] Ripley." The critic also provides a brief overview of Highsmith's career.

Peary, Gerald. "Highsmith." *Sight and Sound* 57, No. 2 (Spring 1988): 104-05.
> Feature article written on the occasion of Highsmith's participation in the 1988 Toronto International Festival of Authors. Peary discusses film adaptations of Highsmith's works.

Symons, Julian. "Life with a Likable Killer." *The New York Times Book Review* (October 18, 1992): 41.
> Negative review of *Ripley under Water*; Symons concludes that "this is the least good of the Ripley books."

Tolkin, Michael. "In Memory of Patricia Highsmith." *Los Angeles Times Book Review* (February 12, 1995): 8.
> Overview of Highsmith's career written on the occasion of her death in 1995.

Wheelwright, Julie. "Fashion Victim." *New Statesman and Society* 8, No. 344 (March 1995): 38.
> Negative review of *Small g: A Summer Idyll* in which Wheelwright calls Highsmith's last book "a disappointment."

Additional coverage of Highsmith's life and career is contained in the following sources published by Gale Research: *Contemporary Authors,* **Vols. 1-4R, 147;** *Contemporary Authors New Revision Series,* **Vols. 20, 48;** *DISCovering Authors Modules: Novelists; DISCovering Authors Modules: Popular Fiction and Genre Authors;* **and** *Major 20th-Century Writers.*

Josephine Jacobsen
1908-

(Born Josephine Winder Boylan) Canadian-born American poet, short story writer, and critic.

The following entry provides an overview of Jacobsen's career through 1996. For further information on her life and works, see *CLC*, Volume 48.

INTRODUCTION

Josephine Jacobsen's poetry is noted for its spare, elegant language and broad range of form and subject matter. She explores such concerns as communication, pain, identity, isolation, and the relationship between the physical and the spiritual in verse often imbued with animal and nature imagery. Although Jacobsen often examines dark and mysterious elements of life, she is regarded as a poet of affirmation who articulates her themes with intelligence and conviction. Critics note that her poetry derives its power from her skillful use of metaphor, irony, and understatement blended with wit and compassion. Jacobsen is also highly regarded for her short fiction, particularly such stories as "A Walk with Raschid," "The Mango Community," and "Nel Bagno."

Biographical Information

Jacobsen was born in Cobourg, Ontario, Canada. Her father died when she was five, and after his death she lived with her mother and brother, both of whom were emotionally unstable. Jacobsen has described her mother as "passionate and intense, either elated or depressed." Her brother was a talented writer and artist but eventually suffered a nervous breakdown. Initially educated by private tutors, Jacobsen later attended Roland Park Country School, graduating in 1926. Although she did not attend college because at the time women were not expected to get a higher education, Jacobsen has stated that "I have wished passionately that I had been to college or that I had had the opportunity to decide if I wanted to go." She married Eric Jacobsen in 1932 and had one son. Jacobsen gained some critical attention with the publication of her first poetry collection, *Let Each Man Remember* (1940), but she remained outside the literary world until 1971, when she was named consultant in poetry to the Library of Congress. She remained in this position until 1973, when she became honorary consultant in American letters, an appointment she held until 1979. Jacobsen has also served as a member of the literature panel for the National Endowment for the Arts from 1970 to 1983 and has belonged to such organizations as the Poetry Society of America and PEN. In addition to winning many literary awards, including an Acad-

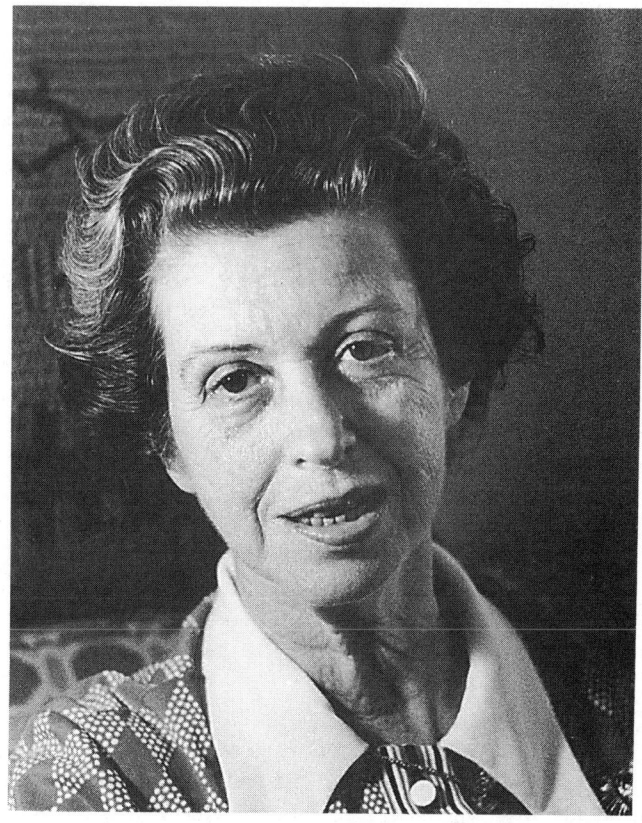

emy of American Poets fellowship, the Lenore Marshall Poetry prize, and numerous O'Henry prizes for her short stories, Jacobsen was inducted into the American Academy of Arts and Letters in 1994.

Major Works

Jacobsen's first poetry collection, *Let Each Man Remember,* features fifteen love sonnets, collected under the title "Winter Castle," and a section of metaphysical lyric poems. *The Human Climate* (1953) contains intensely personal verse in which Jacobsen conveys through direct, personal, and incisive language her views on the injustices and hypocrisies of the world. Jacobsen's next poetry collection, *The Animal Inside* (1966), includes seventy poems dating back to 1953 and displays her range of subject and form. This work contains poems about animals, including a sestina on hummingbirds, as well as meditative pieces probing love and death. In *The Shade-Seller* (1974), Jacobsen further reveals her interest in primitive natural forces and explores such themes as history, travel, and religion. *The Chinese Insomniacs* (1981) examines the role of language in building and maintaining human relationships and community. In many of these poems, Jacobsen employs a detached tone and minimalist structure to emphasize her themes. *The Sisters* (1987) spans fifty years and comprises representative poems from her previous verse collections as well as new works. *In the Crevice of Time* (1995), which includes poems dating from the 1930s to 1994, won the Shelley Memorial Award, the William Carlos Williams award, and was a National Book Award finalist. Jacobsen's short fiction is collected in *A Walk with Raschid and Other Stories* (1978), *Adios, Mr. Moxley* (1986), *On the Island* (1989), and *What Goes without Saying* (1996). Set in such diverse locales as Baltimore, the Caribbean Islands, Mexico, and Morocco, Jacobsen's short stories often end unresolved, leaving the reader to speculate about the future of her characters. In "The Mango Community," for example, an unmarried American couple are caught up in revolutionary politics on the island of Ste. Cecile. "Nel Bagno" is the story of writer Jane Glessner, who, minutes before she is to depart for Italy, finds herself stuck in her bathroom with nothing more than an Italian phrase book. In addition to writing poetry and fiction, Jacobsen has also collaborated with William R. Mueller on two critical studies, *The Testament of Samuel Beckett* (1964) and *Ionesco and Genet* (1968).

Critical Reception

Although Jacobsen's work is not widely read or anthologized, critical reaction to her writings has been positive and enthusiastic. Reviewers have consistently praised her poetry for being disciplined, intelligent, unpretentious, and personal and have compared her verse to that of such noted poets as Elizabeth Bishop, Emily Dickinson, Marianne Moore, Theodore Roethke, and W. H. Auden. Her short stories have also been positively received, with critics lauding her skillful characterization, evocative prose, and use of simple plots to address such complex themes as loss, age and youth, and the conflict between the sexes. Although Jacobsen treats universal themes, critics note that her work is unique and individualistic and is therefore not easily categorized. Jacobsen herself has noted: "I have not involved my work with any clique, school, or other group; I have not been content to repeat what I have already accomplished or to establish any stance which would limit the flexibility of discovery." While praising Jacobsen's commitment and dedication to her craft, critics have suggested that her idiosyncratic approach to writing has contributed to her lack of prominence. In recent years, however, Jacobsen's works have attracted more attention, and critics speculate she will gain the reputation she deserves. Marilyn Hacker, for example, has stated that "the work of Josephine Jacobsen is one of the best-kept secrets of contemporary American literature," and Joe Osterhaus, in a review of *In the Crevice of Time*, has declared that "Jacobsen aspires to the rarest of statures—the poet whose originality and power force us to rethink the accepted categories of poetic excellence."

PRINCIPAL WORKS

Let Each Man Remember (poetry) 1940
For the Unlost (poetry) 1946
The Human Climate: New Poems (poetry) 1953
The Testament of Samuel Beckett [with William R. Mueller] (criticism) 1964
The Animal Inside (poetry) 1966
Ionesco and Genet: Playwrights of Silence [with Mueller] (criticism) 1968
From Anne to Marianne: Some American Women Poets [editor] (poetry) 1972
The Instant of Knowing (lecture) 1974
The Shade-Seller: New and Selected Poems (poetry) 1974
One Poet's Poetry (lecture) 1975
A Walk with Raschid and Other Stories (short stories) 1978
The Chinese Insomniacs: New Poems (poetry) 1981
Adios, Mr. Moxley: Thirteen Stories (short stories) 1986
The Sisters: New and Selected Poems (poetry) 1987
On the Island: New and Selected Stories (short stories) 1989
Distances (poetry) 1991
Collected Poems: New and Collected Poems (poetry) 1995
In the Crevice of Time (poetry) 1995
What Goes without Saying: Collected Short Stories (short stories) 1996

CRITICISM

Josephine Jacobsen with Jacqueline-Tavernier Courbin (interview date 12 October 1979)

SOURCE: "Interview with Josephine Jacobsen," in *THALIA: Studies in Literary Humor*, Vol. II, Nos. 1 & 2, Spring/Fall, 1979, pp. 5-15.

[*In the following interview, which was conducted in New Hampshire on October 12, 1979, Jacobsen discusses such subjects as her critical works—particularly her volume on Samuel Beckett—the nature of poetry, and humor in literature.*]

[*Courbin:*] *You have, over a period of time, produced several volumes of poetry, a couple of books on modern French dramatists, and your latest book is, I believe, the collection of short stories,* **A Walk With Raschid.** *Does this represent a generally widespread interest or a pattern of change or development?*

[Jacobsen:] I don't think it really represents as much a pattern of development as things in which I've always been interested. Years ago I started trying to write some short stories and they were very unsatisfactory. Even I knew that. And I did abandon it at that point, but it was not because I lost interest in writing stories, it was just that I realized I wasn't really doing what I wanted to. The theatre is something in which I've always been extremely interested, but poetry has been and is my main concern. I think of myself as a poet even if I write criticism, even if I write short stories; stories are a major interest but they are not my central interest. So I don't think it's been a sequence as much as it's been something that was always there.

Your critical studies of Beckett and of Ionesco and Genet are distinctive for their poetic insight: that is, in describing the work of these other writers, you seem to be able to analyze without losing sight of the qualitative element. Do you find any difficulty in regarding a writer objectively and at the same time conveying the intrinsic or internal meaning that he has for you? Put another way, can poetry—do you think—be identified logically?

Well, that's a very difficult question and there are many ways of answering it. The simplest thing that I can say would be that one does what one is most interested in, and that is usually what one is most capable of doing. I have never been as interested in the technical analysis of a writer's work as I have been in the quality of the texture and the tone and, above all, what seems to me his intention. There are usually a great many adequate studies of what the writer has actually done. Very often some of them have seemed to me fairly obtuse about what the subject really was saying, what his intent was. That's what I have been most interested in and this, I think, ties in very closely with the idea of poetry; as we all know, you could analyze poetry technically endlessly and still have said nothing about the poem itself.

In your critical studies, you have been quite taken with the Theatre of the Absurd. Do you have any personal definition of the Absurd, not simply in drama but in other literary forms as well?

Of course, the whole business of the absurd became very much of a label and I'm always very nervous with labels and very suspicious of them, particularly definitions which in their turn become labels. I suppose everyone will agree broadly and basically that the Theatre of the Absurd and all the writing which comes under that general heading came about because, perhaps for the first time, the question of whether there was any real significance in human identity, whether there was any real purpose in anyone's life became a central concern. It is, perhaps, in the last 15 or 20 years that for the first time this has become a real preoccupation with writers. What attracted me so much about Beckett was the fact that he is preeminently a poet. He is a very interesting dramatist and certainly a very innovative dramatist, but above all he is a poet. Genet, whom I do not admire and love as I do Beckett, is also a poet, and in his own, somewhat screwy, way I think Ionesco is. It would be very interesting to compare those three from the point of view of poetry. But, certainly, what first attracted me to Beckett was less his philosophy, less his concept of the absurd element in human life than his incredible poetic insight, the fact that he somehow manages, in often the most dismal or grim or scatological language, to produce pure poetry. It's certainly extraordinary. I can go back now and read the novels which are relatively seldom read. People talk a great deal about Beckett and you find they've gone to waiting for Godot or something like that. They haven't read the novels and yet that whole cycle of novels is an extraordinary poetic achievement. So, I think of him less in this rigidly defined school of the absurd than as a poet who is alive with the absurd because of his questioning of certain values, of certain preconceptions. But it's the poetry that, for me, has been the dominant thing.

When you speak of him as a poet, are you thinking of him as a conceiver of scenes, characters, and situations which yield a certain quality of poetic action and vision or as someone who uses language that produces a "poetic" effect?

That's an interesting question because you've defined almost exactly both ways in which I feel he is a poet. His use of language is absolutely magnificent. There is something hypnotizing in Beckett's use of language and also in his use of the opposite, in his concept of silence, and the way he plays those two things against each other. But his entire vision, as you say, his whole approach to the character, the situation, or anything else, obviously, is never realistic. There is nothing you can read in Beckett that you can translate in literal terms. Both his vision and his language label him very much as a poet. An extraordinary thing is that he had so little talent for technical verse—the actual poetry that he's written is basically unintensified. It's curious, James Joyce, who was enormously innovative, wrote very delicate and very conventional lyrics. It's curious how often this happens.

In terms of your own writing, do you find any difficulties with these preconceptions—about how art works, that is, conceptions by which you judge other writers: characteristics or limits of the various genres, that sort of thing?

The relationship between short stories and poetry is very, very strong for me and I think perhaps that I would find great difficulty if I tried to write a novel. Anyone who writes anything and publishes anything is always urged to write a novel. One is snowed by letters from publishers saying, "We loved your story and have you thought of writing a novel and could we see it?" I know enough to know, unlike many people, that I can't write a novel. I don't have that horizontal vision at all. I don't have the underpinned, horizontal, massive, drawn-out vision that I think is required for a novel. I don't feel that being a poet has been in any way a disadvantage in short fiction. In fact, I think it's been a great help. It's a cliché to assert what a close relationship the story has to poetry, but I think that the impression, the intensity, the brief duration that you have to work with is similar in both, and I find it very refreshing to work first on one and then on the other. As I say, I didn't write stories for years, and then, about ten or eleven years ago, I suddenly thought to myself: "I want to write short stories and I don't care if they ever get published. I'm a poet and I'm not going to bother about that, I'm just going to write them for my own satisfaction." I must have learned something in the interim or else publishers' standards have declined—I don't know which—because I began to publish immediately and with very little trouble. It's one of those curious things. So that, now, I think they both work together.

Have you ever had a poem yield a short story?

Yes, absolutely. Sometimes I say to myself, now wait a minute, is this a poem or is this a story? And a great many of my poems have very strong elements of the story in them. A great many of them are rather dramatic or deal with people, a great many deal with people in special circumstances. So that the seed could have grown either way.

> **It's a cliché to assert what a close relationship the short story has to poetry, but I think that the impression, the intensity, the brief duration that you have to work with is similar in both, and I find it very refreshing to work first on one and then on the other.**
> **—Josephine Jacobsen**

Have you ever had a story which directly came out of a poem, or vice versa; have you ever written a story—and ever felt that there was a poem embedded there that you had to dig out?

Well, it's interesting that you ask me that because it hasn't worked quite that way for me, but I have written poems that I know I wouldn't otherwise have written if I hadn't previously written stories. They've come out of it in that sense. It's something that I've learned in the story. For instance, I've written a poem which came out not long ago about the experience of a writer finding his characters coming up with signs of independent life, and rather startling him by making him realize that he did not completely control them. I also wrote a poem recently about dreams in which characters in

stories come and say that they should have been in poems. So there's been a lot of interchange. Usually, though, I *have* made up my mind in the beginning, before I've started. Almost always I say: "This is a poem or this is a story." I can't remember one specifically coming out of the other.

What is there to a story that distinguishes it from a poem in such an instance?

Let me give you an example: One of the cases was quite literally a dream; in the other it was as if the characters had escaped. It was a dream scenario in which characters had wandered out of the story and you got that fragmentary— after all, a story can't be that fragmentary—glimpse of them just walking down a street or listening to something, or standing in a position turning their heads in which this could be a story but it was a small, almost minute, poem in itself. There was a very strong interchange there, very strong.

So, in the story, the character wants more life, a more intense story.

Yes, or sometimes he wants more latitude and more sort of a sequential development than he can get in the poem and he wants to get into a story. Sometimes the writer himself is confused as to where he wants him.

You were speaking about the dramatic quality of poetry, and suddenly it made me think of Robert Frost who wrote, in an introduction to one of his plays, something like this: "Anything written is as good as it is dramatic. It need not express itself in form, but it is drama or nothing."

Well, there's a great deal of drama in Frost's work besides his very famous long poems. A tremendous number of Frost's poems are concerned with drama, with the interaction of people and emotions. People think of him as a nature boy but almost always, if you actually read the poems, the nature is very much tied to the human. It's the human element that is played against it, and there's always that consciousness, of course, of the antagonism between nature, that seems impersonal, and the human being. For instance, there is that marvelous poem where he hears a thing crashing through the underbrush, and he thinks perhaps it's going to be an answer to him, and when it comes out it's a great deer that swims across the river and disappears in the woods; it's that and nothing more, and he has a sense of letdown. There's always that antagonism, almost, between impersonal nature and the human being, so that his poems have great drama.

In fact, Frost's poems could really make beautiful one-act plays couldn't they?

Oh yes, absolutely. He was a very dramatic person himself. In fact, he was a great deal of a ham, Mr. Frost, when he was performing, as anyone who heard him knows. He was a marvelous performer. He had the audience in the palm of his hands. He was very dramatic, he played the audience. He could be coy, he could be dramatic, he was very much an actor. He was a wonderful reader.

Do you feel yourself that it is necessary for poetry to be dramatic?

Only for my own poetry. There's a great deal of poetry that I love, certain kinds of lyric poetry. No, I don't really feel that, in order for a poem to be a beautiful poem or a satisfactory poem, it necessarily has to be dramatic. It is an element that I find in my own work because that's simply the way my mind works, my emotions work, so it is a necessary element in anything I've done. I've done almost no descriptive poetry. Practically none.

Let's get back to Ionesco and Genet. In the **Ionesco and Genet** *book, you say that "the predominant disposition of our time is toward holocaust. It is this temperament which the theatre of the absurd has engraved with precision tooling." Am I right in interpreting this to mean that writers such as Beckett and Genet have, through an art of the absurd, made increasingly clear the impulse of our generation towards compulsive destructiveness?*

Yes, absolutely. I feel that very strongly. And while we are speaking of those books on Genet, Ionesco and Beckett, I would like to emphasize that both those books were written in collaboration with William Mueller who is a splendid writer and a highly perceptive artist. Whatever we accomplished in those books, we've learned much from the joint situation. It was rather interesting because I'd never collaborated before, and I had always regarded that as an impossible thing. I never could understand how people could collaborate. We had to feel before we started those books that we had an almost totally similar reaction to the work of the writers that we were discussing. We both had this feeling that these people spelled out a tremendous absorption—you know, this absorption with destruction is tremendously widespread. I think suicide, for instance, has an almost compulsive fascination for people. Perhaps it always has had but I have noticed, in the case of Sylvia Plath and Anne Sexton, John Berryman and others, that the fact of suicide seems inextricably entangled in people's minds with the work of those writers, that they seem to feel the work is in some way more valuable or more precious to them or more moving because of the dénouement of those lives. So I think that is part of this whole absorption in the destructive situation. Of course, I suppose, there always has been a very high suicide incidence among artists. There certainly was an enormous absorption with suicide in Berryman's work—well, in all three of them, there was a constant, almost obsessive, feeling of death. It is certainly also true of Hemingway, not with the suicidal intent to the extent that you get it in Plath's and Berryman's work, but certainly this preoccupation with death runs through his work. It isn't just hunting in Africa, it isn't just the bullfights, but it's an absorbing, dominating concern.

What about your own work? Is there also an element of despair in it?

I don't think my work is particularly optimistic. Certainly the fiction is not. I've been accused of writing extremely despairing stories. But I don't feel that they are totally so. In fact, I have an ongoing argument about that now with a critic whom I'm fond of. We've been giving points to the stories on how much is positive and how much is negative. I feel that in almost all the stories something emerges that is valuable that wasn't there in the beginning. So I don't consider them as depressing. But my work doesn't reflect any great optimism. I think probably as a person I feel more optimism than the work shows. But I can't really imagine what my work would be like if my entire orientation was changed by some awful occurrence.

In terms of fiction, do you feel that experience is always of value, a positive thing in itself?

It's hard to say that because you see so many incredible experiences around you that are almost impossible to relate to any value. And yet certainly speaking from my own work, I would feel very definitely that experience, any experience that I have had, however painful or however destructive, has certainly left some residue of value. I think it's very easy to say that and I draw back from saying it for other people because I think we're being surrounded by such powers. How can you say, for instance, that what people are going through in Cambodia will leave something of value with them? You know that takes a lot of audacity. I couldn't say experience always leaves value but it has for me. I've been very fortunate I haven't been exposed to the horrors that are all around the world today. I'm simply speaking for myself in what has been a relatively sheltered and happy life.

Do you think that poetry is by nature life-affirming? Do you feel that your own poetry is life-affirming?

I think so. One of the hardest things in the world is to be objective about your own work. One of the tremendous problems that I notice in bad poetry, when young people are trying to learn to write poetry, is that, when you have a concept of a poem you want to write, what you put down on the page ultimately is a very thin shadow of your original impulse. But what confuses a writer is that very often in his own mind he feels that what he has put down on the page is what he did have in his mind and heart. He thinks it's there because it's in his brain. It's terribly hard to see your own work objectively. Is my poetry life-affirming? It's like the ancient argument of the Greeks: is it better to have been born or not to have been born? I would say yes, it is better to have been born, and I think that is a pretty daring decision as you look around. In fact, I would hate to have to sustain it in a debate.

Do you feel that the Absurd is of value only as a corrective? Or does its humor represent a separate, positive value in itself?

I think that humor is one of these things that are absolutely undefinable, but humor in the Absurd is an instrument of its very grimness. There is humor in Beckett; and people say that they can't really see that there is any humor in Beckett because it's so appalling. But there certainly is. We have this whole thing now which is very big of black humor, of the humor of the Absurd, which is basically a destructive humor. A case can be made that all humor, though sometimes quite gentle, is destructive. But this black humor is *massively* destructive. It is trying to destroy shibboleths, it is trying to destroy hypocracies, it is trying to destroy *knee-jerk reactions*. It is wielded as a kind of cleaver and there is a tremendous gap between that and the kind of humor that impregnates a lot of poetry. There is a great deal of humor in Frost's work. There is a great deal of humor in most good poetry but it is far gentler. There is such an enormous range in the word humor that, unless you define the kind of humor, it's very hard to discuss. Someone has said that humor is always cruel. I don't think that is necessarily true but I think perhaps it is always destructive in the sense that it is basically deflating. It pricks a pompousness. You may be laughing at yourself, you may be laughing at someone else. It may be in the gentlest kind of way in the world but it's still, to some degree, a cutting down of some pretension or of some pomposity. Take the basic situation: slipping on a banana peel. If just an ordinary person slips, someone may think that's funny. If a Bishop slips, or some judge in robes, it's much funnier from a crude point of view. In other words, it's the deflating of pretensions and ego that you think of as humor. With the Absurdists, humor has been very terrifying. What I love about Ionesco is that a lot of his vision is also very frightening and, in fact, I'm a tremendous admirer of his plays because he has used humor in a marvelous, marvelous way. It remains very funny. Now with Beckett, I defy anyone to laugh. You're aware that something is funny in a horrible way but you're not going to sit down and laugh. Ionesco is funny in the classic sense of making you laugh. There's a ludicrous element that is very funny. Humor has been used in tremendously different ways by these people, even within the Absurd group themselves. Curiously, Genet in a way is quite lacking in humor. He has tremendous wit, enormous wit, but I associate humor itself in general with a certain warmth. In Genet there's not that basically self-deprecatory attitude that humor is apt to produce. There's more of a—I think of a cerebral kind of wit. Much colder. It's

much less than you would get with a circus clown if you want to get to that kind of humor. Ionesco has a great deal of clown's humor. He loves to maneuver furniture. He loves to make ludicrous effects. He loves to have someone so big, that the body is sticking out of both windows, like Bill the Lizard in *Alice in Wonderland*. He loves these kinds of effects. Genet is much more poetic. He works through wit and poetry, much more than from the ridiculous.

Do you think that your poetry has been influenced very much by your critical insights?

I really doubt it very much, and yet I'm sure, at one remove, it has been. In other words, when I write a poem or even when I go back and work very, very hard over it, I really don't think of it in terms of any critical theories that I possess. I think of it on a very pragmatic basis, probably a very emotional basis: "This doesn't sound right to me, this is not what I was trying to say. This strikes a jarring note. This is slack or is not." I never analyze it by saying this is not my concept of what this type of poem should be. I can do that much better with someone else's work than I can with my own.

In writing of Beckett, you take laughter as a very serious thing. Do you think humor in poetry can be equally serious?

Yes, I certainly do. I think this would make a perfectly fascinating article, or even a book. To discuss the humor in a series of poets. As a matter of fact, I don't recall that it has been done specifically in comparing these particular qualities, and I think of Yeats, just from the top of my head, I think of Auden, I think of Frost. Now all of those have a great deal of humor in their work. But the humor in each is just as different as it could possibly be from the others with almost no similarity whatsoever. You could have very, very serious humor. You are much less apt to have the kind of humor that I'm talking about when I talk about clowns' humor, the kind of humor that Ionesco at his least analytical and his most exuberant has. You don't find much of that in poetry. You find it much more on the stage because it is a visual thing and it's easier to have that kind of humor when it's tangible, when you can see it, when it's part of the human anatomy and the human voice and so on. You don't find that type of humor much in poetry. In poetry you find wit—I suppose wit is in general the most predominant kind of humor in poetry—from Pope, on, or really as far back as you want to go. Lyric poetry is almost innocent of humor except in very rare cases. It's a whole different construction of things.

On the other hand, Keats wrote a lot of dramatic poetry. The interesting thing about Keats is that there is really almost no humor that I'm aware of—I may be way off on this—but I'm a great fan of Keats, and I know his poetry pretty well. I can't think of any real element of humor that is significant in his poetry. And, yet, when you read his letters you realize that he had a very, very warm and very spontaneous sense of humor and was often very funny. The letters are wonderful, particularly the letters that he wrote to his young sister. But he was so awestruck by poetry. His relationship with poetry was so intense that, except in the nonsense verses that he wrote just in his letters, his humor doesn't come through in the work at all.

Something which has always puzzled me in Hemingway is that I've never been able to really find any sense of humor in his work.

Oh I don't think he had any. Don't you think that's why you couldn't find it because it wasn't there? I think he is the most humorless of all the good writers that I know. He took himself profoundly seriously, and the only reason he isn't more irritating is that he also took life and every situation and things like honor and courage so deadly seriously.

I suppose it's the reason why he is parodied so often. As you hear an overly serious view dramatically expounded three or four times, it becomes parody without being defined as such; and then someone simply puts on the label, defines it as parody.

For one thing, it was his style at that time. He changed the concept of prose rhythm a great deal. The very short sentences, the very factual things, such as: "She was chewing her steak, she picked up her glass, she put it down . . ." This kind of thing was a different rhythm and because of the fact that it was so different, it was easily imitated. There have been some marvelous and quite cruel but very, very funny parodies. Well, people who have very distinctive styles are easy to parody. You can do fifth-rate Henry James very, very easily, or a Faulkner for instance. Of course, that would be exhausting. One would have to go on for two pages without taking a breath, so people don't do it as much.

There were many things that were endearing about Hemingway, and that people have come to laugh at now. He did have certain definitions of courage that do seem very simplistic, very unsophisticated, very lacking in any humor. This courage meant a great deal to him. Who was it who told the story about Hemingway sitting at a table during a Second World War bombardment? He and some other people were in an old farmhouse in France near the fighting line. When the shells began falling, everyone dove under the table groping for helmets and making themselves small, but Hemingway just stayed there, sitting at the table, his broad back to the window, eating. His was basically, from the practical point of view, an extremely silly reaction. There is no virtue in sitting at the table while everybody around you is being shot. The thing is to get under the table and stay firmly

there and then get up and do something else. Only someone who has a very unsophisticated sense of priorities could feel otherwise. But as long as he does feel that way, there's something very exhilarating about seeing him sit there because he imposes on this silly action a great deal of dignity because to him it's important.

Back to poetry. Most humorous poetry seems to be second-rate poetry, as poetry, if not as statement. Why is that? Is humor logically prosaic?

As a matter of fact, it's an interesting point. I don't know why. It certainly is true. Absolutely true. But I don't know why it should be. I suppose the only poetry that we can think of where humor is the predominant characteristic that is good would be this rather cold cerebral kind of humor such as Pope's or, not so cold but certainly cerebral, Auden's. I suppose intensity is the one thing humor draws back from. Humor is apt to be slightly debunking and the essense of poetry tends to be intensity; so you have these two characteristics working against each other. As you have more humor you have less intensity, because you're standing off. Isn't it one of the famous differences between comedy and tragedy that, in tragedy, you're involved and, in comedy, you're standing off and looking. And perhaps poetry as we have agreed is basically quite dramatic. It is also, above all things, intense. Don't you think that would probably be the reason?

In a way it's true. And it fits very well with what you were saying earlier that humor is always to a certain extent deflating.

I think so. Exactly.

Do you think that there are certain kinds of humor more suited to poetry than others?

I would think "verbal." Yes, I would think it very important that humor be basically verbal. It should not get into the emotions and into the concepts because if humor gets into the emotional framework it is going to definitely lower the temperature, it's going to lower the intensity. Whereas verbal humor can find a place because it's only skin deep. It's not going into the actual emotional roots of the poem, and I would think the happiest kind of humor in poetry is always verbal humor. It has to do with words, the play of words.

That reminds me of something. As you said, humor of Ionesco's kind is funny; it makes you laugh. Word sounds can delight you, make you happy; if not laugh, at least smile. Can humor include phonetic play? Hopkins, for instance, plays with sound and delights us. Is there some element here that is parallel to, perhaps even synonymous with, humor?

I think there is, absolutely. And I think that's exactly what I was trying myself to say. When I said it would be primarily verbal it would be largely a matter of tempo and sound rather than of content because, God knows, Hopkins' work is certainly serious. Basically it's enormously serious. But he did play with sounds. He loved the repercussions like a wave coming in and then going out and another wave coming in. That was strong rhythm.

One of the characteristics of poetry is that, as you were saying, the intensity is at odds with humor.

Yes. But you don't have to define, you see. I think that's the beauty of it. Word play and a strong rhythm and that kind of thing will at the broadest scope tie something like the Jobberwocky together with Hopkins. The play of sound and of tempos clashing do not invade the purpose or the meaning of the poem and that's probably just where you have the sort of escape hatch with this question of humor in poetry. As long as it doesn't invade the emotional push of the poem, it seems to me that it adds, but once it gets into the mental and emotional part, rather than into the verbal, you begin to get the deflation. With comedy you get the cut-down and with tragedy you get the build-up; you get the large work. Humor always to some extent minimizes in the derogatory sense, but it minimizes in the physical sense. It cuts the enormous and overblown down to size. Whereas tragedy takes an individual thing, it seems to me, and makes it into a great, almost universal sorrow. It's a very interesting relationship. I haven't thought about it much until now.

We use words such as satire, comedy, humor quite indiscriminately at times. How wide a range would you yourself define for humor?

Well, enormous. It could go all the way from the most slapstick comedy, from your clown in a small village circus, all the way up to James Joyce's manipulation of the English language. It would have that wide a range. It has a tremendous range.

Does humor in a literary work presuppose any distinct emotional effect?

I'm not sure I understand exactly what you're asking. Do you mean a person intend an emotional reaction? In other words, is he trying to humiliate or amuse or what is his purpose, what is his intent? Well, I think it can be used as an ax or used as a rapier. The only purpose I can think of at the moment for which humor has been much used in poetry, is for satire. Wouldn't that be the essential, the basic approach if you're going to have humor in poetry, wouldn't it mostly be satirical? I can't think really of other forms of humor that would be apt to be particularly useful or suitable to the poet. If you think of poetry in which humor has played a great part, wouldn't the great satirists be much more apt to come

to your mind than almost any other kind of writer? I would think so. It seems to be one of the natural uses of humor in poetry. And that, of course, again can be benign or can be extremely savage. It can run all the way from someone like Swift, to a much more gentler Ogden Nash. You know, I think that Ogden Nash could have been a very good poet. He had an extraordinary verbal range and capacity. What we were talking about a little earlier about Jabberwocky and so on . . . Some of Nash's poems have an almost inspired sense of word play. Of course, he ground out a great deal of stuff. And a great deal of it is very humdrum and very second-rate. But he had a marvelous ability with words and he wrote a couple of serious poems not long before his death that were extremely good. There was one about his experience in the hospital which combined his rather fey quality with grimness. Very effective. I think he had great possibilities. I wrote him a letter—I knew him very pleasantly but not well. I wrote him a letter about that one poem because I liked it so much. He wrote back and said he appreciated it very much. His wife said to me, "You don't know how pleased Ogden was to get letters from poets saying that they liked that poem." And I thought, well, isn't it extraordinary, that a number of poets might have told him that. It was very good. You know, that's another thing about labels. They're the scariest thing in the world. You pin a label on a man like Ogden Nash which says, well, you know how very clever he is. He had much more scope, much more imagination.

At the end of your Beckett book you say that "he directs his laughter . . . against that which is not good, against that which is not true, against that which mocks suffering." Given some of his protagonists, do you feel that Beckett directs all of his laughter against things? Does he ever direct it towards things; that is, is his laughter positive as well as negative, creative instead of moral?

Well, there are two things that I'd like to distinguish between in that question. I feel that very largely his laughter is against. But this is part of his whole system. One of the fascinating things about his work is that he is able to create an image of what he feels should be by the description of its exact opposite. In other words, he will so completely appeal you by the opposite of that quality he wishes to express—anything to do with beauty or truth or grace or sensitivity—that he inevitably and immediately makes you think of the quality that he is valuing. He does this over and over again. Take his famous sexual scenes, for instance, with the distortions and the hideousness of the grotesque details. His laughter is negative and is against but I think in the end—so I'm having my cake and eating it too,—it is in some mysterious way creative because I think he is saying, "Look at the way this is instead of," and he forces you to supply the "instead of." So that I would say he is negative and creative at the same time.

If the hideous or the horrible creates its opposite, is that opposite defined recognizably in the work?

Well, I suppose it would be the substitution of emotional tenderness—a feeling of love freely given and exchanged—instead of the terrible debility that is no longer able to love or to consummate but that goes through the fumbling, intimate kind of gestures without any of that real ability left that goes with love or goes with the actions of love, except to imitate remotely the gestures.

Wouldn't that wipe out most of his actual protagonists?

Yes, I think it probably would. Well, there are, I think, a few scenes in Beckett, very, very few, that have an almost dreamy quality of beauty, and because they are so contradictory and set in what otherwise is a morass, they are peculiarly beautiful and moving. There are a number of passages that reveal, I think, that he has this feeling for the old. He had a terrible feeling of disfigurement and age and debility. He goes over it again and again and again. But it seems to me he's less concerned with the purely physical fact of this kind of grotesque distortion than he is with the fact that this is the outward and visible sign of an inward debility that people have spiritually to love or feel strongly or, above all, to have trust in their own significance. And you know there is always in Beckett this element of indignation with God, which is very interesting. It's almost a throwback to another age. I remember Mother when she was, well much younger—very young—she wrote an essay about religion and sent it to some magazine and they sent it back with a little note: "La question de Dieu manque d'actualité." This is the general attitude now. I mean, who's excited? It's like Hemingway getting under the table. Whereas Beckett is in a continual rage because nobody's answering, nobody's listening. He's being fed just enough drops of hope here and there to get him going again. It's a personal vendetta going on between him and a God who either is or is not there, and this is really a very unmodern point of view.

Is Beckett really, through his humor, attacking, generally, things which are negative?

Absolutely. You have your two negatives which notoriously make a positive. How discouraging to hear what you write a whole book about put in one sentence. That's very dismaying.

There are really different types of humor, the humor which attacks the negative and the humor which makes fun of the positive.

Oh absolutely. Completely opposed by their very nature. One is sort of a dog-in-the-manger thing. The idea that if you can't be something or have something or do something, you want to destroy the fact that it has any value in the first place. There's a kind of profound cynicism in that. Skepticism is one of the wonderful things in the world and God knows we could use it. But cynicism is the most debilitating thing in the world. And that is the difference, I think, in Beckett. In fact, I'm working on something now about his definition of the three types of laughter. What you just said is absolutely true. What he attacks is something that he would like to see destroyed because it is the opposite of what he feels should be there.

It seems that the modern novel has, on the whole, been far more inclined to humor than has the modern short story. Writers—such as Barth, Pynchon, Vonnegut and others have created comic worlds almost exclusively, while the short story remains essentially climactic and serious. There are, of course, notable exceptions. Is there something inherent, *do you think, in the* seriousness *of* short *literary works?*

That brings us back to some degree to what we were talking about earlier, the relationship between poetry and the short story. Now all those writers you mentioned and particularly Barth and Pynchon of course, go in for tremendously long books and I don't think that's an accident. In other words, they are creating a comic world and then they are exploring it and I think it's no accident that it is related to size. And that brings us back to the poem or short story because I think that when you have an extraordinary limitation of space you've got to make up in intensity what you do not have in space. In other words, you cannot dilute and you cannot go on with ramifications. You are essentially compressed into a rigidly limited form. You don't have 700 pages. And I think it's no accident that poetry and short stories share this. The seriousness is closely related to the form and to the question of intensity. That's a very close relationship.

In a novel, you can create a whole world, and then you show the way in which this world functions, lay out examples of it and then you gradually work this out and you build on it. This is denied to you in a poem or a short story. You haven't got that much space to work with and you've got to have the force to make an impact in that extremely limited climate. You cannot fool around. I think that's why.

Leaving out the unessential and leaving the actual core in is, I think, the way of the short story writer. And that's why this whole business of the enormous created comic world is a very, very tricky one and why I think it's a law of diminishing returns. Take John Barth whom I admire very much. I find him very charming and attractive and I heard him give the most brilliant short talk I think I've heard in twenty years at the Library of Congress. *The Sot Weed Factor* was perfectly fascinating and I thought "my what an enormous original talent." But although I read *Giles Goat-Boy* right through to the last word, it was a constant effort. This is the danger.

By doing one of these marvelous comic worlds, you've done it and it isn't meant to be like life and it doesn't have the self-renewing intensity of life. It's a marvelous fabrication and you've done it and I think it's very dangerous when it gets repetitive.

In a novel, you can create a whole world, and then you show the way in which this world functions, lay out examples of it and then you gradually work this out and you build on it. This is denied to you in a poem or a short story. You haven't got that much space to work with and you've got to have the force to make an impact in that extremely limited climate. You cannot fool around.
                                        —*Josephine Jacobsen*

Talking about intensity, would you agree with Edgar Allan Poe that a poem should not be longer than about one hundred lines?

No. That's a rather restrained order on poetry. I am not able to write long poems. There again I simply come back to my own limitations, my own tastes, my own inclination. I have written very, very few poems over one hundred lines. Very, very few. I would say that for every fifty or one hundred good short poems you're lucky if you find one good long one. Because if intensity, real intensity, is one of the essential elements of poetry it obviously is going to be harder and harder to keep that real poetic impact as you expand and expand and expand. In general I would certainly say that a long poem has to be most exceptional. There's something forbidding, to begin with, about a long poem. Actually more and more we have to be conscious of the fact that photography is a very important factor. When you look at a very long poem it's solid on the page. No space between the lines. Remember *Alice in Wonderland*, when she said that the book had no conversation or pictures and what is the use of the book without conversation or pictures? You feel a little bit this way when you see page after page after page of solid poetry. It's got to be very good. It's got to be the *Iliad* or the *Odyssey* or something like that.

Do you consider the idea of a separate *female consciousness as very relevant in literature?*

Would you accept "differing?" I think I would rather say "differing" than "separate," for separate implies an almost total lack of communication. I do think they *differ*. I would jib a little at the word separate but I think differing, yes.

Do you think that artistic projection can be effectively car-

ried out across the sexes? Can a male writer capture and convey a female consciousness and vice versa?

I think it's hard but it certainly has been done. It's funny, I was thinking about Robert Browning—I think he had a marvelous, intuitive understanding of the female mind. (God help me, I don't want to say that.) Let me say that the women he wrote about in his poetry frequently seemed to be very real, very natural, quite an intuitive leap for a man. I don't know why because he certainly was a highly specialized person himself and I wouldn't have really thought that sensitive but he has made that leap. One curious thing: take someone like D. H. Lawrence. So confusing because many people think he's a terrific male chauvinistic pig. And certainly when you get him into the analytical field he just comes apart anyway. I mean, I think you try to make Lawrence stand up on a strictly intellectual, analytical basis and he just goes to pieces. But intuitively I think some of the women he's written about have been remarkably real.

What do you consider the most difficult part of your writing? Aside from getting the first word on paper!

Oh, that's very hard to answer. I suppose the hard thing is coming to terms with the difference between what I feel I have to say and what I've succeeded in saying. That effort to get down on paper what your whole concept is, what Henry James called your "*donnée,*" without dismembering it or injuring it or having it be but a feeble shadow of what you were trying to say, would be the very hardest part. Any reasonably experienced poet can pull a poem together technically. You can strengthen it and you can make it readable but that isn't what you really care about. I think that would be it. Trying to get everything that you know is possible into that poem said—but then it's a very hard thing to get everything down on paper.

You know, it strikes me that poets, far more than novelists or other writers, are constantly revising their work, in many cases going on with it all through their lifetime, long after its original publication. Yeats did.

Yes. And Auden kept changing. Dylan Thomas used to, also. I haven't changed any published poems but I would not scruple to do it. I can never understand that terrific brouhaha and uproar about Auden altering his published poems. I don't feel that publishing makes them sacred, and I think that, if you can improve a poem, you have a right to do it. I have never tried to do that because, in a curious way—I won't say I lose interest—but I never care as much about the poem once it is in print and gone. I feel that it's on its own feet. It has to survive or not. I'm interested in what I'm doing *now*. But I certainly never send a poem out within a month of the time it's written. I've done two or three versions of it, and when I've done the best I know how, I put it away, and usually, if I go back to it two or three weeks later, I can always alter it, see something wrong that I didn't do, that I left out, that I put in, that was wrong. So yes, I do revise quite a great deal, and I hate it, I absolutely loathe it. Some people love to review, and I hate it. But there is that awful feeling that you have in some way again injured the poem. That you've done something to it. And so I do quite a bit of revision up to the point where it goes into print.

How do you feel about **The Shade-Seller***?*

It's a collection of four previous books and I think that I have less second thoughts about that book than any book I've ever published for the simple reason that there was such a winnowing process. The other poems were poems that I had been doing for a certain number of years. I have a new collection which I hope will be finished within the next six months which will be poems that I have worked on within the last five years. I'm not a prolific writer. I don't publish a book every couple of years. I don't want to. But in that book, I took only perhaps I think six or eight or nine poems from each book or maybe ten poems from each book. So that I winnowed out so much that it's the best I can do and I'm not exalted by it but, on the other hand, there's nothing in it that I'm ashamed of and there's nothing in it that I feel "oh gosh I wish I had that back so I could change it" because it is already an extremely selected group. But I do feel that the few times I've sent a poem off red-hot, when it seemed simply wonderful to me, I've fallen into that thing that I'm just talking about, that I know I should know better, that I am attributing to the poem on paper all the things that are still in my mind. And that becomes mercilessly clear when it has sat around for two or three weeks. But it isn't clear the first twenty four hours. Far from it. And I think all that school of poetry that I call the "that's what happened to me last night" school of poetry are the prime example of people who are attributing to the poem they've written all their own emotions about how marvelous it was to be with Harry or whatever, and they don't see what's down on the paper at all. They think it's enormously significant. That's the hardest thing when you criticize young people's poetry. You don't have the heart to say, "Look, my dear, what you've got down here is so uninteresting and so unimportant and so trivial that nobody should waste their time reading it. But what happened to you was probably very important and not trivial at all and of great significance but it's not here, you know." But you can't say that.

Let me ask you a couple of final questions. First one, other modern poets—do you have any observations about them, good or bad, their influence, that sort of thing?

Alive or dead or what? In the sense of writing now. Well, I am a great admirer of Auden, Yeats, Roethke; Archie Ammons is one of my very, very favorites. Whereas I can't really understand someone getting nothing out of Yeats and getting nothing out of Roethke, I can understand someone getting nothing out of Ammons. I think it's a very special kind of poetry. I happen to love it. Elizabeth Bishop who just died I admired very much. A poet whose work I like very much who is not at all well-known—she is highly respected by other poets but she's not really well-known—is Julia Randell. She's very good. She's a metaphysical poet. It's not fashionable poetry but I think it's marvelous. Very, very good. Well, that's quite a few. Probably I'll find I left out some of my very favorites. I think probably of my contemporaries I would say Roethke, Yeats, Auden and Ammons. And possibly Elizabeth Bishop. I wish I knew more of the English poets.

> A poet has a nasty tendency to just keep on writing poetry, instead of having a good project ahead. I would like to write simpler poetry, more script poetry all the time. I would like to move toward further compression, further intensity, eliminating explanations, having the word explain itself.
> —*Josephine Jacobsen*

Where do you want to go in your writing at this point?

A poet has a nasty tendency to just keep on writing poetry, instead of having a good project ahead. I would like to write simpler poetry, more script poetry all the time. I would like to move toward further compression, further intensity, eliminating explanations, having the word explain itself. I would like to go on writing stories and perhaps—I'll never write a novel, I know—but I would like to write a selection of stories that would in some way impinge or connect with each other and might possibly form a book. This is not a project because I can't do it unless I happen to want to write those stories. But I'm afraid what I really want to do is just go on writing better stories and better poems. I don't have any major projects. I think I'm going to stay off criticism except for a few critical articles. I just had an article published in the *Sewanee Review* and have a couple of other articles coming out. Once in a while I do a book review. But I have very limited time. I have two months a year in which to work, actually: two weeks here in the fall, two weeks here in June and a month when my husband and I go to the Caribbean. I work from when I get up at 5:45 in the morning and work out in the garden from 6 to 8. And those two months are the only time I have really for work during the year. The rest of the time I'm doing readings, seminars, and the summer is totally domestic. Criticism is marvelous and interesting and terribly fun. After all, working on someone else's work is fundamental but I don't think I want to do another book of criticism. I don't have the time or the energy. But beyond that I would just like to better what I'm doing.

Josephine Jacobsen with Evelyn Prettyman (interview date Summer 1987)

SOURCE: "The Mystery of Faith: An Interview with Josephine Jacobsen," in *New Letters*, Vol. 53, No. 4, Summer, 1987, pp. 40-56.

[*In the following interview, Jacobsen discusses such subjects as how her upbringing and background influenced her poetry, the themes in her verse, religion, and poetic technique.*]

[*Prettyman:*] *In your writing, your world is a world of pain, usually because someone else is hurt. How early did that awareness begin?*

[Jacobsen:] That touches on very tender points. . . . My mother was an unhappy person. She had a young husband who was killed tragically in an accident. Personally, she was passionate and intense, either depressed or elated; she had great shifts. She had no ability to handle finances, she was unprepared for it. For us, it was boom or bust.

My brother was humorous and talented; he was a good writer, a fine sculptor and a professional actor. But he had all kinds of serious emotional problems. Eventually he had a series of crackups.

Mother was always worried about finances or her son; her life never had any kind of serenity. I was devoted to both my mother and my brother, and I was aware very soon that I was living with people I loved who were not happy people. I felt responsible. I thought there ought to be something I could do.

It's interesting that you say that your mother and brother always felt in peril, and yet I find you a person who is challenged, even healthily thrilled by danger.

Don't you think that you're either terribly tough or you go under? If you're under tremendous strain as a child, it just tips; you sink, or if you stay on top you develop certain resources in yourself that have got to be called on.

In your poems, you have even equated danger with beauty and joy.

Well, there's the challenge of the ball being in your court. And there's the blissful feeling of serenity when it's out of your hands, what a patient feels going into the operating room, or one can feel just before an automobile accident. And of course there's the physical exhilaration. Our oldest grandson, Ricky, was a racing driver. Then, ironically, he was killed by a truck, run down on a Boston street.

You also equate beauty with pain.

Everyone should be outraged by pain, but if you once accept the mystery of it, that it has some significance that you'll never understand, then it can be purifying; it activates sympathy. It has been associated with rites of purification. If you do come through pain, for you there is a beauty.

Then your childhood was unhappy?

No, I felt that I was loved by my mother and brother. I had a variety of friends; although as soon as I made friends anywhere, we moved away. Mother had the wonderful ability when things were going well to enjoy life, to dress up and look beautiful. She was a person of great charm. So it was never a dreary or loveless atmosphere. There was usually warmth and gaiety, and a certain amount of grace; and then everything would fall in pieces.

What books did you read?

My mother read an enormous amount to me. She read Dickens, *Lorna Doone, Jane Eyre, The Cloister and the Hearth*, among many, many others.

I also grew up on fairy tales. My mother read me fairy tales until I could read them, and then I read *The Red Fairy Book, The Green Fairy Book, The Blue Fairy Book*, Hans Andersen, Grimm, Oscar Wilde. Although I had kind of a weird life, looking back, I don't even know much to regret. Perhaps one regret: I have wished passionately that I had been to college or that I had had the opportunity to decide if I wanted to go. Mother, who was from North Carolina, had that Southern conception that college was a refuge for girls who were having problems, who didn't have a young man on the scene. It was years later, when I had begun to realize that my life might develop along the lines of writing, that I thought, "My God, someone should have told me. I should have gone to college." At times it just lacerates me to think of, oh, if I'd had that experience, the friendships, the contacts, the launching. But then I question that, and I have never made up my mind to this day whether it was a good or a bad thing that I didn't go. Maybe my whole career would have been different. But I concentrated entirely on poetry. That was my life line; it was the only thing I had left. It was my only intellectual contact. It was a fairly rough track for a while.

What did you do between high school and marriage? Did you write poetry?

I had met my husband-to-be by then; and the year I fell in love, I wrote a lot of poetry. That's the poetry that's in *Let Each Man Remember.*

"Winter Castle?"

Yes, exactly. That was the first solid effort at professional poetry that I ever made, and Harriet Monroe took a couple of those for *Poetry.* I just dropped them in the mailbox. I subscribed to *Poetry,* and I thought I'd like to send something in, and I thought, "This is ridiculous, but what can they do to me?" She took two or three sonnets from "Winter Castle." And she used quite a lot of my poetry from then on. That's one thing I'm very proud of, that every single editor of *Poetry* has used my poems.

From what else would you say your happiness has come?

My work. My husband. And the family relationship has always been lucky. We happen to have a son, Erlend, with whom we are extraordinarily congenial. And our daughter-in-law. We had one grandchild, the oldest, to whom we were especially close: Ricky, the one who was killed in that random accident.

Tell me again about the trip you, your husband and Ricky took to Africa.

It was one of the high points of my life, but it was a very simple thing, and I don't want to exaggerate it. When Ricky was a small child we had gone together to see *Born Free.* Oh, several times. And he had said he'd give anything to go and see the animals; and I, in that lighthearted, adult, irresponsible way that one does, said, "Well, tell you what, Ricky, some day we will all go to Africa together." And he believed this implicitly, as you do when you're seven or eight. And almost immediately afterward, I got an attack of devastating guilt, and I thought this is exactly the thing that people do to children all the time—they lie to them. So the first moment I got the job at the Library of Congress, the first thing I thought was that we could make this thing come true.

So it was real. We got to Kilimanjaro on New Year's Eve, camping right at the foot of the mountain; and it was, of course, covered with clouds. You couldn't even see the snows on the top. And everybody said it's almost never in a clear sky. You can look at pictures of it, but you're not going to see the summit.

So we all had a New Year's Eve party, and we were exhausted and went to bed about ten o'clock. We were fast asleep, and all of sudden we heard this pounding on the door. We got up and went to the door, and it was Ricky in a tremendous state of excitement, in his pajamas with a blanket around his shoulders. He said, "Get a blanket, get a blanket!

Come out!" We came out—it was about five minutes of midnight, which was the weird thing—and every cloud had cleared away. The sky was absolutely crystal clear, and there was this moon blazing right on the snows right up at the top. We stayed there looking at it for maybe ten minutes, so that we were there before and after the beginning of the year.

There are so many sources of joy. When I get these awful fits of desolation, I feel guilty.

Was your trip to Africa the beginning of your interest in animals? They're in so much of your writing.

I've always had this animal fascination. I've always been drawn to this mysterious kingdom. Animals have been great mythical figures. You go back in the Bible or in any great literature and you see mythical figures of the lion, and the serpent, the dragon and the scorpion, very potent images. And I think fairy tales had a lot to do with my feelings. There's this huge mysterious world—of which we're such a small, messy, crossed-up part—that is going on without us all the time. For me there's something liberating in that.

Wild animals live their separate lives. They don't know anything about humans; they've never seen them; they don't care about humans. Monkeys are almost a lower human, whereas when you see an elephant or a leopard, a tiger or an antelope, you don't feel that they have tried to become human and failed; you feel they belong to a whole different order.

I think we've lost the sense of mystery and wonder in the world. I think of my grandchildren, and I worry about what is going to be left for them on this marvelous planet. We've turned everything into what can be utilized. We've put up oil derricks to get oil out of the earth, we've cut down the game preserves so that agriculture can go ahead. Gradually we're eliminating all the unconquered, beautiful parts of the planet, all the frontiers.

Tell me how you see fire; it's such a strong image in your poems.

I'm fascinated by the mysterious levels of fire. I build a little fire and warm myself at my hearth, and then I see these devastating forest fires that sweep through thousands of acres and tower up to the sky. I strike a match and it's light, it's fire, a little thing that I can get for a few cents and blow out. And fire went so far back. The hunters used to build fires at night to keep the wolves away, and then there were the sacred fires built on Walpurgis Night, and then we brought the fire inside, the civilized fires. It has been a sacred thing always, in some form.

But not always benign, in your poems, by any means.

No, no, by no means. Absolutely not. Nothing ever is always the same. That's what is so confusing and compelling about life to me. I never see anything in a simple way.

Tell me how you see shadows.

A shadow is a fascinating statement because you can see a man's shadow, for instance, on bright green grass, and you know exactly what it is. It's a man. You can see how tall he is, you can see the shape of his head, his hands and his body, and yet every particular is withheld from you. I mean you don't know the color of his eyes or the expression of his eyes. It's almost as if shadows were the simplest image of almost anything, the thing reduced to its primitive self, the first signal.

And there's something mysterious to me about the way it follows you, and that every single person has this primitive notice, without any details that will modify or explain it. It's like the spirit of someone about which you really know nothing.

Quite a few of your poems deal with the different levels of time.

Time has been almost an obsession with me. I'm conscious of the fact that our ideas of time are so warped. I think we lose the sense of proportion. The proportion is so strange. Two people loving or living in a house, and their voices and their actions, and then you think, ah, that happened 20 years ago. On the other hand, I remember when I went back to our summer house the summer after our grandson's death. I kept finding theater stubs from when we'd gone to the summer theater, or a particular recipe I'd written out because he'd liked it, and it seemed to me that there were hundreds of years between that summer and the summer before. I felt that I couldn't have lived through so much so long.

Archeology and paleontology have always fascinated me. They give me a sense of how far back things reach. My father was an amateur archeologist. He was tremendously interested in it, he did some work in it in Egypt. He translated scarab inscriptions, and he knew hieroglyphics.

But you were only five when he died.

I often wonder if interests don't sometimes run biologically in a family. However, I probably began consciously to think about these things when I read *The Golden Bough*, in my 20s. *The Animal Inside* is just filled with the influence of that book. From then on, I began to be drawn to traces of things. I am always fascinated by cities. I think most people are; look at Atlantis, it's a romantic thing in most people's mind. And I try to remember how much closer Genghis Kahn

is to me today than he was to the period when the equus horse developed.

Religion, or faith, is present in some of your work. Tell me about your early poem, "The Faithful."

The great term in the Mass is "the mystery of faith," and what I'm trying to say is, isn't it really marvelous that people know that these things are going to happen to them, night, winter, death, burial, and they still believe. How *can* men live through life and see how it goes, see that everything that is beautiful dies, that everything that is good goes away, that everyone they love is vulnerable, and still say that they know that they are going to rise from the grave, they know that all is going to be well. How can they?

Is it fair to say that for you the answer to these mysteries lies somewhere in the inscrutability of whatever we mean by the divine?

Yes, yes. I think the whole basis of the thing is probably that the inability to comprehend God sets up a tremendous sense of contradiction. I assume that the inability to comprehend God is universal, and I don't care who tells me that they do comprehend Him, I don't believe it. I have a poem about an optimist who says you can't look at anything in nature without believing in God, by which he means that you can't look at flowers or butterflies; he does not mean you can't look at sharks or hyenas.

It's like your poem about Christmas . . .

Yes, **"Bush Christmas Eve."** That's one of my half-dozen favorite poems that I've ever written, because it more or less postulates all my confusion and the fact that I'm not willing to accept the people who say God is obvious because He created kittens. I say, He also created the praying mantis and the animal that stings something and takes it away and eats it piecemeal. You don't try to falsify that.

I've always had this animal fascination. I've always been drawn to this mysterious kingdom. Animals have been great mythical figures. You go back in the Bible or in any great literature and you see mythical figures of the lion, and the serpent, the dragon and the scorpion, very potent images.
—Josephine Jacobsen

I don't see in your writing that you go much further than wonder at these contradictions.

I wonder . . . It is in me, and I'm wondering why it isn't more reflected in the poems. I think that the tension I have with people who see God's beneficence in the world all the time has kept this confidence out of my work. I do believe in a design, but I would hate to take the case for it in court.

I think I want never to forget that there is a terrible price you pay for believing; that you have to submit your intellect, and the testimony of your senses and your experience, to faith. In other words, you make a great sacrifice when you say, I believe in a design; I believe in an ultimately good and great God. You're making a statement that can be made to ignore all the suffering and all the horror of which life is so often so largely composed.

So if you did say that you believed in a design, you'd also have to say so much more.

Yes, that's what I'm trying to say exactly: that God says, as in my poem **"Mr. McMirty,"** "Don't forget, I am who I am. Don't try to explain this or you'll fall flat on your face."

So, what is your religion?

I come back to the very simple facts. The Eucharist in the Catholic church is the center of my whole belief, because I believe in the inexplicable tangle of body and spirit; the spirit is encased in the physical. If you're going to know God you've got to know Him in physical terms. A lot of people think that the symbols of the Church are so childish, so crude: feeding on the body and blood of Christ, multiplying the fishes; but when they drop that out and get talking about spiritual things, they lose me.

I don't care if you're a philosopher or a king, you've got these things that are going to happen to you: You're going to be born; if you're cut, you're going to bleed; we're all united by this physical presence. And we're even united with the whole animal kingdom by the fact that they can suffer, and fear and be hurt.

Death and pain: In your poems, those are the common denominators that connect us with the human afflicted, including the urban isolates, the urban lost.

I think there's a terrific amount of condescension that creeps into poems about the unfortunate, always as if they were somebody else, as if they were Martians, and they're not; they're just like us. That's what **"Deaf-Mutes at the Ballgame"** finally says: Inside of us sits his own deaf-mute, fingerless. There's something there at the bottom of all of us that we can't tell anybody because it cannot be put into words. So we are all isolated in that sense. There are these dropouts constantly in the human race, people always getting lost,

people whom life completely passes by, especially in the big cities. I just wrote a poem, it isn't even finished yet, about Potter's Field. The sad thing is also that people tend to be overlooked, to get lost, in quite different circumstances, as they become a chore to be with. We tend to cooperate in this isolation by gradually saying to ourselves, "Goodness, I haven't seen so-and-so in a couple of years," but we haven't really tried to find them.

Your poem, "They Never Were Found," about urban isolates, is an illustration of how we are all connected. But there is no explicit statement of connection in that poem. It just describes the lost. What did you mean?

Well, I think of it perhaps as going through a jungle and seeing a path going off in what looks like a very deserted direction, but there is a little sign indicating that something is there. I'd like to tell you something, and I doubt if this has any bearing. My own best friends don't know it, not because I've tried to conceal it but because it's almost meaningless to me. Everybody says, do you have any brothers, do you have any sisters; and I say I had a brother . . . I also had a half sister . . . whom I saw for 15 minutes in my life. She was 30 years older than I. I'm telling you this because I'm wondering if it had anything to do, subliminally, with this feeling. I must say it meant so little in my life except as a sort of shadowy, beautiful thing about my father. When he was a very young doctor, he attended to a woman, a widow, who was 20 years older than he was, and this woman had a retarded child who was dying. She was never going to get beyond nine years old and maybe she was 12 or 13. In any case the child died of scarlet fever. My father had come very close to the mother; he admired very much the way she handled herself, and he had great sympathy for her. He was a young man, and they married. This was his first wife; my mother was his second wife. A second child was born, and she was supposed to have had brain fever, but actually the same thing occurred; there was an arrest in development when she was a small child. Well, the mother died, and my father was left with this teenaged daughter, to whom he was very, very devoted; and he made up his mind that he was going to keep her with him, hoping that an attempt to lead a normal life might possibly make some sort of improvement. Well, obviously, it didn't; and it became more and more difficult for her. As she tried more and more to come up to her age, it became more tragic for her. All my father's family grew up in Italy, my father was brought up in Italy; and he knew of some nuns in Bologna who were lovely, gentle people, and he sent Elsa for holidays with them every year. She became the pet of the convent. I mean, she was the kind of person who could go out and gather bouquets of flowers and bring them in, decorate the altar, be very proud of that, have a plot of garden, learn to sew, learn to sew beautifully.

You only met her for 15 minutes?

This was so many years before I was born. Finally it became obvious that this was the one place where she was really not under pressure, where she was happy. So father made an arrangement for her to live there. He visited her regularly every month, and he would take her away for a day or two.

When she was about 30 years old, my father met my mother, who was a widow with a son from her first marriage, and they fell in love and got married. Father went back every year of his life, twice a year, to spend time in this little village and be with Elsa Louise. To me she was just a name. As a child, I knew she existed. I had a friendly feeling, in fact I had a little picture taken of her, with curls. And she was to me like somebody in a story. Finally when I was 19 years old, my mother and I went over to Italy and Mother wanted to have a conversation with Elsa Louise with nobody else in the room. She was infinitely relieved because Elsa was obviously very happy in an infantile way. Then I was called in and for about 15 minutes we sat there, and they said, "This is your sister, Josephine," and we kissed each other. She died—oh heavens, I guess when I was 26 or 27—so my entire contact with her was when I was 19 with no way to communicate except to say a few friendly things.

What role does your religion play in your feelings about human communication and suffering?

It seems to me that the Christian religion is overwhelmingly right for me, because I cannot conceive of any religion sheltering me that didn't acknowledge *in* its God a degree of human suffering, and, indeed, failure.

That is why the moment on the cross when Christ is supposed to have said, "My God, my God, why have You forsaken me?" is the most important thing that has been said in all the testaments. In other words, they always say that Christ experienced all the sorrow and suffering of being a human being, but if He didn't lose that sense of His own omnipotence, then He didn't experience everything. To me this is something that is priceless. I feel that all my poems have a religious background, in the sense that they spring out of that view of life, yet very few of them deal explicitly with religion, very few.

I'd like you to explain something you once said about the changes in your style of writing. You said that you started out writing rhymed, lyric poetry, and that you changed to a rougher, looser style, and that now you write a more terse, compact form. And you've said that you write according to what the poem demands, which I take to mean according to what you want to say. What has changed about what you want to say?

It's a very interesting question. There's no intention, no theory involved. I deal with each poem according to my own aesthetic impulse of the moment. I started out with rather musical, rhymed poetry, and then I began to feel constrained, to feel that the purely lyric, 19th-century terms didn't seem to express the tangled life that was happening around me.

I have no interest in a poem that just makes a flat statement and has no counter current, because nothing in life goes smoothly from start to finish.
—*Josephine Jacobsen*

In that case, the first stimulus to change your poetic style was primarily a change in your aesthetics rather than an actual change in your personal life. What was it that moved you from the looser style to a more compact one?

As I get older and life gets more complex and more confusing, the expression of it has to get simple. You can't be diverse and wander; you have to take the gist, the seed, the one vital core. My recent poems deal with big issues, maybe inadequately, but big issues. One is about the way body and mind work together. Another, grim poem is about someone who misses a midnight train and gets to Pennsylvania station at 1:30 a.m. and sees this great terminal where most people are milling about, busy, motivated to get somewhere; and old ladies are lying down outside the toilet downstairs—poems concerned with the vital, less and less with the peripheral. When you get to the end of your life, you've got to make decisions about what is important.

A young person looks out at the world and thinks there are five hundred thousand things I can do, and this should be different; but at the end of your life, you ask what shall I save, what are the one or two things that matter?

About technique: You said, mostly in reference to your fiction, that one of the great challenges is how to make your theme clear. There is a sort of inexpensive way in which a writer suppresses all those things that go against the point he's making, so that he's left with a straightforward impact. But you said that for you, you must infuse into the story instead something that is more like real life, contradictions and irrelevancies, against which your theme has to sustain itself.

I believe somebody else said it, it's too good. Did I really say it?

Yes. Do you find that somewhat true about your poetic style, too?

Yes, I do, absolutely. I have no interest in a poem that just makes a flat statement and has no counter current, because nothing in life goes smoothly from start to finish. I just had this impressed on me recently, because I met for the first time in my life a military-career man, with whom I had absolutely no opinion in common, not one single one; but he was a perfectly lovely man. His basic premises were all different from mine, but he was good, kind, gentle, obviously sincere. I wish I could have known him longer. And that's what I think life is like. I get terribly impatient with stories that don't leave something that you can't resolve, a ragged edge.

But poems, the diffuseness and contradictions in poems . . .

I'm much more conscious of what I'm doing in stories; it's a funny thing, in a poem I'm much more at sea on a sea shell. That's one reason I find writing prose such a relief.

Because you know more where you're going?

It's so much easier. Because I can have fun. I develop the characters, and I say it would happen just this way. It's really—I don't want to say escape, because that means escape-writing, which I don't like—but it's much less tearing apart than poetry is.

You've written that writing poems is dangerous. There are many ways you could mean that. How do you mean it?

Just what we've been talking about. You're starting out on a journey in which you don't really know your destination. The chances are that it's not going to come off, that you're never going to get this nebulous, mysterious thing into language at all.

Whereas if you're a professional short-story writer, if you can't get it into language there's something wrong. You may have to work and go back and do it over two or three times, but you've got the material; you've got the language. You ought to be able to get the material into the language.

Do you think what a writer tries to capture in a story is less precious than what he tries for in a poem?

You know, I think I secretly do feel that. I don't want to admit it because I think the short story is a great form, a terribly difficult form. I prefer it to the novel. But in my heart, to me there is nothing that compares to poetry. Because I don't have any confidence that I can do it until I've done it. There's much more to lose here, you see. I never have any confidence until the poem is over that I can capture that beast in the net. It's like a delicate operation. Under certain conditions, you can't go that far in because you get to an organ that is a life source. I feel that with poetry you get closer to that organ; I feel that you're getting as deep as it's possible.

Robert B. Shaw (review date 4 April 1988)

SOURCE: A review of *The Sisters: New and Selected Poems,* in *Poetry* (Chicago), Vol. LLII, No. 1, April 4, 1988, pp. 40-41.

[*In the following positive review, Shaw critic states that "what is striking and admirable in Jacobsen's work is the consistency with which she unites firmness of technique with intelligence and feeling."*]

How many poets do we have who can make a moral point without pomposity? The answer is: Not many. Josephine Jacobsen is one of the few. An especially fine instance of this ability of hers comes in **"An Absence of Slaves,"** when she describes her Greek tour guide boasting that the Parthenon was built with free labor. The poem ends:

> . . . she said: "The city
> sent a slave
> to each man's yoke,
> oil press and furrow,
> to free for toil the free Greek:
>
> the free raised these!" she cried
> to the blue sky and honey-
> veined columns. "This is
> no pyramid." And I saw
> the loins and wrists
> and bones and tendons of those disprized
> who in absence reared the great frieze.

Together with the ethical clarity of this, the beauty of description and the precision of diction are also typical of this poet. (How perfect the word "disprized" is here.) What is striking and admirable in Jacobsen's work is the consistency with which she unites firmness of technique with intelligence and feeling. There is an attractive lack of egotism in her writing; it is distinguished instead for its empathy, its awareness of vulnerabilities we all share. She is so poised in manner, so level in tone, that the reader is recurrently startled by how closely the poems take account of peril, deprivation, and mental or moral darkness. In one of several poems set in the Caribbean [**"The Night Watchman"**], the speaker is awakened by the night watchman's light and muses:

> Dogged as cock or dog, his light will return.
> Protection! Protection? While
> the thin knives of the clock
> shred minute by minute, and the sea
> turns over its bones?

In a much earlier poem, **"The Eyes of Children at the Brink of the Sea's Grasp,"** the children in an "ecstasy of panic" play in the waves:

. . . down the shining
Dark slope of invitation, outward, to the prize
Of shaping danger they go—and widen their eyes
Innocent and voluptuous.

To grow up, of course, is to lose that innocence, and Jacobsen's poems are everywhere touched by the foreboding knowledge which replaces it.

Jacobsen is so poised in manner, so level in tone, that the reader is recurrently startled by how closely the poems take account of peril, deprivation, and mental or moral darkness.
—Robert B. Shaw

Like the children braving the waves, she has been willing to take risks. She has remained open to formal innovation, and each of her volumes had among its contents poems which are fresh and surprising—not exotic, momentarily diverting "experiments," but new and individualized strategies for poetic success. (The macaronic **"Phrases in Common Use,"** the bouncy **"Pondicherry Blues,"** and the monosyllabic **"The Monosyllable"** are examples.) She has taken another risk, where reputation is concerned, in publishing considerably less than many of her contemporaries have done in the span of almost fifty years represented in this book. It contains selections from six previous volumes and a group of new poems, but remains at 132 pages unusually compact as a summing-up. In a society which prizes quantity as much as ours, Jacobsen's choice of writing only when she has had something significant to say has probably cost her some attention. In the long run, though, quality is what counts; and I venture to predict that this book will continue to be taken from the shelves to be read when many another weightier one is taken down only to be dusted.

Michael Heller (review date 12 June 1988)

SOURCE: "Owls, Monkeys and Spiders in Space," in *The New York Times Book Review*, Vol. 93, June 12, 1988, p. 15.

[*In the following excerpt, Heller praises Jacobsen's use of language in* The Sisters: New and Selected Poems.]

Josephine Jacobsen's poetry has always been a matter of the cool ear over the fanciful eye. *The Sisters,* which gathers poems from nearly 50 years, demonstrates not only scrupulous verbal craft but a kind of auditory seriousness, a preference for depth and precision over mere charm or beauty. In **"Winter Castle"** (1940), she conjures up a picture of "the

owl that . . . shall serve as nightingale." In a later poem, she writes of "the shade-seller," a man at a bull-fight who sells one a seat out of the direct glare of sun and blood. Such images hint at Ms. Jacobsen's lyricisms, which seem always adumbrated by night vision.

In her most recent poems, among the strongest she has written, the voice is even deeper and more simplified. It is as though the poet were relying on Browning's "purged Ear," which "apprehends Earth's import." For Ms. Jacobsen, such apprehension means the discovery of both death and renewal, often entwined, as in one poem about swimmers floating over a "necropolis of the fish":

So, out of the deeps of sleep
where they cannot keep company—
chosen, at least—
from the fathoms of memory, one

by one, at morning, they rise
into themselves, into their limbs, the new
sight of the old sun on their sea.
As though they would, always, wake.

One hears in that "always" a half-fleeting stay of the music in the stanza, as if the idea that one were going to live forever had momentarily snagged on truth.

Ms. Jacobsen's theme is often regeneration—but in a minor key, a matter of limited befores and afters or of contraries arising out of the play of the real and the imagined. The witty title poem of this volume pits "*A*" against "*B*," two sides of the poet's psyche who sometimes disagree and are only reconciled by bearing common witness to the world: "amicably they watched the blood orange dip / into water, then stars, larger and brighter than elsewhere. / Before bed, *A* looked at herself in the mirror, using *B*'s eyes."

The poet, who has spent a long life at her craft, is most powerful in splendid, oblique meditations on death:

What must be said of clouds is: they are silent.
Their silence is flawless. . . .

Death is equally silent but does not move.
I think a good thing to see before the quiet that is
motionless, would be the bright soundless motion.

This silence fills the ear like another music.
It appeases. How much time in which to be
grateful is roughly sufficient?

Sound and word are caught in endless refractions in such passages. In Ms. Jacobsen's craft, language seems as flawless as silence.

Steven G. Kellman (review date 27 August 1989)

SOURCE: "The Human Archipelago," in *The New York Times Book Review,* Vol. 94, August 27, 1989, p. 20.

[*The following is a positive review of* On the Island: New and Selected Stories.]

"The distinction between poetry and prose writers," wrote Shelley (in prose), "is a vulgar error." The vulgar fact is that 81-year-old Josephine Jacobsen, the former Consultant in Poetry to the Library of Congress, is known primarily as a writer of poems. One of them, **"Instances of Communication,"** begins with the ambiguous declaration: "Almost nothing concerns me but communication." And, at first glance, the 20 exquisite stories she has collected in *On the Island* seem to concern nothing, almost.

Consider **"The Jungle of Lord Lion,"** which is set, like several other offerings, on an imaginary Caribbean island named Boudina. Fastidious Mrs. Pomeroy's happiness at the guest house called Morne Jaune is marred by the presence of Mrs. Chubb, a boorish bigot who "looked like a nasty sea monster, all blubber and malignancy." Thus Mrs. Pomeroy is stunned when it is she, not the loathsome Mrs. Chubb, who is asked to leave. That is all there is to the plot; nevertheless, Ms. Jacobsen's narrative haiku fits Mrs. Pomeroy's own description of a phrase from Yeats—"the words were as true as bone . . . it was life held up like a transparency to the blaze of loss."

Ms. Jacobsen's osseous truth is pared of fat; she gives us spare, unsparing tales of spiritual tropism. In **"The Night the Playoffs Were Rained Out,"** Mr. and Mrs. Plessy are transformed after watching baseball on a motel television with the obnoxious Luther and Minna Gombrecht. In **"The Wreath,"** a visitor betrays a patient at the Pine Mount clinic by handing the patient's fantasized shopping list to a nurse. In **"Jack Frost,"** the nonagenarian Mrs. Travis, determined to spend another winter alone in her New Hampshire homestead, trips in her garden but manages to crawl inside the house.

> Ms. Jacobsen's osseous truth is pared of fat; she gives us spare, unsparing tales of spiritual tropism in *On the Island.*
> —*Steven G. Kellman*

James Gantry, on his honeymoon in Fez in **"A Walk with Raschid,"** feels contempt for "those dreadful, contrived stories in which at the last moment someone is run over, his mother falls dead, he is arrested, or locked in a windowless room." That is a catalogue of endings for several of the con-

summately contrived stories in *On the Island.* In others, despite Ms. Jacobsen's apparent discomfort with the crudity of merely recounting a story, a terminally ill maid is suffocated by her employer, a Guatemalan peasant severs the index finger of a human-rights investigator, a priest inadvertently backs his car off a Vermont mountain, a man in bed during an idyllic Caribbean vacation is decapitated. But what is sensational about these stories is less the events they rehearse than their delicate designs. They demand to be reread, since Ms. Jacobsen, unlike O. Henry, resolves nothing with her surprise endings.

It is not quite a windowless room into which Jane Glessner is locked, and her claustration occurs at the outset, not the end, of **"Nel Bagno."** Moments before she is to depart for Italy, Mrs. Glessner, a writer, finds herself stuck in her own bathroom with little more than an Italian phrase book, her wits and her words. **"Nel Bagno"** is a parable of the writer's calling, a desperate effort to break out of the isolation into which each of us is locked. Whether in New England, Philadelphia, Baltimore, Acapulco, Central America, Morocco or Boudina, Ms. Jacobsen's characters, like Jane Glessner, inhabit what Wallace Stevens called an island solitude under an old chaos of the sun. Against Dorme's assertion that "no man is an island," the stories in *On the Island* give each one of us in the human archipelago, like Odysseus before the Cyclops, the name of Noman.

Erin McGraw (review date Spring 1991)

SOURCE: "The Landscape of Story," in *Georgia Review,* Vol. 45, No. 1, Spring, 1991, pp. 170-76.

[*In the following excerpt, McGraw positively reviews* On the Island, *praising Jacobsen's treatment of the themes of loss and isolation and her unsentimental characterization.*]

The stories in Josephine Jacobsen's *On the Island* don't fall immediately into overarching categories. The collection is new and selected work published over the past twelve years, and the stories cast a wide net encompassing age and youth, the battles between men and women, and the battles we carry on to know ourselves. But Jacobsen relies on place to a striking degree for activating her stories: actions occur *because* people are where they are—Baltimore, Mexico, the Caribbean—and couldn't happen anywhere else. A tourist, unfamiliar with the undertow of a local beach, is swept out to sea; a man is forced to die within the confines of a world so narrow he is trapped by his own men's club; and even in **"Nel Bagno,"** an odd and comic piece in which a woman is trapped in the bathroom of her own house, it is the confines of the room itself—the small window and smooth tiles—

that hold her back, so that the physical reality of the room becomes her enemy.

Jacobsen deals most frequently with loss, and in particular with unanticipated loss. More broadly, her stories tend toward representations of isolation, and they feature the places that are unfamiliar, where we and the characters are forced to look around carefully. In **"The Mango Community,"** a few Americans staying on a small Caribbean island must determine what to do as the native society around them swells and bristles with coming revolution. Should the visitors stay and declare solidarity? Should they return with their children to their own home, the place of safety? For Jacobsen, identity is formed by action, and the story's deepest question is this: What, finally, is our identity?

Attachment to the land or detachment from it jars these characters into awareness. Feigning ignorance of the dangerous undertows of Mexico, a young husband can lose his beautiful, gentle wife as he reaches for her wanton half sister. Well-meaning Americans can cause boys to be killed in the Caribbean or Morocco, the very wideness of their intended mercy more than the culture can absorb. Or in her own home an aging woman can bring on her own death, seeing the early frost come and knowing what such a frost means, in New Hampshire, to a woman in her nineties and alone.

Jacobsen is known primarily as a poet, and her poet's sense of structure and language are everywhere apparent here. Not only are some of her characters remarkably familiar with contemporary poetry (Father Haggerty, in **"Late Fall,"** has published poems in *Foxfire* and *Lillabulero*, and he quotes Howard Nemerov to his weary pastor), but the language is gorgeous and embellished, filled with little gifts. Beyond the restraining wall "the Caribbean glared and glittered," and an American thinks about feeding the fish she can't see beneath its surface, imagining "the demented maze and flicker of hunger." Metaphors are a part of the terrain of this language: "the marriage split like an old rowboat"; "her hand, like the paw of a starving bear after fish, had darted down"; waves of fatigue curdle over a man.

In a certain sense the stories are also structured like poems, turning on the finest point of near-revelation. Such moments come when characters are closest to seeing themselves in a new light, one cast by strangeness or illness or age. These are moments of epiphany, but Jacobsen makes them tight and compressed—and gone before the characters realize their full import, because in these pieces life is unruly and pushes us along before we're ready. In **"Late Fall,"** for instance, Father Consadine escapes his Nemerov-quoting curate and slips into church:

> He put his hands down and sat back in the pew. For any acknowledgment of his presence, he might have

been back at his desk. It was all wrong; he had lived by personal encounter, by grace or the experience of grace. That encounter, that sense of grace, had become rarer and rarer. Suppose finally it never came again? Well then, he would wait.

> Who was he to be disappointed, to dictate the occasion of meeting?

And the story moves on. As readers, we must be quick on our feet.

On the Island is a rich collection and a large one (twenty stories across 250 pages), reminiscent often of V. S. Pritchett and Graham Greene in the texture of its language. Jacobsen writes with some formality but never with distance, plunging us into the centers of her characters' lives, into the hopes—and the fears—they haven't articulated even to themselves. She has maturity of craft and, more important, of vision. Her lens is wide, clear, and unsentimental; there is room for all of us to play in her stories, for all of our hopes and tragedies. She doesn't shy away from anything, and in the end her collection feels as broad and various as the world.

Dulcy Brainard (review date 24 April 1995)

SOURCE: A review of *In the Crevice of Time*, in *Publishers Weekly*, Vol. 241, No. 17, April 24, 1995, p. 66.

[*Below, Brainard provides a positive review of* In the Crevice of Time.]

One turns to Jacobsen's poems [in *In the Crevice of Time*] not for flashy, egotistical juggling, but as to an old friend, for her dependable, philosophical voice, rich in technique and free from cliché. She imagines eliminating the "monosyllable *love*" from our language in the hope that someone "will enunciate a syllable / of force" to replace it. "What small / metaphors we set / ourselves," she laments elsewhere, and in poem after poem proves this need not be the case. Her gaze is often directed outward, sighting the estranged or deformed: clowns with highly individualized sorrows, deafmutes watching baseball. Whatever handicaps these subjects bear don't generate pity; if anyone seems deficient it will be the reader. Because her poems don't fall into easily recognizable categories—political, confessional, nature, or even formalist poetry (though she writes well in her share of forms)—Jacobsen is seldom anthologized. Yet her work has withstood the test of time better than many of her more-often-read contemporaries from the 1940s and 1950s. Her latest poems are modern and forceful.

FURTHER READING

Criticism

Mason, David. Review of *In the Crevice of Time,* by Josephine Jacobsen. *Hudson Review* 49 (Spring 1996): 168-69.

> Positive review in which Mason states that *"In the Crevice of Time* is worth buying and going back to."

Osterhaus, Joe. Review of *In the Crevice of Time,* by Josephine Jacobsen. *Boston Review* (1997), www-polisci.mit.edu/BostonReview/BR20.6.

> Laudatory review of *In the Crevice of Time.* Osterhaus also discusses Jacobsen's development as a poet.

Review of *What Goes Without Saying,* by Josephine Jacobsen. *Publishers Weekly* 243, No. 47 (November 18, 1996): 64.

> Brief positive review in which the critic calls the short stories in the volume "small, highly polished gems."

Additional coverage of Jacobsen's life and career is contained in the following sources published by Gale Research: *Contemporary Authors,* Vols. 33-36R; *Contemporary Authors Autobiography Series,* Vol. 18; and *Contemporary Authors New Revision Series,* Vols. 23, 48.

Donald Justice
1925-

(Full name Donald Rodney Justice) American poet, short story writer, and editor.

The following entry presents an overview of Justice's career. For further information on his life and works, see *CLC*, Volumes 6 and 19.

INTRODUCTION

Justice is considered one of the foremost American poets of the twentieth century. He has won numerous writing awards, among them the Pulitzer Prize in 1979 for *Selected Poems*. Considered a poet's poet, Justice is known for his attention to form and language, his use of rhyme and meter, and his ability to master many poetic forms. Initially not widely read, Justice's recent awards have brought him greater national attention.

Biographical Information

Justice was born in Miami, Florida, on August 12, 1925, to Vasco Justice, a carpenter, and Mary Ethel Cook Justice. He grew up in Miami, never leaving the South until adulthood. He received a B.A. from the University of Miami in 1945, an M.A. in English from University of North Carolina in 1947, and a Ph.D. from the Writer's Workshop at the University of Iowa in 1954. From 1948 to 1949 he studied under Yvor Winters at Stanford University. In 1947 he married Jean Ross with whom he had one son. Throughout his career Justice has been both student and teacher. At Iowa he worked under John Berryman, Robert Lowell, and Karl Shapiro and he taught Mark Strand, Charles Wright, and Jorie Graham. Justice taught at the University of Iowa, Syracuse, University of California, and other universities before settling at the University of Florida. He has been retired since 1992 but continues to write and publish. His numerous awards include the Lamont Poetry Selection, a nomination for the National Book Award, the Pulitzer Prize, the Bollingen Prize and awards from the Rockefeller and Guggenheim foundations and the National Endowment for the Arts.

Major Works

Justice has not been a prolific writer; he has published only a handful of books, mostly slim volumes of short poems. His first volume, *The Summer Anniversaries* (1960), which won the Lamont Poetry Selection, centered on his childhood experiences in Miami. Justice's distinct voice first emerged in these poems. He is nostalgic without becoming sentimen-

tal or maudlin; he experiments with form, employing difficult structures such as sestina and villanelle; and he writes in a distant, third person, not focusing attention on himself but on others. In *Night Light* (1967) Justice continued to work in this tradition but his viewpoint shifted from childhood to adulthood. The influence of William Carlos Williams can be seen in these poems, both in style and subject. In *Departures* (1973) Justice experimented even more, creating poems by placing words on cards and then shuffling them to create a poem by chance. *The Sunset Maker* (1987) consists of poems, stories, and a memoir. *Selected Poems* (1979) and *A Donald Justice Reader* (1991) reflect Justice's propensity for revision as well as his use of varying poetic structures. Dana Gioia writes about *Selected Poems*, "There are sestinas, villanelles and ballads rubbing shoulders with aleatory poems, surreal odes, and . . . free verse." *New and Selected Poems* (1995), containing fifteen new poems as well as work spanning three decades, reflects the characteristics of Justice's writing style which have made him such a noted poet. He deals with themes of sorrow, loss, and vulnerability in a quiet, understated tone, paying careful attention to word choice and meter, and experimenting widely with structure.

Critical Reception

Throughout his career Justice has not conformed to the tenets of modern poetry, which is typically known for its intensely emotional, energetic tone and free, unstructured form. This has resulted in two critical reactions to his poetry. Critics have claimed that, compared with the vibrant work of his contemporaries, Justice's work is passive and lacks vitality. Calvin Bedient, writing in the *Sewanee Review,* found Justice "an uncertain talent that has not been turned to much account." In the *New Statesman,* Allan Hollinghurst wrote that Justice's poems were hampered "by a weary passivity, a lack of vitality that is unsupported by fastidious formal elegance." Other critics, finding fault with modern poetry, have delighted in Justice's attention to detail, understated voice, and lack of sentimentality. In their introduction in *Verse,* Gioia and William Logan wrote, "Literary culture, for all its whims and sudden moods, loves nothing more than a settled judgement, and is slow to appreciate a poet whose gains and attractions are cumulative, and whose work has never suffered, or contrived, a radical breach."

PRINCIPAL WORKS

The Summer Anniversaries (poetry) 1960; revised edition, 1981
A Local Storm (poetry) 1963
Night Light (poetry) 1967; revised edition, 1981
Four Poets [with Tom McAfee, Donald Drummond, and R. P. Dickey] (poetry) 1968
Sixteen Poems (poetry) 1970
From a Notebook (poetry) 1971
Departures (poetry) 1973
L'Homme qui se ferme/The Man Closing Up [translator] (poetry) 1973
Selected Poems (poetry) 1979
Platonic Scripts (essays) 1984
Tremayne (poetry) 1984
The Sunset Maker: Poems/Stories/A Memoir (poetry, short stories, memoir) 1987
The Death of Lincoln (libretto) 1988
A Donald Justice Reader: Selected Poetry and Prose (poetry) 1991
New and Selected Poems (poetry) 1995

CRITICISM

Donald Justice (essay date 1979)

SOURCE: "Meters and Memory," in *The Structure of Verse: Modern Essays on Prosody,* edited by Harvey Gross, Ecco Press, 1979, pp. 269-76.

[*In the following essay, which is prefaced by commentary from Harvey Gross, Justice discusses the function of meter in poetry.*]

Donald Justice describes himself as "a rationalist defender of the meters." He is primarily concerned with the traditional metrical ordering of English verse and does not touch upon the larger question of rhythm and its significances. He is an eloquent spokesman for the mnemonic function of meter; however, his concept of memory is really a theory of the imagination. Meter serves as stimulus to the processes of creation: the meters "will have called back the thing itself—the subject—that became the poem." But the meters do not only stimulate imagination by helping to recollect the original experience; they also serve to transform and hence fix the "terror or beauty or plain ordinariness of the original event. . . ." Meters are artificial in the Renaissance sense; providing aesthetic distance, their very artifice reminds us "that we are at that remove from life which traditionally we have called art."

Skeptical of the supposed mimetic function of meter, he points out, as does Dr. Johnson, that we often "ascribe to the numbers the effects of the sense." Meters accompany the sense "like a kind of percussion only, mostly noise." (We are reminded of Ransom's characterization of meter as a low-grade musical material.) The function of the meters—apart from their power to set memory and imagination in motion—is architectonic. Like syntax they serve to articulate the words and the larger elements of poetic form.

The poet who uses the meters "may feel as deeply as the non-metrical writer. . . ." A young woman once asked the great pianist and teacher, Artur Schnabel, whether she should play in time or in accordance with her feelings. Schnabel answered, with his usual wit, "Why not feel in time?" Professor Justice, in rejecting the fallacy of imitative form and its corollary that a disorderly world requires a poetry without meter and syntax, argues that the meters help the poet gain mastery of his subject. And by learning to feel in time, his feelings become both understandable to himself and more truly communicable to his audience.

The mnemonic value of meters seems always to have been

recognized. There are, to begin with, the weather saws, counting spells, and the like, which one does more or less get by heart in childhood. But any ornament, however trivial and even meaningless, probably assists the recollection to some degree, if by ornament we mean a device of sound or structure not required by the plain sense of a passage. Repetition obviously functions in this way—anaphora, refrains, even the sort of repetition which involves nothing more than an approximate equivalence of length, as in Pound's Sapphic fragment:

> Spring. . . .
> Too long. . . .
> Gongula. . . .

Likewise with such structural features as parallel parts or syllogistic order, whether in verse or prose. For that matter, fine and exact phrasing alone enables the memory to take hold about as well as anything. A friend of mine, at parties, preferred to recite prose rather than verse, usually, as I recall, the opening paragraph of *A Farewell to Arms*.

The purely mnemonic character of a passage, however, contributes very little to its aesthetic power. Often enough rhymes are more effective mnemonically than meters, and occasionally other devices may prove to be. But the meters, where employed at all, are likely to be the groundwork underlying other figurations, hence basic, if not always dominant. Consider a couplet like "Red sky at morning, / Sailor take warning." Here the meters cooperate with the rhymes to fit the lines to one another, not only as lines of verse but as linked parts of a perception. It is no more than a slight exaggeration to claim that the couplet becomes fixed in memory by reason of this sense of fittedness. But few devices of sound are enough in themselves to ensure recall. Should, for example, the sky of the couplet be changed from red to blue, although neither rhyme nor meter would be affected, I cannot, believe the couplet would survive. Survival in this case has something to do with aptness of observation, with use, that is, as well as cleverness or beauty. The kernel of lore provides a reason for keeping the jingle; the jingle preserves the lore in stable form.

Now all this is to consider memory, as is customary, from the viewpoint of an audience, as if a significant purpose of poetry were simply to put itself in the way of being memorized. For my part, when I am at work on a poem, the memory of an audience concerns me less than my own. While the meters and other assorted devices may ultimately make the lines easier for an audience to remember, they are offering meanwhile, like the stone of the sculptor, a certain resistance to the writer's efforts to call up his subject, which seems always to be involved, one way or another, with memory. (Hobbes somewhere calls imagination the same thing as memory.) In any case, memory is going to keep whatever it

chooses to keep not just because it has been made easy and agreeable to remember but because it comes to be recognized as worth the trouble of keeping, and first of all by the poet. The audience will find it possible to commit to memory only what the poet first recalls for himself. Anything can be memorized, including numbers, but numbers that refer to something beyond themselves, as to the combination of a safe, are the easier to keep in mind for that reason. Something other than themselves may likewise be hidden in the meters, and an aptness to be committed to memory might almost be taken as a sign of this other presence. Pattern is not enough. The trivial and insignificant pass beyond recall, no matter how patterned, discounting perhaps a double handful of songs and nonsense pieces, where the pattern itself has somehow become a part of what is memorable. But such a result is exceptional. What happens in the more serious and ordinary case is that some recollection of a person, of an incident or a landscape, whatever we are willing to designate as subject, comes to seem worth preserving. The question for the poet is how to preserve it.

One motive for much if not all art (music is probably an exception) is to accomplish this—to keep memorable what deserves to be remembered. So much seems true at least from the perspective of the one who makes it. Nor should any resemblance to the more mechanical functions of camera and tape recorder prove embarrassing; like a literary text in the making, film and tape also permit editing, room enough for the artist. Let emotion be recollected, in tranquility or turmoil, as luck and temperament would have it. And then what? Art lies still in the future. The emotion needs to be fixed, so that whatever has been temporarily recovered may become as nearly permanent as possible, allowing it to be called back again and again at pleasure. It is at this point that the various aids to memory, and meter most persistently, begin to serve memory beyond mnemonics. Such artifices are, let us say, the fixatives. Like the chemicals in the darkroom, they are useful in developing the negative. The audience is enabled to call back the poem, or pieces of it, the poet to call back the thing itself, the subject, all that was to become the poem.

The transcription of experience represented by the meters ought not to be confused with the experience itself. At best they can perform no more than a reenactment, as on some stage of the mind. This being so, to object to the meters as unnatural because unrealistic is to miss the point. Like the odd mustaches and baggy pants of the old comedians, they put us on notice that we are at a certain distance from the normal rules and expectations of life. The effect has been variously called a distancing or a framing. Wordsworth described it as serving "to divest language, in a certain degree, of its reality, and thus to throw a sort of half-consciousness of unsubstantial existence over the whole composition." The meters signify this much at least, that we are at that remove from life which traditionally we have called art.

Their very presence seems to testify to some degree of plan, purpose, and meaning. The meters seem always faintly teleological by implication, even in company with an anti-teleological argument, as the case may be. They are proof of the hand and ear of a maker (uncapitalized), even in a poetry which otherwise effaces the self. They seem to propose that an emotion, however uncontrollable it may have appeared originally, was not, in fact, unmanageable. "I don't know why I am crying" becomes "Tears, idle tears, I know not what they mean." The difference seems important to me. The poetic line comes to constitute a sort of paraphrase of the raw feeling, which will only get broken back down close to its original state in some future critic's re-paraphrase. The writer in meters, I insist, may feel as deeply as the non-metrical writer, and the choice whether or not to use meters is as likely to be dictated by literary fashion as by depth of feeling or sincerity. Nevertheless, they have become a conventional sign for at least the desire for some outward control; though their use cannot be interpreted as any guarantee of inner control, the very act of writing at all does usually imply an attempt to master the subject well enough to understand it, and the meters reinforce the impression that such an attempt is being made and perhaps succeeding. Even so, the technology of verse does not of itself affirm a philosophy, despite arguments to the contrary. Certain recent critics have argued that even syntax is now "bogus," since the modern world contains no such order as that implied in an ordinary sentence, much less a metrical one. But the imitation theory underlying this argument seems naive and unhistorical, for it was never the obligation of words or of word-order to imitate conditions so reflexively. Syntax deals, after all, primarily with word-order, not world-order, and even the meters, or so it seems to me, can imitate only by convention.

Let me take a simple case. Yvor Winters once offered his line "The slow cry of a bird" as an example of metrical imitation, not strictly of a birdcall itself but of "the slowness of the cry." The convention would seem to be that two or more strong syllables in succession carry associations of slowness and heaviness, while two or more weak syllables in succession carry contrary associations of rapidity and lightness: melancholy on the one hand, playfulness on the other. But the displacement of a stress from *of* to *cry* in the Winters line, bringing two stresses together, fails to slow the line down, as I hear it. Substitute for this "The *quick* cry of a bird," and the two weak syllables following *cry* can be said to do as much to speed the line up, or as little. But whether the cry is to sound quick or slow, the metrical situation itself remains, practically speaking, identical. If any question of interpretation arises from the reversed foot, the meaning of the reversal must depend on the denotation of the adjective rather than on the particular arrangement of syllables and stresses, for denotation overrides any implication of the meters apart from it. Though apparently agreed on by generations of poets, the minor convention on which Winters

was depending is hardly observed any longer except in criticism or occasionally the classroom. Nor was it, for that matter, observed by Milton in his great melancholy-playful pair. "Il Penseroso" and "L'Allegro," or if observed, then only to be consciously played against. Composers of music for the movies learned early that direct imitation of a visual image through sound was best restricted to comic effects (pizzicati, trombone glissandi, staccato bassoons). Pushed far enough, and that is not very far at all, the results of metrical imitations can seem similarly cartoonlike:

> I sank to the pillow, and Joris, and he;
> I slumbered, Dirck slumbered, we slumbered all
>   three.

In any case, simple imitation by means by rhythm would seem to be more plausible in free verse, with its greater flexibility, and most workable in prose, which is allowed any and every arrangement of syllables. Wordsworth ascribes to the meters a different power, finding in them a "great efficacy in tempering and restraining the passion by an intertexture of ordinary feeling," and, he goes on to add, "of feeling not strictly and necessarily connected with the passion." The meters move along in their own domain, scarcely intersecting the domain of meaning, except in some illusory fashion or by virtue of conventions nearly private. The responsibility they bear to the sense, comic writing aside, is mostly not to interfere. But so effacing themselves they will have accomplished all that they must accomplish in relation to the sense. Speech they can and do imitate, from a little distance, but rarely by quoting, that is to say, by attempting to become speech. Song they perhaps are or can become, their natural inclination; no question in that of imitating anything outside their own nature.

Whether their nature really embodies an imitation of natural processes may be arguable. But I do not think the meters can be, in any such sense, organic. A recognition of this, conscious or not, has been reason enough for their rejection by contemporary organicists, poets and critics both. The meters seem more to resemble the hammer-work of carpenters putting together a building, say, than waves coming in to shore or the parade of seasons. We do inhale and exhale more or less rhythmically, as long as we stay healthy; our hearts do beat without much skipping, for years on end. Breath and heart are the least remote of these similitudes, but any connection between them and the more or less regular alternation of weak and strong syllables in verse seems doubtful to me and, valid or not, need carry no particular prestige. In urban life, far from the Lake Country of 1800, are to be found analogies as appropriate as any from nature, if no more convincing. Signals timed to regulate the flow of traffic not only seem analogous but at times remarkably beautiful, as on a nearly deserted stretch of Ninth Avenue in New York City at three a.m., especially in a mild drizzle. If the meters do represent or imitate anything in general, it may be nothing more (or less) than some psychological compulsion, a sort of counting on the fingers or stepping on cracks, magic to keep an unpredictable world under control.

Where the meters are supposed to possess anything of an imitative character, the implicit purpose must be to bring the poetic text closer to its source in reality or nature by making it more "like" the thing it imitates. Such an illusion may be enhanced if the poet's conviction is strong enough to persuade an audience to share his faith, but such conversions are more likely to be accomplished through criticism than through poetry alone. The twin illusions of control and understanding seem more valuable to me than this illusion of the real or the natural, since it is through these, I suspect, that the meters are more firmly connected to memory. To remember an event is almost to begin to control it, as well as to approach an understanding of it; incapable of recurring now, it is only to be contemplated rather than acted on or reacted to. Any sacrifice of immediate reality is compensated for by these new perspectives. The terror or beauty or, for that matter, the plain ordinariness of the original event, being transformed, is fixed and thereby made more tolerable. That the event can recur only in its new context, the context of art, shears it of some risks, the chief of which may anyhow have been its transitory character.

If for an audience the meters function in part to call back the words of the poem, so for the poet they may help to call the words forth, at the same time casting over them the illusion of a necessary or at least not inappropriate fitness and order. There is a kind of accrediting in the process, a warrant that things are being remembered right and set down right, so long as the meters go on working. In this way the meters serve as a neutral and impersonal check on self-indulgence and whimsy; a subjective event gets made over into something more like an object. It becomes accessible to memory, repeatedly accessible, because it exists finally in a form that can be perused at leisure, like a snapshot in an album. Memory itself tends to act not without craft, but selectively, adding here to restore a gap, omitting the incongruous there, rearranging and shifting the emphasis, striving, consciously or not, to make some sense and point out of what in experience may have seemed to lack either. That other presence of which I spoke earlier—the charge of feeling, let us say, which attaches perhaps inexplicably to the subject, what the psychologist might call its *affect*—is not much subject to vicissitudes and manipulations of this sort, except for a natural enough diminution. It remains, but more than likely beneath the surface.

The meters are worth speculating about because they are so specific to the medium, if not altogether essential. Without them nothing may, on occasion, be lost; with them, on occasion, something may be gained, though whatever that is prob-

ably has little or nothing to do with sense or ostensible subject. This, in fact, appears to be the sticking point, that in themselves the meters signify so little. It seems a mistake for a rationalist defender of the meters to insist on too much meaningfulness. Let us concede that the effects of the meters are mysterious, from moment to moment imprecise, often enough uncertain or ambiguous. Like Coleridge's incense or wine, however, their presence may "act powerfully, though themselves unnoticed." To which he adds an interesting comparison to yeast—"worthless," as he says, "or disagreeable by itself, but giving vivacity and spirit to the liquor" in right combination. Meters do accompany the sense, like a kind of percussion only, mostly noise. Over and above syntax, they bind the individual words together, and the larger structural parts as well, over and above whatever appearance of logic survives in the argument; as a result, the words and parts seem to cohere, more perhaps than in plain fact may be the case. How they assist the recollection is by fixing it in permanent, or would-be permanent, form. This, for the poet, may be the large and rather sentimental purpose which gives force to all their various combining and intersecting functions.

Donald Justice with *The Iowa Review* (interview date Spring-Summer 1980)

SOURCE: "An Interview with Donald Justice," in *The Iowa Review,* Vol. 11, Nos. 2-3, Sprint-Summer, 1980, pp. 1-21.

[*In the following interview, Justice discusses various aspects of his work, including his literary influences and the importance of memory, meter, and music in his poetry.*]

[*The Iowa Review:*] *Let's begin by asking about* **Selected Poems** *because that, after all, is the occasion for this interview. We'd like you to tell us something of how it came together out of your other collections. In the notes at the back you describe its arrangement as a "fair chronological order." That's a curious qualification.*

[Donald Justice:] I didn't realize that would be ambiguous. I meant "approximately." After so long it's difficult to know exactly when you wrote something. I didn't want to say the poems were arranged in chronological order because I couldn't be quite sure of that. But as well as I could reconstruct the history of it these are in order. In some cases I'm positive of the sequence because it meant something to me at the time.

Do you keep notebooks and dated papers?

I do now but I didn't in the past. I've become more compulsive instead of less. In quite a few cases I can remember where or when I wrote a certain poem. One poem I remember writing on Memorial Day, 1954. We were supposed to go to a couple of parties and I kept saying, "Let's wait until I finish this, it won't be long now." It took me all day and well into the night, so we didn't make the parties.

You can probably remember when you wrote a poem more easily than many other things.

Perhaps. But I do generally remember where and when I saw movies, for instance, and I can remember where I read most novels. I read *Madame Bovary* in the railroad station in Portland, Maine.

Sometimes you have remembered very precisely, as with, for example, the poem "Fragment: To a Mirror," which has two dates, '63-'72. Was that one you returned to and finished?

Yes. I had started it in 1963. I keep notes while working on poems—phrases, lines, passages, perhaps only words—if anything at all seems promising in the project. I had gone back to the notes for this one more than once to try to make something out of them. And finally, when preparing *Departures*, I just decided I would do what I could with those old notes, and if I couldn't do anything I'd throw them away. They'd been around long enough. I left out a great deal of the ambitious scaffolding for the poem but did get it whittled down to what I could accept.

When you say you keep notes . . .

I mean all the paper that has been written or scribbled on while working out the poem.

I had a remarkable experience once. I was working on a poem that wasn't going anywhere, but once in a while you can rescue something from the wreckage of the notes. I'd been fiddling with this particular poem off and on for two or three years, and one night I made a little progress. So when I was free to work on it again, three or four nights later, I looked around for the notes containing those small advances. I couldn't find them. I'd spent thirty minutes looking for them, I guess, when I gave up and decided to start back at the point I'd started before. I worked perhaps till midnight and again made a little progress. Well, the next time I came to work on the poem, I found both sets of notes and they were almost identical, almost word for word, including scratchings out. "Oh," I thought, "I'm really doing marvellously well on this poem; I must have found what has to be done." I have a sort of Platonic notion that somewhere ideally exists the poem I'm trying to write, if only I can find it, and here I had this excellent testimony, a sign that I was on the right track. As it happens, I finished the poem and it wasn't very good. I published it, but it's not in *Selected Poems*. I had been mis-

taken, you know; the signs were wrong. Very disappointing, considering all the work I put into it, and the sign.

I picture lots of papers around, in cardboard boxes and desk drawers.

Boxes, and now I have a fine filing cabinet that I've been picking through in preparation for going away for the year. Yes, it has a lot of stuff in it. And I've thrown things away as well.

One of the things you have to do now is decide which poems to take along.

Yes, that's right, and that was interesting. I'm taking five poems and four plays. Plays are what I want to try to work on this year, but I have a few poems too that I haven't quite finished.

Are any of these poems of Tremayne? We've seen three of those, two in Selected Poems and another in The New Yorker. They suggest a series.

That most recent Tremayne poem is one that was left over from *Selected Poems*; I hadn't been able to finish it. There was meant to be a group of four poems, and two of them simply weren't finished in time for the book. In a fourth Tremayne poem, still not done, I have, maybe, twenty versions of the last stanza, and I'm not satisfied. I'd like to get it out of the way. I've spent more than enough time on it already and probably should settle for one of the versions I have, but I know there is something better.

What I seem to have been doing this year is simply trying to finish whatever I could not finish before. Actually that seems to be the condition I'm often in, and not just after a book. There always seem to be notes and bits of things and fragments lying around and I keep trying to complete them, put them together. It's a little bit like—I don't know whether you have this compulsion or not—trying to make the meat and the bread come out together. If you don't, you have to take a little bit more of one or the other. Well, there always seem to be notes spilling over from poems just finished. An endless process, thank goodness.

When did you know the Tremayne poems were going to be a series of four?

Early. Four happens to be one of those literary numbers, like three or nine. I noticed that in the first couple of Tremaynes, seasons were mentioned. And I thought, "Ah ha, one for each season." Someone with the predictable sense of design I have is always looking for ways to make things go together, and a set of seasons adding up to four would make the kind of obvious sense that appeals to me. It turned out that the third one didn't have anything to do with a season; nevertheless that was part of the idea.

It spoke of seasons of the day: "And something starts all over, call it day."

Right but . . . the last one, what I think will be the last one—I don't know, if I enjoy doing them and have another workable idea I wouldn't necessarily keep to my own rule—but the fourth and last one I intend to write is about autumn.

I'm curious about your decision when putting together **Selected Poems** *to move to chronological order as opposed to whatever were the ordering principles of the other volumes. What guided that shift?*

I'm not sure. I know I had organized my other books by considering two factors: subject or theme, and form or type or genre. In the first book, for instance, I put all the sestina-like poems together. In another part I put together a number of poems dealing with madness. That at least was my principle. But in combining three books and the uncollected poems I found myself backtracking again and again to some of the same topics, and I didn't think it would make very good sense to put all the poems on childhood together, say, dating from the early fifties to the late seventies. And I didn't want to put all the rhymed poems together, or all the syllabics together. It seemed wrong somehow. So, it occurred to me that others had arranged their selections in chronological order, and I had really been interested in seeing history unfold itself, so to speak, in their work. I tried it and it seemed to make good sense, even perhaps to reveal something. I have had letters from friends saying that they hadn't seen so clearly before how the books seemed to follow from one another, or how all of them seemed more of a piece than they had supposed. If that's the impression, good; I was lucky to have chosen a chronological order.

That choice touches on your fascination with memory; it allows us to see the book itself as a kind of chronology, less of your life than of your memory.

Yes, I hadn't thought of that and I would be happy if that were true. It may be.

It would seem that one of the ways that you could tamper with things if you're going to make a chronological order is by omission. You could heighten a connection or a sense of thematic closeness by leaving something out.

I didn't leave things out for that reason. I left things out because I didn't like them any longer. They had failed to achieve their intention or were written in a style I had become unwilling to acknowledge as mine.

Obviously that must be true, but it did strike us that the other kind of tinkering could be hovering on the margins of things. To leave the "ABC" poem out of **Departures**, *for example, allowed you to put* "Fragment" *first, which emphasizes a very different theme in that book.*

Not intentionally. "**ABC**" was much influenced by Continental poetry, particularly French. Postwar French poets seemed to have, as I read them, one dominant theme, which was poetry itself. I read a fair amount of the poetry from that period, translated some of it, and became hung up on the theme myself. "**ABC**" is in part a product of that. But it came to seem to me not a theme I wanted much to do with after all. I was grandiloquent in that poem, I thought, and I didn't like that. I left out at least one other poem on the art of poetry, a poem from my first book, entitled "**Thus.**" It was a nice exercise in a way, but it didn't really represent the way I felt about the case. I still have some left-over notes for "**ABC**" around, I think, because that was a poem that took a great many pages to write. Some of the metaphors I generated by whatever means I was using—I was using a variety of means—were unbelievable. At least I couldn't believe in them.

"Variety of means," could you itemize?

Well, one of the things I was doing at the time was using my all too notorious cards.

Chance methods?

Yes. And another thing I was doing—I don't know how to describe this method, if it's a method, and yet it's something others have done too—was conscientiously to mistranslate. I don't know quite how to explain what you do, but you might say that you worry more about getting it interesting than about getting it right. If a word in French suggests a word you like, you're quite willing to use it even though it's not what the French means. It's a way of displacing the mental attention, which I think is often fruitful in composition. If you can look not straight at the object, but from an angle, you see it differently. I had a student in California, a very talented student, who claimed he had nothing to write about. And I asked if he knew French. He did. "Well," I said, "do you know Spanish?" He did not. And I suggested he get a book of poems in Spanish, the language he did not know, and translate *them*. That afternoon he wrote twenty or so poems, and perhaps seven or eight of them were beautiful— I've never seen the method work so well for anybody else. I don't think he uses it any more, but it was like a small revelation, that once. I think it might work for anybody, on a lucky afternoon.

That suggests something about faith in the riches of the mind, doesn't it?

Yes, you have to have something—a certain character, say—to bring to whatever method or process you're using and you have to have a certain facility, but if you've got those you don't have to write *directly* about whatever may seem to be deepest in your soul. Whatever that is, if it is strong and true, will come out anyway.

Can you think of times when you tried to write directly about what you thought was deepest in your soul?

I cannot remember a time when I tried that, I'm sorry to say. Not certainly since adolescence.

We were wondering about changes in **Selected Poems**. *Not only were the poems reordered, several were revised. In* **"The Confession,"** *the first stanza now reads, "You have no name, intimate crime; / There is nothing to whisper. / You have fled across many pillows, / But you leave nothing behind." Originally it was, "You have no name, intimate crime, / Into which I might plunge my hand. / Your knives have entered many pillows, / But you leave nothing behind."*

I found those two images somewhat melodramatic—maybe they were appropriate to the crime itself—but I felt they were mannered in a popularly surreal sense. I wanted to make them quieter while keeping the same argument. Also one or two people who had taken the trouble to speak of that stanza had been slightly confused by the images. I didn't think they were unclear or I wouldn't have written them in the first place, and I might have been willing to simplify in the interest of clarity alone if I had not been even more strongly motivated by this desire to cut down on the melodrama and the manneristic surrealism of the images. I myself think the surreal image is most powerful when it is rooted in the real.

Another revision I wanted to ask you about was **"Sonatina in Yellow,"** *a poem I'm very fond of.*

What did I change, the end?

Right. Originally it was, "Repeat it now, no one was listening. / Repeat it, the air, the variations."

Ah, yes.

Why did you remove the line, "Repeat it, the air, the variations"?

Well, I always had had trouble with what I think of as the coda of this poem, the last little paragraph. Now what it should do, I felt from the start, was repeat or take up again motives, or motifs even, to speak of the question musically, from what had gone before. Now the "air" is a pun on the dead air of summer mentioned earlier in the poem and also on a musical air. That much is obvious. The "variations" would have to

do with musical form as well—also of course with the verbal variations on the phrases and as a consequence on the themes that appear earlier in the poem. In that sense it fitted in the coda, but it seemed to me that it slowed things down a good deal. It was in there merely for a sort of formal reason. It was doing its *job*. And I wanted whatever I had in there at the end to be doing more than its job. I'm glad you like the poem, because I like it too, but I'm worried about some of its features. Particularly there at the end. When I first sent in the text for the book, the "Repeat it now" line was also gone. Finally I thought I needed one "repeat" line but not two. Who knows? Listen, the first time I finished this poem, there were crows flying around through several of the stanzas.

And you got all the crows out.

And kept them out.

It seems like a willful thing to do, putting crows in a sonatina in yellow.

Well, the poem is in a way about death, and they seemed to me, with their blackness, to associate very well with that. Also their harsh music. But they were too symbolical really.

One of the things I was wondering about taking south with me was the notes on this poem. I haven't given up on this. It has a prose commentary intended to accompany the verse text which I haven't shown to anybody. Still, I decided finally to leave all this behind in the filing cabinet. I didn't want to get hung up on that again. I've spent a lot of time on this poem and on the other sonatina and on a couple of others I haven't published. But one day I may get it right, in which case it will have a prose commentary, and that prose commentary will describe a descent into the underworld, a legendary sort of descent. Because that is implied in this poem. The prose commentary will bring out undertones and make them much stronger perhaps. All speculative, of course.

So when you come to offering a prose commentary as in **"Childhood,"** *the last poem in the volume, that's not something that you've just happened upon.*

It's an idea I've wanted to put to work for a long time. Once the notion of a prose commentary enters your head, it's hard to get it out. You'd like not only to write the poems but to write the commentary, you know; don't leave that up to the others, who're likely to get it wrong anyhow.

Do you have models in mind for that kind of writing?

Coleridge, Hart Crane. But I wasn't able to do it as they did it. I wanted to write elevated, mystical, highly charged prose. I just couldn't screw my courage up to that—or my style, more likely.

Prose that would be more rhetorical than the poetry?

Yes, exactly.

And that would serve as some sort of ironic counterpoint to the poetry?

Yes, in the commentaries on the sonatinas which I have, but which I haven't been able to get right, that is indeed the case. I was reading some of *The Bridge* marginalia yesterday and it's a prose much more as I would want it, you know, nicely florid and elevated.

And yet I have to acknowledge that one of the afflictions of American verse at present is the prose poem, and one reason it is an affliction instead of a salvation is that poets allow themselves all sorts of licenses regarding rhetoric, elevation, diction, and foolish ideas that they wouldn't think of allowing themselves in their so-called verse. I've been saying to my students in the last few years, "Your prose has got to be at least as well-written as your poetry," because most of them really do write their poems more conscientiously than they do their prose. Maybe we've come to another historical moment.

You've expressed a conviction that there really is no such thing as organic meters, that you can't imitate the sea, breathing, the heartbeat.

I do think that. I may be wrong, but that is a conviction.

You also believe that music is the one art that does not have as its motive memory.

So far as I can experience the arts that is true.

Given these two convictions, I'm surprised that I find music entering your poetry at the moments of most intense memory.

I knew you were working up to some sort of paradox.

In "Memory of a Porch," "I heard / The thing begin / A thin, skeletal music," or in "Absences," "Like the memory of scales descending the white keys." The sonatinas themselves, especially the "Sonatina in Yellow," are intense poems of memory, I think, and your sonatina form apparently tries to imitate music in language.

I think I can account superficially for what you're pointing out, which I hadn't noticed before. I think it may be because my own memory happens to be rich in memories of music. I have felt very strongly about music at times. So recollections of music come back to me naturally enough sometimes when emotion approaches. I mean quite naturally out of ex-

perience, rather than from any theory, involving hierarchies or distinctions among the arts.

What about the sonatina form then?

The sonatina form is really very simple. I'd wanted to try a quasi-musical form and the simplest of all among the classical possibilities, it seemed, would be the precursor of the sonata form, the sonatina, in which you only really had to have two parts, two themes. I didn't want to get into a complicated sonata-allegro, even if it could be done. I certainly didn't want to get into any sort of complicated set of quasi-musical forms such as you find in the "Four Quartets," or think you have found after reading the criticism. It seemed to me that you might wish to start modestly. The sonatina is a modest classical form which involves an A part and a B part. It involves saying A again and saying B again in a key different from the one it was said in the first time around.

> I hadn't meant when I started "Sonatina in Yellow" to write about my father. But I did have as a general idea in all the sonatinas the mythic or legendary theme of descending into the underworld, and once I began mentally or spiritually or esthetically to descend into the underworld I found my father.
> —Donald Justice

The only thing I had to find was an A thing to say and a B thing to say, and—which was trickier—a way to change the key of B. The form also allows a little freedom; you can either say A B A B or you can say A B B A or you can say A plus transition plus B, you know, or you can put a coda or several codas at the end. There's little flexibility, a little give. I tried to find a change of key, a modulation, which would be linguistic or grammatical rather than musical. So I worked all these schemes out in advance of writing the poem; that was part of the pleasure of the whole business for me at the time. And it seemed to me that one of the ways of modulating, grammatically, would be to change the *tense*; another might be to change the *person*. I've forgotten now, but I worked out four or five of these; I guess one was to change from interrogation to declaration. But then I felt it really wasn't literarily interesting just to repeat A if there were more than two or three lines to it; so I modified A, which also happens in the musical form, at least as it moves toward the sonata-allegro form—you get into development sections.

It becomes analogous to your way of using translation as a mode of invention, not just in fidelity to the original text.

Yes, that's true; to think about something else allowed me to write about what I was interested in, but indirectly, from an angle. I hadn't meant when I started **"Sonatina in Yellow"** to write about my father. But I did have as a general idea in all the sonatinas the mythic or legendary theme of descending into the underworld, and once I began mentally or spiritually or esthetically to descend into the underworld I found my father.

Had he been dead then for some time?

For thirteen years. But I hadn't written any poems about him. So I need not have been surprised to find him there.

Are musical forms generally available to you?

Not so much what I would call forms—but yes, vaguely musical possibilities, though I think "musical" as a critical term referring to effects of sound in poetry is much overused, abused even. I am interested in the musical sounding of the words in some poems, and in a few places I have gone to some trouble to make these sounds linguistically rich; but I haven't loaded up the sonatinas in this way. They're probably a little more musical in this primitive fashion, that is, in the mere sounding of their words, than most of what I would write, but it's the structure of the music that I was interested in imitating, not otherwise the sound. I would be interested in trying to write something in another musical form sometime. I've tried the blues but that's even simpler.

You did that in the "uncollected" section of **Selected Poems***.*

I was using up what I knew about the blues in the two I included in the book and in four or five others I wrote at the same time but didn't publish. I may publish three or four more sometime, but . . .

So you have more blues songs around.

Oh yes, but by now I've almost forgotten which lines come from traditional blues and which ones I've invented. I know they don't sound like Mississippi Delta blues, for instance, but then I didn't want them to, I'm not from the Mississippi Delta. I wanted them to be a sort of "literary blues."

The blues lend themselves more to poetry because they have words built into them.

Yes, that's quite right.

And the sonatina is a much more abstract form.

Absolutely, but I do believe poetry is capable of being structured in terms that can be described abstractly. There may be half a dozen schools of theory which can't entertain that

notion, but not to do so is an historical and esthetic blindness both. Obviously there is room for abstract structure in any esthetic design. There may be no necessity for it, but there is room for it.

But in the case of the sonatina you had some sense of that abstract structure when you began, while in other cases you may discover the structure along the way.

Actually I discovered the sonatina along the way too because although I knew what a musical sonatina was and I'd played many sonatinas on the piano, I didn't know what a sonatina in poetry would be until I had tried to write one. I don't think it turned out to be what I might ideally have imagined a literary sonatina to be, but it's similar. It's as close as I've been able to get, and I think it's as close as anybody's been able to get to a musical form in poetry—musical form, that is, so far as the structural outline goes.

The synesthesia in the titles mixes an aural form with a visual image; why did you add color to the musical structure?

Several reasons, but one was simply to emphasize the abstraction because the colors, musically speaking, must seem abstract. Actually in the text of the poems, there's very little reference to the color; it's background. There would be more reference to color in the prose commentary, but at least once in each of the poems, I think maybe only once, there's a reference to it. Yellow seemed to me eventually to associate with decay. And green with freshness. Not very original associations. The simple practical reason for the titles, however, was that I had bought in the university bookstore a four-color notebook to start writing the poems in, and one of the four colors was green and one was yellow, one was blue and one was pink. Pink was very hard; blue I almost managed, but not pink.

Is a **"Sonatina in Blue"** *one of the sets of notes you're taking along?*

No, I decided not to take it. I've given up on blue.

Are those five poems you're taking along new or old poems?

One goes back to the fall of '74, the one I'm most serious about, but it's very hard and may end up rather long. It's in several parts and I've finished maybe two parts of it, or three. I don't know what will eventually become of it, but I must finish it. And the Tremayne poem I'm still working at I started in the fall of '77. That happened to be dated. All of these are failures, you might say, up to this point. They're poems I haven't been able to get right but that I have had some hopes for.

The same with the plays. One of the plays I started in 1964

and I think the beginning of it is really very good, but it's hard to go on with.

Will the plays be easier to complete than the poems?

No, I don't think so. I know more about writing poems than I do about writing plays, so the poems really are easier.

Can you tell us something about the plays?

I don't think I should spoil them by talking too much about them. But I can say that one of them has to do with Lorca. One of the things I've done so far is to translate some Lorca poems not just into American but into what I think of as a sort of California language of the future. Not of the distant future, but if something like the death of Lorca were to occur in America, California would be the most likely place, wouldn't it? But that's enough on that, I think.

Another play you've been working on is an updating of The Tempest, *isn't it?*

Yes, right.

Is part of your updating that it's no longer verse drama at all?

What I've written of it is definitely not verse, it's prose. The updating amounted to a complete rethinking. *The Tempest* was going to be a king of ideal model in the back of my mind which perhaps no one would ever think of in seeing the play. In the first version—it has now been changed a little—Caliban was going to be the second son of the Prospero character, and was going to be an auto mechanic by occupation and an amateur of the viola da gamba. It really should be Ariel, I guess, who plays this instrument, but I thought Caliban, who speaks so beautifully in the play—"This isle is full of noises"—ought to have it. Well, you know, I was just amusing myself by making false analogies.

Deflected analogies.

Yes, yes, that's better.

You do that all the time.

Well, yes, perhaps so. I don't know whether I'll be able to write these two plays or not but I'm going to try.

You mentioned four plays.

The other two are short, and whether anything will come of them or not I don't know. One is called **"Faust: A Skit"**—a farce, partly in verse. The other is called **"The Whistler"** and is about anti-Semitism.

These are subjects you would not feel like dealing with in poems?

I suppose not. Anti-Semitism, for instance. I don't know quite why, but early in life I was probably too much influenced by Poe's theory of poetry. Poems were not to be didactic, for example. I no longer think that's true, but I must have been affected by it.

I think poetry ought to be capable of dealing with anything. I mean, I do basically believe that. On the other hand, for me, it's very difficult to write a poem about something I could write an essay on.

Maybe it's because in something like anti-Semitism there aren't many permissible views.

Well, the forbidden view has lately begun to become more and more permissible, apparently. Your point is a good one, but I think the unthinkable is becoming acceptable again, and I find that tragic, after the experience of the thirties and forties. This week I've been reading newspapers from the thirties because my wife happened to buy some from an antique dealer a few years ago. They're fascinating. One of the stories that keeps cropping up, on the front page of course, concerns whatever the latest decree of the Nazi government may have been. These decrees are treated just like ordinary news stories. And I remember how horrible it became. And the theme comes around again these days; it begins to matter a lot. Even so, I can't see myself writing a poem directly about it.

> I think poetry ought to be capable of dealing with anything. I mean, I do basically believe that. On the other hand, for me, it's very difficult to write a poem about something I could write an essay on.
> —*Donald Justice*

Can we return once more to "Sonatina in Yellow"?

Yes.

The epigraph is from Rilke, "Your quickly vanishing photograph in my more slowly vanishing hand." That strikes me as applicable to all your work.

I think it might be.

It's applicable for a number of reasons, not the least of which is the reference to photographs. You've talked about poems at their best transmuting subjective experience into an object, and have said that that object at its best would be like a snapshot. It would be a memory captured that you could come back to and deal with because it's there now in an object.

I do believe that, yes.

The experience of many of your poems, for me, is the experience of reading a sensitive description of a snapshot or photograph, a photo that you care for greatly. I wonder how many of your poems actually are based on snapshots.

I don't think any of them are except the one I just finished, and even that wasn't a snapshot; it was a photograph by Walker Evans, a scene in Alabama in the thirties. I do carry around a packet of photographs of my parents and of houses we used to live in and that sort of thing. I've never been able to use them. You might say they have become for me a sort of talisman. I keep thinking they will fructify. But I don't think any poems I've written except this new one, are based on photographs. What they are based on, some of them, is memories of the way something looked at a certain time.

It's as if you were doing a photograph mentally, taking your own snapshot.

Yes, that's right.

So making the poem, then, is more like making a photograph than like describing one?

That's right.

In "Memories of the Depression Years" there are three memories, at three-year intervals, and those are the snapshot-like moments that stand out?

Yes, that's right.

Are there more that you're working on?

I certainly meant to write an endless series, but those were the only three I've managed to finish. I have no other notes on hand. I do mean to remain alert to the possibility of doing others that would fit into such a series, but I haven't got any.

Now that you've written a poem describing the Walker Evans photograph, what's the difference between writing that poem and creating the "photograph" or "snapshot" out of your memory?

I felt more limited in this case. I didn't want to depart from the facts of the photograph, which anybody else could look at too, and check up on. So I think the poem will seem esthetically cooler. I like to think that many of my poems seem objective and well-distanced, but I think this poem may be even more so. I was interested in it as practice, and indeed

I've tried to write others; but I haven't been able to, and I've just about given up on the idea. I wanted to see what the answer would be to the question you just put to me, I think. I did not put as much of myself into it, and my own experience, though the scene was the kind of scene I recall from childhood.

I was going to ask what attracted you to the photograph. It was not a purely esthetic attraction.

No, it wasn't; it made a connection with my own life and the life of my relatives in the South in the thirties. I would like to be able to say, and it would be partly true, that it was like a photograph made of a long-ago part of my life.

This was a farm family?

No, it's a photograph sometimes identified as **"Mule Team and Poster."** It depicts a brick wall of what appears to be a warehouse. It's in Alabama in 1936, but I don't think it's in *Let Us Now Praise Famous Men.* It's just one of the Farm Security Administration photographs; it depicts a brick wall of what appears to be a warehouse in front of which a couple of mules are standing, munching corn shucks on the arid looking earth, and there's a poster of a Silas Green traveling show peeling from the wall. It's really quite beautiful, and I'm sure that one of my interests in it, one of the secrets of its appeal to me, was that the manifest content of the photograph was ugly and unpleasant—and I myself knew that ugliness and unpleasantness because I had been in Alabama in 1936, and in the summertime, and it really was like a photograph of something I could almost remember. My father was from Alabama, farther south than where this photograph was made, and we used to visit our relatives over there, poor farmers and store clerks and so on. There seemed to be a lot of this sort of thing—brick walls and mules standing in front of them, and posters advertising movies of traveling shows. Out of this very unattractive but quite sympathetic scene, an arrangement of great beauty, I thought, and evident art had come forth, through Evans. Art having occurred, I wanted to try to multiply that art.

And then, last week I spent trying to describe another Evans photograph and wasn't able to.

What do you mean? That you found that what you thought to say about it just doesn't interest you once it's said?

In part. I simply was not able to see enough in the photograph to make saying so much worthwhile. The words were not paying off with a high enough quotient of what Aristotle would have called "thought"—what I call "perception." So it just wasn't worth it. I could describe the thing perfectly well, in a somewhat heavy style, as luck would have it, but once I'd done that, it didn't make any difference. It didn't make enough difference. With the first of Evans' photographs I judged, maybe wrongly, that I had seen enough in it to make the saying count.

Had your father grown up on a farm in Alabama?

Yes, he had been born in southern Alabama and then as a youth he moved over to a part of Georgia adjoining Alabama and which looked just like it as far as I could tell. This was a part of my summers growing up, not a part I really liked.

Are you aware much of generations beyond, say, your grandfather?

Not much beyond great-grandfathers, no. I can't account for it, perhaps because we were always poor, but on neither side of my family do recollections go back beyond what would be my great-grandparents—except for a story about a woman ancestor on my father's side who became a stowaway to North Carolina supposedly because she had committed some technical offense against a king or a king's property, a king's forest perhaps. Maybe she poached. But those stories grow to be a little like myths; you don't know how much to credit them. And there aren't many such stories in my family, unhappily. I wish there were.

Have you always been fascinated with family albums and looking at pictures?

I didn't know that I was, but I was; my mother was, and she thrust them upon me from the start.

When you were working on the Evans photograph, did you think of Williams' Pictures from Brueghel?

Absolutely. It would be awfully hard not to. I once tried writing a series of poems on Hopper paintings and they sounded like Williams' Brueghel poems, but defective somehow. Yes, the Williams poems are very powerful; it would be hard to resist them. But I tried to, not quite successfully.

It's interesting that your memory leads to repositories of lore like family albums or the attic (as in "In the Attic" and "Fragments") whereas the more popular American metaphor for examining the past is digging in earth. Archaeological excavations, roots, seem more the clichés of our time.

I hadn't thought of that. I don't know what that means. If you grew up in South Florida as I did, houses had no attics. Or very few houses had attics. If you went to visit a relative somewhat farther north there might be an attic, and you might go up into it. It would have been a privileged place—a repository of the really rather distant past, you know, of strange, exciting objects. Many children must have felt that. I don't think the attic fails to be a kind of cliché too, for a place the past has been left in. Roots may be a more active and dramatic metaphor, but I hadn't thought of the contrast.

The attic is the image of the family past.

That's right.

As opposed to roots and the archaeological past, the tribal past.

Right, and what I write about, I guess, is narrower than archaeology, tribes, and all that. What I can think about seems more limited.

It's personally associated memory rather than historically or pre-historically associated memory.

I couldn't write about bog men, for example, like Heaney. I just can't imagine bog men.

But he lives around bogs.

All right, and I don't so I mustn't write about bog men.

But we could conceivably write about the Hopewell or the Effigy Mound Builders.

If we'd taken part in the digging, perhaps.

There's another kind of memory alive in your poems, that being the memory of a spacious poetic past. In "Ladies by their Windows," which opens Selected Poems, you write, "It is the lurch and slur the world makes, turning. / It is the sound of turning, of a wheel / Or hand-cranked grinder turning." I hear an echo from Conrad Aiken's "Sound of Breaking," where he says "It is a sound of breaking, / The world is breaking, the world is a sound of breaking." There are frequent echoes of this kind in your poems. Did you intend this one?

I was aware when writing it of that one and yet in all the years since no one, till now, has ever mentioned the Aiken poem to me. I'm pleased that you know it. Yes, I discovered that poem when I was about fifteen, I think, at least I remember the summer, reading it on my grandfather's porch. I've always liked it, and I was not sorry to echo it if it could be done gracefully.

Do you find Aiken helpful in other ways?

No, I'm afraid not.

I ask because as I was looking up that poem to hear exactly the lines I was hearing in your poem . . .

It was the sound that I was after, the sound.

I came across "Senlin."

That was a poem I knew, definitely.

I was fascinated because when I read the Tremayne poems again after reading "Senlin," I thought of them as similar types of character.

Maybe as types of character, but I would think the Tremayne poems had more in common with Robinson or perhaps Hardy than with Aiken. Aiken is smoother, the edges are more shorn off. Maybe I'm wrong, but the poems of his that I remember from the period I liked most in him impressed me with their beautiful smoothness. I was unable to write smoothly then. It really is easy once you get the knack of it, but when you don't have that knack, smoothness may come to seem like an overpowering virtue.

Also, when I was young, I was interested in writing very elaborate syntax. Some of the poets I liked a lot were interesting in part because of their syntax. Yeats sometimes has a very elaborate syntax. And I wanted to try that. Even Williams, though he looks simple, has a very elaborate syntax, and this challenged me. But then at some point comes the desire to purify, to simplify, and that has, you know, begun to appeal to me more and more.

One of the things that interests me syntactically now is the use of fragments, as in the last line of **"Thinking about the Past,"** which goes "Dusks, dawns; waves; the ends of songs . . . " I don't know that anybody else likes or ought to like that, but I like the line myself and in part because it's just like little bits of consciousness floating up. Touches of a brush, say. It seems to me that fragments sometimes can have that effect. The first time I recall really liking fragments myself and seeing more powerful possibilities in them was in reading Alberti, who uses fragments beautifully, dramatically. Ever since I've tried to do something with them. Of course I don't at all mean the notational style you see frequently, ever since the Imagists at least, and not only in amateur verses—as if to suppress a verb were to write a line.

Whether we're talking about elaborate or simplified syntax, or about fragments for that matter, we're talking about kinds of technical proficiency.

Yes, there are properties which, I think, belong unarguably to poetry, and one of them is technical virtue. I don't know how else to put that, but without it poetry dies. I think, on the other hand, poetry can live on the strength of technical virtue alone, but it only lives a sort of half life then, like much of Aiken, which I regard as quite beautiful but not whole. When you write, you have to be willing to settle for that, I think, but what you really desire is something whole; large, even. Aiken wanted that too, I'm sure, it's just that he was probably best when he concentrated on lesser goals. A number of poets have been best when they weren't trying too hard.

Poetry at its best, is fulfilling its nature most entirely, when it has a great mastery of form, or technique, and shows considerable, though perhaps a hidden or disguised interest in its own formal or technical character. Otherwise it might as well be prose. I love prose, and it really *might* as well be prose. Now once it has this, it is of course much better if what is said proves interesting and intelligent and intelligible and true and perceptive and has all those virtues one would expect even of expository prose. And of course it becomes even better if the themes it deals with are grand. A seven-line poem ought to be better than a six-line poem, all other things being equal, simply because it contains more. But all those things are not equal, and what is basic and absolutely necessary is formal and technical character; otherwise the poem will be forgotten eventually, or remembered only for something like the personality or history of the poet, or the fact that he may have been the first or the loudest to deal with a certain topic, or something of that sort. Well, that is of a certain interest, too. I don't wish to deny it. But for the art of poetry itself, basic is some formal or technical interest. That does not mean that anyone can or should prescribe the nature of that formal or technical interest in advance of the occasion. That always remains to be defined, or ought always to remain to be defined, for the various occasions, and by the age. But I think it is absolutely essential.

Many poets today would say that memory seeks out its own meter, but in a very real way, with you, meter seeks out memory, right?

Well, I'm willing to go with that version, though it seems an extreme way of putting it.

It's an extreme reversal, but you've talked about meter as a kind of substantiation of your poetry, even as a "fixative" of memory.

If you're working in meter in the first place—you don't have to work in meters, in the kind of meters I'm thinking of—but if you are, then to get it wrong proves to you that you haven't even, as I would suggest, *remembered* it right. If you commit yourself, if you give yourself over to the meters, they have to be right. If you don't, well, that's a different story.

If we think less of meters than of form, much the same thing applies. In "Sonatina in Yellow," you hadn't been seeking out a way to talk about your father in a particular form, but the form you devised gave you the memory of your father.

In a sense that's true, yes. It is a false notion, I am sure, to propose that poetry comes only from subject, is never more than an extension of content, as one might say. Poetry comes from anywhere, and the subject is certainly a major source, probably the major source. If you have something you care a lot about, then you may well write a poem about it, may indeed be driven to do so. But it can come from elsewhere—just as a composition in music may come from merely fooling around. Or from thinking: This time I'll try D minor; or, I like what Handel wrote just there, I think I'll try some variations on it. It comes from anywhere, and as far as I'm concerned, there should be no hierarchy of values in the consideration of this. What matters is the result, not the source, the origin, or the theory.

Your history so far seems to suggest a particular interest in seeking conscious deflections from established forms. I'd see that interest in deflection as central, as you say, to the "formal or technical character" of your work.

I would like to think so.

In "Variation for Two Pianos," for example, were you thinking of the villanelle when you started the poem?

Of course.

And simultaneously thinking of not *doing the villanelle.*

Yes, exactly. The villanelle is practically impossible, at least in English, and I don't know of any villanelle that doesn't have at least one waste stanza in it. There seems to me no obligation to carry on with a proper villanelle when it may mean including one or two stanzas less good than the others. So you may end up with a quasi-or pseudo-villanelle if you're going to do one, unless you happen to be very lucky and get the whole thing. A double villanelle, even. I can imagine that, but it would be hard to find.

What do you mean by "get" and "find"?

"Find" may be the better word for it. I mean something like going on a voyage of discovery in the old days, or prospecting, digging for precious metals.

The sestinas are another example; they avoid the usual sestina metrics.

When I was writing those sestinas, I think all the sestinas that had been written in English before, all that I had read anyway, were in iambic pentameter—or at least in what I would call a casual pentameter, one in which the line might get a little longer or a little shorter, as in Pound's or the two by Kees. But I consciously shortened the lines; I varied the length of the lines. Nowadays anybody may do that. The

Katmandu sestina has a small place in the history of the form, I think.

I want to get to your "Odes" in a moment but by way of "Elsewheres." That seems to be a more sophisticated deflection. "North," "South," "Waiting Room," that's not . . .

It should be the Midwest, say, or the middle of something anyway, right?

You mentioned the checkered fields of the Midwest in that, but that was another attempt, I take it, not to be satisfied with the symmetry you would expect—North and South—but to get outside of it.

That's right.

In addition to specific deflected forms, groups of your poems sometimes deny expectations of patterns. In the gathering of three odes, for example, the "Cool Dark Ode" addresses night and suggests winter night; the "Warm Flesh-Colored Ode" suggests late summer. But what does the "Pale Tepid Ode" suggest? You set up a pattern, then jump track.

Well, on the other hand, it keeps to the track because you have "Cool Dark," "Warm Flesh-Colored" and what's left? Not much.

You reverse the placement of the adjectives—"Pale Tepid" rather than "Tepid Pale."

But that's the way it would be in speech probably; you wouldn't say "tepid pale." If you did it would be like the overcareful Joycean placement of adjectives before a noun. It's just something other than the two that come before it—what's left? That's the way I thought of it. Sort of the bleaching out of colors, of definition. I don't know how to put it, but it seemed to me altogether obvious that "Pale Tepid" followed from "Cool Dark" and "Warm Flesh-Colored." Just set yourself that problem. What pair of adjectives having to do with color and temperature could possibly come next?

Well, given cool and warm, you'd have to say something like. . .

Lukewarm anyway, or pale, or tepid, or . . .

Terribly hot.

Sure, but that's not my style.

I'm fascinated that you say it seemed perfectly natural that that would be the completion. I think it's not perfectly natural to most people.

All right, okay, but I'm asking, well, "terribly hot," yes, all right. But what *color*? After dark and flesh-colored. If you had to have a third.

Well, "flesh-colored" seems mild. I might think of something harsh, say, "dazzling."

"Dazzling" might be good. I may write a fourth, "Hot Dazzling Ode."

If you do, you owe that one to us.

I do indeed. But look, one reason I like series and groups is because once you have a couple of poems connecting somewhere or associating in some way, another may be produced simply by thinking: What would be related, what would come out of, or what would connect with that? Anybody becomes inventive thinking along those lines.

I'm thinking of a pattern suggested by "Unflushed Urinals" and "Sunday Afternoon in Buffalo, Texas."

I consider the Walker Evans poem I spoke of as a third along those lines. They're American scenes, and I really feel I should take a couple more bus trips and see what turns up.

It has to be by bus?

Well, it seems so. The bus still shows you the America of the past. Plane rides, in this respect, don't seem to turn up anything. One of the great experiences of my married life was to take the bus from Albemarle, North Carolina to Palo Alto, California years ago. It was an awful and wonderful experience. Four nights and three days, or three nights and four days; I've forgotten which. And we'll never forget that trip.

Speaking of things American, do you see an American tradition that has influenced your own work, an American tradition in poetry that you look back toward?

I can say whom and what I like, that's about all. In America there is not just one line of evolution, one stream, despite the propaganda. As for American poets of the nineteenth century, I like Emerson; I think he's a good poet, and I like some of Melville's poems. I like Emily Dickinson very much; I think she's a very great poet. I like Trumbull Stickney; Tuckerman. And I respect Whitman, without having the kind of affection for him many people seem to have. The twentieth century begins for me with Edwin Arlington Robinson. And in this century the best poets seem so different from one another that any attempt to define an American tradition ought to involve some strong sense of the variety and the diversity and the going off in all directions. Emerson does not necessarily end up in James Dickey.

Hart Crane?

Hart Crane is a master, yes, in a few lines anyway. Such beauty as I hope not to be forgotten.

Ezra Pound?

Early Pound anyway, yes, a master. Thereafter, I don't know. Thereafter I think he became victimized, as far as I can tell, by ideas. As Emerson might have put it, "Ideas are in the saddle and ride mankind." When that happens with poetry, something goes wrong, I believe, and I believe that happened to Pound. I know that not everyone thinks so, in fact most people probably don't. But just reading him for pleasure and the power of invention or recovery, for the beauty of sound and the shapeliness of his expression, the early poems seem certainly very fine—*Personae*, including of course *Cathay*.

Which of the American poets do you find yourself returning to and reading most?

Williams would be among them, certainly. Williams is so inventive, and he *does* hold up. Stevens of course is another. Eliot remains for me a great model of seriousness. His ideas are another matter, but . . . Well, let's see, Robinson I read frequently with pleasure, and Emily Dickinson. I shouldn't forget Frost, for years my favorite. Those are, I think, the main ones.

Do you subscribe to the separation of the Dickinson and Whitman traditions?

If it's forced upon me, I do. If there were an election in November, I'd go with Dickinson, the one with the more modest scope.

I sometimes hear Dickinson off-rhymes in your poetry.

Maybe so; I think off-rhymes can be very nice, but they may have come as much from incapacity as from remembering Dickinson.

Ransom, Tate, Warren?

Yes, I haven't gone back and read them lately, but they certainly were a formative influence. I wrote my master's thesis on them, and in a way I've always known their work. Ransom is a favorite.

You mentioned once that the first poet of note that you heard read was Robert Frost.

I don't think other poets were reading much in public then. I lived and went to school in Miami where he wintered in the early forties, and he would read at the university. He would say at the end of a reading, "Now what are your favorites, what would you like to hear?" That used to embarrass me. I was studying composition with a composer named Carl Ruggles. At one of those readings, maybe the very first one I went to, Ruggles—who also came down from New England to winter there and who knew Frost—called up one of his favorites and I felt terribly embarrassed for those two great men. It seemed to me, in my juvenile way, not sophisticated. Come to think of it, it still does.

What about the European poets? Obviously the French and Spanish poets.

Mainly them; I don't really read any foreign language with great ease, and certainly I don't speak any. Those are the two that I know best. I worked hard to get acquainted with some poetry in German, postwar poetry, but French and Spanish I feel a little more comfortable with.

Is Alberti the master in that group for you?

Absolutely.

South American poets?

Oh yes, well, my favorite American poet in Spanish is a Mexican poet, Ramon López Velarde.

I don't know of him at all.

Paz calls him the father of Mexican poetry. He died about the time the First World War ended, at an early age, but I think he's a very great poet. H. R. Hays translated some of his poems during the Second World War, and he's been intermittently translated since, but there's never been collection of translations and there should be; he's very good.

Let's go back to the Anglo-American poets briefly. When you go back to Williams, which periods or volumes do you favor?

Well, there are two moments in his career that I particularly like. One is the *Spring and All* period, 1922 or thereabouts. The other is the *Pictures from Brueghel* period, postwar, indeed post-*Paterson*. For me those are the two most moving and instructive passages in his career. I like the historical book, *In the American Grain*, I like much of that very well indeed. The novels have not grabbed me; a few stories. I think he was a major figure in the twentieth century, perhaps in spite of himself.

With your interest in meter and measure, how do you react to Williams' emphasis on measure, on finding an American measure, and his attempts to break a Whitman line into three

parts, to put the Whitman line into a proper measure, his creation of the variable foot, and so on?

Well, very simply and with great respect for Williams, it's this: that his theories about meter are interesting because he writes meters, not because he writes *about* meters. I think that he writes, when he writes critically, too confusingly, too vaguely, which he does not do when he's writing poems.

The direct influence of Williams on your work would be seen in "American Sketches."

I was trying to perform a sort of *homage* to Williams there, but I wouldn't be surprised if I could show . . .

I would think in these snapshot-like pieces, too.

Maybe. What I think happens is that, say, X turns something up, but it really doesn't belong to him or her; it's something that's in the culture, and you are free to deal with it, to try your hand at it too, I think, without becoming an epigone. Now there have been epigones of Williams, but that's a different story.

You wouldn't be mistaken for one of those.

To tell the truth, I don't think that he would have liked me, but that doesn't matter.

He's the one of that generation you read the most.

If I'm looking to learn something, yes, and next to him Stevens. Stevens would be a close second. They are very different, even though they were friends of a sort.

Marianne Moore?

I read her, but I prefer Elizabeth Bishop. I would think that Elizabeth Bishop is Marianne Moore perfected. On the other hand something must be said for Moore because she was in this vein the pioneer. I like reading them both actually, but seeing things historically is important, I believe, for the writer. I have students who don't think so, who think everything was all written at about the same time, usually yesterday. I think it is interesting to know that Elizabeth Bishop comes after Marianne Moore, if only for the sake of accuracy and historical truth. But also for the evolution of an art; the changes, aside from their intrinsic interest, cannot fail to show you something about your own work if you're willing to learn.

That brings us back to **Selected Poems** *and why it's in "fair chronological order."*

Well, I did some things after other writers and some things

before other writers and this ought to lay out the record of which was which. For those who care.

Dana Gioia (review date 1981)

SOURCE: "Three Poets in Mid Career," in *Southern Review,* Vol. 17, No. 3, 1981, pp. 667-74.

[*In the following excerpt, Gioai considers* Selected Poems, *citing Justice's mastery of diverse forms and keen editorial sense as the skills which have helped produce a nearly perfect collection of poetry.*]

From his first book, *Summer Anniversaries*, which won the Lamont Prize in 1959, to his third volume, *Departures*, which was nominated for a National Book Award in 1974, the work of Donald Justice has been consistently well received, and a few of his early poems have already become standard anthology pieces. Yet outside of his many students from the University of Iowa writing program, and a few outspoken critics who have been trying to tell us for years that he is an important poet, Justice has not been a writer who has been widely read.

Justice's work presents a uniquely difficult job in seeing as a whole because the poet has self-consciously tried to write in as many new and different ways as possible. There is not a poet in America who has mastered as many styles as Justice. At times, his most recent book, *Selected Poems*, reads almost like an anthology of the possibilities of contemporary poetry. There are sestinas, villanelles, and ballads rubbing pages with aleatory poems, surreal odes, and Williamsesque free verse. Yvor Winters once observed that Wallace Stevens was the only poet of his generation who could write equally well in both free and metered verse. That remark could be applied to Justice with almost equal exclusivity. This unsurpassed ambidexterity betrays years of discipline and work, but his remarkable technique never calls attention to itself in Justice's understated work. Justice rarely writes when he has nothing new to say. A new technique is often developed, mastered, and exhausted in one unprecedented and unrepeated poem. A new theme is handled definitively in a sequence or a pair of poems. Justice has published very little, but he has also distilled a decade of writing and experimenting in each new volume.

Despite its variety, Justice's poetry has several identifiable characteristics—a sense of form, a tone of understatement, and a high degree of self-consciousness. No matter whether he is working in formal or in open poetry, it is always possible to see an underlying form in Justice's work. Nothing seems arbitrary. Even when he is imitating Williams, his line breaks make a kind of sense his model's never do. His po-

ems are also highly polished. There never seems to be a word uncertain of its place. Just as the form seems controlled, Justice's voice always seems objective and understated.

Under their highly polished surfaces most of Justice's poems deal with basic emotional themes like love, friendship, sorrow, and loss. He is specially concerned with the loss of his childhood world, and many of his best poems present the Miami of his boyhood and are filled with a brooding nostalgia for its lost people and places.

If it is now impossible to misjudge the shape of Justice's career, much of the credit must go to the author's editorial instincts. *Selected Poems* is a model of editorial judgment. Justice has gone over his entire work, from early uncollected poems to new unpublished poems, and rearranged it chronologically. Many of the older poems have been drastically revised. For example, the title poem of his first volume, "**The Summer Anniversaries,**" has only two lines out of thirty-six remaining from the original forty-eight line poem. Likewise Justice has dropped many of the original poems and rearranged and reordered the remaining ones. Many authors revise their early work, but the results are often mixed. Justice is unerring in his revisions.

What Justice has finally achieved through all the revision, rearrangement, and omission is a nearly perfect volume. There are almost no bad poems in his *Selected Poems* and quite a few perfect ones. Surveying Justice's finest work, it is hard to believe that either future readers or anthologists will want to pass up poems like "**On the Death of Friends in Childhood,**" "**But That Is Another Story,**" "**On a Painting by Patient B of the Independence State Hospital for the Insane,**" "**American Sketches,**" "**Men at Forty,**" "**Unflushed Urinals,**" "**Variations on a Text by Vallejo,**" and many others.

If Justice has a remarkably high percentage of successes, he also has his limitations. There are no long poems in his canon, no epics, no dramas, none of those ambitious single poems on which most contemporary reputations are founded, not even any pieces of moderate length. About two pages seems Justice's maximum. Nor are there any extended sequences. Occasionally there is a pair of related poems or a short series like his "Three Odes," but even these groups are usually best read as a series of independent poems informed by the same technique. The decision to eschew longer forms must be deliberate in so talented a poet. Like his English contemporary, Philip Larkin, Justice is content to excel within very definite, self-imposed limits.

Mary Gosselink De Jong (essay date 1985)

SOURCE: "'Musical Possibilities': Music, Memory, and Composition in the Poetry of Donald Justice," in *Concerning Poetry,* Vol. 18, Nos. 1-2, 1985, pp. 57-66.

[*In the essay below, De Jong discusses the significance of music to Justice's poetry, noting his use of rhyme, assonance, consonance, and repetition and the way in which music has served as subject or allegory in his poems.*]

For centuries authors, composers, and critics have been exploring the parallels between the "sister arts" of music and literature. As Calvin S. Brown dryly observes, the study of musico-literary correspondences holds "a fatal attraction for the dilettante, the faddist and the crackpot." To suggest, then, that Pulitzer-Prize-winning poet Donald Justice has been influenced by music is to incur a certain risk. Being called a faddist or a dilettante would fracture no bones, only pride, and an academic becomes accustomed to being thought a crackpot, by students if not by colleagues and social acquaintances. Still, one would prefer other epithets. Moreover, influence cannot be proved, not even (or especially not?) by a writer's own statements about his or her art. In the case of Justice, it is unlikely that absolute "proof" of musical influence would help us to interpret his poems. But an awareness of his use of "musical possibilities" does afford insights into the composing process; it does enhance the reader's experience of Justice's poetry. As a writer and writing teacher, Justice is much concerned with the way in which a work takes shape. His commitment to the appropriate form—the characteristic feature of his poetry—and his use of certain structures, techniques, and metaphors may be traced to his early and continuing interest in music.

Justice has stated that in his youth he "played the piano and a few other instruments," studied musical composition, and aspired to be a composer. Recently asked by an interviewer whether music has influenced his poetry, he replied that it probably has, but he could not specify how. After speaking of poetic and musical rhythms as "roughly analogous," he continued, "There would be a common sensibility in composing music and writing poems; the same sort of . . . creative desire would obviously lie behind virtually any of the arts. But music and poetry are the two that I would know most about from personal experience. In both there is the same kind of joy in working something out. . . ." In another interview, while making the point that poems are not developed only from subjects, Justice again compared composing music and writing poetry. Poetry has various sources, he said, "just as a composition in music may come from merely fooling around. Or from thinking: This time I'll try D minor; or, I like what Handel wrote just there, I think I'll try some variations on it."

His interest in music is immediately obvious in certain titles— **"White Notes," "Sonatina in Green," "Variations for Two Pianos."** In the latter poem he treats pianist Thomas Higgins as a hero for bringing art to the wilderness of Arkansas. Playing Mozart for "his pupils, the birds," Higgins taught them trills and attacks they could not otherwise have learned. But he has moved away, "taking both his pianos," and "There is no music now in all Arkansas." Though his poem is whimsical and well as elegiac, it records a real loss and testifies to Justice's regard for the beauty and order of art.

He is a virtuoso of the sound effects commonly called "musical": rhyme, assonance, consonance, and other kinds of repetition. To be sure, many poets—Algernon Charles Swinburne and Edward Lear, for example—have charmed the ear, but poems should not be called "musical" simply because they are euphonious. One of Justice's fortes is the structural and thematic use of sound patterns. **"Beyond the Hunting Woods,"** composed of two fifteen-line stanzas, is unrhymed, but oral performance brings out recurring consonants and vowels in the end-words:

> I speak of that great house
> Beyond the hunting woods,
> Turreted and towered
> In nineteenth-century style,
> Where fireflies by the hundreds
> Leap in the long grass,
> Odor of jessamine
> And roses, canker-bit,
> Recalling famous times
> When dame and maiden sipped
> Sassafras or wild
> Elderberry wine,
> While far in the hunting woods
> Men after their red hounds
> Pursued the mythic beast.
>
> I ask it of a stranger,
> In all that great house finding
> Not any living thing,
> Or of the wind and the weather,
> What charm was in that wine
> That they should vanish so,
> Ladies in their stiff
> Bone and clean of limb,
> And over the hunting woods
> What mist had maddened them
> That gentlemen should lose
> Not only the beast in view
> But Belle and Ginger too,
> Nor home from the hunting woods
> Ever, ever come?

This repetition, pleasing in itself, tightens each stanza and links it with the other, for certain vowels (short i, long i) are used throughout. **"Presences"** illustrates his use of repetition to unify a work as well as enact its meaning:

> Everyone, everyone went away today.
> They left without a word, and I think
> I did not hear a single goodbye today.
>
> And all that I saw was someone's hand, I think,
> Thrown up out there like the hand of someone drowning,
> But far away, too far to be sure what it was or meant.
>
> No, but I saw how everything had changed
> Later, just as the light had; and at night
> I saw that from dream to dream everything changed.
>
> And those who might have come to me in the night,
> The ones who did come back but without a word,
> All those I remembered passed through my hands like clouds—
>
> Clouds out of the south, familiar clouds—
> But I could not hold onto them, they were drifting away,
> Everything going away in the night again and again.

The recurrence of words and images corresponds with the paradoxical constancy of loss and change; it conveys the presence of absence. In his essay, **"Meters and Memory"** Justice speaks of poetic meters as having no organic relationship to the sense of the poem but functioning to make it orderly. Like a composer of music, he has made such structural use of repetition and variation; as a poet, he can use these techniques to create and convey meaning.

During the 1960s many American poets rather noisily abandoned rhyme and other literary conventions, arguing that poetry must be "natural," "sincere," not "artificial." Justice's first book, *The Summer Anniversaries* (1960), which appeared at the beginning of this poetic revolution, includes a number of sonnets and sestinas. He did not repudiate literary tradition even when it was fashionable to do so, but in the last twenty years he has developed a repertoire of open forms, some departing from established ones, many assuming the shape of their subjects. Some are reminiscent of musical structures. **"Dreams of Water"** (*Night Light*), for instance, has three ten-line 'movements' linked by theme but different in mood; they might be marked Riposato, Misterioso, and Scherzando. The titles and subtitles of certain poems ask us to think of them as musical compositions: **"Variations on a Theme from James," "Improvisations**

on themes from Guillevic," "Variations on a Text by Vallejo,"** and his two **"Sonatinas."** With such titles he acknowledges influences, indicates how we may perceive a poem and the relations between its parts, and presents his work as his contribution to the common enterprise of Art. Epigraphs, allusions, and endnotes identifying his sources associate his work with that of composers and performers in various art-forms.

Justice's poetic statements about his art are often expressed in terms of another medium—sometimes painting, more often music. Richard Howard has called **"Thus,"** first published more than twenty years ago, Justice's "artistic credo." The narrator says that his key "must be minor. / B minor, then, as having passed for noble / On one or two occasions." His one theme, "with variations," will be "spoken outright by the oboe / Without apology of any string" and "without overmuch adornment." Not for him "the major resolution of the minor, / Johann's great signature"; he has no pretensions to the grand style (*The Summer Anniversaries*). The ironic stance and subdued voice are characteristic; some critics have spoken of Justice as a "low-keyed" poet. His one theme, by no means minor, is change—on this he has worked many variations.

> **Justice's poetic statements about his art are often expressed in terms of another medium—sometimes painting, more often music.**
> *—Mary Gosselink De Jong*

"Sonatina in Green," subtitled "for my students," assesses the state of contemporary poetry. Iconoclastic, undisciplined novices who burst into the muse's "boudoir" are contrasted with "We few with the old instruments, / Obstinate, sounding the one string." For the young, art is "ecstatic" utterance, Bacchic revelry; for their elders it means "playing upon worn keys," enamored of a rich literary past and their own accomplishments but not unaware that modern audiences may have no ear for the music of another time. Both kinds of poet, he implies, think too much of themselves as performers. Seeking publicity and publication, they do not really respect their art: "There has been traffic enough / In the boudoir of the muse" (*Departures*). A highly respected teacher of writing, Justice suggests here what he makes explicit elsewhere, that a number of contemporary poets are indifferent craftsmen with too little concern for making the memorable poem. (He has called poetry readings "a kind of vaudeville," "show-biz rather than art.") By speaking of poets as musicians, he asks us to recognize them as performers and reminds us of the ancient unity of poetry and music-not-held 'sacred' by many of today's poets.

The most evocative of his poems about art, **"Sonatina in Yellow,"** explores the relationship between memory and the creative imagination. Justice has stated that the writer's subject "seems always to be involved, in one way or another, with memory" and remarked that some of his own most profound memories are accompanied by music. **"Sonatina in Yellow"** dramatizes the creative process of a pianist, Justice's figure for the poet. Stimulated by a yellowed photography album, he relives a moment from his childhood. He sits at his instrument thinking of and trying to forget the past. But the forgetting is "an exercise requiring further practice." Fingering the keys as he tries to suppress a memory, he seems to hear it as "a difficult exercise, played through by someone else." The recollection assumes a definite shape: the hot, quiet room; the summer sunlight; he is a child; his father, risen from the dead, wakes from a nap, speaks. . . . In the last stanza, which Justice has called the poem's "coda," the artist comes back to himself at the keyboard. He realizes that in reliving, as it were rehearsing, the long-past drama and its attendant emotions, he has also been shaping it: for the creative mind, to remember is not merely to recall. Wishing to hear the 'music' he has been composing, he says, "Repeat it now, no one was listening. / Repeat it, the air, the variations." The man remembers; the artist makes. **"Sonatina in Yellow"** closes with these lines: "So your hand moves, moving across the keys, / And slowly the keys grow darker to the touch" (**Departures**). His father is dead, his youth is gone, the evening of his own life approaches; but in descending into memory he has discovered, controlled, and preserved a part of his past. The poet, then, has not merely experienced and expressed emotion: he has made something. The final image of dark keys is particularly rich for readers familiar with other poems by Justice.

The former pianist uses keys and scales to represent moods and phases of development. **"Absences"** contemplates descending scales played on "the white keys of a childhood piano," snowflakes, drooping flowers, and other luminous and delicate things that can be kept only in memory—or art (**Departures**). If white keys are associated with innocence and loss, black keys suggest the complexity of mature experience. In "Anniversaries," a poem tracing the speaker's loss of certainty about his own destiny, the narrator recalls how unlike other seventeen-year-olds he was: while they played kickball, he pondered the neurosis of the governess in *The Turn of the Screw* and spent a year "lost / Somewhere among the black / Keys of Chopin . . . / Fingering his ripe heart" (*The Summer Anniversaries*).

Piano keys suggest another kind of self-expression in **"The Suicides."** The narrator muses on the life-long masquerade of acquaintances who surprised everyone by destroying themselves. They made certain that their friends would not really know them—yet they must have always been secretly furious at not being known and accepted for what they were.

Speaking for their survivors, the narrator addresses the suicides, now in their coffins, as "musicians of the black keys," as if they were pianists—then, more chillingly, as if, being no longer human, they are boxed-up pianos angrily playing themselves for only themselves in death as they did in life: "At last you compose yourselves. / We hear the music raging / Under the lids we have closed" (*Night Light*). Eyes, cases, and selves are locked shut forever. Who can know the meaning of lives whose music is so muffled?

> **For Justice, poetry, music, and the other fine arts are means for making sense of experience. The artist does this for himself and his audience by composing.**
> —*Mary Gosselink De Jong*

Justice uses the keys image again in **"Homage to the Memory of Wallace Stevens,"** a tribute to a master and farewell to operatic poetry. Human activities and natural processes proceed in a world without Stevens; poets no longer imitate his "French words and postures." Yet "The poet practicing his scales / Thinks of you as his thumbs slip clumsily under and under, / Avoiding the darker notes" (*Departures*). Again the association of music, poetry, and memory. Here the "darker notes" suggest a level of creativity that only the artist with skill, experience, and courage can attempt. Apprentice pianists—and poets—must practice.

For Justice, poetry, music, and the other fine arts are means for making sense of experience. The artist does this for himself and his audience by composing. A poetic form "fixes" an occurrence, insight, or emotion so that it may be apprehended. Justice is convinced that it is not the poet's business to expose himself in verse or other media. His association of the composing process with memory and music has apparently influenced his own techniques of composition and certainly given him a way of writing about his past and his art while maintaining aesthetic distance. A mature artist enjoying the benefits of his early finger exercises, Justice plays the white keys and the black.

Irvin Ehrenpreis (essay date 1989)

SOURCE: "Ashbery and Justice," in *Poetries of America: Essays on the Relations of Character to Style,* edited by Daniel Albright, University Press of Virginia, 1989, pp. 207-14.

[*In the following excerpt, Ehrenpreis focuses on theme in Justice's collection* Departures.]

Donald Justice has some kinship with Ashbery. The master to whom both seem deeply related is Wallace Stevens. But there is some difference between the author of "Peter Quince at the Clavier" and the one whom Jarrell named "G.E. Moore at the spinet." Justice recalls the music, elegance, and passion of Stevens, not his devotion to aesthetics. In Justice's latest book [*Departures*], certainly his best, the poet keeps his old attachment to the community of vulnerable creatures—lovers, children, the old, the weak. And he bestows on them the richness of sound and cadence, the depth of feeling and subtlety of language that he displayed in his earlier collections.

What draws him to such people is not their dependence but their openness to affection and fantasy, to strong emotions and wild thoughts. For Justice, the receptivity of the artist feeds both his creative imagination and his human sympathy, two aspects of one impulse. Conversely, what seems to matter most to him, in the labors of art, is the chance the imagination offers us to keep in touch with those who share our world but not our neighborhood: the dead, the remote, those imprisoned by their frailty or foolishness.

Justice has marvelous poems about the way the creative process goes: the need to be tough, violent, and fearful at the same time ("ABC"); the difficulty of the effort and the littleness of the reward ("Sonatina in Green"). One that exemplifies his power to charm us is "The Telephone Number of the Muse." Here the poet feels his talent is dwindling; his muse has turned to other, younger lovers:

> I call her up sometimes, long distance now.
> And she still knows my voice, but I can hear,
> Always beyond the music of her phonograph,
> The laughter of the young men with their keys.

The unfashionable refinement of the syntax, like the unfashionable purity of the language, is typical of Justice. Both these features are touching contrasts to his pathos when Justice gives in to the elegiac mood and turns to his central concern. This is with the class of people who sink in the trajectory of their wayward natures, who leave the tribe sooner than alter their own essence. I suppose that for him the poets belong to this class.

The circular patterns that Justice loves sound appropriate to the solitary character of such people, turned back on themselves, shut in willingly or unwillingly, caught in irreversible cycles. No wonder he finds so much occupation for mirrors, guitars, pianos, repetitions of words and syllables. Such images and devices, such iterative and musical designs, suit the meditations and recapitulations of the solitary life.

The dead belong here, because our relation with them must be circular. They prepare us for their place, and we have taken it. The hushed tone that marks Justice's voice mounts to reverence as he evokes his relation to his father in "Sonatina in Yellow." Here, the ambiguities, continuities, and repetitions move parallel to memory and forgetfulness, in a sequence impressively like a musical modulation. Love for the dead suggests love for the past, the poet's desire to keep with him the beauty and awfulness of the filiation that he will hand on in his turn; and the imagination then seems our one genuine weapon against mortality:

> The pages of the album,
> As they are turned, turn yellow; a word,
> Once spoken, obsolete,
> No longer what was meant. Say it.
> The meanings come, or come back later,
> Unobtrusive, taking their places.

Solitude falls into loneliness, isolation decays to imprisonment, repression gives way to murder, as Justice travels across his land of self-enclosures. And we meet the neurotic in the sanitarium, longing to get back to the way of life that sent her there ("A Letter"), or the love-hungry poet (not Justice), reliving in his poems his love-hungry youth ("Portrait with Flashlight"). Because he has the habit of understatement and terseness in an era when overexpression is normal, Justice may sound too reserved. But the intensity of vision that directs his work will be evident to those who care to observe it, as when the poet admits his complicity in the terrors he conveys:

> You have no name, intimate crime,
> Into which I might plunge my hand.
> Your knives have entered many pillows,
> But you leave nothing behind.
>
> ("The Confession")

In making these new poems, Justice discarded some of his old traits. He has given up regular meters for free verse. He has enlarged his allotment of dreamlike images and veiled meanings. But his ear and his sense of design are so reliable that the poems remain seductive in sound and shape.

He has not reduced his most engaging feature, the mixture of gentleness with power. The confidence Justice has in his own selfhood enables him to reach out to lives that would unsettle a thinner character; and he can obey his admonition in "ABC":

> Be the statue leaning out from the stone,
> the stone also, torn between past and future,
> and the hammer, whose strength we share.

Robert Mezey (essay date Winter-Spring 1992)

SOURCE: "Of Donald Justice's Ear," in *Verse,* Vols. 8-9, Nos. 3 and 1, Winter-Spring, 1992, pp. 37-8.

[*In the following essay, Mezey praises the power of Justice's imagery and the seeming effortlessness with which it is evoked.*]

In an essay published about ten years ago, Donald Justice wrote: "Words sometimes, through likeness of sound, become bound to one another by ties remotely like those of human kinship. This is not to propose that any *meaning* attaches to the sounds independent of the words. But the interlocking sounds do seem to reinforce and in some curious way to authenticate the meanings of the words, perhaps indirectly to deepen and enlarge them. A part of the very nature of poetry lies in this fact."

For at least one reader, perhaps the essential part. (One can think of poets who have written beautifully without metaphor, without sensuous or concrete diction, without subject or drama, even without intelligence, but none who has done so without an ear.) And I would go further: I would say that the poet who has the requisite power not only discloses the very nature of poetry but seems to penetrate to the very nature of experience. I am not speaking now of onomatopoeia or the various kinds of mimicry, crude and sophisticated, that ingenious poets are capable of. Any poet of sufficient skill can slow down his tempo and articulation "When Ajax strives, some rocks' vast weight to throw," or contrive the flashy magic of Tennyson's moaning doves and murmuring bees. Justice's skill is more than sufficient for such professional illusions as in

> To stand, braced in a swaying vestibule,

or, at somewhat greater length,

> And then a
> Slow blacksnake, lazy with long sunning, slides
> Down from its slab, and through the thick grass,
> and hides
> Somewhere among the purpling wild verbena.

(We shall save the delights of that characteristic rhyme for another occasion.) No, I am thinking rather of something like Wordsworth's "Or the unimaginable touch of Time," something that cannot quite properly be called imitative form but thrills us all the same with its power to evoke, by means of little more, apparently, than a couple of very light accents and a diction almost entirely abstract, an intense, almost physical apprehension of the slow, soundless crumbling of the centuries. Wordsworth calls it unimaginable even as he makes us imagine it. In such lines we have the sensation that words have somehow slipped free from their characters, their shadowy life in the world of signs, and come down, as Yeats

implored his sages to do, to participate in the world of experience. It is as if we are touching, through the medium of language, that constantly receding wonder, reality. We feel that the poem is creating truth itself. Perhaps that is why we cannot do without it, those of us who cannot.

It is not always easy to distinguish between the obvious sorts of verbal mimesis, however fine, and this deeper thing I have been trying to describe. One mark of the distinction may be that the former is likely to be susceptible of analysis and the latter not. For example, in this lovely quatrain about a sofa in a dance teacher's parlor (her "makeshift ballroom"),

> At lesson time, pushed back, it used to be
> The thing we managed somehow just to miss
> With our last-second dips and twirls—all this
> While the Victrola wound down gradually.

I would say that that last line is a particularly beautiful instance of imitation. One could lead a reasonably sensitive student to see how the third line with its vivid lexicon, fluid cadence and short vowels speeds to the dash, to be pulled up short as the last line, beginning with the long "while," almost a syllable and a half, descends to the long vowels in mid-line, the insistent nasals, the juncture that enforces a slight pause between "wound" and the unaccented but long, heavy "down," the faded rhyme, and the limpness, the dying fall, of the adverb with its feeble final accent. (Of course it goes without saying that all such effects depend utterly on the meanings of the words; meters and tropes of sound mean nothing in themselves. So I began my brief analysis by indicating the lexicon, and so Justice was careful to include a similar stipulation in the paragraph I quoted earlier, for there are still many simple souls in the textbooks and classrooms who think that every trochee expresses conflict or resistance and that sibilance in a line of verse signifies evil. One would think that Ransom had laughed such readers off the stage forever; alas, apparently not.)

But how, I wonder, would I analyze the effect of these two lines from an elegy for a friend kicked to death in an alley (a poem, by the way, that has my nomination for the best villanelle in the language)?

> I picture the snow as falling without hurry
> To cover the cobbles and the toppled ashcans
> completely.

How does he do it, and so effortlessly, or so it seems? That calm, steady, almost nerveless line, that dry, cruel phrase, "without hurry," the infinitive that suggests intention without in the least asserting it, the intricate pattern of sound in the second line, subtler than any chiasmus, flakes of vowel and consonant that bond together to cover the fifteen syllables of the five-beater completely—I am waxing impressionistic because I am at a loss to account for the haunting power of these cold-eyed and heartbreaking lines.

Or take the ending of his exquisite version of Rilke's "Letzer Abend," where the doomed officer's jacket hangs across the chair

> Like the coats scarecrows wear
>
> And which the birdshadows flee and scatter from;
> Or like the skin of some great battle-drum.

It is elementary to suggest that the static quality of the trimeter derives partly from the heavy ionic foot, the thick jam of consonants, especially the s juncture, and the internal rhyme, assonance, and alliteration, but it is impossible, at least to me, to tell clearly how the extra syllable of "birdshadows" and the lighter assonance of "-shadows" and "scatter" seem to embody the wild and panicky movement the line describes; it has something to do, surely, with the dramatic preposition that ends the clause and the ominous semi-colon, not to mention the odd force of our realization that we are following not the fleeing birds but their shadows, but now we are trying to explain the inexplicable. And that great last line— yes, only a dullard would fail to feel the reverberation of the internal rhyme (another one!), but what accounts for the power of the final word, a power that lies to some extent in its nearness to and its distance from being a triple rhyme and seems almost to summon up the much more dreadful scattering to come? I don't know.

This is state-of-the-art, as they say. I wish it were truly representative of the state of the art. But, still, it gives some cheer to remember that at the end of the 20th century, when American poetry is drearier and more amateurish than it has been at any time since the end of the 19th, a few writers are "saying the thing once for all and perfectly." The gratitude I feel for **"Last Evening"** and for so many of Donald Justice's poems is the gratitude I feel for any act or gesture of love and loving care. That is, no doubt, "a love that masquerades as pure technique." But it is love.

Bruce Bawer (essay date Winter-Spring 1992)

SOURCE: "'Avec une Élégance Grave et Lente': The Poetry of Donald Justice," in *Verse,* Vols. 8-9, Nos. 3 and 1, Winter-Spring, 1992, pp. 44-9.

[*In the following essay, Bawer defends Justice's work against hostile critics, stating that the negative criticism stems from Justice's reluctance to conform to the styles of his peers.*]

On the American poetry scene these days, the only thing

rarer than a fine poem is a negative review. Yet reviewers of Donald Justice—who has written some of the finest poems of our time—have often been not only negative but surprisingly hostile. Calvin Bedient, assessing Justice's 1979 *Selected Poems* in the *Sewanee Review*, described him as "an uncertain talent that has not been turned to much account." Wrote Gerald Burns: "*Selected Poems* reads like a very thin Tennessee Williams—little poems about obscure Florida people and architecture. . . . As a *career* his, though honest, does not quite make the ascent to poet from racket." And Alan Hollinghurst, appraising the same volume for *The New Statesman*, complained that Justice's poems lacked "vitality . . . urgency . . . colour and surprise," that they suffered from "lassitude," "a weary passivity," and "a habit of elegance which cushions meaning," and that the poems, "formal but *fatigués* . . . create the impression of getting great job-satisfaction without actually doing much work."

What has Justice done to deserve such attacks? Well, he was imprudent enough to begin writing poetry at a time when the Beats were at the height of their popularity and when many readers were unable to see, in his low-decibel traditional verses, anything but an absence of the "vitality and urgency" that they admired in the Beats and in the recognized non-Beat camps of the day: the Black Mountain poets, the New York poets, the confessionalists. Nor did Justice necessarily appeal to the academic admirers of his fellow traditionalists Richard Wilbur and Anthony Hecht; for it was, and is, in the nature of a certain kind of postwar academic critic to feel very much at home with the poems of a Wilbur or a Hecht—many of which seem, by their intricacy and impersonality, to solicit critical attention—while feeling uncomfortable with a plainer and more personal poet such as Justice, to whose sublime and delicate music such a critic may well be deaf and to whose conspicuous and compassionate interest in people's lives and feelings he may be constitutionally incapable of responding except by reflexively and defensively dismissing the poet as sentimental.

Nor has Justice gone out of his way to endear himself to the poetry world. While many poets of his generation have distributed enthusiastic blurbs like Halloween candy, Justice has committed the grave error of saying what he really thinks about his contemporaries. In the interviews collected in *Platonic Scripts*, he scorns the vapid, glibly romantic *idées reçues*—"*Nature is good . . .* government is *bad . . .* [poetry is] *good for the Soul*"—that form the contemporary Poets' Code: in a time when poets pay more attention to politics than to aesthetics, Justice declares that poems should not be didactic; in a time when one of the major prerequisites for an American poet seems to be an endless capacity for self-righteousness about his vocation, Justice observes stingingly that poets today "act as if they believed there were something almost sacred in the name of *poet*." While other poets hesitate to step on toes, he refers bluntly to the "so-called poetry of the Beats." dismisses terms like Olson's "organic form" as so much pretentious blather, and is "appalled" by poets who brag about moving young people to tears, saying that such things are "morally wrong" and that poems should properly be "objects of contemplation." Ultimately, the dismissive reviews of Justice's *Selected Poems* are a reflection not of any failing in the work itself but of the manifold moral and cultural failures of an age in which it has been Justice's peculiar honor to be the apotheosis of the unfashionable poet.

Nor has Justice gone out of his way to endear himself to the poetry world. While many poets of his generation have distributed enthusiastic blurbs like Halloween candy, Justice has committed the grave error of saying what he really thinks about his contemporaries.
—*Bruce Bawer*

Justice's poetry is, it must be said, understated. (He once agreed with an interviewer who remarked that "understatement is to you, practically, a religious principle.") But it does not lack vitality and urgency. What it lacks, rather, are the vulgarity, hysteria, conceit, anarchism, and morbid fixation on madness, drug abuse, grubby sex, and the like that characterize the most extreme Beat and confessional verses and that some readers, alas, equate with vitality and urgency. The urgency of Justice's finest verse is of a thoroughly different order. It is the urgency of deeply controlled feeling about loss and mortality, about the inevitable passing of time and the irrevocable pastness of the past. And while a table of contents that includes such titles as **"Sonnet to My Father"** and **"Tales from a Family Album"** and **"On the Death of Friends in Childhood"** might well strike many a critic as a firm guarantee of a poet's sentimental leanings, Justice's poems are delivered from sentimentality by honest feeling, careful observation, and fresh expression—and by a seemingly stoical resistance to grief. In an age of emotional exhibitionism, Justice rises, time and again, beyond his particular circumstances toward the level of tragic myth. To be sure, many a line from a Justice poem might indeed sound maudlin in other contexts, such as the closing line of one poem: "But already the silent world is lost forever." Yet such a line is maudlin only if it strikes one as false and easy, as having been forced onto a poem rather than having grown out of it. Such is not the case here. On the contrary, the poem positions the reader perfectly for the line, so that it seems true and heartfelt, the inevitable terminus of a very real emotional journey: the poem, in other words, captures with extraordinary precision the tenor of a mind and the rhythms of its thought, and the concluding line comes as the natural reflection on all that has gone before.

It is, to be sure, misleading to speak of Justice's poetry as if it were all of an ilk. His first book, *The Summer Anniversaries* (1960), established the intelligent, composed, and pensive voice with which he is most frequently identified—and established, too, his independence from the accepted poetic modes of the day. For many of his contemporaries, notably his teacher Robert Lowell (whose pivotal *Life Studies* had appeared a year earlier), the breakthrough to using autobiographical material in poetry was coupled with a break with form, a rejection of virtuosity as the ultimate poetic value in favor of sincerity; but though many of the poems of *The Summer Anniversaries* patently concern people and places that are of great personal significance for the poet, none of the poems is in free verse; Justice refuses to join Lowell, Snodgrass, Sexton, et al., in emphasizing sincerity at the expense of formal artistry ("Now that is simply not the kind of poetry I write," he once told an interviewer apropos of Snodgrass). Justice distinguishes between writing about himself, which he tries not to do ("I've always felt it was an author's privilege to leave himself out if he chose," he has said, citing with approval Eliot's now-unfashionable theory of the impersonality of the poet), and writing about people and places that have been important to him. Indeed, though his family and friends proliferate in *The Summer Anniversaries*, Justice attempts to restrict himself to the role of the observer and chronicler, and when he *is* present (or, more accurately, when there is an I in the poem that one tends to identify with the poet), he does his best to objectify his experience, to place mythic elements in the foreground and to exclude the irrelevantly personal.

Justice has said that poems, at their best, transform a subjective experience into an object not unlike a treasured family photograph, an object that preserves a precious moment for readers of present and future generations as well as for the later refreshment of one's own memory, and he has expressed the hope that "some of the poems I've tried to write were treasurable in the sense that I *know* a photograph can be treasurable. Treasured." ("I like it," he has said of his poem **"First Death,"** "because it records something otherwise lost.") Rather than write subjective, anti-literary, free-verse effusions in the manner of the Beats or the confessional poets, then, he seeks to create timeless, unapologetically literary objects—*made* objects ("I think of poetry as making things")—that preserve selected encounters, observations, and reflections. More than one interviewer has seemed bemused by Justice's traditional bent, by his habit of constant revision and his devotion to established forms; one interlocutor even asked if he ever felt the need to "free yourself from this restraint or control?" Justice's reply: "I don't think I feel the need to let go. Nowadays people may think of that as a flaw. I don't." Critics routinely praise the "courage" of an Allen Ginsberg; but there is more pluck in Justice's firm "I don't" than in all of Ginsberg's *Collected Poems*.

Formal though they are, though, Justice's poems do not re-call what he has called the "hard, thuddy iambic pentameter line" of Lowell's dense, formal verses in *Lord Weary's Castle* any more than they recall the more relaxed free-verse rhythms of *Life Studies* and after. Rather, his poems exhibit a limpid lyricism, a gracefully flowing music; trained in his early years as a pianist, Justice himself makes reference to the musical-ity of his poems, prefacing his volume *The Sunset Maker* with several tempo markings from major modern compos-ers: "Sec et musclé" (Milhaud), "Avec une élégance grave et lente" (Debussy), "broadly singing" (Carl Ruggles). Justice's most representative poems do tend to display these characteristics: they are dry, muscular, elegant, grave, and slow (one might mark them *piano* and *andante*), with a fine, smooth, and austere melodic line, as it were, reminiscent of many a modern French composer.

Justice is, moreover, a poet who, even as he pays tribute to the radiant possibilities of human experience and the natural world, associates unalloyed wonder and joy at these things with the innocence of childhood, characterizing life, in **"To a Ten-Months' Child,"** as a state that one enters from a "remote . . . kingdom" and, in **"Song,"** describing a glori-ous dawn with awe and saying that" all that day / Was a fairy tale / Told once in a while / To a good child." To Justice, growing up is a matter of recognizing that life is not the per-fectly sublime affair that one may have believed it to be in one's early years: in **"The Snowfall,"** he refers to the "ter-rible whispers of our elders / Falling softly about our ears / In childhood, never believed till now." The innocence of joy and the terror of knowledge are also themes of the memo-rable **"Sonnet,"** in which the innocents are not children but Adam and Eve:

> The walls surrounding them they never saw;
> The angels, often. Angles were as common
> As birds or butterflies, but looked more human.
> As long as the wings were furled, they felt no awe.
> Beasts, too, were friendly. They could find no
> flaw
> In all of Eden: this was the first omen.
> The second was the dream which woke the
> woman:
> She dreamed she saw the lion sharpen his claw.
> As for the fruit, it had no taste at all.
> They had been warned of what was bound to
> happen;
> They had been told of something called the world;
> They had been told and told about the wall.
> They saw it now; the gate was standing open.
> As they advanced, the giant wings unfurled.

Both in its vision of man and his world and in its means of imparting that vision, this poem is vintage Justice. With one stunning final image—an image that is all the more effec-

tive for the quiet simplicity with which it is presented and for the omission of any reference to Adam and Eve's reac-tion to it—Justice makes one feel the terror of the knowl-edge that comes to all of us when we move beyond the complacent bliss of childhood: the knowledge of our mor-tality, of the world's imperfection, and of our separation from the awful, winged majesty of God and His angels. The irony here, a familiar one in Justice's poetry, is that though the happiness of a child, or of Adam and Eve in Eden, is un-tainted by the adult's bitter knowledge, it is only in that state of knowledge, born of loss, that the irreclaimable joys of creation can be fully appreciated.

A reader of **"Sonnet"**—and of the numerous poems in which Justice refers to saints and angels and heaven—might be ex-cused for concluding that he is a religious man. Yet though he was raised as a Southern Baptist, Justice has said that he lost his faith as a young man. "I don't believe in the spiri-tual," he declared flatly in a 1975 interview. "You know, there is a power in the obvious. That which is hidden I can't see." Yet in these secular times, Justice has a remarkable sense of what one cannot describe as anything other than the sanctity of the quotidian (he writes in **"Unflushed Urinals"** of "The acceptingness of the washbowls, in which we ab-solve ourselves!"): to him, sin and grace manifestly remain vital concepts, and life, for all its deficiencies, has its mo-ments of sublime radiance.

His second and third collections find Justice in territory that one doesn't necessarily think of as his own. These are books of experiment, in which Justice wanders afield from the dis-ciplined forms and elegant musicality of his debut volume to try his hand at blank verse, syllabic verse, and free verse. Both books also contain a number of verses inspired not by personal experience but by the work of other poets; since such poems as **"The Telephone Number of the Muse"** sug-gest that Justice felt abandoned by the Muse, one presumes that imitation and experiment were his way of keeping busy at his craft during her supposed absence. And indeed, though they are far from unaccomplished, the poems of *Night Light* (1967, revised 1981) and *Departures* (1973) represent some-thing of a loosening, a thinning out, a descent into the fine but familiar from the serene and singular music of *The Sum-mer Anniversaries*.

The models for the poems in these two volumes come from all over the map. There is a pair of **"American Sketches"** written in imitation of William Carlos Williams (to whom they are dedicated): there is a poem entitled **"After a Phrase Abandoned by Wallace Stevens"**: and there are several el-liptical, portentous poems, with wildly different line lengths and short, clipped sentences, in imitation of Lorca and Vallejo. These poems, surreal and often deliberately dis-jointed and fragmentary, are quite admirable of their kind, but they strike one as being very much against the grain of

Justice's own native music, which typically casts its spell by means of clear and coherent imagery, elegant and supple language, and delicate variations on the iambic line. Justice's Lorcaesque poems, by contrast, tend to be too metrically varied, too expressionistic, and too loosely conversational in tone and rhythm to satisfy a lover of Justice's best work: conversely, there may well be too much in these poems of Justice to satisfy an ardent admirer of Vallejo or Lorca. The bottom line is that Justice's gently responsive sensibility and strong sense of control don't really lend themselves to the jagged rhythms and erratic thought patterns of a Lorca-type poem; to read Justice's Lorcaesque poems, in fact, is a bit like hearing an opera singer do *Showboat*: it's not great opera and it's not great Kern. Nonetheless, both books show a side of Justice that one cannot but admire: namely, Justice the astute and sensitive student of his art, who has never lost the essential humility, and the willingness to learn, of the earnest young painter copying an Old Master canvas in a museum.

In the new poems included in the Pulitzer Prize-winning *Selected Poems* (1979), Justice leaves Lorca and company behind and writes in what might be described as a sharper, more seasoned version of his *Summer Anniversaries* voice. Indeed, one of the finest poems in *Selected Poems* is "**The Summer Anniversaries**," an alternate version of "**Anniversaries**," the opening poem in his debut volume. The poem charts the speaker's growth from a ten-year-old who, though wheelchair-bound, glories in the bounties of the earth—

> I thought it absurd
> For anyone to have quarreled
> Ever with such a world—
> O brave new planet!—
> And with such music in it.

—to a twenty-one-year-old who sees a balloon "veer crazily off" and compares it to himself. "All sense of direction gone"; to a thirty-year-old who watches

> Through the window beside my desk
> Boys deep in the summer dusk
> Of Iowa, at catch,
> Toss, back and forth, their ball.
> Shadows begin to fall.
> The colors of the day
> Resolve into one dull,
> Unremarkable gray,
> And I watch them go in from their play[,]
> Small figures of some myth
> Now, vanishing up the path.

With extraordinary concision and effectiveness, the poem captures in turn the child's naive enthusiasm about life, the adolescent's confusion and romantic self-pity, and the adult's preoccupation with the prosaic business of existence, which, when he notices young people at all, causes him to think of them—and of his own younger self—as if they were part of some half-remembered legend. The poem is a splendid example, too, of Justice's genius for distancing: as much as any sonnet of Donne, it represents not an indulgence in personality but an escape from personality's restrictions; the specifics take on a symbolic weight, and one does not find oneself wondering (as one does with much confessional verse) about the poem's degree of autobiographical accuracy. (The poem is reminiscent, in particular, of Donne's "A Valediction: Of Weeping," in which three round objects—a ball, a tear, and the earth—are connected imagistically; here, similarly, Justice connects three round objects—a wheelchair wheel, a balloon, a ball—all emblems of the cycle of life.)

The Sunset Maker (1987) displays the music of Justice's poetry at its most elevated and austerely beautiful. In this volume, which contains not only twenty-five poems but two stories and a prose memoir, Justice is more than ever a poet of things past and passing, lamenting his incalculable losses and tendering his most cherished memories—mostly of his parents and of his childhood piano teachers—in language replete with allusions to the fragile beauty of music, to the ever-shifting light and shadow of nature ("The sun seems not to move at all, / Till it has moved on"), and to the tenets and typology of Christianity, with its assurance of an eternal and omnipresent deity (after rain, Justice writes in "**Mule Team and Poster**," the sun returns, "Invisible, but everywhere present, / and of a special brightness, like God"). The echoes of Stevens are more multitudinous than ever: if a line like "Mordancies of the armchair!" (in "**Tremayne**") brings to mind "Sunday Morning," a reference to "the last shade perhaps in all of Alabama" (in "**Mule Team and Poster**") recalls "Anecdote of the Jar." As in earlier volumes, Justice takes somber note of the contrast between the real world and childhood's fanciful view of it, noting that the world a child dreams "is the world we run to from the world."

For the Justice of *The Sunset Maker*, the chief function of art is to preserve what little it can of life. Perhaps the book's two most idiosyncratic items are the poem "**The Sunset Maker**" and its pendant, a story entitled "**Little Elegy for Cello and Piano**"; both works concern the speaker's friendship with a recently deceased and largely forgotten composer named Eugene Bestor, who survives only in a six-note phrase remembered by the speaker:

> The hard early years of study, those still,
> Sequestered mornings in the studio,
> The perfect ear, the technique, the great gift
> All have come down to this one ghostly phrase.
> And soon nobody will recall the sound
> These six notes made once or that there were six.

It is to be hoped—not only for his sake, but for that of American poetry—that Justice's work will be more widely remembered than that of the fictional Bestor. Certainty there is more than one phrase in Justice's verse—plain, unaffected, and gently apocalyptic—that haunts the memory: "Darkness they rise from, darkness they sink back towards." "It is the lurch and slur the world makes, turning." "To shine is to be surrounded by the dark." Justice is the poet of a world in which loss is ubiquitous, sorrow inevitable, and adult joy always bittersweet; a world in which the genuinely heroic act, for a literary artist, is not to thrash about uncontrollably, raising a manic and ugly din, but to fashion a body of work whose beauty and poise and gravity in the face of life's abomination may, one trusts, help it to endure.

William Logan (essay date Winter-Spring 1992)

SOURCE: "The Forces of Nostalgia," in *Verse,* Vols. 8-9, Nos. 3 and 1, Winter-Spring, 1992, pp. 59-66.

[*In the following essay, Logan analyzes the role of nostalgia in Justice's poems.*]

> What a dreadful disease Nostalgia must
> be on the banks of the Missouri.
> —Sydney Smith

> We have heard the chimes at midnight.
> Master Shallow.
>
> —Falstaff

One does not have to be religious to succumb to nostalgia, though in certain individuals nostalgia may supplant the religious instinct. The Christian present pursues its balance between a past of grace freely bestowed, fall, and redemption through blood, and a future of redemption in death, rise from sin, and grace everlasting. As pure philosophy it is progressive, though I am not of the party which believes that the angels will wear togas or holy tunics to protect their modesty. In practice, and in its daily injunctions, it tends to be backward-looking, and in its regressiveness to resemble the common operations of nostalgia.

We think of nostalgia as the vice of maturity, a disease of age, but one does not have to pass forty for nostalgia to press into a life, and even the very young may show signs of its addiction. In *The Oxford Book of Literary Anecdotes,* Ronald Knox is recorded as saying, during a bout of insomnia at the age of four. "I lie awake and think about the past." As a literary theme (rather than, say, as transient concern or rhetorical figure), nostalgia required a notion of the self perhaps impossible before Rousseau. Once the trivial incidents of a life had gained the authority of the poetic lyric, nostal-

gia became another vehicle for certain ancient, governing anxieties: the loss of the past (especially the perfected or romanticized past, an Eden): the forfeit of opportunity and the regret for actions taken or mistaken: the corrupted potential or relative poverty of the present.

There was a feeling before the feeling found a name. When Shallow boasts, in *Henry IV, Part II,* "Jesu, Jesu, the mad days that I have spent! And to see how many of my old acquaintance are dead!", he mingles regret with the consolation of reminiscence, measuring the present on the terms of the past. And Falstaff, somewhile later, detects how reminiscence overwhelms the thin particulars: "I do see the bottom of Justice Shallow. Lord, Lord, how subject we old men are to this vice of lying!"

The burdens of nostalgia are not just an old man's quarrels with truth—for seeing the past, for saying the past, as better than it was. In an unsparing and sensible book called *The Burden of the Past and the English Poet,* Walter Jackson Bate reminds us that the pressures of the past have been felt since antiquity: an Egyptian scribe of 2000 B.C. named Khakheperresenb lamented. "Would I had phrases that are not known, utterances that are strange, in new language that has not been used, free from repetition, not an utterance which has grown stale, which men of old have spoken." The burdens fell differently on Shallow and Khakheperresenb, the literary construction and the literary scribe, but were jointly derived from and jointly determined by the belief that compared to a past of vital originality, the present was a withering or falling away.

The word *nostalgia* is a learned neologism of the late Renaissance. According to the scholar Fred Davis, it can be traced to an obscure 1688 medical tract, by the Swiss physician Johannes Hofer, describing a disorder found among Swiss mercenaries serving abroad in the armies of Europe. Their symptoms included melancholy, despondency, weeping, anorexia, and attempted suicide. They were, in short, desperately homesick. The first use in English is not recorded until almost a century later, and before the present century all *OED* citations retain the sense of the cobbled-up Greek: *nostos,* a return home, and *algos,* pain.

Even used figuratively, the word remained within the pathology of homesickness, as in "That pond has . . . about half-a-dozen trouts, if indeed they have not sickened and died of Nostalgia" (1842). The first citation in the *OED* for our modern sense, for the "regret or sorrowful longing for the conditions of a past age; regretful or wistful memory or recall of an earlier time," does not occur until 1920, in D.H. Lawrence's *The Lost Girl.* No doubt a deeper trawl of literature would drag up earlier examples, but the shift from pathology to *pathétique* comes remarkably late.

It is widely supposed that nostalgia in literature is immitigably bad, that it protects what ought to be examined, falsifies what should be exposed, defends what must be attacked. The nostalgic impulse is thought to derive from the complacency of denial, and therefore to exist wholly within the precincts of sentimentality, of the unexamined indulgence in emotional forms. But nostalgia is not necessarily a wish to return to the past; it is the wish to be privileged to recall it, and to the extent that nostalgia is the admission of a practice, is aware of limit in the character of its longing, it is a gesture of counter-sentiment. Nostalgia is the refuge of poets for whom the current modes of reminiscence have been irremediably stained with sentiment.

The sentimentalities to which our poetry is susceptible contaminate the treatment of private life. The modern poet is an adept of the material or moral condition of his own life—the affect of love takes a poor second to the versification of daily display. When minute episodes are tweezered out and presented in quivering symbolic virtue, the allocating sentiment raises the trivial and adventitious to the virtues of symbol, without the symbol having weight or accidence. What is commonly thought to represent "risk" in contemporary poetry—the revelation of private affairs—requires just that attitude to experience which is most smug and calculating. From this, nostalgia can represent an escape and the radical of a reformation. It is also, of course, peculiarly permeable to sentiment, and every example of nostalgia in its reforming character may be balanced by a dozen examples of sentimental misuse.

I have entertained these general notes before coming to the individual case because I am interested in nostalgia only as anti-sentiment, as the canker within sentiment. Given the rarity of a nostalgia of this condition, the subject of this essay might more usefully have been "The Abuse of Nostalgia," but that would have eliminated consideration of the reforming instance.

The dominating method of Donald Justice's later poetry requires nostalgia, a nostalgia that has little of the emotional consolation of submission and more of the formal economies of engagement. In his arching dark ironies, Justice has long proved an irritant to the simpler taxonomies of American poetry, which find it convenient to ignore whatever lies beyond the margin of immediate comprehension. Justice rarely uses the self as the location of dramatic action, for the great tragedy moving through the little event. In his detachment he is a modern (his most obvious forebears Williams and Stevens) at a time when the sharper reliefs of modernism have been eroded. Modernism's respect for history, for a culture that spans millennia and not just months, has been superseded no less than its cool outward presentation of subject. No longer is modernism's "impersonality" recognized as a matter of tension and tone: when fully employed, tension and tone do not require the outward display of emotion (Eliot's poems, to me at least, are frighteningly emotional).

> **The dominating method of Donald Justice's later poetry requires nostalgia, a nostalgia that has little of the emotional consolation of submission and more of the formal economies of engagement.**
> **—William Logan**

The poetry of Pound and Eliot threw out grappling hooks in all directions; the poetry of Williams and Stevens was, in the main, self-sufficient. Most of Donald Justice's poems are similarly occlusive; they are the horizon of their own reference. They have practiced various strategies of impersonality, and without a side-glancing title or an accommodating note a reader would scarcely be aware of a debt to Vallejo, or Rilke, or Baudelaire. Justice has often made his own what is most foreign (one might see this strategy as a way of *avoiding* the burdens of the self), the foreign landscapes become local, the references to a wider culture made properly private. His poetry is consequent to its limitations (which is not the same as complacent in them): this may be called its modesty. Within that modesty, however, he has discovered—increasingly in the past decade—a richness and lushness located almost entirely within the remove of the past. In his use of nostalgia, nostalgia can no longer be considered a defensive exhaustion—rather it has been a recovered plenitude.

Justice's last new collection, *The Sunset Maker*, is a book of assignations with the past: and it is necessary to stand a little aside from the assignatory character to observe precisely the conditions the artist has made in the fabric of observation. **"Nostalgia of the Lakefronts,"** the poem in which the method most readily implicates the verse technique as well as the verse subject, opens with what seems the destruction of Sodom and Gomorrah: "Cities burn behind us . . . " But the cities burn with lights; these are not the cities of the plain, and the hints of holocaust would be a mild, darkening joke if certain shadows—of the proper end to wicked pleasures, of the punishment for those who look back—did not obtrude.

The poem establishes itself not as a meditation but as a movement through childhood, or through the moment when childhood is "fading to a landscape deep with distance." Neither the moment nor the loss is precise—the poem memorizes, perhaps memorializes, certain summers by a lake, perhaps one certain summer, the summer of 1942, the last before war closed the hotels. The memories have wavered past precision (Justice would have turned seventeen late in the summer of '42), until what is important is not their specific outline but their evocative ghostliness, their "indecipherable blurred harmonies"—the loudspeaker, the distant sad piano, the horn over the water.

> At such times, wakeful, a child will dream the
> world.
> And this is the world we run to from the world.

But in this blurring (the second line sounds like a blurred quotation of Jarrell, whose favorite word was *world*) the world inwardly dreamed and the world outwardly experienced cannot necessarily be kept apart—it is perhaps not the proper burden of the artist to keep them apart:

> Or the two worlds come together and are one
> On dark sweet afternoons of storm and of rain . . .

The child dreaming the world may be the artist in his earliest manifestation, but the fiction of the artist is more devouring than the child's mere dreaming. The past has an achieved coherence, but here the subversion of the present by that past lies in the very innocence of its art, the art of a now vanished moment. The lake, for instance, "is famed among painters for its blues":

> Is their wish not unique—
> To anthropomorphize the inanimate
> With a love that masquerades as pure technique?

Here the artist's impersonality is the condition or cost of his feeling—the feeling guaranteed only by the purity of technique. There are two movements from this question, one through subject and one through form. In the poem the question is not answered but overridden, perhaps overwritten:

> O art and the child are innocent together!

The remainder of the poem chronicles the loss of that innocence—not the child's but the artist's. "Soon now the war will shutter the grand hotels"—this is the loss or corruption nostalgia expects, even revels in (there would be little point in setting up a stone for something that still existed). But there is a ghostlier, more painful loss in the very concept of artistry. I wouldn't wish to press the suggestion too far, at least not past the point where it is merely suggestive; but in poetry as well as painting a certain innocence (some might prefer to call it sophistication) did not survive much longer. The realism which even the Cubists subscribed to, in their way, soon became the province of the amateur only—the line immediately after the exclamation above is, "But landscapes grow abstract . . . ," and its bearing on painting (the collapse in value of draftsmanship, the triumph of Abstract Expressionism over line, the later relegation of figure to the cartoon kitsch of Pop Art) is not wholly compelled by an abstraction of memory. In the final stanza,

> And after a time the lakefront disappears
> Into the stubborn verses of its exiles
> Or a few gifted sketches of old piers.

The verses are stubborn because they *are* verses at a time when metrical verse has long been suspect and "amateur." And those "old piers" sound grimly with the "old peers" whose techniques are vanished issues. I have taken a liberal course with the pun because of the second movement, through form, to which I alluded earlier. The poem's stanzas vary between six and seven lines, but the rhymes are all exact, sometimes a word *with* itself (harmonies/harmonies), but never weaker than a syllable with itself (cockatoo/1942, unique/technique, disappears/piers). The words rhyme not with something like themselves but with themselves; and this violation of the normal prescription of rhyme is not just the calculated echo in language of the past's vibration into the present (at times a little distorted), but the calculated deviation in technique which implies, first, that the artist who would respond *to* tradition must respond *within* tradition, and, second, that the history of poetry is the violation of technique, not the abandonment of it. For the artist. "Then we remember, whether we would or no." Nostalgia is not, not necessarily, the parasitic enactment of the past for its emotion; but the enactment of a responsibility by the measurement of loss.

The past is a series of half-forgotten particulars, but in Justice's poetry, to what I think is an unusual degree, the observer stands aside from the force of the particulars, not immune to them (because continually establishing relations between them) but curiously detached from their access. It is as if a poet were permitted every intimacy with a speaker except intimacy itself: that is, all the stoic intimacies of knowledge but few of feeling. This may seem exactly the reverse of what we expect when the speaker is the poet himself (the question is, of course, more vexed than I have space to allow, but it should not be made *needlessly* difficult—in almost all poems other than dramatic monologues, the speaking voice represents itself as the poet). On reflection, however, the inadequacy of contemporary poetry may seem to lie in its confidence of feeling (even its representation of feeling) and its absence of a knowledge susceptible to anything outside feeling. The determinism of contemporary poetry demands that feelings be enactments of events, perhaps better the performatives of events; that is why the past in most poems is so often on trial. One of the merits of Justice's poetry lies not in its absence of feeling, but in the withholding of confidence from it. The events which suffer this withholding are permitted a range of insinuation more disturbing because less mediated. At a felt distance, the past cannot be revealed or re-enacted, only rendered (for this reason Justice's exclamations, his characteristic mark of exhausted plangency, seem twice lonely). Such a speaker is unreliable because he will not accede to the conventions of sentiment.

The unreliable narrator provides a convenient transition to Jamesian sentiment: that is, a sentiment established and modified by the intimacies of knowing, the intimacies of detail. That Henry James was a sentimentalist I do not think it necessary to establish, as long as I am speaking of the evidence of the letters rather than of the literature. It was a convenience, and he acceded to it, and whether it was for the sake of his friends or of his mental detachment makes little difference. Justice's poem **"American Scenes (1904-1905)"** is a variant instance where the use of nostalgia is formal—that is, has formal value (in the structure or the development of structure) beyond the entablature of "meaning." I take it as an example of how a mind which finds longing a kind of failing, a mind both superbly aware and superbly devious, may counter the reactionary gestures of nostalgia even while seeming to observe them. The indulgence is the satisfaction of an urge, while the countering marks off the grounds of refusal. This is called having it both ways.

The impersonation of James requires a fidelity to external observation, as well as to the internal tones which are impressed by rhyme and meter (the operations by which poetry establishes its difference from prose, and so the most difficult to set in accord with it). The four sections, the four scenes, which are the emphatic form through which the poem sustains its relation to James' original journey, are mere fragments, the shattered recollections of a shattered sensibility: three pairs of quatrains and a sonnet epilogue. This is enough, as a matter of formal responsibility, to invent the intact sensibility, or as much of the whole as applies.

Many of the phrases in the poem fall, unencumbered or unelaborated, from James' notebooks and from one of the saddest books of American travel, *The American Scene*.

CAMBRIDGE IN WINTER

Immense pale houses! Sunshine just now and snow
Light up and pauperize the whole brave show—
Each fanlight, each veranda, each good address.
All a mere paint and pasteboard paltriness!

These winter sunsets are the one fine thing:
Blood on the snow, one last impassioned fling.
The wild frankness and sadness of surrender—
As if our cities ever could be tender!

(*Notebooks*)

The snow, the sunshine, light up and pauperize all the
wooden surfaces, all the mere paint and pasteboard

paltriness. The one fine thing are the winter sunsets, the
blood on the snow, the pink crystal of the west, the wild
frankness, wild sadness(?)—so to speak—*of the surrender.*

Borrowing is the artificial shell around which an obligation accrues. Here the very ease with which the pilfered phrases are united in the tone guarantees, seems to guarantee, the fidelity of the poem's exhausted, translucent passion, even though in James the passages are neither as richly evocative nor as exclamatory. They are reportorial, professionally engrossed, almost dry—they have leaked into style.

It is the aversion from the original, however, that rescues the richness of feeling beneath James' phrasing. I am reminded of the dramatic placements Shakespeare found for the phrases from Holinshed or North's Plutarch, or of the superb Elizabeth Bishop poem, "From Trollope's Journal," funded on a few spare lines from Trollope's *North America*. The reproduction is the supplement to the original, yet it comes to have original force.

James had written to W.D. Howells, before leaving for America. "I *want* to come, quite pathetically and tragically—it is a passion of nostalgia." Here the meaning balances between old and new, in the passion that once was sickly possession, almost ready to detach itself from the pathology of homesickness to become mere yearning for the past. It was the past James came for—he had not visited America in twenty years. He had turned sixty. And everywhere among his old haunts were the vastations and devastations of two decades of unrelieved commerce. Some of the ancient streets behind Boston's statehouse had been cleared, but the house of his childhood was still present, rich in its recollections. He looked upon it, and a month later, when he returned to look again, it had vanished completely—". . . if I had often seen how fast history could be made I had doubtless never so felt that it could be unmade still faster."

I have lingered over these circumstances for their relevance, not to the minor arrangements of the poem, but to the responsibilities that such arrangements assume. Any negotiation with the past, it should be clear from James, is either a surrender or a recovery—each loss of the richness of the past, each triumph of the tawdry or the commercial, freed James from the material aspect of his nostalgia. And yet the very terms of his analysis, of his distaste, were conditioned by a past irretrievably absent. The rage to recover, the "nostalgic rage" as he called it in another context, is thus cruelly limited in its capacities of analysis—that is its pathos. Its triumph is its refusal merely to surrender to the pleasures of recall. The closing lines of the first three sections of Justice's poem mark his wary regard for this temptation, as well as his refusal of its blandishments: "As if our cities ever could be tender!", "Of open gates, of all but bland abysses," "and the South meanwhile / Has only to be tragic to beguile."

In the sonnet epilogue, Justice finally overtakes James:

> EPILOGUE: CORONADO BEACH, CALIFORNIA
>
> In a hotel room by the sea, the Master
> Sits brooding on the continent he has crossed.
> Not that he foresees immediate disaster,
> Only a sort of freshness being lost—
> Or should he go on calling it Innocence?
> The sad-faced monsters of the plains are gone;
> Wall Street controls the wilderness. There's an immense
> Novel in all this waiting to be done,
> But not, not—sadly enough—by him. His talents,
> Such as they may be, want an older theme,
> One rather more civilized than this, on balance.
> For him now always the consoling dream
> Is just the mild dear light of Lamb House falling
> Beautifully down the pages of his calling.

Except for the penultimate line (*Notebooks*: "the mild still light of dear old L<amb> H<ouse>"), the phrases are now all the poet's, and yet the impersonation is complete, having shifted to a manner detached no less fondly, or fixedly, than James' own erasure or self-effacement as "this victim," "the strayed amateur," "the ancient contemplative person," and especially "the restless analyst," as he variously styled himself through *The American Scene*. These scenes this particular book, and this particular author converge in their attractions for a poet himself drawn into the "nostalgic rage." In a poet past sixty, one may read into this epilogue, "sadly enough," a disavowal, perhaps even a farewell, like Prospero's farewell, to certain ambitions (it must be remembered that Justice's poetry has been rather liberal in such disavowals since his forties). But it is also a recognition of the subjects proper to such a talent, and of the home that has been made in the present, rather than the home that has been surrendered to the past.

The beauty of this epilogue is the manner of its refusal, which may be called the judgment of the observations, while the judgments of the form lie in its deviations from and attachments to tradition. The feminine rhymes, for example, are usually considered a weakness: but here they bind the poem to another modern poem of loss (Bishop's villanelle "One Art," with its main rhymes "master" and "disaster") and prepare the gorgeous lambency of the final couplet. Too, it is the subtlety as well as the frequency of the metrical reversals and the spondaic or anapestic substitutions which establish the emphases and delicacies of tone. In these deviations—permissable deviations though they are—the accord with prose alluded to earlier is reached, where, for the poet as well as the novelist, the past is not succumbed to but regarded, not like a yielding but like an availing.

But there, there again, is that register of innocence being lost. James' demonic eye could not help recording the changes of landscape and manner with the most rectifying precision, even while each notation (at least in the nostalgic landscapes—he had not visited the South or West before) drove him further from the fond memories he had inhabited during his decades in England. Further, or more deeply within them, because however much the past is minutely modified by the present, it is never sufficiently vast to sustain itself as a fiction—those who would pretend otherwise must drive themselves to ever more heroic measures of submission. (What is interesting about the past is not of course its vastness, but the narrow channel of episodes to which our memories reduce it. We are likely to recall, in our indulgence, only what we have recalled before: in the repetitive traffic of scene and event, we worry the same wounds and the same pleasures.)

The more Justice has made the past his subject, the more richly textured and tonal his vocabulary has become.
—*William Logan*

The more Justice has made the past his subject, the more richly textured and tonal his vocabulary has become. This purging of earlier dictions is most acutely evident in the long poem "**Childhood**," which closed his *Selected Poems* (and is dedicated, self-protectively, "to the poets of a mythical childhood—Wordsworth, Rimbaud, Hart Crane, and Alberti").

> Winter mornings now, my grandfather.
> Head bared to the mild sunshine, likes to spread
> The Katzenjammers out around a white lawn chair
> To catch the stray curls of citrus from his knife.
> Chameleons quiver in ambush: wings
> Of monarchs beat above bronze turds, feasting. . .

It is difficult to recapture a visual innocence, but then if something can be recaptured it isn't innocent. The detachment of recollection, which is often illicit, is here explicit in the system of *en face* notes which explain some of the less and most of the more obscure references to Miami in the thirties. The notes create that double world which is the sufficient cause of longing: the modalities of pathos lie in the detachment of the present from the past. The notes are the evidence of the present, but in his admission that a distance exists, and cannot be breached, the thwarted wish becomes the pathos and not the longing itself. Here, I would argue, where nostalgia is no longer a succumbing to, it has become a recovery of. The notes are the "smell of ocean longing landward."

In a poem which reveals the logic of its longing as a structural design, there are apt to be traces or accidents of that longing in the verbal play. It is not, or not just, that the reader is more attuned to such accidents by the structure: but that the divided attention of composition prepares, elicits, such slips or tremulations of reference. "Already / I know the pleasure of certain solitudes," the poet says, and we would be more certain that those pleasures were merely *particular* pleasures if we were not made aware that they might also be *assured* pleasures. Similarly, in the "cool arcades" of the shops:

> O counters of spectacles!—where the bored child
> first
> Scans new perspectives squinting through strange
> lenses. . .

These are "a tray of unsorted eyeglasses"—the notes tell us so. And yet the deposition of the note seems insufficient, in a poem which is one long relation of spectacles, from the world beyond the horizon, the distant world of doomed republics and the nearer one where "Westward now, / The smoky rose of oblivion blooms, hangs" (the Everglades afire), to the circumscribed world of the boy's osteomyelitis: "on my knee a small red sun-glow, setting." This world of suffusions—of the globe's "blur of colors," of the "Myriad tiny suns" that "Drown in the deep mahogany polish of the chairarms," of the "soft glow / Of exit signs," of the horizon afire and the knee's "sun-glow"—suggests the inevitable haze, the partial blur, in which the past exists. It is hardly surprising that when the boy catches sight of himself, he is not quite himself:

> Often I blink, re-entering
> The world—or catch, surprised, in a shop window,
> My ghostly image skimming across nude mannequins.

That blink, that ghostly image shimmering in the divided attention for which the structure has prepared us, is the sign of the present as it imposes itself on the past. There has been in Justice's poetry an increasing recognition—a dawning, perhaps—that there will be no hereby, no chance of alternative, and little of change. In this recognition the character of Justice's work has grown gradually Jamesian: for James, fate was only the accrual of sensibility.

If this withholding is the necessary condition for a nostalgia that eludes sentiment, it acts on itself as a loss of innocence, the loss to which these poems have obsessively returned. Those who have been expelled from the garden of the past are doomed to recall it, and all recollections conditioned by the sin of knowledge must be fictional. And what such sinners recreate in the name of the past will be tainted by their own determining circumstance. (This is the retrospective burden: you cannot analyze without being afflicted by the past: you cannot recreate without being afflicted by the present.)

If the wilderness can never recall the garden without some acknowledgment, some trace or fleck must betray what has come after. I am reminded of James himself, having escaped in the middle of his journey, having taken refuge from the disaster of his visit to Richmond in the drafty recesses of George Washington Vanderbilt's mansion, Biltmore. *The American Scene* scarcely alludes to this week of "deviation"; but, in a letter to his nephew Harry, James describes that misappropriation of energy which attends the attempt to create the past within the present:

> I arrived at this place, last P.M. in a driving snow
> storm (the land all buried, and the dreariness and
> bleakness indescribable), and the first thing that has
> happened to me, alas, has been to have a sharp explosion of gout in my left foot. But I hope to make
> this a *short* business . . .: only the conditions, of vast
> sequestered remoteness and "form," pompous machinery that doesn't *work*, are unfavourable to it:
> huge freezing spaces and fantastic immensities of
> *scale* (from point to point) that have been based on
> a fundamental ignorance of comfort and wondrous
> deludedness . . . as to what *can* be the application of
> a colossal French chateau to life in this irretrievable
> niggery wilderness.

That is what the re-invented Eden will suffer, if created without continual suspicion toward its attraction, even its possibility. The knowledge from which nostalgia must descend is that the substances of the past are always a little tawdry, "Forlorn suburbs, but with golden names". That is the final line of **"Childhood."** To go further, and even perhaps too far, nostalgia requires the wish for religious grace compromised by a religious scrutiny.

Dana Gioia (essay date 1992)

SOURCE: "Tradition and an Individual Talent," in *Can Poetry Matter?: Essays on Poetry and American Culture,* Graywolf Press, 1992, pp. 221-36.

[*In the essay below, Gioia argues that Justice creates an intertextual dialogue in his poetry through his conscious borrowing from and response to other writers.*]

Anyone who reads Donald Justice's poetry at length will eventually note how often his poems seem to originate out of other literary texts. While most poems conduct a conversation with the past—if only by employing a form or genre their audience will recognize—authors, especially Americans, often exert immense effort and ingenuity to disguise their literary antecedents. If poetry grows out of the dialectic between innovation and emulation, our literature has always prized originality over continuity. Originality is, after all, America's one strict tradition.

Donald Justice, however, appears unconcerned about revealing the extent to which his poems rely on the literary tradition. *Departures, Selected Poems, The Sunset Maker*, and *A Donald Justice Reader* all end with "Notes" in which the author identifies the sources of particular poems, including some borrowings that even a sophisticated reader would not have detected. Other poems begin with clearly labeled epigraphs that contain images or phrases used later in the text. Even Justice's titles openly advertise their genealogy: **"Sestina on Six Words by Weldon Kees," "Last Days of Prospero," "After a Phrase Abandoned by Wallace Stevens," "Variations on a Text by Vallejo," "Henry James by the Pacific."** Whereas most writers diligently hide their literary debts, Justice practices what accountants call "full disclosure." In this respect he writes as a historian would, carefully crediting all of his predecessors to acknowledge that scholarship—like literature itself—is a collective enterprise. Justice's meticulous notation not only attests to his integrity as a writer, but it also suggests that his borrowings are a conscious and central aspect of his poetics.

> **Anyone who reads Donald Justice's poetry at length will eventually note how often his poems seem to originate out of other literary texts.**
> —*Dana Gioia*

Until going through all of Justice's published poetry, however, even a careful reader may not realize the full extent and diversity of the author's appropriations. Moreover, such an examination also reveals the surprising fact that Justice's conscious employment of other texts for his own imaginative purposes is not part of an early imitative stage but has increased with each collection. Whereas his first volume, *The Summer Anniversaries* (1960), contains only five poems (out of thirty-two total) that have overt literary sources, Justice's second collection, *Night Light* (1967), includes no less than eleven (out of forty). In *Departures* (1973), the ratio increases with ten out of twenty-nine poems openly drawing material from other literary works. In *Selected Poems* (1979), four of the sixteen previously uncollected poems employ borrowed literary models. (This count does not include the Tremayne poems, which show an oblique debt to Kees's Robinson and Berryman's Henry poems). Finally, in *The Sunset Maker* (1987), not only do nine of the twenty-five poems owe debts to other literary works (three are translations), but the last half of the book constitutes two internally referential sequences of poems, stories, and memoir that borrow and develop material from one another.

I do not claim this census is scientific. Another critic might arrive at a slightly different total or make a convincing argument why a particular poem does or does not belong on the list. But by any count, it appears that at least one quarter of Justice's published poems utilize openly borrowed material—even if it is only something as small as a memorable phrase. His appropriations vary from entire poems (like Attila József's 1927 "O Europe," which Justice rewrote about the American landscape as **"1971"**) to borrowed situations and characters (**"Last Days of Prospero"**). He may steal an opening line (as he did from the beginning of John Peale Bishop's "Ode," which now also starts Justice's **"The Grandfathers"**). He may adopt elements of a poet's style (as in his Guillevic homages) or a particular typographical arrangement (like Hart Crane's use of marginal commentary in *The Bridge*, which found its way into one version of Justice's **"Childhood"** before being revised away). He also has reshaped prose passages into verse while keeping much of the original phrasing, as in **"Young Girls Growing Up (1911),"** which recasts an incident from Kafka's diaries. And sometimes he simply quotes an author in a passing allusion. The sheer diversity of his textual appropriations is not only impressive but unusual, as is his habit of underscoring each debt with a conspicuous epigraph or end-note that heightens the reader's awareness of the transaction. One often reads an allusive author unconscious of his borrowings. Justice, a lifelong teacher, intends his allusions to be recognized—whether the reader is prepared for them or not.

When critics discuss the debt one poem owes to another, they usually analyze the relationship in terms of influence. In understanding the nature of Justice's textual appropriations, however, traditional concepts of influence are not especially helpful. Except for a few early poems influenced by Auden (one of which, **"Sonnet,"** is equal to anything in its model, Auden's "In Time of War"), Justice has always had an identifiable tone and manner. His obsession with formal experimentation and his impatience with writing the same kind of poem for very long have given his work an extraordinary stylistic variety out of proportion with its relatively small size. But his poetic signature remains constant—clarity of expression, relentless economy of means, self-conscious formal design, unpretentious intelligence, and quiet but memorable musicality. Reading his work, one always senses an integrating and independent imagination.

Discussing literary influences, one also looks for the critical relationships between an author and one or two dominant predecessors. Reading Blake, one recognizes the crucial importance of Milton as a model. Studying Baudelaire, one considers his obsessive relationship with Poe. A contemporary writer like William Everson, for example, cannot be understood without constant reference to his lifelong master, Robinson Jeffers. Harold Bloom insists that such dominant influences must be seen in Freudian terms as decisive psychic struggles. In order to become strong and mature, a younger poet must assimilate and then overpower his elder authority figures. Such theories, however, do little to clarify Justice's case. Not only does one not sense any psychic wrestling with his three dominant early masters—Stevens, Baudelaire, and Auden—one also doesn't find much evidence of them in his poems outside of a few deliberate homages. Likewise, the broad range of Justice's borrowings—from T.S. Eliot's prose and Hart Crane's marginalia to Duke Ellington's lyrics and Mother Goose's syntax—makes it impossible to discuss dominant single influences. If Justice is, to use Bloom's term, a "strong poet," one aspect of his strength is the ability to draw from the breadth of world literature.

The one critic who provides a helpful model for Justice's appropriations is T.S. Eliot. In his 1920 essay on the Elizabethan dramatist Philip Massinger, Eliot wrote that one could learn a great deal about a poet by understanding the way in which he borrows:

> Immature poets imitate; mature poets steal; bad poets deface what they take, and good poets make it into something better, or at least something different. The good poet welds his theft into a whole of feeling which is unique, utterly different from that from which it was torn; the bad poet throws it into something which has no cohesion. A good poet will usually borrow from authors remote in time, or alien in language, or diverse in interest.

Except in his conscious homages, Justice does not imitate the styles or employ the thematics of the texts from which he draws material. Instead, like Eliot's mature poet, he steals an image or idea, a phrase or pattern to use in a new imaginative context. In **"Counting the Mad,"** for example, Justice borrowed the meter and syntax of the Mother Goose toe-and-finger counting rhyme, "This little pig went to market." But Justice's poem imitates neither the style nor effect of its source:

> This one was put in a jacket,
> This one was sent home,
> This one was given bread and meat
> But would eat none,
> And this one cried No No No No
> All day long.

> This one looked at the window
> As though it were a wall,
> This one saw things that were not there,
> This one things that were,
> And this one cried No No No No
> All day long.

> This one thought himself a bird,
> This one a dog,
> And this one thought himself a man,
> An ordinary man,
> And cried and cried No No No No
> All day long.

The original nursery rhyme (or at least the most common modern variant, which Justice uses as his model) is playful and intimate—as befitting a verbal and tactile game a mother shares with a small child. By keeping the syntactic pattern of the original more or less intact but substituting shocking new subject matter, Justice achieves the double effect of familiarity and dislocation. The harmless market-day adventures of five childlike pigs become a nightmarish tour of an insane asylum. Significantly, Justice formalizes the idiosyncratic rhythms of the original nursery rhyme into a fixed stanza. Repeating this pattern three times, always ending with the staccato cries of the inmate who "thought himself a man, / An ordinary man," Justice creates a formal feeling of confinement analogous to the mad's physical incarceration. Imaginative literature about insanity often tries to re-create the disjunctive mental processes of the mad. This method tends to create complex imitations of the mad's interior monologue. In **"Counting the Mad,"** however, Justice views the insane from a largely exterior perspective. He reproduces what a visitor would see or hear, and in doing so also reproduces the horror a visitor would feel. The only projection into the interior life of the mad is in the final stanza, where he states the central figure's self-image of normality. Although Justice's subject is potentially complex and unknowable, by using the Mother Goose paradigm he makes the finished poem simple, lucid, and accessible.

"Counting the Mad" also illustrates Eliot's point that good poets improve or transform what they take because Justice's poem is both more ambitious than and different from its model. This sort of appropriation is typical of Justice. He takes something from one context and uses it in another. Reading in a newspaper about "a hatbox of old letters" to be sold at auction, he transformed the item into the elegiac poem **"To the Unknown Lady Who Wrote the Letters Found in the Hatbox."** Finding a striking description in a John D. MacDonald detective novel ("One of those men who can be a car salesman or a tourist from Syracuse or a hired assassin"), Justice—who was then living in Syracuse—expands the passage into a menacing, metaphysical poem, mysterious in ways quite alien to MacDonald. Justice's poem **"The Tourist from Syracuse"** ends:

> Shall I confess who I am?
> My name is all names and none.
> I am the used-car salesman,
> The tourist from Syracuse,
>
> The hired assassin, waiting.
> I will stand here forever
> Like one who has missed his bus—
> Familiar, anonymous—
>
> On my usual corner,
> The corner at which you turn
> To approach that place where now
> You must not hope to arrive.

The way Justice elaborates MacDonald's brief description into an independent poem is characteristic of his creative method. **"The Tourist from Syracuse,"** however, illustrates this intertextual procedure at its simplest. Although Justice's poem achieves a degree of linguistic and intellectual complexity beyond MacDonald's original, it nonetheless bears a paraphrasable resemblance to its prose parent. Justice rarely develops borrowed material in so linear a fashion. Usually his appropriations only provide a point of departure toward an imaginative end unforeshadowed in the original.

More typical of Justice's creative method is his **"After a Phrase Abandoned by Wallace Stevens,"** which bears as its epigraph an eight-word fragment from Stevens's notebook ("The alp at the end of the street"). Justice has revised the poem significantly since its first appearance as a three-part sequence. Its most current version reads in full:

> The alp at the end of the street
> Occurs in the dreams of the town.
> Over burgher and shopkeeper,
> Massive, he broods,
> A snowy-headed father
> Upon whose knees his children
> No longer climb;
> Or is reflected
> In the cool, unruffled lakes of
> Their minds, at evening,
> After their day in the shops,
> As shadow only, shapeless
> As a wind that has stopped blowing.
>
> Grandeur, it seems,
> Comes down to this in the end—
> A street of shops
> With white shutters
> Open for business . . .

This poem does bear a family resemblance to Stevens's work. Justice not only borrows the opening line from his Hartford master. He also employs Stevens's characteristic dialectic between the sublime and quotidian suggested by the borrowed phrase. Moreover, Justice uses some Stevensian stock characters, the burgher and the shopkeeper. But no sooner has Justice established this Stevensian scene in the three opening lines than he liberates the town from the elder poet's metaphysics. The new poem uses the contrast between the cold, primal presence of the mountain and the increasingly self-contained, man-made reality of the village to make points quite alien to Stevens. Justice observes the psychological situation of the townspeople, who have banished the paternal image of nature to the boundaries of their consciousness. He postulates no Stevensian struggle with abstractions of reality. Rather than transforming his observations into the premises of a supreme fiction, Justice accepts the loss of mythic consciousness as a condition of modern life. Justice even celebrates—despite the touch of irony in the last stanza—the functional beauty of the burghers' workaday world. Without mocking Stevens's fixation on the loss of religious faith, Justice quietly moves beyond this late romantic concern to create a poem of contemporary consciousness.

Justice's poem acknowledges Stevens as its precursor. It even initiates a subtle ontological discussion between the younger and the elder poet. But there is no Bloomian struggle for displacement. Rather than the anxiety of influence, Justice displays a characteristic confidence and respectful tolerance. "True poetic history," Bloom has asserted, "is the story of how poets as poets have suffered from other poets, just as any true biography is the story of how anyone suffered his own family—of his own displacement of family into lovers and friends." Justice's example demonstrates the sheer inadequacy of such Freudian theories of poetic influence. As a means of apprehending how Justice works his intertextual appropriations, Bloomian displacement offers no more insight than does the simple theory of imitation. It is more helpful here to expand Eliot's notion of the "mature poet." No anguished rebel, Justice is a thoroughly mature writer—stylistically, intellectually, psychologically. His authorial identity meets its precursors with the self-assurance, independence, and discriminating affection found in a fully developed and healthy psyche.

"After a Phrase Abandoned by Wallace Stevens" also demonstrates the unusual manner in which Justice uses borrowed material to generate new poems. There were several distinctive ways in which quotations from other texts were commonly incorporated into Modernist poems. They were, for example, used as decorative devices, arresting local effects to add interest to the surface of the poem. Although Modernist poetics minimized the notion of decorative language, properly proportioned decoration remained one of its fundamental poetic techniques. Marianne Moore frequently employed striking quotations in this manner, as in, for example, the second stanza of "England." Quotation was also used as an emphatic device to add force or authority to a passage. Ezra Pound habitually inserted classical quotations into his poems to achieve this effect. Emphatic quotation became a central technique for his "Hugh Selwyn Mauberley." Quotation was also used as a contrapuntal device to provide an ironic contrast to other elements in a poem. Eliot borrowed lines of poems, songs, prayers, and nursery rhymes to use contrapuntally in *The Waste Land* and "The Hollow Men." Sometimes an author even used borrowed language architecturally, as Nabokov did in several of his novels, using, for instance, Poe's "Annabel Lee" as a recurring emotional scaffold in *Lolita*.

Although one finds examples of decorative, emphatic, and contrapuntal quotation in Justice's work (**"After a Phrase Abandoned by Wallace Stevens,"** for instance, borrows a decorative phrase from Auden's song "Fish in the unruffled lakes"), Justice's characteristic method is to use quotation as a generative device. He coaxes a new poem out of the unrealized possibilities suggested by a borrowed phrase or image. His Stevens poem proceeds directly from the images and ideas of the fragment. **"The Tourist from Syracuse"** likewise uncovers levels of meaning in MacDonald's phrase beyond the normal depth of the detective genre.

In the work of Pound or Eliot, borrowed quotations usually maintain their original identity despite their new context. Even when they are used ironically, one hears them as foreign words imported into the new text. Their quotation marks, as it were, remain intact. The final text often has the texture of a collage in which borrowed and original materials combine to create a novel effect. But in Justice's work, quoted material usually seems totally assimilated into the new poem. Not only does it no longer seem foreign to the text; the new poem appears to have grown organically and seamlessly out of it. One occasionally sees this generative technique in the early modernists, as in the opening section of Eliot's "Ash-Wednesday," which incorporates a line translated from Cavalcanti ("Because I do not hope to turn again"). But even in "Ash-Wednesday," Eliot ends the passage by returning to emphatic quotation. Having stolen a line to begin his poem, Eliot makes public penance by quoting the end of the "Hail Mary" as a self-standing coda.

Although Justice has appropriated other texts with the imaginative rapacity of an Eliot or a Pound, he has never been much drawn to the techniques of collage. The surfaces of his poems reflect such high polish, his syntax unfolds with such architectural assurance, that one suspects he found the disjunctive energy of high-modernist collage unappealing. Even when he began poems out of chance fragments (as in the aleatory poems in *Departures*), he left them with a seamless finish. Generative quotation has been a technique more com-

patible with his tastes, and no American poet has used it more effectively. When Justice titled his third collection *Departures*, he slyly but self-consciously confessed to this obsession. Stylistically the volume was a departure from his earlier formal work, but the book was also built around a series of poems that began as imaginative departures from other texts, some drawn from literary tradition, others from chance methods. Justice's title signals the author's unabashed reliance on the intertextual play between tradition and innovation. Tradition, to tweak Prof. Bloom one last time, is not a threatening father intimidating creation, but a generative matrix for new poems.

The reason why theories of influence as Romantic rebellion have so little applicability to Justice is that he is essentially a post-modern classicist, a contemporary artist who understands the sustaining power of tradition without seeking to stifle innovation and experiment. "Classicist" and "tradition" have often become code words for aesthetic and political reactionism, but Justice is no traditionalist in the narrow sense. As a poet, critic, and translator, he has assimilated the achievements of international modernism, but he has from the beginning also recognized that his historical position comes after that aesthetic revolution ended. Justice's response to the predicament of the post-modern artist is part of his originality. He fostered no illusions of perpetuating the superannuated avant-garde aesthetic (a temptation that ruined many artists of his generation, especially the composers). Instead, he confronted the burden of the past by exploring and consolidating the enduring techniques of modernism to create a style that reconciled the experiments of the previous two generations with the demands of the present.

A central means of achieving this synthesis was to borrow material and techniques from the major Modernists and determine—in practical poetic terms rather than the abstract critical concepts—what remained viable for the contemporary artist. Eliot, Pound, Stevens, James, Williams, Rilke, Crane, Vallejo, Lorca, Kafka, Rimbaud, Baudelaire, József, Alberti, and others provided the material for experiment. The imaginative mission of consolidating the heritage of modernism also explains why, despite his voracious appropriations, Justice so rarely borrows from earlier writers. With only a handful of exceptions, his appropriations begin chronologically with Baudelaire and Rimbaud, at the start of modern poetry. (And even his use of earlier sources like Dante in **"Hell"** often have an Eliotic or Poundian flavor). Contrasting the chronological range of Justice's allusions and quotations with those of a Pound or Eliot, Kees or Lowell demonstrates how closely focused Justice has been on Modernism.

In someone less talented or self-critical, Justice's allusive method might have proved dangerous. To borrow the words of great writers for inclusion in a new poem forces the reader to compare the new text with the original. Poetry so openly intertextual also risks seeming remote or pedantic, something drawn bloodlessly from books rather than learned firsthand from life. The common complaint of "academic formalism" leveled at members of Justice's generation is inadequate to address either the early work or ultimate accomplishments of poets like Richard Wilbur, Louis Simpson, James Merrill, Donald Hall, William Jay Smith, or Adrienne Rich. Nonetheless there does remain—as often is the case with unfair but enduring criticism—an uncomfortable kernel of truth in that generational stereotype. Some of Justice's contemporaries have produced dully learned and pointlessly self-conscious work. Poets are often scholarly creatures, and much intelligence and learning goes into every genuine poem. But intelligence cannot endow a poem with life in the absence of emotion or imagination. Perhaps a poet can never know too much, but a poem can.

Despite the literary models behind many of his poems, Justice rarely seems bookish. Although subtle in language and sophisticated in technique, his work—except for the overtly experimental pieces in *Departures*—is exemplary in its clarity and accessibility. One always senses the emotional impulse driving the poem (which is frequently a painful sense of loss or, more recently, bittersweet nostalgia), and that intuition clarifies all of the other elements, even when they are complex or deliberately ambiguous. But if Justice's language is often tentative, his poems never display the densely allusive or obscure manner of his teachers, Robert Lowell and John Berryman. His learning is assimilated into the total experience of the poem. One need not know the source of his allusions to understand what they mean in their new context. Even writing about literary subjects such as Henry James or the forgotten poet Robert Boardman Vaughn, Justice remains accessible. In this respect, his work reminds one of the poems of Jorge Luis Borges. Despite their formidable learning, Borges's poems are not difficult, because their intellectual content is always integrated into their imaginative and emotional fabric. Borges might have been speaking for Justice when he said, "I am also living when I dream, when I sleep, when I write, when I read." Reading is a natural part of Justice's poetic process because it is an integral part of his life.

Despite the literary models behind many of his poems, Justice rarely seems bookish.
　　　　　　　　　　　　—*Dana Gioia*

Justice has fulfilled Eliot's challenge in "Tradition and the Individual Talent." He has demonstrated what Eliot called a poet's indispensable "historical sense," the ability to perceive the literary past in order to develop his own contemporary identity. Tradition, Eliot maintained, "cannot be inherited,

and if you want it you must obtain it by great labor." Not every poet is willing to make the effort. Most are content to work within a received (and therefore entropic) idea of tradition. Aside from the sheer excellence of his poetry, Justice's importance comes from his determination to explore and redefine the traditions available to contemporary poets. The Modernists accomplished the task for their generation largely in their prose. Justice, however, has conducted his inquiries almost entirely in verse.

Prefacing *Platonic Scripts*, his only prose collection (which includes more pages of interviews than essays), Justice regrets having written so little criticism. "I see now," he remarks, "that criticism can be of enormous value in helping to define and refine one's own thinking." But even while sharing Justice's regret, one must point out that his poems have performed an important critical function in evaluating the heritage of Modernism. Without ever becoming didactic or dully programmatic, they have clarified the possibilities of contemporary poetry. They are intellectually challenging without losing their emotional force. Although his poems pursue an investigative mission, they never forget that their primary purpose is to be good poetry. They are experimental in the happiest sense—experiments that succeed. His achievement has been to synthesize the diverse strands of Modernism into a powerful, new classical style.

Justice's poetry combines the concentration and energy of Modernism with the clarity and accessibility that typify classical styles. Although the tradition out of which he writes is the Modern movement, his sensibility exhibits the chief features of classicism—unity of design and aim, simplicity of means, clarity of expression, and a governing sense of form, all grounded in an informing tradition. There is also a notable element of restraint, but not in the stereotypical sense of excluding violence and emotion, which classical styles do not do (Beethoven, after all, was the apogee of classicism). Instead, classical styles control and balance emotional energy within a total design. Classicism has never had much good press in America. Our nation prefers the technicolor claims of Romanticism. But classicism is not a single style; rather, it is a sensibility that must in each age reinvent its own means of expression. At its best—which in contemporary art is very rare—classicism can achieve a unique balance of accessibility and profundity, of energy and concentration.

To demonstrate how effectively Justice's style achieves classicism's double aims of simplicity and profundity, we will end by examining **"The Grandfathers."** In this short, early poem Justice had already created a style with an accessible surface and complex subtext. Characteristically, he did this by appropriating another poet's words to create a subtle intertextual argument. **"The Grandfathers"** begins with the opening line of "Ode" by John Peale Bishop (a largely forgotten figure who wrote half a dozen of the best American poems of the twenties and thirties). Here is Justice's poem:

THE GRANDFATHERS

Why will they never sleep?
John Peale Bishop

Why will they never sleep,
The old ones, the grandfathers?
Always you find them sitting
On ruined porches, deep
In the back country, at dusk,
Hawking and spitting.
They might have sat there forever,
Tapping their sticks,
Peevish, discredited gods.
Ask the lost traveler how,
At road-end, they will fix
You maybe with the cold
Eye of a snake or a bird
And answer not a word,
Only these blank, oracular
Headshakes or headnods.

On a narrative level **"The Grandfathers"** is a descriptive poem about taciturn country elders, the sort of old men one might observe while traveling backwoods roads. Read as a realistic lyric examining archetypical figures of American folklore, **"The Grandfathers"**—with its quirky irregular rhyme scheme and sharp images—is a haunting poem. Aside from compliments, it does not appear to need much commentary. But if one goes back to its source, Bishop's "Ode," one finds an unexpected poem, which begins:

Why will they never sleep
Those great women who sit
Peering at me with parrot eyes?
They sit with grave knees; they keep
Perpetual stare; and their hands move
As though hands could be aware—
Forward and back, to begin again—
As though on tumultuous shuttles of wind they wove
Shrouds out of air.

Bishop's poem describes a frightening vision of the three Fates, who become symbols for a tragic pagan worldview. The three sisters serve as horrific reminders of man's mortality and the transience of human accomplishment. Bishop has no protection from them because his Christian faith, with its promise of salvation and resurrection, is dead. "Ode" ends:

There was One who might have saved
Me from the grave dissolute stones

And parrot eyes. But He is dead,
Christ is dead. And in a grave
Dark as a sightless skull He lies
And of His bones are charnels made.

Returning to **"The Grandfathers"** after studying Bishop's poem of existential dread, one sees a different text. What seemed like a macabre but naturalistic lyric now also reads as a densely metaphorical examination of how religious anxiety persists even after the religion itself has died. One now notices, for instance, the ambiguity of reference for "they" in the opening line. Does it refer to "the grandfathers," as one might initially have assumed, or to "The old ones," or to something else left unstated (such as the "they" in Bishop's original, quoted in the epigraph)? One also notes that the grandfathers themselves may not be as entirely literal as they as first appeared. These ancient figures consistently operate on both a realistic and metaphorical level. Continuing through the poem, the reader now finds that many of the seemingly realistic details also have sinister, religious meanings. If they are indeed divinities, Justice's "old ones," those "Peevish, discredited gods," may indeed "have sat there forever." Two carefully elaborated levels of meaning coexist in the poem, each becoming a metaphor for the other. On a realistic level, **"The Grandfathers"** is a study of malign but impotent backcountry elders; on the intertextual and metaphorical level, it describes the silent but troubling gods who still haunt the modern psyche. Characteristically, Justice designs the poem so it can be read satisfyingly on the first level alone, but he also creates a mythic subtext that can be understood only by reference to the poem's source. Justice's headnote from Bishop, therefore, isn't only an acknowledgment of the poet's borrowing; it is also a necessary clue to the poem's tradition, which includes not only Bishop's "Ode" but other Modernist poems about the death of religion.

Poems like **"The Grandfathers"** demonstrate the centrality of textual appropriation to Justice's aesthetic. Without understanding the intertextual complexity of his work, one cannot fully read his poems. Placing Justice in his own self-defined Modernist tradition and appreciating the hidden complexity of his sometimes deceptively simple classical style, however, reveals a profound and challenging poet. He has shown that Modernism remains a living tradition for artists strong enough to approach it with imagination and independence.

Robert Richman (review date June 1993)

SOURCE: "Intimations of Inadequacy," in *Poetry*, Vol. CLXII, No. 3, June, 1993, pp. 160-66.

[Below, Richman argues that in Justice's poetry form takes precedence over subject matter.]

Donald Justice is one of our most reticent poets. He may very well be the most reticent poet of his generation—the generation of Richard Wilbur, Anthony Hecht, Louis Simpson, Adrienne Rich, and the late Howard Nemerov. For Justice is even more sparing in output than the notoriously slow-working and slow-to-publish Hecht. "I'm not all that much for increasing the world's population of poems," Justice once said in an interview. Of his four books of all original material—*The Summer Anniversaries* (1960), *Night Light* (1967), *Departures* (1973), and *The Sunset Maker* (1987)—two were fifty-two pages or less. (A 137-page *Selected Poems*, containing seventeen new poems, came out in 1979.) No wonder Justice's 171-page *Reader*, which has seven previously uncollected poems, is as slender as it is.

Justice has been equally restrained with his prose. This too sets him apart from the poets of his generation, who are, for the most part, a critically garrulous bunch. Justice's lone prose volume, *Platonic Scripts* (1984), contains six essays, seven interviews, and ten pages of extracts from a notebook. The *Reader* doesn't exactly ameliorate the situation. The book's prose selections—three essays, two stories, and a memoir of Justice's Miami childhood—are superb, but one yearns for more.

One essay omitted from the *Reader* is the one on his late friend, Henri Coulette. This essay, which was co-written by Robert Mezey, served as an introduction to the 1990 edition of Coulette's *Collected Poems*. This omission is unfortunate because Justice and Coulette are kindred spirits. Both poets, as Justice said about himself in a 1970 interview, seek to "displace the self from the poem—not to remove it entirely, but to displace it, in some degree." In Coulette's work, the displaced self gives way to other selves—actors, double agents, and Jews destined for death camps—who speak for the absent poet. In Justice's case, the standbys are writers, mostly poets.

The writers on whom Justice relies, however, seldom speak in monologues, as do the selves in Coulette's poems. Instead, the words Justice borrows are assimilated into poems that seem to be spoken in Justice's voice. His borrowings from César Vallejo, Weldon Kees, Wallace Stevens, Rilke, Catullus, Baudelaire, Mallarmé, Thomas Wolfe, Henry James, Somerset Maugham, and others are openly acknowledged in titles, epigraphs, and notes.

Justice once observed in an interview that when reading Robert Browning, the master of the dramatic monologue, "you know clearly and definitely it's not Browning talking, and the poem is the better for it . . . [nowadays there is an] unacknowledged confusion of a poet with narrator." Justice continued:

> Aren't you surprised how easy it seems to be to assimilate a great multitude and variety of experience which others have spared us the necessity of acquiring for ourselves, and not only to assimilate but to write about. . . . If you develop . . . a great affection for Chekhov, say . . . then you can invent for yourself Chekhovian characters or situations or even borrow passages from things he wrote and treat them as if they were your own, almost your own. . . . You could feel that way about a hundred others, too, and master their experience as well simply by turning the pages.

Even though Justice abjures dramatic monologues that imaginatively freed poets like Browning and Coulette, the writers' words that Justice "treats as his own" are needed for the same reason: to unchain his imagination. Justice admits his handicap: "neither suffering nor exaltation . . . leads to poetry, at least not for me," Justice writes in the essay **"Bus Stop: Or, Fear and Loneliness on Potrero Hill."** Or, as he writes in **"Variations on a Text in Vallejo":** "When I took out this paper and began to write, / Never before had anything looked so blank, / My life, these words, the paper, the gray Sunday."

None of this is meant to imply that Justice isn't moved by the things of the world. Hardly; but when it comes to consigning those emotions to the page, he often needs the bits and scraps of perfected language to get him going. No doubt there are times when Justice responds without assistance to reality's often paralyzing realm, but if the poems are any proof—**"Sestina on Six Words by Weldon Kees," "Variations on a Theme from James," "After a Phrase Abandoned by Wallace Stevens," "Homage to the Memory of Wallace Stevens"** (in which he writes: "Now all quotations from the text apply, / Including the laughter, including the offstage thunder, / Including even this almost human cry")—he'd just as soon rely on books. Much the way Virgil led Dante, Justice likes to be guided, by his many literary betters, through the inferno of the poem.

Justice, who usually writes in meter and rhyme, claims that his main interest in poetry is form. Although subject-matter is not unimportant, it is a secondary consideration. This would make Justice an Old rather than a New Formalist, since poets of the latter camp emphasize subject-matter over form. "Sincerity," he writes in an essay on Baudelaire, "is saying what the form obliges you to say regardless of whether or not you believe it." No wonder, as Justice notes in the same piece, that a poet's "pose" may paradoxically "be sincere." The sincere poet, Justice writes, "becomes a performer, a charlatan, a great pretender; art is artifice. What he has to be sincere about is his art." Justice would agree with Picasso's remark, "We all know that art is not truth. Art is a lie that makes us realize truth."

It comes as no surprise to learn that as a young man Justice studied the most abstract of the arts, music. From the beginning Justice has been skeptical of a naively mimetic poetry. The difference between poetry and music, of course, is that music is quite forthright about its inability to reproduce physical reality. Poetry, on the other hand, with its seemingly referential statements and images, suggests a closer relationship to reality than it actually possesses.

Justice likes to remind readers of the distance between poetry and life. One way he does this is to write artificially—to use meters. "Like the odd mustaches and baggy pants of the old comedians," Justice writes in the essay **"Meters and Memory,"** meters "put us on notice that we are at a certain distance from the normal rules and expectations of life." Another way to point out the poem's distance from reality is to divulge its literary origins. One more way to show how far poems are from life is to use imagery that suggests it. Justice isn't above a flagrantly self-reflexive remark, like "the *the* has become an *a*" (in **"Homage to the Memory of Wallace Stevens"**). Usually, though, Justice's poems live a double life—as a commentary on life, and as a commentary on the poem's status as a nettlesome aesthetic object.

One poem that leads this kind of double life is **"Children Walking Home from School through Good Neighborhood."** It seems, at any rate, that the "good neighborhood" through which the children walk exists not only in the real cities and towns of our experience, but on the page, as well: a tranquil aesthetic "neighborhood" that is even more serene than the one it evokes:

> They are like figures held in some glass ball,
> One of those in which, when shaken, snowstorms occur;
> But this one is not yet shaken.
>   And they go unaccompanied still,
> Out along this walkway between two worlds,
> This almost swaying bridge.
>   October sunlight checkers their path;
> It frets their cheeks and bare arms now with shadow
> Almost too pure to signify itself.
> And they progress slowly, somewhat lingeringly,
> Independent, yet moving all together,
> Like polyphonic voices that crisscross
> In short-lived harmonies.
>
>   Today, a few stragglers.
> One, a girl, stands there with hands spaced out, so—

> A gesture in a story. Someone's school notebook spills,
> And they bend down to gather up the loose pages.
> (Bright sweaters knotted at the waist; solemn expressions.)
> Not that they would shrink or hold back from what may come,
> For now they all at once run to meet it, a little swirl of colors,
> Like the leaves already blazing and falling farther north.

This poem is the last word in formal polish and grace, but how well does its image of quiet tranquility reflect reality? Not all that well, at least not in Justice's view. Hence his wish to self-reflexively question the mimetic accuracy of an image that appears to be a by-product of the search for formal perfection. The questioning starts with the first line's *held*, which here means, not just *borne*, but *imprisoned*; aptly, for what is being held hostage in the poem's beautiful but inanimate prison is a group of living children. It would appear, at any rate, that the first stage of this poem's composition involved formally following through the initial motivation or spark, and the second stage involved disavowing the posing-as-real images that the heedless aesthetic imagination had wrought.

Not all of the poem's self-reflexive images are so critical of the poem's mimetic claims. For instance, the lines, "And they go unaccompanied still, / Out along this walkway between two worlds," appear to suggest that the children move, not only between the "two worlds" of childhood and adulthood, but between the "two worlds" of art and life, as well. Also not overtly critical are the lines, "Independent, yet moving all together, / Like polyphonic voices that crisscross / In short-lived harmonies," which could conceivably describe both the children and the lines of the poem. Also uncritical is the image of the girl whose movement is described as "a gesture in a story." (Her gesture exists in two stories: Justice's and hers.) Although none of these images casts a shadow on the poem's ability to reflect reality the way *held* does, they do remind us that poetry is as much on Justice's mind as reality.

Also curious is the image of the snowstorm that doesn't occur because the glass ball "is not yet shaken." This seems to suggest that it is wrong to grant the reality's "storms," especially its emotional storms, access into the poem. For allowing these "storms" into posing-as-real poems diminishes and dilutes them. **"First Death,"** a poem about the death of the poet's grandmother, is stripped of strong emotions, one senses, because Justice doesn't want them taking part in the counterfeit life of the poem. It is this counterfeit life that Justice wants to keep us apprised of by means of the self-reflexive images.

Once one knows to keep an eye out for them, Justice's self-reflexive cues pop up everywhere. When he writes, in **"Sonnet to My Father,"** that he is "leaving this likeness only in [his dead father's] place," it is unclear whether "likeness" refers to the poet or to the poem. And in **"Poem,"** Justice writes that the poem in question is "not sad, really, only empty." And in the first section of **"American Scenes (1904-1905)"** (which Justice tells us is culled from James's *Notebooks*), the poet writes: "Each fanlight, each veranda, each good address, / All a mere paint and pasteboard paltriness!" These self-reflexive images are much like the admissions of borrowings in other poems: intimations of inadequacy that this intensely conscientious poet must impart.

In **"Thinking about the Past,"** the poet chides himself for attempting to preserve those moments of the past that will, as he writes, "never change, nor stop being." For to seize the past in verse reduces its vanished abundance to words, all "fixed into place now," as Justice writes, "all rhyming with each other":

> Certain moments will never change, nor stop
> being—
> My mother's face all smiles, all wrinkles soon;
> The rock wall building, built, collapsed then,
> fallen;
> Our upright loosening downward slowly out of
> tune—
> All fixed into place now, all rhyming with each
> other.
> That red-haired girl with the wide mouth—
> Eleanor—
> Forgotten thirty years—her freckled shoulders,
> hands,
> The breast of Mary Something, freed from a white
> swimsuit,
> Damp, sandy, warm; or Margery's, a small, caught
> bird—
> Darkness they rise from, darkness they sink back
> toward.
> O marvellous early cigarettes! O bitter smoke,
> Benton . . .
> And Kenny in wartime whites, crisp, cocky,
> Time a bow bent with his certain failure.
> Dusks, dawns; waves; the ends of songs . . .

In **"Cinema and Ballad of the Great Depression,"** meanwhile, Justice likens the economic indignity of men with the indignity of having been transformed into a lifeless aesthetic object: "We had become a line somehow," gripes the poem's speaker.

In **"Mrs. Snow,"** however, the memory is vivid, the poetic rendering doesn't vex Justice all that much, and the poem is free of self-reflexive omens:

> Busts of the great composers glimmered in niches,
> Pale stars. Poor Mrs. Snow, who could forget her,
> Counting the time out in that hushed falsetto?
> (How early we begin to grasp what kitsch is!)
> But when she loomed above us like an alp,
> We little towns below could feel her shadow.
> Somehow her nods of approval seemed to matter
> More than the stray flakes drifting from her scalp.
> Her etchings of ruins, her mass-production Mings
> Were our first culture: she put us in awe of things.
> And once, with her help, I composed a waltz,
> Too innocent to be completely false,
> Perhaps, but full of marvellous clichés.
> She beamed and softened then.
>   Ah, those were the days.

But just as often the past is fading from view, not coming into focus.

And yet, as alert as Justice is to the representational failings of poetry, and as much as this reticent poet seems to flirt at times with total silence, he never quite washes his hands of poetry. One reason, certainly, as he himself has suggested, is the many formal rewards of verse. It could be argued, in fact, that each poem is a kind of hopeful formal rejoinder to the painful knowledge, expressed in the content, of its many representational shortcomings:

> We shall not ever meet them bearded in heaven,
> Nor sunning themselves among the bald of hell;
> If anywhere, in the deserted schoolyard at twilight,
> Forming a ring, perhaps, or joining hands
> In games whose very names we have forgotten.
> Come, memory, let us seek them there in the
> shadows.
>   ON THE DEATH OF FRIENDS IN CHILD-
> HOOD

But beyond the strictly formal excellence of Justice's work, there is the added marvel of one poet's unrelenting honesty about the boundaries and limitations of art. Donald Justice is one of our finest poets.

FURTHER READING

Criticism

Gioia, Dana, and William Logan, editors. *Certain Solitudes: Essays on the Poetry of Donald Justice.* University of Arkansas Press, 1997: 288 p.

> Laudatory overview of the author's career as a poet and educator.

Hirsch, Edward. "Heroes and Villanelles." *New York Times Book Review* (23 August 1987): 20.
Reviews *The Sunset Maker* and describes Justice as an "elegiac poet" and a "scrupulous tactician of melancholy and loss."

Kirby, Donald. "Refined Craftsman." *American Book Review* 15, No. 1 (April-May 1993): 26.
Reviews *A Donald Justice Reader,* focusing on theme and Justice's place in contemporary American poetry.

Leithauser, Brad. "Getting Things Right," *New York Review of Books* XLIII, No. 14, (19 September 1996): 49-50, 52.
A review of New and Selected Poems in which Leithauser claims that the collection reflects the solid work and skill of Justice's career and that the new poems continue to impress.

Nemerov, Howard. A review of *The Summer Anniversaries,* by Donald Justice. *American Scholar* 29, No. 4 (Autumn 1960): 578.
Describes the principal subject of Justice's poems as "the journey from innocence to experience."

St. John, David. "Scripts and Water, Rules and Riches." *The Antioch Review* 43, No. 3 (Summer 1985): 309-19.
Remarks on the importance of "technical virtue" in Justice's poetry.

Turco, Lewis. "The Progress of Donald Justice." *The Hollins Critic* XXIX, No. 4 (October 1992): 1-7.
Provides a brief survey of Justice's writings, covering the major themes and stylistic development evident in each of his collections.

"Donald Justice Special Feature." *Verse* 8 and 9, Nos. 3 and 1 (Winter-Spring 1992): 3-72.
Collection of essays and other material centering on the work of Donald Justice.

Wright, Charles. "Homage to the Thin Man." *Southern Review* 30, No. 4 (Autumn 1994): 741-44.
Describes Justice as a "contemporary master whose public ink is nowhere near his poetic achievement."

Interview

Fitz Gerald, Gregory, and William Heyen. "Falling into Place: A Conversation with Donald Justice." Edited by Philip L. Gerber and Robert J. Gemmett. *Prairie Schooner* XLVII, No. 4 (Winter 1973-74): 317-24.
Discussion of theme, style, and voice in Justice's poetry.

Additional coverage of Justice's life and career is contained in the following sources published by Gale Research: *Contemporary Authors,* **Vols. 5-8R;** *Contemporary Authors New Revision Series,* **Vols. 26, 54;** *Dictionary of Literary Biography Yearbook,* **1983; and** *DISCovering Authors Modules: Poets.*

Christopher Lasch
1932-1994

American social critic, historian, essayist, and professor.

The following entry presents an overview of Lasch's career through 1995.

INTRODUCTION

A historian and social critic, Lasch was a controversial and often misunderstood theorist of contemporary American culture. Speaking from a position generally sympathetic to the intellectual left, he united political radicalism and social conservatism in his disturbing but thought-provoking analyses of American society, which he viewed as increasingly bureaucratic, consumption-oriented, and politically driven by a "new," elite economic class. His works—including *The New Radicalism in America* (1965), *The Culture of Narcissism* (1977), and *The True and Only Heaven* (1991)—examine how late nineteenth-century capitalism, progressivism, and the consequent social problems of that era evolved during the twentieth century, and demonstrate how traditional institutions and values have been dismantled and replaced by confusion and despair. Although his thought generated strong disagreement as often as high approbation from both rightist and leftist critics, most agree that Lasch brought a fresh perspective to the debate about the American cultural crisis at the end of the twentieth century. Jean Bethke Elshtain has observed: "Christopher Lasch was a man of grace who found much of late modernity graceless; a man of wit who found much of our politics witless; a man of purpose who lamented our culture's frenetic purposelessness; a man of hope who saw in boundless optimism a deep despair."

Biographical Information

Lasch was born June 1, 1932, in Omaha, Nebraska, to Robert and Zora Lasch, a journalist and philosophy professor, respectively. Little is known about his childhood and adolescence until his entrance into Harvard University in 1950, where he was novelist John Updike's roommate. Lasch received a B.A. degree in history in 1954, after which he enrolled at Columbia University for postgraduate studies, earning his master's degree in 1955 and a Ph.D. degree in 1961. While he pursued his doctoral studies, he taught history at Williams College, Columbia, and Roosevelt University and published a number of essays on historical trends in American culture and politics. As a history professor during the 1960s, first at the University of Iowa and later at Northwestern University, Lasch wrote *The American Liberals and the Russian Revolution* (1962), *The New Radicalism in*

America, and *The Agony of the American Left* (1969). In 1970 Lasch accepted an appointment as professor of history at the University of Rochester, where he stayed for the remainder of his life. Following the publication of *The World of Nations* (1973) and *Haven in a Heartless World* (1977), Lasch gained national attention with the best-selling *The Culture of Narcissism*, which received an American Book Award in current interest in 1980. That year, he delivered the Freud Lectures at University College in London. Lasch wrote three more books—*The Minimal Self* (1984), *The True and Only Heaven,* and the posthumously published *Revolt of the Elites and the Betrayal of Democracy* (1995)—before he died of cancer on February 14, 1994.

Major Works

The American Liberals and the Russian Revolution, based in part on Lasch's doctoral dissertation, argues that a blind faith in progress obscured the distressing effects of the communist revolution in Russia in 1917 and suggests that similar consequences await the unrestrained optimism found in modern American liberalism. *The New Radicalism in America* identifies in a series of biographical sketches the early twentieth-century foundations of a socially aware radicalism, tracing its development through mid-century as a force for social and political reform that ultimately produced the American welfare state. These themes emerge again in *Haven in a Heartless World,* which suggests that the industrial revolution produced ideological justifications for state interference in private, family life. *The Agony of the American Left,* comprising five essays on populism, socialism, black power, and students' rights, describes how post-World War I radicalism had co-opted progressive ideology, which has diluted radicalism's political influence. *The World of Nations,* divided into "The Limits of Liberal Reform," "Alternatives to Liberalism," and "The So-Called Post-Industrial Society," contains eighteen essays and book reviews published between 1958 and 1972. Lasch turned from considered aspects of modern society to focus on the modern individual in his next book. *The Culture of Narcissism* examines contemporary narcissism, a personality structure characterized by self-absorption and a stern superego, and analyzes historical and cultural patterns to account for its widespread emergence during the latter half of the twentieth century. *The Minimal Self,* a sequel to *The Culture of Narcissism,* clarifies argumentative points made in the previous book by analyzing the ethic of "survivalism" and radical feminism. Returning to criticism of liberalism, *The True and Only Heaven* rejects the modern ideology of progress in favor of petty-bourgeois values and an acceptance of limits without despair, or "hope." *The Revolt of the Elites* discusses the differences between populism and contemporary "communitarianism" in terms of changes in late twentieth-century capitalism.

Critical Reception

Elshtain has remarked that Lasch "was better at putting the questions than at providing the answers," and most critical commentary on his works has made similar conclusions. As a radical historian in his early career, "his trenchant analysis of modern liberal and radical ideology made Lasch a darling of the New Left," observed Steven Watts. The critical reception of Lasch's social criticism since 1975, however, has been marked by contention and controversy, mainly since his "commentary has defied confident ideological categorization," according to Watts. Watts also has noted that Lasch's "social criticism has raised as many angry rebuttals from ostensible allies on the Left as from evident targets on the Right. . . . Misunderstood more than any other contemporary critic, he has been praised and condemned for all the wrong reasons." Rightist critics generally have endorsed Lasch's writing for upholding traditional values, while leftist critics have accused him of betraying the liberal cause. Some commentators have faulted Lasch's books for lacking humor and assuming a tone of self-righteousness; others have responded to his treatment of gender issues and the cultural meaning of feminine with cries of "authoritarian" and "hal-

lucinatory." Economists also have noticed the vagueness of Lasch's agenda for a return to small-scale production in the face of global competition, questioning its practicality. But Watts has concluded: "The fact that [Lasch] has mystified and infuriated so many only supports the suspicion that he must be on to something."

PRINCIPAL WORKS

The American Liberals and the Russian Revolution (history) 1962
The New Radicalism in America, 1889-1963: The Intellectual as a Social Type (history) 1965
The Agony of the American Left (essays) 1969
The World of Nations (essays) 1973
Haven in a Heartless World: The Family Besieged (social criticism) 1977
The Culture of Narcissism: American Life in an Age of Diminishing Expectations (social criticism) 1977
The Minimal Self: Psychic Survival in Troubled Times (social criticism) 1984
The True and Only Heaven: Progress and Its Critics (social criticism) 1991
The Revolt of the Elites and the Betrayal of Democracy (social criticism) 1995

CRITICISM

Joseph Voelker (review date Spring 1986)

SOURCE: A review of *The Minimal Self,* in *Southwestern Humanities Review,* Spring, 1986, pp. 181-83.

[*In the following review, Voelker compares the themes of* The Minimal Self *to those of* The Culture of Narcissism, *concluding that, while* The Minimal Self *"seems guilty of the same cultural shallowness it sees around it," the book has "occasional sharp observations."*]

There is something meretricious in the title to Christopher Lasch's sequel to his often precise and powerful *The Culture of Narcissism.* A reader unacquainted with Lasch's work who comes across a book sub-titled "Psychic Survival in Troubled Times" is likely to mistake it for a success manual—one of those hot-selling cynical paeans to the very "minimalism" Lasch decries. "Meretricious" is perhaps too strong a term for what is wrong with the rest of *The Minimal Self.* Lasch works in an impressionistic field, extrapolating cultural observation from psychoanalytic terminology, and in *The Culture of Narcissism* he brought a degree of rigor to the application of a much-used word. "Narcissism," Lasch insisted, is not self-love but love rejected that turns back toward the self as hatred. His was a timely reminder that we are not well-served as historians or clinicians when we apply "Narcissism" loosely to all contemporary forms of selfishness. Critics of Narcissism, he wrote,

> fail to explore any of the character traits associated with pathological Narcissism, which in less extreme forms appear in such profusion in the everyday life of our age: dependence on the vicarious warmth provided by others combined with a fear of dependence, a sense of inner emptiness, boundless repressed rage, and unsatisfied oral cravings. Nor do they discuss what might be called the secondary characteristics of Narcissism: pseudo self-insight, calculating seductiveness, nervous, self-deprecatory humor.... For these critics, Narcissism remains at its loosest a synonym for selfishness and at its most precise a metaphor, and nothing more, that describes the state of mind in which the world appears as a mirror of the self.

The only test of the accuracy of a psychoanalytic explanation of cultural tendencies is impressionistic, of course, but *The Culture of Narcissism*'s portrait of the typal personality of our era rang true. Americans of the 1980s do seem trapped in a landscape of insubstantial images, incapable of emotional investment, driven by motives shaped by commercial forces, slavishly respondent to "therapeutic" forms of authority, excessively reliant upon a detached and superficial self-irony.

In comparison, *The Minimal Self* rings hollow. One is generous to credit the book with a thesis. What it has is a rhetoric—a recurrent tone—the loose principle that often yokes the materials of a sequel together. The rhetorical position of *The Minimal Self* is that things are even worse than we thought. Not only is the American soul Narcissistic, it is shrinking. Lasch has always been fond of the catalog of horrors as a device for delighting himself and certain readers with a delicious sense of malaise and impending catastrophe. That rhetorical technique was much in evidence in *The Culture of Narcissism*:

> Today almost everyone lives in a dangerous world from which there is little escape. International terrorism and blackmail, bombings, and hijackings arbitrarily affect the rich and poor alike. Crime, violence, and gang wars make cities unsafe and threaten to spread to the suburbs. Racial violence on the streets and in the schools creates an atmosphere of chronic tensions and threatens to erupt at any time into full scale racial conflict. Unemploy-

ment spreads from the poor to the white-collar class, while inflation eats away the savings of those who hoped to retire in comfort.

It is clearly in the direst catalogs in *The Culture of Narcissism* that the seeds of its sequel were scattered. But in *The Minimal Self,* Lasch's rhetoric achieves its culmination in the millennial utterance:

> People have lost confidence in the future. Faced with an escalating arms race, an increase in crime and terrorism, environmental deterioration, and the prospect of long-term economic decline, they have begun to prepare for the worst, sometimes by building fallout shelters and laying in provisions, more commonly by executing a kind of emotional retreat from the long-term commitments that presuppose a stable, secure, and orderly world.

There is something forcedly hysterical about Lasch when he catalogs reasons for us to be anxious. As Barbara Tuchman has so popularly demonstrated, every age has its terrors. In reading in early Tudor literature, I have repeatedly run into the Turkophobia that infected western Europe in the sixteenth century, when children crawled into bed at night, terrified that a man in women's pants would come in the window, his scimitar gleaming under a crescent moon. True, the Turk might have overrun Europe, and we may die in a nuclear holocaust. But Lasch underestimates people's capacity to carry on with their emotional lives in the meantime.

Besides reiterating its fundamental observation of a collective emotional jettisoning of ethical ideals and altruistic norms, *The Minimal Self* updates Lasch's earlier work by noticing a paradoxical consequence of Narcissism. The Narcissistic self, in its need to deny its dependency, acts in contradictory ways—at one time asserting absolute independence from others, at another longing for ecstatic union, either of which serves to deny autonomy to all that is outside the self. An engaging insight, it unfortunately allows Lasch to cast too broad a net. What action or gesture cannot be classified as an expression of the desire for either union or autonomy? What action or gesture is not a consequence of Narcissism? Like Freudian denial, Narcissism becomes suspect because it accounts both for "P" and "not P."

Thus there is an excessive inclusiveness in *The Minimal Self. The Culture of Narcissism* was certainly expansive. It pursued its central insight across the major arenas of contemporary American life—schooling, the family, sports, sexual relations. *The Minimal Self* is not so much expansive as diffuse. It opens in an engaging series of observations of mass culture that see the electronic revolution as exchanging the solidity of earlier materialistic culture for a fantasy world of ephemeral images. Two chapters on survivalism follow, one of them a string of deeply unnecessary utterances on the Nazi holocaust followed by an assertion of its inappropriateness as a metaphor for everyday life. There is then a chapter on minimalism as a philosophical premise behind the cold, disengaged quality of postwar art and fiction, and three chapters on neo-Freudianism that seem at times to have a wholly internecine agenda, tenuously connected to the subject of the great hunkering-down Lasch sees in contemporary culture.

On the whole, *The Minimal Self* seems guilty of some of the same cultural shallownesses it sees around it. It is at best a ransackable book, where the devotee of Christopher Lasch will be pleased with occasional sharp observations.

Godfrey Hodgson (review date 27 January 1991)

SOURCE: "Liberalism Takes a Licking," in *Los Angeles Times Book Review*, January 27, 1991, pp. 2, 11.

[*In the highly positive review of* The True and Only Heaven *below, Hodgson discusses the book's critique of the ideology of progress and some strategies used by Lasch.*]

From the New Deal until the 1970s, liberalism in all its variants was the public philosophy of the United States. And what brought together a whole coalition of interests, classes and temperaments under the banners of liberalism was a shared belief in the idea, indeed the ideology of progress.

Since the 1970s, with bewildering speed, liberalism has been rudely unseated from that position of hegemony. This is not just a swing of the political pendulum, or of shifting fashions in graduate schools, publishing houses and the editorial pages of newspapers. Liberalism, once arrogantly confident of its solutions for all manner of problems, has turned defensive, and all its enemies have been on the attack.

The most familiar assaults, of course, come from the various tribes of conservatives. Christopher Lasch, the historian and long an adherent of the American Left, does not march under any of their banners. Instead, in this difficult but learned and subtle—perhaps too subtle—book [*The True and Only Heaven*], he digs down to the philosophical foundations of liberalism, and exhumes a whole cluster of rival traditions that always have challenged the liberal assumptions.

At the heart of the liberal tradition, says Lasch, is the idea, the ideology of progress. In its origins in the 18th-Century Enlightenment, this was the noble doctrine of the perfectibility of man and his institutions. At the height of Victorian confidence, liberals saw no contradiction between moral and material progress, and sought to bring the whole world the blessings both of Protestant Christianity and of capitalism. But in the late 20th Century, the liberal idea coarsened until liberals often confused the ideal of progress with the pursuit of economic growth.

In form, therefore, Lasch's book is an essay on the history of ideas, an analytic catalogue of the chief successive enemies of the idea of progress. In the beginning, the idea of infinite progress and perfectibility ran counter to the grand tradition of republicanism, or "civic humanism," as Lasch names it, that traces back through Rousseau, Montesquieu and James Harrington to Machiavelli, whose concepts of "virtue" and "fortune" embodied an awareness of limits that was the antithesis of the liberal confidence in progress.

> In form . . . , Lasch's book [*The True and Only Heaven*] is an essay on the history of ideas, an analytic catalogue of the chief successive enemies of the idea of progress.
> —*Godfrey Hodgson*

Then Lasch looks at a whole series of ideas and traditions in European and American thought that militated against the all-conquering power of progress. There was nostalgia for a Golden Age in the past, whether it was the Arcadian idyll that haunted the Renaissance imagination, the idealized Middle Ages of the pre-Raphaelites or the gentrified Frontier of James Fenimore Cooper.

There was the ideal of "community"—*Gemeindschaft* as opposed to *Gesellschaft*, mere "society" without the communal bonds of obligation and duty—held out by Toennies, Max Weber and the other founders of sociology. And there was the long, stern line of 19th-Century prophets who denounced the false gods of progress, from Thomas Carlyle thundering forth his denunciations of Mammon worship amid the coalsmoke fogs of Victorian London to Emerson and William James in a Boston that felt its puritan heritage just as much threatened by the accelerating machines of the Gilded Age as were its banks by the triumph of New York.

And so Lasch leads the reader on, sure-footedly negotiating the intellectual bogs and potholes of the late 19th- and early 20th-Century Left, never losing sight of the bearing he has drawn on the distinction between those writers who accept, and those who reject, the idea of progress as their guiding star.

It is done with remarkable skill. Lasch's reading is vast, his insight into what a writer is trying to say penetrating. Still, there comes a point where many readers may stop and ask themselves: Why is he telling me all this? Adam Smith and Orestes Brownson, Henry George and Jonathan Edwards,

Georges Sorel and G. D. H. Cole: The menu is so long and many of the dishes so unfamiliar that the reader may find the meal indigestible.

I myself had almost reached the point Winston Churchill had arrived at during the famous dinner party where he is said to have burst out, "Waiter! Take this pudding away; it has no *theme*!" when I began to catch on to what Lasch was about. Two clues hinted to me what Lasch's real purpose is. The first lies in a brief intellectual autobiography he provides early in the book.

Lasch explains that he grew up in the tradition of Middle West progressivism. In the 1970s, he reacted to the excesses and absurdities of the 1960s "New Left" by embracing Marxism, not in its straitjacket form, but as taught by such Western Marxists as Gramsci, Marcuse, Raymond Williams and E. P. Thompson. But in the mid-1970s, influenced by his experience and concerns as a parent, he began to see that most liberals did not really believe that ordinary Americans shared their values.

Thus the use of legalistic strategies to advance the rights of "minorities" (in quotation marks because one group treated by analogy as a minority was "women") both demonstrated how little liberals really trusted the majority of their fellow citizens, and divided liberals from the working-class majority they had been accustomed to lead.

The second clue is closely related. As a former Marxist, Lasch instinctively associates a theory with a particular class. And just as the natural bearers of the ideology of liberalism are the "New Class" of those who live by the word and the idea, so resistance to the idea of progress, Lasch argues, always has been associated with another class, none other than the "petty bourgeoisie," the lower middle class which gave us Margaret Thatcher's father, Ronald Reagan's mother and so many other of the enemies of liberalism.

Lasch is far from praising the lower middle class without reservation. Its characteristic vices, he says with some justice, are envy, resentment and servility. Yet notwithstanding those vices, he goes on, "the moral conservatism of the petty bourgeoisie, its egalitarianism, its respect for workmanship, its understanding of the value of loyalty, and its struggle against the moral temptation of resentment are the materials on which critics of progress"—he means, of the idea of progress—"have always had to rely."

It is a remarkable insight, and his book would be stronger and more satisfying if he had worked it out and followed it out with less literary analysis and more political savvy. For I think I see what he is after:

Liberalism, he is saying—and it is not an original percep-

tion—has lost contact with the working class in America because the working class put other values, not least the survival and happiness of family, neighborhood and children, before progress. "Small proprietors, artisans, tradesmen— more often the victims of 'improvement' than beneficiaries— are unlikely to mistake the promised land of progress for the true and only heaven."

Lasch's strategy is original. He is suggesting that an intelligentsia that wishes well to its fellow citizens ought to abandon the unattainable ideal of unlimited progress and join hands with Middle America in the search for a happier society less obsessed with progress.

What he has not succeeded in doing in [*The True and Only Heaven*], impressive in many ways as it is, is in even sketching out a convincing theoretical basis on which the heirs of the "working stiff" of labor tradition and the corporatized intellectuals of the New Class might join to build a new solidarity.

Louis Menand (review date 11 April 1991)

SOURCE: "Man of the People," in *The New York Review of Books,* Vol. XXXVIII, April, 11, 1991, pp. 39-44.

[*In the following review, Menand surveys Lasch's critique of liberalism throughout his works, including* The True and Only Heaven, *and concludes that Lasch's insightful but sometimes limited cultural criticism neglects the influence of both literature and "the political doctrine of rights" on twentieth-century society.*]

Christopher Lasch began his career as a historian and critic of American liberalism. His analysis of liberalism led him to an analysis of some of the alternatives to liberalism in American political thought and, eventually, to a long excursion into social history and cultural criticism. It is clear from this work that he is unhappy with the dominant political and intellectual traditions in American life, and distressed by the mess he thinks those traditions have gotten us into. But it has not been clear what he thinks we might do to organize our thoughts and our lives more propitiously. With *The True and Only Heaven,* he returns to the criticism of liberalism with which he started, but this time he offers a prescription.

What does he mean by "liberalism"? The term is used to describe such a variety of political views that it has become a vexing one to define. Some people we call liberals—those associated with the War on Poverty in the 1960s, say, or with George McGovern's 1972 presidential campaign—believe that the government should provide, in some measure, for the basic welfare of its citizens. Others—Michael

Dukakis, for instance—think that a vigorous and expanding free-market economy is more likely to produce prosperity. Some liberals want foreign policy to be dictated by a concern for human rights and democratic values, as Jimmy Carter did; others, like Richard Nixon—in this respect a traditionally liberal president—believe that our relations with other nations should be governed by an unsentimental assessment of our own interests.

These disagreements among liberals are not a recent development, a splitting up of what was once a unified core of beliefs. Liberal thought has been divided along similar lines since at least the early years of the century, when liberals argued about America's entry into the First World War, about the growing dominance of large corporations in the American economy, and about the nature of Soviet communism. But in Lasch's view, all liberals, whether they dislike corporate capitalism or welcome it, whether they approve of American intervention in foreign conflicts or deplore it, share a common attitude: they are all optimists, believers in moral and material progress. Liberals believe that as civilization advances (by which, Lasch thinks, liberals usually mean "as people become more liberal"), more wants and desires are satisfied, and fewer prejudices and superstitions inhibit us. Once life was made miserable by bad kings and bad teeth; now we have democracy and dentists, political freedom and physical comfort, and thus, liberals believe, we can say that people have become happier, and that life is improving.

It was this faith in progress, Lasch argued in his first book, *The American Liberals and the Russian Revolution* (1962), that made it so difficult for many liberals in 1917 to understand the Communist revolution in Russia as the malign event it was. For to do so would have meant calling into question this central tenet of liberal faith: that history is a continuous progression from tyranny toward freedom, whose advance is marked by a series of democratic revolutions. Liberals are themselves the heirs of a revolutionary tradition, Lasch pointed out; how were they to accept the fact of a revolution that rejected the liberal ideal? And even if Soviet communism proved to be antiliberal and antidemocratic (as, of course, it did), liberals insisted on regarding its emergence as simply a temporary setback in the advance of progress; in the end, liberalism must triumph even in Russia, because the triumph of liberalism was destined to be universal.

> *The American Liberals and the Russian Revolution* is a detailed study of the political debate during the years of the First World War—from 1914-1919.
> —Louis Menand

The American Liberals and the Russian Revolution is a detailed study of the political debate during the years of the First World War—from 1914 to 1919. But the argument was clearly addressed to the liberals of Lasch's own day. When Lasch wrote that "liberalism in America, no less than communism in Russia, has always been a messianic creed, which staked everything on the ultimate triumph of liberalism throughout the world," he was describing, he thought, not only the liberalism of 1919—of Woodrow Wilson and Walter Lippmann—but the liberalism of the Kennedy administration as well.

This was an ingenious and antithetical point to make. For to describe liberalism as a messianic creed in 1962 was to call the vampire killer a vampire—as the titles of two standard expositions of liberal political theory in the early cold war era suggest: Arthur M. Schlesinger, Jr.'s *The Vital Center* (1949) and Daniel Bell's *The End of Ideology* (1960). Contemporary liberalism, for these writers, was precisely not an absolutist, world-transforming politics. It was a problem-solving, consensus-reaching politics, one that "dedicates itself," as Schlesinger suggested, "to problems as they come." Such pragmatism could only be impeded by prior ideological convictions, which Bell analyzed specifically as displaced religious and messianic impulses. "Ideology, which once was a road to action, has come to be a dead end," he claimed.

> Few serious minds believe any longer that one can set down "blueprints" and through "social engineering" bring about a new utopia of social harmony.

"People who know they alone are right find it hard to compromise," was the way Schlesinger put it; "and compromise is the strategy of democracy." A little utopianism might be fine as a spur to political engagement, but the business of politics lay in fine-tuning the machinery that makes social and economic freedoms possible, and in resisting ideology and messianism wherever they threaten those freedoms. Liberals were not supposed to become obsessed with the ends (or "the end") of history.

It is possible to be messianic in the effort to root out messianism, though. Even pragmatists can suffer from hubris; and Lasch's detection of a self-aggrandizing impulse, a secret determination to convert the world to its own "anti-ideological" ideology, in the ostensibly instrumentalist politics of mid-century liberalism, was an insight whose accuracy was confirmed, for many people, by America's subsequent entanglement, under a series of liberal administrations, in Vietnam. Lasch's accusation was also, of course, one that any liberal disenchanted with the self-righteous certainty of some of his fellow liberals might have made. It need not have led anyone to abandon liberalism. After all, a liberal might reasonably have asked, so long as we don't force people to become like us, why shouldn't we hope that liberal institutions—democratic societies and free markets—become universal?

For Lasch, however, the point had a different consequence. He began to see not only liberalism, but the whole march of "progress" itself as a creeping tyranny of centralized social and political control. Though liberalism was the ascendant political theory of this historical process, even many of the adversaries of liberalism, Lasch concluded, shared its optimism and its passion for transforming people's lives. In *The New Radicalism in America* (1965) and *The Agony of the American Left* (1969), he considered some of these adversaries: the "cultural radicals," such as Mabel Dodge Luhan and Randolph Bourne; the turn-of-the-century populists and socialists; and the leaders of the progressive movement, which, during the first two decades of the century, sought to restore a (somewhat ill-defined) sense of "civic virtue" to American political and economic life. Among these, only populism and socialism—"two broad patterns of opposition to corporate capitalism, occasionally converging but ideologically distinct"—seemed to Lasch to have offered a genuine alternative to the corporate economy and the liberal state; their failure, early in the century, marks for him the death of all real dissent.

For the reformers and cultural radicals were, he decided, in the end only participating in the general effort to "enlighten"—and thus to remold—the citizenry from the top down, through public education and artistic and literary culture; and this was an enterprise so congenial to the liberal mentality that liberals found it easy to adopt the radical style, and to patronize intellectual culture, in a way that rendered those traditions powerless. The Kennedy administration, with its indulgence of artists and intellectuals enthralled by the illusion that they were having an influence on the exercise of political power, represented, for Lasch, the culmination of this process. As for the progressive movement, associated with the early followers of Theodore Roosevelt and with liberal militants such as Herbert Croly, Walter Lippmann, and William Weyl, it was progressive "chiefly in attacking the archaic entrepreneurial capitalism the existence of which impeded the rationalization of American industry," and thus "actually served the needs of the industrial system." In seeking to reform the system rather than to resist it—to discover ways for more people to partake of the material prosperity capitalism provided rather than ways to prevent big business from turning people into well-fed "wage slaves"—the progressives only smoothed capitalism's path. So that by mid-century, Lasch concluded, it had become "almost impossible for criticism of existing policies to become part of political discourse. The language of American politics increasingly resembles an Orwellian monologue."

Having come to the bottom of the political barrel, Lasch turned first to social history and then to jeremiad. *Haven in*

a Heartless World (1977) proposes that the history of modern society can be described as "the socialization of production, followed by the socialization of reproduction." By the first phrase, Lasch meant the division of labor that accompanied the emergence of industrial capitalism, and that, by depriving people of control over their work, deprived them as well of the virtues unalienated labor instills. A day on an assembly line spent fixing the heads on pins, to use Adam Smith's famous example of specialization in *The Wealth of Nations*, is not likely to lead a person to an elevated conception of life, or to give him a sense of independence and self-confidence. (This was a warning about the moral effects of specialization that Smith himself recorded elsewhere in his writings.) By "the socialization of reproduction," Lasch meant the proliferation, beginning in the nineteenth century, of the so-called helping professions: the doctors, psychologists, teachers, child guidance experts, juvenile court officers, and so forth, who, by their constant intervention in people's private lives, "eroded the capacity for self-help and social invention."

> **The Culture of Narcissism was a book of its moment. It appeared at the close of a depressing decade and near the close of an unpopular presidency.**
> **—Louis Menand**

This second development constitutes, in Lasch's view, liberalism's worst betrayal. For liberalism, he argued, had struck a deal: in return for transforming the worker from an independent producer of goods into a fixer of heads on pins, it was agreed that people would be free to pursue happiness and virtue in their private lives in whatever manner they chose. The work place was thus severed from the home, and the family became the "haven in a heartless world." But no sooner was the deal made, Lasch argued, than liberalism reneged. Private life was immediately made prey to the quasi-official helping professions and to the "forces of organized virtue," led by "feminists, temperance advocates, educational reformers, liberal ministers, penologists, doctors, and bureaucrats." "From the moment the conception of the family as a refuge made its historical appearance, the same forces that gave rise to the new privacy began to erode it. . . . The hope that private transactions could make up for the collapse of communal traditions and civic order" was killed by organized kindness.

Modern life, in Lasch's conception, is thus predicated on one basic transaction: the exchange of genuine independence for pseudo-liberation. Liberals and reformers will free us from the repressiveness of the patriarchal family, of the closed ethnic community—even of our own unhappiness. All we have to do is to surrender ourselves to the benevolent paternalism of the sociologists, psychiatrists, educators, and corporate and welfare bureaucrats.

But those "helpers" have effectively destroyed the very institutions, such as the nuclear family, through which character and independence were traditionally instilled. The responsibility for raising children has been lifted from the shoulders of parents (thus discrediting their authority) and been placed in the offices of medical and educational professionals and experts; a pattern of "normal" development is now enforced by the public schools, whose purpose has been reconceived as socialization—turning people into good citizens on the liberal model, rather than simply introducing them to knowledge. "Liberating" people has meant, in short, converting them into permanent dependents of the modern state and its "human science" apparatchiks.

Lasch's argument, at this point in his work, had begun to show some similarity to that of Michel Foucault, whose analysis of modern institutional benevolence as a tyrannical system of social controls Lasch has written about approvingly. Perhaps a stronger, or more immediate, influence was Philip Rieff's notion of "the triumph of the therapeutic"—the idea that the twentieth-century belief in personal liberation has created a new culture organized around a new type of human being, whom Rieff called "psychological man." It was Lasch's development of this argument of Rieff's that yielded the work for which he is famous.

The Culture of Narcissism (1979) was a book of its moment. It appeared at the close of a depressing decade and near the close of an unpopular presidency. Lasch was, in fact one of the luminaries invited to Camp David to help Jimmy Carter organize his thoughts for the speech claiming that Americans were suffering a "malaise," and this well-publicized distinction no doubt helped put the book on the best-seller list. Its argument is a little more complicated than many readers may remember. Lasch proposed that the modern developments he had examined in his earlier work—the demise of the family and the erosion of private life generally—had produced "a new form of personality organization." If (as he thought) people were behaving and feeling differently, it was because a fundamental change had taken place not only in beliefs and values—in what people thought moral, or permissible, or desirable—but in the structure of the mind itself. Our "social arrangements live on," he proposed, "in the individual, buried in the mind below the level of consciousness."

The principal evidence for this assertion—beyond sociological observations about a "sense of inner emptiness," the "decline of the play spirit," and so forth—were psychiatric reports on contemporary personality disorders, which were (Lasch claimed) increasingly assuming a "narcissistic" pattern. Lasch was not, as some of his more casual readers may

have assumed, using "narcissism" in the everyday sense of "self-centered" or "hedonistic." He was using the term in a clinical sense that had been developed in a psychoanalytic tradition arising out of Freudian theory—in the work of Heinz Kohut, Otto Kernberg, and the object-relations psychologist Melanie Klein. In this literature, a "narcissist" is not someone with an overweening sense of self, but, on the contrary, someone with a very weak sense of self.

In order to make the psychoanalytic data he had assembled fit the case he was making about the emergence of a new personality type in society at large, Lasch made one further assumption: that "pathology represents a heightened version of normality"—that is, that a clinically disordered personality, of the kind reported in psychoanalytic studies, is representative of the current "normal" personality type.

This made for a rather elaborate theoretical contraption. The reader was being called upon to make the following assumptions, any one of which is clearly vulnerable to challenge: that changes in education, the role of the family, the nature of work, and so on are capable of producing fundamental changes, "below the level of consciousness," in people's psychological makeup; that the changes in American life over the last hundred years have been extensive and monolithic enough to create an entire population consisting of this new personality type; that the pathological personality does indeed represent a version of the normal personality; and that the particular examples of narcissistic behavior adduced by Lasch in 1979—among them the Manson Family killings, the kidnapping of Patty Hearst, the attack on theatrical illusion in contemporary drama, "the fascination with oral sex," and the streaker craze—are evidence of long-term personality disintegration, rather than isolated responses to a confusing but transitory social moment. (There was also the problem that a writer who had elsewhere suggested that psychiatry was, in the hands of some of its practitioners at least, one of the corrupting forces in modern life was relying rather heavily on a psychiatric conception of the "normal.")

The Culture of Narcissism was thus an easy book to misunderstand. Lasch was not saying that things were better in the Fifties, as conservatives offended by countercultural permissiveness probably took him to be saying. He was not saying that things were better in the Sixties, as former activists disgusted by the "me-ism" of the Seventies are likely to have imagined. He was diagnosing a condition that originated, he believed, in the nineteenth century.

The Minimal Self (1984) was written to correct the misapprehensions of the earlier book's admirers. The "narcissistic" self, Lasch explained, was really a type of what he was now calling the "minimal" self—"a self uncertain of its own outlines, [yet] longing either to remake the world in its own image" (as in the case of technocratic reformers and other acolytes of "progress") "or to merge into its environment in a blissful union" (as in the case of counterculturalists, feminists, and ecological utopians). Authentic selfhood lies between these extremes, he wrote—in an acceptance of limits without despair. But the conditions in which such a self might be forged were being destroyed.

What is distinctive about Lasch's criticism of modern life, besides its unusually broad scope, is its moral and personal intensity. For it is one thing—and not an uncommon thing among academic intellectuals—to analyze modern democratic society as a system of social controls masquerading as personal freedoms, without concluding anything more radical (or less banal) than that all societies must hold themselves together somehow, and that an officially "open" society will find means for doing so that are designed to appear as uncoercive as possible. But Lasch has shown no interest in this kind of analytic detachment, which he regards as just the kind of superior sociological "expertise" he associates with the bureaucratic and professionalist mentality he abhors. He is (or he gives, in his work, the impression of being) a man who believes he has caught "the modern project"—his phrase for the group of social and political tendencies he has analyzed—in an enormous lie, and who cannot rest until the lie has been exposed. There is an invasion-of-the-body-snatchers urgency about his writing; and this has given it, over the years, an increasingly aggrieved, and sometimes paranoid, tone. It has also drawn him to a style of relentless and contentious assertion which can be, to put it gently, extremely off-putting. It is an unusual style for a scholar to resort to, and I think he means it, quite deliberately, to be offensive: an affront to the modern taste for cool and logically seamless forms of persuasion. If he does mean it this way, it works.

The True and Only Heaven is the first place in which Lasch has tried to suggest, with some degree of comprehensiveness, a way out of the regrettable condition he thinks the modern liberal view has left us in. It is much the longest of his books, and it suffers from many of the faults one has come to associate with Lasch's work: it lingers pedantically on minor matters and dashes through major ones; it makes much of points almost everyone would concede and ignores obvious objections to its more controversial assertions; and it is written from a position that has hardened into something like dogmatism. This is, after all, a writer who, over the last fifteen years, has argued that "all medical technology has done is to increase patients' dependence on machines and the medical experts who operate [them]"; that "new ideas of sexual liberation—the celebration of oral sex, masturbation, and homosexuality—spring from the prevailing fear of heterosexual passion, even of sexual intercourse itself"; that the reliance on medical intervention during pregnancy "helped women in their campaign for voluntary motherhood by raising the cost of pregnancy to their husbands—not only

the financial cost but the emotional cost of the doctor's intrusion into the bedroom, his usurpation of the husband's sexual prerogatives"; that the imposition of child labor laws "obscured the positive possibility of children working alongside their parents at jobs of recognized importance"; and that "the prison life of the past looks in our time like liberation itself."

Like all of Lasch's books, *The True and Only Heaven* is clearly responsive to contemporary anxieties—in this case, to concern about the ecological dangers that are bound, it seems, to accompany the spread of capitalist economies across the globe. Lasch thinks that if we continue to believe, as the religion of progress encourages us to believe, that somehow everyone in the world can be given the standard of living of a middle-class American, the planet will be used up long before we ever arrive at that dubious utopia. He is not the first person to sound this warning, but he has, as usual, sounded it in a provocative manner.

> **Lasch thinks that if we continue to believe, as the religion of progress encourages us to believe, that somehow everyone in the world can be given the standard of living of a middle-class American, the planet will be used up long before we ever arrive at that dubious utopia.**
> **—Louis Menand**

Lasch now regards the belief in progress not as simply an interesting paradox in twentieth-century liberal thought, but as the dominant ideology of modern history. It is in the name of progress, he thinks, that traditional sources of happiness and virtue—work, faith, the family, even an independent sense of self—are being destroyed; and he begins his book with an analysis of the false values of the modern liberal outlook, proposing, for each value or attitude he rejects, an alternative. This discussion is filled with references to various thinkers and ideas, as is the case throughout *The True and Only Heaven;* but references to specific policies or social arrangements are scarce, so that the analysis has a theoretical or abstract cast. Lasch's purpose, evidently, is to establish a vocabulary.

Lasch says, as he had in his first book nearly thirty years ago, that liberals are optimists: they believe in an unlimited ability to provide for an ever-expanding array of human wants. A worthier sentiment, he feels, is "hope"—an acceptance of limits without despair (as he had described it in *The Minimal Self*). Liberals espouse a kind of Enlightenment universalism; they regard their truths as self-evident to all reasonable people, and therefore as applicable to everyone. He recommends instead an emphasis on particularism—a recognition of the persistence of national and ethnic loyalties. Nostalgia, he argues, is progress's "ideological twin," since it is a way of thinking about the past that makes it seem irrecoverable, and change seem inevitable. He proposes "memory" as an alternative, a way of seeing the past and present as continuous. Instead of the modern conception of people as consumers, working only to provide themselves with the means to satisfy material wants, he suggests a conception of people as producers, working in order to acquire the virtues labor instills—among them independence, responsibility, and self-sufficiency. And in place of "self-interest," which defines the economic man of liberal individualism, he proposes "virtue," which defines the citizen ready to take an active part in community life.

This much of Lasch's argument, directed at the mentality, certainly recognizable, that sees no limits to economic growth, and that understands the ends of social and economic policy to be simply the creation and satisfaction of more consumers, has a timely appeal. The collapse of the communist economies has been greeted in some quarters, as Lasch in 1962 suggested it would, as evidence of the inevitable global triumph of liberalism—the theoretically predicted "end of history," in the catchphrase made popular a few years ago by Francis Fukuyama. And on these matters, as Lasch quite rightly points out, there is no longer an appreciable difference in mainstream American political thought between "liberals" and "conservatives." The "New Right," in this respect, has proved a sham: Ronald Reagan is no less a worshiper of progress—no less an optimist, a nostalgist, and a global crusader for the American way—than any classic liberal Lasch might name.

Much of the attention Lasch's book has already received has therefore, as might be expected, been preoccupied with its attack on the "progressive" world view; and the general terms that define the substitute world view he proposes as a substitute are plainly attractive. Who would want to defend "optimism" against "hope," "nostalgia" against "memory," "self-interest" against "virtue"? So long as the discussion remains at this level of abstraction, there is very little to argue. But Lasch has a broader purpose: he has undertaken to reconstruct a political and moral tradition in which his "alternative" values are rooted. This tradition he calls "populism," and it is not possible to engage his argument in a serious way without confronting the challenges that tradition makes (or Lasch understands it to make) to modern liberal assumptions.

Lasch means by "populism" something more than the late-nineteenth-century political movement the term ordinarily denotes; indeed, the book contains very little discussion of William Jennings Bryan, for instance, or of the Southern populist leader Tom Watson. The populist tradition Lasch describes has been transmitted through an oddly assorted sequence of thinkers. These thinkers all share one attitude, of course: an antagonism to the modern liberal outlook as Lasch has defined it. This may express itself in an appreciation for the "civic virtues"—the virtues derived from personal independence, political participation, and genuinely productive labor; in an acceptance of "fate" (one of Lasch's key terms in this book) and of the idea of limits; or in an admiration for a set of characteristics Lasch identifies with lower-middle-class, or "petty-bourgeois," culture: moral conservatism, egalitarianism, loyalty, and the "struggle against the moral temptation of resentment" (that is, the capacity for forgiveness).

Among the social and political critics Lasch regards as populists are writers who defend small-scale producers (farmers, artisans, and so forth), who despise creditors, and who oppose the culture of uplift and universal philanthropy because of its disruptive intervention in personal and family life. These sentiments are, he thinks, particularly strongly expressed in the writings of Tom Paine; the English radical William Cobbett; the nineteenth-century editor, transcendentalist, and controversialist Orestes Brownson; and the author of the classic of populist political economy, *Progress and Poverty* (1879), Henry George. Two labor-movement theorists from the turn of the century are important to Lasch's tradition as champions of small-scale producers: the French syndicalist Georges Sorel, whose *Reflections on Violence* (1908) was admired by critics of the Third Republic in France and of liberalism in England, and the British guild socialist G. D. H. Cole. By proposing to restore control over production to the worker, Lasch argues, syndicalism and guild socialism represented genuine alternatives to corporate capitalism. What socialists and the labor movement generally ended up settling for, he feels (and Cole is his example), was a top-down welfare system that turned the worker into a consumer, and left him, though more secure in his job, even more dependent.

This tradition of political and economic criticism is complemented, Lasch argues, by a parallel tradition of moral criticism—and this proposal is the chief novelty of his book. The major figure in this line is Emerson, whose recognition, in the late essay on "Fate" (1860), that "freedom lies in the acceptance of necessity" Lasch regards as the philosophical centerpiece of populist thought. Emerson's fatalism has been ignored, he thinks, by the Emersonians—"those professional Pollyannas,"—and he proposes to restore us to a proper understanding, principally by reading Emerson by the lights of the Puritan divine Jonathan Edwards. Two other writers, both readily associated with Emerson, are said to share the populist moral vision: Thomas Carlyle, in *Sartor Resartus* (1834) and the essays on heroes and hero worship, published in 1841, and William James, in the discussion of the "twice-born" in *The Varieties of Religious Experience* (1902) and in the essay "The Moral Equivalent of War" (1910).

Lasch traces the course of populist ideals in a group of twentieth-century American writers: Josiah Royce, Randolph Bourne, Herbert Croly, Waldo Frank, John Dewey, the New Dealer Thurman Arnold, and Reinhold Niebuhr. In some of these cases, he is reconsidering writers whose ideas he had once criticized. Croly, for instance, whose book *The Promise of American Life* (1910) Lasch once regarded as a typical example of the progressive's naive understanding of the nature of corporate power, is now praised for recognizing, in a later book *Progressive Democracy* (1914), the importance of endowing the worker with a sense of responsibility—and for perceiving that the specialization required by big business and mass production would destroy the possibilities of meaningful work. Niebuhr (one of the heroes of Schlesinger's *The Vital Center*) was attacked by Lasch in ***The New Radicalism in America*** for taking an uncritical and Manichean view of the struggle between American liberal democracy and Soviet totalitarianism—for assuming too readily the inherent virtue of the American way and the monolithic evil of Soviet communism. In ***The True and Only Heaven,*** though, Niebuhr is seen as a critic of liberalism. His defense of "particularism"—of the innate desire of groups to protect their difference and autonomy against the liberal inclination to force compromises on competing interests—now seems to Lasch to make him a misunderstood antagonist of liberal ideology.

Niebuhr is also important to the populist tradition, as Lasch interprets it, because of his insistence on the desirability of forgiveness, and the futility of resentment, in struggles for social justice; and Lasch's consideration of this aspect of Niebuhr's thought leads directly to the only political success story in the book: Martin Luther King, Jr.'s leadership of the Southern civil rights movement. King succeeded, Lasch believes, by appealing to the populist virtues of lower-middle-class communities in the South—both black and white—and by preaching the doctrine of "spiritual discipline against resentment." Blacks in King's movement did not seek revenge for the injustices they had suffered, since they understood (or King, who had studied Niebuhr as a divinity student, understood) Niebuhr's teaching that to combat injustice and coercion with more injustice and coercion is only to perpetuate a cycle of conflict. But, Lasch argues, when King and his associates attempted to mobilize victims of poverty in the inner cities of the North, they could no longer appeal, as they had in the South, to communities of people who understood the value of forgiveness. Resentment against the powerful became instead the motivating emotion of the struggle, with disastrous results.

Lower-middle-class virtues persist, Lasch thinks, but as an endangered moral species, preyed upon by the social-engineering schemes of the liberal professional classes. The controversy between suburban liberals and working-class city residents over the busing of school children to achieve racial integration and the struggle over abortion rights are, he suggests, recent instances of liberal imperialism. In the Boston busing wars, and in the struggles for open housing in the suburbs of Chicago, lower-middle-class white communities were reviled, and even demonized, by liberals; yet their "only crime," Lasch says, "so far as anyone could see, was their sense of ethnic solidarity." The populist solution, apparently, would have entailed an attempt to transform the inner city into a "real community," rather than to compel people to ignore their ethnic and racial differences—though Lasch is vague about how this transformation would take place.

In the case of abortion rights, one might imagine that pro-choice advocates, because of their insistence that the decision to have an abortion should be left to the individual woman rather than foreclosed by the state, would have the stronger case for Lasch. But Lasch regards the procedure of abortion itself as an instance of technological intrusion into the natural process of reproduction, and he accuses the proponents of abortion rights of advocating social engineering—of trying to use medical advances to eliminate the "unwanted" in the name of social improvement. (This view of the pro-choice mentality derives mainly from a single sociological study, Kristin Luker's *Abortion and the Politics of Motherhood* [1984].)

And yet in these cases there is at least some engagement between the classes. In general, Lasch thinks, "neither left-nor right-wing intellectuals . . . seem to have much interest in the rest of American society." A revived populist tradition, he concludes, would challenge the ideologues of progress, and help to answer "the great question of twentieth-century politics": how we are to restore a spirit of civic virtue to our lives.

This does not mean that Lasch is proposing a resurrection of the populist political and economic program (though his lengthy and often quarrelsome elaboration of that program sometimes makes it appear otherwise). As he concedes, much of populist economic theory—with its hatred of creditors and landlords, its monetary gimmicks and paper money schemes, its call for a return to small-scale production—was anachronistic even in the nineteenth century. Many populist political convictions are similarly outdated: the belief that armed conflict breeds virtue in the citizenry, for example, surely died in the Battle of the Somme. Lasch is not suggesting that all the facts of modern history can be repealed, or that someday we can all become yeoman farmers, with our ancestral rifles hanging next to the fireplace—though he would perhaps like us to think more respectfully of yeoman farmers.

The real argument of the book is a more philosophical one, having to do with the juxtaposition of populist economic theory, such as it is, with the tradition of moral criticism Lasch finds in Edwards, Emerson, Carlyle, James, Niebuhr, and others. His point seems to be that we need a political economy that matches the moral economy (as Lasch believes those writers understand it) of the universe. The universe, in this conception, is a place in which we earn our way, and do so in part by recognizing that there are limits to how far we can go, and forces militating against us which we cannot control. Character is built by striving to perform the role fate has assigned us, and a society that recognized this truth would be one which understood that conditions a modern person finds oppressive—obedience to family discipline, acceptance of the restrictions of place and class, military conscription, demanding or unremunerative work—are really the conditions that make a full and independent life possible.

The reason populists give for agitating against capitalists, creditors, and landlords is that those are classes of people who profit without producing. In doing so, they violate the principles of an economics based on a labor theory of value—the foundation of not only populist and Marxist, but even liberal economic theory in the nineteenth century. More than that, though, they violate the universe's moral principle of just compensation. You must give something to get something back. Only if we are producers will we deserve to consume. And to be a "producer" in the larger, moral sense means to feel oneself responsible for all of what one does in one's life.

This is not an unattractive philosophical conception. But what happens when it touches ground in the thought and practice of a particular "populist" writer? Consider the case of Georges Sorel, whose militant version of socialist syndicalism appeals to Lasch because of its rejection of both liberal and Marxist utopianism. Among the less attractive features of Sorel's thought, Lasch notes in passing, is "probably" anti-Semitism. But a man who compared France's struggle against the Jews to America's against the "Yellow Peril," who wrote that "the French should defend their state, their customs, and their ideas against the Jewish invaders" and that "the so-called excesses of the Bolsheviks were due to the Jewish elements that had penetrated the movement," and who referred, in two of the works Lasch cites, *Reflections on Violence* and *The Illusion of Progress*, to "big Jew bankers" is not only "probably" an anti-Semite. Nor was Sorel's anti-Semitism simply a detachable element of his general outlook. It was the obvious, if not the unavoidable, consequence of an economic theory that demonized financiers and creditors.

And this side of populist thought is of a paranoid piece throughout: the dislike of professional armies, as an instance of specialization that deprives citizens of the virtue-making activity of war; the dislike of those who lend the state the money to pay its armies, and who therefore supposedly find it in their interest to foment war; the defense of local religious and ethnic communities—these are all classic sources of anti-Semitism.

They are also among the sources of fascism, particularly in France. "The intellectual father of fascism," one French admirer called Sorel in the 1920s; and although Lasch notes Sorel's close association with the Action Française and his enthusiastically reciprocated admiration for Mussolini (later complemented by an equally fervent admiration for Lenin), he does not explain why this aspect of Sorel's thought, of which he plainly does not approve, should be regarded as irrelevant to the aspects he praises. And the same is true of the racism, jingoism, and demagoguery associated with populist political movements generally: Lasch acknowledges these tendencies, but asks us to ignore them—occasionally by the discreditable tactic of throwing our suspicions back in our faces. He addresses the question of Sorel's connections to fascism, for instance, simply by remarking that "liberals' obsession with fascism . . . leads them to see 'fascist tendencies' or 'proto-fascism' in all opinions unsympathetic to liberalism." This may or may not be true, but it is not an argument.

The True and Only Heaven will provoke—and is, one assumes, intended to provoke—many such arguments about the selective readings and unorthodox interpretations of various figures. But there are two larger criticisms I think Lasch invites, and they have application not only to this book, but to his work generally.

> **At the core of Lasch's condemnation of liberalism is the familiar charge that liberalism is effectively without content—that "liberal man" is a wind-up contraption that chases its own short-term interests.**
> **—*Louis Menand***

Of the many peculiarities about the moral tradition Lasch has constructed, the most astonishing is the omission of Freud—a writer who has played an important part in Lasch's thinking in the past and is still, one presumes, a figure he admires. For surely the Freudian notion of psychic economy involves exactly the principle of compensation, and exactly the tragic sense of life, that Lasch so passionately admires in thinkers of far smaller intellectual stature. But a writer like Freud cannot figure in Lasch's account, because Freud has already been accepted as one of the heroes of modern culture. And this is also, it seems to me, why the writers who do have a prominent place in Lasch's tradition are either minor and eccentric figures, like Brownson and Sorel, or major ones who are supposed to have been misread by everyone else, like Emerson and Niebuhr. For to concede that the "populist" moral conception is simply a limited and somewhat cranky version of a moral conception we find everywhere in modern culture would mean conceding that values modern society is supposed to have made obsolete are actually to be found at the very heart of modern life.

If, as Lasch suggested in his work on the family, there is a "deal" on which the modern liberal society was founded, it is that we shall have the freedom to criticize the conditions in which we live. This bargain has given us an enormous body of literary and intellectual work, fiercely protected by liberal institutions, whose moral intention is to complicate all the issues that traditional liberal theory makes too simple. Lionel Trilling wrote a famous book to make this point; but *The Liberal Imagination* is not mentioned by Lasch. He seems, and not only on the evidence of *The True and Only Heaven,* simply deaf to literature. "Misgivings were destined to be confined to a shadowy half-life on the fringes of debate," he writes of the spread of specialization and the division of labor in the early years of the Industrial Revolution. It is as though Wordsworth and Dickens had never written, or their books been read.

At the core of Lasch's condemnation of liberalism is the familiar charge that liberalism is effectively without content—that "liberal man" is a wind-up contraption that chases its own short-term interests, and the liberal state a night watchman that only keeps the streets clean and the fights fair (or, at least, "efficient"). But liberalism does have a moral conception of the self, which is expressed in the political doctrine of rights. There is virtually no mention of rights in Lasch's attack on the elements of the modern liberal outlook, or in his analysis, in this book, of particular political events, such as the disputes about busing and abortion. Elsewhere, he has linked modern feminism's attachment to medical technology to the eighteenth-century idea of individual rights: the progressive mentality, he thinks, regards access to reproductive technology as an enhancement of the woman's right to choose whether to bear children. And it is clear that, like many other critics of liberalism, he would replace talk of rights in our political vocabulary with talk of duties—talk of what we owe to our society and to each other, rather than what is owed to us. "Rights-bearers," he claims in a recent symposium on the subject, "are regarded as autonomous individuals, and that is precisely the style of thinking we are trying to avoid."

This seems to me to be an insufficient account of rights. It is insufficient historically because the recognition of individual rights figures crucially in the liberal idea of what counts as progress. And it is insufficient morally, as well, since our notion of exactly what a right entails—to speak freely, or to bear arms, or to travel or own property—and under what circumstances it must give way to other claims, is the subject of continual debate. The history of United States Supreme Court decisions alone is ample evidence of the intellectual and moral complexity of the idea of rights. It is true that from one perspective rights appear to uphold private interests against public goods—to protect my desire to publish obscene material, for example, against the community's desire to maintain standards of good taste. But from another perspective, a system of enumerated rights against the state, such as the Bill of Rights provides, is precisely an acknowledgment of the *general* claim of the society as a whole against the individual. This was the view taken by liberal contemporaries of Lasch's turn-of-the-century populists, such as the younger Oliver Wendell Holmes: that it is only because we recognize the legitimacy of society's claims generally that we undertake to respect the desire of people to be exempted from those claims in specified kinds of behavior.

Because the subject is dismissed altogether from *The True and Only Heaven,* rights have no place in the book's account of the Southern civil rights movement, and this seems to me to be a telling omission. For what saves Lasch's populist tradition from being merely a souvenir of the values left strewn in the wake of progress is his contention that the populist spirit continues to have a life in real communities. Since the South has been the breeding ground for many populist politicians in this century, and since the South was itself a classic example of antiliberal "particularism"—"the preindustrial society par excellence," as Lasch has called it—one would expect him to give special attention to the character of Southern life. But prominent Southern populists go almost unmentioned in *The True and Only Heaven.* Huey Long's name, for example, appears only twice, in lists of the sort of people liberals unfairly associate with populism. George Wallace turns up more often; but although Lasch seems to disapprove of the politics of resentment Wallace practiced during his days as a segregationist, his remarks on Wallace are otherwise not unkind, and Wallace's eventual acceptance of racial integration is noted approvingly as testimony to the ability of one local ethnic constituency—lower-middle-class Southern whites—to respond to a moral appeal from another.

It is true that the Montgomery bus boycott of 1955, which is where the modern civil rights movement began, is one of the noblest political events in our history, and that it was made possible by the religious faith of a lower-middle-class ethnic community—Southern blacks—essentially untouched by legalistic ways of thinking. But it is not true, as Lasch suggests it is, that the boycotters' victory, or the victories in other civil rights campaigns in the South, came about because lower-middle-class Southern whites understood the justice of the blacks' moral appeal. Southern whites did not take a notable part in the Montgomery protest, except to oppose it and to humiliate and harass its participants. The protest succeeded because on the day a local judge issued the injunction that would have broken the boycott, the Supreme Court ruled that the black citizens of Montgomery had the right to sit where they chose on city buses. There was no "local solution" to the problem of racial segregation in the South because the principle at stake was not a local principle.

Lasch is at his most acerbic in his criticism of middle-class liberals who impose the values of their culture on lower-middle-class communities and families, and he has much to say in his discussion of the busing controversy and the contemporary abortion debate about the attitude of moral superiority some liberals assume toward the less articulate and less educated people who oppose them. There is indeed some ugliness in the middle-class attitudes he describes; but to take note of that ugliness does not dispose of the matter.

Back in the 1960s, a group of film makers, Drew Associates, was invited by the Kennedy administration to film its enforcement of the court-ordered desegregation of the University of Alabama—the incident that culminated in George Wallace's famous "stand in the schoolhouse door." The film that was produced, *Crisis: Behind a Presidential Commitment*, covers events both at the White House and in Alabama. It is sometimes shown on public television, and it dramatizes the cultural friction Lasch writes about. Robert Kennedy, in the White House, and his deputy Nicholas DeB. Katzenbach, in Alabama—Ivy League liberals, supremely assured of their virtue—are seen discussing their strategy for handling Wallace as though Wallace were an inconvenient road hazard, a man, in their calculus, of no moral account whatever. And Wallace is seen arriving at the university and accepting expressions of support from the people waiting to greet him with the easy familiarity of a man who knows them and is part of a genuine community.

Wallace was as successful a populist politician as the postwar era produced, and the Kennedy administration was undoubtedly the incarnation of the modern liberal mentality as Lasch conceives it. There is something slightly chilling about the confrontation, as there is when you watch any ancient and deeply rooted thing smoothly and expertly obliterated by the forces of "progress." But Kennedy and Katzenbach were right, and Wallace was wrong.

Steven Watts (review date Fall 1992)

SOURCE: "Sinners in the Hands of an Angry Critic: Christopher Lasch's Struggle with Progressive America," in *American Studies*, Vol. 33, No. 2, Fall, 1992, pp. 113-20.

[*In the review below, Watts summarizes the themes of and the critical responses to Lasch's works from the mid-1970s to the early 1990s, offering a general assessment of the weaknesses and strengths of his arguments.*]

In the volatile cultural politics of late twentieth-century America, the only thing worse than an opponent is a traitor. In many ways, Christopher Lasch has acquired precisely that image. He began his career as a radical historian in the 1960s—one of his essays, for instance, appeared alongside those of Eugene Genovese and Staughton Lynd in the 1969 dissenting manifesto *Towards a New Past*—and his trenchant analysis of modern liberal and radical ideology made him a darling of the New Left. Within a few years, however, the young critic began heading off in a direction quite alarming to many of his admirers. The transforming nature of his view of American life brought growing controversy in its wake.

Beginning in the mid-1970s and continuing over the next decade and a half, Lasch would publish four highly contentious books. They examined a number of crucial issues in modern America: the disintegration of the family as part of a larger crisis of culture, the corrosive psychological effects accruing to modern consumer capitalism, the powerful but insidious impact of the notion of "progress" upon American ideology. In all of these texts there emerged a critique that ran across the grain of his earlier radicalism. As Lasch has explained in a long biographical section of his most recent work, his intellectual odyssey began with a growing sense that the exhaustion of 1960s dissent had been richly deserved. Self-criticism produced disillusionment with the doctrines of Marxism and the New Left, but it did not culminate in a neo-conservative reaction. Instead, it produced a unique body of radical writing notable for two things. First, Lasch's work since 1975 has abandoned academic scholarship almost entirely to enter the realm of social criticism. He has become more a public intellectual than a professional historian. Second, and more importantly, Lasch's commentary has defied confident ideological categorization. His social criticism has consistently raised as many angry rebuttals from ostensible allies on the Left as from evident targets on the Right. This flows from the depressingly deceptive state of contemporary political culture, where, on one side, the Reactionary Right offers a marriage of untethered corporate greed and a highly sentimentalized vision of bourgeois domestic life, while on the other side the Liberationist Left presents a companionate relationship of socioeconomic quietism and pietistic identity politics. Lasch's challenging analysis at least gets beyond all that. His central message, along with the curiously tangled reaction it has provoked, tell us much about the massive problems besetting American life in the late twentieth century.

Lasch's recent criticism has gone through three topical stages that overlap in terms of analysis. *Haven in a Heartless World: The Family Besieged* (1977), his initial effort in this genre, explored the plight of the American family under modern capitalist culture. It combined a critique of the "second industrial revolution" in twentieth-century America with a critique of the sociological formulation of family life offered by social scientists. It also offered a blistering attack on the "helping professions"—therapists, counselors, bureaucratic agencies, child-rearing and family "experts"—as a therapeutic arm of the corporate liberal state. The intervention of these groups, Lasch argued, promoted a subtle form of social regulation that undermined family efficacy and authority. But this state of affairs with the modern family, he carefully noted, was tied to a larger crisis of authority in modern capitalism: a massive quest for therapeutic self-fulfillment in consumer society that made *any* authority that questioned gratification suspect. And in the most controversial part of the book, he attacked feminism for its ironic reinforcement of the dominant culture. This movement, he argued, had gone beyond the notion of equal rights to offer up the family as a sacrifice on the altar of individualist gratification.

In the late 1970s and early 1980s, Lasch wrote two books that burrowed deeper into modern capitalist culture to illuminate its dominant personality type. The picture was not a pretty one. *The Culture of Narcissism: American Life in an Age of Diminishing Expectations* (1979) exposed the debilitating psychological effects of modern consumer society. This scathing attack pictured the dominance of a "therapeutic culture of narcissism" full of childlike dependence and grandiose agendas for self-fulfillment. In particular, Lasch focused on a "new paternalism" where therapeutic discourse and institutions manufactured "fantasies of total gratification." Advertising, success ideology, the helping professions and an obsession with "health" all fed this leviathan. Such developments dangerously eroded people's capacity for self-reliance, competence and moral responsibility. In advanced capitalist society where the producer had become the consumer, and where the citizen had become the client, Lasch argued, the individual was encouraged to embrace "a narcissistic preoccupation with self."

> *The Culture of Narcissism: American Life in an Age of Diminishing Expectations* **exposed the debilitating psychological effects of modern consumer society.**
> —*Steven Watts*

A few years later Lasch extended this line of argument in *The Minimal Self: Psychic Survival in Troubled Times* (1984). Here he developed a full-scale diagnosis of the pathology of capitalist culture to explain how the old "imperial self" of the nineteenth century had steadily atrophied into a "minimal self" by the late twentieth. A survival mentality, he contended, now comprised the parameters of personal endeavor. Life was defined as a series of crises, the self was seen as a victim of outside forces, and psychological identities had become mere masks to use and discard according to

the needs of survival. Even public life had retracted into cultural disputes over a "politics of the psyche" between conservative defenders of the superego, liberal advocates of the ego, and radical enthusiasts for the libido. With democracy degenerating into an "exercise of consumer preference," and selfhood becoming "the ability to play a variety of roles and to assume an endless variety of freely chosen identities," the desperate condition of bureaucratic, consumer society had become obvious. The degradation of labor was now matched by the attenuation of civic life and the constriction of private endeavor.

Lasch has reached the latest stage of his cultural criticism with the recent publication of *The True and Only Heaven: Progress and its Critics* (1991). Stepping back for a broader look at the vicissitudes of contemporary America, he focuses on the notion of progress that lay at the heart of modern Western development for nearly three centuries. This examination, one might also note, fleshes out the historical context for many of his earlier arguments. Progress, as Lasch sees it, has deep roots both in Western ideas and institutions since the 1600s. Adam Smith's "rehabilitation of desire," an Enlightenment ethos of instrumental reason, and commercializing trends that accompanied market development all combined to produce a steadily growing emphasis on gratification, consumption and material abundance that seems to have culminated in modern America. The resulting progressive ideology has carved out a wide mainstream of modern sociopolitical thought—it includes figures like Thomas Spencer and Thomas Macauley, Progressives, Keynesian welfare statistics, liberals and conservatives of many stripes, even most Marxists—that converges around ideals of economic growth, bureaucratic organization and centralized planning. This tradition uses the comforting notion of "progress" much as the drunk uses the lamppost: more for support than illumination. But alongside this ideological juggernaut, Lasch insists, has developed a minor tradition of criticism. A populist, or petty bourgeois, sensibility has expressed skepticism about the progressive platitudes of the dominant culture. Opposing the division of labor, unrestrained desire, and compulsive consumption, this camp has included Thomas Paine and William Cobbett, Ralph Waldo Emerson and Thomas Carlyle, the Populists and the Syndicalists. In Lasch's view, this coalition has defended producerism, craft, property ownership and personal independence as a precondition for citizenship. It has opposed the "new class" of bureaucratic experts, corporate managers and elitist technocrats from the multiversity in the name of community integrity and individual competence. It has battled the invasion of consumer capitalism and its ironically destructive logic of progress.

Throughout his writings Lasch has supplemented his critical analysis with a carefully developed corrective ideology. It is based on a number of broad principles. At the most basic level, he has called for social reorganization to sustain a "small producer" ethic. This is crucial to challenging the bureaucratic organizations and scientific management of modern capitalism, he insists, since its schemes replaced the dignity of labor with the imperatives of production in the mid-nineteenth century and those of consumption in the twentieth. Work, Lasch contends, mediates the human relationship to nature, and its moral value and creativity are abandoned only at enormous cost. The "moral discipline" of a "calling," the "competence" conferred by craft, and the community cohesion of "democratic proprietorship" cannot be easily replaced by the drudgery of industrial labor or the gaudy attractions of consumption. Consumerism, Lasch has passionately insisted, has become the ideological twin of degraded labor, and only a restructuring of work can return that activity to its rightful place at the center of human existence.

At another level in his books, Lasch has encouraged the rooting and cultivation of several ideological principles. First, he suggests that a grasp of human limitation—as opposed to fantasies of self-fulfillment—must be the watchword of a genuinely reformist ideology. A more "modest assessment of the economic aspirations appropriate to human beings," a "humbler set of expectations than . . . access to a proliferating supply of goods," as Lasch has put it in *The True and Only Heaven* is essential to stalling the exploitive momentum of consumer capitalism. Second, the principle of "hope"—as opposed to the flaccid progressive optimism that too easily degenerates into despair—must regain renewed loyalty. Hope, in the words of this critic, "trusts life without denying its tragic character." It demands a strenuous definition of the good life, and the disciplined pursuit of justice in facing the future, but assumes neither of those are inevitable or entitlements. Third, Lasch asserts that "authority"—as opposed to the power to compel obedience—must find a new legitimacy in a just society. This authority would be based not only upon loyalty to the moral consensus of a community, but also upon the self-restraints of character to which it is linked. It would articulate the difference between right and wrong rather than sinking into the swamp of moral relativism. By posing respect for legitimate authority as the antidote to the search for private gratification, a reformed society would thus avoid the present dilemma of the modern capitalist order: a twisted situation where therapeutic manipulation and police power must desperately work in tandem to control the very self-indulgent behavior it has created.

Finally, for the psychological lifeblood of social regeneration, Lasch has urged a transfusion of what he terms "genuine selfhood." This notion neither elevates the self to narcissistic heights according to the therapeutic logic of self-fulfillment, nor envelops the self in nature according to the airy demands of New Age consciousness. Instead, genuine selfhood would be based on, in the words of this critic, "a critical awareness of man's divided nature. . . . [and] the

painful awareness between human aspirations and human limitations." It would recognize the simultaneous dependence and separation of human beings, and ground selfhood on the very struggle of psychological division, emotional tension, and moral conflict. According to Lasch, this individualism stems from the best in the Judaeo-Christian tradition rather than the capitalist acquisitive individualism which twists and parodies it. Its modern possibilities, as this critic contends in a wonderfully unfashionable phrase from *The Minimal Self,* constitute "the case for a guilty conscience."

All four of Lasch's books have prompted howls of outrage from the self-proclaimed forces of liberation, as the sense of betrayal mentioned earlier has surfaced with a vengeance.
—*Steven Watts*

Predictably, Lasch's provocative and wide-ranging social critique has brought heated reactions more noted for their passion than their insight. Misunderstood more than any other contemporary critic, he has been both praised and condemned for all of the wrong reasons. Many figures on the Right, for example, have endorsed his writings for upholding traditional values (family, work, self-restraint, moral responsibility), while conveniently overlooking the radical condemnation of modern consumer capitalism that provides the ideological basis for his position. The reaction of the Left has been even less restrained, and even more confused. All four of Lasch's books have prompted howls of outrage from the self-proclaimed forces of liberation, as the sense of betrayal mentioned earlier has surfaced with a vengeance. It is as if Tom Hayden, by virtue of some high-tech ideological special effects, had melted and transformed into William Bennett. From this direction Lasch has been condemned, rather than acclaimed, for upholding traditional values. Without bothering to grasp his argument about the link between consumerism and self-gratification, many Leftists have pictured him as an authoritarian opposing human liberation and particularly female liberation. They have termed him a reactionary who romanticizes the bourgeois family, patriarchal power, and bourgeois character of self-control. They have waxed indignant about this intellectual killjoy who wants to dampen choice and freedom, and yearns to replace the free-flowing identity of modern life with conformity and repression.

One might note that Lasch's acerbic comments about the greed and stupidity of the Right and the tantrums of the "infantile left" have not exactly helped matters. If conservatives have been relatively straightforward in their incomprehension of the consequences of endless abundance, he suggests scornfully, both cultural radicals and corporate liberals have appeared even worse in their penchant for self-delusion. These groups share a smug and elitist "politics of the civilized minority," in Lasch's assessment, and he describes the sheltered position of "new class" managers, experts, university professors, professionals and technocrats in *The True and Only Heaven:*

> Their educated jargon had lost touch with everyday spoken language and no longer served as a repository of the community's common sense. Academic discourse had achieved a certain analytical precision . . . at the expense of vividness and evocative power; while in fields like psychiatry, sociology, and social work, it merely distinguished insiders from outsiders. . . . The bureaucratization of language indicated what was happening to intellectual culture as a whole. . . . The people who stood at the forefront of the "communications age" had lost the ability to communicate with anyone but themselves. . . . The cosmopolitanism of educated specialists overcame the old barriers of local, regional, and even national identity but insulated them from ordinary people and ordinary human experience.

With an abundance of such passages, it is a wonder that Lasch has any friends at all.

Ultimately, the attacks on Lasch from so many directions reinforce the explanatory power of his central argument, namely that *both* the Left and Right in modern America are mirror images of one another in their common devotion to progress, abundance and self-gratification. The great strength of Lasch's critique lies in several profound insights that flow from this contention. First, by showing that the conventional categories of American political life are simplistic and superficial, Lasch has illuminated the hegemony of modern consumer capitalism and its therapeutic creed of self-fulfillment. Second—and here the argument parallels those of many critics both from the 1960s New Left and the 1980s Neoconservative movement—he has argued persuasively that the dominant ideology of modern America has been shaped by a "new class" of managers and experts in the corporate welfare state. These technocrats have shaped a consensus within the larger confines of progressive discourse. Debating only the *means* to growth and gratification rather than their fundamental validity, bureaucratic experts from the Left and Right have basically converged. Significantly, Lasch also reveals how even so-called "radical" solutions from the agenda of the contemporary Left—"the personal is political," private liberation and self-discovery, therapeutic identity, "narrative" conversion experiences—are cast in the very language and assumptions of the dominant culture. In other words, his criticism has revealed much about the public malaise that has gripped the American republic at the end of the twentieth century and produced a pervasive despair and disgust with our common life.

All of this does not imply, however, that Lasch's social criticism is without weakness. Several difficulties mar his efforts. Lasch is a marvelous polemicist with a gift for the biting turn of phrase or the deflating jibe, and an inspiration to those of us with a weakness for such activity. But at the same time, a lack of humor in his writing and a frequent tone of self-righteousness prove annoying while undermining the real moral strength of his argument. Occasionally, he seems to be in danger of becoming the "Church Lady" of the American Left. In addition, the intellectualist tendencies of Lasch's analysis appear occasionally unsettling. He is incredibly well-read and erudite, but sometimes to the point of suspicion. His criticism tends to inhabit a world of books that is several steps removed from actual people and their historical experience. In *The True and Only Heaven,* for instance, Lasch consistently examines not so much socioeconomic change itself as the great ideas and books *about* such change. Social experience and the thought of common people—in other words, their reaction to historical development—tend to fall into the background as broad theory and elite thinkers bear the brunt of analysis. Thus while Lasch ranges widely and deeply into an amazing array of texts from the last three centuries of Western experience, one often gets an unsettling sense of disembodied intellectual history at work. Viewing history from the top down, one suspects, provides a curious basis for a populist sensibility.

The issue of gender also gnaws at Lasch's criticism. While his accusation that much of the feminist movement has been caught up in the dominant-culture discourse of self-fulfillment and gratification may be on target—a position that is not that different from certain "second wave" feminist theorists—this does little to address the deeper, legitimate concerns about the meaning of feminine in our culture and the place of women in our society. Lasch's confusion about gender politics and their powerful resonance in modern life continuously crops up, most notably in his recent suggestion that the Constitution be amended to prohibit divorce between couples with children under the age of twenty-one. This eye-rubbing comment goes beyond authoritarianism. It is hallucinatory. In an age where traditional sex roles have changed irrevocably and for very complicated reasons, a critic of Lasch's shrewdness owes us more. To put the issue succinctly, his insistence about what feminism should not be tells us too little about what it *should* be.

Finally, Lasch appears frustratingly vague about the creation, or recreation, of a society of small producers in the context of a national and international economy that seems to be galloping hard in the direction of expanding global markets and proliferating consumer goods. Lasch's critique, powerful and hard-nosed as it may be, betrays a faint scent of romanticism. While the indictment of modern bureaucracy and growth may be intellectually compelling and emotionally satisfying, it may also appear irrelevant if left in the realm of theory. In practical terms, how exactly can an America of small-producers coalesce and survive in a world of international corporations, European economic consolidation, and global statist support for large-scale economic development? To be fully persuasive, an agenda for social, economic and cultural downsizing requires specifics, although the landslide of recent revolutionary events in the former Soviet bloc should give pause for reflection about the seeming imperviousness of bureaucratic power to radical reform.

In the final analysis, however, Lasch's critical writings constitute an impressive achievement. If nothing else, he has forced us to reconsider the possibilities of civic life in an age where a shallow narcissism reigns supreme.

—*Steven Watts*

In the final analysis, however, Lasch's critical writings constitute an impressive achievement. If nothing else, he has forced us to reconsider the possibilities of civic life in an age where a shallow narcissism reigns supreme. His linking of traditional cultural values—a commitment to family, community, tradition, moral struggle, human limitation—with a radical attack on the bureaucratic forms of consumer capitalism has shaped a position that strikes at the heart of a modern America in disarray. The fact that he has mystified and infuriated so many only supports the suspicion that he must be on to something. Lasch's populist sensibility has unmasked the complacency and convergence of both the mainstream Left and Right in contemporary America. He has revealed, simultaneously, the cynical evasiveness of a corporate "thousand points of light" and the self-indulgent solipsism of a liberationist "thousand points of spite."

Cutting through the therapeutic fog of modern identity politics, the disingenuous babble of bureaucratic expertise, the adolescent whine of victimization, and the trivial promises of consumerism, Christopher Lasch has recalled us to larger and nobler goals: a sense of place, the joys of purposeful work, moral struggle which alone produces justice, and an individualism that accepts the limitations of the human condition. His agenda of "populism for the twenty-first century" holds out the possibility of commitments beyond the self, of a regenerated public life, and of a planet saved from the ravages of progress. It also suggests an enormously provocative idea for those struggling with the dominations and degradations of modern American life: a convergence of cultural conservatism and political radicalism may indicate the clearest road to real reform.

Jeffrey Isaac and Christopher Lasch (essay date Winter 1992)

SOURCE: "Modernity and Progress: An Exchange," in *Salmagundi*, Vol. 9, No. 3, Winter, 1992, pp. 82-116.

[*Below, each writer separately explains the themes of* The True and Only Heaven. *In the first essay Isaac offers a point-by-point analysis of Lasch's social criticism in his book, concentrating on what he perceives as omissions and dismissals in Lasch's otherwise astute observations. In the second essay Lasch responds to specific criticisms of his book made by several reviewers, focusing especially on those by Isaac about Lasch's treatment of "the problem of democracy."*]

I. On Christopher Lasch

> Both the facts which justified my indignation and the moral motives which demanded it stemmed directly from the district where I was born. This explains . . . why everything I shall ever write, although I have traveled and lived abroad, is concerned solely with this same district or more precisely with the part of it which can be seen from the house where I was born. . . . It is a district, like the rest of the Abruzzi, poor in secular history and almost entirely Christian and medieval in its formation. . . . The conditions of human existence have always been particularly difficult there; pain has always been accepted there among the laws of nature, and the Cross welcomed and honored because of it. . . . The ashes of skepticism have never suffocated, in the hearts of those who suffered most, the ancient hope of the Kingdom of God on earth. . . . And this is a fact of enormous, fundamental importance; in a disappointed, arid, exhausted, weary country such as ours, it constitutes its real riches, it is a miraculous reserve.

Ignazio Silone wrote these words in 1949, reflecting back upon a political odyssey that had brought him full circle, from the simple dignities of his peasant upbringing in Southern Italy, to the "scientific" radicalism of the Communist Party, "living like a foreigner in my own country," to his eventual return to the initial sources of his rebellion: "an extension of the ethical impulse from the restricted individual and family sphere to the whole domain of human activity, a need for effective brotherhood, an affirmation of the superiority of the human person over all the economic and social mechanisms which oppress him." Silone testifies to the "real riches" of locale and tradition, a "miraculous reserve" unrecognized by science and political ideology.

Christopher Lasch's *The True and Only Heaven: Progress and its Critics* sounds a very similar theme. In the Introduction, possibly the most moving and revealing part of this long and fascinating book, Lasch offers an autobiographical sketch of his own political evolution from Midwestern progressivism to Marxist radicalism toward disenchantment with politics and a new appreciation for "the forbidden topic of limits." Written in the wake of eight years of Reaganism, the book is motivated by an effort to understand the appeal of right-wing populism and its critique of cultural modernism. A major theme of the book is that "the civilized minority" of left-liberals have failed to appreciate the value of lower middle class culture and its concern with family, neighborhood, and religion. While Lasch traces this failure to the deepest roots of modern thought, he indicates that for him this became apparent during his participation in the sixties New Left. Perhaps more decisive, however, has been Lasch's experience as a husband and father, seeking to sustain friendships and instill moral values in his children, yet confronting a world driven by technology, consumerism, and a disregard for particularity and limit. All that is solid melts into air, all that is holy is profaned . . .

This book is an effort to articulate some intellectual foundations for a more humane society, to discern some mooring to which we can anchor our need for meaning in our lives. As the subtitle makes clear, for Lasch the problem is progress itself. More precisely, it is a distinctively modern faith in technology, seen as a means of both expanding and satisfying human wants. Lasch argues that this view of the infinite elasticity of human demands and of nature as an object of ceaseless appropriation is rooted in the Scottish Enlightenment writings of Adam Smith, and is shared by liberals and Marxists alike. Writing in a distinctively Anglo-American idiom, Lasch echoes some of the arguments of Nietzsche, Heidegger, the Frankfurt School, and many current "postmodern" writers, that the problem of our time is humanism—a nihilistic faith in human power that underwrites the subjugation of otherness. But, as we will see, Lasch will have nothing of a radicalized or "post" modernism; his is a distinctively anti-modernist brand of social criticism.

Lasch convincingly identifies the mythical character of this humanism which, in its self-assured optimism about the future, refuses to recognize the contingent and provisional quality of all temporal things. Yet having done so Lasch refuses the easy way out—a pastoral appeal to restore traditional community. One of his more interesting arguments is that what he calls "nostalgia" is simply the obverse of a faith in progress—while progressives operate with an unrealistically sanguine view that everything is alterable, nostalgia represents an "abdication of memory," an idealization of a past that never was, a past invested with the same unambiguous goodness and innocence that progressives invest in the future. Against this Lasch insists, as Albert Camus once noted, that "the only paradises are those we have lost."

Rejecting both "progress" and "nostalgia," Lasch holds out for what he calls "hope," an attitude of common decency and perseverance, resting on an "unshakable conviction" that "the wicked will suffer, that wrongs will be made right, that the underlying order of things is not flouted with impunity." The remainder of the book is an effort to delineate what Lasch calls a tradition of populist social criticism based upon such hope. He locates this tradition in "the moral conservatism of the petty bourgeoisie, its egalitarianism, its understanding of the value of loyalty, and its struggle against the moral temptation of resentment." Lasch's excavation of this tradition draws upon diverse sources—the producer ethic of Thomas Paine, William Cobbett, and Orestes Brownson; the late nineteenth century American populist "campaign against improvement"; the neo-Calvinist moral criticism of Ralph Waldo Emerson, Thomas Carlyle and William James; the syndicalism of Georges Sorel and the guild socialism of G. D. H. Cole.

For Lasch this loose idiom of criticism culminates in "the spiritual discipline against resentment" articulated in mid-twentieth century America by Reinhold Niebuhr and Martin Luther King. Protestant ministers and social critics/activists, both supported the struggle against injustice, but also maintained that the human world was intrinsically imperfect and ridden with partiality and antagonism. Their writings join a deep dedication to moral values with a spiritually ingrained discipline against resentment towards antagonists. Both thus supported a vigorous political radicalism based upon a principled commitment to non-violent forms of empowerment. In presenting these figures as exemplars of his populism, Lasch is able to suggest that it is both ethically sensitive and politically efficacious, that the respect for limits is not a call for quiescence but for a certain kind of revolt, one epitomized by the civil rights movement in the American South.

Having made his case for such a "populism," Lasch returns in the final chapters to his critique of liberalism and socialism, arguing that the dirty little secret of twentieth century leftism is its hostility toward the lower middle class and its values. Contemptuous of populism's defense of localism and its hostility to progress, the left has recoiled from "public opinion" and has sought refuge in technocracy and anti-majoritarian institutions like the bureaucracy and the Supreme Court. Here Lasch's argument converges with neoconservative criticism, holding that the liberal-left intelligentsia constitutes a "new class" whose rarified programs of sexual liberation and social reform are advanced through its undemocratic hold on the strategic levers of cultural power. Yet Lasch sharply dissents from neoconservatism in his vigorous insistence that the roots of our cultural "decay" lie in a faith in progress shared by socialists and capitalists alike. Whereas neoconservatism is only ambiguously antimodern, criticizing the cultural but not the economic contradictions of capitalism, Lasch is unambiguously critical of modernism in culture *and* economics. Indeed a deep aversion to corporate power and the homogenizing tendencies of the capitalist market is a major component of his argument.

This is an extraordinarily rich and important book. While I have my doubts about the coherence of the "tradition of populist social criticism" that Lasch seeks to delineate, there is no doubt that his effort displays much creativity and ingenuity. He is certainly right that a distinctive feature of modernity is its faith in the link between human power and human freedom, and that this faith has been dashed by the events of the twentieth century—two world wars, totalitarianism, Holocaust, environmental degradation. The cultural malaise of our time goes beyond the physical and political nihilism of our faith in progress. It affects deeper questions about the meaning of life itself. Toward what ends should human power be exercised? What are the appropriate limits of human power? How can we discern and sustain value in a world whose relentless technological and economic progress seems to empty everything around us of value? How can we cultivate our distinctive differences in a world of ever more homogenizing economic and political imperatives? To simply enumerate these questions is to suggest the impoverishment of our politics, which seems unable to generate any effective public policy much less a compelling moral vision. As a result our political discourse seems strangely removed from the concerns of everyday life, and citizenship has become an experience of powerlessness before the seemingly inexorable imperatives of economic and political systems. There is thus much that is attractive in Lasch's arguments in favor of a sense of limits, and in defense of the importance of family, friends, neighborhood, and religion. For they no doubt touch on some of the most pressing needs experienced by many inhabitants of the modern world, who seek some worldly permanence, some haven in a heartless world.

Lasch's portrait of the Enlightenment . . . is at best a caricature and at worst a travesty of Enlightenment thinking.
—*Jeffrey Isaac*

And yet I find the overall thrust of Lasch's argument deeply disturbing. While he goes to great lengths to argue for hope against progress and nostalgia, it is frequently difficult for me to discern the difference between his "hope" and nostalgia. It is hard to avoid the suspicion that his critique of modernity is too easy, and that he ultimately seeks solace in a world that we have lost, a world, furthermore, that we should be *happy* to have lost. In short, in his compelling critique of an unrealistic faith in progress he indiscriminately refuses the possibility—indeed, the reality—of progress itself. Once we recognize, with Lasch, that a certain Promethean optimism characteristic of modern humanism is deeply flawed,

we must still acknowledge, as he does not, that humanism is a good thing, and that the modern world at least holds out the promise of becoming a better place than the world that preceded it.

Lasch's portrait of the Enlightenment, for example, is at best a caricature and at worst a travesty of Enlightenment thinking. He describes the cosmopolitanism of eighteenth century Europe as "arrogant" and "naive," and notes derisively that Kant "detached morality from its ordinary social context." In underscoring the blindness of Enlightenment thinkers to questions of particularity, he simply ignores the enormous importance of the universalistic perspective articulated so vigorously by thinkers like Kant. After all, the ordinary social context of eighteenth century Europe from which Kant detached morality was hardly hospitable to freedom for most of its participants. What are we to make of Lasch's oversimplified contention that Enlightenment cosmopolitanism "rested on the assumption that human beings are all alike . . . [which] sometimes gave rise to sweeping reforms untempered by the slightest doubt about the ability of enlightened legislators to prescribe for all"? Lasch is undoubtedly correct to associate enterprises like Bentham's Panopticon and the French Revolution with an enthusiastic faith in Reason bordering on authoritarianism. But what about such "sweeping" measures as press freedom, abolition of slavery, penal reform, the elimination of torture, and the expansion of suffrage? Lasch seems to cast indiscriminate suspicion upon all aspects of Enlightenment universalism. What he derisively calls "the assumption of uniformity" can only with great difficulty be construed as the ingenuous idea that all people are alike in all respects. Instead what one finds in examining the writings of thinkers like Locke, Rousseau and Kant, is a growing conviction that people, as members of a common human species, are fundamentally alike as regards their capacities for autonomy, and they are thus deserving of equal moral and political status as citizens. Voltaire, whom Lasch quotes, put it well: "They all have the same vital organs, sensibility, and movement." This is why, presumably, we can say with confidence that it is no more justified to torture or maim a Malaysian tribeswoman than it is to torture or maim a member of the local Midwestern community in which we happen to live. Without such an idea the notion of universal human rights would make no sense. Is it not progress that we no longer live in such a world?

Lasch's dismissiveness toward the Enlightenment extends beyond its egalitarian universalism to its more general valuation of reason. In discussing the similarities between the writings of Augustine and Machiavelli, he notes perceptively that both writers emphasize the inscrutability of the workings of the world. Lasch observes that "whatever the conceptual deficiencies in this way of understanding history, at least it did not expose . . . [us] to the delusion that man can control history for his own purposes or build a new kind of social order that will withstand the corrosive effects of time." The remark about "conceptual deficiencies" is made in passing, yet by failing to dwell on it Lasch is able to avoid coming to terms with a major aspect of modernity—science itself. As an eminent historian Lasch surely knows that the idea that an inscrutable Providence or Fortuna governs the universe is *profoundly* "deficient." But were he to acknowledge the importance, indeed the truth value, of modern, scientific, causal explanation, then he would also have to acknowledge that we *can* understand a great deal about the way the world works. Further, while we cannot subjugate history to our purposes or obviate the mortality of our creations and ourselves, we *can* employ our knowledge to shape the world in accordance with our purposes. We *do* make history, though not under circumstances of our own choosing, nor usually with all of the results that we intend. The alternative to believing this would be to believe that God, or that vengeful woman called Fortuna, makes our history for us behind our backs. It is doubtful that Lasch believes this, but it is clear that if he does he makes no effort to defend it.

Lasch often seems to valorize the sense of "mystery" about the universe that pervaded the pre-modern era. The great virtue of his book is its recognition of the danger of modernity, which strips away this veil of ignorance, and substitutes scientific knowledge, about physics, biology, politics, gender. In demystifying the world, modern reason deprives us of our quiescence, and encourages us to understand more, and to do more, to expand our horizons in every sense of the term. The humanistic idea that man is the center of the universe has certainly produced many pyrrhic victories but, as Max Weber recognized long ago, we simply cannot go back to a world we have lost. We live in a disenchanted world, and it can be no other way. What this means is that we must learn to live with our dangerous truths, especially the most dangerous and frightening truth of all—that we humans are enormously powerful creatures, and that only we can limit ourselves. Lasch's account skirts these truths. It fails to confront the fact that they are the achievements of modern enlightenment. And it draws its force from a neo-Calvinist conception of original sin and inherent human deficiency that is both undefended and deeply problematic.

This is how Lasch scornfully describes "the new class": "As the heir to the critical traditions of the scientific revolution and the Enlightenment, the new class pins its hopes on the eventual triumph of critical intelligence over superstition, cosmopolitanism over provincialism, man over nature, abundance over scarcity." But here he effaces the true dialectic of the Enlightenment. For of course many of us endorse reason over superstition, universalism over provincialism. Could Lasch possibly propose that we do otherwise? Would he have us close our eyes to the truths about evolution, as did William Jennings Bryan, or consider foreigners barbarians, as

did Aristotle? Lasch is correct in insisting that the vision of limitless technological and economic progress needs to be abandoned, in the name of a natural and an ethical ecology. But is this insight anything more than a more sensitive application of critical intelligence, advanced in the interest of the human species as a whole? Instead of arguing that the tradition of Enlightenment is simply a dangerous expression of hubris, Lasch should acknowledge that the tools of enlightenment need to be brought to bear upon enlightenment itself, that a reasoned consideration of our condition ought to instruct us about our own limits as partial, moral creatures inhabiting a finite and elusive universe.

We must limit ourselves. But in doing so we cannot rely upon the aid of any *deux ex machina*, nor can we take solace in the mysteries of Providence or Fortune. Here Lasch again fails to appreciate the dialectic of modernity. He sees that modern political ideologies, whether liberal, democratic, or socialist, have been wedded to an untenable faith in progress and an equally unrealistic underappreciation of the importance of particularity and difference. But he fails to see that these same ideologies have been indispensable agencies for the expansion of freedom in the modern world. Lasch has few kind words for liberalism. While attentive to its deficiencies as an economic doctrine he says little about its support for civil and political liberties. He is careful to say that Bayle's defense of religious toleration "made a certain kind of sense" at the time, and to insist (though not convincingly) that Orestes Brownson's critique of the separation of religion and politics, which he endorses, was not a call for religious establishment. But if Lasch appreciates the importance of religious toleration his defense is muted.

Perhaps the most disturbing line in the book is a vague and hostile reference to "the propaganda for unlimited abortion." In his discussion of this complex issue Lasch refuses to recognize that the movement in favor of a woman's right to choose is not driven by narcissism or selfishness but a concern for the autonomy of women and for the quality of life. Lasch writes that: "The objection that sex and procreation cannot be severed without losing sight of the mystery surrounding both struck liberals as the worst kind of theological obscurantism," leaving no doubt that he sympathizes with this objection. Now Lasch may be right that liberals have failed to understand the authenticity of what Lasch calls "lower middle class" beliefs. But it is also clear that most anti-abortion crusaders make no effort at all to understand what drives the pro-choice movement. Further, can Lasch deny that talk about the "mystery" of sex and procreation is anything but obscurantism, theological or otherwise? Does he really believe that we should ignore what we know through science, endorse a feminine mystique, abandon family planning and use the coercive powers of the state to force women to carry fetuses to term against their will?

> **In his discussion of this complex issue Lasch refuses to recognize that the movement in favor of a woman's right to choose is not driven by narcissism or selfishness but a concern for the autonomy of women and for the quality of life.**
> *—Jeffrey Isaac*

Nowhere does Lasch acknowledge that modern liberalism has established a certain sphere of personal liberty and privacy that is indispensable to freedom. Lasch is highly sensitive to those respects in which these liberties may be exercised irresponsibly. Yet while I would agree that a public philosophy requires more than a doctrine of individual liberties, I would also insist that no public philosophy suited to the conditions of modernity is possible without such a doctrine. We may not always like the choices our fellow citizens make, but the only way to eliminate such possibilities is to extinguish their freedom in the name of our own particular ethical or religious conceptions, a recipe for enormous cruelty and injustice.

Lasch's dismissiveness extends to social democracy as well, which for him is much like liberalism in its concern with economic growth and the individual consumer choices it brings. Here again his criticisms are incisive. Yet he fails to convince that consumption is all that has mattered to the socialist tradition, and in choosing to focus exclusively on the weaknesses of socialism he ignores its important contributions—its support of worker rights, minimum wage laws, social security, public health, education, housing, and family assistance for the poor. It is true that the bureaucratization of the welfare state is morally alienating and politically disempowering. But, especially given the ravages of the capitalist marketplace that Lasch himself discusses, is it possible to deny that the establishment of these social rights represents progress? On the book's final page Lasch indicates that populism "has generated very little in the way of an economic or political theory—its most conspicuous weakness." But he fails to draw the proper conclusion from this—that the ideal of small-scale proprietorship and freeholder independence is deeply anachronistic, whatever its virtues once were. The producer ethic of hard work and care may still have an important place, but in today's global economy it must be embedded in a system of economic regulations and welfare rights if it is to help foster freedom. Lasch seems unwilling to make such concession to contemporary reality. There is no ambivalence in his account, no appreciation of the necessary relation between the limits of modern liberalism, or socialism, and their essential *achievements*.

The most telling indication of this is the absence of serious attention to the problem of democracy in the book. It would,

I think, be unfair to read the book as a critique of democratic politics. Yet it seems worth noting that many of the writers from whom Lasch draws inspiration, particularly Emerson and Carlyle, can hardly be noted for their democratic sensibilities. After detailing Progressive criticisms of mass society Lasch disappointingly spends only two pages dismissing John Dewey's *The Public and its Problems*, one of the most important statements of democratic theory in the twentieth century. Most disturbing, perhaps, is Lasch's treatment of Georges Sorel. Challenging a number of criticisms normally levelled against Sorel, Lasch writes that: "Even his scorn for parliamentary democracy has to be removed from the indictment against Sorel, unless we can show that democracy embodies a demanding, morally elevating standard of conduct."

Here we arrive at the deepest weakness of Lasch's argument as a piece of political criticism. Can Lasch really mean that unless democracy can be shown to embody an elevated standard of conduct it deserves our scorn? This is not clear, but it is clear that for Lasch, like Sorel, democracy is symptomatic of the failings of modernity in the weak demands it makes upon solidarity and specific moral commitment. Democracy universalizes, it homogenizes, it includes, it tolerates. But it is hard to see these as weaknesses of democracy given what we know about the modern world. I would submit that democracy's openness and toleration is its great strength as a form of government appropriate to modernity. Much to the chagrin of neo-Calvinist populism, it is a feature of modernity that we can no longer rely upon an overarching cosmology to ground our political culture and provide us with a "morally elevating" conception of the good life. As thinkers as diverse as Michael Walzer and Jürgen Habermas have insisted, modernity is distinguished not simply by a disenchantment of the universe but by a corresponding pluralism of ethical commitments. How should I dress? What should I eat? Whom should I marry? How should I live? With whom should I associate? Once we abandon the naive view that it is possible to provide a single right answer to these questions derived from Nature, History, or God, we must acknowledge that there are a plurality of possible responses depending upon the particular cultural heritage with which one identifies. Catholics will answer these questions differently than Protestants; Muslims, differently than Jews; heterosexuals will answer differently than gays, African-Americans differently than white Americans. . . . The great virtue of democracy is that it provides a legal framework that accommodates and secures these differences at the same time that it provides a framework for dialogue and negotiation about common interests.

In this respect the ideal of democracy does indeed embody "a demanding, morally elevating standard of conduct"—the standard of critical intelligence and openness to difference. Jürgen Habermas has made this point emphatically: "Under the unrelenting moralizing gaze of the participant in discourse this totality [of particularistic ethical commitments] has lost its quality of naive acceptance, and the normative power of the factual has weakened. Familiar institutions can be transformed into so many instances of problematic justice." This "moralizing gaze" of democratic discourse, by allowing diverse ethical perspectives to come into contact with each other, encourages toleration and respect for difference. In coming to see how others ascribe value differently than we do, we come to appreciate the contingency of our own particular values. On the one hand this allows us to appreciate these values all the more precisely because they are distinctively ours, and ours because we choose to accept them as such rather than ascribe them to the mystery of nature. On the other hand, an awareness of the contingency of all values problematizes them, leaving nothing immune from the question of justice.

Thus, as a Jew, someone born into the Jewish tradition and raised as a Jew in a secular, multi-cultural environment, who has *chosen* to identify as Jewish, my views about how I should live my life will differ from those of most Protestants. In a modern democratic society it becomes possible for me to appreciate the contingency of my Jewish identity, and to prize it all the more as I respect the existence of other equally contingent ethnic and religious identities. Democratic secularism and universalism allow particular traditions to thrive, but they also set limits upon them in criminal and civil matters, prohibiting certain forms of physical abuse and allowing such procedures as civil divorce and geographical mobility. And democratic freedom of association, in allowing us to identify with the range of existing communities, also allows us to forge our own alternative lifestyles and communities. There is nothing in a democratic ethos that requires us all to live our lives in the same ways. But there is a commitment to mutual respect, and to participation in a larger common world that makes the retreat into insularity difficult if not impossible. Ideally we can learn to respect our differences and to robustly join together as citizens in order to shape broader forms of public identity.

Because we are all members of many overlapping communities and because we are all citizens of a common public world as well, identity formation and ethical commitment in a modern pluralistic democracy are complex matters indeed. We seem to lack the security of ethical conviction that can come only from inhabiting a closed moral universe; it is difficult to find a single home for ourselves in this heartless world, and it is impossible for us all to converge on the same places of shelter. But it is hard to imagine any alternative given the diversity of culture, religion, and association characteristic of the modern world.

Lasch is not unaware of this. But his book curiously insists on banishing it to the margins. Thus he concedes in the Pref-

ace that "I have no intention of minimizing the narrowness and provincialism of lower-middle-class culture; nor do I deny that it has produced racism, nativism, anti-intellectualism, and all the other evils so often cited by liberal critics." A similar caveat garnishes the next to last page of the book. But in between there is no discussion of this seamy side of what Lasch calls "populism," nor of the virtues of modern democratic theory and practice in supporting what I can only call more rational, hospitable politics. In this regard the unabashedly male Protestant tonality of the book is deceptive, for it would almost have us forget that profound ethnic, racial, and gender antagonisms are defining features of our cultural landscape, and that any compelling idiom of social thought needs to deal with them directly. Ironically, while Lasch chastises modern political theory for its supposed "assumption of uniformity," it is he who fails to acknowledge that only modern democracy has proven itself consistent with the very facts of human difference to which he appeals.

At the heart of my criticisms of the book lies one more fundamental question, regarding Lasch's genre of populist criticism itself. Lasch writes that "a sense of limits [is] the unifying thread of the following narrative." The great strength of the book is in fact the way it hammers away at this theme, intelligently invoking figures as diverse as Thomas Carlyle and Abraham Lincoln to underscore the tragic and provisional character of the human condition. But Lasch ignores the fact that his narrative of limits is not the only one we might construct. Despite its reliance upon a number of writers whose probing skepticism can only be described as modernist, the book's narrative articulates a distinctively *limited* conception of limits, one tied to petty bourgeois proprietorship, a conception of closeness to the land and acceptance of the cycles of nature, and a distinctly religious temper. Lasch encapsulates this temper when he quotes Martin Luther King's comment that: "We are gravely mistaken to think that religion protects us from the pain and agony of mortal existence. Life is not a euphoria of unalloyed comfort and untroubled ease. . . . To be a Christian one must take up his cross," approvingly noting King's affirmation of "the rightness of a world full of unmerited hardship."

Here Lasch seems to collapse two very different ideas. One is the belief that everything human is limited, finite, and mortal, that we can never have unalloyed faith in our aspirations or projects. The other is the belief that our difficulties are not simply inevitable but right, that they accord with some mysterious properties of the universe that we cannot understand and to which we should thus submit. This submission is not really a social or political so much as a *metaphysical* submission, an aversion to forms of inquiry or practice that might explode the horizons of our settled ways of living, our soulful havens. Compare this with Albert Camus: "Revolt is the certainty of a crushing fate without the resignation that ought to accompany it." Camus endorses Lasch's first insight, but resolutely defies the second. A cultural modernist, for whom the world was thoroughly disenchanted, he squarely confronted the limits of the human condition while simultaneously endorsing a ceaseless rebellion. "Rebellion is born of the spectacle of irrationality, confronted with an unjust and incomprehensible condition. But its blind impulse is to demand order in the midst of chaos, and unity in the very heart of the ephemeral. It protests, it demands, it insists that the outrage be brought to an end, and that what has up to now been built on shifting sands should henceforth be founded on rock. Its preoccupation is to transform. . . . Therefore it is absolutely necessary that rebellion find its reasons within itself, since it cannot find them elsewhere." Camus sees that there is no protection from the pain and agony of mortal existence, but he refuses to accept the essential rightness of suffering. He partakes of much of the sensibility shared by Lasch and King; but he is unable to share the religious conception of a higher purpose that underwrites it. As a creature of modern reason, he refuses such a leap of faith, believing, as he once put it, that "man is always a prey to his truths."

I mention Camus because he belonged to what James Wilkinson has called "the resistance generation" of political intellectuals forced to sustain meaning in their lives through their resistance to totalitarianism. People like Camus, Silone, Hannah Arendt, Dwight Macdonald, and Nicola Chiaromonte all appreciated the dangerous hubris at the heart of twentieth century politics and society. They shared an awareness of the power of what Lasch calls Nemesis, the compensatory force of the unanticipated that recommends moderation. They also sought to forge a political "third way" between capitalism and socialism based on this awareness. What distinguished them from Lasch's populist critics, however, was a refusal to take refuge in the shade of any mystique about the universe. As Camus put it, the sense of the absurd approaches "those waterless deserts where thought reaches its confines . . . the real effort is to stay there . . . in so far as that is possible, and to examine closely the odd vegetation of those distant regions."

Lasch tries to do this. In opposing both progress and nostalgia he tries to resist a too easy comfort. And he intermittently writes about the "ambivalence" warranted by modernity. But this effort to stay in the desert seems halfhearted. His hope seems empty. Camus offers us another, more satisfactory way of grappling with the problem of modern homelessness. Like Silone, he too retained a profound sense of the value of ordinary life, kinship, and locale, what he called, in his laudatory review of Silone's *Bread and Wine*, the "return from an abstract philosophy of the revolution to the bread and wine of simplicity." His writings are laced with reflections on his youthful experience of the Mediterranean and its importance to him. He wrote, echoing Silone, that: "a man's work is nothing but this slow trek to rediscover,

through the detours of art, those two or three great and simple images in whose presence his heart first opened." In his writings on the Algerian crisis he epitomized what Lasch calls the "remembrance" of the values of lower middle-class life, recalling "the story of the men of my family who, being poor and free of hatred, never exploited or oppressed anyone." He argued, against naive universalism, that "the way to human society passes through national society." Yet he also insisted, against blind particularism, that "national society can be preserved only by opening it up to a universal perspective."

This for me is the key—opening up particular traditions of ethnicity, family, religion, to a universal perspective. Like Silone, Camus's appreciation of particularity involves a *return from* the naive optimism of humanism to what can only be described as a chastened humanism. He saw that the values of family, religion, and ethnicity have their place. He appreciated the plain decency and sense of limits of traditional lower middle-class life. But he also appreciated the insufficiency of this way of life, its closed-mindedness, its danger of tribalism. Camus thus supported the effort not to assimilate or insulate these ways of life, but to open them up, to reappropriate them so that their ethical virtues, and the sense of meaning that they afford their participants, can be preserved in a modern, critical, universalist setting. This is not an easy thing for a modern intellectual to do. It involves a paradoxically rationalist and modernist effort to revalorize traditional ways of life. This is bound to satisfy neither hard-core traditionalists, by whom one will invariably be considered a traitor to his people, nor hard-core modernists, who seek to destroy all idols and level all traditions. It is easier either to retreat into tradition, or to disavow its value entirely. But this is simply another way of saying that the modern intellectual cannot help being an exile, a pariah of his or her many allegiances, and that this is a hard thing.

Lasch's book is a fascinating, provocative, and brave effort to explore this condition of homelessness. Yet while he powerfully indicts blind worship before the altar of progress, and insists that nostalgia is not the answer, Lasch falters in his failure to acknowledge the undeniable achievements, the progress, of modernity. Uncomfortable with the role of pariah, he resorts to an organic intellectualism of the American lower middle-class at the expense of his own modernist intelligence. While I can sympathize with much of Lasch's social criticism, I cannot join him in his indiscriminate dismissal of modern humanism. He would do better to embrace the deep and never-ending tension between the achievements of modernity, due to the expansion of human cognitive and organizational powers, and the danger that these achievements pose when we cease to be vigilant and critical of them. There is certainly great ambiguity and risk involved in this, and no small degree of anxiety and uncertainty. But there is,

I fear, no safe haven to which we can escape from these difficulties.

II. A Reply to Jeffrey Isaac

Reviews of *The True and Only Heaven* tend to support my contention that neither the left nor the right has much to contribute to political discussion. Both ideologies are now so rigid that new ideas make little impression on their adherents. The faithful, having sealed themselves off from arguments and events that might call their own convictions into question, no longer attempt to engage their adversaries in debate. Their reading consists for the most part of works written from a point of view identical with their own. Instead of engaging unfamiliar arguments, they are content to classify them either as orthodox or heretical. The exposure of ideological deviation, on both sides, absorbs energies that might better be invested in self-criticism—the waning capacity for which is the surest sign of a moribund intellectual tradition.

Left-wing reviewers predictably insist that I belong heart and soul to the right. The *Progressive's* hatchet-man, Matthew Rothschild, says that my book is the work of a "peculiar kind of right-wing crank." The only reason to bother with the thing at all is that "we need to take our adversaries seriously." What this means becomes clear when Rothschild proceeds to warn readers against the book's insidiously "fascistic appeal." The task of criticism evidently extends no farther than classification—the search for the right label. Once adversaries have been correctly identified as such, readers will know what to avoid. In case there is any doubt in my case, Rothschild reels off a list of ideological crimes: a "telling scorn for 'personal freedom'"; a "cavalier attitude about fascism"; an indulgent view of the lower middle class (which has "traditionally furnished the foot soldiers of fascism, racism, and nativism"); hostility to "liberation," and many more.

> **Reviews of *The True and Only Heaven* tend to support my contention that neither the left nor the right has much to contribute to political discussion.**
> —*Christopher Lasch*

Rothschild's outrage typifies the left-wing response to my recent writings; but right-wing reviewers are equally sensitive to the smell of heresy. Rothschild's prediction that the book will "please the powerful" and appeal to the "George Wills of the world" has proved no more accurate, alas, than other predictions issued by the left over the years. Reviewers on the right can recognize an adversary just as quickly as reviewers on the left, and they share the left's understanding of what it means to take adversaries seriously. Roger

Kimball's pompous polemic in the *New Criterion* is designed to leave no doubt that my environmentalism ("eco-angst," in Kimball's phrase), together with my attack on capitalism ("the most dazzlingly productive engine of wealth ever devised"), makes my work unacceptable to right-thinking conservatives. Kimball deplores even my attack on the idea of progress. As an antidote, he recommends Robert Nisbet's *History of the Idea of Progress*, passing over in silence my detailed examination of this very book and making no effort to answer my objections to it.

Kimball is not alone among right-wing reviewers in condemning *The True and Only Heaven*. Indeed he is far more restrained than most. In the *National Review*, Bruce Frohnen accuses me of leading unsuspecting readers down the familiar "road to serfdom." The academic left, Frohnen says, may take exception to passages questioning the wisdom of affirmative action, but it has nothing to fear from me after all; my concern with social justice (which is non-existent, according to Rothschild) gives the game away. "It is his fixation on 'wage slavery,' along with his tiresome leftist 'alternative' (the equal distribution of material goods), which keeps Mr. Lasch on the safe and beaten path of academic orthodoxy." Llewellyn H. Rockwell, Jr., writing in *Chronicles* has no more hesitation than Frohnen in classifying me as an unreconstructed social democrat—a "paleoleftist," in Rockwell's finely honed terminology. Ignoring my critical analysis of consumerism and distributive democracy, and bowdlerizing the several pages I wrote in specific criticism of John Maynard Keynes, Rockwell declares that I "embrace" Keynes's "immoral economics"—"mass theft through inflation and other forms of redistribution." Like Kimball, Rockwell puts in a good word for progress. "Socialists to the contrary, material improvement cannot be evil." (Did I say it was?) To argue against progress is to place oneself beyond the pale not just of left-wing opinion but of acceptable conservative opinion as well. According to Rockwell, my talk of limits betrays a continuing allegiance to the left. It amounts to the "Green-socialist agenda in a nutshell."

In the introduction to *The True and Only Heaven,* I noted that ideologues of the right and left, instead of addressing the social and political developments that tend to call conventional pieties into question, prefer to exchange accusations of fascism and socialism—this in spite of the obvious fact that neither fascism nor socialism represents the wave of the future. My reviewers have obligingly confirmed the accuracy of this observation by conferring both labels on the very same author, whose work they find (for opposite reasons) politically suspect. That much, as I say, was easy to foresee. What I did not foresee is the general reluctance, even on the part of reviewers less rigid in their ideological commitments than those I have mentioned, to explore the historical interpretations at the heart of my argument. Again and again, reviewers discuss the book as if it were itself an ideological manifesto, a fully developed set of political recommendations intended to rally the country to the banner of populism. Thus Jeffrey Isaac chides me for holding to a "deeply anachronistic" ideal of "small-scale proprietorship and freeholder independence," as if I am advocating an immediate return to the small workshop and the family farm. That is of course not my purpose, though it ought to be noted in passing that small proprietorship has by no means disappeared from industrial economies, and there is even some reason to hope (as Piore and Sabel have argued in their analysis of post-Fordist production) that it will become increasingly important as those economies move beyond mass production. The idea that small-scale production is "deeply anachronistic" is anachronistic in its own right; it belongs to the conventional wisdom of the recent past. Those who make a great point of bravely facing up to modern homelessness, like Isaac, often seem to be the last to hear of social and economic changes that are making conventional definitions of modernity obsolete. Not only the decline of mass production (which is being replaced by flexible production for specialized markets) but the breakup of overgrown nation-states and the rise of movements for regional autonomy indicate that the historical tide is no longer running in the direction of economic and political centralization. The latest news from what was formerly called the Soviet Union leaves no doubt about the future of centralized structures of all kinds. The collapse of these structures carries dangers of its own, but they are not the dangers Isaac has in mind when he accuses me of nostalgia for a "deeply anachronistic" ideal of localism and decentralized control.

But *The True and Only Heaven* is only indirectly and tentatively concerned with the future; its main concern is with the past. This is not to deny that it is also a "piece of political criticism" or that it should be judged accordingly. In this case, however, political criticism issues from historical interpretations that have to be understood on their own terms before political judgment can properly begin. The question I raised was not whether it would be a good idea to return to a pre-market economy but what people said about democracy when it became evident, in the latter half of the nineteenth century, that small property was disappearing. Could the virtues once associated with proprietorship be preserved, in some other form, under economic conditions that seemed to make proprietorship untenable? I reminded readers that democracy had once been linked, both in theory and in practice, to a broad distribution of property ownership. Before the Civil War it was generally agreed, across a broad spectrum of political opinion, that democracy had no future in a nation of hirelings. The emergence of a permanent class of wage-earners, after the war, was a profoundly disturbing development, which troubled commentators on American politics far more widely than we have realized. The agrarian movements that came to a climax in the People's party were not alone in their attempt to preserve small-scale production

through cooperative buying and selling. Liberals like E. L. Godkin, influential editor of the *Nation* and the New York *Evening Post*, also supported cooperative movements, until they discovered that their success depended on governmental regulation of credit and banking. In the early years of the twentieth century, syndicalists and guild socialists in Europe proposed bold and imaginative (if ultimately unworkable) solutions to the problem of wage labor, at a time when social democrats were capitulating to the "logic of history"—the allegedly inexorable movement toward centralization and the corresponding reduction of the citizen to a consumer. Even in the United States, which never developed a strong syndicalist movement, the issues raised by syndicalists nevertheless generated a good deal of speculation during the so-called progressive era. Progressive thought was lively and suggestive precisely because so much of it resisted the political orthodoxies associated with the idea of progress. A number of important progressives refused to accept the division of society into a learned and a laboring class as the price of progress. Nor did they embrace the welfare state as the only way of protecting workers' interests. They admitted the force of the conservative objection that welfare programs would promote a "sense of dependence," in Herbert Croly's words, but they rejected conservatives' claim that "the wage-earner's only hope is to become a property owner." Some of the responsibility for "operating the business mechanism of modern life," Croly maintained, would have to be transferred to the working class—or rather, wrested by the workers from their employers, since their "independence . . . would not amount to much" if it was "handed down to them by the state or by employers' associations."

Conventional wisdom has it that we live in an interdependent society, in which the virtue of self-reliance has become just as anachronistic as small-scale production. The populist tradition, as I understand it, took issue with this view. Independence, not interdependence, was the populist watchword. Populists regarded self-reliance (which of course does not preclude cooperation in civic and economic life) as the essence of democracy, a virtue that never went out of demand. Their quarrel with large-scale production and political centralization was that they weakened the spirit of self-reliance and discouraged people from taking responsibility for their actions. That these misgivings are more cogent than ever is suggested by the cult of the victim and its prominence in recent campaigns for social reform. It was the strength of the civil rights movement, which can best be understood as part of the populist tradition, that it consistently refused to claim a privileged moral position for the victims of oppression. Martin Luther King was a liberal in his theology but a populist in his insistence that black people had to take responsibility for their lives and in his praise of the petty bourgeois virtues: hard work, sobriety, self-improvement. If the civil rights movement was a triumph for democracy, it was because King's leadership transformed a degraded people into active, self-respecting citizens, who achieved a new dignity in the course of defending their constitutional rights.

In view of my attempt to rethink the democratic tradition—in particular, to distinguish participatory from distributive democracy, the democracy of active and independent citizens from the democracy of consumers—Isaac's curious complaint that I fail to give "serious attention to the problem of democracy" becomes almost incomprehensible (though I will try to explain it). The extent of my interest in democracy cannot be measured by the amount of attention given to Carlyle and Sorel, unless Isaac wants us to believe that democracy has nothing to learn from its critics. As for John Dewey, it is quite misleading to say that I "dismiss" *The Public and Its Problems*. I simply point out the inadequacy of Dewey's reply to Walter Lippmann, who maintained that public opinion is necessarily ill-informed and that government is best left to specialists. In opposition to Lippmann, Dewey rightly took issue with the idea that democracy meant nothing more than universal access to the good things of life. In Dewey's view, it had to rest on the "assumption of responsibility" by ordinary men and women—on a "stable and balanced development of mind and character." What he failed to explain was just how responsibility could thrive in a world dominated by giant organizations and mass communications. Classical theorists of democracy doubted whether self-government could work very effectively beyond the local level—which is why they favored as much localism as possible. Dewey himself hoped for a "return movement . . . into the local homes of mankind," but he could not tell his readers how such a return was to come about, since he took the inevitability of centralization for granted, together with the "disintegration of the family, church, and neighborhood."

Dewey's exchange with Lippmann raises one of the questions that puzzles Isaac—the question of whether democracy implies high standards of personal conduct. Dewey clearly thought it did. Isaac, who doesn't—but who claims to admire Dewey as a great democratic theorist—should ask himself whether Dewey's entire program of education wasn't intended precisely to promote the "solidarity" and "specific moral commitment" that he himself finds so threatening. In the book Isaac thinks he admires, *The Public and Its Problems*, Dewey noted with alarm that "the loyalties which once held individuals, which gave them support, direction, and unity of outlook on life, have well-nigh disappeared." The problem to which his title referred was how to reconstitute them. Like other progressive thinkers, notably Charles H. Cooley, Dewey was bent on refuting critics of democracy who claimed that it fostered mediocrity, self-indulgence, an excessive love of comfort, sloppy workmanship, and a timid conformity to prevailing opinion. The idea that democracy is incompatible with excellence, that high standards are inherently elitist (or as we would say today, sexist, racist, and

so on) has always been the best argument against it. Unfortunately many democrats secretly (or not so secretly) share this belief and are therefore unable to answer it. Instead they fall back on the claim that democratic men and women make up in tolerance what they lack in the way of character. The latest variation on this familiar theme, its *reductio ad absurdum*, is that a respect for cultural diversity forbids us to impose the standards of privileged groups on the victims of oppression. This is so clearly a recipe for universal incompetence (or at least for a disastrous split between the competent classes and the incompetent) that it is rapidly losing whatever credibility it may have had when our society (because of its abundance of land and other natural resources, combined with its chronic shortage of labor) offered a more generous margin for incompetence. The mounting evidence of widespread inefficiency and corruption, the decline of American productivity, the pursuit of speculative profits at the expense of manufacturing, the deterioration of our country's material infrastructure, the squalid conditions in our crime-ridden cities, the alarming and disgraceful growth of poverty, and the widening disparity between poverty and wealth, which is morally obscene and politically explosive as well—these developments, the ominous import of which can no longer be ignored or concealed, have reopened the historical debate about democracy. At the moment of its dazzling triumph over communism, democracy is coming under heavy fire at home, and criticism is bound to increase if things continue to fall apart at the present rate. Formally democratic institutions do not guarantee a workable social order, as we know from the example of India and Latin America. As conditions in American cities begin to approach those of the Third World, democracy will have to prove itself all over again.

Liberals have always taken the position that democracy can dispense with civic virtue. According to this way of thinking, it is liberal institutions, not the character of citizens, that make democracy work. As Isaac puts it, democracy "provides a legal framework" that makes it possible for people to live with their differences. The impending crisis of competence and civic trust, however, casts a heavy pall of doubt over the agreeable assumption that institutions, as opposed to character, provide all the virtue democracy needs. The crisis of competence suggests the need for a revisionist interpretation of American history, one that stresses the degree to which liberal democracy has lived off the borrowed capital of moral and religious traditions antedating the rise of liberalism. A second element in this revisionism is a heightened respect for hitherto neglected traditions of thought, deriving from classical republicanism and early Protestant theology, that never had any illusions about the unimportance of civic virtue. The more we come to appreciate the loyalties that once gave individuals "support, directions, and unity of outlook on life," the more we will need to look for guidance to thinkers who understood that democracy has to stand for something more demanding than enlightened self-interest, "openness," and toleration.

It isn't simply a question of whether democracy can survive. That alone is enough to give new urgency to the issues that people like Isaac have always been so eager to avoid, notwithstanding their ostensible interest in the "problem of democracy." But the deeper question, of course, is whether democracy deserves to survive. For all its intrinsic attractions, democracy is not an end in itself. It has to be judged by its success in producing superior goods, superior works of art and learning, a superior type of character. "Democracy can never prove itself beyond cavil," Walt Whitman wrote in *Democratic Vistas*, "until it founds and luxuriously grows its own forms of art," its own "religious and moral character," the "perfect personalities" that will make "our western world a nationality superior to any hither known." The test of democracy, Whitman thought, was whether it could produce an "aggregate of heroes, characters, exploits, sufferings, prosperity or misfortune, glory or disgrace, common to all, typical of all."

For Isaac and his kind, peace-loving academics who cherish the ideal of the open mind (even if it turns out to be an empty mind), this talk of heroes, exploits, glory, and disgrace is automatically suspect—frightening, in fact. The call for models of heroism "common to all" seems to threaten the "pluralism of ethical commitments," as Isaac puts it, that democracy is obliged to protect. In the absence of common standards, however, tolerance becomes indifference, and cultural pluralism degenerates into an aesthetic spectacle in which the curious folkways of our neighbors are savored with the relish of the connoisseur but our neighbors themselves, as individuals, are never held up to any kind of judgment. The suspension of ethical judgment, in the conception or misconception of pluralism now current, makes it inappropriate to speak of "ethical commitments" at all. Aesthetic appreciation is all that can be achieved under current definitions of cultural diversity. The questions to which there is no "single right answer," according to Isaac, turn out to be lifestyle questions, in the jargon of the day. "How should I dress? What should I eat? Whom should I marry? With whom should I associate?" In this context, the question that really matters—"how should I live?"—also becomes a matter of taste, of idiosyncratic personal preference, at best of religious or ethnic identification. But the question, rightly understood, requires us to speak of impersonal virtues like fortitude, workmanship, moral courage, honesty, and respect for adversaries. If we believe in these things, moreover, we must be prepared to recommend them to everyone, as the moral preconditions of a good life. To refer everything to a "plurality of ethical commitments" means that we make no demands on anyone and acknowledge no one's right to make any demands on ourselves. The suspension of judgement logically condemns us to solitude. Unless we are prepared to

make demands on each other, we can enjoy only the most rudimentary kind of common life.

Even if we can't agree on the definition of a good life—and it could be argued that we have not yet seriously made the effort—we can surely agree on minimal standards of workmanship, literacy, and general competence. Without these, we have no basis on which either to demand respect or to grant it. Common standards are absolutely indispensable to a democratic society. Societies organized around a hierarchy of privilege can afford multiple standards, but a democracy cannot. Double standards mean second-class citizenship.

The recognition of equal rights is a necessary but insufficient condition of democratic citizenship. Unless everyone has equal access to the means of competence (as we might speak of them), equal rights will not confer self-respect. That is why it is a mistake to base the defense of democracy on the sentimental fiction that people are all alike. Isaac faults me for attributing this view to the Enlightenment, only to adopt it himself a few lines later on: "People, as members of a common human species, are fundamentally alike as regards their capacities for autonomy, and . . . are thus deserving of equal moral and political status as citizens." But in fact people are not alike in their capacities (which of course does not prevent us from imaginatively entering the lives of others). As Hannah Arendt has pointed out, the Enlightenment got it backward. It is citizenship that confers equality, not equality that creates a right to citizenship. Sameness is not equality, and "political equality, therefore, is the very opposite of the equality before death," Arendt says, ". . . or of equality before God." Political equality—citizenship—equalizes people who are otherwise unequal in their capacities, and the universalization of citizenship therefore has to be accompanied not only by formal training in the civic arts but by measures designed to assure the broadest distribution of economic and political responsibility, the exercise of which is even more important than formal training in teaching good judgement, clear and cogent speech, the capacity for decision, and the willingness to accept the consequences of our actions. It is in this sense that universal citizenship implies a whole world of heroes. Democracy requires such a world if citizenship is not to become an empty formality.

Democracy also requires a more invigorating ethic than tolerance. Tolerance is a fine thing, but it is only the beginning of democracy, not its destination. In our time, democracy is more seriously threatened by indifference than by intolerance or superstition. We have become too proficient in making excuses for ourselves—worse, in making excuses for the "disadvantaged." We are so busy defending our rights (rights conferred, for the most part, by judicial decree) that we give little thought to our responsibilities. We seldom say what we think, for fear of giving offense. We are determined to respect everyone, but we have forgotten that respect has to be earned. Respect is not another word for tolerance or the appreciation of "alternative lifestyles and communities," in Isaac's revealing phrase. This is a tourist's approach to morality. Respect is what we experience in the presence of admirable achievements, admirably formed characters, natural gifts put to good use. It entails the exercise of discriminating judgment, not indiscriminate acceptance.

Our society labors in the grip of two great, paralyzing fears: fanaticism and racial warfare. Having belatedly discovered the contingency of all belief-systems and ideologies, we are obsessed with the terrors that arise when partial truths are taken as universal. In a century dominated by fascism and communism, this fear is understandable; but by this time it is surely possible to argue, without being accused of complacency, that the totalitarian menace is receding. Nor is Islamic fundamentalism an equivalent danger, as we are so often told. Those who worry overmuch about ideological fanaticism often fall into a complacency of their own, which we see especially in liberal intellectuals. It is as if they alone understood the danger of misplaced universality, the relativity of truth, the need for suspended judgment. They see themselves, these devoutly open-minded intellectuals, as a civilized minority in a sea of fanaticism. Priding themselves on their emancipation from religion, they misunderstand religion as a set of definitive, absolute dogmas resistant to any kind of intelligent appraisal. They miss the discipline against fanaticism in religion itself. The "quest for certainty", as Dewey called it, is nowhere condemned with such relentless passion than in the prophetic tradition common to Judaism and Christianity, which warns again and again against idolatry, the idolatry of the church included. Like many other intellectuals, Isaac assumes that religion satisfies the need for a "safe haven"—which shows only that he doesn't know what he is talking about. There are limits, it seems, even to the openness of the open mind—limits quickly revealed when the conversation turns to religion.

The problem of racial intolerance is closely linked to fanaticism. Here again, there is a good deal of complacency and self-righteousness mixed up in the fear of intolerance. Liberal intellectuals seem to labor under the delusion that they alone have overcome racial prejudice. The rest of their country, in their view, remains incorrigibly racist. Their eagerness to drag every conversation back to race is enough in itself to invite the suspicion that their investment in this issue exceeds anything that is justified by the actual state of race relations. Monomania is not a sign of good judgment. But whether it springs from self-righteousness or panic or a mixture of the two, the assumption that most Americans remain racists at heart cannot stand up to close examination. The improvement of racial attitudes is one of the few positive developments of recent decades. Not that racial conflict has subsided; but it is a serious mistake to interpret every conflict as evidence of the retrograde outlook of ordinary

Americans—as a revival of the historic intolerance that has played so large a part in our country's history. The new racism is reactive rather than residual, let alone resurgent. It is a response, however inappropriate and offensive, to a double standard of racial justice that strikes most Americans as unreasonable and unfair. Since opposition to an "affirmative" double standard is routinely dismissed as racist, one reaction to this insult, from working-and lower middle-class people harassed by affirmative action and busing, and now from college students harassed by attempts to enforce politically correct language and thought, is to accept "racism" as a badge of honor—to flaunt it, with studied provocation, in the face of those who want to make racism and minority rights the only subject of public discussion.

From the point of view of liberals single-mindedly obsessed with racism and ideological fanaticism, the "problem of democracy," as Isaac calls it, can only mean one thing—the defense of what they call cultural diversity. As I have already indicated, their respect for diversity is better understood as a form of aesthetic appreciation, but in any case it gets in the way of more important issues—the crisis of competence, the spread of apathy and a suffocating cynicism, the moral paralysis of those who value "openness" above all. In the 1870's, Walt Whitman wrote: "Never was there, perhaps, more hollowness at heart than at present, and here in the United States. Genuine belief seems to have left us." Those words are as timely as ever. When will we be ready to listen to them?

Robert B. Westbrook (essay date March 1995)

SOURCE: "Christopher Lasch, *The New Radicalism,* and the Vocation of Intellectuals," in *Reviews in American History,* Vol. 23, No. 1, March, 1995, pp. 176-91.

[*In the essay below, Westbrook examines the influence of* The New Radicalism in America *on the American intellectual community .*]

> ***The New Radicalism*** is really a brilliant book, a book of such importance that people will be talking about it as long as they are talking about 20th Century history. It is an unconventional book, because it is based not on massing evidence but on *thinking* about history, an endeavor that has largely gone out of fashion.
>
> —William Leuchtenburg to Christopher
> Lasch, July 5, 1965.

In a foreword to the twenty-fifth anniversary edition of Richard Hofstadter's *American Political Tradition* (1973), Christopher Lasch paid tribute to the late historian and teacher who, above all others, had provided a model for his own vocation.

> Even though his career was cut short in its prime, leaving us immeasurably impoverished by the loss, Richard Hofstadter left a full and rounded body of work, not merely one or two important books, which is the best that most historians can hope for.... Hofstadter's imagination never rested for long, and his thought ranged widely, embracing political, social, and cultural history—he was impatient with such distinctions—and extending to all periods of American history. Yet his ideas constantly return to certain central preoccupations stated at the outset of his career.

In the wake of Lasch's own untimely death in February 1994, a certain eeriness settles over these words, for they apply as well to Lasch as to Hofstadter. Moreover, Lasch shared many of Hofstadter's "central preoccupations," including a concern for the role of the intellectual in modern American society and culture. It was this concern that animated *The New Radicalism in America,* the book that established Lasch's reputation at a young age as a penetrating and controversial social critic. *The New Radicalism* was also the book that made Lasch a figure of commanding importance for the generation of historians that followed his. For those of us middle-age who now find ourselves standing in something of the same relation to Lasch as he stood to Hofstadter, a relation at once admiring and contentious, *The New Radicalism* is the book with which a retrospective view of the life and work of Christopher Lasch must begin.

In an American Historical Association convention session honoring Lasch shortly before his death, Richard Fox recalled his first encounter with Lasch's writing, offering what seems to me to be a representative account of the experience of those of us who found a lodestar in *The New Radicalism.* As Fox said:

> Each of us, if we are lucky, encounters in adolescence or early manhood some writer, some artist, some musician, who seems to speak as much from us as to us, who gives voice to thoughts or feelings we may well not yet have articulated, but which we recognize immediately, mysteriously, as our own, as coming from us too. To encounter such a writer when we are passing from one regime of selfhood to another is startling, enthralling, transformative. Such a meeting gives us a model to emulate, and it gives us more: the realization that we have been invited to take up a calling and to join a community. [Lasch's] *New York Review* essays in 1969 had that sort of impact on me. They led me to *The New Radicalism in America,* the reading of which quite liter-

ally changed my life course by tipping the scales and persuading me to become an historian, not the journalist I was thinking about being.... [Lasch's] prose in the whole book sounded like music and felt like revelation. I wanted to know what he knew, and write as he wrote.

As Fox suggests, those of us with intellectual aspirations struggling to figure out what sort of life to make for ourselves amidst the political turmoil of the late sixties found in *The New Radicalism* an "assertion of the intellectual vocation" quite at odds with that proffered by our liberal elders or most of our radical contemporaries, an assertion centered in Lasch's effort to defend a role for intellectuals as social critics at once detached and engaged. If we (like many of his critics) were more certain of Lasch's view of the irresponsibilities of the intellectuals whose careers he surveyed in his book than of the alternative he wished to hold out to us, we strained to grasp his point and to learn from the manner in which he practiced his ideals in the pages of the *New York Review of Books* and other journals of opinion. Because Lasch so forcefully made the responsibilities of the intellectual one of his preoccupations, those of us who hoped also to exercise those responsibilities looked to him—and continued to look to him—for instruction in their practice, even when we found ourselves at odds with the substance of his arguments.

This is not to say, especially in retrospect, that *The New Radicalism* was not the confusing, ill-conceived, and sometimes wrong-headed book that its critics said it was. If the book was not, as Arthur Mann charged in a scathing review, "flawless in its failure," it was, in important respects, weak. And its shortcomings need not be obscured in order to appreciate its persistent virtues.

Something of the book's weaknesses can be suggested simply by describing its argument and method. The "main argument" of the book, Lasch said, was that "modern radicalism or liberalism can best be understood as a phase in the social history of intellectuals." In the United States in particular, "the rise of the new radicalism coincided with the emergence of the intellectual as a distinctive social type." Although intellectuals—people "for whom thinking fulfills at once the function of work and play"—had long existed in literate societies, only since the turn of the century had they constituted a self-conscious subculture, a class or status group that stood apart from and at odds with bourgeois culture. This development was part of a larger process, "the cultural fragmentation that seems to characterize industrial and postindustrial societies." The subculture of intellectuals was symptomatic of the decline of community and the emergence of a "mass society" which tended "to break down into its component parts, each having its own autonomous culture and maintaining only the most tenuous connections with the general life of society—which as a consequence has almost ceased to exist."

The newness of the new radicalism, Lasch contended, lay in its "confusion of politics and culture," a promiscuous mixing of political and cultural means and ends in which political reform came to be conceived as an instrument of cultural renewal and cultural change as a form of political action. "The new radicalism differed from the old," he said, "in its interest in questions which lay outside the realm of conventional politics":

> It was no longer his political allegiance alone which distinguished the radical from the conservative. What characterized the person of advanced opinions in the first two decades of the twentieth century—and what by and large continues to characterize him at the present time—was his position with regard to such issues as childhood, education, and sex; sex above all. Politics by comparison was almost immaterial, if by politics one refers to the traditional business of government and statecraft: taxes, tariffs, treaties. But the new radicals had not so much abandoned politics as redefined it, bringing to political debate questions formerly reserved to art and letters.

This shifting of the terrain of politics to spheres of experience once regarded as private, Lasch argued, reflected the anxieties and ambitions of intellectuals at once cut off from middle-class society and yet eager to reconstruct it.

In the identification of many new radicals with social outcasts such as "women, children, proletarians, Indians, and Jews," Lasch saw further evidence that the new radicalism was tied to the emergence of intellectuals themselves in exile from middle-class society. In revolt against the "overcivilized" households in which they were raised, radical intellectuals looked for countercultural inspiration in repressed instincts, buried levels of the self, and the "uncivilized" lives of primitive peoples and lower classes. Yet, he observed, the new radicals were hardly content with their marginal role or at ease with social conflict. Their new brand of "cultural politics" with its essentially "educational" program for social transformation betrayed its origins in the will to power of a newly self-conscious intelligentsia by suggesting that men and women of learning ought to occupy "the strategic loci of social control" from which they might foster the "adjustment" to modernity of their fellow Americans, including those outcasts with whom they sometimes identified. "The new radicals," Lasch remarked, "were torn between their wish to liberate the unused energies of the submerged portions of society and their enthusiasm for social planning, which led in practice to new and subtler forms of repression."

> *The New Radicalism* was also the book that made Lasch a figure of commanding importance for the generation of historians that followed his.
> —*Robert B. Westbrook*

For Lasch the most troubling feature of this effort of the new radicals to overcome their social and cultural isolation was the loss of the detachment it entailed, a detachment that he regarded as essential to the vocation of the intellectual. The intellectual, he said, is "a person whose relationship to society is defined, both in his eyes and in the eyes of the society, principally by his presumed capacity to comment upon it with greater detachment than those more directly caught up in the practical business of production and power." Because detached social criticism was the business of intellectuals, their relationship to the rest of society was "never entirely comfortable." This discomfort, Lasch implied, was something intellectuals would have to live with if they were to be true to their vocation. But all too often the new radicals sought to relieve their discomfort by abandoning their detachment. At their worst, they gave in to an "outraged envy" of men of power and went in search of a piece of the action for themselves. One could see this envy, he said, "in the discontent of intellectuals not only with the old conception of culture but with intellectual life itself; in their eagerness to escape from the isolation to which intellectuality seemed to condemn them; in the self-effacement and self-contempt which made them yearn to put their abilities at the service of the community." For the new radicals, "disinterested inquiry and speculation could no longer suffice"; they "could find comfort and meaning, it appeared, only in large, encompassing movements of masses of people, of which they could imagine themselves a part."

Lasch sought to make this argument by means of a series of biographical essays, portraits of "progressive intellectuals" whom he took to be exemplary new radicals. Jane Addams, Randolph Bourne, Mabel Dodge Luhan, Lincoln Colcord, Colonel Edward House, and Lincoln Steffens received chapter-length treatment, while more thematic chapters on feminism, "politics as social control," and the response of *The New Republic* to World War I rested on shorter sketches of the work of, among others, Robert Herrick, Charlotte Perkins Gilman, Fremont Older, John Dewey, Edward A. Ross, and Walter Lippmann. The book's final chapter, "The Anti-Intellectualism of the Intellectuals," examined the legacy of the new radicalism after 1920, finding its characteristic features and flaws in both the "hard-boiled" liberalism of the likes of Reinhold Niebuhr, Sidney Hook, and Arthur Schlesinger, Jr., and in the "increasingly shrill, increasingly desperate, and increasingly bizarre" radicalism of intellectuals such as Dwight Macdonald. The book ends (in "a clatter of loud Wagnerian chords," Lasch told a friend) with a portrayal of Norman Mailer as the apotheosis of the new radicalism.

> With Norman Mailer, the body of ideas and assumptions which I have called the new radicalism achieved some kind of final and definitive statement. The confusion of power and art, the effort to liberate the social and psychological "underground" by means of political action, the fevered pursuit of experience, the conception of life as an experiment, the intellectual's identification of himself with the outcasts of society—these things could be carried no further without carrying them to absurdity. Perhaps Mailer had carried them past that point already.

As this brief summary suggests, Lasch assembled a peculiar cast of characters in *The New Radicalism*. Holding them together in a single book with a singular argument, especially one as sweeping as that which Lasch advanced, proved difficult. As William Leuchtenburg told Lasch, he had undertaken "a kind of high wire act."

> It just is not possible, one says, for you to put together such incongruous people or to rest such bold assertions on so few footnotes—and one thanks God that you have gotten away with it in this chapter only to be unnerved to see that you are trying something still more difficult in the next chapter until finally comes the climax when a book on Jane Addams ends with Norman Mailer—and you shudder and say O my God he's not really going to bring in Norman Mailer—only to see you carry that off triumphantly too. . . . You make reading the book not something to be commented upon at a distance but something to be lived through and experienced.

Unlike Leuchtenburg, others were certain that Lasch had fallen off the wire. "Even the most credulous reader," Mann sniffed, "is likely to question an interpretation that Jane Addams set ideas in motion that culminated in the fantasies of Norman Mailer." Yet even if one finds Lasch's fine thread of argument connecting Addams and Mailer and finds it persuasive, one is still not quite sure what to make of his odd assortment of characters, for he offered no rationale for his selection of subjects. He himself admitted that "it is not possible to write about these people as a group, since they weren't, most of them having not had contact with each other at all." Lasch's new radicals cohere as a group only in the pages of *The New Radicalism,* and to some critics it appeared that he had chosen his subjects to exemplify rather than test his general argument. As Max Beloff put it, "while one can illustrate a sociological argument with instances, one cannot build one on them."

Having read through Lasch's papers from the early 1960s, I believe the explanation for the peculiar congregation in *The New Radicalism* is more mundane. This was a book for which, in a sense, Lasch did little fresh research. Although it is filled with material from manuscript sources, this research and most of the work in published sources evident in the book had been done in the course of work on four other projects: Lasch's doctoral dissertation (published in 1962 as *American Liberals and the Russian Revolution*), a short book on Jane Addams (never published), a book on the history of American women and feminism he planned to write with William Taylor (aborted), and a textbook on the period 1877-1914 that was to be published in a series that he and Taylor put together (abandoned). And much of what he had to say in the final chapter of *The New Radicalism* drew on his initial ventures as a public intellectual in the early sixties in journals such as the *Nation* in which he began to break from the "realism" of George Kennan that had shaped his thinking in the 1950s and to articulate a critique of Cold War liberalism. While Lasch was apparently thinking about writing "a social history of the American intellectual from about 1880 to the present" as early as the fall of 1961 and some of the arguments in *The New Radicalism* begin to emerge then in his correspondence and in lectures at the University of Iowa, he does not seem to have committed himself to a book like *The New Radicalism* until the spring of 1963. At that time, he and his family decided to spend a year's leave from teaching in England, and with Hofstadter's encouragement, he went to work there on a book of biographical essays based on material that he had gathered largely for other purposes. The general argument Lasch advanced in *The New Radicalism* was one that seemed to make sense of the wide, deep, but unsystematic and even inadvertent research he had already done. In important respects, the book was the peculiar sort of book it was because it was a book written in haste, the kind of book that he (unlike most of us) could write quickly in a relatively isolated Cambridgeshire cottage. Although he made use of a little writing he had already done, Lasch wrote most of *The New Radicalism* in nine months.

If Lasch was willing to acknowledge that his new radicals were "a motley crew if I ever saw one," he nicely evaded the charge that they were "unrepresentative" men and women. If these intellectuals were not "typical of their times," they were, he argued, representative or, perhaps better, symptomatic of their times in that their experience "could only have happened at a particular place at a particular time." But this was a claim that he did little to substantiate, and a number of critics pointed out the similarities between his interpretation of the world of progressive intellectuals and that offered by Stanley Elkins in his book, *Slavery* (1959), of the "anti-institutional" reformers of the antebellum period. Lasch responded weakly to this criticism and admitted that "the strongest criticisms of my book are those which argue that the new radicalism was not new after all."

Lasch's failure to establish conclusively the newness of the new radicalism reflected a more substantial weakness of his book, for far from empirically working up the social context behind the emergence of American intellectuals as a self-conscious status group, he merely deduced that context from the theory of mass society that informed his analysis, locating the collapse of "community," the erosion of "patriarchy," and the emergence of "mass man" and isolated "subcultures" in the late nineteenth century when his subjects came of age. The deficiencies of this argument are perhaps most apparent in Lasch's portrait of the world that was lost, the world of communities in which "in a sense, the private life did not exist at all, in a setting in which so much emphasis was placed upon the duties and responsibilities of life, so little upon its opportunities for new forms of experience." Here, he continued, "what one owed to others was always so much more apparent than what one owed to oneself. All the details of personal intercourse, moreover, were circumscribed by elaborate forms and conventions, as if to emphasize their quasi-public character; and under those conditions there was little opportunity for the naked embrace of the spirit which the modern world has since learned to understand as the essence of love and friendship, the essence of life itself." Whether this terribly abstract formulation accurately described nineteenth-century American communities was very much open to dispute, and Lasch provided little evidence to suggest it did, only lyrical reworkings of what had already become sociological clichés.

Lasch's focus on the cultural radicalism of modern American intellectuals slighted the considerable energy they had invested in what he regarded as persistent forms of the "old radicalism." As William Phillips complained, Lasch had little or nothing to say about "the Socialists, the IWW, the Communists, Norman Thomas, Eugene Debs, the civil rights movement, Marxism, the pacifists, the anarchists, Students for a Democratic Society. . . . There is one reference to Trotsky, as there is to Frank Sinatra." While Lasch could rightly deny that this sort of radical politics was his concern, he missed a good bet in saying so little about it. A solid case could be made that the same anti-intellectualism and will to power that he saw infecting the new radicalism of the intellectuals was apparent as well in their embrace of the newer forms of the old radicalism. At the very least, Lasch might have saved himself some of the abuse he suffered from such anticommunist stalwarts as John Roche and Arthur Schlesinger, Jr., had he pointed out at greater length than he did that when it came to whoring after power, the intellectuals in and around the Communist party could hold their own with Cold War liberals (some of whom picked up their disposition for hard-boiled "realism" in the CP and its environs).

One might also contend, as none of Lasch's critics did when *The New Radicalism* appeared, that he was too quick to attribute the discontents and enthusiasms evident among his subjects to members of an isolated subculture alone. In important respects, the "new radicalism" was more of a popular movement than he indicated, more "typical" than he imagined. The attack on a desiccated, overcivilized, and repressive bourgeois culture, the mobilization of political energies on the cultural terrain of education and sexual behavior, and the effort to invest power and social control in the hands of experts were initiatives hardly confined to intellectuals in the early twentieth century. Indeed, since the publication of *The New Radicalism* a number of historians have found in the "consumer culture" of the urban bourgeoisie, which emerged alongside his new radicalism, much the same "quest for 'real life'" that Lasch believed was "evidently destined to remain the exclusive possession of a small minority." And Lasch himself would eventually extend criticisms he made of the new radicals to the culture as a whole. For example, one can see in Lasch's portrait of the sexual politics of Mabel Dodge Luhan an anticipation of the much broader indictment of the "sociopsychology of the sex war" he would draw up in *The Culture of Narcissism* (1978). Luhan's "intensely analyzed emotional life," Lasch argued, was "a result of the withering away of the larger social context of existence, which causes people in their loneliness to seek an intimacy even in casual friendships which hitherto was expected only of a few special relationships, if indeed it was expected at all." She celebrated sex as a "communion of souls," but afflicted with the "habit of seeing all human relations as a form of politics," she conceived of her own sexual life as a battle of wills, a "struggle for mastery." In the *Culture of Narcissism,* Lasch described a widespread "cult of intimacy" that concealed a "growing despair of finding it" and fueled "sexual combat" between enraged women and fearful men. In this context, Luhan seemed less the marginalized eccentric than the harbinger of wider sexual warfare. From this perspective, much of the new radicalism was less adversarial, or at least less obviously adversarial, than Lasch thought. Many of its elements were less the property of an isolated intellectual subculture than the stock-in-trade of a rapidly growing new middle class.

The New Radicalism remains a book worth reading and re-reading today less for its "main argument" than for the subsidiary arguments that accompany it. This was Hofstadter's view, and he put it to Lasch quite nicely. "Actually, though I think the greater part of your general argument is valid, or persuasive at least," he wrote, "I think the most valuable thing about your book is the steady flow of marginal insight, about the people you've chosen, the intellectual life as vocation, and the development of our culture." Drawing on Isaiah Berlin's famous distinction between the fox who knows many things and the hedgehog who knows one big thing, Hofstadter suggested that Lasch was, in the end, more fox than hedgehog. "This," he said, "is why the book can be read with great pleasure and profit by someone who happens not to agree with your central point, and why I think you will still find people reading it when you are an old man."

Among the foxy aspects of *The New Radicalism* that make it a great and enduring book, I would put first the sheer brilliance of the portraits of its subjects. In both substance and style they remain models of the biographer's art, combining an acute sensitivity to the dynamics of the inner life of some very complicated individuals with a novelist's eye for the telling detail. Often one finds *The New Radicalism* most engaging at those points at which Lasch wandered away from pressing his organizing thesis and examined the lives of his subjects in leisurely detail. Each of his extended portraits (and some of the briefer sketches) immediately became essential reading for students of the careers of these figures. And it remains the case that one cannot write about Addams, Bourne, Luhan, or Steffens without confronting Lasch's treatment of them.

As he indicated in his preface, Lasch was well aware of the political risks he ran in exploring the motives of radical intellectuals. To some, he remarked, his efforts to understand where the new radicalism came from would seem "an insidious attempt to discredit the ideas of radicals and reformers by 'psychologizing' them away." At least one reader, his friend Staughton Lynd, had been raising this objection to him for years, worrying that Lasch was joining forces with Hofstadter by launching *ad hominem* inquiries that ended up "questioning the validity of radical action by exploring its psychic origins." Lasch had indeed defended Hofstadter from critics such as Norman Pollack, whom he regarded as terrible simplifiers, but he did not see why the sort of psychological analysis which Hofstadter practiced and which he admired need entail the conservative consequences Lynd feared. In any case, he was not himself in search of sordid "hidden motives," for he took his cues from the explicit accounts that Jane Addams and others offered of their own motives. "The real choice," he wrote Lynd in the summer of 1962, "is not so much between looking for hidden motives on the one hand and discounting almost automatically what people say just because it was said, and on the other, discounting everything which does not appear in black and white on paper, as it is between recognition of the difficulty of understanding what people mean when they say something and assuming that it is really quite simple. . . . At its best, [psychological analysis] pays much more attention to what people say than those who attack it." But Lynd remained unmoved, and the debate became increasingly acrimonious. Finally, after Lynd once again charged Lasch with psychologizing away Jane Addams's radicalism in the manuscript of the first chapter of *The New Radicalism,* Lasch exploded. "I continue to be disturbed by your willingness to exchange analysis for propaganda," he wrote. "I consider it my job to try to understand Jane Addams, not to dilate endlessly on the truth and beauty of her works. But in any case under-

standing how such a woman came to spend her life the way she did does not necessarily detract from the validity of her works. Why should it? But this is the point on which you cannot be convinced. To you the radical tradition is sacred and must not be analyzed, except to murmur approvingly."

> **Often one finds *The New Radicalism* most engaging at those points at which Lasch wandered away from pressing his organizing thesis and examined the lives of his subjects in leisurely detail.**
> **—*Robert B. Westbrook***

This dispute with Lynd points to what I take to be the other fox-like feature of *The New Radicalism* that lends it persistent power: Lasch's attack on the anti-intellectualism of his intellectuals and his attempt to work out an ideal of "detached engagement" for intellectuals that was not oxymoronic. Shortly before he died, Lasch told me that in the course of a number of interviews he gave in his last months, he had at last realized what *The New Radicalism* was really about. As he put it in one of those interviews, it was "a book about intellectuals who weren't content to be intellectuals but wanted to be something else—movers and shakers, or the power behind the throne, or revolutionaries, or Indians or members of some allegedly simple culture that enjoyed a direct, unmediated connection with nature." Although Lasch disclaimed any desire to write "another *Trahison des Clercs,*" that is precisely what he did. Much of the force of *The New Radicalism* lies in Lasch's cataloguing of the various ways in which he believed American intellectuals had gone about betraying the intellectual vocation and in his struggle to articulate and defend his own complex notion of that vocation.

The principal voice in the book of Lasch's alternative is Benjamin Ginzburg, an obscure philosopher and socialist. Writing in 1931 at a moment at which liberal and radical intellectuals were beginning an extended stint of the "old" radicalism, Ginzburg warned them against a "messianism" that "sets up social reforms as prior to intellectual faith and political action as prior to cultural activity." For intellectuals, "the messianic inversion of values leads to a depreciation of their intellectual crafts in favor of a mysticism of social action." The role of intellectuals, he argued, lay first and foremost in "the cultivation of intellectual values," but few American intellectuals seemed satisfied with this. Anticipating Lasch's argument, he observed that "in no country is the intellectual so preoccupied with affecting the course of politics to the exclusion of his intellectual interests. The less power he has of determining conditions, the more passionate, it would seem, is his will-o'-the-wisp quest of political influence." Ironically, Ginzburg concluded, the real power of intellectuals lay not in political action conventionally conceived but in "clarification of political and social ideals" and above all in "the cultivation of a cultural-intellectual conscience whence these values derive." Ginzburg, Lasch emphasized, was not calling upon intellectuals to retreat from politics altogether but rather urging them to recognize that what political power they had could best be exercised indirectly by shaping values. "Ginzburg's radicalism," he said, centered on "a recognition that intellectuals had more influence over politics as *intellectuals* than as political activists in their own right."

Few of Lasch's readers grasped his (or Ginzburg's) argument. Nearly all saw him advising intellectuals to make an irresponsible retreat from politics. Liberals bristled at his criticisms of their service to the national security state, of their love affair with the Kennedy administration, and of their insistence that one must "choose the West" in the Cold War, as if that conflict could be reduced to such simple (and "messianic") terms. On the other hand, radicals took him to be promoting "alienation" at a time when they sought "commitment." Once again, these issues were ones that Lasch debated privately with Lynd long before he wrote *The New Radicalism*. While Lynd shared Lasch's contempt for Cold War academics, he saw the alternative for intellectuals in a radical activism toward which Lasch was a good deal more skeptical. "As you say," Lasch wrote Lynd in 1962, "the universities are strongholds of anti-radicalism":

> The man who throws himself into radical politics is better off, unquestionably. But I think he is better off insofar as his radical activism represents a form of withdrawal and detachment from the values that prevail in the university and in society in general. I don't think his advantage lies in the commitment he makes to radicalism, as opposed to the lack of commitment of the ordinary professor. The trouble with the latter is surely not that he lives in an ivory tower but that he is so pathetically far from living in one, because he is committed, often in a very immediate way, to the current consensus. In the bigger schools this commitment more and more takes the immediate and tangible form of working for the government as a technical advisor; helping the government find new ways of blowing people up, or find new ways of persuading Africans to be on our side. Well, it may be that a man has to become a radical and an activist in order to avoid being drawn into this miserable academic routine. If he can't keep his detachment within the academic setting, and I'm quite willing to concede that he can't, then by all means let him be an activist. The only trouble with the radical movement that I can see is that it often seems to impose a conformity of its own. I sense this in the writings of some of the people associated with radi-

cal movements—a kind of glibness, and the unquestioning acceptance of assumptions which need to be questioned and argued; all of which is just as destructive of independence of mind as conformity to the clichés current in academia.

It is not surprising that Lasch found himself misunderstood, for he was urging intellectuals to be both detached and engaged, which, to many, was plainly contradictory advice. But as Lasch saw it, detachment, which he distinguished from indifference and alienation, was essential to effective social criticism. Engaged intellectuals had to remain detached or they ceased to be intellectuals. And, for him, being detached was in the end less a matter of institutional location than of perspective. As he put it to Leuchtenburg (who was at once his most enthusiastic reader and his most perceptive critic):

> I only ask that [intellectuals] act like intellectuals. It isn't really a matter, necessarily, of whether or not to engage in practical politics; if that is really the course in which one thinks he can do the most good, I see no reason why he should not take it. I don't think one automatically ceases to be an intellectual when he gets on the inside of things. . . . But the point is that most of the intellectuals engaged in this enterprise are not speaking for intellectual values at all. When they try to speak a language which powerful people can understand, they soon forget that there is any other language. Again, I do not attribute this simply to the act of getting into power. It is a state of mind which pervades the intellectual community, including those who do not have power. . . . I am not advocating a fashionable cult of "alienation" and demanding symbolic gestures of withdrawal and rejection. I am only demanding what the new radicals promised but drew back from, trying to see middle-class society from the outside in, and then using this perspective to analyze, criticize, argue, persuade, in one's "work" or in one's polemics, it makes no difference. In other words, some perspectives seem to me more fruitful for intellectual work than others, and I would like to see more people cultivate those perspectives. But the work is still intellectual.

The principal threat to intellectual independence, Lasch argued, was "a manipulative habit of mind," which was easier to cultivate within the corridors of power but was not confined there. Indeed, as he had earlier complained to Lynd, intellectuals in the emerging New Left were sometimes as guilty of anti-intellectualism as the liberals they attacked. There, too often, "one forsakes the language of criticism, the Western tradition of rational discourse for the obscurantist jargon of the 'movement.' And this seems as bad in its way as the language of power."

> Between *The New Radicalism* and *The True and Only Heaven* (1991) one can discern a basic rethinking of what might be termed the epistemological (even metaphysical) underpinnings of the intellectual's role and the development of a perspective quite different from that of Benjamin Ginzburg, the presiding spirit of the earlier book.
> —*Robert B. Westbrook*

"Detached engagement" was an understanding of the vocation of the intellectual to which Lasch continued to hold for the rest of his life. But his rendering of this complicated and seemingly contradictory notion shifted in important ways, becoming less abstract and consequently, I would say, more attractive. Between *The New Radicalism* and *The True and Only Heaven* (1991) one can discern a basic rethinking of what might be termed the epistemological (even metaphysical) underpinnings of the intellectual's role and the development of a perspective quite different from that of Benjamin Ginzburg, the presiding spirit of the earlier book. Ginzburg's argument, which he termed "rational intellectualism" or "rational critical religion," seems to have been grounded in a universalism and rationalism (even Platonism) of the sort we have come to call "foundationalist" in that it sought to provide intellectuals with a transcendent standpoint outside of the contingencies of history and culture. It is not altogether clear if Lasch shared this philosophy when he wrote *The New Radicalism,* but he does not challenge Ginzburg in this respect and his own invocation of "intellectual values" and "the Western tradition of rational discourse" suggests that he found Ginzburg's foundationalism attractive. By the 1980s Lasch was sharply critical of such rationalism, and he tried to fashion a defense of the critical independence of the intellectual which dispensed with such foundations. Just because it was impossible to achieve a rationalist "view from nowhere" on one's society, he argued, did not preclude a significant measure of detachment. It was possible for intellectuals to be *in* without being *of* their culture.

Hence, at the end of his life, Lasch found Michael Walzer's conception of the "rooted" or "connected" intellectual an attractive one. On the face of it, Walzer's conception is at odds with Lasch's earlier defense of "detachment." As Lasch said in an interview:

> One type of social critic, according to Walzer, tries to stand outside his society and to see it as an outsider, the way an anthropologist studies a primitive tribe. This kind of criticism stands in relation to the society in question in a position of complete detachment, as if the critic's only allegiance were to justice and truth in the abstract. The critic adopts the point of view of an outcast or stranger. Connected critics stand within the society under criticism. Their position is one of provisional loyalty. They hold society up to its own highest standards, appeal to its own traditions in order to show how far its practice falls short of its principles.

Here, quite literally, detachment and alienation are one: the detached intellectual is one who takes the view of an alien. But absent a transcendent realm from which to hail, this alien perspective is a view not from nowhere but from somewhere else, that is, loyalty to another community. Without rationalist foundations, wholesale detachment is impossible; one must choose one's fellows. And in his last years Lasch connected himself to American culture in profound fashion, finding (some would say constructing) an indigenous, "populist" tradition to which he gave his provisional loyalty.

But if connected criticism forbids wholesale detachment, it does not thwart a more modest distancing of intellectuals from the practices of their society. For the connected critic, as Walzer says, "what is crucial is the critic's independence, his freedom from governmental responsibility, religious authority, corporate power, party discipline. He is an oppositional figure, and he must remain independent if he is to sustain his opposition." Thus if Lasch, in an important sense, abandoned "detachment," he never relinquished a defense of critical independence, which is often precisely what he meant by "detachment" in *The New Radicalism*.

No one can doubt Lasch's own critical independence. Having raised the hackles of ideologues on the right and left in 1965, he persisted in making both camps uncomfortable for the rest of his life. His ideal of the intellectual's vocation is a difficult one to grasp, and it is the sort of ideal that is understood less by trying to define it than by pointing to its exemplary practice. And no one practiced it better in the thirty years following the publication of *The New Radicalism* than Christopher Lasch himself. No matter how well we may have learned the lessons he had to teach us, our culture and our politics are much the poorer without him.

Jean Bethke Elshtain (essay date Spring-Summer 1995)

SOURCE: "The Life and Work of Christopher Lasch: An American Story," in *Salmagundi*, Nos. 106-107, Spring-Summer, 1995, pp. 146-61.

[*Below, Elshtain, a personal friend of Lasch, relates Lasch's thought to his character, reminiscing about and illuminating Lasch's observations of contemporary American life.*]

Christopher Lasch was my friend. That means I called him "Kit." When he died on Valentine's Day, 1994, the loss was a personal one enveloped by a patina of public concern. Who, I fretted sadly, will take his place? I found it hard to imagine a world without Kit's voice, a very particular voice, quintessentially American, rooted in the soil of this strange and wonderful country with its vast and lurching empathies and antipathies. Lasch believed in the responsibility—shorn of condescension and vanguardist elitism—of the intellectual to and for his or her particular time and place. Sadly contemplating a world without Kit, I recalled the words of Susan B. Anthony when she learned that her great friend and indefatigable colleague, Elizabeth Cady Stanton, had died. "Well," she said, "it is a great hush." It will, I decided, be a great hush. There is no other voice quite like his.

Lasch courted controversy. He once told me that he thought the "jeremiad" as a form of public expression was worth recuperating—he was thinking of Jonathan Edwards. There were those who hissed at the sound of his name. Most, who did not know him, were utterly perplexed when they encountered him in the flesh. Their image was that of a fire-breathing figure of the sort who strides to center stage and dominates the situation. Instead, the audience beheld a rather slight man curled around a podium, speaking softly, obviously unaware of, or unconcerned by, the contrast he in "real life" might present to those expecting to be riled and roused to a pitch of intense animus. Lasch compelled the audience to come to him, to listen attentively, in order to appreciate the full force of his words and his arguments. I was charmed by this fact, in part because one of Kit's most endearing characteristics was the intense concentration he gave to those he was listening to. Before I knew him well, I wondered if his silences betokened disagreement, or consternation, or perplexity. I decided instead that he was doing that most rare of all things in our speeded up, careless time: he was actually paying attention, taking things in, keeping his own counsel, musing on what he was hearing, filing observations for future consideration.

Lasch not only preached rectitude and modesty. He exemplified these and other homey, old-fashioned virtues conspicuous by their near obliteration in contemporary American public and, increasingly, private life. Consider Lasch's reaction to the death sentence he received in late May, 1993, when he was told that a cancer the doctors had assured him had been successfully excised with surgery, had returned "with a vengeance," in Kit's words. With characteristic modesty and that economy of style he himself called "plain," he wrote (in a letter circulated to his friends): "If I can avoid it, I'd like not to make a career of cancer; I don't want to become a kind of hostage to the medical profession. I'm not afraid of death, if that's what fate has decreed, and I despise the cowardly clinging to life, purely for the sake of life, that seems so deeply ingrained in the contemporary American

temperament." Never one to let the "helping professions" off the hook, he added: "The medical profession, it seems to me, has contributed to this attitude by interpreting its mission not as the relief of suffering but as the indefinite prolongation of life by any means possible." Instead, Kit enjoined *amor fati*: we must love our fates, for only from this love is it possible to say, as he did, "Please be assured that I'm in good spirits." His daughter, Elisabeth Lasch-Quinn, a historian, told me that what made it possible for his close circle of friends and his family to carry on through the nine months of his dying was that "Dad made what was extraordinary seem ordinary. He turned it into another family event, a routine. I don't know how we could have borne it otherwise."

> **If I can avoid it, I'd like not to make a career of cancer; I don't want to become a kind of hostage to the medical profession. I'm not afraid of death, if that's what fate has decreed, and I despise the cowardly clinging to life, purely for the sake of life, that seems so deeply ingrained in the contemporary American temperament.**
> **—*Christopher Lasch***

This recalls what used to be called "dying well." In my remarks at Kit's memorial service, I reflected on the fact that there is a lot of loose talk these days about "dying with dignity," much of it involving technical interventions (both assisted suicide and extraordinary measures to keep living) of the sort Kit disdained. Dying well, by contrast, means something different. It means reaffirming and strengthening ties of family and friendship and collegiality. It means leaving behind a gift of courage and clear-sightedness. What sort of man, then, was Christopher Lasch? Or, perhaps better put, what concatenation of familial, scholarly, and political forces helped to give rise to such a man and can account, therefore, for the widespread grief at his loss coupled, as it is, with a recognition that he was one of the premier American public intellectuals of the last quarter century?

Christopher Lasch was born in 1932 into a cultivated, liberal family. His father, Robert Lasch, was a newspaper editor. His mother, Zora Schaupp Lasch, had attended Bryn Mawr College, receiving a Ph.D. in 1925. When Lasch was a child, his mother did part-time social work and volunteered for civic-minded, progressive organizations. He breathed in Midwestern Progressivism, shorn of religious training and commitment, as a formative, and lasting influence. ("Both my parents were militant secularists—another part of my inheritance.") In an interview with historians Casey Blake and Christopher Phelps, Lasch mused that his father, now in his nineties, was "puzzled by my attacks on liberalism." But, Lasch added, a tradition, including the liberal tradition, "isn't some settled body of dogma but something you argue with or against; in that respect I'm unavoidably part of the political tradition in which I was raised. Some would probably say I was more of a renegade against it." He then made a critical point, one bound to be missed by partisans whose idea of public discourse is to line up opposing teams in clearly identified jerseys and to permit no defection from either side, when he averred that those positions to which one is most committed are those most in need of critical scrutiny. "If I seem to spend a lot of time attacking liberalism and the Left, that should be taken more as a mark of respect than one of dismissal. You don't bother to argue against positions that aren't worth arguing with."

Reared in a "very political household," Lasch's political instincts were well-honed. He remained politically engaged throughout his life but with a growing sense of unease and something akin to despair. I recall his early hopefulness about Bill Clinton's candidacy for the Democratic nomination in 1992. I was visiting Rochester at the time and staying with the Lasch's, and Kit asked me if I wouldn't mind if we stopped off so that he could vote in the Democratic primary. He applauded Clinton's talk of a "social covenant." But he grew disillusioned rapidly and by December 18, 1992, in a letter to me, he wrote: "The Clintonians, without any question, are going to prove insufferable. I've been getting a refreshing perspective on the best and brightest from some of my undergraduates who have a healthy hatred of the baby boomers with their ideological enthusiasms, their self-righteous lectures to their juniors deploring their alleged apathy, and their self-importance. This new generation takes a very caustic view of its betters."

With the Clintonians, as with others before them, most especially the Kennedy Camelot crew who, for Lasch, embodied a particularly obnoxious form of opportunistic Cold Warrioring, Lasch mistrusted, even despised, the feckless and the opportunistic as well as the ideologically inflamed—two political types who began to flourish, he believed, in the 1960s, although the roots of resentment and cynicism go very deep in the American political tradition: in this and other matters he was shaped by the work of Richard Hofstadter. Lasch spoke variously of "the historic imagination" and murmured mischievously of the professionalization and trivialization of history, a development he repudiated. He described what he did as "social criticism," an activity "deeply informed by a study of history, literature, philosophy, and the social sciences. It is less concerned with public policy, strictly speaking, or with day-to-day commentary on party politics or administrative detail. A social critic tries to catch the general drift of the times, to show how a particular incident or policy or a distinctive configuration of sentiments holds up a mirror to society, revealing patterns that otherwise might go undetected." The social critic, Lasch insisted, must pass judgement. He or she cannot let things pass away

as in a dream. There is a world beyond that of the professional associations with their gate-keepers and purveyors of standards, keepers of the keys to tenure and academic success.

As a social critic, Lasch recognized that no single school of thought or tradition offered a "panacea for all the ills that afflict the modern world." But a tradition worth mining helps us to ask "the right questions." Such a tradition draws us away from "fantasies of omnipotence" into a more complex world. One strong characteristic of Lasch's work, from *The New Radicalism in America*, the 1965 book that first drew him to public attention, to *The True and Only Heaven*, his "baggy monster" of 1991, is his incisive determination to make distinctions. In other words, he exhibited in an exemplary way that faculty the political theorist, Hannah Arendt, called the most important of all the *political* faculties of the human mind: the ability to make judgements. To evoke prejudice and to make a judgement are two very different human possibilities; indeed, the more we proliferate prejudices, the less capable we are of judging. A "prejudice" is a universal, sweeping, *a priori* expression immune to concrete evidence. Judging, on the other hand, consists in "thinking the particular," according to Arendt. An engagement with "the particular" in all its complexity is one of the most compelling qualities of Lasch's work.

> One strong characteristic of Lasch's work, from *The New Radicalism in America,* the 1965 book that first drew him to public attention, to *The True and Only Heaven,* his "baggy monster" of 1991, is his incisive determination to make distinctions.
> —*Jean Bethke Elshtain*

That the capacity to make critical judgments is at something of a nadir among us is of a piece with that decline in the affairs of men and women I believe Lasch detected in America's story as we approach the end of this tormented century. To say that Lasch feared we had lost our moral bearings is to understate. Consider, for example, the "victimization ideology" rampant at the present. This craze, with its insistence that it is wrong to make moral judgements, gestures toward something truly alarming: the possibility that we might, as a society, no longer generate the sorts of human beings who recognize what judging is all about and what we are called upon to do, or not to do, in light of our faculty of judgement. Judging makes it possible for us to make our way with some firmness of purpose and thought rather than lurching from one situation to the next, flotsam and jetsam on the surging sea of cultural freneticism.

Mind you, I didn't always agree with Lasch's particular evaluations. I was, for example, surprised at how strongly he separated his "populist" position, as articulated in *The True and Only Heaven*, from a "communitarian" one. From my point of view, the differences were not as great as he made them out to be. But one strong characteristic of his work—all his work, from beginning to end—was his incisive clarity and his restless and stubborn insistence that he must call things by their correct names. In an era in which we are invited to be as flabby-minded as possible, to make grand pronouncements, and to mistake decibel level for courage, Kit's doggedness in saying, "No, that isn't really it. It is more like this," or, "This isn't what it claims to be," or, "Let's look at the implications of holding this apparently benign view," is a great tonic.

One persistent way in which Lasch was perhaps not so much misunderstood as understood all-too-well by those who accused him of nostalgia and priggishness and harshness and "Puritanism," that all-purpose bugaboo, was his stalwart resistance to quasi-therapeutic subjectivism of the "I'm okay, you're okay," variety. This, for Lasch, was a cop-out, a way to stop forming and expressing moral judgments altogether. The strange suspension of specific moments of judgement often goes hand-in-glove, of course, with a violent rhetoric of condemnation of whole categories of persons, past and present—that all purpose villain, the Dead White European Male here comes to mind. To Lasch, this was a rotten deal all the way around, a way to promote and to deepen the worst trends and tendencies of our increasingly tawdry time. Ruling that "anything goes" means that what will go is our ability to assess what is going on: of this Lasch was convinced and he knew that this was not a matter to be adjudicated on the level of pure thought, no matter how clever, but on the streets and in the homes and neighborhoods of America.

The optimistic, progressivist world-view in its specific American incarnation that Lasch challenged holds that the more we change, and the more we have, the better things are bound to become. A complex, troubled trajectory characterized by a series of continuing engagements—from liberal realism (associated with Reinhold Niebuhr and George Kennan), to and through Marxism and the Frankfurt School, to Freud, Melanie Klein, and other psychoanalytic thinkers, and, from beginning to end, to an American counter-tradition (Randolph Bourne, Orestes Brownson, and a mordant version of Ralph Waldo Emerson are exemplars)—became for Lasch a way to proffer checks on our tendencies toward uncritical optimism. At the end, Christopher Lasch wrote of both "limits and hope." These words, he concluded, "sum up the lines of argument I have tried to weave together." His work taken as a whole was such a weaving, an exploration of our follies and our aspirations, our decent achievements and our shameless ambition. There is an "experience of loss and defeat," Kit insisted, that "makes up so much of the tex-

ture of daily life," and he cited Orestes Brownson, "Are there no calamities in history? Nothing tragic?"

Lasch's insistence on limits spoke to his recognition of human vulnerability and finiteness and to his conviction that an ever expanding culture of productivity must eventually spiral downward into a terrible cultural entropy. For the more we produce and the more we consume, the faster we must run, and the sooner we will exhaust ourselves and the natural world upon which we depend. How, then, would Lasch urge us to cultivate that on which we depend? What habits of mind must be constructed and cherished in order that limits be acknowledged and a genuine rather than a false and illusory political hope be kept ever fresh? It must be said that he, and, I daresay, anyone who goes against the cultural grain in this way, was better at putting the questions than at providing answers. But he gave us strong markers, maps of a terrain at once scholarly and moral, whether in his scholarly exegeses or his many occasional pieces and polemical forays.

Take one brief example of the way Lasch simultaneously shocked *and* illumined, for those prepared to go beyond their initial reaction of consternation. In a forum in *Harper's Magazine*, Lasch stunned many, including his fellow interlocutors, when he delivered himself up of the view that divorce should be made very difficult, if not more or less forbidden, if young children were involved. Cries of outrage poured into the magazine. What Lasch's critics failed to understand was that the point he was here making, in his characteristically forthright way, was that we Americans should have greater patience learning to live with our mistakes and that we might, in fact, discover—with such persistence—that it wasn't such a mistake after all. That is, he feared that Americans had lost a sense of perspective and persistence. That we had become quick on the trigger and short on the ability to realize that the current moment will not last forever; that, perhaps, the habit of living with one another over time, over the long haul, will build layer upon layer of attentiveness and respect that current unhappiness and inconvenience cannot even imagine. And it is only patience that sustains marriages, communities, and even polities. This, of course, is what social scientists call a "best case scenario" and Lasch surely knew it. As well, the matter is difficult and none of us would dare to insist that persons trapped in brutal marriages remain trapped in order to demonstrate that patience survives in an impatient world. There is a severity to Lasch's judgement in this instance that could well be ameliorated without losing, at the same time, his central point. Recasting that point, I would argue that what might be called a widespread "culture of divorce" imperils marriages by encouraging a sentimentalism about relationships that ignores the hard work that sustaining any relationship over time requires. In our avid enthrallment with the beckoning green light at the end of Daisy's dock we denude ourselves of the textured richness of what it means to perdure. That this is a lesson well lost on the vast majority of Americans was not a lesson lost on Lasch: it helps to account for his gloominess about our prospects.

Lasch was a seeker who never stopped searching for secular sources that might offer occasion for the stories of human sin and redemption, the coming to grips with evil in oneself and the world generally, the possibilities for grace and awe found in religion or, to be more precise, in the Christian narrative. I think his turn to Freud can, in part, be understood in this way. For Freud, too, is a thinker who restlessly and ceaselessly insisted on limits to enlightenment, limits to projects of transcendence, limits to what finite and mortal human beings can do confronted with the great and inexorable force of necessity. Lasch was offended by the sleight-of-hand pulled by certain cultural 'Freudians' (Marcuse comes to mind) when they tried to turn Freud into a totem of 'liberationism.' One way they did this was by translating— by just simply altering—Freud's texts, substituting "scarcity" for Freud's "necessity," as if "necessity," for Freud, was primarily an economic category. But it was not. It was the great and inexorable goddess of Fate in the very ancient, very Greek sense. This was not something that could be overcome with a superabundance of goods of every kind and a growing superfluity and optimism. For Freud, this sort of thinking represented an illusion and a dangerous one at that. Unsurprisingly, then, Lasch's Freud was the Freud who reminded us, over and over again, that we were limited and mortal and that while there might be defensible grounds for hope there were no good grounds at all for optimism.

If Lasch is right that alienation "is the normal condition of human existence," much of American thought of the optimistic, booster variety becomes a beguiling exercise in self-deception. The religious story is one in which the human being renounces what Lasch called the "comfortable belief" that the world is made for our convenience or cut to our design. It is not. Lasch believed that some people understood this, those he called "Middle Americans," the stalwart backbone of America, people who worked hard and tried to do their best for their children. By contrast to the "unbearably smug and superior" attitude of latter-day progressives, Lasch's "populist" Americans were worriers, people who fretted about "the future their children were going to inherit." He continued: "My study of the family suggested a broader conclusion: that the capacity for loyalty is stretched too thin when it tries to attach itself to the hypothetical solidarity of the whole human race. It needs to attach itself to specific people and places, not to an abstract ideal of universal human rights. We love particular men and women, not humanity in general." This concrete love, with its specificity in time and place, its everyday burdens and joys, is "flesh and blood," not one of the airy abstractions so much bandied about by folks who consider themselves superior to the local, the ev-

eryday, the small gestures of everyday life. Of course, such a man was bound to offend. He never let people forget that they lived in bodies that sickened and grew old and finally died. He never let people forget that perhaps bringing the neighbor a pot of soup when she was sequestered with a sick child might mean more than trotting off on an ideological junket to some foreign place in order to put one's radical bona fides in order.

Perhaps I may be permitted a story, this one at my own expense. I tell it because it says something about Kit Lasch's concern for small gestures and offers insight into his civility and decency and humor. One cold January in Rochester, following my participation in an event at the University with Kit, I spent the evening as a dinner guest of the Lasch's. The night grew very late. Drinks had been plentiful. At one point I felt emboldened to ask Kit to take Mozart off the stereo and to put Bob Dylan on! (Lasch was pretty well immunized against American popular culture and I saw myself as an ambassador in behalf of the best of it.) At about 2 a.m. it seemed prudent, to say the least, to call it a night as I had an early morning flight. Kit and I lurched out into the cold for the ride to my motel, both of us animated and chatting nonstop. He dropped me off. I rushed to my room and plunged in the general direction of the bed, remembering to leave a 5 a.m. wake-up call. When the call came, all too soon, I went through a minimalist morning ritual, threw some things into my bag, went to my closet for my coat—but there was no coat. I searched frantically for a few moments and then realized that I had obviously left the coat hanging at the Lasch's. There was no time to call and ask Kit to bring it over, and I was too embarrassed at that moment to have done so, in any case. I thought that forgetting a coat in January in Rochester was probably a pretty clear sign that I had been in a rather giddy state the night—or just a few hours—before. So I hailed a cab to the airport, the cabby querying me about my lack of outerwear; arrived at Bradley Airport in Hartford where my husband picked me up and where his first words were: "Where on earth is your coat?" I called Kit when I got home and said, rather abashedly, "I'm afraid I left my coat hanging in the hall closet." He said he had already noticed and had put it in the mail. Several days later the coat arrived. Rather than being stuffed into a nondescript mailer, it had been gift wrapped. Kit had folded it neatly; put it in a department store gift box, nestled it in tissue paper, and tied it with a ribbon. That gesture bears a world within it, a sign of gentlemanliness—I know not what else to call it—the handiwork of one determined to keep alive small signs of decorum and civility. Rumpled I may have been when I left the Lasch home that night. But the evening, like the returned coat, was a gift.

Lasch's daughter, Betsy, tells a story along similar lines. At a panel held in her Father's honor at the American Historical Association Meeting, she noted that her father had made a book "for our family every year for the last 25 years and presented as a gift to my mother every Christmas—*A Christmas Garland*. He made the book in its entirety, sewing the pages, binding it, covering it with beautiful cloth. Inside he pasted all the little evidences of our family life, a life of unbelievable richness and creativity. In these volumes, which sit quietly on a shelf between living room and kitchen, one finds photographs, tickets, passports, notecards with jottings from work and fun, defaced *New Yorker* cartoons, doodles, jokes, parodies, letters from imaginary friends and pets, report cards, concert programs, letters of congratulations, letters of rejection, programs to the University of Rochester commencement, letters from friends and family members, people in ads with balloons coming out from them and messages that they could never have said originally. Leafing through these volumes makes people laugh out loud."

Reading Betsy Lasch-Quinn's reminiscence reminded me of Milan Kundera's comments about the creation of "intimate life" in the West. Kundera tells a chilling tale. In a 1984 interview with Philip Roth, Kundera notes a "magic border" between "intimate life and public life . . . that can't be crossed with impunity." Kundera goes on to recall the tragedy of a friend, a writer named Jan Prochazka, whose intimate "kitchen table" talks were recorded by the state police in pre-1989 Czechoslovakia and assembled into a "program" broadcast on state radio. Kundera writes of Prochazka: "He finds himself in a state of complete humiliation: the secret eye observes him even when he kisses his wife in the bedroom or stands in front of the toilet bowl. Such a man can only die." Prochazka did, tormented by this violent intrusion into his life and the harm the making public of his intimate conversation did to his family and friends. According to Kundera, intimate life, a creation of European civilization "during the last 400 years," understood as "one's personal secret, as something valuable, inviolable, the basis of one's originality," is now in jeopardy everywhere, not just in statist societies with a secret police apparatus.

Some such recognition lay behind Lasch's continuing criticism of the "helping professions." Interpreted as callous by some, certainly as "anti-progressive," what Kit wanted to address were the many ways in which intrusive "do-gooders" wind up doing harm. The secret police of Kundera's tale are clearly malign. But social workers and others are good people, are they not? Yes, most are, but they are up to no-good, on Lasch's view, because they too readily adopt a stance of paternalism (or maternalism) toward those they aim to reform. Reform means a whipping into shape to some foreordained standard. The avid reformer suspects privacy, knowing that people hatch all kinds of attitudes and dispositions on their own that may not comport with the forward march of history. There is more than a little self-aggrandizement in all of this, a sense that one knows better than those one "helps" how they ought to think and to live. Thus, in *Haven in a*

Heartless World, an ironic title, Lasch talks of "the family besieged," closed in on from all sides, constantly interfered with in ways that erode people's "capacity for self-help and social invention." Why, he suggests, should we take for granted that space we call "intimate life"? It might well disappear and those small saving graces of human love and interaction with it.

Here I am reminded of another story I told Kit, one that I believe illustrates many of his concerns about the rise of a managerial, pseudoscientific way of thinking that believes it has a divine mission to overtake and to supplant "traditional" ways of doing things. Kit liked this story and agreed that it was an example, in miniature, of the broad social forces and processes he documented and lamented. When I was a sophomore in high school in a small town in Colorado in the late 1950s, I was required, as were all female students, to take a course in "home economics." The home economics movement had emerged out of progressive reform concerns to "scientize" a hitherto amateur activity. The complicated tasks of mothering and homemaking were now to follow managerial, time-flow innovations already instituted in other spheres, like the industrial work-place. I recall filling out charts in which meal preparation was divided and sub-divided and sub-divided again into micro-management tasks of precise refinement. 3:30, wash and snap string beans. 3:52, start water to boil. 4:00, put snapped, washed beans into boiling water. 4:03, after beans have come to a boil cover and simmer. That sort of thing. One had to check off each task as it was completed and to note any variation on the time chart. Somehow a meal often resulted from all this. But the poor, beleaguered scientific cook, more often than not, had lost her appetite. Not to worry: she was a pioneer. The experts had designed this for us, we were told, to protect innocent husbands and children from the ministrations of the ill-informed amateur cook.

One day, a day of great excitement at Cache La Poudre High School, a *real expert*, all the way from Washington, D.C., was sent our way. She was a visiting Home Economics consultant from the (then) Department of Health, Education and Welfare, come to the benighted provinces. She was going to do us the honor of presenting the latest scientific research on child management. All we eager or not-so-eager home economics students were enjoined to bring our mothers to the event. Indeed, our instructor made it very clear that it would be a blot on our records if our mothers failed to attend. I, by then, was an enthusiastic booster of scientifically managed households. (This became a handy bludgeon for many of us to use against our 'old-fashioned' mothers.) Mothers and daughters sat together in the home economics room, awaiting the arrival of the Expert. When she walked in, I stared. I had never seen a "professional woman" before. She smelled of perfume or deodorant soap and her heels clicked smartly on the freshly waxed floor. Her hair was all in place and smooth, like a swirly ice cream cone, and she had two perfectly drawn lines where eyebrows usually are. Her skin was pale and smooth, quite unlike that of the ruddier, weather-worn complexions of Colorado women who spent quite a bit of time working outdoors, whether they were farm women or not.

Her talk was: "New Scientific Theories of Child Rearing." I don't remember what those theories were. I just remember feeling impressed at how impressed I felt. My mother, on the other hand, started tapping her right foot, always a bad sign. When the Expert had finished she asked, smartly, for questions with a benign and self-certain expression on her face. My mother raised her hand. I sank into my chair. "Do you have children of your own?" queried mother. "No, I don't have children, but I have studied." My mother continued, "Well, I don't think you have very much to teach us then." She got up and left. I was humiliated. Red-faced, I sat in my chair, wondering if I should apologize for my mother's shockingly anti-progressive, anti-science stance. I did not. Instead I grew sullen and remained so for days.

My mother, of course, was right. Not right because, in current lingo, she was "privileging" her own experience—certainly my mother would have countenanced many stories of child rearing told by women in diverse circumstances who had some hands-on experience of the task of caring. There was not one universal child-rearing experience. But what she could not tolerate was the presumption of the managerial mentality on display in that classroom on that particular afternoon, promulgated by one who thought she knew more than the undereducated who were actually doing the childrearing, farming, sewing, and food preparation. But under the presumption that such activities required streamlining and managing, those Lasch criticized so vehemently in his work moved in to eviscerate forms of local knowledge, and to fight tradition, always backward, always that which must be defeated. Women were often big losers in this fight as their generations old streams of practical reason were brought under pressure to succumb to the superior force of scientific management in all its guises—medicinal, educational, nutritional.

The reason I offer up this vignette is simple: I use it to flesh out one of Lasch's concerns. Perhaps I can put it rather more fancily: it is a mistake, sometimes a mistake for which real people in real situations pay the price, for any of us to too readily equate the rhythms of intellectual life with the rhythms of social and political life. It is far easier to seize and abandon epistemological positions, or to take up or refute categorical stances, in intellectual life than when one is dealing with the density of lived life. When we no longer tend to local knowledges and lived lives our politics grows eerily abstract and too easily becomes impositional. This, I think, helps to account for the congealment of current political de-

bates. Positions harden and become ever more abstracted, ever more disassociated from their points of origin or concern. They return as alienated constructions—imposed on, rather than flowing from, the rhythms of everyday life. My mother understood this. The Expert did not and never will.

I first encountered the writing of Christopher Lasch when I, one of that plentiful, notorious, and now wiser (I hope) "60s generation," discovered him in *The New York Review of Books*. His were the only pieces I routinely tore out, stapled together, and saved. I was fascinated by his range. So much lay within his purview: revisionist history about the origins of the Cold War; American foreign policy in light of America's self-understanding; the generous beginnings and fateful turnings of the student movement; the contrast between a statist liberalism and a robust, because more local and community based, democratic politics; the fateful alliances forged between feminist reformers and 'social hygienists,' whether doctors or Calvinist ministers; psychoanalysis and feminism; the American character, and so on. I clipped and filed and learned. I never stopped learning from Christopher Lasch. Now his works are, for us, part of a complex tradition we will continue to engage. For engage it we must, no matter how thoroughly we are dismayed by the irresoluteness, frivolity, chicanery, and sheer shamelessness of our time. Kit traced the turn on the left (or pseudo-left) to the view that there is nothing but power; that all points of view are similarly power-ridden and ideological. That, he suggested, in an interview with Robb Westbrook and Richard Fox, stops serious argument dead in its tracks.

Lasch also mourned what he called the "lost art of argument." Failure to understand argument represents a confusion about democracy itself. Argument is the "very essence" of a democratic political culture, by contrast to closed-minded ideological rigidity, on the one hand, or supine "niceness," on the other. Why can't we have "good, impersonal" arguments any more, Lasch asked? And he answered: Because, overtaken by a pop-therapeutic worldview, we over-personalize everything; we are offended easily; we make no distinction between our identities and our ideas or, perhaps better said, we conflate the two. Lasch recalled Dietrich Bonhoeffer's experience at Union Theological Seminary in the 1930s. "He said, 'Why is everyone so nice to everyone around here? How come in passing each other in the hallway you have to smile and say hello? Why can't we have any good arguments?'" When the "art of argument" is lost, a democratic idiom falters and with it we stand in danger of losing as well a "democratic character," defined by Lasch as "a willingness not to confuse one's feelings with one's ideas." This character requires "institutions like schools that will teach that [impersonal argument] rather than foreclose that by teaching this sort of touchy-feely notion."

Lasch also mourned what he called the "lost art of argument." Failure to understand argument represents a confusion about democracy itself.
—*Jean Bethke Elshtain*

Christopher Lasch was a man of grace who found much of late modernity graceless; a man of wit who found much of our politics witless; a man of purpose who lamented our culture's frenetic purposelessness; a man of hope who saw in boundless optimism a deep despair. From the beginning of his work to the end, he marked those "fantasies of omnipotence" that underscored America's intellectual elite and threatened to swamp the culture itself. There were times when he grew gloomy about our prospects. In one of his letters to me, he expressed the fear that "we are winning the argument but losing the culture." If that, in fact, is not to be our fate, we will owe Kit an even greater debt than the one many of us now rightly feel. For he would have us persevere. The "better angels of our nature" might yet be rekindled and America brought back to what Kit considered her richest prospects (not measured by wealth) and her truest ideals (not measured by power.) In thought, word, and deed, Christopher Lasch was a critic, a moralist, a historian, a citizen who saw in recognition of limits the beginning of hope. Only in that recognition lies a freedom worthy of the name. Only in that recognition lies a community worthy of devotion. Only in that recognition lies a culture worthy of free citizens.

"Hope," he wrote, "is the rejection of envy and resentment and all that invites them. It's not difficult to see why those would always seem to be compelling moral postures, because we live in a world that doesn't seem arranged for human convenience. It's a world in which human happiness is not the overriding goal, and our plans go awry, and there are terrible limitations on what we can know and understand and control. And in any case our lives are very short. The fact of death is always there, haunting our imagination. All of which seems to justify a renunciation of any belief in the possibility that the world, in spite of all these facts, is good, just, beautiful. Hope is a grateful disposition that acknowledges everything that justifies its absence. None of this, of course, implies that this is the best of all possible worlds or that the struggle against injustice ought to be suspended on the grounds that whatever is, is right."

FURTHER READING

Criticism

Beatty, Jack. "Beyond Narcissism." *Washington Post Book World* (16 December 1984): 6.
Finds *The Minimal Self* "a book stronger in ad hoc criticism than in sustained argument."

Bentley, James. "Looking after Number One." *New Statesman* (5 July 1985): 28.
Focuses on Lasch's attitudes about victimization and survival in *The Minimal Self.*

Brinkley, Alan. "Putting the Community First." *Times Literary Supplement* (20 September 1991): 24.
Concludes that "*The True and Only Heaven,* for all its intelligence, erudition, and passion, evades [the] crucial obligation" to explain the rationale for "the relative weakness of the values [Lasch] is devaluing."

Clare, Anthony. "Hidden Dependence." *Times Literary Supplement* (13 September 1985): 1006.
Analyzes the new concept of selfhood that seems to emerge in *The Minimal Self.*

Fraser, C. Gerald. A review of *The Minimal Self. The New York Times Book Review* (29 September 1985): 54.
Briefly notes "the unrelieved negativism of [Lasch's] diagnosis of our time."

Gallagher, Bernard J. "Breaking Up Isn't Hard to Do: Stephen King, Christopher Lasch, and Psychic Fragmentation." *Journal of American Culture* 10, No. 4 (Winter 1987): 59-67.
Uses King's fiction to illuminate key points of Lasch's social criticism in *The Culture of Narcissism,* demonstrating similarities of both writers' approaches to psychic fragmentation.

Harper, Kenneth. "Ever Wonder What Freud Might Think about Life in the 1980s?" *Christian Science Monitor* (2 January 1985): 21-2.
Reviews *The Minimal Self* in Freudian terms.

Herman, David. "The Rich Are Different." *New Statesman and Society* 8, No. 344 (17 March 1995): 39-40.
Discusses the debate about community in *The Revolt of the Elites,* treating the range of subjects, tones, and moral values addressed by Lasch.

Johnson, George. A review of *The True and Only Heaven. The New York Times Book Review* (8 September 1991): 38.
Short notice, stating that "the book is required reading for any student of social criticism and cultural history."

Kakutani, Michiko. "Sounding Like Quayle Blasting Cultural Elites." *The New York Times* CXLIV, No. 49940 (13 January 1995): C32.
Suggests that *The Revolt of the Elites* "never [transcends] the simplistic realm of complaint."

Kirn, Walter. "Beat the Elite." *New York* 28, No. 2 (9 January 1995): 50-1.

> Examines *The Revolt of the Elites* as "a fogyish jeremiad," noting that the book "starts out as sociology, but it ends as theology."

A review of *The True and Only Heaven. The New Yorker* LXVI, No. 52 (11 February 1991): 96.

> Calls the book "stimulating, though what it principally stimulates is skepticism about the pretensions of all social theory, including the author's."

Nieli, Russell. "Social Conservatives of the Left: James Lincoln Collier, Christopher Lasch, and Daniel Bell." *The Political Science Reviewer* XXII (1993): 198-292.

> Summarizes the contents of *Haven in a Heartless World,* *The Culture of Narcissism, The Minimal Self,* and *The True and Only Heaven,* noting that Lasch's account of "the narcissistic personality of our time is illuminating, sometimes brilliantly so."

North, James. "State of the Union." *Chicago Tribune Books* (29 January 1995): 3.

> Praises *The Revolt of the Elites* as "the last work of one of the truly original American thinkers of our time."

Ryan, Alan. "The Middling Sort." *London Review of Books* 17, No. 10 (25 May 1995): 13-14.

> Places *The Revolt of the Elites* in the context of Lasch's others works, finding his thought "a terrific antidote to the blather of the communitarians and the lies of the laissez-faire Right."

Additional coverage of Lasch's life and career is contained in the following sources published by Gale Research: *Contemporary Authors,* Vols. 73-76, 144; *Contemporary Authors New Revision Series,* Vol. 25; and *Major 20th-Century Writers.*

Nicanor Parra

1914-

[Born San Fabián de Aliceo] Chilean poet and physicist.

The following entry presents an overview of Parra's career. For further information on his life and works, see *CLC*, Volume 2.

INTRODUCTION

Parra is known as the founder of antipoetry, a term used by the poet himself to overcome the concepts of poet as prophet and poetry as having some mystical power. Antipoetry is the poetry of everyday life experience and language. Parra's work influenced a generation of poets, and of the Chilean poets of his generation, he is the only one to have established a school.

Biographical Information

Parra was born on September 5, 1914, in Chillán, Chile, to Nincanor P. and Clara S. (Navarette) Parra. His childhood was a difficult one filled with uncertainty and poverty, but he managed to concentrate on his studies and perform well in school. He obtained degrees in mathematics and physics from the University of Chile in 1938. He then taught secondary school until 1943 when he left to study advanced mechanics at Brown University. In 1948 he became the director of the School of Engineering at the University of Chile. From 1949 to 1951 he studied cosmology at Oxford University. He worked as a professor of theoretical physics at the University of Chile until his retirement in 1991. Parra has been married twice: his first marriage to Ana Troncoso was dissolved and his second marriage to Inga Palmen resulted in seven children. In addition to his work as a scientist, Parra has been writing poetry since the late 1930s and began publishing in 1937. Parra's most significant work was his first collection of antipoems, *Poemas y antipoemas* (1954). Parra has won numerous literary awards including the City of Santiago prize in 1937 and 1954, Writers' Union prize in 1954, National Literature Prize in 1969, a Guggenheim fellowship in 1972, and the Juan Rulfo prize in 1991.

Major Works

Parra's earlier work, written as a teenager and a young man, was heavily surrealist. His first collection, *Cancionero sin nombre* (1937), was written before Parra had developed an idea of what poetry should be. *Poemas y antipoemas* was Parra's first attempt at antipoetry. In this and subsequent works, Parra was trying to demystify the form of poetry. Parra wanted to remake poetry from purely ornamental to an ev-

eryday expression. In these poems Parra fights against literary tradition in order to find his own original voice. The reader is typically drawn into this battle as representing tradition. Many of Parra's poems from *Poemas y antipoemas* include a hostile dialogue between the poet and the reader. In *Versos de salón* (1962) Parra parodies our everyday forms of communication such as tests, questionnaires, and advertising and campaign slogans. With *Artefactos* (1972) he added his use of street language and everyday jargon into his poetry. The poems from this collection have the informal rhythm of everyday conversations. Nostalgia is a common theme running throughout Parra's poetry, and he tries to infuse it in his work in waves. Parra's work is also filled with desperation at the chaos in the world and the human condition. Parra uses his antipoetry to destroy the utopian images of poetry and replace them with the reality of the world. An outspoken opponent of social and political oppression, Parra did not hold to any one ideology. His only consistent response to the chaos of the world and the helplessness of the human condition was humor.

Critical Reception

Parra's *Poemas y antipoemas* brought him his international reputation. Many reviewers praise the ease of Parra's language with its almost prose-like quality. Critics often point out that while Parra's antipoetry illuminates the problems of human existence, it offers no solutions. Some critics find his work limited in this respect. Some critics find his later poems from *Sermones y prédicas del Cristo de Elqui* (1977) weaker than his original antipoetry. Reviewers often comment on the humor, irony, and irreverence common in Parra's poetry. Critics agree that his version of antipoetry has influenced a generation of poets.

PRINCIPAL WORKS

Cancionero sin nombre (poetry) 1937
Poemas y antipoemas (poetry) 1954
La cueca larga (poetry) 1958
Anti-Poems (poetry) 1960
Versos de salón (poetry) 1962
La cueca larga y otros poemas [edited by Margarita Aguirre] (poetry) 1964
Poesía soviética rusa [editor] (poetry) 1965
Canciones rusas (poetry) 1967
Fundamentos de la física [translator] (nonfiction) 1967
Poems and Antipoems [edited by Miller Williams] (poetry) 1967
Poesía rusa contemporanea (poetry) 1967
Obra gruesa (poetry) 1969
Poemas (poetry) 1969
Los profesores (poetry) 1971
Antipoemas: antologia 1944-1969 (poetry) 1972
Artefactos (poetry) 1972
Sermones y prédicas del Cristo de Elqui (poetry) 1977
Nuevos sermones y prédicas del Cristo de Elqui (poetry) 1979
El anti-Lázaro (poetry) 1982
Poema y antipoema a Eduardo Frei (poetry) 1982
Chistes para desorientar a la poliesía (poetry) 1983
Coplas de navidad (poetry) 1983
Poesí a política (poetry) 1983
Antipoems: New and Selected [edited by David Unger] (poetry) 1985
Hojas de Parra [edited by David Turkeltaub] (poetry) 1985
Fotopoemas sobre textos de Nicanor Parra (poetry) 1986
Nicanor Parra: biografía emotiva [edited by Efrain Szmulewicz] (poetry) 1988

CRITICISM

Frank MacShane (essay date 19 November 1977)

SOURCE: "A Breath of Satire in Chile," in *The Nation,* Vol. 325, No. 17, November 19, 1977, p. 535.

[*In the following essay, MacShane discusses a controversial performance of Parra's* Hojas de Parra *in Chile.*]

For years Nicanor Parra has kept silent. Then, some months ago, his poetry was heard again in Chile. The occasion was a theatrical performance based on his work called ***Hojas de Parra***—or ***Pages from Parra.*** It opened on February 24 in a circus tent erected in Providencia, a residential section of Santiago. Subtitled "A Fatal Leap in One Act," it was a collage of circus and theatre, poetry reading and happening, deriving from his poems, some of them never before heard in public.

Two Chilean actors, José Manuel Salcedo and Jaime Vadell, were responsible for the production. Salcedo described it in the newspaper *El Cronista* as "an experimental work which tries to resolve scenically the metaphysical problem that lies between life and death." But with the actors dressed as clowns, trapeze artists and jugglers, a good deal of humor also made its way into the performance. Parra's satirical skills emerge in scenes such as one devoted to an imaginary political rally in a Presidential campaign. The name of the candidate is Nadie (Nobody), and here are some of the slogans and responses by his supporters as reported in the magazine *Ercilla*:

> Nobody will put an end to inflation
> Nobody will fix the balance of payments
> Nobody will respect our rights
> Who will realize our dreams?
> > Nobody
> Who really says what he thinks?
> > Nobody
> Who really thinks what he says?
> > Nobody
> Who will give us a raise?
> > Nobody
> Who will lower the rents?
> > Nobody
> Who will increase production?
> > Nobody
> Let's every one vote for Nobody
> Elect Nobody
> Nobody for President

The scene closes with a sardonic echo of the Cuban revolutionary slogan: "*Ambiguidad o muerte, ¡Venceremos!*"— "Ambiguity or death. We shall overcome!"

Pages from Parra also contains a scene in which the playing space for a circus act is gradually reduced as grave diggers bring in corpses for burial and set up gravestones and crosses in the arena. There is a banquet in honor of the Unknown Poet which also involves invocations and responses. It begins with a roll call for dead poets but soon leads to other things:

> Gabriela Mistral?
> > Present
> Pablo Neruda?
> > Present
> Filet mignon with mushrooms?
> > Absent
> A political constitution for the state?
> > We'll see about it.
> Human rights?
> > Present
> Rights for humans?
> > Absent

Pages from Parra, whose Spanish title is also a play on words that can be translated best as "Fig Leaves," was attended by many notables, including the former minister of education, the former Mayor of Santiago and the former rector of the University of Chile. The reviewer in *El Cronista* noted that whether one liked it or not, "no one could be indifferent to it." The notices were mixed, but the consensus of those interviewed after the opening night production was that "the play not only made them laugh, it made them think."

One notable exception to the generally favorable reception of the piece was published in the newspaper *La Tercera* under a page-one headline that read: "Infamous Attack on the Government." The reviewer asserted that the production was "a clear message of criticism of the present government" and said that it was "not constructive but Sibylline criticism." He revealed his own political point of view by putting in a good word for the regime, for he noted that "the fact that this work was presented shows once more that there is liberty in Chile."

According to *Ercilla,* this hostile review made the production. Thousands of people began to buy tickets and *Pages from Parra* became an overnight hit. On March 1, *Las Ultimas Noticias* observed that the negative review had created a storm, but quoted Salcedo and Vadell as saying they had no intention of attacking the junta. Four days later the Mayor of Providencia renewed the play's license, but a few hours thereafter the theatre was closed under orders of the National Health Service. *El Mercurio* explained that the circus tent had been shut down because of a lack of toilets, washrooms and fire extinguishers. For its part, *La Tercera* quoted the head of the Health Service as saying that "if the sanitary requirements are met, the tent theatre will reopen."

On March 11, *El Mercurio* announced that the sanitary objections had been met and that the play was reopening, but

next day the Mayor of Providencia reversed his position and revoked the license. According to *La Tercera*, he explained that the neighbors had objected to "the offensive allusions to the government that appear in the work." He was also reported as saying that "possible hostile demonstrations" might take place and have "lamentable consequences." This reasoning was questioned by *Que Pasa* which observed that demonstrations of all kinds were forbidden in Chile.

At that point in the debate, all verbal arguments became academic: at 2:30 in the morning of March 12, well after the curfew, two unknown men drove up and threw gasoline bombs at the tent. Within a few minutes it was in flames. Firemen arrived and managed to put out the fire, but not before the theatre was half-destroyed. Two newspapers claimed that members of the company had set the fire, but with financial losses estimated at $15,000, most of the other papers agreed with *Ercilla* that it was an act of arson by hostile persons.

On March 17, *Que Pasa* printed an interview with José Manuel Salcedo. He said that the fire which finally closed the theatre had given it "a solemnity that goes with historic works of art." Next day, President Pinochet himself observed in another context that legal means must always be employed "to prevent irresponsible or subversive actions by those who, consciously or unconsciously, are capable of bringing about a return of chaos."

Karen S. Van Hooft (essay date 1982)

SOURCE: "Vipers, Victims, and Virgins: Women and Their Relationships with Men in the Poetry of Nicanor Parra," in *Theory and Practice of Feminist Literary Criticism,* edited by Gabriela Mara and Karen S. Van Hooft, Bilingual Press, 1982, pp. 256-78.

[*In the following essay, Van Hooft analyzes the role of women in Parra's poetry and their relationship to the male protagonists of his poems. She asserts that Parra attacks social institutions and the human condition, not simply the role of women.*]

One aspect of the work of the Chilean poet Nicanor Parra that has been insufficiently studied is the role played by women and the related themes of love and sex. This is surprising, for even a superficial examination of Parra's works from *Poemas y antipoemas* (1954) to the controversial *Artefactos* (1972) reveals a considerable preoccupation with women and with men's relationships to them.

The typical analysis of this theme in Parra's poetry has focused on his misogynic portrayal of women and his negative attitude toward love and sex. Indeed, there is considerable textual basis for such an analysis. However, a closer and more balanced reading of the poet's works, one which relates his treatment of women to other central themes in his poetry, gives a somewhat different picture. In this reading, women are seen *in their relationships* with men, and one is obliged to conclude that the latter are not portrayed in a particularly more sympathetic light. Parra's men are seen to be as hindered in the quest for fulfillment by sexual stereotypes and role playing as the women they relate to and as incapable of finding a satisfactory solution to the resulting war between the sexes.

The problem thus becomes one of understanding Parra's critical attitude toward innumerable facets of contemporary life, from sexual stereotyping and role playing to the over-reliance on Freudian psychology, and so on. I shall attempt to show that Parra's treatment of women is part of a larger assault on our most cherished institutions and mental habits; it is basically the attack of an anarchistic poetic *persona* who delights in the evidence of decay around him but who offers no real solutions. To single out the poet's misogynic treatment of women without considering these other factors is to distort his basic intent.

The principal poems I will analyze are from *Poemas y antipoemas,* although some reference will be made to poems from other works. There are two reasons for this selectivity: (1) the poems in the first volume adequately reveal the attitudes found in the entire body of Parra's poetry, and (2) while the subject of women and love is continuously present, a considerable change in stylistic treatment occurs in the course of Parra's poetic development. In *Poemas y antipoemas* the subject is dealt with extensively in poems of a confessional nature such as **"La víbora"**; in later works (*La camisa de fuerza, Otros poemas,* the new poems of *Emergency Poems,* and especially the *Artefactos*) the subject is treated much more fragmentarily. This change in treatment corresponds to the variations observable in Parra's poetic *personae*. In his first volume the *persona* is most often a passive, suffering voice who narrates his erotic (mis)adventures with bitter irony, whereas in the later works the narrative aspect is almost completely lost and the attitudes are usually expressed as psychic outbursts of a different type of poetic protagonist, the *energúmeno*. And finally, in the *Artefactos* this latter tendency is developed to the extreme, and the *persona* becomes something akin to the anonymous writer of graffiti.

The obvious place to begin an analysis of the subject of women, love, and sex in Parra's work is with the poem **"La víbora"** (*Poemas y antipoemas*), for this is the most complete expression of the attitudes I will be discussing.

Durante largos años estuve condenado a adorar a
una mujer despreciable
Sacrificarme por ella, sufrir humillaciones y burlas
sin cuento,
Trabajar día y noche para alimentarla y vestirla,
Llevar a cabo algunos delitos, cometer algunas
faltas,
A la luz de la luna realizar pequeños robos,
Falsificaciones de documentos comprometedores,
So pena de caer en descrédito ante sus ojos
fascinantes.

In the title and introduction we are presented with the essential facts: the speaker of the poem informs us that the woman in question is "a viper" and "una mujer despreciable." Furthermore, he states that he was "condemned" to "adore" her, an interesting combination of the vocabulary of love with a word suggesting imprisonment, and finally he reveals that this imprisonment, with its serious consequences of suffering, sacrifice, and crime, was involuntary, for he was trapped by the viper's "fascinating eyes." One of Parra's critics has noted that this last element may refer to the traditional belief that snakes can hypnotize their victims. While this is certainly one level of meaning present here, there are several other levels, both more simple and more complex, which contribute to the total impact. For example, the idea of a man being trapped by a woman's captivating eyes is an everyday commonplace, and the expression "ojos fascinantes" can be simply related to the banal vocabulary of advertisements for eye makeup and the like. The use of colloquial language related to common experience is a striking feature of Parra's poetry and has been amply studied elsewhere. If one wishes to continue the search for additional levels of meaning, one can also refer to the Biblical story of the Fall, in which the serpent, closely identified with the female, Eve, seduces Adam and causes the expulsion from the Garden and the condemnation of humanity to work, suffering, and sacrifice.

Parra's use of irony as an important element of his poetic technique, which has also been extensively studied, is visible in the opening section of the poem. It is in fact supremely ironic for the poetic protagonist to state that he was trapped in a life of personal suffering, humiliation, and petty crime by something so apparently trivial as a pair of captivating eyes. Of course, the reader sees beyond this lame excuse and begins to suspect some deeper cause of the speaker's suffering.

In the next section of the poem the *persona* refers to the "horas de comprensión" between himself and the viper when they would have their picture taken together in the park or would go to a club, "Donde nos entregábamos a un baile desenfrenado / Que se prolongaba hasta altas horas de la madrugada." The first of these activities suggests the falsity of their "understanding," for what the reader sees is not any real togetherness or communication but rather a posture that substitutes for it (posing for a picture). It is as if the lovers are trying to capture their togetherness by creating some proof that it exists. This idea, the lack of true contact and communication between human beings and the futility of attempts to achieve it, is an important motive in Parra's poetry. The second activity, the "baile desenfrenado," introduces the motive of the erotic dance and the idea, suggested by "desenfrenado," of uncontrolled, orgiastic activity associated with sex.

The protagonist continues:

> Largos años viví prisionero del encanto de aquella
> mujer
> Que solía presentarse a mi oficina completamente
> desnuda
> Ejecutando las contorsiones más difíciles de
> imaginar
> Con el propósito de incorporar mi pobre alma a su
> órbita
> Y, sobre todo, para extorsionarme hasta el último
> centavo.
> Me prohibía estrictamente que me relacionase con
> mi familia,
> Mis amigos eran separados de mí mediante libelos
> infamantes
> Que la víbora hacía publicar en un diario de su
> propiedad.

In the first line of this section the imprisonment motive is repeated, this time in association with the word "encanto," giving a similar ironic contrast to that seen previously. Of course, "encanto" has several levels of meaning; on one level is the commonplace idea of being trapped by a woman's "charms" and on another that of being the victim of an evil hypnotic spell. This second level is strengthened by the reader's previous understanding that the viper is a contemptible woman. The following lines emphasize this point, for the woman's intent is apparently to control the man's soul and extort his last cent. She intends to possess him so completely that he is separated from his family and friends by her manipulations.

At the same time another motive is developed, that of the woman's aggressive and exaggerated sexuality and her exploitation of the man.

> Apasionada hasta el delirio no me daba un instante
> de tregua,
> Exigiéndome perentoriamente que besara su boca
> Y que contestase sin dilación sus necias preguntas
> Varias de ellas referentes a la eternidad y a la vida
> futura

> Temas que producían en mi un lamentable estado
> de ánimo,
> Zumbidos de oídos, entrecortadas náuseas,
> desvanecimientos prematuros
> Que ella sabía aprovechar con ese espíritu práctico
> que la caracterizaba
> Para vestirse rápidamente sin pérdida de tiempo
> Y abandonar mi departamento dejándome con un
> palmo de narices.

At this point the reader begins to associate the previous labeling of the woman as a viper with the obvious symbolic possibilities present. For example, the viper can be seen as a phallic symbol, thereby suggesting that her aggressive sexuality is "masculine." And this idea can then be related to the myth of the Fall, for in one interpretation the serpent symbolizes sexuality and what it offers Eve is sexual knowledge, which she in turn uses to seduce Adam.

After describing the viper's attempts to seduce him, the poetic protagonist refers to her "necias preguntas" of a metaphysical nature and his resulting "lamentable estado de ánimo" and physical malaise. The close association of her sexual advances with these metaphysical questions (note the apparent reversal of roles) serves to suggest that his symptoms of illness are not entirely caused by the questions. In fact, the speaker indicates that the final result is really impotence and frustration on all levels, physical and mental, which the woman compounds by her calculated flight.

In the next section of the poem we are informed that the affair with the viper went on for more than five years, a seemingly incredible amount of time to endure such suffering. During some of this time they lived together, ". . . en una pieza redonda / Que pagábamos a medias en un barrio de lujo cerca del cementerio." Here the prison, disguised as a love nest, takes the form of a round room—a female symbol in Freudian terms. It is, significantly, near a cemetery, thereby associating their relationship with death, another important motive in Parra. In a typical use of irony, this living arrangement is called a "honeymoon" and then the image is immediately deflated by describing their battle with "las ratas que se colaban por la ventana."

Next we are informed of other details relating to the viper's exploitative nature, particularly her intent to take economic advantage of her victim. She accuses her lover of ruining her youth, and with "flashing eyes" (another commonplace but suggestive description) she threatens to take him to court to collect the money he owes her. One begins to wonder who is exploiting whom! We remember that early in the poem the speaker claims to work night and day to feed and clothe the viper, but later he states that they share the rent in the round room, and now he is apparently borrowing money from her. Obviously he means to indicate that she is causing his ruin, for next he must live on charity and is reduced to sleeping on park benches.

> Felizmente aquel estado de cosas no pasó más
> adelante,
> Porque cierta vez en que yo me encontraba en una
> plaza también
> Posando frente a una cámara fotográfica
> Unas deliciosas manos femeninas me vendaron de
> pronto la vista
> Mientras una voz amada para mi me preguntaba
> quién soy yo.
> Tú eres mi amor, respondí con serenidad.
> ¡Angel mío, dijo ella nerviosamente,
> Permite que me siente en tus rodillas una vez más!
> Entonces pude percatarme de que ella se
> presentaba ahora provista de un pequeño
> taparrabos.

The scene of the viper's reappearance is full of "notas discordantes": the protagonist posing for a picture while living on charity; the woman showing up dressed in a loincloth, playing a child's game with her former victim and asking to sit on his lap; and the male reacting with the hackneyed phrases "deliciosas manos femeninas," "voz amada," and "tú eres mi amor." The juxtaposition of this banal love vocabulary with the "discordant" description of the viper's appearance again provides an ironic contrast that underscores the true nature of the relationship.

The speaker next discovers that the viper has new plans for them:

> Me he comprado una parcela, no lejos del
> matadero, exclamó,
> Allí pienso construir una especie de pirámide
> En la que podamos pasar los últimos días de
> nuestra vida.
> Ya he terminado mis estudios, me he recibido de
> abogado,
> Dispongo de un buen capital;
> Dediquémonos a un negocio productivo, los dos,
> amor mío, agregó,
> Lejos del mundo construyamos nuestro nido.

Significantly, the plot of land is near the slaughterhouse and the new love nest will be a pyramid, both things again suggesting that their love is akin to death. Furthermore, the plan is to structure their new relationship as a business deal, emphasizing the viper's materialistic nature and the baseness of their love. But the protagonist rejects her plans and finally begins to demand something real and necessary from her: that she give him water and food, if she is to give him anything. He flatly states that the affair is over: "No puedo trabajar más para ti, / Todo ha terminado entre nosotros." He

is at last unwilling to go on allowing her to imprison him. However, it is clear that this affirmative decision is not all that hopeful for him, for he is old and "profundamente agotado."

In summary, the attitudes present in this poem toward love, women, and sex are decidedly negative. Love here is an exploitative relationship in which the woman imprisons the man, causing physical and mental suffering and his eventual perdition. Furthermore, it is seen as a death-trap which must ultimately be rejected. The sexual component of love participates quite virulently in these characteristics; sex is seen as being little more than an uncontrolled, orgiastic, and finally futile and frustrating activity. The failure in sex, then, is indicative of the more general failure to establish a satisfying and communicating relationship.

The woman in the poem, the viper, does not correspond to the conventional female stereotype of the passive "homebody," for she appears both sexually and intellectually aggressive. However, the description the poetic voice gives us in fact contains a number of contradictions. In spite of the viper's supposed ability to support herself (we are told that she owns a daily newspaper), she still demands at the beginning that the man provide for her or at least collaborate in her maintenance. Her aggressive sexuality, which the reader sees in an obviously exaggerated form, threatens the protagonist's established masculine role and renders him impotent. Still, the viper makes rather traditional demands for affection. Finally, her metaphysical questionings of him suggest an underlying intellectual passivity stereotypically associated with women. The reader notes that she asks questions, seemingly looking to the male for guidance, rather than expressing or asserting her own ideas. In other words, the viper partially usurps the traditional masculine role, but not completely. But for the male this is sufficient to make her deadly; she is able to entrap and manipulate him, ostensibly against his will. She ultimately contributes to his impotence on all levels.

The protagonist himself is shown to be powerless and easily duped. Trapped by this aggressive woman who definitely represents a threat to his well-being and whom he is unable to handle, he has neither the will nor the ability to escape until the end, when it may be too late. While she is presented as being truly malevolent, he is not any better a person, for he is not only incapable of communicating with the woman, whom he views in purely sexual terms, but he is also deluded as to the true cause of his suffering—his own inability to take the action necessary to free himself from her clutches.

The poem following **"La víbora"** in *Poemas y antipoemas,* **"La trampa,"** presents a complementary view of the themes elaborated above. Whereas in the first poem the most visible motive is that of frustration and ruin due to female malevolence and exploitation, here it is that of intellectual and sexual failure caused by the inability to communicate successfully. The imprisonment motive is also important, as is indicated by the title. The viper's trap was presented as being a hypnotic spell cast by her enchanting eyes; here the trap is objectively represented by a telephone.

The first part of the poem is a description of the poetic protagonist's mental imprisonment. He is unable to cope with "las escenas demasiado misteriosas" and his "pensamientos atrabiliarios," so he flees social contact, preferring to remain at home. Although he states that "En la soledad poseía un dominio absoluto sobre mí mismo, / Iba de un lado a otro con plena conciencia de mis actos," the reader is soon aware that this is not true, for one proceeds to observe the protagonist's aimless pursuits: ". . . dilucidando algunas cuestiones / Referentes a la reproducción de las arañas"; "O también en mangas de camisa, en actitud desafiante, / Solía lanzar iracundas miradas a la luna"; "O me tendí entre las tablas de la bodega / A soñar, a idear mecanismos. . . ."

The speaker of the poem next admits that these attempts at avoidance are futile. He cannot escape his desire to establish communication with someone. But he fails in his attempt.

> Comenzaba a deslizarme automáticamente por una
> especie de plano inclinado,
> Como un globo que se desinfla mi alma perdía
> altura,
> El instinto de conservación dejaba de funcionar
> Y privado de mis prejuicios más esenciales
> Caía fatalmente en la trampa del teléfono
> Que como un abismo atrae a los objetos que lo
> rodean
> Y con manos trémulas marcaba ese número
> maldito
> Que aún suelo repetir automáticamente mientras
> duermo.
> De incertidumbre y de miseria eran aquellos
> segundos
> En que yo, como un esqueleto de pie delante de
> esa mesa del infierno
> Cubierta de una cretona amarilla,
> Esperaba una respuesta desde el otro extremo del
> mundo,
> La otra mitad de mi ser prisionera en un hoyo.

This part of the poem is introduced with the images of sliding and falling, and Edith Grossman's analysis of it summarizes the main points:

> . . . the second half of the poem, dealing with the protagonist's tortured eroticism as he slips into the chasm of frustrated sexuality is, significantly, conceived of as the fall. In the intellectual abyss, the protagonist avoids contact through withdrawal; in the sexual abyss, he avoids profound sexual contact through the removed communication of the telephone, through false and unsatisfied stimulation, through meetings in public places.

We see here the now familiar association of sexuality with imprisonment and with the Fall, and again there is the suggestion of death in the use of the words "esqueleto" and "infierno." The reader also notes that the subject suffers symptoms of physical malaise as did the protagonist of **"La víbora"**: "manos trémulas," "incertidumbre y miseria," "comenzaba a transpirar y tartamudear," "Me producía malestares difusos / Perturbaciones locales de angustia. . . ." And finally these symptoms become directly sexual in the form of "incipientes erecciones y . . . una sensación de fracaso." The theme of frustrated communication is also found in the lines following the section quoted above, as is another reference to death:

> Mi lengua parecida a un beefsteak de ternera
> Se interponía entre mi ser y mi interlocutora
> Como esas cortinas negras que nos separan de los
> muertos.

The woman whom the subject is speaking to is hardly described at all, but when she *is* referred to it is in terms of her attempts to be overly intimate (she calls him by his first name, "En ese tono de familiaridad forzada") and her sexuality (the protagonist refers to her excited state as "efervescencia pseudoerótico"). Again the reader receives the impression of a clinging, overly erotic female whose reactions are identified by the subject as a cause of his "feeling of failure."

Finally, the speaker admits that he is left in a state of mental prostration ("aquellas catástrofes tan deprimentes para mi espíritu"). This prostration is so closely connected with his statements of purely physical symptoms as to make the sexual failure inseparable from it. At the end of the poem no solution is in sight, for the "stupid idyll" will continue: the man has arranged to see the woman the next day at a soda fountain or the door of a church, both public places that will again frustrate the desire for intimate communication. Of note is that the protagonist in this poem is somewhat more aware that his own weakness is a cause of his suffering: "Yo no deseaba sostener esas conversaciones demasiado íntimas / Que, sin embargo, yo mismo provocaba en forma torpe."

A third important poem in *Poemas y antipoemas* is **"Recuerdos de juventud."** It begins with a statement by the speaker that, unlike the *persona* of **"La trampa,"** he has no illusions of being in control of himself:

> Lo cierto es que yo iba de un lado a otro,
> A veces chocaba con los árboles,

Chocaba con los mendigos,
Me abría paso a través de un bosque de sillas y
mesas.

But his attempts to find his way through this "forest of chairs and tables" are futile: "Cada vez me hundía más y más en una especie de jalea." The image of sinking recalls the sliding and falling of **"La trampa,"** and the jelly has a possible sexual connotation. The poetic voice continues:

La gente se reía de mis arrebatos,
. . . .
Y las mujeres me dirigían miradas de odio
Haciéndome subir, haciéndome bajar,
Haciéndome llorar y reír en contra de mi voluntad.

The word "arrebatos," which closely follows upon the image of sinking into the jelly, recalls the "desenfreno"—the uncontrolled, orgiastic activity—in **"La víbora"** and strengthens the possible sexual connotation. And the next three lines cited are a direct statement of the protagonist's victimization by women, who manipulate him both emotionally (the references to laughing and crying) and sexually (the suggestive use of "subir" and "bajar") against his will.

"De todo esto resultó un sentimiento de asco," states the *persona*. Since this line follows the section on women, the reader suspects that a large part of the repulsion is sexual, although the character at first states that it manifested itself as ". . . una tempestad de frases incoherentes, / Amenazas, insultos, juramentos. . . ." However, the next section confirms the original suspicion:

Resultaron unos movimientos agotadores de
caderas,
Aquellos bailes fúnebres
Que me dejaban sin respiración
Y que me impedían levantar cabeza durante días,
Durante noches.

The sexual reference could not be clearer. Sex is seen as a dance, recalling the erotic dance in **"La víbora,"** and is associated again with physical prostration and death ("fúnebre"). Therefore sexual activity is presented here as both a causal factor in the protagonist's situation and as a desperate attempt to resolve it, one which only leads to further repulsion and alienation.

The protagonist's next attempts to escape are intellectual rather than sexual: "Con una hoja de papel y un lápiz yo entraba en los cementerios / Dispuesto a no dejarme engañar." We note that this effort involves writing as a form of communication (a possible biographical reference) and that it takes place in cemeteries, relating it to the death motive. Following this is a description of other intellectual endeav-

ors and attempts to communicate in classrooms, literary circles and private houses, but all efforts fail:

Con el filo de la lengua traté de comunicarme con
los espectadores:
Ellos leían el periódico
O desaparecían detrás de un taxi.

The last two lines of the poem reflect the protagonist's complete despair: "Yo pensaba en un trozo de cebolla visto durante la cena / Y en el abismo que nos separa de los otros abismos." The startling first line signals the continuation of his disconcerted mental state and the second his awareness of the futility of his attempts to communicate with others, who are as trapped in the abyss as he is.

Other poems from *Poemas y antipoemas* that belong to the same thematic unit, in that they express the same attitudes, are **"El túnel," "El peregrino,"** and **"Notas de viaje."** In **"El túnel"** there is another version of the imprisonment theme, this time presenting a protagonist who is considerably younger. Interestingly, the figures who trap and manipulate him are his aunts, "tres ancianas histéricas," "temibles damas"; they oblige him to work for them and deceive him cruelly by feigning helplessness in the form of illness and paralysis. The imprisonment here is referred to in terms of the tunnel of the title, the "interior de una botella de mesa," a "malla impenetrable," and a "campana de vidrio." The first two of these, especially, in association with the figures of the aunts and the imprisonment motive, can be seen as symbolically representing female malevolence (comparable to the round room in **"La víbora"**).

The young protagonist in **"El túnel"** has essentially the same problems as the previous *personae*. At the hands of his aunts he suffers a constant martyrdom, revulsion, anguish, and finally ruin and misery, which he attempts to escape by another type of flight, that of playing a role to please them: ". . . angustia que yo trataba de disimular al máximo / Con el objeto de no despertar curiosidad en torno a mi persona." He experiences the same failures of understanding and communication seen previously, for he has a distorted perception of reality ("Yo lo veía todo a través de un prisma") and he is isolated from others:

Un joven de escasos recursos no se da cuenta de
las cosas.
El vive en una campana de vidrio que se llama
Arte
Que se llama Lujuria, que se llama Ciencia
Tratando de establecer contacto con un mundo de
relaciones
Que sólo existen para él y para un pequeño grupo
de amigos.

"**El peregrino**" again refers to the sexual and intellectual abyss in which the protagonist lives and his abortive attempts to communicate with other people:

> Un alma que ha estado embotellada durante años
> En una especie de abismo sexual e intelectual
> Alimentándose escasamente por la nariz
> Desea hacerse escuchar por ustedes.
> Deseo que se me informe sobre algunas materias,
> Necesito un poco de luz. . . .

Finally, in "**Notas de viaje**" the *persona* tries to flee the abyss by abandoning his job and travelling. In spite of his flight, however, he still attempts to communicate superficially with others by "exchanging impressions." The dance motive is present again and is related to thoughts of "cosas absurdas" and "cosas fantásticas relacionadas con mi familia," which bring to mind the "desenfreno" seen previously in reference to the dance. And the image of the boat entering the river ". . . a través de un banco de medusas" has suggested to one critic a concretely sexual picture. This vision affects the protagonist's spirit, obliging him to resort to a self-imposed imprisonment.

The remaining poems examined in this paper offer somewhat different stylistic treatments of the subject of women, love, and sex. Nevertheless, most of these poems express attitudes that are the same or complementary to those already discussed, while only a few appear to offer contradictory views.

The poem "**Canción**" presents a different type of woman from that seen previously.

> Quién eres tú repentina
> Doncella que te desplomas
> Como la araña que pende
> Del pétalo de una rosa.
>
> Tu cuerpo relampaguea
> Entre las maduras pomas
> Que el aire arranca
> Del árbol de la centolla.
>
> Caes con el sol, esclava
> Dorada de la amapola
> Y lloras entre los brazos
> Del hombre que te deshoja.

This is not the sexually domineering and manipulating woman of "**La víbora**" and other poems. Instead she is virginal, receptive, and submissive. The term "esclava" refers to the fact that she is bound both to her nascent, uncontrolled passions and, to a lesser degree, to the man who deflowers her.

> Herida en lo más profundo
> Del cáliz, te desenrollas,
> Gimes de placer, te estiras,
> Te rompes como una copa.
>
> Mujer parecida al mar,
> —Violada entre ola y ola—
> Eres más ardiente aún
> Que un cielo de nubes rojas.
>
> La mesa está puesta, muerde
> La uva que te trastorna
> Y besa con ira el duro
> Cristal que te vuelve loca.

In contrast with previous poems, it is the woman who is here associated with imagery of physical and emotional distress and pain related to sex ("te desplomas," "herida," "Te rompes," "violada"; "lloras," "gimes," "ira"). Similar to the "unhinged" male protagonists seen earlier, she has lost control ("La uva que te trastorna," "Cristal que te vuelve loca"); this contrasts with the consciously manipulative sexual extravagances of "**La víbora**."

Therefore in this poem the roles are reversed. Whereas previously woman has been the manipulator and sexual aggressor, now she is manipulated (and thus a potential victim); where previously she caused suffering, now she suffers, albeit for the "higher" purpose of sexual initiation. Both types of women are presented in the poems in such a way as to be ultimately negative: the one because she controls and effectively castrates the male, and the other because she is at the mercy of unbridled instincts that do her physical violence and cast her in the unenviable and limited role of submissive receptacle of the phallus.

A poem that deals with the theme of male victimization of woman is "**Las tablas**." This poem has many different levels of meaning, and the following brief analysis is only one possible reading.

> Soñé que me encontraba en un desierto y que
> hastiado de mí mismo
> Comenzaba a golpear a una mujer.
> Hacía un frío de los demonios; era necesario hacer
> algo,
> Hacer fuego, hacer un poco de ejercicio;
> Pero a mí me dolía la cabeza, me sentía fatigado
> Sólo quería dormir, quería, morir.

The poem begins with the familiar idea of the protagonist not being able to stand himself or cope with the world; this time he seeks an escape through action in the form of sexual violence. We next discover that he is, in fact, beating his mother: "'Por qué maltratas a tu madre' me preguntaba entonces una piedra." The poetic *persona* is plagued by accusatory voices and visions ("Y veía la imagen de ese ídolo / Mi dios que me miraba hacer estas cosas") and he reacts by trembling, biting his nails, and attempting to divert his thoughts.

All of this is useless, for the voices return in other forms: the "tablets of the law" and the birds that will record his crimes. He soon becomes bored with listening to the voices, and failing to be rid of them:

> Entonces y me volví de nuevo a mi dama
> Y le empecé a dar más firme que antes.
> Para mantenerse despierto había que hacer algo
> Estaba en la obligación de actuar.

Finally he makes one last effort ("Y decidí quemar el busto del dios"), only to discover that in ridding himself of his guilt he has also lost the one thing he may successfully take out his frustration on: "Mi madre me había abandonado." Because of his actions he is cut off from any human contact, with further action of any kind frustrated ("Ya no podía más"). He has destroyed the "tablets of the law," the norms of social behavior, and is therefore excluded from society.

"Las tablas" complements the negative view of sexuality seen elsewhere, and the inclusion of the mother figure adds a new dimension. The poem may be understood on one level as an expression of sexual loathing, the type of expression that often takes its strongest form in dreams such as this. The mother figure's humiliation suggests the whole question of familial relations and their effect on male and female sexual behavior (e.g., sadistic and masochistic behavior, respectively).

It should be noted that there are generally few negative references to the family in Parra's poetry, and these usually relate to the wife rather than to mother, sisters, or daughters. For example, in **"Lo que el difunto dijo de sí mismo"** (*Versos de salón*), the *persona* reacts violently to a question regarding his abandonment of his wife: "Respondí con un golpe en el pupitre / 'Esa mujer se abandonó a sí misma.'" In **"Vida de perros"** (*Versos de salón*) we see the following: "El hogar es un campo de batalla. / La mujer se defiende con las piernas."

In other poems extremely positive attitudes toward female family members are present. **"Catalina Parra"** (*Poemas y antipoemas*) is a nostalgic and affectionate poem about the poet's daughter. **"Defensa de Violeta Parra"** (*Otros poemas*) is a poem of praise, admiration, and respect for the poet's sister, the most positively drawn female in any of Parra's poems.

Two poems from *Poemas y antipoemas* provide a strange contrast with the others analyzed to this point. These are **"Es olvido"** and **"Cartas a una desconocida."** Their strangeness results from their unusually nostalgic, melancholic, and even somewhat romantic tone, a rarity in Parra's work, though it does appear elsewhere (See **"Aromos"** and other poems in *Canciones rusas*).

"Es olvido" is a lament on the death of a young girl whom the poet belatedly discovers was in love with him. She is presented in what is almost the classic vocabulary of romantic love poems: she is described as "una joven pálida y sombría," recalling the pale and sad princesses of Darío and others; she is also "una joven triste y pensativa," "múltiple rosa inmaculada," "una lámpara legítima," "una paloma fugitiva." Furthermore, the protagonist's relationship with her is partially expressed in similar tones: "Mas moriré llamándola María," "Y una que otra mención de golondrinas"; her death causes ". . . tal desengaño / Que derramé una lágrima al oírla." All of this is not to say that the irony so typical of Parra is not present; the last line cited is followed by "Una lágrima, sí, ¡quién lo creyera! / Y eso que soy persona de energía." The poem is really a mixture of romantic and ironic elements.

Significantly, the protagonist affirms that for him this relationship meant little or nothing, for he cannot even remember the girl's real name. He indeed insists on this point:

> Debo creer, sin vacilar un punto,
> Que murió con mi nombre en las pupilas,
> Hecho que me sorprende, porque nunca
> Fue para mi otra cosa que una amiga
> . . . .
> . . . jamás vi en ella otro destino
> Que el de una joven triste y pensativa.
> . . . .
> Puede ser que una vez la haya besado
> ¡Quién es el que no besa a sus amigas!
> Pero tened presente que lo hice
> Sin darme cuenta bien de lo que hacía.
> No negaré, eso sí, que me gustaba
> Su immaterial y vaga compañía
> . . . .
> Mas, a pesar de todo, es necesario
> Que comprendan que yo no la quería.

Aside from noting that her importance to him, and indeed his vision of her as a person, is rather limited, we may conclude that this is basically another example of a failure of communication. The girl offers him love and happiness, but he does not see it until it is too late. The protagonist actually admits this frustrated communication in the line "Nada más que palabras y palabras." The fact that he has forgotten her, "Como todas las cosas de la vida" is a sad reflection of the transitory nature of human experience.

Another melancholic and semi-romantic poem is the short **"Cartas a una desconocida."**

> Cuando pasen los años, cuando pasen
> Los años y el aire haya cavado un foso
> Entre tu alma y la mía; cuando pasen los años
> Y yo sólo sea un hombre que amó, un ser que se detuvo
> Un instante frente a tus labios,
> Un pobre hombre cansado de andar por los jardines,
> ¿Dónde estarás tú? ¡Dónde
> Estaraás, oh hija de mis besos!

The title is important, for the woman is "una desconocida." The speaker's contact with her was brief, he does not really know her, and he sees that time and distance will destroy even his memory of her. The use of the word "foso" recalls the abyss of poems such as **"Recuerdos de juventud"**; the combined effect of the presentation of the unknown woman and the abyss again suggests isolation and non-communication. And the activity of "walking through gardens" reminds the reader of the aimless pursuits of the various protagonists elsewhere. Finally, the reader notes that in spite of the tone of the poem, the language is generally commonplace rather than elevated, contrasting with the usual language of love poetry. Therefore Parra here complements the view seen previously by emphasizing the mediocrity of human communication and feeling and the hopelessness of aspiring to the ideal of a lasting love relationship.

To expand the discussion of our subject, reference could be made to many other poems from Parra's later works. However, most of these poems deal with the same attitudes already discussed, although the particular treatment may vary the stress. One poem that should be examined is **"Mujeres"** (*Versos de salón*). This poem exemplifies the tendency to define women according to a limited or narrow framework; here they are categorized on the basis of their sexual attitudes or sexual behavior, or simply on the basis of appearance.

> La mujer imposible,
> La mujer de dos metros de estatura,
> La señora de mármol de Carrara
> Que no fuma ni bebe,
> La mujer que no quiere desnudarse
> Por temor a quedar embarazada,
> La vestal intocable
> Que no quiere ser madre de familia
> . . . .
> La que sólo se entrega por amor
> La doncella que mira con un ojo,
> La que sólo se deja poseer
> En el diván, al borde del abismo,
> La que odia los órganos sexuales,
> La que se une sólo con su perro,
> La mujer que se hace la dormida.

While there is considerable variation in the types presented, this is of course a limited and limiting view of women as people.

A related motive in Parra's poetry is that of the search for some type of "ideal" woman, a search which is inevitably frustrated. (In the poem **"Vida de perros"** in *Versos de salón,* the poet cries "¡Dónde encontrar a la mujer precisa!"). It is never really clear what this ideal might be; it is certainly neither the aggressive, manipulating woman nor the submissive virgin. At the end of **"Mujeres"** the poet indicates his frustration and his ultimate inability to deal with any of the women he has described in such limiting and stereotypical terms.

> Todas estas walkirias
> Todas estas matronas respetables
> Con sus labios mayores y menores
> Terminarán sacándome de quicio.

The dislike—or even fear—of the sexually aggressive woman and the resultant impotence of the male are also present in **"Mujeres,"** where the poet rejects

> La mujer que camina
> Virgen hacia la cámara nupcial
> Pero que reacciona como hombre.

This idea is also very clear in **"Conversación galante"** (*Versos de salón*), where the woman is the aggressor and the man is incapable of responding:"—Pero entonces, ¿por qué no reaccionas? / Tócalos, aproveca la ocasión. / —No me gusta tocarlos a la fuerza." And finally, "Cartas del poeta que duerme en una silla" (*Otros poemas*) presents a disguised statement of this attitude in the form of a dream. (Note the references to death, physical and mental suffering, war, and insanity.)

> Toda la noche sueño con mujeres
> Unas se ríen ostensiblemente de mí
> Otras me dan el golpe del conejo.
> No me dejan en paz.
> Están en guerra permanente conmigo.
>
> Me levanto con cara de trueno.
> De lo que se deduce que estoy loco
> O por lo menos que estoy muerto de susto.

Other important poems are (1) **"Se me ocurren ideas luminosas"** (*Versos de salón*), where the emphasis is on role playing and the failure of verbal and sexual communication;

(2) **"La doncella y la muerte"** (*Versos de salón*), which pictures woman as *femme fatale* or temptress and associates sexuality with death; and (3) **"Como les iba diciendo"** (*Emergency Poems*), in which the protagonist brags of his sexual prowess.

It is hardly necessary to state that this is a generally dreadful picture of love and sex and women. In the world of Parra's poetry, love is impossible, sex is frustrating, and the women presented are certainly not people one would want to have relationships with. A superficial reader might dismiss these attitudes as misogynic, sick, perverted, or whatever; it is also possible, of course, that the reader might identify with these attitudes. Their dismissal is not so easy when they are taken in the total context of Parra's poetry. In fact, an understanding of these attitudes as an integral part of the poet's larger vision does much to clarify exactly what this vision is.

In the world of Parra's poetry, love is impossible, sex is frustrating, and the women presented are certainly not people one would want to have relationships with.
—Karen S. Van Hooft

Parra's poetry presents a profoundly critical attack on the decaying world we live in and the poverty of the values we live by. Humanity in general is seen as being imprisoned by its cherished attitudes and mental habits, by its faulty perception of reality, and by its inability to communicate its despair or take positive action to remedy the situation. As José M. Ibáñez-Langlois aptly states:

> Los poemas de Nicanor Parra, en su caótico flujo, subvierten inveterados hábitos mentales de nuestra herencia filosófica, cultural, política. Toda una visión convencional del mundo, toda una estructura lógica del pensamiento, todo un edificio verbal que sustenta el orden establecido, todo un conjunto de seguridades tácitas que defienden el "paraíso del pequeño burgués", es revelado en su vacuidad y corroído desde su interior por el impacto de las descargas antipoéticas.

As this quotation indicates, Parra employs a varied arsenal of weapons in his attack. Perhaps the most powerful of these are his use of irony and occasionally parody and the use of colloquial, anti-metaphorical language rather than traditionally "poetic" language. Both of these techniques serve to demythologize or deflate the importance of traditional habits of thought, patterns of behavior, and values.

To accomplish this poetic deflation Parra first signals his targets. This paper has analyzed one such target: the attitudes toward women, sex, and love. This and other targets are catalogued in the poem **"Los vicios del mundo moderno"** (*Poemas y antipoemas*):

> Los vicios del mundo moderno:
> El automóvil y el cine sonoro,
> Las discriminaciones raciales,
> El exterminio de los pieles rojas,
> Los trucos de la alta banca,
> La catástrofe de los ancianos,
> . . . .
> El auto-erotismo y la crueldad sexual
> . . . .
> El endiosamiento del falo,
> . . . .
> La destrucción de los ídolos,
> . . . .
> Las gotas de sangre que suelen encontrarse entre
> las sábanas de los recién desposados.

In sum, Parra's vision takes on all our cherished myths, our political and financial institutions, our social behavior, and even the gadgets, conveniences, and diversions of our daily life.

Parra's treatment of the subject of love and women has been seen to present, or at least allude to, the myth of the Fall, the impossibility of experiencing romantic love, and the stereotyping of both the male and the female along traditional lines. The use of the myth of the Fall is particularly revealing. In this myth and related ones such as that of Pandora's box, the female is assigned the unenviable role of being the cause of human suffering, knowledge, and sin. It is still an important foundation of our sexual attitudes, as is witnessed by the popular conception of the *femme fatale*, the sexual temptress. These attitudes are clearly present in poems such as **"La víbora."** Nevertheless, Parra deflates the validity of this myth by revealing his protagonists to be at least partially responsible for their own suffering. In other words, the evil female is no more to blame for the situation than the man.

The myth of romantic love is also destroyed by its negative presentation. The use of irony, of hackneyed colloquial language, and the stress on the motives of failed communication, distance, and sexual frustration demonstrate the emptiness of traditional love as a form of human communion. This point is related to the stereotyping of male and female behavior. The playing of traditional sexual roles, roles that are defined by the stereotypes, is shown to be ultimately negative, for such roles are clearly very limiting. For example, if woman conforms to the ideal of physical and intellectual passivity, thereby casting the male in the role of the aggressor, her destiny is to be raped and the male becomes a rapist. If the reverse occurs, and woman becomes the aggressor, the male is left impotent. Neither of these is satisfactory, of course, and there is the strong suggestion that sexual role playing is closely linked to disastrous male-female relationships.

Most importantly, Parra's critical vision even attacks our ways of thinking about the world and analyzing our experience. Our "inveterados hábitos mentales" and our "estructura lógica del pensamiento" referred to by Ibáñez-Langlois are systematically undermined in poems such as **"Siegmund Freud"** (*Otros poemas*). The particular point of this poem is to challenge the tendency in our culture to view the world in psychoanalytic terms, e.g., our exaggerated ability to see phallic symbols and the like everywhere. After a masterful parody in which the poet lists the numerous phallic possibilities, he concludes the poem with a section referring to himself visiting a factory in China and relating all he sees to sex organs. The use of the words "delirar" and "locura" indicates the distortion of reality resulting from reliance on this or any limited mode of thought. The end of the poem openly asserts that it is futile to try to understand human experience in such terms and that the system will eventually bring on its own destruction:

> El laberinto no tiene salida.
>
> El Occidente es una gran pirámide
> Que termina y empieza en una psiquiatra:
> La pirámide está por derrumbarse.

The realization that even one's way of thinking is being challenged has a disconcerting effect on the reader of Parra's poems. We realize that we too are caught in the trap of conventional thinking. This problem certainly affects the analysis presented here, for it has been difficult to avoid speaking in terms of "themes" and "motives" and other traditional literary jargon. The references to sexual symbolism (for example, the female symbolism of the tunnel) were consciously made with tongue in cheek, for one wonders if the poet has not intentionally laid a trap for the reader by using such symbols.

A final question to examine is whether or not the poet presents any solution. The world is in a shambles, humanity is trapped by its conventions, and we are on the verge of self-destruction. Is there any hope? It might be claimed that the mere perception of the human situation, the acceptance of it, and the insight into the reasons for it, represent a type of hope: in other words, that knowledge and understanding are the first step in a cure. But we have seen that for the poet our supposed "knowledge" and "understanding" are actually part of the trap, so the answer must basically be negative.

Ibáñez-Langlois presents a convincing argument for viewing the religious questioning of Parra's poems as a possible element of hope. But, as this critic also notes, in poems such

as **"La cruz"** (*La camisa de fuerza*), religious revelation is a future possibility, not a present hope for the solution of humanity's dilemma.

One poem that seems to offer an immediate solution is **"Los vicios del mundo moderno"**:

> Tratemos de ser felices, recomiendo yo, chupando
> la miserable
> costilla humana.
> Extraigamos de ella el líquido renovador,
> Cada cual de acuerdo con sus inclinaciones
> personales.
> ¡Aferrémonos a esta piltrafa divina!
> Jadeantes y tremebundos
> Chupemos estos labios que nos enloquecen;
> La suerte está echada.
> Aspiremos este perfume enervador y destructor
> Y vivamos un día más la vida de los elegidos:
> De sus axilas extrae el hombre la cera necesaria
> para forjar el rostro de sus ídolos.
> Y del sexo de la mujer la paja y el barro de sus
> templos.

Edith Grossman has suggested that this is a somewhat sardonic description of women (i.e., sex) as the salvation of humanity. It is certainly sardonic, but it is difficult to see that "salvation" is the goal, especially for the female half of humanity. Rather, this would seem to be simply a desperate recipe for male survival, for, after all, "la suerte está echada."

This section of the poem has also been seen to suggest that humanity simply try to maintain the illusion of happiness by clinging to what it has, impoverished and rotten as it is, and by continuing to "suck" and "extract" from life all that it has to offer. Implicit in this extraction is the continuation of the exploitation of others.

However, the sexual references are too clear to ignore (or perhaps, again, too clear to take seriously!). The "costilla humana" can be seen to refer to woman by association with the Biblical story of the creation of Eve from Adam's rib. The subsequent references to sucking on "maddening lips" and to breathing the "enervating and destructive perfume" also appear to be female references. And finally, the statement that man extracts the straw and mud for his temples from woman's sex is the clearest reference to the exploitation of women, and suggests to this reader the often observed commonplace that men, not women, create our official culture; woman is seen as being creative only through the product of her sexuality.

Therefore this solution to the dilemma is also a false one, at least as long as humanity clings to its condition so tenaciously. Perhaps, then, the only true hope for Parra is in the destruction of this condition, in the "crumbling of the pyramid." But no, for we are told in **"Soliloquio del individuo"** (*Poemas y antipoemas*) that this is a vain wish:

> Mejor es tal vez que vuelva a ese valle,
> A esa roca que me sirvió de hogar,
> Y empiece a grabar de nuevo,
> De atrás para adelante grabar
> El mundo al revés.
> Pero no: la vida no tiene sentido.

In the end, then, the only hope for Parra would seem to be the acceptance of the situation ("la vida no tiene sentido") and the ability to laugh, or at least smile, at the insanity of it all.

> Por todo lo cual
> Cultivo un piojo en mi corbata
> Y sonrío a los imbéciles que bajan de los árboles.
> "Los vicios del mundo moderno."

Marjorie Agosin (essay date 1984)

SOURCE: "Pablo Neruda and Nicanor Parra: A Study of Similarities," *poesis*, Vol. 6, No. 1, 1984, pp. 51-60.

[*In the following essay, Agosin asserts that Parra's* Poems and Anti-poems *influenced Pablo Neruda's* Extravagaria.]

Contemporary Chilean poetry represents a rich and vital lyric within Spanish American letters. A few names bear witness to this fact: Vicente Huidobro, Gabriela Mistral, Pablo Neruda and Nicanor Parra. Furthermore, Neruda as much as Parra has exerted an influence on the Spanish American poets that have come after them. Nonetheless, contemporary criticism has rarely pointed out the marked influence that Nicanor Parra has on Pablo Neruda in his book *Extravagaria,* published in 1958.

We consider it important to illustrate how Pablo Neruda was spurred by Parra's *Poems and Anti-poems* (1954) to reevaluate his own poetry and the function of the poet as well. This study will center on observations of how Parra's anti-poetry influenced Neruda's *Extravagaria*. Examples in the work of each of these poets show that they are not as radically different as they are thought to be and that the poet from the Coast, Neruda, is similar to the poet of the Andes, Parra.

The term *anti-poet* was coined by Vicente Huidobro in the celebrated epic poem *Altazor*. Huidobro was the founder of the creationist movement in Spanish American literature, a movement that shares the impulse of modern surrealism towards autonomous imaginative worlds and emphasizes, fol-

lowing its title, "The creation of new worlds that never existed before and that only the poet can discover." This discovery proceeds of course from a profoundly creative sense of *word*: "Rivers and jungles all ask me / What's new? How are you doing? / and while stars and waves have something to say / It's through my mouth they'll say it." The poet is the magician, the verbal alchemist who by means of his word invents a new reality.

In *Altazor,* the image of a windmill serves to focus the poetic theory of Huidobro. Like grain in the mill, words in the language are recreated, transformed in poetry: "And wheat comes and goes, from earth to heaven." Thus as Vicente Huidobro uses the term "anti-poet" in order to indicate the constructor of a new poetic language, Nicanor Parra, many years later, attempts a new elaboration of the poetic language of his period through the dismantling of the poetic culture that preceded him.

By definition anti-poetry, or to be more precise the anti-poem, exists only in a dialectic relation to the "poem," that is, the poem of the poetry previous to Parra's:

> We repudiate
> the poetry of dark glasses
> cloak and dagger
> plumed hat.
> We propose instead
> poetry with a naked eye
> bare chest
> and uncovered head.

Anti-poetry rejects rhetorical, solemn, grandiloquent, or nebulous poetry that reaches only a small elite. Parra accordingly insists that "the splendors of poetry / must reach everyone equally / against the poetry in the clouds / we object." Anti-poetry is by nature a poetry with its feet on solid ground. The language of the anti-poem is nourished by the attrition of a poetic tradition that is perishable and incompatible with the conventions framing the role of the poet and poetry as a highly specialized production of an intellectual elite.

For José Miguel Ibáñez Langlois, a noted critic of Parra, "The anti-poem is a possible answer: a word can no longer sing of nature, nor celebrate mankind, nor glorify God or the gods because everything has become problematic, beginning with the language itself." The language of the anti-poem is colloquial, immediate, and prosaic. The language is fed by irony, commonplace topics, ready-made phrases, and the compressed headlines of journalistic jargon: "Motorbike Plague in Santiago? Sagan takes a car ride / Earthquake in Iran: 600 victims?" All of these elements serve as instruments for the demythologizing of daily actions. Thus life itself is apparently as serious as death: "Still Death has not answered" and

"only one thing is clear / that the flesh gets full of worms."
These images are the target of anti-poetic language in which
the lyric voice itself can be its own victim: "I am a ridiculous sort / in the light of the sun / the plague of soda foun-
tains / I am dying of rage."

Parra's anti-poetry in effect demythologizes the culture and
language of preceding poetry. Recognizing that verbal signs
fulfill a function within a system of conventions, his writing
imposes his own significant order, transforming the direction of older poetic codes. The lyric voice makes sense of
the world since language is what defines it. Committed to a
comprehensible idiom, "We speak / in the language of every
day / we do not believe in cabalistic symbols." Anti-poetry
penetrates through all corners of accessible and comprehensible speech. Edith Grossman defines this idea clearly: "The
aim of anti-poetry is to cut away the poetic accretions—especially the charged words, obscure vocabulary, imagery and
metaphors—and to free and simplify literary language by
returning it to popular roots of the spoken idiom."

Neruda, too, in his works previous to *Extravagaria, Odas*
(Odes), *Odas elementales* (Elemental Odes) 1954, *Nuevas
odas elementales* (New Elemental Odes) 1956, and *Tercer
libro de las Odas* (Third Book of Odes) 1957, attempts to
simplify his language, reach the plain folk, and renew a
friendship between his earthly voice, which at times is grandiloquent, and the simple and accessible speech of the common tongue. There is also in these three books a desire on
the part of the poet to transform or convert poetry into a
useful object within everyone's grasp: "I want everything /
to have a handle / everything to be / cup or tool."

With the publication of *Poems and Anti-poems* by Nicanor
Parra, Neruda seems to resolve both his problems: achieving a lyric voice rooted in common culture, and transforming the apparently commonplace, say an artichoke or an
onion, into a distinct and unique *objet d'art*. But anti-poetry's
influence on Neruda becomes especially evident with the
appearance of *Extravagaria*. This title suggests an extrava-
ganza that at times results in confusion for the reader, since
the powerful vatic voice disappears; likewise the poet who
earlier proposed to speak for all others: "I come to speak
through your dead mouth / Come into my blood and my
veins." He rejects the role of bard and is above all a man like
any other:

> They once asked me
> why I wrote so obscurely
> they can ask the night
> the minerals and the roots
> I didn't know what to answer

The poet who previously had an answer regarding the ad-
versities in society "does not know what to answer." His

whole poetic posture changes here, and we observe a humbler Neruda, more like the anti-poet Parra. In **"Forward to
the Reader,"** Parra tells us that "The author has no answer
for the hardship that his writing can cause." In addition, as
the speaker of the anti-poems, Neruda comes down to earth:
"I am a professor of life / A vague student of death / and if
what I know is no use / I have said nothing and everything."

Extravagaria is not only an important book within the poetic trajectory of Neruda's work, for its revisionist and liberating course with respect to his previous production, but also
because it breaks down the Nerudian version of poet as
prophet. For the first time, we see an indication of the poet
as anti-poet, that is, one who analyzes himself: "And so, in
these brief passing days / I shall not take them into account /
I shall open up / and imprison myself / with my most treacherous enemy / Pablo Neruda."

An interesting counterpoint to this poem is formed by **"Epitaph"** where Parra talks about himself, disencumbered of
the omnipotence of earlier poets, including Neruda: "Through
a light somewhere between ironic and treacherous / not very
clever / nor utterly very silly / I was what I was / a mixture of
vinegar and oil / a sausage made of angel and beast."

The brief examples cited here are meant to point up our central theme: the anti-poetry shaped by Parra which forcefully
invades Latin American verse in the 50's acts as a model of
inspiration to Neruda's *Extravagaria*. What is more, these
lyric similarities would contradict the idea that Neruda and
Parra represent antitheses within Latin American poetry. On
the contrary, they share a common root, attempting to recover a unifying colloquial language which the poet speaks
not as a prophet who solves the crises of the modern world
but as a man like any other.

> Now I don't want to be
> forgetful or respectful
> to continue to give them counsel
> or reproach them for their madness
> I cannot claim independence
> I am lost in so much foliage
> should I leave or enter
> travel or linger
> buy cats or tomatoes?

René de Costa, one of the few critics who admits Parra's
influence on Neruda's work, makes a clear characterization
of this force: "One of the fundamental breakthrough concepts of Parra's anti-poetry that Neruda has made his own in
Extravagaria is the recognition that poetry like other literary genres, need not be solemn." One essential aspect of this
"anti-solemnity" which would be a good thing to study in
future criticism is the anti-solemnity of the language that
Parra utilizes. Let us not forget that throughout the *Anti-*

poems Parra is the great theoretician obsessed with explaining how he constructs his poetry: "As the Phoenicians, I will create my own alphabet." It is precisely in this shaping or renaming of things that the transcendental sense of the poems lies.

Among the strategies used in the language of anti-poetry, we find experiments with images that are unlike and incongruent: "I do not give anyone the right / I adore a piece of rag / I move tombs from their resting places." These unusual images, apparently unconnected, have the feature of surprising the reader and making him use his imagination in order to decipher the enigma encoded in the poetic image: "Perhaps the flies are angels / I'm a communist / I'm a conservative / I am a motionless dancer in the air." Like Parra, Neruda uses these apparently discordant images to lend a humoristic and playful tone to the majority of the poems in the work:

> So gentlemen, I am going
> to converse with a horse;
> let the poetess excuse me,
> the professor give me leave
> I shall be busy all week
> I have to listen incessantly
> What was the cat's name?

> (*Extravagaria*, 274)

Note the playful humor of the poem, especially that of the play on words. The poet says "oír a borbotones" (listen incessantly) instead of "hablar a borbortones" (speaks incessantly), the more usual expression. The end is as unusual as the unmatched images of the anti-poems: "What was the cat's name?" In Parra's **"Rompecabezas" ("Riddles")**, we observe the use of the technique of an incongruent question at the end, just as Neruda has done in the poem above: "Who are these stomachs for? / Who made this mishmash?" *Poems and Anti-poems,* like *Extravagaria*, surprises and excites with its marked humor and playful tone. The first poem of *Extravagaria* gives us on its first page

> need
> you
> sky
> the
> to
> rise
> To

Only by turning the page do we learn what it is one needs: "two wings / a violin / and so many things / incalculable things, things without a name." In giving the definition of the anti-poem, Parra, too, plays with the reader: "What is anti-poetry? / A tempest in a tea cup / a spot of snow on a rock? / a kerosene coffin / A funeral home without a body / Put an X beside / the definition you consider correct."

Both examples indicate an eagerness on the part of the lyric voice to make the reader participate in the poetic experience. Thus, the act of reading poetry is converted into a continual dynamic in which the poet, reader, and text are entwined and regain life by means of the word. In an interesting and revealing poem in *Extravagaria* Neruda writes: "I have a mind to confuse things / unite them, make them newborn / mix them up, undress them, until all light in the world / has the oneness of the ocean / a generous, vast wholeness, a crackling living fragrance." Confusing things is another way of enunciating a poetic manifesto which rejects the categories of acceptable and unacceptable. Parra perhaps suggests that the best way to confuse things is by modernizing this ceremony, a ceremony involved with turning back from the rhetorical word, adorned and luxurious, to the realm of the commonplace and the speech of the common man. In the same poem, Neruda uses the idea of "making them newborn" which obviously implies the start of things which, in turn, signifies the beginning of a new language.

We have observed that these poets, apparently quite unlike, are joined and have a similar objective: that their poetry, in a complex sense, reach everyone. The concept of poetry brought down to the level of life experience and spoken language is Parra's legacy to the Neruda of *Extravagaria,* and in addition, to all the poets that follow Parra, since this master obliges them to revise the traditional concepts of poetry and the role of the poet in contemporary society.

Publishers Weekly (review date 23 August 1985)

SOURCE: A review of *Antipoems: New and Selected,* in *Publishers Weekly,* Vol. 228, No. 8, August 23, 1985, p. 70.

[*In the following review, the critic praises Parra's* Antipoems: New and Selected *for reading as naturally as prose.*]

In any age, poetry, by its solitary and elitist nature, produces few heroes or celebrities, but Parra bids to break the barrier between the poem and the public. Born in Chile in 1914 and educated at Brown and Oxford as a physicist, Parra introduced the idea of the antipoem in 1954, "antipoem" being an ironic contradiction in terms and the signal of an attempt to demystify the form. Initially influenced by such plainspeakers as Whitman, Williams and Auden, Parra has brought an iconoclastic humor and playfulness to poetry that reached its apotheosis in his *Jokes to Mislead the Police* and *Ecopoems,* both published in 1983. The short poems from those collections border on the category of graffiti. He has, at the same time, the passion and commitment of his elder countryman Pablo Neruda. His *obra* defies the received notion of a difficult, elegant, obscurantist, and worst of all, pretty poetry in favor of the earthy, Rabelaisian spirit of a universal art. Though he is already a highly influential poet, this regrettably abbreviated bilingual sampler still has the potential to startle and inspire both old and new readers. Parra reads as naturally as prose, and makes what we already know intuitively about the awful, funny human condition newly available in the compressed and pithy shorthand of poetry.

Stephen Corey (review date Fall 1985)

SOURCE: A review of *Sermons and Homilies of the Christ of Elqui,* in *The Georgia Review,* Vol. XXXIX, No. 5, Fall, 1985, pp. 673-74.

[*In the following review, Corey asserts that Parra's* Sermons and Homilies of the Christ of Elqui *"is far more satisfying as a whole than for its individual parts."*]

Sometime in the 1920's, Domingo Zarate Vega left his job as a construction worker and became an itinerant preacher in his homeland of Chile. He claimed to have had visions following the death of his mother, and in response he dedicated the rest of his life—more than twenty years—to her memory and to sharing his radical views with the poor and suppressed. For his efforts he became a folk legend and an unofficial saint, dubbed "The Christ of Elqui" by his followers.

Nicanor Parra (b. 1914), the elder statesman among contemporary Chilean poets, was moved by these historical facts to render an imaginative version of the Christ of Elqui's teachings. The resulting sequence of sixty-three poems, while more consistent in voice than in poetic quality, makes for a powerful, entertaining, and often quirky reading experience. The range of the Christ's concerns includes the difficulty, in human terms, of his adopted vocation ("if I told it all it'd be an endless story / mockery humiliation and horselaughter / seeing me dressed in this humble sackcloth"); practical advice for daily living ("breakfast as lightly as possible / a cup of hot water should be sufficient / you don't want your shoes to fit too tightly"); political rabble-rousing ("may General Ibáñez forgive me / in Chile they don't respect human rights / freedom of the press does not exist here / the multimillionaires run everything"); sexual counseling ("Husbands should take a correspondence course / if they aren't brave enough to lean firsthand / about the genital organs of a woman / there is serious ignorance in that area"); priest-baiting ("There are certain despicable priests / who present themselves to say mass / wearing gaudy eyeshadow / and—I might

as well speak frankly— / makeup all over their cheeks and lips"); and the general timidity of people in the face of institutions ("Now hear the challenges of the Christ of Elqui: / . . . I'll bet not one of you has the guts / to yank a page out of the Holy Bible / when you run out of toilet paper / See? See? I'll bet nobody would dare / to go up and spit on the Chilean flag").

Sermons and Homilies is far more satisfying as a whole than for its individual parts, since the most memorable quality of this Christ is his flamboyant personality and opinions rather than his way with words. To be sure, he has his flashes of verbal power, but sometimes we are acutely aware of his merely talking, filling us in, with an almost perfunctory prosaic voice: "On 5 February 1927 / I happened to be working in the North / as a construction foreman / for a North American firm / I wanted to save a little money / so I could help my progenitors / who were really in a bad way."

Translator Sandra Reyes speaks in her introduction of the difficulties caused by Parra's use of Protean diction and attitudes to capture the paradoxical nature of the common man-philosopher-satirist who was the Christ of Elqui. Reyes has gone far toward giving us Parra's unusual sound—if I had to equate him with some American voice, I would call him a free-verse John Berryman—but she too often settles for an English cliché when what she ought to have found was a colloquialism or plainness. In one extreme instance, a ten-line passage contains all of the following: "I felt the blood grow cold in my veins," "I suspected the worst," "sorry to say," "I couldn't believe my eyes," and "when I finally came to my senses." From my own reading of the facing Spanish text, I am convinced that Parra sometimes works harder than his translator.

Still, this version of *Sermons and Homilies* is an important addition to the available body of Parra's work in English, and a rousing (though sometimes infuriating) primer for those who have not encountered him in the past. The volume is the winner of the first annual Richard Wilbur Award, cosponsored by the University of Missouri Press and the American Literary Translators Association.

Thom Tammaro (review date 1 October 1985)

SOURCE: A review of *Antipoems: New and Selected,* in *Library Journal,* Vol. 110, No. 16, October 1, 1985, p. 103.

[*In the following review, Tammaro praises Parra's* Antipoems: New and Selected.]

Chilean poet and physicist Parra comes from the great tradition of Latin American writers who are outspoken opponents of social and political oppression. His "antipoems" are full of black humor, irony, irreverence ("Torture doesn't have to be / bloody / Take an intellectual for example— / just hide his glasses"). They strip the human condition naked and place it before a mirror, exposing arrogance, pomposity, and foibles. Often epigrammatic and aphoristic, they shame us into recognition of our barbarity: "Good news! / in a million years the earth / will be whole again / We'll be the ones long gone." A generous sampling of early and recent work, and recommended for larger and foreign language poetry collections.

Adelaida Lopez Mejia (essay date July-December 1990)

SOURCE: "Nicanor Parra and the Question of Authority," in *Latin American Literary Review*, Vol. XVIII, No. 36, July-December, 1990, pp. 59-77.

[*In the following essay, Lopez Mejia traces Parra's attitude toward authority as expressed in his poetry.*]

In the years between 1954 and 1968, Nicanor Parra published various poems that refer to the humorous, aggressive, and deliberately mundane nature of his own "antipoetry". During that same period many European and North American artists were gravitating towards what is currently termed a postmodern aesthetic, in what Fredric Jameson describes as a reaction "against the established forms of high modernism". In Spanish American literary criticism, "high modernism" proves a confusing and awkward term. Parra's "antipoetry" came as an exasperated response, not to the *modernista* school of Rubén Darío, but to the visionary, surrealist voices of the 1920's and 1930's in Spanish American poetry, most notably those of Pablo Neruda and César Vallejo. Parra's early "ars poetica" pieces have more in common with the iconoclastic strain of the twentieth-century European avant-garde than with the style of aesthetic production called postmodern in the First World today. Poems such as **"Warning to the Reader"** and **"Roller Coaster"** impose a normative aesthetic on their audience, vociferously proclaiming the need for a new poetic language. Postmodernist thought, on the other hand, tends to suspect any form of totalizing discourse, and many contemporary artists associated with the movement do not fetishize innovation for they fail to experience the past as oppressive. Nonetheless, the debate surrounding postmodernism raises issues that are quite pertinent to the poetry Parra published during the late 1960's and early 1970's, and I find that the complex rubric of "postmodern" effectively characterizes the work he wrote after 1968. My intent is to analyze the shifting figurations of authority in his writing, focussing initially on his "ars poetica" pieces, and to describe that change in

the context of a transition from surrealist to postmodern in Spanish American poetry.

Two of Parra's commentators interpret **"Warning to the reader"**, **"Name changes"**, and **"Manifesto"** as parodical echoes of the serious "ars poetica" poems of Vicente Huidobro and Pablo Neruda, as well as of the manifestoes of Dada and Surrealism. Self-referential parody, cited by Linda Hutcheon as a definitive characteristic of late twentieth-century literature, makes an undeniably early appearance in Parra's antipoetry. His first "ars poetica" poems, however, primarily re-enact the familiar drama of a young poet struggling to achieve and establish his originality. They locate authority and repression in literary tradition and the reader, and participate in and continue the Western avant-garde rejection of the past. During the late 1960's, coinciding with the emergence of the notion of the postmodern in North America, the Chilean poet begins to inscribe more specifically political figures of authority in his work. When Parra grows increasingly attentive to the drama of Chilean politics during the early 1970's, the paradoxical coordinates of postmodernism as they are defined by Hutcheon, namely a self-conscious parodical urge and a nervous attention to history, combine in and mark the antipoet's work.

"Warning to the reader" first appeared in *Poems and Antipoems* (1954), the book that brought Parra his international reputation after Alan Ginsberg and Lawrence Ferlinghetti translated it in 1958. The poem promises aesthetic innovation in the same breath with which it brandishes a series of admonitions:

> The word rainbow can't be found anywhere
> Much less the word sorrow.
> Sure there's a swarm of chairs and tables.
> Coffins. Desk supplies.

The antipoet contests the authority of literary tradition when he decides to exclude sublime images and tragic subjects from his writing. By censoring rainbows, the poet prevents his text from becoming a vehicle for the representation of beauty. By expurgating sorrow, he devalues expressions of emotional depth or private anguish. He claims no privileged or transcendent meaning for his utterances; he will write only about utilitarian objects related to everyday experience. This speaker seems determined to incorporate poetry into the fabric of ordinary human existence, to graft that everyday experience onto the leisure time of reading, so that the act of reading poetry, too, takes on the quotidian significance of doing the laundry, brewing coffee, or eating lunch. Parra's later poem **"Manifesto"** underscores the intention that underlies most of his work: that of replacing the notion of poetry as ornament with one of poetry as utilitarian, everyday utterance.

For the old folks
Poetry was a luxury item.
But for us
It's an absolute necessity.
We cannot live without poetry.

Here Parra's poetics echoes the European avant-garde's call to break the barriers between art and everyday experience, to force art back into the praxis of life.

Although **"Warning to the Reader"** does not promise to transport us out of or refine everyday experience, its speaker gropes for the precise words, the correct diction, to convey the ordinariness of a new "antipoetic" experience. Parra's struggle to write a new kind of poetry surfaces in the lines: "like the Phoenicians / I'm trying to develop my own alphabet." Arguably, in Harold Bloom's terms, this is the voice of a "strong" poet at the crossroads when he undertakes the task of shaking off tradition. To develop a personal alphabet implies a rejection of the communal institution of language, and **"Warning to the Reader"** defiles traditional poetry by transforming it into a corpse in need of burial. First, the speaker compares himself to the birds in Aristophanes' play that "buried the corpses of their parents / in their own heads". After evoking this gesture of cannibalistic incorporation of parental identity, he threatens to "bring this ritual up-to-date": to "bury my quill in the heads of my readers". Again, the antipoet's provocative belligerence affiliates him with the avant-garde artist, who, according to Hal Foster, acts as the "defiler" of civilization. More importantly, Parra represents the poet's quill as a modernized, transformed parental corpse. When the antipoet buries his writing instrument in the heads of his readers, we become sepulchres of an object that is both weapon and burden, for it both alters and perpetuates poetic tradition. The murderous gesture with which the antipoet victimizes his audience also paradoxically invests us with judgmental authority and bequeaths us the prestigious legitimacy of the cultural past.

Parra's pugilistic speaker also assaults his audience in **"Roller Coaster"** (1962); in this poem, the figurative amusement-park ride of antipoetry leaves the conventional reader bruised and bleeding. Here Parra, like the Italian Futurists, relates aesthetic effect to notions of speed and collision. In **"Roller Coaster"**, the poem's ability to shock becomes a measure of its worth, and Parra shows contempt for readers who might find experimental art more jarring than exhilarating.

Go up, if you feel like it.
It's not my fault if you come down
Bleeding from your nose and mouth.

This text casts its readers as the stuffy enemies of the innovative writer, as the wardens of a stifling literary tradition. The European avant-garde, when addressing a bourgeois audience, adopted a similarly insulting stance. By mocking his audience's purportedly conventional expectations, Parra implies that readers of poetry, like poets themselves, must be prepared to take risks. The Chilean author finds the hostile dialogue between poet and audience pleasurable; in a recorded interview he states, quite emphatically, that needling the reader prolongs the aesthetic delight of his work.

Yet the antipoet does not always emerge victorious from his duel with the audience. Uneasy with the reader's power of judgment over his text, the speaker in Parra's poetry oscillates between aggressive attacks on tradition and a deceptively self-emasculating insistence on his own poetic impotence. I have argued that in **"Warning to Reader"**, the writer who victimizes his audience also invests us with the authority of a judge. In **"I Take Back Everything I've Said"**, the poet grovels before a reader who is deferred to, asked for forgiveness, entreated to burn the author's work. With mock-humility, the antipoet ingratiates himself with the perceived representative of literary tradition: his own audience. Instead of ranting against an unspecified, authoritative poetry, the speaker self-consciously adopts conventional standards of literary value when he asks to be punished for his writing's failure to transform emotion into art: "In spite of the fact that it was written with blood / It's not what I wanted to say". In this poem Parra plays at surrendering the fate of his poetry to the faceless audience he treats elsewhere with overt disdain. In the uneasy drama of his first "ars poetica" poems, now the poet, now the audience, occupies the coveted, potentially sadistic space of power.

In a direct, metaphorless language that accentuates his sense of himself as an artistic failure, the defeated speaker of **"Tres Poesías"** (**"Three poems"**; 1962) abdicates his authority almost before he begins to speak.

I have nothing left to say
Everything that I had to say
Has already been said many times.

Although Parra eventually comes to challenge the notion of originality, in this poem he represents its absence as his own inadequacy and shame. Purportedly crushed by the weight of tradition, he dwells compulsively on his sense of incompetence. Parra's readers often encounter a voice insisting it has nothing new to say and cannot say anything well, an apologetic persona for whom both the classical myth of the virtues of imitation and the Romantic myth of originality have run dry. Both the antipoet's battering of an implicitly conventional reader and his occasional exhibitionist insistence on failure reveal a competitive relation to tradition that is not yet postmodern.

The self-denigrating tone of **"Three Poems"** and **"I Take Back Everything I've Said"** accompanies a certain unresolved attachment to metaphor as a poetic device. The writer begs for punishment from his reader in the very poems most devoid of figurative speech, as if his metaphorless language were the source of his worthlessness and shame. Furthermore, although José Miguel Ibáñez-Langlois argues that Parra's avoidance of metaphor lies at the heart of his antipoetry, I find that the early Parra playfully but strategically uses metaphor in many texts where he defines and proposes a new aesthetic. In **"Puzzle"** (1954), the poet admits to a lack of confidence in his verbal ability:

> I'm the one who can't say what he means
> I stutter
> Thinking one thing I say something else.

Although the speaker deliberately refuses to cast himself as a verbal wizard, he has not exactly banished metaphor from his utterances. The last verse is markedly ambiguous: it might be heard as the voice of a poet attempting to name things in his own way. Miller Williams translates "Yo digo una cosa por otra" by "Thinking one thing / I say something else"; a more literal translation would be "I say one thing for another". Perhaps the antipoet acknowledges that his works serve no communicative purpose precisely because he "says one thing for another", because he still speaks as poets have traditionally spoken, obscurely and metaphorically.

In **"Changes of Name"** (1962), Parra ironically invokes the Aristotelian dictum that great poets must be the masters of metaphor.

> My position is this:
> The poet is not true to his word
> If he doesn't change the names of things.
> . . . Know that from this day forth
> Shoes shall be called coffins
> . . . Every fool who respects himself
> Has to have his own dictionary

Were this poem merely parodical of the fetishized status of symbol in Western poetry, it might unequivocally indicate Parra's postmodern rejection of metaphor as a decadent poetic device. I hear little irony, however, in the statement that only poets who change the names of things are true to their words. Just as in **"Warning to the reader"**, the speaker wanted his own alphabet, in **"Changes of Name"** he needs his own dictionary. Even an antipoet, then, needs a private storehouse of language, a stash of unique metaphors; this speaker strives for a personal and self-generated language. Undeniably, however, he also turns symbolic utterance into willful play. The antipoet's humor transforms the solemn, authoritative device of metaphor into a comic game. When Parra calls the sun a cat and refers to shoes as coffins, he no longer speaks as a privileged visionary who uncovers hidden resemblances between apparently unrelated phenomena.

The poet's coded language, no longer divinatory or sacred, reveals a childlike love of confusing labels, of stripping words of their denotative value and revealing their arbitrary value as signs.

It is no accident that images of corpses, tombs, and coffins predominate in the very poems where Parra set out to deride traditional poetry and conventional audiences. The antipoet inscribes a comic funereal imagery into his critique of an oppressively serious literary tradition. **"Warning to the reader"** and **"Changes of Name"** both include references to coffins; the speaker in **"Puzzle"** declares "I shift tombs back and forth". Similar funeral images crisscross Parra's well-known poem **"Test"**. This parody of multiple-choice tests begins with the question "What is an antipoet?"; one of the eighteen definitions that follow states that he is "someone who deals in coffins and urns". Several of the answers to a second question, "What is antipoetry?", play on variations of the image of a coffin:

> A jet-propelled coffin
> A coffin in centrifugal orbit
> A coffin run on kerosene
> A funeral parlor without a corpse

Whereas in **"Warning to the Reader"**, the image of the quill as a dead parent suggested the burdensome authoritativeness of literary tradition, in **"Test"**, antipoetry disposes of an absent, unnamed corpse. With the iconoclastic and regenerative spirit characteristic of the avant-garde, Parra's metapoems represent tradition as a dead body, as both the burden and the plaything of his own writing.

In two somewhat more personal "ars poetica" pieces, Parra conducts an understatedly passionate defense of the value of humor in poetry while recreating a conventional agonistic struggle between death and the voice of the poet. The figure of the audience still wields considerable authority in the first of these poems, but the speaker's hostility towards literary tradition seems tempered, and the primary threat to his identity now seems to be his own mortality. In **"What the Deceased Had to Say About Himself"**, the voice of a fictive dead poet declares that humor was one of the cornerstones of his technique, a lure, in fact, to catch his readers' attention.

> I wished to startle my readers
> Through humor
> But I made a most unfortunate impression.

Since a sardonic wit characterizes Parra's own antipoetry, these lines read like a wry, self-reflecting commentary on the Chilean writer's work. With the self-disparaging admission that his humor failed to dazzle his audience during his lifetime, the antipoet casts readers as judges whose approval he strove to attain. **"What the Deceased Had to Say About Himself"** implicitly distinguishes between readers who rejected the speaker's humor when he was alive, and the potentially appreciative audience of this pseudo-posthumous "ars poetica", to whom the dead poet appeals from beyond the grave. Because he can still speak about his poetry, death fails to decenter the poet's comic, ghostly voice.

In **"Absolute Zero"** (1968), humor provides the speaker no reprieve from the silence death imposes. Quite conventionally, Parra depicts death as a judge whose final verdict no one can escape. To inscribe death as a somber figure of authority hardly constitutes a novel *topos* in Western poetry; more striking is the high value Parra's poem places on humor as a heroic human attribute. The speaker locates the origin of laughter in the human awareness of death and suggests that humor arises out of the recognition of our own mortality. Sigmund Freud, too, described humor as a method "which the human mind has constructed in order to evade the compulsion to suffer". In **"Absolute Zero"**, laughter emerges as a defense against the fear of death, as a stoical response to its threatening inevitability.

> Death doesn't even respect genuine humor
> for him every joke falls flat
> even though it was Death
> who taught us to laugh in the first place

The poem also implicitly invokes comedy as a literary tradition worthy of imitation, a significant gesture in the work of an author often hostile to tradition. Artists whose work provokes laughter possess a greater right to immortality than other men or women.

> Take the case of Aristophanes
> kneeling on his own knees
> laughing like an energumen
> in the very face of Death:
> I would have spared that priceless life
> if it had been up to me

The dramatist most closely associated with the origins of Western comedy refuses to be cowed by the contemplation of his mortality, and his laughter reaffirms life. By pointing to Aristophanes as a paragon of courage, Parra represents humor as a dignified reaction to the humbling vulnerability of the human condition. The poem's reference to the Attic comedian as an "energumen", an epithet Parra and his speakers often use to describe themselves, also indirectly affiliates the antipoet with the Greek playwright. In **"Absolute Zero"**, Parra provides a defense of and commentary on his own humorous poetry.

Comic verbal artistry manifests itself more often in drama than in lyric poetry, and Parra tellingly prefers to think of his poems as "parlamentos dramáticos", as works that must be spoken publicly to gain artistic validity. Similarly, he insists that he wants his work to reflect the informal rhythms of street conversation. Indeed, the opening verses of **"Letters from the Poet Who Sleeps in a Chair"** (1968), one of Parra's most puzzling metapoems, privilege speech over written language.

> I call a spade a spade
> . . . The only choice given us
> is to learn to speak correctly

This long poem lacks the aggressive, formally wrought closure of **"Warning to the Reader"**, **"Roller Coaster"**, and other earlier metapoems. **"Letters From the Poet Who Sleeps in a Chair"** offers no totalizing, unified view of poetry. The disconcertingly fragmented development of its seventeen disjointed stanzas undermines the validity of the text's initial, provisional description of poetic practice.

The title of **"Letters From the Poet Who Sleeps in a Chair"** probably alludes to the long tradition of poets writing letters of advice concerning their craft to younger ones: Horace, Schiller, and Rilke are illustrious examples. At the same time, the title's humorous reference to a sleeping poet subverts the reader's sense of any firm authorial control over the text. The poem begins with a reference to a "correct" manner of speaking, but this dogmatic notion of a "correct" poetry collapses when, in the fifth stanza, the voice of an apparently aging writer addresses younger poets and encourages all forms of aesthetic experimentation:

> Young poets
> Say whatever you want
> . . . You can do anything in poetry

These verses negate the first stanza's more prescriptive mandate, so that the text can no longer be said to originate from a cohesive, centered artistic identity. A trembling, increasingly incoherent voice slowly takes the place of the optimistic speaker of the first stanza; this fissure in the identity of the speaking subject suggests the heterogeneity of voices associated with postmodernism. As the poem unfolds, the poet's initial self-assured lucidity gives way to a series of increasingly disconnected statements on illness, physical decrepitude, and death. In part three, the speaker wonders at a God who abandons his creatures to old age; part four consists of the single, morosely ironic line "I am one of those who greet the hearse". Parra's funereal images operate somewhat differently here from those in his earlier "ars poetica" poems: most references to death in **"Letters From the Poet Who Sleeps in a Chair"** seem deliberately unmetaphorical. Even the hearse functions less as a comical trope for a defunct literary tradition than as a metonymical reminder of the poet's mortality. Thematically as well as formally, Parra thwarts his readers' attempt to locate a stable, authoritative source of meaning in the speaker. The passage of time, traced by the very development of the poem, alters and finally silences poetic discourse. In the last stanza, the inevitable victory of death and disease over the human body renders writing a futile gesture.

> Only death tells the truth
> Even poetry convinces no one
> . . . Old age is a fact of life

In **"Letters From the Poet Who Sleeps in a Chair"**, as in **"Absolute Zero"**, the speaker who contemplates his own mortality concedes death the space of ultimate power and authority.

The fragmented structure of **"Letters From the Poet Who Sleeps in a Chair"** suggests a postmodern renunciation of the desire for autotelic aesthetic forms. Furthermore, Parra sets aside his avant-garde idealization of originality when he re-utilizes lines of verse from previously published texts and inserts them into different sections of the long seventeen-stanza poem. In the already-cited exhortation to young poets, Parra virtually repeats several lines from **"Jóvenes"** (**"Youngsters"**), a poem he had published in 1966:

> Write as you will
> . . . Too much blood has run under the bridge
> To go on believing
> That only one road is right
> In poetry everything is permitted

He reworks a second fragment from the same 1966 poem when, in 1968, he writes in stanza thirteen: "The poet's job is / To improve on the blank page / I don't think that's possible". Through self-quotation, inserting pre-existent poems into new ones, devouring his own texts and transforming the material he finds there into a different work, the antipoet begins to question notions of poetic originality. Foster has criticized analogous trends in the visual arts, in which "old and new modes and styles . . . are retooled and recycled". **"Letters From the Poet Who Sleeps in a Chair"** engages in a similar postmodern recycling of previously produced, already consumed poetic material: it uses metapoetic aphorisms from Parra's earlier work with very minor modifications.

The Marxist perspective on postmodernism, exemplified by Jameson and Foster, condemns the work of several contemporary North American artists for nostalgically mourning antiquated stereotypes. Both critics expound the need for a resistant postmodernism, or as Foster writes, for "a critique of origins, not a return to them". A mix of nostalgia and critical parody certainly informs Parra's representation of the artist in **"Letters From the Poet Who Sleeps in a Chair"**.

Readers tread a shifting ground as the poem alternatively awakens and undermines our sympathy for the figure of a suffering artist, a stereotype often invoked, according to Foster, by conservative postmodern artists. Parra grafts a clown-like, drowsy figure onto the pathos-laden background of conventional Christian iconography: "The poet asleep on the cross / greets you with tears of blood". The reference to sleep neutralizes any potential empathetic response to the crucified artist. The concluding lines, "Reading my poems makes me drowsy / And yet they were written in blood", appear to perpetuate the Romantic and Modernist identification of suffering as the source of art. Nonetheless, the ridiculous figure of the nodding poet exposes and undercuts the sentimentality of the reference to an *oeuvre* "written in blood". Readers of Parra's poetry may remember that those last lines echo an earlier poem, **"I Take Back Everything I've Said"**, where the poet asked his audience to burn a book "written in blood" because it was not what he "wanted to say". Once again, the insertion of old verses into new poems suggests a postmodern questioning of the validity of the notion of originality.

Although **"Manifesto"**, too, was published in the watershed year of 1968, that poem resists the diffident plurality of voices which informs **"Letters From a Poet Who Sleeps in a Chair"**. **"Manifesto"** offers an unwaveringly self-confident description of the role poetry should play in an ideal society. The poem's title openly invokes the European avant-garde as legitimating precursor, especially since the speaking voice defines itself exclusively in terms of its rupture with the past. In **"Letters From the Poet Who Sleeps in a Chair"**, a fragmented speaking voice moves the text towards its own silence. In **"Manifesto"**, a monolithic group of poets stridently attempts to censor the writing of the past. A collective voice stoutly proclaims its belief in a writing uncluttered by arcane metaphors ("We don't believe in cabalistic signs"). This militant stance necessarily silences an older, rival group of traditional poets for whom poetic meaning is best left veiled. In previous "ars poetica" poems, Parra often pitted the "I" of the speaker against the judgmental "you" of his readers. In **"Manifesto"**, the speaker's quarrel is no longer with his audience. The poem undeniably urges us to choose a poetry of direct statement over one predicated on symbol and allusion, but the primary confrontation takes place among writers.

In **"Manifesto"**, the ideal of an egalitarian society motivates the speaker's advocacy of a poetry of straightforward utterances. In certain ways, the poem's optimistic description of a society where poetry addresses the everyday concerns of men and women lacks Parra's characteristic irony. Another of the text's anomalies lies in its strategic use of the first-person plural pronoun "nosotros" ("we"), as opposed to Parra's earlier, individualistic persona who bemoaned his creative sterility or vaunted the shock-value of his texts.

Whether the antipoet spoke as a self-doubting novice or as an "enfant terrible", he raised a private, individual voice. **"Manifesto"**'s "we" implies a public community of poets with a socially conscious aesthetic not unlike Bertolt Brecht's. For the first time, Parra suggests that poets might have a didactic responsibility in society: "The poet is there / to see to it the tree does not grow crooked". Such an overtly ethical stance sets the poem apart from the Chilean poet's earlier work, in which the intention seemed more iconoclastic than moral. By the 1980's, legitimizing a new form of writing came to preoccupy Parra less than voicing the possibilities of nuclear and ecological catastrophe. In **"Manifesto"**, the antipoet's desire for literary legitimacy still takes precedence over the inscription of the political choices that face his community. Nonetheless, the poem's focus on the social responsibilities of a poet presages the quizzical political voice that surfaces in Parra's later work.

The contrast between the centered, political subject of **"Manifesto"** and the doddering, self-contradictory speaker in **"Letters From the Poet Who Sleeps in a Chair"** may serve to mark the Chilean antipoet's arrival at the aesthetic crossroads of the late 1960's. The former poem, with its avantgarde rejection of the past, suggests Parra's lingering attachment to a Latin American surrealist aesthetic. **"Letters From the Poet Who Sleeps in A Chair"**, on the other hand, with its fragmented structure and its parodic recycling of the author's own past work, bears the imprint of postmodernism. Parra's publications after 1968 also provide increasingly frequent signs of a growing tendency to repeat and quote himself. **"Absolute Zero"**, **"Manifesto"** and **"Letters From the Poet Who Sleeps in a Chair"** appear in print in *Emergency Poems* (1972) for the third time; these "ars poetica" poems already had been reprinted in his collected works *Obra gruesa* (1969). Perhaps significantly, in 1972 Parra did not reprint **"Test"** and **"I Take Back Everything I've Said"**. In **"Test"**, the antipoet anarchically entrusted the definition of poetry to his readers, in effect nihilistically abdicating much of his own authority over the text and conceding us significant power. In **"I Take Back Everything I've Said"**, a punitive audience sat ready to judge the masochistic, self-deprecating speaker. The authorial exclusion of these two "ars poetica" pieces from *Emergency Poems* indicates that the antipoet no longer intended to place his reader in the figurative space of power. By 1972, Parra had silenced the more self-disparaging strains of his poetic persona, a result, perhaps, of his new and liberating lack of concern with the task of measuring up to tradition.

The shift that occurs in Parra's location of authority coincides with a period when his production of "ars poetica" poems dwindles. In the only new piece in *Emergency Poems* that offers a direct commentary on poetry, the poet has donned the mask of a self-aggrandizing braggart. He constructs his claims to originality with the devious, self-perpetuating rhetoric of arbitrary power. **"As I Was Saying"** reads like a list of farcical boasts: the speaker claims he was the first bishop, the first hatmaker, and one of the first filmmakers in Chile. In a crude identification of virility and artistic creativity, the speaker combines boasts concerning his sexual exploits with claims to Gargantuan contributions to Chilean culture. After engaging in erotic reminiscences ("once I got a baby sitter / to come seventeen consecutive times"), the sexist speaker insists on his literary pre-eminence ("before me no one knew anything about poetry") and claims to have discovered Gabriela Mistral. This last claim sounds chillingly cynical; historically, it was Mistral who helped Parra when he was a young poet. The speaker's repeated and exaggerated insistence on origins, on being the "first", eventually exposes his words as a comic series of lies. The text shatters any notion of poetry as a privileged vehicle of expression for communal or personal truths. Not only does the poem suggest the endless ways in which language and rhetoric fabricate untruth, the speaker's exaggerated claims to originality make a grotesque travesty of the figure of the artist as heroic innovator. Swollen with self-importance, the poet presents himself as a pioneer of his culture; he no longer has any quarrel with the past because he has pervertedly identified himself with origins and national tradition. By making a caricature of his speaker's claims to innovation, by inscribing the ways in which power uses language to conveniently recreate and distort reality, Parra strips the notion of originality of its legitimacy and divests himself from its debilitating.

During the late 1960's, the antipoet sets aside his grudge against literary tradition and the reader. As he begins to contest the authority located in the notion of the State, Parra listens carefully to the language of politics, particularly the everyday expression of political opinion, and humorously incorporates it into his poetry. In **"Warnings"**, **"The Discourse of the Good Thief"**, and **"The Last Battle"**, originally published in *The Straitjacket* (1968) but reprinted in *Emergency Poems,* the poet directs his satire against various social and political institutions. **"Warnings"** appropriates the syntax of public street signs and ridicules the language with which society displays its arbitrary regulations and prohibitions: "No praying aloud, no sneezing". This poem highlights the coercive, repressive potential of language and depicts social rules not as rational incentives to order but as rationalized objectifications of power. Similarly, **"The Discourse of the Good Thief"** denounces the empty rhetoric of Latin American bureaucracy and questions the power and status conferred on men and women by official titles. Appropriating the voice of the good thief next to Christ on the cross, the speaker drones on in a litany of requests for a worldly position; the reader witnesses the grotesque spectacle of a man grasping for social influence and prestige, even when close to death. Official titles, like patronymics, often legitimize and provide a stable sense of identity. In the bureaucratic society evoked by Parra's poem, any official appointment seems better than none, as the speaker's absurd final request attests: "If it comes down to it / Put me in as Superintendent of Graveyards". The title of the poem cunningly represents State bureaucrats as thieves; the ensuing monotonous list of official titles inscribes the meaningless complexity of most bureaucratic systems. Finally, the closing verses effect a satiric representation of those systems as a corrupt and deathly space.

A postmodern appropriation of the conventions of the media is particularly evident in Parra's poem **"The Last Battle"**. This witty imitation of the syntax and graphic design of newspaper headlines describes a futuristic clash between a force of police-like robots and a group of "energumens". The latter group, figures of that instinctual irreverence towards authority that characterizes much of Parra's poetry, identify funeral parlors as emblematic sites of culture's repressive artificiality. Heirs to the cultural nihilism of Dada, invoking a familiar opposition between culture (funerals) and nature (death), the energumens chant the absurd slogan: "death sí / funerals no!". The street demonstrations of the 1960's probably provide a reference for the poem. A demonstration against the social ritual of funerals seems more than a little puerile; nonetheless, the closing reference to police brutality during a pacificist protest suggests that, at the time the poem was written, Parra's political sympathies lay with the radical student movement.

In the older texts of *Emergency Poems,* Parra's representation of political authority remains safely vague. Bureaucracy, language, police-robots: these constitute unpolemical targets. The new pieces, however, inscribe critical historical developments in Latin America, often by appropriating popular culture's pat representation of politics and history. An upsurge of radical social movements marked the late 1960's and early 1970's, but Parra's poems from that period question the effectiveness of political action and commitment. When the untrustworthy speaker of **"As I Was Saying"** boasts that he foresaw Che Guevara's death in Bolivia, a hyperbolic claim to prophetic vision frames and perhaps trivializes the reference to a real, dramatic failure of revolutionary idealism in Latin America. Since the details of Guevara's death remain incompletely understood, Parra's choice of historical event enforces a postmodern notion of the inaccessibility and unrepresentability of the past. The poem's reductive allusion to the asthmatic *guerrillero* appears to reproduce consumer culture's neutralization of the man whose face became a safe, domesticated symbol of dissident idealism.

With the exception of the dead, mythologized Guevara, few Marxist figures escape the barbs of Parra's irony in *Emergency Poems.* The book was published during the socialist presidency of Salvador Allende (1970-73), in a political cli-

mate necessarily wary of or even inimical to the antipoet's anarchist sensibility. Ricardo Yamal has interpreted the strongly anti-Marxist rhetoric of the volume as parodical of Latin American bourgeois conservatism. Without intending to minimize Parra's irony, I shall argue that the acerbic critique of twentieth-century socialism in *Emergency Poems* is not intended as parodic play. The Chilean poet's characteristically anti-establishment writing could not resist taunting his country's fragile socialist government; Parra turns Marxist political leaders and intellectuals into the primary targets of an often bitter critique. The tone of **"Viva Stalin"**, for example, recalls the antipoet's deceptive subservience towards that earlier figure of authority, the reader. A dead man's voice recounts his humiliating last moments in front of a Stalinist firing squad, in an enunciative strategy identical to that of **"What the Deceased Had to Say About Himself"**. There, the tranquil voice of a dead poet wryly recalled the lack of appreciative response to his humor. In **"Viva Stalin"**, where State repression silences the fictive speaking voice, Parra no longer addresses issues of poetic technique. Instead, he gives voice to the dead victims of a political terror unleashed and legitimized by Marxist ideals of revolution.

Parra's critique of socialism did not confine itself to the predictable example of Stalinist Russia as the nadir of Marxist regimes. In one poem, Parra appropriates and twists the slogan used by Allende in his 1970 campaign ("la vía pacifica hacia el socialismo") [the peaceful road to socialism]. The title's play on words, "I don't believe in the peaceful way", sardonically questions the effectiveness of the elected socialist government. The title of a second poem, **"If the Pope Doesn't Break with the U.S.A."**, satirically upholds the figure of the Pope as a stereotyped exemplar of morality. The speaker then exposes the Left's frequently dogmatic insistence on ideological purity and points to the political contradictions within the Left itself: "if the Kremlin doesn't break with the USA / . . . why the hell am I supposed to do it?". The dogmas of the Communist party, Parra suggests, are as inflexible as those of the Catholic Church. In the speaker's shrill reaction to crude Marxist representations of the United States as a demonic villain, readers might hear Parra's angry response to real attacks levelled at him by the Latin American Left when he accepted an invitation to the White House. The poet's satirical use of the Kremlin and the Pope as cultural icons again effects a reduction of complex institutions and systems of belief into stereotyped popular images.

Resistant to the coercive demands of both socialism and capitalism, the fickle speaker of *Emergency Poems* refuses to participate in either system's moralistic dichotomies; according to Hutcheon, a similar ideological ambivalence distinguishes most postmodern literature. In **"Modern Times"**, the antipoet rejects the dogmas and rhetoric of dialectical materialism, ironically signalling the abuse of the word "contradition" in certain forms of Marxist discourse. Whether the poet speaks or remains silent, an unnamed, implicitly socialist spectator finds his stance politically evasive, tacitly pro-imperialist.

> you can't speak without committing a contradic-
> tion
> or keep quiet without complicity with the Penta-
> gon.
> Everyone knows there's no alternative possible
> all roads lead to Cuba
> but the air is dirty
> breathing is a futile act.

By implying that the ideological stalemate between socialism and capitalism obscures the ecological plight of the planet, Parra voices the salient political concern of his later *Ecopoemas* (*Ecopoems*; 1983). The poet frames his reference to the Cuban revolution in the mnemonic form of a proverb, reworking the proverbial "all roads lead to Rome" into the contentious motto "all roads lead to Cuba". His formulation wryly concedes the 1959 revolution its significance in modern Latin American history, yet questions its enshrinement among Latin American Marxists as an iconic event.

Emergency Poems exploits many of contemporary culture's simplistic representations of global political conflict. In **"Well Then"**, the proper names of the Kremlin and New York encode and simplify the references to competing political systems. The poem also nostalgically invokes the notion of a subjectivity that transcends cultural parameters, as the speaker locates his sense of identity outside language, culture, or political system.

> hearing mass in a chapel of the Kremlin
> or eating a hot dog
> in a New York airport
>
> I'm the same person both places
> although it seems absurd I'm the same person

This detached yet apparently centered subject claims ultimate immunity from cultural and political difference, insisting that whether he stands at the center of the Communist world or at the threshold of the capitalist, his identity remains invariable. Poststructuralist thought, of course, takes this humanist notion of an immanent identity to task. Perhaps Parra's ironic (though tentative) reference to the absurdity of just such a notion marks his burgeoning postmodern awareness of the social and cultural circumscription of subjectivity.

The figure that occupies the space of power in Parra's poetry, I suggest, undergoes various metamorphoses. The "ars poetica" poems of the 1950's and 60's, where a self-reflect-ing poetic voice deciphers its own artistic technique, provide a useful locus in which to analyze the first manifestations of the antipoet's complex and belligerent relation to authority. In many ways, the early Parra casts his audience in the role of a judgmental, authoritative figure. Confronted by the weight of the literary past, the threatened poet displaces his hostility onto the figure of the reader. His playful, elliptic representation of literary tradition as an unburied corpse repeats the Western avant-garde attempt to immolate the traces of its cultural past. Occasionally, in texts that reflect upon Parra's own comic aesthetic, the antipoet arms himself with the fragile weapon of humor and confronts the threat posed by his own mortality. Perhaps late twentieth-century culture's loss of faith in totalizing systems of thought accounts for the paucity of Parra's "ars poetica" poems after 1972. During the late 1960's, Parra begins to direct his irony at social institutions and to parody the language that represents and encodes political conflict. At this point, Parra's writing appropriates the peculiarities of mass-media syntax, in a postmodern embrace of consumer culture that continues to honor the formal techniques of the avant-garde. In the early twentieth century, the practice of collage quietly subverted the notion of art as an autonomous, privileged realm of the imagination. Parra achieved this collage-effect in his poetry by parodically incorporating the stereotyped, formulaic language of political slogans, newspaper headlines, advertisements, and other public forms of writing and speech. These stylistic strategies document the impact of the media on postmodern culture.

During the early 1970's, the antipoet's habitual rejection of another's authority took as its object the ill-fated government of Allende. Many lines in *Emergency Poems* mock the political rhetoric of the socialist state. To readers with the advantage of hindsight, to those who view Salvador Allende as a tragic figure of Latin American history, Parra's mockery of the brief socialist experiment in Chile is jarring. His rejection of socialism seems particularly virulent in *Artefactos* (*Artifacts*; 1972), a disturbing collection of epigrams that is beyond the scope of this argument. Parra's reactionary critique of his country's socialist government during a politically incandescent period in Latin America develops out of his early antagonistic stance towards all forms of authority. Foster's scathing indictment of postmodernist visual art during the 1970's and 1980's, for its neo-conservative recuperation of history and its "flight from the present", does not strictly apply to the Chilean poet. Parra does not ignore the tensions of his historical present. Significantly, however, a figure like Che Guevara appears in *Emergency Poems* and in *Artifacts* as the cliché he has become for us: a handsome martyr to his idealism. Jameson rebukes contemporary culture for its production of precisely such stereotyped representations; Hutcheon, often impatient with Marxist critiques of postmodern artists, recognizes the movement's double ideological edge. Even when Parra mocks the utterances of conformist political opinion, he runs the postmodern risk of perpetuating them. Perhaps the conservative implications of postmodern formal techniques in First World art find their analogue in the unfortunate political implications of Parra's work during the early 70's. His anarchistic questioning of authority unwittingly allied him, during Salvador Allende's government, with those who worked towards the socialist president's downfall. The coup of September 11, 1973, ushered in the most repressive regime of Chilean history. In *Jokes to Mislead the Police* and *Sermons and Homilies of the Christ of Elqui,* under a brutal military dictatorship, Parra began to reassess the implications of his own previously indiscriminate, anarchistic opposition to all institutions of authority.

W. Nick Hill (review date Winter 1995)

SOURCE: A review of *Poemas para combatir la calvicie: Muestra de antipoesía,* in *World Literature Today,* Vol. 69, No. 1, Winter, 1995, p. 107.

[*In the following review, Hill asserts that Parra's* Poemas para combatir la calvicie *"makes painfully clear that the antipoet's latest work does not stand up to antipoetry."*]

The occasion of having won a major literary award, the first Juan Rulfo Prize, is an appropriate moment to publish a retrospective collection of a poet's work. The operative premise for *Poemas para combatir la calvicie,* for this "sampling of antipoetry," would appear to be to provide general readers, who may have a broad appreciation of antipoetry (i.e., "conversational" poetry), with an overview of the work that set the tone in the first place. The well-known critic and writer Julio Ortega, a jury member for the prize, has collected poems that span the lifetime of Nicanor Parra's work and provides a brief but polemical *prólogo* and a basic bibliography.

Collected here are the commonly anthologized and best-known texts from *Poemas y antipoemas, Versos de salón, Canciones rusas,* and *Otros poemas.* This is the corpus of antipoetry that was collected in English in the late sixties by New Directions. These are the pieces that, like the proverbial breath of fresh air, spun Spanish American poetry around and gave it a new orientation. Also here, in the next half of the volume, are more recent offerings: among others, the entirety of the wise rantings of Domingo Zarate, the self-proclaimed Christ from Elqui (*Sermones y prédicas del Cristo de Elqui* and *Nuevos sermones*), a handful of

"Artefactos," eco-poems, and the entire poem / text of *Mai Mai Peñi,* Parra's acceptance speech for the Rulfo Prize.

Such an occasion as this invites reconsideration of a poet's work—and, in this case, "antipoetry." The compilation leaves me feeling ambivalent. Who can imagine contemporary Spanish American poetry without Parra's "canonical" antipoetry, and then all that has followed from it, including questions about what "antipoetry" really is, how it differs from "conversational" poetry or "exteriorist" poetry. However, Domingo Zarate, as speaker and persona, may enunciate a parable of the whole epoch, according to Ortega, but he could also seem like a "born-again" Rimbaud. The ultimate test for an antipoet is to make him a sacred cow. What is an antipoet? "A quién dedicar este premio? / . . . A Dios señor rector / exista o no exista / gracias / . . . / a mí me carga la literatura / tanto o + que la antiliteratura / si tuviera 20 años más me iría al Africa / a comerciar en estupefacientes" (*Mai mai peñi*).

Poemas para combatir la calvicie makes painfully clear that the antipoet's latest work does not stand up to antipoetry. Such a pass might have been avoided by making more judicious selections—for example, not incorporating the entire acceptance/poem in which the antipoet kneels and intones witticisms before the forces at which he once thumbed his nose. Ortega's prologue appears to establish the basis for such editorial decisions, and he makes several interesting points. However, he also makes claims that need more elaboration than he chooses to give: for instance, that Parra's exploration of diction compares only to Vallejo's urban colloquial. As a result, the prologue and the selection seem more a justification than an explanation.

FURTHER READING

Criticism

Agosin, Marjorie. "Contemporary Poetry of Chile." *Concerning Poetry* 17, No. 2 (Fall 1984): 43-53.
  Asserts that while there are two streams of contemporary Chilean poetry, both use the language of antipoetry.

Flores, Angel. "Nicanor Parra." *Spanish American Authors.* New York: The H.W. Wilson Company, 1992, 654-55.
  Analyzes Parra's impact on Hispanoamerican poetry.

A review of *Antipoems: New and Selected. The Virginia Quarterly Review* 62, No. 2 (Spring 1986): 61.
  Calls Parra's collection, *Antipoems: New and Selected,* his "most solid production."

Additional coverage of Parra's life and career is contained in the following sources published by Gale Research: *Contemporary Authors,* Vol. 85-88; *Contemporary Authors New Revision Series,* Vol. 32; *DISCovering Authors Modules: Multicultural Authors; Hispanic Literature Criticism; Hispanic Writers;* and *Major Twentieth-Century Writers.*

Michel Tremblay
1942-

French Canadian dramatist, novelist, screenwriter, autobiographer, librettist, and short story writer.

The following entry presents an overview of Tremblay's career through 1990. For further information on his life and works, see *CLC,* Volume 29.

INTRODUCTION

Acknowledged as one of the most important playwrights of French Canada, Tremblay has achieved international recognition for the power and originality of his dramatic art. Most of his plays use the impoverished popular speech of urban Quebec, or *joual,* as their dramatic idiom, and they are mainly set in the narrow world of Montreal's working-class slums. His best-known play, *Les Belles-soeurs* (1968), is considered a landmark production that initiated the transition from "French Canadian" to genuine "québécois" theater. An innovator in language and dramatic technique, Tremblay also has written several novels featuring autobiographical elements and connections to the characters and situations of his plays. In addition, he has produced two musical comedies, a historical opera, several screenplays, and translations and adaptations of other dramatists' plays, ranging from Aristophanes to Anton Chekhov. As Leonard E. Doucette remarked: "Prolific and versatile, [Tremblay] continues to voice the frustrations and the aspirations of his native Quebec even as he formulates a universal human search for values in an apparently inhumane world."

Biographical Information

Born June 25, 1942, Tremblay was raised on Rue Fabre in the "Plateau Mont-Royal" section of east Montreal. He won a scholarship to a collège classique, but left after three months and enrolled at the Institut des Arts Graphiques, where he studied graphic arts and, like his father, became a linotype operator. Tremblay's first play, *Le Train* (1964), won first prize in the young amateurs contest of Radio-Canada, and he published his first fiction, the short story collection *Contes pour buveurs attardés* (*Stories for Late Night Drinkers*) in 1966. With the popular success of *Les Belles-soeurs* Tremblay established his theatrical career and reputation, which enabled him to devote himself to writing full-time. Tremblay continued with a group of plays collectively known as "Les Cycle des *Belles-soeurs,*" which concluded with *Damnée Manon, sacrée Sandra* (1977). After this play-cycle, Tremblay directed his attention to a series of novels collectively known as "Les Chroniques du Plateau Mont-Royal,"

including *Le Premier quartier de la lune* (1989; *The First Quarter of the Moon*). Tremblay also produced several independent works, most notably the plays *L'Impromptu d'Outremont* (1980; *The Impromptu of Outremont*), which satirizes bourgeois cultural values, *Les Anciennes Odeurs* (1981; *Remember Me*), a psychological study of a homosexual couple, and *Albertine in cinq temps* (1984; *Albertine in Five Times*), a technical masterpiece focusing on one character in dialogue with herself at different ages; the opera *NELLIGAN* (1990); and the autobiographical sketches and fiction of *Les Vues animées* (1990). Throughout his career, Tremblay has received numerous literary awards and academic honors, and many of his plays have been staged in the United States, Europe, Japan, and New Zealand.

Major Works

Tremblay's work blends psychological realism, structural experimentation, and political expression. "Les Cycle des *Belles-soeurs*" is comprised of the plays *Les Belles-soeurs,* *En Pièces détachées* (1969; *Like Death Warmed Over*), *La Duchesse de Langeais* (1970), *À toi, pour toujours, ta Marie-*

Lou (1971; *Forever Yours, Marie-Lou*), *Hosanna* (1973), *Bonjour, là, bonjour* (1974), *Sainte-Carmen de la Main* (1976; *Saint Carmen of the Main*), and *Damnée Manon, sacrée Sandra,* and well as the plays *Berthe, Johnny Mangano and His Astonishing Dogs,* and *Gloria Star,* published collectively as *Cinq* in 1966. Peopled by social misfits, transvestites, and homosexuals, each play presents a different aspect of life in Montreal's Plateau Mont-Royal district, a milieu of economic and social despair centered around two distinct areas—the residential Rue Fabre and the red-light district known as The Main. *Les Belles-soeurs* centers on Germaine, who has won a million trading stamps in a contest. As a group of neighborhood women gather in Germaine's squalid flat to help her paste them into booklets for redemption, each woman reflects on her frustrations. In the end Germaine's neighbors steal every booklet, leaving Germaine more desperate than ever. Some of the other plays in Tremblay's dramatic cycle portray similar domestic tragedies on Rue Fabre, including *Bonjour, là, bonjour,* which examines a father-son relationship; *Like Death Warmed Over,* which focuses on the children of Robertine, alcoholic Thérèse and insane Marcel; and *Forever Yours, Marie-Lou,* which presents a harsh portrait of family life in impoverished Montreal. The rest of the plays in the cycle feature disillusioned characters who have left Rue Fabre for further disappointment as drag queens, prostitutes, and homosexuals on The Main. *La Duchesse de Langeais* depicts a deluded transvestite prostitute rejected by a young client she loves, and *Hosanna* centers on a crisis in the relationship between a drag queen and "her" male lover. The children of *Forever Yours, Marie-Lou* assume the title roles in Tremblay's last plays in the cycle, *Saint Carmen of the Main,* in which Carmen is murdered for trying to free her transvestite and prostitute friends, and *Damnée Manon, sacrée Sandra,* which juxtaposes the religious ecstasy sought by Manon with the sexual cravings of "Sandra," a male transvestite. The novels of "Les Chroniques du Plateau Mont-Royal"—comprised of *La Grosse Femme d'à côté est enceinte* (1978; *The Fat Woman Next Door Is Pregnant*), *Thérèse et Pierrette à l'école des Saints-Agnes* (1980; *Therese and Pierrette and the Little Hanging Angel*), *La Duchesse et le roturier* (1982), *Des Nouvelles d'Édouard* (1984), *Le Cœur découvert, roman d'amours* (1986; *The Heart Laid Bare: Making Room*), and *The First Quarter of the Moon*—serve as complements to Tremblay's dramatic cycle, providing a social and familial context for central characters in the plays and fleshing out minor characters.

Critical Reception

Regarded as the leading playwright of Quebec, Tremblay has been admired for his innovative and provocative dramas. Although initial criticism of *Les Belles-soeurs* interpreted the play principally as a political statement, it has since become a "classic" of québécois literature, considered the most original play composed in Quebec, and has been translated into more than twenty languages. Critics often have discussed *Les Belles-soeurs* in the context of Quebec's cultural "Quiet Revolution," analyzing the profound influence exerted on the movement by Tremblay's drama. Catherine McQuaid has observed that Tremblay "contributed to a general movement out of colonial, into a tribal Canadian theatre." Both critics and readers have generally hailed his novels, especially *The Fat Woman Next Door Is Pregnant,* but subsequent novels in the series have been less well received. Nonetheless, commentators have "[connected] the ethos of the plays with the world views attributed to the characters in the novels who are associated with the dramatic protagonists, even if these characters do not appear in the plays," as Pierre Gobin remarked. "Tremblay's works . . . [refuse] to sever [their] ties with the community in the name of an apprehension of others, however precise, in which the collective experience of the community plays no part," Bruce Serafin concluded. "And it is precisely because they do justice to this experience that Tremblay's works occupy a special place in Quebec literature."

PRINCIPAL WORKS

Le Train (drama) 1964

Messe Noir (drama) 1965

*Cinq (dramas) 1966; adapted for television as *Trois Petits tours*

Contes pour buveurs attardés [*Stories for Late Night Drinkers*] (short stories) 1966

†*Les Belles-soeurs* (drama) 1968

La Cité dans l'œuf (novel) 1969

C't'à ton tour, Laura Cadieux (novel) 1969

†*En Pièces détachées* [*Like Death Warmed Over*] (drama) 1969

†*La Duchesse de Langeais* (drama) 1970

†*À toi, pour toujours, ta Marie-Lou* [*Forever Yours, Marie-Lou*] (drama) 1971

Demain Matin Montréal m'attend (drama) 1972

†*Hosanna* (drama) 1973

Il était une fois dans l'est [with André Brassard] (screenplay) 1973

†*Bonjour, là, bonjour* (drama) 1974

Les Héros de mon enfance (drama) 1975

Surprise! Surprise! (drama) 1975

‡*La Duchesse de Langeais and Other Plays* (dramas) 1976

Parlez-Vous d'amour (screenplay) 1976

†*Sainte-Carmen de la Main* [*Saint Carmen of the Main*] (drama) 1976

†*Damnée Manon, sacrée Sandra* (drama) 1977

Le Soleil se lève en retard (screenplay) 1977

§*La Grosse Femme d'à côté est enceinte* [*The Fat Woman Next Door Is Pregnant*] (novel) 1978

L'Impromptu d'Outremont [*The Impromptu of Outremont*]
(drama) 1980

§*Thérèse et Pierrette à l'école des Saints-Agnes* [*Therese and Pierrette and the Little Hanging Angel*] (novel) 1980

Les Anciennes Odeurs [*Remember Me*] (drama) 1981

Les Grandes Vacances (drama) 1981

§*La Duchesse et le roturier* (novel) 1982

Albertine in cinq temps [*Albertine in Five Times*] (drama) 1984

§*Des Nouvelles d'Édouard* (novel) 1984

Le Cœur découvert (screenplay) 1986

§*Le Cœur découvert, roman d'amours* [*The Heart Laid Bare; Making Room*] (novel) 1986

Le Vrai Monde? [*The Real World?*] (drama) 1987

Le Grand Jour (screenplay) 1988

§*Le Premier quartier de la lune* [*The First Quarter of the Moon*] (novel) 1989

La Maison suspendue (drama) 1990

NELLIGAN: livret d'opéra (libretto) 1990

§§*Les Vues animées* (autobiography, novella and drama) 1990

Le Vrai Monde? (screenplay) 1991

*This volume contains the plays *Berthe, Johnny Mangano and His Astonishing Dogs,* and *Gloria Star,* and is part of "Les Cycle des *Belles-soeurs.*"

†These works comprise "Les Cycle des *Belles-soeurs.*"

‡This volume includes *Cinq, En Pieces détachées, La Duchesse de Langeais,* and *Surprise! Surprise!*

§These works comprise "Les Chroniques du Plateau Mont-Royal."

§§This volume features autobiographical sketches, the novella *Les Loups se managent entre eux,* and the play *Le Train.*

CRITICISM

Catherine McQuaid (essay date Fall 1976)

SOURCE: "Michel Tremblay's Seduction of the 'Other Solitude,'" in *Canadian Drama,* Fall, 1976, pp. 217-23.

[*In the following essay, McQuaid explains Tremblay's success in English Canada by examining the social concerns, "highly" theatrical nature, and indigenous québécois qualities of his plays.*]

In 1970, anglophone Canadians suddenly learned that the québécois were serious about conserving their heritage and that meant more than the old sections of Montréal and Québec city. Two years later, the Tarragon theatre produced *A Toi Pour Toujours, ta Marie-Lou,* to be followed by *Hosanna* and *Les Belles Soeurs* in 1974. We all read the critics and

noted that Tremblay was daring to write in "joual", so we sought out the French scripts, if we considered ourselves competent in the language. However, most of us were not familiar enough with a Montréal accent to comprehend Tremblay's notation of the celebrated "joual", so we reverted to English.

The critics also told us that Tremblay borrowed theatrical techniques from Brecht, Tennessee Williams and Beckett. We nodded approvingly, because, after all, we were still suffering from colonial inferiority complexes.

So, we went to the Tarragon to see this new wonder who came from that unknown land, and who came so highly recommended. Once in the theatre, we no longer had the impression that we were watching something foreign to us. We were gripped by our mores—Puritan, if you please, as opposed to Jansenist, which shows how similar the two codes are. We were shown realistic/theatrical characters, we heard outraged demands for change. It was only when we were released from an immediate emotional response to Tremblay, that we fit his play back into its original Eastern Montréal context.

Tremblay has had an historical advantage, writing when he did, because Québec's demands for cultural autonomy served as an example for wavering self-determinating efforts in English Canada. That is not to discredit him, merely to say that he chrystalized similar concerns in both cultures. He portrayed characters who were struggling with the same things many Canadians were—poverty, inferiority complexes vis-à-vis Europeans, alienation, especially among women in urban settings, restrictive moral codes inherited from an even more rigid age. Things were changing rapidly socially and when we were confronted with these problems in the theatre, they had a great impact. Thus, Tremblay served as an emissary between the "two solitudes" and demonstrated, inadvertently, that we were struggling with similar problems.

Evocative theatrical techniques also helped to bridge that gap. Excluding their social implications, Tremblay's creations are compelling. Yet, once again, what Tremblay does so well—demystification of the theatre was starting to happen to English Canada. Especially at the Tarragon theatre, James Reaney, for instance, was using homely objects and regional accents, to reduce the sacred nature of theatre which has always existed.

Along with demystification, Tremblay's plays have a tribal unity, both in form within each of the plays and as an entire body of works. Many of the characters re-appear, as is well demonstrated in *Il était une fois dans l'ést,* the film presentation of the Tremblay/Brassard world.

So, there are three factors which aided Tremblay to succeed

in English Canada: social concerns, in which English Canadians were implicated, the highly theatrical nature of each play and a simultaneous movement in both cultures, out of colonial, into indigenous (or tribal) theatre. An examination of Tremblay's texts will serve as an elaboration of these points.

English Canadians are implicated in the social problems which are dealt with. Essentially, the three plays produced at the Tarragon, concern women in revolt. The feminist movement had been getting a lot of publicity, it is true, but, more important, women's roles were being re-evaluated, by both men and women. Tremblay's women question their responsibilities, but within a context which is far enough removed from the comfortable housewife/part-time career women of most English Canadian women who go to the theatre, to avoid making us feel uncomfortable.

Tremblay's women are literally enclosed in the house, with their still-large families. Large families are a cultural phenomenon associated with Québec. Yet, neither the children nor the neglectful husbands are shown on-stage, so the criticism is not to be directed at them, but at the women themselves. The women in *Les Belles Soeurs* and Marie Louise, notate the repetitive drudgery of their lives. Each has her own way of escape: accusing her husband of ruining her life, as Marie-Louise does; dreaming of how to "spend" her stamps, for Germaine Lauzon, and alcohol for Hélène, in *En Pièces Détachées.*

The women are alone in the house and within this theatrically, as well as literally limited space, they are forced into confrontation with each other. Tremblay's most brutal metaphor for spiteful, despairing women, is the Gold Bond Stamp party in *Les Belles Soeurs*. A party turns into a manifestation of jealousy and cruelty. *Who's Afraid of Virginia Woolf* uses the same vehicle. The effects of a hermetic environment explode into aggression in both instances.

The women revolt against their suppressive ethical and financial environment. Marie-Louise is the most outstanding example of the generation of women for whom sexual relations were disgusting. Robertine in *En Pièces Détachées* and the older women in *Les Belles Soeurs,* belong to the same generation. Part of their disgust comes from a rigid Jansenist morality (substitute "Puritan" for English translations) and the other half of it was the risk of pregnancy. The women knew that another child meant financial hardship.

The second generation of women were actively liberating themselves from their mother's hardships. Carmen, Linda Lauzon and Hélène, are the representatives of this generation. Carmen accepts her limitations and doesn't delude herself about her career. Yet, as she says to Manon, her sister,

the most important thing for her is to have reacted and to have escaped from the "marde" in which she was born.

Hélène and Linda Lauzon have not as successfully freed themselves as Carmen has, but they are trying to escape from the situations which cause their mothers so much frustration.

> **Along with demystification, Tremblay's plays have a tribal unity, both in form within each of the plays and as an entire body of works.**
> —*Catherine McQuaid*

With both morality and financial conditions conspiring against them, the families of these women are not very happy either. There is alienation between all members of the family, as a result of no communication. They watch television or the husband spends the evening in the tavern. He is just as dissatisfied as the women are. The only two men in all of Tremblay's repertoire—Henri and Léopold—are exploited and unhappy in the factory. They have their respective avenues of escape; beer and/or compensation payments. All the other men are absent, because, as Tremblay says, "There are no men in Québec."

These problems implicate English Canadians as well. The breakdown of the family unit, labour unrest, dissatisfied women are world problems. Yet, specifically in English Canadian theatre at this time, the same problems were being treated. David French's *Leaving Home* had created a sensation and his main concern is also antagonism within the family. It may be considered that English Canada was even predisposed by David French, to accept Tremblay's examination of problems within a family.

However, that is not the only aspect of Tremblay which made him a success. Social comment is presented in a highly theatrical style, which is extremely compelling. This aspect of his plays needs no translation, because they are so fundamentally theatrical. *Hosanna,* which was successful even outside of Canadian context, is the most theatrical of all of Tremblay's works. It is a drama-within-a-drama, with Hosanna functioning on three levels—Elisabeth Taylor/Cleopatra, Hosanna and Claud; an often-neglected sense in the theatre, the sense of smell, personalizes Hosanna through her cheap, cloying perfume.

The play begins "in medias res", a dependable theatrical gambit, with Hosanna in her Cleopatra costume. From then on, the play is literally a prolonged striptease. It is a metaphorical striptease as well, paralleling the lovers' progression towards honesty. Hosanna's costumes, as well as her lover's costume of the "beau gars", is a disguise, in addition to being a borrowed theatrical personality. Thus, Hosanna is twice-removed from Cleopatra.

Tremblay uses essentially the same theatrical pretext in *La Duchesse de Langeais.* La Duchesse is impersonating La Grande Dame at the beginning of the play. She speaks directly to the audience, addressing us as "ma fille". A dramatic monologue has to be a delicate balance between dramatic impersonation and sympathetic honesty with the audience. That is where la Duchesse succeeds. She gives us a magnanimous mental striptease, yet still retains a fundamental dignity.

En Pièces Détachées is an example of another style which Tremblay uses, which is the statuesque, borrowed from Greek drama. The characters seldom speak to each other and they are very static visually on the stage. The same quality of the statuesque is found in *Marie-Lou, Les Belles Soeurs* and *Bonjour Là, Bonjour,* but *En Pièces Détachées* is a refinement of this style.

Within the reduced realism of the set, which allows free movement, Robertine and Henri remain static. Around them moves Hélène, sometimes drunkenly. The neighbour functions as a Chorus, leading the characters in the family in their chant "Chus pus capable de rien faire", "I am no longer able to do anything". All of the characters are literally immobile at the conclusion of the play.

There is very little action on the stage in any of Tremblay's plays. This is a stage metaphor for the theme of this play—entrapment, whether physical or psychological. It may be an interesting technique for experienced theatre audiences, but why was *Les Belles Soeurs,* for instance, such a success with drama departments in universities?

Tremblay had dared to use the language of his characters and of his environment. The language itself is a form of revolt, even within Québec theatre. In good English translation, the violence of Tremblay's language is conveyed. Therefore, it is only at the verbal level which his theatre could be called a "theatre of revolt". English Canadians were just beginning to talk about anti-americanism and nationalism, with residue sentiment sparked by Expo '67. They were, however, very curious to see Québec in the theatre, since visiting Québec is always so charming.

Tremblay did not portray the habitant and folk characters, which, until this time, was the image perpetuated by the bonhomme and ceintures fléchées of the Québec Winter Carnival. No, Québec and the theatrical experience in general was undergoing demystification. It was startling to realize that québécois were suffering from the same social

problems as we were; to be shown that within families everywhere, there was alienation and non-communication.

David French's success in English Canadian theatre has already been mentioned. His theatre also dealt with the problem of the disintegrating family unit. The fact that French was a Newfoundlander who wrote good plays may have predisposed us to listen to another playwright, also from a relatively mystifying province.

In addition to a genuine desire to get to know each other as Canadians and to do away with stereotypes, there was a general movement away from colonialism in the theatre. We had seen all of Neil Simon's and Bernard Shaw's plays. Canadians want to encourage native talent. Docu-dramas and collective creations were producing a new theatrical form as well as informing Canadians of the variety of our experiences. Thus, Tremblay was fortunate to arrive at the peak of the Canadian awareness movement. That is not, however, to denigrate Tremblay, it is merely to say that he was part of the new interest in information about all things Canadian. His plays have a tribal unity which inspired and focussed Canadian nationalism within English Canada.

Many of the characters reappear, creating an impression of a tribe. La Duchesse is mentioned in *En Pièces Détachées,* Carmen's career is followed in *Ste Carmen de la Main.* There are three generations present within Tremblay's world and each generation has its specific qualities, which contribute to a sense of seeing an entire society. Like Margaret Laurence, Tremblay writes out of a microcosm which implicates all humanity.

Tribalism is manifested in another way. When Lisette de Courval in *Les Belles Soeurs* displays an attitude of superiority because she has visited Europe, or when Hélène in *En Pièces Détachées* resents the Frenchman who comes into the restaurant, a tribal reaction is elicited. A threat from the outside immediately unites a tribe.

Tremblay elicits a tribal response outside of Québec simply by virtue of being a very good playwright. "Discovered" Canadian talents always occasion a national pride. In strictly theatrical techniques, that is involved in the action on-stage through the use of chants, a ritualistic device, and the rhythmic pace of the plays. The acts in *Bonjour Là, Bonjour* are even designated as a vocal selection of music would indicate different groupings of singers. Duo, Trio and Quattor signal the number of actors in the scene. There is a musical quality in the hypnotic chants. *Les Belles Soeurs* accompany their chants with beating of feet as the québécois always do when folk music is played. Tremblay uses every theatrical trick to spellbind his audience.

It was not only the "other solitude" which Tremblay seduced.

It must be remembered that Québec was also suffering from "colonialism" in the arts when Tremblay started to write. Jean-Claude Germain, in *Canadian Theatre Review*, Spring, 1976, uses this term specifically in his article on Québec's struggle against foreign domination in theatre. So, Tremblay's success in New York and in Paris produces a gleeful tribal pride at the reversal of this state of affairs.

Beyond an immediate reaction in the theatre, where Tremblay plays upon audience reaction as surely as any musician, he represents the first Canadian playwright to break through the language barrier of the French, even when, ironically, he writes in "joual", the most indigenous and inaccessible language of Canada. He has also contributed to a general movement out of colonial, into a tribal Canadian theatre.

Bruce Serafin (essay date Summer 1978)

SOURCE: "Five Short Plays by Tremblay," in *Essays on Canadian Writing*, Summer, 1978, pp. 248-59.

[*In the essay below, Serafin discusses how Tremblay's use of language affects the theatricality, characterization, humor, and dialogue of the five plays comprising* La Duchesse de Langeais, and Other Plays.]

In her story "Copenhagen Season" Isak Dinesen tells of an artist who was "feted in society, but feared as well, because he would at times sit without saying a word, taking in the face and figure of a lady until she felt that she had no clothes on, and at other times, when once set upon a theme, would go on talking forever." Nothing could be more appropriate than the fact that Dinesen places this figure in an aristocratic milieu. After all, in what other milieu could one find individuals given to the fastidious and absorbed contemplation that this artist bestows not only on the women who catch his eye but also on the topic to which he later turns his attention? The ruminative genius has always found a refuge in the aristocracy, if not a home. And this has been so right into recent times. Proust, for example, presented a perfect copy of the type that Dinesen ironically summons up in her story. As one critic notes, Proust "alarmed his friends, who dreaded and longed for the moment when the writer would suddenly appear in their drawing rooms long after midnight—*brisé de fatigue* and for just five minutes, as he said—only to stay till the grey of dawn, too tired to get out of his chair or interrupt his conversation." That this behaviour was reflected in his writing is well known. Again and again, one comes across in Proust sentences that go on for interminable, exhausting lengths, so reluctant is the author to let his topic go until it blesses him. It is clear, however, that language which seeks to impulsively touch its listeners cannot afford to cling to its theme in this way. Rather, it must be playful, constantly changing, giving itself up to the most ephemeral subject. That this is so is demonstrated in the work which opens Tremblay's collection.

While *La Duchesse de Langeais* is a monologue, it is not a contemplative voice that we hear, but an ecstatic one.
—*Bruce Serafin*

While *La Duchesse de Langeais* is a monologue, it is not a contemplative voice that we hear, but an ecstatic one. La Duchesse possesses the ecstacy of the creature; she almost literally vibrates with her awareness of herself. Talonbooks has supplied a picture of Claude Gai in the role: the jewelry, voracious mouth and brilliant eyes of this Duchesse bring to mind those habitués of Vancouver's Davie Street bars whose tight white blouses often reveal a startlingly hairy inch of belly and whose Roman-cut hair and shrill voices seem so in accord with their archly mobile faces that one can without effort imagine them as the subject of a Daumier sketch. Like these homosexuals, la Duchesse is garrulous to an extreme, talking as though she had never spent more than three minutes without companions. Her monologue has no inward quality; instead, it is stuccoed with impulsive phrases, as if at every moment she wanted to lean over and pinch an arm or kiss somebody on the lips. To be sure, this language, like a flapping coat, occasionally reveals a bright lining of pain. Nevertheless, these glimpses are far from having a sobering effect. In fact, considering the flushed and uncontrolled nature of her speech, it is surprising that it should be the delicacy which this creature brings to her reminiscences that makes them so vivid. Suffused with delight, la Duchesse harks back to an old lover:

> . . . He used to play at being the poor suffering poet and while la Vaillancourt would tear your ticket, he'd tear your heart out! Hah! All he needed was a pair of big ears and he'd have made a perfect Gérard Philippe . . . Oh, what was his name? . . . Don't dig too deeply, hein, you'll get me all excited . . .

> *She laughs.*

> At your age! Tsk, tsk, tsk! You're so pretentious!

> *A wink, a little squeal and a wiggle of the hips.*

> I called him, "my lover with the brazen shaft." I don't know why. Guess I thought it sounded nice. God knows, that's the only thing about him that was the least bit hard . . . And I was stuck with the little pisspot for two whole months . . . He couldn't do a thing! Nothing! Had to show him everything! Toute!

From beginning to end! Mon Dieu, the crazy things
I've done in my life. No one in Montréal has had
more "aventures stupides" than me. I could tell you
about them for weeks, my darlings . . .

Perhaps a backdrop of cherubs could do justice to this—certainly such a backdrop would be in line with la Duchesse's intoxicated, defenceless vulgarity. This vulgarity is an attribute of the purely spoken word that differentiates it from speech which has been profoundly touched by the reading of books, and since the introspective person is usually a bookworm as well, this includes all speech which ignores its audience for the sake of those interminable, enchanting sentences we mentioned before. What distinguishes it from the speech of la Duchesse is therefore easy to recognize, and why there can be no confusing the two: for those whose involvement with language begins and ends with the sentence the whole area of language that expresses the ecstacy of the creature must remain more or less inaccessible.

Actually, it is in this connection that Tremblay's use of the vernacular becomes most attractive. For that which in language is the receptacle of warmth, ecstacy, bliss—the colloquial utterance, the exclamation, the cry of creaturely abandon that completes itself not with a period but with a slap, a nudge, a kiss—is the very thing that his audience is to a perhaps predominant extent barred from expressing even while being drawn to its presence in others as if to the presence of genius. And it is indeed the genius of language which lives only to ensure communion between individuals that Tremblay has made his own in *La Duchesse de Langeais*. Many of the play's features—the abundant use of question marks and exclamation points, the short, utterly colloquial outbursts—flow from this fact.

There is no denying the jubilantly theatrical context in which this vernacular places itself. Not only is this the context in which la Duchesse's speech may be most fruitfully discussed, but it appears in nearly all the other of Tremblay's works as well, including the others in this collection. The innumerable uncorseted minutes in the lives of Tremblay's characters, the impulsive—one might also say, the improvised—nature of their lives and the concomitant emotional reversals and changes of fortune which again and again overcome them all go hand in hand with a tendency towards unabashed display, theatricality for the sake of theatricality. Tremblay reveals the heaven of his figures to be a theatre in which every moment can be turned into an opportunity to display oneself. And precisely this is reflected in the vernacular as in a mirror. To plan, to think ahead, to discipline oneself—essentially, this means to hold something in reserve, the very reserve whose excluding, distancing power on the social level finds its linguistic counterpart in the dignity of the completed sentence. Pure display of the self, on the other hand, is instantaneous. It gives itself without reservation to

the moment, lives in the moment, and vanishes once the moment has vanished. Like the language that lends it voice, it is in its very essence lyrical. It must be admitted, however, that the creaturely attractiveness that accompanies this lyricism and which is overwhelmingly apparent in such Tremblay figures as la Duchesse is shot through with an element of helplessness. One is reminded of the charm which the wild young men who fill the jails display in the eyes of the social workers who deal with them. "It cannot be guilt that makes them attractive," Kafka once wrote of figures who are distant cousins to those that appear in Tremblay's works, "nor can it be the just punishment that makes them attractive in anticipation . . . so it must be the mere charges brought against them that somehow show on them."

This attractiveness is usually represented by Tremblay in a figure who is charged with a version of the very theatricality discussed above and in whose appeal helplessness and defiance are intertwined. *Hosanna* and *En pièces détachées* provide striking examples of such a figure, and in this collection, too, Tremblay turns his attention to this prototype. *Berthe* details the struggles of a nightclub cashier to free herself of the swamp of daydreams in which she wallows. It is no accident that this woman sits in her box "reading a movie magazine" and wearing glasses "made of blue plastic and shaped like cat's eyes"; they are the attributes one might expect of the kind of dreamy bungler whose home is oblivion. This is Berthe's home, and the fact that this is so is perhaps most appropriately seen as a judgement on her. This judgement marks her unmistakably. The bungled, the useless, the lost—they are the most removed from the times in which they find themselves, and the smaller and more inconspicuous they are, the more they bear, in a concentrated form, as it were, the marks of judgement that the times deal out to whomever has lost touch with them.

To perceive these marks of judgement, to perceive the peculiar beauty which oblivion bestows on individuals, is one of Tremblay's gifts, and explains his sensitivity to the eccentric and grandiose features of his characters. The fact that he presents these features in a humourous light should not obscure the recognition that he does so with a full awareness that they are symptomatic features, just as the garish dress of an isolated individual in a big city is symptomatic of the anxiety his situation causes him to feel. Hosanna's involvement with Elizabeth Taylor is an example of this symptomatic element, as is Berthe's image of herself as a Hollywood star. "I'm the greatest actress in the world, and I get a million bucks per movie!" Berthe says. "I'm not locked up in this box!" Nevertheless, there is precisely the admission of failure which one might expect from a prisoner:

I know it's too late. I know there's nothing I can do.
Everyone's been telling me for years. But let them
say what they want. I'm not that crazy! "You're noth-

ing but a bloody dreamer," they tell me. "All you're good for is making up crazy stories that don't make any sense! We never know if your telling the truth or if you're dreaming out loud. If you keep going like that, you're going to find yourself without any friends, Berthe. One of these days you're going to wind up all alone. All by yourself!" Do something, Berthe. Do something!

A long silence

But I never did anything.

A long silence.

I don't ask for much now . . . Just let me have my dreams. Leave me in peace and let me dream! That's all I've got left. 'Cause I do know how to dream. Ha! Do I ever! Maybe I'm dumb, but that doesn't keep me from making up stories. I know I don't look it, but I can make up, all for myself, the real life of a real Hollywood star. I'm not too smart, but I know how to make myself think I am. So what if I look stupid sitting here. I could have done something with my life if I'd wanted to.

She pauses.

But I never did anything. I just sat here in my box.

It does not take much effort to discern the bewilderment which this creature feels when it comes to reflecting on herself. Actually, there is a dialectics of bewilderment, an oscillation between despondency and rage which Berthe sums up in words that might serve as a motto for her monologue. "If I can't dream, I'm gonna suffocate," she more than once says, and quite palpably, dreaming here takes the place of the real understanding of the situation which is denied her.

In an interview in one of those weekly magazines that appear in the newspapers, Tremblay fervently denounced the addiction to daydreaming that characterizes his subjects, and it is clear that this attitude has played a part in his representation of this figure. Yet it is this very ability to daydream with an almost rhapsodic intensity which is one of the most attractive features of Tremblay's characters. If one thinks back to the passage from *La Duchesse de Langeais,* it is easy to see that one of the most significant components of this monologue lies in the brilliant excessiveness of the reminiscences. Stories flow from Berthe as well. But here it is the other side of the lyricism that makes la Duchesse such a charming figure which is revealed—the utter inadequacy of this lyricism when it comes to productive, cold-blooded reflection on existence. For Berthe, happiness lies in the blissful glamour which communion with friends spreads over life;

isolated in her box, she is at times frantically restless. Indeed, one might go even further and say that it is nothing but pure and simple homesickness which Berthe experiences. For the vernacular is like those tropical birds which lose their brilliant colour when they are taken out of their natural environment; it languishes and wilts in isolation. Unlike la Duchesse, who is drunk enough to surround herself with imaginary companions, Berthe must suffer her loneliness. Her garrulity, one might say, is a short rope against which she continually pits herself in an attempt to take hold of her experience, only to be continually jerked back. And the silences which stud her monologue are loud with the perplexed and painful panting of this creature.

Berthe is in some respects an exhausted older version of those female figures in Tremblay's works whose chief characteristic might be described as an irritated voluptuousness. They are women who eat, smoke cigarettes and talk at the same time, who brush out their hair in front of mirrors as if they hated it and often make abrupt and unarguable statements, as though seeking to unsettle the boring world that has so little time for their dreams. If one were vindictive, one would call them ham actors. Certainly they love to display that "dancer's calf" that Roland Barthes speaks of. The glasses Berthe wears are an example of this, as are the theatrically straight back and sensual kick of the foot which one associates with Hélène in *En pièces détachées,* for instance. Usually one cannot fail to notice the sexuality of these women. They have the flushed, slightly hysterical expressiveness of von Jawlensky's *Spanish Girl*. In this case, however, all that is left of their high, flaunty, nervous colour is a loud, somewhat self-conscious polemicism. The acutely alien isolation in which Berthe finds herself forces her monologue to take on the barren nature of prattle. She is like the sinners in hell who irritate and bore their tormentors because their agony forbids them an adequate language with which to express it. When one considers the extent to which it is her frustrated theatricality that lies at the root of her problems, it stands to reason that it should be the actual theatre which is presented as the way out of the everyday hell in which she finds herself. And this is indeed the case.

In the companion pieces to *Berthe—Gloria Star* and *Johnny Mangano and His Astonishing Dogs*—Tremblay gives us an image of the theatre both as a family setting and as a scene of redemption.
—*Bruce Serafin*

In the companion pieces to *Berthe—Gloria Star* and *Johnny Mangano and His Astonishing Dogs*—Tremblay gives us an image of the theatre both as a family setting and as a scene of redemption. These works are, so to speak, detailed and revealing doodles in the margins of his longer plays. What they present that is most their own is not so much what is explicit in them as it is a buried image—that of the illuminated body, made sumptuous and expressive by the fact that the least of its movements is staged and lit by spotlights. The presence of this image explains the characteristic light in which the backstage argument of the Manganos is bathed, a light which combines the depressive hues of a kitchen sink drama with the pastels of those Cocteau scenes in which little girls dressed in pink tights with round red spots on their cheeks and artificially arched and blackened eyebrows hiss and snarl at each other. In the same way Johnny and Carlotta retain an actor's gaiety even as they quarrel, and just as the above mentioned scenes are usually set in what appear to be attic rooms in which cats, bird cages and old, heavy silk dresses abound, so here, too, the couple argue in a milieu of tights, spangles, make-up and pink poodles.

As is often the case with Tremblay, it is the very perversity of this milieu which both causes their argument and enlivens, lights up its play. For in the realm of acting no less than in the realm of the family which we shall discuss presently, perversion and redemption are so closely contiguous as to be inseparable from each other. Thus, while it is nothing but the actor's bitterness over his "difference" that Carlotta expresses in this play, she reveals her calling by the fact that her flourishes of rhetoric are really a form of self-intoxication that allows her to consume her fate in one swallow, as it were, so as to encounter in its dregs the experience which awaits her onstage. Perhaps it is this experience that Tremblay has attempted to present in the figure of Gloria Star. "I offer you the greatest innovation of the twentieth century!" says Gloria Star's producer—known in the play as "the woman"—to a stage manager busy with his lights.

> The greatest dancers, the greatest strippers have been in my hands and they have known what Gloria Star knows today. Glory! And it's thanks to their bodies. The human body is the masterpiece of creation. . . . Look at the Greeks. I've spent my life showing masterpieces to the public. . . . But . . . young man, women also want to be provoked and transported. . . . I see a large open space. . . . The orchestra playing some savage piece. . . . Yes, we'll work it out so that you won't have too much trouble taking off your clothes. . . . You'll appear dressed as an Arab. . . . in the midst of your women, slaves and animals. Superb women, thinly veiled, shiny black slaves and . . . camels! And slowly you begin to undress. . . . You take off your burnous, your caftan, you unlace your sandals before an audience of delirious women!

The manager laughs. "But don't stop," he says, "I'm listening with one ear."

The role which marginal figures like the stage manager play in Tremblay's works is worth examining. Unmistakably, they are outsiders, individuals who are only incidentally connected to the circle of figures we have heretofore discussed. And like sons who have developed reserved and orderly lives and are no longer capable of the display of feeling that a deep family tie makes possible, they demonstrate by their shadowy existence how ready is the milieu that draws Tremblay's attention to consign to the attic everyone who has escaped into the larger world. (It is worth noting that only the theatrical successes who have the intensely domestic quality of fairytale figures are exempt from such a consignment.) In the above scene, the woman is clearly tempting the manager to step inside this realm. Abbreviating drastically, one may say that what he hears in her speil is the siren song of Tremblay's families. It tempts him to detach himself from the crowd whose members are all strangers to each other by promising him the piercing pleasure of a difference which is not merely exposed but flaunted, just as the "wink perverse" of la Duchesse flaunts the difference which she turns to such ecstatically theatrical account. The fact that Tremblay appears to equate the unabashed intimacy of his families with the theatricality of those who, like la Duchesse, are stigmatized by their difference determines one of the most illuminating features of his work. Berthe, Hosanna, la Duchesse, the bunglers and perverted ones, crowd together, comfort and protect each other. This is why their silliness is so valuable, and why even the element of depravity that inheres in them is suffused with the image of redemption. Tremblay expresses this in the concluding scenes of *Gloria Star,* the only place where the dancer makes her appearance:

> Suddenly, out of the darkness there appears an extraordinarily beautiful dancer. Striptease music begins. The dancer starts her act. The stage manager seems hypnotized. Little by little, the dancer's act becomes a kind of ritual combining dance steps with slow, disquieting gestures.
>
> The woman begins to laugh loudly. The dancer goes toward Carlotta and with a flick of her hand makes her disappear. The same with Berthe. The dancer turns toward the stage manager, gesturing for him to follow her. He goes toward her dancing.
>
> *The woman laughs more and more loudly.*

As the stage manager breaks into dance, he enters a world apart—the seductive world in which Tremblay's most fully realized creatures are at home. His sister is Hélène, who curses her neighbours and drunkenly challenges her seedy, broken-down husband to an arm wrestle. "Do you wanna have an arm wrestle with me, Henri? Do you wanna have an arm wrestle? Eh? Do you . . . ??" The voluptuous hysteria which Hélène gives voice to here finds an echo in the woman's laughter which is the most significant of the ritual elements that accompany the manager's transformation. This laughter, incidentally, recalls those places in Tremblay's longer works where the women join together in "chorus lines" whose function is not so much to provide a commentary on events as it is to produce a state of enchantment through what might be described as the mortification of events, the abrupt stiffening of what occurs on stage into ritualistic, significant patterns. The fact that this ritual delimiting of meaning here proceeds by way of hysterical laughter seems especially appropriate when one considers the affinity of such laughter to the sensual possibilities inherent in the various forms of display. For the ritual joke which explodes into convulsive laughter is not the least of the ways by which these possibilities are realized.

Tremblay is never very far away from such laughter. In a recent radio interview, he admitted to being raised "in front of cartoons and theatre," and anyone who is familiar with the large, lower-class households of French Canada will know what is meant by this juxtaposition of terms and what the connection is to that magnificent humour which runs through all of Tremblay's works. As a child, Tremblay may not only have jumped off an armchair with a towel tied around his neck like Superman, but also mimicked the laughing, screaming, lamenting housewives who have again and again claimed his attention. The creaturely display beloved by these women feeds on the gasping laughter and crude jokes in which Tremblay still partakes, and one can imagine that the hiding places from which the little boy looked out on their playacting were not so very different from the front row seats that he coveted at a later age. For the intoxicating memorability of such scenes is as dependent on physical presence as is the language which animates them; indeed, it would be difficult to imagine Tremblay's mimetic gifts developing apart from prolonged immersion in the physical reality he writes of. Incidentally, this may help explain his reluctance to write for television. When asked about this reluctance in the above mentioned radio interview, Tremblay replied, "I have a great deal of lyricism in me," adding by way of elucidation that "an opera is boring on television." This last statement is especially interesting. Far from insisting on the reproductive accuracy which tends to be associated with the mimetic effort exemplified by his work, Tremblay implicitly compares his figures to those of opera. Nor is it hard to see why. In both cases, the presence of living persons on the stage is a major source of the intoxication felt by the audience. We say of a person that he has presence. What is operatic about Tremblay's work is in fact the heightened presence of its figures. The grace notes and trills of the *coloratura* have an obvious analogue in the colloquial flourishes of Tremblay's characters; both amplify the aura of the figures involved by allowing them to display themselves with a greater intensity. For many readers, the word "aura" will bring Walter Benjamin to mind. His insights regarding the contemporary decline of the aura, in which "photography is decisively implicated," illuminate Tremblay's resistance to television, as well as his need to enhance the presence of his figures in the ways that have been described.

"If, while resting on a summer afternoon," Benjamin says,

> you follow with your eyes a mountain range on the horizon or a branch which casts its shadow over you, you experience the aura of those mountains, of that branch. This image makes it easy to comprehend the social bases of the contemporary decay of the aura. It rests on two circumstances, both of which are related to the increasing significance of the masses in contemporary life. Namely, the desire of contemporary masses to bring things 'closer' spatially and humanly, which is just as ardent as their bent toward overcoming the uniqueness of every reality by accepting its reproduction. Every day the urge grows stronger to get hold of an object at very close range by way of its likeness, its reproduction. . . . To pry an object from its shell, to destroy its aura, is the mark of a perception whose 'sense of the universal equality of things' has increased to such a degree that it extracts it even from a unique object by means of reproduction.

Since television is the medium which enables one to experience the loss of the aura at its sharpest, it may seem surprising that in the last play in this collection, *Surprise, Surprise,* Tremblay should present us with a slapstick situation of the kind which is the stock-in-trade of television comedies—the very place where the uniqueness and authority of the living person shrivels into nothing. To understand this, it is worthwhile to take a closer look at these comedies. What characterizes the situation comedy on television is its continual delineation of a joke which is continually fed by the performance of the actors. Every movement presented by the camera ideally either anticipates the joke or underlies it—in other words, makes it as obvious and effective as possible. This deeply affects the nature of the characters who are shown on the screen. Popular figures, such as Archie Bunker and his wife, are really a bundle of unchanging idiosyncracies which provide immediate visual and dramatic gratification when presented by the camera. The wife's shrill, enthusiastic entrances, and Archie's expressive way of looking at someone who displeases him are examples of these idiosyncracies; their well-nigh inevitable appearance on each show demonstrates that the ambiguous, constantly changing presence of an actual living person would be out of place in a situation in which the joke is to be continually fed.

The nature of the dialogue is affected as well. At no point in these comedies can the characters speak eloquently or at length. This is because language plays a decisive role in establishing the aura of the human creature and in a very literal sense would impede the joke's effectiveness if it were allowed free play. As a result, one finds dialogue formulated down to the least intonation and presented in short bursts which pace the action in such a way as to allow the camera to continually move in for close-ups—either to anticipate the joke, as when Archie looks with disgust at his son-in-law, or to emphasize it, as when Archie's face visually embroiders the sarcasm he unleashes on this same son-in-law. The camera's reproduction of the situation resembles that which his binoculars permit the opera-goer; both turn the actor's living person into material feeding an obsessive outside interest.

To a certain extent, Tremblay also injects an idiosyncratic element into his characters; indeed, his popular appeal is probably due to his willingness to accommodate the television experience which has become part and parcel of the experience of the community which is the real source of his creativity. However, to the delight found in the delineation of the pure joke, Tremblay adds the intoxication inherent in creaturely ecstasy pushed to its limits. Hence the overwhelming presence of his figures, the degree of which casts into relief the limitations of television, and at the same time renders these figures unsuitable for representation by that medium. "I can see it now," says one of the characters in *Surprise, Surprise*:

> I can see it now . . . I come into the restaurant. They're all there, having their party for that stinking corpse, Madeleine Simard! I hide behind a flower pot like a panther. I leap out at their table so fast they don't know what hit them. "Surprise!" And then . . . Down we go, Madeleine's head right in the cake! Her ugly puss all covered with cream! Then I pull off her wig, whack her across the face with it two or three times and smear it around in the other's plates! What else could I do to her? What? I'll slap her face! That's it, some nice big slaps across her face! POW! POW! POW! Maybe I'll take some Javex and wash out her mouth . . . Or a shotgun! Or maybe a butcher knife! That's it, a butcher knife, and I'll mix her blood around in buckets full of Bar B-Q sauce! . . .

If, to paraphrase Benjamin, we designate as aura the poetic associations which tend to cluster around the object of a perception, then its analogue here is the linguistic experience that makes palpable the creaturely ecstasy of this figure. The camera simply cannot do justice to an experience so essentially tied to a unique, individual presence. One need only think of the reaction of an animated family gathering to someone who wishes to take their picture: the uneasiness, even hostility which greets the camera demonstrates how completely it forces one to abandon the display of the self which alone permits communion with others and which is analogous to the above-mentioned experience in order to face up to the test that the camera proposes.

It is precisely this communion with others which is central to the mimic, and nothing illuminates Tremblay's creativity more than the realization that his highly developed sense of community is what gave rise to his mimetic gifts. For what distinguishes mimicry is the fact that it takes for granted the existence of a community. Only when it can draw on a shared linguistic and gestural repertoire can such an impulsive, creaturely art be successful. It is hardly an accident that a large part of Tremblay's appeal lies in the fact that his characters express not only themselves, but also the linguistic genius of their community—that they are, in other words, "operatic" from the start. One senses the mimic's affection and enthusiasm in the heightened expressiveness of even the least of these creatures. Perhaps this is why the soliloquy is unknown to Tremblay. Even where he deals with a disturbed creature like Hosanna or Berthe, the *solitude* of such a figure has nothing in common with the isolation that characterizes Hamlet's contemplation of suicide, for example. In Shakespeare's great soliloquies the thought wears the language which gives it expression as if it were a rich but frightening mask. This makes it easy to see what differentiates these soliloquies from the speech of a figure like Hosanna. While the former are *discourses* which may occasionally take their audience bodily, and, as it were, gasping, straight into the chilly forecourts of language, the latter is lyrical and ecstatic *conversation*, and thus lends itself to mimicry, which by its very nature must communicate the experience of a figure in the most natural and immediate way that comes to hand.

This kind of representation is and will always be opposed to that of the camera. For it bears in its substance traces of the very community which made possible the experience it offers, just as a Navajo rug bears in its crudities and imperfections the stamp of the community which permitted its creation. And the perception of these traces—the experience offered by Tremblay's works—is none other than that of the aura which disappears in technical reproduction, whether it be as a mass-produced rug, or as a figure represented by technical, mechanical means. The lyricism that gives Tremblay's works their beauty and authenticity is the result of a creativity that refuses to sever its ties with the community in the name of an apprehension of others, however precise, in which the collective experience of the community plays no part. And it is precisely because they do justice to this experience that Tremblay's works occupy a special place in Quebec literature.

Pierre Gobin (essay date 1983)

SOURCE: "Michel Tremblay: An Interweave of Prose and Drama," translated by Richard Deshaies, in *Yale French Studies*, No. 65, 1983, pp. 106-23.

[*In the following essay, Gobin elucidates the relationship between the plays and the novels in the series "Le Cycle des Belles-soeurs" and "Les Chroniques du Plateau Mont-Royal," stressing that "it is only by coming to know the plays that one can have an idea of what is being woven in the novels."*]

Although still young—he was born in 1942—the Montréalais writer Michel Tremblay has already produced a considerable amount of work: a dozen or more original plays have been staged; four novels, a work of science fiction, and a collection of short stories have been published; he has also translated into French four contemporary American plays, produced an adaptation of Aristophanes's *Lysistrata* (1969), and coproduced a movie, *Il était une fois dans l'Est* (1974), with André Brassard, his favorite director. Well received by the Québécois public, Tremblay has also succeeded in attracting a large audience outside of his native province, especially in France and English-speaking Canada. He has been recognized by the critics and is clearly a force to be reckoned with. General agreement dates the birth of *Québécois* theater from the first performance of *Les Belles-soeurs* in 1968; before that date there was French-Canadian theater, to be sure, but it was the success and the scandal of *Les Belles-soeurs* that "launched" a theater which was truly Québécois in its form as well as its thematics. Moreover, Tremblay has succeeded in gaining recognition without giving up experimentation, and in becoming a sort of classic whose themes, subjects, and writing are grounded in marginality. At the hinge of the readerly (*lisible*) and the writerly (*scriptible*), Tremblay's texts can be seen at one and the same time as *representative* (since they lend themselves to an explanatory study), *exemplary* in their operation (requiring them to be considered in the light of their own uniqueness), and *subversive* because their very entrance onto the literary "scene" prompts a reexamination of all the ideological postulates of culture of Québec. These quasi masterpieces owe their status and their power as constant reminders of the impossibility of masterpieces to a paradox: Tremblay, the idiot-sage, forces the reader-spectator to consider the most commonplace problems of daily existence, those most closely linked to the preoccupations of all of us, by presenting characters and situations which at first might seem uncommon, odd, deviant, or bizarre. It may well be his Brecht-like ability to "discover the exception in the rule"—and in return to make his audience reconsider the rule after they have reacted to his portrayal of the apparent exception—which explains the unexpected relevance of his works.

However, I should like to examine here another characteristic feature of the theater and novels of Tremblay, namely the *internal intertextuality* of his works. By this I mean the "interrelation (*croisement*) of utterances taken from other texts" *by the same writer*. It is not a question of quotations, excerpts, transpositions, or rewriting from "exterior or synchronic utterances" (of which one can find many examples in Tremblay's work), but of the reactivation of elements drawn from the same corpus. This procedure would be far from original or peculiar if the activated elements were at different levels of textual elaboration: every writer uses over and over again more or less the same motifs, the same obsessive metaphors, and the same structures (in the organization of syntax itself, as well as in the narrative and/or actantial structures, indeed even on the scale of microelements, along with the verbal tics of writing itself); every writer has recourse to notes, notebooks, "logbooks," and papers, in short to his work in progress.

> General agreement dates the birth of *Québécois* theater from the first performance of *Les Belles-soeurs* in 1968; before that date there was French-Canadian theater, to be sure, but it was the success and the scandal of *Les Belles-soeurs* that "launched" a theater which was truly Québécois in its form as well as its thematics.
>
> —*Pierre Gobin*

But Tremblay has formulated certain aspects of his own fundamental myth, an activity in itself less than common. Success in such an undertaking presupposes a sustained effort, a vigilant observation of the outer world and the self's own universe, whether the texts produced appear to be discontinuous (Mallarmé) or more or less continuous (the great novelistic frescoes of Balzac and Zola; those sagas bathed in myth such as Faulkner's Yoknapawtha county or Hardy's Wessex). The texts resulting from this complex form of internal intertextuality are developed in reduced spatial and temporal dimensions; that is why it has been possible to study them in terms of "histories" or "geographies" of the imaginary (e.g. André Ferré on Marcel Proust or more recently, Pierre L'Hérault's study of the Québécois writer Jacques Ferron). Tremblay's literary production also lends itself to this type of study. Nevertheless, I shall not deal with work of a transtextual nature at the heart of a collected ensemble of which all parts are of the same general category (i.e., a collection of poetry, a series of novels, a theater-cycle, etc.), any more than work of a "pretextual" nature on texts that are at different levels of composition (i.e., sketches, rough drafts, projects, *avant-textes*, extratextual material, etc.). Rather, what is at stake is a very specific form of internal intertextuality in which we are dealing with utterances by the same writer at the same level of textual development, but belonging to different genres.

To put it more precisely, these texts do not present themselves as translations of one and the same raw material nor as different developments of the same "hypotextual" outline, such as the ones that are found, for example, in Cocteau's work in which "Le coup de poing sur des boules de neige / Que donne la beauté vite au coeur en passant" ["A blow of the fist on mounds of snow / That beauty quickly delivers to the heart in passing"] is taken up in the poetry of the theater, the poetry of the novel, and the poetry of the cinema, or, in a more systematic but also more limited fashion, in Courteline's work, when he rewrites short stories into comedies (*La Hache/La Peur des coups*). In Tremblay's work, at least in the case of the group of plays that he calls "Le Cycle des *Belles-soeurs*" and the series of novels called "Les Chroniques du Plateau Mont-Royal," we are dealing with a *sustained and coherent internal intertextuality, in which the utterances are not parallel,* "osculatory" in the mathematical sense, or resulting from bifurcations, *but truly interwoven* in every sense of the word, since rewriting is more detectable at the point of their intersection than at the point of their convergence. It is as if the plays formed the woof (*trame*) of an intertextual weave whose warp (*chaîne*)—long since woven, though revealed only afterwards—would be given in the novel cycle.

A strange paradox has been created by the current usage of the term *trame*. In fact, its derived meanings, ("a group of details that form a kind of background, an entire groundwork upon which conspicuous events stand out," and in the graphic arts, "a squared grid . . . that changes the unbroken design of the original . . . into a series of dotted lines), seem to have combined the original meanings of warp and woof (*warp*: "group of regularly spaced parallel threads that are distributed lengthwise in a piece of fabric"; *woof*: "group of threads that weavers interlace, by means of a shuttle, with the threads of the warp already fixed in place on a loom"). Classical French usage substituted outright the term *trame* for *chaîne* in expressions like that of Bossuet (which *Le Grand Larousse* cites as an example): "il a coupé ma trame dès le commencement de mes jours" [he cut off the fabric of my life at the very beginning of my days]. Now it seems to me that the paradox involved in the use of these terms illuminates the relationship between the plays and the novels in the two parts of Tremblay's work which are the objects of this study.

The dramatic texts crisscross the span of the *oeuvre*, already forming, as if superimposed onto the unbroken design of experiences and observations, the framework on which certain types of characters will stand out, perceptible only from dialogue which appears fragmented. Tremblay accentuates this characteristic of his theater by his handling of dialogue:

as in the improvisations of a jazz ensemble, he leaves room for the chorus, counterpoint, and the "break," that virtuoso solo in which a performer reveals himself isolated from his partners. The playwright insists equally on the capacity of the frame to allow for embellishments of the *here* and *now*, and on the unity of tone, atmosphere, and action that the frame establishes. Evocations of somewhere else, projections toward the past and into the future that are allowed for by the dialogue in *La Duchesse de Langeais* or the *mise en scène* of *A toi, pour toujours, ta Marie-Lou* impart to this theater a dimension other than itself, but one which is necessarily made manifest by a series of ruptures. All in all, the works of Tremblay confirm what the entire modern theater repertoire leads us to understand, and what the theory and practice of the well-constructed play or the well-spun plot attempted to hide: the marvelous ability of the theater to partake of the arts of time and space (as "spectacle" in Kowzan's terms, as "a density of signs" in Barthes's); an ability which no other literary genre can claim, for it can only be practiced in a format of discontinuity. Drama only finds its continuity in an imaginary reconstruction; its subject matter is masked by conspicuous events—dramatic ones—which stand out against this backdrop. Furthermore, the threads of the woof can only become a reality when woven on the support of those warp threads already in place, which they in turn hide and are hidden by.

Thus, the narrative threads (*chaîne*) are an inescapable necessity for his theater; this, however, does not explain their appearances (except in those cases where the drama is presented as a chronicle, giving precedence to temporal development, or as a tableau, giving precedence to progression in space). On the contrary, the novel readily develops chronicle and tableau alike (in a consecutive manner, by a syntagmatic linking), by following a linear course. The very title of Tremblay's novel cycle is revealing in this respect: we are dealing with a distinct day by day *chronicle*—dates head each section of *La Grosse femme d'à côté est enceinte* (May 2, 1942, etc.) as well as *Thérèse et Pierrette à l'école des Saints-Anges* and *La Duchesse et le roturier*—of the life of a group of people occupying a precise, though relatively large, geographical area: le plateau Mont-Royal, a sizeable area north of le Parc Lafontaine, a working-class section of Montréal which can be recognized by several crucial streets, la rue Fabre (N-S) with the street that runs parallel it to the east, la rue Papineau, and, cutting them both at right angles, la rue Gilford and le boulevard St-Joseph.

Other indications confirm that Tremblay is sensitive to the specificity of prose texts in general, and to those which he is in the process of writing in particular. The presence right beside the "realistic" characters, in the house next door to the one in which the fat woman and her relatives live (notably Victoire, the fat woman's mother-in-law, Victoire's descendants, Albertine, whose husband is away at war, the latter's children Thérèse and the strange little Marcel, and fat Edouard, a confirmed bachelor), of three old maids (Rose, Violette and Mauve) and their mother Florence—all of whom are invisible except to poets, the crazy, and the dying—this "presence" then establishes a fantastic element and acts as a catalyst for the heterogeneous, the sacred, the strange. However, the fantastic element also furnishes the reader with links between episodes (the four women harbor little Marcel and give him back his cat, Duplessis, restored to life; they appear to old Josaphat-le-Violin who "makes the moon rise" with his music), and reminds us metaphorically of the structure of the novels: seated on the front porch, the three daughters knit baby clothes destined for all those who are to be born on la rue Fabre, beginning with the child of the fat woman; they establish the status of characters who are still curled up in their mothers' wombs by superimposing the thread of destiny onto the umbilical cords. They need neither to spin nor to cut this thread of destiny; by winding it into skeins, by hooking it onto their spindles and knitting needles, by weaving it into fabric destined to adorn "live" bodies, the knitters assume the role of the Fates—frank, discrete, charitable, but also disquieting.

All the main characters of Tremblay's theater were born or are going to be born on la rue Fabre. Now it is there that Tremblay himself came into the world on "June 25, 1942." It is also there that *Les Belles-soeurs, En Pièces détachées,* and *A toi, pour toujours, ta Marie-Lou* take place. And it is also there that the metaphorical chain of destiny, which restores liberty to those whom it binds, is linked or has been linked, in the novels as in the plays. It is by virtue of this bond that the aging Victoire finds the courage necessary to face death at the end of *Thérèse et Pierrette*: "Pour-quoi c'que je mourrais? Pour quelle raison j'me laisserais aller de même, sans me défendre? Parce que la folie s'en vient? Qu'a vienne! C'est toujours ben mieux que de finir dans un trou" [Why should I die? Why should I let myself go like that, without defending myself? Because I'm going crazy? Then let it be! It's better than ending up in a hole], thus repeating/announcing the challenge of her grandson Marcel at the end of *En Pièces détachées*. To all of his relatives who complain, "Chus pus capable de rien faire!" [I can't do anything anymore], he proclaims: "Moé j'peux toute faire! J'ai toutes [sic] les pouvoirs" [I can do anything, man, I am all-powerful].

The novels recreate after the fact a kind of prehistory of the characters who appear in the plays, as well as a geography of their activities and dreams, defining on the basis of "real" coordinates the precise location of the staging, and of the "other stage." The novels are centered around dates which are well anchored in the domain of the referential, but which also allow the staging of the temporality of dramatic, as well as mnemonic and imaginary re-presentation. The novels of the (fictional) *plateau* underpin the actions played out on the (theatrical) *plateau* and their structure brings to light an important part of any theatrical production.

> **The novels recreate after the fact a kind of prehistory of the characters who appear in the plays, as well as a geography of their activities and dreams.**
> —*Pierre Gobin*

In other words, the narrative threads (*la chaîne*), implicit or presumed in the plays, or which at least are revealed in them only by means of certain contrivances (stories or the analyses of situations, flashbacks, *mises en abyme*, intervening breaks), are set in place in the novels, and their continuity is initiated and announced to us (by means of complementary strategies, such as forward projections, a widening of the field of action, and suggestive parallels that would necessitate a detailed study in and of itself). By establishing or making explicit the narrative threads, the novels have recourse to certain *effets de réel* that propel the fictional elements in the direction of the referential, whereas the plays effect an "iconic leap" toward the "as if." It is precisely this leap that allows for a practical closure in the theater and the unity of the plays in terms of their individual plots (*trame*). That is not to say that the *trame* is not present in a novelistic work (which, by unfolding a continuous chronicle also effects a deictic actualization of characters in one time and one place). However, in Tremblay's work theater and the novel are presented as complementary, and they give a privileged place, respectively, to the woof and the warp of a complex fabric whose production and composition it is now appropriate to examine.

Tempted by the numerous comparisons that can be drawn between the frame of Tremblay's own life experiences and the one which he assigns to his characters, one could of course infer that the chronicles are more or less autobiographical, and, like the memoirs of Goldoni for example, explicitly narrate and define episodes or circumstances already treated by the plays. But the Québécois playwright is at one and the same time too cunning to hand over his professional and personal secrets in such a naïve way, and too modern to be duped by the referential illusion or even to accept any kind of mimetic reductionism. He teases and entices his audience by implying that the physical and moral striptease in which so many of his theatrical characters indulge themselves may well be just a (barely disguised) transposition of the author's own scenario. But he escapes identification in his theater by a mythic reinforcement of character (for example, the Duchesse de Langeais) and by a series of artifices and what Sartre calls *tourniquets*, by the arrangement of corresponding voices (Claude and his lover Cuirette in *Hosanna*; the separated homosexual couple in *Les Anciennes odeurs*

[1981]). This is also true of his entire work by the introduction of variations and substitutes (privileged relationships between brother and sister in *Bonjour, là, bonjour*; or between sister and brother in *En Pièces détachées* and in the novel cycle where Thérèse, so clearly distinct from her creator, seems to be stealing the show) or by making use of the fantastic, either global (*La Cité dans l'oeuf* [1969]) or accessory, favorable to a flight toward oneiric and marginal speculations.

Furthermore, Tremblay warns the reader of *Thérèse et Pierrette* twice that the chronicle in question is imaginary. In the epigraph of the novel he quotes John Irving's *The World According to Garp*: "Imagining something is better than remembering something." And in the dedication: "To Denise Filiatrault, Michelle Rossignol and Amulette Garneau, whom I tried to imagine as children for the parts of Thérèse, Pierrette, and Simone," he goes even further. In fact, the three women to whom he pays homage are the actresses who already brought to the stage the *adult* characters whom the young girls of the novel have/will become.

During the second running of *Les Belles-soeurs* (at Le Théâtre du Rideau Vert in 1971), the action of which is set in 1965, Michelle Rossignol played the part of Pierrette Guérin, the sister of the protagonist Germaine Lauzon, Rose Ouimet, and Gabrielle Jodoin. Pierrette is regarded as a kind of black sheep because she works for a nightclub on "La Main," "une maison malfarmée"; however, in spite of her misfortunes ("damn Johnny" who seduced her has just "dropped her like a hot potato" after "making her lose ten years of her life, the bastard!"), she is the only one who tries to defend Germaine in the face of all the "virtuous" women who steal as many of her green stamps as they can get hands on. The dedication therefore suggests that through the (real life) spokesman of a fictitious dramatic character of marginal status of a tolerant morality, Tremblay is attempting to imagine in his novel what will be the destiny of a special child, both more intelligent and more sensitive than those of her own family.

Among other roles, Amulette Garneau has taken that of Bec-de-Lièvre in *Sainte Carmen de la Main,* the little wardrobe keeper who is "damned" (she is a lesbian), disinherited (because of the scar that disfigures her upper lip), rejected, and cruelly treated by her brother Maurice, who has become a leader of the institutionalized underworld. Here again we are dealing with a character from a damned milieu who nevertheless remains loyal to the sacred heroine, Carmen, the country-and-western singer who, because she wanted to compose her own lyrics, assume responsibility for her own destiny, free her female companions, and enlighten an entire nation of wretches (*paumés*), will be murdered by an unfeeling and impotent assassin of the underworld. In *Thérèse et Pierrette,*

little Simone, who has just undergone surgery in order to correct her harelip, finds herself in the middle of conflicts that are tearing apart a respectable religious community; she is intimidated by the authoritarian and narrow-minded mother superior and protected by Soeur Sainte Catherine, an intelligent and charitable woman. Once again we are dealing with a character who is representative, yet marked by her peculiarity. In the novel, Simone is a paradoxical child who wants to affirm her newly found beauty but who suffers the persecutions entailed by that affirmation. She is caught in the middle of a trio of young girls, surrounded by friends who are at the same time jealous and protective of her. Simone does not get a big part in the Corpus Christi tableau put on by the sisters, nor is she included in the title of the novel. In the play she is torn between loyalty to her brother Maurice, a persecutor and profiteer, and her platonic adoration for Carmen, liberator and martyr.

As for Denise Filiatrault, although she brought to the stage several important characterizations in Tremblay's repertoire (in particular, that of Rose Ouimet in *Les Belles-soeurs,* and that of Lola Lee in *Demain Matin*), the part of Thérèse in *En Pièces détachées* was not entrusted to her. However, Denise Filiatrault does constitute a kind of myth in Tremblay's universe. In *Les Héros de mon enfance,* la Fée Carabosse, who terrorizes all the other heroes, appears under her guise:

> Dans le rôle de Lola Lee et celui de Rose Ouimet
> Dans le rôle de Carlotta et celui d'Pierrette
> Elle était tellement bonne la grande Filiatrault
> Que tous disaient? Allons, Denise, vraiment c'est trop!

> In the part of Lola Lee and in that of Rose Ouimet
> In the part of Carlotta and in that of Pierrette
> She was so tremendous the great Filiatrault
> That everyone said: Come on, Denise, you're really too much!

Now for Tremblay, Carabosse is not the hideous old witch whom she traditionally represents but a being who is both fascinating and dangerous, wicked yet unhappy, of great beauty yet shameful, supremely intelligent yet dissatisfied. Like Thérèse in the televised version of *En Pièces détachées* and in the novels, she lives on the border between dreams and nightmares: She is a fairy who resembles a witch, just as Thérèse is an angel who to a large extent resembles a devil. The following is the way in which the chorus of neighbors describes her on her wedding day:

> *Mme Lheureux:* ça faisant ben drôle, une mariée en velours bleu avec les cheveux rouges!
> *Mme Tremblay:* A l'avait pas l'air d'un ange, a l'avait l'air d'un démon!

Mme Monette: Pis on s'est pas gêné pour y dire, nous autres, les femmes!

Les femmes, *en variant:* Maudite démonne!

Mme Lheureux: It looked real funny, a bride with red hair, dressed in blue velour!

Mme Tremblay: Didn't look like an angel, looked like a demon!

Mme Monette: And we weren't bashful in telling 'er, us ladies!

The ladies, in *different voices:* To hell with her!

Like the Fairy and like Thérèse, Denise Filiatrault has an inordinate talent ("Elle était tellement bonne" [She was so tremendous]) that can trigger catastrophes ("vraiment c'est trop" [really that's too much]): in short, she runs the risk of shifting from the gestural representation of a character who is a prey to Hubris, to the incorporation (*actualisation*) of that arrogance into her own personality following the mechanism of possession described in Sartre's *Saint Genet comédien et martyr.*

Thérèse's misfortunes, her social and physical degradation, the humiliation which she experiences as she attempts to escape through *divertissement* and alcohol, and her descent into despair only appear in the plays. But many of the personality traits of this woman appeared in the young girl of the novels. In them she is already a proud being, defiant and secretive, sensitive to the power struggles at the heart of society yet oblivious to what they really imply, extremely talented yet poorly educated. Eleven-year-old Thérèse is already like Thérèse at age forty, precariously perched between good and evil, wrenched between the homogeneous world of school and work on the one hand, and the heterogeneous universe of shady pleasures, whether they be those offered in le parc Lafontaine or on "la Main," on the other. Above all, she is already the mouthpiece for characters without a future, "all screwed up" (*pognés*), and trapped in their cramped milieu, for individuals marked by the seal of insanity—artists like her great-uncle Josaphat-le-Violin or eccentrics like Marcel, her younger brother.

By the choice which Tremblay made of the three people to whom he dedicated *Thérèse et Pierrette,* one can see that he associates the iconic and deictic re-creation of his plays (work and play on the *trame*) with a process of diegetic invention aimed at producing *effets de réel* (putting in place the narrative threads of *la chaîne*). Other indications can be found in the novels where one sees at work a strange kind of circuit in which the interior and the exterior, metalanguage and the poetic message are combined in order to formulate yet another type of interweave. However, I shall limit myself to the intersection of the threads in the two generic parts of the work sharing the same status. Nor shall I study the manner in which the "realistic and fantastic intermingle," except to

sketch a description of their topical composition, for I shall limit my analysis to the way in which "Tremblay recreates certain characters with whom we have already become familiar in his previous work," to cite once again the back cover of *La Grosse femme.*

We have already noticed that in his novels Tremblay does not have his characters come back to life "downstream," namely in a subsequent state of their lives; rather he places them "upstream," much closer to their wellspring as if the course of their lives flowed down the slopes of le plateau Mont-Royal toward the "waterfall" that plunges them dramatically into the maelström of "la Main," or on the contrary loses itself in the swamps of the East End not far from their point of departure. The use of such hydrographic metaphors—which reminds one of a parodic *Carte de Tendre*—could perhaps account for the space and the time lived by the characters in the novels as well as the impression of catastrophic haste produced by the plays (the tragic plays of "la Main" with their catatonic depressions; the plays about the East End with their "infratragic" tendencies). It would allow equally for questions concerning the destinies of the characters that are interiorized in their ethos or psyche ("Tu peux sortir la fille de l'est, mais pas l'est de la fille: [You can take the girl out of the East End, but you can't take the East End out of the girl]). However, it would not draw our attention to the *production,* that twofold textual work: the construction, by the interweaving of threads and of bunches of threads, both horizontally and vertically, of a fabric, a cultural artifact, a kind of megasignifier whose signified would be Tremblay's poetic universe.

The characters in the novels are brought back to life again in a very peculiar fashion, one that resembles *A la recherche du temps perdu* more closely than *Vingt ans après* or *Le Vicomte de Bragelonne.* Similarly, if the realistic and the fantastic intermingle in Tremblay's novels, it is not by chance or even contingently, but according to a well-defined plan. The realistic narrative threads are sometimes associated with the fantastic narrative threads, as in those passages where we are shown the fantasies of Victoire, the old woman who has resisted the Fates all her life but who eventually becomes conscious, at first in an anguished way, and then in a liberated manner, of the presence of her faithful neighbors, thus crossing—before her death—the border between realism and fantasy, between everyday homogeneity and sacred heterogeneity.

Generally the areas or zones affected by the fantastic and the characters associated with it do not become confused with the realistic areas; the Fates are the neighbors of Victoire's family, and even those to whom they appear must visit them (little Marcel and Duplessis the cat) or greet them (old Josaphat). The Fates do not haunt the area of realism; instead they accompany it like a shadow, or better still, like a beam of light. Their presence bestows a different texture onto the ensemble yet without interfering in the chronicle of the homogeneous.

Along with the series of realistic threads—the most important because it is between these strands that the threads of the plays will be interlaced—and the fantastic series which sometimes serves in a parallel fashion as its lining or adornment, it would also be appropriate to recall a legendary series that goes beyond the initially woven threads which form the plots of the novels and which have a quasi-dramatic nature.

The disclosures and hints of recognition of characters in *La Grosse femme* at the time of their encounters on la rue Fabre or in le Parc Lafontaine at the beginning of May, 1942, as well as the telltale conflicts in *Thérèse et Pierrette* surrounding little Simone, l'Ecole des Saints-Anges and the Feast of Corpus Christi in June of the same year, are, in fact, already arranged crosswise to the chronicle of the families whose members are identified with the pattern (*trame*) of those actions that are specifically theatrical (e.g. the evening of premium stamp pasting in *Les Belles-soeurs,* the crisis in *Marie-Lou* and the retrospective view of that crisis, etc.) Tremblay is perfectly conscious of the parallelism of these structures and chooses to emphasize it, as for example in the remarks of Dr. Sanregret concerning the Corpus Christi street altar which for him is no more than a pagan mascarade. One could even consider that the woof threads in the chronicles already dramatize that which will be made explicit in the plays, but which remains implicit in the novels (e.g. Thérèse's loss of innocence, Marcel's transition to madness) or which remains in the mythical form of a recreated primary scene.

Be that as it may, the dramas that are inscribed in the novels—the first threads of the textual fabric—postulate as contiguous to the realist threads strung together by the chronicles but preceding them a mythical series, a repertory of popular legends. Examples would be the tales told by Josaphat-le-Violin, which recall a mysterious family history, the secrets that old Victoire confides to her son Edouard, and the story of Ti-Lou, "La Louve d'Ottawa" who howls her last, defiant cry in the face of death at the very moment two other characters assume their destinies, namely when Béatrice, a whore without style, becomes Betty Bird, the grandest callgirl in all Montréal and when Edouard, a bashful homosexual transforms himself into a stunning transvestite, la Duchesse de Langeais.

Thus, along with the realistic and fantastic developments (the family and convent chronicles and their association with the Fates), the narrative threads contain elements from exemplary or mythical accounts that bolster the narrative and its double. In addition to the action of the plays, these interweaving threads include in the very framework of the novels' dramas, in a more or less potential form, that could well be regarded, after the fact, as the beginnings of the actual plays.

If some of the characters presented in the novels do not appear in the plays (although sometimes their talk, as in the case of Dr. Sanregret, furnishes a kind of ideological and aesthetic commentary on the entire *oeuvre*), and if others function only as *variants* of other more complex figures (Béatrice/Betty Bird, who, parodied by La Duchesse in *Demain matin,* serves as the model for Lola Lee and her sister Lyla Jasmin), there are also other characters who are developed and whose dramatic careers in and of themselves form a complete cycle, such as Edouard/La Duchesse, whose monologue constitutes an entire play (no doubt the most remarkable of the entire corpus), who reappears in *Demain matin,* is evoked or invoked again in *A toi, pour toujours* and *Hosanna,* and whose murder foretells and foreshadows that of the heroine in *Sainte Carmen de la Main.* In Edouard's case, it is his prehistory before he "comes out" as la Duchesse that we find in the chronicles. The same goes for the children whose lives are "invented" or recreated by the narrative threads and who, when adults, function as key dramatic characters: Thérèse, Pierrette, Simone, little Marcel, and, to a lesser extent, Maurice, Simone's brother. The novels originate a type of predramatic woof for all these characters that is not noteworthy when considering the adult characters in the novels for whom the dies are already cast. When these latter characters have important parts in the plays, they are passive "infradramatic" figures, such as the Guérin sisters in *Les Belles-soeurs* or Robertine in *En Pièces détachées,* for they are too entrenched in their resentment or too contorted by their frustrations to attempt to alter the course of events.

There are, however, several exceptions which deserve to be considered: on the one hand, Marie-Lou Brassard and her husband Léopold, whose confrontation in *A toi, pour toujours* is intense and overt and ends up in violence; Gabriel (named after the archangel-messenger), the husband of the fat woman, whom we rediscover as a positive character in *Bonjour, là, bonjour* and as an inspiration in *Les Anciennes odeurs.* But before examining their function in the novels and plays in which they appear, it may be useful to draw attention once again to a third group of characters, alongside the future but as yet unproclaimed heroes and of those for whom *les jeux sont faits:* the reader may have surmised that this group is comprised of the seven children to be born to the women portrayed in *La Grosse femme d'à côté est enceinte.*

Some of these awaited babies do not appear to have any subsequent dramatic career (although their presence supplies Tremblay with a reservoir of characters and situations which he can tap if he wishes to come back to "le cycle des *Belles-soeurs*"): those expected by Germaine Lauzon, Rose Ouimet, and Gabrielle Jodoin are at the very most topical allusions in *Les Belles-soeurs,* or they are mentioned in the remarks made by the neighbors in *En Pièces détachées*; the baby Claire Lemieux is expecting disappears altogether; Laura Cadieux's furnishes us with some indirect glimpses, and functions as an adventurous adjunct to the mother's reflections and ruminations in the novel *C'tà ton tour Laura Cadieux.* But Marie-Louise Brassard's pregnancy lays the foundation for a complex dramatic cycle, since the story of Carmen (the child expected in *La Grosse femme*) will be "constructed" on the basis of *A toi, pour toujours, ta Marie-Lou* and *Sainte Carmen de la Main* to which will be added *Damnée Manon, sacrée Sandra* (since Manon is Carmen's younger sister). As for the pregnancy of the fat woman herself, it seems to provide the key for the entire work if, as I believe to be the case, the child to be born is Michel Tremblay himself.

It is worth noting that the pregnancies of Marie-Lou and the fat woman are the only ones that are *marked* to the extent that their characteristic traits could be contrasted word for word. Already the mother of two children, the fat woman knows "what is awaiting her." On the contrary, Marie-Louise is almost unbelievably ignorant: despite the doctor's explanations, she believes that her child will come into the world by bursting through her navel, since otherwise the birth would be an excretion. The fat woman has chosen to be pregnant; her condition seems beautiful to her ("elle avait voulu cet enfant, elle en avait besoin, et elle était belle") [she had wanted this child; she needed it, and she was beautiful], and she greets her unborn child by singing. Marie-Louise detests "le fruit de (sa) nuit de noces, la seule (passée avec son mari), horrible" [the fruit of (her) wedding night, the only one (spent with her husband), horrible], and she utters an atrocious incantation: "va-t-en, va-t-en, p'tit fatigant ta mère te veut pas, pis ton père est un fou . . ." [go away, go away, you little tiring thing your mother doesn't want you and your father's a jerk . . .]. The fat woman enjoys love, life, and people; she dreams of faraway lands as marvelous horizons; she submerges herself in books; she welcomes everyone (it is at her invitation that the six other pregnant women gather together with her on the balcony at the end of the novel); she opens herself up to the universe. Marie-Louise withdraws into herself, afraid and bored to death; she rejects her husband's every advance; in short, the life that surrounds her "chokes her like an asphalt cape." For one, expecting a child is a truly blessed event; it is a participation in the cosmos and an experience of the divine; for the other, it is a defilement, a damnation, a foretaste of the torments of hell. One can suppose that the world view of children carried under these circumstances will be based on this inheritance, accepted (the "author" himself) or rejected (Carmen whose life will be a continual rebellion and a conquest of freedom). In contrast to *Sainte Carmen*, who rediscovers purity through a dialectical rejection of her mother's puritanical nature, corresponds

a *wise* Michel, who accepts his congenial heritage while transcending its limitations.

The husbands of the two women also react to these attitudes toward pregnancy and their reactions undoubtedly explain their roles in the plays. A disappointed Léopold will withdraw into himself, taking refuge in alcohol, and once on the verge of insanity will look for a means of escape in confronting Marie-Lou. However, when she spurns him, he speeds toward his death, taking her and their son with him, by smashing their car "into a concrete post on Metropolitan Boulevard." What we have here is a catastrophic dramaturgy, but one which is *enclosed* in a "dubious liberation," to use Raymond Joly's expression. The Gabriel in *Bonjour, là bonjour,* widowed at an early age with five children (and here we are dealing with four girls—a fact that is not literally consonant with the sequence of events in the chronicles where he at first has two sons and expects a third), is portrayed as awkward and timid in dealing with his children and rude with those of his own generation. He seeks refuge in a tavern "pour y régler le sort du monde" [in order to determine the fate of the world] (like the Gabriel of *La Grosse femme*); he uses his deafness as an alibi for his misanthropy. However, in the end he succeeds in exchanging words of trust and understanding with his son Serge, the youngest of his children. When the curtain falls, the play opens up with an ambiguous greeting—all the more ambiguous since the Québécois use *Bonjour* upon leave-taking and also since the title can be interpreted as a translation of *Ave atque vale!*— but one that nevertheless represents the starting point of an exemplary step toward communication.

A study of Tremblay's theater has everything to gain by being coupled with the study of his "chronicles." Such a study allows one to resituate the characters in view of their "prehistory" and their "mental geography" (both being subject to retouchings, since they are quasi-referential constructions of the imaginary). It is possible to connect the ethos of the plays with the world views attributed to the characters in the novels who are associated with the dramatic protagonists, even if these characters do not appear in the plays. We begin to perceive how the events of the plays rely upon the narrative threads told in the chronicles, which the plays could only relate in a fragmentary manner (cf. Bec-de-Lièvre's monologue in *Sainte Carmen,* the commentaries by the chorus of neighbors in *En Pièces détachées*). We also discover that the apparent action (*trame manifeste*) performed on the stage often parallels a hidden action that runs through the novels (Thérèse's "fall" and her discovery of coquettishness; the career of La Duchesse and the encounters of Edouard).

On the other hand, it is only by familiarizing himself with the plays that the reader can appreciate the irony contained in the novels as well as all that interrupts the continuity of the storyline: evocations of faraway places (the fat woman's daydreams of Acapulco will be adapted to *La Duchesse de Langeais*), sequences of improbable events (the powers of the Fates will be claimed by a child), and philosophical reflections (the doctor's comparison of the street-altar to a brothel explains Pierrette's religious reverence for "la Main" and the mystification of the characters in *Demain matin*). In short, it is only by coming to know the plays that one can have an idea of what is being woven in the novels.

The coherence of Tremblay's work, which rests on the internal intertextual intersection of two groups of texts that are at the same level of elaboration but belonging to different genres, is thus quite extraordinary. The formula that he has adopted, and which I believe to be unique, deserves to be placed next to those used by Zola and Galsworthy (a treelike expansion in which the structure of the work follows that of genealogical development), Balzac and Faulkner (tapestries of the imaginary woven on a loom borrowed from reality), Henry James and Proust, Mallarmé and Cocteau (the construction of armillary spheres in order to locate imaginary constellations), to illustrate the production of literary texts whose vocation is the pursuit of totality.

Jane Moss (review date Winter 1984)

SOURCE: "School Days," in *Canadian Literature*, Vol. 103, Winter, 1984, pp. 123-25.

[*In the favorable review below, Moss summarizes the plot and themes of* Thérèse et Pierrette.]

Shelia Fischman has performed another valuable service for Anglophones in translating Michel Tremblay's 1980 novel, *Thérèse et Pierrette à l'école des Saints-Anges*. Best known as the playwright who revolutionized Quebec theatre by using joual in *Les Belles Soeurs* (1968), Tremblay has since 1978 devoted himself to the Balzacian task of re-creating Montreal in the 1940's in his "Chroniques du Plateau Mont Royal." Tremblay's Montreal is a personalized fictional world in which the characters of his plays act out their past in the author's old neighbourhood near la rue Fabre. The second volume of this "comédie humaine montréalaise" focuses on a trio of eleven-year-old girls who will play lead roles in the elaborate Corpus Christi celebration put on for the Saint Stanislas de Kostka parish during the first week of June 1942.

Divided into four movements like the Brahms Fourth Symphony named as inspirational background music, the novel's action begins with the school day on Monday morning, June 1, and reaches its climax during the Corpus Christi procession on Thursday evening, June 4. During those four days, a number of events occur which change the lives of the char-

acters and foreshadow the major transformation of Quebec Society during the Quiet Revolution of the 1960's. The plot is set in motion by Simone Côté's return to school after an operation to correct the harelip which had marked her life as well as her face. Her best friends, Thérèse (the future alcoholic waitress of *En pièces détachées*) and Pierrette (the worn-out prostitute of *Les Belles Soeurs*) welcome Simone back joyfully. The school principal, Mother Benoîte, a mean-spirited tyrant whose harsh discipline has earned her the nickname Mother Dragon Devil, takes note of Simone's improved looks by angrily threatening to expel her from school. Her anger stems from the incorrect assumption that the Côté family had paid for the cosmetic surgery after years of claiming they were too poor to pay extra school fees. The principal's overreaction provokes others to rebel against the religious educational system she represents. Simone's teacher becomes insubordinate in her defence of the girl and is threatened with banishment from the school. Sister Sainte-Catherine's dispute with Mother Dragon Devil disrupts the entire school community, and her eventual decision to become a lay teacher presages the demise of the Church's monolithic control over education. Simone's mother reacts by verbally assaulting the nun who humiliated her daughter, and the whole system which teaches shame and hypocrisy. Madame Côté's outburst, witnessed in silent approval by the humanitarian doctor who paid for the harelip operation, is an anachronistically early version of the virulent anticlerical attacks of the 1960's. Despite the unsettling events of Monday, the preparations continue for the gaudy repository which has brought fame to Saint Stanislas de Kostka parish. Sister Sainte-Catherine oversees the pageant, making sure that costumes, statues, and props are all readied and choosing the Grade Six students who will figure in the tableau vivant. Pierrette is named to play the Virgin's role with Thérèse as Bernadette Soubirous at her feet and Simone as an angel suspended by a rope over her head. As the procession nears, tension and excitement mount in the neighbourhood, in the community of nuns, and in the three little girls. Just as the parish priest is about to begin mass a tremendous storm breaks, soaking everyone, destroying the repository, and terrifying the little hanging angel.

> **Best known as the playwright who revolutionized Quebec theatre by using joual in *Les Belles Soeurs* (1968), Tremblay has since 1978 devoted himself to the Balzacian task of re-creating Montreal in the 1940's in his "Chroniques du Plateau Mont Royal."**
>
> —*Jane Moss*

Within a tightly structured chronological sequence of events, Tremblay follows the three girls back and forth from home to school in a way that allows him to present a realistic tableau of the life of average Montrealers during the war years, a fantasy world accessible to a chosen few, and a mordant satire of Quebec Catholicism. Thérèse's homelife is already familiar to the readers of *La Grosse Femme d'à côté est enceinte* (1978), the first volume of Tremblay's "Chroniques." In this second volume, her aunt the Fat Lady is in a hospital Maternity Ward, grandmother Victoire is slowly dying, and Thérèse discovers sexuality in her encounters with the handsome but dull-witted Gérard Bleau. Those familiar with Tremblay's play, *En pièces détachées,* will remember Gérard as Thérèse's cartoon-loving husband and her brother, Marcel, as a madman. In *Thérèse and Pierrette,* the four-year-old Marcel enters the invisible realm of madness by visiting the empty house next door peopled by Rose, Mauve, Violette, and Florence (the knitting Québécois Fates) and the resuscitated cat, Duplessis. Beyond the mixture of realism and fantasy which characterizes life on la rue Fabre as he remembers and imagines it, Tremblay is interested in denouncing the Catholic Church's repressive control over the collective conscience of Quebec. Beneath the satiric comedy of his portrayal of the school nuns and the vulgar Corpus Christi repository, readers sense that Tremblay shares Charlotte Côté's anger. The religious procession becomes a symbol of the shallow ritualism and base hypocrisy of an institution concerned mainly with conserving its own power. But if the Church was all powerful in real life, the author is omnipotent in fiction and Tremblay uses his power to send the winds and rain which ruin the celebration. Building toward this cataclysmic finale, Tremblay skilfully combines numerous characters, subplots, and themes into a unified work, delightful to read.

Sheila Fischman has done an admirable job in translating the novel into English. Rather than translating word for word the often ungrammatical, often obscene, and blasphemous "joual" dialogue, Fischman chooses to make the characters speak the kind of colloquial language that lower-class anglophone Montrealers might have spoken in 1942. Thus, "maudite marde" becomes "shoot," "Mon Dieu" becomes "jeepers" or "Holy Cow," and "chus pas mal tannée" is translated "what a drag!" Purists could quibble over a few awkward expressions, but the overall effect is exceedingly good. Once again, Sheila Fischman has given English-speaking Canadians an opportunity to read a brilliant novel which depicts Quebec society on the verge of change. Tremblay himself metaphorically announces the end of the old era at the beginning of *Thérèse and Pierrette* when one of the girls says: "The lilacs are finished, but the / bleeding hearts'll be out soon. / I like bleeding hearts better."

Volker Strunk (review date January-February 1986)

SOURCE: "Sins of the Father," in *Books in Canada,* Vol. 15, No. 1, January-February, 1986, pp. 20-2.

[*In the following review, Strunk finds* Remember Me *"a fine monodramatic miniature."*]

[**Remember Me** is the translation] of Michel Tremblay's *Les Anciennes Odeurs* (1981), a one-act piece that explores the anxieties of two homosexual but not very gay ex-lovers ambushed by their mid-life crisis and the growing suspicion of their mediocrity. The mode is, or appears to be, relentlessly confessional: if it weren't for the pregnant silences that would have done Harold Pinter proud, the two figures would have talked themselves to death. Visually highlighting the confessional mode is the focal point of the piece, a large, wornout leather armchair in and in front of which Luc and Jean-Marc alternatively sit and kneel as they demonstrate that the need for affection is mutual.

The two had been living together for several years until the younger one, Luc, tired of being Jean-Marc's "cute little joyboy" and "disciple," decided to spread his wings. Evidently he didn't get very far; just back to "that darkness you'd hauled me out of," and *that* wasn't all fun and games. The setting he evokes smacks of Baal's ("I keep moving like a river, discharging my refuse into the sea!"), but unlike Brecht's amoral, polymorphous, perverse degenerate in search of orgiastic wriggles, Tremblay's Luc finds no celestial bliss in radical hedonism, since his pleasures in the gutter are circumscribed by his need to belong. That's why this bird returns to his former prison, his "big cage."

The master/slave relationship in this cage is acted out with an Oedipal vengeance since Jean-Marc, the dominant lover, college teacher by profession, also doubles as a father figure. In a gesture designed to signify his independence from his "father," Luc had moved out, though it's not long after re-entering his former prison that he feels "as if I'm talking to you like a son to his father . . . once again. It's true when all's said and done, you would have made a good father." In due course the prodigal son cries on "daddy's" shoulder and implores him to "Tell me a story like you did when I used to get depressed. Pretend you're my father one last time. When he's dead, I won't ask you again."

"He" is Luc's terminally ill *real* father, reportedly incapable of attending to his son's "stories," yet craving a proper send-off from Luc's lover. As a solution to parental despotism this is of course bound to fail, but the ending is not all bleak because Jean-Marc conveniently undermines his own status as surrogate father by becoming a fellow sufferer, a "brother," as it were, and thereby seems to prepare the ground for true companionship.

All this is about as undramatic as it can get, since the real conflict between Luc and his surrogate father just withers away as Jean-Marc discovers that he, too, is tired of playing games. But is this really what the play is all about? Has Tremblay been writing a silly little naturalistic milieu study demonstrating that not all is well in fairyland? Not one bit. Although the play can be approached as a realistic specimen, it makes its far greater impact as a rather sinister monodrama.

The prospect of a happy ending to this many-mirrored play is somewhat diminished by the fact that the place of the action—Jean-Marc's basement study—is a spatial pretext and that Luc's entry ("My goodness, a ghost!") is that of an unappeased ghost in the subconscious. The translator must have known what he was doing when he chose the title **Remember Me,** which recalls the ghost of Hamlet's father. The title is appropriate in a different sense, too. The man whom we see in the beginning marking papers has left no other mark. Rapidly approaching 40, the teacher/writer with one "utterly boring," "utterly useless" novel to his credit, yearns "to leave some indelible mark on the world, whereas in fact nobody will remember me, they'll just remember my 'disciples'—as you so snidely refer to them, since you're one yourself."

The "rotating" confessional mode the play adopts serves as the great leveller: in the realm where all are mediocre, none is, and that could be the premise of a renewed friendship. But a somewhat different picture begins to emerge if we see Luc's confessions—indeed his whole character—as the *projection* of the man in the basement who had always wanted to become what Luc is: an actor. Instead he has become a spectator, or more precisely, since he is self-conscious to a fault, a voyeur of himself. He used to get through the worst moments of his childhood by "watching myself on an imaginary screen playing my own role in an endless adventure film." But that doesn't work any longer, because "Whenever I try to recapture that state of grace which once did wonders for me, it's you I see, playing my role." And how does one cope with such an apparition, how does one accommodate one's envy of "the other" who has left his mark on the world? Well, one turns this mark into a stain—or better still, lets Luc himself turn the mark and imprint he made into a "stain," a "blemish." And finally one reduces him to the non-entity of one's mirror image: at the end we see Luc at Jean-Marc's desk, marking papers and repeating Jean-Marc's opening line, "Two mistakes in the title alone. . . . Incredible!"

Remember Me is a fine monodramatic miniature. One would like to see this translation performed soon, though one would also like to see the playwright break out of the miniature mold.

Catherine A. Paul (review date Winter 1988)

SOURCE: A review of *Albertine in Five Times,* in *Queen's Quarterly,* Vol. 95, No. 4, Winter, 1988, pp. 967-68.

[*In the following review, Paul comments on Tremblay's critique of patriarchy in* Albertine in Five Times.]

The chief difficulty in translating [*Albertine in Five Times*], originally published in French in 1984, stems from the fact that Tremblay's play was written in *joual.* Thus, much of the colourful charm and poetic forcefulness of the language is lost in the English translation. Although disappointing, this departure from the original text may have been unavoidable. In the Canadian context, it would certainly have been problematic (but not impossible) to find an English-language dialect that could serve as an equivalent to *joual.* The end result is that the standard English of *Albertine in Five Times* reads smoothly enough on its own but it does seem somewhat flat and unevocative when compared to the original French text.

> **The chief difficulty in translating [*Albertine in Five Times*], originally published in French in 1984, stems from the fact that Tremblay's play was written in *joual.*
> —Catherine A. Paul**

Linguistic considerations aside, it must be said that the English version of this play clearly reflects the complex character-structuring of the original. The key to this unusual structure lies in the main character who is deflected into five different roles, representing Albertine at five different stages of her life. Thus, on stage, we have the bizarre situation of five actresses each playing the part of Albertine at a different phase of her life (30, 40, 50, 60, and 70 years of age). The only other character in the play is Madeleine who, in her role as confidant to the five Albertines, performs a precise function in the dynamics of the play. It is her role which holds the disparate strands of dialogue together in a tentative but coherent fashion. The result is quite remarkable on stage, given that the bits and pieces of dialogue span a 50-year period and several different locations.

The thematics of Tremblay's penetrating *rendez-vous* with the five faces of Albertine are not uplifting. For Albertine, there is no evolution to a finer state of being, only nuances of her despair. There is a strong social commentary as the causes of Albertine's misery and rage unfold, fragmented, through the warp of time. We are faced with the ugliness of patriarchy from a woman's perspective—physical and sexual abuse, exhaustion, drugs—and an expanding anger that is ultimately tranquillized and thus leads nowhere. Even the fragile edifice of Albertine's brief spell of happiness is broken asunder by her daughter's death and the mother's subsequent feelings of guilt and responsibility. Thus Albertine must expiate her decision to give primacy to her own life.

Initially, I was astounded by the perspicacity and sensitivity of Tremblay's evocation of Albertine's situation. However, the action in the play is ultimately cyclical; Albertine's anger is exhausted, transforming itself into a hollow despair. Thus, despite the innovative qualities of *Albertine in Five Times,* the play has much in common with the theatre of the absurd. There are no images of creation, no spirals to evoke the possibility of constructive change. The five Albertines are really joining hands in the same fate; they represent variants of the same woman who throughout her life remains caged in the webs of patriarchy. Ultimately, Albertine's sense of failure and nothingness is a problem belonging only to herself: "I've raised two kids for nothing and I feel guilty because I know I did it badly. That's my problem."

Tremblay's play is nonetheless brilliant in its conception and characterization. Certain feminist concerns are delicately presented, inasmuch as they play a part in Albertine's life at different stages. However, the play is confined by its realism. Albertine is still struggling in vain within the limits of a male order. Her anger leads only to an overwhelming sense of powerlessness. On the contrary, in feminist writing, we tend to find characters who are not trapped but empowered to establish the validity of their own values.

In *Albertine in Five Times,* we are witness to the different shades of hopelessness and impossibility throughout the main character's life span. Ultimately, Albertine at 70 is left with nothing: "Nothing will happen now . . . Mind you, that's just as well . . . an empty woman in front of an empty television in an empty room that doesn't smell good. Is this what you call a full life?" It seems that Tremblay is following the tradition of *Waiting for Godot,* only this time the protagonists are women and the original text is in joual.

Eva-Marie Kroller (review date Spring 1991)

SOURCE: A review of *Le Premier quartier de la lune,* in *Canadian Literature,* Vol. 128, Spring, 1991, pp. 229-30.

[*In the favorable review below, Kroller relates the plot of* Le Premier quartier de la lune.]

Le Premier quartier de la lune concludes Tremblay's five-volume "Chroniques du Plateau Mont-Royal," a monumental achievement which sustains the imagination and historical sweep initiated by *La Grosse Femme d'à côté est enceinte* from beginning to end. The cover of *Le Premier Quartier* is adorned by a child's drawing of a cat, smiling craftily like the Cheshire Cat. The similarity with Lewis Carroll's feline is not accidental; Marcel, who reassures himself of his friend's elusive presence by drawing his portrait over and over, suddenly finds his works riddled with holes. Together with Duplessis, the Fates are about to disappear and leave the apparently abandoned house which has been Marcel's refuge for many years. Marcel himself has evolved from the enchanting four-year-old in *La Grosse Femme* to a sweaty adolescent unfit for school and tormented by the other children. He is also given to epileptic seizures, an illness which his family shamefully tries to conceal from the neighbours. At the same time, he partakes of a world of fantasy and dream which remains largely closed to his cousin, "l'enfant de la grosse femme"—Michel Tremblay himself. A star student, "l'enfant" still senses his limitations, and the day covered by this book, June 20, 1952, painfully reveals some of them as he writes his end-of-year examinations. As in the previous books, *Thérèse et Pierrette à l'école des Saints-Anges* in particular, school is above all the place where the power of language is taught, but also often abused. As her son agonizes over his French test, "la grosse femme" graduates from reading to television, an invention she considers capable of breaking through the reader's and radio-listener's solitude, particularly extreme in her sister-in-law Albertine, "renfermée, buckée, bougonne." Here, Tremblay may locate the origins of his own fascination with television as a potentially effective popular art form: recent statistics have confirmed that popular serials are the top-ranking shows in Québec, compared to sports broadcasts in English Canada. This day in 1952 may also be Tremblay's awakening to the importance of *joual* as he watches his classmates yawn at their teacher's assurance that "le français . . . c'était une langue passionnante dont il fallait être fier, que les règles, compliquées au début, se simplifaient au fur et à mesure qu'on les comprenait . . ." This book is a chronicle of despair then, as Marcel and "l'enfant" relinquish their childhood dreams, and Marcel attempts to mark his grief with an apocalyptic burning of the Fates' abandoned house. At the same time, this day marks a beginning, "le premier quartier de la lune," and the book concludes with a brilliant evocation of the images of flight which permeate the "Chroniques" as a whole, whether it be the "chasse-galérie" in *La Grosse Femme* or the little hanging angel in *Thérèse et Pierrette:* "Au creux du croissant de lune, un petit garçon était étendu, bras dernière la tête, jambe croisées; il semblait rêver; au bout, suspendu dans le vide par le col de sa chemise qui risquait de déchirer à tout moment, était accroché un adolescent qui se débattait."

Kathy Mezei (review date Winter 1992)

SOURCE: "Poet's Dilemma," in *Canadian Literature,* Vol. 135, Winter, 1992, pp. 130-31.

[*In the review below, Mezei faults Tremblay's "cliched and tainted" libretto for* NELLIGAN, *finding that his "lines do not rise to his usual exuberant eloquence."*]

There is no doubt that Emile Nelligan, Québec's "national poet," has not loosened his hold on the Québec imagination. As I write this review, a major commemorative conference, "Colloque Nelligan: 50 ans après sa mort" is taking place in Ottawa. It will culminate in the launching of "l'édition critique de l'oeuvre nelliganienne."

Nelligan's poems, which are unquestionably evocative and moving, echo the Symbolists he admired, and with a few, striking exceptions are set in an oneiric rather than a localized world. His renowned sonnet, "Le vaisseau d'or," which sinks "dans l'abîme du rêve" has been set to music, choreographed, and used as the name of a restaurant operated by former Montreal mayor, Jean Drapeau. As Jean Larose's astute study, *Le mythe de Nelligan,* pointed out, Nelligan, handsome, tortured, perfectly symbolized a national schizophrenia—French patrimonie versus anglophone North American context. His was the sad story of a young man devoted to poetry, who wrote fervently from age 16 to 19 (1896 to 1899), at which point he was incarcerated in mental institutions for 42 years and thereby forever silenced. He prefigured many Quebec literary heroes who dreamed heroically, but failed, sinking dismally, like Nelligan's ship of gold, like his own youthful spirit. Think of Hubert Aquin's protagonists.

It was therefore a splendid idea to create an opera about Nelligan, and most appropriate that Michel Tremblay, by now another Quebec "mythe," produce the libretto. The well known Quebec composer, André Gagnon, wrote the score and collaborated with Tremblay. The debut of this opera was eagerly anticipated and surrounded by lavish publicity. Performed by the Opera of Montreal, it opened first in Quebec City in February 1990, and then in March in Montreal. Always interested in the twists and turns of "le mythe de Nelligan" I had wanted to hear the Opera. Luckily fate brought me to Montreal at the right moment.

As a spectacle, *NELLIGAN* was an inspired performance—rich costumes, a simple but powerfully choreographed set, an impressive cast including Louise Forestier (Emilie, Nelligan's mother) and Renée Claude (Françoise). But although the performers were impassioned in their delivery, the opera was a disappointment. Quite simply, Gagnon's music, Tremblay's libretto and presentation of the story were cliched and tainted by a superficial and unconvincing nineteenth-century veneer. A stronger sense of Nelligan's milieu, and indeed of his troubled personality could have been developed (what comes through are merely childish petulance and adolescent alcoholism). Instead, we were presented only with the banal threads of a tragic story, which is still

not fully understood, since by Quebec law psychiatric records are not open to the public.

Tremblay's libretto opens, effectively enough, with a professor come to visit the elderly Nelligan just before his death in the hôpital Saint-Jean-de-Dieu. Nelligan then obligingly and pathetically attempts to recite "Le vaisseau d'or," but falters, misremembering his own lines. (Tremblay draws his material from Paul Wycznynski's detailed biography, *Nelligan, 1879-1941,* and from Bernard Courteau's more idiosyncratic *Nelligan n'était pas fou*). Then while the elderly Nelligan watches, the last few months before the young Nelligan's incarceration are enacted. These unfortunately are stylized, predictable set pieces, redeemed only by the pathos of the older Nelligan observing events roll to their ineluctable end, and trying vainly to intervene. A series of scenes involve his mother, Emilie, a Quebecoise with whom Nelligan has a particularly close relationship (though she was much troubled by the direction of his poems and may have destroyed some), his father, David, who speaks mainly in English (he was played by a former American, Jim Corcoran), his two sisters, his bohemian friends, Charles Gill and Arthur de Bussières, the priest, Eugène Seers (later Louis Dantin, who posthumously published Nelligan's poems), and Françoise, a journalist and kindred spirit.

Tremblay's lines do not rise to his usual exuberant eloquence, they remain pedestrian, hobbled by flat end rhymes: for example, listen to Emilie: "Pourquoi nommez-vous folie / ce qui n'est que mélocolie / d'un poète." These lines reflect banal notions of a tormented poetic soul. Most disturbing, however, is the tremendous importance of the French-English/mother-father conflict in Nelligan's unhappy life. Tremblay carries Philip Larkin's "they fuck you up, your mum and dad" to simplistic, annoying extremes. David Nelligan is forced to sing idiotic lines like "I don't want this son of mine to destroy everything. I worked hard all my life! A poet! For God's sake! Why not a murderer! Why not Jack the Ripper!" The young Nelligan responds later, equally inanely, with "La seule chose que vous me dites en français, c'est que je suis fou. . . ." While obviously librettos are constrained by the need for repetition, often exacerbated by hackneyed end rhymes, surely Tremblay with his wonderful ear for the cadence of speech, could have been more inventive. This opera was produced in the midst of Quebec's language war, but to present Nelligan's sad fate as a consequence of the conflict with his *English*-speaking (and pugnaciously philistine) father, and of the quarrel between French (mother) and English (father) seems to me by now a battered platitude. This disappointing interpretation is all the more puzzling since there seems to be an autobiographical element in Tremblay's portrayal of Nelligan. He obviously identifies with the poet's dilemma—the absent father who works in English, the mother to whom he is warmly attached, and the defiant embracing of a career as writer. Nelligan's psychosis and his undiminished significance to the people of Quebec deserved better. Alas.

Renate Usmiani (essay date Spring 1995)

SOURCE: "The Bingocentric Worlds of Michel Tremblay and Tomson Highway, *Les Belles-Soeurs* vs. *The Rez Sisters*," in *Canadian Literature*, Vol. 144, Spring, 1995, pp. 126-40.

[*In the following essay, Usmiani compares* Les Belles-soeurs *to Tomson Highway's* The Rez Sisters, *demonstrating how both plays parallel aspects of postmodern theater but express a different spirit.*]

The emergent theatre of Native peoples offers theatre scholars and historians a unique opportunity to observe the fusion of cultures in the making. While contemporary postmodern theatre represents just one more link in a long chain of historical evolution that goes back two and a half millennia, contemporary Native playwrights are forced to work in a genre without direct antecedent in their culture—although theatrical elements are present, of course, in many aspects of traditional ritual and story-telling. In the best plays to emerge so far, the authors have successfully grafted the techniques of Euramerican postmodern theatre onto this traditional matrix of ritual and storytelling. The result is a theatre which shares all the surface aspects of Western postmodernism, but differs essentially in spirit. A comparative study of Tomson Highway's *The Rez Sisters* (1988) and Michel Tremblay's *Les Belles-soeurs* (1968) illustrates this point vividly, because of the exceptionally close parallels between these two sister plays.

The parallels are immediately apparent on the levels of subject matter and dramatic techniques; there are also less apparent parallels with respect to the authors. Both *Les Belles-soeurs* and *The Rez Sisters* are first productions which catapulted their young authors, and with them the society they represent, into the spotlight of national and international attention; both plays marked the beginning of a new and original dramaturgy, the "nouveau théâtre québecois" in the case of Tremblay, Native Canadian theatre in that of Highway.

Both plays focus exclusively on female characters. In both plays, these characters are closely related, as indicated by the respective titles. In both plays, the characters are struggling against poverty, as indicated by the respective settings: East Montreal in one case, the Wasaychigan Hill reserve in the other. In each play, Bingo represents a central experience in the characters' lives.

The critical statements which were made about *The Rez Sis-*

ters not surprisingly parallel many comments made earlier about *Les Belles-soeurs*. Daniel David Moses, for example, points to "the spiritual malaise which is the subject of the play"—a clear parallel to Tremblay's much-commented "maudite vie plate" motif. Moses also states that "The accomplishment of *The Rez Sisters* is that it focusses on a variety of such undervalued lives and brings them up to size" —a point much emphasized in the reception of *Les Belles-soeurs*. Finally, the two plays share a central image: Bingo, symbol and illustration of the consumerism of the women represented and the spiritual emptiness of their lives.

Dramatic Techniques

Both playwrights have developed an original and highly effective way of combining bold superrealism, verbal and nonverbal, with theatrical techniques, most importantly, the use of spotlit inner monologues and surrealistic effects. Dramatic structures in both cases reflect the two authors' passionate interest in music. Tremblay's *Les Belles-soeurs* has been referred to as an oratorio, his *Forever Yours, Marie Lou* as a string quartet, *Sainte Carmen of the Main* as an "opéra parlé." Similarly, Daniel David Moses says of Highway's plays: "He structures his theatre pieces according to models of musical composition. He uses characters like themes and thinks of character conflict in terms of counterpoint and contrast." Pennie Petrone states that Highway combines his "knowledge of Indian reality in this country with classical structure, artistic language. It amounted to applying sonata form to the spirit and mental situation of a street drunk"— words that catch Tremblay's mixture of lyricism and naturalism exactly.

Given the fact that Highway himself has stated his admiration for the work of Michel Tremblay, one might be tempted to look upon *The Rez Sisters* as a purely derivative work. Nothing could be more wrong. On the contrary: close analysis shows that the surface similarities actually help to bring out more dramatically the deep seated differences between the two works. These are, of course, rooted in the basic difference in Weltanschauung on which the plays are based: *Les Belles-soeurs* reflects the negativism, nihilism and spiritual void of Western postmodern society; *The Rez Sisters,* in spite of the similarity of its dramatic matrix, reflects the essential humanism, life-affirming and hopeful world view of Native peoples.

The striking parallels between the two plays might therefore seem paradoxical. However they can perhaps be explained by the fact that, historically, both works stand as early monuments to postcolonial emancipation and self-assertion, each appearing in the wake of a—more or less—"quiet revolution": that of Quebec in the 1960s, that of native people in the 1980s. Politically, Native demands for self-government echo Québécois demands for separation. Just as Tremblay's use of the *joual* was in itself a political act in 1968, the very emergence of a Native dramaturgy represented a political act in 1988. The choice of all female characters in both cases underlines the oppression of the respective societies and their desire for empowerment. Each play brought in its wake a veritable explosion of theatrical activity—in the 1970s in Quebec, in the 1980s with Native people. The political impact of these cultural revolutions became clearly manifest in a change of nomenclature from colonial to independently assertive: "French-Canadian" to "Québécois", "Indian" (the colonizers' term) to "Native" or "Aboriginal." An oft expressed and deep-seated nostalgia for the precolonial heroic past accompanies the cultural and political revolution in both cases. In Quebec, it is a nostalgia for the pioneering glories of the period before the British conquest; with Native peoples, it is the memory of pre-contact lifestyles, free from the psychological tutelage and social and physical ills imported by the colonizers. One might offer the hypothesis, then, that obvious similarity in the "moment" within the historical evolution at which the two plays were written accounts for their many parallels, while the equally obvious essential differences between the two societies living through this "moment," would account for the differences. Let us proceed to an examination of these two aspects of the "sister plays."

Parallels

1. *The Bingo Game*

In both plays, the authors focus on a group of disadvantaged women whose lives revolve around bingo. In *The Rez Sisters,* "THE BIGGEST BINGO IN THE WORLD" actually provides the axis on which the action of the play revolves, from news of the impending event, to preparations for the trip to Toronto, to the event itself and its aftermath. In the earlier play, the importance of bingo in the women's lives is presented more subtly, through one of the two stylized Odes which create the leitmotifs for each act. In act one, it is the *Maudite Vie plate* recitation, a summary of the belles-soeurs' frustrated and meaningless lives. In act two, the *Ode to Bingo* mobilizes all of the women's latent energy and enthusiasm. For one brief moment, hostilities cease and they are all united in their common panegyric to the supreme stimulant of their lives. Even senile old Olivine Dubuc is overcome with excitement at the mention of the word "bingo."

The women's bingo mania gives both authors a wonderful opportunity for satirizing their cheap consumerism and materialistic attitudes. In the Tremblay play, the high point of this satire occurs with Germaine's litany of all the household goods she will be able to order, now that the entire catalogue is within reach of her unlimited greed. Highway outdoes the vulgarity of Germaine's monologue by focussing on the particular wish fantasy of one woman, Philomena:

"Myself, I'm gonna go to every bingo and I'm gonna

hit every jackpot between here and Espanola and I'm gonna buy me that toilet I'm dreaming about at night . . . big and wide and white"; and after she has won the money to make her dream come true: ". . . But the best, the most wonderful, my absolute most favorite part is the toilet bowl itself. First of all, it's elevated, like on a sort of . . . pedestal, so that it makes you feel like . . . the Queen . . . And the bowl itself, white, spirit white—is of such a shape, such an exquisitely soft, perfect oval shape that it makes you want to cry. Oh!!! and it's so comfortable you could just sit on it right up until the day you die!"

Women waxing rhapsodic over the shape of a toilet bowl or the Mickey Mouse pattern on their wallpaper obviously lack ordinary emotional, physical or spiritual fulfilment. Bingo represents the ultimate escape—more pathetic even in the case of the belles-soeurs whose rewards seem hardly worth getting worked up about ("plaster dogs, floor lamps") than for the rez sisters, who are true gamblers at heart, always expecting the big jackpot that will take them out of their misery. Neither Tremblay nor Highway chose to present an actual bingo game realistically on stage. The stylization of the *Ode to Bingo,* and surrealistic quality of THE BIGGEST BINGO IN THE WORLD clearly emphasize the preeminently psychological reality of bingo in the lives of the women.

2. *Use of Language*

For both Tremblay and Highway, the creation of a dramatic idiom represents a political statement of self-assertion and identity. Each play mirrors the language spoken by the people, rather than the literary idiom. Tremblay actually created his own idiosyncratic spelling to transcribe an oral language to the printed page. His use of *joual,* highly controversial at the time, forced a breakthrough in Quebec dramaturgy and brought about the evolution of a new stage idiom, totally different from "literary" French. Highway's problems in creating a dramatic idiom are obviously even more difficult than those faced by Tremblay. Like other Native writers, he finds himself trapped between the desire to express himself in his own language, which he loves and admires, and the practical need to use the language of the colonizer ("forced appropriation") in order to have his plays produced before a wider audience. In *The Rez Sisters,* he has achieved a double compromise: small portions of the dialogue are actually written in Cree and Ojibway, with English translations in footnotes; the bulk of the dialogue however, reproduces the "village English" spoken on the reserve, an idiom whose relationship to literary English parallels the relationship of joual to literary French. Although Highway is clearly more reticent than Tremblay about abandoning "correct" grammatical structures, his choice of vocabulary and sentence patterns do convey the feeling of spoken English; his abundant use of swear words amply matches the *sacres* found in Tremblay. Tremblay discovered the poetic qualities of his own vernacular early on in his career and has defended it from the start: "Le joual est très pres de la musique, très lyrique. . . ." Native writers sometimes find it difficult to dare embrace this non-literary type of language. As Maria Campbell says:

> A lot of my writing now is in very broken English. I find that I can express myself better that way. I can't write in our language, because who would understand it? So I've been using the way I spoke when I was at home, rather than the way I speak today . . . what linguists call "village English." It's very beautiful . . . very lyrical, but it took me a long time to realize that . . . it's more like oral tradition.

3. *Superrealism*

Both authors use superrealism—a grotesque extension of naturalism—verbally and as part of the action. With Tremblay, it is the combination of faulty grammar, mispronunciations, clichés, formulas, and swearwords—especially those with religious connotations, the *sacres*—which give the dialogue a superrealistic quality; in the Highway play, it is the totally uninhibited use of offensive language. To give just one example, Emily Dictionary's outburst during the riot scene [in *The Rez Sisters*]:

> Emily: (to Philomena). So damned bossy and pushy and sucky. You make me sick. Always wanting your own way. (To Veronique.) Goddamed trouble-making old crow. (To Pelajia.) Fuckin' self-righteous old bitch. (To Marie-Adèle.) Mental problems, that's what you got, princess. I ain't no baby. I'm the size of a fucking church. (To Annie.) You slippery little slut. Brain the size of a fuckin' pea. Fuck, man, take a Valium.

Violence, scatology and sex as part of the stage performance are the hallmarks of superrealism. Because of the absence of men in the plays under discussion, sex is not shown, although verbal references are made quite frequently. Violence on stage, however, appears prominently in both plays. In *Les Belles-soeurs,* the physical violence is mainly centered around the helpless, pathetic Olivine Dubuc. This unfortunate old lady takes a tumble down three flights of stairs in her wheelchair, an additional fall in Germaine's kitchen afterwards, and is mercilessly beaten over the head by her "saintly" daughter-in-law Thérèse. None of the other women expresses the slightest sympathy for her. General violence erupts at the end of the play, when the "sisters" finally openly admit their rage at Germaine's good luck and not only reveal all the booklets of stamps they have stolen, but start fighting for more stamps among each other like a horde of wild animals, with the old lady gleefully riding her wheelchair amidst their vicious antics.

The most striking examples of superrealism in *The Rez Sisters* occur in act one, as the women meet at the store. Philomena is shown sitting on the toilet, at the back of the store, in full view of the audience; later, she comes forward, slowly pulling her clothes back on. The riot scene that follows exceeds the violence of the riot scene in *Les Belles-soeurs,* which is fully mimed; in *The Rez Sisters,* physical aggression is matched by verbal aggression, as illustrated in the quotation mentioned earlier.

4. *Theatricalism*

Again, the type of theatrical techniques used in the two plays are strikingly similar: both plays focus on individual characters with stylized, spotlit monologues, and on key motifs with highly stylized scenes. In *Les Belles-soeurs,* the stylized monologues reveal the deepest concerns of the women, concerns they are unable and unwilling to verbalize and share: Yvette's obsession with her daughter's wedding and obvious craving for a closer relationship; Mademoiselle Des-Neiges Verrette's secret, hopeless love for the brush salesman; Lisette de Courval's snobbery and disdain for the other women; Rhéauna and Angéline's obsession with illness and death; Angéline's admission of her only, and sinful, pleasures at the "club"; and Rose's bitter denunciation of marriage and her husband's unending demand for his sexual "dues."

In *Les Belles-soeurs,* the stylized monologues reveal the deepest concerns of the women, concerns they are unable and unwilling to verbalize and share
—*Renate Usmiani*

Highway uses stylized, spotlit monologues in act one, spotlit duologues in act two. The speeches in act one, by Annie, Marie-Adèle, and Veronique are all framed by the refrain WHEN I WIN THE BIGGEST BINGO IN THE WORLD, and express each woman's greatest dream. For Annie, it is to be able to buy records, and to sing with the band of her idol, Fritz the Katz; Marie-Adèle fantasizes about a lovely island of her own; and Veronique sees total bliss in a new kitchen stove, just like the one used by Madame Benoit on television. Similarly, Highway uses characters isolated by spotlight in act two; however, here, in the van en route to Toronto, the women do not speak singly, but in pairs revealing themselves to each other in moments of total intimacy: Annie with Marie-Adèle, Philomena with Pelijia, Emily with Annie and Marie-Adèle. Thus, we learn about their underlying troubles, fears and anxieties, not normally mentioned: Marie-Adèle's fear of what will happen to her husband and children after her death from cancer; the trauma of Philomena's past, the white man who left her, the child she had to abandon; Emily's tragic loss of her best friend in a motorcycle accident.

Unlike the spotlit monologues and duologues, which reveal the thoughts and feelings of individual characters, the stylized scenes illustrate their collective concerns. In *Les Belles-soeurs* these take the form of choral recitations: the *Maudite vie plate* chorus in act 1, the *Ode to Bingo* in act two. In the *Maudite vie plate recitation,* by five women, a solo voice alternates with the chorus in a litany enumerating the endlessly repetitive daily chores of everyday life in a loveless family setting. The entire piece is framed by the play's leitmotif, the "maudite vie plate" refrain. "Chus tannée de mener une maudite vie plate! Une maudite vie plate! Une maudite vie plate! Une maudite vie plate! Une maud. . . ." The *Ode to Bingo* is similarly set in a leitmotif frame: "Moé, l'aime ça, le bingo! Moé, j'adore le bingo! Moé, y'a rien au monde que j'aime plus que le bingo!" The recitation itself is done by a chorus of four voices, with four other women shouting out bingo numbers in rhythmic counterpoint.

While Tremblay's stylized scenes operate entirely on the verbal level, Highway's are based exclusively on movement and sound. As in *Les Belles-soeurs,* each act features one major stylized scene. In act one, the superrealistic scene in the store fades into a highly theatrical, mimed finale, accompanied by sound effects:

> The seven women have this grand and ridiculous march to the band office, around the set and all over the stage area, with Pelajia leading them forward heroically, her hammer just a-swinging in the air. Nanabush (the Trickster figure) trails merrily along in the rear of the line. They reach the "band office"— standing in one straight line square in front of the audience. The "invisible" chief "speaks": cacophonous percussion for about seven beats, the women listening more and more incredulously. Finally, the percussion comes to a dead stop.
>
> PELAJIA: No?
>
> Pelajia raises her hammer to hit the "invisible" chief, Nanabush shrugs a "don't ask me, I don't know," Emily fingers a "fuck you, man." Blackout.

A similar pattern appears in act two. Following the women's (realistic) planning session in Pelajia's basement, a series of highly theatrical sequences—seven "beats"—illustrates their superhuman fundraising efforts for the trip to Toronto. Musical effects accompany their frantic activities, mimed at ever accelerating speed:

> And the women start their fundraising activities with a vengeance. The drive is underlined by a wild rhyth-

mic beat from the musician, one that gets wilder and wilder with each successive beat, though always underpinned by this persistent, almost dance-like pulse. The movement of the women covers the entire stage area, and like the music, gets wilder and wilder, until by the end it is as if we are looking at an insane eight-ring circus. . . . Pelajia's basement simply dissolves into the madness of the fundraising drive.

As a final, and obvious, parallel, the theatrical, rather than realistic, conclusions to both plays must be mentioned: Tremblay's surrealistic rain of gold bond stamps to the tune of "O Canada," Highway's Trickster figure Nanabush in a triumphant dance on the roof of Pelajia's house. Both authors have thus chosen to end their basically realistic play on a highly unrealistic finale. However, the feeling we are left with in each case is totally different. Underneath the surface parallels, the two sisters plays are poles—or rather, cultures—apart.

Differences

The rain of gold bond stamps at the end of *Les Belles-soeurs* reinforces the consumerism which is being satirized throughout the play. It also serves to make a political statement: material bliss (unlimited stamps) is linked to toe-ing the patriotic party line (singing of *O Canada*). On both levels, the author's cynicism is complete and absolute. In contrast, the appearance of the Nanabush character at the end of *The Rez Sisters,* not just dancing, but dancing "triumphantly," points to the underlying spirituality, affirmation of life and joie de vivre which characterize the play as a whole—a far cry from the spiritual and emotional aridity of *Les Belles-soeurs.* This essential difference between the Quebecois and the Native "sisters" play can be easily demonstrated by examining the different treatment of settings, representation of characters and representation of religion and morality in the two works.

1. *Settings*

The obvious difference here is the single setting of Tremblay as opposed to the multiple settings of Highway. Tremblay achieves the oppressive atmosphere of his play largely through classical concentration. Not only does all the action take place within the confined space of Germaine's kitchen; concentration of time is also used, to the point where acting time in fact parallels real time. Even the division into two acts is carefully engineered so as not to break this unity: the beginning of act two reiterates the final lines of act one, so that the linkage is complete.

Corresponding to the greater spirit of freedom in the Highway play, a variety of settings is used, both indoor and outdoor: on the roof of Pelajia's house, in front of Marie-Adèle's, inside Emily's store and Pelajia's basement; in the "van," the bingo hall, by the "graveside." Some of these are realistic, others, such as the van, the bingo scene and the grave scene, only indicated. Some of the transitions take the form of conventional scene changes, others are built into the action in such a way that imaginary settings are created through mime and movement on stage: the march to the store, the march to the band office, the shift from van to bingo hall and from bingo hall to Marie-Adèle's porch and graveside. Tomson deals as freely with time as he does with space. Time zones are telescoped and crossed as he cuts from one scene to the next without transition. These technical differences in dramatic structure create a diametrically opposed "atmosphere" for each of the two plays. In, *Les Belles-soeurs* the audience is drawn into the oppressive, almost claustrophobic ambiance in which the characters conduct their lives; with *The Rez Sisters,* we feel a sense of fluidity, movement and greater freedom.

The rain of gold bond stamps at the end of *Les Belles-soeurs* reinforces the consumerism which is being satirized throughout the play.
—*Renate Usmiani*

---

2. *Characters*
The essential difference between the two plays becomes even more apparent if we take a closer look at the depiction of the characters. The "sisters" of the two plays differ considerably in their attitude towards each other. Tremblay's belles-soeurs detest each other with a vengeance; although they try hard to maintain a facade of polite behavior, their underlying hostility, envy, and aggression shows through at all times, occasionally erupting into vicious quarrels and bouts of insults. The only time they seem to be able to act in unison is in a collective act of disloyalty as they embezzle all of Germaine's gold bond stamps. The rez sisters, too, have their often violent disagreements and their anger often flares up. However, an underlying spirit of cooperation and genuine sisterhood permeates the play. The women work together, rather than against each other, and thus manage to carry out their ambitious project of going to Toronto.

Highway has chosen not to deal with the generational conflict in his play. Tremblay, on the other hand, includes three young women to illustrate the tragic mother/daughter relationship among his belles-soeurs. The play opens with dialogue between Germaine and her daughter Linda, and the antiquated form of address they use (Linda says "vous" to her mother, Germaine "tu" to her daughter) already indicates the existence of a hierarchical relationship that can only lead to tension. Intolerance and total lack of comprehension on the part of the older generation creates resentment, rebellion and often, as in the case of Lise, despair for the younger

women. Both playwrights have included a black sheep in their roster of characters. In *Les Belles-soeurs,* it is the unfortunate Pierrette, who works in a "club"; in *The Rez Sisters,* the infamous Gazelle Nataways, "who's got them legs of hers wrapped around big Joey day and night." The rez sisters look upon Gazelle with a certain amount of amused disgust; but the belles-soeurs, rejoicing in their moral superiority and Pierrette's inevitable eternal damnation, feel justified in ostracising her fully and refusing all help, even when she reveals her desperate situation. Their lack of tolerance is absolute.

A similar pattern applies in the treatment of the old and handicapped, nonagenarian Olivine Dubuc in *Les Belles-soeurs,* Zhaboonigan Peterson, the 24-year old mentally retarded adopted daughter of Veronique in *The Rez Sisters.* Tremblay's vitriolic representation of the women's heartless treatment of the old lady contrasts sharply with the rez sisters' friendly acceptance and mothering of Zhaboonigan. The belles-soeurs' uncharitable attitude is further aggravated by their hypocrisy. Although they are all exasperated by the presence of the senile old woman, only Rose, the most outspoken of the group, openly voices what they secretly think: "Est assez vieille! Est pus bonne à rien!" Meanwhile the others vie with each other in their hypocritical encouragement of Thérèse's self-indulgent martyr complex:

> GERMAINE: Mon Dieu, Thérèse, que j'vous plains donc!
>
> Des-Neiges Verrette: Vous êtes trop bonne, Thérèse!
>
> GABRIELLE: C'est vrai, ca, vous êtes ben que trop bonne!
>
> THÉRÈSE: Que voulez-vous, y faut ben gagner son ciel!
>
> MARIE-ANGE: On pourra dire que vous l'avez gagné, vot'ciel, vous!
>
> THÉRÈSE: Ah! Mais, j'me plains pas! J'me dis que le bon Dieu est bon, pis qu'y va m'aider à passer à travers!
>
> LISETTE: C'est ben simple, vous m'émouvez jusqu'aularmes!
>
> THÉRÈSE: Voyons donc, Madame de Courval, prenez sur vous!
>
> Des-Neiges Verrette: J'ai rien qu'une chose à vous dire, Madame Dubuc, vous êtes une sainte femme!

Nobody objects, of course, when the object of their adulation administers vigorous blows to the old woman's head, her normal method of keeping Madame Dubuc senior in line. Zhaboonigan, too, often makes a nuisance of herself; but one of the women invariably finds a way to distract and control her in a casual and friendly manner. There is little self-pity on Veronique's part, and certainly no undue praise given by the other women.

Intolerant, narrow-minded and emotionally stunted, Tremblay's women are naturally unable to form intimate relationships with each other. We learn of their real lives only through the stylized monologues. In contrast, Highway, by spotlighting not only single characters, but also pairs, emphasizes the openness and intimacy between the women.

In both plays, the consumerism of the women depicted is heavily satirized. However, even here there is a difference. In *The Rez Sisters,* crass materialism is tempered by some more humane ideals: Veronique dreams of a shiny new kitchen stove, but she also plans to use it to cook for all the motherless orphans on the reserve; Marie-Adèle's utopic private island will provide an ideal spot to bring up a happy family. In contrast, the belles-soeurs' greed is unmitigated: Germaine has no intention of sharing a single item of her windfall with anyone.

In the pursuit of their materialistic goals, the two groups of women also show essential differences. The belles-soeurs live in a state of resignation. They may curse their "maudite vie plate," but do nothing to improve their lot. They can only count on good luck to improve their fate: a windfall of gold bond stamps, or maybe a win at bingo. The rez sisters, too, set all their hopes on the chance of winning at bingo. However, once they find out about THE BIGGEST BINGO IN THE WORLD, they display enormous energy to get what they want (the fundraising drive). In fact, the author emphasizes his characters' active, resolute commitment to self-help by beginning and ending the play with the image of Pelajia, hammer in hand, repairing the roof of her house. The conclusions of the two plays also sharply contrast the belles-soeurs' inertia with the practical, no-nonsense approach of the rez sisters. At the end of Tremblay's play, nothing has changed for his group of women. At the end of *The Rez Sisters,* a number of positive developments have taken place: Philomena has the coveted new toilet; Annie gets to sing backup with the band of Fritz the Cat; Emily is carrying a child; Véronique cooks for the widowed Eugene and his fourteen children. Just like the differences in dramatic structures, the differences in the depiction of the characters reveal the almost polar opposition in attitude between the two cultures.

3. *Religion and Morality*

Both plays depict societies which have retained just a faint echo of the profound spirituality of the past; and where winning at bingo, rather than religious ecstasy, has become the ultimate metaphysical experience. However, the way the two authors deal with this loss of spirituality is essentially different. Tremblay puts on stage the ossified remains of a defunct Catholicism to which the belles-soeurs still adhere, oblivious to the emptiness of their religious practices: novenas and rosaries at home, faithful attendance at all parish events outside. Tremblay's regular stage designer, André Brassard, captured this spirit of excessive, but spiritually bankrupt, religiosity in his stage set for the original production of *Les Belles-soeurs:* Germaine's kitchen appeared cluttered with cheap plaster saints and holy pictures, in cynical counter-point to the less than Christian behavior of the assembled parish ladies.

In contrast, Highway's rez sisters show no interest in organized religion—other than Church-run bingo games, of course. But the author has chosen to give them a steady, if largely unrecognized, spiritual companion, Nanabush, the Trickster figure of Native mythology. Looking at the two plays under discussion, one must agree with his own basic distinction between native and non-native theatre: "The use of underlying native mythology is the distinctive feature. Native mythology is so alive, electric, passionate . . . the relationship in Christian mythology is so academic by comparison . . . [in] native theatre that spirituality is there. It is magic." The Nanabush figure in *The Rez Sisters* indeed conveys that sense of magic. According to the author's production notes, he is to be played by a male dancer, "modern, ballet or traditional." He appears in three guises: a white bird (joy); a black bird (death); and as the glittering bingo master (wish fulfilment). Only Zhaboonigan, the retarded girl, and Marie-Adèle, sick with cancer and close to death, have some inkling of the spirit within the bird. When Nanabush first appears, a white seagull outside Marie-Adèle's house, the author immediately makes the connection between native mythology and native language: Marie-Adèle addresses him in Cree in the longest Native language passage of the play. Subsequently, Nanabush appears in his multiple roles. As a joyous, comic trickster, he accompanies the women on their march to the store, to the band office, and playfully joins his own antics to their frantic fundraising efforts. In a moving scene with Zhaboonigan, he proves the only confidante to whom she is able to tell the story of her traumatic childhood experiences. Full of trust, she concludes with a childlike: "Nice white birdie you." In the surrealistic bingo scene, Nanabush becomes the glitzy bingo master who, however, fails to call out the much-wanted number, B14. Nanabush as the black bird visits Marie-Adèle, and finally comes to take her away in the midst of the bingo riot:

> And out of this chaos emerges the calm, silent image of Marie-Adèle waltzing romantically in the arms of the Bingo Master. The Bingo Master says "Bingo" into her ear. And the Bingo Master changes, with sudden, bird-like movements, into the nighthawk,

Nanabush in dark feathers. Marie-Adèle meets Nanabush.

Nanabush, then, stands for the joyful, life-affirming spirit of Native mythology, as well as for a calm and fearless attitude to death. As Highway points out, contrasting these attitudes to the Christian ones, "One super-hero is stating that we are here to suffer and the other basically says we are here to have a helluva good time ... One was crucified, the other wasn't; so we have absolutely nothing to feel guilty about. . . ." The two plays provide a perfect illustration of these basic differences. All the women of the older generation in *Les Belles-soeurs* are deeply steeped in a sense of sin and guilt. Trying to have a bit of innocuous fun at a club brings tragic consequences for Angéline Sauvé, as she is told "mais c'est péché mortel" and "le club, mais c'est l'enfer" by her self-righteous best friend Rhéauna. Angéline's spotlit monologue reveals the full pathos of such oppressive Puritanical attitudes, as she comments on her joyless upbringing: "J'ai été élevée dans des salles paroissiales par des soeurs qui faisaient c' qu'y pouvaient mais qui connaissaient rien, les pauvres! J'ai appris à rire à cinquante-cinq ans! Comprenez-vous! J'ai appris à rire à cinquante-cinq ans!" Similarly, the belles-soeurs show total intolerance and lack of compassion for any young girl who has "fallen" from the straight and narrow path. Lise Paquette is driven to the edge of suicide by their vicious self-righteousness, summed up by Rose, speaking for all of them: "Non, pour moé là, les filles-mères c'est des vicieuses, qui courent aprés les hommes." The problem does not arise in *The Rez Sisters*; even Emily Dictionary, the toughest of them all, accepts the fact of her pregnancy quite stoically.

Just as the excessively developed sense of sin and guilt leads to a total condemnation of all pleasures, it brings with it an almost hysterical fear of death and the threat of eternal damnation. This is well demonstrated in *Les Belles-soeurs* as Rhéauna and Angéline contemplate their own death on their return from the funeral parlour:

> ANGÉLINE: ... J'veux mourir dans mon lit ... avoir le temps de me confesser ...
>
> RHÉAUNA: Pour ça, non, j'voudrais pas mourir sans me confesser! Angéline, promets-moé que tu vas faire v'nir le prêtre quand j'vas me sentir mal! Promets-le moé!
>
> ANGÉLINE: Ben oui, ben oui, ça fait cent fois que tu me le demandes ...
>
> RHEAUNA: J'ai tellement peur de mourir sans recevoir les derniers sacrements!

The contrast to the attitudes about death in *The Rez Sisters* is

absolute. Marie-Adèle's last words, spoken, significantly, in Cree, convey only trust and serenity:

> U-wi-nuk u-wa? U-wi-nuk u-wa? Eugene? Neee. U-wi-nuk ma-a oo-ma kee-tha? Ka. Kee-tha i-chi-goo-ma so that's who you are ... at rest upon the rock . . . the master of the game ... the game ... it's me ... nee-tha ... come ... come ... don't be afraid ... as-tum ... come ... to ... me ... ever soft wings ... beautiful soft ... soft ... dark wings ... here ... take me ... as-tum ... as-tum ... pee-na-sin ... wings ... here ... take me ... take ... me ... with ... pee-na-sin ...;
>
> Who are you? Who are you? Eugene? Nee. Then who are you really? Oh. It's you, so that's who you are ... at rest upon the rock ... the master of the game ... the game ... it's me ... me ... come ... come ... don't be afraid ... come ... come ... to ... me ... ever soft wings ... beautiful soft ... soft ... dark wings ... here ... take me ... come ... come ... come and get me ... wings here ... take me ... take me ... with ... come and get me.

In conclusion, we see how Michel Tremblay and Tomson Highway, writing at similar points in the historical evolution of their society, and choosing a similar dramatic matrix, have created two totally dissimilar plays, each reflecting its own culture. Tremblay's cynical treatment of the topic echoes Western postmodern nihilism; Highway's idealization of characters and retention of a humanistic value system indicates a society in which hope has not yet died. Highway sums it all up in the funeral speech, given by Pelijia at Marie-Adèle's grave:

> Well, sister, guess you finally hit the big jackpot. Best bingo game we've ever been to in our lives, huh? You know, life's like that, I figure. When all is said and done. Kinda silly, innit, this business of living? But. What choice do we have? ... I figure we gotta make the most of it while we're here. You certainly did. And I sure as hell am giving it one good try. For you. For me. For all of us. Promise. Really. See you when that big bird finally comes for me.

FURTHER READING

Criticism

Fogel, Melanie. Review of *The Heart Laid Bare*. *CM* XVIII, No. 1 (January 1990): 27-28.

    Suggests that "superlatives to describe Tremblay's work

were exhausted a long time ago. Let's just say that with *The Heart Laid Bare* he lives up to his reputation."

Freeman, Mark. "Affairs that Start Out All Wrong." *Lambda Book Report* 2 (September, 1991): 29.
Admires *Making Room,* claiming that "we haven't heard such truth in much gay fiction."

Johnson, Ann. Review of *Hosanna* and *La Maison suspendue. Books in Canada* 21, No. 1 (February, 1992): 29.
Favorably assesses *La Maison suspendue* and a re-issue of *Hosanna.*

Kellaway, Kate. Review of *The Fat Woman Next Door Is Pregnant. Observer Review* (27 January 1991): 58.
Notes that "it's impossible not to warm to [Tremblay's] world; the problem is there is so little to support exuberant characters who badly need the narrative equivalent of a corset."

Manguel, Alberto. Review of *Albertine in Five Times,* by Michel Tremblay. *Books in Canada* 16, No. 4 (May, 1987): 22.
Considers the relevance of memory in *Albertine in Five Times.*

McGrath, Carmelita. "Caught in Suspension." *Books in Canada* 24, No. 2 (March, 1995): 38.
Review of *The First Quarter of the Moon,* observing that "Tremblay's particular gift . . . [is] to simultaneously enlarge a day into a world, and compress a world into a day."

Messenger, Ann P. Review of *La Duchesse de Langeais and Other Plays. Canadian Literature* 76 (Spring 1978): 101-04.
Briefly considers the various ways Tremblay uses the opportunities afforded by the short play genre.

Mitchell, Constantine. "Vues Animées." *Canadian Literature* 134 (Autumn, 1992): 171-73.
Finds *Les Vues animées* "an important contribution to understanding Tremblay's mature works."

O'Connor, John J. "Tremblay's Troupe." *Canadian Literature* 98 (Autumn 1983): 76-9.
Reviews translated editions of *The Fat Woman Next Door Is Pregnant, The Impromptu of Outremont, Damnée Manon Sacrée Sandra,* and *Sainte-Carmen of the Main.* Also includes positive review of *Les Anciennes Odeurs.*

Parker, Peter. "Sebastien Lives with Matthieu and Jean-Marc." *The Listener* 123, No. 3152 (15 February 1990): 34.
Denigrates *Making Room* as "sentimental, cliché-strewn and hollow."

Salmonson, Jessica Amanda. Review of *Stories for Late Night Drinkers. Fantasy Review* 9, No. 5 (May 1986): 25.
Praises the collection's "[wide] variety of characters" and "finely-honed construction and phrasing."

Solomon, Charles. Review of *Making Room. Los Angeles Times Book Review* (7 April 1991): 14.
Comments briefly on four-year-old Sebastien's role in the novel.

Townsend, Martin. Review of *The Real World?. Quill & Quire* 55, No. 3 (March 1989): 77.
Claims that *"The Real World?* reads a lot like Pirandello mired in melodrama."

Yhap, Beverly. Review of *La Maison suspendue. Quill & Quire* 58, No. 1 (January 1992): 28.
Finds the play "a brilliant accomplishment . . . but its brilliance is heightened further when seen in the context of a marvellous body of work."

Additional coverage of Tremblay's life and career is contained in the following sources published by Gale Research: *Contemporary Authors,* **Vols. 116 and 128;** *DISCovering Authors: Canadian; DISCovering Authors Modules: Most-Studied Authors; Dictionary of Literary Biography,* **Vol. 60; and** *Major Twentieth-Century Writers.*

☐ Contemporary Literary Criticism

Indexes

How to Use This Index

The main references

> Camus, Albert
> 1913-1960 . . . . CLC 1, 2, 4, 9, 11, 14,
> 32, 69; DA; DAB; DAC; DAM DRAM,
> MST, NOV; DC2; SSC 9; WLC

list all author entries in the following Gale Literary Criticism series:

BLC = *Black Literature Criticism*
CLC = *Contemporary Literary Criticism*
CLR = *Children's Literature Review*
CMLC = *Classical and Medieval Literature Criticism*
DA = *DISCovering Authors*
DAB = *DISCovering Authors: British*
DAC = *DISCovering Authors: Canadian*
DAM = *DISCovering Authors Modules*
  DRAM = *dramatists;* *MST* = *most-studied*
  authors; *MULT* = *multicultural authors;* *NOV* =
  novelists; *POET* = *poets;* *POP* = *popular/genre*
  writers; *DC* = *Drama Criticism*
HLC = *Hispanic Literature Criticism*
LC = *Literature Criticism from 1400 to 1800*
NCLC = *Nineteenth-Century Literature Criticism*
PC = *Poetry Criticism*
SSC = *Short Story Criticism*
TCLC = *Twentieth-Century Literary Criticism*
WLC = *World Literature Criticism, 1500 to the Present*

The cross-references

> See also CA 89-92; DLB 72; MTCW

list all author entries in the following Gale biographical and literary sources:

AAYA = *Authors & Artists for Young Adults*
AITN = *Authors in the News*
BEST = *Bestsellers*
BW = *Black Writers*
CA = *Contemporary Authors*
CAAS = *Contemporary Authors Autobiography Series*
CABS = *Contemporary Authors Bibliographical Series*
CANR = *Contemporary Authors New Revision Series*
CAP = *Contemporary Authors Permanent Series*
CDALB = *Concise Dictionary of American Literary Biography*
CDBLB = *Concise Dictionary of British Literary Biography*

DLB = *Dictionary of Literary Biography*
DLBD = *Dictionary of Literary Biography Documentary Series*
DLBY = *Dictionary of Literary Biography Yearbook*
HW = *Hispanic Writers*
JRDA = *Junior DISCovering Authors*
MAICYA = *Major Authors and Illustrators for Children and Young Adults*
MTCW = *Major 20th-Century Writers*
NNAL = *Native North American Literature*
SAAS = *Something about the Author Autobiography Series*
SATA = *Something about the Author*
YABC = *Yesterday's Authors of Books for Children*

Literary Criticism Series
Cumulative Author Index

Appleman, Philip (Dean) 1926- .... **CLC 51**
  See also CA 13-16R; CAAS 18; CANR 6, 29,
  56
Appleton, Lawrence
  See Lovecraft, H(oward) P(hillips)
Apteryx
  See Eliot, T(homas) S(tearns)
Apuleius, (Lucius Madaurensis) 125(?)-175(?)
  CMLC 1
Aquin, Hubert 1929-1977 .... **CLC 15**
  See also CA 105; DLB 53
Aragon, Louis 1897-1982 .. **CLC 3, 22; DAM
  NOV, POET**
  See also CA 69-72; 108; CANR 28; DLB 72;
  MTCW
Arany, Janos 1817-1882 .... **NCLC 34**
Arbuthnot, John 1667-1735 .... **LC 1**
  See also DLB 101
Archer, Herbert Winslow
  See Mencken, H(enry) L(ouis)
Archer, Jeffrey (Howard) 1940- ..... **CLC 28;
  DAM POP**
  See also AAYA 16; BEST 89:3; CA 77-80;
  CANR 22, 52; INT CANR-22
Archer, Jules 1915- .... **CLC 12**
  See also CA 9-12R; CANR 6; SAAS 5; SATA
  4, 85
Archer, Lee
  See Ellison, Harlan (Jay)
Arden, John 1930- **CLC 6, 13, 15; DAM DRAM**
  See also CA 13-16R; CAAS 4; CANR 31; DLB
  13; MTCW
Arenas, Reinaldo 1943-1990 . **CLC 41; DAM
  MULT; HLC**
  See also CA 124; 128; 133; DLB 145; HW
Arendt, Hannah 1906-1975 .... **CLC 66, 98**
  See also CA 17-20R; 61-64; CANR 26; MTCW
Aretino, Pietro 1492-1556 .... **LC 12**
Arghezi, Tudor .... **CLC 80**
  See also Theodorescu, Ion N.
Arguedas, Jose Maria 1911-1969 **CLC 10, 18**
  See also CA 89-92; DLB 113; HW
Argueta, Manlio 1936- .... **CLC 31**
  See also CA 131; DLB 145; HW
Ariosto, Ludovico 1474-1533 .... **LC 6**
Aristides
  See Epstein, Joseph
Aristophanes 450B.C.-385B.C.**CMLC 4; DA;
  DAB; DAC; DAM DRAM, MST; DC 2;
  WLCS**
  See also DLB 176
Arlt, Roberto (Godofredo Christophersen)
  1900-1942**TCLC 29; DAM MULT; HLC**
  See also CA 123; 131; HW
Armah, Ayi Kwei 1939-**CLC 5, 33; BLC; DAM
  MULT, POET**
  See also BW 1; CA 61-64; CANR 21; DLB 117;
  MTCW
Armatrading, Joan 1950- .... **CLC 17**
  See also CA 114
Arnette, Robert
  See Silverberg, Robert
Arnim, Achim von (Ludwig Joachim von
  Arnim) 1781-1831 .... **NCLC 5**
  See also DLB 90
Arnim, Bettina von 1785-1859 .... **NCLC 38**
  See also DLB 90
Arnold, Matthew 1822-1888**NCLC 6, 29; DA;
  DAB; DAC; DAM MST, POET; PC 5;
  WLC**
  See also CDBLB 1832-1890; DLB 32, 57
Arnold, Thomas 1795-1842 .... **NCLC 18**
  See also DLB 55

Arnow, Harriette (Louisa) Simpson 1908-1986
  CLC 2, 7, 18
  See also CA 9-12R; 118; CANR 14; DLB 6;
  MTCW; SATA 42; SATA-Obit 47
Arp, Hans
  See Arp, Jean
Arp, Jean 1887-1966 .... **CLC 5**
  See also CA 81-84; 25-28R; CANR 42
Arrabal
  See Arrabal, Fernando
Arrabal, Fernando 1932- .... **CLC 2, 9, 18, 58**
  See also CA 9-12R; CANR 15
Arrick, Fran .... **CLC 30**
  See also Gaberman, Judie Angell
Artaud, Antonin (Marie Joseph) 1896-1948
  TCLC 3, 36; DAM DRAM
  See also CA 104; 149
Arthur, Ruth M(abel) 1905-1979 ...... **CLC 12**
  See also CA 9-12R; 85-88; CANR 4; SATA 7,
  26
Artsybashev, Mikhail (Petrovich) 1878-1927
  TCLC 31
Arundel, Honor (Morfydd) 1919-1973**CLC 17**
  See also CA 21-22; 41-44R; CAP 2; CLR 35;
  SATA 4; SATA-Obit 24
Arzner, Dorothy 1897-1979 .... **CLC 98**
Asch, Sholem 1880-1957 .... **TCLC 3**
  See also CA 105
Ash, Shalom
  See Asch, Sholem
Ashbery, John (Lawrence) 1927-**CLC 2, 3, 4,
  6, 9, 13, 15, 25, 41, 77; DAM POET**
  See also CA 5-8R; CANR 9, 37; DLB 5, 165;
  DLBY 81; INT CANR-9; MTCW
Ashdown, Clifford
  See Freeman, R(ichard) Austin
Ashe, Gordon
  See Creasey, John
Ashton-Warner, Sylvia (Constance) 1908-1984
  CLC 19
  See also CA 69-72; 112; CANR 29; MTCW
Asimov, Isaac 1920-1992 **CLC 1, 3, 9, 19, 26,
  76, 92; DAM POP**
  See also AAYA 13; BEST 90:2; CA 1-4R; 137;
  CANR 2, 19, 36; CLR 12; DLB 8; DLBY
  92; INT CANR-19; JRDA; MAICYA;
  MTCW; SATA 1, 26, 74
Assis, Joaquim Maria Machado de
  See Machado de Assis, Joaquim Maria
Astley, Thea (Beatrice May) 1925- ... **CLC 41**
  See also CA 65-68; CANR 11, 43
Aston, James
  See White, T(erence) H(anbury)
Asturias, Miguel Angel 1899-1974 **CLC 3, 8,
  13; DAM MULT, NOV; HLC**
  See also CA 25-28; 49-52; CANR 32; CAP 2;
  DLB 113; HW; MTCW
Atares, Carlos Saura
  See Saura (Atares), Carlos
Atheling, William
  See Pound, Ezra (Weston Loomis)
Atheling, William, Jr.
  See Blish, James (Benjamin)
Atherton, Gertrude (Franklin Horn) 1857-1948
  TCLC 2
  See also CA 104; 155; DLB 9, 78
Atherton, Lucius
  See Masters, Edgar Lee
Atkins, Jack
  See Harris, Mark
Atkinson, Kate .... **CLC 99**
Attaway, William (Alexander) 1911-1986**CLC
  92; BLC; DAM MULT**

See also BW 2; CA 143; DLB 76
Atticus
  See Fleming, Ian (Lancaster)
Atwood, Margaret (Eleanor) 1939-**CLC 2, 3,
  4, 8, 13, 15, 25, 44, 84; DA; DAB; DAC;
  DAM MST, NOV, POET; PC 8; SSC 2;
  WLC**
  See also AAYA 12; BEST 89:2; CA 49-52;
  CANR 3, 24, 33, 59; DLB 53; INT CANR-
  24; MTCW; SATA 50
Aubigny, Pierre d'
  See Mencken, H(enry) L(ouis)
Aubin, Penelope 1685-1731(?) .... **LC 9**
  See also DLB 39
Auchincloss, Louis (Stanton) 1917-**CLC 4, 6,
  9, 18, 45; DAM NOV; SSC 22**
  See also CA 1-4R; CANR 6, 29, 55; DLB 2;
  DLBY 80; INT CANR-29; MTCW
Auden, W(ystan) H(ugh) 1907-1973**CLC 1, 2,
  3, 4, 6, 9, 11, 14, 43; DA; DAB; DAC; DAM
  DRAM, MST, POET; PC 1; WLC**
  See also AAYA 18; CA 9-12R; 45-48; CANR
  5; CDBLB 1914-1945; DLB 10, 20; MTCW
Audiberti, Jacques 1900-1965**CLC 38; DAM
  DRAM**
  See also CA 25-28R
Audubon, John James 1785-1851 .. **NCLC 47**
Auel, Jean M(arie) 1936-**CLC 31; DAM POP**
  See also AAYA 7; BEST 90:4; CA 103; CANR
  21; INT CANR-21; SATA 91
Auerbach, Erich 1892-1957 .... **TCLC 43**
  See also CA 118; 155
Augier, Emile 1820-1889 .... **NCLC 31**
August, John
  See De Voto, Bernard (Augustine)
Augustine, St. 354-430 .... **CMLC 6; DAB**
Aurelius
  See Bourne, Randolph S(illiman)
Aurobindo, Sri 1872-1950 .... **TCLC 63**
Austen, Jane 1775-1817 **NCLC 1, 13, 19, 33,
  51; DA; DAB; DAC; DAM MST, NOV;
  WLC**
  See also AAYA 19; CDBLB 1789-1832; DLB
  116
Auster, Paul 1947- .... **CLC 47**
  See also CA 69-72; CANR 23, 52
Austin, Frank
  See Faust, Frederick (Schiller)
Austin, Mary (Hunter) 1868-1934 . **TCLC 25**
  See also CA 109; DLB 9, 78
Autran Dourado, Waldomiro
  See Dourado, (Waldomiro Freitas) Autran
Averroes 1126-1198 .... **CMLC 7**
  See also DLB 115
Avicenna 980-1037 .... **CMLC 16**
  See also DLB 115
Avison, Margaret 1918- **CLC 2, 4, 97; DAC;
  DAM POET**
  See also CA 17-20R; DLB 53; MTCW
Axton, David
  See Koontz, Dean R(ay)
Ayckbourn, Alan 1939- **CLC 5, 8, 18, 33, 74;
  DAB; DAM DRAM**
  See also CA 21-24R; CANR 31, 59; DLB 13;
  MTCW
Aydy, Catherine
  See Tennant, Emma (Christina)
Ayme, Marcel (Andre) 1902-1967 .... **CLC 11**
  See also CA 89-92; CLR 25; DLB 72; SATA 91
Ayrton, Michael 1921-1975 .... **CLC 7**
  See also CA 5-8R; 61-64; CANR 9, 21
Azorin .... **CLC 11**
  See also Martinez Ruiz, Jose

Blacklin, Malcolm
See Chambers, Aidan

Blackmore, R(ichard) D(oddridge) 1825-1900
TCLC 27
See also CA 120; DLB 18

Blackmur, R(ichard) P(almer) 1904-1965
CLC 2, 24
See also CA 11-12; 25-28R; CAP 1; DLB 63

Black Tarantula
See Acker, Kathy

Blackwood, Algernon (Henry) 1869-1951
TCLC 5
See also CA 105; 150; DLB 153, 156, 178

Blackwood, Caroline 1931-1996 **CLC 6, 9, 100**
See also CA 85-88; 151; CANR 32; DLB 14;
MTCW

Blade, Alexander
See Hamilton, Edmond; Silverberg, Robert

Blaga, Lucian 1895-1961 .... **CLC 75**

Blair, Eric (Arthur) 1903-1950
See Orwell, George
See also CA 104; 132; DA; DAB; DAC; DAM
MST, NOV; MTCW; SATA 29

Blais, Marie-Claire 1939- **CLC 2, 4, 6, 13, 22;**
DAC; DAM MST
See also CA 21-24R; CAAS 4; CANR 38; DLB
53; MTCW

Blaise, Clark 1940- .... **CLC 29**
See also AITN 2; CA 53-56; CAAS 3; CANR
5; DLB 53

Blake, Nicholas
See Day Lewis, C(ecil)
See also DLB 77

Blake, William 1757-1827. **NCLC 13, 37, 57;**
DA; DAB; DAC; DAM MST, POET; PC
12; WLC
See also CDBLB 1789-1832; DLB 93, 163;
MAICYA; SATA 30

Blake, William J(ames) 1894-1969 ...... **PC 12**
See also CA 5-8R; 25-28R

Blasco Ibanez, Vicente 1867-1928 **TCLC 12;**
DAM NOV
See also CA 110; 131; HW; MTCW

Blatty, William Peter 1928- **CLC 2; DAM POP**
See also CA 5-8R; CANR 9

Bleeck, Oliver
See Thomas, Ross (Elmore)

Blessing, Lee 1949- .... **CLC 54**

Blish, James (Benjamin) 1921-1975. **CLC 14**
See also CA 1-4R; 57-60; CANR 3; DLB 8;
MTCW; SATA 66

Bliss, Reginald
See Wells, H(erbert) G(eorge)

Blixen, Karen (Christentze Dinesen) 1885-1962
See Dinesen, Isak
See also CA 25-28; CANR 22, 50; CAP 2;
MTCW; SATA 44

Bloch, Robert (Albert) 1917-1994 .... **CLC 33**
See also CA 5-8R; 146; CAAS 20; CANR 5;
DLB 44; INT CANR-5; SATA 12; SATA-Obit
82

Blok, Alexander (Alexandrovich) 1880-1921
TCLC 5
See also CA 104

Blom, Jan
See Breytenbach, Breyten

Bloom, Harold 1930- .... **CLC 24**
See also CA 13-16R; CANR 39; DLB 67

Bloomfield, Aurelius
See Bourne, Randolph S(illiman)

Blount, Roy (Alton), Jr. 1941- .... **CLC 38**
See also CA 53-56; CANR 10, 28; INT CANR-
28; MTCW

Bloy, Leon 1846-1917 .... **TCLC 22**
See also CA 121; DLB 123

Blume, Judy (Sussman) 1938- .. **CLC 12, 30;**
DAM NOV, POP
See also AAYA 3; CA 29-32R; CANR 13, 37;
CLR 2, 15; DLB 52; JRDA; MAICYA;
MTCW; SATA 2, 31, 79

Blunden, Edmund (Charles) 1896-1974 **C L C**
2, 56
See also CA 17-18; 45-48; CANR 54; CAP 2;
DLB 20, 100, 155; MTCW

Bly, Robert (Elwood) 1926- **CLC 1, 2, 5, 10, 15,**
38; DAM POET
See also CA 5-8R; CANR 41; DLB 5; MTCW

Boas, Franz 1858-1942 .... **TCLC 56**
See also CA 115

Bobette
See Simenon, Georges (Jacques Christian)

Boccaccio, Giovanni 1313-1375 ... **CMLC 13;**
SSC 10

Bochco, Steven 1943- .... **CLC 35**
See also AAYA 11; CA 124; 138

Bodenheim, Maxwell 1892-1954 .... **TCLC 44**
See also CA 110; DLB 9, 45

Bodker, Cecil 1927- .... **CLC 21**
See also CA 73-76; CANR 13, 44; CLR 23;
MAICYA; SATA 14

Boell, Heinrich (Theodor) 1917-1985 **CLC 2,**
3, 6, 9, 11, 15, 27, 32, 72; DA; DAB; DAC;
DAM MST, NOV; SSC 23; WLC
See also CA 21-24R; 116; CANR 24; DLB 69;
DLBY 85; MTCW

Boerne, Alfred
See Doeblin, Alfred

Boethius 480(?)-524(?) .... **CMLC 15**
See also DLB 115

Bogan, Louise 1897-1970. **CLC 4, 39, 46, 93;**
DAM POET; PC 12
See also CA 73-76; 25-28R; CANR 33; DLB
45, 169; MTCW

Bogarde, Dirk .... **CLC 19**
See also Van Den Bogarde, Derek Jules Gaspard
Ulric Niven
See also DLB 14

Bogosian, Eric 1953- .... **CLC 45**
See also CA 138

Bograd, Larry 1953- .... **CLC 35**
See also CA 93-96; CANR 57; SAAS 21; SATA
33, 89

Boiardo, Matteo Maria 1441-1494 .... **LC 6**

Boileau-Despreaux, Nicolas 1636-1711. **LC 3**

Bojer, Johan 1872-1959 .... **TCLC 64**

Boland, Eavan (Aisling) 1944- .. **CLC 40, 67;**
DAM POET
See also CA 143; DLB 40

Bolt, Lee
See Faust, Frederick (Schiller)

Bolt, Robert (Oxton) 1924-1995 **CLC 14; DAM**
DRAM
See also CA 17-20R; 147; CANR 35; DLB 13;
MTCW

Bombet, Louis-Alexandre-Cesar
See Stendhal

Bomkauf
See Kaufman, Bob (Garnell)

Bonaventura .... **NCLC 35**
See also DLB 90

Bond, Edward 1934- **CLC 4, 6, 13, 23; DAM**
DRAM
See also CA 25-28R; CANR 38; DLB 13;
MTCW

Bonham, Frank 1914-1989 .... **CLC 12**
See also AAYA 1; CA 9-12R; CANR 4, 36;

JRDA; MAICYA; SAAS 3; SATA 1, 49;
SATA-Obit 62

Bonnefoy, Yves 1923-... **CLC 9, 15, 58; DAM**
MST, POET
See also CA 85-88; CANR 33; MTCW

Bontemps, Arna(ud Wendell) 1902-1973 **C L C**
1, 18; BLC; DAM MULT, NOV, POET
See also BW 1; CA 1-4R; 41-44R; CANR 4,
35; CLR 6; DLB 48, 51; JRDA; MAICYA;
MTCW; SATA 2, 44; SATA-Obit 24

Booth, Martin 1944- .... **CLC 13**
See also CA 93-96; CAAS 2

Booth, Philip 1925- .... **CLC 23**
See also CA 5-8R; CANR 5; DLBY 82

Booth, Wayne C(layson) 1921- .... **CLC 24**
See also CA 1-4R; CAAS 5; CANR 3, 43; DLB
67

Borchert, Wolfgang 1921-1947 .... **TCLC 5**
See also CA 104; DLB 69, 124

Borel, Petrus 1809-1859 .... **NCLC 41**

Borges, Jorge Luis 1899-1986 **CLC 1, 2, 3, 4, 6,**
8, 9, 10, 13, 19, 44, 48, 83; DA; DAB; DAC;
DAM MST, MULT; HLC; SSC 4; WLC
See also AAYA 19; CA 21-24R; CANR 19, 33;
DLB 113; DLBY 86; HW; MTCW

Borowski, Tadeusz 1922-1951 .... **TCLC 9**
See also CA 106; 154

Borrow, George (Henry) 1803-1881 **NCLC 9**
See also DLB 21, 55, 166

Bosman, Herman Charles 1905-1951 **T C L C**
49

Bosschere, Jean de 1878(?)-1953 ... **TCLC 19**
See also CA 115

Boswell, James 1740-1795. **LC 4; DA; DAB;**
DAC; DAM MST; WLC
See also CDBLB 1660-1789; DLB 104, 142

Bottoms, David 1949- .... **CLC 53**
See also CA 105; CANR 22; DLB 120; DLBY
83

Boucicault, Dion 1820-1890 .... **NCLC 41**

Boucolon, Maryse 1937(?)-
See Conde, Maryse
See also CA 110; CANR 30, 53

Bourget, Paul (Charles Joseph) 1852-1935
TCLC 12
See also CA 107; DLB 123

Bourjaily, Vance (Nye) 1922- .... **CLC 8, 62**
See also CA 1-4R; CAAS 1; CANR 2; DLB 2,
143

Bourne, Randolph S(illiman) 1886-1918
TCLC 16
See also CA 117; 155; DLB 63

Bova, Ben(jamin William) 1932- ...... **CLC 45**
See also AAYA 16; CA 5-8R; CAAS 18; CANR
11, 56; CLR 3; DLBY 81; INT CANR-11;
MAICYA; MTCW; SATA 6, 68

Bowen, Elizabeth (Dorothea Cole) 1899-1973
CLC 1, 3, 6, 11, 15, 22; DAM NOV; SSC 3
See also CA 17-18; 41-44R; CANR 35; CAP 2;
CDBLB 1945-1960; DLB 15, 162; MTCW

Bowering, George 1935- .... **CLC 15, 47**
See also CA 21-24R; CAAS 16; CANR 10; DLB
53

Bowering, Marilyn R(uthe) 1949- .... **CLC 32**
See also CA 101; CANR 49

Bowers, Edgar 1924- .... **CLC 9**
See also CA 5-8R; CANR 24; DLB 5

Bowie, David .... **CLC 17**
See also Jones, David Robert

Bowles, Jane (Sydney) 1917-1973 **CLC 3, 68**
See also CA 19-20; 41-44R; CAP 2

Bowles, Paul (Frederick) 1910- **CLC 1, 2, 19,**
53; SSC 3

Bustos, F(rancisco)
See Borges, Jorge Luis
Bustos Domecq, H(onorio)
See Bioy Casares, Adolfo; Borges, Jorge Luis
Butler, Octavia E(stelle) 1947-**CLC 38; DAM MULT, POP**
See also AAYA 18; BW 2; CA 73-76; CANR 12, 24, 38; DLB 33; MTCW; SATA 84
Butler, Robert Olen (Jr.) 1945-**CLC 81; DAM POP**
See also CA 112; DLB 173; INT 112
Butler, Samuel 1612-1680 .... **LC 16**
See also DLB 101, 126
Butler, Samuel 1835-1902 . **TCLC 1, 33; DA; DAB; DAC; DAM MST, NOV; WLC**
See also CA 143; CDBLB 1890-1914; DLB 18, 57, 174
Butler, Walter C.
See Faust, Frederick (Schiller)
Butor, Michel (Marie Francois) 1926-**CLC 1, 3, 8, 11, 15**
See also CA 9-12R; CANR 33; DLB 83; MTCW
Buzo, Alexander (John) 1944- .... **CLC 61**
See also CA 97-100; CANR 17, 39
Buzzati, Dino 1906-1972 .... **CLC 36**
See also CA 33-36R; DLB 177
Byars, Betsy (Cromer) 1928- .... **CLC 35**
See also AAYA 19; CA 33-36R; CANR 18, 36, 57; CLR 1, 16; DLB 52; INT CANR-18; JRDA; MAICYA; MTCW; SAAS 1; SATA 4, 46, 80
Byatt, A(ntonia) S(usan Drabble) 1936- **C L C 19, 65; DAM NOV, POP**
See also CA 13-16R; CANR 13, 33, 50; DLB 14; MTCW
Byrne, David 1952- .... **CLC 26**
See also CA 127
Byrne, John Keyes 1926-
See Leonard, Hugh
See also CA 102; INT 102
Byron, George Gordon (Noel) 1788-1824 **NCLC 2, 12; DA; DAB; DAC; DAM MST, POET; PC 16; WLC**
See also CDBLB 1789-1832; DLB 96, 110
Byron, Robert 1905-1941 .... **TCLC 67**
C. 3. 3.
See Wilde, Oscar (Fingal O'Flahertie Wills)
Caballero, Fernan 1796-1877 .... **NCLC 10**
Cabell, Branch
See Cabell, James Branch
Cabell, James Branch 1879-1958 .... **TCLC 6**
See also CA 105; 152; DLB 9, 78
Cable, George Washington 1844-1925 **T C L C 4; SSC 4**
See also CA 104; 155; DLB 12, 74; DLBD 13
Cabral de Melo Neto, Joao 1920- ... **CLC 76; DAM MULT**
See also CA 151
Cabrera Infante, G(uillermo) 1929-.. **CLC 5, 25, 45; DAM MULT; HLC**
See also CA 85-88; CANR 29; DLB 113; HW; MTCW
Cade, Toni
See Bambara, Toni Cade
Cadmus and Harmonia
See Buchan, John
Caedmon fl. 658-680 .... **CMLC 7**
See also DLB 146
Caeiro, Alberto
See Pessoa, Fernando (Antonio Nogueira)
Cage, John (Milton, Jr.) 1912- .... **CLC 41**
See also CA 13-16R; CANR 9; INT CANR-9
Cahan, Abraham 1860-1951 .... **TCLC 71**

See also CA 108; 154; DLB 9, 25, 28
Cain, G.
See Cabrera Infante, G(uillermo)
Cain, Guillermo
See Cabrera Infante, G(uillermo)
Cain, James M(allahan) 1892-1977**CLC 3, 11, 28**
See also AITN 1; CA 17-20R; 73-76; CANR 8, 34; MTCW
Caine, Mark
See Raphael, Frederic (Michael)
Calasso, Roberto 1941- .... **CLC 81**
See also CA 143
Calderon de la Barca, Pedro 1600-1681 .. **L C 23; DC 3**
Caldwell, Erskine (Preston) 1903-1987**CLC 1, 8, 14, 50, 60; DAM NOV; SSC 19**
See also AITN 1; CA 1-4R; 121; CAAS 1; CANR 2, 33; DLB 9, 86; MTCW
Caldwell, (Janet Miriam) Taylor (Holland) 1900-1985**CLC 2, 28, 39; DAM NOV, POP**
See also CA 5-8R; 116; CANR 5
Calhoun, John Caldwell 1782-1850**NCLC 15**
See also DLB 3
Calisher, Hortense 1911-**CLC 2, 4, 8, 38; DAM NOV; SSC 15**
See also CA 1-4R; CANR 1, 22; DLB 2; INT CANR-22; MTCW
Callaghan, Morley Edward 1903-1990**CLC 3, 14, 41, 65; DAC; DAM MST**
See also CA 9-12R; 132; CANR 33; DLB 68; MTCW
Callimachus c. 305B.C.-c. 240B.C. **CMLC 18**
See also DLB 176
Calvin, John 1509-1564 .... **LC 37**
Calvino, Italo 1923-1985**CLC 5, 8, 11, 22, 33, 39, 73; DAM NOV; SSC 3**
See also CA 85-88; 116; CANR 23; MTCW
Cameron, Carey 1952- .... **CLC 59**
See also CA 135
Cameron, Peter 1959- .... **CLC 44**
See also CA 125; CANR 50
Campana, Dino 1885-1932 .... **TCLC 20**
See also CA 117; DLB 114
Campanella, Tommaso 1568-1639 .... **LC 32**
Campbell, John W(ood, Jr.) 1910-1971 **C L C 32**
See also CA 21-22; 29-32R; CANR 34; CAP 2; DLB 8; MTCW
Campbell, Joseph 1904-1987 .... **CLC 69**
See also AAYA 3; BEST 89:2; CA 1-4R; 124; CANR 3, 28; MTCW
Campbell, Maria 1940- .... **CLC 85; DAC**
See also CA 102; CANR 54; NNAL
Campbell, (John) Ramsey 1946-**CLC 42; SSC 19**
See also CA 57-60; CANR 7; INT CANR-7
Campbell, (Ignatius) Roy (Dunnachie) 1901-1957 .... **TCLC 5**
See also CA 104; 155; DLB 20
Campbell, Thomas 1777-1844 .... **NCLC 19**
See also DLB 93; 144
Campbell, Wilfred .... **TCLC 9**
See also Campbell, William
Campbell, William 1858(?)-1918
See Campbell, Wilfred
See also CA 106; DLB 92
Campion, Jane .... **CLC 95**
See also CA 138
Campos, Alvaro de
See Pessoa, Fernando (Antonio Nogueira)
Camus, Albert 1913-1960**CLC 1, 2, 4, 9, 11, 14, 32, 63, 69; DA; DAB; DAC; DAM DRAM,**

MST, NOV; DC 2; SSC 9; WLC
See also CA 89-92; DLB 72; MTCW
Canby, Vincent 1924- .... **CLC 13**
See also CA 81-84
Cancale
See Desnos, Robert
Canetti, Elias 1905-1994**CLC 3, 14, 25, 75, 86**
See also CA 21-24R; 146; CANR 23; DLB 85, 124; MTCW
Canin, Ethan 1960- .... **CLC 55**
See also CA 131; 135
Cannon, Curt
See Hunter, Evan
Cape, Judith
See Page, P(atricia) K(athleen)
Capek, Karel 1890-1938 ... **TCLC 6, 37; DA; DAB; DAC; DAM DRAM, MST, NOV; DC 1; WLC**
See also CA 104; 140
Capote, Truman 1924-1984**CLC 1, 3, 8, 13, 19, 34, 38, 58; DA; DAB; DAC; DAM MST, NOV, POP; SSC 2; WLC**
See also CA 5-8R; 113; CANR 18; CDALB 1941-1968; DLB 2; DLBY 80, 84; MTCW; SATA 91
Capra, Frank 1897-1991 .... **CLC 16**
See also CA 61-64; 135
Caputo, Philip 1941- .... **CLC 32**
See also CA 73-76; CANR 40
Card, Orson Scott 1951-**CLC 44, 47, 50; DAM POP**
See also AAYA 11; CA 102; CANR 27, 47; INT CANR-27; MTCW; SATA 83
Cardenal, Ernesto 1925- .... **CLC 31; DAM MULT, POET; HLC**
See also CA 49-52; CANR 2, 32; HW; MTCW
Cardozo, Benjamin N(athan) 1870-1938 **TCLC 65**
See also CA 117
Carducci, Giosue 1835-1907 .... **TCLC 32**
Carew, Thomas 1595(?)-1640 .... **LC 13**
See also DLB 126
Carey, Ernestine Gilbreth 1908- .... **CLC 17**
See also CA 5-8R; SATA 2
Carey, Peter 1943- .... **CLC 40, 55, 96**
See also CA 123; 127; CANR 53; INT 127; MTCW; SATA 94
Carleton, William 1794-1869 .... **NCLC 3**
See also DLB 159
Carlisle, Henry (Coffin) 1926- .... **CLC 33**
See also CA 13-16R; CANR 15
Carlsen, Chris
See Holdstock, Robert P.
Carlson, Ron(ald F.) 1947- .... **CLC 54**
See also CA 105; CANR 27
Carlyle, Thomas 1795-1881 . **NCLC 22; DA; DAB; DAC; DAM MST**
See also CDBLB 1789-1832; DLB 55; 144
Carman, (William) Bliss 1861-1929 **TCLC 7; DAC**
See also CA 104; 152; DLB 92
Carnegie, Dale 1888-1955 .... **TCLC 53**
Carossa, Hans 1878-1956 .... **TCLC 48**
See also DLB 66
Carpenter, Don(ald Richard) 1931-1995**C L C 41**
See also CA 45-48; 149; CANR 1
Carpentier (y Valmont), Alejo 1904-1980**CLC 8, 11, 38; DAM MULT; HLC**
See also CA 65-68; 97-100; CANR 11; DLB 113; HW
Carr, Caleb 1955(?)- .... **CLC 86**
See also CA 147

See also CA 13-16; 41-44R; CAP 1; SATA 10
Chase, Nicholas
See Hyde, Anthony
Chateaubriand, Francois Rene de 1768-1848
NCLC 3
See also DLB 119
Chatterje, Sarat Chandra 1876-1936(?)
See Chatterji, Saratchandra
See also CA 109
Chatterji, Bankim Chandra 1838-1894**NCLC 19**
Chatterji, Saratchandra .... **TCLC 13**
See also Chatterje, Sarat Chandra
Chatterton, Thomas 1752-1770 . **LC 3; DAM POET**
See also DLB 109
Chatwin, (Charles) Bruce 1940-1989**CLC 28, 57, 59; DAM POP**
See also AAYA 4; BEST 90:1; CA 85-88; 127
Chaucer, Daniel
See Ford, Ford Madox
Chaucer, Geoffrey 1340(?)-1400 **LC 17; DA; DAB; DAC; DAM MST, POET; PC 19; WLCS**
See also CDBLB Before 1660; DLB 146
Chaviaras, Strates 1935-
See Haviaras, Stratis
See also CA 105
Chayefsky, Paddy .... **CLC 23**
See also Chayefsky, Sidney
See also DLB 7, 44; DLBY 81
Chayefsky, Sidney 1923-1981
See Chayefsky, Paddy
See also CA 9-12R; 104; CANR 18; DAM DRAM
Chedid, Andree 1920- .... **CLC 47**
See also CA 145
Cheever, John 1912-1982 **CLC 3, 7, 8, 11, 15, 25, 64; DA; DAB; DAC; DAM MST, NOV, POP; SSC 1; WLC**
See also CA 5-8R; 106; CABS 1; CANR 5, 27; CDALB 1941-1968; DLB 2, 102; DLBY 80, 82; INT CANR-5; MTCW
Cheever, Susan 1943- .... **CLC 18, 48**
See also CA 103; CANR 27, 51; DLBY 82; INT CANR-27
Chekhonte, Antosha
See Chekhov, Anton (Pavlovich)
Chekhov, Anton (Pavlovich) 1860-1904**TCLC 3, 10, 31, 55; DA; DAB; DAC; DAM DRAM, MST; SSC 2; WLC**
See also CA 104; 124; SATA 90
Chernyshevsky, Nikolay Gavrilovich 1828-1889
NCLC 1
Cherry, Carolyn Janice 1942-
See Cherryh, C. J.
See also CA 65-68; CANR 10
Cherryh, C. J. .... **CLC 35**
See also Cherry, Carolyn Janice
See also DLBY 80; SATA 93
Chesnutt, Charles W(addell) 1858-1932
TCLC 5, 39; BLC; DAM MULT; SSC 7
See also BW 1; CA 106; 125; DLB 12, 50, 78; MTCW
Chester, Alfred 1929(?)-1971 .... **CLC 49**
See also CA 33-36R; DLB 130
Chesterton, G(ilbert) K(eith) 1874-1936
TCLC 1, 6, 64; DAM NOV, POET; SSC 1
See also CA 104; 132; CDBLB 1914-1945; DLB 10, 19, 34, 70, 98, 149, 178; MTCW; SATA 27
Chiang Pin-chin 1904-1986
See Ding Ling

See also CA 118
Ch'ien Chung-shu 1910- .... **CLC 22**
See also CA 130; MTCW
Child, L. Maria
See Child, Lydia Maria
Child, Lydia Maria 1802-1880 .... **NCLC 6**
See also DLB 1, 74; SATA 67
Child, Mrs.
See Child, Lydia Maria
Child, Philip 1898-1978 .... **CLC 19, 68**
See also CA 13-14; CAP 1; SATA 47
Childers, (Robert) Erskine 1870-1922 **T C L C 65**
See also CA 113; 153; DLB 70
Childress, Alice 1920-1994**CLC 12, 15, 86, 96; BLC; DAM DRAM, MULT, NOV; DC 4**
See also AAYA 8; BW 2; CA 45-48; 146; CANR 3, 27, 50; CLR 14; DLB 7, 38; JRDA; MAICYA; MTCW; SATA 7, 48, 81
Chin, Frank (Chew, Jr.) 1940- .... **DC 7**
See also CA 33-36R; DAM MULT
Chislett, (Margaret) Anne 1943- ...... **CLC 34**
See also CA 151
Chitty, Thomas Willes 1926- .... **CLC 11**
See also Hinde, Thomas
See also CA 5-8R
Chivers, Thomas Holley 1809-1858**NCLC 49**
See also DLB 3
Chomette, Rene Lucien 1898-1981
See Clair, Rene
See also CA 103
Chopin, Kate TCLC 5, 14; DA; DAB; SSC 8; WLCS
See also Chopin, Katherine
See also CDALB 1865-1917; DLB 12, 78
Chopin, Katherine 1851-1904
See Chopin, Kate
See also CA 104; 122; DAC; DAM MST, NOV
Chretien de Troyes c. 12th cent. -.. **CMLC 10**
Christie
See Ichikawa, Kon
Christie, Agatha (Mary Clarissa) 1890-1976
CLC 1, 6, 8, 12, 39, 48; DAB; DAC; DAM NOV
See also AAYA 9; AITN 1, 2; CA 17-20R; 61-64; CANR 10, 37; CDBLB 1914-1945; DLB 13, 77; MTCW; SATA 36
Christie, (Ann) Philippa
See Pearce, Philippa
See also CA 5-8R; CANR 4
Christine de Pizan 1365(?)-1431(?) .... **LC 9**
Chubb, Elmer
See Masters, Edgar Lee
Chulkov, Mikhail Dmitrievich 1743-1792**LC 2**
See also DLB 150
Churchill, Caryl 1938- ..... **CLC 31, 55; DC 5**
See also CA 102; CANR 22, 46; DLB 13; MTCW
Churchill, Charles 1731-1764 .... **LC 3**
See also DLB 109
Chute, Carolyn 1947- .... **CLC 39**
See also CA 123
Ciardi, John (Anthony) 1916-1986 . **CLC 10, 40, 44; DAM POET**
See also CA 5-8R; 118; CAAS 2; CANR 5, 33; CLR 19; DLB 5; DLBY 86; INT CANR-5; MAICYA; MTCW; SATA 1, 65; SATA-Obit 46
Cicero, Marcus Tullius 106B.C.-43B.C.
CMLC 3
Cimino, Michael 1943- .... **CLC 16**
See also CA 105
Cioran, E(mil) M. 1911-1995 .... **CLC 64**

See also CA 25-28R; 149
Cisneros, Sandra 1954-**CLC 69; DAM MULT; HLC**
See also AAYA 9; CA 131; DLB 122, 152; HW
Cixous, Helene 1937- .... **CLC 92**
See also CA 126; CANR 55; DLB 83; MTCW
Clair, Rene .... **CLC 20**
See also Chomette, Rene Lucien
Clampitt, Amy 1920-1994 ..... **CLC 32; PC 19**
See also CA 110; 146; CANR 29; DLB 105
Clancy, Thomas L., Jr. 1947-
See Clancy, Tom
See also CA 125; 131; INT 131; MTCW
Clancy, Tom .... **CLC 45; DAM NOV, POP**
See also Clancy, Thomas L., Jr.
See also AAYA 9; BEST 89:1, 90:1
Clare, John 1793-1864 **NCLC 9; DAB; DAM POET**
See also DLB 55, 96
Clarin
See Alas (y Urena), Leopoldo (Enrique Garcia)
Clark, Al C.
See Goines, Donald
Clark, (Robert) Brian 1932- .... **CLC 29**
See also CA 41-44R
Clark, Curt
See Westlake, Donald E(dwin)
Clark, Eleanor 1913-1996 ....**CLC 5, 19**
See also CA 9-12R; 151; CANR 41; DLB 6
Clark, J. P.
See Clark, John Pepper
See also DLB 117
Clark, John Pepper 1935- ...... **CLC 38; BLC; DAM DRAM, MULT; DC 5**
See also Clark, J. P.
See also BW 1; CA 65-68; CANR 16
Clark, M. R.
See Clark, Mavis Thorpe
Clark, Mavis Thorpe 1909- .... **CLC 12**
See also CA 57-60; CANR 8, 37; CLR 30; MAICYA; SAAS 5; SATA 8, 74
Clark, Walter Van Tilburg 1909-1971**CLC 28**
See also CA 9-12R; 33-36R; DLB 9; SATA 8
Clarke, Arthur C(harles) 1917-**CLC 1, 4, 13, 18, 35; DAM POP; SSC 3**
See also AAYA 4; CA 1-4R; CANR 2, 28, 55; JRDA; MAICYA; MTCW; SATA 13, 70
Clarke, Austin 1896-1974 .... **CLC 6, 9; DAM POET**
See also CA 29-32; 49-52; CAP 2; DLB 10, 20
Clarke, Austin C(hesterfield) 1934-**CLC 8, 53; BLC; DAC; DAM MULT**
See also BW 1; CA 25-28R; CAAS 16; CANR 14, 32; DLB 53, 125
Clarke, Gillian 1937- .... **CLC 61**
See also CA 106; DLB 40
Clarke, Marcus (Andrew Hislop) 1846-1881
NCLC 19
Clarke, Shirley 1925- .... **CLC 16**
Clash, The
See Headon, (Nicky) Topper; Jones, Mick; Simonon, Paul; Strummer, Joe
Claudel, Paul (Louis Charles Marie) 1868-1955
TCLC 2, 10
See also CA 104
Clavell, James (duMaresq) 1925-1994**CLC 6, 25, 87; DAM NOV, POP**
See also CA 25-28R; 146; CANR 26, 48; MTCW
Cleaver, (Leroy) Eldridge 1935- ..... **CLC 30; BLC; DAM MULT**
See also BW 1; CA 21-24R; CANR 16
Cleese, John (Marwood) 1939- .... **CLC 21**

See also Monty Python
See also CA 112; 116; CANR 35; MTCW
Cleishbotham, Jebediah
See Scott, Walter
Cleland, John 1710-1789 .... **LC 2**
See also DLB 39
Clemens, Samuel Langhorne 1835-1910
See Twain, Mark
See also CA 104; 135; CDALB 1865-1917; DA;
DAB; DAC; DAM MST, NOV; DLB 11, 12,
23, 64, 74; JRDA; MAICYA; YABC 2
Cleophil
See Congreve, William
Clerihew, E.
See Bentley, E(dmund) C(lerihew)
Clerk, N. W.
See Lewis, C(live) S(taples)
Cliff, Jimmy .... **CLC 21**
See also Chambers, James
Clifton, (Thelma) Lucille 1936- **CLC 19, 66;
BLC; DAM MULT, POET; PC 17**
See also BW 2; CA 49-52; CANR 2, 24, 42;
CLR 5; DLB 5, 41; MAICYA; MTCW; SATA
20, 69
Clinton, Dirk
See Silverberg, Robert
Clough, Arthur Hugh 1819-1861 ... **NCLC 27**
See also DLB 32
Clutha, Janet Paterson Frame 1924-
See Frame, Janet
See also CA 1-4R; CANR 2, 36; MTCW
Clyne, Terence
See Blatty, William Peter
Cobalt, Martin
See Mayne, William (James Carter)
Cobbett, William 1763-1835 .... **NCLC 49**
See also DLB 43, 107, 158
Coburn, D(onald) L(ee) 1938- .... **CLC 10**
See also CA 89-92
Cocteau, Jean (Maurice Eugene Clement) 1889-
1963 **CLC 1, 8, 15, 16, 43; DA; DAB; DAC;
DAM DRAM, MST, NOV; WLC**
See also CA 25-28; CANR 40; CAP 2; DLB
65; MTCW
Codrescu, Andrei 1946- **CLC 46; DAM POET**
See also CA 33-36R; CAAS 19; CANR 13, 34,
53
Coe, Max
See Bourne, Randolph S(illiman)
Coe, Tucker
See Westlake, Donald E(dwin)
Coetzee, J(ohn) M(ichael) 1940- **CLC 23, 33,
66; DAM NOV**
See also CA 77-80; CANR 41, 54; MTCW
Coffey, Brian
See Koontz, Dean R(ay)
Cohan, George M. 1878-1942 .... **TCLC 60**
See also CA 157
Cohen, Arthur A(llen) 1928-1986 . **CLC 7, 31**
See also CA 1-4R; 120; CANR 1, 17, 42; DLB
28
Cohen, Leonard (Norman) 1934- **CLC 3, 38;
DAC; DAM MST**
See also CA 21-24R; CANR 14; DLB 53;
MTCW
Cohen, Matt 1942- .... **CLC 19; DAC**
See also CA 61-64; CAAS 18; CANR 40; DLB
53
Cohen-Solal, Annie 19(?)- .... **CLC 50**
Colegate, Isabel 1931- .... **CLC 36**
See also CA 17-20R; CANR 8, 22; DLB 14;
INT CANR-22; MTCW
Coleman, Emmett

See Reed, Ishmael
Coleridge, Samuel Taylor 1772-1834 **NCLC 9,
54; DA; DAB; DAC; DAM MST, POET;
PC 11; WLC**
See also CDBLB 1789-1832; DLB 93, 107
Coleridge, Sara 1802-1852 .... **NCLC 31**
Coles, Don 1928- .... **CLC 46**
See also CA 115; CANR 38
Colette, (Sidonie-Gabrielle) 1873-1954 **T C L C
1, 5, 16; DAM NOV; SSC 10**
See also CA 104; 131; DLB 65; MTCW
Collett, (Jacobine) Camilla (Wergeland) 1813-
1895 .... **NCLC 22**
Collier, Christopher 1930- .... **CLC 30**
See also AAYA 13; CA 33-36R; CANR 13, 33;
JRDA; MAICYA; SATA 16, 70
Collier, James L(incoln) 1928- **CLC 30; DAM
POP**
See also AAYA 13; CA 9-12R; CANR 4, 33;
CLR 3; JRDA; MAICYA; SAAS 21; SATA
8, 70
Collier, Jeremy 1650-1726 .... **LC 6**
Collier, John 1901-1980 .... **SSC 19**
See also CA 65-68; 97-100; CANR 10; DLB
77
Collingwood, R(obin) G(eorge) 1889(?)-1943
TCLC 67
See also CA 117; 155
Collins, Hunt
See Hunter, Evan
Collins, Linda 1931- .... **CLC 44**
See also CA 125
Collins, (William) Wilkie 1824-1889 **NCLC 1,
18**
See also CDBLB 1832-1890; DLB 18, 70, 159
Collins, William 1721-1759 **LC 4; DAM POET**
See also DLB 109
Collodi, Carlo 1826-1890 .... **NCLC 54**
See also Lorenzini, Carlo
See also CLR 5
Colman, George
See Glassco, John
Colt, Winchester Remington
See Hubbard, L(afayette) Ron(ald)
Colter, Cyrus 1910- .... **CLC 58**
See also BW 1; CA 65-68; CANR 10; DLB 33
Colton, James
See Hansen, Joseph
Colum, Padraic 1881-1972 .... **CLC 28**
See also CA 73-76; 33-36R; CANR 35; CLR
36; MAICYA; MTCW; SATA 15
Colvin, James
See Moorcock, Michael (John)
Colwin, Laurie (E.) 1944-1992 **CLC 5, 13, 23,
84**
See also CA 89-92; 139; CANR 20, 46; DLBY
80; MTCW
Comfort, Alex(ander) 1920- **CLC 7; DAM POP**
See also CA 1-4R; CANR 1, 45
Comfort, Montgomery
See Campbell, (John) Ramsey
Compton-Burnett, I(vy) 1884(?)-1969 **CLC 1,
3, 10, 15, 34; DAM NOV**
See also CA 1-4R; 25-28R; CANR 4; DLB 36;
MTCW
Comstock, Anthony 1844-1915 ...... **TCLC 13**
See also CA 110
Comte, Auguste 1798-1857 .... **NCLC 54**
Conan Doyle, Arthur
See Doyle, Arthur Conan
Conde, Maryse 1937- ...... **CLC 52, 92; DAM
MULT**
See also Boucolon, Maryse

See also BW 2
Condillac, Etienne Bonnot de 1714-1780 **L C
26**
Condon, Richard (Thomas) 1915-1996 **CLC 4,
6, 8, 10, 45, 100; DAM NOV**
See also BEST 90:3; CA 1-4R; 151; CAAS 1;
CANR 2, 23; INT CANR-23; MTCW
Confucius 551B.C.-479B.C. . **CMLC 19; DA;
DAB; DAC; DAM MST; WLCS**
Congreve, William 1670-1729 **LC 5, 21; DA;
DAB; DAC; DAM DRAM, MST, POET;
DC 2; WLC**
See also CDBLB 1660-1789; DLB 39, 84
Connell, Evan S(helby), Jr. 1924- **CLC 4, 6, 45;
DAM NOV**
See also AAYA 7; CA 1-4R; CAAS 2; CANR
2, 39; DLB 2; DLBY 81; MTCW
Connelly, Marc(us Cook) 1890-1980 .. **CLC 7**
See also CA 85-88; 102; CANR 30; DLB 7;
DLBY 80; SATA-Obit 25
Connor, Ralph .... **TCLC 31**
See also Gordon, Charles William
See also DLB 92
Conrad, Joseph 1857-1924 **TCLC 1, 6, 13, 25,
43, 57; DA; DAB; DAC; DAM MST, NOV;
SSC 9; WLC**
See also CA 104; 131; CDBLB 1890-1914;
DLB 10, 34, 98, 156; MTCW; SATA 27
Conrad, Robert Arnold
See Hart, Moss
Conroy, Donald Pat(rick) 1945- **CLC 30, 74;
DAM NOV, POP**
See also AAYA 8; AITN 1; CA 85-88; CANR
24, 53; DLB 6; MTCW
Constant (de Rebecque), (Henri) Benjamin
1767-1830 .... **NCLC 6**
See also DLB 119
Conybeare, Charles Augustus
See Eliot, T(homas) S(tearns)
Cook, Michael 1933- .... **CLC 58**
See also CA 93-96; DLB 53
Cook, Robin 1940- .... **CLC 14; DAM POP**
See also BEST 90:2; CA 108; 111; CANR 41;
INT 111
Cook, Roy
See Silverberg, Robert
Cooke, Elizabeth 1948- .... **CLC 55**
See also CA 129
Cooke, John Esten 1830-1886 .... **NCLC 5**
See also DLB 3
Cooke, John Estes
See Baum, L(yman) Frank
Cooke, M. E.
See Creasey, John
Cooke, Margaret
See Creasey, John
Cook-Lynn, Elizabeth 1930-.. **CLC 93; DAM
MULT**
See also CA 133; DLB 175; NNAL
Cooney, Ray .... **CLC 62**
Cooper, Douglas 1960- .... **CLC 86**
Cooper, Henry St. John
See Creasey, John
Cooper, J(oan) California .... **CLC 56; DAM
MULT**
See also AAYA 12; BW 1; CA 125; CANR 55
Cooper, James Fenimore 1789-1851 **NCLC 1,
27, 54**
See also AAYA 22; CDALB 1640-1865; DLB
3; SATA 19
Coover, Robert (Lowell) 1932- **CLC 3, 7, 15,
32, 46, 87; DAM NOV; SSC 15**
See also CA 45-48; CANR 3, 37, 58; DLB 2;

Eiseley, Loren Corey 1907-1977 .... **CLC 7**
  See also AAYA 5; CA 1-4R; 73-76; CANR 6
Eisenstadt, Jill 1963- .... **CLC 50**
  See also CA 140
Eisenstein, Sergei (Mikhailovich) 1898-1948
    TCLC 57
  See also CA 114; 149
Eisner, Simon
  See Kornbluth, C(yril) M.
Ekeloef, (Bengt) Gunnar 1907-1968 **CLC 27;**
    DAM POET
  See also CA 123; 25-28R
Ekelof, (Bengt) Gunnar
  See Ekeloef, (Bengt) Gunnar
Ekwensi, C. O. D.
  See Ekwensi, Cyprian (Odiatu Duaka)
Ekwensi, Cyprian (Odiatu Duaka) 1921-**CLC**
    4; BLC; DAM MULT
  See also BW 2; CA 29-32R; CANR 18, 42; DLB
    117; MTCW; SATA 66
Elaine .... **TCLC 18**
  See also Leverson, Ada
El Crummo
  See Crumb, R(obert)
Elia
  See Lamb, Charles
Eliade, Mircea 1907-1986 .... **CLC 19**
  See also CA 65-68; 119; CANR 30; MTCW
Eliot, A. D.
  See Jewett, (Theodora) Sarah Orne
Eliot, Alice
  See Jewett, (Theodora) Sarah Orne
Eliot, Dan
  See Silverberg, Robert
Eliot, George 1819-1880 **NCLC 4, 13, 23, 41,**
    49; DA; DAB; DAC; DAM MST, NOV;
    WLC
  See also CDBLB 1832-1890; DLB 21, 35, 55
Eliot, John 1604-1690 .... **LC 5**
  See also DLB 24
Eliot, T(homas) S(tearns) 1888-1965**CLC 1, 2,**
    3, 6, 9, 10, 13, 15, 24, 34, 41, 55, 57; DA;
    DAB; DAC; DAM DRAM, MST, POET;
    PC 5; WLC 2
  See also CA 5-8R; 25-28R; CANR 41; CDALB
    1929-1941; DLB 7, 10, 45, 63; DLBY 88;
    MTCW
Elizabeth 1866-1941 .... **TCLC 41**
Elkin, Stanley L(awrence) 1930-1995 **CLC 4,**
    6, 9, 14, 27, 51, 91; DAM NOV, POP; SSC
    12
  See also CA 9-12R; 148; CANR 8, 46; DLB 2,
    28; DLBY 80; INT CANR-8; MTCW
Elledge, Scott .... **CLC 34**
Elliot, Don
  See Silverberg, Robert
Elliott, Don
  See Silverberg, Robert
Elliott, George P(aul) 1918-1980 .... **CLC 2**
  See also CA 1-4R; 97-100; CANR 2
Elliott, Janice 1931- .... **CLC 47**
  See also CA 13-16R; CANR 8, 29; DLB 14
Elliott, Sumner Locke 1917-1991 ..... **CLC 38**
  See also CA 5-8R; 134; CANR 2, 21
Elliott, William
  See Bradbury, Ray (Douglas)
Ellis, A. E. .... **CLC 7**
Ellis, Alice Thomas .... **CLC 40**
  See also Haycraft, Anna
Ellis, Bret Easton 1964- .. **CLC 39, 71; DAM**
    POP
  See also AAYA 2; CA 118; 123; CANR 51; INT
    123

Ellis, (Henry) Havelock 1859-1939 **TCLC 14**
  See also CA 109
Ellis, Landon
  See Ellison, Harlan (Jay)
Ellis, Trey 1962- .... **CLC 55**
  See also CA 146
Ellison, Harlan (Jay) 1934- ... **CLC 1, 13, 42;**
    DAM POP; SSC 14
  See also CA 5-8R; CANR 5, 46; DLB 8; INT
    CANR-5; MTCW
Ellison, Ralph (Waldo) 1914-1994 . **CLC 1, 3,**
    11, 54, 86; BLC; DA; DAB; DAC; DAM
    MST, MULT, NOV; SSC 26; WLC
  See also AAYA 19; BW 1; CA 9-12R; 145;
    CANR 24, 53; CDALB 1941-1968; DLB 2,
    76; DLBY 94; MTCW
Ellmann, Lucy (Elizabeth) 1956- ...... **CLC 61**
  See also CA 128
Ellmann, Richard (David) 1918-1987**CLC 50**
  See also BEST 89:2; CA 1-4R; 122; CANR 2,
    28; DLB 103; DLBY 87; MTCW
Elman, Richard 1934- .... **CLC 19**
  See also CA 17-20R; CAAS 3; CANR 47
Elron
  See Hubbard, L(afayette) Ron(ald)
Eluard, Paul .... **TCLC 7, 41**
  See also Grindel, Eugene
Elyot, Sir Thomas 1490(?)-1546 .... **LC 11**
Elytis, Odysseus 1911-1996 **CLC 15, 49, 100;**
    DAM POET
  See also CA 102; 151; MTCW
Emecheta, (Florence Onye) Buchi 1944-**C L C**
    14, 48; BLC; DAM MULT
  See also BW 2; CA 81-84; CANR 27; DLB 117;
    MTCW; SATA 66
Emerson, Ralph Waldo 1803-1882 . **NCLC 1,**
    38; DA; DAB; DAC; DAM MST, POET;
    PC 18; WLC
  See also CDALB 1640-1865; DLB 1, 59, 73
Eminescu, Mihail 1850-1889 .... **NCLC 33**
Empson, William 1906-1984**CLC 3, 8, 19, 33,**
    34
  See also CA 17-20R; 112; CANR 31; DLB 20;
    MTCW
Enchi Fumiko (Ueda) 1905-1986 ...... **CLC 31**
  See also CA 129; 121
Ende, Michael (Andreas Helmuth) 1929-1995
    CLC 31
  See also CA 118; 124; 149; CANR 36; CLR
    14; DLB 75; MAICYA; SATA 61; SATA-
    Brief 42; SATA-Obit 86
Endo, Shusaku 1923-1996 **CLC 7, 14, 19, 54,**
    99; DAM NOV
  See also CA 29-32R; 153; CANR 21, 54; DLB
    182; MTCW
Engel, Marian 1933-1985 .... **CLC 36**
  See also CA 25-28R; CANR 12; DLB 53; INT
    CANR-12
Engelhardt, Frederick
  See Hubbard, L(afayette) Ron(ald)
Enright, D(ennis) J(oseph) 1920-**CLC 4, 8, 31**
  See also CA 1-4R; CANR 1, 42; DLB 27; SATA
    25
Enzensberger, Hans Magnus 1929- .. **CLC 43**
  See also CA 116; 119
Ephron, Nora 1941- .... **CLC 17, 31**
  See also AITN 2; CA 65-68; CANR 12, 39
Epicurus 341B.C.-270B.C. .... **CMLC 21**
  See also DLB 176
Epsilon
  See Betjeman, John
Epstein, Daniel Mark 1948- .... **CLC 7**
  See also CA 49-52; CANR 2, 53

Epstein, Jacob 1956- .... **CLC 19**
  See also CA 114
Epstein, Joseph 1937- .... **CLC 39**
  See also CA 112; 119; CANR 50
Epstein, Leslie 1938- .... **CLC 27**
  See also CA 73-76; CAAS 12; CANR 23
Equiano, Olaudah 1745(?)-1797**LC 16; BLC;**
    DAM MULT
  See also DLB 37, 50
Erasmus, Desiderius 1469(?)-1536 ...... **LC 16**
Erdman, Paul E(mil) 1932- .... **CLC 25**
  See also AITN 1; CA 61-64; CANR 13, 43
Erdrich, Louise 1954- ..... **CLC 39, 54; DAM**
    MULT, NOV, POP
  See also AAYA 10; BEST 89:1; CA 114; CANR
    41; DLB 152, 175; MTCW; NNAL; SATA
    94
Erenburg, Ilya (Grigoryevich)
  See Ehrenburg, Ilya (Grigoryevich)
Erickson, Stephen Michael 1950-
  See Erickson, Steve
  See also CA 129
Erickson, Steve .... **CLC 64**
  See also Erickson, Stephen Michael
Ericson, Walter
  See Fast, Howard (Melvin)
Eriksson, Buntel
  See Bergman, (Ernst) Ingmar
Ernaux, Annie 1940- .... **CLC 88**
  See also CA 147
Eschenbach, Wolfram von
  See Wolfram von Eschenbach
Eseki, Bruno
  See Mphahlele, Ezekiel
Esenin, Sergei (Alexandrovich) 1895-1925
    TCLC 4
  See also CA 104
Eshleman, Clayton 1935- .... **CLC 7**
  See also CA 33-36R; CAAS 6; DLB 5
Espriella, Don Manuel Alvarez
  See Southey, Robert
Espriu, Salvador 1913-1985 .... **CLC 9**
  See also CA 154; 115; DLB 134
Espronceda, Jose de 1808-1842 ..... **NCLC 39**
Esse, James
  See Stephens, James
Esterbrook, Tom
  See Hubbard, L(afayette) Ron(ald)
Estleman, Loren D. 1952-**CLC 48; DAM NOV,**
    POP
  See also CA 85-88; CANR 27; INT CANR-27;
    MTCW
Eugenides, Jeffrey 1960(?)- .... **CLC 81**
  See also CA 144
Euripides c. 485B.C.-406B.C.**CMLC 23; DA;**
    DAB; DAC; DAM DRAM, MST; DC 4;
    WLCS
  See also DLB 176
Evan, Evin
  See Faust, Frederick (Schiller)
Evans, Evan
  See Faust, Frederick (Schiller)
Evans, Marian
  See Eliot, George
Evans, Mary Ann
  See Eliot, George
Evarts, Esther
  See Benson, Sally
Everett, Percival L. 1956- .... **CLC 57**
  See also BW 2; CA 129
Everson, R(onald) G(ilmour) 1903- . **CLC 27**
  See also CA 17-20R; DLB 88
Everson, William (Oliver) 1912-1994 **CLC 1,**

40

Fisher, Rudolph 1897-1934. **TCLC 11; BLC; DAM MULT; SSC 25**
  See also BW 1; CA 107; 124; DLB 51, 102
Fisher, Vardis (Alvero) 1895-1968 ...... **CLC 7**
  See also CA 5-8R; 25-28R; DLB 9
Fiske, Tarleton
  See Bloch, Robert (Albert)
Fitch, Clarke
  See Sinclair, Upton (Beall)
Fitch, John IV
  See Cormier, Robert (Edmund)
Fitzgerald, Captain Hugh
  See Baum, L(yman) Frank
FitzGerald, Edward 1809-1883 .... **NCLC 9**
  See also DLB 32
Fitzgerald, F(rancis) Scott (Key) 1896-1940
  TCLC 1, 6, 14, 28, 55; DA; DAB; DAC; DAM MST, NOV; SSC 6; WLC
  See also AITN 1; CA 110; 123; CDALB 1917-1929; DLB 4, 9, 86; DLBD 1, 15; DLBY 81, 96; MTCW
Fitzgerald, Penelope 1916- ... **CLC 19, 51, 61**
  See also CA 85-88; CAAS 10; CANR 56; DLB 14
Fitzgerald, Robert (Stuart) 1910-1985 **CLC 39**
  See also CA 1-4R; 114; CANR 1; DLBY 80
FitzGerald, Robert D(avid) 1902-1987 **CLC 19**
  See also CA 17-20R
Fitzgerald, Zelda (Sayre) 1900-1948 **TCLC 52**
  See also CA 117; 126; DLBY 84
Flanagan, Thomas (James Bonner) 1923-
  CLC 25, 52
  See also CA 108; CANR 55; DLBY 80; INT 108; MTCW
Flaubert, Gustave 1821-1880 **NCLC 2, 10, 19, 62; DA; DAB; DAC; DAM MST, NOV; SSC 11; WLC**
  See also DLB 119
Flecker, Herman Elroy
  See Flecker, (Herman) James Elroy
Flecker, (Herman) James Elroy 1884-1915
  TCLC 43
  See also CA 109; 150; DLB 10, 19
Fleming, Ian (Lancaster) 1908-1964 . **CLC 3, 30; DAM POP**
  See also CA 5-8R; CANR 59; CDBLB 1945-1960; DLB 87; MTCW; SATA 9
Fleming, Thomas (James) 1927- .... **CLC 37**
  See also CA 5-8R; CANR 10; INT CANR-10; SATA 8
Fletcher, John 1579-1625 .... **LC 33; DC 6**
  See also CDBLB Before 1660; DLB 58
Fletcher, John Gould 1886-1950 .... **TCLC 35**
  See also CA 107; DLB 4, 45
Fleur, Paul
  See Pohl, Frederik
Flooglebuckle, Al
  See Spiegelman, Art
Flying Officer X
  See Bates, H(erbert) E(rnest)
Fo, Dario 1926- .... **CLC 32; DAM DRAM**
  See also CA 116; 128; MTCW
Fogarty, Jonathan Titulescu Esq.
  See Farrell, James T(homas)
Folke, Will
  See Bloch, Robert (Albert)
Follett, Ken(neth Martin) 1949- ..... **CLC 18; DAM NOV, POP**
  See also AAYA 6; BEST 89:4; CA 81-84; CANR 13, 33, 54; DLB 87; DLBY 81; INT CANR-33; MTCW
Fontane, Theodor 1819-1898 .... **NCLC 26**

See also DLB 129
Foote, Horton 1916- **CLC 51, 91; DAM DRAM**
  See also CA 73-76; CANR 34, 51; DLB 26; INT CANR-34
Foote, Shelby 1916- **CLC 75; DAM NOV, POP**
  See also CA 5-8R; CANR 3, 45; DLB 2, 17
Forbes, Esther 1891-1967 .... **CLC 12**
  See also AAYA 17; CA 13-14; 25-28R; CAP 1; CLR 27; DLB 22; JRDA; MAICYA; SATA 2
Forche, Carolyn (Louise) 1950- **CLC 25, 83, 86; DAM POET; PC 10**
  See also CA 109; 117; CANR 50; DLB 5; INT 117
Ford, Elbur
  See Hibbert, Eleanor Alice Burford
Ford, Ford Madox 1873-1939 **TCLC 1, 15, 39, 57; DAM NOV**
  See also CA 104; 132; CDBLB 1914-1945; DLB 162; MTCW
Ford, John 1895-1973 .... **CLC 16**
  See also CA 45-48
Ford, Richard .... **CLC 99**
Ford, Richard 1944- .... **CLC 46**
  See also CA 69-72; CANR 11, 47
Ford, Webster
  See Masters, Edgar Lee
Foreman, Richard 1937- .... **CLC 50**
  See also CA 65-68; CANR 32
Forester, C(ecil) S(cott) 1899-1966 ... **CLC 35**
  See also CA 73-76; 25-28R; SATA 13
Forez
  See Mauriac, Francois (Charles)
Forman, James Douglas 1932- .... **CLC 21**
  See also AAYA 17; CA 9-12R; CANR 4, 19, 42; JRDA; MAICYA; SATA 8, 70
Fornes, Maria Irene 1930- .... **CLC 39, 61**
  See also CA 25-28R; CANR 28; DLB 7; HW; INT CANR-28; MTCW
Forrest, Leon 1937- .... **CLC 4**
  See also BW 2; CA 89-92; CAAS 7; CANR 25, 52; DLB 33
Forster, E(dward) M(organ) 1879-1970 **C L C 1, 2, 3, 4, 9, 10, 13, 15, 22, 45, 77; DA; DAB; DAC; DAM MST, NOV; SSC 27; WLC**
  See also AAYA 2; CA 13-14; 25-28R; CANR 45; CAP 1; CDBLB 1914-1945; DLB 34, 98, 162, 178; DLBD 10; MTCW; SATA 57
Forster, John 1812-1876 .... **NCLC 11**
  See also DLB 144
Forsyth, Frederick 1938- **CLC 2, 5, 36; DAM NOV, POP**
  See also BEST 89:4; CA 85-88; CANR 38; DLB 87; MTCW
Forten, Charlotte L. .... **TCLC 16; BLC**
  See also Grimke, Charlotte L(ottie) Forten
  See also DLB 50
Foscolo, Ugo 1778-1827 .... **NCLC 8**
Fosse, Bob .... **CLC 20**
  See also Fosse, Robert Louis
Fosse, Robert Louis 1927-1987
  See Fosse, Bob
  See also CA 110; 123
Foster, Stephen Collins 1826-1864 **NCLC 26**
Foucault, Michel 1926-1984 . **CLC 31, 34, 69**
  See also CA 105; 113; CANR 34; MTCW
Fouque, Friedrich (Heinrich Karl) de la Motte 1777-1843 .... **NCLC 2**
  See also DLB 90
Fourier, Charles 1772-1837 .... **NCLC 51**
Fournier, Henri Alban 1886-1914
  See Alain-Fournier
  See also CA 104
Fournier, Pierre 1916- .... **CLC 11**

See also Gascar, Pierre
  See also CA 89-92; CANR 16, 40
Fowles, John 1926- **CLC 1, 2, 3, 4, 6, 9, 10, 15, 33, 87; DAB; DAC; DAM MST**
  See also CA 5-8R; CANR 25; CDBLB 1960 to Present; DLB 14, 139; MTCW; SATA 22
Fox, Paula 1923- .... **CLC 2, 8**
  See also AAYA 3; CA 73-76; CANR 20, 36; CLR 1, 44; DLB 52; JRDA; MAICYA; MTCW; SATA 17, 60
Fox, William Price (Jr.) 1926- .... **CLC 22**
  See also CA 17-20R; CAAS 19; CANR 11; DLB 2; DLBY 81
Foxe, John 1516(?)-1587 .... **LC 14**
Frame, Janet 1924- ... **CLC 2, 3, 6, 22, 66, 96**
  See also Clutha, Janet Paterson Frame
France, Anatole .... **TCLC 9**
  See also Thibault, Jacques Anatole Francois
  See also DLB 123
Francis, Claude 19(?)- .... **CLC 50**
Francis, Dick 1920- **CLC 2, 22, 42, 102; DAM POP**
  See also AAYA 5, 21; BEST 89:3; CA 5-8R; CANR 9, 42; CDBLB 1960 to Present; DLB 87; INT CANR-9; MTCW
Francis, Robert (Churchill) 1901-1987 **C L C 15**
  See also CA 1-4R; 123; CANR 1
Frank, Anne(lies Marie) 1929-1945 **TCLC 17; DA; DAB; DAC; DAM MST; WLC**
  See also AAYA 12; CA 113; 133; MTCW; SATA 87; SATA-Brief 42
Frank, Elizabeth 1945- .... **CLC 39**
  See also CA 121; 126; INT 126
Frankl, Viktor E(mil) 1905- .... **CLC 93**
  See also CA 65-68
Franklin, Benjamin
  See Hasek, Jaroslav (Matej Frantisek)
Franklin, Benjamin 1706-1790 .. **LC 25; DA; DAB; DAC; DAM MST; WLCS**
  See also CDALB 1640-1865; DLB 24, 43, 73
Franklin, (Stella Maraia Sarah) Miles 1879-1954 .... **TCLC 7**
  See also CA 104
Fraser, (Lady) Antonia (Pakenham) 1932-
  CLC 32
  See also CA 85-88; CANR 44; MTCW; SATA-Brief 32
Fraser, George MacDonald 1925- ...... **CLC 7**
  See also CA 45-48; CANR 2, 48
Fraser, Sylvia 1935- .... **CLC 64**
  See also CA 45-48; CANR 1, 16
Frayn, Michael 1933- **CLC 3, 7, 31, 47; DAM DRAM, NOV**
  See also CA 5-8R; CANR 30; DLB 13, 14; MTCW
Fraze, Candida (Merrill) 1945- .... **CLC 50**
  See also CA 126
Frazer, J(ames) G(eorge) 1854-1941 **TCLC 32**
  See also CA 118
Frazer, Robert Caine
  See Creasey, John
Frazer, Sir James George
  See Frazer, J(ames) G(eorge)
Frazier, Ian 1951- .... **CLC 46**
  See also CA 130; CANR 54
Frederic, Harold 1856-1898 .... **NCLC 10**
  See also DLB 12, 23; DLBD 13
Frederick, John
  See Faust, Frederick (Schiller)
Frederick the Great 1712-1786 .... **LC 14**
Fredro, Aleksander 1793-1876 .... **NCLC 8**
Freeling, Nicolas 1927- .... **CLC 38**

See also CA 138

Gray, Francine du Plessix 1930- ..... **CLC 22; DAM NOV**
See also BEST 90:3; CA 61-64; CAAS 2; CANR 11, 33; INT CANR-11; MTCW

Gray, John (Henry) 1866-1934 ...... **TCLC 19**
See also CA 119

Gray, Simon (James Holliday) 1936- **CLC 9, 14, 36**
See also AITN 1; CA 21-24R; CAAS 3; CANR 32; DLB 13; MTCW

Gray, Spalding 1941- **CLC 49; DAM POP; DC 7**
See also CA 128

Gray, Thomas 1716-1771 ... **LC 4; DA; DAB; DAC; DAM MST; PC 2; WLC**
See also CDBLB 1660-1789; DLB 109

Grayson, David
See Baker, Ray Stannard

Grayson, Richard (A.) 1951- .... **CLC 38**
See also CA 85-88; CANR 14, 31, 57

Greeley, Andrew M(oran) 1928- ..... **CLC 28; DAM POP**
See also CA 5-8R; CAAS 7; CANR 7, 43; MTCW

Green, Anna Katharine 1846-1935 **TCLC 63**
See also CA 112

Green, Brian
See Card, Orson Scott

Green, Hannah
See Greenberg, Joanne (Goldenberg)

Green, Hannah 1927(?)-1996 .... **CLC 3**
See also CA 73-76; CANR 59

Green, Henry 1905-1973 .... **CLC 2, 13, 97**
See also Yorke, Henry Vincent
See also DLB 15

Green, Julian (Hartridge) 1900-
See Green, Julien
See also CA 21-24R; CANR 33; DLB 4, 72; MTCW

Green, Julien .... **CLC 3, 11, 77**
See also Green, Julian (Hartridge)

Green, Paul (Eliot) 1894-1981 **CLC 25; DAM DRAM**
See also AITN 1; CA 5-8R; 103; CANR 3; DLB 7, 9; DLBY 81

Greenberg, Ivan 1908-1973
See Rahv, Philip
See also CA 85-88

Greenberg, Joanne (Goldenberg) 1932- **C L C 7, 30**
See also AAYA 12; CA 5-8R; CANR 14, 32; SATA 25

Greenberg, Richard 1959(?)- .... **CLC 57**
See also CA 138

Greene, Bette 1934- .... **CLC 30**
See also AAYA 7; CA 53-56; CANR 4; CLR 2; JRDA; MAICYA; SAAS 16; SATA 8

Greene, Gael .... **CLC 8**
See also CA 13-16R; CANR 10

Greene, Graham 1904-1991 **CLC 1, 3, 6, 9, 14, 18, 27, 37, 70, 72; DA; DAB; DAC; DAM MST, NOV; WLC**
See also AITN 2; CA 13-16R; 133; CANR 35; CDBLB 1945-1960; DLB 13, 15, 77, 100, 162; DLBY 91; MTCW; SATA 20

Greer, Richard
See Silverberg, Robert

Gregor, Arthur 1923- .... **CLC 9**
See also CA 25-28R; CAAS 10; CANR 11; SATA 36

Gregor, Lee
See Pohl, Frederik

Gregory, Isabella Augusta (Persse) 1852-1932 **TCLC 1**
See also CA 104; DLB 10

Gregory, J. Dennis
See Williams, John A(lfred)

Grendon, Stephen
See Derleth, August (William)

Grenville, Kate 1950- .... **CLC 61**
See also CA 118; CANR 53

Grenville, Pelham
See Wodehouse, P(elham) G(renville)

Greve, Felix Paul (Berthold Friedrich) 1879-1948
See Grove, Frederick Philip
See also CA 104; 141; DAC; DAM MST

Grey, Zane 1872-1939 .. **TCLC 6; DAM POP**
See also CA 104; 132; DLB 9; MTCW

Grieg, (Johan) Nordahl (Brun) 1902-1943 **TCLC 10**
See also CA 107

Grieve, C(hristopher) M(urray) 1892-1978 **CLC 11, 19; DAM POET**
See also MacDiarmid, Hugh; Pteleon
See also CA 5-8R; 85-88; CANR 33; MTCW

Griffin, Gerald 1803-1840 .... **NCLC 7**
See also DLB 159

Griffin, John Howard 1920-1980 ..... **CLC 68**
See also AITN 1; CA 1-4R; 101; CANR 2

Griffin, Peter 1942- .... **CLC 39**
See also CA 136

Griffith, D(avid Lewelyn) W(ark) 1875(?)-1948 **TCLC 68**
See also CA 119; 150

Griffith, Lawrence
See Griffith, D(avid Lewelyn) W(ark)

Griffiths, Trevor 1935- .... **CLC 13, 52**
See also CA 97-100; CANR 45; DLB 13

Grigson, Geoffrey (Edward Harvey) 1905-1985 **CLC 7, 39**
See also CA 25-28R; 118; CANR 20, 33; DLB 27; MTCW

Grillparzer, Franz 1791-1872 .... **NCLC 1**
See also DLB 133

Grimble, Reverend Charles James
See Eliot, T(homas) S(tearns)

Grimke, Charlotte L(ottie) Forten 1837(?)-1914
See Forten, Charlotte L.
See also BW 1; CA 117; 124; DAM MULT, POET

Grimm, Jacob Ludwig Karl 1785-1863 **NCLC 3**
See also DLB 90; MAICYA; SATA 22

Grimm, Wilhelm Karl 1786-1859 .... **NCLC 3**
See also DLB 90; MAICYA; SATA 22

Grimmelshausen, Johann Jakob Christoffel von 1621-1676 .... **LC 6**
See also DLB 168

Grindel, Eugene 1895-1952
See Eluard, Paul
See also CA 104

Grisham, John 1955- .... **CLC 84; DAM POP**
See also AAYA 14; CA 138; CANR 47

Grossman, David 1954- .... **CLC 67**
See also CA 138

Grossman, Vasily (Semenovich) 1905-1964 **CLC 41**
See also CA 124; 130; MTCW

Grove, Frederick Philip .... **TCLC 4**
See also Greve, Felix Paul (Berthold Friedrich)
See also DLB 92

Grubb
See Crumb, R(obert)

Grumbach, Doris (Isaac) 1918- **CLC 13, 22, 64**

See also CA 5-8R; CAAS 2; CANR 9, 42; INT CANR-9

Grundtvig, Nicolai Frederik Severin 1783-1872 **NCLC 1**

Grunge
See Crumb, R(obert)

Grunwald, Lisa 1959- .... **CLC 44**
See also CA 120

Guare, John 1938- . **CLC 8, 14, 29, 67; DAM DRAM**
See also CA 73-76; CANR 21; DLB 7; MTCW

Gudjonsson, Halldor Kiljan 1902-
See Laxness, Halldor
See also CA 103

Guenter, Erich
See Eich, Guenter

Guest, Barbara 1920- .... **CLC 34**
See also CA 25-28R; CANR 11, 44; DLB 5

Guest, Judith (Ann) 1936- **CLC 8, 30; DAM NOV, POP**
See also AAYA 7; CA 77-80; CANR 15; INT CANR-15; MTCW

Guevara, Che .... **CLC 87; HLC**
See also Guevara (Serna), Ernesto

Guevara (Serna), Ernesto 1928-1967
See Guevara, Che
See also CA 127; 111; CANR 56; DAM MULT; HW

Guild, Nicholas M. 1944- .... **CLC 33**
See also CA 93-96

Guillemin, Jacques
See Sartre, Jean-Paul

Guillen, Jorge 1893-1984 .... **CLC 11; DAM MULT, POET**
See also CA 89-92; 112; DLB 108; HW

Guillen, Nicolas (Cristobal) 1902-1989 **C L C 48, 79; BLC; DAM MST, MULT, POET; HLC**
See also BW 2; CA 116; 125; 129; HW

Guillevic, (Eugene) 1907- .... **CLC 33**
See also CA 93-96

Guillois
See Desnos, Robert

Guillois, Valentin
See Desnos, Robert

Guiney, Louise Imogen 1861-1920 **TCLC 41**
See also DLB 54

Guiraldes, Ricardo (Guillermo) 1886-1927 **TCLC 39**
See also CA 131; HW; MTCW

Gumilev, Nikolai Stephanovich 1886-1921 **TCLC 60**

Gunesekera, Romesh .... **CLC 91**

Gunn, Bill .... **CLC 5**
See also Gunn, William Harrison
See also DLB 38

Gunn, Thom(son William) 1929- **CLC 3, 6, 18, 32, 81; DAM POET**
See also CA 17-20R; CANR 9, 33; CDBLB 1960 to Present; DLB 27; INT CANR-33; MTCW

Gunn, William Harrison 1934(?)-1989
See Gunn, Bill
See also AITN 1; BW 1; CA 13-16R; 128; CANR 12, 25

Gunnars, Kristjana 1948- .... **CLC 69**
See also CA 113; DLB 60

Gurdjieff, G(eorgei) I(vanovich) 1877(?)-1949 **TCLC 71**
See also CA 157

Gurganus, Allan 1947- . **CLC 70; DAM POP**
See also BEST 90:1; CA 135

Gurney, A(lbert) R(amsdell), Jr. 1930- . **C L C**

See also CA 102; 89-92

Harris, MacDonald .... **CLC 9**
See also Heiney, Donald (William)

Harris, Mark 1922- .... **CLC 19**
See also CA 5-8R; CAAS 3; CANR 2, 55; DLB 2; DLBY 80

Harris, (Theodore) Wilson 1921- ..... **CLC 25**
See also BW 2; CA 65-68; CAAS 16; CANR 11, 27; DLB 117; MTCW

Harrison, Elizabeth Cavanna 1909-
See Cavanna, Betty
See also CA 9-12R; CANR 6, 27

Harrison, Harry (Max) 1925- .... **CLC 42**
See also CA 1-4R; CANR 5, 21; DLB 8; SATA 4

Harrison, James (Thomas) 1937- **CLC 6, 14, 33, 66; SSC 19**
See also CA 13-16R; CANR 8, 51; DLBY 82; INT CANR-8

Harrison, Jim
See Harrison, James (Thomas)

Harrison, Kathryn 1961- .... **CLC 70**
See also CA 144

Harrison, Tony 1937- .... **CLC 43**
See also CA 65-68; CANR 44; DLB 40; MTCW

Harriss, Will(ard Irvin) 1922- .... **CLC 34**
See also CA 111

Harson, Sley
See Ellison, Harlan (Jay)

Hart, Ellis
See Ellison, Harlan (Jay)

Hart, Josephine 1942(?)-**CLC 70; DAM POP**
See also CA 138

Hart, Moss 1904-1961**CLC 66; DAM DRAM**
See also CA 109; 89-92; DLB 7

Harte, (Francis) Bret(t) 1836(?)-1902**TCLC 1, 25; DA; DAC; DAM MST; SSC 8; WLC**
See also CA 104; 140; CDALB 1865-1917; DLB 12, 64, 74, 79; SATA 26

Hartley, L(eslie) P(oles) 1895-1972**CLC 2, 22**
See also CA 45-48; 37-40R; CANR 33; DLB 15, 139; MTCW

Hartman, Geoffrey H. 1929- .... **CLC 27**
See also CA 117; 125; DLB 67

Hartmann von Aue c. 1160-c. 1205**CMLC 15**
See also DLB 138

Hartmann von Aue 1170-1210 ...... **CMLC 15**

Haruf, Kent 1943- .... **CLC 34**
See also CA 149

Harwood, Ronald 1934- .... **CLC 32; DAM DRAM, MST**
See also CA 1-4R; CANR 4, 55; DLB 13

Hasek, Jaroslav (Matej Frantisek) 1883-1923 **TCLC 4**
See also CA 104; 129; MTCW

Hass, Robert 1941- ... **CLC 18, 39, 99; PC 16**
See also CA 111; CANR 30, 50; DLB 105; SATA 94

Hastings, Hudson
See Kuttner, Henry

Hastings, Selina .... **CLC 44**

Hathorne, John 1641-1717 .... **LC 38**

Hatteras, Amelia
See Mencken, H(enry) L(ouis)

Hatteras, Owen .... **TCLC 18**
See also Mencken, H(enry) L(ouis); Nathan, George Jean

Hauptmann, Gerhart (Johann Robert) 1862-1946 .... **TCLC 4; DAM DRAM**
See also CA 104; 153; DLB 66, 118

Havel, Vaclav 1936- ... **CLC 25, 58, 65; DAM DRAM; DC 6**
See also CA 104; CANR 36; MTCW

Haviaras, Stratis .... **CLC 33**
See also Chaviaras, Strates

Hawes, Stephen 1475(?)-1523(?) .... **LC 17**

Hawkes, John (Clendennin Burne, Jr.) 1925- **CLC 1, 2, 3, 4, 7, 9, 14, 15, 27, 49**
See also CA 1-4R; CANR 2, 47; DLB 2, 7; DLBY 80; MTCW

Hawking, S. W.
See Hawking, Stephen W(illiam)

Hawking, Stephen W(illiam) 1942- .. **CLC 63**
See also AAYA 13; BEST 89:1; CA 126; 129; CANR 48

Hawthorne, Julian 1846-1934 .... **TCLC 25**

Hawthorne, Nathaniel 1804-1864 **NCLC 39; DA; DAB; DAC; DAM MST, NOV; SSC 3; WLC**
See also AAYA 18; CDALB 1640-1865; DLB 1, 74; YABC 2

Haxton, Josephine Ayres 1921-
See Douglas, Ellen
See also CA 115; CANR 41

Hayaseca y Eizaguirre, Jorge
See Echegaray (y Eizaguirre), Jose (Maria Waldo)

Hayashi Fumiko 1904-1951 .... **TCLC 27**
See also DLB 180

Haycraft, Anna
See Ellis, Alice Thomas
See also CA 122

Hayden, Robert E(arl) 1913-1980 . **CLC 5, 9, 14, 37; BLC; DA; DAC; DAM MST, MULT, POET; PC 6**
See also BW 1; CA 69-72; 97-100; CABS 2; CANR 24; CDALB 1941-1968; DLB 5, 76; MTCW; SATA 19; SATA-Obit 26

Hayford, J(oseph) E(phraim) Casely
See Casely-Hayford, J(oseph) E(phraim)

Hayman, Ronald 1932- .... **CLC 44**
See also CA 25-28R; CANR 18, 50; DLB 155

Haywood, Eliza (Fowler) 1693(?)-1756 **LC 1**

Hazlitt, William 1778-1830 .... **NCLC 29**
See also DLB 110, 158

Hazzard, Shirley 1931- .... **CLC 18**
See also CA 9-12R; CANR 4; DLBY 82; MTCW

Head, Bessie 1937-1986... **CLC 25, 67; BLC; DAM MULT**
See also BW 2; CA 29-32R; 119; CANR 25; DLB 117; MTCW

Headon, (Nicky) Topper 1956(?)- ..... **CLC 30**

Heaney, Seamus (Justin) 1939- **CLC 5, 7, 14, 25, 37, 74, 91; DAB; DAM POET; PC 18; WLCS**
See also CA 85-88; CANR 25, 48; CDBLB 1960 to Present; DLB 40; DLBY 95; MTCW

Hearn, (Patricio) Lafcadio (Tessima Carlos) 1850-1904 .... **TCLC 9**
See also CA 105; DLB 12, 78

Hearne, Vicki 1946- .... **CLC 56**
See also CA 139

Hearon, Shelby 1931- .... **CLC 63**
See also AITN 2; CA 25-28R; CANR 18, 48

Heat-Moon, William Least .... **CLC 29**
See also Trogdon, William (Lewis)
See also AAYA 9

Hebbel, Friedrich 1813-1863**NCLC 43; DAM DRAM**
See also DLB 129

Hebert, Anne 1916-**CLC 4, 13, 29; DAC; DAM MST, POET**
See also CA 85-88; DLB 68; MTCW

Hecht, Anthony (Evan) 1923- **CLC 8, 13, 19; DAM POET**

Hecht, Ben 1894-1964 .... **CLC 8**
See also CA 85-88; DLB 7, 9, 25, 26, 28, 86

Hedayat, Sadeq 1903-1951 .... **TCLC 21**
See also CA 120

Hegel, Georg Wilhelm Friedrich 1770-1831 **NCLC 46**
See also DLB 90

Heidegger, Martin 1889-1976 .... **CLC 24**
See also CA 81-84; 65-68; CANR 34; MTCW

Heidenstam, (Carl Gustaf) Verner von 1859-1940 .... **TCLC 5**
See also CA 104

Heifner, Jack 1946- .... **CLC 11**
See also CA 105; CANR 47

Heijermans, Herman 1864-1924 .... **TCLC 24**
See also CA 123

Heilbrun, Carolyn G(old) 1926- .... **CLC 25**
See also CA 45-48; CANR 1, 28, 58

Heine, Heinrich 1797-1856 .... **NCLC 4, 54**
See also DLB 90

Heinemann, Larry (Curtiss) 1944- ... **CLC 50**
See also CA 110; CAAS 21; CANR 31; DLBD 9; INT CANR-31

Heiney, Donald (William) 1921-1993
See Harris, MacDonald
See also CA 1-4R; 142; CANR 3, 58

Heinlein, Robert A(nson) 1907-1988**CLC 1, 3, 8, 14, 26, 55; DAM POP**
See also AAYA 17; CA 1-4R; 125; CANR 1, 20, 53; DLB 8; JRDA; MAICYA; MTCW; SATA 9, 69; SATA-Obit 56

Helforth, John
See Doolittle, Hilda

Hellenhofferu, Vojtech Kapristian z
See Hasek, Jaroslav (Matej Frantisek)

Heller, Joseph 1923-**CLC 1, 3, 5, 8, 11, 36, 63; DA; DAB; DAC; DAM MST, NOV, POP; WLC**
See also AITN 1; CA 5-8R; CABS 1; CANR 8, 42; DLB 2, 28; DLBY 80; INT CANR-8; MTCW

Hellman, Lillian (Florence) 1906-1984**CLC 2, 4, 8, 14, 18, 34, 44, 52; DAM DRAM; DC 1**
See also AITN 1, 2; CA 13-16R; 112; CANR 33; DLB 7; DLBY 84; MTCW

Helprin, Mark 1947-**CLC 7, 10, 22, 32; DAM NOV, POP**
See also CA 81-84; CANR 47; DLBY 85; MTCW

Helvetius, Claude-Adrien 1715-1771 ..**LC 26**

Helyar, Jane Penelope Josephine 1933-
See Poole, Josephine
See also CA 21-24R; CANR 10, 26; SATA 82

Hemans, Felicia 1793-1835 .... **NCLC 29**
See also DLB 96

Hemingway, Ernest (Miller) 1899-1961 **C L C 1, 3, 6, 8, 10, 13, 19, 30, 34, 39, 41, 44, 50, 61, 80; DA; DAB; DAC; DAM MST, NOV; SSC 25; WLC**
See also AAYA 19; CA 77-80; CANR 34; CDALB 1917-1929; DLB 4, 9, 102; DLBD 1, 15; DLBY 81, 87, 96; MTCW

Hempel, Amy 1951- .... **CLC 39**
See also CA 118; 137

Henderson, F. C.
See Mencken, H(enry) L(ouis)

Henderson, Sylvia
See Ashton-Warner, Sylvia (Constance)

Henley, Beth .... **CLC 23; DC 6**
See also Henley, Elizabeth Becker
See also CABS 3; DLBY 86

Henley, Elizabeth Becker 1952-

See Trumbo, Dalton

Jackson, Sara
See Wingrove, David (John)

Jackson, Shirley 1919-1965 . **CLC 11, 60, 87; DA; DAC; DAM MST; SSC 9; WLC**
See also AAYA 9; CA 1-4R; 25-28R; CANR 4, 52; CDALB 1941-1968; DLB 6; SATA 2

Jacob, (Cyprien-)Max 1876-1944 .... **TCLC 6**
See also CA 104

Jacobs, Jim 1942- .... **CLC 12**
See also CA 97-100; INT 97-100

Jacobs, W(illiam) W(ymark) 1863-1943 **TCLC 22**
See also CA 121; DLB 135

Jacobsen, Jens Peter 1847-1885 .... **NCLC 34**

Jacobsen, Josephine 1908- .... **CLC 48, 102**
See also CA 33-36R; CAAS 18; CANR 23, 48

Jacobson, Dan 1929- .... **CLC 4, 14**
See also CA 1-4R; CANR 2, 25; DLB 14; MTCW

Jacqueline
See Carpentier (y Valmont), Alejo

Jagger, Mick 1944- .... **CLC 17**

Jakes, John (William) 1932- .. **CLC 29; DAM NOV, POP**
See also BEST 89:4; CA 57-60; CANR 10, 43; DLBY 83; INT CANR-10; MTCW; SATA 62

James, Andrew
See Kirkup, James

James, C(yril) L(ionel) R(obert) 1901-1989 **CLC 33**
See also BW 2; CA 117; 125; 128; DLB 125; MTCW

James, Daniel (Lewis) 1911-1988
See Santiago, Danny
See also CA 125

James, Dynely
See Mayne, William (James Carter)

James, Henry Sr. 1811-1882 .... **NCLC 53**

James, Henry 1843-1916 **TCLC 2, 11, 24, 40, 47, 64; DA; DAB; DAC; DAM MST, NOV; SSC 8; WLC**
See also CA 104; 132; CDALB 1865-1917; DLB 12, 71, 74; DLBD 13; MTCW

James, M. R.
See James, Montague (Rhodes)
See also DLB 156

James, Montague (Rhodes) 1862-1936 **T C L C 6; SSC 16**
See also CA 104

James, P. D. .... **CLC 18, 46**
See also White, Phyllis Dorothy James
See also BEST 90:2; CDBLB 1960 to Present; DLB 87

James, Philip
See Moorcock, Michael (John)

James, William 1842-1910 .... **TCLC 15, 32**
See also CA 109

James I 1394-1437 .... **LC 20**

Jameson, Anna 1794-1860 .... **NCLC 43**
See also DLB 99, 166

Jami, Nur al-Din 'Abd al-Rahman 1414-1492 **LC 9**

Jandl, Ernst 1925- .... **CLC 34**

Janowitz, Tama 1957- .. **CLC 43; DAM POP**
See also CA 106; CANR 52

Japrisot, Sebastien 1931- .... **CLC 90**

Jarrell, Randall 1914-1965 **CLC 1, 2, 6, 9, 13, 49; DAM POET**
See also CA 5-8R; 25-28R; CABS 2; CANR 6, 34; CDALB 1941-1968; CLR 6; DLB 48, 52; MAICYA; MTCW; SATA 7

Jarry, Alfred 1873-1907 .. **TCLC 2, 14; DAM DRAM; SSC 20**
See also CA 104; 153

Jarvis, E. K.
See Bloch, Robert (Albert); Ellison, Harlan (Jay); Silverberg, Robert

Jeake, Samuel, Jr.
See Aiken, Conrad (Potter)

Jean Paul 1763-1825 .... **NCLC 7**

Jefferies, (John) Richard 1848-1887 **NCLC 47**
See also DLB 98, 141; SATA 16

Jeffers, (John) Robinson 1887-1962 **CLC 2, 3, 11, 15, 54; DA; DAC; DAM MST, POET; PC 17; WLC**
See also CA 85-88; CANR 35; CDALB 1917-1929; DLB 45; MTCW

Jefferson, Janet
See Mencken, H(enry) L(ouis)

Jefferson, Thomas 1743-1826 .... **NCLC 11**
See also CDALB 1640-1865; DLB 31

Jeffrey, Francis 1773-1850 .... **NCLC 33**
See also DLB 107

Jelakowitch, Ivan
See Heijermans, Herman

Jellicoe, (Patricia) Ann 1927- .... **CLC 27**
See also CA 85-88; DLB 13

Jen, Gish .... **CLC 70**
See also Jen, Lillian

Jen, Lillian 1956(?)-
See Jen, Gish
See also CA 135

Jenkins, (John) Robin 1912- .... **CLC 52**
See also CA 1-4R; CANR 1; DLB 14

Jennings, Elizabeth (Joan) 1926- . **CLC 5, 14**
See also CA 61-64; CAAS 5; CANR 8, 39; DLB 27; MTCW; SATA 66

Jennings, Waylon 1937- .... **CLC 21**

Jensen, Johannes V. 1873-1950 ...... **TCLC 41**

Jensen, Laura (Linnea) 1948- .... **CLC 37**
See also CA 103

Jerome, Jerome K(lapka) 1859-1927 **TCLC 23**
See also CA 119; DLB 10, 34, 135

Jerrold, Douglas William 1803-1857 **NCLC 2**
See also DLB 158, 159

Jewett, (Theodora) Sarah Orne 1849-1909 **TCLC 1, 22; SSC 6**
See also CA 108; 127; DLB 12, 74; SATA 15

Jewsbury, Geraldine (Endsor) 1812-1880 **NCLC 22**
See also DLB 21

Jhabvala, Ruth Prawer 1927- **CLC 4, 8, 29, 94; DAB; DAM NOV**
See also CA 1-4R; CANR 2, 29, 51; DLB 139; INT CANR-29; MTCW

Jibran, Kahlil
See Gibran, Kahlil

Jibran, Khalil
See Gibran, Kahlil

Jiles, Paulette 1943- .... **CLC 13, 58**
See also CA 101

Jimenez (Mantecon), Juan Ramon 1881-1958 **TCLC 4; DAM MULT, POET; HLC; PC 7**
See also CA 104; 131; DLB 134; HW; MTCW

Jimenez, Ramon
See Jimenez (Mantecon), Juan Ramon

Jimenez Mantecon, Juan
See Jimenez (Mantecon), Juan Ramon

Joel, Billy .... **CLC 26**
See also Joel, William Martin

Joel, William Martin 1949-
See Joel, Billy
See also CA 108

John of the Cross, St. 1542-1591 .... **LC 18**

Johnson, B(ryan) S(tanley William) 1933-1973 **CLC 6, 9**
See also CA 9-12R; 53-56; CANR 9; DLB 14, 40

Johnson, Benj. F. of Boo
See Riley, James Whitcomb

Johnson, Benjamin F. of Boo
See Riley, James Whitcomb

Johnson, Charles (Richard) 1948- **CLC 7, 51, 65; BLC; DAM MULT**
See also BW 2; CA 116; CAAS 18; CANR 42; DLB 33

Johnson, Denis 1949- .... **CLC 52**
See also CA 117; 121; DLB 120

Johnson, Diane 1934- .... **CLC 5, 13, 48**
See also CA 41-44R; CANR 17, 40; DLBY 80; INT CANR-17; MTCW

Johnson, Eyvind (Olof Verner) 1900-1976 **CLC 14**
See also CA 73-76; 69-72; CANR 34

Johnson, J. R.
See James, C(yril) L(ionel) R(obert)

Johnson, James Weldon 1871-1938 **TCLC 3, 19; BLC; DAM MULT, POET**
See also BW 1; CA 104; 125; CDALB 1917-1929; CLR 32; DLB 51; MTCW; SATA 31

Johnson, Joyce 1935- .... **CLC 58**
See also CA 125; 129

Johnson, Lionel (Pigot) 1867-1902 **TCLC 19**
See also CA 117; DLB 19

Johnson, Mel
See Malzberg, Barry N(athaniel)

Johnson, Pamela Hansford 1912-1981 **CLC 1, 7, 27**
See also CA 1-4R; 104; CANR 2, 28; DLB 15; MTCW

Johnson, Robert 1911(?)-1938 .... **TCLC 69**

Johnson, Samuel 1709-1784 **LC 15; DA; DAB; DAC; DAM MST; WLC**
See also CDBLB 1660-1789; DLB 39, 95, 104, 142

Johnson, Uwe 1934-1984 .. **CLC 5, 10, 15, 40**
See also CA 1-4R; 112; CANR 1, 39; DLB 75; MTCW

Johnston, George (Benson) 1913- ..... **CLC 51**
See also CA 1-4R; CANR 5, 20; DLB 88

Johnston, Jennifer 1930- .... **CLC 7**
See also CA 85-88; DLB 14

Jolley, (Monica) Elizabeth 1923- **CLC 46; SSC 19**
See also CA 127; CAAS 13; CANR 59

Jones, Arthur Llewellyn 1863-1947
See Machen, Arthur
See also CA 104

Jones, D(ouglas) G(ordon) 1929- ...... **CLC 10**
See also CA 29-32R; CANR 13; DLB 53

Jones, David (Michael) 1895-1974 **CLC 2, 4, 7, 13, 42**
See also CA 9-12R; 53-56; CANR 28; CDBLB 1945-1960; DLB 20, 100; MTCW

Jones, David Robert 1947-
See Bowie, David
See also CA 103

Jones, Diana Wynne 1934- .... **CLC 26**
See also AAYA 12; CA 49-52; CANR 4, 26, 56; CLR 23; DLB 161; JRDA; MAICYA; SAAS 7; SATA 9, 70

Jones, Edward P. 1950- .... **CLC 76**
See also BW 2; CA 142

Jones, Gayl 1949- .... **CLC 6, 9; BLC; DAM MULT**
See also BW 2; CA 77-80; CANR 27; DLB 33; MTCW

NCLC 11
See also DLB 97
Knapp, Caroline 1959- .... **CLC 99**
See also CA 154
Knebel, Fletcher 1911-1993 .... **CLC 14**
See also AITN 1; CA 1-4R; 140; CAAS 3;
CANR 1, 36; SATA 36; SATA-Obit 75
Knickerbocker, Diedrich
See Irving, Washington
Knight, Etheridge 1931-1991 **CLC 40; BLC;
DAM POET; PC 14**
See also BW 1; CA 21-24R; 133; CANR 23;
DLB 41
Knight, Sarah Kemble 1666-1727 .... **LC 7**
See also DLB 24
Knister, Raymond 1899-1932 .... **TCLC 56**
See also DLB 68
Knowles, John 1926- . **CLC 1, 4, 10, 26; DA;
DAC; DAM MST, NOV**
See also AAYA 10; CA 17-20R; CANR 40;
CDALB 1968-1988; DLB 6; MTCW; SATA
8, 89
Knox, Calvin M.
See Silverberg, Robert
Knox, John c. 1505-1572 .... **LC 37**
See also DLB 132
Knye, Cassandra
See Disch, Thomas M(ichael)
Koch, C(hristopher) J(ohn) 1932- .... **CLC 42**
See also CA 127
Koch, Christopher
See Koch, C(hristopher) J(ohn)
Koch, Kenneth 1925- ..... **CLC 5, 8, 44; DAM
POET**
See also CA 1-4R; CANR 6, 36, 57; DLB 5;
INT CANR-36; SATA 65
Kochanowski, Jan 1530-1584 .... **LC 10**
Kock, Charles Paul de 1794-1871 . **NCLC 16**
Koda Shigeyuki 1867-1947
See Rohan, Koda
See also CA 121
Koestler, Arthur 1905-1983 **CLC 1, 3, 6, 8, 15,
33**
See also CA 1-4R; 109; CANR 1, 33; CDBLB
1945-1960; DLBY 83; MTCW
Kogawa, Joy Nozomi 1935- .. **CLC 78; DAC;
DAM MST, MULT**
See also CA 101; CANR 19
Kohout, Pavel 1928- .... **CLC 13**
See also CA 45-48; CANR 3
Koizumi, Yakumo
See Hearn, (Patricio) Lafcadio (Tessima Carlos)
Kolmar, Gertrud 1894-1943 .... **TCLC 40**
Komunyakaa, Yusef 1947- .... **CLC 86, 94**
See also CA 147; DLB 120
Konrad, George
See Konrad, Gyoergy
Konrad, Gyoergy 1933- .... **CLC 4, 10, 73**
See also CA 85-88
Konwicki, Tadeusz 1926- .... **CLC 8, 28, 54**
See also CA 101; CAAS 9; CANR 39, 59;
MTCW
Koontz, Dean R(ay) 1945- ..... **CLC 78; DAM
NOV, POP**
See also AAYA 9; BEST 89:3, 90:2; CA 108;
CANR 19, 36, 52; MTCW; SATA 92
Kopit, Arthur (Lee) 1937- **CLC 1, 18, 33; DAM
DRAM**
See also AITN 1; CA 81-84; CABS 3; DLB 7;
MTCW
Kops, Bernard 1926- .... **CLC 4**
See also CA 5-8R; DLB 13
Kornbluth, C(yril) M. 1923-1958 .... **TCLC 8**

See also CA 105; DLB 8
Korolenko, V. G.
See Korolenko, Vladimir Galaktionovich
Korolenko, Vladimir
See Korolenko, Vladimir Galaktionovich
Korolenko, Vladimir G.
See Korolenko, Vladimir Galaktionovich
Korolenko, Vladimir Galaktionovich 1853-
1921 .... **TCLC 22**
See also CA 121
Korzybski, Alfred (Habdank Skarbek) 1879-
1950 .... **TCLC 61**
See also CA 123
Kosinski, Jerzy (Nikodem) 1933-1991 **CLC 1,
2, 3, 6, 10, 15, 53, 70; DAM NOV**
See also CA 17-20R; 134; CANR 9, 46; DLB
2; DLBY 82; MTCW
Kostelanetz, Richard (Cory) 1940- .. **CLC 28**
See also CA 13-16R; CAAS 8; CANR 38
Kostrowitzki, Wilhelm Apollinaris de 1880-
1918
See Apollinaire, Guillaume
See also CA 104
Kotlowitz, Robert 1924- .... **CLC 4**
See also CA 33-36R; CANR 36
Kotzebue, August (Friedrich Ferdinand) von
1761-1819 .... **NCLC 25**
See also DLB 94
Kotzwinkle, William 1938- ..... **CLC 5, 14, 35**
See also CA 45-48; CANR 3, 44; CLR 6; DLB
173; MAICYA; SATA 24, 70
Kowna, Stancy
See Szymborska, Wislawa
Kozol, Jonathan 1936- .... **CLC 17**
See also CA 61-64; CANR 16, 45
Kozoll, Michael 1940(?)- .... **CLC 35**
Kramer, Kathryn 19(?)- .... **CLC 34**
Kramer, Larry 1935- .... **CLC 42; DAM POP**
See also CA 124; 126
Krasicki, Ignacy 1735-1801 .... **NCLC 8**
Krasinski, Zygmunt 1812-1859 .... **NCLC 4**
Kraus, Karl 1874-1936 .... **TCLC 5**
See also CA 104; DLB 118
Kreve (Mickevicius), Vincas 1882-1954 **TCLC
27**
Kristeva, Julia 1941- .... **CLC 77**
See also CA 154
Kristofferson, Kris 1936- .... **CLC 26**
See also CA 104
Krizanc, John 1956- .... **CLC 57**
Krleza, Miroslav 1893-1981 .... **CLC 8**
See also CA 97-100; 105; CANR 50; DLB 147
Kroetsch, Robert 1927- **CLC 5, 23, 57; DAC;
DAM POET**
See also CA 17-20R; CANR 8, 38; DLB 53;
MTCW
Kroetz, Franz
See Kroetz, Franz Xaver
Kroetz, Franz Xaver 1946- .... **CLC 41**
See also CA 130
Kroker, Arthur 1945- .... **CLC 77**
Kropotkin, Peter (Aleksieevich) 1842-1921
TCLC 36
See also CA 119
Krotkov, Yuri 1917- .... **CLC 19**
See also CA 102
Krumb
See Crumb, R(obert)
Krumgold, Joseph (Quincy) 1908-1980 **C L C
12**
See also CA 9-12R; 101; CANR 7; MAICYA;
SATA 1, 48; SATA-Obit 23
Krumwitz

See Crumb, R(obert)
Krutch, Joseph Wood 1893-1970 ...... **CLC 24**
See also CA 1-4R; 25-28R; CANR 4; DLB 63
Krutzch, Gus
See Eliot, T(homas) S(tearns)
Krylov, Ivan Andreevich 1768(?)-1844 **N C L C
1**
See also DLB 150
Kubin, Alfred (Leopold Isidor) 1877-1959
TCLC 23
See also CA 112; 149; DLB 81
Kubrick, Stanley 1928- .... **CLC 16**
See also CA 81-84; CANR 33; DLB 26
Kumin, Maxine (Winokur) 1925- **CLC 5, 13,
28; DAM POET; PC 15**
See also AITN 2; CA 1-4R; CAAS 8; CANR 1,
21; DLB 5; MTCW; SATA 12
Kundera, Milan 1929- . **CLC 4, 9, 19, 32, 68;
DAM NOV; SSC 24**
See also AAYA 2; CA 85-88; CANR 19, 52;
MTCW
Kunene, Mazisi (Raymond) 1930- .... **CLC 85**
See also BW 1; CA 125; DLB 117
Kunitz, Stanley (Jasspon) 1905- **CLC 6, 11, 14;
PC 19**
See also CA 41-44R; CANR 26, 57; DLB 48;
INT CANR-26; MTCW
Kunze, Reiner 1933- .... **CLC 10**
See also CA 93-96; DLB 75
Kuprin, Aleksandr Ivanovich 1870-1938
TCLC 5
See also CA 104
Kureishi, Hanif 1954(?)- .... **CLC 64**
See also CA 139
Kurosawa, Akira 1910- **CLC 16; DAM MULT**
See also AAYA 11; CA 101; CANR 46
Kushner, Tony 1957(?)- **CLC 81; DAM DRAM**
See also CA 144
Kuttner, Henry 1915-1958 .... **TCLC 10**
See Vance, Jack
See also CA 107; 157; DLB 8
Kuzma, Greg 1944- .... **CLC 7**
See also CA 33-36R
Kuzmin, Mikhail 1872(?)-1936 ...... **TCLC 40**
Kyd, Thomas 1558-1594 **LC 22; DAM DRAM;
DC 3**
See also DLB 62
Kyprianos, Iossif
See Samarakis, Antonis
La Bruyere, Jean de 1645-1696 .... **LC 17**
Lacan, Jacques (Marie Emile) 1901-1981
CLC 75
See also CA 121; 104
Laclos, Pierre Ambroise Francois Choderlos de
1741-1803 .... **NCLC 4**
Lacolere, Francois
See Aragon, Louis
La Colere, Francois
See Aragon, Louis
La Deshabilleuse
See Simenon, Georges (Jacques Christian)
Lady Gregory
See Gregory, Isabella Augusta (Persse)
Lady of Quality, A
See Bagnold, Enid
**La Fayette, Marie (Madelaine Pioche de la
Vergne Comtes** 1634-1693 .... **LC 2**
Lafayette, Rene
See Hubbard, L(afayette) Ron(ald)
Laforgue, Jules 1860-1887 **NCLC 5, 53; PC 14;
SSC 20**
Lagerkvist, Paer (Fabian) 1891-1974 **CLC 7,
10, 13, 54; DAM DRAM, NOV**

POP; WLC
See also AAYA 3; CA 81-84; CANR 33; CDBLB 1945-1960; CLR 3, 27; DLB 15, 100, 160; JRDA; MAICYA; MTCW; SATA 13

Lewis, Janet 1899- .... **CLC 41**
See also Winters, Janet Lewis
See also CA 9-12R; CANR 29; CAP 1; DLBY 87

Lewis, Matthew Gregory 1775-1818**NCLC 11, 62**
See also DLB 39, 158, 178

Lewis, (Harry) Sinclair 1885-1951 . **TCLC 4, 13, 23, 39; DA; DAB; DAC; DAM MST, NOV; WLC**
See also CA 104; 133; CDALB 1917-1929; DLB 9, 102; DLBD 1; MTCW

Lewis, (Percy) Wyndham 1882(?)-1957**TCLC 2, 9**
See also CA 104; 157; DLB 15

Lewisohn, Ludwig 1883-1955 .... **TCLC 19**
See also CA 107; DLB 4, 9, 28, 102

Leyner, Mark 1956- .... **CLC 92**
See also CA 110; CANR 28, 53

Lezama Lima, Jose 1910-1976**CLC 4, 10, 101; DAM MULT**
See also CA 77-80; DLB 113; HW

L'Heureux, John (Clarke) 1934- .... **CLC 52**
See also CA 13-16R; CANR 23, 45

Liddell, C. H.
See Kuttner, Henry

Lie, Jonas (Lauritz Idemil) 1833-1908(?) **TCLC 5**
See also CA 115

Lieber, Joel 1937-1971 .... **CLC 6**
See also CA 73-76; 29-32R

Lieber, Stanley Martin
See Lee, Stan

Lieberman, Laurence (James) 1935- **CLC 4, 36**
See also CA 17-20R; CANR 8, 36

Lieksman, Anders
See Haavikko, Paavo Juhani

Li Fei-kan 1904-
See Pa Chin
See also CA 105

Lifton, Robert Jay 1926- .... **CLC 67**
See also CA 17-20R; CANR 27; INT CANR-27; SATA 66

Lightfoot, Gordon 1938- .... **CLC 26**
See also CA 109

Lightman, Alan P. 1948- .... **CLC 81**
See also CA 141

Ligotti, Thomas (Robert) 1953-**CLC 44; SSC 16**
See also CA 123; CANR 49

Li Ho 791-817 .... **PC 13**

Liliencron, (Friedrich Adolf Axel) Detlev von 1844-1909 .... **TCLC 18**
See also CA 117

Lilly, William 1602-1681 .... **LC 27**

Lima, Jose Lezama
See Lezama Lima, Jose

Lima Barreto, Afonso Henrique de 1881-1922 **TCLC 23**
See also CA 117

Limonov, Edward 1944- .... **CLC 67**
See also CA 137

Lin, Frank
See Atherton, Gertrude (Franklin Horn)

Lincoln, Abraham 1809-1865 .... **NCLC 18**

Lind, Jakov .... **CLC 1, 2, 4, 27, 82**
See also Landwirth, Heinz

See also CAAS 4

Lindbergh, Anne (Spencer) Morrow 1906- **CLC 82; DAM NOV**
See also CA 17-20R; CANR 16; MTCW; SATA 33

Lindsay, David 1878-1945 .... **TCLC 15**
See also CA 113

Lindsay, (Nicholas) Vachel 1879-1931 **TCLC 17; DA; DAC; DAM MST, POET; WLC**
See also CA 114; 135; CDALB 1865-1917; DLB 54; SATA 40

Linke-Poot
See Doeblin, Alfred

Linney, Romulus 1930- .... **CLC 51**
See also CA 1-4R; CANR 40, 44

Linton, Eliza Lynn 1822-1898 .... **NCLC 41**
See also DLB 18

Li Po 701-763 .... **CMLC 2**

Lipsius, Justus 1547-1606 .... **LC 16**

Lipsyte, Robert (Michael) 1938-**CLC 21; DA; DAC; DAM MST, NOV**
See also AAYA 7; CA 17-20R; CANR 8, 57; CLR 23; JRDA; MAICYA; SATA 5, 68

Lish, Gordon (Jay) 1934- ... **CLC 45; SSC 18**
See also CA 113; 117; DLB 130; INT 117

Lispector, Clarice 1925-1977 .... **CLC 43**
See also CA 139; 116; DLB 113

Littell, Robert 1935(?)- .... **CLC 42**
See also CA 109; 112

Little, Malcolm 1925-1965
See Malcolm X
See also BW 1; CA 125; 111; DA; DAB; DAC; DAM MST, MULT; MTCW

Littlewit, Humphrey Gent.
See Lovecraft, H(oward) P(hillips)

Litwos
See Sienkiewicz, Henryk (Adam Alexander Pius)

Liu E 1857-1909 .... **TCLC 15**
See also CA 115

Lively, Penelope (Margaret) 1933- .. **CLC 32, 50; DAM NOV**
See also CA 41-44R; CANR 29; CLR 7; DLB 14, 161; JRDA; MAICYA; MTCW; SATA 7, 60

Livesay, Dorothy (Kathleen) 1909-**CLC 4, 15, 79; DAC; DAM MST, POET**
See also AITN 2; CA 25-28R; CAAS 8; CANR 36; DLB 68; MTCW

Livy c. 59B.C.-c. 17 .... **CMLC 11**

Lizardi, Jose Joaquin Fernandez de 1776-1827 **NCLC 30**

Llewellyn, Richard
See Llewellyn Lloyd, Richard Dafydd Vivian
See also DLB 15

Llewellyn Lloyd, Richard Dafydd Vivian 1906-1983 .... **CLC 7, 80**
See Llewellyn, Richard
See also CA 53-56; 111; CANR 7; SATA 11; SATA-Obit 37

Llosa, (Jorge) Mario (Pedro) Vargas
See Vargas Llosa, (Jorge) Mario (Pedro)

Lloyd Webber, Andrew 1948-
See Webber, Andrew Lloyd
See also AAYA 1; CA 116; 149; DAM DRAM; SATA 56

Llull, Ramon c. 1235-c. 1316 .... **CMLC 12**

Locke, Alain (Le Roy) 1886-1954 .. **TCLC 43**
See also BW 1; CA 106; 124; DLB 51

Locke, John 1632-1704 .... **LC 7, 35**
See also DLB 101

Locke-Elliott, Sumner
See Elliott, Sumner Locke

Lockhart, John Gibson 1794-1854 .. **NCLC 6**
See also DLB 110, 116, 144

Lodge, David (John) 1935- .... **CLC 36; DAM POP**
See also BEST 90:1; CA 17-20R; CANR 19, 53; DLB 14; INT CANR-19; MTCW

Loennbohm, Armas Eino Leopold 1878-1926
See Leino, Eino
See also CA 123

Loewinsohn, Ron(ald William) 1937-**CLC 52**
See also CA 25-28R

Logan, Jake
See Smith, Martin Cruz

Logan, John (Burton) 1923-1987 .... **CLC 5**
See also CA 77-80; 124; CANR 45; DLB 5

Lo Kuan-chung 1330(?)-1400(?) .... **LC 12**

Lombard, Nap
See Johnson, Pamela Hansford

London, Jack . **TCLC 9, 15, 39; SSC 4; WLC**
See also London, John Griffith
See also AAYA 13; AITN 2; CDALB 1865-1917; DLB 8, 12, 78; SATA 18

London, John Griffith 1876-1916
See London, Jack
See also CA 110; 119; DA; DAB; DAC; DAM MST, NOV; JRDA; MAICYA; MTCW

Long, Emmett
See Leonard, Elmore (John, Jr.)

Longbaugh, Harry
See Goldman, William (W.)

Longfellow, Henry Wadsworth 1807-1882 **NCLC 2, 45; DA; DAB; DAC; DAM MST, POET; WLCS**
See also CDALB 1640-1865; DLB 1, 59; SATA 19

Longley, Michael 1939- .... **CLC 29**
See also CA 102; DLB 40

Longus fl. c. 2nd cent. - .... **CMLC 7**

Longway, A. Hugh
See Lang, Andrew

Lonnrot, Elias 1802-1884 .... **NCLC 53**

Lopate, Phillip 1943- .... **CLC 29**
See also CA 97-100; DLBY 80; INT 97-100

Lopez Portillo (y Pacheco), Jose 1920- . **C L C 46**
See also CA 129; HW

Lopez y Fuentes, Gregorio 1897(?)-1966**C L C 32**
See also CA 131; HW

Lorca, Federico Garcia
See Garcia Lorca, Federico

Lord, Bette Bao 1938- .... **CLC 23**
See also BEST 90:3; CA 107; CANR 41; INT 107; SATA 58

Lord Auch
See Bataille, Georges

Lord Byron
See Byron, George Gordon (Noel)

Lorde, Audre (Geraldine) 1934-1992**CLC 18, 71; BLC; DAM MULT, POET; PC 12**
See also BW 1; CA 25-28R; 142; CANR 16, 26, 46; DLB 41; MTCW

Lord Houghton
See Milnes, Richard Monckton

Lord Jeffrey
See Jeffrey, Francis

Lorenzini, Carlo 1826-1890
See Collodi, Carlo
See also MAICYA; SATA 29

Lorenzo, Heberto Padilla
See Padilla (Lorenzo), Heberto

Loris
See Hofmannsthal, Hugo von

See also CA 73-76; CANR 54; DLB 111

Meynell, Alice (Christina Gertrude Thompson)
1847-1922 ....
TCLC 6
See also CA 104; DLB 19, 98

Meyrink, Gustav .... **TCLC 21**
See also Meyer-Meyrink, Gustav
See also DLB 81

Michaels, Leonard 1933- **CLC 6, 25; SSC 16**
See also CA 61-64; CANR 21; DLB 130;
MTCW

Michaux, Henri 1899-1984 .... **CLC 8, 19**
See also CA 85-88; 114

Michelangelo 1475-1564 .... **LC 12**

Michelet, Jules 1798-1874 .... **NCLC 31**

Michener, James A(lbert) 1907(?)- **CLC 1, 5,**
11, 29, 60; DAM NOV, POP
See also AITN 1; BEST 90:1; CA 5-8R; CANR
21, 45; DLB 6; MTCW

Mickiewicz, Adam 1798-1855 .... **NCLC 3**

Middleton, Christopher 1926- .... **CLC 13**
See also CA 13-16R; CANR 29, 54; DLB 40

Middleton, Richard (Barham) 1882-1911
TCLC 56
See also DLB 156

Middleton, Stanley 1919- .... **CLC 7, 38**
See also CA 25-28R; CAAS 23; CANR 21, 46;
DLB 14

Middleton, Thomas 1580-1627 **LC 33; DAM**
DRAM, MST; DC 5
See also DLB 58

Migueis, Jose Rodrigues 1901- .... **CLC 10**

Mikszath, Kalman 1847-1910 .... **TCLC 31**

Miles, Jack .... **CLC 100**

Miles, Josephine (Louise) 1911-1985 **CLC 1, 2,**
14, 34, 39; DAM POET
See also CA 1-4R; 116; CANR 2, 55; DLB 48

Militant
See Sandburg, Carl (August)

Mill, John Stuart 1806-1873 .... **NCLC 11, 58**
See also CDBLB 1832-1890; DLB 55

Millar, Kenneth 1915-1983 .... **CLC 14; DAM**
POP
See also Macdonald, Ross
See also CA 9-12R; 110; CANR 16; DLB 2;
DLBD 6; DLBY 83; MTCW

Millay, E. Vincent
See Millay, Edna St. Vincent

Millay, Edna St. Vincent 1892-1950 **TCLC 4,**
49; DA; DAB; DAC; DAM MST, POET;
PC 6; WLCS
See also CA 104; 130; CDALB 1917-1929;
DLB 45; MTCW

Miller, Arthur 1915- **CLC 1, 2, 6, 10, 15, 26, 47,**
78; DA; DAB; DAC; DAM DRAM, MST;
DC 1; WLC
See also AAYA 15; AITN 1; CA 1-4R; CABS
3; CANR 2, 30, 54; CDALB 1941-1968;
DLB 7; MTCW

Miller, Henry (Valentine) 1891-1980 **CLC 1, 2,**
4, 9, 14, 43, 84; DA; DAB; DAC; DAM
MST, NOV; WLC
See also CA 9-12R; 97-100; CANR 33; CDALB
1929-1941; DLB 4, 9; DLBY 80; MTCW

Miller, Jason 1939(?)- .... **CLC 2**
See also AITN 1; CA 73-76; DLB 7

Miller, Sue 1943- .... **CLC 44; DAM POP**
See also BEST 90:3; CA 139; CANR 59; DLB
143

Miller, Walter M(ichael, Jr.) 1923- **CLC 4, 30**
See also CA 85-88; DLB 8

Millett, Kate 1934- .... **CLC 67**
See also AITN 1; CA 73-76; CANR 32, 53;
MTCW

Millhauser, Steven 1943- .... **CLC 21, 54**
See also CA 110; 111; DLB 2; INT 111

Millin, Sarah Gertrude 1889-1968 ... **CLC 49**
See also CA 102; 93-96

Milne, A(lan) A(lexander) 1882-1956 **TCLC 6;**
DAB; DAC; DAM MST
See also CA 104; 133; CLR 1, 26; DLB 10, 77,
100, 160; MAICYA; MTCW; YABC 1

Milner, Ron(ald) 1938- **CLC 56; BLC; DAM**
MULT
See also AITN 1; BW 1; CA 73-76; CANR 24;
DLB 38; MTCW

Milnes, Richard Monckton 1809-1885 **N C L C**
61
See also DLB 32

Milosz, Czeslaw 1911- **CLC 5, 11, 22, 31, 56,**
82; DAM MST, POET; PC 8; WLCS
See also CA 81-84; CANR 23, 51; MTCW

Milton, John 1608-1674 ..... **LC 9; DA; DAB;**
DAC; DAM MST, POET; PC 19; WLC
See also CDBLB 1660-1789; DLB 131, 151

Min, Anchee 1957- .... **CLC 86**
See also CA 146

Minehaha, Cornelius
See Wedekind, (Benjamin) Frank(lin)

Miner, Valerie 1947- .... **CLC 40**
See also CA 97-100; CANR 59

Minimo, Duca
See D'Annunzio, Gabriele

Minot, Susan 1956- .... **CLC 44**
See also CA 134

Minus, Ed 1938- .... **CLC 39**

Miranda, Javier
See Bioy Casares, Adolfo

Mirbeau, Octave 1848-1917 .... **TCLC 55**
See also DLB 123

Miro (Ferrer), Gabriel (Francisco Victor) 1879-
1930 .... **TCLC 5**
See also CA 104

Mishima, Yukio 1925-1970 **CLC 2, 4, 6, 9, 27;**
DC 1; SSC 4
See also Hiraoka, Kimitake
See also DLB 182

Mistral, Frederic 1830-1914 .... **TCLC 51**
See also CA 122

Mistral, Gabriela .... **TCLC 2; HLC**
See also Godoy Alcayaga, Lucila

Mistry, Rohinton 1952- .... **CLC 71; DAC**
See also CA 141

Mitchell, Clyde
See Ellison, Harlan (Jay); Silverberg, Robert

Mitchell, James Leslie 1901-1935
See Gibbon, Lewis Grassic
See also CA 104; DLB 15

Mitchell, Joni 1943- .... **CLC 12**
See also CA 112

Mitchell, Joseph (Quincy) 1908-1996 **CLC 98**
See also CA 77-80; 152; DLBY 96

Mitchell, Margaret (Munnerlyn) 1900-1949
TCLC 11; DAM NOV, POP
See also CA 109; 125; CANR 55; DLB 9;
MTCW

Mitchell, Peggy
See Mitchell, Margaret (Munnerlyn)

Mitchell, S(ilas) Weir 1829-1914 ... **TCLC 36**

Mitchell, W(illiam) O(rmond) 1914- **CLC 25;**
DAC; DAM MST
See also CA 77-80; CANR 15, 43; DLB 88

Mitford, Mary Russell 1787-1855 ... **NCLC 4**
See also DLB 110, 116

Mitford, Nancy 1904-1973 .... **CLC 44**
See also CA 9-12R

Miyamoto, Yuriko 1899-1951 .... **TCLC 37**
See also DLB 180

Mizoguchi, Kenji 1898-1956 .... **TCLC 72**

Mo, Timothy (Peter) 1950(?)- .... **CLC 46**
See also CA 117; MTCW

Modarressi, Taghi (M.) 1931- .... **CLC 44**
See also CA 121; 134; INT 134

Modiano, Patrick (Jean) 1945- .... **CLC 18**
See also CA 85-88; CANR 17, 40; DLB 83

Moerck, Paal
See Roelvaag, O(le) E(dvart)

Mofolo, Thomas (Mokopu) 1875(?)-1948
TCLC 22; BLC; DAM MULT
See also CA 121; 153

Mohr, Nicholasa 1935- **CLC 12; DAM MULT;**
HLC
See also AAYA 8; CA 49-52; CANR 1, 32; CLR
22; DLB 145; HW; JRDA; SAAS 8; SATA 8

Mojtabai, A(nn) G(race) 1938- **CLC 5, 9, 15,**
29
See also CA 85-88

Moliere 1622-1673 . **LC 28; DA; DAB; DAC;**
DAM DRAM, MST; WLC

Molin, Charles
See Mayne, William (James Carter)

Molnar, Ferenc 1878-1952 .. **TCLC 20; DAM**
DRAM
See also CA 109; 153

Momaday, N(avarre) Scott 1934- **CLC 2, 19,**
85, 95; DA; DAB; DAC; DAM MST,
MULT, NOV, POP; WLCS
See also AAYA 11; CA 25-28R; CANR 14, 34;
DLB 143, 175; INT CANR-14; MTCW;
NNAL; SATA 48; SATA-Brief 30

Monette, Paul 1945-1995 .... **CLC 82**
See also CA 139; 147

Monroe, Harriet 1860-1936 .... **TCLC 12**
See also CA 109; DLB 54, 91

Monroe, Lyle
See Heinlein, Robert A(nson)

Montagu, Elizabeth 1917- .... **NCLC 7**
See also CA 9-12R

Montagu, Mary (Pierrepont) Wortley 1689-
1762 .... **LC 9; PC 16**
See also DLB 95, 101

Montagu, W. H.
See Coleridge, Samuel Taylor

Montague, John (Patrick) 1929- **CLC 13, 46**
See also CA 9-12R; CANR 9; DLB 40; MTCW

Montaigne, Michel (Eyquem) de 1533-1592
LC 8; DA; DAB; DAC; DAM MST; WLC

Montale, Eugenio 1896-1981 **CLC 7, 9, 18; PC**
13
See also CA 17-20R; 104; CANR 30; DLB 114;
MTCW

Montesquieu, Charles-Louis de Secondat 1689-
1755 .... **LC 7**

Montgomery, (Robert) Bruce 1921-1978
See Crispin, Edmund
See also CA 104

Montgomery, L(ucy) M(aud) 1874-1942
TCLC 51; DAC; DAM MST
See also AAYA 12; CA 108; 137; CLR 8; DLB
92; DLBD 14; JRDA; MAICYA; YABC 1

Montgomery, Marion H., Jr. 1925- .... **CLC 7**
See also AITN 1; CA 1-4R; CANR 3, 48; DLB
6

Montgomery, Max
See Davenport, Guy (Mattison, Jr.)

Montherlant, Henry (Milon) de 1896-1972
CLC 8, 19; DAM DRAM
See also CA 85-88; 37-40R; DLB 72; MTCW

Monty Python

See Chapman, Graham; Cleese, John (Marwood); Gilliam, Terry (Vance); Idle, Eric; Jones, Terence Graham Parry; Palin, Michael (Edward)
    See also AAYA 7
Moodie, Susanna (Strickland) 1803-1885 **NCLC 14**
    See also DLB 99
Mooney, Edward 1951-
    See Mooney, Ted
    See also CA 130
Mooney, Ted .... **CLC 25**
    See also Mooney, Edward
Moorcock, Michael (John) 1939- **CLC 5, 27, 58**
    See also CA 45-48; CAAS 5; CANR 2, 17, 38; DLB 14; MTCW; SATA 93
Moore, Brian 1921- **CLC 1, 3, 5, 7, 8, 19, 32, 90; DAB; DAC; DAM MST**
    See also CA 1-4R; CANR 1, 25, 42; MTCW
Moore, Edward
    See Muir, Edwin
Moore, George Augustus 1852-1933 **TCLC 7; SSC 19**
    See also CA 104; DLB 10, 18, 57, 135
Moore, Lorrie .... **CLC 39, 45, 68**
    See also Moore, Marie Lorena
Moore, Marianne (Craig) 1887-1972 **CLC 1, 2, 4, 8, 10, 13, 19, 47; DA; DAB; DAC; DAM MST, POET; PC 4; WLCS**
    See also CA 1-4R; 33-36R; CANR 3; CDALB 1929-1941; DLB 45; DLBD 7; MTCW; SATA 20
Moore, Marie Lorena 1957-
    See Moore, Lorrie
    See also CA 116; CANR 39
Moore, Thomas 1779-1852 .... **NCLC 6**
    See also DLB 96, 144
Morand, Paul 1888-1976 .... **CLC 41; SSC 22**
    See also CA 69-72; DLB 65
Morante, Elsa 1918-1985 .... **CLC 8, 47**
    See also CA 85-88; 117; CANR 35; DLB 177; MTCW
Moravia, Alberto 1907-1990 **CLC 2, 7, 11, 27, 46; SSC 26**
    See also Pincherle, Alberto
    See also DLB 177
More, Hannah 1745-1833 .... **NCLC 27**
    See also DLB 107, 109, 116, 158
More, Henry 1614-1687 .... **LC 9**
    See also DLB 126
More, Sir Thomas 1478-1535 .... **LC 10, 32**
Moreas, Jean .... **TCLC 18**
    See also Papadiamantopoulos, Johannes
Morgan, Berry 1919- .... **CLC 6**
    See also CA 49-52; DLB 6
Morgan, Claire
    See Highsmith, (Mary) Patricia
Morgan, Edwin (George) 1920- .... **CLC 31**
    See also CA 5-8R; CANR 3, 43; DLB 27
Morgan, (George) Frederick 1922- ... **CLC 23**
    See also CA 17-20R; CANR 21
Morgan, Harriet
    See Mencken, H(enry) L(ouis)
Morgan, Jane
    See Cooper, James Fenimore
Morgan, Janet 1945- .... **CLC 39**
    See also CA 65-68
Morgan, Lady 1776(?)-1859 .... **NCLC 29**
    See also DLB 116, 158
Morgan, Robin 1941- .... **CLC 2**
    See also CA 69-72; CANR 29; MTCW; SATA 80
Morgan, Scott

See Kuttner, Henry
Morgan, Seth 1949(?)-1990 .... **CLC 65**
    See also CA 132
Morgenstern, Christian 1871-1914 . **TCLC 8**
    See also CA 105
Morgenstern, S.
    See Goldman, William (W.)
Moricz, Zsigmond 1879-1942 .... **TCLC 33**
Morike, Eduard (Friedrich) 1804-1875 **NCLC 10**
    See also DLB 133
Mori Ogai .... **TCLC 14**
    See also Mori Rintaro
Mori Rintaro 1862-1922
    See Mori Ogai
    See also CA 110
Moritz, Karl Philipp 1756-1793 .... **LC 2**
    See also DLB 94
Morland, Peter Henry
    See Faust, Frederick (Schiller)
Morren, Theophil
    See Hofmannsthal, Hugo von
Morris, Bill 1952- .... **CLC 76**
Morris, Julian
    See West, Morris L(anglo)
Morris, Steveland Judkins 1950(?)-
    See Wonder, Stevie
    See also CA 111
Morris, William 1834-1896 .... **NCLC 4**
    See also CDBLB 1832-1890; DLB 18, 35, 57, 156, 178
Morris, Wright 1910- ...... **CLC 1, 3, 7, 18, 37**
    See also CA 9-12R; CANR 21; DLB 2; DLBY 81; MTCW
Morrison, Arthur 1863-1945 .... **TCLC 72**
    See also CA 120; 157; DLB 70, 135
Morrison, Chloe Anthony Wofford
    See Morrison, Toni
Morrison, James Douglas 1943-1971
    See Morrison, Jim
    See also CA 73-76; CANR 40
Morrison, Jim .... **CLC 17**
    See also Morrison, James Douglas
Morrison, Toni 1931- **CLC 4, 10, 22, 55, 81, 87; BLC; DA; DAB; DAC; DAM MST, MULT, NOV, POP**
    See also AAYA 1, 22; BW 2; CA 29-32R; CANR 27, 42; CDALB 1968-1988; DLB 6, 33, 143; DLBY 81; MTCW; SATA 57
Morrison, Van 1945- .... **CLC 21**
    See also CA 116
Morrissy, Mary 1958- .... **CLC 99**
Mortimer, John (Clifford) 1923- **CLC 28, 43; DAM DRAM, POP**
    See also CA 13-16R; CANR 21; CDBLB 1960 to Present; DLB 13; INT CANR-21; MTCW
Mortimer, Penelope (Ruth) 1918- .... **CLC 5**
    See also CA 57-60; CANR 45
Morton, Anthony
    See Creasey, John
Mosher, Howard Frank 1943- .... **CLC 62**
    See also CA 139
Mosley, Nicholas 1923- .... **CLC 43, 70**
    See also CA 69-72; CANR 41; DLB 14
Mosley, Walter 1952- **CLC 97; DAM MULT, POP**
    See also AAYA 17; BW 2; CA 142; CANR 57
Moss, Howard 1922-1987 **CLC 7, 14, 45, 50; DAM POET**
    See also CA 1-4R; 123; CANR 1, 44; DLB 5
Mossgiel, Rab
    See Burns, Robert
Motion, Andrew (Peter) 1952- .... **CLC 47**

See also CA 146; DLB 40
Motley, Willard (Francis) 1909-1965 **CLC 18**
    See also BW 1; CA 117; 106; DLB 76, 143
Motoori, Noringa 1730-1801 .... **NCLC 45**
Mott, Michael (Charles Alston) 1930- **CLC 15, 34**
    See also CA 5-8R; CAAS 7; CANR 7, 29
Mountain Wolf Woman 1884-1960 .. **CLC 92**
    See also CA 144; NNAL
Moure, Erin 1955- .... **CLC 88**
    See also CA 113; DLB 60
Mowat, Farley (McGill) 1921- **CLC 26; DAC; DAM MST**
    See also AAYA 1; CA 1-4R; CANR 4, 24, 42; CLR 20; DLB 68; INT CANAR-24; JRDA; MAICYA; MTCW; SATA 3, 55
Moyers, Bill 1934- .... **CLC 74**
    See also AITN 2; CA 61-64; CANR 31, 52
Mphahlele, Es'kia
    See Mphahlele, Ezekiel
    See also DLB 125
Mphahlele, Ezekiel 1919- **CLC 25; BLC; DAM MULT**
    See also Mphahlele, Es'kia
    See also BW 2; CA 81-84; CANR 26
Mqhayi, S(amuel) E(dward) K(rune Loliwe) 1875-1945 **TCLC 25; BLC; DAM MULT**
    See also CA 153
Mrozek, Slawomir 1930- .... **CLC 3, 13**
    See also CA 13-16R; CAAS 10; CANR 29; MTCW
Mrs. Belloc-Lowndes
    See Lowndes, Marie Adelaide (Belloc)
Mtwa, Percy (?)- .... **CLC 47**
Mueller, Lisel 1924- .... **CLC 13, 51**
    See also CA 93-96; DLB 105
Muir, Edwin 1887-1959 .... **TCLC 2**
    See also CA 104; DLB 20, 100
Muir, John 1838-1914 .... **TCLC 28**
Mujica Lainez, Manuel 1910-1984 ... **CLC 31**
    See also Lainez, Manuel Mujica
    See also CA 81-84; 112; CANR 32; HW
Mukherjee, Bharati 1940- **CLC 53; DAM NOV**
    See also BEST 89:2; CA 107; CANR 45; DLB 60; MTCW
Muldoon, Paul 1951- **CLC 32, 72; DAM POET**
    See also CA 113; 129; CANR 52; DLB 40; INT 129
Mulisch, Harry 1927- .... **CLC 42**
    See also CA 9-12R; CANR 6, 26, 56
Mull, Martin 1943- .... **CLC 17**
    See also CA 105
Mulock, Dinah Maria
    See Craik, Dinah Maria (Mulock)
Munford, Robert 1737(?)-1783 .... **LC 5**
    See also DLB 31
Mungo, Raymond 1946- .... **CLC 72**
    See also CA 49-52; CANR 2
Munro, Alice 1931- .... **CLC 6, 10, 19, 50, 95; DAC; DAM MST, NOV; SSC 3; WLCS**
    See also AITN 2; CA 33-36R; CANR 33, 53; DLB 53; MTCW; SATA 29
Munro, H(ector) H(ugh) 1870-1916
    See Saki
    See also CA 104; 130; CDBLB 1890-1914; DA; DAB; DAC; DAM MST, NOV; DLB 34, 162; MTCW; WLC
Murasaki, Lady .... **CMLC 1**
Murdoch, (Jean) Iris 1919- **CLC 1, 2, 3, 4, 6, 8, 11, 15, 22, 31, 51; DAB; DAC; DAM MST, NOV**
    See also CA 13-16R; CANR 8, 43; CDBLB 1960 to Present; DLB 14; INT CANR-8;

MTCW

Murfree, Mary Noailles 1850-1922 ... **SSC 22**
See also CA 122; DLB 12, 74

Murnau, Friedrich Wilhelm
See Plumpe, Friedrich Wilhelm

Murphy, Richard 1927- .... **CLC 41**
See also CA 29-32R; DLB 40

Murphy, Sylvia 1937- .... **CLC 34**
See also CA 121

Murphy, Thomas (Bernard) 1935- ... **CLC 51**
See also CA 101

Murray, Albert L. 1916- .... **CLC 73**
See also BW 2; CA 49-52; CANR 26, 52; DLB 38

Murray, Les(lie) A(llan) 1938-**CLC 40; DAM POET**
See also CA 21-24R; CANR 11, 27, 56

Murry, J. Middleton
See Murry, John Middleton

Murry, John Middleton 1889-1957 **TCLC 16**
See also CA 118; DLB 149

Musgrave, Susan 1951- .... **CLC 13, 54**
See also CA 69-72; CANR 45

Musil, Robert (Edler von) 1880-1942 **T C L C 12, 68; SSC 18**
See also CA 109; CANR 55; DLB 81, 124

Muske, Carol 1945- .... **CLC 90**
See also Muske-Dukes, Carol (Anne)

Muske-Dukes, Carol (Anne) 1945-
See Muske, Carol
See also CA 65-68; CANR 32

Musset, (Louis Charles) Alfred de 1810-1857 **NCLC 7**

My Brother's Brother
See Chekhov, Anton (Pavlovich)

Myers, L(eopold) H(amilton) 1881-1944 **TCLC 59**
See also CA 157; DLB 15

Myers, Walter Dean 1937- ..... **CLC 35; BLC; DAM MULT, NOV**
See also AAYA 4; BW 2; CA 33-36R; CANR 20, 42; CLR 4, 16, 35; DLB 33; INT CANR-20; JRDA; MAICYA; SAAS 2; SATA 41, 71; SATA-Brief 27

Myers, Walter M.
See Myers, Walter Dean

Myles, Symon
See Follett, Ken(neth Martin)

Nabokov, Vladimir (Vladimirovich) 1899-1977 **CLC 1, 2, 3, 6, 8, 11, 15, 23, 44, 46, 64; DA; DAB; DAC; DAM MST, NOV; SSC 11; WLC**
See also CA 5-8R; 69-72; CANR 20; CDALB 1941-1968; DLB 2; DLBD 3; DLBY 80, 91; MTCW

Nagai Kafu 1879-1959 .... **TCLC 51**
See also Nagai Sokichi
See also DLB 180

Nagai Sokichi 1879-1959
See Nagai Kafu
See also CA 117

Nagy, Laszlo 1925-1978 .... **CLC 7**
See also CA 129; 112

Naipaul, Shiva(dhar Srinivasa) 1945-1985 **CLC 32, 39; DAM NOV**
See also CA 110; 112; 116; CANR 33; DLB 157; DLBY 85; MTCW

Naipaul, V(idiadhar) S(urajprasad) 1932- **CLC 4, 7, 9, 13, 18, 37; DAB; DAC; DAM MST, NOV**
See also CA 1-4R; CANR 1, 33, 51; CDBLB 1960 to Present; DLB 125; DLBY 85; MTCW

Nakos, Lilika 1899(?)- .... **CLC 29**

Narayan, R(asipuram) K(rishnaswami) 1906- **CLC 7, 28, 47; DAM NOV; SSC 25**
See also CA 81-84; CANR 33; MTCW; SATA 62

Nash, (Frediric) Ogden 1902-1971 . **CLC 23; DAM POET**
See also CA 13-14; 29-32R; CANR 34; CAP 1; DLB 11; MAICYA; MTCW; SATA 2, 46

Nathan, Daniel
See Dannay, Frederic

Nathan, George Jean 1882-1958 .... **TCLC 18**
See also Hatteras, Owen
See also CA 114; DLB 137

Natsume, Kinnosuke 1867-1916
See Natsume, Soseki
See also CA 104

Natsume, Soseki 1867-1916 .... **TCLC 2, 10**
See also Natsume, Kinnosuke
See also DLB 180

Natti, (Mary) Lee 1919-
See Kingman, Lee
See also CA 5-8R; CANR 2

Naylor, Gloria 1950- **CLC 28, 52; BLC; DA; DAC; DAM MST, MULT, NOV, POP; WLCS**
See also AAYA 6; BW 2; CA 107; CANR 27, 51; DLB 173; MTCW

Neihardt, John Gneisenau 1881-1973**CLC 32**
See also CA 13-14; CAP 1; DLB 9, 54

Nekrasov, Nikolai Alekseevich 1821-1878 **NCLC 11**

Nelligan, Emile 1879-1941 .... **TCLC 14**
See also CA 114; DLB 92

Nelson, Willie 1933- .... **CLC 17**
See also CA 107

Nemerov, Howard (Stanley) 1920-1991**CLC 2, 6, 9, 36; DAM POET**
See also CA 1-4R; 134; CABS 2; CANR 1, 27, 53; DLB 5, 6; DLBY 83; INT CANR-27; MTCW

Neruda, Pablo 1904-1973**CLC 1, 2, 5, 7, 9, 28, 62; DA; DAB; DAC; DAM MST, MULT, POET; HLC; PC 4; WLC**
See also CA 19-20; 45-48; CAP 2; HW; MTCW

Nerval, Gerard de 1808-1855**NCLC 1; PC 13; SSC 18**

Nervo, (Jose) Amado (Ruiz de) 1870-1919 **TCLC 11**
See also CA 109; 131; HW

Nessi, Pio Baroja y
See Baroja (y Nessi), Pio

Nestroy, Johann 1801-1862 .... **NCLC 42**
See also DLB 133

Netterville, Luke
See O'Grady, Standish (James)

Neufeld, John (Arthur) 1938- .... **CLC 17**
See also AAYA 11; CA 25-28R; CANR 11, 37, 56; MAICYA; SAAS 3; SATA 6, 81

Neville, Emily Cheney 1919- .... **CLC 12**
See also CA 5-8R; CANR 3, 37; JRDA; MAICYA; SAAS 2; SATA 1

Newbound, Bernard Slade 1930-
See Slade, Bernard
See also CA 81-84; CANR 49; DAM DRAM

Newby, P(ercy) H(oward) 1918- . **CLC 2, 13; DAM NOV**
See also CA 5-8R; CANR 32; DLB 15; MTCW

Newlove, Donald 1928- .... **CLC 6**
See also CA 29-32R; CANR 25

Newlove, John (Herbert) 1938- .... **CLC 14**
See also CA 21-24R; CANR 9, 25

Newman, Charles 1938- .... **CLC 2, 8**

See also CA 21-24R

Newman, Edwin (Harold) 1919- .... **CLC 14**
See also AITN 1; CA 69-72; CANR 5

Newman, John Henry 1801-1890 .. **NCLC 38**
See also DLB 18, 32, 55

Newton, Suzanne 1936- .... **CLC 35**
See also CA 41-44R; CANR 14; JRDA; SATA 5, 77

Nexo, Martin Andersen 1869-1954 **TCLC 43**

Nezval, Vitezslav 1900-1958 .... **TCLC 44**
See also CA 123

Ng, Fae Myenne 1957(?)- .... **CLC 81**
See also CA 146

Ngema, Mbongeni 1955- .... **CLC 57**
See also BW 2; CA 143

Ngugi, James T(hiong'o) .... **CLC 3, 7, 13**
See also Ngugi wa Thiong'o

Ngugi wa Thiong'o 1938-**CLC 36; BLC; DAM MULT, NOV**
See also Ngugi, James T(hiong'o)
See also BW 2; CA 81-84; CANR 27, 58; DLB 125; MTCW

Nichol, B(arrie) P(hillip) 1944-1988 **CLC 18**
See also CA 53-56; DLB 53; SATA 66

Nichols, John (Treadwell) 1940- .... **CLC 38**
See also CA 9-12R; CAAS 2; CANR 6; DLBY 82

Nichols, Leigh
See Koontz, Dean R(ay)

Nichols, Peter (Richard) 1927- **CLC 5, 36, 65**
See also CA 104; CANR 33; DLB 13; MTCW

Nicolas, F. R. E.
See Freeling, Nicolas

Niedecker, Lorine 1903-1970 .... **CLC 10, 42; DAM POET**
See also CA 25-28; CAP 2; DLB 48

Nietzsche, Friedrich (Wilhelm) 1844-1900 **TCLC 10, 18, 55**
See also CA 107; 121; DLB 129

Nievo, Ippolito 1831-1861 .... **NCLC 22**

Nightingale, Anne Redmon 1943-
See Redmon, Anne
See also CA 103

Nik. T. O.
See Annensky, Innokenty (Fyodorovich)

Nin, Anais 1903-1977 **CLC 1, 4, 8, 11, 14, 60; DAM NOV, POP; SSC 10**
See also AITN 2; CA 13-16R; 69-72; CANR 22, 53; DLB 2, 4, 152; MTCW

Nishiwaki, Junzaburo 1894-1982 .... **PC 15**
See also CA 107

Nissenson, Hugh 1933- .... **CLC 4, 9**
See also CA 17-20R; CANR 27; DLB 28

Niven, Larry .... **CLC 8**
See also Niven, Laurence Van Cott
See also DLB 8

Niven, Laurence Van Cott 1938-
See Niven, Larry
See also CA 21-24R; CAAS 12; CANR 14, 44; DAM POP; MTCW

Nixon, Agnes Eckhardt 1927- .... **CLC 21**
See also CA 110

Nizan, Paul 1905-1940 .... **TCLC 40**
See also DLB 72

Nkosi, Lewis 1936- .... **CLC 45; BLC; DAM MULT**
See also BW 1; CA 65-68; CANR 27; DLB 157

Nodier, (Jean) Charles (Emmanuel) 1780-1844 **NCLC 19**
See also DLB 119

Nolan, Christopher 1965- .... **CLC 58**
See also CA 111

Noon, Jeff 1957- .... **CLC 91**

See also CA 148
Norden, Charles
   See Durrell, Lawrence (George)
Nordhoff, Charles (Bernard) 1887-1947
   TCLC 23
   See also CA 108; DLB 9; SATA 23
Norfolk, Lawrence 1963- .... **CLC 76**
   See also CA 144
Norman, Marsha 1947-**CLC 28; DAM DRAM**
   See also CA 105; CABS 3; CANR 41; DLBY
   84
Norris, Benjamin Franklin, Jr. 1870-1902
   TCLC 24
   See also Norris, Frank
   See also CA 110
Norris, Frank
   See Norris, Benjamin Franklin, Jr.
   See also CDALB 1865-1917; DLB 12, 71
Norris, Leslie 1921- .... **CLC 14**
   See also CA 11-12; CANR 14; CAP 1; DLB 27
North, Andrew
   See Norton, Andre
North, Anthony
   See Koontz, Dean R(ay)
North, Captain George
   See Stevenson, Robert Louis (Balfour)
North, Milou
   See Erdrich, Louise
Northrup, B. A.
   See Hubbard, L(afayette) Ron(ald)
North Staffs
   See Hulme, T(homas) E(rnest)
Norton, Alice Mary
   See Norton, Andre
   See also MAICYA; SATA 1, 43
Norton, Andre 1912- .... **CLC 12**
   See also Norton, Alice Mary
   See also AAYA 14; CA 1-4R; CANR 2, 31; DLB
   8, 52; JRDA; MTCW; SATA 91
Norton, Caroline 1808-1877 .... **NCLC 47**
   See also DLB 21, 159
Norway, Nevil Shute 1899-1960
   See Shute, Nevil
   See also CA 102; 93-96
Norwid, Cyprian Kamil 1821-1883 **NCLC 17**
Nosille, Nabrah
   See Ellison, Harlan (Jay)
Nossack, Hans Erich 1901-1978 .... **CLC 6**
   See also CA 93-96; 85-88; DLB 69
Nostradamus 1503-1566 .... **LC 27**
Nosu, Chuji
   See Ozu, Yasujiro
Notenburg, Eleanora (Genrikhovna) von
   See Guro, Elena
Nova, Craig 1945- .... **CLC 7, 31**
   See also CA 45-48; CANR 2, 53
Novak, Joseph
   See Kosinski, Jerzy (Nikodem)
Novalis 1772-1801 .... **NCLC 13**
   See also DLB 90
Nowlan, Alden (Albert) 1933-1983 **CLC 15;**
   DAC; DAM MST
   See also CA 9-12R; CANR 5; DLB 53
Noyes, Alfred 1880-1958 .... **TCLC 7**
   See also CA 104; DLB 20
Nunn, Kem 19(?)- .... **CLC 34**
Nye, Robert 1939- .. **CLC 13, 42; DAM NOV**
   See also CA 33-36R; CANR 29; DLB 14;
   MTCW; SATA 6
Nyro, Laura 1947- .... **CLC 17**
Oates, Joyce Carol 1938-**CLC 1, 2, 3, 6, 9, 11,**
   15, 19, 33, 52; DA; DAB; DAC; DAM MST,
   NOV, POP; SSC 6; WLC

See also AAYA 15; AITN 1; BEST 89:2; CA 5-
   8R; CANR 25, 45; CDALB 1968-1988; DLB
   2, 5, 130; DLBY 81; INT CANR-25; MTCW
O'Brien, Darcy 1939- .... **CLC 11**
   See also CA 21-24R; CANR 8, 59
O'Brien, E. G.
   See Clarke, Arthur C(harles)
O'Brien, Edna 1936- **CLC 3, 5, 8, 13, 36, 65;**
   DAM NOV; SSC 10
   See also CA 1-4R; CANR 6, 41; CDBLB 1960
   to Present; DLB 14; MTCW
O'Brien, Fitz-James 1828-1862 ..... **NCLC 21**
   See also DLB 74
O'Brien, Flann .... **CLC 1, 4, 5, 7, 10, 47**
   See also O Nuallain, Brian
O'Brien, Richard 1942- .... **CLC 17**
   See also CA 124
O'Brien, (William) Tim(othy) 1946- . **CLC 7,**
   19, 40; DAM POP
   See also AAYA 16; CA 85-88; CANR 40, 58;
   DLB 152; DLBD 9; DLBY 80
Obstfelder, Sigbjoern 1866-1900 ... **TCLC 23**
   See also CA 123
O'Casey, Sean 1880-1964**CLC 1, 5, 9, 11, 15,**
   88; DAB; DAC; DAM DRAM, MST;
   WLCS
   See also CA 89-92; CDBLB 1914-1945; DLB
   10; MTCW
O'Cathasaigh, Sean
   See O'Casey, Sean
Ochs, Phil 1940-1976 .... **CLC 17**
   See also CA 65-68
O'Connor, Edwin (Greene) 1918-1968**CLC 14**
   See also CA 93-96; 25-28R
O'Connor, (Mary) Flannery 1925-1964 **C L C**
   1, 2, 3, 6, 10, 13, 15, 21, 66; DA; DAB;
   DAC; DAM MST, NOV; SSC 1, 23; WLC
   See also AAYA 7; CA 1-4R; CANR 3, 41;
   CDALB 1941-1968; DLB 2, 152; DLBD 12;
   DLBY 80; MTCW
O'Connor, Frank .... **CLC 23; SSC 5**
   See also O'Donovan, Michael John
   See also DLB 162
O'Dell, Scott 1898-1989 .... **CLC 30**
   See also AAYA 3; CA 61-64; 129; CANR 12,
   30; CLR 1, 16; DLB 52; JRDA; MAICYA;
   SATA 12, 60
Odets, Clifford 1906-1963**CLC 2, 28, 98; DAM**
   DRAM; DC 6
   See also CA 85-88; DLB 7, 26; MTCW
O'Doherty, Brian 1934- .... **CLC 76**
   See also CA 105
O'Donnell, K. M.
   See Malzberg, Barry N(athaniel)
O'Donnell, Lawrence
   See Kuttner, Henry
O'Donovan, Michael John 1903-1966**CLC 14**
   See also O'Connor, Frank
   See also CA 93-96
Oe, Kenzaburo 1935- **CLC 10, 36, 86; DAM**
   NOV; SSC 20
   See also CA 97-100; CANR 36, 50; DLB 182;
   DLBY 94; MTCW
O'Faolain, Julia 1932- .... **CLC 6, 19, 47**
   See also CA 81-84; CAAS 2; CANR 12; DLB
   14; MTCW
O'Faolain, Sean 1900-1991 **CLC 1, 7, 14, 32,**
   70; SSC 13
   See also CA 61-64; 134; CANR 12; DLB 15,
   162; MTCW
O'Flaherty, Liam 1896-1984**CLC 5, 34; SSC 6**
   See also CA 101; 113; CANR 35; DLB 36, 162;
   DLBY 84; MTCW

Ogilvy, Gavin
   See Barrie, J(ames) M(atthew)
O'Grady, Standish (James) 1846-1928**T C L C**
   5
   See also CA 104; 157
O'Grady, Timothy 1951- .... **CLC 59**
   See also CA 138
O'Hara, Frank 1926-1966 . **CLC 2, 5, 13, 78;**
   DAM POET
   See also CA 9-12R; 25-28R; CANR 33; DLB
   5, 16; MTCW
O'Hara, John (Henry) 1905-1970**CLC 1, 2, 3,**
   6, 11, 42; DAM NOV; SSC 15
   See also CA 5-8R; 25-28R; CANR 31; CDALB
   1929-1941; DLB 9, 86; DLBD 2; MTCW
O Hehir, Diana 1922- .... **CLC 41**
   See also CA 93-96
Okigbo, Christopher (Ifenayichukwu) 1932-
   1967 .... **CLC 25, 84; BLC; DAM MULT,**
   POET; PC 7
   See also BW 1; CA 77-80; DLB 125; MTCW
Okri, Ben 1959- .... **CLC 87**
   See also BW 2; CA 130; 138; DLB 157; INT
   138
Olds, Sharon 1942- .... **CLC 32, 39, 85; DAM**
   POET
   See also CA 101; CANR 18, 41; DLB 120
Oldstyle, Jonathan
   See Irving, Washington
Olesha, Yuri (Karlovich) 1899-1960 .. **CLC 8**
   See also CA 85-88
Oliphant, Laurence 1829(?)-1888 .. **NCLC 47**
   See also DLB 18, 166
Oliphant, Margaret (Oliphant Wilson) 1828-
   1897 .... **NCLC 11, 61; SSC 25**
   See also DLB 18, 159
Oliver, Mary 1935- .... **CLC 19, 34, 98**
   See also CA 21-24R; CANR 9, 43; DLB 5
Olivier, Laurence (Kerr) 1907-1989 . **CLC 20**
   See also CA 111; 150; 129
Olsen, Tillie 1913-**CLC 4, 13; DA; DAB; DAC;**
   DAM MST; SSC 11
   See also CA 1-4R; CANR 1, 43; DLB 28; DLBY
   80; MTCW
Olson, Charles (John) 1910-1970**CLC 1, 2, 5,**
   6, 9, 11, 29; DAM POET; PC 19
   See also CA 13-16; 25-28R; CABS 2; CANR
   35; CAP 1; DLB 5, 16; MTCW
Olson, Toby 1937- .... **CLC 28**
   See also CA 65-68; CANR 9, 31
Olyesha, Yuri
   See Olesha, Yuri (Karlovich)
Ondaatje, (Philip) Michael 1943-**CLC 14, 29,**
   51, 76; DAB; DAC; DAM MST
   See also CA 77-80; CANR 42; DLB 60
Oneal, Elizabeth 1934-
   See Oneal, Zibby
   See also CA 106; CANR 28; MAICYA; SATA
   30, 82
Oneal, Zibby .... **CLC 30**
   See also Oneal, Elizabeth
   See also AAYA 5; CLR 13; JRDA
O'Neill, Eugene (Gladstone) 1888-1953**TCLC**
   1, 6, 27, 49; DA; DAB; DAC; DAM DRAM,
   MST; WLC
   See also AITN 1; CA 110; 132; CDALB 1929-
   1941; DLB 7; MTCW
Onetti, Juan Carlos 1909-1994 ... **CLC 7, 10;**
   DAM MULT, NOV; SSC 23
   See also CA 85-88; 145; CANR 32; DLB 113;
   HW; MTCW
O Nuallain, Brian 1911-1966
   See O'Brien, Flann

See also CA 21-22; 25-28R; CAP 2

Oppen, George 1908-1984 ...... **CLC 7, 13, 34**
See also CA 13-16R; 113; CANR 8; DLB 5, 165

Oppenheim, E(dward) Phillips 1866-1946 **TCLC 45**
See also CA 111; DLB 70

Origen c. 185-c. 254 .... **CMLC 19**

Orlovitz, Gil 1918-1973 .... **CLC 22**
See also CA 77-80; 45-48; DLB 2, 5

Orris
See Ingelow, Jean

Ortega y Gasset, Jose 1883-1955 .... **TCLC 9; DAM MULT; HLC**
See also CA 106; 130; HW; MTCW

Ortese, Anna Maria 1914- .... **CLC 89**
See also DLB 177

Ortiz, Simon J(oseph) 1941- .. **CLC 45; DAM MULT, POET; PC 17**
See also CA 134; DLB 120, 175; NNAL

Orton, Joe .... **CLC 4, 13, 43; DC 3**
See also Orton, John Kingsley
See also CDBLB 1960 to Present; DLB 13

Orton, John Kingsley 1933-1967
See Orton, Joe
See also CA 85-88; CANR 35; DAM DRAM; MTCW

Orwell, George . **TCLC 2, 6, 15, 31, 51; DAB; WLC**
See also Blair, Eric (Arthur)
See also CDBLB 1945-1960; DLB 15, 98

Osborne, David
See Silverberg, Robert

Osborne, George
See Silverberg, Robert

Osborne, John (James) 1929-1994**CLC 1, 2, 5, 11, 45; DA; DAB; DAC; DAM DRAM, MST; WLC**
See also CA 13-16R; 147; CANR 21, 56; CDBLB 1945-1960; DLB 13; MTCW

Osborne, Lawrence 1958- .... **CLC 50**

Oshima, Nagisa 1932- .... **CLC 20**
See also CA 116; 121

Oskison, John Milton 1874-1947 .. **TCLC 35; DAM MULT**
See also CA 144; DLB 175; NNAL

Ossoli, Sarah Margaret (Fuller marchesa d') 1810-1850
See Fuller, Margaret
See also SATA 25

Ostrovsky, Alexander 1823-1886**NCLC 30, 57**

Otero, Blas de 1916-1979 .... **CLC 11**
See also CA 89-92; DLB 134

Otto, Whitney 1955- .... **CLC 70**
See also CA 140

Ouida .... **TCLC 43**
See also De La Ramee, (Marie) Louise
See also DLB 18, 156

Ousmane, Sembene 1923- .... **CLC 66; BLC**
See also BW 1; CA 117; 125; MTCW

Ovid 43B.C.-18(?)**CMLC 7; DAM POET; PC 2**

Owen, Hugh
See Faust, Frederick (Schiller)

Owen, Wilfred (Edward Salter) 1893-1918 **TCLC 5, 27; DA; DAB; DAC; DAM MST, POET; PC 19; WLC**
See also CA 104; 141; CDBLB 1914-1945; DLB 20

Owens, Rochelle 1936- .... **CLC 8**
See also CA 17-20R; CAAS 2; CANR 39

Oz, Amos 1939-**CLC 5, 8, 11, 27, 33, 54; DAM NOV**

See also CA 53-56; CANR 27, 47; MTCW

Ozick, Cynthia 1928- **CLC 3, 7, 28, 62; DAM NOV, POP; SSC 15**
See also BEST 90:1; CA 17-20R; CANR 23, 58; DLB 28, 152; DLBY 82; INT CANR-23; MTCW

Ozu, Yasujiro 1903-1963 .... **CLC 16**
See also CA 112

Pacheco, C.
See Pessoa, Fernando (Antonio Nogueira)

Pa Chin .... **CLC 18**
See also Li Fei-kan

Pack, Robert 1929- .... **CLC 13**
See also CA 1-4R; CANR 3, 44; DLB 5

Padgett, Lewis
See Kuttner, Henry

Padilla (Lorenzo), Heberto 1932- ..... **CLC 38**
See also AITN 1; CA 123; 131; HW

Page, Jimmy 1944- .... **CLC 12**

Page, Louise 1955- .... **CLC 40**
See also CA 140

Page, P(atricia) K(athleen) 1916- **CLC 7, 18; DAC; DAM MST; PC 12**
See also CA 53-56; CANR 4, 22; DLB 68; MTCW

Page, Thomas Nelson 1853-1922 .... **SSC 23**
See also CA 118; DLB 12, 78; DLBD 13

Paget, Violet 1856-1935
See Lee, Vernon
See also CA 104

Paget-Lowe, Henry
See Lovecraft, H(oward) P(hillips)

Paglia, Camille (Anna) 1947- .... **CLC 68**
See also CA 140

Paige, Richard
See Koontz, Dean R(ay)

Paine, Thomas 1737-1809 .... **NCLC 62**
See also CDALB 1640-1865; DLB 31, 43, 73, 158

Pakenham, Antonia
See Fraser, (Lady) Antonia (Pakenham)

Palamas, Kostes 1859-1943 .... **TCLC 5**
See also CA 105

Palazzeschi, Aldo 1885-1974 .... **CLC 11**
See also CA 89-92; 53-56; DLB 114

Paley, Grace 1922- **CLC 4, 6, 37; DAM POP; SSC 8**
See also CA 25-28R; CANR 13, 46; DLB 28; INT CANR-13; MTCW

Palin, Michael (Edward) 1943- .... **CLC 21**
See also Monty Python
See also CA 107; CANR 35; SATA 67

Palliser, Charles 1947- .... **CLC 65**
See also CA 136

Palma, Ricardo 1833-1919 .... **TCLC 29**

Pancake, Breece Dexter 1952-1979
See Pancake, Breece D'J
See also CA 123; 109

Pancake, Breece D'J .... **CLC 29**
See also Pancake, Breece Dexter
See also DLB 130

Panko, Rudy
See Gogol, Nikolai (Vasilyevich)

Papadiamantis, Alexandros 1851-1911**T C L C 29**

Papadiamantopoulos, Johannes 1856-1910
See Moreas, Jean
See also CA 117

Papini, Giovanni 1881-1956 .... **TCLC 22**
See also CA 121

Paracelsus 1493-1541 .... **LC 14**
See also DLB 179

Parasol, Peter

See Stevens, Wallace

Pareto, Vilfredo 1848-1923 .... **TCLC 69**

Parfenie, Maria
See Codrescu, Andrei

Parini, Jay (Lee) 1948- .... **CLC 54**
See also CA 97-100; CAAS 16; CANR 32

Park, Jordan
See Kornbluth, C(yril) M.; Pohl, Frederik

Parker, Bert
See Ellison, Harlan (Jay)

Parker, Dorothy (Rothschild) 1893-1967**C L C 15, 68; DAM POET; SSC 2**
See also CA 19-20; 25-28R; CAP 2; DLB 11, 45, 86; MTCW

Parker, Robert B(rown) 1932-**CLC 27; DAM NOV, POP**
See also BEST 89:4; CA 49-52; CANR 1, 26, 52; INT CANR-26; MTCW

Parkin, Frank 1940- .... **CLC 43**
See also CA 147

Parkman, Francis, Jr. 1823-1893 .. **NCLC 12**
See also DLB 1, 30

Parks, Gordon (Alexander Buchanan) 1912- **CLC 1, 16; BLC; DAM MULT**
See also AITN 2; BW 2; CA 41-44R; CANR 26; DLB 33; SATA 8

Parmenides c. 515B.C.-c. 450B.C. **CMLC 22**
See also DLB 176

Parnell, Thomas 1679-1718 .... **LC 3**
See also DLB 94

Parra, Nicanor 1914- ...... **CLC 2, 102; DAM MULT; HLC**
See also CA 85-88; CANR 32; HW; MTCW

Parrish, Mary Frances
See Fisher, M(ary) F(rances) K(ennedy)

Parson
See Coleridge, Samuel Taylor

Parson Lot
See Kingsley, Charles

Partridge, Anthony
See Oppenheim, E(dward) Phillips

Pascal, Blaise 1623-1662 .... **LC 35**

Pascoli, Giovanni 1855-1912 .... **TCLC 45**

Pasolini, Pier Paolo 1922-1975**CLC 20, 37; PC 17**
See also CA 93-96; 61-64; DLB 128, 177; MTCW

Pasquini
See Silone, Ignazio

Pastan, Linda (Olenik) 1932- **CLC 27; DAM POET**
See also CA 61-64; CANR 18, 40; DLB 5

Pasternak, Boris (Leonidovich) 1890-1960 **CLC 7, 10, 18, 63; DA; DAB; DAC; DAM MST, NOV, POET; PC 6; WLC**
See also CA 127; 116; MTCW

Patchen, Kenneth 1911-1972 ... **CLC 1, 2, 18; DAM POET**
See also CA 1-4R; 33-36R; CANR 3, 35; DLB 16, 48; MTCW

Pater, Walter (Horatio) 1839-1894 .. **NCLC 7**
See also CDBLB 1832-1890; DLB 57, 156

Paterson, A(ndrew) B(arton) 1864-1941 **TCLC 32**
See also CA 155

Paterson, Katherine (Womeldorf) 1932-**C L C 12, 30**
See also AAYA 1; CA 21-24R; CANR 28, 59; CLR 7; DLB 52; JRDA; MAICYA; MTCW; SATA 13, 53, 92

Patmore, Coventry Kersey Dighton 1823-1896 **NCLC 9**
See also DLB 35, 98

DLBY 82

Pinta, Harold
See Pinter, Harold

Pinter, Harold 1930-CLC **1, 3, 6, 9, 11, 15, 27, 58, 73; DA; DAB; DAC; DAM DRAM, MST; WLC**
See also CA 5-8R; CANR 33; CDBLB 1960 to Present; DLB 13; MTCW

Piozzi, Hester Lynch (Thrale) 1741-1821 **NCLC 57**
See also DLB 104, 142

Pirandello, Luigi 1867-1936**TCLC 4, 29; DA; DAB; DAC; DAM DRAM, MST; DC 5; SSC 22; WLC**
See also CA 104; 153

Pirsig, Robert M(aynard) 1928-CLC **4, 6, 73; DAM POP**
See also CA 53-56; CANR 42; MTCW; SATA 39

Pisarev, Dmitry Ivanovich 1840-1868 **NCLC 25**

Pix, Mary (Griffith) 1666-1709 .... **LC 8**
See also DLB 80

Pixerecourt, Guilbert de 1773-1844**NCLC 39**

Plaatje, Sol(omon) T(shekisho) 1876-1932 **TCLC 71**
See also BW 2; CA 141

Plaidy, Jean
See Hibbert, Eleanor Alice Burford

Planche, James Robinson 1796-1880**NCLC 42**

Plant, Robert 1948- .... **CLC 12**

Plante, David (Robert) 1940- CLC **7, 23, 38; DAM NOV**
See also CA 37-40R; CANR 12, 36, 58; DLBY 83; INT CANR-12; MTCW

Plath, Sylvia 1932-1963 CLC **1, 2, 3, 5, 9, 11, 14, 17, 50, 51, 62; DA; DAB; DAC; DAM MST, POET; PC 1; WLC**
See also AAYA 13; CA 19-20; CANR 34; CAP 2; CDALB 1941-1968; DLB 5, 6, 152; MTCW

Plato 428(?)B.C.-348(?)B.C. .... CMLC **8; DA; DAB; DAC; DAM MST; WLCS**
See also DLB 176

Platonov, Andrei .... **TCLC 14**
See also Klimentov, Andrei Platonovich

Platt, Kin 1911- .... **CLC 26**
See also AAYA 11; CA 17-20R; CANR 11; JRDA; SAAS 17; SATA 21, 86

Plautus c. 251B.C.-184B.C. .... **DC 6**

Plick et Plock
See Simenon, Georges (Jacques Christian)

Plimpton, George (Ames) 1927- .... **CLC 36**
See also AITN 1; CA 21-24R; CANR 32; MTCW; SATA 10

Pliny the Elder c. 23-79 .... **CMLC 23**

Plomer, William Charles Franklin 1903-1973 **CLC 4, 8**
See also CA 21-22; CANR 34; CAP 2; DLB 20, 162; MTCW; SATA 24

Plowman, Piers
See Kavanagh, Patrick (Joseph)

Plum, J.
See Wodehouse, P(elham) G(renville)

Plumly, Stanley (Ross) 1939- .... **CLC 33**
See also CA 108; 110; DLB 5; INT 110

Plumpe, Friedrich Wilhelm 1888-1931**TCLC 53**
See also CA 112

Poe, Edgar Allan 1809-1849**NCLC 1, 16, 55; DA; DAB; DAC; DAM MST, POET; PC 1; SSC 1, 22; WLC**
See also AAYA 14; CDALB 1640-1865; DLB

3, 59, 73, 74; SATA 23

Poet of Titchfield Street, The
See Pound, Ezra (Weston Loomis)

Pohl, Frederik 1919- .... CLC **18; SSC 25**
See also CA 61-64; CAAS 1; CANR 11, 37; DLB 8; INT CANR-11; MTCW; SATA 24

Poirier, Louis 1910-
See Gracq, Julien
See also CA 122; 126

Poitier, Sidney 1927- .... **CLC 26**
See also BW 1; CA 117

Polanski, Roman 1933- .... **CLC 16**
See also CA 77-80

Poliakoff, Stephen 1952- .... **CLC 38**
See also CA 106; DLB 13

Police, The
See Copeland, Stewart (Armstrong); Summers, Andrew James; Sumner, Gordon Matthew

Polidori, John William 1795-1821 . **NCLC 51**
See also DLB 116

Pollitt, Katha 1949- .... **CLC 28**
See also CA 120; 122; MTCW

Pollock, (Mary) Sharon 1936-CLC **50; DAC; DAM DRAM, MST**
See also CA 141; DLB 60

Polo, Marco 1254-1324 .... **CMLC 15**

Polonsky, Abraham (Lincoln) 1910- **CLC 92**
See also CA 104; DLB 26; INT 104

Polybius c. 200B.C.-c. 118B.C. ...... **CMLC 17**
See also DLB 176

Pomerance, Bernard 1940- .... CLC **13; DAM DRAM**
See also CA 101; CANR 49

Ponge, Francis (Jean Gaston Alfred) 1899-1988 **CLC 6, 18; DAM POET**
See also CA 85-88; 126; CANR 40

Pontoppidan, Henrik 1857-1943 .... **TCLC 29**

Poole, Josephine .... **CLC 17**
See also Helyar, Jane Penelope Josephine
See also SAAS 2; SATA 5

Popa, Vasko 1922-1991 .... **CLC 19**
See also CA 112; 148; DLB 181

Pope, Alexander 1688-1744 LC **3; DA; DAB; DAC; DAM MST, POET; WLC**
See also CDBLB 1660-1789; DLB 95, 101

Porter, Connie (Rose) 1959(?)- .... **CLC 70**
See also BW 2; CA 142; SATA 81

Porter, Gene(va Grace) Stratton 1863(?)-1924 **TCLC 21**
See also CA 112

Porter, Katherine Anne 1890-1980**CLC 1, 3, 7, 10, 13, 15, 27, 101; DA; DAB; DAC; DAM MST, NOV; SSC 4**
See also AITN 1; CA 1-4R; 101; CANR 1; DLB 4, 9, 102; DLBD 12; DLBY 80; MTCW; SATA 39; SATA-Obit 23

Porter, Peter (Neville Frederick) 1929-CLC **5, 13, 33**
See also CA 85-88; DLB 40

Porter, William Sydney 1862-1910
See Henry, O.
See also CA 104; 131; CDALB 1865-1917; DA; DAB; DAC; DAM MST; DLB 12, 78, 79; MTCW; YABC 2

Portillo (y Pacheco), Jose Lopez
See Lopez Portillo (y Pacheco), Jose

Post, Melville Davisson 1869-1930 **TCLC 39**
See also CA 110

Potok, Chaim 1929- . CLC **2, 7, 14, 26; DAM NOV**
See also AAYA 15; AITN 1, 2; CA 17-20R; CANR 19, 35; DLB 28, 152; INT CANR-19; MTCW; SATA 33

Potter, (Helen) Beatrix 1866-1943
See Webb, (Martha) Beatrice (Potter)
See also MAICYA

Potter, Dennis (Christopher George) 1935-1994 **CLC 58, 86**
See also CA 107; 145; CANR 33; MTCW

Pound, Ezra (Weston Loomis) 1885-1972 **CLC 1, 2, 3, 4, 5, 7, 10, 13, 18, 34, 48, 50; DA; DAB; DAC; DAM MST, POET; PC 4; WLC**
See also CA 5-8R; 37-40R; CANR 40; CDALB 1917-1929; DLB 4, 45, 63; DLBD 15; MTCW

Povod, Reinaldo 1959-1994 .... **CLC 44**
See also CA 136; 146

Powell, Adam Clayton, Jr. 1908-1972CLC **89; BLC; DAM MULT**
See also BW 1; CA 102; 33-36R

Powell, Anthony (Dymoke) 1905-CLC **1, 3, 7, 9, 10, 31**
See also CA 1-4R; CANR 1, 32; CDBLB 1945-1960; DLB 15; MTCW

Powell, Dawn 1897-1965 .... **CLC 66**
See also CA 5-8R

Powell, Padgett 1952- .... **CLC 34**
See also CA 126

Power, Susan .... **CLC 91**

Powers, J(ames) F(arl) 1917-CLC **1, 4, 8, 57; SSC 4**
See also CA 1-4R; CANR 2; DLB 130; MTCW

Powers, John J(ames) 1945-
See Powers, John R.
See also CA 69-72

Powers, John R. .... **CLC 66**
See also Powers, John J(ames)

Powers, Richard (S.) 1957- .... **CLC 93**
See also CA 148

Pownall, David 1938- .... **CLC 10**
See also CA 89-92; CAAS 18; CANR 49; DLB 14

Powys, John Cowper 1872-1963CLC **7, 9, 15, 46**
See also CA 85-88; DLB 15; MTCW

Powys, T(heodore) F(rancis) 1875-1953 **TCLC 9**
See also CA 106; DLB 36, 162

Prager, Emily 1952- .... **CLC 56**

Pratt, E(dwin) J(ohn) 1883(?)-1964 CLC **19; DAC; DAM POET**
See also CA 141; 93-96; DLB 92

Premchand .... **TCLC 21**
See also Srivastava, Dhanpat Rai

Preussler, Otfried 1923- .... **CLC 17**
See also CA 77-80; SATA 24

Prevert, Jacques (Henri Marie) 1900-1977 **CLC 15**
See also CA 77-80; 69-72; CANR 29; MTCW; SATA-Obit 30

Prevost, Abbe (Antoine Francois) 1697-1763 **LC 1**

Price, (Edward) Reynolds 1933-CLC **3, 6, 13, 43, 50, 63; DAM NOV; SSC 22**
See also CA 1-4R; CANR 1, 37, 57; DLB 2; INT CANR-37

Price, Richard 1949- .... CLC **6, 12**
See also CA 49-52; CANR 3; DLBY 81

Prichard, Katharine Susannah 1883-1969 **CLC 46**
See also CA 11-12; CANR 33; CAP 1; MTCW; SATA 66

Priestley, J(ohn) B(oynton) 1894-1984CLC **2, 5, 9, 34; DAM DRAM, NOV**
See also CA 9-12R; 113; CANR 33; CDBLB

1914-1945; DLB 10, 34, 77, 100, 139; DLBY 84; MTCW
Prince 1958(?)- .... **CLC 35**
Prince, F(rank) T(empleton) 1912- .. **CLC 22**
See also CA 101; CANR 43; DLB 20
Prince Kropotkin
See Kropotkin, Peter (Aleksieevich)
Prior, Matthew 1664-1721 .... **LC 4**
See also DLB 95
Pritchard, William H(arrison) 1932- **CLC 34**
See also CA 65-68; CANR 23; DLB 111
Pritchett, V(ictor) S(awdon) 1900-1997 **C L C 5, 13, 15, 41; DAM NOV; SSC 14**
See also CA 61-64; 157; CANR 31; DLB 15, 139; MTCW
Private 19022
See Manning, Frederic
Probst, Mark 1925- .... **CLC 59**
See also CA 130
Prokosch, Frederic 1908-1989 ...... **CLC 4, 48**
See also CA 73-76; 128; DLB 48
Prophet, The
See Dreiser, Theodore (Herman Albert)
Prose, Francine 1947- .... **CLC 45**
See also CA 109; 112; CANR 46
Proudhon
See Cunha, Euclides (Rodrigues Pimenta) da
Proulx, E. Annie 1935- .... **CLC 81**
Proust, (Valentin-Louis-George-Eugene-) Marcel 1871-1922 **TCLC 7, 13, 33; DA; DAB; DAC; DAM MST, NOV; WLC**
See also CA 104; 120; DLB 65; MTCW
Prowler, Harley
See Masters, Edgar Lee
Prus, Boleslaw 1845-1912 .... **TCLC 48**
Pryor, Richard (Franklin Lenox Thomas) 1940- **CLC 26**
See also CA 122
Przybyszewski, Stanislaw 1868-1927**TCLC 36**
See also DLB 66
Pteleon
See Grieve, C(hristopher) M(urray)
See also DAM POET
Puckett, Lute
See Masters, Edgar Lee
Puig, Manuel 1932-1990**CLC 3, 5, 10, 28, 65; DAM MULT; HLC**
See also CA 45-48; CANR 2, 32; DLB 113; HW; MTCW
Purdy, Al(fred Wellington) 1918-**CLC 3, 6, 14, 50; DAC; DAM MST, POET**
See also CA 81-84; CAAS 17; CANR 42; DLB 88
Purdy, James (Amos) 1923- **CLC 2, 4, 10, 28, 52**
See also CA 33-36R; CAAS 1; CANR 19, 51; DLB 2; INT CANR-19; MTCW
Pure, Simon
See Swinnerton, Frank Arthur
Pushkin, Alexander (Sergeyevich) 1799-1837 **NCLC 3, 27; DA; DAB; DAC; DAM DRAM, MST, POET; PC 10; SSC 27; WLC**
See also SATA 61
P'u Sung-ling 1640-1715 .... **LC 3**
Putnam, Arthur Lee
See Alger, Horatio, Jr.
Puzo, Mario 1920-**CLC 1, 2, 6, 36; DAM NOV, POP**
See also CA 65-68; CANR 4, 42; DLB 6; MTCW
Pygge, Edward
See Barnes, Julian (Patrick)

Pym, Barbara (Mary Crampton) 1913-1980 **CLC 13, 19, 37**
See also CA 13-14; 97-100; CANR 13, 34; CAP 1; DLB 14; DLBY 87; MTCW
Pynchon, Thomas (Ruggles, Jr.) 1937-**CLC 2, 3, 6, 9, 11, 18, 33, 62, 72; DA; DAB; DAC; DAM MST, NOV, POP; SSC 14; WLC**
See also BEST 90:2; CA 17-20R; CANR 22, 46; DLB 2, 173; MTCW
Pythagoras c. 570B.C.-c. 500B.C. . **CMLC 22**
See also DLB 176
Qian Zhongshu
See Ch'ien Chung-shu
Qroll
See Dagerman, Stig (Halvard)
Quarrington, Paul (Lewis) 1953- ..... **CLC 65**
See also CA 129
Quasimodo, Salvatore 1901-1968 ..... **CLC 10**
See also CA 13-16; 25-28R; CAP 1; DLB 114; MTCW
Quay, Stephen 1947- .... **CLC 95**
Quay, The Brothers
See Quay, Stephen; Quay, Timothy
Quay, Timothy 1947- .... **CLC 95**
Queen, Ellery .... **CLC 3, 11**
See also Dannay, Frederic; Davidson, Avram; Lee, Manfred B(ennington); Marlowe, Stephen; Sturgeon, Theodore (Hamilton); Vance, John Holbrook
Queen, Ellery, Jr.
See Dannay, Frederic; Lee, Manfred B(ennington)
Queneau, Raymond 1903-1976 **CLC 2, 5, 10, 42**
See also CA 77-80; 69-72; CANR 32; DLB 72; MTCW
Quevedo, Francisco de 1580-1645 .... **LC 23**
Quiller-Couch, Arthur Thomas 1863-1944 **TCLC 53**
See also CA 118; DLB 135, 153
Quin, Ann (Marie) 1936-1973 .... **CLC 6**
See also CA 9-12R; 45-48; DLB 14
Quinn, Martin
See Smith, Martin Cruz
Quinn, Peter 1947- .... **CLC 91**
Quinn, Simon
See Smith, Martin Cruz
Quiroga, Horacio (Sylvestre) 1878-1937 **TCLC 20; DAM MULT; HLC**
See also CA 117; 131; HW; MTCW
Quoirez, Francoise 1935- .... **CLC 9**
See also Sagan, Francoise
See also CA 49-52; CANR 6, 39; MTCW
Raabe, Wilhelm 1831-1910 .... **TCLC 45**
See also DLB 129
Rabe, David (William) 1940- ... **CLC 4, 8, 33; DAM DRAM**
See also CA 85-88; CABS 3; CANR 59; DLB 7
Rabelais, Francois 1483-1553**LC 5; DA; DAB; DAC; DAM MST; WLC**
Rabinovitch, Sholem 1859-1916
See Aleichem, Sholom
See also CA 104
Rachilde 1860-1953 .... **TCLC 67**
See also DLB 123
Racine, Jean 1639-1699 . **LC 28; DAB; DAM MST**
Radcliffe, Ann (Ward) 1764-1823**NCLC 6, 55**
See also DLB 39, 178
Radiguet, Raymond 1903-1923 ...... **TCLC 29**
See also DLB 65
Radnoti, Miklos 1909-1944............. **TCLC 16**
See also CA 118

Rado, James 1939- .... **CLC 17**
See also CA 105
Radvanyi, Netty 1900-1983
See Seghers, Anna
See also CA 85-88; 110
Rae, Ben
See Griffiths, Trevor
Raeburn, John (Hay) 1941- .... **CLC 34**
See also CA 57-60
Ragni, Gerome 1942-1991 .... **CLC 17**
See also CA 105; 134
Rahv, Philip 1908-1973 .... **CLC 24**
See also Greenberg, Ivan
See also DLB 137
Raine, Craig 1944- .... **CLC 32**
See also CA 108; CANR 29, 51; DLB 40
Raine, Kathleen (Jessie) 1908- ...... **CLC 7, 45**
See also CA 85-88; CANR 46; DLB 20; MTCW
Rainis, Janis 1865-1929 .... **TCLC 29**
Rakosi, Carl .... **CLC 47**
See also Rawley, Callman
See also CAAS 5
Raleigh, Richard
See Lovecraft, H(oward) P(hillips)
Raleigh, Sir Walter 1554(?)-1618 . **LC 31, 39**
See also CDBLB Before 1660; DLB 172
Rallentando, H. P.
See Sayers, Dorothy L(eigh)
Ramal, Walter
See de la Mare, Walter (John)
Ramon, Juan
See Jimenez (Mantecon), Juan Ramon
Ramos, Graciliano 1892-1953 .... **TCLC 32**
Rampersad, Arnold 1941- .... **CLC 44**
See also BW 2; CA 127; 133; DLB 111; INT 133
Rampling, Anne
See Rice, Anne
Ramsay, Allan 1684(?)-1758 .... **LC 29**
See also DLB 95
Ramuz, Charles-Ferdinand 1878-1947**T C L C 33**
Rand, Ayn 1905-1982**CLC 3, 30, 44, 79; DA; DAC; DAM MST, NOV, POP; WLC**
See also AAYA 10; CA 13-16R; 105; CANR 27; MTCW
Randall, Dudley (Felker) 1914-**CLC 1; BLC; DAM MULT**
See also BW 1; CA 25-28R; CANR 23; DLB 41
Randall, Robert
See Silverberg, Robert
Ranger, Ken
See Creasey, John
Ransom, John Crowe 1888-1974**CLC 2, 4, 5, 11, 24; DAM POET**
See also CA 5-8R; 49-52; CANR 6, 34; DLB 45, 63; MTCW
Rao, Raja 1909- ...... **CLC 25, 56; DAM NOV**
See also CA 73-76; CANR 51; MTCW
Raphael, Frederic (Michael) 1931-**CLC 2, 14**
See also CA 1-4R; CANR 1; DLB 14
Ratcliffe, James P.
See Mencken, H(enry) L(ouis)
Rathbone, Julian 1935- .... **CLC 41**
See also CA 101; CANR 34
Rattigan, Terence (Mervyn) 1911-1977**CLC 7; DAM DRAM**
See also CA 85-88; 73-76; CDBLB 1945-1960; DLB 13; MTCW
Ratushinskaya, Irina 1954- .... **CLC 54**
See also CA 129
Raven, Simon (Arthur Noel) 1927- .. **CLC 14**

Rowe, Nicholas 1674-1718 .... **LC 8**
  See also DLB 84
Rowley, Ames Dorrance
  See Lovecraft, H(oward) P(hillips)
Rowson, Susanna Haswell 1762(?)-1824
    NCLC 5
  See also DLB 37
Roy, Gabrielle 1909-1983 **CLC 10, 14; DAB;**
    DAC; DAM MST
  See also CA 53-56; 110; CANR 5; DLB 68;
    MTCW
Rozewicz, Tadeusz 1921- .. **CLC 9, 23; DAM**
    POET
  See also CA 108; CANR 36; MTCW
Ruark, Gibbons 1941- .... **CLC 3**
  See also CA 33-36R; CAAS 23; CANR 14, 31,
    57; DLB 120
Rubens, Bernice (Ruth) 1923- .... **CLC 19, 31**
  See also CA 25-28R; CANR 33; DLB 14;
    MTCW
Rubin, Harold
  See Robbins, Harold
Rudkin, (James) David 1936- .... **CLC 14**
  See also CA 89-92; DLB 13
Rudnik, Raphael 1933- .... **CLC 7**
  See also CA 29-32R
Ruffian, M.
  See Hasek, Jaroslav (Matej Frantisek)
Ruiz, Jose Martinez .... **CLC 11**
  See also Martinez Ruiz, Jose
Rukeyser, Muriel 1913-1980**CLC 6, 10, 15, 27;**
    DAM POET; PC 12
  See also CA 5-8R; 93-96; CANR 26; DLB 48;
    MTCW; SATA-Obit 22
Rule, Jane (Vance) 1931- .... **CLC 27**
  See also CA 25-28R; CAAS 18; CANR 12; DLB
    60
Rulfo, Juan 1918-1986 ...... **CLC 8, 80; DAM**
    MULT; HLC; SSC 25
  See also CA 85-88; 118; CANR 26; DLB 113;
    HW; MTCW
Rumi, Jalal al-Din 1297-1373 .... **CMLC 20**
Runeberg, Johan 1804-1877 .... **NCLC 41**
Runyon, (Alfred) Damon 1884(?)-1946**T C L C**
    10
  See also CA 107; DLB 11, 86, 171
Rush, Norman 1933- .... **CLC 44**
  See also CA 121; 126; INT 126
Rushdie, (Ahmed) Salman 1947- **CLC 23, 31,**
    55, 100; DAB; DAC; DAM MST, NOV,
    POP; WLCS
  See also BEST 89:3; CA 108; 111; CANR 33,
    56; INT 111; MTCW
Rushforth, Peter (Scott) 1945- .... **CLC 19**
  See also CA 101
Ruskin, John 1819-1900 .... **TCLC 63**
  See also CA 114; 129; CDBLB 1832-1890;
    DLB 55, 163; SATA 24
Russ, Joanna 1937- .... **CLC 15**
  See also CA 25-28R; CANR 11, 31; DLB 8;
    MTCW
Russell, George William 1867-1935
  See Baker, Jean H.
  See also CA 104; 153; CDBLB 1890-1914;
    DAM POET
Russell, (Henry) Ken(neth Alfred) 1927-**C L C**
    16
  See also CA 105
Russell, Willy 1947- .... **CLC 60**
Rutherford, Mark .... **TCLC 25**
  See also White, William Hale
  See also DLB 18
Ruyslinck, Ward 1929- .... **CLC 14**

See also Belser, Reimond Karel Maria de
Ryan, Cornelius (John) 1920-1974 ..... **CLC 7**
  See also CA 69-72; 53-56; CANR 38
Ryan, Michael 1946- .... **CLC 65**
  See also CA 49-52; DLBY 82
Ryan, Tim
  See Dent, Lester
Rybakov, Anatoli (Naumovich) 1911-**CLC 23,**
    53
  See also CA 126; 135; SATA 79
Ryder, Jonathan
  See Ludlum, Robert
Ryga, George 1932-1987**CLC 14; DAC; DAM**
    MST
  See also CA 101; 124; CANR 43; DLB 60
S. S.
  See Sassoon, Siegfried (Lorraine)
Saba, Umberto 1883-1957 .... **TCLC 33**
  See also CA 144; DLB 114
Sabatini, Rafael 1875-1950 .... **TCLC 47**
Sabato, Ernesto (R.) 1911-**CLC 10, 23; DAM**
    MULT; HLC
  See also CA 97-100; CANR 32; DLB 145; HW;
    MTCW
Sacastru, Martin
  See Bioy Casares, Adolfo
Sacher-Masoch, Leopold von 1836(?)-1895
    NCLC 31
Sachs, Marilyn (Stickle) 1927- .... **CLC 35**
  See also AAYA 2; CA 17-20R; CANR 13, 47;
    CLR 2; JRDA; MAICYA; SAAS 2; SATA 3,
    68
Sachs, Nelly 1891-1970 .... **CLC 14, 98**
  See also CA 17-18; 25-28R; CAP 2
Sackler, Howard (Oliver) 1929-1982 **CLC 14**
  See also CA 61-64; 108; CANR 30; DLB 7
Sacks, Oliver (Wolf) 1933- .... **CLC 67**
  See also CA 53-56; CANR 28, 50; INT CANR-
    28; MTCW
Sade, Donatien Alphonse Francois Comte 1740-
    1814 .... **NCLC 47**
Sadoff, Ira 1945- .... **CLC 9**
  See also CA 53-56; CANR 5, 21; DLB 120
Saetone
  See Camus, Albert
Safire, William 1929- .... **CLC 10**
  See also CA 17-20R; CANR 31, 54
Sagan, Carl (Edward) 1934-1996 ..... **CLC 30**
  See also AAYA 2; CA 25-28R; 155; CANR 11,
    36; MTCW; SATA 58; SATA-Obit 94
Sagan, Francoise .... **CLC 3, 6, 9, 17, 36**
  See also Quoirez, Francoise
  See also DLB 83
Sahgal, Nayantara (Pandit) 1927- .... **CLC 41**
  See also CA 9-12R; CANR 11
Saint, H(arry) F. 1941- .... **CLC 50**
  See also CA 127
St. Aubin de Teran, Lisa 1953-
  See Teran, Lisa St. Aubin de
  See also CA 118; 126; INT 126
Sainte-Beuve, Charles Augustin 1804-1869
    NCLC 5
**Saint-Exupery, Antoine (Jean Baptiste Marie
    Roger) de** 1900-1944**TCLC 2, 56; DAM
    NOV; WLC**
  See also CA 108; 132; CLR 10; DLB 72;
    MAICYA; MTCW; SATA 20
St. John, David
  See Hunt, E(verette) Howard, (Jr.)
Saint-John Perse
  See Leger, (Marie-Rene Auguste) Alexis Saint-
    Leger
Saintsbury, George (Edward Bateman) 1845-

1933 .... **TCLC 31**
  See also DLB 57, 149
Sait Faik .... **TCLC 23**
  See also Abasiyanik, Sait Faik
Saki .... **TCLC 3; SSC 12**
  See also Munro, H(ector) H(ugh)
Sala, George Augustus .... **NCLC 46**
Salama, Hannu 1936- .... **CLC 18**
Salamanca, J(ack) R(ichard) 1922-**CLC 4, 15**
  See also CA 25-28R
Sale, J. Kirkpatrick
  See Sale, Kirkpatrick
Sale, Kirkpatrick 1937- .... **CLC 68**
  See also CA 13-16R; CANR 10
Salinas, Luis Omar 1937- ...... **CLC 90; DAM**
    MULT; HLC
  See also CA 131; DLB 82; HW
Salinas (y Serrano), Pedro 1891(?)-1951
    TCLC 17
  See also CA 117; DLB 134
Salinger, J(erome) D(avid) 1919-**CLC 1, 3, 8,**
    12, 55, 56; DA; DAB; DAC; DAM MST,
    NOV, POP; SSC 2; WLC
  See also AAYA 2; CA 5-8R; CANR 39; CDALB
    1941-1968; CLR 18; DLB 2, 102, 173;
    MAICYA; MTCW; SATA 67
Salisbury, John
  See Caute, David
Salter, James 1925- .... **CLC 7, 52, 59**
  See also CA 73-76; DLB 130
Saltus, Edgar (Everton) 1855-1921 . **TCLC 8**
  See also CA 105
Saltykov, Mikhail Evgrafovich 1826-1889
    NCLC 16
Samarakis, Antonis 1919- .... **CLC 5**
  See also CA 25-28R; CAAS 16; CANR 36
Sanchez, Florencio 1875-1910 .... **TCLC 37**
  See also CA 153; HW
Sanchez, Luis Rafael 1936- .... **CLC 23**
  See also CA 128; DLB 145; HW
Sanchez, Sonia 1934- ..... **CLC 5; BLC; DAM**
    MULT; PC 9
  See also BW 2; CA 33-36R; CANR 24, 49; CLR
    18; DLB 41; DLBD 8; MAICYA; MTCW;
    SATA 22
Sand, George 1804-1876**NCLC 2, 42, 57; DA;**
    DAB; DAC; DAM MST, NOV; WLC
  See also DLB 119
Sandburg, Carl (August) 1878-1967**CLC 1, 4,**
    10, 15, 35; DA; DAB; DAC; DAM MST,
    POET; PC 2; WLC
  See also CA 5-8R; 25-28R; CANR 35; CDALB
    1865-1917; DLB 17, 54; MAICYA; MTCW;
    SATA 8
Sandburg, Charles
  See Sandburg, Carl (August)
Sandburg, Charles A.
  See Sandburg, Carl (August)
Sanders, (James) Ed(ward) 1939- .... **CLC 53**
  See also CA 13-16R; CAAS 21; CANR 13, 44;
    DLB 16
Sanders, Lawrence 1920-**CLC 41; DAM POP**
  See also BEST 89:4; CA 81-84; CANR 33;
    MTCW
Sanders, Noah
  See Blount, Roy (Alton), Jr.
Sanders, Winston P.
  See Anderson, Poul (William)
Sandoz, Mari(e Susette) 1896-1966 .. **CLC 28**
  See also CA 1-4R; 25-28R; CANR 17; DLB 9;
    MTCW; SATA 5
Saner, Reg(inald Anthony) 1931- .... **CLC 9**
  See also CA 65-68

Sannazaro, Jacopo 1456(?)-1530 .... **LC 8**

Sansom, William 1912-1976 **CLC 2, 6; DAM NOV; SSC 21**
See also CA 5-8R; 65-68; CANR 42; DLB 139; MTCW

Santayana, George 1863-1952 .... **TCLC 40**
See also CA 115; DLB 54, 71; DLBD 13

Santiago, Danny .... **CLC 33**
See also James, Daniel (Lewis)
See also DLB 122

Santmyer, Helen Hoover 1895-1986 . **CLC 33**
See also CA 1-4R; 118; CANR 15, 33; DLBY 84; MTCW

Santoka, Taneda 1882-1940 .... **TCLC 72**

Santos, Bienvenido N(uqui) 1911-1996 . **C L C 22; DAM MULT**
See also CA 101; 151; CANR 19, 46

Sapper .... **TCLC 44**
See also McNeile, Herman Cyril

Sapphire 1950- .... **CLC 99**

Sappho fl. 6th cent. B.C.- ...... **CMLC 3; DAM POET; PC 5**
See also DLB 176

Sarduy, Severo 1937-1993 .... **CLC 6, 97**
See also CA 89-92; 142; CANR 58; DLB 113; HW

Sargeson, Frank 1903-1982 .... **CLC 31**
See also CA 25-28R; 106; CANR 38

Sarmiento, Felix Ruben Garcia
See Dario, Ruben

Saroyan, William 1908-1981 **CLC 1, 8, 10, 29, 34, 56; DA; DAB; DAC; DAM DRAM, MST, NOV; SSC 21; WLC**
See also CA 5-8R; 103; CANR 30; DLB 7, 9, 86; DLBY 81; MTCW; SATA 23; SATA-Obit 24

Sarraute, Nathalie 1900- **CLC 1, 2, 4, 8, 10, 31, 80**
See also CA 9-12R; CANR 23; DLB 83; MTCW

Sarton, (Eleanor) May 1912-1995 **CLC 4, 14, 49, 91; DAM POET**
See also CA 1-4R; 149; CANR 1, 34, 55; DLB 48; DLBY 81; INT CANR-34; MTCW; SATA 36; SATA-Obit 86

Sartre, Jean-Paul 1905-1980 **CLC 1, 4, 7, 9, 13, 18, 24, 44, 50, 52; DA; DAB; DAC; DAM DRAM, MST, NOV; DC 3; WLC**
See also CA 9-12R; 97-100; CANR 21; DLB 72; MTCW

Sassoon, Siegfried (Lorraine) 1886-1967 **C L C 36; DAB; DAM MST, NOV, POET; PC 12**
See also CA 104; 25-28R; CANR 36; DLB 20; MTCW

Satterfield, Charles
See Pohl, Frederik

Saul, John (W. III) 1942- **CLC 46; DAM NOV, POP**
See also AAYA 10; BEST 90:4; CA 81-84; CANR 16, 40

Saunders, Caleb
See Heinlein, Robert A(nson)

Saura (Atares), Carlos 1932- .... **CLC 20**
See also CA 114; 131; HW

Sauser-Hall, Frederic 1887-1961 ...... **CLC 18**
See also Cendrars, Blaise
See also CA 102; 93-96; CANR 36; MTCW

Saussure, Ferdinand de 1857-1913 **TCLC 49**

Savage, Catharine
See Brosman, Catharine Savage

Savage, Thomas 1915- .... **CLC 40**
See also CA 126; 132; CAAS 15; INT 132

Savan, Glenn 19(?)- .... **CLC 50**

Sayers, Dorothy L(eigh) 1893-1957 **T C L C 2, 15; DAM POP**
See also CA 104; 119; CDBLB 1914-1945; DLB 10, 36, 77, 100; MTCW

Sayers, Valerie 1952- .... **CLC 50**
See also CA 134

Sayles, John (Thomas) 1950- . **CLC 7, 10, 14**
See also CA 57-60; CANR 41; DLB 44

Scammell, Michael 1935- .... **CLC 34**
See also CA 156

Scannell, Vernon 1922- .... **CLC 49**
See also CA 5-8R; CANR 8, 24, 57; DLB 27; SATA 59

Scarlett, Susan
See Streatfeild, (Mary) Noel

Schaeffer, Susan Fromberg 1941- **CLC 6, 11, 22**
See also CA 49-52; CANR 18; DLB 28; MTCW; SATA 22

Schary, Jill
See Robinson, Jill

Schell, Jonathan 1943- .... **CLC 35**
See also CA 73-76; CANR 12

Schelling, Friedrich Wilhelm Joseph von 1775-1854 .... **NCLC 30**
See also DLB 90

Schendel, Arthur van 1874-1946 ... **TCLC 56**

Scherer, Jean-Marie Maurice 1920-
See Rohmer, Eric
See also CA 110

Schevill, James (Erwin) 1920- .... **CLC 7**
See also CA 5-8R; CAAS 12

Schiller, Friedrich 1759-1805 **NCLC 39; DAM DRAM**
See also DLB 94

Schisgal, Murray (Joseph) 1926- .... **CLC 6**
See also CA 21-24R; CANR 48

Schlee, Ann 1934- .... **CLC 35**
See also CA 101; CANR 29; SATA 44; SATA-Brief 36

Schlegel, August Wilhelm von 1767-1845 **NCLC 15**
See also DLB 94

Schlegel, Friedrich 1772-1829 .... **NCLC 45**
See also DLB 90

Schlegel, Johann Elias (von) 1719(?)-1749 **L C 5**

Schlesinger, Arthur M(eier), Jr. 1917- **CLC 84**
See also AITN 1; CA 1-4R; CANR 1, 28, 58; DLB 17; INT CANR-28; MTCW; SATA 61

Schmidt, Arno (Otto) 1914-1979 ...... **CLC 56**
See also CA 128; 109; DLB 69

Schmitz, Aron Hector 1861-1928
See Svevo, Italo
See also CA 104; 122; MTCW

Schnackenberg, Gjertrud 1953- .... **CLC 40**
See also CA 116; DLB 120

Schneider, Leonard Alfred 1925-1966
See Bruce, Lenny
See also CA 89-92

Schnitzler, Arthur 1862-1931 **TCLC 4; SSC 15**
See also CA 104; DLB 81, 118

Schopenhauer, Arthur 1788-1860 . **NCLC 51**
See also DLB 90

Schor, Sandra (M.) 1932(?)-1990 ...... **CLC 65**
See also CA 132

Schorer, Mark 1908-1977 .... **CLC 9**
See also CA 5-8R; 73-76; CANR 7; DLB 103

Schrader, Paul (Joseph) 1946- .... **CLC 26**
See also CA 37-40R; CANR 41; DLB 44

Schreiner, Olive (Emilie Albertina) 1855-1920 **TCLC 9**
See also CA 105; DLB 18, 156

Schulberg, Budd (Wilson) 1914- ... **CLC 7, 48**
See also CA 25-28R; CANR 19; DLB 6, 26, 28; DLBY 81

Schulz, Bruno 1892-1942 **TCLC 5, 51; SSC 13**
See also CA 115; 123

Schulz, Charles M(onroe) 1922- .... **CLC 12**
See also CA 9-12R; CANR 6; INT CANR-6; SATA 10

Schumacher, E(rnst) F(riedrich) 1911-1977 **CLC 80**
See also CA 81-84; 73-76; CANR 34

Schuyler, James Marcus 1923-1991 **CLC 5, 23; DAM POET**
See also CA 101; 134; DLB 5, 169; INT 101

Schwartz, Delmore (David) 1913-1966 **CLC 2, 4, 10, 45, 87; PC 8**
See also CA 17-18; 25-28R; CANR 35; CAP 2; DLB 28, 48; MTCW

Schwartz, Ernst
See Ozu, Yasujiro

Schwartz, John Burnham 1965- .... **CLC 59**
See also CA 132

Schwartz, Lynne Sharon 1939- .... **CLC 31**
See also CA 103; CANR 44

Schwartz, Muriel A.
See Eliot, T(homas) S(tearns)

Schwarz-Bart, Andre 1928- .... **CLC 2, 4**
See also CA 89-92

Schwarz-Bart, Simone 1938- .... **CLC 7**
See also BW 2; CA 97-100

Schwob, (Mayer Andre) Marcel 1867-1905 **TCLC 20**
See also CA 117; DLB 123

Sciascia, Leonardo 1921-1989 . **CLC 8, 9, 41**
See also CA 85-88; 130; CANR 35; DLB 177; MTCW

Scoppettone, Sandra 1936- .... **CLC 26**
See also AAYA 11; CA 5-8R; CANR 41; SATA 9, 92

Scorsese, Martin 1942- .... **CLC 20, 89**
See also CA 110; 114; CANR 46

Scotland, Jay
See Jakes, John (William)

Scott, Duncan Campbell 1862-1947 **TCLC 6; DAC**
See also CA 104; 153; DLB 92

Scott, Evelyn 1893-1963 .... **CLC 43**
See also CA 104; 112; DLB 9, 48

Scott, F(rancis) R(eginald) 1899-1985 **CLC 22**
See also CA 101; 114; DLB 88; INT 101

Scott, Frank
See Scott, F(rancis) R(eginald)

Scott, Joanna 1960- .... **CLC 50**
See also CA 126; CANR 53

Scott, Paul (Mark) 1920-1978 .... **CLC 9, 60**
See also CA 81-84; 77-80; CANR 33; DLB 14; MTCW

Scott, Walter 1771-1832 **NCLC 15; DA; DAB; DAC; DAM MST, NOV, POET; PC 13; WLC**
See also AAYA 22; CDBLB 1789-1832; DLB 93, 107, 116, 144, 159; YABC 2

Scribe, (Augustin) Eugene 1791-1861 **N C L C 16; DAM DRAM; DC 5**

Scrum, R.
See Crumb, R(obert)

Scudery, Madeleine de 1607-1701 .... **LC 2**

Scum
See Crumb, R(obert)

Scumbag, Little Bobby
See Crumb, R(obert)

Seabrook, John
See Hubbard, L(afayette) Ron(ald)

Sealy, I. Allan 1951- .... **CLC 55**

Shields, David 1956- .... **CLC 97**
See also CA 124; CANR 48
Shiga, Naoya 1883-1971 ...... **CLC 33; SSC 23**
See also CA 101; 33-36R; DLB 180
Shilts, Randy 1951-1994 .... **CLC 85**
See also AAYA 19; CA 115; 127; 144; CANR
45; INT 127
Shimazaki, Haruki 1872-1943
See Shimazaki Toson
See also CA 105; 134
Shimazaki Toson 1872-1943 .... **TCLC 5**
See also Shimazaki, Haruki
See also DLB 180
Sholokhov, Mikhail (Aleksandrovich) 1905-
1984 .... **CLC 7, 15**
See also CA 101; 112; MTCW; SATA-Obit 36
Shone, Patric
See Hanley, James
Shreve, Susan Richards 1939- .... **CLC 23**
See also CA 49-52; CAAS 5; CANR 5, 38;
MAICYA; SATA 46; SATA-Brief 41
Shue, Larry 1946-1985 **CLC 52; DAM DRAM**
See also CA 145; 117
Shu-Jen, Chou 1881-1936
See Lu Hsun
See also CA 104
Shulman, Alix Kates 1932- .... **CLC 2, 10**
See also CA 29-32R; CANR 43; SATA 7
Shuster, Joe 1914- .... **CLC 21**
Shute, Nevil .... **CLC 30**
See also Norway, Nevil Shute
Shuttle, Penelope (Diane) 1947- .... **CLC 7**
See also CA 93-96; CANR 39; DLB 14, 40
Sidney, Mary 1561-1621 .... **LC 19, 39**
Sidney, Sir Philip 1554-1586 **LC 19, 39; DA;**
DAB; DAC; DAM MST, POET
See also CDBLB Before 1660; DLB 167
Siegel, Jerome 1914-1996 .... **CLC 21**
See also CA 116; 151
Siegel, Jerry
See Siegel, Jerome
Sienkiewicz, Henryk (Adam Alexander Pius)
1846-1916 .... **TCLC 3**
See also CA 104; 134
Sierra, Gregorio Martinez
See Martinez Sierra, Gregorio
Sierra, Maria (de la O'LeJarraga) Martinez
See Martinez Sierra, Maria (de la O'LeJarraga)
Sigal, Clancy 1926- .... **CLC 7**
See also CA 1-4R
Sigourney, Lydia Howard (Huntley) 1791-1865
NCLC 21
See also DLB 1, 42, 73
Siguenza y Gongora, Carlos de 1645-1700 **L C**
8
Sigurjonsson, Johann 1880-1919 ... **TCLC 27**
Sikelianos, Angelos 1884-1951 .... **TCLC 39**
Silkin, Jon 1930- .... **CLC 2, 6, 43**
See also CA 5-8R; CAAS 5; DLB 27
Silko, Leslie (Marmon) 1948- **CLC 23, 74; DA;**
DAC; DAM MST, MULT, POP; WLCS
See also AAYA 14; CA 115; 122; CANR 45;
DLB 143, 175; NNAL
Sillanpaa, Frans Eemil 1888-1964 ... **CLC 19**
See also CA 129; 93-96; MTCW
Sillitoe, Alan 1928- ... **CLC 1, 3, 6, 10, 19, 57**
See also AITN 1; CA 9-12R; CAAS 2; CANR
8, 26, 55; CDBLB 1960 to Present; DLB 14,
139; MTCW; SATA 61
Silone, Ignazio 1900-1978 .... **CLC 4**
See also CA 25-28; 81-84; CANR 34; CAP 2;
MTCW
Silver, Joan Micklin 1935- .... **CLC 20**

See also CA 114; 121; INT 121
Silver, Nicholas
See Faust, Frederick (Schiller)
Silverberg, Robert 1935- **CLC 7; DAM POP**
See also CA 1-4R; CAAS 3; CANR 1, 20, 36;
DLB 8; INT CANR-20; MAICYA; MTCW;
SATA 13, 91
Silverstein, Alvin 1933- .... **CLC 17**
See also CA 49-52; CANR 2; CLR 25; JRDA;
MAICYA; SATA 8, 69
Silverstein, Virginia B(arbara Opshelor) 1937-
CLC 17
See also CA 49-52; CANR 2; CLR 25; JRDA;
MAICYA; SATA 8, 69
Sim, Georges
See Simenon, Georges (Jacques Christian)
Simak, Clifford D(onald) 1904-1988 **CLC 1, 55**
See also CA 1-4R; 125; CANR 1, 35; DLB 8;
MTCW; SATA-Obit 56
Simenon, Georges (Jacques Christian) 1903-
1989 .. **CLC 1, 2, 3, 8, 18, 47; DAM POP**
See also CA 85-88; 129; CANR 35; DLB 72;
DLBY 89; MTCW
Simic, Charles 1938- .... **CLC 6, 9, 22, 49, 68;**
DAM POET
See also CA 29-32R; CAAS 4; CANR 12, 33,
52; DLB 105
Simmel, Georg 1858-1918 .... **TCLC 64**
See also CA 157
Simmons, Charles (Paul) 1924- .... **CLC 57**
See also CA 89-92; INT 89-92
Simmons, Dan 1948- ..... **CLC 44; DAM POP**
See also AAYA 16; CA 138; CANR 53
Simmons, James (Stewart Alexander) 1933-
CLC 43
See also CA 105; CAAS 21; DLB 40
Simms, William Gilmore 1806-1870 **NCLC 3**
See also DLB 3, 30, 59, 73
Simon, Carly 1945- .... **CLC 26**
See also CA 105
Simon, Claude 1913- **CLC 4, 9, 15, 39; DAM**
NOV
See also CA 89-92; CANR 33; DLB 83; MTCW
Simon, (Marvin) Neil 1927- **CLC 6, 11, 31, 39,**
70; DAM DRAM
See also AITN 1; CA 21-24R; CANR 26, 54;
DLB 7; MTCW
Simon, Paul (Frederick) 1941(?)- ..... **CLC 17**
See also CA 116; 153
Simonon, Paul 1956(?)- .... **CLC 30**
Simpson, Harriette
See Arnow, Harriette (Louisa) Simpson
Simpson, Louis (Aston Marantz) 1923- **CLC 4,**
7, 9, 32; DAM POET
See also CA 1-4R; CAAS 4; CANR 1; DLB 5;
MTCW
Simpson, Mona (Elizabeth) 1957- .... **CLC 44**
See also CA 122; 135
Simpson, N(orman) F(rederick) 1919- **CLC 29**
See also CA 13-16R; DLB 13
Sinclair, Andrew (Annandale) 1935- . **CLC 2,**
14
See also CA 9-12R; CAAS 5; CANR 14, 38;
DLB 14; MTCW
Sinclair, Emil
See Hesse, Hermann
Sinclair, Iain 1943- .... **CLC 76**
See also CA 132
Sinclair, Iain MacGregor
See Sinclair, Iain
Sinclair, Irene
See Griffith, D(avid Lewelyn) W(ark)
Sinclair, Mary Amelia St. Clair 1865(?)-1946

See Sinclair, May
See also CA 104
Sinclair, May .... **TCLC 3, 11**
See also Sinclair, Mary Amelia St. Clair
See also DLB 36, 135
Sinclair, Roy
See Griffith, D(avid Lewelyn) W(ark)
Sinclair, Upton (Beall) 1878-1968 **CLC 1, 11,**
15, 63; DA; DAB; DAC; DAM MST, NOV;
WLC
See also CA 5-8R; 25-28R; CANR 7; CDALB
1929-1941; DLB 9; INT CANR-7; MTCW;
SATA 9
Singer, Isaac
See Singer, Isaac Bashevis
Singer, Isaac Bashevis 1904-1991 **CLC 1, 3, 6,**
9, 11, 15, 23, 38, 69; DA; DAB; DAC; DAM
MST, NOV; SSC 3; WLC
See also AITN 1, 2; CA 1-4R; 134; CANR 1,
39; CDALB 1941-1968; CLR 1; DLB 6, 28,
52; DLBY 91; JRDA; MAICYA; MTCW;
SATA 3, 27; SATA-Obit 68
Singer, Israel Joshua 1893-1944 .... **TCLC 33**
Singh, Khushwant 1915- .... **CLC 11**
See also CA 9-12R; CAAS 9; CANR 6
Singleton, Ann
See Benedict, Ruth (Fulton)
Sinjohn, John
See Galsworthy, John
Sinyavsky, Andrei (Donatevich) 1925- **CLC 8**
See also CA 85-88
Sirin, V.
See Nabokov, Vladimir (Vladimirovich)
Sissman, L(ouis) E(dward) 1928-1976 **CLC 9,**
18
See also CA 21-24R; 65-68; CANR 13; DLB 5
Sisson, C(harles) H(ubert) 1914- .... **CLC 8**
See also CA 1-4R; CAAS 3; CANR 3, 48; DLB
27
Sitwell, Dame Edith 1887-1964 **CLC 2, 9, 67;**
DAM POET; PC 3
See also CA 9-12R; CANR 35; CDBLB 1945-
1960; DLB 20; MTCW
Sjoewall, Maj 1935- .... **CLC 7**
See also CA 65-68
Sjowall, Maj
See Sjoewall, Maj
Skelton, Robin 1925- .... **CLC 13**
See also AITN 2; CA 5-8R; CAAS 5; CANR
28; DLB 27, 53
Skolimowski, Jerzy 1938- .... **CLC 20**
See also CA 128
Skram, Amalie (Bertha) 1847-1905 **TCLC 25**
Skvorecky, Josef (Vaclav) 1924- **CLC 15, 39,**
69; DAC; DAM NOV
See also CA 61-64; CAAS 1; CANR 10, 34;
MTCW
Slade, Bernard .... **CLC 11, 46**
See also Newbound, Bernard Slade
See also CAAS 9; DLB 53
Slaughter, Carolyn 1946- .... **CLC 56**
See also CA 85-88
Slaughter, Frank G(ill) 1908- .... **CLC 29**
See also AITN 2; CA 5-8R; CANR 5; INT
CANR-5
Slavitt, David R(ytman) 1935- ...... **CLC 5, 14**
See also CA 21-24R; CAAS 3; CANR 41; DLB
5, 6
Slesinger, Tess 1905-1945 .... **TCLC 10**
See also CA 107; DLB 102
Slessor, Kenneth 1901-1971 .... **CLC 14**
See also CA 102; 89-92
Slowacki, Juliusz 1809-1849 .... **NCLC 15**

Tartt, Donna 1964(?)- .... CLC 76
   See also CA 142
Tasso, Torquato 1544-1595 .... LC 5
Tate, (John Orley) Allen 1899-1979CLC 2, 4,
   6, 9, 11, 14, 24
   See also CA 5-8R; 85-88; CANR 32; DLB 4,
   45, 63; MTCW
Tate, Ellalice
   See Hibbert, Eleanor Alice Burford
Tate, James (Vincent) 1943- ..... CLC 2, 6, 25
   See also CA 21-24R; CANR 29, 57; DLB 5,
   169
Tavel, Ronald 1940- .... CLC 6
   See also CA 21-24R; CANR 33
Taylor, C(ecil) P(hilip) 1929-1981 .... CLC 27
   See also CA 25-28R; 105; CANR 47
Taylor, Edward 1642(?)-1729 ..... LC 11; DA;
   DAB; DAC; DAM MST, POET
   See also DLB 24
Taylor, Eleanor Ross 1920- .... CLC 5
   See also CA 81-84
Taylor, Elizabeth 1912-1975 ..... CLC 2, 4, 29
   See also CA 13-16R; CANR 9; DLB 139;
   MTCW; SATA 13
Taylor, Henry (Splawn) 1942- .... CLC 44
   See also CA 33-36R; CAAS 7; CANR 31; DLB
   5
Taylor, Kamala (Purnaiya) 1924-
   See Markandaya, Kamala
   See also CA 77-80
Taylor, Mildred D. .... CLC 21
   See also AAYA 10; BW 1; CA 85-88; CANR
   25; CLR 9; DLB 52; JRDA; MAICYA; SAAS
   5; SATA 15, 70
Taylor, Peter (Hillsman) 1917-1994CLC 1, 4,
   18, 37, 44, 50, 71; SSC 10
   See also CA 13-16R; 147; CANR 9, 50; DLBY
   81, 94; INT CANR-9; MTCW
Taylor, Robert Lewis 1912- .... CLC 14
   See also CA 1-4R; CANR 3; SATA 10
Tchekhov, Anton
   See Chekhov, Anton (Pavlovich)
Tchicaya, Gerald Felix 1931-1988 .. CLC 101
   See also CA 129; 125
Tchicaya U Tam'si
   See Tchicaya, Gerald Felix
Teasdale, Sara 1884-1933 .... TCLC 4
   See also CA 104; DLB 45; SATA 32
Tegner, Esaias 1782-1846.................. NCLC 2
Teilhard de Chardin, (Marie Joseph) Pierre
   1881-1955 .... TCLC 9
   See also CA 105
Temple, Ann
   See Mortimer, Penelope (Ruth)
Tennant, Emma (Christina) 1937-CLC 13, 52
   See also CA 65-68; CAAS 9; CANR 10, 38,
   59; DLB 14
Tenneshaw, S. M.
   See Silverberg, Robert
Tennyson, Alfred 1809-1892 . NCLC 30; DA;
   DAB; DAC; DAM MST, POET; PC 6;
   WLC
   See also CDBLB 1832-1890; DLB 32
Teran, Lisa St. Aubin de .... CLC 36
   See also St. Aubin de Teran, Lisa
Terence 195(?)B.C.-159B.C. CMLC 14; DC 7
Teresa de Jesus, St. 1515-1582 .... LC 18
Terkel, Louis 1912-
   See Terkel, Studs
   See also CA 57-60; CANR 18, 45; MTCW
Terkel, Studs .... CLC 38
   See also Terkel, Louis
   See also AITN 1

Terry, C. V.
   See Slaughter, Frank G(ill)
Terry, Megan 1932- .... CLC 19
   See also CA 77-80; CABS 3; CANR 43; DLB 7
Tertz, Abram
   See Sinyavsky, Andrei (Donatevich)
Tesich, Steve 1943(?)-1996 .... CLC 40, 69
   See also CA 105; 152; DLBY 83
Teternikov, Fyodor Kuzmich 1863-1927
   See Sologub, Fyodor
   See also CA 104
Tevis, Walter 1928-1984 .... CLC 42
   See also CA 113
Tey, Josephine .... TCLC 14
   See also Mackintosh, Elizabeth
   See also DLB 77
Thackeray, William Makepeace 1811-1863
   NCLC 5, 14, 22, 43; DA; DAB; DAC; DAM
   MST, NOV; WLC
   See also CDBLB 1832-1890; DLB 21, 55, 159,
   163; SATA 23
Thakura, Ravindranatha
   See Tagore, Rabindranath
Tharoor, Shashi 1956- .... CLC 70
   See also CA 141
Thelwell, Michael Miles 1939- .... CLC 22
   See also BW 2; CA 101
Theobald, Lewis, Jr.
   See Lovecraft, H(oward) P(hillips)
Theodorescu, Ion N. 1880-1967
   See Arghezi, Tudor
   See also CA 116
Theriault, Yves 1915-1983 .... CLC 79; DAC;
   DAM MST
   See also CA 102; DLB 88
Theroux, Alexander (Louis) 1939- CLC 2, 25
   See also CA 85-88; CANR 20
Theroux, Paul (Edward) 1941- CLC 5, 8, 11,
   15, 28, 46; DAM POP
   See also BEST 89:4; CA 33-36R; CANR 20,
   45; DLB 2; MTCW; SATA 44
Thesen, Sharon 1946- .... CLC 56
Thevenin, Denis
   See Duhamel, Georges
Thibault, Jacques Anatole Francois 1844-1924
   See France, Anatole
   See also CA 106; 127; DAM NOV; MTCW
Thiele, Colin (Milton) 1920- .... CLC 17
   See also CA 29-32R; CANR 12, 28, 53; CLR
   27; MAICYA; SAAS 2; SATA 14, 72
Thomas, Audrey (Callahan) 1935-CLC 7, 13,
   37; SSC 20
   See also AITN 2; CA 21-24R; CAAS 19; CANR
   36, 58; DLB 60; MTCW
Thomas, D(onald) M(ichael) 1935- . CLC 13,
   22, 31
   See also CA 61-64; CAAS 11; CANR 17, 45;
   CDBLB 1960 to Present; DLB 40; INT
   CANR-17; MTCW
Thomas, Dylan (Marlais) 1914-1953TCLC 1,
   8, 45; DA; DAB; DAC; DAM DRAM,
   MST, POET; PC 2; SSC 3; WLC
   See also CA 104; 120; CDBLB 1945-1960;
   DLB 13, 20, 139; MTCW; SATA 60
Thomas, (Philip) Edward 1878-1917 . TCLC
   10; DAM POET
   See also CA 106; 153; DLB 19
Thomas, Joyce Carol 1938- .... CLC 35
   See also AAYA 12; BW 2; CA 113; 116; CANR
   48; CLR 19; DLB 33; INT 116; JRDA;
   MAICYA; MTCW; SAAS 7; SATA 40, 78
Thomas, Lewis 1913-1993 .... CLC 35
   See also CA 85-88; 143; CANR 38; MTCW

Thomas, Paul
   See Mann, (Paul) Thomas
Thomas, Piri 1928- .... CLC 17
   See also CA 73-76; HW
Thomas, R(onald) S(tuart) 1913- CLC 6, 13,
   48; DAB; DAM POET
   See also CA 89-92; CAAS 4; CANR 30;
   CDBLB 1960 to Present; DLB 27; MTCW
Thomas, Ross (Elmore) 1926-1995 ... CLC 39
   See also CA 33-36R; 150; CANR 22
Thompson, Francis Clegg
   See Mencken, H(enry) L(ouis)
Thompson, Francis Joseph 1859-1907TCLC 4
   See also CA 104; CDBLB 1890-1914; DLB 19
Thompson, Hunter S(tockton) 1939-. CLC 9,
   17, 40; DAM POP
   See also BEST 89:1; CA 17-20R; CANR 23,
   46; MTCW
Thompson, James Myers
   See Thompson, Jim (Myers)
Thompson, Jim (Myers) 1906-1977(?)CLC 69
   See also CA 140
Thompson, Judith .... CLC 39
Thomson, James 1700-1748 LC 16, 29; DAM
   POET
   See also DLB 95
Thomson, James 1834-1882 NCLC 18; DAM
   POET
   See also DLB 35
Thoreau, Henry David 1817-1862NCLC 7, 21,
   61; DA; DAB; DAC; DAM MST; WLC
   See also CDALB 1640-1865; DLB 1
Thornton, Hall
   See Silverberg, Robert
Thucydides c. 455B.C.-399B.C. .... CMLC 17
   See also DLB 176
Thurber, James (Grover) 1894-1961 . CLC 5,
   11, 25; DA; DAB; DAC; DAM DRAM,
   MST, NOV; SSC 1
   See also CA 73-76; CANR 17, 39; CDALB
   1929-1941; DLB 4, 11, 22, 102; MAICYA;
   MTCW; SATA 13
Thurman, Wallace (Henry) 1902-1934T L C
   6; BLC; DAM MULT
   See also BW 1; CA 104; 124; DLB 51
Ticheburn, Cheviot
   See Ainsworth, William Harrison
Tieck, (Johann) Ludwig 1773-1853 NCLC 5,
   46
   See also DLB 90
Tiger, Derry
   See Ellison, Harlan (Jay)
Tilghman, Christopher 1948(?)- .... CLC 65
Tillinghast, Richard (Williford) 1940-CLC 29
   See also CA 29-32R; CAAS 23; CANR 26, 51
Timrod, Henry 1828-1867 .... NCLC 25
   See also DLB 3
Tindall, Gillian 1938- .... CLC 7
   See also CA 21-24R; CANR 11
Tiptree, James, Jr. .... CLC 48, 50
   See also Sheldon, Alice Hastings Bradley
   See also DLB 8
Titmarsh, Michael Angelo
   See Thackeray, William Makepeace
Tocqueville, Alexis (Charles Henri Maurice
   Clerel Comte) 1805-1859 .... NCLC 7
Tolkien, J(ohn) R(onald) R(euel) 1892-1973
   CLC 1, 2, 3, 8, 12, 38; DA; DAB; DAC;
   DAM MST, NOV, POP; WLC
   See also AAYA 10; AITN 1; CA 17-18; 45-48;
   CANR 36; CAP 2; CDBLB 1914-1945; DLB
   15, 160; JRDA; MAICYA; MTCW; SATA 2,
   32; SATA-Obit 24

See Strindberg, (Johan) August

Ulibarri, Sabine R(eyes) 1919-**CLC 83; DAM MULT**
See also CA 131; DLB 82; HW

Unamuno (y Jugo), Miguel de 1864-1936
TCLC 2, 9; DAM MULT, NOV; HLC; SSC 11
See also CA 104; 131; DLB 108; HW; MTCW

Undercliffe, Errol
See Campbell, (John) Ramsey

Underwood, Miles
See Glassco, John

Undset, Sigrid 1882-1949**TCLC 3; DA; DAB; DAC; DAM MST, NOV; WLC**
See also CA 104; 129; MTCW

Ungaretti, Giuseppe 1888-1970**CLC 7, 11, 15**
See also CA 19-20; 25-28R; CAP 2; DLB 114

Unger, Douglas 1952- .... **CLC 34**
See also CA 130

Unsworth, Barry (Forster) 1930- ..... **CLC 76**
See also CA 25-28R; CANR 30, 54

Updike, John (Hoyer) 1932-**CLC 1, 2, 3, 5, 7, 9, 13, 15, 23, 34, 43, 70; DA; DAB; DAC; DAM MST, NOV, POET, POP; SSC 13, 27; WLC**
See also CA 1-4R; CABS 1; CANR 4, 33, 51; CDALB 1968-1988; DLB 2, 5, 143; DLBD 3; DLBY 80, 82; MTCW

Upshaw, Margaret Mitchell
See Mitchell, Margaret (Munnerlyn)

Upton, Mark
See Sanders, Lawrence

Urdang, Constance (Henriette) 1922-**CLC 47**
See also CA 21-24R; CANR 9, 24

Uriel, Henry
See Faust, Frederick (Schiller)

Uris, Leon (Marcus) 1924- **CLC 7, 32; DAM NOV, POP**
See also AITN 1, 2; BEST 89:2; CA 1-4R; CANR 1, 40; MTCW; SATA 49

Urmuz
See Codrescu, Andrei

Urquhart, Jane 1949- .... **CLC 90; DAC**
See also CA 113; CANR 32

Ustinov, Peter (Alexander) 1921- .... **CLC 1**
See also AITN 1; CA 13-16R; CANR 25, 51; DLB 13

U Tam'si, Gerald Felix Tchicaya
See Tchicaya, Gerald Felix

U Tam'si, Tchicaya
See Tchicaya, Gerald Felix

Vaculik, Ludvik 1926- .... **CLC 7**
See also CA 53-56

Vaihinger, Hans 1852-1933 .... **TCLC 71**
See also CA 116

Valdez, Luis (Miguel) 1940- .. **CLC 84; DAM MULT; HLC**
See also CA 101; CANR 32; DLB 122; HW

Valenzuela, Luisa 1938-**CLC 31; DAM MULT; SSC 14**
See also CA 101; CANR 32; DLB 113; HW

Valera y Alcala-Galiano, Juan 1824-1905
TCLC 10
See also CA 106

Valery, (Ambroise) Paul (Toussaint Jules) 1871-1945 ..... **TCLC 4, 15; DAM POET; PC 9**
See also CA 104; 122; MTCW

Valle-Inclan, Ramon (Maria) del 1866-1936
TCLC 5; DAM MULT; HLC
See also CA 106; 153; DLB 134

Vallejo, Antonio Buero
See Buero Vallejo, Antonio

Vallejo, Cesar (Abraham) 1892-1938**TCLC 3,**

56; **DAM MULT; HLC**
See also CA 105; 153; HW

Vallette, Marguerite Eymery
See Rachilde

Valle Y Pena, Ramon del
See Valle-Inclan, Ramon (Maria) del

Van Ash, Cay 1918- .... **CLC 34**

Vanbrugh, Sir John 1664-1726 **LC 21; DAM DRAM**
See also DLB 80

Van Campen, Karl
See Campbell, John W(ood, Jr.)

Vance, Gerald
See Silverberg, Robert

Vance, Jack .... **CLC 35**
See also Kuttner, Henry; Vance, John Holbrook
See also DLB 8

Vance, John Holbrook 1916-
See Queen, Ellery; Vance, Jack
See also CA 29-32R; CANR 17; MTCW

Van Den Bogarde, Derek Jules Gaspard Ulric Niven 1921-
See Bogarde, Dirk
See also CA 77-80

Vandenburgh, Jane .... **CLC 59**

Vanderhaeghe, Guy 1951- .... **CLC 41**
See also CA 113

van der Post, Laurens (Jan) 1906-1996**CLC 5**
See also CA 5-8R; 155; CANR 35

van de Wetering, Janwillem 1931- ... **CLC 47**
See also CA 49-52; CANR 4

Van Dine, S. S. .... **TCLC 23**
See also Wright, Willard Huntington

Van Doren, Carl (Clinton) 1885-1950 **TCLC 18**
See also CA 111

Van Doren, Mark 1894-1972 .... **CLC 6, 10**
See also CA 1-4R; 37-40R; CANR 3; DLB 45; MTCW

Van Druten, John (William) 1901-1957**TCLC 2**
See also CA 104; DLB 10

Van Duyn, Mona (Jane) 1921- **CLC 3, 7, 63; DAM POET**
See also CA 9-12R; CANR 7, 38; DLB 5

Van Dyne, Edith
See Baum, L(yman) Frank

van Itallie, Jean-Claude 1936- .... **CLC 3**
See also CA 45-48; CAAS 2; CANR 1, 48; DLB 7

van Ostaijen, Paul 1896-1928 .... **TCLC 33**

Van Peebles, Melvin 1932- **CLC 2, 20; DAM MULT**
See also BW 2; CA 85-88; CANR 27

Vansittart, Peter 1920- .... **CLC 42**
See also CA 1-4R; CANR 3, 49

Van Vechten, Carl 1880-1964 .... **CLC 33**
See also CA 89-92; DLB 4, 9, 51

Van Vogt, A(lfred) E(lton) 1912- .... **CLC 1**
See also CA 21-24R; CANR 28; DLB 8; SATA 14

Varda, Agnes 1928- .... **CLC 16**
See also CA 116; 122

Vargas Llosa, (Jorge) Mario (Pedro) 1936-
CLC 3, 6, 9, 10, 15, 31, 42, 85; DA; DAB; DAC; DAM MST, MULT, NOV; HLC
See also CA 73-76; CANR 18, 32, 42; DLB 145; HW; MTCW

Vasiliu, Gheorghe 1881-1957
See Bacovia, George
See also CA 123

Vassa, Gustavus
See Equiano, Olaudah

Vassilikos, Vassilis 1933- .... **CLC 4, 8**
See also CA 81-84

Vaughan, Henry 1621-1695 .... **LC 27**
See also DLB 131

Vaughn, Stephanie .... **CLC 62**

Vazov, Ivan (Minchov) 1850-1921 . **TCLC 25**
See also CA 121; DLB 147

Veblen, Thorstein (Bunde) 1857-1929 **TCLC 31**
See also CA 115

Vega, Lope de 1562-1635 .... **LC 23**

Venison, Alfred
See Pound, Ezra (Weston Loomis)

Verdi, Marie de
See Mencken, H(enry) L(ouis)

Verdu, Matilde
See Cela, Camilo Jose

Verga, Giovanni (Carmelo) 1840-1922**TCLC 3; SSC 21**
See also CA 104; 123

Vergil 70B.C.-19B.C. ... **CMLC 9; DA; DAB; DAC; DAM MST, POET; PC 12; WLCS**

Verhaeren, Emile (Adolphe Gustave) 1855-1916
TCLC 12
See also CA 109

Verlaine, Paul (Marie) 1844-1896**NCLC 2, 51; DAM POET; PC 2**

Verne, Jules (Gabriel) 1828-1905**TCLC 6, 52**
See also AAYA 16; CA 110; 131; DLB 123; JRDA; MAICYA; SATA 21

Very, Jones 1813-1880 .... **NCLC 9**
See also DLB 1

Vesaas, Tarjei 1897-1970 .... **CLC 48**
See also CA 29-32R

Vialis, Gaston
See Simenon, Georges (Jacques Christian)

Vian, Boris 1920-1959 .... **TCLC 9**
See also CA 106; DLB 72

Viaud, (Louis Marie) Julien 1850-1923
See Loti, Pierre
See also CA 107

Vicar, Henry
See Felsen, Henry Gregor

Vicker, Angus
See Felsen, Henry Gregor

Vidal, Gore 1925-**CLC 2, 4, 6, 8, 10, 22, 33, 72; DAM NOV, POP**
See also AITN 1; BEST 90:2; CA 5-8R; CANR 13, 45; DLB 6, 152; INT CANR-13; MTCW

Viereck, Peter (Robert Edwin) 1916- . **CLC 4**
See also CA 1-4R; CANR 1, 47; DLB 5

Vigny, Alfred (Victor) de 1797-1863**NCLC 7; DAM POET**
See also DLB 119

Vilakazi, Benedict Wallet 1906-1947**TCLC 37**

Villiers de l'Isle Adam, Jean Marie Mathias Philippe Auguste Comte 1838-1889
NCLC 3; SSC 14
See also DLB 123

Villon, Francois 1431-1463(?) .... **PC 13**

Vinci, Leonardo da 1452-1519 ....**LC 12**

Vine, Barbara .... **CLC 50**
See also Rendell, Ruth (Barbara)
See also BEST 90:4

Vinge, Joan D(ennison) 1948-**CLC 30; SSC 24**
See also CA 93-96; SATA 36

Violis, G.
See Simenon, Georges (Jacques Christian)

Visconti, Luchino 1906-1976 .... **CLC 16**
See also CA 81-84; 65-68; CANR 39

Vittorini, Elio 1908-1966 .... **CLC 6, 9, 14**
See also CA 133; 25-28R

Vizinczey, Stephen 1933- .... **CLC 40**

Literary Criticism Series
Cumulative Topic Index

This index lists all topic entries in Gale's *Classical and Medieval Literature Criticism, Contemporary Literary Criticism, Literature Criticism from 1400 to 1800, Nineteenth-Century Literature Criticism,* and *Twentieth-Century Literary Criticism.*

Topic Index

Topic Index

Topic Index

Contemporary Literary Criticism
Cumulative Nationality Index

Nationality Index

Nationality Index

Nationality Index

Nationality Index

CLC-102 Title Index

Title Index

ISBN 0-7876-1192-1

90000

9 780787 611927